CRITICAL SURVEY OF

Young Adult Literature

CRITICAL SURVEY OF

Young Adult Literature

Editor

Amy Pattee

Simmons College

SALEM PRESS
A Division of EBSCO Information Services, Inc.
Ipswich, Massachusetts

GREY HOUSE PUBLISHING

Publisher's Cataloging-In-Publication Data
(Prepared by The Donohue Group, Inc.)

Names: Pattee, Amy, editor.
Title: Critical survey of young adult literature / editor, Amy Pattee, Simmons College.
Other Titles: Young adult literature
Description: [First edition]. | Ipswich, Massachusetts : Salem Press, a division of EBSCO Information Services, Inc. ; Amenia, NY : Grey House Publishing, [2016] | Series: Critical survey | Includes bibliographical references and index.
Identifiers: ISBN 978-1-61925-971-3 (hardcover)
Subjects: LCSH: Young adult literature, American–History and criticism. | Young adult literature, English–History and criticism. | Young adult literature, American–Film adaptations–History and criticism. | Young adult literature, English–Film adaptations–History and criticism. | Authors, American–Biography. | Authors, English–Biography.
Classification: LCC PS490 .C75 2016 | DDC 810.9/9283–dc23

PRINTED IN THE UNITED STATES OF AMERICA

Contents

FILM ADAPTATIONS OF YOUNG ADULT LITERATURE

THEMES IN YOUNG ADULT LITERATURE

GENRES OF YOUNG ADULT LITERATURE

About This Volume

Young adult literature has carved out a place for itself in libraries and bookstores since its emergence as a bona fide literary category, having attained the level of respect and permanence in academia held by its counterpart, adult prose. This new Salem Press title, *Critical Survey of Young Adult Literature* aims to offer the most representative young adult work that forms today's canon for academic coursework and library collection development, with over 300 essays of clear, concise, and accessible analysis. This collection includes classic young adult titles like *The Outsiders*, popular series like *Divergent*, plus a variety of significant themes, film adaptations and other sections important to the popular young adult category.

Young adult literature that emphasizes young protagonists dealing with issues of adolescent concern—whether in real or imagined settings—forms the backbone of this volume. Designed for both popular and scholarly arenas and collections, this series provides unique insight and analysis into the most influential and widely read young adult literature with the emphasis on establishing the medium as an important academic discipline. Researchers and general readers alike will gain a deeper understanding of these works as the literary nature is presented in a critical format.

Critical Survey of Young Adult Literature is the most recent title in Salem Press's Critical Survey series. With more than 300 essays on the evolution of young adult literature from its idiosyncratic beginnings to widespread appeal and acceptance as a legitimate category worthy of critical examination, it covers the unique development of books about teenagers to books for teenagers. Historic overviews track the complex development of this important literary form, while the survey of key themes and genres–albeit far from exhaustive–will help define major milestones and provide an important foundation for future research.

Scope and Coverage

This single volume comprises biographies, plot summaries, film adaptations, themes and genres of young adult literature with dozens of images of authors or book jackets of influential works. The collection cuts across a wide swath of content with essays on well-loved authors such as Judy Blume as well as trailblazers, like David Levithan in brand new sub-genres. Genres covered include science fiction, romance, thriller, coming-of-age, dystopia and more. Themes include family life, gender and sexuality as well as nature and survival.

This work also provides insight into trends in young adult literature and charts the worldwide phenomenon of several successful series, both in books and film adaptations, while assessing the role of the young adult publishing industry and the crossover titles that have attracted adult readers in large numbers.

Organization and Format

The essays in *Critical Survey of Young Adult Literature* are organized into five sections: biographies, plot summaries, film adaptations, themes, and genres.

- **Biographies**—covers 61 young adult authors, focusing on their principal works and life story, with a bibliography and section for further reading
- **Plot Summaries**—includes authorship, principal characters and story line of 88 works, with a section on critical evaluation and further reading
- **Film Adaptations**—includes 68 young adult titles that have been made into films, offering film analysis and significance
- **Themes**— each of 25 themes are examined through three works, offering thematic overview and conclusions
- **Genres**—examines 23 genres by analyzing three young adult works within it, offering a genre overview and conclusions

Supplemental Features

Additional tools for further research and points of access to the wealth of information contained in *Critical Survey of Young Adult Literature* include:

- **Timeline** which charts significant events in the development of young adult literature and is punctuated by news, award winners, notable books and media adaptations to give readers and researchers a clear idea of the historic development of the form.

- **Guide to online resources** with links for further subject study of particular works or authors, organized by type of reference into the following sections:

  - Young Adult Literature Overviews, Encyclopedias, and Reference Works
  - Young Adult Literature Textbooks
  - International Awards Recognizing Young Adult Literature
  - U.S. Awards Recognizing Young Adult Literature

  - Blogs Addressing Themes and Topics in Young Adult Literature

- **General bibliography** which provides a comprehensive list for researching students to access source material used throughout the volume, and an index by subject and name.

Acknowledgments

Salem Press is grateful for the expertise, professionalism and good cheer of Amy Pattee, who played the role of general editor to this volume.

List of Contributors

Pegge Bochynski, MA

Patrick G. Cooper

Joy Crelin

Robert C. Evans, PhD

Jack Ewing

Stephanie Finnegan

T. Fleischmann, MFA

Molly Hagan

Gina Hagler, MBA

Aaron Horton, MA

Raymond Pierre Hylton, PhD

M. Lewandowski, MA

R. C. Lutz, PhD

Alexandra McBride, MA

Amy Pattee

Julia A. Sienkewicz

Amy Sisson, MS, MLS

Theresa L. Stowell, PhD

Editor's Introduction

Young adult literature is a relatively new genre. While literature of adolescence—novels known as "Bildungsroman" that describe an adolescent protagonist's growth from late childhood to early adulthood—has been part of the literary spectrum since the 18th century, these books are typically written by adults for adults. Though teenagers may be part of the reading audience for these books, this "literature of adolescence" is not directed at teens, exclusively. Young adult literature written for and marketed to an expressly teenaged audience is a 20th century development.

The growth and development of young adult literature can be linked to the growth and development of the concept of the "teenager." As critic Roberta Seelinger Trites and others have observed, the concept of adolescence did not solidify in America until the twentieth century. Although people between the ages of 12 and 18 certainly existed before the twentieth century, they weren't thought of as "teenagers." Depending on their social position and responsibilities, these young people were considered either "children" or "adults." This changed with the 1904 publication of a groundbreaking book: psychologist G. Stanley Hall's *Adolescence: Its Psychology and Its Relations to Physiology, Anthropology, Sociology, Sex, Crime, Religion, and Education.* Hall's book argued that the period between childhood and adulthood was a time of "storm and stress" and described adolescence as a period of intense personal growth and identity development influenced by the physical changes wrought by puberty. To better understand adolescents, Hall recommended that adults pay attention to literature written about them and encouraged the development of more of this literature (Kidd).

Soon after Hall's book appeared, early twentieth century child labor laws, mandatory education laws, and the recognition that more education and training were necessary to compete in an increasingly industrialized world led to increasing numbers of students enrolling in and completing high school. These students also benefitted from specialized training and extracurricular programs developed for their edification. As they prepared to enter a more technological world of work, these adolescents took on an almost mythic status. Teenagers represented the nation's hope for the future and were both idealized and feared. At the same time, within the walls of the nation's high schools, a teenage culture began to develop. Marketers recognized the potential spending power of this newly acknowledged demographic and created new products, including specialized reading material, targeting this new consumer.

Among these new teen-targeted products were novels written and published expressly for young adults. While there is disagreement as to what book represents the first young adult novel, Maureen Daly's 1942 novel, *Seventeenth Summer*, is a primary contender. Written when the author was in college and published when she was twenty-one, *Seventeenth Summer* describes seventeen-year-old Angie's first serious romance. Told from Angie's first-person perspective, Daly's novel treated Angie's feelings and experiences with a seriousness not typically found in the novels for young people published at that time. Describing *Seventeenth Summer* as a novel that "perhaps captures better than any other novel the spirit of adolescence," Dwight L. Burton, writing in 1951 for *The English Journal*, argued that Daly's novel validated adolescent experiences and relationships (363). This characteristic would come to distinguish young adult novels as works of literature that legitimize and find value in adolescence itself.

The young adult novels that followed the publication of *Seventeenth Summer* were clearly influenced by both Daly's novel and the popular juvenile series books published during the same period. These "junior novels"—critic Michael Cart notes that the term "young adult literature" was not adopted until the 1960s—depicted the experiences and inner worlds of adolescents, describing high school life, family quarrels, and romantic relationships. Like the juvenile series books popular during the same period (think: "Nancy Drew" and the "Hardy Boys"), the new junior novels were divided along traditional gender lines. Books featuring female protagonists (like Betty Cavanna's *Going on Sixteen* [1945] and Rosamund du Jardin's *Practically Seventeen* [1949]) were marketed to girls and consisted primarily of stories revolving around romance and popularity. Novels with male protagonists (like Clair Bee's *Touchdown Pass* [1948] and Henry Gregor Felsen's *Hot Rod* [1950]) dealt with more active interests and described sporting triumphs and teenage car culture. Mostly set in what Cart calls "a *Saturday Evening Post* world of white faces and white picket fences surrounding small-town, middle-class lives" (20), these first young adult novels painted a romantic and idealized picture of adolescent life.

In 1951, almost ten years following the publication of the first young adult book, a novel was published that would affect and redirect the young adult literature published in its wake: J.D. Salinger's *The Catcher in the Rye*. Salinger's novel of adolescence was widely read by adults and teens alike and its protagonist Holden's cynical first-person narration became a model for young adult literature to come. The novel, which concludes by revealing that Holden is narrating his story from a psychiatric hospital, depicts and laments the loss of innocence that *The Catcher in the Rye* associates with adolescence. As it does so, it constructs a new and more realistic kind of adolescent protagonist that would become a prototype for future young adult novels.

Salinger's novel was a clear influence on S.E. Hinton's *The Outsiders* (1967), a novel many critics identify as the book that established a period of "new realism" in young adult literature. Written by Hinton when she was a teenager and told from the first-person perspective of Ponyboy, a fourteen-year-old "greaser" from the wrong side of the tracks, *The Outsiders* "blends romance with realism, focusing on the class divide between the 'greasers' and the 'socs'" (Kidd 170). Although the conflicts these characters face are realistic, Cart describes Hinton's greasers as "impossibly romanticized" and "romantically idealized" (48, 49). While the greaser heroes of Hinton's novel may be unbelievable "tuff" guys with hearts of gold, *The Outsiders* still offered a significant challenge to the young adult literature that came before it. By depicting adolescence in more complex terms and dramatizing the experiences of urban young people outside the middle-class, Hinton's novel confronted the romantic image of adolescence that early young adult novels worked to establish and maintain.

Published in 1974, Robert Cormier's *The Chocolate War* paints an even bleaker picture of adolescent life than the one Hinton imagined. The story of Jerry Renault, a student at an all-boys Catholic school, Cormier's novel depicts the unintended consequences of Jerry's refusal to sell chocolates as part of what is revealed as a corrupt school fundraiser. Critics called the *Chocolate War* "an important book" and "a disturbing book," pointing out the way the novel's lack of a happy ending "depresses many adult readers who are accustomed to thinking that adolescent novels will at least end happily" (Nilsen 80). Cormier's novel revolutionized young adult literature

by challenging this happy ending mandate, offering instead an intensely realistic conclusion that, more so than *The Outsiders* and even *The Catcher in the Rye*, broke from the literary conventions established by the young adult novels of the past.

Critics call the ten-year period following the publication of *The Outsiders* and *The Chocolate War* the "golden age" of young adult literature during which literature for adolescents came of age. Writing for *The English Journal*, Linda Bachelder and others argued that the young adult novels of the late 1960s and early 1970s were the first to "treat subjects of real depth," including "profound social and personal problems" (86) like teen drug and alcohol use and abuse, mental illness, and teen sex. During this time, a number of ambitious, demanding, and boundary-breaking young adult novels were published that are today considered classics of the genre. These classic novels include many of the works of Judy Blume, whose books for young adults (including *Then Again Maybe I Won't* [1971], *Deenie* [1973], and *Forever* [1975]) dealt frankly with puberty, masturbation, and sexual activity; and Lois Duncan, whose novels (including *I Know What You Did Last Summer* [1973] and *Daughters of Eve* [1979]) offered both thrills and social commentary. Meanwhile, African American authors Virginia Hamilton (*The Planet of Junior Brown* [1971]), Sharon Bell Mathis (*A Teacup Full of Roses* [1972]), and Alice Childress (*A Hero Ain't Nothin' But a Sandwich* [1973]) were blazing a trail for young adult authors of color with their realistic novels of Black American experience.

As Johnny, quoting the poet Robert Frost, says to Ponyboy in a pivotal scene in *The Outsiders*, "nothing gold can stay;" and the literary backlash following the twentieth century "golden age" of young adult literature is proof. After what Cart calls "a decade-long emergence of realism, with its relatively unsparing—and unrelenting—focus on life's darker aspects" (98), young adult publishing returned to its roots and romance novels reminiscent of the early junior novels reemerged in the 1980s. These romance novels were published as parts of branded collections like "Sweet Dreams" or "Wildfire," or as part of soap opera-like series, like "Sweet Valley High." The "new" teen romances returned their adolescent protagonists to the safety of the suburbs and reestablished romantic relationship as their primary concern. These books were criticized for "present[ing] a new, revised version of the 1950s romance stories" (Murray 198); however, in spite of—or perhaps even because of—adult disdain for the popular novels, young people purchased and read these books in unprecedented numbers. In fact, in 1985, a "super edition" of the "Sweet Valley High" series, called *Perfect Summer*, became the first young adult book to ever appear on the *New York Times* best sellers' list.

The young adult literature of the 1990s offered a response to the romance of the 1980s in the form of the popular teen horror thriller and the resurrection of young adult realism. Influenced by the thrillers popularized by Lois Duncan in the 1970s, authors R.L. Stine and Christopher Pike rebelled against the teen romance novels of the 1980s with their "Fear Street" series (Stine) and stand-alone novels (Pike) depicting adolescent life and high school as horrific rather than idyllic. These genre novels symbolically addressed what the realistic fiction published during the same period confronted directly: complex issues like physical and sexual abuse, mental illness, eating disorders, and substance abuse. Like the novels of realism associated with the young adult literary "golden age," the realistic novels of the 1990s featured endings that were "ambiguous at best" and offered "no happy conclusions" (Brown and DiMarzo 120).

While some adult critics worried that the realistic novels of the 1990s were too grim, this period in young adult literature also produced some ambitiously literary fare. The *New York Times* called these books "tales of raw misery for ages 12 and up" (Lewin); however, many of these "outstandingly dark" (Brown and DiMarzo 120) novels won national awards. These award-winning titles included the 1997 National Book Award nominee *The Facts Speak for Themselves*, by Brock Cole, a novel told from the perspective of an unreliable thirteen-year-old narrator who witnesses the murder of her adult lover by her mother's boyfriend, and National Book Award winner *Dancing on the Edge*, by Han Nolan, which captures the thoughts of a girl with mental illness who sets herself on fire. Other award-winning titles of the decade include Walter Dean Myers' *Monster* (1999), a National Book Award nominee, Coretta Scott King honor book, and winner of the Michael L. Printz award that depicts the trial of a teenage boy charged with murder.

Young adult literature published since the millennium reflects the influences of the genre's diverse past, as well as the successes of more recently published blockbuster series like J.K. Rowling's "Harry Potter," Stephanie Meyer's "Twilight," Suzanne Collins's "Hunger Games," and Veronica Roth's "Divergent." Popular authors of contemporary realistic fiction John Green and Rainbow Rowell owe a debt to S.E. Hinton for establishing the realistic tradition in young adult literature, while the "Caster Chronicles" series by Kami Garcia and Margaret Stohl reflects the influences of both the horror novels of the 1990s and the supernatural romance hybrid popularized by Stephanie Meyer.

While young adult literature has matured since its origination in 1942, it still has some growing up to do. Although contemporary young adult novels are only getting more innovative, the world of young adult literature has remained homogeneous in terms of its representation of people of color, people with disabilities, and people who identify as LGBTQ. The history of young adult literature features notable exceptions to this lack of diversity, including Nancy Garden's *Annie on My Mind*, a 1982 novel known as the "first GLBTQ love story with a positive ending" (Cart and Jenkins 76); the works of Walter Dean Myers, Jacqueline Woodson, and Sharon M. Draper, the only three African American writers to win the Margaret A. Edwards award honoring young adult authors' lifetime achievement; and Cynthia Voigt's 1986 novel *Izzy, Willy-Nilly*, which described the changes to a popular teenager's life following the amputation of her leg. While these books and authors are remarkable and influential, young adult novels reflecting diversity in meaningful ways still remain the exception, rather than the rule.

Today, more people—including adults—are reading young adult literature than ever before. While some critics, like Ruth Graham, writing for *Slate*, argue that young adult fiction "presents the teenage experience in a fundamentally uncritical way" and "indulge[s] in the kind of endings . . . adult readers ought to reject as far too simple," champions of young adult literature disagree. "Things made for teenagers are not inherently less worthy of our time, attention, and critical consideration, simply because they're for and about teens," Julie Beck writes in *The Atlantic*. Beck's words have strong implications when considered in terms of the parallel development and cultural conception of "the adolescent" and the body of literature described as "young adult." If the twenty-first century celebration of young adult literature signifies a new appreciation for stories once considered "too immature" for serious adult reading, perhaps this change of heart also represents a new appreciation for the real teenagers young adult literature represents.

Amy Pattee

Bibliography

Bachelder, Linda, Patricia Kelly, Donald Kenney, and Robert Small. "Young Adult Literature: Looking Backward: Trying to Find the Classic Young Adult Novel." *The English Journal* 69.6 (Sept. 1980): 86–89.

Beck, Julie. "The Adult Lessons of YA Fiction." *The Atlantic*. The Atlantic Monthly Group, 9 June 2014. Web. 28 February 2016.

Brown, Jennifer M. and Cindi DiMarzo. "Why So Grim?" *Publishers Weekly* 245.7 (16 February 1998): 120–124.

Burton, Dwight L. (1951). "The Novel for the Adolescent." *The English Journal,* 40.7 (1951): 363 – 369

Cart, Michael. *From Romance to Realism: 50 Years of Growth and Change in Young Adult Literature*. NY: Harper Collins, 1996.

Cart, Michael and Christine A. Jenkins. *The Heart Has Its Reasons: Young Adult Literature with Gay/Lesbian/Queer Content, 1969–2004*. Lanham, MD: Scarecrow Press, 2006. Print.

Graham, Ruth. "Against YA." *Slate*. The Slate Group, 5 June 2014. Web. 28 February 2016.

Kidd, Kenneth. *Freud in Oz: At the Intersections of Psychoanalysis and Children's Literature*. Minneapolis, MN: University of Minnesota Press, 2011.

Lewin, Tamar. "Tales of Raw Misery for Ages 12 and Up." *New York Times* 30 July 2000. ProQuest Historical Newspapers. Web. 27 February 2016.

Murray, Gail S. *American Children's Literature and the Construction of Childhood*. NY: Twayne, 1998.

Nilsen, Alleen Pace. "Books for Young Adults: Grandly Revolutionary? Or Simply Revolting?" *The English Journal* 64.6 (September 1975): 80–83.

Trites, Roberta Seelinger. *Disturbing the Universe: Power and Repression in Adolescent Literature*. Iowa City, IA: University of Iowa Press, 2000.

BIOGRAPHIES

Laurie Halse Anderson

Date of birth: October 23, 1961
Place of birth: Potsdam, New York

Principal Works

Young Adult Literature
Speak (1999)
Fever 1793 (2000)
Catalyst (2002)
Prom (2005)
Twisted (2007)
Seeds of America trilogy (2008–)
Wintergirls (2009)
The Impossible Knife of Memory (2014)
Children's Literature
Ndito Runs (1996)
Turkey Pox (1996)
No Time for Mother's Day (1999)
Vet Volunteers series (2000–2013)
The Big Cheese of Third Street (2002)
The Hair of Zoe Fleefenbacher Goes to School (2009)
Nonfiction
Thank You, Sarah! The Woman Who Saved Thanksgiving (2002)
Independent Dames (2008)

© Joyce Tenneson

Biography

Laurie Halse Anderson is an American writer known for her young adult novels, including *Speak* (1999), *Catalyst* (2002), *Wintergirls* (2009), and *The Impossible Knife of Memory* (2014). Her novels, which tend to discuss difficult and often taboo topics that are nonetheless of significant concern to many teens, have received critical acclaim as well as various awards. Anderson is also the author of a variety of children's books.

Born Laurie Beth Halse on October 23, 1961, in Potsdam, New York, Anderson was the first of two daughters born to Frank and Joyce Halse. Her father was a minister who served for a time as chaplain at Syracuse University. As a child, Anderson initially had some trouble with reading, but she soon became an avid reader and particularly enjoyed the fantasy works of J. R. R. Tolkien. A poetry lesson in elementary school taught her about the ability of words to convey emotion, a lesson that was key to her development as a writer.

Several of Anderson's experiences during her early life would have a significant influence on her later writing. Her novel *Speak*, which chronicles a teenager's trauma and recovery following a sexual assault, draws some emotional inspiration from Anderson's own assault at the age of thirteen. The novel *The Impossible Knife of Memory*, which focuses on a teenager's experience with her veteran father's post-traumatic stress disorder (PTSD), is similarly personal. During World War II, Anderson's father was drafted into the US Army and stationed in Germany, where he witnessed the horrors of the Dachau concentration camp. In later life he, much like the father in the novel, struggled with PTSD and alcohol abuse because of his wartime experiences.

Anderson attended Fayetteville-Manlius High School in upstate New York and spent her senior year studying abroad in Denmark. After completing high school, she attended Onondaga Community College for a time before transferring to Georgetown University in Washington, DC. She graduated from Georgetown in 1984 with a bachelor's degree in languages and linguistics. Following graduation she worked a variety of jobs and exercised her love of writing as a freelance journalist.

In 1996 Anderson published her first book, the children's picture book *Ndito Runs*, about a young Kenyan girl who runs to school each day. She continued to write books for children, including some nonfiction books about notable women in American history. In 1999 she published *Speak*, her first young adult novel. She followed *Speak* with a number of other novels, including the historical novel *Fever 1793* (2000), *Prom* (2005), and *Twisted* (2007).

Laurie Halse Anderson married computer programmer Greg Anderson while still in college. They had two daughters, Stephanie and Meredith, and eventually divorced. Anderson later married carpenter Scot Larrabee, a childhood friend who has two children from a previous relationship. Anderson and Larrabee live in Mexico, New York, where Anderson writes in a secluded cottage built by her husband.

Major Works

Many of Anderson's works deal with subject matter that, though considered controversial by some parents and conservative activist groups, nevertheless reflects realistic challenges faced by teens, including Anderson herself during her youth. *Speak*, which focuses on the aftermath of protagonist Melinda's rape, presents a powerful portrayal of trauma and the damaging effects of the silence that often surrounds the topic of sexual assault. The book has been used in many schools to start conversations about the importance of consent and to encourage students who may have had similar experiences to speak up without fear or shame. *The Impossible Knife of Memory* likewise calls attention not only to the challenges faced by many American veterans, but also to the ways in which their PTSD affects their loved ones. Anderson's other young adult novels also deal with difficult topics: *Catalyst* focuses on the pressure to be successful; *Wintergirls* deals with eating disorders; and *Twisted*, her first novel told from a male perspective, confronts the idea of twenty-first-century masculinity.

Historical themes are also prevalent in Anderson's novels. The novel *Fever 1793* follows a young woman who lives in Philadelphia during the 1793 yellow fever epidemic. In *Chains* (2008) and *Forge* (2010), the first two installments in Anderson's Seeds of America series, young slaves seek their freedom during the Revolutionary War. Anderson's devotion to historical settings and detailed research extends even to her children's books, several of which present the stories of historical women whose exploits are not widely known.

Joy Crelin

Further Reading

Anderson, Laurie Halse. "Laurie." *Laurie Halse Anderson*. Anderson, n. d. Web. 12 May 2015. <http://madwomanintheforest.com/laurie>.

Glenn, Wendy J. *Laurie Halse Anderson: Speaking in Tongues*. Lanham: Scarecrow, 2010. Print.

Lew, Kristi. *Laurie Halse Anderson*. New York: Rosen, 2014. Print.

Bibliography

Anderson, Laurie Halse. "Author Revealed." *Simon & Schuster*. Simon, n. d. Web. 12 May 2015. <http://authors.simonandschuster.com/Laurie-Halse-Anderson/1791921/revealed>.

Anderson, Laurie Halse. "Q & A with Laurie Halse Anderson." Interview by Sally Lodge. *Publishers Weekly*. PWxyz, 5 Dec. 2013. Web. 12 May 2015. <http://www.publishersweekly.com/pw/by-topic/authors/interviews/article/60266-q-a-with-laurie-halse-anderson.html>.

Anderson, Laurie Halse. "#Speak4RAINN: An Interview with Author Laurie Halse Anderson." Interview by Becca Rose. *HelloGiggles*. HelloGiggles, 18 Apr. 2013. Web. 12 May 2015. <http://hellogiggles.com/speak4rainn-an-interview-with-author-laurie-halse-anderson>.

"Biography: Laurie Halse Anderson." *Scholastic*. Scholastic, n. d. Web. 12 May 2015. <http://www.scholastic.com/teachers/contributor/laurie-halse-anderson>.

Mirabito, Roger. "Stories of Inspiration: Laurie Halse Anderson, '81." *Continuum*. Onondaga Community College, 30 Jan. 2015. Web. 12 May 2015. <http://news.sunyocc.edu/2015/01/30/laurie-halse-anderson-81>.

M. T. Anderson

Date of birth: November 4, 1968
Place of birth: Cambridge, Massachusetts

Principal Works
Young Adult Literature
Thirsty (1997)
Burger Wuss (1999)
Feed (2002)
The Game of Sunken Places (2004)
The Astonishing Life of Octavian Nothing, Traitor to the Nation, Volume I: The Pox Party (2006)
The Astonishing Life of Octavian Nothing, Traitor to the Nation, Volume II: The Kingdom on the Waves (2008)
The Suburb Beyond the Stars (2010)
The Empire of Gut and Bone (2011)
The Chamber in the Sky (2012)
Nonfiction
Symphony for the City of the Dead: Dmitri Shostakovich and the Siege of Leningrad (2015)

© Deborah Noyes 2007

Biography

M. T. Anderson is the author of the Octavian Nothing saga; the first book of the series, *The Astonishing Life of Octavian Nothing, Traitor to the Nation, Volume I: The Pox Party*, earned the 2006 National Book Award for young people's literature. Set before and during the American Revolution, the twin volumes tell the story of an African American teenager named Octavian. Before publishing the Octavian Nothing series, Anderson was best known for his science fiction novels and picture books. Inspired by his upbringing in historic Cambridge, Massachusetts, Anderson decided to focus on telling a tale about slavery, hypocrisy, and the ambiguous concept of liberty. Some reviewers have noted that Anderson's books seem more sophisticated than most young adult novels, but Anderson dismisses the compliment. "It's insulting to believe that teens should have a different kind of book than an adult should," he told Bob Thompson for the *Washington Post*. "They can tell when a book is simplifying life."

Matthew Tobin Anderson was born in Cambridge, Massachusetts, on November 4, 1968, and grew up in the rural town of Stow. For a few years when he was young, Anderson and his family lived in Italy while his father worked on a radar system at a US Army base. Anderson explored old monasteries and Roman ruins—"the sights I saw in those years changed me completely," Anderson wrote on his website. Anderson described his childhood to Thompson as happy but isolated. He began writing as a teenager and completed his first book when he was seventeen; fifteen years later, Anderson revised the story and published it as *The Game of Sunken Places* in 2004.

After high school, Anderson won a scholarship to spend a year at a boarding school in England where he studied Anglo-Saxon history and English poetry. He then enrolled at Harvard University, only to drop out and take a job at a retail store. He then enrolled at Cambridge University in England, graduating with a degree in English literature. Anderson returned to the United States and began working as an editorial assistant at Candlewick Press in Cambridge, Massachusetts, and as a classical music reviewer for the *Improper Bostonian*. In 1997, Candlewick published his first novel, *Thirsty*, about teenage vampires. At the age of twenty-six, he enrolled in the MFA creative writing program at Syracuse University in New York. He graduated in 1998 and began teaching at the MFA program for writing for children and young adults at Vermont College. In 1999, he published a satirical novel about love and fast food called *Burger Wuss*, but it was his next book, *Feed* (2002), that was his first major success. The science fiction novel is a sharp satire of consumer culture. In it, all humans have a "feed" (similar to a social media newsfeed) implanted in their brain. *Feed* won the Los Angeles Times Book Prize and was a finalist for the National Book Award.

Major Works

Anderson's novel *The Astonishing Life of Octavian Nothing, Traitor to the Nation, Volume I: The Pox Party* was published in 2006. Written in dense, eighteenth-century English, the book purports to be the actual journals of a boy named Octavian Nothing. (Anderson spent six years researching the writing style of the time to get the tone and cadence exactly right.) Octavian and his mother, an African princess, live a life fit for royalty in 1760s Boston. They share their home, the Novanglian College of Lucidity, with philosophers and scientists and dress in wigs and fine clothes. Octavian receives a first-rate education, but as a teenager, he discovers that he is a part of an elaborate experiment to test the intelligence capacity of the African race—and he and his mother are not actually royalty but instead are slaves. The book received the National Book Award in 2006.

The second book of the Octavian Nothing saga, *The Astonishing Life of Octavian Nothing, Traitor to the Nation, Volume II: The Kingdom on the Waves*, was published in 2008. In it, Octavian has run away from the college with plans of joining the British army. He accepts the call of Lord Dunmore, who offers emancipation to any slave who joins his Ethiopian Regiment to fight the colonists. Eventually, after many misadventures including a deadly bout of smallpox, Dunmore sells half of his army back into slavery. The American Library Association named *The Kingdom on the Waves* a 2009 Printz Honor Book.

Molly Hagan

Further Reading

Davidson, Jenny. "Slave to Science." Rev. of *The Astonishing Life of Octavian Nothing, Traitor to the Nation, Volume I: The Pox Party*, by M. T. Anderson. *Sunday Book Review*. New York Times, 12 Nov. 2006. Web. 7 May 2015. <http://www.nytimes.com/2006/11/12/books/review/Davidson.t.html?_r=0>.

Griswold, Jerry. "The War for Independence." Rev. of *The Astonishing Life of Octavian Nothing, Traitor to the Nation, Volume II: The Kingdom on the Waves*, by M. T. Anderson. *Sunday Book Review*. New York Times, 7 Nov. 2008. Web. 7 May 2015. <http://www.nytimes.com/2008/11/09/books/review/Griswold-t.html?pagewanted=all>.

Ragusea, Adam. "Visionaries: Author M. T. Anderson, Pioneer of Smart Young Adult Fiction." *WBUR*. Boston U, 1 May 2012. Web. 7 May 2015. <http://www.wbur.org/2012/05/01/m-t-anderson>.

Thompson, Bob. "Profile: M. T. Anderson Challenges Young Adults With Complex Narratives." *Washington Post*. Washington Post, 29 Nov. 2008. Web. 7 May. 2015. <http://www.washingtonpost.com/wp-dyn/content/article/2008/11/28/AR2008112802766.html>.

Bibliography

Anderson, M. T. "Him." *MT-Anderson*. M. T. Anderson, n.d. Web. 7 May 2015. <http://www.mt-anderson.com>.

Anderson, M. T. "Q & A with M. T. Anderson." Interview by John A. Sellers. *Publisher's Weekly*. PWxyz, 16 Oct. 2008. Web. 7 May 2015. <http://www.publishersweekly.com/pw/by-topic/authors/interviews/article/9085-q-a-with-m-t-anderson.html>.

Francesca Lia Block

Date of birth: December 3, 1962
Place of birth: Los Angeles, California

Principal Works
Young Adult Literature
Dangerous Angels series (1989–2012)
Ecstasia (1993)
The Hanged Man (1994)
Primavera (1994)
I Was a Teenage Fairy (1998)
Violet and Claire (1999)
Echo (2001)
Wasteland (2003)
Ruby (2006)
Psyche in a Dress (2006)
Blood Roses (2008)
The Waters and the Wild (2009)
Pretty Dead (2009)
The Frenzy (2010)
House of Dolls (2010)
The Elementals (2012)
Love in the Time of Global Warming (2013)
Teen Spirit (2014)
The Island of Excess Love (2014)

Maria Andreotti Photography, via Wikimedia Commons

Adult Literature
Quakeland (2008)
Beyond the Pale Motel (2014)
How to (Un)Cage a Girl (2008)
Short Stories
The Rose and the Beast: Fairy Tales Retold (2000)

Biography

Francesca Lia Block is a young adult writer best known for her Dangerous Angels series, which focuses on the lives of quirky Weetzie Bat and her friends in a magical version of Los Angeles, California. The author of more than twenty-five novels as well as many short stories and poems, Block often incorporates themes of magic, sexuality, and coming of age into her work. Her books have received numerous awards but have also been the focus of challenges by conservative activist groups that object to her frequent depictions of topics such as homosexuality, premarital sex, eating disorders, and drug use.

Block was born on December 3, 1962, in the Hollywood district of Los Angeles, the city that would become the magical, otherworldly setting of the majority of her later work. Her parents, Irving and Gilda Block, were both deeply involved in the arts; Irving was a writer and painter, and Gilda was a poet. Growing up in Los Angeles, Block began telling stories at an early age, and her parents read her myths and fairy tales that made a great impression on her. She composed poetry as a teenager, and in 1978 she published her first poetry collection, *Moon Harvest*.

After graduating from North Hollywood High School, Block attended the University of California, Berkeley, from which she earned her bachelor's degree in 1986. While at Berkeley, Block began writing what would become her first published novel, *Weetzie Bat*. In writing the book, which follows the adventures of the titular young woman and her friends in Los Angeles, Block drew on her own experiences growing up in Los Angeles as well as her love of mythology and folklore and her knowledge of magical realism in literature. *Weetzie Bat* was published in 1989 to significant critical acclaim, and over the following years, Block wrote a number of sequels focused on Weetzie and various members of her found family; the books collectively came to be known as the Dangerous Angels series. Although not initially intended for teenagers, the Dangerous Angels books came to be considered young adult literature and have been credited with sparking major changes in the genre. Block's later books, including *Violet and Claire* (1999),

Echo (2001), *The Waters and the Wild* (2009), and *Love in the Time of Global Warming* (2013), likewise proved popular with young adult audiences. In 2005 Block received the Margaret A. Edwards Award for lifetime achievement from the *School Library Journal*.

In 1998 Block married actor Chris Schuette; they later divorced. Block lives in Los Angeles with her two children, Jasmine and Samuel. In addition to writing her own novels and short stories, she teaches classes on writing and publishing at a variety of colleges and writing workshops.

Major Works

Although Block has written more than twenty-five novels over the course of her long career, she remains best known for the Dangerous Angels series, which consists of the books *Weetzie Bat* (1989), *Witch Baby* (1991), *Cherokee Bat and the Goat Guys* (1992), *Missing Angel Juan* (1993), *Baby Be-Bop* (1995), *Necklace of Kisses* (2005), and *Pink Smog* (2012). Set in an otherworldly version of Los Angeles, the books feature a variety of magical beings and focus on the protagonists' search for love, belonging, and family. Block's lyrical style and rendering of Los Angeles as a character in its own right further fuel the magical realism of the series, making the books unique examples of the young adult genre.

The novels in the Dangerous Angels series won significant praise from critics and proved popular with many young adult readers. However, they also met with negative responses from conservative activist groups dedicated to monitoring the content of books found in schools and public libraries. The Dangerous Angels books tackle topics often considered taboo in young adult literature, such as sexuality and drug use, as do many of Block's standalone works: *The Hanged Man* (1994), for instance, examines sexual abuse, while *Echo* deals with terminal illness and eating disorders. As Block's most popular works, however, the books in the Dangerous Angels series, particularly *Weetzie Bat* and the gay coming-of-age story *Baby Be-Bop*, have faced frequent challenges, bans, and even attempted burnings. Despite these controversies, Block remains committed to tackling difficult or controversial topics in her writing, noting in interviews that she is less interested in being deliberately controversial than she is in simply depicting the world and the people in it as they truly are.

Joy Crelin

Further Reading

Block, Francesca Lia. *Francesca Lia Block*. Author, 2015. Web. 31 Mar. 2015. <http://www.francescalia-block.com/>.

Block, Francesca Lia. "An Interview with Francesca Lia Block." Interview by Abigail Welhouse. *Toast*. Toast, 31 Dec. 2013. Web. 31 Mar. 2015. <http://the-toast.net/2013/12/31/interview-with-francesca-lia-block/>.

Smith, Dinitia. "Writing Frankly, Young adult Author Pushes Limits." *New York Times*. New York Times, 23 Feb. 2005. Web. 31 Mar. 2015. <http://www.ny-times.com/2005/02/23/books/23bloc.html>.

Bibliography

Block, Francesca Lia. "A Conversation with Francesca Lia Block." Interview by Alan Fox. *Rattle*. Rattle Foundation, 5 Mar. 2014. Web. 31 Mar. 2015. <http://www.rattle.com/poetry/a-conversation-with-francesca-lia-block/>.

Block, Francesca Lia. "Empathy, Love and the LGBT Characters in My Books." *Huffington Post*. TheHuffingtonPost.com, 23 Oct. 2013. Web. 31 Mar. 2015. <http://www.huffingtonpost.com/francesca-lia-block/francesca-lia-block_b_3804983.html>.

Block, Francesca Lia. "An Interview with *Weetzie Bat* Author Francesca Lia Block." Interview by Denise Hamilton. *Los Angeles Times*. Los Angeles Times, 15 Nov. 2008. Web. 31 Mar. 2015. <http://www.latimes.com/world/europe/la-et-francesca-lia-block15-2008nov15-story.html>.

Block, Francesca Lia. "The Rumpus Interview with Francesca Lia Block." Interview by Lauren Eggert-Crowe. *Rumpus*. Rumpus, 4 Aug. 2014. Web. 31 Mar. 2015. <http://therumpus.net/2014/08/the-rumpus-interview-with-francesca-lia-block/>.

Brodesser-Akner, Taffy. "Francesca Lia Block and Her Post-Apocalyptic Year." *Los Angeles Times*. Los Angeles Times, 22 Aug. 2013. Web. 31 Mar. 2015. <http://articles.latimes.com/2013/aug/22/entertainment/la-ca-jc-francesca-lia-block-20130825>.

Salzer, Maureen. "Francesca Lia Block." *Popular Contemporary Writers*. Ed. Michael D. Sharp. Vol. 2. Tarrytown: Marshall, 2006. 209–18. Print.

Judy Blume

Date of birth: February 12, 1938
Place of birth: Elizabeth, New Jersey

Principal Works
Children's Literature
The One in the Middle Is the Green Kangaroo (1969)
Iggie's House (1970)
Freckle Juice (1971)
The Fudge series (1972–2002)
The Pain and the Great One series (1974–2008)
Blubber (1974)
Starring Sally J. Freedman as Herself (1977)
Just as Long as We're Together (1987)
Young Adult Literature
Are You There God? It's Me, Margaret (1970)
Then Again, Maybe I Won't (1971)
It's Not the End of the World (1972)
Deenie (1973)
Forever (1975)
Tiger Eyes (1981)
Here's to You, Rachel Robinson (1993)
Adult Literature
Wifey (1978)
Smart Women (1983)
Summer Sisters (1998)
In the Unlikely Event (2015)

Carl Lender derivative work: Solid State Survivor, CC BY 2.0, via Wikimedia Commons

Biography

Judy Blume is the author of numerous popular novels for middle-grade and young adult readers as well as a variety of children's books and adult novels. She is best known for her novels in which young women come of age and face issues such as bullying, parental pressures, menstruation, sexuality, and religious confusion. Blume has never shied away from discussing potentially controversial subjects in her work, and as a result, her books have frequently been challenged by parents and conservative activist groups as well as banned from some schools and public libraries.

Judy Blume was born Judith Sussman in Elizabeth, New Jersey, on February 12, 1938. She was the second of two children born to Rudolph Sussman, a dentist, and Esther Rosenfeld Sussman, a homemaker. She had an older brother named David. As a child, Blume amused herself by making up stories but never committed them to paper. An avid reader, she particularly enjoyed the Betsy-Tacy series by Maud Hart Lovelace, which follows a Minnesota girl named Betsy as she matures from a child into an adult during the early twentieth century.

Blume attended schools in Elizabeth and Miami Beach, Florida, where most of the family lived for a time. After graduating from Battin High School, a single-sex school in Elizabeth, Blume enrolled in Boston University; however, she returned to New Jersey early in the semester after being diagnosed with mononucleosis. Following her recovery, Blume enrolled in New York University, from which she earned her bachelor's degree in education in 1961. While in college, Blume met and married John Blume. The couple had two children, Randy and Lawrence, before divorcing in 1975.

A storyteller from an early age, Blume began writing for publication in the mid-1960s, when her children were still young. She published her first book, the picture book *The One in the Middle Is the Green Kangaroo*, in 1969. Over the following decades, Blume published numerous books for young readers, including *Freckle Juice* (1971) and the Fudge series (1972–2002). She also penned several novels for adults, including *Wifey* (1978) and *Smart Women* (1983). Her most popular works, however, were her novels aimed at preteens and teenagers, which included *Are You There God? It's Me, Margaret* (1970), *Forever* (1975), and *Tiger Eyes* (1981). Although the category of young adult literature had not yet been fully established at the time, Blume's books proved to be classics of the genre and shaped the field for decades after their publication.

Blume married Thomas Kitchens, a physicist, in 1976; they divorced several years later. In 1979, Blume met George Cooper, a Columbia University law professor. They married in 1987. Blume and Cooper live primarily in Key West, Florida.

Major Works

Although Blume has written a number of children's picture books and chapter books as well as several novels for adult readers, she is best known as a writer of young adult novels, realistic coming-of-age stories that are true to the challenges and dilemmas teenagers regularly face. As a writer devoted to presenting life as it actually is, Blume frequently writes about difficult or potentially controversial subjects. Many of her books deal with the body or sexuality; *Are You There God? It's Me, Margaret* includes frank discussions of the onset of menstruation, while *Forever* presents a teenage couple's decision to have sex in a healthy and positive light. Other difficult topics featured in Blume's books include bullying (*Blubber*, 1974), racism (*Iggie's House*, 1970), the death of a parent (*Tiger Eyes*), and divorce (*It's Not the End of the World*, 1972). As one of the first notable American authors to write about such topics in books for teenagers, Blume played a significant role in the development of the young adult genre and has been cited as a particular inspiration by numerous later writers.

Although popular among both teenagers and adults, Blume's books, particularly *Forever*, have often been challenged or banned by individuals and organizations concerned about their content. As a result, Blume is regularly included in lists of the top ten most frequently challenged or banned authors. An opponent of literary censorship, Blume is a member of the board of directors of the National Coalition Against Censorship and has donated time and money to various organizations that oppose censorship and promote reading among children and young adults.

Joy Crelin

Further Reading

Blume, Judy. Interview. *Reading Rockets*. WETA Public Broadcasting, 2015. Web. 31 Mar. 2015. <http://www.readingrockets.org/books/interviews/blume/transcript>.

Blume, Judy. *Judy Blume on the Web*. Blume, 2015. Web. 31 Mar. 2015. <http://www.judyblume.com/home.php>.

Tracy, Kathleen. *Judy Blume: A Biography*. Westport: Greenwood, 2008. Print.

Bibliography

Blume, Judy. "Judy Blume: Often Banned, but Widely Beloved." Interview by Neal Conan. *Talk of the Nation*. NPR, 28 Nov. 2011. Web. 31 Mar. 2015. <http://www.npr.org/2011/11/28/142859819/judy-blume-banned-often-but-widely-beloved>.

Gottlieb, Amy. "Judy Blume." *Jewish Women's Archive*. Jewish Women's Archive, 2015. Web. 31 Mar. 2015. <http://jwa.org/encyclopedia/article/blume-judy>.

Karolides, Nicholas J., Lee Burress, and John M. Kean, eds. *Censored Books: Critical Viewpoints*. Lanham: Scarecrow, 2001. Print.

Richards, Linda. "Judy Blume: On Censorship, Enjoying Life, and Staying in the Spotlight for 25 Years." *January Magazine*. January Magazine, n.d. Web. 31 Mar. 2015. <http://januarymagazine.com/profiles/blume.html>.

Whitworth, Melissa. "Judy Blume's Lessons in Love." *Telegraph*. Telegraph Media Group, 3 Feb. 2008. Web. 31 Mar. 2015. <http://www.telegraph.co.uk/culture/books/3670951/Judy-Blumes-lessons-in-love.html>.

Coe Booth

Place of birth: New York, New York

Principal Works

Tyrell (2006)
Kendra (2008)
Bronxwood (2011)
Kinda Like Brothers (2014)

Biography

Coe Booth is an American young adult fiction and short story writer. She is best known for her first novel, *Tyrell* (2006), which won the Los Angeles Times Book Prize the same year it was published. Booth was born and raised in the Bronx. She attended public school and was involved in dancing, music, and sports as a child. Although she was involved with many different extracurricular activities from a young age, writing was always her passion. She started writing stories when she was in the second grade and continued to write while she was in school, although generally on her own time and only for her friends and family.

Booth graduated from college with a bachelor's degree in psychology in 1996 and went on to receive a master's degree in psychology in 1998. She worked in a crisis center helping teens and their families. She spent much of her time during this period working with teenagers who were involved with gangs, addicted to drugs, and victims of abuse and neglect. As emotionally difficult as the work sometimes was, Booth used her experience at the center as an inspiration for her writing. Soon after her work with the crisis center, she enrolled in a writing for children MFA program at the New School in New York City. She received her MFA in 2005 and published *Tyrell* the following year.

Booth still lives in the Bronx and works as a part-time writing teacher at the Vermont College of Fine Arts, teaching in the MFA program in Writing for Children and Young Adults.

Major Works

Since the publication of her first novel, *Tyrell*, Booth has become known for her realistic portrayal of African American young adults living in urban environments, usually New York City. *Tyrell* is narrated from the point of view of a fifteen-year-old boy living in Brooklyn who dreams of one day living with his girlfriend but finds himself frustrated in the face of major challenges before him. Tyrell is homeless, living with his mother and brother in a small motel room, and the events of the novel focus on his struggles to make money while also doing the right thing.

Reviewers have praised Booth for her rendering of Tyrell, an African American teen protagonist who tells his own story, in his own voice, in a way that rings true. While race is certainly present in the novel, it is not the primary focus of Booth's narrative. *Tyrell* shows the struggles of a lower-class, inner-city teen whose family is just barely holding together. While issues of broken families, divorce, jail, and even violence are common in young adult narratives, stories dealing with class issues are relatively rare in young adult literature.

Booth's second novel, *Kendra* (2008), follows a similar narrative structure to *Tyrell*. Narrated in the first person from the point of view of the title character, *Kendra* uses the same tone and style that impressed critics in *Tyrell*. Swearing and foul language appear frequently in Booth's novels; however, reviewers generally agree that this adds credibility to the characters rather than detracting from the literary value of her work or its appropriateness for younger audiences.

Kendra follows the life of a girl who lives in the Bronx with her grandmother and has a relationship with her irresponsible but emotionally supportive father while her mother, who has just received her PhD, wants little to do with her. *Kendra* is also similar to *Tyrell* in the way that the protagonists' romantic relationships take precedence over all other relationships. Kendra's relationship with her boyfriend is the most important thing in her life, but she soon finds out that family ties matter too as she works to reconnect with her mother again.

Bronxwood (2011) takes the issue of emotional survival and the need for personal relationships to an even further level. A sequel to *Tyrell*, the novel focuses on the importance of family relationships by showing Tyrell's struggle to reestablish his family bonds. At the start of *Bronxwood*, the family that barely held together in Booth's first book has disintegrated even further, and Tyrell finds himself trying to connect with his recently released father while his younger brother is in foster care because his mother has given up trying to raise children.

Although there is a certain isolation that Booth's characters face as they work to keep their personal relationships together, it is the importance that is placed on these relationships that adds authenticity to Booth's writing. While her characters might not face the same challenges that many young adult protagonists do, in the end, many of the same values are upheld. Booth simply emphasizes the importance of these relationships in different ways, which is why she has become a unique voice in young adult fiction. Her books have appeared on "best of" lists for the American Library Association, and *Tyrell* won the 2006 Los Angeles Times Book Prize for young adult fiction and was selected as one of New York Public Library's Books for the Teen Age in 2007.

Aaron Horton, MA

Further Reading

Blasingame, James, Jr. "What a Man Do: Coe Booth and the Genesis of *Tyrell*." *ALAN Review* 34.2 (2007): 28–33. Web. 31 Oct. 2015. <https://scholar.lib.vt.edu/ejournals/ALAN/v34n2/blasingame.pdf>.

Booth, Coe. "Honoring the Voices of Today's Youth: Interview with Coe Booth." *Voice of Youth Advocates* Aug. 2010: 204+. Print.

Booth, Coe. "Keeping It Real: An Interview with Coe Booth." Interview by Julie Prince. *Teacher Librarian* Apr. 2009: 62–63. *Academic Search Complete*. Web. 31 Oct. 2015. <http://search.ebscohost.com/login.aspx?direct=true&db=a9h&AN=37792488&site=ehost-live>.

Bibliography

Booth, Coe. "A Bronx Tale." Interview by Rick Margolis. *School Library Journal* Feb. 2007: 32. *Academic Search Complete*. Web. 31 Oct. 2015. <http://search.ebscohost.com/login.aspx?direct=true&db=a9h&AN=23962092&site=ehost-live>.

Booth, Coe. "Everything You Need to Know about Me (Well, Not Really!)." *Coe Booth*. Author, 2014. Web. 29 Sept. 2015. <http://coebooth.com/about/>.

Dobrez, Cindy. Rev. of *Kendra*, by Coe Booth. *Booklist* 1 Nov. 2008: 34. *Literary Reference Center*. Web. 19 Sept. 2015. <http://search.ebscohost.com/login.aspx?direct=true&db=lfh&AN=35119402&site=lrc-live>.

Rev. of *Kinda Like Brothers*, by Coe Booth. *Kirkus Reviews* 12 July 2014: 1. *Academic Search Complete*. Web. 31 Oct. 2015. <http://search.ebscohost.com/login.aspx?direct=true&db=a9h&AN=97045599&site=ehost-live>.

S., R. Rev. of *Kendra*, by Coe Booth. *Horn Book Magazine* Nov.–Dec. 2008: 696–97. *Literary Reference Center*. Web. 19 Oct. 2015. <http://search.ebscohost.com/login.aspx?direct=true&db=lfh&AN=34874866&site=lrc-live>.

Smith, Robin. Rev. of *Tyrell*, by Coe Booth. *Horn Book Magazine* Jan.–Feb. 2007: 62–63. *Literary Reference Center*. Web. 19 Oct. 2015. <http://search.ebscohost.com/login.aspx?direct=true&db=lfh&AN=23337108&site=lrc-live>.

Sutton, Roger. Rev. of *Bronxwood*, by Coe Booth. *Horn Book Magazine* Nov.–Dec. 2011: 93–94. *Literary Reference Center*. Web. 19 Oct. 2015. <http://search.ebscohost.com/login.aspx?direct=true&db=lfh&AN=67090976&site=lrc-live>.

Libba Bray

Date of birth: March 11, 1964
Place of birth: Montgomery, Alabama

Principal Works
Gemma Doyle trilogy (2003–7)
Going Bovine (2009)
Beauty Queens (2011)
The Diviners (2012)

Biography
Libba Bray is the *New York Times* best-selling young adult author of the Gemma Doyle trilogy, about a Victorian teenager with magical powers. In 2009, her surreal novel about a boy dying from mad cow disease, titled *Going Bovine*, won the Michael L. Printz Award for young adult literature. Bray's stories are united by her eccentric brand of humor and a beguiling strangeness rooted in her love of mystery and horror. In Bray's world, killer beauty queens, wizards, and Norse gods-turned-garden gnomes live in chaotic harmony.

Bray was born Martha Elizabeth Bray (Libba is short for Elizabeth) in Montgomery, Alabama, on March 11, 1964. Her family moved to West Virginia briefly before settling in Corpus Christi, Texas, when Bray was three years old. Her father was a Presbyterian minister who came out as a gay man when she was fourteen years old. Her mother, Nancy, was a high school English teacher who recalls that when Bray was a child, she wrote a family newspaper called the *Daily Blah*. When Bray was eleven, her family moved to Denton, Texas.

As an adolescent, Bray was obsessed with the Star Wars movies, New Wave punk, and *The Rocky Horror Picture Show*. Her favorite book was J. D. Salinger's *Catcher in the Rye* (1951). A popular student at Denton High School, she was a cheerleader and a community theater actress. Three weeks following graduation in 1982, Bray was involved in a serious car accident after dropping her father off at the airport. The impact caused devastating damage to her face, the loss of her left eye, and two broken legs. It took six years and thirteen surgeries for doctors to reconstruct her face. She notes on her website that writing saved her life during that period.

Bray attended the University of Texas at Austin, where she earned a bachelor's degree in drama in 1988. She began writing plays, including *High Hopes and Heavy Sweatshirts*, a debut collection of monologues from a group of women living in a small Texas town.

After graduation, Bray moved to New York City with only six hundred dollars and her grandmother's punch bowl. She worked in the publicity department at Penguin Putnam before moving to Spier, an advertising agency, where she wrote copy for exercise guru Richard Simmons. In 2001, Bray sent a pitch for a novel that would become *A Great and Terrible Beauty* (2003) to an editor she had met while writing for a book packager. Since its publication, she has focused solely on her own writing.

Bray met her husband, Barry Goldblatt, a literary agent, in the early 1990s. They have a son named Josh and live in Brooklyn. She is also part of a cover band called Tiger Beat, which consists of all young adult authors.

Major Works
While some young adult authors often pick a genre and stick to it throughout the majority of their fiction, especially if there is a successful trend captivating readers, Bray has been known for her ability to jump from one type of plot to another rather effortlessly. Though Bray employs a variety of settings and other literary devices to convey her different stories, they do typically share the universal young adult theme of the struggle for identity.

Bray's first young adult novel, *A Great and Terrible Beauty* (2003) was the first in a trilogy about a nineteenth-century teenager named Gemma Doyle. After her mother dies a mysterious death in British India, Gemma's father ships her off to a boarding school in England. But Gemma is plagued by visions, eventually discovering that she has occult powers and the ability to communicate with the spirit world. In addition to ghostly scares, Bray depicts the fright of living as a woman in repressive, Victorian society. The book became a *New York Times* best seller, along with the sequels *Rebel Angels* (2005), in which Gemma must contend with the evil forces she accidentally unleashed in *Terrible Beauty*, and *The Sweet Far Thing* (2007), which chronicles her struggles with responsibility, trust, and friendship as she tries to understand her role.

While Bray's next novel also included elements of the fantastic, it is darker and focuses on more of an existential quest, departing from her previous works. *Going Bovine* (2009) became Bray's most lauded novel, winning the Printz Award. With *Beauty Queens* (2011), she ventured even further from her earlier subject matter, writing a sarcastic satire of the worlds of reality television and obsessive beauty. Her 2012 book *The Diviners* is the first of a planned trilogy set in 1920s New York City. Amid the flappers and the dancing Ziegfeld girls, seventeen-year-old Evie O'Neill must help her uncle, the owner of a museum of the occult, find a vicious, supernatural serial killer. Paramount Pictures bought the film rights to *The Diviners*, with an anticipated premiere date of the adaptation in 2015. The second book of the trilogy, *Lair of Dreams*, is scheduled for release in August 2015.

Molly Hagan

Further Reading
Bray, Libba. "The Booklist Printz Interview: Libba Bray." Interview by Gillian Engberg. *Booklist* 1 Mar. 2010: 62. *Literary Reference Center*. Web. 7 Apr. 2015. <http://search.ebscohost.com/login.aspx?direct=true&db=lfh&AN=48639584&site=lrc-live>.

Corbett, Sue. "It Takes a Village to Finish a Trilogy." *Publishers Weekly* 12 Nov. 2007: 24. *Literary Reference Center*. Web. 7 Apr. 2015. <http://search.ebscohost.com/login.aspx?direct=true&db=lfh&AN=28026558&site=lrc-live>.

Rev. of *A Great and Terrible Beauty*, by Libba Bray. *Kirkus Reviews* 15 Nov. 2003: 1358. *Literary Reference Center*. Web. 7 Apr. 2015. <http://search.ebscohost.com/login.aspx?direct=true&db=lfh&AN=11476857&site=lrc-live>.

Bibliography
Bray, Libba. "About Libba." *Libba Bray*. Libba Bray, n.d. Web. 7 Apr. 2015. <http://libbabray.com/about-libba>.

Breeding, Lucinda. "Fantastic Voyages." *Denton Record Chronicle* [TX] 18 Apr. 2004: 4A+. PDF File. <http://inthenews.unt.edu/sites/default/files/PDF/2004/4/18/04_18_2004_DRC_FantasticVoyages.pdf>.

Corbett, Sue. "What's New in YA? Mashups." *Publishers Weekly* Oct. 2012: 24–31. *Literary Reference Center*. Web. 14 Apr. 2015. <http://search.ebscohost.com/login.aspx?direct=true&db=lfh&AN=82205886&site=lrc-live>.

Heppermann, Christine M. Rev. of *Beauty Queens*, by Libba Bray. *Horn Book Magazine* 87.4 (2011): 140–41. *Literary Reference Center*. Web. 14 Apr. 2015. <http://search.ebscohost.com/login.aspx?direct=true&db=lfh&AN=62033448&site=lrc-live>.

Yin, Maryann. "Libba Bray Reveals Title & Release Date for *The Diviners* Sequel." *GalleyCat*. AdWeek, 23 Mar. 2015. Web. 14 Apr. 2015. <http://www.adweek.com/galleycat/libba-bray-reveals-title-release-date-for-the-diviners-sequel/100887>.

White, Claire E. "A Conversation with Libba Bray." *Internet Writing Journal*. Writers Write, Feb. 2004. Web. 7 Apr. 2015. <http://www.writerswrite.com/journal/feb04/a-conversation-with-libba-bray-2042>.

Meg Cabot

Date of birth: February 1, 1967
Place of birth: Bloomington, Indiana

Principal Works
Children's Literature
Moving Day (2008)
From the Notebooks of a Middle School Princess (2015)

Thesupermat, CC BY-SA 3.0, via Wikimedia Commons

Adult Literature
Where Roses Grow Wild (as Patricia Cabot, 1998)
Portrait of My Heart (as Patricia Cabot, 1999)
An Improper Proposal (as Patricia Cabot, 1999)
A Little Scandal (as Patricia Cabot, 2000)
Lady of Skye (as Patricia Cabot, 2001)
Educating Caroline (as Patricia Cabot, 2001)

She Went All the Way (2002)

The Boy Next Door (2002)

Queen of Babble (2006)

Young Adult Literature

Shadowland (2000)

The Princess Diaries (2000)

Ninth Key (2001)

Reunion (2001)

Darkest Hour (2001)

When Lightning Strikes (2001)

Nicola and the Viscount (2002)

All American Girl (2002)

Victoria and the Rogue (2003)

Haunted (2003)

Teen Idol (2004)

Avalon High (2005)

Twilight (2005)

How to Be Popular (2006)

Pants on Fire (2007)

Jinx (2007)

Airhead (2008)

Being Nikki (2009)

Ransom My Heart (as Mia Thermopolis, 2009)

Abandon (2011)

Biography

Meg Cabot is a best-selling American writer of novels for young adult readers. The author of series such as 1-800-WHERE-R-U? series (also known as the Vanished series) and the Mediator series, she is best known for her Princess Diaries series, which proved incredibly popular among readers and inspired the films *The Princess Diaries* (2001) and *The Princess Diaries 2: Royal Engagement* (2004). In addition to her young adult novels, Cabot has also written several books for younger readers as well as numerous novels, primarily romances, for adults.

Meggin Patricia Cabot was born on February 1, 1967, in Bloomington, Indiana. Her father taught computer science at the local university, while her mother worked as an illustrator. As a child, she developed a deep love of writing, which her mother encouraged. She wrote her first short story at the age of seven and went on to write both original works and fan fiction based on characters and settings from the Star Wars films. Cabot was an avid reader and particularly enjoyed reading fantasy books by authors such as Lloyd Alexander and Susan Cooper.

Cabot attended Bloomington High School South and later enrolled in Indiana University in Bloomington,

where she studied studio arts. Although she preferred creative writing, she feared that majoring in the discipline would have a negative effect on her love of writing. Cabot earned her bachelor's degree from Indiana University in 1991.

After college, Cabot moved to New York City with the intention of finding work as an illustrator. However, she ultimately took a position as an assistant residence hall director at New York University (NYU). Cabot began to pursue writing seriously while working at NYU, and in 1998 she published her first book, the romance novel *Where Roses Grow Wild*, under the pseudonym Patricia Cabot. She went on to publish numerous romances under that name over the next several years.

Cabot published her first novel for young adults, *The Princess Diaries*, in 2000. The novel proved popular among teenage readers, and the Princess Diaries series eventually came to encompass more than fifteen novels and companion books. The first installment in the series intended for adult readers, *Royal Wedding*, was published in 2015. Although Cabot continued to write books for adult readers, the success of her young adult novels established her as a major writer in that field. In addition to the Princess Diaries series, she received significant critical and popular acclaim for works such as the Mediator series (2000–15) and the 1-800-WHERE-R-U? series (2001–6; later republished as the Vanished series). The first four books of both series were written under the pseudonym Jenny Carroll and later republished under Cabot's real name. Cabot has also authored several standalone young adult novels, such as *Teen Idol* (2004) and *Jinx* (2007).

Cabot married her husband, Benjamin Egnatz, in 1993. Cabot and Egnatz live in Key West, Florida.

Major Works

Although Cabot's young adult novels are similar in that they are intended for a teenage female audience and typically focus on protagonists in that demographic, her various series and standalone books encompass a diverse array of subgenres and themes. Perhaps her most famous novels, those in the Princess Diaries series, are written in journal format and thus belong to the trend of epistolary fiction in young adult literature that arose during the first decade of the twenty-first century. Those novels and others, such as *All American Girl* (2002) and its sequel *Ready or Not* (2005), are set in the real world and feature numerous references to American popular culture. Other novels, such as those in the 1-800-WHERE-R-U? series and the Abandon trilogy (2011–13), fall within the paranormal genre, while the Airhead trilogy (2008–10) incorporates science-fiction elements.

Romance often plays a significant role in her protagonists' lives, and a number of her novels also feature mysteries. As is the case in much young adult literature, Cabot's novels are frequently coming-of-age stories that chronicle the growth and maturation of her heroines, who often struggle to fit in within their families or at school. Cabot has noted that some of her protagonists' struggles are based in part on her own experiences, which lends an additional degree of emotional realism to her work.

Joy Crelin

Further Reading

Cabot, Meg. *Meg Cabot*. Cabot, 2015. Web. 9 June 2015. <http://www.megcabot.com>.

Cabot, Meg. "My Family Values." Interview by Kate Hilpern. *Guardian*. Guardian News and Media, 28 Nov. 2008. Web. 9 June 2015. <http://www.theguardian.com/lifeandstyle/2008/nov/29/my-family-values-meg-cabot>.

Cabot, Meg. "The New 'Princess Diaries' Book May or May Not Include Sex in the Throne Room." Interview by Eliza Thompson. *Cosmopolitan*. Hearst Communications, 13 May 2015. Web. 9 June. <http://www.cosmopolitan.com/entertainment/books/q-and-a/a40446/meg-cabot-royal-wedding-interview>.

Bibliography

Cabot, Meg. "Author Chat with Meg Cabot." Interview. *New York Public Library*. New York Public Library, 25 Aug. 2005. Web. 9 June 2015. <http://www.nypl.org/author-chat-meg-cabot>.

Cabot, Meg. "Children's Bookshelf Talks with Meg Cabot." Interview by Sue Corbett. *Publishers Weekly*. PWxyz, 17 Jan 2008. Web. 9 June 2015. <http://www.publishersweekly.com/pw/by-topic/authors/interviews/article/11164-children-s-bookshelf-talks-with-meg-cabot.html>.

Cabot, Meg. Interview. *Readers Read*. Writers Write, 2015. Web. 9 June 2015. <http://www.readersread.com/features/interview-with-meg-cabot-100120011>.

Cabot, Meg. Interview. *YARN*. Young Adult Review Network, 19 Apr. 2010. Web. 9 June 2015. <http://yareview.net/2010/04/interview-with-meg-cabot>.

Cabot, Meg. "Meg Cabot: Find Out What Meg Cabot Was Like at Seventeen." *Seventeen*. Hearst Communications, 25 Dec. 2007. Web. 31 May. 2015.

Corbett, Sue. "Meg Cabot in Margaritaville." *Publishers Weekly*. PWxyz, 14 July 2006. Web. 9 June 2015. <http://www.publishersweekly.com/pw/print/20060717/18387-meg-cabot-in-margaritaville.html>.

Lawler, Kelly. "Book Buzz: Meg Cabot Returns to 'Princess Diaries' World." *USA Today*. Gannett, 5 May 2014. Web. 9 June 2015. <http://www.usatoday.com/story/life/books/2014/05/05/meg-cabot-returns-to-the-world-of-the-princess-diaries/8722877>.

"Meg Cabot." *Teen Reads*. Book Report Inc., 2015. Web. 9 June 2015. <http://www.teenreads.com/authors/meg-cabot>.

Orson Scott Card

Date of birth: August 24, 1951
Place of birth: Richland, Washington

Principal Works

Ender's Game (1985)
Speaker for the Dead (1986)
Xenocide (1991)
Seventh Son (1987)
Red Prophet (1988)
Prentice Alvin (1989)
Alvin Journeyman (1995)
Heartfire (1998)
Ender's Shadow (1999)
Shadow of the Hegemon (2001)
Pathfinder (2010)

Biography

Orson Scott Card is the author of the popular science fiction novel *Ender's Game* (1985), which won both the 1985 Nebula Award and the 1986 Hugo Award for best science fiction novel. In addition, he won these same prestigious awards for *Speaker for the Dead* (1986), the first sequel to *Ender's Game*, in 1986 and 1987. He is the only author in history to win both awards in two consecutive years. Almost two decades later, he won the

Margaret A. Edwards Award for lifetime achievement in young adult literature. *Ender's Game* spawned several more books about Andrew "Ender" Wiggin and his world, and, in 2013, a major motion picture of the same name. However, the press surrounding the film made Card's long-held views about homosexuality public. Card's opinions are not new, nor were they exactly a secret—he had written a statement in 1990 in support of laws against sodomy. Regardless, when Card's opinions were pushed into the mainstream, they were met with a boycott of the film and a public debate about whether one could separate one's enjoyment of a piece of fiction from the views of the artist who made it.

Card was born on August 24, 1951, in Richland, Washington, but he grew up in Santa Clara, California. Card and his family are devout Mormons, descended from Brigham Young himself. He was an avid reader as a child and devoured history books. Card attended Brigham Young High School, graduating during his junior year with a Presidential Scholarship to Brigham Young University. While he enrolled as an archeology major, the love for theater that he had developed as a child pulled him into the drama department. During his senior year, he put his studies on hold to complete a two-year mission for the Mormon Church in Brazil. Upon his return, he finished his bachelor's degree in theater in 1975. After beginning to produce his plays with a small repertory company, he quickly realized that he could not financially sustain the company.

In 1977, Card published a short story titled "Ender's Game" in *Analog* magazine. It won him the John W. Campbell Award for best new writer. He then earned a master's degree in English from the University of Utah in 1981. Four years later, he adapted his short story into what became his first novel. After the success of *Ender's Game*, Card became one of the most celebrated and prolific writers in the science fiction genre. Over the years, he gained wider audiences, including more young adults, through the publication of books in series such as Tales of Alvin Maker and Pathfinder. In 2006, he founded an award-winning online magazine called the *Intergalactic Medicine Show*.

Card married Kristine Allen in 1977. Residing in Greensboro, North Carolina, they have had five children together.

Major Works

An influential part of the emerging trend of dystopian literature in the 1980s, *Ender's Game* tells the story of Andrew "Ender" Wiggin, an extraordinarily gifted six-year-old living in a future in which humans are at war with a bug-like race of creatures from another planet called "buggers." He is eventually chosen as a recruit for battle school and, for the first time in his life, manages to make a few friends. However, at every turn, Ender is forced to commit violence to save himself—and the guilt of his actions only makes him angrier. Eventually, he is fast-tracked to Command School, where he is trained by a famous commander who defeated the buggers in the first battle. Ender commands elaborate simulations against the buggers that grow increasingly impossible; in his last, he decides to commit a war crime in order to win. His teachers celebrate and explain to him that the simulations were not really simulations at all, and that by blowing up the buggers' planet in the "simulation," he has destroyed the entire bugger race.

Ender's Game is about empathy, genocide, tortured adolescence, child soldiers, and, in a very prescient way, drone warfare. Such complex topics have led Card's books to inspire legions of writers and readers. Card is known for using the elements of science fiction and fantasy to highlight the kinds of very real issues that young adults struggle with every day. Both the Tales of Alvin Maker and the Pathfinder series feature young protagonists who must confront morality and demonstrate responsibility. However, the story of *Ender's Game*, the most beloved and expanded story in Card's oeuvre, lost some of its moral value for many readers following the public announcement of the seemingly hypocritical view that its author holds regarding homosexuality. For some fans and critics, those beliefs clash with the book's themes of empathy and tolerance.

Molly Hagan

Further Reading

Decker, Kevin, ed. Ender's Game *and Philosophy: The Logic Gate Is Down*. Malden: Wiley, 2013. Print.

Edidin, Rachel. "Orson Scott Card: Mentor, Friend, Bigot." *Wired*. Condé Nast, 31 Oct. 2013. Web. 2 June 2015. <http://www.wired.com/2013/10/enders-game/>.

Silman, Anna. "A Primer on Orson Scott Card and the *Ender's Game* Controversy." *Vulture*. New York Media, 31 Oct. 2013. Web. 2 June 2015. <http://www.vulture.com/2013/10/primer-orson-scott-card-enders-game-controversy.html>.

Bibliography

Shippey, Tom. "Orson Scott Card's Three-Decade Run." *Wall Street Journal*. Dow Jones, 22 Jan. 2011. Web. 2 June 2015. <http://www.wsj.com/articles/SB100014 24052748703954004576089884087115742>.

Snow, Shane. "Orson Scott Card Talks Ender's Game in Rare Interview." *Wired*. Condé Nast, 31 Oct. 2013. Web. 2 June 2015. <http://www.wired.com/2013/10/cardqa/>.

Tyson, Edith S. *Orson Scott Card: Writer of the Terrible Choice*. Lanham: Scarecrow, 2003. Print.

"Who is Orson Scott Card?" *Hatrack River*. Hatrack River Enterprises, n.d. Web. 2 June 2015. <http://www.hatrack.com/osc/about.shtml>.

Aidan Chambers

Date of birth: December 27, 1934
Place of birth: Chester-le-Street, England

Principal Works
Young Adult Literature
Breaktime (1978)
Dance on My Grave: A Life and Death in Four Parts (1982)
Now I Know (1987)
The Toll Bridge (1992)
Postcards from No Man's Land (1999)
This Is All: The Pillow Book of Cordelia Kenn (2005)
Dying to Know You (2012)
Short Stories
The Kissing Game (2011)

Biography

Aidan Chambers is an award-winning young adult author and playwright. He has also written books for children. His best-known work is the six-book young adult series Dance Sequence. The series includes the novels *Dance on My Grave* and *Postcards from No Man's Land*, which won the prestigious Carnegie Medal in 2000. A former monk and schoolteacher, Chambers has an unusual life history that has informed various aspects of his work. Though he writes about young adults, Chambers does not shy away from adult themes such as sex and grief. His understanding of the teenage psyche has grown more complex over his forty-plus years of writing, and his novel *Dying to*

Know You explores the similarities between youth and old age.

Aidan Chambers was born on December 27, 1934, in Chester-le-Street, County Durham, England. His father was a woodworker and his mother was a homemaker. When he was ten, his family moved to another town, leaving behind his only childhood friend, Marion. Chambers believes that the trauma of this youthful separation has informed the themes of his novels.

Chambers did poorly in school and struggled to learn to read until he was nine years old. His family moved again, this time to Darlington, where Chambers befriended an enthusiastic reader named Alan. The boys took books out of the public library every week, but Chambers preferred to go to the cinema and a weekly variety show. At age thirteen, he was transferred to Queen Elizabeth I Grammar School, where he met an English teacher named Jim Osborn who changed his life. Osborn introduced him to Shakespeare, theater, and great literature. At fifteen, Chambers read D. H. Lawrence's *Sons and Lovers* (1913) and decided to become a writer himself.

When he was seventeen, Chambers began his two years of compulsory service in the Royal Navy. He served as a clerk in the Supply and Secretariat division in Portsmouth. After that, he enrolled at a teaching college through London University and wrote his first play. In 1957, he was hired as an English teacher and head of drama at the Westcliff High School for Boys in the holiday destination Southend-on-Sea. Chambers enjoyed his post and sailed his own dinghy. One day, he capsized and almost drowned, a harrowing scene that he later included in his novel *Dancing on My Grave*.

In the early 1960s, Chambers, previously a nonbeliever, converted to Christianity, moved to a monastic order in Stroud, Gloucestershire, and became a monk. He would later mine this experience in his novel *Now I Know*. As Brother Aidan, he took a teaching job and began to write, publishing his first books and plays. In 1967 Chambers realized that he was still a nonbeliever at heart. He quit his teaching job in 1968 and began working as a freelance writer.

Chambers married an American magazine editor named Nancy Lockwood in 1968. Together, the couple founded a publishing company called Thimble Press and a magazine about young adult literature called *SIGNAL* in 1969. They were jointly awarded the 1982 Eleanor Farjeon Award for outstanding services to children's books. In 2002, Chambers became the first

Briton to receive the international Hans Christian Andersen Award for his contributions to literature for children and young adults. He lives in Gloucestershire, England.

Major Works

In 1975 Chambers began writing *Breaktime*, the first novel of what would become his Dance Sequence series. The novel, published in 1978, is about a young boy's holiday and explores the convergence of fact and fiction. In 1982 he published what is perhaps his most famous novel: *Dance on My Grave*, a coming-of-age love story between two boys in Southend. While writing *Dance on My Grave*, Chambers decided that the Dance Sequence series would include six books. The stories are related "like members of a family," Chambers wrote on his personal website. Each explores a particular aspect of adolescence. His third book, *Now I Know* (1987), explores religious belief and rational thought. *The Toll Bridge* (1992), which won the Dutch Silver Pencil Award in 1993, explores the deep intimacy of platonic friendship.

In 1999, Chambers published his other famous novel, *Postcards from No Man's Land*. The novel features two interwoven stories, set fifty years apart. The first story is about the love between a young Dutch woman and a wounded English soldier. The second story is narrated by the soldier's grandson, who is visiting Amsterdam for the commemoration of the Battle of Arnhem. *Postcards from No Man's Land* won several honors, including the prestigious Carnegie Medal (1999), the Printz Award (2003), and the Italian Andersen Prize for best youth novel of the year (2000).

The final book in Chambers's Dance Sequence is called *This Is All: The Pillow Book of Cordelia Kenn* (2005). The novel is experimental; Cordelia, nineteen and pregnant, compiles fragments of her life according to an ancient Japanese form. She hopes to gift her pillow book to her unborn daughter when she turns sixteen. In 2011, Chambers published a book of short stories for teens called *The Kissing Game,* and in 2012, he published a young adult novel called *Dying to Know You*, about the friendship between an eighteen-year-old boy and seventy-five-year-old author whose wife has just died. The book explores both youth and old age, a rarity for young adult novels.

In addition to his books for young adults, Chambers has written two children's novels: *Seal Secret*

(1980), which won the Dutch Silver Pencil Award in 1985, and *The Present Takers* (1983), which won the same award in 1986. He has also written a number of plays, including the award-winning *De Tolbrug*, a Dutch-language adaptation of his novel *The Toll Bridge*.

Molly Hagan

Further Reading

Brace, Alison. "Shock Tactics." *Guardian*. Guardian News and Media, 10 July 2000. Web. 15 Feb. 2015. <http://www.theguardian.com/education/2000/jul/11/schools.booksforchildrenandteenagers>.

Gill, S. David. "Aidan Chambers: Monk, Writer, Critic." *ALAN Review* 25.1 (1997): n. pag. Web. 15 Feb. 2015. <http://scholar.lib.vt.edu/ejournals/ALAN/fall97/gill.html>.

Meek, Margaret, and Victor Watson. *Coming of Age in Children's Literature.* New York: Continuum, 2003. Print.

Bibliography

"Aidan Chambers." *British Council: Literature*. British Council, 2011. Web. 18 Feb. 2015. <http://literature.britishcouncil.org/aidan-chambers>.

"Biography." *Aidan Chambers*. Aidan Chambers, 2011. Web. 18 Feb. 2015. <http://www.aidanchambers.co.uk/bio.htm>.

Chambers, Aidan. "Reading: 'The Heart of English'; An Interview with Aidan Chambers." Interview by Anne Fairhall. *English Drama Media* Feb. 2011: 35–42. *Literary Reference Center*. Web. 27 Feb. 2015. <http://search.ebscohost.com/login.aspx?direct=true&db=lkh&AN=60126180&site=lrc-plus>.

Rev. of *Dying to Know You*, by Aidan Chambers. *Horn Book Magazine* May–June 2012: 78–79. *Literary Reference Center*. Web. 18 Feb. 2015. <http://search.ebscohost.com/login.aspx?direct=true&db=lfh&AN=74608491&site=lrc-live>.

Greenway, Betty. *Aidan Chambers: Master Literary Choreographer*. Lanham: Scarecrow, 2006. Print.

Rev. of *The Kissing Game*, by Aidan Chambers. *Kirkus* 15 Feb. 2011: 304. *Literary Reference Center*. Web. 15 Feb. 2015. <http://search.ebscohost.com/login.aspx?direct=true&db=lfh&AN=59517086&site=lrc-live>.

Ness, Patrick. Rev. of *Dying to Know You*, by Aidan Chambers. *Guardian*. Guardian News and Media, 15

Jun. 2012. Web. 15 Feb. 2015. <http://www.theguardian.com/books/2012/jun/15/dying-to-know-you-aidan-chambers-review>.

Stephen Chbosky

Date of birth: January 25, 1970
Place of birth: Pittsburgh, Pennsylvania

Principal Works
Young Adult Literature
The Perks of Being a Wallflower (1999)
Screenplays
The Four Corners of Nothing (1995)
Rent (2005)
Jericho (2006–8)
The Perks of Being a Wallflower (2012)

Biography
Stephen Chbosky is a screenwriter and the author of the classic young adult novel *The Perks of Being a Wallflower* (1999). He wrote and directed a film version of the book, which was released in 2012 and stars Logan Lerman, Emma Watson, and Ezra Miller. Told through a series of letters addressed to an unknown pen pal, the book is about an awkward high school freshman named Charlie.

Chbosky was born on January 25, 1970, and grew up in Upper St. Clair, a suburb outside of Pittsburgh, Pennsylvania. As a teenager, Chbosky's list of favorite books included J. D. Salinger's *The Catcher in the Rye* (1951), F. Scott Fitzgerald's *The Great Gatsby* (1925), J. R. R. Tolkien's *The Hobbit* (1937), Harper Lee's *To Kill a Mockingbird* (1960), and Stephen King's *The Shining* (1977), but he also enjoyed Arthur Miller's play *Death of a Salesman* (1949) and William Shakespeare's classic play *Hamlet* (ca. 1600).

When he was a seventeen-year-old senior at Upper St. Clair High School, Chbosky met his mentor, screenwriter Stewart Stern, who wrote the classic James Dean film *Rebel Without a Cause* (1955). Chbosky was visiting the University of Southern California (USC) in Los Angeles, trying to decide whether he wanted to go to the USC School of Cinematic Arts, when he heard Stern give a seminar. He was so enthralled by Stern that after the seminar was over, he decided to attend to USC. Shortly after that, Stern (who died in 2015) suffered a heart attack. Chbosky penned an anonymous letter to Stern, explaining the impact Stern had on his life. Chbosky also sent him a mix tape. Stern tracked him down a year and a half later and, many years after that, was the first person to read Chbosky's screenplay adaptation of *The Perks of Being a Wallflower*. Chbosky based the character Bill, the English teacher who takes Charlie under his wing, on Stern, and his initial interaction with Stern inspired him to have Charlie tell his story through anonymous letters.

Chbosky graduated from USC in 1992. He later said in interviews that he drew on experiences from college to write *The Perks of Being a Wallflower*. "It's not like 'coming of age' stops after you graduate high school," he told Jacqueline Mansky for the USC *Daily Trojan*. A few years after graduating from USC, Chbosky wrote and directed an independent comedy called *The Four Corners of Nothing* (1995), which premiered at the Sundance Film Festival. After writing and publishing the novel *The Perks of Being a Wallflower* in 1999, Chbosky returned to film and television, penning the screenplay for the film adaptation of the Broadway musical *Rent* in 2005. In 2006, he co-produced and wrote for the CBS television series *Jericho*. The postapocalyptic drama starring Skeet Ulrich won a fervent but small viewership. CBS cancelled the show after the first season, but fans petitioned the network to bring it back, which they did for seven episodes before the show was cancelled again in 2008. Chbosky lives in Los Angeles with his wife, Liz, and daughter.

Major Works
Charlie, the main character in Chbosky's *The Perks of Being a Wallflower* (1999), is still reeling over the suicide of his best friend as he begins his high school career. He is also extremely socially awkward—the only student who takes any notice of him during his first week of school is a senior bully. Soon, however, he meets two other misfits named Patrick and Sam (short for Samantha), two senior step-siblings who take Charlie under their wing. Charlie is an unlikely addition to their clique of vampire-lovers and music nerds, but he quickly settles in. He learns about masturbating and smoking pot; he learns how to kiss, date, and break-up; and he learns how to stand in the bed of a pickup truck while it is speeding through a tunnel (one of the book's

most iconic scenes). At its heart, *The Perks of Being a Wallflower* is about finding real love and happiness, and why good people allow themselves to be treated poorly. It became one of the most popular young adult novels of the 1990s and early 2000s. In 2012, Chbosky wrote and directed the film adaptation of the novel. He shot it on location in Pittsburgh. The movie was well received by audiences and critics.

Molly Hagan

Further Reading

Chbosky, Stephen. "Interview with Stephen Chbosky, Author of *The Perks of Being a Wallflower*." Interview by Ann Beisch. *LA Youth*. L.A. Youth, Nov. 2001. Web. 5 June 2015. <http://web.archive.org/web/20110215225037/http://www.layouth.com/interview-with-stephen-chbosky-author-of-the-perks-of-being-a-wallflower/>.

Chbosky, Stephen. "'Wallflower' Film Puts Adolescence on Screen." Interview by Linda Wertheimer. *Weekend Edition*. NPR, 23 Sept. 2012. Web. 5 June 2015. <http://www.npr.org/2012/09/23/161638564/wallflower-film-puts-adolescence-on-screen>.

Vancheri, Barbara. "The Perks of Being Stephen Chbosky: Upper St. Clair Native Talks about His Novel and New Film." *Pittsburgh Post-Gazette*. PG, 26 Sept. 2012. Web. 5 June 2015. <http://www.post-gazette.com/ae/movies/2012/09/26/The-perks-of-being-Stephen-Chbosky-Upper-St-Clair-native-talks-about-his-novel-and-new-film/stories/201209260184>.

Bibliography

Ebert, Roger. Rev. of *The Perks of Being a Wallflower*, dir. by Stephen Chbosky. *RogerEbert.com*. Ebert Digital, 26 Sept. 2012. Web. 5 June 2015. <http://www.rogerebert.com/reviews/the-perks-of-being-a-wallflower-2012>.

Isenberg, Robert. "The Perks of Being a Pittsburgher." *Pittsburgh Magazine*. Wiesner Media, 3 Oct. 2012. Web. 5 June 2015. <http://www.pittsburghmagazine.com/Pittsburgh-Magazine/October-2012/The-Perks-of-Being-a-Pittsburgher/>.

Mansky, Jacqueline. "Perk Creator Credits Versatility to USC." *Daily Trojan*. U of Southern California, 2 Oct. 2012. Web. 5 June 2015. <http://dailytrojan.com/2012/10/02/perks-creator-credits-versatility-to-usc/>.

"Screenwriter and Novelist Stephen Chbosky: Rebel with a Cause." *Script Magazine*. FW, 21 Sept. 2012. Web. 5 June 2015. <http://www.scriptmag.com/features/writer-profiles/screenwriter-noveliststephen-chbosky-rebel-with-a-cause-2>.

Cassandra Clare

Born: July 27, 1973
Place of birth: Tehran, Iran

Principal Works

The Mortal Instruments series (2007–14)
The Infernal Devices series (2010–13)
The Shadowhunter's Codex (2013; with Joshua Lewis)
The Bane Chronicles (2014; with Sarah Rees Brennan and Maureen Johnson)
The Magisterium series (2014–; with Holly Black)

Biography

Cassandra Clare is a writer of young adult urban fantasy novels, most notably the Mortal Instruments series and the Infernal Devices series. Her best-selling novels have been nominated for various awards, and in 2013 the first Mortal Instruments book was adapted into a film, *The Mortal Instruments: City of Bones*.

Clare was born Judith Rumelt on July 27, 1973, in Tehran, Iran. Her father, Richard, is a professor of business strategy at the University of California, Los Angeles's Anderson School of Management, and her mother, Elizabeth, is a social worker. Clare's parents divorced when she was a teenager and later remarried other people, and she has noted in interviews that a stepfather-like character in her Mortal Instruments series is based in part on her own stepfather.

The family moved frequently during Clare's childhood, and she ultimately spent time in Iran, England, France, and various other countries. When Clare was a teenager, the family settled in California, and she attended high school in Los Angeles. Clare studied creative writing and wrote extensively in high school, but dissatisfying college fiction-writing courses led her to pursue a career in journalism instead. After graduating from college, Clare wrote for entertainment publications such as the *Hollywood Reporter*. In 2001, she moved to New York City, which would become the setting and inspiration for many of her later novels.

Clare initially gained popular attention as a writer of fan fiction, stories based on characters or settings from existing works. She was particularly well known for her novel-length works based on the Harry Potter series as well as her parodies of characters from *The Lord of the Rings*, which she posted online under the name Cassandra Claire. Although Clare remained open about her fan writing after being professionally published, she nevertheless opted to delete her fan fiction from Internet archives prior to the publication of her first novel, *City of Bones*. She also changed the spelling of her pseudonym from Claire to Clare, retaining her name recognition while somewhat distancing herself from her earlier work.

In 2004, Clare began work on *City of Bones*, the first installment in the Mortal Instruments series. The novel was ultimately published in 2007. Clare followed the book with five more installments in the Mortal Instruments series, as well as a prequel series and various companion books. In 2014 she published *The Iron Trial*, the first installment in the Magisterium series, a new series cowritten with novelist Holly Black.

Clare married Joshua Lewis in 2010. The two live in Amherst, Massachusetts. Clare and Lewis cowrote *The Shadowhunter's Codex*, a companion book to the Mortal Instruments series, published in 2013.

Major Works

During the first decade of the twenty-first century, urban fantasy and paranormal romance became prevalent genres in young adult fiction, spurred on in large part by the commercial success of Stephenie Meyer's Twilight series. The publication of Clare's novels may be considered part of this trend, with their focus on teenage heroes who battle supernatural foes and find romance in magic-infused versions of real-world urban environments. Additionally, these fantastical elements serve effectively as a vehicle to explore common young adult themes, such as friendship, love, and self-identity. The Mortal Instruments series, which began with the 2007 publication of *City of Bones* and concluded with *City of Heavenly Fire* in 2014, follows the adventures of teenager Clary Fray and her friends, many of whom are members of a secret organization of demon slayers known as Shadowhunters. The Infernal Devices series (2010–13), a prequel set in Victorian England, builds on Clare's urban fantasy world and its overarching mythology.

As a writer who first gained popularity in the intensely collaborative world of fan fiction, in which writers often build upon the work of professionally published authors and frequently receive extensive reader feedback on their in-progress works, it seems fitting that Clare's writing process often includes contributions by her fellow young adult writers. Clare has credited the members of her writing group as essential contributors to her success, often thanking them in the acknowledgements sections of her novels. In addition to receiving feedback, Clare has also collaborated extensively with other writers; her book *The Bane Chronicles* (2014), a companion to the Mortal Instruments series, collects short stories written not only by Clare but also by popular young adult writers Sarah Rees Brennan and Maureen Johnson. Clare has also cowritten a book with her husband, Joshua Lewis, and in 2014 she published the first book in the Magisterium series, cowritten with young adult author and longtime friend Holly Black. Through such collaborations, Clare has expanded the scope of her urban fantasy world while remaining close to her writing roots.

Joy Crelin

Further Reading

Alter, Alexandra. "The New Queen of Fantasy: Cassandra Clare's Breakout." *Wall Street Journal*. Dow Jones, 15 June 2012. Web. 4 Mar. 2015. <http://www.wsj.com/articles/SB10001424052702303734204577464593388416630>.

Springen, Karen. "Cassandra Clare Talks 'Mortal Instruments,' Movie Releases, and More." *Publishers Weekly*. PWxyz, 2 Aug. 2013. Web. 4 Mar. 2015. <http://www.publishersweekly.com/pw/by-topic/childrens/childrens-authors/article/58553-city-of-bestsellers.html>.

Bibliography

Clare, Cassandra. "Q&A: Cassandra Clare." Interview by Angelina Benedetti. *Library Journal* 1 June 2013: 66. Print. <http://search.ebscohost.com/login.aspx?direct=true&db=lfh&AN=87800459&site=lrc-live>.

Gresh, Lois H. *The Mortal Instruments Companion: City of Bones, Shadowhunters, and the Sight*. New York: St. Martin's, 2013. Print.

Kaplan, David A. "A Most Unusual Father-Daughter Professional Pairing." *Fortune*. Time, 29 Aug. 2012. Web. 4 Mar. 2015. <http://fortune.com/2012/08/29/a-most-unusual-father-daughter-professional-pairing>.

Spencer, Liv. *Navigating the Shadow World: The Unofficial Guide to Cassandra Clare's The Mortal Instruments*. Toronto: ECW, 2013. Print.

Suzanne Collins

Date of birth: August 10, 1962
Place of birth: Hartford, Connecticut

Principal Works

Children's Literature
Gregor the Overlander (2003)
Gregor and the Prophecy of Bane (2004)
Gregor and the Curse of the Warmbloods (2005)
Gregor and the Marks of Secret (2006)
Gregor and the Code of Claw (2007)
Fire Proof (1999)
When Charlie McButton Lost Power (2005)
Year of the Jungle (2013)

Young Adult Literature
The Hunger Games (2008)
Catching Fire (2009)
Mockingjay (2010)

David Shankbone, via Wikimedia Commons

Biography

Suzanne Collins is the author of the popular Hunger Games trilogy, which began in 2008 with the publication of *The Hunger Games* and concluded with the publication of *Mockingjay* in 2010. The novels were adapted into films between 2012 and 2015. In addition to the Hunger Games novels, Collins has written a series of middle-grade novels known as the Underland Chronicles (2003–7) and several books for younger readers.

Suzanne Marie Collins was born on August 10, 1962, in Hartford, Connecticut. She was the youngest of four children born to Jane and Michael Collins. Her father was an officer in the United States Air Force, and as a result, Collins and her family moved frequently. The family settled in Indiana in the late 1960s, but her father was soon sent to serve in the Vietnam War. After his return, the family moved several times, living in various states on the East Coast and later in Belgium.

Collins began high school in Belgium and later attended the Alabama School of Fine Arts, graduating in 1980. After high school, she enrolled in Indiana University, where she double-majored in telecommunications and theater and drama. She completed her bachelor's degree in 1985 and two years later moved to New York City to pursue graduate studies in dramatic writing at New York University. She earned her master's degree in 1989. Collins later found work as a television writer, writing for series such as *Clarissa Explains It All* (1991–94) and *Generation O!* (2000–1). Although she largely stopped working as a television writer after beginning her career as a novelist, she wrote a number of episodes of the educational children's series *Wow! Wow! Wubbzy!* (2006–10) in 2008 and 2009.

In 1999 Collins published her first book, *Fire Proof*, a tie-in to the Nickelodeon series *The Mystery Files of Shelby Woo* (1996–98), for which she wrote several episodes between 1997 and 1998. Her first book based on an original concept, *Gregor the Overlander*, was published in 2003. The novel is a work of fantasy about a preteen boy who discovers an underground realm populated by strange humans and sentient animals. *Gregor the Overlander* ultimately became the first installment in the five-part Underland Chronicles series, which concluded in 2007 with the publication of *Gregor and the Code of Claw*.

Collins published her first young adult book, *The Hunger Games*, in 2008. The dystopian novel follows teenager Katniss as she fights for her life in a brutal death match organized by her country's corrupt government. *The Hunger Games* proved incredibly popular among readers, and Collins followed the novel with two sequels, *Catching Fire* (2009) and *Mockingjay* (2010). The series was soon adapted for the screen, with the film version of *The Hunger Games* premiering in 2012. Drawing from her experience as a television writer, Collins cowrote the screenplay for that first film. *The Hunger Games: Catching Fire* was released in 2013, while the final installment, *The Hunger Games: Mockingjay*, was split into two parts and released in 2014 and 2015.

In addition to the Underland Chronicles and the Hunger Games trilogy, Collins is the author of the children's books *When Charlie McButton Lost Power* (2005) and *Year of the Jungle* (2013). The latter, an autobiographical work, is based on her experiences while her father was deployed in Vietnam.

Collins and her husband, Cap Pryor, have two children. They live in Connecticut.

Major Works

Collins was an avid reader as a child and young adult, and her early interest in the fantasy and science-fiction genres has had a significant influence on her work. She has noted in interviews that she was particularly inspired by Greek mythology and has likened the protagonist of the Hunger Games trilogy, Katniss, to the legendary hero Theseus, who is said to have killed the monstrous Minotaur to end the sacrifice of Athenian youth. Greek mythological references are also prominent in the Underland Chronicles. In addition to its literary influences, the Hunger Games series was also inspired by several facets of Collins's personal life, including her father's experiences during the Vietnam War and her observations of the strange juxtaposition between television coverage of the then-ongoing Iraq War and reality programming.

As overwhelmingly popular dystopian novels, the Hunger Games books signaled a trend toward dystopian fiction in young adult literature. Although young adult bookshelves had previously been filled with paranormal fiction, which remained common thanks to the enduring popularity of Stephenie Meyer's Twilight series (2005–8) about vampires, the number of dystopian young adult novels increased significantly during the height of Collins's popularity. The success of the film adaptations of the Hunger Games novels likewise prompted the adaptation of other successful dystopian novels, among them the books in Veronica Roth's Divergent trilogy (2011–13).

Joy Crelin

Further Reading

"Biography." *Suzanne Collins*. Collins, n.d. Web. 8 June 2015. <http://www.suzannecollinsbooks.com/bio.htm>.

Cunningham, John M. "Suzanne Collins." *Encyclopaedia Britannica*. Encyclopaedia Britannica, 20 Nov. 2014. Web. 8 June 2015. <http://www.britannica.com/EBchecked/topic/1854139/Suzanne-Collins>.

Dominus, Susan. "Suzanne Collins's War Stories for Kids." *New York Times Magazine*. New York Times, 8 Apr. 2011. Web. 8 June 2015. <http://www.nytimes.com/2011/04/10/magazine/mag-10collins-t.html?_r=0>.

Bibliography

Collins, Suzanne. Interview with James Blasingame. *Journal of Adolescent & Adult Literacy* 52.8 (May 2009): 726–27. Print.

Collins, Suzanne. "A Killer Story: An Interview with Suzanne Collins, Author of 'The Hunger Games.'" Interview with Rick Margolis. *School Library Journal*. School Library Journal, 1 Sept. 2008. Web. 8 June 2015. <http://www.slj.com/2008/09/interviews/under-cover/a-killer-story-an-interview-with-suzanne-collins-author-of-the-hunger-games>.

Dominus, Susan. "Suzanne Collins's War Stories for Kids." *New York Times Magazine*. New York Times, 8 Apr. 2011. Web. 8 June 2015. <http://www.nytimes.com/2011/04/10/magazine/mag-10collins-t.html?_r=0>.

Henthorne, Tom. *Approaching the Hunger Games Trilogy: A Literary and Cultural Analysis*. Jefferson: McFarland, 2012. Print.

"'Hunger Games' Author Suzanne Collins Graduated from IU." *IU News Room*. Indiana U, 22 Mar. 2012. Web. 8 June 2015. <http://newsinfo.iu.edu/news/page/normal/21670.html>.

Robert Cormier

Date of birth: January 17, 1925
Place of birth: Leominster, Massachusetts
Date of death: November 2, 2000
Place of death: Boston, Massachusetts

Principal Works

The Chocolate War (1974)
I Am the Cheese (1977)
We All Fall Down (1991)
Tenderness (1997)

Biography

Robert Cormier, who died in 2000, was one of the best-known young adult authors in the United States for his 1974 book *The Chocolate War*, a dark take on power and corruption at a prep school. The book is one of the most frequently banned in the country but also one of the most admired. Cormier wrote fourteen books for young adults, among them the thrillers *I Am the Cheese* (1977) and *We All Fall Down* (1991) as well as a novel titled *Tenderness* (1997) about a teenage girl who falls in love with a serial killer. In 1991 he received the Margaret A. Edwards Award for his contribution to young adult literature. The iconic author never shied away from difficult characters and themes (such as sex, murder, manipulation, power, betrayal, and physical abuse), which put him at odds with adults who defined the merit of a young adult book by the clear-cut moral provided at the end of it. However, the complexity of his stories is exactly what has helped them endure decades after they were written. To date, four of his novels have been adapted for film, including *I Am the Cheese* in 1983, *The Chocolate War* in 1988, *The Bumblebee Flies Anyway* (1983) in 1999, and *Tenderness* in 2009.

Cormier was born on January 17, 1925, in Leominster, Massachusetts—the town in which he would live his entire life. His neighborhood, French Hill, was working class and largely French Canadian. The second of eight children, Cormier was bruised by early brushes with death. His three-year-old brother died of pneumonia and a cousin died very young, as did a friend after falling from a cliff. At school, he was tormented by bullies but found a home in the local library. He began writing when he was just twelve. Cormier graduated from St. Cecilia's School in 1938 and from Leominster High School in 1942. Rejected from military service during World War II, he attended Fitchburg State College, where he was the president of his class, from 1943 to 1944. He wrote radio commercials before taking up a career in journalism in 1948, writing for the *Worcester Telegram* and then the *Fitchburg Sentinel*.

After writing his first novel, *Now and at the Hour*, in 1960, and successfully publishing *The Chocolate War* and *I Am the Cheese*, he quit his job as a reporter in 1978. Cormier had been in the local news business for exactly thirty years, allowing him to draw inspiration from the people of Leominster and French Hill. His novels are even set in a similar neighborhood called Frenchtown.

In 1948, Cormier married Constance Senay, a woman from Leominster. Together they had four children, including a son named Peter, who served as the inspiration for the protagonist of *The Chocolate War*. Cormier died at age seventy-five in Boston following complications from a blood clot on November 2, 2000. According to his obituary in the *New York Times*, he listed his real phone number in his novel *I Am the Cheese*, and for years after its publication, he accepted phone calls from young fans "who felt lonely or distraught."

Major Works

Cormier has been widely praised and admired for his uniquely honest, real, and relatable treatment of young adult topics at a time when the genre did not quite exist yet—especially not in its modern form. Famous for claiming that no subject, handled well, was too taboo despite the audience, he consistently strove to remain faithful to his vision with every book that he published. Therefore, he also became known for refusing to sacrifice the authenticity of such important issues by wrapping up the story in a neat and happy conclusion.

When Cormier's son, Peter, was a freshman in high school, he refused to participate in his school's candy sale. *The Chocolate War* features Jerry Renault, a freshman at a boy's prep school called Trinity High, where a secret society known as the Vigils lords over the social pecking order. Jerry is told to refuse, for two weeks, to participate in the school's chocolate sale. For reasons that are unclear to Jerry himself, he continues the prank passed its appointed end date, earning the ire of the Vigils themselves. *The Chocolate War* is a bleak tale about power, peer pressure, and psychological warfare. It was lauded for extracting terror from familiar surroundings and subverting the ubiquitous happy ending of young adult literature.

Cormier's other well-known works include *I Am the Cheese*, a psychological thriller told from the point of view of an unreliable narrator in the form of a twelve-year-old boy bicycling from Massachusetts to Vermont to reach his father. *We All Fall Down*, told from various perspectives, focuses on an incident in which a group of teenage boys vandalize a family's house and push a young girl down the stairs, putting her in a coma. "Parents want to protect their children and so there's a tendency to have books with happy endings, to white-wash things," Cormier said in a May 5, 1985, interview with Merri Rosenberg for the *New York Times*. "But the kids can absorb my kind of book because they know this kind of thing happens in life."

Molly Hagan

Further Reading

Roney-O'Brien, Susan. "Robert Cormier Lived Next Door." *Worcester Review* 29 (2008): 43–47. *Literary Reference Center*. Web. 2 June 2015. <http://search.ebscohost.com/login.aspx?direct=true&db=lfh&AN=36400972&site=ehost-live&scope=site>.

Woo, Elaine. "Robert Cormier; Author Gave Dark Touch to Juvenile Fiction." *Los Angeles Times*. Los Angeles Times, 11 Nov. 2000. Web. 2 June 2015. <http://articles.latimes.com/2000/nov/11/local/me-50378>.

Bibliography

Campbell, Patricia J. *Robert Cormier: Daring to Disturb the Universe*. New York: Delacorte, 2006. Print.

Cormier, Robert. Interview by Anita Silvey. Rpt. *Horn Book Magazine* 16 Aug. 2013: n. pag. *Horn Book*. Web. 11 June 2015. <http://www.hbook.com/2013/08/authors-illustrators/interviews/an-interview-with-robert-cormier>.

Gardner, Lyn. "Robert Cormier." *Guardian*. Guardian News and Media, 5 Nov. 2000. Web. 2 June 2015. <http://www.theguardian.com/news/2000/nov/06/guardianobituaries.books>.

Gavin, Adrienne E., ed. *Robert Cormier*. New York: Palgrave, 2012. Print.

Honan, William H. "Robert E. Cormier, 75, Author of Enduring Books for Teenagers." *New York Times*. New York Times, 5 Nov. 2000. Web. 2 June 2015. <http://www.nytimes.com/2000/11/05/nyregion/robert-e-cormier-75-author-of-enduring-books-for-teenagers.html>.

"On Robert Cormier's The Chocolate War." *PEN America*. PEN American Center, 15 Oct. 2012. Web. 11 June 2015. <http://www.pen.org/nonfiction/robert-cormier%E2%80%99s-chocolate-war>.

Rosenberg, Merri. "Children's Books; Teen-Agers Face Evil." *New York Times*. New York Times, 5 May 1985. Web. 2 June 2015. <http://www.nytimes.com/1985/05/05/books/children-s-books-teen-agers-face-evil.html>.

Cath Crowley

Date of birth: 1971
Place of birth: Victoria, Australia

Principal Works

The Life and Times of Gracie Faltrain (2004)
Chasing Charlie Duskin (2005)
Gracie Faltrain Takes Control (2006)
Gracie Faltrain Gets It Right (Finally) (2008)
A Little Wanting Song (2010)
Graffiti Moon (2010)

Biography

Cath Crowley is an award-winning children's and young adult author from Australia. She has written more than half a dozen novels, among them her well-received Gracie Faltrain series, about an adolescent soccer star during her high school years.

Crowley was born in rural Victoria, Australia, in 1971. She grew up with three brothers and was not interested in writing for most of her early life, until she was inspired by the work of her brother, playwright Anthony Crowley. When she was in her late twenties, she moved to Europe and began writing letters to Anthony, who turned the experiences in her letters into a musical called *The Journey Girl* (1998).

Seeing her brother's work performed on stage, Cath began writing down her own stories and published her first book, *The Life and Times of Gracie Faltrain*, in 2004. Her next novel, *Chasing Charlie Duskin* (2005), was released in the United States as *A Little Wanting Song* in 2010. Because the US release took place nearly five years after the original publication, Crowley was able to edit the original novel, making Charlie a stronger character and adding details such as song lyrics to give more depth to the supporting characters.

Major Works

While Cath Crowley's literary corpus is relatively small to date, her work as a whole has been received well by critics in Australia and around the world. Crowley typically writes from a first-person perspective while filtering the narration of the story through multiple points of view. For example, the Gracie Faltrain series focuses on the life of the title character, and the majority of the story is told from her point of view; however, other narrators, including Gracie's teammates and other students at her school, adults, and even Gracie's own parents, tell their own sides of the story. This narrative technique continues in *Gracie Faltrain Takes Control* (2006) and *Gracie Faltrain Gets It Right* (2008), the latter of which was recognized by the Children's Book Council of Australia Book of the Year Awards in 2009

Crowley's other novels use the same technique, but they tend not to have quite the same range of perspective. Instead they are generally told from the two main characters' perspectives. In *A Little Wanting Song*, for example, the two female protagonists, friends Charlie and Rose, tell the story in alternating first-person chapters. This technique of multiple perspectives, particularly those of adults within a young adult novel, has been received well by adolescent audiences. The technique is not unique to Crowley's works; young adult authors such as American writer Todd Strasser have used a similar multiple-narrator style to good effect.

Crowley's novel *Graffiti Moon* (2010) is also told from the perspective of two central narrators, Ed and Lucy. Lucy enlists Ed to help her search for a mysterious graffiti artist called Shadow who has been leaving messages all around her town, and soon a relationship begins to grow between them. What makes *Graffiti Moon* unique is the inclusion of another perspective, that of Poet (also known as Leopold Green), Shadow's "partner in art," in the words of *Booklist* reviewer Pam Holley Spencer. Poet's sections appear somewhat randomly and include poetry and poetry assignments.

What these poetic interludes add to the narrative is up for debate, but it is clear that they are one way in which *Graffiti Moon* challenges traditional literary values. Crowley's work is known for having a moderate amount of swearing, sexual content, and violence, but *Graffiti Moon* goes beyond the limits of simple prose, into the more experimental world of the verse novel. The book is Crowley's most critically acclaimed work to date. It has received many honors, including being shortlisted for four literary awards and, in 2011, winning the New South Wales Premier's Literary Awards Ethel Turner Prize and the Prime Minister's Literary Award for young adult fiction.

Aaron Horton, MA

Further Reading

Crowley, Cath. Interview. *RollerCoaster*. ABC, 2009. Web. 2 Oct. 2015. <http://www.abc.net.au/rollercoaster/therap/interviews/s1593482.htm>.

Rev. of *A Little Wanting Song*, by Cath Crowley. *Kirkus Reviews* 1 May 2010: 414. *Literary Reference Center*. Web. 14 Oct. 2015. <http://search.ebscohost.com/login.aspx?direct=true&db=lfh&AN=50449455&site=lrc-live>.

Bibliography

Carton, Debbie. Rev. of *A Little Wanting Song*, by Cath Crowley. *Booklist* 1 May 2010: 77. *Literary Reference Center*. Web. 16 Oct. 2015. <http://search.ebscohost.com/login.aspx?direct=true&db=lfh&AN=50656189&site=lrc-live>.

"Cath Crowley Biography." *BookBrowse*. BookBrowse, 26 Aug. 2010. Web. 31 Oct, 2015. <https://www.bookbrowse.com/biographies/index.cfm/author_number/1932/cath-crowley>.

Rev. of *Graffiti Moon*, by Cath Crowley. *Publishers Weekly* 19 Dec. 2011: 54. *Literary Reference Center*. Web. 14 Oct. 2015. <http://search.ebscohost.com/login.aspx?direct=true&db=lfh&AN=71874917&site=lrc-live>.

Spencer Holley, Pam. Rev. of *Graffiti Moon*, by Cath Crowley. *Booklist* 15 May 2012: 70. *Literary Reference Center*. Web. 14 Oct. 2015. <http://search.ebscohost.com/login.aspx?direct=true&db=lfh&AN=76352501&site=lrc-live>.

Chris Crutcher

Date of birth: July 17, 1946
Place of birth: Dayton, Ohio

Principal Works
Running Loose (1983)
Stotan! (1986)
Athletic Shorts: Six Short Stories (1991)
Staying Fat for Sarah Byrnes (1993)
Ironman (1995)
Whale Talk (2001)
The Sledding Hill (2005)
Deadline (2007)
Period 8 (2013)

Biography
Chris Crutcher is an award-winning young adult novelist. He began publishing books relatively late in life—at the age of thirty-five—but has published more than a dozen novels and two collections of short stories

since his first novel, *Running Loose*, appeared in 1983. In 2000, Crutcher received the Margaret A. Edwards Award from the Young Adult Library Services Association (YALSA), a division of the American Library Association (ALA), for lifetime achievement in writing for young adults. Crutcher's stories often mirror his own upbringing in a small Idaho town. Many of his characters are teenage athletes—usually boys—who must reckon with adult problems such as death, terminal disease, suicide, bullying, or mental illness. Crutcher's work has been criticized as melodramatic and didactic, but he remains enormously popular teenagers who identify with his striving, alienated characters.

Crutcher was born on July 17, 1946, in Dayton, Ohio. His father, John, whose nickname was Crutch, was a former bomber pilot in the US Air Force during World War II. His father ran a service station and oil business while Crutcher was growing up. His mother, Jewel, was a homemaker and, as Crutcher later described her, a functioning alcoholic. Crutcher and his two siblings, older brother John and younger sister Candy, were raised in rural Cascade, Idaho. In high school, Crutcher played football and basketball, ran track, and competed on the swim team. He attributes his interest in sports more to boredom in a small town than to natural ability, though athletics often play a significant role in Crutcher's books. Crutcher was an admittedly lazy student who hated reading—on his personal website, he writes that he was deemed "most likely to plagiarize" in high school. By the time he graduated, he had only read one classic novel—Harper Lee's *To Kill a Mockingbird* (1960). Crutcher attended Eastern Washington State College, where he earned a bachelor's degree in sociology and psychology in 1968. Soon after, he obtained his teaching certificate.

Crutcher taught in Washington State and northern California, and in the early 1970s, he served as the director of the Lakeside School, an alternative, racially diverse K–12 school in Oakland, California. His time there inspired him to write his first novel for young adults, called *Running Loose*. Crutcher left the school in 1981 and moved to Spokane, Washington. He took a job with the Spokane Community Health Center and Child Protection team as a family therapist and child protection advocate. Even after becoming a prolific and published author, he continued to serve these roles. He also travels around the world giving lectures to students.

Major Works

Crutcher's first novel, *Running Loose* (1983), came out of his experiences working with teenagers and explores issues of sportsmanship, racism, sexual discovery, and death. Although the book, about a star high school football player who must reckon with his racist coach and the death of his girlfriend, features a teenage protagonist, Crutcher did not realize that he had written a young adult novel until it was accepted as such by a publisher. The book also established Crutcher's reputation as a "controversial" writer for teens. Despite the book's heavy subject matter, it drew criticism from parents for an episode involving sex and a juvenile prank involving the main character's penis. Many of Crutcher's later books have been censored or banned in some US schools, including a short story called "In the Time I Get," which appears in the collection *Athletic Shorts: Six Short Stories* (1991), because it features a gay character who is dying from acquired immune deficiency syndrome (AIDS).

Crutcher published his second novel, *Stotan!*, about a grueling period of training on a high school swim team, in 1986. His next book, *The Crazy Horse Electric Game* (1987), is about a high school baseball star named Willie Weaver, who is maimed in a horrible accident. Unable to play baseball and feeling ostracized by his family and friends, Willie runs away. Similar themes—such as body image and alienation—are explored in another of Crutcher's most famous books, *Staying Fat for Sarah Byrnes* (1993). In *Sarah Byrnes*, an overweight teenager nicknamed Moby befriends a fellow misfit, Sarah Byrnes, who has severe burn scars on her face and hands. Moby, a high school swimmer, eventually sheds his weight—though he desperately tries to gain it back to keep her friendship—and must try to help Sarah Byrnes as she battles mental illness and an abusive father.

"I want to be remembered as a storyteller, and I want to tell stories that seem real so that people will recognize something in their own lives and see the connections," Crutcher said in an interview with Christine McDonnell for the *Horn Book Magazine* (333). His brand of realism is characterized by truth-telling; Crutcher utilizes the wisdom gained from his years as a counselor to tackle such contemporary issues as homosexuality, teenage violence, and race. "We don't do anywhere near enough to address [racism], though some schools are making big jumps in that area," he said in a July 24, 2002, live chat for the New York Public Library. In

2001, Crutcher published a well-received and surprisingly triumphant novel called *Whale Talk*, about a biracial swimmer who overcomes adversity to found his own high school swim team. (Even more surprisingly, the book, which Crutcher began writing before the horrific Columbine High School massacre, was originally about a school shooting. Crutcher pulled the manuscript and rewrote the book, using the same characters to tell a different tale.) Crutcher's later novels include *Deadline* (2007), about a teenager who suffers from a rare blood disease, and *Period 8* (2013), a thriller about a missing teenager.

Molly Hagan

Further Reading

Smith, Louisa. "Limitations on Young Adult Fiction: An Interview with Chris Crutcher." *Lion and the Unicorn* 16.1 (1992): 66–74. Print.

Rev. of *Staying Fat for Sarah Byrnes*, by Chris Crutcher. *Publishers Weekly*. PWxyz, 1 Apr. 1993. Web. 18 Mar. 2015. <http://www.publishersweekly.com/978-0-688-11552-4>.

Rev. of *Whale Talk*, by Chris Crutcher. *Kirkus*. Kirkus, 30 Apr. 2001. Web. 18 Mar. 2015. <https://www.kirkusreviews.com/book-reviews/chris-crutcher/whale-talk>.

Bibliography

Banned Books Resource Guide, Robert P. Doyle, and ALA. "Why Have These Books Been Banned/Challenged?" *American Library Association*. ALA, 2007. Web. 18 Mar. 2015. <http://www.ala.org/Template.cfm?Section=bbwlinks&Template=/ContentManagement/ContentDisplay.cfm&ContentID=164710>.

Crutcher, Chris. Interview. "Author Chat with Chris Crutcher—Transcript of Live Chat." *New York Public Library*. New York Public Lib., 24 July 2002. Web. 18 Mar. 2015. <http://www.nypl.org/author-chat-chris-crutcher>.

Greenway, Betty. "Chris Crutcher—Hero or Villain?" *ALAN Review* 22.1 (1994): n. pag. Web. 18 Mar. 2015. <http://scholar.lib.vt.edu/ejournals/ALAN/fall94/Greenway.html>.

"New Brief Biography." *ChrisCrutcher.com*. ChrisCrutcher.com, n.d. Web. 18 Mar. 2015. <http://www.chriscrutcher.com/biography.html>.

McDonnell, Christine. "New Voices, New Visions: Chris Crutcher." *Horn Book Magazine* 64 (May 1988): 332–335.

Sharon M. Draper

Date of birth: August 21, 1948
Place of birth: Cleveland, Ohio

Principal Works
Hazelwood High trilogy (1994–2001)
Copper Sun (2006)
Out of My Mind (2010)
Stella by Starlight (2015)

Biography
Sharon M. Draper is the award-winning author of more than twenty books for children and young adults. Among her best-known works is the Hazelwood High trilogy, which includes the novels *Tears of a Tiger* (1994), *Forged by Fire* (1997), and *Darkness before Dawn* (2001). *Forged by Fire* won a 1998 Coretta Scott King Book Award. A former high-school teacher—she was named national teacher of the year in 1997—Draper initially became known for her realistic portrayal of contemporary teenage life, but a trip to Ghana inspired her to write a historical fiction novel about the Middle Passage and American slavery, which became *Copper Sun* (2006). Draper's 2010 novel, *Out of My Mind*, was a *New York Times* best seller and included in *Time* magazine's list of one hundred best young adult books of all time. Draper has won the Coretta Scott King Book Award five times and received the Margaret A. Edwards Award for lifetime achievement in young adult literature in 2015.

Sharon M. Draper was born Sharon Renee Mills in Cleveland, Ohio, on August 21, 1948, the oldest of three siblings. Her father, Victor, worked as a maître d' at a Cleveland hotel, and her mother, Catherine, was a manager of classified advertisements at the now-defunct *Cleveland Press*. Draper was a voracious reader—by the time she was eleven, she had read every children's book at her local library—and excelled in school from an early age. She recalls the influence of her fifth-grade teacher, who read Shakespeare to the class and taught black history in an era when doing so was not required, or even widely accepted. The woman inspired Draper to become a teacher herself. Draper was a National Merit Scholar and, after graduating from John Adams High School in 1966, enrolled at Pepperdine University in Los Angeles, California. She earned a BA in English with high honors in 1969.

Turning down an offer to remain at Pepperdine and pursue her master's degree, Draper returned to Ohio and began teaching at Princeton Junior High School in Cincinnati. She earned her MA in English, graduating summa cum laude from Miami University in Oxford, Ohio, in 1974, and began teaching at Walnut Hills High School in Cincinnati in 1978. As a teacher she was both respected and feared; her year-end senior research paper was a notoriously difficult assignment. Students who did well were given T-shirts that read "I Survived the Draper Paper." In 1990, one of her students challenged her to write something herself. He handed her an ad for a short-story contest through *Ebony* magazine. Draper took the ad but thought nothing of it. That night, she stopped at the grocery store and was struck by a cruel exchange between a mother and her young son. Disturbed, Draper found herself writing a story about the boy called "One Small Torch." She mailed it off to the contest and, four months later, received a call telling her that she had won. The contest launched her writing career and earned her praise from one of her favorite writers, Alex Haley, the author of the Pulitzer Prize–winning book *Roots: The Saga of an American Family* (1976). In 1994, Draper published her first novel, *Tears of a Tiger*, which would become the first of her award-winning Hazelwood High trilogy.

Draper met her husband, Larry, when she was in high school. The couple were married in 1970 and have four children. Draper retired from teaching in 2000.

Major Works

Draper's debut novel, *Tears of a Tiger*, is about a teenage boy named Andy who accidentally kills his best friend while driving drunk. Andy is tortured by guilt and considers committing suicide to assuage his pain. Told from the perspectives of various characters, the book ends in another tragedy. Despite its lack of a happy ending, *Tears of a Tiger* remains one of Draper's most popular books. In 1997, she wrote a sequel about some of the characters, called *Forged by Fire*, this time dealing with issues such as drugs and child abuse. The book proved so popular with readers that Draper wrote a third and final book, *Darkness before Dawn* (2001), about a toxic relationship between an older man and a teenage girl at Hazelwood High.

In addition to penning realistic novels on serious problems faced by contemporary teens, Draper has also branched out into the genre of historical fiction. In 2006, after ten years of research, Draper published her first historical fiction novel, *Copper Sun*, about a young African girl named Amari who is sold into slavery. After crossing the Middle Passage, Amari is sold to a family in South Carolina, where she endures a number of horrors. *Copper Sun* was critically well received, as were Draper's subsequent novels, *Out of My Mind* (2010) and *Stella by Starlight* (2015). *Out of My Mind*, about a girl with cerebral palsy, became a *New York Times* best seller and, as of 2015, was slated to be adapted for film. *Stella by Starlight*, aimed at a middle-grade audience, is set in North Carolina in the 1930s. In it, the oppression of Jim Crow laws and the Ku Klux Klan define the life of a young, budding writer named Stella, who finds solace in her community and church.

Molly Hagan

Further Reading

Draper, Sharon M. "Sharon M. Draper: Reaching Reluctant Readers." Interview by KaaVonia Hinton-Johnson. *ALAN Review* 36.2 (2009): 89–93. PDF file.

Draper, Sharon M. "Q&A with Sharon M. Draper." Interview by Felicia Pride. *Publishers Weekly*. PWxyz, 25 June 2009. Web. 16 June 2015. <http://www.publishersweekly.com/pw/by-topic/authors/interviews/article/17713-q-a-with-sharon-m-draper.html>.

Hinton-Johnson, KaaVonia. *Sharon M. Draper: Embracing Literacy*. Lanham: Scarecrow, 2009. Print.

Bibliography

"Biography." *SharonDraper.com*. Draper, n.d. Web. 16 June 2015. <http://sharondraper.com/biography.asp>.

Castellitto, Linda M. "Sharon M. Draper: This Is the Sound of Courage." *BookPage*. BookPage, Jan. 2015. Web. 16 June 2015. <http://bookpage.com/interviews/17616-sharon-m-draper#.VWS1MCT4vFI>.

Goldberg-Sloan, Holly. "'Stella by Starlight' and 'Moonpenny Island.'" Rev. of *Stella by Starlight*, by Sharon M. Draper. *New York Times*. New York Times, 6 Feb. 2015. Web. 16 June 2015. <http://www.nytimes.com/2015/02/08/books/review/stella-by-starlight-and-moonpenny-island.html>.

McNary, Dave. "Sharon Draper's 'Out of My Mind' YA Novel Set for Movie Adaptation." *Variety*. Variety Media, 27 Apr. 2015. Web. 16 June 2015. <http://variety.com/2015/film/news/out-of-my-mind-movie-sharon-draper-1201480508>.

Draper, Sharon M. "Interview with Award-Winning and Bestselling Author Dr. Sharon M. Draper." Interview by Bianca Shulze. *Children's Book Review*. Children's Book Review, 22 Aug. 2013. Web. 16 June 2015. <http://www.thechildrensbookreview.com/weblog/2013/08/interview-with-award-winning-and-bestselling-author-dr-sharon-m-draper.html>.

Wittenberg, Ed. "Award-Winning Author Sharon Draper Helps Celebrate Newly Renovated Library at Memorial Junior High School in South Euclid." *Sun Messenger* [Cleveland]. Plain Dealer and Northeast Ohio Media, 3 Mar. 2011. Web. 16 June 2015. <http://blog.cleveland.com/sunmessenger/2011/03/award-winning_author_sharon_dr.html>.

Lois Duncan

Date of birth: April 28, 1934
Place of birth: Philadelphia, Pennsylvania

Principal Works
Young Adult Literature
Debutante Hill (1958)
Ransom (1966)
I Know What You Did Last Summer (1973)
Down a Dark Hall (1974)
Killing Mr. Griffin (1978)
Stranger with My Face (1981)
The Third Eye (1984)
Locked in Time (1985)
The Twisted Window (1987)
Don't Look behind You (1989)
Gallows Hill (1997)
Children's Literature
Hotel for Dogs (1971)
News for Dogs (2009)
Movies for Dogs (2010)

Biography
Lois Duncan is an award-winning author of young adult novels as well as children's literature and picture books. Hailed as a true innovator of the modern young adult thriller, she won the Margaret A. Edwards Award for her body of work in 1992. In her books, teenagers, most often teenage girls, reckon with killers, keep and discover nasty secrets, possess supernatural powers, and plan wicked pranks only to watch them go horribly awry.

Over fifty years after the publication of her first novel, Duncan still has loyal readers; she is also enjoying a renaissance through new editions (with updated technological references) of her books and film adaptations. Her 1973 novel *I Know What You Did Last Summer* launched a horror film franchise in 1997, and the plot of her 1978 novel *Killing Mr. Griffin* was adapted as a made-for-television film that aired on a major network channel earlier that same year. *Down a Dark Hall*, her 1974 supernatural suspense novel, was acquired by the Lionsgate Films in 2014, with Stephenie Meyer, the author of the Twilight series, signed on as coproducer.

Lois Duncan Steinmetz was born on April 28, 1934, in Philadelphia and grew up in Sarasota, Florida. Her parents, Lois and Joseph Steinmetz, were famous magazine photographers. Duncan knew she wanted to be a writer as a child, and she sold her first story to the magazine *Calling All Girls* when she was thirteen years old. She continued to write for magazines, including *Seventeen*, throughout high school. After graduating from Sarasota High School in 1952, she enrolled at Duke University in North Carolina. Although she was unhappy there, she met a man named Joseph "Buzz" Cardozo, and she dropped out of school at age nineteen when they married after her freshman year. By 1956, Duncan had given birth to two daughters, Robin and Kerry, and had finished her first novel, *Debutante Hill* (1958), after a year-long bout of writer's block.

Duncan gave birth to a son, Brett, in 1960, around the same time that she found out that Cardozo was in love with another woman. The marriage dissolved, and Duncan moved to Albuquerque, New Mexico, with her children. To make money, she anonymously wrote pulpy "true confessions" for magazines. She eventually parlayed this work into other articles and a job teaching journalism at the University of New Mexico. She married Don Arquette in 1965 and published her first young adult suspense novel, *Ransom* (1966), about a group of high school students who are kidnapped off their school bus and held for ransom.

Duncan had two more children with Arquette. In 1989, her youngest daughter, Kaitlyn, was murdered. The case remains unsolved. Devastated by the loss, Duncan did not write another novel for eight years. She eventually published *Gallows Hill* in 1997.

Major Works
In 1973, Duncan published *I Know What You Did Last Summer*, a novel about a group of teenagers involved

in a hit-and-run that killed a young boy. The plot of the book is markedly different from its big-screen adaptation. Most notably, the book does not feature a serial killer. Duncan was appalled by the 1997 slasher film's seeming commercialization of violence and murder. The senseless violence of the film was at odds with Duncan's entire canon, in which she employs violence only in the service of a larger moral or philosophical point. In *Last Summer*, for instance, the teens decide that living with their guilt is no way to live at all, so they turn themselves in. In *Killing Mr. Griffin* (1978), a group of high school students formulate a plot to kidnap their strict English teacher. When Mr. Griffin dies, the students are forced to reckon with their crime in a similar way.

Duncan is also interested in classic gothic horror. In *Down a Dark Hall* (1974), the first of Duncan's novels to delve into the occult, a teenager named Kit enrolls at a strange private school (there are only four students) only to discover that she has psychic powers that allow her to communicate with the dead. In *Stranger with My Face* (1981), a teenager named Laurie discovers that she has an evil twin. However, even when Duncan's plots test the bounds of realism, she keeps her characters rooted in real-life young adult problems. Though Duncan has updated a few of the plot points in several of her books—adding the Internet and cell phones, for example—she believes her teenage heroines still ring true emotionally.

Molly Hagan

Further Reading

Campbell, Kimberly. *Lois Duncan: Author of* I Know What You Did Last Summer. Berkeley Heights: Enslow, 2009. Print.

Duncan, Lois. "Q&A with Lois Duncan." Interview by Sue Corbett. *Publishers Weekly*. PWxyz, 13 Aug. 2013. Web. 7 Apr. 2015. <http://www.publishersweekly.com/pw/by-topic/authors/interviews/article/58693-q-a-with-lois-duncan.html>.

Stelloh, Tim. "Who Killed Lois Duncan's Daughter?" *BuzzFeed*. BuzzFeed, 30 May 2014. Web. 7 Apr. 2015. <http://www.buzzfeed.com/timstelloh/who-killed-lois-duncan-s-daughter>.

Bibliography

Billard, Mary. "Lois Duncan: Revisiting the Classics of an Earlier Generation." *New York Times*. New York Times, 2 Oct. 2013. Web. 7 Apr. 2015. <http://www.nytimes.com/2013/10/03/fashion/lois-duncan-revisiting-the-classics-of-an-earlier-generation.html>.

Duncan, Lois. "An Interview with Lois Duncan." Interview by Joan Kaywell. *Journal of Adolescent & Adult Literacy* 52.6 (2009): 545–47. *Literary Reference Center*. Web. 7 Apr. 2015. <http://search.ebscohost.com/login.aspx?direct=true&db=lfh&AN=37012205&site=lrc-live>.

Lippman, Laura. "The Story behind *Last Summer* Writer: Lois Duncan Will Use the Film Version of Her Book, *I Know What You Did Last Summer*, to Draw Attention to the Murder of Her Daughter." *Baltimore Sun*. Tribune Interactive, 19 Nov. 1997. Web. 7 Apr. 2015. <http://articles.baltimoresun.com/1997-11-19/features/1997323052_1_lois-duncan-kait-duncan-wrote>.

Gayle Forman

Date of birth: June 5, 1970
Place of birth: Los Angeles, California

Principal Works
If I Stay (2009)
Just One Day (2013)
Just One Year (2013)
I Was Here (2015)

Biography

Gayle Forman is the best-selling author of the novel *If I Stay* (2009), which was adapted into a 2014 film starring Chloë Grace Moretz. The novel is based in part on a terrible car accident in which Forman's best friends, a married couple, and their two small boys were killed. Forman is also the author of a popular series about a traveler named Allyson, whose experiences are culled from Forman's early life, and a swaggering Dutch actor named Willem. The series includes the novels *Just One Day* (2013) and *Just One Year* (2013) and the novella *Just One Night* (2014). Forman writes about tenacious young people facing intense moments of emotional growth. Whether they are exploring the world or fighting to survive, Forman's characters emerge from their experiences reborn. In 2015 Forman published the novel *I Was Here* and announced that her first book for adults, tentatively titled *Bypass*, would be published in 2016.

Forman was born on June 5, 1970, in Los Angeles, California. She writes on her website that as a child she wanted to grow up to be the sun. She was a self-described weird girl who was into thrift shopping and punk music before those interests were considered cool. When she was sixteen, she spent a year in England as an exchange student and earned her diploma from an experimental academy in Countesthorpe, Leicestershire, where there were neither classrooms nor structured classes.

After graduation, Forman traveled. She made her way through Europe working odd jobs, making friends with street performers in Florence and selling flowers in Paris. After three years of traveling, she went to college, where she considered studying medicine but wound up studying journalism instead. She moved to New York City and got a job as a senior writer for *Seventeen* magazine. As part of her job, Forman continued to travel, covering stories about child soldiers in Sierra Leone and the Troubles in Northern Ireland.

Forman and her husband, Nick, embarked on a year-long trek around the world in early 2002. Stories from their adventure, including Forman's brief gig as a Bolly-wood extra, are collected in her first book, a travelogue called *You Can't Get There From Here: A Year on the Fringes of a Shrinking World* (2005). When Forman returned to the United States, she and her husband settled in Brooklyn and began a family. Her interest in travel waned, and a friend suggested that she write a novel. Forman began writing *Sisters in Sanity* (2007), a novel based on an article she had written for *Seventeen* about troubled teen girls in rough rehabilitation treatment centers. After its publication, Forman devoted all of her energies to her new career as a novelist.

Major Works

After *Sisters in Sanity*, Forman wrote *If I Stay*. According to Forman, the main character, a seventeen-year-old cellist named Mia, popped into her head one day and demanded to be written. Mia has an ordinary life, but a terrible accident places her in a realm between life and death. She must decide if she wants to return to a life that has been destroyed or let it all go and die. Forman was always haunted by a similar accident that had killed her friends and their two young children. She heard that one of the boys survived the accident only to die in the hospital, and she always wondered if he knew what had happened to his family and consciously decided to give up his fight. Writing the novel was Forman's way of communicating with her friends and exploring the boy's

last moments. *If I Stay* became a *New York Times* best seller and was adapted into a major film, released in 2014. Forman wrote a sequel to the novel, called *Where She Went*, which was published in 2011. The book is told from the perspective of Adam, Mia's boyfriend, who three years after her accident has become a rock star.

In 2013, Forman published *Just One Day*, a novel inspired by her European travels. An American traveler named Allyson meets a Dutch actor named Willem. The book was sold as a romance, but it blossoms into a tale of personal growth, reviewer Priscilla Gilman wrote for the *New York Times*. The same year, Forman published a sequel, *Just One Year*, featuring the same characters but told from Willem's perspective. Willem's tale is also one of self-exploration. As Forman herself did, he travels to India and experiences an important moment of emotional growth. In 2014, Forman released an e-novella called *Just One Night*. The novella reunites Allyson and Willem and concludes their saga. Forman's next novel, *I Was Here* (2015), is a mystery that explores the suicide of a college freshman named Meg. In it, Meg's best friend, Cody, is left to piece together why Meg killed herself while dealing with her own grief.

Molly Hagan

Further Reading

Fielding, Ellen Wilson. "Young Death in Fiction and Fact." *Human Life Review* 40.4 (2014): 22–30. *Academic Search Complete*. Web. 8 Oct. 2015. <http://search.ebscohost.com/login.aspx?direct=true&db=a9h&AN=10055321&site=ehost-live>.

Forman, Gayle. "In a Balm of Space and Time, Healing." *New York Times*. New York Times, 7 Aug. 2014. Web. 14 Sept. 2015. <http://www.nytimes.com/2014/08/10/fashion/Modern-love-In-a-Balm-of-Space-and-Time-Healing.html>.

Meyer, Susan. *Gayle Forman*. New York: Rosen, 2016. Print.

Bibliography

Biedenharn, Isabella. "Gayle Forman to Write First Novel for Adults—Exclusive." *Entertainment Weekly*. Entertainment Weekly, 23 June 2015. Web. 14 Sept. 2015. <http://www.ew.com/article/2015/06/22/gayle-forman-first-novel-adults>.

Crutcher, Paige. "Gayle Forman Concludes *Just One Day* and *Just One Year* with the E-Novella *Just One*

Night." *Publishers Weekly*. PWxyz, 6 May 2014. Web. 14 Sept. 2015. <http://www.publishersweekly.com/pw/by-topic/childrens/childrens-book-news/article/62175-gayle-forman-concludes-just-one-day-and-just-one-year-with-the-e-novella-just-one-night.html>.

Forman, Gayle. Interview by Mike French. *The View from Here*. View from Here, 1 Nov. 2014. Web. 14 Sept. 2015. <http://www.viewfromheremagazine.com/2009/04/interview-with-gayle-forman-part-1-of-2.html>.

Forman, Gayle. "Q&A with Gayle Forman." Interview by Sue Corbett. *Publishers Weekly*. PWxyz, 30 Apr. 2009. Web. 14 Sept. 2015. <http://www.publishersweekly.com/pw/by-topic/authors/interviews/article/13595-q-a-with-gayle-forman.html>.

Gilman, Priscilla. "Midnight in Paris." Rev. of *Just One Day*, by Gayle Forman. *New York Times*. New York Times, 11 Jan. 2013. Web. 14 Sept. 2015. <http://www.nytimes.com/2013/01/13/books/review/just-one-day-by-gayle-forman.html>.

Gilman, Priscilla. Rev. of *Just One Year*, by Gayle Forman. *Kirkus Reviews* 1 Oct. 2013: 201. *Literary Reference Center*. Web. 14 Sept. 2015. <http://search.ebscohost.com/login.aspx?direct=true&db=lfh&AN=90554135&site=lrc-live>.

"Making Her Presence Known." *Publishers Weekly* 9 Feb. 2015: 14. *Literary Reference Center*. Web. 8 Oct. 2015. <http://search.ebscohost.com/login.aspx?direct=true&db=lfh&AN=100934836&site=lrc-live>.

Tackett MacDonald, Jessica. Rev. of *I Was Here*, by Gayle Forman. *Horn Book Magazine* 1 Jan. 2015: 80–81. *Literary Reference Center*. Web. 8 Oct. 2015. <http://search.ebscohost.com/login.aspx?direct=true&db=lfh&AN=99998109&site=lrc-live>.

John Green

Date of birth: August 24, 1977
Place of birth: Indianapolis, Indiana

Principal Works
Looking for Alaska (2005)
An Abundance of Katherines (2006)
Paper Towns (2008)
The Fault in Our Stars (2012)

Courtesy of Marina Waters

Biography
John Green is an award-winning writer of young adult novels. Thanks to word-of-mouth momentum, his 2012 novel *The Fault in Our Stars*—which became a *New York Times* best seller and a hit film in 2014—made Green one of the most popular YA writers in the business. In a genre that is often divided by gender and age, Green enjoys a diverse following of teenagers and adults. His first novel, *Looking for Alaska* (2005), won the Michael L. Printz Award in 2006. In 2009, he won the Edgar Award for best young adult novel for his book *Paper Towns* (2008)—which was also adapted for film.

Green was born on August 24, 1977, in Indianapolis, Indiana, and grew up in Orlando, Florida, where his father, Mike, worked as the state director of the Nature Conservancy and his mother, Sydney, was a homemaker before joining the staff of a nonprofit called the Healthy Community Initiative. Green did poorly—both academically and socially—in middle school. When he was fifteen, his parents enrolled him in a Birmingham, Alabama, boarding school called Indian Springs. The school fostered a love of books and academia. At Indian Springs, Green fell in love with the works of authors such as J. D. Salinger, Kurt Vonnegut, and Toni Morrison, and made a number of friends who shared his love of literature, though he remained a mediocre student.

In 1995, Green graduated from high school and enrolled at Kenyon College in Gambier, Ohio, where he double-majored in religion and literature. He took a writing class with the novelist P. F. Kluge, though he failed to make the cut for Kluge's advanced-writing course. In 2000, Green graduated and considered going to divinity school. He spent six months as an apprentice chaplain at a children's hospital in Columbus, Ohio. It was a terribly sad experience for him (though one he mined to comic effect in *The Fault in Our Stars*), and he decided not to pursue a career in religion.

Instead, Green moved to Chicago, where he took a job in data entry for the American Library Association (ALA) magazine *Booklist*. He quickly made friends with the magazine's editors and began writing book reviews. After *Looking for Alaska* was published in 2005, he quit his job to focus on writing, though he soon found that he did not enjoy the solitude of a writer's life. In 2006, Green and his younger brother Hank started making YouTube videos for each other as a way to keep in touch. The videos—which feature Green and his brother riffing on obscure, funny, or wonky topics—garnered an enormous following. Fans developed a lingo based on Green's own idiosyncratic way of speaking and dubbed themselves the Nerdfighters, after a word Green used in one of his videos. The Green brothers—and Green's wife, Sarah—run the Vlogbrothers, the original name for the correspondence endeavor, as a video-blog business, featuring other channels devoted to science and art.

Green met his wife, Sarah Urist, an art gallerist and Indian Springs alum, while he was living in Chicago. They live in Indianapolis with their two children.

Major Works

Green's most famous novel, *The Fault in Our Stars* (2012), is about two teenagers with terminal cancer. The book's premise springs from Green's brief work as a chaplain, but its protagonist, Hazel Grace Lancaster, is loosely based on an early Nerdfighter named Esther, who suffered from thyroid cancer (like Hazel in the book) and died at the age of sixteen. Green wanted to write a book about Esther and the kids he had known that embraced their full humanity and that did not treat those who are ill or dying as Other. Hazel, and her boyfriend, August, are dynamic and unique characters with strengths and weaknesses fundamentally separate from their illnesses. Hazel, the book's whip-smart narrator, has a biting sense of humor that masks her fear of dying. She brightens when she meets August, the charming former basketball player with an amputated leg. August

can spar with Hazel on her intellectual level, but he is wrapped up in a performance of "himself" and is consumed by a desire to be remembered. Therefore, he needs Hazel to remind him that enjoying his own life is more important than what he leaves behind. Despite its saccharine-sounding themes, *The Fault in Our Stars* actively resists sentimentality, even in its depiction of one main character's unpleasant death.

The novel is a perfect example of Green's writing style, which reflects his own personality: gregarious, intellectual, playful, and a bit verbose. His books appeal to a wide audience because he does not "talk down" to his young characters or his young audience. "[Green] writes *for* youth, rather than *to* them," Rachel Syme wrote for National Public Radio.

Molly Hagan

Further Reading

Brockes, Emma. "John Green: Teenager, Aged 36." *Intelligent Life*. Economist Newspaper, 1 May 2014. Web. 15 Apr. 2015. <http://moreintelligentlife.com/content/features/emma-brockes/john-green?page=full>.

Miller, Laura. "'The Fault in Our Stars' Has Been Unfairly Bashed by Critics Who Don't Understand It." *Salon*, Salon Media Group, 6 June 2014. Web. 15 Apr. 2015. <http://www.salon.com/2014/06/06/the_fault_in_our_stars_has_been_unfairly_bashed_by_critics_who_dont_understand_it>.

Talbot, Margaret. "The Teen Whisperer." *New Yorker*. Condé Nast, 9 June 2014. Web. 15 Apr. 2015. <http://www.newyorker.com/magazine/2014/06/09/the-teen-whisperer>.

Bibliography

"John Green's Biography." *JohnGreenBooks.com*. John Green Books, n.d. Web. 15 Apr. 2015.

Syme, Rachel. "'The Fault in Our Stars': Love in a Time of Cancer." Rev. of *The Fault in Our Stars*, by John Green. *NPR Books*. Natl. Public Radio, 17 Jan. 2012. Web. 15 Apr. 2015.

Rosen, Rebecca J. "How John Green Wrote a Cancer Book but Not a 'Bulls—— Cancer Book.'" *Atlantic*. Atlantic Monthly, 25 Feb. 2013. Web. 15 Apr. 2015.

Woodley, Shailene. "The 100 Most Influential People: John Green." *Time*. Time, 23 Apr. 2014. Web. 17 Apr. 2015.

Sonya Hartnett

Date of birth: March 23, 1968
Place of birth: Melbourne, Australia

Principal Works

Young Adult Literature
Trouble All the Way (1984)
The Glass House (1990)
Wilful Blue (1994)
Sleeping Dogs (1995)
Black Foxes (1996)
Princes (1997)
Of a Boy (2000; *What the Birds See*, 2003)
Forest (2001)
Thursday's Child (2002)
The Silver Donkey (2004)
Surrender (2005)
The Midnight Zoo (2010)
Nonfiction
Life in Ten Houses (2012)
Short Stories
There Must Be Lions: Stories about Mental Illness (with Nick Earls and Heide Seaman, 1998)
Children's Literature
Sadie and Ratz (2008)

Biography

Sonya Hartnett is an Australian writer of children's, young adult, and adult fiction and nonfiction. She has won numerous awards throughout her extended career and has had many of her books shortlisted for major literary awards in Australia and internationally. Born in Melbourne, Australia, in 1968, Sonya began writing from an early age. She took up the task of writing a novel seriously at the age of thirteen; in 1984, at the age of fifteen, she published her first book, *Trouble All the Way*.

Many consider Hartnett's most important and well-written book to be *Sleeping Dogs* (1995), which she wrote while in her early twenties. She has also published a handful of books for children under the age of twelve and several novels written for an adult audience, as well as a memoir of her life, *Life in Ten Houses* (2012). Hartnett's body of literature is extensive, consisting of more than two dozen works. While these texts have received generally favorable reviews and a few have found high praise, she is recognized most for her contributions to the young adult genre.

Major Works

Hartnett wrote the first two of her young adult novels when she was still an adolescent herself. These two books were generally well received, but not until the publication of *The Glass House* (1990) did critics start taking her writing seriously. As Hartnett matured, so did her writing, and *Wilful Blue* (1994), for which she had received a writer's fellowship from the Literature Board of the Australian Council in 1992, elevated her status even higher, earning her the Ena Noel Award in 1996. Moving away from writing for very young audiences, Hartnett wrote *Sleeping Dogs*, which was awarded the Victorian Premier's Literary Award, known as the Sheaffer Pen Prize for Young Adult Fiction. The book was also recognized, and often criticized, for its distinctly bleak outlook on life.

Sleeping Dogs, along with *Black Foxes* (1996), seemed to mark another change in Hartnett's style. Her subsequent books have had a distinctly dark tone, often dealing with morbid themes and sometimes unhappy endings. *Princes* (1997) stands out for its strong use of horror conventions and explicit details of death, murder, and other macabre subject matter. While Hartnett's style has been marked by this often dark tone, her novels are generally found within the realistic genre of young adult fiction. She focuses on real-life situations with protagonists who are often set apart from the majority their peers. This loneliness and isolation helps intensify the subject matter and tone.

While the situations in which Hartnett's main characters find themselves are painfully realistic, her writing also has a fantastical side. Often, the fantastical elements of Hartnett's narratives come through in the form of her character's imaginations. Through these elements the stories can acquire a softer edge, toning down the harshness of reality with doses of fantasy. However, the main characters, as well as the readers, are often brought back, sometimes abruptly, to the harsh realities that permeate the novels. For example, *Of a Boy* (2000) focuses on the life of an isolated child who lives with his grandmother after being taken from his mother. Troubled and lonely, he is obsessed with unsettling thoughts, primarily the recent disappearance of three children from a neighborhood near his home. The story ends tragically, as the main character goes out in search for the lost children. Yet despite the mature subject matter and tone, *Of a Boy* won the Age Book of the Year Award and the Commonwealth Writers' Prize in 2003.

Sonya Hartnett has been widely recognized for her many contributions to literature in her own country, but she is also an internationally recognized author. Her novels sell and are received well in countries across the world, including the United States. In 2008, she received the Astrid Lindgren Memorial Award, known being the children's literature award with the world's largest payout—five million Swedish kronor.

Aaron Horton, MA

Further Reading

"The Case for *The Ghost's Child* by Sonya Hartnett." *The Conversation*. Conversation US, 25 Mar. 2014. Web. 26 Sept. 2015. <http://theconversation.com/the-case-for-the-ghosts-child-by-sonya-hartnett-24055>.

Eccleshare, Julia. "Dig a Little Deeper." *Guardian*. Guardian News and Media, 12 Oct. 2002. Web. 26 Sept. 2015. <http://www.theguardian.com/books/2002/oct/12/featuresreviews.guardianreview32>.

"Sonya Hartnett: Love and Loss." *Book Trust*. Arts Council England, n.d. Web. 26 Sept. 2015. <http://www.booktrust.org.uk/books/children/authors/128>.

Bibliography

Beauchamp, Emma. Rev. of *The Midnight Zoo*, by Sonya Hartnett. Sept.–Oct. 2011: 61. *Literary Reference Center*. Web. 19 Sept. 2015. <http://search.ebscohost.com/login.aspx?direct=true&db=lfh&AN=65470493&site=lrc-live>.

Gross, Claire E. Rev. of *Butterfly*, by Sonya Hartnett. *Horn Book Magazine* July–Aug. 2010: 108–9. *Literary Reference Center*. Web. 19 Sept. 2015. <http://search.ebscohost.com/login.aspx?direct=true&db=lfh&AN=52482519&site=lrc-live>.

Knoth, Maeve Visser. Rev. of *Sleeping Dogs*, by Sonya Hartnett. *Horn Book Magazine* Mar.–Apr. 1996: 207. *Literary Reference Center*. Web. 15 Oct. 2015. <http://search.ebscohost.com/login.aspx?direct=true&db=lfh&AN=9603203716&site=lrc-live>.

"Sonya Hartnett." *Literature Matters*. British Council of Lit., 2011. Web. 26 Sept. 2015. <http://literature.britishcouncil.org/sonya-hartnett>.

"Sonya Hartnett Wins £400,000 Prize for Children's Writing." *Bookseller* 6 June 2008: 8. *Literary Reference Center*. Web. 15 Oct. 2015. <http://search.ebscohost.com/login.aspx?direct=true&db=lfh&AN=32670332&site=lrc-live>.

S. E. Hinton

Date of birth: July 22, 1948
Place of birth: Tulsa, Oklahoma

Principal Works

The Outsiders (1967)
That Was Then, This Is Now (1971)
Rumble Fish (1975)
Tex (1979)
Taming the Star Runner (1988)

Biography

S. E. Hinton is the author of the classic 1967 novel *The Outsiders*. The coming-of-age tale about a group of working-class boys in 1950s Oklahoma was her first novel and is widely considered a major influence in the development of the young adult genre due to its frank, nonidealized look at the lives of teenagers and its confrontation of serious subject matter. Hinton went on to write other well-known novels for teens, including *Rumble Fish* (1975), *Tex* (1979), and *Taming the Star Runner* (1988). In 1983, Hinton teamed up with the director of *The Godfather* (1972), Francis Ford Coppola, to create a movie adaptation of *The Outsiders*; the film was recut and rereleased in 2005. The pair adapted *Rumble Fish* the same year. Director Tim Hunter adapted *Tex* for film in 1982, and Christopher Cain made *That Was Then, This Is Now* (based on Hinton's 1971 novel of the same title) in 1985. Hinton won the Margaret A. Edwards award for lifetime achievement in young adult literature in 1988.

Susan Eloise Hinton was born on July 22, 1948, in Tulsa, Oklahoma. She grew up in a working-class neighborhood on Tulsa's North Side. Her father, Grady, was a door-to-door salesman, and her mother, Lillian, worked on an assembly line. Hinton did not get along with her parents, and has described her mother as physically and emotionally abusive. At home, she kept to herself, writing stories about horses. As a teenager, Hinton attended Will Rogers High School, where the poor "Greasers" duked it out with the wealthy "Socs" (short for "social"). The violent conflict between the two social classes would provide the basis for *The Outsiders*, which she began after one of her friends was badly beaten by a gang of Socs while walking home from school. It was a difficult period in Hinton's life; her father was dying of a brain tumor, but Hinton grew her story draft by draft. When she was seventeen, she showed her manuscript to a friend's mother, a writer who was connected to a literary agent in New York. The agent loved the manuscript, and sold it to Viking, the second publisher that read it.

The Outsiders was not an immediate best seller. The novel fared poorly when it was marketed as a drugstore paperback, but Viking noticed that teachers appeared to be buying the book to teach in their classrooms and began marketing it directly to young adults. Hinton was not the first to write about teenagers smoking, drinking, and engaging in gang violence, but previous books and movies of the sort had been marketed to adults, not to teenagers themselves. Books actually aimed at the teenage audience tended to be lighter, less realistic, and, Hinton felt, less interesting—her dissatisfaction with the books available for young adults was part of what spurred her to write her own.

Meanwhile, Hinton suffered a short period of writer's block and depression. She met her future husband, David Inhofe, in a freshman biology class at the University of Tulsa, and has said that he helped her to start writing again. She published *That Was Then, This Is Now* in 1971 and *Rumble Fish* in 1975. By 1979, the same year she published the best-selling novel *Tex*, *The Outsiders* had sold over ten million copies.

Hinton continues to write. She lives in Tulsa with her husband, who is a software engineer. They have an adult son named Nick.

Major Works

The Outsiders takes place in the Tulsa of Hinton's youth, and is told from the perspective of a fourteen-year-old Greaser named Ponyboy. Both of Ponyboy's parents are dead, and he lives with his older brothers, Sodapop and Darry. Outside of his immediate kin, Ponyboy counts the handful of Greasers—among them Two-Bit, Dally, Steve, and Johnny—as his extended family. When Ponyboy is walking home from school one day, he is attacked by a group of Socs wielding a switchblade, but his Greaser family comes to his rescue. Later, when Ponyboy unwittingly captures the attention of a pretty, popular girl named Cherry, Cherry's Soc boyfriend, Bob, and his gang try to drown Ponyboy by holding his head underwater at a park fountain. Afraid that Ponyboy might die, Johnny stabs Bob and kills him. The two boys become fugitives, and with Dally's help, try to make a life for themselves hiding in an abandoned church. The plot continues to twist—one could argue, in increasingly implausible directions—but the enduring appeal of the novel lies in Ponyboy's own journey to find what is good in himself and in others and hold onto those things in a cruel world. Those themes have continued to resonate with teenagers throughout the decades following the book's publication.

Tex, published in 1979, is Hinton's favorite among her own novels. The book looks a lot like *The Outsiders* on the surface, with a restless teenage boy, a small town beset by rural poverty, and absent parents. Tex lives with his older brother, Mason, and the two boys become entangled with a drug dealer and an escaped murderer. Like *The Outsiders* and *Rumble Fish*, *Tex* is about finding value in people whom society has deemed valueless.

Molly Hagan

Further Reading

Lang, George. "S. E. Hinton Recalls 'The Outsiders' 45 Years Later—E-book Due in Spring 2013." *Oklahoman*. NewsOK.com, 26 Apr. 2013. Web. 23 May 2015. <http://newsok.com/s.e.-hinton-recalls-the-outsiders-45-years-later-e-book-due-in-spring-2013/article/3770291>.

Michaud, Jon. "S. E. Hinton and the Y. A. Debate." *New Yorker*. Condé Nast, 14 Oct. 2014. Web. 23 May 2015. <http://www.newyorker.com/culture/cultural-comment/hinton-outsiders-young adult-literature>.

Peck, Dale. "'The Outsiders:' 40 Years Later." *New York Times*. New York Times, 23 Sept. 2007. Web. 23 May 2015. <http://www.nytimes.com/2007/09/23/books/review/Peck-t.html>.

Bibliography

Carter, Ally. "Rich Kids, Greasers and the Life-Changing Power of 'The Outsiders.'" *National Public Radio*. NPR, 28 Jan. 2013. Web. 25 May 2015. <http://www.npr.org/2013/01/28/151966146/rich-kids-greasers-and-the-life-changing-power-of-the-outsiders>.

Michaud, Jon. "That Was Then, This Is Now: S. E. Hinton in the Twitter Age." *New Yorker*. Condé Nast, 8 Nov. 2013. Web. 23 May 2015. <http://www.newyorker.com/books/page-turner/that-was-then-this-is-now-s-e-hinton-in-the-twitter-age>.

Smith, Dinitia. "An Outsider, Out of the Shadows." *New York Times*. New York Times, 7 Sept. 2005. Web. 23 May 2015. <http://www.nytimes.com/2005/09/07/movies/MoviesFeatures/07hint.html>.

Rev. of *Tex*, by S. E. Hinton. *Kirkus Reviews*. Kirkus Media, 1 Oct. 1980. Web. 25 May 2015. <https://www.kirkusreviews.com/book-reviews/se-hinton/tex/>.

Alaya Dawn Johnson

Date of birth: 1982
Place of birth: Washington, DC

Principal Works
Children's Literature
The Goblin King (2009)
Detective Frankenstein (2011)
Young Adult Literature
Spirit Binders series (2007–10)
Zephyr Hollis series (2010–12)
The Summer Prince (2013)
Love Is the Drug (2014)

Biography
Alaya Dawn Johnson is a critically acclaimed author of novels for adult and young adult readers. She is perhaps best known for her novels *Moonshine* (2010) and *Wicked City* (2012), urban fantasy books for adults set in the 1920s, as well as her critically acclaimed young adult novels *The Summer Prince* (2013) and *Love Is the Drug* (2014). In addition to her novels, Johnson is the author of two graphic novels for children, *The Goblin King* (2009) and *Detective Frankenstein* (2011), as well as various short stories. Johnson's work has been nominated for numerous awards, including the Nebula Award and the Andre Norton Award.

Johnson was born in Washington, DC, in 1982. Her father, Ford T. Johnson Jr., was the petitioner in the 1963 court case *Johnson v. Virginia*, which ultimately led to the desegregation of Virginia's courtrooms. Johnson grew up in Potomac, Maryland, and attended private school in Washington, DC. Her parents valued storytelling and encouraged Johnson's love of writing, which she developed at an early age. An avid reader, she enjoyed the fantasy and science-fiction works of writers such as Diana Wynne Jones, Ursula K. Le Guin, and Octavia Butler. After graduating from high school, Johnson went on to Columbia University, where she studied East Asian languages and culture.

She earned her bachelor's degree from the university in 2004.

In December of that year, Johnson published her first short story, "Who Ever Loved," in *Arabella Magazine*. She went on to publish numerous stories in well-known speculative-fiction venues such as *Strange Horizons*, *Interzone*, and the *Magazine of Fantasy and Science Fiction*. In 2007 she published her first novel, *Racing the Dark*, the first installment in her Spirit Binders trilogy. She followed that novel with *Burning City* (2010), the second in the series, as well as two novels featuring protagonist Zephyr Hollis. Set in a 1920s New York City populated by both humans and vampires, the Zephyr Hollis novels, *Moonshine* (2010) and *Wicked City* (2012), earned Johnson significant attention from readers. Johnson also authored two graphic novels, *The Goblin King* (2009) and *Detective Frankenstein* (2011). Published by the imprint Graphic Universe as part of its Twisted Journeys line, the graphic novels are choose-your-own-adventure stories intended for middle-grade readers.

In 2013 Johnson published *The Summer Prince*, a young adult novel set in a futuristic, somewhat dystopian version of Brazil. Johnson earned significant praise for the novel, which was included in the long list for the 2013 National Book Award for young people's literature. Her next publication, the novel *Love Is the Drug*, was published in 2014. *Love Is the Drug* follows teenager Emily Bird, who, upon awakening in the hospital with no memory of how she got there, struggles to regain her lost memories amid a deadly virus outbreak and a government conspiracy. A critically acclaimed novel, *Love Is the Drug* was awarded the Andre Norton Award for young adult science-fiction and fantasy in 2015.

Major Works
One of the most notable features of Johnson's novels is their settings, which she fuses with the novels' specific genre elements to form unique, effective, and fully realized worlds. Her Zephyr Hollis novels, for instance, merge the historical setting of 1920s New York City with the trappings of urban fantasy, creating a city that is intriguing on multiple levels. This trend is perhaps most apparent in *The Summer Prince*, which is set in Brazil, in the futuristic pyramid city of Palmares Três, four hundred years after nuclear war devastated much of the world. Johnson, who was inspired to write the novel in part by

a visit to Brazil, incorporates numerous seemingly disparate elements into her story, from innovative urban planning designs to the history of the African diaspora in Brazil to the Mesopotamian *Epic of Gilgamesh*. This wide range of influences renders the world of the novel rich and layered, creating an effective backdrop for the novel's events. The Washington, DC, setting of *Love Is the Drug*, on the other hand, ostensibly falls within the real world, or close to it; however, the novel's high-stakes action transforms the real-life city into something greater than itself, instilling in the novel a sense of heightened reality that renders it an entertaining and effective thriller.

Joy Crelin

Further Reading

"About." *Alaya Dawn Johnson*. Johnson, 2015. Web. 30 Nov. 2015. <http://www.alayadawnjohnson.com/about>.

Gross, Claire E. Rev. of *The Summer Prince*, by Alaya Dawn Johnson. *Horn Book Magazine* 89.2 (2013): 107–8. *Literary Reference Center*. Web. 1 Dec. 2015. <http://search.ebscohost.com/login.aspx?direct=true&db=lfh&AN=85726421&site=lrc-live>.

Johnson, Alaya Dawn. "Day 3: Alaya Dawn Johnson." *Brown Bookshelf*. Brown Bookshelf, 3 Feb. 2013. Web. 30 Dec. 2015. <http://thebrownbookshelf.com/2013/02/03/day-3-alaya-dawn-johnson>.

Bibliography

Johnson, Alaya Dawn. "Alaya Dawn Johnson: Dreaming Stories." *Locus Online*. Locus, 18 Mar. 2011. Web. 30 Nov. 2015. <http://www.locusmag.com/Perspectives/2011/03/alaya-dawn-johnson-dreaming-stories>.

Johnson, Alaya Dawn. "Alaya Dawn Johnson: The Interfictions 2 Interview." Interview by Christian Desrosiers. *Interstitial Arts Foundation*. Interstitial Arts Foundation, 2009. Web. 30 Nov. 2015. <http://www.interstitialarts.org/projects/about-interfictions/interfictions-2/interfictions-2-interviews/alaya-dawn-johnson-the-interfictions-2-interview>.

Johnson, Alaya Dawn. "All Futures Are Political: A Q&A with Spec-Fic Author Alaya Dawn Johnson." Interview by Vann R. Newkirk II. *Gawker*. Gawker Media, 12 May 2015. Web. 30 Nov. 2015. <http://review.gawker.com/all-futures-are-political-a-q-a-with-spec-fic-author-a-1703637208>.

Johnson, Alaya Dawn. Interview. *Lightspeed*. Lightspeed, Aug. 2013. Web. 30 Nov. 2015. <http://www.lightspeedmagazine.com/nonfiction/interview-alaya-dawn-johnson>.

Johnson, Alaya Dawn. "Interview with Alaya Dawn Johnson: Transcript." *Gay YA*. Gay YA, 23 Oct. 2014. Web. 30 Nov. 2015. <http://www.gayya.org/?p=1326?>.

Johnson, Alaya Dawn. "Questions for Alaya Dawn Johnson, Author of 'The Summer Prince.'" Interview by Petra Mayer. *NPR Books*. NPR, 15 Feb. 2013. Web. 30 Nov. 2015. <http://www.npr.org/2013/02/15/172032734/questions-for-alaya-dawn-johnson-author-of-the-summer-prince>.

Johnson, Alaya Dawn. "#TTBF14 Interview: Alaya Dawn Johnson." *Texas Teen Book Festival*. Texas Teen Book Festival, 18 Oct. 2014. Web. 30 Nov. 2015. <http://texasteenbookfestival.org/ttbf14-interview-alaya-dawn-johnson>.

Johnson, Alaya Dawn, and Carole McDonnell. "Multicultural Fantasists Alaya Dawn Johnson and Carole McDonnell." Interview by K. Tempest Bradford. *Fantasy Magazine*. Fantasy Magazine, 2007. Web. 30 Nov. 2015. <http://www.fantasy-magazine.com/nonfiction/articles/multicultual-fantasists-alaya-dawn-johnson-and-carole-mcdonnell>.

Angela Johnson

Date of birth: June 18, 1961
Place of birth: Tuskegee, Alabama

Principal Works
Poetry
The Other Side: Shorter Poems (1998)
Running Back to Ludie (2001)
Children's Literature
Tell Me a Story, Mama (1989)
Do Like Kyla (1990)
When I Am Old with You (1990)
One of Three (1991)
The Leaving Morning (1992)
Julius (1993)
Joshua's Night Whispers (1994)
Joshua by the Sea (1994)
Shoes Like Miss Alice's (1995)
The Aunt in Our House (1996)
The Rolling Store (1997)

Courtesy of the John D. and Catherine T. MacArthur Foundation, via Wikimedia Commons

Daddy Calls Me Man (1997)
The Wedding (1999)
Down the Winding Road (2000)
Violet's Music (2004)
Just Like Josh Gibson (2004)
A Sweet Smell of Roses (2005)
Lottie Paris Lives Here (2011)
Lottie Paris and the Best Place (2013)
Young Adult Literature
Toning the Sweep (1993)
Humming Whispers (1995)
Heaven (1998)
Looking for Red (2002)
A Cool Moonlight (2003)
The First Part Last (2003)
Sweet, Hereafter (2010)
A Certain October (2012)
Short Stories
Gone from Home: Short Takes (1998)
Maniac Monkeys on Magnolia Street (1999)
When Mules Flew on Magnolia Street (2000)

Biography

Poet and writer Angela Johnson has authored more than forty books for children and young adults. She has been the recipient of the Ezra Jack Keats New Writer Award, three Coretta Scott King Author Awards, and the Michael L. Printz Award. Johnson's books depict African American families and the common experiences that children and teens have growing up. Her books also chronicle African American histories and struggles for civil rights. In 2003 Johnson was named a MacArthur Fellow.

Johnson was born in Tuskegee, Alabama. She grew up in Alabama and Ohio. As a child, Johnson spent a lot of time listening to stories. Her teacher would read stories to the students after lunch, making the characters "come to life," as Johnson put it in an interview for the website Brown Bookshelf. It was then that Johnson knew that she wanted to be a writer. Johnson's father and grandfather were storytellers, too. Their funny stories made Johnson realize that storytelling made life into theater. During her teenage years, Johnson's writing became a way of expressing feelings like frustration and alienation. When a high school teacher introduced her to the experimental Beat poets of the 1950s, Johnson became interested in reading poetry and nonfiction. In college and beyond, Johnson would go on to read and admire poetry by Nikki Giovanni, Amiri Baraka, Rita Dove, and others. In her teenage years, Johnson also discovered that she enjoyed reading stories about people's lives, including books about Janis Joplin and Malcolm X.

Johnson attended Kent State University and worked in child development for Volunteers in Service to America. In early adulthood, Johnson began to focus on her writing. In 1989 she published her first picture book, *Tell Me a Story, Mama*, which won the 1991 Ezra Jack Keats New Writer Award. Johnson went on to publish more children's picture books, and in 1993 she published her first young adult novel, *Toning the Sweep*. The novel, which received the 1994 Coretta Scott King Author Award, is a coming-of-age story about fourteen-year-old Emma, who must navigate the hardship of her grandmother Ola's terminal illness. Johnson went on to author the novel *Heaven* (1998), in which young Marley learns that her parents are also her aunt and uncle and that her Uncle Jack is really her biological father. Johnson received the 1999 Coretta Scott King Author Award for the book. In 2003 Johnson published a prequel to *Heaven*, titled *The First Part Last*, about a teen father. Among other awards, the novel won the 2004 Coretta Scott King Author Award as well as the 2004 Michael L. Printz Award for excellence in young adult literature.

Major Works

In her young adult novels, Johnson addresses real-life issues that teens face. Her first novel, *Toning the Sweep* (1993), is narrated by three women: teenaged Emily, her mother, Diane, and her grandmother Ola. When Ola is diagnosed with terminal cancer, she invites Emily and Diane to help her pack up her home in the California desert. In a letter to Emily, Ola simply writes, "Come to the desert and smell the flowers" (2). As Emily and Diane help Ola get ready to move back to Cleveland with them, they must reckon with Ola's decision to forgo cancer therapy and die peacefully. In the process, all three women learn more about each other. Emily develops a greater appreciation for her grandmother's resilience in the face of hardship. In the novel, Johnson writes in compressed, lyric prose. The characters' narratives are often personal, idiosyncratic recollections: "Mama says that in 1964 she sang Supremes songs so much, Grandmama threatened to take her radio" (3). But they also evoke larger, shared histories like the civil rights movement: "Alabama got too big for Mama in 1964—everything happening in that state got too big" (4). In this way, Johnson brings the personal to the political, and vice versa.

In her later novel *The First Part Last*, Johnson tells the story of a sixteen-year-old dad. The novel, narrated from the perspective of the teen father, Bobby, juxtaposes the "then" of childhood with the "now" of adulthood responsibilities. *The First Part Last* challenges traditional assumptions about gender roles in its depiction of a young man's struggle to parent his infant child. Written in a style that is both lyrical and colloquial, the novel paints Bobby as thoughtful and complex. Bobby speculates, "I figure if the world were really right, humans would live life backward and do the first part last. They'd be all knowing in the beginning and innocent in the end" (4). Bobby's voice is casual and honest, but it is also philosophical. In encountering Bobby's complexity, readers also learn about how complicated it is to move from childhood to adulthood.

Johnson has also published poetry and short stories. Her collection of poems, *The Other Side*, features a fourteen-year-old narrator who speaks of her small town in Alabama. The collection was designated a 1999

Coretta Scott King Author Honor Book. Johnson's collection of linked stories, *Gone from Home* (1999), address the types of losses that many teens face, including homelessness, violence, and terminal illness.

M. Lewandowski, MA

Further Reading
Johnson, Angela. "The Booklist Interview: Angela Johnson." Interview by Gillian Engberg. *Booklist* 15 Feb. 2004: 1074. Print.
Johnson, Dianne. "She's Grown Dreadlocks: The Fiction of Angela Johnson." *World Literature Today* Sept.–Dec. 2004: 75–78. Print.

Bibliography
"Angela Johnson." *MacArthur Foundation.* John D. and Catherine T. MacArthur Foundation, 5 Oct. 2003. Web. 1 Dec. 2015. <https://www.macfound.org/fellows/711>.
Johnson, Angela. Interview. *Brown Bookshelf.* Brown Bookshelf, 8 Feb. 2009. Web. 1 Dec. 2015. <http://thebrownbookshelf.com/2009/02/08/angela-johnson>.
Johnson, Angela. "Real Moments: An Interview with Angela Johnson." Interview by Andrea Maxworthy O'Brien. *Cooperative Children's Book Center.* Friends of the CCBC, U of Wisconsin-Madison, 2005. Web. 1 Dec. 2015. <https://ccbc.education.wisc.edu/authors/experts/ajohnson.asp>.
"2004 Printz Award." *YALSA.* Amer. Lib. Assn., 2004. Web. 8 Dec. 2015. <http://www.ala.org/yalsa/booklistsawards/bookawards/printzaward/previous-winners/04print>.

M. E. Kerr

Date of birth: May 27, 1927
Place of birth: Auburn, New York

Principal Works
Young Adult Literature
Dinky Hocker Shoots Smack! (1972)
If I Love You, Am I Trapped Forever? (1973)
Gentlehands (1978)
Night Kites (1986)
Deliver Us from Evie (1994)

Adult Nonfiction

We Walk Alone (as Ann Aldrich, 1955)

We, Too, Must Love (as Ann Aldrich, 1955)

Me Me Me Me Me: Not a Novel (as M. J. Meaker, 1983)

Highsmith: A Romance of the 1950s (as M. J. Meaker, 2003)

Marijane Meaker, CC-BY-SA-3.0, via Wikimedia Commons

Biography

M. E. Kerr, who was born Marijane Meaker, is an award-winning young adult author. She has been written and published books for over fifty years under various pen names, including M. E. Kerr, Ann Aldrich, Mary James, and Vin Packer. Meaker has written crime novels, non-fiction accounts of the lesbian subculture in Greenwich Village in the 1950s, and books for children—but she has been most prolific as a writer for young adults. She won the 1993 Margaret A. Edwards Award from the Young Adult Library Services Association for her contributions in young adult literature.

Marijane Agnes Meaker was born on May 27, 1927, to Ellis R. and Ida T. Meaker. Ellis, Meaker's father, was son of a respected grocer and the owner of a mayonnaise factory. Meaker grew up in Auburn, New York, where she attended the now defunct Fulton Avenue School before enrolling at Stuart Hall boarding school in Staunton, Virginia. (Her 1975 novel, *Is That You, Miss Blue?*, is based on her boarding school experience.) She was an avid reader but, as she recalls in her autobiography *Me Me Me Me Me: Not a Novel* (1983), a troublemaker as well. At boarding school, Meaker tacked pictures of the school's faculty to the wall and encouraged her friends to use the headmistress's image as a bull's eye for throwing darts. When the school found out, Meaker was expelled. Her mother appealed the decision, and Meaker was allowed to finish out her senior year. After graduation in 1944, she attended Vermont Junior College for a year before enrolling at the University of Missouri, where she studied English literature. She graduated in 1949 and moved to New York City with some college friends. As an aspiring writer—and a lover of multiple identities—Meaker used her given name to pose as a writing agent and claimed to represent the myriad writers that were actually all her. She sold her first piece of writing, an article under the name Laura Winston, to *Ladies Home Journal* in April 1951.

Unlike most writers with pen names, Meaker created entire alter egos for her "writers." For example, a completely imaginary elderly couple named Edgar and Mamie Stone were enormously successful selling true-confession stories—so much so, that Meaker told those who might want to meet them that the couple never left their home in Maine. Meaker's first truly successful alter ego, however, was a mystery and suspense writer named Vin Packer. Several of Packer's novels were positively reviewed by Anthony Boucher for the *New York Times* in the 1950s. Meaker also published several classic non-fiction books about lesbians in the 1950s, '60s, and '70s under the name Ann Aldrich. The series includes the classics *We Walk Alone* (1955) and *We, Too, Must Love* (1955). In the 1960s, Meaker published three books under the name M. J. Meaker, including a novel called *Hometown* in 1967. She also published—and continues to publish—under her own name. In 2003, she wrote *Highsmith: A Romance of the 1950s*, about her two-year love affair with the famed literary crime novelist, Patricia Highsmith. Meaker lives in East Hampton, New York, where she occasionally teaches writing.

Major Works

In the early 1970s, Meaker was encouraged to write a book for young adults. For that endeavor, she chose the name, M. E. Kerr, a play on her real last name, Meaker; she writes middle-grade children's books under the name Mary James, a play on her real first name,

Marijane. She published her first YA novel, *Dinky Hocker Shoots Smack!*, in 1972. The book, full of idiosyncratic characters (one is a compulsive rhymer), is about an overweight teenage girl named Susan "Dinky" Hocker and her small, and similarly troubled, group of friends. *Dinky Hocker* explores societal attitudes toward appearance, but also parent-child relationships. Dinky's mother ignores her in favor of the drug-rehabilitation program that she is involved in—while immersing herself in the pain of others, she has failed to recognize the pain of her own daughter. Critics such as Dale Carlson for the *New York Times* noted Meaker's ear for spoken language and her ability to get to the core of real-life problems. The story was later adapted for television and aired as an ABC afterschool special in 1978.

Meaker's other well-known novels include *Gentlehands* (1978), *Night Kites* (1986), and *Deliver Us from Evie* (1994). *Gentlehands* features a present-day romance between a wealthy girl and a lower-middle-class boy—themes of class and class differences are prevalent in this and much of Meaker's work—but the story revolves around events that took place in World War II and the identity of a Nazi killer. In *Night Kites*, Erick Rudd enjoys a coming-of-age romance with a girl named Nicki Marr only to discover that his older brother Pete is gay and dying of AIDS. Meaker explored sexual orientation and discrimination again in the book *Deliver Us from Evie*. Narrated by Evie Burrman's brother Parr, the book chronicles the romance between Evie and the much-wealthier Patsy Duff, as well as his family's denial of the girls' relationship.

Molly Hagan

Further Reading

Kerr, M. E. "Long Island Opinion: View from a Windowless School." *New York Times*. New York Times, 6 Dec. 1987. Web. 30 Mar. 2015. <http://www.nytimes.com/1987/12/06/nyregion/long-island-opinion-view-from-a-windowless-school.html>.

Nilsen, Alleen Pace. *Presenting M.E. Kerr*. New York: Twayne, 1997. Print.

Ricci, Michael. "Auburn Author M.E. Kerr a Model of Literary Ambition." *Citizen*. Auburn Citizen [NY], 16 July 2014. Web. 30 Mar. 2015. <http://auburnpub.com/lifestyles/ricci-auburn-author-m-e-kerr-a-model-of-literary/article_516e1f26-7969-5d1d-8c6c-5dd85f038234.html>.

Bibliography

Carlson, Dale. Rev. of *Dinky Hocker Shoots Smack!*, by M. E. Kerr. *New York Times* 11 Feb. 1973: BR36. Web. 31 Mar. 2015. <http://query.nytimes.com/gst/abstract.html?res=9B00E4D91730E63ABC4952DFB4668388669EDE>.

Kerr, M. E. Interview by Terry Gross. *Fresh Air*. NPR, 19 June 2003. Web. 3 Apr. 2015. <http://www.npr.org/templates/story/story.php?storyId=1303128>.

Kerr, M. E. "M.E. Kerr (A.K.A. Mary James & Vin Packer)." *Balkin Buddies*. Catherine Balkin, n.d. Web. 30 Mar. 2015. <http://balkinbuddies.com/kerr/index.html>.

Kerr, M. E. *Me Me Me Me Me: Not a Novel*. New York: HarperCollins, 1983. Print.

Silvey, Anita, ed. *Children's Books and Their Creators*. New York: Houghton, 1995. Print.

Madeleine L'Engle

Date of birth: November 29, 1918
Place of birth: New York, New York
Date of death: September 6, 2007
Place of death: Litchfield, Connecticut

Principal Works
Young Adult Literature
The Small Rain (1945)
And Both Were Young (1949)
Camilla (1951)
Meet the Austins (1960)
The Arm of the Starfish (1965)
Dragons in the Waters (1976)
A House Like a Lotus (1984)
Many Waters (1986)
An Acceptable Time (1989)
Children's Literature
A Wrinkle in Time (1962)
A Wind in the Door (1973)
A Swiftly Tilting Planet (1978)
Adult Literature
The Other Side of the Sun (1971)
A Severed Wasp (1982)
Certain Women (1992)
A Live Coal in the Sea (1996)
The Joys of Love (2008)

Nonfiction

A Circle of Quiet (1972)

The Summer of the Great-Grandmother (1974)

Walking on Water: Reflections on Faith and Art (1980)

The Glorious Impossible (1990)

The Rock That Is Higher (1993)

Penguins and Golden Calves: Icons and Idols (1996)

Bright Evening Star (1997)

Friends for the Journey (with Luci Shaw, 1997)

Madeleine L'Engle Herself: Reflections on a Writing Life (with Carole Chase, 2001)

Biography

Madeleine L'Engle was an American writer of fiction for adults and younger readers whose career spanned six decades. She is best known for several series for children and young adults that combine themes such as family, faith, and grief with fantastic or science-fictional elements, among them the Time Quintet and the Austin Family series. In addition to her many novels, L'Engle wrote numerous works of nonfiction as well as poetry.

L'Engle was born Madeleine L'Engle Camp on November 29, 1918, in New York City. She was the only child born to Charles and Madeleine Camp. L'Engle was surrounded by writing from an early age, as her father worked as a journalist and reviewer for the *New York Sun*. She began writing fiction as a young child and soon began to write poetry and keep journals as well. Although she struggled somewhat at school, her parents encouraged her literary efforts. An avid reader, L'Engle particularly enjoyed the works of Canadian writer L. M. Montgomery and identified strongly with the protagonist of Montgomery's novel *Emily of New Moon* (1923).

In 1930 L'Engle and her family moved to the French Alps in an attempt to improve her father's health. She attended the École Le Châtelard, an English-speaking boarding school in Switzerland, for two years before returning to the United States. Her family settled in Florida, and L'Engle traveled to South Carolina to attend the boarding school Ashley Hall. After completing her education at Ashley Hall, she enrolled in Smith College in Northampton, Massachusetts, where she studied English. L'Engle graduated with honors from the college in 1941.

After college, L'Engle moved to New York, where she found work as a stage actor. She pursued writing seriously during that time and in 1945 published her first novel, *The Small Rain*. The novel, the first of two books about protagonist Katherine Forrester, is a realistic coming-of-age story that incorporates some autobiographical elements. Despite her previous success, L'Engle struggled with writing during the 1950s, receiving numerous rejection letters from publishers, and at one point seriously considered giving up the profession.

The following decade brought numerous achievements, beginning with the publication of *Meet the Austins* in 1960. The success of that book, which chronicles the family life of protagonist Vicky Austin, led to the publication of further books in the series, which ultimately took on a more fantastical tone. L'Engle perhaps became best known for her novel *A Wrinkle in Time* (1962), which, along with the other books in her Time Quintet (*A Wind in the Door*, 1973; *A Swiftly Tilting Planet*, 1978; *Many Waters*, 1986; *An Acceptable Time*, 1989) and the subsequent related series focusing on the O'Keefe family, greatly influenced the development of science fiction and fantasy literature for children and young adults. In addition to those novels, she went on to write various other works as fiction as well as numerous nonfiction works, many of which feature L'Engle's musings on her life and religious faith.

L'Engle married actor Hugh Franklin in 1946. The couple had three children, Josephine, Bion, and Maria. In addition to writing, L'Engle served for decades as a librarian for the Cathedral of St. John the Divine in New York City. L'Engle died on September 6, 2007, in Litchfield, Connecticut.

Major Works

L'Engle's major works for young adults share a number of common themes and concerns, many of which were deeply relevant to the author's own life. Although she spent many of her formative years in boarding schools, family remained of great importance to L'Engle, and many of her novels focus on the strength of family relationships. The Austin family series, for instance, follows the lives and adventures of the members of the family, while *A Wrinkle in Time* focuses on protagonist Meg's quest to find her missing father. L'Engle's novels are likewise deeply personal in regard to their use of religious themes. She was a devout Christian, but she objected to many elements of organized religion, particularly the emphasis some denominations placed on eternal damnation, which she found to be entirely incompatible with her personal conception of the Christian god. Many of L'Engle's novels, particularly those in the Time Quintet, draw heavily from Christian theology as well as from her own understanding of her faith. This is perhaps most obvious in *Many Waters* (1986), the fourth novel in the Time Quintet, which features biblical figures such as Noah. The author's personal interest in science likewise played a critical role in the development of her novels; although L'Engle did not have a scientific background, she enjoyed reading about scientific topics such as quantum theory and at times incorporated such topics into her work.

Joy Crelin

Further Reading

Marcus, Leonard S. *Listening for Madeleine: A Portrait of Madeleine L'Engle in Many Voices*. New York: Farrar, 2012. Print.

Rosenberg, Aaron. *Madeleine L'Engle*. New York: Rosen, 2006. Print.

Bibliography

"About Madeleine L'Engle." *Madeleine L'Engle*. Crosswicks, n.d. Web. 4 June 2015. <http://www.madeleinelengle.com/madeleine-lengle>.

L'Engle, Madeleine. "Madeleine L'Engle." Interview by Bob Abernethy. *Religion and Ethics Newsweekly*. WNET, 10 Feb. 2012. Web. 4 June 2015. <http://www.pbs.org/wnet/religionandethics/2012/02/10/november-17-2000-madeleine-lengle/3639>.

Martin, Douglas. "Madeleine L'Engle, Writer of Children's Classics, Is Dead at 88." *New York Times*. New York Times, 8 Sept. 2007. Web. 4 June 2015. <http://www.nytimes.com/2007/09/08/books/07cnd-lengle.html?hp&_r=1&>.

Sharp, Michael D., ed. *Popular Contemporary Writers*. Vol. 7. Tarrytown: Marshall, 2006. Print.

Justine Larbalestier

Date of birth: 1967
Place of birth: Sydney, Australia

Principal Works

Magic or Madness trilogy (2005–7)
How to Ditch Your Fairy (2008)
Liar (2009)
Team Human, cowritten with Sarah Rees Brennan (2012)
Razorhurst (2014)
My Sister Rosa (2016)

Biography

Australian American author Justine Larbalestier is a young adult novelist and short story writer. Her novels include the Magic or Madness fantasy trilogy and the popular novel *Liar* (2009), a psychological thriller. In 2007 *Magic or Madness*, the first book in the trilogy, won the Andre Norton Award for Young Adult Science Fiction and Fantasy. Larbalestier is also the author of a book of literary criticism, *The Battle of the Sexes in Science Fiction* (2002), about the role of women and feminism in American science fiction.

Larbalestier was born in Sydney. Because both of her parents were anthropologists, Larbalestier had the opportunity to live in different parts of Australia, including Newcastle, Canberra, and two Aboriginal settlements in the Northern Territory. According to Larbalestier, she has been writing fiction for as long as she has been able to write. Larbalestier's first publication was a poem she wrote when she was nine years old. It appeared in the *Newcastle Morning Herald* and later in the feminist magazine *Refractory Girl*. Before becoming a young adult novelist, Larbalestier worked in academia. Her critical book *The Battle of the Sexes in Science Fiction* examines the influence of 1920s to 1970s feminism on contemporary feminist science fiction.

In 2005 Larbalestier published *Magic or Madness*, her first young adult novel. The novel tells the story of fifteen-year-old Reason Cansino and her grandmother, Esmeralda, who practices magic. The novel won an Andre Norton Award and was shortlisted for the Ethel Turner Prize for Young People's Literature. In 2006 and 2007, Larbalestier published *Magic Lessons* and *Magic's Child,* completing the trilogy. In the years that followed, she published *How to Ditch Your Fairy* (2008), *Liar* (2009), and *Razorhurst* (2014). *Razorhurst* is a historical thriller set in 1932 in a fictional neighborhood of Sydney, where rival gangs dominate and fight using razor blades. It features two female protagonists. According to Larbalestier, she performed extensive research for the novel. But while Larbalestier capitalized on her research skills in the writing of *Razorhurst*, she has said in interviews that she has no intention of revisiting an academic career. Larbalestier lives with her husband, young adult writer Scott Westerfeld. The couple spends half of the year living in Sydney and half in New York.

Major Works

Larbalestier's Magic or Madness trilogy, originally published between 2005 and 2007, tells the story of teenager Reason Cansino and her grandmother, Esmeralda, who is said to be a wicked witch. When Reason's mother, Sarafina, has a mental breakdown, Reason is sent to live with Esmeralda in Sydney. There Reason discovers a magic door. Upon walking through it, she finds herself halfway around the world in New York City. In New York, Reason befriends Jay-Tee. When Esmeralda comes to their rescue at one point, the two begin to trust the older woman and learn from her about magic. *Magic or Madness* is told in a close third person that focuses on Reason's perspective. The language of the novel is descriptive, merging detailed realist accounts of Sydney and New York with supernatural encounters and events. In this way, the novel suspends readers in a place between reality and fantasy. Through Reason, readers are brought into the fantastical world of the novel. The novel explores issues like the development of identity and autonomy in adolescence, the dangerous, even predatory adult world, and the false dichotomy of good versus evil.

In Larbalestier's later novel *Liar* (2009), the compulsive liar and unreliable narrator Micah Wilkins is the lens through which readers experience the action. Micah is seventeen years old and biracial. She lives in New York City with her parents. At the beginning of the novel, Micah's boyfriend, Zach, is found murdered in the park, and Micah is considered a potential suspect. In the opening pages of the book, Micah tells readers, "I will tell you my story and I will tell it straight. No lies, no omissions." But as the novel progresses, Micah takes back or corrects previous claims. Readers begin to wonder increasingly whether any of Micah's narrative is true. The novel juxtaposes nonlinear narratives of "Before" and "After" the murder and intersperses "Family History" and "History of Me." The novel's structure contributes to the complexity of Micah's character and the tension and suspense of the plot. *Liar* won a number of awards, including the 2009 Carl Brandon Kindred Award, the 2010 Davitt Award for the Best Young Adult Crime Novel, and the 2009 Western Australia (WA) Premier's Young Adult Prize.

M. Lewandowski, MA

Further Reading

Anderson, Kristine J. "Justine Larbalestier. The Battle of the Sexes in Science Fiction." *Utopian Studies* 14.1 (2003): 223–25. Print.

Larbalestier, Justine. *The Battle of the Sexes in Science Fiction*. Middletown: Wesleyan UP, 2002. Print.

Bibliography

Clark, Noelene. "Gory *Razorhurst* by Justine Larbalestier Mixes Noir and Ghosts." Rev. of *Razorhurst* by Justine Larbalestier. *Los Angeles Times*. Tribune, 12 March, 2015. Web. 21 Dec. 2015. <http://www.latimes.com/books/jacketcopy/la-ca-jc-justine-larbalestier-20150315-story.html>.

"Justine Larbalestier." *JustineLarbalestier.com*. Web. December 15, 2015. <http://justinelarbalestier.com/>.

"Liar." Rev. of *Liar* by Justine Larbalestier. *Publisher's Weekly*. PWxyz, n.d. Web. December 15, 2015. <http://www.publishersweekly.com/978-1-59990-305-7>.

Walton, Jo. "Australian Fantasy: Justine Larbalestier's *Magic or Madness*." *Tor.com*. Macmillan, 12 Apr. 2013. Web. 21 Dec. 2015. <http://www.tor.com/2013/04/12/australian-fantasy-justine-larbalestiers-magic-or-madness/>.

Ursula K. Le Guin

Date of birth: October 21, 1929
Place of birth: Berkeley, California

Principal Works
Children's Literature
The Catwings Collection (1988–99)
Young Adult Literature
Earthsea series (1968–2001)
Very Far Away from Anywhere Else (1976)
The Beginning Place (1980)
The Annals of the Western Shore series (2004–7)
Lavinia (2008)
Adult Literature
Hainish Cycle (1966–2000)
The Lathe of Heaven (1971)
Malafrena (1979)
Always Coming Home (1985)

Biography
Ursula K. Le Guin is an influential American writer of science fiction and fantasy. In the realm of young adult

literature, she is perhaps best known for her Earthsea series, published between 1968 and 2001. In addition to that series, she is the author of the young adult novel *Very Far Away from Anywhere Else* (1976) as well as the three novels comprising the Annals of the Western Shore (2004–7). An award-winning and critically acclaimed writer, Le Guin has also written numerous novels for adults and various books for children.

Le Guin was born Ursula Kroeber on October 21, 1929, in Berkeley, California. She was the youngest of four children born to Alfred and Theodora Kroeber, both of whom were anthropologists. Her parents fostered her love of reading from an early age, and she grew up reading both mainstream literature and pulp science fiction. A storyteller since early childhood, Le Guin submitted her first short story to a magazine at the age of eleven, although it was not published.

In 1947 Le Guin enrolled in Radcliffe College to study French and Italian literature. She earned her bachelor's degree in 1951 and proceeded to Columbia University, from which she received her master's degree the following year. Planning to pursue further studies, she traveled to France on a Fulbright grant. However, after marrying and settling in Portland, Oregon, Le Guin opted to pursue a career in writing rather than academia. Over the following years, she wrote several novels and numerous short stories but faced frequent rejections from publishers and fiction magazines. She sold her first short story in 1962 and published her first novel for adults, *Rocannon's World*, in 1966. The novel was the first book in her Hainish Cycle, which would come to include the influential novels *The Left Hand of Darkness* (1969) and *The Dispossessed* (1974).

Le Guin's first novel for young adult readers, *A Wizard of Earthsea*, was published in 1968. The novel was the first of several installments in the Earthsea series, which also includes the novels *The Tombs of Atuan* (1971), *The Farthest Shore* (1972), *Tehanu* (1990), and *The Other Wind* (2001). The Earthsea novels are set in a fantasy world that first appeared in Le Guin's 1964 short story "The Word of Unbinding." A Sci Fi Channel television special based on the series, titled *Legend of Earthsea*, aired in 2004, while Studio Ghibli, a Japanese animation studio, released the film *Tales from Earthsea* in 2006. However, Le Guin was disappointed in both adaptations and felt that they did not represent her work, particularly citing the portrayal of her dark-skinned characters as white and the increased focus on violent battles between good and evil rather than personal struggles.

In addition to the Earthsea novels, Le Guin has written several other books for young adults, including *Very Far Away from Anywhere Else*, a work of realistic fiction published in the 1970s. She also published three novels known collectively as the Annals of the Western Shore—*Gifts* (2004), *Voices* (2006), and *Powers* (2007)—which follow young people as they discover their magical gifts in a fantasy world. In 2004, Le Guin won the American Library Association's Margaret A. Edwards Award for her lifetime contribution to young adult literature.

Le Guin met her husband, Charles A. Le Guin, on a boat while traveling to France to pursue her studies in literature. They married in 1953 and later had three children. Le Guin lives in Portland, Oregon.

Major Works

Although Le Guin's best-known adult novels fall within the science-fiction genre, her most popular young adult novels do not. The Earthsea series is firmly rooted in fantasy and takes place in a world in which magic plays a key role in most cultures; the protagonist of the first novel in the series, Ged, is a wizard in training. Magic similarly plays a crucial role in the Annals of the Western Shore, as the protagonists of each novel discover magical gifts and use them to overcome challenges. Le Guin's young adult novel *Very Far Away from Anywhere Else*, on the other hand, takes place in the United States and is realistic in nature. Despite their different genres, Le Guin's works tend to share a number of themes. Coming-of-age themes are prominent in her young adult novels, and characters' personal development is often tied to their development as magic users. She is likewise interested in setting fantasy novels in fictional versions of non-European societies and has noted on numerous occasions that she objects to the Eurocentrism of much mainstream fantasy. Themes of gender and feminism are also prevalent in Le Guin's work. This wide range of genres and themes demonstrates Le Guin's versatility as a writer in both her adult and young adult fiction.

Joy Crelin

Further Reading

Freeman, John. "Ursula Le Guin: She Got There First." *Boston Globe*. Boston Globe Media, 22 Nov. 2014. Web. 10 June 2015. <https://www.bostonglobe.com/arts/books/2014/11/22/ursula-guin-she-got-there-first/aQURr2fiFuKjxf1Fv6zW3O/story.html#>.

Justice, Faith L. "Ursula K. Le Guin." *Salon*. Salon Media, 23 Jan. 2001. Web. 10 June 2015. <http://www.salon.com/2001/01/23/le_guin>.

Le Guin, Ursula K. "About Ursula K. Le Guin." *Ursula K. Le Guin*. Le Guin, 2015. Web. 10 June 2015. <http://www.ursulakleguin.com/MenuContentsList.html#AboutUKL>.

Bibliography

Bernardo, Susan M., and Graham J. Murphy. *Ursula K. Le Guin: A Critical Companion*. Westport: Greenwood, 2006. Print.

Freedman, Carl, ed. *Conversations with Ursula K. Le Guin*. Jackson: UP of Mississippi, 2008. Print.

Le Guin, Ursula K. Interview by John Wray. *Paris Review*. Paris Review, 2013. Web. 10 June 2015. <http://www.theparisreview.org/interviews/6253/the-art-of-fiction-no-221-ursula-k-le-guin>.

Le Guin, Ursula K. "Ursula K. Le Guin: Still Battling the Powers That Be." Interview by John Joseph Adams and David Barr Kirtley. *Wired*. Condé Nast, 25 July 2012. Web. 10 June 2015. <http://www.wired.com/2012/07/geeks-guide-ursula-k-le-guin>.

Liptak, Andrew. "The Left and Right Hands of Ursula K. Le Guin." *Kirkus*. Kirkus Media, 14 Aug. 2014. Web. 11 June 2015. <https://www.kirkusreviews.com/features/left-and-right-hands-ursula-k-le-guin>.

David Levithan

Date of birth: September 7, 1972
Place of birth: Short Hills, New Jersey

Principal Works
Young Adult Literature
Boy Meets Boy (2003)
Nick and Norah's Infinite Playlist (with Rachel Cohn, 2006)
Will Grayson, Will Grayson (with John Green, 2009)
The Lover's Dictionary (2011)
Every Day (2012)
Two Boys Kissing (2013)
Another Day (2015)

Biography
David Levithan is an award-winning young adult author whose 2006 novel *Nick and Nora's Infinite Playlist*, cowritten with fellow young adult novelist Rachel

Jake Hamilton

Cohn, was adapted into a successful film starring Kat Dennings and Michael Cera in 2008. In addition to being a prolific author and innovative collaborator, partnering with writers such as Cohn, John Green, and Brian Selznick, Levithan is also the executive editorial director at Scholastic Press and manages his own young adult imprint called PUSH. Levithan champions stories about gay teenagers, particularly stories that challenge the tortured "coming out" narrative. In his novel *Two Boys Kissing* (2013), for example, two teenage boys try to set a world record for longest kiss; for the *Los Angeles Review of Books*, Jonathan Alexander described *Two Boys Kissing* as a celebration of "everyday queerness," focusing on the excitement of sexual discovery rather than the agony of trying to fit into a straight world. The book is a thematic extension of Levithan's first book, *Boy Meets Boy* (2003), which is set in a veritable gay utopia: two boys fall in love at a high school where the quarterback of the football team is also a drag queen. Levithan published a book about adults called *The Lover's Dictionary* in 2011.

Levithan was born in Short Hills, New Jersey, on September 7, 1972, to parents Beth and Allen Levithan. He was a happy child and teenager who was always reading. He attended Millburn High School, where as a student he used to write the names of his favorite authors, including Margaret Atwood, Philip Roth, and young adult writer Cynthia Voigt, on his jeans. He graduated from Brown University with dual degrees in political science and English in 1994.

As a college student, Levithan interned at Scholastic and worked on the best-selling Babysitter's Club series. Serendipitously, his boss's assistant had recently left, so the nineteen-year-old Levithan was able to take on more work than would regularly be afforded to an intern—he even helped develop plot. Levithan wound up staying with the company, where he became an executive editorial director in 2006. He founded his own publishing imprint called PUSH in February 2002. With PUSH, Levithan adopted a mission of honesty. Scholastic readers craved real stories about their lives, so Levithan set out to find writers who could offer fresh perspectives on being a teenager. The material was a lot edgier than anything Scholastic had published in the past; one early book was about tripping on acid (*Pure Sunshine*, by Brian James), and another was about growing up homeless (Coe Booth's *Tyrell*). Since then, in his capacity as editor and publisher, Levithan has worked with such authors as Suzanne Collins (*The Hunger Games*), fantasy writer Garth Nix, Alice Hoffman (*Practical Magic*), and historical fiction author M. T. Anderson.

Major Works

Levithan published his first novel, *Boy Meets Boy*, in 2003. The book was inspired by a short story he wrote for his friends as a Valentine's Day present. The love story is set in a suburban high school where gay and lesbian teenagers are not social outcasts but rather the most popular kids in school. Levithan said that he wrote the book because it was the kind of story he always hoped to come across as an editor but never did. He then teamed up with another young adult writer, Rachel Cohn, to write *Nick and Norah's Infinite Playlist*, published in 2006. Cohn wanted to write a book about two teenagers named Nick and Norah (named after the bantering Nick and Nora Charles of the *Thin Man* movies in the 1930s) but felt self-conscious writing from a male's perspective. She contacted Levithan, and the two concocted a story about two music-loving teenagers who fall in love. They wrote the book chapter by chapter, alternating between Nick and Norah's perspectives. The book was so popular that it was made into a film in 2008. Levithan and Cohn also wrote *Naomi and Ely's No Kiss List* (2007) and *Dash & Lily's Book of Dares* (2010).

In 2006 Levithan collaborated with author and illustrator Brian Selznick, author of *The Invention of Hugo Cabret* (2007), to write an illustrated Valentine's Day retelling of Charles Dickens's *A Christmas Carol* (1843). Levithan has also collaborated with John Green, the best-selling author of *The Fault in Our Stars* (2011); the two cowrote *Will Grayson, Will Grayson* (2009), a novel about two boys with the same name who meet in a porn shop. Levithan explored themes of identity through an innovative new angle in his novel *Every Day* (2012), about a teenager named A who wakes up in the body of a new person every day. A falls in love with a girl named Rhiannon after he inhabits the body of her unappreciative boyfriend, Justin. As time goes on, he must find his way back to her, wooing her as whomever he happens to be that day. In 2013 Levithan published *Two Boys Kissing*, based on a true story about two boys who broke a world record for world's longest kiss in 2011. The book, like *Boy Meets Boy* before it, is playful but with an added layer of poignancy. Narrated by a chorus of men who died of AIDS in the 1980s and early 1990s, the book marvels at the social changes a generation can bring but also notes how far gay and lesbian acceptance has yet to go. In *Another Day*, the 2015 companion novel to *Every Day*, Levithan presents Rhiannon's quest to find the truth about love.

Molly Hagan

Further Reading

Elejalde-Ruiz, Alexia. "Author's Focus: Soul, but No Body." *Chicago Tribune* 19 Sept. 2012. Web. 13 Sept. 2015. <http://articles.chicagotribune.com/2012-09-19/features/sc-ent-0919-books-david-levithan-20120919_1_david-levithan-gender-or-race-body>.

Garcia, Antero. *Critical Foundations in Young Adult Literature: Challenging Genres*. Rotterdam: Sense, 2013. *eBook Academic Collection*. Web. 7 Oct. 2015. <http://search.ebscohost.com/login.aspx?direct=true&db=e000xww&AN=668597&site=eds-live>.

Levithan, David. "One Thing Leads to Another: An Interview with David Levithan." Interview by Julie Bartel. *Hub*. YALSA, 29 Aug. 2013. Web. 13 Sept. 2015. <http://www.yalsa.ala.org/thehub/2013/08/29/one-thing-leads-to-another-an-interview-with-david-levithan/>.

Levithan, David, and Rachel Cohn. "The Real Couple behind the *Infinite Playlist*." Interview by Alex Cohen. *NPR*. NPR, 3 Oct. 2008. Web. 13 Sept. 2015. <http://www.npr.org/templates/transcript/transcript.php?storyId=95335682>.

Bibliography

Alexander, Jonathan. "The Career of David Levithan: It Gets Better and Better." *Los Angeles Review of Books*. LARB, 22 Apr. 2014. Web. 13 Sept. 2015. <https://lareviewofbooks.org/essay/career-david-levithan-gets-better-better>.

Bruni, Frank. "Bodies and Souls." Rev. of *Every Day*, by David Levithan. *New York Times*. New York Times, 23 Aug. 2012. Web. 13 Sept. 2015. <http://www.nytimes.com/2012/08/26/books/review/every-day-by-david-levithan.html>.

Deahl, Rachel. "David Levithan: The Happy Editor-Writer." *Publisher's Weekly*. PWxyz, 18 Feb. 2008. Web. 13 Sept. 2015. <http://www.publishersweekly.com/pw/by-topic/new-titles/adult-announcements/article/12792-david-levithan-the-happy-editor-writer.html>.

Friedman, Robin. "The Write Stuff: A Young Adult Author's (Almost) Infinite Playlist." *New Jersey Jewish News*. New Jersey Jewish News, 2 July 2009. Web. 13 Sept. 2015. <http://njjewishnews.com/njjn.com/070209/ltDavidLevithan.html>.

Minkel, Elizabeth. "[Heart] for the 'The Lover's Dictionary.'" *New Yorker*. Condé Nast, 14 Feb. 2011. Web. 13 Sept. 2015. <http://www.newyorker.com/books/page-turner/for-the-lovers-dictionary>.

Rosen, Michael. "Lizzie McGuire Meets Queer as Folk." Rev. of *Boy Meets Boy*, by David Levithan. *Guardian*. Guardian News and Media, 15 Apr. 2005. Web. 13 Sept. 2015. <http://www.theguardian.com/books/2005/apr/16/featuresreviews.guardianreview29>.

Schwartzapfel, Beth. "Two Teens, One Name." *Brown Alumni Magazine*. Brown Alumni Magazine, 1 July 2010. Web. 13 Sept. 2015. <http://www.brownalumnimagazine.com/content/view/2605/40/>

C.S. Lewis

Date of birth: November 29, 1898
Place of birth: Belfast, Ireland (now in Northern Ireland)
Date of death: November 22, 1963
Place of death: Oxford, England

Principal Works

Children's Literature
The Chronicles of Narnia (1950–56)

Adult Literature
The Pilgrim's Regress (1933)
The Space Trilogy (1938–45)
The Screwtape Letters (1942)
The Great Divorce (1946)
Till We Have Faces (1956)

Biography

C. S. Lewis was the author of numerous novels and nonfiction works, many of them dealing with Christianity, mythology, and literature. He is best known for his Chronicles of Narnia, a series of fantasy novels for young readers that encompasses *The Lion, the Witch, and the Wardrobe* (1950); *Prince Caspian* (1951); *The Voyage of the Dawn Treader* (1952); *The Silver Chair* (1953); *The Horse and His Boy* (1954); *The Magician's Nephew* (1955); and *The Last Battle* (1956).

Clive Staples Lewis was born in Belfast, in what is now Northern Ireland, on November 29, 1898, the second of Albert and Florence Lewis's two children. After his brother, Warren, was sent to boarding school, Lewis was educated at home by his parents and governess, and he spent a great deal of time reading. Florence died when Lewis was nine, and soon after, he was sent to the Wynyard School, a boarding school in Watford, England. He went on to study at Campbell College in Belfast and Cherbourg House in Malvern, England, before enrolling in Malvern College in late 1913. He did not remain at the school long, however, and in 1914, he traveled to Great Bookham, England, to study with W. T. Kirkpatrick, the retired headmaster of Lurgan College, Albert Lewis's alma mater. Kirkpatrick's tutelage prepared Lewis well for university, and in April 1917, he began his studies at University College, Oxford.

By the fall of 1917, Great Britain was deeply entrenched in World War I, and Lewis left university to enlist in the army as an officer. With his battalion, Lewis traveled to France, where he was injured in a battle near the Western Front. Following the war he returned to University College, where he studied English, Greek, and Latin literature, philosophy, and ancient history. After completing his studies in 1924, Lewis became a philosophy tutor at University College before taking a position as an English language and literature tutor at Magdalen College, Oxford. He remained in the position for nearly thirty years. While in Oxford Lewis became a member of the Inklings, an informal group of writers and academics that also included Lord of the Rings (1954–55) author J. R. R. Tolkien. It was during this period that Lewis also developed the strong Christian faith that would shape most of his literary works.

Many of Lewis's early published writings were academic in nature, focusing on such topics as religion, education, and literature. He also wrote and published poetry. Lewis published his first novel, *The Pilgrim's Regress*, in 1933. The novel, the title of which calls to mind the seventeenth-century *The Pilgrim's Progress,* is an allegorical work that explores the philosophies prevalent in Lewis's world. Lewis went on to write various other novels dealing with religion and philosophy, including *The Screwtape Letters* (1942) and *The Great Divorce* (1946). Among many readers, however, Lewis became best known as the author of the Chronicles of Narnia, which began in 1950 with the publication of *The Lion, the Witch, and the Wardrobe* and concluded with the 1956 publication of *The Last Battle*. Intended for young readers, the Narnia books were soon considered classics of British children's literature.

In 1954, Lewis took the position of chair of medieval and Renaissance literature at Cambridge University. While at Cambridge, he married Joy Davidman, an American writer whom he had first met several years before. Her death in 1960 had a profound effect on Lewis, who wrote the book *A Grief Observed* (1961) about the experience. Lewis himself died of kidney disease in Oxford on November 22, 1963.

Major Works

As a member of the Inklings, Lewis had access to a host of colleagues with whom to discuss literature and writing. He received extensive feedback from his writer friends, and their input, particularly that of Tolkien, had a great influence on the development of both Lewis's spiritual worldview and his fiction. Many of his novels for adults present religious and philosophical concepts through the form of allegory and take place in either a version of his contemporary world or in his conception of heaven or hell. However, Lewis also notably explored his themes of interest through speculative fiction, creating worlds greatly removed from his own. The novels in his Space Trilogy—which includes *Out of the Silent Planet* (1938), *Perelandra* (1943), *That Hideous Strength* (1945)—for example, are works of science fiction that draw heavily from Lewis's interest in religion and mythology and take place largely on other planets.

Lewis's series of novels for young readers, the Chronicles of Narnia, builds upon the themes and literary devices used in his adult novels, presenting an allegorical fantasy world that both reflects and contrasts with the real one. In the majority of the novels, children from England are transported into a fantastical land filled with magic, mythological and fairy-tale creatures, and an ongoing struggle between good and evil. The land is under the protection of the lion Aslan, a Christlike figure who, in *The Lion, the Witch, and the Wardrobe*, is betrayed, killed, and resurrected. The Christian allegory becomes clearest in the final book, *The Last Battle*, in which both the real world and the world of Narnia come to an end, and the characters ultimately deemed good are welcomed into a heavenly plane of which the old Narnia and England were merely a dim reflection. The Chronicles of Narnia ultimately came to encapsulate many of Lewis's chief spiritual and philosophical themes while also drawing from his academic history and broad knowledge of British literary traditions.

Joy Crelin

Further Reading

McGrath, Alister. *C. S. Lewis—A Life: Eccentric Genius, Reluctant Prophet.* Carol Stream: Tyndale House, 2013. Print.

Wilson, A. N. *C. S. Lewis: A Biography.* New York: Harper, 2005. Print.

Bibliography

Caughey, Shanna. *Revisiting Narnia: Fantasy, Myth and Religion in C. S. Lewis' Chronicles.* Dallas: BenBella, 2005. Print.

Lewis, C. S. *Surprised by Joy: The Shape of My Early Life.* 1955. New York: Mariner, 2012. Print.

"The Life of C. S. Lewis Timeline." *CSLewis.org.* C. S. Lewis Foundation, 2015. Web. 25 Feb. 2015. <http://www.cslewis.org/resource/chronocsl>.

Malinda Lo

Date of birth: 1974
Place of birth: China

Principal Works

Ash (2009)
Huntress (2011)
Adaptation series (2012–13)

Biography

Malinda Lo is the award-winning author of several science-fiction and fantasy novels for young adults. Perhaps best known for her novel *Ash* (2009), a retelling of the Cinderella story, and its companion novel, *Huntress* (2011), she is also the author of the Adaptation series and various short stories. Lo is deeply committed to promoting diversity within the young adult genre and is a co-founder of the website *Diversity in YA*, which publishes book lists, author interviews, and statistics related to that cause.

Born in China in 1974, Lo moved to the United States with her family when she was three years old. She began writing at an early age and published her first poem at the age of twelve with the encouragement of her grandmother Ruth Earnshaw Lo, herself a published writer. Lo also began to write novels, completing three during her teen years. A fan of fantasy literature, she was particularly inspired by novelists such as Robin McKinley and Madeleine L'Engle.

After graduating from Centaurus High School in Lafayette, Colorado, Lo enrolled in Wellesley College, where she majored in economics with the goal of becoming an investment banker. She earned her bachelor's degree from the college in 1996. Following college, Lo worked as an editorial assistant for Ballantine Books for a couple of years. She later went on to earn a master's degree in East Asian studies from Harvard University, where she researched Chinese cookbooks in the United States. She next enrolled in Stanford University to pursue a PhD in cultural and social anthropology but left the university before completing her degree. Her doctoral research concerned the science-fiction television show *The X-Files*, which she has noted greatly influenced some of her later work. She began a career as a freelance writer after leaving Stanford and in 2002 began writing for the website *After Ellen*, which had been founded by a college friend. Lo served as an entertainment reporter and managing editor of the site, which focuses on lesbian and bisexual popular culture, until leaving to focus on her fiction-writing career in 2008.

Lo published her first novel, *Ash*, in 2009. A reimagining of the Cinderella story and a young adult coming-of-age tale, the novel was nominated for numerous awards, including the Andre Norton Award for excellence in young adult science-fiction and fantasy and the Lambda Literary Award for best LGBT children's or young adult book. *Huntress*, a novel set in the same world but featuring different characters, was published in 2011. Lo is also the author of the science-fiction novel *Adaptation* (2012), its sequel, *Inheritance* (2013), and a companion novella, *Natural Selection* (2013), as well as a variety of short stories. In addition to her writing, she has been an influential voice in the movement toward diversity in young adult literature. In 2011, Lo and Cindy Pon, a fellow young adult author, collaborated to create the website *Diversity in YA*, which promotes all forms of diverse young adult literature.

Major Works

As a writer of fantasy and science-fiction for young adult readers, Lo engages with various works that came before, reshaping elements from such works into something new. *Ash*, for example, is in many ways a retelling of the traditional Cinderella fairy tale, in which a girl who is mistreated by her cruel stepmother ultimately catches the attention of a handsome prince. However, Lo reinterprets this narrative in her own style, creating a rich world in which the realm of the fairies exists alongside a forested human land inspired by Northern California, where Lo lived for many years. While the novel's protagonist, Aisling, known as Ash, does gain the attention of a prince, she ultimately falls in love with the huntress Kaisa. Her later works likewise reinterpret and reinvent familiar narratives; *Adaptation*, Lo's first science-fiction novel, features aliens and government conspiracies somewhat reminiscent of *The X-Files*. Indeed, Lo has commented in interviews that the novel is in many ways a love letter to that show, which she had studied in depth during her time at Stanford.

Lo is an outspoken proponent of diversity in young adult fiction, and her own work reflects that in many ways. In addition to featuring same-sex relationships, her fantasy novels blend elements of multiple cultures, featuring European, American, and Asian influences. The Adaptation series of science-fiction novels initially seems to set up a love triangle, a plot device that is common in young adult fiction; the popular Twilight and Hunger Games series, for instance, both feature prominent and polarizing love triangles. In *Inheritance*, however, protagonist Reese resolves her love triangle not by choosing one prospective love interest or the other but by entering into a polyamorous, bisexual relationship, a far less common resolution to that romantic dilemma. In this way, Lo not only provides a fresh take on a genre cliché but also provides a welcome depiction of typically underrepresented identities.

Joy Crelin

Further Reading

"Bio." *Malinda Lo*. Lo, 2015. Web. 30 Nov. 2015. <http://www.malindalo.com/bio>.

Lo, Malinda, and Cindy Pon, comps. *Diversity in YA*. Diversity in YA, 2015. Web. 30 Nov. 2015. <http://www.diversityinya.com>.

Bibliography

Lo, Malinda. "One Thing Leads to Another: An Interview with Malinda Lo." Interview by Julie Bartel. *Hub*. Amer. Lib. Assn., 27 June 2013. Web. 30 Nov. 2015. <http://www.yalsa.ala.org/thehub/2013/06/27/one-thing-leads-to-another-an-interview-with-malinda-lo>.

Lo, Malinda. "Q & A with Malinda Lo." Interview by Donna Freitas. *Publishers Weekly*. PWxyz, 7 Apr. 2011. Web. 30 Nov. 2015. <http://www.publishersweekly.com/pw/by-topic/authors/interviews/article/46762-q-a-with-malinda-lo.html>.

Springen, Karen. "Fall 2009 Flying Starts: Malinda Lo." *Publishers Weekly*. PWxyz, 21 Dec. 2009. Web. 30 Nov. 2015. <http://www.publishersweekly.com/pw/by-topic/authors/profiles/article/53221-fall-2009-flying-starts-malinda-lo.html>.

Welsh, Kate Linnea. "How to Make Young Adult Fiction More Diverse." *Atlantic*. Atlantic Monthly, 2 June 2011. Web. 30 Nov. 2015. <http://www.theatlantic.com/entertainment/archive/2011/06/how-to-make-young adult-fiction-more-diverse/239795>.

E. Lockhart

Date of birth: September 13, 1967
Place of birth: New York, New York

Principal Works
Children's Literature
The Secret Life of Billie's Uncle Myron (with Len Jenkin, 1996)
Young Adult Literature
The Boyfriend List (2005)

The Disreputable History of Frankie Landau-Banks (2008)
Treasure Map of Boys (2009)
Real Live Boyfriends (2010)
We Were Liars (2014)

Biography

E. Lockhart is an award-winning author of books for children and young adults. Her novel *The Disreputable History of Frankie Landau-Banks* was a finalist for the National Book Award for Young People's Literature in 2008 and for the prestigious Michael L. Printz Award for Excellence in Young Adult Literature in 2009. It also won the Cybils Award for best young adult novel in 2009. Lockhart is the author of a number of children's books, including the Toys series featuring illustrations by Paul O. Zelinsky and the Invisible Inkling series featuring illustrations by Harry Bliss. She began writing books for young adults in 2005. Her 2014 novel, a mystery called *We Were Liars*, was a *New York Times* best seller. Lockhart has a PhD in English literature and a passion for old tales. *We Were Liars*, despite its contemporary setting, draws on fairy-tale tropes as well as the plots of Shakespeare's *King Lear* and Emily Brontë's *Wuthering Heights*.

Lockhart was born Emily Jenkins—Lockhart is her middle name and her maternal grandmother's maiden name—on September 13, 1967, in New York City. Her father, Len Jenkin, is an award-winning playwright. (Father and daughter teamed up in 1996 to write a novel for children called *The Secret Life of Billie's Uncle Myron*.) Lockhart's mother worked as a preschool teacher and added an *s* to the family's surname after consulting a numerologist in the 1970s. Lockhart was raised in Boston and Seattle and grew up watching rehearsals for her father's plays. He read her classic books like *Alice's Adventures in Wonderland* and *Huckleberry Finn* and recounted for her the plots of Shakespearean plays. She also read on her own and, at the age of eight, began writing novel-length stories based on her favorite books. Lockhart briefly tried acting, but by the time she enrolled at Vassar College, her ambition was to become a writer. She developed an interest in picture books through one of her professors, Nancy Willard, a Newbery Award–winning children's book author. Willard introduced her to the artist Barry Moser, whom Lockhart interviewed for her senior thesis. During her time at Vassar, Lockhart was a student assistant in the school's lab preschool and, after graduation, worked as an assistant teacher at a Montessori school in Chicago.

In 1998, while earning her PhD in English literature at Columbia University, Lockhart (under her real name) published a book of essays about body politics called *Tongue First: Adventures in Physical Culture*. Throughout the 1990s and early 2000s, Lockhart wrote essays for the online magazine *Salon*, where her subjects included the pseudonymous author of the Nancy Drew mysteries and a critique of celebrity-penned children's books. She also wrote for the New York *Village Voice* and continues to occasionally review children's books for the *New York Times Book Review*. In 2002, Lockhart (again as Emily Jenkins) published a well-received adult novel called *Mister Posterior and the Genius Child*. She lives in Brooklyn with her family. She writes every day and teaches online in the low-residency MFA program in writing for children and young adults at Hamline University in St. Paul, Minnesota.

Major Works

Lockhart began writing books for young adults at the behest of an editor named Donna Bray, who thought that Lockhart's familiarity with young people—showcased in *Tongue First*—made her a good fit for a YA audience. Lockhart published *The Boyfriend List*, the first novel in a four-book series about a teenager named Ruby Oliver, in 2005. (She began using the pseudonym E. Lockhart to give her new career as a YA author a fresh start.) The plot is inspired by Lockhart's teenage self—she began writing the book after stumbling upon an old notebook in which she wrote down all the boys she kissed in high school. Ruby, however, begins to keep a notebook detailing all of her boyfriends and crushes on the recommendation of her new therapist and in the process learns more about herself than any of her beaus. The second book in the series is *The Boy Book* (2006), followed by *Treasure Map of Boys* (2009) and *Real Live Boyfriends* (2010).

Lockhart's most celebrated novel to date is *The Disreputable History of Frankie Landau-Banks* (2008), about a high school sophomore named Frankie and her journey from a studious and unassuming good girl to, as Lockhart calls her, a "near-criminal mastermind." Barred from her prep school's all-male secret society—of which her boyfriend is a member—Frankie embarks on a series of pranks to rival the society's old masters. The book is funny and "playful," Donna Freitas wrote

in her August 15, 2008, review for the *New York Times*, but Lockhart's story touches on something deeper. Freitas noted its "biting social commentary throughout—not the kind that deadens a story but the kind that gives it punch." For instance, Frankie, whom Freitas deemed "independent and fearless," is punished for the same clever antics that were celebrated when the perpetrator was assumed to be a boy.

In 2014, Lockhart published a best-selling mystery novel called *We Were Liars*, about a wealthy teenage foursome that vacations on a private island in New England. The protagonist is Cadence Sinclair Eastman, who suffers a strange and debilitating brain injury at fifteen that leaves her with chronic migraines and temporary amnesia. The nature of the accident is the novel's major dramatic question. The book, which also features a host of beguiling and greedy adult characters, was successfully marketed as a "crossover" book for both young adults and adults who enjoy reading YA. Like *Disreputable History* before it, *We Were Liars* is interested in larger themes, including class and social inequality.

Molly Hagan

Further Reading

Corbett, Sue. "YA Novelist E. Lockhart's Sleight of Hand." *Publishers Weekly*. PWxyz, 21 Feb. 2014. Web. 1 Mar. 2015. <http://www.publishersweekly.com/pw/by-topic/authors/profiles/article/61148-ya-novelist-e-lockhart-s-sleight-of-hand.html>.

Rosoff, Meg. "Fantasy Island." Rev. of *We Were Liars*, by E. Lockhart. *New York Times*. New York Times, 9 May 2014. Web. 1 Mar. 2015. <http://www.nytimes.com/2014/05/11/books/review/we-were-liars-by-e-lockhart.html>.

Rev. of *We Were Liars*, by E. Lockhart. *Kirkus Reviews*. Kirkus Media, 17 Mar. 2014. Web. 1 Mar. 2015. <https://www.kirkusreviews.com/book-reviews/e-lockhart/we-were-liars/>.

Bibliography

Freitas, Donna. "How to Be Bad." Rev. of *The Disreputable History of Frankie Landau-Banks*, by E. Lockhart. *New York Times*. New York Times, 15 Aug. 2008. Web. 1 Mar. 2015. <http://www.nytimes.com/2008/08/17/books/review/Freitas-t.html>.

Lockhart, E. "Biography." *E. Lockhart*. E. Lockhart, 2014. Web. 1 Mar. 2015. <http://www.emilylockhart.com/bio>.

Winfrey, Kerry. "Ruby Oliver Rules: 'The Boyfriend List' by E. Lockhart." *Hello Giggles*. HelloGiggles, 24 Aug. 2013. Web. 1 Mar. 2015. <http://hellogiggles.com/ruby-oliver-rules-the-boyfriend-list-by-e-lockhart>.

Lois Lowry

Date of birth: March 20, 1937
Place of birth: Honolulu, Hawaii

Principal Works
A Summer to Die (1977)
Autumn Street (1980)
Anastasia series (1979–95)
Rabble Starkey (1987)
Number the Stars (1989)
The Giver Quartet (1993–2012)

Biography

Lois Lowry is the author of several classic young adult novel series, including the Anastasia Krupnik series (1979–95) and the Giver Quartet (1993–2012). Lowry is perhaps best known for the first book of the Giver Quartet, *The Giver* (1993), about a young boy living in a dystopian society in which people do not experience love or pain. The book—as well as her 1990 novel *Number the Stars*, about the Nazi invasion of Denmark—won the prestigious Newbery Medal. Lowry, who published her first young adult novel in 1977, is beloved by young readers, but some of her works have been considered controversial or even banned. *The Giver* is one of the most frequently challenged young adult books in print. Critics cite violence as the reason why they think the book is problematic, but Lowry has other ideas about why her book is so often disputed in schools. "What I think [adults are] really objecting to is the fact that a young person is rejecting the authority and wisdom of the governing body," she told Dan Kois for the *New York Times*. "That's unnerving to them."

Lowry was born in Honolulu, Hawaii, on March 20, 1937. Her birth name was Cena Hammersberg, but she was baptized as Lois Ann Hammersberg. She was the second of three children and, by her own admission, a solitary child who preferred her own imagination to the company of others. Because her father was an army dentist, Lowry's family moved often. She began school at Berkeley Institute in Brooklyn, New York, in the early 1940s and can still recall practicing air raid drills with her kindergarten class after the bombing of Pearl Harbor in 1941. She writes about life during World War II in her 1980 novel *Autumn Street*. When her father was summoned aboard a hospital ship during the war, Lowry and her mother and siblings moved in with her grandparents in Carlisle, Pennsylvania. When Lowry was in seventh grade, the family moved to Tokyo. She later graduated from high school in New York City. Lowry attended Pembroke College at Brown University but left to marry Donald Grey Lowry, a naval officer, after her sophomore year. Her new military family moved just as much as her parents had: in fewer than five years, Lowry and her husband had four children and lived in five cities.

Lowry's husband left the military to attend Harvard Law School. The family settled in Maine after he graduated with a law degree. In the 1960s Lowry returned to college. She finished her bachelor's degree in English literature at the University of Southern Maine in 1972, went to graduate school, and began to write professionally. She wrote her first young adult novel, called *A Summer to Die* about the death of her older sister Helen, when she was in her twenties and published it in 1977. That same year her marriage ended and Lowry met Martin Small, who remained her partner for over thirty years until his death in 2011. Lowry divides her time between her house in Cambridge, Massachusetts, and an eighteenth-century farmhouse in Maine.

Much of Lowry's writing—the heart of her stories, if not their actual plots—is culled from experiences in her own life. In 1995, her son Grey, an air force flight instructor, died in a training accident. In 2012 she published a book called *Son*, the final novel in a quartet of books that include her most famous novel, *The Giver* (1993). Though she told Kois that she did not realize it when she was writing it, *Son* is an expression of her pervasive longing to have her own son back.

Major Works

Lowry's novel *The Giver* is the first in a series of four books that include *Gathering Blue* (2000), *Messenger* (2004), and *Son* (2012). Together the books are called the Giver Quartet, and they are all set in a dystopian world. In *The Giver*, humans have embraced a harmonious mode of living called Sameness, in which everything is planned. There is no color, pain, or competition. Spouses, children, and careers are chosen by a committee of elders, and all aspects of life are governed by rules. Those who break the rules are "released," or euthanized. Twelve-year-old Jonas is assigned by the elders to become the community's Receiver. As Receiver, Jonas is the keeper of the community's collective memory—which he receives from the current Receiver, who passes the memories along as the Giver. Jonas alone feels the emotions denied to his family and friends. Before writing *The Giver*, Lowry was best known for *Number the Stars* (1989) a novel about the Holocaust told from the perspective of a young Danish girl, and a series of humorous novels about a girl named Anastasia Krupnik. Writing for the *New York Times*, Karen Ray marveled at Lowry's capacity to capture the disturbing nuances of Sameness. Ray wrote that *The Giver* was "haunting and unpredictable," "powerful and provocative." After winning the Newbery Medal, the book quickly became a classic—both in spite of and because of the controversy surrounding its content. It was adapted for film in 2014.

Though *The Giver* has been compared to other, later young adult dystopian novels, including *The Hunger Games* (2008) and *Divergent* (2011), it more closely resembles books like George Orwell's *Nineteen Eighty-Four*, in which a supreme authority regulates those things which make humans human. To paraphrase Kois describing Lowry's book *Son*, the final installment of the Giver Quartet, Lowry's characters are not violent but wield love and empathy as weapons against oppression.

Molly Hagan

Further Reading

D'Addario, Daniel. "Lois Lowry: The Dystopian Fiction Trend Is Ending." *Salon*. Salon Media Group, 10 July 2014. Web. 26 Mar. 2015. <http://www.salon.com/2014/07/10/lois_lowry_the_dystopian_fiction_trend_is_ending>.

Lowry, Lois. Interview by Linda M. Castellitto. *Indie Bound*. Amer. Booksellers Assn., 1 Nov. 2000. Web. 27 Mar. 2015. <http://www.indiebound.org/author-interviews/lowry>.

Ray, Karen. "Children's Books: The Giver." Rev. of *The Giver*, by Lois Lowry. *New York Times*. New York Times, 31 Oct. 1993. Web. 30 Mar. 2015. <http://www.nytimes.com/1993/10/31/books/children-s-books-335293.html>.

Bibliography

Blatt, Ben. "Why Do So Many Schools Try to Ban *The Giver*?" *Slate*. Slate Group, 14 Aug. 2014. Web. 30 Mar. 2015. <http://www.slate.com/blogs/browbeat/2014/08/14/the_giver_banned_why_do_so_many_parents_try_to_remove_lois_lowry_s_book.html>.

Doll, Jen. "Reading Lois Lowry's 'The Giver' as an Adult." *Wire*. Atlantic Monthly Group, 23 Aug. 2012. Web. 30 Mar. 2015. <http://www.thewire.com/entertainment/2012/08/reading-lois-lowrys-giver-adult/56114/>.

"Lois Lowry." *Biography Today* (2010): 1. *Biography Reference Center*. Web. 13 Apr. 2015. <http://search.ebscohost.com/login.aspx?direct=true&db=b6h&AN=34934019&site=brc-live>.

Lowry, Lois. Interview. *Reading Rockets*. WETA Public Broadcasting, 2015. Web. 27 Mar. 2015. <http://www.readingrockets.org/books/interviews/lowry/transcript>.

Tehereh Mafi

Date of birth: November 9, 1988
Place of birth: Connecticut

Principal Works
The Juliette Chronicles (2011–14)

Biography
Tahereh Mafi is an American author of young adult fiction. She is known for her Juliette Chronicles, a dystopian series that focuses on the life of teenage protagonist Juliette Ferrars, who is initially imprisoned due to her power to kill people with a single touch. The first novel in the series, *Shatter Me* (2011), was published when Mafi was just twenty-three years old.

Mafi was born Tahereh Haddadi in a small town in Connecticut on November 9, 1988. She is the youngest of five children born to Iranian immigrants. When she was twelve years old, her family moved to California, first to Northern California and then to Orange County. She attended Soka University of America, a small liberal arts college in Aliso Viejo, California, and spent a semester abroad in Barcelona, Spain.

Growing up, Mafi was always an avid reader, but she never once considered becoming a writer. After graduating from college in 2009, she found herself reading a lot of young adult literature and rekindling her previous love of the genre. In an interview by Tatin Yang for the *Philippine Daily Inquirer*, she explained, "I knew I wanted to live in that world and I thought the best way to do that would be to immerse myself in it. That was the first time I ever thought maybe I could write a book of my own."

When Mafi did find the impetus to write and finish her first novel, *Shatter Me*, it was not immediately published. The book was rejected hundreds of times before it was finally accepted for publication. Mafi describes herself as an obsessive writer and claims that she wrote *Unravel Me* (2013), the second book in the series, in just two weeks of nonstop writing. To date, the books of the Juliette Chronicles, also known as the Shatter Me series, are Mafi's only published works. In addition to the third book in the trilogy, *Ignite Me* (2014), the series also includes two companion novellas, *Destroy Me* (2012) and *Fracture Me* (2013), written to complement the first and second novels, respectively.

Mafi married fellow young adult author Ransom Riggs in September 2013. The couple live in Santa Monica, California.

Major Works

When *Shatter Me* was first published in 2011, it met with mixed but overall favorable reviews. Critics found the novel to be an interesting example of storytelling within the young adult genre, particularly the subgenre of young adult dystopian literature. While it treaded some familiar territory, it also included enough unique aspects, such as crossed-out sections of narration, to set it apart from its predecessors. Some reviewers noted structural faults and a tendency toward overly dramatic writing, but the novel was generally praised by readers and critics as a flawed but ultimately rewarding read.

Shatter Me begins by establishing the traditional conventions of the dystopian genre. First, the organization that is exerting its totalitarian control over the world, known as the Reestablishment, seems to have control over every aspect of the lives of its citizens and does not look well upon personal expression. For example, the boy Juliette is forced to share a cell with has been picked up for what appears to be his countercultural style: he is covered in tattoos, and a ring was removed from his eyebrow before incarceration.

As the story continues, details of the state of the new world are gradually revealed, piece by piece, and conventions of the young adult genre become more apparent. When Juliette's roommate is introduced to her cell, she is horrified that he is a boy. She has difficulty dealing with her own emotions as she finds herself embarrassed, confused, and angry at the new arrival. Eventually, love will become a major part of the novel and Juliette's life, but before this she must face many difficult decisions, some shared by many adolescents and others unique to her story.

Juliette is different from other teenagers because she can drain the energy from any living thing with her touch; she was imprisoned for the accidental death of a man who came in direct contact with her. She is demonized by the reestablishment and made to feel inferior for her power. However, she eventually finds herself having to make the personal, moral decision of how she will use her power. As Juliette begins to find perspective on her life and rethink how she has been labeled by society, she learns to see herself differently, to empower herself and turn her curse into a weapon for survival. At the same time, she must deal with dating and her relationships with those around her. In the end, the novel blends the conventions of several young adult genres, including paranormal romance, dystopian literature, and the superhero genre.

The Juliette Chronicles are distinguished not just by Mafi's genre blending but also by the manner in which they were published. Before writing the second book in the trilogy, *Unravel Me*, Mafi released an e-book novella, *Destroy Me*, borrowing from the tradition of serialized novels popular in the nineteenth and early twentieth centuries. The novella takes place between *Shatter Me* and *Unravel Me* and is told from the point of view of another character, Aaron Warner, who begins the series as an antagonist before falling in love with Juliette. Another e-book novella, *Fracture Me*, was released between *Unravel Me* and *Ignite Me*; this one retells the ending of *Unravel Me* and explores its aftermath from the point of view of Adam Kent, Juliette's childhood love interest. Though both novellas were originally available only in digital form, they were later published together in print in a single volume called *Unite Me* (2014).

It is clear from Mafi's writing is that she is aware of and educated in the conventions of young adult literature, but she has reshaped and repurposed these conventions in an attempt to create something new. Critics and young adult readers alike have praised the new perspective that Mafi has brought to young adult literature. Her voice and style are unique enough that she has been recognized in a subgenre—fantasy young adult fiction—that has become overpopulated with new writers attempting to recreate the success of such wildly popular young adult series as J. K. Rowling's Harry Potter series (1997–2007) and Suzanne Collins's Hunger Games trilogy (2008–10).

Aaron Horton, MA

Further Reading
Rev. of *Ignite Me*, by Tahereh Mafi. *Kirkus Reviews* 15 Jan. 2014: 188. *Literary Reference Center*. Web. 27 Oct. 2015. <http://search.ebscohost.com/login.aspx?direct=true&db=1fh&AN=93684772&site=lrc-live>.

Mafi, Tahereh. *Grab a Pen*. Blogger, 22 June 2012. Web. 27 Oct. 2015. <http://stiryourtea.blogspot.com/>.

Rev. of *Shatter Me*, by Tahereh Mafi. *Kirkus Reviews* 15 Apr. 2011: 37. *Literary Reference Center*. Web. 27 Oct. 2015. <http://search.ebscohost.com/login.aspx?direct=true&db=1fh&AN=60526867&site=lrc-live>.

Bibliography
Mafi, Tahereh. "Meet *Shatter Me* Author Tahereh Mafi." *Seventeen*. Hearst Communications, 12 Jan. 2012. Web. 27 Oct. 2015. <http://www.seventeen.com/life/a17070/tahereh-mafi-shatter-me-author-interview/>.

Mafi, Tahereh. "Not Just for Kids: Author Tahereh Mafi Discusses *Shatter Me*." Interview by Susan Carpenter. *Jacket Copy*. Los Angeles Times, 28 Nov. 2011. Web. 30 Oct. 2015. <http://latimesblogs.latimes.com/jacketcopy/2011/11/shatter-me.html>.

Mafi, Tahereh. "Unraveling Tahereh Mafi." Interview by Tatin Yang. *Inquirer.net*. Inquirer.net, 16 Mar. 2013. Web. 30 Oct. 2015. <http://lifestyle.inquirer.net/94433/unraveling-tahereh-mafi>.

Ramos, Miguel. "10 Things You Did Not Know about Tahereh Mafi." *Philippine Star*. Philstar, 10 Mar. 2013. Web. 27 Oct. 2015. <http://www.philstar.com/sunday-life/2013/03/10/917688/10-things-you-did-not-know-about-tahereh-mafi>.

Melina Marchetta

Date of birth: March 25, 1965
Place of birth: Sydney, Australia

Principal Works
Looking for Alibrandi (1992)
Saving Francesca (2003)
On the Jellicoe Road (2006)
Finnikin of the Rock (2008)
Jellicoe Road (2008)
The Piper's Son (2010)
Froi of the Exiles (2011)
Quintana of Charyn (2012)

Biography
Melina Marchetta is an award-winning Australian author. In 1992 she published her first novel, *Looking for Alibrandi*. The book became one of the highest-selling debut novels from an Australian author and was adapted into a successful film in 2000. Ten years after *Looking for Alibrandi* was released, Marchetta published her second novel, *Saving Francesca* (2003), followed by *On the Jellicoe Road* (2006), which was published as *Jellicoe Road* in the United States in 2008 and won the prestigious Michael L. Printz Award in 2009. Her later novels include the multivolume Lumatere Chronicles; *The Piper's Son*, a companion novel to *Saving Francesca*; and *The Gorgon in the Gully*, a novel for middle-grade readers.

Marchetta was born to an Italian Australian family on March 25, 1965, and was raised in Marrickville, a suburb of Sydney. When she was a child, she wanted to be a librarian. She was a decent student, and she read and watched movies ferociously. She loved history and devoured books about the ill-fated Romanov family in imperial Russia. She has said that she decided she wanted to spend her life telling stories after watching the 1981 Indiana Jones film *Raiders of the Lost Ark*. She has cited K. M. Peyton, Ivan Southall, and Paul Zindel as some of her favorite authors as a child.

Marchetta left school when she was fifteen years old because she thought that she would fail her senior exams. She took a job as a teller at a bank—where she used her work computer to work on early drafts of *Looking for Alibrandi*—and then at a travel consultancy. When she was in her early twenties, *Looking for Alibrandi* was accepted for publication. Marchetta worked with her editors for several years before the book was published in 1992, just after she began her bachelor's degree in education at the Australian Catholic University. After graduation, she taught at Killara High School and then spent ten years teaching at St. Mary's Cathedral College, a private secondary school for boys in Sydney, before she began writing full time.

Major Works

Marchetta spent nearly seven years writing and re-writing *Looking for Alibrandi*. The book was published in October 1992, and its first printing was sold out by late December that year. The novel follows a teenage girl named Josephine Alibrandi who, like Marchetta, feels torn between her Italian heritage and her Australian upbringing. *Looking for Alibrandi* was unique among Australian young adult literature at the time because it explored issues of ethnicity and gender and the sense of isolation inherent in being different. The book was so popular that Marchetta wrote the screenplay for the 2000 film adaptation, for which she won awards from the Australian Film Institute and the Film Critics Circle of Australia for best adapted screenplay. She spent nearly a decade working on a follow-up novel. In 2003 she published *Saving Francesca*, about teenage girl making her way in predominantly boys' school (in the book, the academy has just begun to admit girls). The story was inspired by Marchetta's time working at an all-boys school as well as a dark period during her teenage years when her mother slipped into a depression. The book was well received, as was its companion, *The Piper's Son*, which was published in 2010. Set five years later, *The Piper's Son* follows Francesca's friend, Tom Mackee, who has turned to drugs after his uncle's death in a terrorist attack.

Marchetta spent years plotting her third novel, an intricately structured mystery called *On the Jellicoe Road* (2006). The novel was published as *Jellicoe Road* in the United States in 2008, where it won the American Library Association's prestigious Michael L. Printz Award for excellence in young adult literature in 2009. The book focuses on a teenager named Taylor who struggles to find her guardian, Hannah, after she mysteriously disappears. The book operates from multiple points of view and jumps forward and backward in time; a reviewer for the Melbourne *Age* likened the plot to a satisfying jigsaw puzzle. Following the success of *Jellicoe Road*, Marchetta began working on a screenplay adaptation of the book.

In 2008 she published the first book of an epic fantasy series called the Lumatere Chronicles inspired in part by her love of the Romanovs. In *Finnikin of the Rock*, Finnikin, the only surviving member of the royal family of Lumatere, must free his land from evil occupation. *Finnikin of the Rock* won the Aurealis Award for best young adult novel. Adventures in Lumatere continue with *Froi of the Exiles* (2012), in which a former slave named Froi is asked to assassinate the king of Charyn. The series concludes with *Quintana of Charyn* (2013), in which a queen goes into hiding to protect her child. Reviewers praised the series for its complex characters, particularly Quintana, whose story plays an important role in tying together the plots involving Finnikin and Froi.

Molly Hagan

Further Reading

Austin, Keith. "The Girl Most Unlikely to . . ." *Sydney Morning Herald*. Fairfax Media, 5 Apr. 2003. Web. 15 Sept. 2015. <http://www.smh.com.au/articles/2003/04/04/1048962924056.html>.

Marchetta, Melina. "One Thing Leads To Another: An Interview with Melina Marchetta." Interview by Julie Bartel. *Hub*. Young Adult Library Services Assn., 30 May 2013. Web. 15 Sept. 2015. <http://www.yalsa.ala.org/thehub/2013/05/30/one-thing-leads-to-another-an-interview-with-melina-marchetta/>.

Webb, Carolyn. "Looking beyond Alibrandi." *Age*. Age, 28 Mar. 2003. Web. 15 Sept. 2015. <http://www.theage.com.au/articles/2003/03/27/1048653798346.html>.

Bibliography

Atkinson, Frances. Rev. of *On the Jellicoe Road*, by Melina Marchetta. *Age*. Age, 13 Oct. 2006. Web. 15 Sept. 2015. <http://www.theage.com.au/news/book-reviews/on-the-jellicoe-road/2006/10/13/1160246311285.html>.

Marchetta, Melina. Interview by Cris Menendez. *El Templo de las Mil Puertas*. El Templo de las Mil Puertas, Dec. 2012. Web. 15 Sept. 2015. <https://www.kirkusreviews.com/book-reviews/melina-marchetta/jellicoe-road>.

Marchetta, Melina. Interview by Judith Ridge. *Viewpoint: On Books for Young Adults*. Misrule.com.au,

1992. Web. 15 Sept. 2015. <http://misrule.com.au/wordpress/interviews/melina-marchetta-interview/>.

Rev. of *Froi of the Exiles*, by Melina Marchetta. *Kirkus*. Kirkus, 18 Jan. 2012. Web. 15 Sept. 2015. <https://www.kirkusreviews.com/book-reviews/melina-marchetta/froi-exiles/>.

Rev. of *Jellicoe Road*, by Melina Marchetta. *Kirkus*. Kirkus, 20 May 2010. Web. 15 Sept. 2015. <https://www.kirkusreviews.com/book-reviews/melina-marchetta/jellicoe-road>.

Rev. of *Saving Francesca*, by Melina Marchetta. *Publisher's Weekly*. PWxyz, n.d. Web. 15 Sept. 2015. <http://www.publishersweekly.com/978-0-375-82982-6>.

John Marsden

Date of birth: September 27, 1950
Place of birth: Victoria, Australia

Principal Works
Children's Literature
Checkers (1996)
Prayer for the Twenty-First Century (1997)
Norton's Hut (1998)
The Rabbits (1998)
Millie (2002)
Home and Away (2008)
Young Adult Literature
So Much to Tell You (1987)
The Journey (1988)
Out of Time (1990)
Letters from the Inside (1991)
Take My Word for It (1992)
Tomorrow Series (1993–99)
Ellie Chronicles (2003–6)

Biography
Australian writer John Marsden is a best-selling author of children's books and young adult novels. His first novel for teens, *So Much to Tell You*, was published in 1987 and sold record numbers, launching his career. Since then he has written many more books, including *The Rabbits* (1998), which was named the 1999 CBCA Children's Picture Book of the Year. Among other honors, Marsden received the Australian Book Industry Awards' Lloyd O'Neil Award in 2006, as well as a nomination for the prestigious Astrid Lindgren Memorial Award in 2008.

Marsden grew up in Kyneton, Victoria, and Devonport, Tasmania. In his early childhood, he developed a love of books. Some of his early favorites were *Robinson Crusoe* and works by Nan Chauncy and Enid Blyton. In an interview, Marsden recalls the moment it occurred to him that he was a writer. When he and a friend started their own newspaper in the fourth grade, Marsden would write articles and poems for it. Marsden remembers wanting his readers to be able to experience the lives of others and gain empathy as a result. At age ten, Marsden moved to Sydney with his family. Later he attended Sydney University but dropped out to receive treatment for depression. According to Marsden, his hospital experience taught him about the primacy of emotions and enabled him to begin building a new life. In his twenties, Marsden began teaching, first sports and then English.

When he started writing fiction for young adults, Marsden decided not to worry about editing along the way. As a result, Marsden was able to write his first novel in just three weeks. Published in 1987, *So Much to Tell You* is the story of a traumatized teen, Marina, who goes on a personal journey to find her voice again. The novel won both the Christopher Medal and the Victorian Premier's Award, among other honors. Marsden wrote many more books, including the Tomorrow Series and Ellie Chronicles. His works explore themes like war, violence, imperialism, and child abuse. In Marsden's own words, they are also about the "nobility you can find in ordinary people." In 2006 Marsden founded Candlebark, an alternative school just outside of Melbourne. The school enrolls only 150 students and espouses a philosophy of creative and lively learning.

Major Works
Originally published from 1993 to 1999, Marsden's Tomorrow Series includes seven young adult novels and tells the story of teenager Ellie Linton and her friends. The group must wage guerrilla war on enemy soldiers when Australia is invaded by a foreign power and all of their friends and family are captured. The books in the series, first published by Pan Macmillan, have been reprinted sixteen times. In the first book, *Tomorrow, When the War Began*, Ellie and her friends go camping. When they return a week later, they find their

hometown, Wirrawee, completely deserted. The teens decide to work together to ensure their survival and stand up to enemy invaders. The story is narrated in the first person. It reads like a journal; Ellie's voice is conversational, confessional, and honest. Ellie admits right away, "I don't know if I'll be able to do this. I might as well say so now." She continues, "Writing it down means we might be remembered. . . . That makes me think that I should be writing this like a history book, in a very serious language, all formal. But I can't do that." Through Ellie's eyes, readers experience the suspense, action, and horror of war. Readers also witness as the teens are transformed from normal adolescents with ordinary hopes and anxieties into adults who are forced to make difficult decisions.

Marsden followed the Tomorrow Series with a sequel series, the Ellie Chronicles, published from 2003 to 2006. In this later series, Ellie struggles to regain a sense of normalcy while living on her family's farm in the years following the war. But peacetime is short lived, and soon Ellie is thrown back into a war zone. In the first book of the series, *While I Live*, Ellie, her adopted brother Gavin, and her friend Homer hear gunshots near her home. The three young people return to find that Ellie's parents have been killed in a raid. In what follows, Ellie must defend her property and home from a lawyer who wants to take it from her. She must also raise Gavin, who has his own complicated past. Like the Tomorrow Series, the Ellie Chronicles feature Ellie's observant, passionate, mature, and often humorous voice. At one point Ellie says, "When you decide you won't think about something you can think of nothing else. It's like Tolstoy's brothers telling him that the secrets of the universe would be revealed if he stood in the corner of the room without thinking of a white horse."

M. Lewandowski, MA

Further Reading

Marsden, John. *Marsden on Marsden: The Stories behind John Marsden's Bestselling Books*. Sydney: Pan, 2000. Print.

Michaels, Wendy. "The Realistic Turn: Trends in Recent Australian Young Adult Fiction." *Papers: Explorations into Children's Literature* 14.1 (2004): 49–59. Print.

Moore, John N. *John Marsden: Darkness, Shadow, and Light*. Lanham: Scarecrow, 2011. Print.

Bibliography

Hutcheon, Jane. "Australian Author and Educator John Marsden on Children, Parents and Relationships." *ABC News: One plus One*. ABC, 21 May 2015. Web. 14 Dec. 2015. <http://www.abc.net.au/news/2015-05-22/australian-author-and-educator-john-marsden-on/6488196>.

Sheckels, Theodore: "The Complex Politics and Rhetoric of John Marsden's 'Tomorrow' Series." *Antipodes* 28.2 (2014): 436–49. *Literary Reference Center*. Web. 17 Dec. 2015. <http://search.ebscohost.com/login.aspx?direct=true&db=lfh&AN=102345530&site=lrc-live>.

Tan, Monica. "John Marsden Is Reminded of His Reply to the Fan Letter I Sent Him When I Was 14." *Guardian*. Guardian News and Media, 12 Feb. 2015. Web. 14 Dec. 2015. <http://www.theguardian.com/books/2015/feb/13/john-marsden-is-reminded-of-his-reply-to-the-fan-letter-i-sent-him-when-i-was-14>.

Anne McCaffrey

Date of birth: April 1, 1926
Place of birth: Cambridge, Massachusetts
Date of death: November 21, 2011
Place of death: County Wicklow, Ireland

Principal Works

Restoree (1967)
Dragonriders of Pern series (with Todd McCaffrey, 1968–2012)
Doona series (with Jody Lynn Nye, 1969–94)
Brainship series (with Margaret Ball, Mercedes Lackey, and S. M. Stirling, 1969–96)
The Mark of Merlin (1971)
Ring of Fear (1971)
Pegasus series (1973–2000)
The Kilternan Legacy (1975)
Dinosaur Planet series (1978–84)
Crystal Singer series (1982–92)
Stitch in Snow (1984)
The Year of the Lucy (1986)
The Lady (1987)
Planet Pirates series (with Elizabeth Moon and Jody Lynn Nye, 1990–91)
Tower and the Hive series (1990–99)

Petaybee series (with Elizabeth Ann Scarborough, 1993–95)

Catteni Sequence (1995–2002)

Black Horses for the King (1996)

Acorna series (with Margaret Ball and Elizabeth Ann Scarborough, 1997–2004)

Nimisha's Ship (1998)

Acorna's Children series (with Elizabeth Ann Scarborough, 2005–7)

Twins of Petaybee series (with Elizabeth Ann Scarborough, 2006–8)

Barque Cats series (with Elizabeth Ann Scarborough, 2009–10)

Biography

Anne McCaffrey was the author of the popular Dragonriders of Pern series of science-fiction novels, which follows the adventures of human heroes and their telepathically bonded dragon companions. The first woman to win the prestigious Hugo Award in any fiction category, McCaffrey was an influential figure in the science-fiction community and beyond. She was inducted into the Science Fiction Hall of Fame in 2005.

Anne Inez McCaffrey was born in Cambridge, Massachusetts, on April 1, 1926, the second child of George and Anne McCaffrey. Her father was a colonel in the US Army, and her mother worked as a real estate agent. McCaffrey and her two brothers grew up primarily in Montclair, New Jersey, a suburban community northwest of New York City.

As a teenager, McCaffrey attended Stuart Hall, a boarding school in Staunton, Virginia, for a time and ultimately graduated from Montclair High School in 1943. She went on to study Slavonic languages and literature at Radcliffe College (now part of Harvard University) and in 1947 completed her bachelor's degree. After college, McCaffrey initially pursued a career as an actor, singer, and director, specializing in opera, and also worked as a copywriter. In 1950 she married Horace Wright Johnson, with whom she would have three children, Alec, Todd, and Georgeanne. The couple divorced in 1970. Following her divorce, McCaffrey immigrated to Ireland, where she raised horses and focused on her writing career.

McCaffrey published her first short story, "Freedom of the Race," in 1953, in the magazine *Science-Fiction Plus*. Her first novel, *Restoree*, followed in 1967. That year she also published her first two novellas set in the world of Pern, "Weyr Search" and "Dragonrider," in the magazine *Analog*. The two novellas earned McCaffrey

the prestigious Hugo Award (1968) and Nebula Award (1968), respectively. Over the subsequent decades, McCaffrey became a prolific and beloved writer of science fiction and fantasy for teens and adults, publishing more than twenty Pern novels as well as more than ten unrelated series and numerous stand-alone novels. She also served as editor of anthologies and cookbooks and cowrote several nonfiction books about the Pern series.

McCaffrey died at Dragonhold-Underhill, her home in Ireland's County Wicklow, on November 21, 2011, following a stroke.

Major Works

McCaffrey is best known for her Dragonriders of Pern series of novels, which began in 1968 with the publication of *Dragonflight*; the novel incorporated and built upon her 1967 Pern novellas, "Weyr Search" and "Dragonrider." Between 1968 and her death in 2011, McCaffrey published more than twenty Pern novels as well as various short stories, novellas, and related works. The Pern novel *Sky Dragons*, a collaboration between McCaffrey and her son Todd, was published posthumously in 2012.

The Pern novels provide examples of many of the common aspects of McCaffrey's work, perhaps most notably her commitment to world building and her habit of collaborating extensively with fellow writers. The world of Pern is one that in many ways seems close to the pretechnological world of many fantasy novels; however, the novels make it clear that the planet was in fact colonized by spacefaring settlers from Earth, and the unique circumstances in which those settlers found themselves influenced the development of human society on Pern and its dependence on intelligent, genetically modified dragons. Such complex world building is evident in many of McCaffrey's works, including her Crystal Singer series, in which singers mine valuable crystals using their voices, and the Tower and the Hive series, in which technology is used in concert with telepathy. McCaffrey collaborated with her son Todd on many of the later Pern books, and that spirit of collaboration is evident in several of her other series as well. McCaffrey frequently cowrote books with writers such as Jody Lynn Nye, Elizabeth Ann Scarborough, and others, transforming writing from a solitary pursuit into a collaborative effort.

Over the course of McCaffrey's publishing career, many readers classified her Pern series and other novels as falling into the realm of fantasy, often in part because they prominently feature dragons, creatures typically found in that genre, as well as settings and aesthetics often associated with fantasy. McCaffrey, however, was adamant that her novels are science-fictional works and noted on her official website that while fantasy worlds are based on magic, the worlds in her novels are based on Newtonian logic. McCaffrey's habit of mixing science-fiction foundations with some of the hallmarks of fantasy proved influential to later writers, many of whom rejected traditional genre boundaries in favor of innovative new forms of speculative fiction.

Joy Crelin

Further Reading

McCaffrey, Todd, ed. *Dragonwriter: A Tribute to Anne McCaffrey and Pern*. New York: BenBella, 2013. Digital file.

McCaffrey, Todd, and Anne McCaffrey. *The Worlds of Anne McCaffrey*. McCaffrey, 2014. Web. 24 Feb. 2015. <http://pernhome.com/aim>.

Roberts, Robin. *Anne McCaffrey: A Life with Dragons*. Jackson: UP of Mississippi, 2007. Print.

Bibliography

Clute, John. "McCaffrey, Anne." *The Encyclopedia of Science Fiction*. Ed. John Clute, David Langford, Peter Nicholls, and Graham Sleight. Gollancz, 13 Nov. 2014. Web. 24 Feb. 2015. <http://www.sf-encyclopedia.com/entry/mccaffrey_anne>.

Fox, Margalit. "Anne McCaffrey, Author of 'Dragonriders' Fantasies, Dies at 85." *New York Times*. New York Times, 24 Nov. 2011. Web. 22 Feb. 2015. <http://www.nytimes.com/2011/11/24/arts/anne-mccaffrey-dragonriders-author-dies-at-85.html>.

"In Memoriam: Anne McCaffrey (1926–2011)." *SFWA*. Science Fiction and Fantasy Writers of America, 22 Nov. 2011. Web. 24 Feb. 2015. <http://www.sfwa.org/2011/11/anne-mccaffrey-1926-2011>.

Stephanie Meyer

Date of birth: December 24, 1973
Place of birth: Hartford, Connecticut

Principal Works
Young Adult Literature
Twilight series (2005–8)
The Short Second Life of Bree Tanner (2010)

Adult Literature
The Host (2008)

Biography

Stephenie Meyer is an American writer of novels for young adult and adult readers. She is best known as the author of the Twilight series, a four-book paranormal series for young adults that began in 2005 with the publication of *Twilight* and concluded in 2008 with the publication of the final installment, *Breaking Dawn* (2008). The series became a global phenomenon and was adapted into a five-part film series between 2008 and 2012. In addition to the Twilight novels, Meyer has written a novella set in the world of Twilight, *The Short Second Life of Bree Tanner* (2010), and the adult science-fiction novel *The Host* (2008).

Meyer was born Stephenie Morgan on December 24, 1973, in Hartford, Connecticut. She was one of six children born to Stephen and Candy Morgan. Meyer spent her first years in Connecticut, but when she was about four, her traditionally Mormon family moved to Arizona.

As a child, Meyer spent a great deal of time looking after her four younger siblings. She was an avid reader, and her love of books was encouraged strongly by her parents; her father recommended she read his favorite fantasy books, while her mother promoted classic works by writers such as Jane Austen. Meyer was a storyteller from a young age as well, but while she enjoyed making up stories to entertain herself, she rarely wrote them down.

Meyer attended Chaparral High School, from which she graduated in 1992. She was somewhat unhappy in school and has noted that she drew on some of her experiences as a teenager when writing about Twilight protagonist Bella's awkward teen years. After completing high school, Meyer enrolled in Brigham Young University in Provo, Utah, where she majored in English. She married while in college and dedicated herself primarily to taking care of her young children following her graduation.

In 2003, Meyer began working on *Twilight*, the first novel in her best-selling series. She later told journalists that the novel was inspired by dream she had about a conversation between a teenage girl and a vampire. *Twilight* follows a teenager named Bella, who, after moving from Arizona to a small town in Washington, learns that several of the town's residents are vampires and pursues a romance with one of them, the handsome Edward. The two characters' romance continues to develop throughout the subsequent books, *New Moon* (2006) and *Eclipse* (2007), and culminates in their marriage in *Breaking Dawn* (2008). The Twilight series proved incredibly popular with readers worldwide and was adapted into a series of films. The first installment in the film series premiered in 2008 and was followed by *The Twilight Saga: New Moon* (2009) and *The Twilight Saga: Eclipse* (2010). The adaptation of the final novel was split into two separate films, released in 2011 and 2012, respectively.

In addition to the books in the Twilight series, Meyer also wrote a companion novella to the series, *The Short Second Life of Bree Tanner*. The novella tells the story of a minor vampire character introduced in *Breaking Dawn*. Meyer is also the author of *The Host*, a romantic science-fiction novel marketed primarily toward adults. The novel was adapted into a film in 2013.

Meyer married her husband, Christian, in 1994. They have three sons and live in Cave Creek, Arizona.

Major Works

As the author of the internationally popular Twilight novels, Meyer was responsible for helping to usher in a major trend in young adult publishing. Although novels featuring paranormal and romantic themes had long been popular among teenage readers, the Twilight series has a particular blend of such themes that sparked the publication of numerous similar novels, many featuring romances between young human women and supernatural beings. The popularity of such novels further revitalized the young adult publishing industry as a whole, despite the difficulties faced by many publishing companies during the global recession that began in 2007. The popularity of the Twilight films likewise spurred on the trend of adapting young adult novels for the screen, and numerous films based on young adult properties premiered during the height of the Twilight films' popularity. The adaptation of Meyer's science-fiction novel, *The Host*, could be said to be part of this trend; although the novel was marketed toward adults, Meyer's popularity among teens likely contributed to the film's success at the box office.

The Twilight novels generated a degree of controversy following their publication, in large part because of the depiction of their female protagonist and her relationship with Edward. Some critics objected to aspects of Bella's personality and frequent need to be rescued by male characters and noted that elements of her relationship with Edward could be considered abusive. However, Meyer argued that the power differentials noted by some critics were the result of the novels' paranormal elements, such as the inherent vulnerability of humans as compared to vampires. Some

of the young adult novels published in Twilight's wake reproduced such dynamics, while others sought to subvert the tropes popularized by the Twilight series.

Joy Crelin

Further Reading

Blasingame, James, Kathleen Deakin, and Laura A. Walsh. *Stephenie Meyer: In the Twilight*. Lanham: Scarecrow, 2012. Print.

Meyer, Stephenie. *The Official Website of Stephenie Meyer*. Meyer, n.d. Web. 4 June 2015. <http://stepheniemeyer.com/bio.html>.

Shapiro, Marc. *Stephenie Meyer*. New York: St. Martin's, 2009. Print.

Bibliography

Cochrane, Kira. "Stephenie Meyer on *Twilight*, Feminism and True Love." *Guardian*. Guardian News and Media, 11 Mar. 2013. Web. 4 June 2015. <http://www.theguardian.com/books/2013/mar/11/stephenie-meyer-twilight-the-host>.

Kokkola, Lydia. "Virtuous Vampires and Voluptuous Vamps: Romance Conventions Reconsidered in Stephenie Meyer's 'Twilight' Series." *Children's Literature in Education* 42.2 (2011): 165–79. *Literary Reference Center*. Web. 16 June 2015. <http://search.ebscohost.com/login.aspx?direct=true&db=lfh&AN=60529020&site=lrc-live>.

Laing, Olivia. "Stephenie Meyer: A Squeaky-Clean Vampire Queen." *Guardian*. Guardian News and Media, 14 Nov. 2009. Web. 4 June 2015. <http://www.theguardian.com/books/2009/nov/15/profile-stephenie-meyer-vampire-queen>.

Meyer, Stephenie. "Interview with Vampire Writer Stephenie Meyer." Interview by Gregory Kirschling. *Entertainment Weekly*. Entertainment Weekly, 5 July 2008. Web. 4 June 2015. <http://www.ew.com/article/2008/07/05/interview-vampire-writer-stephenie-meyer>.

L. M. Montgomery

Date of birth: November 30, 1874
Place of birth: Clifton (now New London), Canada
Date of death: April 24, 1942
Place of death: Toronto, Canada

Principal Works

Anne of Green Gables series (1908–39)
Kilmeny of the Orchard (1910)
The Story Girl series (1911–13)
Emily series (1923–27)
The Blue Castle (1926)
Magic for Marigold (1929)
A Tangled Web (1931)
Pat of Silver Bush series (1933–35)
Jane of Lantern Hill (1937)

Biography

L. M. Montgomery was a Canadian writer best known for her young adult novels set in rural communities on Prince Edward Island, Canada. The most famous of her novels are those in her Anne of Green Gables series, which follows a young orphan as she finds a new home and forms lasting friendships. In addition to that series, Montgomery was the author of numerous other novels as well as hundreds of short stories and various poems and nonfiction works.

Lucy Maud Montgomery was born on November 30, 1874, in the village of Clifton in the Canadian province of Prince Edward Island. She was the only child born to Hugh and Clara Montgomery. Following Clara's death in 1876, Hugh Montgomery sent his young daughter to live with her maternal grandparents in Cavendish, a coastal community near her birthplace. Montgomery developed a love of reading and writing at an early age, and she likewise came to enjoy exploring the beaches and other outdoor environments around Cavendish.

Montgomery attended a small local schoolhouse and also studied for a time in Prince Albert, in the central Canadian province of Saskatchewan, where her father lived with his second wife and their son. A writer since childhood, Montgomery also published her first poem in 1890, in the Charlottetown *Patriot* newspaper. After completing her primary education, she attended Prince of Wales College, from which she obtained a teaching license in 1894. Montgomery found work at several schools on Prince Edward Island and later put her teaching career on hold to take classes at Dalhousie University in Nova Scotia. She resumed teaching in her home province in 1896, and the following year she returned to her grandparents' home to take care of her grandmother following her grandfather's death. Over the next decade she worked intermittently, with stints as a newspaper copy editor and an assistant postmaster, but she spent much of her time writing and looking after her grandmother.

In 1905 Montgomery completed her first novel, *Anne of Green Gables*; however, it was not published until 1908. The book proved extremely popular among readers, and she soon published several sequels, including *Anne of Avonlea* (1909) and *Anne of the Island* (1915). Later novels, such as *The Story Girl* (1911), *Emily of New Moon* (1923), and *Pat of Silver Bush* (1933), were also popular and brought Montgomery further renown as a writer. Even after finding fame as a novelist, she continued to write short stories, publishing several hundred in all.

After two previous courtships, Montgomery married Ewan Macdonald, a minister, in July of 1911. The couple settled in Leaskdale, Ontario, where Montgomery continued to write and Macdonald served as minister at a local Presbyterian church. They had three sons, Chester, Hugh, and Stuart; Hugh died the day he was born, an event that had a significant effect on Montgomery's psyche. The family later moved to Norval, Ontario, and eventually to Toronto, where Montgomery spent the last years of her life. Montgomery died at her home in Toronto on April 24, 1942. Although some family members and later biographers believed that she had committed suicide, the official cause of death was listed as coronary thrombosis.

Major Works

The majority of Montgomery's best-known works—including the Anne of Green Gables series and the Emily series—are coming-of-age tales set in rural Prince Edward Island communities. The young heroines of Montgomery's works tend to grow both physically and emotionally over the course of the novels, transforming from young, idealistic girls into mature adult women with fulfilling careers. Often, the details of these characters' lives and coming-of-age experiences mirror those of Montgomery herself, lending her novels a large degree of autobiographical significance.

Montgomery's use of real-life inspiration is most evident in the Anne of Green Gables series, by far her most popular novels. An orphan, young Anne is sent to live with elderly siblings Marilla and Matthew Cuthbert; Montgomery was not an orphan but was nevertheless sent to live with elderly relatives following her mother's death. Anne's imaginative nature, love of the outdoors, and strong friendships likewise reflect Montgomery's own experiences, and by the end of *Anne of Green Gables*, the teenage Anne has, much like the author, obtained her teaching license but put aside her dreams of further education to care for her female guardian. In *Anne of the Island*, Anne studies at a Nova Scotia college based on Montgomery's alma mater. The Emily series likewise shows autobiographical influences, particularly in regard to Emily's career. By the third and final book of the series, *Emily's Quest* (1927), the titular protagonist has succeeded in becoming a published novelist, much like her creator. In drawing from her own life and experiences, Montgomery gave her novels a sense of realism that makes her protagonists' journeys all the more powerful.

Joy Crelin

Further Reading

"Her Life." *L. M. Montgomery Institute*. U of Prince Edward Island, n.d. Web. 1 May 2015. <http://www.lm-montgomery.ca/aboutlmm/herlife>.

Mah, Ann. "Searching for 'Anne of Green Gables' on Prince Edward Island." *New York Times*. New York Times, 21 Aug. 2014. Web. 1 May 2015. <http://www.nytimes.com/2014/08/24/travel/searching-for-anne-of-green-gables-on-prince-edward-island.html>.

Rubio, Mary Henley. *Lucy Maud Montgomery: The Gift of Wings*. Toronto: Anchor, 2008. Print.

Bibliography

"About Maud." *The Official Website of the Lucy Maud Montgomery Society of Ontario*. LMMSO, n.d. Web. 1 May 2015. <http://lucymaudmontgomery.ca/about-maud>.

L. M. Montgomery Research Centre. U of Guelph, 12 Mar. 2009. Web. 1 May 2015. <http://www.lmmrc.ca>.

Montgomery, Lucy Maud. *The Alpine Path: The Story of My Career*. Don Mills: Fitzhenry, 1974. Print.

Walter Dean Myers

Date of birth: August 12, 1937
Place of birth: Martinsburg, West Virginia
Date of death: July 1, 2014
Place of death: New York, New York

Library of Congress, via Wikimedia Commons

Principal Works

Scorpions (1988)
Fallen Angels (1988)
Somewhere in the Darkness (1992)
Monster (1999)
Autobiography of My Dead Brother (2005)
Lockdown (2010)

Biography

Walter Dean Myers was the award-winning author of more than one hundred books for children and young adults. He won the Coretta Scott King Award five times and received Newbery Honors for his books *Scorpions* (1988) and *Somewhere in the Darkness* (1992). One of his best-known novels, *Monster* (1999), won the first Michael L. Printz Award and was a finalist for the National Book Award in 1999. Myers was a finalist for the prestigious award again in 2005 for his book *Autobiography of My Dead Brother* (2005) and in 2010 for *Lockdown* (2010). He won the Margaret A. Edwards Award for lifetime achievement in young adult literature in 1994. Despite a turbulent adolescence, Myers was always a voracious reader. He has explained that his first real encouragement to write his own inspirational stories came after reading a short story called "Sonny's Blues" (1957) by James Baldwin, who often wrote about what it was like to grow up as an African American man in the mid-twentieth century. Afterward, Myers became an advocate for young adults through the publication of books that honestly depict African American youths dealing with real and significant issues.

Walter Milton Myers was born on August 12, 1937, in Martinsburg, West Virginia. He was the fourth of five children. His mother died when he was eighteen months old, and Myers's father sent him to live with his first wife and her husband in Harlem, New York. His adoptive mother taught him how to read at an early age, and as he got older, books and writing became his refuge. Myers had a speech impediment and did poorly in school, though a high school English teacher encouraged him to keep writing. He dropped out of Stuyvesant High School and joined the army on his seventeenth birthday. He served for three years before beginning to work in construction and doing other odd jobs. Although he drank rather heavily, he was also writing. Myers contributed stories for Alfred Hitchcock's mystery magazine, and when his half brother, Wayne, was killed in Vietnam, he wrote a piece about him for *Essence* magazine. In 1969, he published his first book, *Where Does the Day Go?* (1969), which won the Council on Interracial Books for Children Award.

Myers spent the rest of his life building a canon to make up for what the literature of his youth so desperately lacked. The dearth of black characters and depictions of the African American experience drove him to tell stories born of his own experience over and over again. Myers wrote about the wars in Vietnam and Iraq as well as gangs in Harlem and the unfairness of the justice system. In 2012, the Library of Congress appointed Myers as its third national ambassador for young people's literature.

Myers was married to his wife, Constance, for nearly fifty years before his death on July 1, 2014, at the age of seventy-six. He lived in Jersey City, New Jersey, where he and his wife raised three children: Michael, Christopher, and Karen.

Major Works

Critics have continuously praised Myers's literary efforts and his ability to write about gritty, risky subjects that resonate with readers while also offering a sense of hope. Myers published a novel titled *Fallen Angels* (1988) about a Harlem teenager who is sent to fight in the Vietnam War. Like Myers himself, seventeen-year-old Richie Perry enlists in the Army when he realizes that he has little chance of going to college. While Myers did not go to Vietnam, he served in the Army in the 1950s. Myers's account of Perry's life in war is bleak but truthful to the generation that the book seeks to portray. *Fallen Angels* was the first in Myers's unofficial war trilogy that includes *Sunrise over Fallujah* (2008), which is about Iraq, and *Invasion* (2013), which is about World War II. The books follow three generations of fighting men in the Perry family. Myers's most famous novel, *Monster*, is about a fight of a different kind. In it, a teenager named Steve Harmon is on trial for felony murder. The story is uniquely written as a screenplay (Steve is an aspiring filmmaker) and includes excerpts of Steve's diary. Steve fights to prove his innocence and reckons with his own self-image.

Myers's novel *Lockdown* is based on his experiences speaking with children in juvenile-detention centers. Reese, the novel's protagonist, is a fourteen-year-old African American coming of age behind bars. Through a work-release program, he meets an elderly man named Mr. Hooft, who was in a Japanese internment camp during World War II. *Lockdown* is about freedom, confinement, and survival. Like a lot of the characters in Myers's books, Reese is subject to forces outside of his control: a drug-addicted mother, poverty, and a system of justice stacked against young African American men.

Molly Hagan

Further Reading

Horner, Shirley. "Author Seeks to Inspire Black Youth." *New York Times*. New York Times, 21 Aug. 1988. Web. 10 June 2015. <http://www.nytimes.com/1988/08/21/nyregion/author-seeks-to-inspire-black-youth.html>.

Lee, Felicia R. "Walter Dean Myers Dies at 76; Wrote of Black Youth for the Young." *New York Times*. New York Times, 3 July 2014. Web. 10 June 2015. <http://www.nytimes.com/2014/07/04/arts/walter-dean-myers-childrens-author-dies-at-76.html>.

Tucker, Neely. "Walter Dean Myers: Bad Boy Makes Good." *Washington Post*. Washington Post, 20 Jan. 2012. Web. 10 June 2015. <http://www.washingtonpost.com/lifestyle/style/walter-dean-myers-bad-boy-makes-good/2012/01/16/gIQANnUCEQ_story.html>.

Bibliography

Dean Myers, Walter. "The Importance of Literacy: A Q&A with Author Walter Dean Myers." Interview by Earl Martin Phalen. *Huffington Post*. HuffingtonPost.

com, 10 May 2012. Web. 10 June 2015. <http://www.huffingtonpost.com/earl-martin-phalen/the-importance-of-literac_b_1504905.html>.

Dean Myers, Walter. "Talking with Walter Dean Myers." Interview by Cyndi Giorgis. *Booklist* 1 Jan. 2014: 16–19. *Literary Reference Center*. Web. 10 June 2015. <http://search.ebscohost.com/login.aspx?direct=true&db=lfh&AN=93652659&site=ehost-live&scope=site>.

Dean Myers, Walter. "Walter Dean Myers: *Lockdown*." Interview by Eisa Ulen. *National Book Foundation*. Natl. Book Foundation, n.d. Web. 10 June 2015. <http://www.nationalbook.org/nba2010_ypl_deanmyers_interview.html>.

Patrick Ness

Date of birth: October 17, 1971
Place of birth: Fort Belvoir, Virginia

Principal Works
Adult Literature
The Crash of Hennington (2003)
Topics About Which I Know Nothing (2005)
The Crane Wife (2014)
Young Adult Literature
Chaos Walking trilogy (2008–10)
A Monster Calls, illustrated by Jim Kay (2011)
More Than This (2014)
The Rest of Us Just Live Here (2015)

Biography
An award-winning author of books for adults and young adults, Patrick Ness was born in Fort Belvoir, Virginia, in 1971. The son of a U.S. Army officer, Ness spent his youth in Hawaii and Washington, moving to California to attend college. Ness studied English Literature at the University of Southern California in Los Angeles and spent time working as a corporate writer in California before moving to the United Kingdom, where he currently lives.

After moving to the U.K., Ness taught creative writing at Oxford University for several years and wrote for a number of British newspapers, including *The Daily Telegraph* and *The Guardian*. In 2009, Ness served as Booktrust's online writer in residence, where he contributed a series of posts about writing to the organization's blog.

Of his writing process, Ness has noted, "When I'm working on a first draft, all I write is 1000 words a day, which isn't that much (I started out with 300, then moved up to 500, now I can do 1000 easy). And if I write my 1000 words, I'm done for the day, even if it only took an hour (it usually takes more, of course, but not always)." ("Patrick Ness's Biography").

Ness had written two books for adults—a novel and a collection of short stories—when his agent submitted the first pages of the novel that would become *The Knife of Never Letting Go* to Walker Books, an independent publisher of books for young people. This first novel in the Chaos Walking trilogy was published in 2008, followed by the second book in the series, *The Ask and the Answer* in 2009, and the series' conclusion, *Monsters of Men* in 2010. Each book in the trilogy has received critical acclaim and accolades, with *Monsters of Men* winning the prestigious CILIP Carnegie medal in 2011. Following the Chaos Walking trilogy, Ness wrote and published three more books for young people in four years: *A Monster Calls*, in 2011; *More Than This*, in 2014; and *The Rest of Us Just Live Here*, in 2015.

Ness is a strong supporter of and advocate for young people. During his speech accepting the Carnegie medal for *Monsters of Men*, Ness criticized the British government—and education minister Michael Gove, in particular—for lamenting youth illiteracy while failing to support libraries. In 2015, Ness led an appeal to raise money for the humanitarian organization Save the Children's efforts to aid refugees in Europe, agreeing to match £10,000 in donations. Children's and young adult authors from around the world, including Americans John Green and Rainbow Rowell, contributed as well, offering their own matching donations in similar amounts.

On Feb. 10, 2015, Ness announced on his blog that he would be the creator, sole writer, and co-executive producer of a *Doctor Who* spin-off series called *Class*, set at the Coal Hill school and aimed at an audience of young people. The show is scheduled to be broadcast on BBC in 2016.

Ness married his partner on their seventh anniversary, shortly after the British Civil Partnership act, which affords same sex couples the rights and privileges associated with civil marriage, was put into effect.

Major Works

The Chaos Walking trilogy represents Patrick Ness's first published work for young people. Set on a distant planet called New World on which all men are bombarded with "Noise," the audible thoughts of one another and of all living creatures, *The Knife of Never Letting Go* begins when the series protagonist, Todd, discovers a surprising source of blessed silence. Having been told that a germ is the source of the Noise that has plagued the men and killed the planet's women, when Todd learns that this silence emanates from a girl, he begins to uncover a web of lies that seems to exist to maintain the New World's despotic authority. Writing for the *Horn Book* magazine, Jonathan Hunt called the series as a whole a "significant contribution to science fiction" (99). Michael Cart, writing for *Booklist*, agreed, characterizing the Chaos Walking trilogy as "an extraordinary exercise in dystopian fiction" (42).

Ness was commissioned to write *A Monster Calls*, his fourth book for young people, when he was asked by his publisher to write a novel drawn from the notes created by author Siobhan Dowd, who had died before she could complete the story. Illustrated by Jim Kay, the novel describes the relationship between 13-year-old Conor and the monster that visits him and brokers an agreement to exchange three of his stories for a single story of Conor's. Conor's mother is suffering from a terminal illness and, as the monster's stories seem to bleed into Conor's real life, he begins to face the reality of his mother's impending death.

A Monster Calls was the first book to win both the Carnegie medal and the Greenaway medal (awarded to Jim Kay for his illustration). When Ness was awarded the Carnegie, he became the second person to win this award two years in a row (he was first awarded the medal for *Monsters of Men*). Quoted in *The Guardian*, awards judge Rachel Levy asserted, "It was mind-blowing to find a book that so perfectly captured the spirit of both awards . . . Patrick Ness's story is exquisitely told with not a word out of place. Jim Kay's bold, haunting illustrations beautifully complement, and even expand the text . . . It is, quite simply, one of the defining books of its generation" (Flood).

More Than This begins with the death of Seth, its 16-year-old protagonist. When Seth inexplicably awakens, he finds himself in a deserted town that resembles the place where he and his family spent his youth. There, he allies himself with two other young people as the three try to determine where, exactly, they all are and why they have been brought to this place. *Kirkus Reviews* considered this stand-along novel "characteristic" of Ness, noting that the book "delves into the stuff of nightmares for an existential exploration of the human psyche" (Rev. of *More Than This* 107).

Ness's most recent novel, *The Rest of Us Just Live Here*, debuted at #2 on the *New York Times* list of best selling young adult novels and was described by Sarah Crown, writing for *The Guardian*, as "a fantastically witty send-up of the "chosen one" conceit that's dominated young adult fiction for so long . . . [the] novel gives voice to the 99.9% of us who aren't special; who only crop up in crowd scenes." Protagonist Mikey and his friends, are, with the notable exception of a god of cats, exceedingly normal in a world populated by teenage saviors (think: Buffy, the vampire slayer or Katniss Everdeen) with supernatural or otherwise remarkable powers; however, this lack of distinction doesn't mean that this normal clique isn't without "typical" teenage problems.

In an interview with *The Guardian*, Ness said of *The Rest of Us Just Live Here*, "The restaurant Mikey works in, in *The Rest of Us Just Live Here*, is a lightly fictionalised version of the one I used to work in, and at the time I had OCD so bad that I did what Mikey does: I washed my hands so often I washed the oil out, so the skin cracks. I look back at my teenage self and think: you should have got help. When I'm writing for teenagers, I'm writing for him" (Crown).

Amy Pattee

Further Reading

Chaos Walking Short Stories. Walker Books, 2013. Web. 5 February 2016. <http://www.chaoswalking-stories.com/>

More Than This Website. Walker Books, 2013. Web. 5 February 2016. <http://www.morethanthisbook.com/>

Ness, Patrick. *Patrick Ness.* Web. 5 February 2016. <http://patrickness.com/>

Bibliography

Brown, Cat. "Authors raise 200,000 for refugees in 24 hours." *The Telegraph*. Telegraph Media Group Limited, 4 September 2015. Web. 5 February 2016.

Cart, Michael. "Making noise about chaos." *Booklist* 107.5 (2010): 42.

Corbett, Sue. "In praise of 'chaos.'" *Publishers Weekly* 257.28 (2010 July 19): 26 – 27. Print.

Crown, Sarah. "You're 10, a refugee in a foreign country. What the hell do you do?" *The Guardian*. Guardian, 18 December 2015. Web. 5 February 2016.

Flood, Allison. "Patrick Ness wins Carnegie medal for second year running. *The Guardian*. Guardian, 14 June 2012. Web. 5 February 2016.

Horn, Caroline. "Carnegie winner attacks Gove." *Bookseller* 5486 (2011): 10. Business Source Complete. Web. 5 Feb. 2016.

Hunt, Jonathan. Rev. of *Monsters of Men*, by Patrick Ness. *Horn Book* Nov./Dec. 2010: 99. Print.

Jones, Nicolette. "Whole truth for teenagers: Patrick Ness's novels have attracted acclaim, awards—and censure." *Independent*. Independent, 23 June 2011. Web. 5 February 2016.

Ness, Patrick. *Patrick Ness*. Web. 5 February 2016.

Ness, Patrick. "We two boys together clinging." *The Guardian*. Guardian, 23 June 2006. Web. 5 February 2016.

"Ness, Patrick 1971–." *Something About the Author*, 2013. Print.

"Patrick Ness's Biography." *Scholastic*. Scholastic, n.d. Web. 5 February 2016.

"Patrick Ness writing new Doctor Who spinoff series called Class." *Writers Write*. Writers Write, Inc., 3 October 2015. Web. 5 February 2016.

Rev. of *More Than This*, by Patrick Ness. *Kirkus Reviews* 81.17 (2013): 107.

Scott O'Dell

Date of birth: May 23, 1898
Place of birth: Los Angeles, California
Date of death: October 15, 1989
Place of death: Mount Kisco, New York

Principal Works
Island of the Blue Dolphins (1960)
The Black Pearl (1967)
Sing Down the Moon (1970)

Biography

Scott O'Dell was the award-winning author of several young adult novels. He received the Newbery Medal for *Island of the Blue Dolphins* in 1961 and Newbery Honors for *The King's Fifth* (1966), *The Black Pearl* (1967), and *Sing Down the Moon* (1970). In 1972, he received what many believe to be the most distinguished award in children's literature: the Hans Christian Anderson Award. *Island of the Blue Dolphins* was made into a successful feature film in 1964, and *The Black Pearl* was adapted for film in 1977. In 1982, O'Dell established the annual Scott O'Dell Award for Historical Fiction. The author told tales in which characters, often women, triumphed over adversity. "The only reason I write is to say something," he told Conrad Wesselhoeft for the *New York Times*. "I've forsaken adults because they're not going to change, though they may try awfully hard. But children can and do change."

Scott O'Dell was born Odell Gabriel Scott in Los Angeles, California, on May 23, 1898. O'Dell was a descendent of Sir Walter Scott, the author of *Ivanhoe* (1820), and excelled in school from a young age. After graduation, he attended Occidental College in California, the University of Wisconsin, Stanford University, and the University of Rome, though he never earned a degree. In 1918, he enlisted in the US Army but did not complete training in time to serve in World War I. After college, O'Dell critiqued scripts for Paramount Studios and worked as a cameraman and technical director. It was the era of silent films, and O'Dell worked on the classic films *Ben Hur* (1925) and *The Sheik* (1921). For the next thirty years, O'Dell worked a variety of different jobs as an editor for the *Los Angeles Daily News* and a book reviewer for the *Los Angeles Times*. He wrote novels for adults (his first, *Woman of Spain*, was published in 1934) and even tried his hand as an orange farmer. While writing a history of California called *Country of the Sun* (1957), O'Dell came across the story of a girl named Juana Maria, or the "Lone Woman of San Nicholas Island," who was a member of the Nicoleño tribe. She served as the inspiration for his most famous novel, *Island of the Blue Dolphins* (1960). After the success of *Island of the Blue Dolphins*, O'Dell devoted his career to writing novels for young adults.

O'Dell began going by "Scott O'Dell" after a typesetter accidently applied that name to an article he had written. O'Dell liked it and then had it legally changed in the early 1920s. He married Elizabeth Hall, a psychologist, writer, and magazine editor, in the 1960s. Hall completed and published O'Dell's unfinished manuscript, *Thunder Rolling in the Mountains* (1992) after O'Dell died of prostate cancer on October 15, 1989. O'Dell and Hall had two children and seven grandchildren.

Major Works
O'Dell did not set out to write a book for children. His idea for *Island of the Blue Dolphins* was born from a story he had read about a young American Indian girl called Juana Maria and his own anger at a growing number of hunters killing off the wildlife in the California community in which he lived. He wanted to tell a story that brought together themes of reverence for all life and forgiveness. In O'Dell's story, a twelve-year-old Nicoleño girl named Karana and her brother escape their tribe's massacre, but her brother soon dies after being attacked by feral dogs. Karana learns to survive on her own on a desert island off the coast of Southern California. Although she tries to destroy the pack of dogs that killed her brother, when one dog refuses to die, she decides to forgive the animal and nurse it back to health. Over the ensuing years, she develops special abilities that allow her to communicate with animals, and eighteen years after her exile, she sees a ship approaching her island and feels compelled to return to the mainland.

The story of the real Juana Maria is more ambiguous, but O'Dell's fictional rendering of Juana Maria's life was an immediate best seller, and what his account lacked in historical accuracy, it made up for in a different kind of truth. O'Dell was able to take stories from the past—from a pearl diver in Mexico to the story of a young Navaho girl escaping Spanish slavers in *Sing Down the Moon* (1970)—and make them immediate and compelling to modern readers.

Molly Hagan

Further Reading
Crawford, Richard. "'Island of the Blue Dolphins' Was Spawned near Julian." *San Diego Yesterday*. San Diego Union-Tribune, 19 Mar. 2011. Web. 25 May 2015. <http://www.sandiegoyesterday.com/wp-content/uploads/2010/12/ScottODell.pdf>.
McDowell, Edwin. "Scott O'Dell, a Children's Author of Historical Fiction, Dies at 91." *New York Times*. New York Times, 17 Oct. 1989. Web. 25 May 2015. <http://www.nytimes.com/1989/10/17/obituaries/scott-o-dell-a-children-s-author-of-historical-fiction-dies-at-91.html>.
Wesselhoeft, Conrad. "'Blue Dolphins' Author Tells Why He Writes for Children." *New York Times*. New York Times, 15 Apr. 1984. Web. 25 May 2015. <http://www.nytimes.com/1984/04/15/nyregion/blue-dolphins-author-tells-why-he-writes-for-children.html>.

Bibliography
"Elizabeth Hall: Author, Psychologist, Voyager." *Elizabethhall*. Elizabeth Hall, 11 June 2009. Web. 25 May 2015. <http://www.elizabethhall.net/biography.htm>.
Folkart, Burt A. "Scott O'Dell, 91: 'Writer of Books That Children Read.'" *LA Times*. Los Angeles Times, 18 Oct. 1989. Web. 25 May 2015. <http://articles.latimes.com/1989-10-18/news/mn-50_1_o-dell-books>.
McNamee, Gregory. "Appreciations: Scott O'Dell's 'Island of the Blue Dolphins.'" *Kirkus*. Kirkus, 12 Feb. 2014. Web. 25 May 2015. <https://www.kirkusreviews.com/features/appreciations-scott-odells-island-blue-dolphins/#continue_reading_post>.
Reynolds, Christopher. "Once Upon a Time: There Was a Little Girl Stranded on a Channel Island." *LA Times*. Los Angeles Times, 13 Dec. 1990. Web. 25 May 2015. <http://articles.latimes.com/1990-12-13/news/vl-8616_1_channel-islands>.

Ellen Oh

Place of birth: South Korea

Principal Works
Young Adult Literature
Prophecy (2013)
Warrior (2013)
King (2015)
Short Stories
"The Last Day" in the anthology *Diverse Energies* (edited by Tobias S. Buckell and Joe Monti, 2012)

Biography
Korean American writer Ellen Oh is the author of the young adult Prophecy trilogy, published by

HarperCollins. The trilogy is about a young female warrior, Kira, who serves as the bodyguard for a crown prince in a mythical world called the Seven Kingdoms. Oh is also the cofounder and president of We Need Diverse Books, an organization that advocates for changes in the publishing industry to reflect the diversity of young readers and the life experiences of all young people.

Born in South Korea, Oh grew up in Brooklyn, New York. In elementary school, Oh experienced bullying, an issue that would later figure prominently into her Prophecy trilogy. Oh attended New York University and Georgetown University Law Center in Washington, DC. After law school, Oh practiced corporate and entertainment law. She worked at private law firms, at the Corporation for Public Broadcasting, and at the National Wildlife Federation.

In 2000 Oh started writing fiction. Her interest in fiction writing emerged at the same time as her interest in learning about Korean history. According to Oh, she read a biography of Genghis Khan and became fascinated with ancient Asia. Oh's research inspired her to write. Before publishing her first book, titled *Prophecy*, Oh pitched it to a number of editors. In 2010 Oh began to work with the agent Joe Monti and submitted her book to HarperCollins. In December of that year, just two weeks after she had submitted the manuscript, Oh received a three-book deal from the publisher.

Although Oh did not start publishing young adult novels until she was in her forties, she recalls being encouraged to pursue her creative writing in high school. According to Oh, a high school English teacher once told her that she had a talent for writing. As a child, Oh wrote creatively and would fill notebooks with her ideas. But it was not until Oh started researching ancient Asian history that she became serious about her creative writing. Oh decided to write a fantasy novel that blended Korean history, mythology, and legend. In preparation, she immersed herself in Korean history, reading books and watching films and documentaries on the subject. Being the mother of three daughters also inspired Oh to write novels. Oh wanted to write books featuring Korean American characters for her daughters and other girls to read. She observed that while books like *The Hunger Games* featured strong female protagonists, not many featured strong female protagonists of color, and she wanted her daughters to

have fictional role models who shared their cultural background.

Major Works

In Oh's book *Prophecy* (2013), the first novel in a trilogy that goes by the same name, readers are introduced to the young woman warrior Kira, known as the "demon slayer" and an outcast in her fictional hometown of Hansong. Kira, renowned for her yellow eyes and fierce fighting skills, is the only woman warrior in the king's army. When Hansong is invaded by demons, Kira must run away with the prince, her first cousin, and keep him safe while searching for an ancient treasure. Along the way, she fights demons, imps, shamans, hobgoblins, and even the Demon Lord. Oh constructs a rich and textured mythical world through the incorporation of myriad details. Kira has the special ability to sniff out demons. At one point Oh describes how Kira breathes in "the familiar waft of demon stink." Through description of sensory experiences like this one, Oh brings Kira's world to life for readers. Oh also provides readers with details about Kira's thoughts and feelings during her adventures through third-person limited narration. She dramatizes Kira's anxieties, emotions, and self-doubt as Kira strives to meet her goals. Despite the fact that her world is a fictional one, Kira becomes a complex, relatable character for young adult readers.

In the second book, *Warrior* (2013), Kira's adventures continue. When Hansong is thrown into chaos, Kira must continue to fight demons and search for ancient treasure. In the novel Oh further develops the world of the Seven Kingdoms. She also further develops her protagonist, now a seventeen-year-old young woman. In *Warrior*, Kira has a love interest, a handsome young man named Jaewon. Through the events of the book, Kira learns adult lessons about trusting yourself, trusting other people, and forgiveness. As in the earlier book, in *Warrior* Oh also incorporate details from Korean history and folklore.

The third installment of the Prophecy trilogy, *King*, was published in March 2015. In it, Kira continues her quest to unearth lost treasure and unite the Seven Kingdoms, in the process learning more about herself and her own power.

M. Lewandowski, MA

Further Reading

Goo, Maurene. "The Wayward Bound: How a Doctor and Lawyer Became Young Adult Novelists." *Hyphen Magazine* 28 (2014): 44–5. Print.

Qureshi, Bilal. "#WeNeedDiverseBooks Campaign Comes to Inaugural Bookcon." *NPR Code Switch.* NPR, 2 June 2014. Web. 11 Dec. 2015. <http://www.npr.org/sections/codeswitch/2014/06/02/318098926/-weneeddiversebooks-campaign-comes-to-inaugural-bookcon>.

Bibliography

"Bio." *Ellen Oh.* Author, n.d. Web. 11 Dec. 2015. <http://ellenoh.com/bio>.

"FAQ." *We Need Diverse Books.* We Need Diverse Books, n.d. Web. 11 Dec. 2015. <http://weneeddiversebooks.org/faq>.

Hong, Terry. "Ellen Oh's Prophecy Trilogy and Why #WeNeedDiverseBooks." *Bloom.* Bloom, 8 Sept. 2014. Web. 9 Dec. 2015. <http://bloom-site.com/2014/09/08/ellen-ohs-prophecy-trilogy-and-why-weneeddiversebooks>.

Lovelace, Sunnie. "Warrior: A Prophecy Novel." Rev. of *Warrior*, by Ellen Oh. *School Library Journal* 60.2 (2014): 110. Print.

Oh, Ellen. Interview by Natalie Aguirre. *Literary Rambles.* Literary Rambles, 7 Jan. 2013. Web. 9 Dec. 2015. <http://www.literaryrambles.com/2013/01/ellen-oh-interview-and-prophecy-giveaway.html>.

Sette, Sunnie. Rev. of *Prophecy*, by Ellen Oh. *School Library Journal* 59.2 (2013): 111. Print.

Rev. of *Warrior*, by Ellen Oh. *Kirkus Reviews* 81.21 (2013): 37. *Literary Reference Center.* Web. 14 Dec. 2015. <http://search.ebscohost.com/login.aspx?direct=true&db=lfh&AN=91760832&site=lrc-live>.

Gary Paulsen

Date of birth: May 17, 1939
Place of birth: Minneapolis, Minnesota

Principal Works

Tucket Adventures series (1969–2000)
Dogsong (1985)
Hatchet (1987)
The Winter Room (1989)
Woodsong (1990)
The River (1991)
Alida series (1991–2004)
Nightjohn (1993)
Woods Runner (2010)

Biography

Gary Paulsen has written approximately two hundred of books during his career, including, perhaps most famously, the 1987 survival classic *Hatchet*, about a thirteen-year-old boy who survives a plane crash. He has been a finalist for the Newbery Medal three times. An adventurer, Paulsen eschews human company (outside of his wife and children) for the solitude of the wilderness, the thrill of dog racing, or the open sea. Among his many adventures, Paulsen participated in the Alaskan Iditarod and rode his Harley-Davidson motorcycle from New Mexico to Alaska when he was sixty (which he chronicled in the 1997 memoir *Zero to Sixty: The Motorcycle Journey of a Lifetime*). Paulsen imbues his characters—from *Hatchet*'s Brian Robeson to a real-life slave-turned-field marshal named Bass Reeves—with prodigious survival skills and a focus on self-reliance.

Paulsen was born on May 17, 1939, in Minneapolis, Minnesota. He grew up in Chicago; Manila, Philippines, where his father was stationed after World War II; and, later, on a chicken farm in Thief River Falls, Minnesota. His parents, Oscar and Eunice, were poor, and they drank and fought incessantly. They were also tough: when a drunk tried to molest Paulsen when he was four, his mother kicked the drunk to death. (His first nine years were so eventful—often horrifically so—that he wrote a book about them in 1993 called *Eastern Sun, Winter Moon*.) Early on, Paulsen learned to fend for himself. He pretended to sell newspapers in bars to steal money from patrons when they were too drunk to notice. Sometimes he would run away to a relative's house or simply into the woods, where (like his characters) he would hunt and scavenge to survive.

Paulsen was a voracious reader as a teen, though he hated school. At seventeen, he forged his father's signature to join the Army, where he studied electrical engineering. In 1962, he tested missiles in White Sands, New Mexico. In 1965, he left his first wife and two children to move to Hollywood. He wrote dialogue for the television series *Mission Impossible* (1966–73) and the film *The Reivers* (1969) starring Steve McQueen. In

1966, with his second wife Pam, he moved to an isolated cabin in Minnesota and wrote his first book, a collection of essays about the missile industry called *Some Birds Don't Fly* (1968).

After his second book was published, Paulsen left his wife and moved to Taos, New Mexico. For six years he drank and got into fights. Eventually, he met an artist named Ruth Wright, whom he later married and with whom he had a son, Jim. (Ruth Wright Paulsen has illustrated some of Paulsen's books for children.) The couple moved to a remote cabin in Minnesota. Paulsen sobered up and began to write prolifically, producing nearly seven books a year throughout the 1970s. In 1983, he ran his first Iditarod, and he participated in his last in 2006 at the age of sixty-five. His book about the race, called *Dogsong* (1985), effectively made his career. Published in 1990, *Woodsong* is a nonfiction account of the Iditarod. The publication of Paulsen's most famous novel, *Hatchet*, in 1987 changed the quality of his family's life forever. He and his family moved to a house with a washer, dryer, and running toilet near the small town of Bemidji. Paulsen keeps a cabin in Minnesota, a house in Alaska, and another in New Mexico; he also spends time in the Pacific Ocean on his boat.

Major Works

Paulsen's most famous novel is *Hatchet*, about a thirteen-year-old survivor of a plane crash named Brian. It has remained one of the bestselling YA books in print. It received a Newbery Honor, meaning that it was a finalist for the prestigious Newbery Medal. His other two Newberry Honor books are *Dogsong* (1985) and *The Winter Room* (1989), about two boys who live on a farm. In *Hatchet*, Brian must learn to fend for himself in the unforgiving Canadian wilderness with only a hatchet. A classic of survival literature, the book demonstrates the cruelty of nature and the resourcefulness of man. Paulsen's writing is escapist as well. *Hatchet* was the first of a series called Brian's Saga. Paulsen's other series include the Tucket Adventures series (1969–2000), about a boy on the Oregon Trail who is captured by Pawnee Indians; the Alida series (1991–2004), about a boy living on his grandmother's farm; and a Western series for adults centered on a character named Murphy (1987–1996).

Molly Hagan

Further Reading

Royte, Elizabeth. "Grumpy Old Man and the Sea: Adventures with Gary Paulsen." *Outside Online*. Outside, 23 May 2013. Web. 2 Mar. 2015. <http://www.outsideonline.com/outdoor-adventure/media/books/Gary-Paulsen-Grumpy-Old-Man-and-the-Sea.html>.

Schmitz, James A. "Gary Paulsen: A Writer of His Time." *ALAN Review* 22.1 (1994). Web. 2 Mar. 2015. <http://scholar.lib.vt.edu/ejournals/ALAN/fall94/Schmitz.html>.

Sides, Anne Goodwin. "On the Road and Between the Pages, an Author Is Restless for Adventure." *New York Times*. New York Times, 26 Aug. 2006. Web. 1 Mar. 2015. <http://www.nytimes.com/2006/08/26/books/26paul.html>.

Bibliography

Corbett, Sue. *Gary Paulsen*. New York: Cavendish, 2014. *eBook Collection (EBSCOhost)*. Web. 23 Mar. 2015.

Paulsen, Gary, and Jim Paulsen. Interview by Sally Lodge. "Q&A with Gary Paulsen and Jim Paulsen." *Publisher's Weekly*. PWxyz, 6 Dec. 2012. Web. 3 Mar. 2015. <http://www.publishersweekly.com/pw/by-topic/authors/interviews/article/55019-q-a-with-gary-paulsen-and-jim-paulsen.html>.

Somers, Joseph Michael. "Gary Paulsen." *Magill's Survey of American Literature*. Rev. ed. Ipswich: Salem, 2006. *Biography Reference Center*. Web. 23 Mar. 2015.

Wheeler, Jill C. *Gary Paulsen*. [N.p.]: ABDO, 2015. *eBook Collection (EBSCOhost)*. Web. 23 Mar. 2015.

Richard Peck

Date of birth: April 10, 1934
Place of birth: Decatur, Illinois

Principal Works

Don't Look and It Won't Hurt (1972)
Close Enough to Touch (1981)
A Long Way from Chicago (1998)
A Year Down Yonder (2000)
A Season of Gifts (2009)

Biography

Richard Peck is an American writer who is perhaps best known for his young adult Newbery Medal–winning novel *A Year Down Yonder* (2000), the sequel to Peck's *A Long Way from Chicago* (1998), a Newbery Honor book in 1999. At age thirty-seven, Peck quit his teaching career to become a writer and publish his first novel *Don't Look and It Won't Hurt* (1972). Peck told Heather Vogel Frederick for *Publisher's Weekly*, "I would never have been a writer if I hadn't been a teacher first." Since then, he has written more than thirty books for young adults. Peck received the Margaret A. Edwards Award for lifetime achievement in 1990, and in 2002, he was the first children's book author to receive a National Humanities Medal from the White House.

Peck was born on April 10, 1934, in Decatur, Illinois. He lived with his mother, who was a dietitian, and his father, who was a salesman. He attended DePauw University in Greencastle, Indiana, and in 1955, when Peck was a junior, he traveled to the United Kingdom to spend a year studying at the University of Exeter. The students there, Peck recalled to Jennifer M. Brown for *Publisher's Weekly*, were "a generation who had grown up under the tables and in the bomb shelters of World War II. To Peck, his classmates seemed "immensely tempered," while he felt "so big and wholesome and untried." Back in Indiana, Peck graduated from DePauw in 1956, and after graduation was drafted into military service and sent to West Germany. While there he ghostwrote sermons for his company's nondenominational chaplain.

When Peck returned to the United States he enrolled in graduate school at Southern Illinois University Carbondale and worked as a graduate teaching assistant, while earning his master's degree. He began teaching English at Glenbrook North High School in Northbrook, Illinois, in 1961. Later, the school would provide Peck with an idea for the setting in his 1981 novel *Close Enough to Touch*. In 1963 he took a job with a textbook publishing company in Chicago, and in 1965 he moved to New York City to become an English instructor at Hunter College and Hunter College High School. By chance, Peck was asked to work with another instructor to compile a book of essays, which included author Jack Kerouac and anthropologist Margaret Mead. Compiling the book was Peck's first foray into the exclusive world of New York publishing; he credits his students and the contacts he made at the school for giving him the courage to pursue a writing career. Peck first met George Nicholson, an editor at Dell Paperbacks, when Peck was an English teacher at Hunter College. Peck turned in his first novel for young adults to Nicholson, who was then working at Holt Publishing. Peck quit his teaching job in 1971, and his first book *Don't Look and It Won't Hurt* was published in 1972. Peck lives on New York's Upper East Side.

Major Works

After teaching, Peck felt he had a better understanding of teenagers and determined that he wanted to write for the thoughtful, quiet students who are often overlooked. Peck's two most popular books for young adults are *A Long Way from Chicago* (1998) and *A Year Down Yonder* (2000). The first is a novel told in a series of vignettes spanning thirteen years. Peck's readers are introduced to a boy named Joey, and his little sister, Mary Alice. In the book, Peck focuses on the duo's summertime adventures with their Grandmother Dowdel, who lives in rural southern Illinois. In the last story, Joey, on his way to war, visits his grandmother when his train makes a stop nearby. The *Kirkus Review* wrote, "Peck weaves a wry tale that ranges from humorous to poignant," he "deftly captures the spirit of the times." The review called the book "remarkable and fine."

The sequel, *A Year Down Yonder* (2000), takes place during the so-called Roosevelt recession in 1937. In this book, Joe and Mary Alice's parents struggle to get back on their feet, while fifteen-year-old Mary Alice spends a year living with Grandma Dowdel, and Joey joins the Civilian Conservation Corps and heads west. A reviewer for *Publisher's Weekly* wrote that *A Year Down Yonder* "reveals a marshmallow heart inside Grandma's rock-hard exterior and adroitly exposes the mutual, unspoken affection she shares with her granddaughter." Peck's folksy tale-telling skills in the Grandma Dowdel series reflect his affection for where he grew up. "I find the Midwest very underrepresented in fiction," Peck told Frederick, "and the older I get, the more meaningful those childhood memories are."

Molly Hagan

Further Reading

Brown, Jennifer M. "Richard Peck: A Long Way from Decatur." *Publisher's Weekly*. PWxyz, 21 July 2003. Web. 7 May 2015. <http:www.publishersweekly.com/pw/print/20030821/22661-richard-peck-a-long-way-from-decatur.html>.

Gallo, Donald R., and Wendy J. Glenn. *Richard Peck: The Past Is Paramount*. Lanham: Scarecrow P, 2009. Print.

Peck, Richard. "Interview with Newbery Award-Winning 'A Year Down Yonder' Author Richard Peck." Interview by Henry Herz. *Examiner.com*. Examiner.com, 25 Feb. 2014. Web. 7 May 2015. <http://www.examiner.com/article/interview-with-newbery-award-winning-a-year-down-yonder-author-richard-peck>.

Bibliography

"Author Richard Peck '56 Wins Coveted Newbery Medal." *DePauw University*. DePauw University, 16 Jan. 2001. Web. 7 May 2015. <http://www.depauw.edu/news-media/latest-news/details/11380/>.

"A Long Way from Chicago." Rev. of *A Long Way from Chicago*, by Richard Peck. *Kirkus*. Kirkus, 1 Sept. 1998. Web. 8 May 2015. <https://www.kirkusreviews.com/book-reviews/richard-peck/a-long-way-from-chicago/>.

"A Long Way from Chicago: A Novel in Stories." Rev. of *A Long Way from Chicago*, by Richard Peck. *Publisher's Weekly*. PWxyz, 1 Sept. 1998. Web. 8 May 2015. <htttp://www.publishersweekly.com/978-0-8037-2290-3>.

"A Year Down Yonder." Rev. of *A Year Down Yonder*, by Richard Peck. *Publisher's Weekly*. PWxyz, 1 Oct. 2000. Web. 8 May 2015. <http://www.publishersweekly.com/978-0-8037-2518-8>.

"Q&A with Richard Peck." Interview by Heather Vogel Frederick. *Publisher's Weekly*, PWxyz, 24 Sept. 2009. Web. 7 May 2015. <http://www.publishersweekly.com/pw/by-topic/authors/interviews/article/28-q-a-with-richard-peck.html>.

Julie Anne Peters

Date of birth: January 16, 1952
Place of birth: Jamestown, New York

Principal Works
Children's Literature
The Stinky Sneakers Contest (1992)
B. J.'s Billion Dollar Bet (1994)
Short Stories
grl2grl: Short Fictions (2007)
grl2grl 2: Short Fictions (2011)

Young Adult Literature
Risky Friends (1993)
How Do You Spell G-E-E-K? (1996)
Revenge of the Snob Squad (1998)
Romance of the Snob Squad (1999)
Love Me, Love My Broccoli (1999)
Define "Normal" (2000)
A Snitch in the Snob Squad (2001)
Keeping You a Secret (2003)
Luna (2004)
Far from Xanadu (2005; republished as *Pretend You Love Me*, 2011)
Between Mom and Jo (2006)
Rage: A Love Story (2009)
By the Time You Read This, I'll Be Dead (2010)
She Loves You, She Loves You Not . . . (2011)
It's Our Prom (So Deal with It) (2012)
Lies My Girlfriend Told Me (2014)

Biography

Julie Anne Peters was born in Jamestown, New York, a small city in the westernmost portion of the state. When she was five years old, she moved with her family to a suburb of Denver, Colorado, where she was raised with her older brother, John, and younger sisters, Jeanne and Susan. She earned her first college degree in elementary education from Colorado Women's College in 1974, but after one year in the field, Peters decided to change careers. She went back to school and earned a bachelor of science degree in business and computer science. Ultimately, she found that working with computers was not right for her either, so she began to write. According to Peters, she was in her late thirties when she published her first two books: *The Stinky Sneakers Contest* (1992), a children's book, and *Risky Friends* (1993), which was marketed toward middle schoolers.

In the late 1990s Peters built on the popularity of *Risky Friends* among middle-school-age children and published a series of books about "the Snob Squad." After the publication and success of some of her earlier humorous books, she published an essay on comic devices for children's writing, "When You Write Humor for Children." In 2003 the young adult novel *Keeping You a Secret*, about two high school girls who fall in love, was released. A year later *Luna* was published. It is a story about a transgender teen who faces the challenge of coming out to family and friends. The novel, a National Book Award finalist, was named an

American Library Association Best Book for Young Adults.

Peters continued to tackle difficult topics not typically addressed in young adult literature, including queer identity, abuse, destructive relationships, and suicide. Her book *By the Time You Read This, I'll Be Dead* (2010), follows Daelyn, an unhappy teen who is tired of being bullied and plans to commit suicide. In an interview, Peters explained that letters from young readers describing the bullying they experienced in school for coming out as gay were an inspiration to write the book. Peters has also published short fiction in *grl2grl* (2007) and *grl2grl 2* (2011), which all feature stories featuring young LGBTQ (lesbian, gay, bisexual, transgender, and queer) protagonists. Peters lives in Colorado with Sherri, her partner of many years. Peters works full time with the Colorado Reading Corps, helping children improve their reading skills.

Major Works

Julie Anne Peters is an author of young adult books, many of which address LGBTQ issues. Her books have received many honors, including the Stonewall Honor Book award and a Lambda Literary Award. *Luna* (2004), the first mainstream published young adult novel with a transgender character, was a 2004 National Book Award finalist, and Lynn Evarts for the *Lambda Book Report* called it one of the most important young adult books to be published in a decade. In it Peters tells the story of Regan and her older sibling, Liam, who is transgender. At night, Liam sneaks into Regan's room to become Luna, and with the help of Regan's wigs, clothes, and makeup, Luna is able to then express her true identity. She chooses her name because, in her own words, she is "a girl who can only be seen by moonlight." The novel is narrated from the perspective of Regan, who grapples with the complexity of her relationship to Luna. "I loved her," Regan admits. "I couldn't help it. She was my brother." Regan struggles with the ways in which Liam's coming out as transgender complicates her own life. The novel is interspersed with Regan's memories of her childhood with Liam, bickering, for example, over who gets to play the role of the mommy when they play house. These memories, which feel relatable and mostly ordinary to readers, are punctuated by moments that begin to reveal Liam's true gender identity. Regan's memories are often starkly juxtaposed with the harsher reality that is her adolescence

with Liam. Over the course of the novel, the two siblings support each other through trying times, confront their parents about Luna's true identity, and, in the end, learn to let go of each other as they enter adulthood.

In 2009 Peters published *Rage: A Love Story*, which was another finalist for a National Book Award. The novel tells the story of two young women: reliable Johanna and emotionally unstable Reeve. When Johanna starts tutoring Reeve's autistic twin brother, Robbie, she has a chance to get closer to her crush. But as Johanna becomes more involved with Reeve, she begins to learn about Reeve's violent home life with a mother who is a drug addict and an uncle who is abusive. When Reeve begins to abuse Johanna, Johanna justifies staying in the relationship because she believes that Reeve loves her. The novel chronicles Johanna's difficult journey to realization that what she shares with Reeve is not love. The book, told from Johanna's perspective, features visceral details and descriptions of abuse, and readers are forced to reckon with the realities of domestic violence and abusive relationships. At times the violence depicted in the book may seem extreme to readers. But critics have praised Peters for her skillful handling of troubling, ambitious material.

M. Lewandowski, MA

Further Reading

Alter, Alexandra. "Transgender Children's Books Fill a Void and Break a Taboo." *New York Times*. New York Times, 6 June 2015. Web. 17 Dec. 2015. <http://www.nytimes.com/2015/06/07/business/media/transgender-childrens-books-fill-a-void-and-break-a-taboo.html?_r=0>.

Rockefeller, Elsworth. "The Genre of Gender: the Emerging Canon of Transgender-Inclusive YA Literature." *Horn Book*. Lifestyle Theme on Genesis Framework, 1 Sept. 2007. Web. 17 Dec. 2015. <http://www.hbook.com/2007/09/choosing-books/hornbook-magazine/genre-of-gender/#_>.

Bibliography

Evarts, Lynn. "Trans by the Light of the Moon." *Lambda Book Report* 13.3 (2004): 13. *Academic Search Complete*. Web. 17 Dec. 2015. <http://search.ebscohost.com/login.aspx?direct=true&db=a9h&AN=15374832>.

Hill, Rebecca A. "GLBT Young Adult Fiction." *School Library Monthly* 27.8 (2011): 20–21. *Academic*

Search Complete. Web. 17 Dec. 2015. <http://search.ebscohost.com/login.aspx?direct=true&db=a9h&AN=60797073>.

Molland, Judy. "How Many Young Adult Novels Feature Transgender Characters?" *Care2.* Care2.com, 15 June 2015. Web. 17 Dec. 2015. <http://www.care2.com/causes/how-many-young adult-novels-feature-transgender-characters.html>.

Pekoll, Kristin. "Why Gay Characters Matter." *Huffington Post.* TheHuffingtonPost.com, 22 Sept. 2014. Web. 17 Dec. 2015. <http://www.huffingtonpost.com/kristin-pekoll/why-gay-characters-matter_b_5851516.html>.

Peters, Julie Anne. *Julie Anne Peters.* Julie Anne Peters, 2000. Web. 17 Dec. 2015. <http://www.julieannepeters.com/>.

Sir Terry Pratchett

Date of birth: April 28, 1948
Place of birth: Beaconsfield, England
Date of death: March 12, 2015
Place of death: Broad Chalke, England

Principal Works
Children's Literature
The Carpet People (1971)
The Nome Trilogy, or the Bromeliad Trilogy (1989–90)
Johnny Maxwell series (1992–96)
Dodger (2012)
Young Adult Literature
Nation (2008)
Tiffany Aching books of the Discworld series (2005–15)
Adult Literature
The Dark Side of the Sun (1976)
Strata (1981)
Discworld series (1983–2015)
Good Omens (with Neil Gaiman, 1990)
The Long Earth series (with Stephen Baxer, 2012–15)

Biography
Sir Terry Pratchett was an English author known primarily for his works of fantasy fiction. He published more than forty books in his long-running Discworld series, as well as numerous companion books about the Discworld's characters, culture, and geography. Although many of his novels were marketed primarily to adults, they are typically considered appropriate for younger readers as well, and several Discworld novels were specifically marketed toward young adult audiences. In addition to the Discworld series, Pratchett wrote several unrelated novels for adults and children as well as numerous short stories, essays, and related works.

Terence David John Pratchett was born on April 28, 1948, in Beaconsfield, England, to David and Eileen Pratchett. As a young child, Pratchett initially hated reading and would read a book only if his mother bribed him with a small amount of money. However, he quickly developed a love of reading and became a devoted patron of the local library, to which he attributed the bulk of his education. Pratchett also developed an interest in astronomy, which led him to read a great deal of science fiction.

After completing primary school, Pratchett attended High Wycombe Technical High School. Already a writer, he published his first short story in the school magazine at the age of thirteen. Pratchett left school in 1965, at the age of seventeen, to take a position with the *Bucks Free Press* newspaper in Buckinghamshire. In addition to working as a journalist, he wrote short children's stories for the newspaper as well. He later worked for South West England's *Western Daily Press* and the *Bath Evening Chronicle* before taking a position in the Central Electricity Generating Board's publicity department.

Pratchett published his first book, the children's fantasy novel *The Carpet People*, in 1971. After publishing the adult science-fiction novels *The Dark Side of the Sun* (1976) and *Strata* (1981), he began what would become his most famous series with the publication of *The Colour of Magic* in 1983. The novel was the first installment in the Discworld series; the final installment, *The Shepherd's Crown*, was published posthumously in 2015. Although most of the Discworld novels are typically considered appropriate for young adult readers, a select few were specifically marketed to children or teenagers, including *The Amazing Maurice and His Educated Rodents* (2001), *The Wee Free Men* (2003), *A Hat Full of Sky* (2004), *Wintersmith* (2006), *I Shall Wear Midnight* (2010), and *The Shepherd's Crown*. Expanding on the world of his novels, Pratchett also published a number of companion books to the Discworld series, many of which provided further information about its people, history, and culture.

Although best known for his Discworld novels, Pratchett was a prolific writer outside of that series as well. He published the unrelated standalone young adult novel *Nation* in 2008, as well as a number of other books for children. He also cowrote several other science-fiction and fantasy novels for adults, including *Good Omens* (1990), with Neil Gaiman, and the Long Earth series (2012–15), with Stephen Baxter. In recognition of his contributions to British literature, Pratchett was made an officer of the Most Excellent Order of the British Empire (OBE) in 2009.

Pratchett married Lyn Purves in 1968. The couple had one daughter, Rhianna, born in 1976. In 2007, Pratchett was diagnosed with posterior cortical atrophy, a type of Alzheimer disease. Over the following years, he became an advocate for both Alzheimer research and the legalization of assisted suicide, though he preferred the term "assisted death." Pratchett died of complications from his disease at his home in Broad Chalke, England, on March 12, 2015.

Major Works

The most famous of Pratchett's numerous works, the Discworld series consists of forty-one humorous fantasy novels set on a flat, disc-shaped world supported on the backs of four giant elephants, which in turn stand on the shell of a massive spacefaring turtle known as the Great A'Tuin. Within the series are several unofficial subseries that follow a number of recurring characters, including a coven of rural witches, the guards of the City Watch, the wizards of the Unseen University, and Death and his granddaughter, Susan. Other novels in the series stand on their own, though most include familiar elements—such as recurring background characters or references to the events of other books—that make the vast, sprawling universe of the Discworld feel more cohesive.

The Discworld novels share a number of features common to Pratchett's work as a whole. As humorous fantasy works, they combine the fantastic elements found in many of his other books with an offbeat sense of humor and a strong satirical bent. The idea of a flat world featured in a previous novel, *Strata*, although the Discworld series explores the concept and how it might function in significantly more depth. In addition, while the novels are rife with fantastic elements, they incorporate aspects of real-world cultures, attitudes, and historical and technological developments as well, evoking a sense of recognition in the reader that Pratchett frequently used as a

platform for indirect social commentary and occasional philosophy.

As both popular and critically well-regarded works, the Discworld books were frequently adapted into other media. Several television movies and miniseries based on the novels aired on British television, and a number of radio adaptations were produced as well.

Joy Crelin

Further Reading

Smythe, Colin. "Terry Pratchett Biography." *L-Space Web*. L-Space Librarians, 2011. Web. 4 June 2015. <http://www.lspace.org/about-terry/biography.html>.

Terry Pratchett. Transworld, 31 May 2015. Web. 4 June 2015. <http://www.terrypratchett.co.uk>.

Weber, Bruce. "Terry Pratchett, Novelist, Dies at 66." *New York Times*. New York Times, 12 Mar. 2015. Web. 4 June 2015. <http://www.nytimes.com/2015/03/13/books/terry-pratchett-popular-fantasy-novelist-dies-at-66.html>.

Bibliography

Eldridge, Alison. "Terry Pratchett." *Encyclopaedia Britannica*. Encyclopaedia Britannica, 12 Mar. 2015. Web. 4 June 2015. <http://www.britannica.com/EBchecked/topic/1854183/Terry-Pratchett>.

Flood, Alison. "A Life in Writing: Terry Pratchett." *Guardian*. Guardian News and Media, 14 Oct. 2011. Web. 4 June 2015. <http://www.theguardian.com/culture/2011/oct/14/terry-pratchett-life-writing>.

Grice, Elizabeth. "Sir Terry Pratchett: 'I Thought My Alzheimer's Would Be a Lot Worse than This by Now.'" *Telegraph*. Telegraph Media Group, 10 Sept. 2012. Web. 4 June 2015. <http://www.telegraph.co.uk/lifestyle/9532983/Sir-Terry-Pratchett-I-thought-my-Alzheimers-would-be-a-lot-worse-than-this-by-now.html>.

Pratchett, Terry. "Terry Pratchett: My Case for a Euthanasia Tribunal." *Guardian*. Guardian News and Media, 1 Feb. 2010. Web. 4 June 2015. <http://www.theguardian.com/society/2010/feb/02/terry-pratchett-assisted-suicide-tribunal>.

Pratchett, Terry. "Terry Pratchett Interview: A Fantasy Writer Facing Reality." Interview by Tom Chivers. *Telegraph*. Telegraph Media Group, 12 Mar. 2015. Web. 4 June 2015. <http://www.telegraph.co.uk/culture/books/authorinterviews/10396286/Terry-Pratchett-interview-a-fantasy-writer-facing-reality.html>.

Philip Pullman

Date of birth: October 19, 1946
Place of birth: Norwich, England

Principal Works
Children's Literature
Count Karlstein (1982)
The Wonderful Story of Aladdin and the Enchanted Lamp (1993)
Thunderbolt's Waxwork (1994)
The Gasfitter's Ball (1995)
The Firework-Maker's Daughter (1995)
Clockwork; or, All Wound Up (1996)
Mossycoat (1998)
I Was a Rat! (1999)
Puss in Boots (2000)
The Scarecrow and His Servant (2004)
Fairy Tales from the Brothers Grimm (2012)
Young Adult Literature
Ruby in the Smoke (1985)
The Shadow in the North (1986)
How to Be Cool (1987)
The Tiger in the Well (1990)
The Tin Princess (1994)
The Golden Compass (1995)
The Subtle Knife (1997)
The Amber Spyglass (2000)
Lyra's Oxford (2003)
Once Upon a Time in the North (2008)
Adult Literature
The Haunted Storm (1972)
Galatea (1979)
The Good Man Jesus and the Scoundrel Christ (2010)

Biography
Philip Pullman is a British author best known for his novels for young adult readers. Among his best-known young adult novels are the books in the His Dark Materials series and the Sally Lockhart series as well as the standalone novels *The Broken Bridge* (1990) and *The White Mercedes* (1992; republished as *The Butterfly Tattoo* in 1998). In addition to his young adult fiction, Pullman is the author of numerous children's books, primarily retellings of popular fairy tales, and several novels for adults.

Philip Nicholas Pullman was born on October 19, 1946, in Norwich, England, the first of two sons born to Alfred and Audrey Pullman. He grew up in the United Kingdom and in what is now Zimbabwe, where his father, a pilot in the Royal Air Force (RAF), was stationed for a time. Alfred Pullman died in 1953, during the Mau Mau Uprising in Kenya. After his death, Pullman's mother married another RAF pilot, and the family moved to Australia.

As a child, Pullman was an avid reader and particularly enjoyed both the popular superhero comic books published by DC Comics and Arthur Conan Doyle's tales of Sherlock Holmes. Pullman eventually returned to the United Kingdom to attend school, and his family later settled in northern Wales, where he attended secondary school at Ysgol Ardudwy. After completing his secondary education, Pullman enrolled in Exeter College, Oxford, where he studied English.

After completing his undergraduate degree, Pullman worked briefly as a librarian before beginning a teaching career. After more than a decade of teaching English to preteens and young teenagers in Oxford, Pullman became a senior lecturer at Westminster College, a teacher training college and part of the University of Oxford. He remained at the college until the late 1990s. While working as a teacher, Pullman wrote numerous plays for his students, some of which he later adapted into children's books. He published his first novel for adults, *The Haunted Storm*, in 1972. Ultimately disappointed in the book, Pullman typically avoided discussing it later in his career.

Pullman's first novel for younger readers, *The Ruby in the Smoke*, was published in 1985. The novel, set in the Victorian era, became the first installment in the four-volume Sally Lockhart series. The first two books in the series, *The Ruby in the Smoke* and *The Shadow in the North* (1986; originally *The Shadow in the Plate*), were later adapted into television films and aired on the BBC in 2006 and 2007, respectively. Pullman went on to write several standalone young adult books during the 1980s and 1990s, including *How to Be Cool* (1987) and *The Broken Bridge* (1990).

During the early 1990s, Pullman began work on *Northern Lights*, the first book in the His Dark Materials series. The novel was published in the United Kingdom in 1995 and in the United States the following year, under the title *The Golden Compass*. The novel received significant critical acclaim, as did the next two novels in the trilogy, *The Subtle Knife* (1997) and *The Amber Spyglass* (2000), and the companion novellas *Lyra's Oxford* (2003) and *Once upon a Time in the North* (2008). The first book in the series was adapted into a film, *The Golden Compass*, in 2007.

Pullman married his wife, Judith Speller, in 1970. They have two sons, Jamie and Tom.

Major Works

An avid reader from an early age, Pullman drew inspiration from a number of classic works in creating his most popular young adult novels. His love of the Sherlock Holmes stories he read as a child likely played a significant role when he was constructing the Victorian milieu of the Sally Lockhart novels, which combine elements of mystery with period-appropriate settings and plot elements. The His Dark Materials series, in which conflicts among humans and seemingly divine beings play a crucial role, was inspired in part by seventeenth-century poet John Milton's epic *Paradise Lost* (1667), which Pullman first read in secondary school. Building upon such classic influences, Pullman constructs rich settings for his protagonists' adventures.

Although absent from many of Pullman's works, religious themes are prevalent in the His Dark Materials series, which criticizes religious oppression and elements of organized religion. The novels have generated controversy because of those themes, and their use in libraries and schools is frequently challenged by parents and activist groups that object to their content. However, some prominent religious thinkers have praised the novels for their antioppression message and supported their use as teaching tools.

Joy Crelin

Further Reading

"About Philip Pullman." *Philip Pullman*. Pullman, 2015. <http://www.philip-pullman.com/about-philip-pullman>.

Dowd, Siobhan. "Philip Pullman." *Encyclopaedia Britannica*. Encyclopaedia Britannica, 5 June 2014. Web. 4 June 2015. <http://www.britannica.com/EBchecked/topic/973773/Philip-Pullman>.

Mitchison, Amanda. "The Art of Darkness." *Telegraph*. Telegraph Media Group, 3 Nov. 2003. Web. 4 June 2015. <http://www.telegraph.co.uk/culture/donotmigrate/3605857/The-art-of-darkness.html>.

Bibliography

Brown, Helen. "Page in the Life: Philip Pullman." *Telegraph*. Telegraph Media Group, 17 Oct. 2011. Web. 4 June 2015. <http://www.telegraph.co.uk/culture/books/authorinterviews/8824867/Page-in-the-Life-Philip-Pullman.html>.

La Bella, Laura. *Philip Pullman*. New York: Rosen, 2014. Print.

McCrum, Robert. "Dæmon Geezer." *Guardian*. Guardian News and Media, 27 Jan, 2002. Web. 4 June 2015. <http://www.theguardian.com/books/2002/jan/27/whitbreadprize2001.costabookaward>.

Pullman, Philip. "The Inventory: Philip Pullman." Interview with Hester Lacey. *FT Magazine*. Financial Times, 16 Mar. 2012. Web. 4 June 2015. <http://www.ft.com/intl/cms/s/2/10f13e1e-6d6f-11e1-b6ff-00144feab49a.html#axzz1pe6frZ43>.

Pullman, Philip. "Philip Pullman: A Life in Writing." *Guardian*. Guardian News and Media, 3 Mar. 2011. Web. 4 June 2015. <http://www.theguardian.com/culture/2011/mar/03/philip-pullman-life-in-writing>.

Rick Riordan

Date of birth: June 5, 1964
Place of birth: San Antonio, Texas

Principal Works

Children's Literature
The Maze of Bones (2008)
Vespers Rising (with Peter Lerangis, Gordon Korman, and Jude Watson, 2011)
Young Adult Literature
Percy Jackson and the Olympians series (2005–09)
The Kane Chronicles (2010–12)
The Heroes of Olympus (2010–14)
Percy Jackson's Greek Gods (2014)
Percy Jackson's Greek Heroes (2015)
Magnus Chase and the Gods of Asgard series (2015–present)
Adult Literature
The Tres Navarre series (1997–2007)
Short Stories
The Demigod Files (2009)

Biography

Rick Riordan is an American author of fiction for middle-grade and young adult readers. His best-known work is the series Percy Jackson and the Olympians, which follows the adventures of the eponymous Percy, a seemingly ordinary boy who learns that he is truly the son of Poseidon and thus a demigod. In addition to that bestselling series, Riordan is the author of several further series that draw from ancient mythology and a number of companion books. He has also published a series of mystery novels for adults.

Richard Russell Riordan was born on June 5, 1964, in San Antonio, Texas. His parents, Rick and Lyn, were teachers who divorced when Riordan was still young. As a child, Riordan disliked reading and was especially bored by the books he was assigned to read in school. His outlook changed, however, when he discovered fantasy literature in middle school, becoming a devoted fan of J. R. R. Tolkien's *Lord of the Rings*. He developed a strong interest in mythology thanks to his eighth-grade English teacher, who also encouraged him to write stories and submit them for publication.

After high school, Riordan enrolled in North Texas State University to study guitar. He later transferred to the University of Texas at Austin, where he studied English and history. During the summers, he worked at a camp that would later inspire Camp Half-Blood, one of the key settings of the Percy Jackson and the Olympians series. After obtaining his teaching certification at the University of Texas in San Antonio, Riordan found work as a middle-school English teacher. He taught for fifteen years, in both Texas and California, before deciding to quit teaching and write full time.

While working as a teacher, Riordan published his first novel, *Big Red Tequila*, in 1997. The novel became the first of seven mystery novels featuring private detective Tres Navarre. He began working on *The Lighting Thief*, the first novel in the Percy Jackson and the Olympians series, early in the next decade. The novel originated as a story he told his eldest son, to whom he had previously told versions of numerous Greek myths as bedtime stories. The character of Percy was inspired in part by Riordan's son, who has attention deficit hyperactivity disorder (ADHD) as well as dyslexia; Percy struggles with both but learns that they are in fact the result of his demigod heritage. Published in 2005, the novel proved very successful and led to the publication of four additional books in the series as well as several companion books, including *The Demigod Files* (2009) and *Percy Jackson's Greek Gods* (2014). *The Lightning Thief* and the second installment in the series, *The Sea of Monsters* (2006), were adapted into films in 2010 and 2013, respectively.

Following the success of that series, Riordan began writing the Heroes of Olympus series (2010–14),

set in the same world. Diversifying his novels' mythological backgrounds, he also published the Egyptian myth–based Kane Chronicles, beginning with *The Red Pyramid* (2010), and the Norse myth–inspired Magnus Chase and the Gods of Asgard series, beginning with *The Sword of Summer* (2015). Riordan has also written two books for younger readers, *The Maze of Bones* (2008) and *Vespers Rising* (2011), as part of the multi-author 39 Clues series.

Riordan and his wife, Becky, have two sons, Haley and Patrick. They live in Boston, Massachusetts.

Major Works

Perhaps the most prominent feature of Riordan's novels for middle-grade and young adult readers is their recurring use of mythological characters, settings, and motifs, which in many ways are defining features of his work and help differentiate his novels from the various other fantasy series that are popular with young adults, such as J. K. Rowling's Harry Potter series. Figures from mythology play a significant role in Riordan's novels: Poseidon, the Greek god of the sea, is Percy's absentee father, while the protagonist of the Heroes of Olympus series, Jason, is the son of the chief god Zeus. Similarly, the novels in the Kane Chronicles feature appearances by numerous Egyptian gods, including Isis, Osiris, and Set.

Like many middle-grade and young adult novels, Riordan's books often have strong coming-of-age themes. Riordan has commented in interviews that his works, particularly those in the Percy Jackson series, tend to follow a traditional framework in which a hero must prove himself or herself by going on a quest and overcoming challenges to come of age. This framework, articulated as the hero's journey in famed mythologist Joseph Campbell's *Hero with a Thousand Faces* (1949), has roots in ancient myth and folklore. Riordan's novels, then, are connected to the myths that inspired them not merely through characters and settings but also on a deeper narrative level.

Joy Crelin

Further Reading

Parker, Dan. "If the Name Rick Riordan Sounds Familiar—It Should." *Port Aransas South Jetty*. Port Aransas South Jetty, 25 Aug. 2011. Web. 31 May 2015. <http://www.portasouthjetty.com/news/2011-08-25/

Front_Page/If_the_name_Rick_Riordan_sounds_fa-
miliar__it_shoul.html>.

Riordan, Rick. "About." *Rick Riordan*. Riordan, 2015.
Web. 31 May 2015. <http://www.rickriordan.com/
about/biography>.
Riordan, Rick. "Transcript of an Interview with Rick
Riordan." *AdLit.org*. WETA, n.d. Web. 31 May 2015.
<http://www.adlit.org/transcript_display/29098>.

Bibliography

"In 'Red Pyramid,' Kid Heroes Take on Ancient
Egypt." *NPR Books*. NPR, 19 Dec. 2012. Web.
31 May 2015. <http://www.npr.org/2012/12/19/
167547891/in-red-pyramid-kid-heroes-take-on-
ancient-egypt>.
Riordan, Rick, ed. *Demigods and Monsters: Your Favorite Authors on Rick Riordan's Percy Jackson and
the Olympians Series*. Expanded ed. Dallas: Benbella,
2013. Print.
Riordan, Rick. "Rick Riordan Answers All Your Questions." *Guardian*. Guardian News and Media, 3 May
2011. Web. 31 May 2015. <http://www.theguardian.
com/childrens-books-site/2011/may/03/rick-riordan-
percy-jackson>.
Riordan, Rick. "Talking with Rick Riordan." Interview
by Jeanette Larson. *ALA*. Amer. Library Assn., May
2009. Web. 31 May 2015. <http://www.ala.org/offic-
es/resources/riordan>.
Williams, Sally. "Percy Jackson: My Boy's Own Adventure." *Guardian*. Guardian News and Media, 8
Feb. 2010. Web. 31 May 2015. <http://www.the-
guardian.com/lifeandstyle/2010/feb/08/percy-jack-
son-rick-riordan>.

Veronica Roth

Date of birth: August 19, 1988
Place of birth: New York

Principal Works
Young Adult Literature
Divergent (2011)
Insurgent (2012)
Allegiant (2013)
Four: A Divergent Collection (2014)

Short stories
"Hearken" in *Shards and Ashes*, edited by Melissa Marr
and Kelley Armstrong (2013)

Biography

Born in New York in 1988, Veronica Roth is the youngest of three children; she has an older sister, Ingrid,
and an older brother, Karl. Roth's father was an energy
trader, and her early life involved travel to Hong Kong
and Germany with her family in support of his job.
When Roth was five years old, her parents divorced.
Her mother, a painter, has since remarried and Roth
has described her relationship with her stepfather as
close.

Roth grew up in Barrington, Illinois, attended
Carlton College (in Northfield, MN) as a freshman,
and then transferred to Northwestern University,
where she received her BA in 2010. She wrote *Divergent*, the first book in her best-selling Divergent
series, while she was still a student at Northwestern
and sold it to a publisher at the age of 21. As an article on the Northeastern University's online news site
describes it, "Roth wrote a novel over winter break,
revised it in January, started looking for literary representation in February and signed with an agent in
March. By April, she had a contract with HarperCollins" (Leopold). The process was clearly a whirl-
wind; according to an article in *New York* magazine,
Divergent "sold quickly—after four days, to the first
editor who finished reading it" (Dobbins). The film
rights to *Divergent* were sold quickly as well; Summit Entertainment purchased the rights to the novel
prior to its publication, paying an "undisclosed sum"
for the property (Crowder). After signing the book
deal with HarperCollins, Roth celebrated by filling
her bathtub with 42 bags of mini marshmallows and
sitting in it.

Roth's series, which is set in post-apocalyptic
Chicago, describes a society divided into factions that
organizes its citizens based on their values, talents, and
abilities. While citizens may be born into a particular
faction, when each reaches the age of sixteen, they complete an aptitude test that recommends an optimal faction to join. After Tris, the series' heroine, discovers that
the results of her aptitude test reveal an affinity for not
one but three factions, she is cautioned to keep these
results a secret as the inconclusive results mark her "Divergent," an identity too dangerous to reveal.

Written on the heels of the Suzanne Collins's best-selling dystopian Hunger Games series, Roth's Divergent series has drawn numerous comparisons to Collins's novels. Both series feature strong, brave, and daring teenaged female protagonists who are in conflict with the dystopian societies in which they live, and both offer an element of tense romance.

While Hunger Games may be one clear influencer of the Divergent series, Roth has asserted that she has always been a science fiction reader and fan. She has spoken of her affection for Lois Lowry's *The Giver*, Madeleine L'Engle's *A Wrinkle in Time*, Orson Scott Card's *Ender's Game*, and Frank Herbert's *Dune* and these books' interest in both speculative fiction and personal strength are reflected Roth's novels.

Much of the first novel in the Divergent series describes Tris's training and initiation into the Dauntless faction she ultimately chooses to join. As part of this training, initiates must enter a simulated world to face and battle their greatest fears. On her blog and in numerous interviews, Roth has said that this aspect of the novel was influenced by her interest in exposure therapy, a therapeutic technique that involves progressive exposure to the source of a patient's anxiety.

Roth has been open about her struggles with anxiety and her Divergent heroine, Tris, represents an attempt to imagine herself with more confidence. In an interview with the *Chicago Tribune*, Roth stated, "Because of the anxiety, my own life felt repressive. So just as Tris makes bold moves and leaves her repression, I did bold things: I got married young. I moved to Romania for a while. I cut my hair short. Like Tris, I am trying to be a richer, fuller version of myself." (Borrelli).

Roth identifies as a Christian and has mentioned that a high school boyfriend's invitation to a Bible study led her to the faith. While she is up front about her Christianity and how her faith has informed some of her opinions and decisions, she is also insistent that the Divergent series does not represent an attempt to profess a particular set of religious values. As she told Christopher Borrelli in an interview for the *Chicago Tribune*, "People assume there's some weird indoctrination thing hidden in these books, because the assumption is if you're Christian, you're preachy. But that would be a horrible thing to do to kids."

Roth's first novel and the trilogy it began have brought the author significant popularity and financial success. In 2015, *Forbes* magazine named her one of the world's top earning authors of the year; Roth earned $25 million in 2015, second to John Green, who earned $26 million. Roth and Green represented two of four authors for young people (Jeff Kenney and J.K. Rowling were also included on the list) included in the top ten list of high earners and were, with James Patterson (number one on the list), in the top three.

With the Divergent series completed, Roth is currently working on a new novel that she describes on her blog as "a sci-fi fantasy story set in a time of extreme political unrest." The book is scheduled to be published in 2017.

Major Works

Veronica Roth's first published novel, *Divergent*, was also the first in the series for which she would become known. The series is set in a dystopian society that has divided its citizens into five factions based on their essential beliefs: Abnegation, who value selflessness; Amity, who value peace; Candor, who value honesty; Dauntless, who value bravery; and Erudite, who value intelligence. The youth of the divided society are raised in the faction of their parents; however, every year, all citizens who have reached the age of sixteen complete an aptitude test that determines the faction for which they are best suited. After learning the results of the test, these young people are free to join whatever faction they wish.

Beatrice Prior, the Divergent series' heroine, was born into Abnegation; however, she never felt that she completely embodied the value of selflessness the others of her faction hold dear. When her aptitude test reveals that she is suited to three factions—Abnegation, Dauntless, and Erudite—and, as a result, is considered "Divergent," she is warned to keep this identity a secret, as a society based on fundamental differences among its citizens cannot tolerate those who diverge from its categories.

On "Choosing Day," the day on which society's sixteen-year-olds choose the factions they will join, Beatrice chooses to join Dauntless, and, during the initiation phase, begins calling herself Tris. As Tris participates in the Dauntless initiation, she develops a relationship with Four, a Dauntless instructor known for his fearlessness.

After Tris is initiated into Dauntless, a war between the factions is begun and, as the series continues, Tris and Four find themselves at the center of the conflict.

Reviews of *Divergent* were mostly positive, with reviewers noting that, "fans of [Suzanne] Collins, dystopias, and strong female characters will love this novel" (Norton 133). Reviews of *Insurgent* were less positive; *Booklist* argued that "this sequel is more for hard-core fans" (Kraus 59) and *School Library Journal* called the novel "a very good read, despite its difficulties" (Sachs 136).

Divergent debuted on the *New York Times* best-seller list at #6 and, by 2014—after the entire trilogy had been published and the first of four movies based on the series had premiered—the trilogy occupied the top three places on the *USA Today* list of best-selling novels (Sims). All three volumes in the series were named on Nielsen's list of best-selling books of 2014, with *Divergent* coming in at #3, *Insurgent* at #4, and *Allegiant* at #6 (Swanson).

Readers were decidedly more enthusiastic than the reviewers about Roth's series. In 2011, *Divergent* was named Goodreads' "Best Book of 2011" and "Best Young Adult Fantasy and Science Fiction" novel ("Best Books of 2011"). Goodreads also named *Insurgent* and *Allegiant* "Best Young Adult Fantasy and Science Fiction" books in the years they were published ("Best Books of 2012," "Best Books of 2013"). *Divergent* was chosen by teens as a "Teens' Top Ten" book in 2012, and was named a "Best Book for Young Adults" by the Young Adult Library Services Association in the same year (ALA, YALSA, "2012"). *Insurgent* was also chosen as a "Teens' Top Ten" book in 2013 (YALSA, "2013").

Both *Divergent* and *Insurgent* have been made into movies starring Shailene Woodley as Tris and Theo James as Four. *Divergent* was released in 2014 and *Insurgent* premiered in 2015. *Allegiant* will be presented as two movies—*Divergent Series: Allegiant* and *Divergent Series: Ascendant*.

Amy Pattee

Further Reading

Roth, Veronica. *Veronica Roth* [Veronica Roth's Tumblr]. <http://theartofnotwriting.tumblr.com/>

Summit Entertainment. *Divergent The Movie.* <http://divergentthemovie.com/>

Bibliography

ALA. "Teens Choose Divergent as Their Favorite Book in YALSA's Teens' Top Ten." *ALA.* ALA, 15 October 2012. Web. 20 February 2016. <http://www.ala.org/news/press-releases/2012/10/teens-choose-divergent-their-favorite-book-yalsa%E2%80%99s-teens%E2%80%99-top-ten>

"Best Books of 2011." *Goodreads.* Goodreads, n.d. Web. 20 February 2016. <http://www.goodreads.com/choiceawards/best-books-2011>

"Best Books of 2012: Results for Best Young Adult Fantasy and Science Fiction." *Goodreads.* Goodreads, n.d. Web. 20 February 2016. <http://www.goodreads.com/choiceawards/best-young-adult-fantasy-books-2012>

"Best Books of 2013 Winners: Results for Best Young Adult Fantasy and Science Fiction." *Goodreads.* Goodreads, n.d. Web. 20 February 2016. <http://www.goodreads.com/choiceawards/best-young-adult-fantasy-books-2013>

Borrelli, Christopher. "Veronica Roth the next literary superstar?" *Chicago Tribune.* Chicago Tribune, 21 October 2013. Web. 8 February 2016. <http://articles.chicagotribune.com/2013-10-21/entertainment/chi-veronica-roth-profile-20131021_1_veronica-roth-allegiant-anderson>

Crowder, Courtney. "Chicago Novelist Sells Film Rights." *Chicago Tribune.* Chicago Tribune, 20 April 2011. Web. 16 February 2016. <http://www.chicagotribune.com/lifestyles/books/ct-books-0423-veronica-roth-20110422-story.html>

Dobbins, Amanda. "Chasing Katniss: Divergent Author Veronica Roth Builds Her Dystopian Empire." *New York* 7 October 2013. Academic One File. Web. 16 February 2016.

Fry, Erin. "Veronica Roth." *Publishers Weekly* 258.25 (2011): 25. Business Source Complete. Web. 16 February 2016.

Kidd, James. "'I don't want smut on the page:' Divergent author Veronica Roth on sex and teen fiction. *The Independent*. The Independent, 4 January 2014. Web. 8 February 2016. <http://www.independent.co.uk/arts-entertainment/books/features/i-dont-want-smut-on-the-page-divergent-author-veronica-roth-on-sex-and-teen-fiction-9035852.html>

Kraus, Daniel. Rev. of *Insurgent*. *Booklist* 108.14 (15 March 2012): 59.

Leopold, Wendy. "A book contract already!" *Northwestern University News*. Northwestern University, 10 May, 2010. Web. 8 February 2016. <http://www.northwestern.edu/newscenter/stories/2010/05/roth.html>

Norton, Eric. Rev. of *Divergent*. *School Library Journal* 57.6 (June 2011): 133.

Sachs, Nina. Rev. of *Insurgent*. *School Library Journal* 58.6 (June 2012): 136.

Robehmed, Natalie. "The World's Top-Earning Authors." *Forbes* 17 August 2015. Business Source Complete. Web. 16 February 2016.

Roth, Veronica. "FAQs: About that next book." *Veronica Roth*. n.p., 4 December 2015. Web. 8 February 2016. <http://theartofnotwriting.tumblr.com/>

Roth, Veronica. "How Many Drafts Did You Go Through . . . ?" *Veronica Roth*. n.p., 14 October 2015. Web. 8 February 2016. <http://theartofnotwriting.tumblr.com/>

Sims, Andrew. "'Divergent' Trilogy Holds Top Three Places on *USA Today*'s Best-Selling Books List." *Hypable*. Hypable, 9 January 2014. Web. 20 February 2016. <http://www.hypable.com/divergent-book-sales-usa-today-best-selling-list/>

Swanson, Clare. "The Bestselling Books of 2014." *Publishers Weekly*. PWxyz, LLC, 2 January 2015. Web. 20 February 2016. <http://www.publishersweekly.com/pw/by-topic/industry-news/bookselling/article/65171-the-fault-in-our-stars-tops-print-and-digital.html>

"Veronica Roth." *Contemporary Authors Online*. Detroit: Gale, 2015. Literature Resource Center. Web. 8 February 2016.

Wainwright, Natalie. "'Divergent:' A best-seller built in Evanston." *Evanston Round Table*. Evanston Round Table, LLC, 2011 July 5. Web. 8 February 2016. <http://evanstonroundtable.com/main.asp?-SectionID=4&SubSectionID=4&ArticleID=4435>

YALSA. "2012 Best Fiction for Young Adults." *YALSA*. ALA, n.d. Web. 20 February 2016. <http://www.ala.org/yalsa/bfya/2012>

YALSA. "2012 Teens' Top Ten." *YALSA*. ALA, n.d. Web. 20 February 2016. <http://www.ala.org/yalsa/2012-teens-top-ten>

YALSA. "2013 Teens' Top Ten." *YALSA*. ALA, n.d. Web. 20 February 2016. <http://www.ala.org/yalsa/2013-teens-top-ten>

Rainbow Rowell

Date of birth: 1973
Place of birth: Omaha, Nebraska

Principal Works
Young Adult Literature
Eleanor & Park (2013)
Fangirl (2013)
Carry On (2015)
Adult Literature
Attachments (2011)
Landline (2014)

Biography
Rainbow Rowell is the best-selling author of the young adult novel *Eleanor & Park*, which is about two teenage misfits falling in love over comic books and mixtapes in 1986. Rowell began her career as a newspaper columnist and started writing her first novel, *Attachments*, as a hobby. Since its publication in 2011, Rowell has written additional young adult novels, a novel for adults called *Landline*, a fantasy novel called *Carry On*, and a screenplay adaptation of *Eleanor & Park*. Many young adult authors write series and sequels, hewing close to their original stories and voice, but Rowell is an anomaly in this regard. She wrote her first novel on a whim, and all of her subsequent projects have been informed by the same spirit of discovery.

Rowell was born in 1973 in Omaha, Nebraska. She was raised by her mother in rural Nebraska in a house without electricity or a telephone. Her father was rarely around, but when he was, he was abusive. Later, Rowell and her family moved to the city, where they were on welfare. Books became her solace; she recalls reading *The Lion, the Witch and the Wardrobe* (1950) by C. S. Lewis, and the works of Beverly Cleary. Rowell had a difficult time during her teenage years, and she explored her feelings of isolation during that time through her first young adult novel, *Eleanor & Park* (2013). Like the characters in the book, Rowell loved comic books and used to sift through the discount bins at her local comic store to find them. Though her own love story is a little bit different from the one shared by Eleanor and Park, Rowell did meet her future husband in middle school. Rowell and her husband married after she graduated from the University of Nebraska in Lincoln.

Rowell began her writing career as a metro columnist for her hometown newspaper, the *Omaha World-Herald*. After ten years, Rowell felt she needed a change and took a job as an advertising copy editor and creative director at a local ad agency. She also began writing a novel, but she set it aside after her first child was born. Two years passed before Rowell picked up the manuscript again. About a young IT employee working at a newspaper who is assigned to secretly read employees' emails, *Attachments* fared better than Rowell expected; its success allowed her two pursue novel writing full time. Rowell lives and writes in Omaha with her husband and two sons.

Major Works

After the success of *Attachments*, Rowell wrote prolifically, churning out three books in about two years. She wrote *Eleanor & Park*, a love story between a fierce, overweight girl nicknamed Big Red and a Korean American comic-book lover named Park, though she did not realize initially that she had written a young adult book. Best-selling author John Green gave it a glowing review in the *New York Times*, and the sad love story become a best seller. In 2014 DreamWorks optioned the film rights to the book, and Rowell wrote the first draft of the screenplay. In 2013 Rowell published a novel called *Fangirl*, though she had actually written the book before she had written *Eleanor & Park*. *Fangirl* is both a celebration of Rowell's love for fan fiction and a love story. In it, a college girl named Cath is obsessed with a character (based on Harry Potter) named Simon Snow, and she writes elaborate stories about him while trying to navigate the changing landscape of her own life.

In 2014 Rowell published an adult novel called *Landline*, about a failing marriage. Georgie, the novel's protagonist, is an ambitious sitcom writer who appears to have outgrown her once-passionate marriage with her househusband, Neal. Rowell explores what could have been for the relationship through the device of a time-traveling landline phone. *New York Times* book critic Janet Maslin praised the simplicity of the story and the tenderness of its telling. *Carry On* is a fantasy novel—though fans of Rowell will recognize its subject, the magician Simon Snow, from *Fangirl*. Unique among novels, Rowell's could be described as self-written fan fiction.

Molly Hagan

Further Reading

Acree, Cat. "Rainbow Rowell: Young Love and Fortune's Fools." *BookPage*. BookPage, 1 Mar. 2013. Web. 14 Sept. 2015. <http://bookpage.com/interviews/8912-rainbow-rowell#.Vfcr-ST4vFJ>.

Ford, Ashley C. "How Rainbow Rowell Turned a Bomb into a Best-Selling Novel." *BuzzFeed Books*. BuzzFeed, 7 Aug. 2014. Web. 14 Sept. 2015. <http://www.buzzfeed.com/ashleyford/how-rainbow-rowell-turned-a-bomb-into-a-best-selling-novel#.kmqr2WwYe>.

Green, John. "Two against the World." Rev. of *Eleanor & Park*, by Rainbow Rowell. *New York Times*. New York Times, 8 Mar. 2013. Web. 14 Sept. 2015. <http://www.nytimes.com/2013/03/10/books/review/eleanor-park-by-rainbow-rowell.html>.

Bibliography

Breznican, Anthony. "'Eleanor & Park': DreamWorks Picks up Film Rights to Rainbow Rowell Novel." *Entertainment Weekly*. Entertainment Weekly, 2 Apr. 2014. Web. 14 Sept. 2015. <http://www.ew.com/article/2014/04/02/eleanor-park-dreamworks-picks-up-film-rights-to-rainbow-rowell-novel-exclusive>.

Charaipotra, Sona. "*Eleanor & Park* Author Rainbow Rowell Talks about Her Latest Novel, *Fangirl*." *Parade*. Athlon Media Group, 11 Sept. 2013. Web. 14 Sept. 2015. <http://parade.com/154939/sonacharaipotra/eleanor-park-author-rainbow-rowell-talks-about-her-latest-novel-fangirl/>.

Green, Amanda. "How Rainbow Rowell Went from Newspaper Reporter to Superstar Novelist." *Mental Floss*. Mental Floss, 1 Sep. 2014. Web. 14 Sep. 2015. <http://mentalfloss.com/article/58469/how-rainbow-rowell-went-newspaper-reporter-superstar-novelist>.

Maslin, Janet. "Marriage Gone Sour? Go Home to Ma Bell." Rev. of *Landline*, by Rainbow Rowell. *New York Times*. New York Times, 9 July 2014. Web. 14 Sept. 2015. <http://www.nytimes.com/2014/07/10/books/in-rainbow-rowells-landline-magic-may-fix-things.html?_r=0>.

Rowell, Rainbow. Interview by Julie Bartel. "One Thing Leads to Another: An Interview with Rainbow Rowell." *Hub*. Young Adult Library Services Association, 27 Feb. 2014. Web. 14 Sept. 2015. <http://www.yalsa.ala.org/thehub/2014/02/27/one-thing-leads-to-another-an-interview-with-rainbow-rowell/>.

Rowell, Rainbow. Interview by Nolan Feeney. "*Eleanor & Park* Author Rainbow Rowell Talks *Fifty Shades* and Franzen." *Time*. Time, 19 Feb. 2015. Web. 14 Sept. 2015. <http://time.com/3714753/rainbow-rowell-interview/>.

Rowell, Rainbow. Interview by Amanda Green. "The Rumpus Interview with Rainbow Rowell." *Rumpus*. Rumpus, 17 Oct. 2014. Web. 14 Sept. 2015. <http://therumpus.net/2014/10/the-rumpus-interview-with-rainbow-rowell/>.

J. K. Rowling

Date of birth: July 31, 1965
Place of birth: Yate, England

Principal Works
Children's Literature
Harry Potter series (1997–2007)
Fantastic Beasts and Where to Find Them (2001; as Newt Scamander)
Quidditch through the Ages (2001; as Kennilworthy Whisp)
The Tales of Beedle the Bard (2008)
Adult Literature
The Casual Vacancy (2012)
The Cuckoo's Calling (2013; as Robert Galbraith)
The Silkworm (2014; as Robert Galbraith)

Biography
Known as the creator of young wizard Harry Potter, J. K. Rowling is the author of the seven-book series dedicated to her iconic character's adventures. The Harry Potter series' worldwide popularity led to the publication of several companion books, real-life versions of works mentioned in the series. Following the conclusion of the series, Rowling next found success as a writer of adult fiction, although she remains best known for her works for younger readers.

Joanne Rowling was born on July 31, 1965, in Yate, England. She was the first of two children born to Peter and Anne Rowling, an engineer and a homemaker who had met while serving in the British navy. As a child, Rowling developed a love of reading with the encouragement of her mother, and she enjoyed making up and reciting stories to her younger sister, Dianne.

Daniel Ogren, CC BY 2.0, via Wikimedia Commons

After completing her primary schooling at St. Michael's Church of England Primary School and Tutshill Church of England Primary School, Rowling enrolled in the Wyedean School, a comprehensive secondary school in Sedbury, England, in 1976. Rowling graduated with honors from the Wyedean School in 1983 and went on to study classics and French at Exeter University. After earning her bachelor's degree in 1986, she took a position with the humanitarian organization Amnesty International. Reading accounts of torture and political murders and meeting refugees and displaced dissidents had a profound effect on Rowling, and she has noted that the experience shaped her understanding of the human capacity for both evil and good.

The core idea of the Harry Potter series came to Rowling in 1990, while she was traveling from Manchester to London by train. She worked on the first book in the series, *Harry Potter and the Philosopher's Stone* (known in the United States as *Harry Potter and the Sorcerer's Stone*), over the next several years. During that time, she taught English in Portugal, where she met and married her first husband, journalist Jorge Arantes, and gave birth to a daughter, Jessica. Following Rowling and Arantes's separation, she and her daughter moved to Edinburgh, Scotland. Although Rowling struggled with both financial difficulties and depression during that period, she was nevertheless able to complete her first novel, which was ultimately published in 1997. Believing that boys would be reluctant to read a book by an identifiably female author, Rowling's publishers urged her to publish under her initials rather than her first name. As she did not have a middle name, she took the middle initial K. from her paternal grandmother's name, Kathleen.

Harry Potter and the Philosopher's Stone was a tremendous success in the United Kingdom and was published to significant acclaim in the United States the following year. Building upon the story line begun in that novel, Rowling went on to publish six more books in the series as well as several companion books that shed further light on the wildlife, sports, and folktales of the wizarding world. Although Rowling found fame as a writer of books for children and young adults, she began publishing adult fiction following the conclusion of the Harry Potter series; her first adult novel, *The Casual Vacancy*, was published in 2012. In the summer of 2013, the British press revealed that the detective novel *The Cuckoo's Calling*, published several months earlier and ostensibly the debut work of former military investigator Robert Galbraith, was in fact the work of Rowling. She published a second book under that pseudonym, *The Silkworm*, in 2014.

Rowling married Neil Murray, a doctor and a friend of her sister, in 2001. In addition to Jessica, Rowling and Murray have two children together, David and Mackenzie. The family lives in Scotland.

Major Works

Rowling's best-known creation is the globally popular Harry Potter series, which encompasses the novels *Harry Potter and the Philosopher's Stone* (1997; *Harry Potter and the Sorcerer's Stone*, 1998), *Harry Potter and the Chamber of Secrets* (1998), *Harry Potter and the Prisoner of Azkaban* (1999), *Harry Potter and the Goblet of Fire* (2000), *Harry Potter and the Order of the Phoenix* (2003), *Harry Potter and the Half-Blood Prince* (2005), and *Harry Potter and the Deathly Hallows* (2007). In many ways the series tells an extended coming-of-age narrative, documenting not only Harry's life between the ages of eleven and seventeen and the friendships, romances, and school experiences that take place during that period but also his magical growth as a wizard and evolution into a hero. The conflict between good and evil is central to the series, and although the novels are intended for young readers, Rowling does not shy away from demonstrating the consequences of such conflict. Themes of grief, fear, depression, and trauma make the stakes of the novels' conflict concrete, despite the whimsy that pervades Rowling's wizarding world.

One of the defining characteristics of the Harry Potter series is its extensive world building; the wizarding world, though existing parallel to—and sometimes lurking invisibly within—the real world, is a complex society with history, culture, and mores all its own. Rowling's companion books to the series further expand upon that world, giving a more in-depth view of wizarding culture than the main novels would allow. *Fantastic Beasts and Where to Find Them* (2001) expands the reader's knowledge of the many magical beings seen, mentioned, or hinted at in the novels, while *Quidditch through the Ages* (2001) explores the history of the titular magical sport. *The Tales of Beedle the Bard* (2008) differs somewhat in that its contents are presented not as wizarding facts but as folktales that shed light on some of the lesser-known aspects of wizarding culture. The companion books to the Harry Potter series, all of which are mentioned within the novels, thus provide interesting background information about the series while also inviting their readers to experience some of the magic for themselves.

Joy Crelin

Further Reading

"Biography." *JKRowling.com*. Rowling, 2014. Web. 31 Mar. 2015. <http://www.jkrowling.com/en_GB/#/about-jk-rowling>.

Errington, Philip W. *J. K. Rowling: A Bibliography 1997–2013*. London: Bloomsbury, 2015. Print.

Bibliography

Biddlecombe, Sarah. "J. K. Rowling: Life after Harry Potter." *Telegraph*. Telegraph Media Group, 1 Feb. 2015. Web. 31 Mar. 2015. <http://www.telegraph.co.uk/culture/books/booknews/11371823/J-K-Rowling-life-after-Harry-Potter.html>.

Parker, Ian. "Mugglemarch: J. K. Rowling Writes a Realist Novel for Adults." *New Yorker*. New Yorker, 1 Oct. 2012. Web. 31 Mar. 2015. <http://www.newyorker.com/magazine/2012/10/01/mugglemarch>.

Rowling, J. K. "The Fringe Benefits of Failure, and the Importance of Imagination." *Harvard Magazine*. Harvard Magazine, 5 June 2008. Web. 31 Mar. 2015. <http://harvardmagazine.com/2008/06/the-fringe-benefits-failure-the-importance-imagination>.

Sexton, Colleen A. *J. K. Rowling*. Minneapolis: Twenty-First Century, 2008. Print.

Louis Sachar

Date of birth: March 20, 1954
Place of birth: East Meadow, New York

Principal Works

Children's Literature
The Wayside School series (1978–95)
Johnny's in the Basement (1981)
Someday Angeline (1983)
Sixth Grade Secrets (1987)
There's a Boy in the Girls' Bathroom (1987)
The Boy Who Lost His Face (1989)
Dogs Don't Tell Jokes (1991)
Marvin Redpost series (1992–2000)
Monkey Soup (1992)

Young Adult Literature
Holes (1998)
Stanley Yelnats' Survival Guide to Camp Green Lake (2003)
Small Steps (2006)
The Cardturner (2010)
Fuzzy Mud (2015)

Biography

Louis Sachar is an American writer who is perhaps best known for his award-winning young adult novel *Holes* (1998), about a teenage boy who is sent to a desert camp for juvenile offenders after being wrongfully convicted of theft. Sachar is also the author of numerous books for children, including the Wayside School series and the Marvin Redpost series, as well as the young adult novels *Small Steps* (2006) and *The Cardturner* (2010).

Sachar was born on March 20, 1954, in East Meadow, New York. His family lived on Long Island until he was nine years old, when they moved to Tustin, California. Growing up, Sachar developed a love of reading and storytelling, and he also enjoyed solving puzzles and playing chess with his older brother, Andy. He sometimes had the opportunity to watch his parents play bridge, although he rarely played himself. As an adult, he became an avid fan of the game, which would inspire the writing of his novel *The Cardturner*.

After high school, Sachar enrolled in Antioch College in Yellow Springs, Ohio. He attended the college only briefly, leaving school following his father's death during his freshman year. After a stint as a door-to-door salesperson, he enrolled in the University of California, Berkeley. While attending Berkeley, Sachar worked

for a time as a classroom aide and recess supervisor at a local elementary school. This job not only earned him college credits but also provided the inspiration for his Wayside School series of children's books. Sachar graduated from Berkeley in 1976 with a degree in economics.

Following his graduation, Sachar began writing the first book in the Wayside School series, *Sideways Stories from Wayside School*. The book was published in 1978, while Sachar was studying at the University of California Hastings College of the Law. After completing law school in 1980 and passing the state bar exam, Sachar continued to write, balancing his literary and legal careers throughout the next decade. He published more than fifteen books for children during the 1980s and 1990s, including several further installments in the Wayside School series.

During the 1990s Sachar and his family moved from California to Texas. Sachar was awestruck by the high-temperature records of the Texas heat, and he began to write a novel inspired, in part, by his observations. This novel, which became known as *Holes*, was published in 1998. The book was received well by both readers and critics and earned numerous awards, including a National Book Award and a Newbery Medal. In 2003, in conjunction with the release of the film adaptation of *Holes*, Sachar published *Stanley Yelnats' Survival Guide to Camp Green Lake* (2003), a companion book. Sachar then published the novel *Small Steps* (2006), which focuses on two of *Holes*' secondary characters. Inspired by his love of bridge, which he plays competitively, Sachar published *The Cardturner* (2010), a young adult novel about a teenager and his bridge-playing great-uncle.

Sachar married Carla Askew in 1985. Their daughter, Sherre, was born in 1987. The Sachars live in Austin, Texas.

Major Works

As a writer, Sachar is well-known for the offbeat sense of humor that characterizes many of his children's books, especially the Wayside School series. His novels, aimed at a somewhat older audience, combine that signature humor with more serious themes such as poverty, racism, immigrant identity, fate, and the importance of family. The way in which his novels balance humor and important lessons makes them a popular teaching tool. *Holes*, in particular, is frequently assigned reading in schools. It has been challenged by parents who deem the subject matter and language inappropriate; however, teachers and librarians have typically been successful in demonstrating that it is a useful and appropriate text.

Like many writers, Sachar often incorporates details from his own life into his novels and children's books. *Sideways Stories from Wayside School*, for instance, was inspired by the children he met while working as a teacher's aide, and the character of Louis the yard teacher, who appears throughout the series, is a fictionalized version of Sachar himself. Sachar likewise incorporates elements of his life into his young adult novels. *Holes* was initially inspired by his experience with Texas's extreme heat, while *Small Steps* is set in Austin, where Sachar and his family settled. *The Cardturner* draws from Sachar's many years as an avid bridge player. By incorporating such details, Sachar has created unique novels that have received significant acclaim from both critics and young readers.

Joy Crelin

Further Reading

Sachar, Louis. "Author Bio." *Louis Sachar*. Sachar, 2002. Web. 30 Apr. 2015. <http://www.louissachar.com/Bio.htm>.

Sachar, Louis. "Louis Sachar." *Macmillan*. Macmillan, 2014. Web. 30 Apr. 2015. <http://us.macmillan.com/author/louissachar>.

Bibliography

Greene, Meg. *Louis Sachar*. New York: Rosen, 2004. Print.

Sachar, Louis. "An Interview with Louis Sachar." Interview by Julie Just. *New York Times*. New York Times, 15 Jan. 2006. Web. 30 Apr. 2015. <http://www.nytimes.com/2006/01/15/books/review/sachar-interview.html?_r=0>.

Sachar, Louis. "Louis Sachar Interview Transcript." *Scholastic*. Scholastic, 23 Feb. 2006. Web. 30 Apr. 2015. <http://www.scholastic.com/teachers/article/louis-sachar-interview-transcript>.

Sachar, Louis. "Q & A with Louis Sachar." *Publishers Weekly*. PWxyz, 6 May 2010. Web. 30 Apr. 2015. <http://www.publishersweekly.com/pw/by-topic/authors/interviews/article/43086-q-a-with-louis-sachar.html>.

Sachar, Louis. "Younger Audiences." Interview by Elizabeth Farnsworth. *PBS Newshour*. Newshour Productions, 25 Nov. 1998. Web. 30 Apr. 2015. <http://www.pbs.org/newshour/bb/entertainment-july-dec98-sacher_11-25>.

Benjamin Alire Saenz

Date of birth: August 16, 1954

Principal Works
Poetry
Calendar of Dust (1991)
Dark and Perfect Angels (1995)
The Book of What Remains (2010)
Children's Literature
A Gift from Papa Diego (1998)
The Dog Who Loved Tortillas (2009)
Young Adult Literature
Sammy and Juliana in Hollywood (2004)
He Forgot to Say Goodbye (2008)
Last Night I Sang to the Monster (2009)
Aristotle and Dante Discover the Secrets of the Universe (2012)

Larry D. Moore, CC BY-SA 3.0, via Wikimedia Commons

Short Stories
Flowers for the Broken (1992)
Everything Begins and Ends at the Kentucky Club (2012)

Biography

Benjamin Alire Sáenz is a prolific writer of poetry, short stories, children's books, and novels for teenagers and adults. In 2013, he became the first Hispanic writer to win the prestigious PEN/Faulkner Award for Fiction for his book of short stories *Everything Begins and Ends at the Kentucky Club* (2012). Sáenz was raised in the American Southwest, and the area—"la frontera," or the US-Mexican borderland—figures heavily into his work. Sáenz was fifty-four years old and married to a woman when he realized that he was gay. His struggle with own sexual orientation manifests itself in his award-winning young adult novel *Aristotle and Dante Discover the Secrets of the Universe* (2012).

Sáenz was born the fourth of seven children on August 16, 1954, in Old Picacho, New Mexico. He was raised on a small cotton farm in Las Cruces, forty-five miles northwest of El Paso. Sáenz was drawn to art and books, but when he was in the fourth grade his parents lost their farm, and he began working, painting apartments and performing other manual tasks. Sáenz and his father shared a strained relationship; his brothers were treated like little men. Always left home on hunting trips, Sáenz was closer with his mother. He graduated from Las Cruces High School in 1972 and entered the seminary, beguiled by the notion that God was a leader of the poor. He earned his BA degree at St. Thomas Seminary in Denver, Colorado, and then attended the University of Louvain in Belgium. He spent a summer in Tanzania, where he decided he did not want to become a missionary. After he was ordained, he returned to El Paso; however, he quit the priesthood after three years, in 1984. Sáenz had been working on a novel and decided that he was meant to become a writer.

Sáenz worked as a waiter in Louisiana and Houston, Texas, and saved money to go back to school. He earned his master's degree in creative writing at the University of Texas at El Paso (UTEP) and began work on his doctorate at the University of Iowa; after a year, however, he was contacted by Stanford University, which offered him the prestigious Wallace Stegner Fellowship

for poetry. He returned to El Paso in 1994 and began teaching at UTEP—eventually, he became the chair of the MFA creative-writing program, the only bilingual writing program in the country. Despite his growing success, Sáenz was haunted by sexual abuse he had suffered at the hands of a family member as a child. He was married for fifteen years to a family court judge, but in 2008, he realized through therapy that he was gay. He and his wife divorced in 2009. He embraced his new single life and started abusing recreational drugs before becoming sober. In 2011, his mother became sick and died. Her death deeply traumatized Sáenz, who relapsed and began to abuse drugs again; several months after the funeral, a friend helped him check into a rehabilitation program. Through it all, Sáenz continued to write and publish his work. He is single and lives in El Paso.

Major Works

Sáenz began his writing career as a poet. His first book of poems, the 1991 collection *Calendar of Dust*, won the American Book Award in 1992. But Sáenz, a writer with an intense desire to share his experience and the experiences of those living on *la frontera*, recognizes that poetry has a relatively small readership. Though he has published subsequent poetry collections—including *The Book of What Remains* in 2010—he has focused mostly on prose. After publishing a handful of short stories and two adult novels, Sáenz wrote *A Gift from Papa Diego* (1998), a bilingual book for children about a young aspiring superhero who longs to see his grandfather across the border in Mexico. In 2004, Sáenz published his first young adult novel, *Sammy and Juliana in Hollywood*. The book was a finalist for the Los Angeles Book Prize and was named one of the top ten books of the year by the American Library Association. Based on Sáenz's own high school experience the story is about two teens from a tough barrio, called Hollywood, in New Mexico in 1969.

In 2008, Sáenz published his second young adult novel, *He Forgot to Say Goodbye*, which intertwines two stories about lost fathers. His third young adult novel, *Last Night I Sang to the Monster*, about an alcoholic teen battling memories of an early trauma, was published in 2009. In 2012, Sáenz published a book about the love between two teenage boys called *Aristotle and Dante Discover the Secrets of the Universe*. The book won a slew of awards including the Pura Belpré Award, for depicting the Latino cultural experience; the Stonewall Book Award, for depicting LGBT experience;

and the Michael L. Printz Honor for writing in teen literature. The disparate categories in which it was recognized reflect Sáenz's identity.

Also in 2012, Sáenz published his most celebrated work to date. His short-story collection *Everything Begins and Ends at the Kentucky Club* won the prestigious PEN/Faulkner Award for Fiction in 2013. The stories in the collection revolve around a famous bar in Juárez called the Kentucky Club. Once a celebrity watering hole, the bar (which claims to have invented the margarita) fell on hard times during the drug-cartel conflicts that have made the city one of the most violent in the world. Sáenz's sorrow for his "dying city" and his own personal trauma inspired his writing.

Molly Hagan

Further Reading

Ballí, Cecilia. "The Passion of Benjamin Sáenz: A Border Poet Rises from the Ashes." *Texas Monthly* 1 Aug. 2013. Web. 23 Feb. 2015. <http://www.texasmonthly.com/story/the-messy-visionary-passionate-life-of-benjamin-s%C3%A1enz>.

Mermann-Jozwiak, Elisabeth, and Nancy Sullivan. *Conversations with Mexican American Writers: Languages and Literatures in the Borderlands*. Jackson: U of Mississippi P, 2009. Print.

Sáenz, Benjamin Alire. "Between Violence and Tenderness: Aristotle and Dante Author Sáenz Talks to SLJ." Interview by Karyn M. Peterson. *School Library Journal* 31 Jan. 2013. Web. 23 Feb. 2015. <http://www.slj.com/2013/01/authors-illustrators/interviews/between-violence-and-tenderness-aristotle-and-dante-author-saenz-talks-to-slj/#_>.

Bibliography

Ramirez, Cindy. "El Paso Author Benjamin Alire Sáenz Wins PEN/Faulkner Award for Fiction." *El Paso Times*. El Paso Times, 19 Mar. 2013. Web. 16 Feb. 2015. <http://www.elpasotimes.com/ci_22823132/el-paso-author-benjamin-alire-saenz-honored-his-border-stories>.

Rentería, Ramón. "Author Ben Saenz Transcends, Inspires." *El Paso Times*. El Paso Times, 5 Mar. 2010. Web. 23 Feb. 2015. <http://www.elpasotimes.com/ci_14517101>.

Sáenz, Benjamin Alire. "Discovering Sexuality through Teen Lit." Interview by Michel Martin. *NPR Books.* NPR, 20 Feb. 2013. Web. 16 Feb. 2015. <http://www.npr.org/2013/02/20/172495550/discovering-sexuality-through-teen-lit>.

Sáenz, Benjamin Alire. "Just This Side of Tragic: An Interview with Benjamin Alire Sáenz." Interview by Daniel Olivas. *Los Angeles Review of Books*. Los Angeles Review of Books, 6 May 2013. Web. 23 Feb. 2015. <http://lareviewofbooks.org/interview/just-this-side-of-tragic-an-interview-with-benjamin-alire-saenz>.

Andrew Smith

Date of birth: 1959
Place of birth: California

Principal Works
Young Adult Literature
Ghost Medicine (2008)
In the Path of Falling Objects (2009)
The Marbury Lens (2010)
Stick (2011)
Passenger (2012)
Winger (2013)
Grasshopper Jungle (2014)
100 Sideways Miles (2014)
The Alex Crow (2015)
Stand-Off (2015)
Short Stories
King of Marbury (2012)

Biography
Andrew Anselmo Smith is an American young adult author and essayist. His first book, *Ghost Medicine* (2008), was included in the American Library Association's 2009 list of best books for young adults. Smith is probably best known for his 2014 novel *Grasshopper Jungle*.

Born in California in 1959, Smith was interested in writing from an early age. He served as the editor of his school newspaper at Newbury Park High School and wrote during his spare time. After graduating from California State University, Northridge, where he studied journalism and political science, Smith started a short career in journalism but was ultimately not interested in nonfiction writing. Fulfilling a desire to travel, he worked various jobs around the world before finally returning to settle in California. In the early 1990s, he began teaching at Canyon High School in Santa Clarita and eventually married.

Smith wrote fictional prose for himself for most of his adult life, but he had no intention of publishing his work until he was finally pushed to do so by his friend Kelly Milner Halls, a young adult nonfiction writer. After being published, he continued to work as a high school instructor. He lives in Southern California near Lake Elizabeth. He and his wife, Jocelyn, have a son, Trevin, and a daughter, Chiara.

Major Works

Since the publication of his first novel in 2008, Andrew Smith has continued to publish novels and short stories for a young adult audience. While Smith's work is aimed at an adolescent audience, his work often deals with very serious situations. He is known as an author who tests the limits of the young adult genre by including situations in his novels that are traditionally reserved for a more adult audience. *Ghost Medicine*, for example, a novel that follows many conventions of the western genre, focuses on a summer in the lives of four teenage protagonists and includes themes of attempted rape, violence, and death. Following the mantra on his personal website to "keep YA weird," Smith has continued to publish books that test traditional boundaries.

While Smith's books tend to focus on graphic violence, his young protagonists usually encounter difficulties within narratives that most teenagers face in the real world. The majority of Smith's novels are written within the subgenre of realistic fiction, and often the most important aspects of his characters' lives are family and personal relationships. His second novel, *In the Path of Falling Objects* (2009), follows the lives of two brothers as they set out on their own to find what is left of their family. As they embark on a road trip with a young couple, the brothers encounter new experiences that test them but also teach them about love and loyalty. Similarly, *Winger* (2013) focuses on the life of a teenage boy, Ryan Dean West, who must negotiate the problems he faces in boarding school, including bullying, teen romance, and underage drinking. However, he must find something new within himself when his best friend Joey, an openly gay rugby player, is the victim of a hate crime.

Identity is another important theme in the varied lives of Smith's young characters. As the brothers of *In the Path of Falling Objects* search for their older brother, who is serving in the Vietnam War, they are also looking to make sense of their own lives through learning about their family. In *100 Sideways Miles* (2014), Finn Easton has been severely and permanently injured after being crushed under the weight of a dead horse. Finn's father has written a story about a young scarred alien named Finn who wants to be a normal human boy, and although he is told the alien is not him, Finn struggles to separate himself and his own identity from his father's creation.

While Smith's characters grapple with real-world problems, the fantastic is also a major part of a number of his celebrated novels. He often includes elements of fantasy and science fiction in books that appear to be simply realistic at the beginning. *The Marbury Lens* (2010) was Smith's first speculative fiction work. The male protagonist, struggling to find his own way through life at sixteen, goes to London and finds a pair of glasses that allow him to see a bleak and violent world known as Marbury. This alternate world was also the subject of the sequel, *Passenger* (2012). However, Smith's most shocking novel is also his most critically acclaimed. *Grasshopper Jungle* (2014) begins in what seems a normal, everyday world, until the protagonist suddenly finds himself involved in a plan for world domination by way of giant praying mantises.

There has been some debate over the appropriateness of Smith's novels for a young audience, but his work has received more commendation than criticism. *100 Sideways Miles* was shortlisted for the National Book Award, and *The Marbury Lens*, *Winger*, and *In the Path of Falling Objects* were all recognized as top reads by organizations such as the American Library Association, Amazon, and *Publishers Weekly*. *Grasshopper Jungle*, Smith's most honored book, received the 2015 Michael L. Printz Award and the 2014 Boston Globe–Horn Book Award and was included on the long list for the Carnegie Medal.

Aaron Horton, MA

Further Reading

Huneven, Michelle. Rev. of *100 Sideways Miles*, by Andrew Smith. *New York Times*. New York Times, 7 Nov. 2014. Web. 22 Oct. 2015. <http://www.nytimes.com/2014/11/09/books/review/100-sideways-miles-by-andrew-smith.html>.

Smith, Andrew. "An Interview with YA Author Andrew Smith." Interview by Melissa Albert. *B&N Reads*. Barnes & Noble, 19 Sept. 2014. Web. 22 Oct. 2015.

<http://www.barnesandnoble.com/blog/an-interview-with-ya-author-andrew-smith>.

Smith, Andrew. "Q & A with Andrew Smith." Interview by Michael Levy. *Publishers Weekly*. PWxyz, 23 Oct. 2012. Web. 22 Oct. 2015. <http://www.publishersweekly.com/pw/by-topic/childrens/childrens-authors/article/54476-q-a-with-andrew-smith.html>.

Bibliography

Breznican, Anthony. "Author Andrew Smith Keeps YA Weird with *Grasshopper Jungle* and *The Alex Crow*." *Entertainment Weekly*. Entertainment Weekly, 5 Mar. 2015. Web. 22 Oct. 2015. <http://www.ew.com/article/2015/03/05/author-andrew-smith-keeps-ya-weird-'grasshopper-jungle'-and-'-alex-crow'>.

Corbett, Sue. "Writing for Risk Takers: Andrew Smith." *Publishers Weekly*. PWxzy, 13 Feb. 2015. Web. 22 Oct. 2015. <http://publishersweekly.com/pw/by-topic/authors/profiles/article/65602-writing-for-risk-takers-andrew-smith.html>.

Rev. of *Grasshopper Jungle*, by Andrew Smith. *Publishers Weekly* 4 Nov. 2013: 68. *Literary Reference Center*. Web. 22 Oct. 2015. <http://search.ebscohost.com/login.aspx?direct=true&db=lfh&AN=91924113&site=lrc-live>.

Rev. of *Passenger*, by Andrew Smith. *Kirkus Reviews* 2 Dec. 2012: 80–81. *Literary Reference Center*. Web. 22 Oct. 2015. <http://search.ebscohost.com/login.aspx?direct=true&db=lfh&AN=84296088&site=lrc-live>.

Smith, Andrew. "One Thing Leads to Another: An Interview with Andrew Smith." Interview by Julie Bartel. *Hub*. YALSA, 9 Oct. 2014. Web. 22 Oct. 2015. <http://www.yalsa.ala.org/thehub/2014/10/09/one-thing-leads-to-another-an-interview-with-andrew-smith/>.

Maggie Stiefvater

Date of birth: November 18, 1981
Place of birth: Harrisonburg, Virginia

Principal Works

Book of Faerie series (2008–present)
Wolves of Mercy Falls series (2009–11)
Raven cycle (2012–present)
Hunted (2014)

Pip Bartlett's Guide to Magical Creatures (with Jackson Pearce, 2015)

Biography

Best known for paranormal series novels, Maggie Stiefvater appeared on the young adult fiction scene in 2008 when she, along with two partners, began publishing a blog containing short stories. This led to more writing, and she soon published *Lament: The Faerie Queen's Deception* (2008). This first book, which was listed among the American Library Association's 2010 popular paperbacks for young adults and 2010 best books for young adults, began a prolific career in young adult literature.

Maggie Stiefvater was born Heidi Hummel on November 18, 1981, in Harrisonburg, Virginia. Her father, Dr. Keith Bydler Hummel, was in the navy, and her mother, Penella Hummel, was an artist and musician. The family spent a good portion of her childhood moving, so her formal education was difficult. By the time she had reached sixth grade, the family decided to homeschool. Stiefvater moved quickly through school, and she received a General Equivalency Diploma (GED) when she was sixteen. She also changed her name to Margaret Hummel, in tribute to British prime minister Margaret Thatcher. Stiefvater attended the University of Mary Washington in Fredericksburg, Virginia, where she pursued a degree in early British history. She graduated in 2003.

As a recent college graduate, she worked at an office job for a short time before becoming a full-time artist. In 2008 she returned to writing, a passion she had pursued since childhood. Stiefvater credits many authors as influential on her own desire to become a professional writer. Some of her favorite childhood books included Marguerite Henry's Misty books, Susan Cooper's Dark Is Rising series, C. S. Lewis's Chronicles of Narnia, and Lloyd Alexander's Black Cauldron series. Though she had written many unpublished novels before college, she had moved away from writing while an artist. After starting the *Merry Sisters of Fate* blog with friends Tessa Gratton and Brenna Yovanoff, Stiefvater began *Lament*. A second book, *Ballad*, followed a year later. Her first major success, however, appeared with the publication of *Shiver*, the first novel in the Wolves of Mercy Falls trilogy.

Firmly established as a successful young adult writer, Stiefvater felt able to return to a slightly different kind of novel she had begun years earlier, *The Scorpio Races*, which was published in 2011. Stiefvater continues to write even while traveling the world to promote her books and speak about writing. She and her husband, Edward, have two children, Victoria and Will, and live in Virginia.

Major Works

Stiefvater's career has been prolific. She has written three series and several standalone books. Starting with *Lament*, her works have continually been named as notable on prestigious lists, such as the American Library Association best books, the Young Adult Library Services Association best fiction for young adults, and the *New York Times* list of best-selling books. The paranormal themes of the novels are integrated with popular everyday teen issues, such as peer pressure and romance, and often incorporate elements of mythology and folklore.

Lament was the first book in the Books of Faerie series; it was followed by *Ballad* (2009). In *Lament*, Stiefvater incorporates Celtic folklore in the story of Dierdre Monaghan, a gifted musician who is pulled into an ancient war between the faeries. Romance appears in the form of Luke Dillon, who has been sent to kill Dierdre before her talent is noticed by the wrong figures. However, Luke is not the only person to want Dierdre dead, and her life becomes more complicated than she could ever imagine. She must protect her family and her best friend, James, while fighting a romantic attraction to the dangerous Luke. *Ballad* continues with James's story, and the battle with the faeries comes to a head as he fights to save not only his life but that of his muse. A third book, *Requiem*, is anticipated.

Stiefvater's most notable series, the Wolves of Mercy Falls, followed these first two novels. This series includes *Shiver* (2009), *Linger* (2010), and *Forever* (2011). This paranormal trilogy traces the stories of Grace and Sam, two teens who fall in love despite the overwhelming problems that result from the fact that Sam is a werewolf. As they strive to stay together, despite the odds, the young lovers are torn by changes that will affect their lives forever. Questions left at the end of the series are somewhat answered in *Sinner* (2014), a companion novel that follows the story of Isabel Culpeper and Cole St. Clair, characters introduced in the trilogy.

Published the same year as *Forever*, *The Scorpio Races* is a standalone novel hailed as a paranormal romance. However, instead of faeries or werewolves, the supernatural element in this novel is the little-known water horse, drawn from Celtic myth, and the islanders in the book follow traditions and practices that blend Catholic and pagan beliefs. In it, teenagers Sean Kendrick and Puck Connolly compete in the Scorpio Races, a rough-and-tumble contest that spells death for some of its participants and that holds the promise of a better future for the winner.

Stiefvater's creative mind continues to impress with the Raven Cycle books. This series includes *The Raven Boys* (2012), *The Dream Thieves* (2013), *Blue Lily, Lily Blue* (2014), and *The Raven King* (forthcoming). Focusing on Welsh folklore, the cycle tells the story of five young people from a fictional Virginia town. Romance and friendship become two of the central themes as readers follow Blue Sargent's struggle to come to terms with her role in a prophecy that her true love will die.

Pip Bartlett's Guide to Magical Creatures (2015), cowritten with Jackson Pearce, marks a change in direction for Stiefvater. Though the book continues with a magical focus, the intended audience is much younger. In addition to her role in writing this book, Stiefvater returns to her artistic roots by illustrating it as well.

Theresa L. Stowell, PhD

Further Reading

Bodart, Joni Richards. *They Suck, They Bite, They Eat, They Kill: The Psychological Meaning of Supernatural Monsters in Young Adult Fiction*. Lanham: Scarecrow, 2012. Print.

Staley, Erin. *Maggie Stiefvater*. New York: Rosen, 2014. Print.

Bibliography

MaggieStiefvater.com. Maggie Stiefvater, 2015. Web. 11 Dec. 2015. <http://maggiestiefvater.com>.

Stiefvater, Maggie. "One Thing Leads to Another: An Interview with Maggie Stiefvater." Interview by Julie Bartel. *Hub*. YALSA, 9 Jan. 2014. Web. 11 Dec. 2015. <http://www.yalsa.ala.org/thehub/2014/01/09/one-thing-leads-to-another-an-interview-with-maggie-stiefvater>.

Stiefvater, Maggie. "Q & A with Maggie Stiefvater." Interview by Sue Corbett. *Publishers Weekly*. PWxyz, 6 Oct. 2011. Web. 11 Dec. 2015.

Ned Vizzini

Date of birth: April 4, 1981
Place of birth: New York, New York
Date of death: December 19, 2013
Place of death: Brooklyn, New York

Principal Works

Teen Angst? Naaah . . . A Quasi-Autobiography (2000)
Be More Chill (2004)
It's Kind of a Funny Story (2006)
House of Secrets series (with Chris Columbus, 2013–16)
The Other Normals (2012)

Biography

Ned Vizzini was best known for his young adult novels about the struggles of being a teenager, but he also cowrote a series of fantasy books for younger readers, a variety of nonfiction essays, and several screenplays. Vizzini's career started at the age of fifteen when he wrote a series of columns for the *New York Press*. Some of those columns later became the basis for his autobiographical first book, *Teen Angst? Naaah*, published when he was nineteen. Vizzini's novels have been lauded for their twisted and humorous look inside the lives of teenagers who often struggle with emotional problems, peer pressure, dating, and family relationships.

Vizzini was born Edison Price Vizzini on April 4, 1981, in New York, New York. His father, James D. Vizzini, and his mother, Emma Vizzini, both worked in the business world. He was the oldest of three children. He graduated from New York's Stuyvesant High School in 1999 and received his bachelor of science degree from Hunter College in 2003.

Vizzini's writing career began during high school after winning an essay contest and becoming a regular columnist for the *New York Press*, which then led to being invited to write an article for the *New York Times Magazine*. Vizzini's first novel, *Teen Angst? Naaah* (2000), incorporated much of his material from his columns and article. He wrote three additional novels that deal with teen problems from a mature yet funny point of view. In the mid-2000s, he collaborated on the House of Secrets trilogy with film director Chris Columbus. Vizzini also wrote screenplays for several television episodes, most notably on the shows *Teen Wolf* and *Last Resort*.

Vizzini struggled with depression throughout his life, about which he spoke openly and which he incorporated into his young adult fiction. His depression was compounded by a self-imposed pressure to succeed, to write the next masterpiece, and to emotionally connect with his fans. Vizzini admitted himself to a mental hospital when he was twenty-three, and he used this experience as a basis for his 2006 novel *It's Kind of a Funny Story*. Vizzini's novels have been noted for their candid and mature approach to the challenges faced by teens, something that he freely shared as he traveled around the country talking about mental health issues.

Vizzini was married to writer Sabra Embury, and the two had one child, Felix. In December of 2013, Vizzini's lifelong battle with depression ended in suicide.

Major Works

Teen Angst? Naaah . . . A Quasi-Autobiography was Vizzini's first book and is a compilation of his earlier essays. The stories are organized according to his high school year and contain glimpses into the experiences of a self-proclaimed nerd. The tone is self-deprecating and humorous, making the book relatable for teen and adult readers alike.

Be More Chill (2004), Vizzini's second book, tells the story of Jeremy Heere, a high school nerd who does not fit in and has no chance with the girl of his dreams. Jeremy's life changes, however, when he is introduced to a pill that is actually a supercomputer. When he takes that pill, he becomes cool. This first novel presents a sharp and mature look at the problems of an outcast teen.

Vizzini's next novel, *It's Kind of a Funny Story* (2006), is his most notable work. It is based on his own experiences in the adult mental health ward of a Brooklyn, New York, hospital. Craig Gilner, the protagonist, is so focused on his future that he tries to commit suicide when he realizes that he is not a genius. While in the hospital, Craig learns that his experiences are not as difficult as what others are going through, and he begins to come to terms with the pressures that led to his breakdown. This novel was particularly influential to teen readers who had struggled with mental health issues or could empathize with Gilner's character. As Vizzini's friend writer Marty Beckerman explained, "Most writers are lucky if we entertain people; Ned was saving them." A film adaptation by the same name was released in 2010.

Vizzini also cowrote the first book in a series of fantasy novels featuring the Walker children.

Fifteen-year-old Cordelia, twelve-year-old Brendan, and nine-year-old Eleanor are thrust into an alternate reality when their parents move into a historic home in San Francisco, California. Previously owned by the writer of dime-store novels, Kristoff House becomes a vessel to carry the children into those books where the original owner's daughter, who has turned into a witch, forces them to search for *The Book of Doom and Desire*, an evil magical tome. The children must overcome a variety of fictional villains and their own desires if they are to survive the experience. The *House of Secrets* (2013) is followed by two books that continue the story: *Battle of the Beasts* (2014) and *Clash of the Worlds* (2016). Both of these books were published after Vizzini's death, and although the series maintains Vizzini's tone and humor, the content is significantly different from his other novels.

The last novel Vizzini wrote is *The Other Normals* (2012). Drawing from his own teenage involvement in role-playing games, this book follows Peregrine "Perry" Eckert's exile to summer camp after his parents worry about his limited social experiences. It combines Vizzini's wit and social awkwardness with the fantasy genre to create an entertaining and relatable piece.

Theresa L. Stowell, PhD

Further Reading

"Ned Vizzini." *Famous Authors.* FamousAuthors.org, n.d. Web. 15 Dec. 2015. <http://www.famousauthors.org/ned-vizzini>.

Vizzini, Ned. Interview by James Blasingame. *Journal of Adolescent & Adult Literacy* 50.7 (2007): 607–08. *Academic Search Complete.* Web. 15 Dec. 2015. <http://search.ebscohost.com/login.aspx?direct=true&db=a9h&AN=24572516>.

Vizzini, Ned. *Rockets in the Night—A Metaphor.* Live Journal, 5 May 2008–21 Apr. 2013. Web. 15 Dec. 2015. <http://ned-vizzini.livejournal.com>.

Bibliography

Beckerman, Marty. "A Year without Ned Vizzini: Brilliant YA Author, 'Teen Wolf' Writer, and My Best Friend.'" *MTV.* Viacom International, 18 Dec. 2014. Web. 11 Dec. 2015. <http://www.mtv.com/news/2021698/ned-vizzini-tribute>.

Crutcher, Chris. "Godspeed Ned Vizinni." *Huffington Post.* TheHuffingtonPost.com, 31 Dec. 2013. Web. 15 Dec. 2015. <http://www.huffingtonpost.com/chris-crutcher/godspeed-ned-vizinni_b_4513216.html>.

Wigginton, Catherine. "Too Hot to Handle." *Village Voice.* Village Voice, 7 Nov. 2006. Web. 15 Dec. 2015. <http://www.villagevoice.com/arts/too-hot-to-handle-7157872>.

Yardley, William. "Ned Vizzini, 32, Dies; Wrote Teenage Novels." *New York Times.* New York Times, 20 Dec. 2013. Web. 11 Dec. 2015. <http://www.nytimes.com/2013/12/21/books/ned-vizzini-author-of-teenage-novels-dies-at-32.html?_r=0>.

Cynthia Voigt

Date of birth: February 25, 1942
Place of birth: Boston, Massachusetts

Principal Works
Children's Literature
Stories about Rosie (1986)
The Rosie Stories (2003)
Angus and Sadie (2005)

Courtesy of Cynthia Voigt

Young Fredle (2011)
Mister Max series (2013–)
Young Adult Literature
Tillerman Cycle (1981–89)
Tell Me If the Lovers Are Losers (1982)
The Callender Papers (1983)
Building Blocks (1984)
Kingdom series (1985–99)
Izzy, Willy-Nilly (1986)
Tree by Leaf (1988)
The Vandemark Mummy (1991)
David and Jonathan (1992)
Orfe (1993)
When She Hollers (1994)
Bad Girls series (1996–2006)

Biography

Cynthia Voigt is the award-winning author of a number of novels for young adults, including the seven-volume Tillerman Cycle, about a family of four abandoned children living in New England in the 1980s. The first novel in the series, *Homecoming* (1981), was nominated for an American Book Award in 1982, and a television film adaptation starring Anne Bancroft was released in 1996. The second novel in the series, *Dicey's Song* (1982), won the prestigious Newbery Medal in 1983, and the third, *A Solitary Blue* (1983), won a 1984 Newbery Honor award. Voigt is also the author of the Kingdom series (1985–99), the Bad Girls series (1996–2006), and a handful of stand-alone novels and children's books. In 1995, she won the Margaret Edwards Award for her body of work, and in 1998, she received the Tulsa Library Trust's Anne V. Zarrow Award for Young Readers' Literature. In 2003, the Maine Library Association awarded Voigt the Katahdin Award for lifetime achievement in children's literature.

Voigt was born Cynthia Irving in Boston, Massachusetts, on February 25, 1942. She was the second of five children. Her father was a corporate executive, and she enjoyed a comfortable, upper-middle-class upbringing in southern Connecticut. As a child, she learned to play the piano, dance tap and ballet, and type. She enjoyed reading and writing from a young age. Later, Voigt attended the Dana Hall School, an all-girls boarding school in Wellesley, Massachusetts.

After graduating from Smith College in 1963, Voigt moved to New York City's Greenwich Village and found a job at the J. Walter Thompson advertising agency. She wrote her first book during this time, but she lost the manuscript and later claimed not to even remember the title. In 1964, Voigt married her first husband and moved with him to Santa Fe, New Mexico, where she earned her teaching certificate at St. Michael's College (now the Santa Fe University of Art and Design). The couple later moved to Annapolis, Maryland, where Voigt gave birth to their daughter, Jessica. She taught English at the Key School in Annapolis and at a high school in nearby Glen Burnie. It was during this time that she began writing again. In 1971, she became chair of the Key School's English Department.

She divorced in 1972 and, two years later, married fellow Key School teacher Walter Voigt, who taught Latin and Greek. Voigt became pregnant again not long after, at which point she switched to teaching part time so she could focus more on her writing. Her son, Peter, was born in 1977.

In the late 1980s, Voigt and her family moved to Minnesota, eventually settling in the small town of Deer Isle. In 2013, Voigt published the first book of a new series, *Mister Max: The Book of Lost Things*. The second book, *Mister Max: The Book of Secrets*, was published in September 2014.

Major Works

Voigt began writing her first young adult novel in 1977, while she was pregnant with her son. That summer, she completed the first draft of what would eventually become *The Callender Papers*, a mystery set in mid-nineteenth-century Massachusetts. It was not published until 1983, however, at which point she already had three published works to her name.

Voigt's first published novel was *Homecoming* (1981), the first in her celebrated Tillerman Cycle, in which four children are abandoned in a parking lot by their alcoholic mother. The resourceful foursome embark on a journey to a relative's house to start their lives anew, but their destination turns out not to be the safe haven they had hoped, engendering a larger odyssey to their grandmother's house farther away. "The bleak fundamentals of the children's situation may be strong stuff for many young readers," Kathleen Leverich wrote in a review for the *New York Times*, "but for those who have the resilience to take it, the accomplishments of this feisty band of complex and, in contrast to the adults, sympathetically conceived kids makes for an enthralling journey to a gratifying end." (par. 4). *Homecoming*, which is set in Connecticut and Maryland in the 1980s, explores themes of poverty, survival, and, as the title suggests, alternative concepts of home.

The second book in the Tillerman Cycle, *Dicey's Song*, was published in 1982. The novel focuses on thirteen-year-old Dicey, the oldest of the Tillerman children. After leading her siblings on an epic journey through New England to their grandmother's farm, Dicey must reconcile her role as caretaker with her life as a child. *Dicey's Song* won the 1983 Newbery Medal, a prestigious literary award from the American Library Association (ALA) Association for Library Service to Children. *A Solitary Blue* (1983), Voigt's fifth book and the third in the series, focuses on Dicey's friend Jeff Greene; it was a 1984 Newbery Honor Book, a designation given to Newbery Medal runners-up. The Tillerman Cycle continued with *The Runner* (1985), *Come a Stranger* (1986), and *Sons from Afar* (1987) before ending with *Seventeen against the Dealer*, published in 1989. Altogether, the saga follows the family through almost ten years of trial and triumph.

While working on the Tillerman Cycle, Voigt also published *Jackaroo* (1985), the first book of what would later be known as the Kingdom series, a historical fantasy about a kingdom in which reading is banned for the lower classes. Despite being Voigt's first foray into the fantasy genre, *Jackaroo* deals with real-world themes of societal discrimination, which Voigt would continue to explore in subsequent books. *Come a Stranger* is the coming-of-age tale of Dicey's friend Mina Smiths, an African American girl dealing with issues of racism and her own growing social awareness; the stand-alone novel *Izzy Willy-Nilly*, also published in 1986, follows a fifteen-year-old girl readjusting to life after a car accident in which she lost her right leg. *David and Jonathan* (1992) is a historical novel exploring the survivor's guilt of a teenage boy who lived through the Holocaust, and *When She Hollers* (1994) is about a teenage girl whose adoptive father sexually abuses her. In a critical analysis of Voigt's work for the *ALAN Review*, the journal of the National Council of Teachers of English (NCTE) Assembly on Literature for Adolescents, Jaime Hylton argues that Voigt successfully rides the razor's edge separating fiction for young people and adults, writing, "There is a richness to her work that transcends topical stories with teen-oriented, identity-focused themes" (50).

Molly Hagan

Further Reading

Drew, Bernard A. *The 100 Most Popular Young Adult Authors: Biographical Sketches and Bibliographies.* Rev. ed. Englewood: Libs. Unltd., 1997. Print.

Gopnik, Adam. "Disappearing Act." Rev. of *Mister Max: The Book of Lost Things*, by Cynthia Voigt. *New York Times*. New York Times, 13 Sept. 2013. Web. 6 Mar. 2015. <http://www.nytimes.com/2013/09/15/books/review/mister-max-the-book-of-lost-things-by-cynthia-voigt.html>.

Irving, Elsie K., and Jessica Voigt. "Profiles of Cynthia Voigt." Aug. 1983. *Horn Book*. Lib. Jour., 16 Sept. 2013. Web. 6 Mar. 2015. <http://www.hbook.com/2013/09/choosing-books/horn-book-magazine/profiles-cynthia-voigt>.

Bibliography

Hylton, Jaime. "Exploring the 'Academic Side' of Cynthia Voigt." *ALAN Review* 33.1 (2005): 50–55. PDF file.

Leverich, Kathleen. "Children's Books." Rev. of *Homecoming*, by Cynthia Voigt. *New York Times*. New York Times, 10 May 1981. Web. 6 Mar. 2015. <http://www.nytimes.com/1981/05/10/books/children-s-books-112153.html>.

Voigt, Cynthia. "Author Biography." *Cynthia Voigt*. Author, n.d. Web. 6 Mar. 2015. <http://www.cynthia-voigt.com/biography.php>.

Voigt, Cynthia. "A Chat with Cynthia Voigt." Interview by Raymond Baartmans. *Time for Kids*. Time, 16 Oct. 2013. Web. 6 Mar. 2015. <http://www.timeforkids.com/news/chat-cynthia-voigt/114961>.

Voigt, Cynthia. "Biography: Cynthia Voigt." *Scholastic*. Scholastic, n.d. Web. 6 Mar. 2015. <http://www.scholastic.com/teachers/contributor/cynthia-voigt>.

Voigt, Cynthia. "Cynthia Voigt Interview Transcript." *Scholastic*. Scholastic, n.d. Web. 6 Mar. 2015. <http://www.scholastic.com/teachers/article/cynthia-voigt-interview-transcript>.

Voigt, Cynthia. "Cynthia Voigt Learns the Rhythms of a Different Life." Interview by Eugenia Williamson. *Boston Globe*. Boston Globe Media Partners, 27 Dec. 2014. Web. 6 Mar. 2015. <http://www.bostonglobe.com/arts/2014/12/27/new-england-writers-work-cynthia-voigt/JsMDuJ3vsJbPoUf0ONrquJ/story.html>.

John Corey Whaley

Date of birth: January 19, 1984
Place of birth: Springhill, Louisiana

Principal Works
Where Things Come Back (2011)
Noggin (2014)

Public domain, via Wikimedia Commons;
Courtesy of John Corey Whaley (both credits listed; one on each spreadsheet)

Biography
John Corey Whaley began writing award-winning
young adult novels when he was scarcely older than
a young adult himself. His first novel, *Where Things
Come Back*, was published in 2011, when he was just
twenty-seven; the following year, it won both the
William C. Morris YA Debut Award for best debut
young adult novel and the Michael L. Printz Award
for best book written for teenagers. Also in 2011, the
National Book Foundation named Whaley one of
their "5 under 35" writers to watch. He was the first
young adult author to receive the honor. His second novel, *Noggin* (2014), about a teenager whose
head was cryogenically frozen after his death and
then reattached to a stranger's body, was a finalist for
the 2014 National Book Award for Young People's
Literature.

John Corey Whaley was born on January 19, 1984 in
Springhill, Louisiana. He knew from a young age that
he wanted to write stories about kids who, like himself, felt trapped and isolated by their rural surroundings. Whaley felt like an outsider in his small hometown, and after high school, he left to attend Louisiana
Tech University in the comparatively large city of Rus-
ton. He earned a bachelor's degree in English in 2006
and a master's degree in secondary education in 2009.
After graduation, he took a job teaching advanced
eighth-grade English at Youree Drive Middle School in
Shreveport, Louisiana.

Whaley got the idea for *Where Things Come Back*
in 2005, when he was still an undergraduate. He heard
a report on National Public Radio (NPR) about a town
called Brinkley, Arkansas, where ornithologists claimed
to have spotted an ivory-billed woodpecker, a bird previously thought to have been extinct. Tourists rushed
to the small town to see the bird, though conclusive
evidence of its existence proved elusive. Whaley was
struck by the scenario, and though he had previously
struggled to turn story ideas into completed works, he
knew that a novel based on the Brinkley bird would be
one he could finally finish.

Major Works
Whaley finished writing his first novel, at the time called
Good God Bird, in 2007, but he had trouble finding an
agent to represent him. The manuscript was rejected
more than fifty times, even though it was one of one
hundred semifinalists for the first Amazon Breakthrough
Novel Award in 2008. Finally, a Facebook friend suggested that he try WEbook, a social network that connects writers with agents. In October 2009, Whaley was
put in touch with Ken Wright at Writer's House, who
agreed to read *Good God Bird* within the next six weeks.
In less than a week, Wright had finished the book and
agreed to represent Whaley. The manuscript was sold
to Simon & Schuster's Atheneum imprint two months
later. Whaley worked closely with his editor to turn his
novel into the award-winning finished product, which
was published two years later to great acclaim.

Where Things Come Back tells the story of a teenager named Cullen Witter, whose younger brother,
Gabriel, has disappeared. Cullen's tiny town is unconcerned with Gabriel's disappearance, too busy enjoying
the onslaught of the tourists who have come to view a
bird that was thought to have been extinct. A secondary
plot follows a young missionary named Benton Sage.
Though Cullen lives in Arkansas and Benton is stationed in Ethiopia, Whaley weaves their stories together

until they intersect to answer to the question of Gabriel's disappearance.

Whaley's second book, *Noggin*, was originally titled *The Defenestration of Abbott*. He finished the first draft of the book before the success of *Where Things Come Back* and spent the next several years editing it. In *Noggin*, a teenager named Travis Coates dies of leukemia when he is sixteen—but his death is only the start of his story. Travis's head is cryogenically frozen; five years later, medical technology has advanced far enough to allow it to come out of the freezer and be attached to a whole new (and wholly different) body. Travis picks up where he left off—as a sophomore in high school—but his friends and his girlfriend have already moved on to college and altogether different lives. *Noggin* is not a novel about science; rather, it is about feeling stuck in time and feeling like a stranger in one's own body.

Molly Hagan

Further Reading

Jacobs, A. J. "Out-of-Body Experience." Rev. of *Noggin*, by John Corey Whaley. *New York Times*. New York Times, 9 May 2014. Web. 22 Oct. 2015. <http://www.nytimes.com/2014/05/11/books/review/noggin-by-john-corey-whaley.html>.

Roper, Ingrid. "Spring 2011 Flying Starts: John Corey Whaley." *Publisher's Weekly*. PWxyz, 20 June 2011. Web. 22 Oct. 2015. <http://www.publishersweekly.com/pw/by-topic/authors/interviews/article/47656-spring-2011-flying-starts-john-corey-whaley.html>.

Bibliography

"John Corey Whaley—Who Is This Guy?" *John Corey Whaley, Author & Friend*. Author, 2013. Web. 22 Oct. 2015. <http://johncoreywhaley.com/about/>.

Rev. of *Noggin*, by John Corey Whaley. *Publishers Weekly* 20 Jan. 2014: 58. *Literary Reference Center*. Web. 22 Oct. 2015. <http://search.ebscohost.com/login.aspx?direct=true&db=lfh&AN=94004836&site=lrc-live>.

Whaley, John Corey. "Author Interview: John Corey Whaley." Interview by Kate Pickett. *Hub*. Young Adult Lib. Services Assn., 12 Jan. 2012. Web. 22 Oct. 2015. <http://www.yalsa.ala.org/thehub/2012/01/12/author-interview-john-corey-whaley/>.

Whaley, John Corey. "Flying High: The Improbable True Tale of Debut Novelist John Corey Whaley." Interview by Ed Spicer. *School Library Journal*. Lib. Jours., 1 May 2012. Web. 22 Oct. 2015. <http://www.slj.com/2012/05/teens-ya/flying-high-the-improbable-true-tale-of-debut-novelist-john-corey-whaley/>.

Whaley, John Corey. "John Corey Whaley, 28, Discusses His Printz Award and What's Next." Interview by Susan Carpenter. *Los Angeles Times*. Tribune, 23 Jan. 2012. Web. 22 Oct. 2015. <http://latimesblogs.latimes.com/jacketcopy/2012/01/201printz-john-corey-whaley.html>.

Whaley, John Corey. "Printz Award Winner John Corey Whaley Talks *Noggin*. Also, See the Cover—Exclusive." Interview by Stephan Lee. *EW.com*. Entertainment Weekly, 13 June 2013. Web. 17 Sept. 2015. http://www.ew.com/article/2013/06/13/john-corey-whaley-noggin-cover

Whaley, John Corey. "Wouldn't You Like to Know . . . John Corey Whaley." Interview by Stacey Hayman. *VOYA*. VOYA, 21 July 2015. Web. 22 Oct. 2015. <http://www.voyamagazine.com/2015/07/21/wouldnt-you-like-to-know-john-corey-whaley/>.

Rev. of *Where Things Come Back*, by John Corey Whaley. *Kirkus Reviews* 15 Apr. 2011: 702. *Literary Reference Center*. Web. 22 Oct. 2015. <http://search.ebscohost.com/login.aspx?direct=true&db=lfh&AN=60526765&site=lrc-live>.

Jacqueline Woodson

Date of birth: February 12, 1963
Place of birth: Columbus, Ohio

Principal Works
Children's Literature
Last Summer with Maizon (1990)
Miracle's Boys (2000)
Hush (2002)
Nonfiction
Brown Girl Dreaming (2014)

Biography

Jacqueline Woodson is the award-winning author of more than two dozen books for children and young adults. In 2014, she received the National Book Award for young people's literature for *Brown Girl Dreaming*, a memoir of her childhood and adolescence in South Carolina and Brooklyn, written in verse. The book went on

© Marty Umans

to win the 2015 Coretta Scott King Award (Woodson's second) and a Newbery Honor (her fourth). In 2005, she won the Young Adult Library Services Association's Margaret A. Edwards Award for lifetime achievement in writing for young adults.

Woodson grew up in both the segregated south and Brooklyn, New York, and writes about adolescents struggling with issues of identity, class, race, and homosexuality. Still, Woodson does not characterize her books as "issue" novels. "Race and economic class and sexuality—these were always issues that were a part of my life," she told Jennifer M. Brown for *Publishers Weekly* in February 2002. "The idea of writing stories that didn't deal with them just seemed so unrealistic and not true."

Woodson was born on February 12, 1963, in Columbus, Ohio. According to family tradition, the Woodsons trace their lineage back to Sally Hemings, the slave mistress of President Thomas Jefferson. After her parents separated, Woodson and her siblings moved with her mother to Nicholtown, a small black community in Greenville, South Carolina. Though Jim Crow was theoretically over, people still lived very segregated lives in South Carolina, Woodson has said. Living with her maternal grandparents, Woodson and her siblings were raised as Jehovah's Witnesses. Her family moved to the Bushwick neighborhood of Brooklyn, New York, when she was seven; she left the Jehovah's Witness faith when she was fifteen. Growing up, Woodson was fascinated by language, though she was a slow reader. She was interested in the mechanics of words and stories and copied down advertising jingles and popular songs until she had them memorized. In high school, she fell in love with the work of James Baldwin.

Woodson studied English at Adelphi University in New York and came out as a lesbian in her early twenties. She began writing her first book, *Last Summer with Maizon*, but set the manuscript aside to take a job with Kirchhoff/Wohlberg, a children's publishing company, after graduation. For her job, Woodson helped develop a standardized reading test. She used an excerpt from *Maizon* that caught the attention of her boss, children's book agent Liza Pulitzer-Voges. Woodson enrolled in a children's book writing class at the New School in New York City, through which she met her first editor, Wendy Lamb. *Maizon*, about two adolescent girls growing up together in Brooklyn, was published in 1990. "I feel like I owe so much to Wendy because I had this idea of what the children's book world was, even though I'd read . . . all these books that were not happily-ever-after stories," Woodson told Brown. "But I had this idea that there were certain things you couldn't say. And Wendy said, basically, 'Nothing you can do is wrong.'"

Woodson lives with her partner, physician Juliet Widoff, and children, Toshi and Jackson-Leroi, in Brooklyn's Park Slope neighborhood.

Major Works

After the success of the novels *From the Notebooks of the Melanin Sun* (1995), about a young boy whose mother is a lesbian, and *If You Come Softly* (1998), an interracial love story, Woodson published a book called *Miracle's Boys* (2000). *Miracle's Boys* tells the story of three Harlem brothers struggling to take care of each other and make ends meet after the death of their parents. The book won the Coretta Scott King Award and was adapted into a six-part miniseries directed by Spike Lee in 2005. A review in *Publishers Weekly* called it an "intelligently wrought, thought-provoking story," but Woodson had her doubts about the authenticity of the book before it was published. It was the first time she had written a cast exclusively made up of male characters; she rewrote the book in its entirety twenty-five times. In 2002, Woodson's novel *Hush*, about a family that has to enter the Witness Protection Program, was nominated for the National Book Award for young people's literature, as was *Locomotion*, about a budding poet in Brooklyn, in 2003. Woodson received Newbery Honors for her books *Show Way* (2005), *Feathers*

(2007), and *After Tupac and D Foster* (2008), but she is best known for her free-verse memoir, *Brown Girl Dreaming* (2014), which won the National Book Award in 2014. After writing for over two decades about the neighborhoods in which she had lived and the people she had known growing up, it seemed fitting that Woodson would win the most prestigious award of her career to date for the story of her own life. "The triumph of 'Brown Girl Dreaming' is not just in how well Woodson tells us the story of her life, but in how elegantly she writes words that make us want to hold those carefully crafted poems close, apply them to our lives, reach into the mirror she holds up and make the words and the worlds she explores our own," Veronica Chambers wrote in her review for the *New York Times* in August 2014.

Molly Hagan

Further Reading
Warrell, Laura. "Jacqueline Woodson's Windows." *Writer*. Madavor, 2 Dec. 2014. Web. 19 Mar. 2015. <http://www.writermag.com/2014/12/02/jacqueline-woodsons-windows>.

Woodson, Jacqueline. "Newsmaker: Jacqueline Woodson." Interview by Mariam Pera. *American Libraries*. ALA, 2 Mar. 2015. Web. 18 Mar 2015. <http://americanlibrariesmagazine.org/2015/03/02/newsmaker-jacqueline-woodson>.

Woodson, Jacqueline. "The Pain of the Watermelon Joke." *New York Times*. New York Times, 28 Nov. 2014. Web. 18 Mar. 2015. <http://www.nytimes.com/2014/11/29/opinion/the-pain-of-the-watermelon-joke.html>.

Bibliography
Brown, Jennifer M. "From Outsider to Insider." *Publishers Weekly*. PWxyz, 11 Feb. 2002. Web. 19 Mar. 2015. <http://www.publishersweekly.com/pw/print/20020211/40294-from-outsider-to-insider.html>.

Chambers, Veronica. "Where We Enter." Rev. of *Brown Girl Dreaming*, by Jacqueline Woodson. *New York Times*. New York Times, 22 Aug. 2014. Web. 18 Mar. 2015. <http://www.nytimes.com/2014/08/24/books/review/jacqueline-woodsons-brown-girl-dreaming.html>.

Rev. of *Miracle's Boys*, by Jacqueline Woodson. *Publishers Weekly*. PWxyz, 24 Apr. 2000. Web. 19 Mar.

2015. <http://www.publishersweekly.com/978-0-399-23113-1>.

Woodson, Jacqueline. "Jacqueline Woodson on Growing Up, Coming Out and Saying Hi to Strangers." Interview by Terry Gross. *Fresh Air*. NPR, 10 Dec. 2014. Web. 18 Mar. 2015. <http://www.npr.org/templates/transcript/transcript.php?storyId=369736205>.

Gene Luen Yang

Date of birth: August 9, 1973
Place of birth: California

Principal Works
Animal Crackers (2004)
American Born Chinese (2006)
The Eternal Smile (2009)
Prime Baby (2010)
Level Up (2011)
Boxers & Saints (2013)
The Shadow Hero (2014)

Biography
The author of numerous comics and graphic novels for young adult readers, Gene Luen Yang is best known as the author and illustrator of the award-winning graphic novel *American Born Chinese* (2006), in which three seemingly divergent stories combine to form a thought-provoking exploration of race, assimilation, and Chinese identity in the United States. He is also the author of *Boxers & Saints* (2013), a pair of graphic novels that chronicle the diverging lives of two young people during China's Boxer Rebellion. Yang's works have received significant critical recognition both within and outside of the comics industry, and he has been the recipient of multiple Eisner Awards, which recognize excellence in comic books and graphic novels. He has also received recognition from organizations such as the American Library Association and the National Book Foundation. *American Born Chinese* was the first graphic novel to be nominated for the National Book Award.

Yang was born on August 9, 1973, in Alameda County, California. The child of parents who had immigrated to the United States from Taiwan and Hong Kong, Yang endured race-based bullying and struggled with his identity as an American-born person of Chinese descent during his early life, experiences that influenced his later work. His parents' stories were a memorable part of his childhood, and he began writing and drawing comics at an early age. Yang soon became an avid reader of comics, particularly superhero titles.

After graduating from high school, Yang enrolled in the University of California, Berkeley, where he majored in computer science and minored in creative writing. He later attended California State University, East Bay, from which he earned his master's degree in education. After college Yang initially took a software engineering position, a role he found unfulfilling. After two years, he ultimately decided to leave his job to become a teacher and work on comics in his spare time.

Yang soon began self-publishing short comics, establishing the publishing company Humble Comics. He first found success in 1997 with the publication of *Gordon Yamamoto and the King of the Geeks*, a comic published in several installments in which a teenager has a life-changing encounter with a tiny alien. He followed that work with *Loyola Chin and the San Peligran Order*, a comic set in the same universe; the two were collected and published in a single volume, titled *Animal Crackers*, in 2004.

It was Yang's next major work that brought him significant acclaim from both the comics industry and the wider literary community. Published in 2006, *American Born Chinese* features three stories that are ultimately deeply connected and provide a thoughtful portrait of the protagonist's experiences as the American-born son of Chinese immigrants. Yang also illustrated the graphic novel, which became the first such work to win the Michael L. Printz Award for excellence in young adult literature from the American Library Association. Following the success of *American Born Chinese*, Yang went on to write various other graphic novels, including *Level Up* (2011), *Boxers & Saints*, and *The Shadow Hero* (2014). *Boxers & Saints* was a finalist for the 2013 National Book Award and the winner of the Los Angeles Times Book Prize for young adult literature. Yang also wrote several graphic novels set in the world of the animated television series *Avatar: The Last Airbender* (2005–8), chronicling the continuing adventures of the characters after the end of the series.

In addition to his work in comics, Yang taught computer science at Bishop O'Dowd High School in Oakland, California, for more than ten years. In 2012, he joined the faculty of Hamline University as a creative writing teacher in the school's master of fine arts program. He lives in northern California's Bay Area with his wife, Theresa, and their two children.

Major Works

Yang is best known for *American Born Chinese*, a complex graphic novel that weaves together the stories of a Chinese American boy who seeks acceptance in his predominantly white school, a white American teen whose life is sent into upheaval when his Chinese cousin comes to visit, and the Monkey King, a deity who wants to be perceived as something other than his true self. Incorporating elements of Chinese literature and American popular culture, *American Born Chinese* examines themes of immigrant identity, assimilation, and self-acceptance. Yang returns to such themes in some of his later works, including the superhero graphic novel *The Shadow Hero*, about a Chinese American teenager in the 1930s who becomes a costumed crime fighter.

A devout Catholic, Yang often considers the subject of religious faith in his graphic novels. Christianity plays a small but significant role in *American Born Chinese*, in which the story of the Monkey King, a figure from Chinese literature, is somewhat Christianized. Yang likewise engages with both Chinese culture and Christianity in *Boxers & Saints*; as two companion volumes, *Boxers* follows a Chinese boy who opposes Western imperialism during the Boxer Rebellion of 1899–1901, while *Saints* follows a Chinese girl who converts to Catholicism and faces persecution during the same period. Through such works, Yang explores the importance of religion, and especially Christianity, to many people of Chinese descent.

Joy Crelin

Further Reading

"About." *Gene Luen Yang*. Gene Luen Yang, n.d. Web. 31 Oct. 2015. <http://geneyang.com/about>.

Chen, Alice C. "The Humble Comic." *SFGate*. Hearst Communications, 11 May 2008. Web. 31 Oct. 2015. <http://www.sfgate.com/magazine/article/The-Humble-Comic-3214214.php>.

Bibliography

"Announcing New Faculty." *Hamline University*. Hamline U, 2012. Web. 31 Oct. 2015. <http://www.hamline.edu/HUContent.aspx?pageid=2147517472>.

Mayer, Petra. "'Boxers & Saints' & Compassion: Questions for Gene Luen Yang." *NPR Books*. NPR, 22 Oct.

2013. Web. 31 Oct. 2015. <http://www.npr.org/2013/10/22/234824741/boxers-saints-compassion-quesions-for-gene-luen-yang>.

"The Michael L. Printz Award for Excellence in Young Adult Literature." *ALA*. Amer. Lib. Assn., 2007. Web. 31 Oct. 2015. <http://www.ala.org/Template.cfm?Section=bookmediaawards&template=/ContentManagement/ContentDisplay.cfm&ContentID=148145>.

Peitzman, Louis. "Gene Luen Yang: Teacher, Dad, Graphic Novelist." *SFGate*. Hearst Communications, 29 Apr. 2010. Web. 31 Oct. 2015. <http://www.sfgate.com/thingstodo/article/Gene-Luen-Yang-Teacher-dad-graphic-novelist-3265852.php>.

Markus Zusak

Date of birth: June 23, 1975
Place of birth: Sydney, Australia

Principal Works

The Underdog (1999)
Fighting Ruben Wolfe (2001)
The Messenger (2002; *I Am the Messenger*, 2005)
Getting the Girl (2003)
The Book Thief (2006)
Bridge of Clay (2011)
Underdogs (2011)

Biography

Markus Zusak is an Australian author best known for his novel *The Book Thief* (2006). The book, based on the experiences of Zusak's German-born parents, is about two teenagers living outside of Munich during World War II. *The Book Thief* was marketed for adults in Australia, but was labeled a young adult novel in the United States. It became a best seller in both genres and was made into a movie starring Geoffrey Rush and Emily Watson in 2013. "A loved book is a loved book, no matter where it comes from or the category it is placed in," Zusak told Victoria Burrows for the *South China Morning Post*. "You just have to trust readers and hope that the book finds its way into the right hands." In 2014, Zusak received the lifetime achievement Margaret A. Edwards Award for his contributions to young adult literature.

Zusak was born in Sydney, Australia, on June 23, 1975. His mother, Lisa, was six years old and in foster care in Munich, Germany, when it was bombed by the British during the war. She then lived for a time in Dachau, Germany, near the notorious concentration camp. Zusak's father, Helmut, was a member of the Hitler Youth in Austria. Their stories intrigued Zusak growing up, and he did not consider writing them down until later. Zusak's parents spoke no English when they came to Australia but were determined their children would be proficient in the language. Zusak learned to read at an early age, but when he was sixteen something changed, and he began reading books for enjoyment. "I had that feeling of turning pages and you don't even notice, you are just so caught up in it—that's one of the best feelings you can have," he told Rod Moran for the Perth *West Australian*. "I thought, 'That's what I want to do with my life.'"

Zusak was twenty-three when he published his first novel, *The Underdog*, in 1999. The book is narrated by the character Cameron Wolfe, who serves as the protagonist of Zusak's next two books, *Fighting Ruben Wolfe* (2001) and *Getting the Girl* (2003), which won the Queensland Premier's Literary Award. The Wolfe trilogy was published as a collection titled *Underdogs* in the United States in 2011. The personalities of the protagonists in the story, two working-class brothers, Cameron and Ruben, are based on Zusak and his own brother. In the second book in the trilogy, Cameron and Ruben begin boxing in order to earn money, and in the third book, *Getting the Girl*, Cameron pursues his brother's ex-girlfriend. Like *The Book Thief*, the Wolfe trilogy is about survival and "fighting, both physical and metaphorical," Susan Carpenter wrote for the *Los Angeles Times*. "It's the hardscrabble life of the working class, for which there's little joy or hope of escape, yet Cameron's voice offers glimmers of redemption."

Zusak, his wife, Dominika, and their daughter live in Sydney.

Major Works

Zusak's novel *The Messenger* (2002) won the New South Wales Premier's Literary Award. It was published as *I Am the Messenger* in the United States in 2005 and received a Michael L. Printz Honor the same year. The book centers around an underage cabdriver turned vigilante and was Zusak's first commercial success, but his most celebrated novel remains *The Book Thief*, a book about war, survival, and the power of stories. Set in a small town outside of Nazi-occupied Munich in 1939, the story is narrated by Death, who is "telling this story to prove to himself that humans are actually worth it,"

Zusak told Moran. Liesel Meminger—a feisty school-girl who acts out by stealing books after the death of her family—is taken in by Rosa and Hans Hubermann. The Hubermanns are a kind couple who later take in a Jewish teenager named Max Vandenburg and hide him in their basement. The book finds whimsy and even beauty in a horrific chapter of history. Some reviewers criticized the book as overstuffed, but even its critics agree that Zusak captures moments of sharp truth. Janet Maslin for the *New York Times* wrote, "At its most effective, the book's tone can be terrifyingly matter of fact. 'For the book thief, everything was going nicely,' Death observes, as the extermination camps flourish in the summer of 1942. 'For me, the sky was the color of Jews.'"

The Book Thief spent over four years on the New York Times Best Seller list, and in 2013 it was made into a successful film. The score, composed by veteran composer John Williams, was nominated for an Academy Award.

Molly Hagan

Further Reading

Carpenter, Susan. "Not Just for Kids: 'UnderDogs' by Markus Zusak." *LA Times.* Los Angeles Times, 14 Aug. 2011. Web. 6 May 2015. <http://articles.latimes.com/2011/aug/14/entertainment/la-ca-markus-zusak-20110814>.

Carstensen, Angela. "On Top of His Game: Margaret A. Edwards Award Winner Markus Zusak Talks about Finding His Voice, His Responsibility to Readers, and His Obsession with Getting Things Right." *School Library Journal* 60.6 (2014): 26. Print.

Green, John. "Fighting for Their Lives." *New York Times.* New York Times, 14 May 2006. Web. 6 May 2015. <http://www.nytimes.com/2006/05/14/books/review/14greenj.html>.

Maslin, Janet. "Stealing to Settle a Score with Life." *New York Times.* New York Times, 27 Mar. 2006. Web. 7 May 2015. <http://www.nytimes.com/2006/03/27/books/27masl.html?_r=0>.

Bibliography

Burrows, Victoria. "Rolling with the Punches." *South China Morning Post* 1 Mar. 2009: 3. Print.

Crowley, Cath. "Cameron Wolfe, Lost and Found." *Age* 14 May 2003: 5. Print.

Kinson, Sarah. "Why I Write—Markus Zusak." *Guardian.* Guardian News and Media, 28 Mar. 2008. Web. 6 May 2015. <http://www.theguardian.com/books/2008/mar/28/whyiwrite>.

Moran, Rod. "Beauty amid the Carnage." *West Australian* 16 Oct. 2006: 10. Print.

PLOT SUMMARIES

The Absolutely True Diary of a Part-time Indian

Author: Sherman Alexie (b. 1966)
First published: 2007
Type of work: Novel
Type of plot: Bildungsroman
Time of plot: 2006
Locale: Wellpinit, Spokane Indian Reservation; Reardan, Washington

Principal characters

Arnold Spirit Jr., a teenage Spokane Indian cartoonist
Rowdy, his best friend, an angry, violent teenager on the reservation
Mary Spirit, his older sister
Penelope, his white girlfriend at Reardan High School
Gordy, an intelligent Reardan student

The Story

Arnold Spirit Jr., known as Junior, is a fourteen-year-old Spokane Indian boy who was born with extra cerebrospinal fluid on his skull, which gave him a large head, seizures, a lisp, and other physical issues. He lives on the Spokane Indian Reservation, where many of the other children mock him, calling him Globe or Orbit because of his head size. His family is very poor, so much so that when his dog becomes sick, they cannot afford medical care and have to shoot it. Junior's closest friend is Rowdy, a boy his age whose father physically abuses him. Rowdy is much tougher than Junior and often stands up for his friend when others beat him up. Junior hopes to eventually become a comic artist or writer.

When Junior starts high school, he is assigned a math book that formerly belonged to his mother. After realizing that this means the reservation is too poor to afford new books even after thirty years, he becomes angry and throws it at his teacher, Mr. P., breaking his nose. Junior is immediately suspended, although Mr. P. meets with him during the suspension, saying he is not mad. Instead, he encourages Junior to go to nearby Reardan High School, a wealthy school off the reservation, where he will get a better education.

When Junior transfers to Reardan, he finds that the only other Indian at the school is the school mascot. When he tells Rowdy of his choice, Rowdy, feeling dejected, punches him in the face, and many of the other neighbors on the reservation ostracize him. At Reardan, however, Junior is happy to develop a friendship (and a crush) on a pretty girl named Penelope as well as a friendship with a smart boy named Gordy. Junior largely convinces everyone his family is well-off financially, but Penelope learns how poor he is when they begin dating and he takes her to the winter dance.

When Junior joins the varsity basketball team, he finds himself playing games against the reservation school, and his former best friend, Rowdy, elbows him so hard that he is knocked unconscious. The audience even boos Junior, which heightens the divide he feels between his home life and school life. When the next game against the reservation school team comes, Junior pushes ahead to help his new team win but feels awful once he sees that his former classmates are dejected.

Junior's concerns at school suddenly seem less urgent when he experiences a number of losses. His grandmother is hit by a drunk driver and dies, his father's best friend is shot in the face and also dies, and, perhaps most tragically, his sister, Mary, perishes in a fire. All the deaths come about because of alcohol abuse. Junior is devastated and begins to focus his energy on seeing whatever joy in life he can, making lists of happy things in his notebook.

Following the accidents, Junior and Rowdy get together to play basketball and end their feud. Rowdy says that he has accepted Junior as a traveler, not someone who has left him behind, and tells Junior to send postcards from wherever he goes. Junior hopes that he can forgive himself some day for leaving the reservation. As they continue shooting basketball, they do not keep score.

Critical Evaluation

While Junior is a charming, hopeful, and engaging narrator, the details of his story are often quite dark. He faces the violent deaths of multiple loved ones, experiences physical and emotional abuse, confronts racism and ostracism in all of his communities, and struggles with poverty. Stating that he has gone to forty-two funerals in his short life, he wryly notes, "That's really the biggest difference between Indians and white people."

How, then, does Sherman Alexie infuse so much humor and hope into a novel exploring such depressing topics? In part, this is accomplished by the first-person narration. Readers are told the story directly by Junior, and as such, the teenager's voice strongly guides their understanding of any situation. The fact that he is able to find humor in the fact that he gets beat up constantly (stating he's a member of the "Black-Eye-of-the-Month-Club") allows the reader to also see the humor in the violent circumstance, his laughter giving readers permission to laugh, his hope giving permission for readers to find hope. Junior also identifies himself as someone who loves words and recognizes the power of language, identifying literature as a way that he might achieve a better life. If words will save him later, there is no reason they cannot start doing so now, as the lists of joyful things demonstrate throughout.

If words are important to Junior, so too are drawings, and Alexie's text is filled with cartoon illustrations (meant to be Junior's creations) by Ellen Forney. Junior describes these drawings as "tiny little life boats" that help him survive life—indeed, they often take the more violent aspects of the narrative and make them approachable through the cartoon style and Junior's humor. Combined with the fast-moving, short chapters, the drawings allow the book to jump quickly between a large number of social and personal issues, with the voice and drawing style providing insight into Junior's condition. While the context of racism and poverty seems inescapable, then, the strength of Junior's voice and his trust in language allow both the main character and the audience to realize that even those traumas can be transcended.

T. Fleischmann, MFA

Further Reading

Alexie, Sherman. Interview by Margo Rabb and Leon Lewis. *Critical Insights: Sherman Alexie* (2011): 394–403. *Literary Reference Center*. Web. 19 Feb. 2015. <http://search.ebscohost.com/login.aspx?direct=true&db=lfh&AN=70841001&site=ehost-live>.

Wahpeconiah, Tammy, and Leon Lewis. "Navigating the River of the World: Collective Trauma in *The Absolutely True Diary of a Part-Time Indian.*" *Critical Insights: Sherman Alexie* (2011): 35–52. *Literary Reference Center*. Web. 19 Feb. 2015. <http://search.ebscohost.com/login.aspx?direct=true&db=lfh&AN=70840982&site=ehost-live>.

All the Truth That's in Me

Author: Julie Berry (b. 1974)
First published: 2013
Type of work: Novel
Type of plot: Historical fiction
Time of plot: Late eighteenth century
Locale: New England

Principal characters

Judith Finch, an eighteen-year-old girl who has been shunned by her community
Lucas Whiting, Judith's twenty-two-year-old love interest
Darrel Finch, Judith's brother
Mrs. Finch, Judith's mother
Ezra Whiting, Lucas's father
Lottie Pratt, a teenage girl who is abducted and later found dead
Abijah Pratt, Lottie's father
Rupert Gillis, a schoolmaster

The Story

The narrative of *All the Truth That's in Me* is told through the perspective of Judith Finch, an eighteen-year-old girl living in New England sometime in the late eighteenth century. Written in the form of a journal addressed to the young man she is in love with, Lucas Whiting, and without dates, the novel tells the story of a social outcast living in a small Puritan community as it struggles to survive in the wilderness of early America. While love is the central-most theme in the story, it is also about a young woman's struggle to find a place and her own identity after a terrible incident that has left her shunned by the community.

The story begins as Judith recalls childhood memories that involved Lucas. When she was eight, for example, she would collect earthworms from her mother's garden and give them to Lucas to use when he went fishing. Because of this he gave her the nickname Ladybird. Judith has carried her crush for Lucas, who was four years her senior, from an early age, and while he acknowledged her, he never recognized her in the way that she wanted.

When Judith was twelve, Lucas's father, Ezra, had an emotional breakdown and burned down his house and the town armory. He then disappeared. Lucas lived with the Finches for a year until his house was rebuilt, and then he moved out on his own. Two years later tragedy struck the village when a teenage girl named Lottie Pratt disappeared. Within days, Judith was also abducted, and soon after the townspeople found Lottie's lifeless body naked and in the river. Judith, however, is abducted by Ezra, whom the entire town assumed was dead but who has been living outside of town in a small shack near the hills. Ezra holds Judith hostage for two years, preventing her from escaping numerous times until her spirit is finally broken. Ultimately, he cuts out her tongue and sends her back to the community.

Upon her return, the townspeople assume Judith has been raped and is no longer a virgin, so she is shunned and becomes a pariah to everyone, including her mother and brother. Without the ability to talk, she leads a life of marginalized subservience to her family. One day British Loyalist soldiers known as Homelanders attack the town. Without an armory to support them, the defenses of the town are quickly overrun. However, Judith knows that not only is Ezra Whiting alive, but he also has a large store of gunpowder and munitions from the old armory. She returns to the hut and pleads with Ezra in order to save Lucas's life. He agrees and in a display of bravery that ultimately burns and then sinks the Homelanders' ships, Ezra gives his life defending the town.

This is only the beginning of trouble for Judith and Lucas. As Lucas is charged with keeping the whereabouts of his father a secret and is then cast off from the village, Judith realizes that she can still have a voice and an identity. Although she teaches herself to read and write and becomes more integrated into the lives of community members, she is still not treated as an equal member of the community. In the end, Judith realizes that she must find her voice and the courage to stand up to those people who have shunned and ignored her. She must also defend the lives of those who have become dearest to her and right the wrongs of the community in order to bring the guilty to justice.

Critical Evaluation

While *All the Truth That's in Me* is essentially a love story, the plot of which often overwhelms other essential themes, it is also a story of identity, marginalization, and overcoming trauma.

Judith confides on the opening page of the novel that she cannot share the whole story because she is forbidden from telling it. The Puritan-esque, early American religious community that Berry builds around Judith resonates with young adult readers who often feel constrained by their perceptions of culturally imposed rules. Although the novel is a period piece set several

centuries in the past, Berry's focuses on aspects of early-American life that her contemporary readers can relate to. Many of Judith's worries and fears are relevant to modern young adult readers. The feeling of being marginalized or cast out by others, for example, is a ubiquitous emotion for young adults. While readers may not identify with the severity of Judith's shunning, it is easy to identify with being on the outskirts of a group one desperately wants to be a part of. Furthermore, being judged by one's attitude, appearance, speech, or interactions with others is also something that Berry's readers may empathize with.

Berry's book, which was very well received by critics in its initial printing, is credited as being a unique voice within young adult literature because it informs readers about early American history while addressing issues that are important to adolescent and adult readers alike.

Aaron Horton, MA

Further Reading

Brabander, Jennifer M. Rev. of *All the Truth That's in Me*, by Julie Berry. *Horn Book* Nov.–Dec. 2013: 87–88. *Literary Reference Center*. Web. 21 Dec. 2015. <http://search.ebscohost.com/login.aspx?direct=true&db=lfh&AN=91621854&site=lrc-live>.

Swan, Jennifer Hubert. "Without a Voice" Rev. of *All the Truth That's in Me*, by Julie Berry. *New York Times*. New York Times, 8 Nov. 2013. Web. 18 Dec. 2015. <http://www.nytimes.com/2013/11/10/books/review/all-the-truth-thats-in-me-by-julie-berry.html>.

American Born Chinese

Author: Gene Luen Yang (b. 1973)
First published: 2006
Type of work: Graphic Novel
Type of plot: Coming-of-Age
Time of plot: The early twenty-first century and a legendary past
Locale: United States and China

Principal characters

Jin Wang, an American-born boy of Chinese descent
Wei-Chen Sun, a boy in Jin's class who has recently emigrated from Taiwan

Suzy Nakamura, a Japanese American girl in Jin's class

Amelia Harris, a white American girl, Jin's crush

Danny, a white American teenager

Chin-Kee, Danny's cousin and the embodiment of numerous Chinese stereotypes

Melanie, a white American girl, Danny's crush

The Monkey King, a deity and the ruler of Flower-Fruit Mountain

Tze-Yo-Tzuh, the creator of the universe

Wong Lai-Tsao, a Chinese monk

The Story

Gene Luen Yang's award-winning graphic novel *American Born Chinese*, published in 2006, tells three stories that initially appear to have little to do with each other; however, the three individual tales are ultimately revealed to be intensely intertwined, forming a single cohesive narrative. The first tale is that of the Monkey King, a Chinese literary character perhaps best known from the sixteenth-century Ming dynasty novel *Journey to the West*. At the beginning of his story, the Monkey King, a deity and the ruler of Flower-Fruit Mountain, attempts to attend a dinner party in heaven. Upon arriving at the party, however, he is denied entry because he is not wearing shoes. His arguments prove ineffective, and after being told that he is just a monkey, he grows angry and attacks the partygoers.

After returning to Flower-Fruit Mountain, he commands his monkey subjects to wear shoes and embarks on an intensive kung fu training program, eventually taking on a larger, more humanoid form and declaring he must now be known as the Great Sage, Equal of Heaven. While he is now able to defeat numerous mythological figures, he is unable to impress Tze-Yo-Tzuh, the creator, who tells him that despite his attempts to change himself, he was created to be and always will be a monkey. As punishment for defying the god, the Monkey King is trapped under a pile of rocks for five hundred years, until a monk named Wong Lai-Tsao encourages him to return to his original monkey form. The Monkey King joins Wong Lai-Tsao, whom Tze-Yo-Tzuh has tasked with delivering three packages to the newborn Jesus, on his journey and later becomes the emissary of Tze-Yo-Tzuh. When his firstborn son wants to become an emissary as well, the Monkey King sends him to live among humans for forty years as a test of virtue.

In the second story, a boy named Jin Wang begins to attend elementary school in a new town. One of the few children of Asian descent in his school, Jin, who was born in the United States and previously lived in a community with more Asian American residents, faces various forms of racism in his daily life. Seeking to be accepted by his classmates, he avoids his Japanese American classmate Suzy Nakamura and initially resists becoming friends with Wei-Chen Sun, a Taiwanese boy who enrolls in the school after him. A few years later, Jin develops a crush on his white classmate Amelia Harris, with whom he goes on a date. After the date, a classmate named Greg tells Jin not to ask Amelia out again, as he believes that spending time with Jin will damage Amelia's reputation. Upset about this, Jin impulsively kisses Suzy, who is dating Wei-Chen, and consequently has a falling out with the other boy. Consumed by his desire to fit in, Jin goes to bed that night and awakens in the morning, transformed.

The third story is that of Danny, a blond-haired, blue-eyed teenager who is dismayed when his Chinese cousin Chin-Kee comes for a visit. Chin-Kee, who embodies countless offensive stereotypes, proceeds to embarrass Danny in front of his friends and classmates, behaving inappropriately toward Danny's crush, Melanie, and even urinating in Danny's friend's drink. Angered by Chin-Kee's behavior, Danny hits his cousin. After a long fight, Chin-Kee's head flies off, revealing the Monkey King's visage underneath. Having revealed his true self, the Monkey King encourages Danny to do the same, and Danny is revealed to be Jin. The Monkey King explains that he is attempting to act as Jin's conscience and began to visit Jin after Wei-Chen, who is truly the Monkey King's son, turned his back on his mission. Having learned a lesson about self-acceptance from the Monkey King, Jin next seeks out Wei-Chen, rekindling their friendship.

Critical Evaluation

Through its three connected stories, *American Born Chinese* tells a complex coming-of-age tale in which acceptance of oneself is the key to happiness. The Monkey King and Jin both desire to be perceived as someone other than who they are, at the expense of their true selves. Jin's transformation into Danny serves as a literal depiction of his attempt at assimilation: in trying to fit in with his white classmates, he physically transforms until he resembles them. Both Jin and Wei-Chen are shown with Transformers toys, which likewise underscore the narrative's themes of transformation, assimilation, and identity.

In writing and drawing *American Born Chinese*, Yang drew heavily from both Chinese culture and historical depictions of people of Asian descent in the United States. The tale of the Monkey King was popularized by the novel *Journey to the West*, believed to have been composed in the sixteenth century CE by the writer Wu Cheng'en. Yang follows that original story relatively closely, though he also incorporates elements that reflect his own Christian faith, demonstrating the importance of Christianity among portions of the Asian American community; for example, the Monkey King's journey echoes that of the biblical Wise Men, and the Buddha, a crucial figure in *Journey to the West*, is replaced with Tze-Yo-Tzuh, a figure who is more similar to the Christian god.

In addition to Chinese and Chinese American culture, Yang engages with the stereotypical depictions of Asian Americans that permeated much of American popular culture for centuries. The character of Chin-Kee is an outlandish caricature whose name references a racial slur and who embodies many stereotypes prominent in the early twentieth century and beyond: he has exaggerated features such as buck teeth and a long braid, speaks in a heavy accent, and at one point is portrayed eating cat gizzards. Yang likewise references more contemporary incarnations of those stereotypes; in one scene, Chin-Kee loudly sings the pop song "She Bangs" in a manner similar to that of William Hung, a Chinese American man who became the subject of ridicule after singing the song during his audition for the competitive reality show *American Idol* in 2004. Through this character, Yang calls attention to the stereotypes plaguing the Asian American community and the ways in which some individuals may be tempted to escape that painful legacy through self-transformation.

Joy Crelin

Further Information

Chen, Alice C. "The Humble Comic." *SFGate*. Hearst Communications, 11 May 2008. Web. 31 Oct. 2015. <http://www.sfgate.com/magazine/article/The-Humble-Comic-3214214.php>.

Davis, Rocío G. "Childhood and Ethnic Visibility in Gene Yang's American Born Chinese." *Prose Studies* 35.1 (2013): 7–15. *Literary Reference Center*. Web. 3 Nov. 2015. <http://search.ebscohost.com/login.aspx?direct=true&db=lfh&AN=87070527&site=lrc-live>.

"The Michael L. Printz Award for Excellence in Young Adult Literature." *ALA*. Amer. Lib. Assn., 2007. Web. 31 Oct. 2015. <http://www.ala.org/Template.cfm?Section=bookmediaawards&template=/ContentManagement/ContentDisplay.cfm&ContentID=148145>.

Annie on My Mind

Author: Nancy Garden (1938–2014)
First Published: 1982
Type of Work: Novel
Type of Plot: Realism
Time of Plot: 1980s
Locales: New York City (Manhattan and Brooklyn)

Principal Characters

Eliza "Liza" Winthrop, seventeen-year-old student at Foster Academy; careful and logical, Liza wants to study at MIT to become an architect

Annie Kenyon, seventeen-year-old public school student, Annie is passionate and imaginative and wants to study music at the University of California at Berkeley

Ms. Isabelle Stevenson, an art teacher at Liza's school, Foster Academy, and Ms. Widmer's partner

Ms. Katherine Widmer, an English teacher at Liza's school, Foster Academy, and Ms. Stevenson's partner

The Story

Annie on My Mind is told primarily from the point of view of Eliza "Liza" Winthrop, who is recalling the relationship with Annie Kenyon that defined her senior in high school from her dorm room at MIT. As Liza struggles to draft a letter in response to the many she has received—and never answered—from Annie, she remembers their first meeting and the development of their relationship.

A class officer at her private school, Liza dreams of attending MIT and becoming an architect. On a visit to the Metropolitan Museum of Art meant to inspire her work on a model of a solar house she is building as her senior project, Liza encounters a girl singing in an empty exhibit room. The girl introduces herself as Annie Kenyon and the two explore the museum together. Although Liza is, at first, taken aback by Annie's enthusiasm, particularly when she encourages Liza to engage in a pantomime jousting match in the Hall of Arms and Armor, she finds herself thinking about Annie after they part and is excited to learn that Annie has called her the next day.

Annie and Liza begin a close friendship and spend their free time together exploring the city. They visit museums and take long walks during which they often engage in imaginative play. During their Thanksgiving break from school, Annie and Liza spend every day together and, on the last day of their vacation, walk on a beach near Coney Island where they share their first kiss.

Uncertain as to what this new development in their relationship means, Liza wonders if she might be gay. Annie confesses that she is pretty certain that she is gay and, as Liza's and Annie's relationship becomes more physical, Liza struggles to make sense of this identity.

When two of her teachers, Ms. Stevenson and Ms. Widmer, ask Liza to house- and cat-sit while they are away during their school's spring break, Liza and Annie ensconce themselves in the teachers' home and eventually consummate their relationship. Coincidentally, as they explore their teachers' house, they discover that they, too, are gay and in a relationship with one another.

On the day before Ms. Stevenson and Ms. Widmer are to return home, Liza and Annie are discovered by a neighbor, Ms. Baxter, who also works at Liza's school. Presuming that the teachers have corrupted Annie and Liza, Ms. Baxter reports them all to the school where Liza is threatened with expulsion and Ms. Stevenson and Ms. Widmer are asked to resign.

Liza and Annie's relationship cools after both leave New York to attend college. While Annie is prepared to live as an "out" lesbian, Liza is less certain. At the end of the novel, after Liza has relived their relationship, she decides to call Annie and the two make plans to see one another. "I'm free now," Liza tells Annie, suggesting that she, too, is willing to claim her gay identity.

Critical Evaluation

Although other stories of same-sex romantic relationships had appeared in young adult literature before *Annie on My Mind* was published in 1982, Nancy Garden's novel is considered a young adult LGBTQ classic. As Michael Cart and Christine Jenkins write, *Annie on My Mind* represents the "first GLBTQ love story with a positive ending" (76). LGBTQ-themed young adult novels that came before *Annie* typically featured protagonists agonizing over their sexualities, facing discrimination and violence, and often concluded in tragedy. Notably, none of these pre-*Annie* novels ever rejoiced in their protagonists' same-sex romances. Garden's novel's willingness to depict Liza and Annie's relationship in romantic terms became, in this context, significant. In a 2007 essay revisiting the novel, Roger Sutton wrote: "Forget the gay angle: that *Annie on My Mind* was a love story is possibly the true breakthrough here" (546).

Garden's novel is also noteworthy for its depiction of two generations of same-sex relationships. After Liza

and Annie discover that Ms. Stevenson and Ms. Widmer are gay, the four discuss their experiences and the older women offer advice. While Ms. Stevenson and Ms. Widmer are honest about the challenges they faced—and continue to face—as a same-sex couple, the novel depicts their relationship and love for one another in positive and affirming terms. Cart and Jenkins praise the novel's inclusion of such a model couple, arguing that these adult characters represent a queer community that, then as now, offers extra-familial support to LGBTQ people.

In 2000, *Annie on My Mind* was named one of the "100 Books That Shaped the Century" by *School Library Journal*. In the annotation that accompanied the mention, *School Library Journal* described Garden's novel as "one of the first to deal honestly with girls discovering their interest in a same-sex relationship." Three years after *Annie on My Mind* was included on the *School Library Journal* list of influential titles, the book's author was honored with the American Library Association's Margaret A. Edwards Award. The award recognizes an author for his or her contribution to the young adult literary world and the citation describing the selection of Garden as the 2003 winner mentions *Annie on My Mind* specifically.

Current status as an LGBTQ classic notwithstanding, *Annie on My Mind* has been the subject of numerous challenges since its publication in 1982. Garden's novel was number 44 on the ALA's list of "100 Most Frequently Challenged Books: 1990 – 1999." It is worth noting that the novel is not featured on the 2000 – 2010 list; however, *And Tango Makes Three* (2005), a picturebook based on the true story of two male penguins who raise an orphaned penguin chick at the Central Park Zoo, is in the top five of books challenged during the first decade of the twenty-first century. This history of challenge, and the continued challenges to which books about same-sex relationships are subject, demonstrate that, although the LGBTQ movement has come a long way since *Annie on My Mind* was written and published, books for the young featuring LGBTQ characters and stories remain controversial.

Amy Pattee

Further Reading

Brownworth, Victoria. "In Remembrance: Nancy Garden." *Lambda Literary*. Lambda Literary Foundation, 24 June 2014. Web. 23 February 2016. http://www.

lambdaliterary.org/features/rem/06/24/in-remembrance-nancy-garden/

Smith, Cynthia Leitich. "Interview with Children's and YA Book Author Nancy Garden." *Children's and YA Literature Resources*. Cynthia Leitich Smith, June 2001. Web. 23 February 2016. http://www.cynthialeitichsmith.com/lit_resources/authors/interviews/NancyGarden.html

Bibliography

"100 Books That Shaped the Century." *School Library Journal*. Media Source, Inc, 1 January 2000. Web. 23 February 2016.

Cart, Michael and Christine A. Jenkins. *The Heart Has Its Reasons: Young Adult Literature with Gay/Lesbian/Queer Content, 1969 – 2004*. Lanham, MD: Scarecrow Press, 2006. Print.

Office for Intellectual Freedom of the American Library Association. "100 Most Frequently Challenged Books: 1990 – 1999." *OIF/ALA*. ALA, n.d. Web. 23 February 2016.

Sutton, Roger. "A Second Look: Annie on My Mind." *Horn Book* 83.5 (Sept./Oct. 2007): 543 – 546. Print.

Young Adult Library Association. "2003 Margaret A. Edwards Award Winner." *YALSA*. ALA, n.d. Web. 23 February 2016.

Aristotle and Dante Discover the Secrets of the Universe

Author: Benjamin Alire Sáenz (b. 1954)
First published: 2012
Type of work: Novel
Type of plot: Realism
Time of plot: 1987
Locale: El Paso, Texas

Principal characters

Aristotle "Ari" Mendoza, an angry but loveable fifteen-year-old
Liliana "Lilly" Mendoza, Ari's mother
Santiago "Jaime" Mendoza, Ari's father
Dante Quintana, Ari's friend; an outgoing, intelligent, and eccentric fifteen-year-old
Sam Quintana, Dante's father
Soledad Quintana, Dante's mother

Courtesy of Simon & Schuster Books for Young Readers

The Story

Aristotle Mendoza, nicknamed Ari, is a Mexican American teenager who lives with his mother and father, a Vietnam veteran, in El Paso, Texas. He is the only child in his family still living at home, where he feels restricted and smothered. His twin sisters are twelve years older than he, and his brother, who is eleven years older, is in jail.

In the summer of 1987, when Ari is fifteen, he escapes to the public swimming pool each day, although he does not know how to swim. One day at the pool, he meets an outgoing boy named Dante Quintana. They connect immediately with one another and start meeting at the pool every day. As they become better friends over the course of the summer, they begin to learn more about each other's families. Both boys are Mexican American, but Dante, the more inquisitive of the two, is constantly questioning what exactly this term means and how important aspects of their cultural background are.

Ari, who is angry with his life, his parents, and the lack of any communication in his family, is generally not interested in the ideas of identity, reality, society, and culture that push Dante. However, as their friendship deepens, Ari starts to think about these issues as well. Together they begin to explore what it means to be Mexican Americans who live near the US-Mexico border in the late 1980s.

The relationship between the boys comes to its first significant moment during one of their walks when they see a couple of boys shooting birds with a BB gun. Ari's anger rears up and he chases the boys away, taking one of their guns, only to discover that they have already killed a bird. Dante and Ari bury the bird, reflecting on their own culture as "sparrows falling from the sky." The next day, Ari contracts a horrible fever and Dante comes by, bringing books of poetry and his own personal sketches in hopes that it will make him feel better. This brings them even closer together, although the anger that resides in Ari is always present. His anger keeps him distant from Dante, as it has distanced him from everyone in his life.

Once Ari recovers, the boys spend all their time together during the summer days finding things to occupy their time. One day, after a particularly strong hailstorm, Dante finds another hurt bird in the road. As he bends down to pick it up, a car comes around the bend at him. Ari jumps into the road and pushes his friend out of danger, but at the same time is hit by the car, breaking both of his legs. Dante now feels an even closer connection to Ari and shows this even more, something that Ari appreciates and yet deeply hates at the same time. Nevertheless, the two families also become close through the boys' friendship, and by the end of the summer both sets of parents have become friends as well.

Unfortunately, the Quintanas have to move to Chicago in the fall for Dante's father's job. The boys sustain their friendship for the next year through written letters. As each boy experiences new things such as kissing, drinking, drugs, and sexuality, Dante learns that he is gay. He embraces this and comes out to Ari, who is still unsure about most things in his life, especially his own sexual desires. He is sure, however, that he does not want to kiss boys. When Dante returns, their friendship is tested on a new level as Dante continues to embrace who he is and his deep connection to Ari, while Ari is still confused about his relationship with his family and with himself. It is through the attention and care of both sets of parents that Ari and Dante are able to come back together and find out more about the world than they could have done on their own.

Critical Evaluation

Among the traditional conventions that make up the young adult genre, there is perhaps nothing more important than the theme of identity. Adolescents of every age and from every culture and society face an important change in their lives as they move away from childhood and find their own individual identities as free, autonomous adults. During this time, one of the most important changes for teenagers is the development of sexuality. In his novel Alire Sáenz is quite adept at showing how integral sexuality is to identity.

Set in 1987, the novel has the potential to be outdated very quickly as attitudes toward sexuality, technology, and world cultures change rapidly. However, Alire Sáenz does not rely on period details to drive his narrative. With the exception of the absence of cellular phones or the Internet, this story could take place at any time. Instead, the author's introspective narrative is propelled by the complications and conflicts that arise as the main characters explore their friendship and multiple, interconnected facets of their personal identities. While readers see Ari and Dante's strong sense of a shared history and culture, as well as the ethnocentrism and prejudice they encounter, readers also see the struggle that Dante and Ari face with respect to their own sexuality. For example, when Dante writes to Ari and tells him about kissing a girl and liking it, Ari wonders himself what that will feel like for him. It is not until the end of the book, when each character is honest with himself about his sexuality, that both protagonists are able take the next step toward adulthood.

Aaron Horton, MA

Further Reading

"From Border Life to Len/Faulkner." *Foreword Reviews* 16.3 (2013): 14–15. *Literary Reference Center*. Web. 16 Dec. 2015. <http://search.ebscohost.com/login.aspx?direct=true&db=lfh&AN=87991509&site=lrc-live>.

Hunt, Jonathan. Rev. of *Aristotle and Dante Discover the Secrets of the Universe*, by Benjamin Alire Sáenz. *Horn Book Magazine* 1 Mar. 2012: 120. *Literary Reference Center*. Web. 17 Dec. 2015. <http://search.ebscohost.com/login.aspx?direct=true&db=lfh&AN=71797938&site=lrc-live>.

Smith, Roger. "Benjamin Alire Sáenz." *Guide to Literary Masters & Their Works* (2007): 1. *Literary Reference Center*. Web. 16 Dec. 2015. <http://search.ebscohost.com/login.aspx?direct=true&db=lfh&AN=103331LM66229790306491&site=lrc-live>.

The Astonishing Life of Octavian Nothing, Traitor to the Nation

Author: M. T. Anderson (b. 1968)
First published: *Volume I: The Pox Party* (2006)
   Volume II: The Kingdom on the Waves (2008)
Type of work: Novel
Type of plot: Historical Fiction
Time of plot: 1759–76
Locales: Boston, Massachusetts; Cambridge, Massachusetts; Norfolk, Virginia

Principal characters

Octavian, an enslaved African American teenager who is being educated
Cassiopeia, Ocatvian's mother, who was transported from West Africa
Dr. Trefusis, Ocatvian's tutor
Mr. Josiah Gitney, the head of the Novanglian College of Lucidity
Pro Bono, a fellow slave who befriends Octavian, later a soldier fighting for the British Army
Mr. Richard Sharpe, a businessman and slave owner
Private Evidence Goring, a militiaman whom Octavian befriends

The Story

Octavian is raised by his mother, Cassiopeia, and a group of scientists and thinkers who train him in math, literature, music, and other topics of classical education. They call their project the Novanglian College of Lucidity. The men, led by Mr. Josiah Gitney, also conduct cruel experiments on animals and refuse to let Octavian enter one room in the house. The bizarre nature of this living situation makes Octavian shut down often, trying not to feel any emotions. The mother and son found themselves there after Cassiopeia, who had been a princess in the West African empire of Oyo, was exiled from her home and eventually forced to the United States. The men of the college had offered to take her in, but only if they could educate Octavian. Eventually, Octavian learns that he is a slave and that the men are experimenting to determine whether African people are less intelligent and skilled than European people. While he longs to be free, he also recognizes that his childhood is fairly stable, filled with music and learning even as the rumblings of the American Revolution occur outside

his door in Boston. After the benefactor of the college dies, his heir, Lord Cheldthorpe, comes to visit and flirts with Cassiopeia and bonds with Octavian. When Cassiopeia gets into an argument with him, however, she and Octavian are whipped publically and the college loses its funding.

Octavian is deeply disturbed by the whipping. A new benefactor, Mr. Richard Sharpe, comes to the college and intends to change everything. Octavian's arts education is cut off, and he is put to work as a house servant, facing regular whippings. Another slave, Pro Bono, helps him navigate this new life. Mr. Sharpe makes Octavian play the violin to a paying audience while dressed as the devil one night, then whips him for not being cheerful enough. More prewar violence erupts in Boston, and Octavian learns that Mr. Sharpe actually wants him to fail the experiment in order to prove his opinion that slavery is moral. The people of the college flee the city in fear of violence, and Bono is given away to bribe a benefactor. Mr. Gitney throws a pox party to give everyone smallpox vaccine, and young men with guns watch over the event. Finally, Octavian learns the white people are worried the British have convinced the slaves to rebel. He then finds a key to the house, hidden for him by Bono. As the war spreads, Cassiopeia succumbs to smallpox and dies. When Octavian learns she is being dissected, he escapes the house.

Octavian struggles to find work or food as a runaway. He then joins the militia that is fighting the British, playing music for them and befriending a man named Private Evidence Goring, but remains depressed. Bono has also escaped from his new home. When Octavian's militia finally does battle, the men end up confused and hiding in a ditch. Eventually, Octavian walks into the middle of the shooting, clearly not caring whether he lives or dies, but Goring manages to save him. The company travels to Cambridge, where they rest and wait for the next battle. Octavian works tirelessly building defenses, believing that his work is fighting for freedom. Goring and Octavian split up, as Octavian joins a company of other black men and Irish men. After a bloody encounter, Octavian briefly rejoins Goring, playing music to raise the crowd's spirits. Goring then finds an opportunity for Octavian to become a spy, but when Octavian agrees, it turns out to be a trick, with Mr. Sharpe capturing him again.

Bound in painful devices back at the college, Octavian turns his body off to pain and thinks philosophically about his situation. He refuses to eat and drink for several days and thinks about the fact that many slaves were fighting in the war, but they probably would not receive their freedom. Mr. Sharpe, Mr. Gitney, and others summon Octavian to interview him, and Octavian argues with Mr. Sharpe about slavery. When things escalate, however, Dr. Trefusis (one of Octavian's tutors) serves tea, which turns out to be drugged. As the others faint, he and Octavian make their escape. Although Octavian does not know how he will survive, exactly, he knows that he is heading to freedom.

Octavian escapes to Boston, which is ruled by the British, and decides that joining the British army is the best way to ensure his freedom. Dr. Trefusis is ill and possibly dying, and the two of them find shelter with an older, impoverished woman. Desperate for food, Octavian takes a job with an orchestra, playing concerts in a city surrounded by violence and fires. When rebel attacks escalate nearby, however, Octavian tracks down the governor of Virginia, Lord Dunmore. In exile, the governor has promised freedom to any slave who fights the rebels, and Octavian joins the Royal Ethiopian Regiment in Norfolk, where he encounters Bono once more. The men in this group wear shirts declaring "Liberty to Slaves."

The men call Octavian "Buckra," which is slang for a white person, because he is able to read and write. From them, he learns about different African spiritual and cultural traditions for the first time, and he begins recording their stories. He also meets someone from the same nation as his mother. When Norfolk is attacked and burned, however, Dunmore takes shelter in his ship while smallpox rapidly spreads. As the black soldiers run out of food, they have no choice but to head back to shore, becoming violent in their starvation. Soon, word spreads that not all the men will receive freedom, but instead many of them will be sent to the Caribbean sugar plantations. Octavian contemplates what the term "liberty" means in a world like this, then heads off into the territories to find a new life.

Critical Evaluation

In terms of content, literary style, narrative structure, vocabulary, and nearly every other aspect of the two-part series, The Astonishing Life of Octavian Nothing, Traitor to the Nation is markedly more challenging than most young adult novels. Readers must have a basic knowledge of the colonial history of the United States (including the ability to read eighteenth-century

English), follow regular switches in perspective and setting, and read long stretches of philosophy and history within the fast-moving plot.

For many readers, however, perhaps one of the biggest challenges will be the stance that the novel takes toward the history of the United States. While historical narratives have increasingly taken a more honest accounting of the travesties rooted in the founding of the United States (most notably, the horrific slave trade and the genocide of Native American populations), the complexity with which this series approaches its topic is rare, especially in literature for young adults. In the series, even white leaders who might claim they have the best interests of the enslaved black population in mind prove to be selfish and cruel, and there is no government or ruling class that can be trusted to look out for more than its own interests in the long run. The violence of whipping, of the plague of smallpox, of cruel medical experiments on living humans, of the separation of families—all of these historically accurate atrocities are written in unflinching language, the novel refusing to shelter its readers from the horrors of its moment.

While it may seem that the novel makes a lot of demands on its readers, the demands work together for an engrossing and challenging literary experience. To face such dark subject matter without the full force of literary styles and techniques available—that is, to use simplified language or easy plot devices in order to craft this story—would be to sell short the complexities it explores. It is because of this that the final moment of the novel is as powerful and evocative as it is. Octavian, having realized the deception of Lord Dunmore and the violent fate that awaits him yet again, turns toward the western United States, heading off alone once more in search of freedom. Readers know, of course, that an end will not come in his lifetime, just as readers know that the westward movement in the United States was actually a further spreading of violence and genocide. When readers reach this closing scene, then, they can both appreciate and share Octavian's hope while also knowing the tragedy that reality will likely bring. The novel never accepts easy answers, just as Octavian refuses to give up the intellect and imagination that have helped him survive. This is why a story of violence and slavery can still search for freedom, placed in that historical moment when the outcomes now known have yet to be written. Moreover, while the details of Octavian's ordeal are particular to his circumstance and may seem removed from modern daily life, certain of his experiences, such as the scrutiny Octavian undergoes by those examining his intellect and the revelation that the world as he has known it is not as it seemed, are likely to be familiar to the novel's intended audience of older adolescents.

T. Fleischmann, MFA

Further Reading

Anderson, M. T. "Author M.T. Anderson on Octavian Nothing." Interview by Farai Chideya. *Morning Edition*. NPR, 25 Jan. 2007. Web. 4 Mar. 2015. <http://www.npr.org/templates/story/story.php?storyId=7060904>.

Griswold, Jerry. "The War for Independence." Rev. of *The Astonishing Life of Octavian Nothing*, by M. T. Anderson. *Sunday Book Review*. New York Times, 7 Nov. 2008. Web. 4 Mar. 2015. <http://www.nytimes.com/2008/11/09/books/review/Griswold-t.html?pagewanted=all>.

Ulanowicz, Anastasia. "American Adam, American Cain: Johnny Tremain, Octavian Nothing, and the Fantasy of American Exceptionalism." *Lion & The Unicorn* 35.3 (2011): 267–95. *MLA International Bibliography*. Web. 12 Mar. 2015. <http://search.ebscohost.com/login.aspx?direct=true&db=mzh&AN=2012025655&site=eds-live>.

Baby Be-Bop

Author: Francesca Lia Block (b. 1962)
First published: 1995
Type of work: Novella
Type of plot: Fantasy; Realism
Time of plot: Unspecified
Locale: Los Angeles, California

Principal characters

Dirk McDonald, a gay teenager
Pup Lambert, Dirk's best friend
Grandma Fifi, Dirk's grandmother and guardian
Gazelle Sunday, Dirk's great-grandmother
Dirby "Be-Bop" McDonald, Dirk's father, a beat poet
Just Silver, Dirk's mother
Duck Drake, Dirk's future love interest

The Story

Dirk McDonald has always known he is gay, but he has never told anyone, instead adopting a tough persona to avoid harassment. Dirk lives with his Grandma Fifi, but is essentially a loner until he meets Pup Lambert, who introduces Dirk to cigarettes, marijuana, and petty theft. The boys are inseparable until Dirk tries to confess his love; Pup, struggling with internalized homophobia, rejects Dirk and breaks off their friendship.

Emotionally numb, Dirk becomes a loner again. When he turns sixteen, Grandma Fifi gives him her antique convertible, which has a golden lamp as a hood ornament. Now sporting a Mohawk haircut and black clothes, Dirk drives all over Los Angeles to various punk rock and slam dance clubs. One night some white supremacists call Dirk a "faggot" and then brutally beat him. The pain makes Dirk want to die, but he staggers home with the lamp hood ornament and collapses.

Dirk wakes in his room and sees an elderly woman named Gazelle Sunday, who agrees to tell Dirk the story of her unusual dress if he will dance with her. Gazelle was raised by a grim aunt who kept her locked in their apartment working as a seamstress, until one day when a stranger asked Gazelle to make a beautiful satin dress for his beloved. When the dress was finished, he gave it to Gazelle herself, along with a mysterious golden lamp. Shortly thereafter Gazelle learned that she was pregnant and gave birth to a daughter named Fifi.

Astonished to learn that Gazelle is his great-grandmother, Dirk asks her to tell him more. Gazelle describes Fifi's childhood, including Fifi's friendship with two gay men and her eventual marriage to Derwood McDonald, who died when their son Dirby was only five years old. To support Dirby, Fifi took a job as a film studio animator and was given Gazelle's lamp as a going-away present. Gazelle then ends her story, and Dirk dances with her before she fades away.

When Dirk next opens his eyes, his guitar begins to play itself and his father, Dirby, materializes. Dirby relates how ostracized he felt until he discovered jazz music and the beat poetry scene. When he finally recited his own poetry, he enthralled the crowds with both his words and the telekinetic effect he had on the objects around him. Dirby fell in love with a woman named Just Silver, who soon became pregnant with Dirk himself. Dirby and Just Silver liked taking long drives to escape civilization, until one night they "gave up on life." Dirby tells Dirk they did not consciously commit suicide, but they also did not fight to live. Dirby urges Dirk to do things differently.

Dirk's mother, Just Silver, then appears and encourages Dirk to tell his own story into the golden lamp. As Dirk begins to speak, a genie emerges, whom Dirk recognizes as Gazelle's strange benefactor. Dirk and the genie fly to a little white house by the ocean, where a new story about a young surfer named Duck Drake unfolds. Like Dirk, Duck is afraid to tell his family he is gay, and he despairs of ever finding true love. Dirk realizes that the genie is showing him his future lover, which gives him a reason to live. Dirk then wakes up in the hospital with Grandma Fifi by his side, and she tells Dirk that they have been trading stories of the past, present, and future.

Critical Evaluation

Written at a time when gay teenagers rarely felt they could be open about their sexuality, *Baby Be-Bop* provides a poignant examination of the psychological and physical threats these teens faced—and continue to face in the twenty-first century. The narrative, consisting of interweaving tales filled with colorful and evocative details, conveys that the power of stories can be restorative for both storyteller and listener, especially those who initially feel they do not have interesting stories of their own to tell. *Baby Be-Bop* also emphasizes the importance of family communication: for instance, once Dirk learns that Fifi's two best friends in her young adulthood were gay men, he knows that he can tell her about his own homosexuality without fear. Had he learned more about her life earlier, he might have spared himself much anxiety.

Another theme the author explores is that of finding one's place in the world. Dirk learns that both his father Dirby and his future lover Duck had to struggle to find communities in which they felt natural and accepted; this gives Dirk hope that he too will someday be surrounded by many loving friends and family members. This heartfelt message will be particularly appealing to young adult readers.

Although a standalone work, *Baby Be-Bop* also functions as part of the author's award-winning series beginning with her debut book, *Weetzie Bat* (1989). In that novel, a slightly older Dirk is Weetzie's best friend and is now openly gay. *Baby Be-Bop* serves as Dirk's backstory, yet also furthers the author's ongoing exploration of the curative power of art that began in *Weetzie Bat* and continues in several additional novels. The surreal nature of these books, including Dirk's visions while he lies unconscious, can also be considered a precursor to the increasingly popular magic realism subgenre of young adult literature.

Amy Sisson, MS, MLS

Further Reading

Dorning, Anne-Marie. "Library Book Riles Small Wisconsin Town." *ABC News*. ABC News, 19 June 2009. Web. 1 Apr. 2015. <http://abcnews.go.com/US/story?id=7874866>.

Knoth, Maeve Visser. "Baby Be-Bop." *Horn Book Magazine* 72.2 (1996): 202–03. *Literary Reference Center*. Web. 30 Mar. 2015. <http://search.ebscohost.com/login.aspx?direct=true&db=lfh&AN=9603203707&site=lrc-live>.

Trites, Roberta S. *Disturbing the Universe: Power and Repression in Adolescent Literature*. Iowa City: U of Iowa P, 2000. Print.

Ball Don't Lie

Author: Matt de la Peña
First published: 2005
Type of work: Novel
Type of plot: Realism
Time of plot: 1990s
Locale: East Los Angeles, California; Venice, California

Principal characters

Travis "Sticky" Reichard, a seventeen-year-old high-school basketball player
Annie, Sticky's sixteen-year-old girlfriend
Dante, Sticky's teammate at the Lincoln Rec Center
Dave, Sticky's friend and teammate
Sin, Sticky's friend and teammate

The Story

The narrative of *Ball Don't Lie* begins with a broadly focused look at the basketball games that take place at the fictional Lincoln Rec Center, where young men gather to play with and against each other on the courts. As the narrator describes the intricacies and details of the games and the players, one teen in particular emerges from the crowd with his duct-taped Walkman: Travis Reichard, who has been known most of his life as Sticky. At seventeen, Sticky seems to care only about girls and basketball, and if he is not on the court, he is usually with his

Courtesy of Penguin Random House

girlfriend, Anh-thu, whom everyone calls Annie. The story's narrative centers mostly around Sticky and relates how the traumatic events from his past, which are told to readers through Sticky's memories, affect who Sticky is at seventeen as well as how life-altering events in his present will determine his future.

When the story opens, Sticky is living in the latest in a series of foster homes. He has been in foster care since his mother committed suicide when he was six years old, and through a series of flashbacks, Sticky shares his memories, both good and bad, of several of the foster families he has lived with. Francine, a widow with three grown children, was Sticky's first foster mother and provided a loving and stable environment for the boy. When she was diagnosed with cancer, however, Sticky had to leave her home and was assigned to another foster family. In one those homes, his foster father burned the back of Sticky's ear with a cigarette because he had knocked the man's marijuana onto the carpet. Sticky would live in two other foster homes by the time readers are introduced to him.

Sticky has survived a great deal in his short life, but he pushes aside his memories of his drug-addicted mother and her abusive boyfriend, their struggle to live, and his mother's suicide. He develops obsessive compulsive

disorder (OCD), which makes him engage in frequent and repeated rituals such as tying and untying his shoes and constantly washing his hands. A positive side effect of the disorder, however, is that he practices basketball incessantly, and it is on the basketball courts at school and at the Lincoln Rec Center that he finally develops a connection to what becomes a surrogate family for him. One of Sticky's teammates at the center, Dante, is tough and everyone knows not to mess with him. Sticky's two closest school friends, Dave and Sin, are confidants. Despite being one of the few white people in the poorer areas of his city, Sticky finds that he can truly express himself and earn respect on the basketball courts.

On Sticky and Annie's six-month anniversary, Sticky steals champagne in order to celebrate with her. As they start talking about their future, Sticky tells Annie that he has been invited to attend a basketball camp. Although Annie is worried she will not see him much over the summer, he reassures her that attending the camp means can lead to college basketball, which means they can live together while he goes to school. Both are excited at the prospect of improving their lives, but later in the summer in a desperate attempt to do something nice for Annie, Sticky robs a man with a knife. The man is a drug dealer, and after Sticky buys Annie a stuffed bear, he is hunted down by the man who then shoots Sticky in the hand and ends Sticky's dreams of playing college basketball and any hope for the future. Without his physical gift or his outlet for negative emotions, Sticky must find a way to deal with life on its own terms, but first he must learn to accept himself and his past.

Critical Evaluation

Ball Don't Lie is a traditional young adult novel in many respects. It is a coming-of-age novel that follows a teenage boy as he tries to determine who he is and what life means to him. As someone who has experienced a traumatic and dysfunctional early childhood and who has been moved around in foster-care, Sticky does not have a strong sense of self nor a healthy connection to his past. His life at seventeen is a result of a number of failed living situations with foster parents, and he struggles to find a positive life path. Basketball and the other teenagers he plays with at school and at the community center help to fill that void and help him to develop an inner knowledge and purpose. It is through Sticky's connection to the game and his chosen family of teammates that de la Peña creates a narrative that is traditional yet not entirely conventional.

This type of storyline is common among many of de la Peña's young adult novels. Within the framework of traditional young adult themes and conventions, de la Peña adds details and constructs perspectives and voices that are unconventional within the current genre. The use of an inner-city dialect has become more common in young adult novels in the twenty-first century, but what makes de la Peña's characters unique are their idiosyncrasies. For example, Sticky is not just an inner-city basketball player. His obsessive-compulsive disorder creates other limitations for him but also creates myriad ways for readers to view and connect to his situation. The characters and storyline within *Ball Don't Lie* create various and relatable perspectives within the traditional conventions of the young adult genre.

Aaron Horton, MA

Further Reading

Hayman, Stacey. "Wouldn't You Like to Know . . . Matt de la Peña." *Voya.* VOYA, 28 Sept. 2014. Web. 18 Dec. 2015. <http://www.voyamagazine.com/2014/09/28/wouldnt-you-like-to-know-matt-de-la-pena/>.

Ribay, Randy. "What Makes a Good YA Urban Novel?" *Horn Book Magazine* 89.6 (2013): 48–53. *Academic Search Complete.* Web. 18 Dec. 2015. <http://search.ebscohost.com/login.aspx?direct=true&db=a9h&AN=91621806>.

Beautiful Creatures

Authors: Kami Garcia (b. 1972) and Margaret Stohl (b. 1967)
First published: 2009
Type of work: Novel
Type of plot: Paranormal
Time of plot: Early 2000s
Locale: Gatlin, South Carolina

Principal characters

Ethan Wate, the narrator of the story, a teen boy who has recently lost his mother
Lena Duchannes, a new girl in town and a Caster with supernatural powers, Ethan's love interest
Amarie "Amma" Treadeau, Ethan's main caretaker
Macon Ravenwood, Lena's reclusive uncle
Marian Ashcroft, a librarian at the Lunae Libri
Wesley "Link" Lincoln, Ethan's best friend

The Story

Ethan Wate thinks his hometown of Gatlin, South Carolina, is the most boring place on earth, and he cannot wait to leave. However, his sophomore year in high school reveals how wrong he is. As he begins the narration of the story in the middle of that year, he foreshadows that the story he is about to tell will take an unexpected turn.

In Ethan's dreams, he is holding onto a beautiful girl, but one of them falls, and he is devastated. He knows there is something special about these dreams, but he has no idea what they mean. Then, on his first day of school, he finds out that Macon Ravenwood, the town recluse, has moved his niece to town. The new girl, Lena Duchannes, is the girl from his dreams.

A connection is formed between the teens when Ethan stands up for Lena after some of the popular girls in his grade pick on her. He quickly realizes that Lena can talk to him without anyone else hearing. Though everyone warns against starting a relationship with Lena, he sees something special in her. That trait reveals itself as Ethan pursues her despite the opinions of others. Understanding that Ethan is different, Lena reveals her secret: she and her family members are all supernatural beings known as Casters.

The two are further tied together when they find an antique locket and are transported through time to relive a doomed romance between their ancestors, Genevieve Duchannes and Ethan Carter Wate. The romance was cursed, so Ethan and Lena have to fight that curse as they learn what happened to the earlier couple. The novel follows the pair as they fight the townspeople, dark magic, and the people who should most closely protect them. Lena dreads her approaching sixteenth birthday, when she will be claimed by either Light or Dark Caster force.

The story culminates on Lena's sixteenth birthday. At the claiming hour, Lena refuses to choose Dark or Light, but she almost loses Ethan after her Dark mother stabs him. She invokes the power of *The Book of Moons*, the same book that cursed their ancestors Genevieve and Ethan, and the book's price for saving Ethan is Macon's life, leaving Lena racked with guilt.

Critical Evaluation

One of the main themes of the novel is the way people deal with change. Ethan starts his narration by telling readers, "Nothing ever changed. . . . There were no surprises in Gatlin County." However, Ethan's life has been full of change in the last year, starting with his mother's death. After the loss of his mother, Ethan's father retreats to his study and avoids interaction with anyone, even the son who needs him. Another major change comes when Lena Duchannes arrives in town, and Ethan realizes they have been connected and cursed across generations.

Soon after this new girl walks into school, Ethan recognizes her as the girl from his dreams, literally. The dream connection leads to his discovery of a whole new world, a world where magic exists in the form of Casters. He learns that his family members, including his beloved Amma, have hidden things from him—important people, activities, and fears. One change he must confront is his father's behavior. While his father has spent the months following his wife's death hiding in a study, Ethan has had to move on with his life. Ethan believes that his father has been writing in his study. However, Ethan finds out that his father has not been writing anything. He has only been hiding. Ethan also learns that his family has a secret relative, another Ethan Wate. More important, he discovers his mother's involvement in the magical world that has remained hidden from most of the population of Gatlin. These changes turn Ethan's world upside down.

The fight between good and evil, characterized by Light and Dark Casters, is the central thematic idea of the novel. Lena knows that she will come into her full power at sixteen, and she spends most of the year before that birthday worrying whether she will be claimed as a Light Caster or a Dark one. If she becomes a Light Caster, she will continue to be a part of her family working to protect magic. However, she is deeply concerned that she will claimed as Dark because her mother, Sarafine, is one of the most powerful Dark Casters of the time, and her cousin Ridley was claimed by the Dark just months earlier. The Duchannes family curse that has been carried down through the generations since the Civil War also hangs over her head, and she struggles throughout the novel with control over her powers. Through this struggle, Lena and Ethan learn that their choices are more powerful than the destiny they have been told will control their fate. *Beautiful Creatures* is the first book in the four-part Caster Chronicles series.

Theresa L. Stowell, PhD

Further Information

Rev. of *Beautiful Creatures*, by Kami Garcia and Margaret Stohl. *Kirkus* 1 Dec. 2009: 95. *Literary Reference Center*. Web. 9 Nov. 2015. <http://search.ebscohost.com/login.aspx?direct=true&db=lfh&AN=47077576&site=lrc-live>.

Garcia, Kami, and Margaret Stohl. "*Beautiful Creatures* Authors: In Defense of Young Adult Paranormal Genre Fiction." Interview by Lily Rothman. *Time*. Time, 13 Feb. 2013. Web. 9 Nov. 2015. <http://entertainment.time.com/2013/02/13/beautiful-creatures-authors-in-defense-of-young-adult-paranormal-genre-fiction>.

Perez, Lidia. Rev. of Beautiful Creatures, by Kami Garcia and Margaret Stohl. *Journal of Adolescent & Adult Literacy* 54.2 (2010): 154. *Literary Reference Center*. Web. 9 Nov. 2015. <http://search.ebscohost.com/login.aspx?direct=true&db=lfh&AN=54303707&site=lrc-live>.

Better Nate than Ever

Author: Tim Federle (b. 1980)
First published: 2013
Type of work: Novel
Type of plot: Humorous
Time of plot: Early 2010s
Locale: Jankberg, Pennsylvania; New York City

Principal characters

Nathan "Nate" Foster, a short, hefty thirteen-year-old with aspirations of performing on Broadway
Libby Jones, Nate's best friend
Anthony Foster, Nate's sixteen-year-old brother, who is a jock and a jerk
Jordan Rylance, Libby's Facebook friend and an aspiring performer
Aunt Heidi, Nate's mother's younger sister, who lives and works in New York
Freckles, Heidi's roommate, a bartender at an oyster bar

The Story

Nate Foster and his best friend, Libby Jones, are such avid fans of musical theater that they use the titles of failed Broadway shows as epithets: the bigger the flop, the worse the curse. While his parents are away and his brother Anthony is supposed to be caring for him, Nate and Libby hatch a plan. They conspire to have Nate travel to New York City from his small home town in western Pennsylvania, where he is constantly bullied for his short stature and pudgy shape. Although he is still undecided about his own sexuality, he is continually ridiculed and called antigay slurs—even by his brother. In Manhattan, he hopes to audition for the lead role of Elliott in a Broadway musical adaptation of *E.T.: The Extra-Terrestrial*. With his escape kit (extra underwear, a water bottle, deodorant, his older brother's fake ID, cash, and his mother's ATM card in his school bookbag), he boards a Greyhound bus and heads east on his own.

Arriving in the city, Nate finds the studio where casting for the musical is taking place. Among the thousands of hopeful actors, he runs into Jordan Rylance, Libby's long-distance friend, who is there with his overbearing stage mother. After filling out an application, on which Nate lies about his age, he is about to be eliminated from consideration because he is unaccompanied by an adult, when his Aunt Heidi, his mother's estranged younger sister who dabbles in show business, shows up and vouches for him.

Thus allowed to audition among a group of one hundred aspirants, Nate meets the casting director, Rex Rollins, Sammy the pianist, choreographer Garret Charles, and other members of the creative group behind the show. Nate sings a tune and recites an original monologue—the speech he devised to overcome possible objections to why a minor would be buying a bus ticket, which impresses the creatives, and he is given pages of the script to memorize. When it is his turn to perform, Nate recites and acts out not only the lead role, but all the parts, complete with different voices and mannerisms. The creative team asks him to remain in the city for a few days for a possible callback.

Wondering where he will stay until the studio calls, Nate wanders the city, using subterfuge and glibness to dine on free chips and salsa at a Mexican restaurant. He calls Libby on his ancient cell phone and learns she is stalling his parents, who have threatened to call the police. With few other options available, Nate meanders past gay bars and shady neighborhoods to the Aw Shucks oyster bar where Heidi works to seek her help. She is not pleased to see him. Her good-looking roommate, Freckles, the male bartender, however, treats Nate kindly. Heidi grudgingly allows Nate to sleep on the futon of her small apartment. He finds Heidi's album containing show-biz photos; they talk and she reveals she has been dating a guy named Troy for seven years, wants to get married, and have kids.

Early the following morning, Nate's mother Sherrie, shows up drunk to collect her son and confronts Heidi. Freckles takes Nate to breakfast and during their conversation admits he is gay. The studio calls to tell Nate he did not make the cut for the role of Elliott, though Heidi encourages him by saying anything could still happen. As the two sisters reconcile a long-held grudge, Nate receives a call from the studio again.

Critical Evaluation

Narrated in first-person present tense by eighth-grader Nate, who is by turns self-deprecating and self-confident, *Better Nate than Ever* is a lighthearted and exuberant story about the value of being oneself, ignoring detractors, and following a dream.

The first in what may turn out to be a series (a sequel, *Five, Six, Seven, Nate*, was published in 2014), *Better Nate than Ever* introduces a main character with a distinctive voice and a personality still in flux. Middle-grade readers should be able to easily identify with Nate's multiple concerns about who he really is and what he truly wants from life. Readers of any age will appreciate Nate's whimsically skewed viewpoint, his half-sophisticated and half-naïve outlook, and his dogged determination to overcome a series of obstacles along the path toward achievement.

Humor plays a large part in softening the sharp edges of some of the many issues dealt with in the novel: being the target of bullies, the difficulties of growing up in a dysfunctional family, questions of sexual orientation, and the great gaps in understanding between adolescents and adults. Clever chapter headings—"A Salsa Crawl is Not a Dance Move," "A Couch That Thinks It's an Envelope," "A Boy Soprano with a Ballsy Chest Voice"— add to the fun both by describing the action and Nate's current state of mind. For ambitious readers who might hope, like Nate, to eventually pursue a career in acting or a related field in the performing arts, the novel contains a wealth of details and subtle hints about the casting process to whet any would-be thespian's appetite.

Jack Ewing

Further Reading

Balaban, Bob. "Rising Stars." Rev. of *Better Nate than Ever*, by Tim Federle, and *I Represent Sean Rosen*, by

Jeff Baron. *Sunday Book Review*. New York Times, 8 Mar. 2013. Web. 9 Sept. 2015. <http://www.nytimes.com/2013/03/10/books/review/better-nate-than-ever-and-i-represent-sean-rosen.html?_r=0>.

Wong, Curtis M. "Tim Federle's 'Better Nate than Ever' Is a Glittering Love Letter to Broadway, Bullied Gay Teens." *Huffpost Gay Voices*. TheHuffingtonPost.com, 30 Mar. 2013. Web. 9 Sept. 2015. <http://www.huffingtonpost.com/2013/03/12/tim-federle-better-nate-than-ever-broadway-gay_n_2860050.html>.

Between Shades of Grey

Author: Ruta Sepetys (b. 1967)
First published: 2011
Type of work: Novel
Type of plot: Historical fiction
Time of plot: 1941–42
Locale: Lithuania; Russia; Siberia

Principal characters

Lina Vilkas, an artistic fifteen-year-old girl
Elena Vilkas, Lina's Russian-speaking humanitarian mother
Jonas Vilkas, Lina's ten-year-old brother
Andrius Arvydas, a resourceful seventeen-year-old boy
Nikolai Kretzsky, an NKVD guard

The Story

The Vilkas family—father Kostas, a university provost; mother Elena; teenager Lina; and young boy Jonas—have lived since 1939 under Russian occupation in Lithuania. In mid-1941, Soviet secret police come to collect those considered to be anti-regime: doctors, teachers, lawyers, and intellectuals, along with their families. Some will be permanently eliminated. Others will be imprisoned. Many will be deported to toil at forced labor camps.

Kostas has already been spirited away separately, as Elena, Lina and Jonas hastily pack their belongings. They are marched at bayonet point along with dozens of other unfortunates to waiting trucks, driven to a train station, and herded into cattle cars. While other families are split up, Elena bribes guards to keep her children with her. Some of the people crowded into one car along with the Vilkas family are familiar, while others are strangers. Lina meets handsome Andrius Arvydas,

and secretly sketches his portrait. While waiting for their train to leave, Lina and Jonas slip away to explore another, newly arrived train and discover their father is aboard. From behind a locked door, he tells them the two trains will be connected and taken to Siberia.

Finally, the train begins to move, traveling eastward for many days. Each day, the train stops and a guard hands over two buckets, one filled with water for drinking, one with animal feed for eating. Over the course of the journey, people begin to die, and their bodies are unceremoniously thrown out. After six weeks, the train stops, and some prisoners are sold to local inhabitants as slaves. The captives learn that Russia is at war with Germany.

The remaining prisoners are eventually delivered to a collective potato and beet farm in Altai, Siberia, where they live in tumbledown shacks in the harsh, unforgiving environment and work long hours at various chores under the control of sadistic guards—although Kretzsky, a young guard, seems sympathetic. Lina's artistic skills come in handy when the secret police employ her to sketch portraits and maps. Andrius's mother becomes a prostitute to earn extra privileges and food, and other prisoners bribe locals to send messages to loved ones from a nearby village. The prisoners begin to suspect one another of becoming spies for the Soviets. Jonas falls ill from scurvy and malnourishment, but Andrius saves his life by feeding him stolen food.

After many months, certain prisoners, including the Vilkas family, are winnowed out and placed on another train that travels north and east. At the Angara River, they board barges for weeks of travel, crossing the Arctic Circle, before arriving at the Laptev Sea. The prisoners are to build guard barracks, a bakery, and a fish factory, and they must meanwhile live in deplorable conditions in huts hand-built from scraps of wood and other debris. They suffer from frostbite, dysentery, and typhus, and many die from disease, suicide, exposure, or execution. Finally, a Russian civilian doctor arrives and orders that the sick prisoners be fed soup and raw fish in an effort to improve their health. The spirits of those who survive are uplifted with the arrival of spring.

An epilogue, dated 1995, reveals Lina's ultimate fate. Construction workers unearth a box containing her writings and drawings, buried in 1954 after she returned home following twelve years' imprisonment, only to find the Soviets still in control and ready to persecute those who mention what transpired during their captivity. She buried her work, like a time capsule, in the hope that someone would find it and tell the world what happened.

Critical Evaluation

Among other honors, *Between Shades of Gray* was named one of 2011's best children's books by *Publishers Weekly*, won the International Literacy Association's 2012 Children's and Young Adults' Book Award for young adult fiction, and was a finalist for the 2012 William C. Morris YA Debut Award. The novel tells a story reminiscent of the many fictional and nonfictional works written in the wake of the Holocaust that detail horrors surrounding the persecution and extermination of Jews, gypsies, Communists, the mentally ill, homosexuals, and other groups of people deemed undesirable in Nazi Germany. However, Ruta Sepetys's novel lays bare an equally awful and largely unknown historical event that began during the same time period and was overshadowed by the massive scale of Nazi Germany's final solution. As the author, who is of Lithuanian heritage, notes at the end, untold thousands of Lithuanians, Latvians, and Estonians were subjected to the terror of Soviet domination for a half century.

The story is told in first person through the eyes of impressionable, artistic Lina Vilkas, who represents a typical individual swept up in Soviet suppression. Incidents are reported starkly, via matter-of-fact narration in brief chapters, like black-and-white snapshots whose images linger in the reader's memory. A young woman, still bloody from giving birth, is hustled aboard a truck along with her newborn baby, both considered property of the state. The body of a man is pinned to a cabin wall with a stake for a minor transgression. An old man has his teeth yanked out with pliers for stealing a beet. Frozen bodies, stacked like cordwood, are partially eaten by foxes. Lina draws such scenes to preserve them for future generations.

At the same time, to preserve her own sanity, Lina's mind often escapes to better times in the past. Such scenes reveal bits of Lithuanian tradition and culture, and the credo by which the Vilkas family lives: to stand for what is right, without expectation of gratitude or reward. The novel's title refers to the observation that people, whether Lithuanian or Russian, are neither all good nor all bad—neither black nor white, but of varying shades of gray.

Jack Ewing

Further Reading

Barclay, Alegria. "Ruta Sepetys: Up Close and Personal." *Hub.* YALSA, 28 Mar. 2014. Web. 24 Sept. 2015. <http://www.yalsa.ala.org/thehub/2014/03/28/ruta-sepetys-up-close-and-personal/>.

Driscoll, Molly. "*Between Shades of Gray*—Probably Not the Book You're Thinking of." Rev. of *Between Shades of Gray*, by Ruta Sepetys. *Christian Science Monitor*. Christian Science Monitor, 3 May 2012. Web. 24 Sept. 2015. <http://www.csmonitor.com/Books/chapter-and-verse/2012/0503/Between-Shades-of-Gray-probably-not-the-book-you-re-thinking-of>.

Schneider, Dean. Rev. of *Between Shades of Gray*, by Ruta Sepetys. *Horn Book Magazine* 1 May 2011: 103. *Literary Reference Center*. Web. 9 Oct. 2015. <http://search.ebscohost.com/login.aspx?direct=true&db=lfh&AN=60126142&site=lrc-live>.

Brown Girl Dreaming

Author: Jacqueline Woodson (b. 1963)
First published: 2014
Type of work: Poetry
Type of plot: Memoir
Time of plot: Early 1960s to 1970s
Locales: South Carolina; Ohio; Brooklyn, New York

Principal characters

Jacqueline "Jackie" Woodson, a young African American girl, the speaker
Daddy Gunnar, Jackie's maternal grandfather
Mary Anne Irby, Jackie's mother
Odella "Dell" Woodson, Jackie's older sister
Hope Woodson, Jackie's older brother
Maria, Jackie's best friend, a Puerto Rican girl
Robert Irby, Jackie's maternal uncle
Caroline "Kay" Irby, Jackie's maternal aunt

The Story

Jacqueline Woodson is born in 1963, in the midst of the civil rights movement. Hers is one of the only black families in their Ohio town. Her mother, however, comes from South Carolina and always considers the South home. When Jacqueline is only three months old, her mother brings her and her siblings, Hope and Dell, there to meet their grandparents. Her mother teaches the children that one has to behave differently around white people in the South. Not long after, her mother leaves their father, and the family relocates to South Carolina.

There, the children begin to call their kind grandfather Daddy, and while their mother is happy, she misses her sister, Caroline "Kay," who has moved to New York City. Her grandmother gets a job cleaning houses to help support them. Jacqueline's brother Hope becomes sluggish from the southern weather and depressed, and when the children begin to use southern words like "ain't" and "ma'am," their mother punishes them, wanting them to sound northern. Meanwhile, their mother goes to civil rights marches, their grandfather tells them about the importance of fighting for their rights, and Jacqueline hears women talking about white men spitting on them. Her mother begins to plan a move to New York City and eventually takes a bus there, promising to return for the children.

With her mother gone, Jacqueline begins to appreciate every moment of the South for the future memory it will become. The black high school is burned down by white people angry that the students are protesting, and their grandmother begins to raise them as Jehovah's Witnesses. Daddy, however—who seems to cough more every day—says that he does not believe in his wife's god. Finally, Jacqueline's mother writes and says that she is coming to get them, and also that she is pregnant again. Jacqueline wishes she could be in both New York and the South.

In the city, Jacqueline attends public school, and her mother continues to raise the children as Jehovah's Witnesses, even though it is not her own religion. Uncle Robert moves to New York and visits the children often, encouraging Jacqueline's habit of making up stories. She barely thinks of Ohio anymore but has forgotten the South, and Uncle Robert takes the children to visit there for the summer. They get to enjoy nature again, although the new baby, Roman, stays behind, sick from eating lead paint off the walls.

In the city, Jacqueline excels at athletic pursuits, becoming a tomboy, and finds a new best friend named Maria. She struggles in school with writing and reading, even though she still loves telling stories. The next summer Roman gets to visit South Carolina, but Daddy is so sick he barely leaves bed. In New York, Jacqueline starts writing a volume of poems about butterflies. She wants to grow an Afro, although her mother refuses to let her, and begins to listen to funk music. Uncle Robert

is arrested, and when the children go to visit him in prison upstate, it seems as though he is not the same person.

In the spring, the children go to the South again, arriving just before Daddy dies. After that, their grandmother moves to New York City. Jacqueline finally starts to write as well as she can tell stories, and when her uncle returns home, he inspires her with stories of revolution. She starts to see activists like Angela Davis and the Black Panthers in the news and feels stronger because of them. A teacher at school tells her that writing can be a way for her to make the world better. Jacqueline realizes that with all the different worlds she has lived in, she can also decide what kind of world she is going to make.

Critical Evaluation

"Memory is strange," Woodson states in her author's note, and it is the strangeness of memory that forms much of her memoir. Any recollection of childhood relies on memory, just as any fiction relies on imagination. The fact that Woodson writes her memoir in verse rather than prose, however, uniquely highlights both the strangeness of memory and the unique, dreamy, and sometimes fractured feelings of childhood.

By structuring the narrative through a succession of brief poems, Woodson is able to avoid the heavy emphasis on plot that defines most memoirs. While there is a clear sense of cause and effect between some events, and while the narrative does build, there is just as much room for brief, fleeting impressions—moments of insight and memory that are allowed to stand on their own merit. One clear example of this is the recurring section titled "How to Listen." Always only three lines long, "How to Listen" offers quick and succinct images, as in, "Kids are mean, Dell says. / Just turn away. Pretend we / know better than that." This dialogue is freed from the context of scene—readers do not know when Dell said this or what exactly prompted the moment. What readers do know is that this bit of wisdom resonated with Woodson, earning a spot in her memory that is ultimately more important the scene that surrounds it.

The experience of growing up (and of accessing one's memories of childhood) often feels this way—a collection of images, insights, and emotions that flow in and out of each other. Woodson regularly moves to new locations and faces the complexities of mid-century American politics, including the inspiration of revolution and protest and the horror of racism and violence. By embracing the poetic form, she is able to provide a memoir that mimics this period, both culturally and personally. There is not always clear logic here, nor always an apparent reason why things occur. Instead, there is an accumulation, a gathering of experiences that transform the child of the book into the adult author so beautifully rendering this story.

T. Fleischmann, MFA

Further Reading

Chambers, Veronica. "Where We Enter." Rev. of *Brown Girl Dreaming*, by Jacqueline Woodson. *Sunday Book Review*. New York Times, 22 Aug. 2014. Web. 4 Mar. 2015. <http://www.nytimes.com/2014/08/24/books/review/jacqueline-woodsons-brown-girl-dreaming.html>.

Woodson, Jacqueline. "Jacqueline Woodson on Growing Up, Coming Out and Saying Hi to Strangers." Interview by Terry Gross. *Fresh Air*. Natl. Public Radio, 10 Dec. 2014. *Points of View Reference Center*. Web. 28 Feb. 2015. <http://search.ebscohost.com/login.aspx?direct=true&db=pwh&AN=6XN2014121 01201&site=ehost-live>.

Bruiser

Author: Neal Shusterman (b. 1962)
First published: 2010
Type of work: Novel
Type of plot: Fantasy; Realism
Time of plot: 2011
Locale: United States

Principal characters

Brewster "Bruiser" Rawlins, sixteen-year-old boy
Tennyson Sternberger, Bruiser's friend and twin brother to Brontë
Brontë Sternberger, Bruiser's girlfriend and twin sister to Tennyson
Cody Rawlins, Bruiser's eight-year-old brother
Uncle Hoyt, Bruiser's alcoholic uncle
Katrina, Tennyson's girlfriend
Ozzie, the school bully

The Story

The story begins with Tennyson Sternberger, whose family is in flux. Tennyson's parents are struggling after an affair. Though they are still together, they argue constantly and neglect their parenting duties. This leaves Tennyson and his twin sister, Brontë, laboring to cope with the dysfunction in what was once a solid family life. Tennyson is protective of his sister, but his concern over Brewster "the Bruiser" Rawlins as her romantic interest is a reflection of his prejudice against Brewster's social standing. Once Tennyson sees Brewster in the locker room without a shirt, his views begin to change. Brewster's back is covered with injuries, and Tennyson understands that Brewster's nickname of the Bruiser has been earned, and that he "got that way from being the human receptacle of someone else's brutality." A few days later, Tennyson follows Bruiser home and witnesses first-hand his classmate's home life. The two teens begin to bond when Tennyson observes some strange details of Bruiser's reality.

Brontë does not care what Tennyson thinks of Brewster. She likes him, though she admits "my brother, Tennyson, was right about what first attracted me to Brewster. It was the stray dog thing. I've always had a dangerously unguarded place in my heart for strays." Once she becomes attracted to this shy boy, she wants to get to know him better, and she quietly pursues him, which is a new experience for Brewster. He has always kept himself separate from other people, and as the story progresses, his reasoning is revealed.

Brewster was born different. He takes on the pain and emotions of those he loves. Before he become involved with Brontë, this was limited to his brother Cody and his Uncle Hoyt. Once he begins to allow himself to care for Brontë, he opens himself up to both his girlfriend and her brother. When she hurts her ankle while on a picnic with Brewster, he takes the pain and heals her. When he attends a lacrosse game to watch Tennyson play, he absorbs the injuries immediately after Tennyson receives them. When Uncle Hoyt beats Cody, Bruiser feels the pain and bears the wounds. When Uncle Hoyt has a stroke, Bruiser almost dies. It is only as Brewster realizes that he is dying and must cut himself off that he saves himself.

Uncle Hoyt's death brings complications to Bruiser's and Cody's lives. Brontë and Tennyson talk their parents into fostering the boys, and the Sternbergers' home life improves as Bruiser's presence appears to heal the family and peace returns. The problem is that Bruiser has started to care for more people: the twins, their parents, and a few school friends. His body is battered, and his emotions are in constant turmoil as the blanket of tranquility that he creates shrouds the damage that he absorbs.

Once Brontë realizes this damage, she goes to the local pool to swim in order to work out her worries. She realizes "blame didn't shine on an individual. It was a floodlight cast on all of us." She works too hard in the pool, though, and just as she is trying to get out, she slips, bumps her head, and falls back in. Brewster and Tennyson find Brontë in time to save her from drowning, but part of her salvation happens because Bruiser takes on her critical situation.

As the family waits for Bruiser to come out of the ensuing coma, the twins recognize that he will never heal unless they take responsibility for their own emotions. It is a painful process, but they are able to care enough for him to pull their own damage back into themselves. With this show of unconditional love, which is what Brewster has always demonstrated for others, the twins again experience life as it is meant to be experienced, and Brewster returns to them because of their sacrifice.

Critical Evaluation
Shusterman uses a unique first-person narrator format for this novel. Though this point of view is commonly used in young adult literature, Shusterman changes readers' expectations by rotating through characters to tell the story from a variety of first-person perspectives. The novel starts with Tennyson as narrator, then it moves to Brontë, Brewster, and Cody. Once each of these characters has shared part of the story as it is perceived by them, the novel alternates between them and the story is told from each character's viewpoint as the plot unfolds

Beyond breaking the major format of the novel into sections based on these four characters, each section is broken further into short chapters. The chapter titles are single words and are based on a Sternberger family tradition—the vocabulary curse—which reflects the desire of the twins' literature professor parents to introduce their children to new words on a daily basis. Words like "symbiosis," "howlingly," "injurious," "trajectory," and "embolism" give insight into the characters and foreshadow the issues that will be expanded on in each chapter.

The most important theme of the novel is unconditional love, which is symbolized in Brewster's injuries. The injuries are a result the damages absorbed by Brewster from people he had a relationship with, and are not only physical but also emotional. Though he has been bombarded with pain intended for other people, he struggles with the aftereffects of the pain. It is only when other characters begin to realize that they must take responsibility for their own issues and

actions—thus showing Brewster the same unconditional love he has shown for them—that the young man begins to heal. This lesson about selfishness versus selflessness is a key element of the story.

Theresa L. Stowell, PhD

Further Reading
Cart, Michael. *Young Adult Literature: From Romance to Realism*. Chicago: American Library Assoc., 2010. Print.

Drew, Bernard A. *100 More Popular Young Adult Authors: Biographical Sketches and Bibliographies*. Westport: Libraries Unlimited, 2002. Print.

Rutan, Lynn. Rev. of *Bruiser*, by Neal Shusterman. *Booklist* 1 May 2010: 76. *Literary Reference Center Plus*. Web. 29 May 2015. <http://search.ebscohost.com/login.aspx?direct=true&db=lkh&AN=50656179&site=lrc-plus>.

Chaos Walking (Series)

Author: Patrick Ness (b. 1971)
First published: *The Knife of Never Letting Go* (2008)
The Ask and the Answer (2009)
The New World (2009)
Monsters of Men (2010)
The Wide, Wide Sea (2013)
Snowscape (2013)
Type of work: Novel
Type of plot: Science Fiction; Dystopian Fiction
Time of plot: Future
Locale: Space

Principal characters
Todd Hewitt, a young man who must discover his inner strength
Ben Logan, Todd's guardian and father figure
Viola Eade, a shipwrecked girl who becomes Todd's greatest support
The Return (1017), the Spackle Todd saved, the eventual leader of the alien race
Mayor Prentiss, the manipulative and evil leader of the male army
Mistress Coyle, a healer from Haven who becomes the leader of the rebellion forces
Davy Prentiss, son of Mayor Prentiss
The Sky, the leader of the Spackle

The Story

The Chaos Walking series is made up of three novels and three short stories. The series begins with a short-story prequel called "The New World" (2009), intended to accompany the first novel. In this story, a family is chosen to scout the planet toward which their troop of starships has been traveling for decades. On the eve of Viola Eade's thirteenth birthday, her parents reveal that they are the chosen family. Angry and frightened but also dutiful, Viola is not as sure of this new place as the adults. She struggles to find "hope" in the idea of this new place. Viola's fears about the elusive nature of hope are not unfounded. Something goes terribly wrong when her family's ship enters the planet's atmosphere, which is thicker than anticipated. The turbulence causes the ship to catch fire and crash, killing both of her parents. Viola is left alone.

The Knife of Never Letting Go (2008) begins almost immediately after Viola's crash landing. The main character in this novel is Todd Hewitt, a thirteen-year-old boy on the cusp of adulthood. The youngest member of a community of men, Todd lives with his guardians, Cillian and Ben, in Prentisstown. Todd's town, the last settlement on the planet as far as he knows, is full of men whose every thought can be heard by everyone—this phenomenon is known as the Noise.

In Prentisstown, boys achieve adulthood through the forced killing of a man within their community. Knowing the damage this will do to Todd and fearing for his life as he approaches his fourteenth birthday, his guardians send him away with a cryptic message to run to the next settlement. Todd's world is challenged with this order. He is about to discover that everything he has been told has been a lie. He believes Prentisstown contains the last survivors of the Spackle War, a battle between the humans who had sought refuge on the planet and the alien race that lived there. He has been told that the Noise is a result of a germ the Spackle—a supposedly horrible, aggressive race—used as a kind of biological warfare that also killed all of the women. Todd will discover along his journey that there are several other towns; that women are alive and well in other places; and that unless provoked, the Spackle are actually gentle creatures.

As he flees, Todd discovers Viola hiding in the swamp near his farm. Viola is the first female Todd can remember meeting, and he is shocked and curious about her lack of noise. The town preacher, Aaron, has also discovered Viola, but he has nefarious ideas about the

girl. Todd rescues Viola and takes her as he runs away from something he does not understand.

The novel follows the teens as they both seek refuge from an army that has amassed in Prentisstown and search for a place where Viola can contact her colony. They head for Haven, the largest and most technologically advanced city in the New World. Just when they think they have escaped both Aaron and the army, Viola is shot. Todd carries Viola toward Haven. When they arrive, they are greeted by Mayor Prentiss, who has taken over the city. It seems Todd and Viola's chaotic journey has been for nothing.

The second novel, *The Ask and the Answer* (2009), picks up within hours of the first novel's end. Todd and Viola have been separated. Mayor Prentiss has taken over Haven, dubbing it New Prentisstown and declaring himself President Prentiss. Viola is sent to a house of healing, where she will eventually be trained to join the medical ranks, while Todd is imprisoned by Prentiss.

Todd is forced to work alongside Davy Prentiss, the mayor's son. Their work is menial: guarding and farming a large group of Spackle. Todd grows angry over the treatment of the aliens, and he attempts to care for them as gently as possible. His kindness affects Davy, changing the other boy's attitude and beginning an unlikely friendship.

Mayor Prentiss's leadership is cruel. He has not only imprisoned the Spackle but also locked most of the town's women away. His followers mistreat the women, and one night one of his soldiers kills a young woman who is helping Viola send a message to her ships. This sets rebellion into action, and a group of women leave the city. The faction, which has dubbed themselves the Answer, is led by Mistress Coyle, a healer and former leader of Haven.

The events that follow create chaos for the town as well as for Todd and Viola. The children are used by both Prentiss and Mistress Coyle. The Answer bombs the city, including the communications tower, and all but one of the Spackle are shot. Todd is led to believe that the Answer has committed the murder of the aliens. As the bombing continues, Mayor Prentiss creates the Ask, a name for his followers. His headquarters include a torture chamber where he forces Todd to watch while women and rebellious men are interrogated about the Answer.

Todd and Viola eventually are able to join forces. They confront the mayor, who subsequently kills his own son to prove a point. Just as they begin to subdue him, a landing party from Viola's group swoops over the town. Todd sends Viola to intercept them before Mistress Coyle can. It seems that the civil unrest may be at end, but then an army of Spackle comes into view. Mayor Prentiss reveals his plot to make Todd the face of hatred for the aliens. So, believing it is his only choice, Todd reluctantly frees the ruthless leader.

The next piece in the series is the short story "The Wide, Wide Sea" (2013). This story takes readers back in time to before Todd and Viola were born and foreshadows the events that happen during the third novel.

The final novel, *Monsters of Men* (2010), brings the conflict to a close. It begins with the words "'War . . . at last,'" from Mayor Prentiss. Todd has freed him, knowing this was both the worst and his only possible action. The novel follows the two groups of humans and the Spackle army as they battle for supremacy of the planet. Neither of the human groups, led by Mayor Prentiss and Mistress Coyle, respectively, has the best for the future at heart, though Mistress Coyle believes she does.

Tragedy and triumph overtake Todd and Viola's lives. Viola almost dies from infection as a result of the armband she voluntarily wears, but she is saved by the mayor. Todd struggles to control his noise, almost to a point where he might lose Viola. Then, when the world seems lost, Ben (one of Todd's surrogate fathers) returns, having been found and saved by the Spackle, and Todd experiences true happiness again.

Just when peace seems to be achievable, though, Mistress Coyle realizes she has lost her leadership and commits suicide, with the idea that she will take Mayor Prentiss with her. However, he survives. The series concludes with a short story titled "Snowscape" (2013), which takes place after the ending of the last novel.

Critical Evaluation

The chronology of the Chaos Walking stories is fairly straightforward. The prequel is a series of snapshots in time. It starts as the family approaches the planet and then jumps back and forth between the approach in the present and Viola's memories of the time leading up to the present. The flashbacks provide important information about Viola and foreshadow the thematic focus on the idea of hope that Viola must learn to accept throughout the series.

The novels follow a fairly consistent chronological pattern. *The Knife of Never Letting Go* tells the story of Todd and Viola's flight from Prentisstown to Haven. *The Ask and the Answer* traces the teens' experiences in Haven after the first novel. *Monsters of Men*, brings the chaos to a conclusion.

The narrative format of the novels varies to allow readers different perspectives. *The Knife of Never Letting Go* is told from Todd's first-person perspective. *The Ask and the Answer* also uses first-person narration but splits it between Todd and Viola. *Monsters of Men* also goes back and forth between Todd and Viola, but it also contains snippets of narration from 1017, the lone surviving Spackle from the slaughter in *The Ask and the Answer*. The single focused speaker in the first book sets up the story from Todd's perspective, creating a development of characterization based on the one male from Prentisstown who has retained his humanity. The mixed narration in the second novel sets up the conflict between the men and the women, between Mayor Prentiss and Mistress Coyle (as Todd and Viola are manipulated by these faction leaders), and between the Ask and the Answer groups. The third novel accepts the importance of the alien race in the fight for the planet's survival, adding the viewpoint of one of the aliens.

Thematically, the book centers on the idea of chaos. The planet is ruled by chaos from the very beginning, as the original settler ships, holding Todd's parents and others, land on a world where men's thoughts are immediately broadcast for everyone to hear. Because the Prentisstown men cannot handle the inability to hear what the women are thinking, they wipe out the female population of their community. As a result, they are exiled from the rest of the colonists. This leads to the formation of the army that eventually becomes the Ask. For Todd, who has grown up in this outpost of banished men, bedlam rules: he must rethink his life, his purpose, and the only surviving person he loves. Viola's turmoil begins even before the wreck that killed her parents. Being sent on the mission has upset her life, and the loss of her parents leaves her reeling. Life does not get any less chaotic for these teens as they flee the army, fight to overcome two warped adult leaders, and struggle to survive with their hearts and lives intact.

The idea of hope is also central to the stories. Despite young Viola's trepidation about life on a new planet, in "The New World," her father tells her, "'I've got lots of hope,'" to which she thinks, "And there it is. That word I'm so completely sick of." But hope is the one thing to which Todd and Viola must cling as they seek Haven in the first novel; deal with separation, manipulation, and battle in the second novel; and try to overcome obstacles in the third. The series ends with the short story

"Snowscape," in which Viola's friend Lee must hold onto hope that the human and alien civilizations can be rebuilt together.

Finally, the series is a bildungsroman (a story that traces a person's development from childhood to adulthood) for both Todd and Viola. Their stories begin with innocence but build as they are forced to endure hardships throughout their journeys. The adult decisions they must make show that they have matured. Viola becomes the image of peace for the humans on the planet. Her intelligent decisions make her a strong leader for the Answer even when she does not want the responsibility. Todd's journey is more difficult. The fact that he spends the majority of the second and third novels under the influence of the mayor complicates his development. Even when Todd thinks he is having a good effect on the mayor's behavior and thought processes, he is wrong. He discovers his own lack of power as the novels draw to a close.

Theresa L. Stowell, PhD

Further Reading

Balaka, Basu, Katherine R. Broad, and Carrie Hintz. *Contemporary Dystopian Fiction for Young Adults: Brave New Teenagers*. New York: Routledge, 2013. Print.

Brown, Patricia. "Chaos Walking." *Library Media Connection* 27.5 (2009): 71. *Literary Reference Center*. Web. 9 June 2015. <http://search.ebscohost.com/login.aspx?direct=true&db=lfh&AN=37588667&site=ehost-live&scope=site>.

Kertzer, Adrienne. "Pathways' End: the Space of Trauma in Patrick Ness's 'Chaos Walking." *Bookbird* 50.1 (2012): 10–19. *MLA International Bibliography*. Web. 9 June 2015. <http://search.ebscohost.com/login.aspx?direct=true&db=mzh&AN=2013305533&site=ehost-live&scope=site>.

Charm & Strange

Author: Stephanie Kuehn (b. 1973)
First published: 2013
Type of work: Novel
Type of plot: Psychological Fiction
Time of plot: Early 2010s
Locale: Vermont; Virginia; Massachusetts; New Hampshire

Principal characters

Andrew Winston Winters (also known as Win and Drew), a troubled sixteen-year-old boy
Siobhan Winters, Win's younger sister
Keith Winters, Win's older brother
Lex Emil, Win's former roommate at boarding school
Jordan Herrera, a boyish, dark-haired girl at the school

The Story

Andrew Winston Winters is a severely conflicted teenager. Originally from Virginia, he has, for the past four years, attended an upscale boarding school in Vermont, far from his home, where a family tragedy occurred and was sensationally reported in the media. Meanwhile, a tragedy of startling nature has also recently occurred in Vermont: a man was brutally killed, virtually ripped apart, and partially eaten in the woods nearby. Andrew worries that he may be the killer, because he feels there is a ravening wolf inside him, impatient to burst free on nights when the moon is high and full.

In the present, Andrew is known as Win, a brilliant but alienated student and cross-country track star. A loner, his few friends include former roommate Lex Emil and a new transfer student, Jordan Herrera, a girl with short dark hair. Lex drinks too much—Win saved his life when he was comatose from alcohol poisoning—and knows too much about Win, such as the fact that Win sometimes hurts himself. Jordan, who wears clunky boots and dresses in boyish fashion, is of Mexican heritage, and, like Win, is an outcast.

In the past, Andrew was known as Drew. A child plagued by extreme motion sickness from an inner-ear defect, he had to be heavily drugged when his wealthy family drove on excursions. Drew is close to his kindly older brother Keith and his friendly younger sister Siobhan. Even as a nine-year-old, Drew was an outstanding tennis player, but he had violent tendencies. He once smashed an opponent in the face with his racket, breaking the boy's jaw.

On the night of a full moon, Win/Drew relives events of the past in the company of Lex and Jordan at a clandestine party the boarding-school students stage at a secret mountain clearing in the woods, known as Eden. While other students drink, cavort around a roaring bonfire, play strip poker and neck, Win, Jordan, and a tipsy Lex sit and talk. Win privately recalls the summer he was ten years old. He and his siblings were sent to Massachusetts, to visit their grandparents and hang out with their three female cousins, sixteen-year-old Anna, fourteen-year-old Charlotte (called Charlie), and eleven-year-old Phoebe. Keith makes out with Charlie, and Drew has an unrequited crush on beautiful, dark-haired Anna. When Drew mentions to Phoebe that he thinks it is wrong for cousins to be attracted to one another, she casually mentions that his parents were also cousins. It was in Massachusetts—and later while staying at a luxurious family cabin in the White Mountains of New Hampshire—that images of the wolf seemingly lurking inside Drew first began to be felt. He remembers throwing a tantrum, breaking dishes, and attempting to slash his own throat.

Back at Eden, Win strips naked and runs howling through the woods. Concerned, Lex follows with Jordan and persuades Win to stay until sunrise. Afterward, clothed again, Lex drives Win to a psychiatric hospital, where he is admitted for evaluation.

Critical Evaluation

The structure of *Charm & Strange* is crucial both to maintaining suspense in the telling of the story and in the process of revealing to the reader what really happens to the main character and why he is so disturbed. As the story unfolds, it becomes apparent Win/Drew is exhibiting symptoms of schizophrenia, a mental disorder characterized by confusion, hallucinations, emotional detachment, and an inability to distinguish between what is real and what is imagined. The reader, like Andrew, is likewise challenged to examine the character's two disparate halves, to separate fact from delusion, to piece together the clues that illuminate the family tragedy that ultimately unhinged him and sent him spiraling out of control.

Underscored by themes of fragile friendship and fractured family, the novel is divided into two parts, entitled "Before" and "After." In part one, chapters are alternately subtitled "matter" and "antimatter." In matter mode, Andrew is Win, living his lonely, isolated existence at boarding school in the present; in antimatter mode, he is violent Drew from Virginia, in the past. The subtitles do double duty. In one sense, they concern what is important—what matters—in the main character's current life, in contrast with the memories of past events that should not matter as much as they do, but which remain influential. In another sense, matter and antimatter suggest particle physics, in which subatomic materials of opposite electrical charges collide and annihilate one another.

In part two, the annihilation is complete. Win and Drew have canceled each other, and in the new vacuum, a fresh entity, Andrew, can be constructed. After psychiatric therapy, the character can objectively view the incidents of his past and present life and actually plan for the future. He can appreciate the visits of Jordan and Lex—who give him the solution to the mysterious killing that opened the novel—and is able to notice things that do not affect him directly, like the evidence that his two friends are now dating. In the end he is able to accept a Tolstoyan truth: every unhappy family is unique, with its own combination of good and bad qualities, of charm and strangeness.

Jack Ewing

Further Reading
Bircher, Katie. "Charm & Strange." *Horn Book Magazine* 89.6 (2013): 98–99. *Literary Reference Center.* Web. 7 Oct. 2015. <http://search.ebscohost.com/login.aspx?direct=true&db=lfh&AN=91621872&site=lrc-live>.

Kuehn, Stephanie. Interview by Julie Bartel. "One Thing Leads to Another: An Interview with Stephanie Kuehn." *The Hub.* YALSA. 8 Aug. 2014. Web. 24 Sept. 2015. <http://www.yalsa.ala.org/thehub/2014/08/07/one-thing-leads-to-another-an-interview-with-stephanie-kuehn/>

Chinese Handcuffs

Author: Chris Crutcher (b. 1946)
First published: 1989
Type of work: Novel
Type of plot: Coming-of-Age
Time of plot: 1980s
Locale: Three Forks, Washington

Principal characters
Dillon Hemingway, an athletic, anti-conformist high school student
Jennifer Lawless, Dillon's best friend, a star athlete
Preston Hemingway, Dillon's deceased brother
John Caldwell, Dillon's high school principal
Stacy Ryder, Preston's former girlfriend
T.B., Jennifer's stepfather
Kathy Sherman, Jennifer's basketball coach

The Story

Dillon Hemingway wants only to maintain his grades and graduate from high school in peace, but he is haunted by memories of his deceased brother, Preston; his lingering feelings for Preston's former girlfriend, Stacy; and concerns for his best friend, Jennifer, who appears to be struggling with demons of her own. Dillon is also plagued by Mr. Caldwell, his high school principal, who continually harasses him for not joining the school's sports teams despite his obvious athletic ability. To relieve his feelings, Dillon writes letters to Preston, alternately telling his brother how much he misses him and how angry he is that he killed himself (by gunshot, while forcing Dillon to watch). Dillon also trains for triathlons, with the goal of someday competing for the Ironman race, and acts as trainer for the girls' basketball team.

Dillon's friend Jennifer Lawless, the high school's star basketball player, similarly uses sports as an escape. When Jennifer suffers a concussion during a game, she is terrified that staying in the hospital overnight will leave her younger sister alone with their stepfather, so she asks her basketball coach, Kathy Sherman, to keep her sister for the night. Flashbacks reveal that not only has Jennifer's stepfather been molesting her for years but her biological father had also done so when she was very young. Jennifer's report of her father's behavior resulted in her parents' divorce, but she is frightened enough of her stepfather that she remains silent.

Gradually, additional information about Dillon, Preston, Stacy, and Jennifer emerges. After an awkward date, Jennifer finally tells Dillon about being molested, but she makes him promise not to take any action, in large part because she has already tried to report her stepfather to the authorities. He was able to use his legal knowledge of the system to make it look as though she were lying, and then he killed her dog in retaliation and threatened to do the same to her mother and sister if she tried to report him again.

Around the same time that Jennifer finally begins to open up to him, Dillon realizes that the baby that Stacy's parents suddenly adopted is actually Stacy and Preston's biological child, and therefore Dillon's nephew. Unsure how to handle all of this confusing new information, Dillon turns to the girls' basketball coach, Coach Sherman, for advice. Ultimately Dillon decides to introduce Stacy and Jennifer to one another in the hope that they will all be able to help each other.

The situation comes to a climax when Jennifer leaves in the middle of an important basketball game. Dillon follows, and when he sees that she is climbing the town's water tower, he realizes that she intends to kill herself. He barely manages to stop her. Jennifer tells him that her mother is pregnant with another baby girl, whom she feels she will not be able to protect from her stepfather.

Desperate to help, Dillon seriously considers killing her stepfather, since the man seems beyond the reach of the authorities. Instead, however, Dillon borrows an infrared camera and captures T.B.'s abuse of Jennifer on film. He uses the footage to blackmail T.B. into leaving town permanently, making sure T.B. knows that if any "accidents" befall anyone in Dillon's or Jennifer's families, the tape will be released to the police and the news.

Initially infuriated by Dillon's interference and humiliated by the idea of her abuse being filmed, Jennifer eventually decides that having T.B. on the other side of the country, but still at liberty, is not good enough, and she reports him to the police herself. Dillon realizes that he and Jennifer may or may not have a romantic relationship in the future, but she needs time to heal, and the best thing he can do is be her friend.

Critical Evaluation

Crutcher's fourth novel for young adults, *Chinese Handcuffs* employs a variety of perspectives to show that many of life's problems do not have easy answers. The novel's title is derived from Dillon's memory of Stacy showing him a "Chinese handcuff" finger puzzle. To solve it, the person cannot pull away, but must instead go against instinct and let the puzzle revert to its loosened state. This idea is echoed in Coach Sherman's advice to Dillon: she tells him that people can control only how they respond to people and events. By letting go of the idea of control, people actually gain more control over their own lives.

More concretely, *Chinese Handcuffs* explores several themes for which the author has become known. Sports play a central role in this novel; they are portrayed as an effective means for achieving focus and discipline, as long as they are not blindly equated with patriotism and superiority. In addition, Crutcher does not shy away from serious issues such as rape, teenage pregnancy, drug abuse, suicide, and violent tendencies, and he recognizes that the social safety nets meant to deal with these problems are not always effective. Finally, in what has become one of the author's trademarks, he juxtaposes two types of authority figures in order to contrast them: the supportive coach who encourages students to think through problems for themselves, and the rigid school administrator who, as Dillon observes, claims to want respect from students while actually trying to instill fear in them. By the end of the novel, readers can sense how all of these experiences and influences, both good and bad, will continue to shape the evolution of Dillon's character.

Amy Sisson, MS, MLS

Further Reading

Follos, Allison M. G. "Author Profile: The '3 C's' of Chris Crutcher." *Library Media Connection* Nov.–Dec. 2006: 40–43. *Literary Reference Center*. Web. 31 Oct. 2015. <http://search.ebscohost.com/login.aspx?direct=true&db=lfh&AN=22924186&site=lrc-live>.

Schafer, Elizabeth D. "Chris Crutcher." *Guide to Literary Masters & Their Works*. Pasadena: Salem, 2007. N. pag. *Literary Reference Center*. Web. 9 Oct. 2015. <http://search.ebscohost.com/login.aspx?direct=true&db=lfh&AN=103331LM23309790301789&site=lrc-live>.

Code Name Verity

Author: Elizabeth Wein (b. 1964)
First published: 2012
Type of work: Novel
Type of plot: Historical Fiction
Time of plot: 1943
Locale: France; England

Principal characters

Julia "Queenie" Beaufort-Stuart, a Scottish interrogator and spy for the Allied forces
Margaret "Maddie" Brodatt, Julia's best friend and a pilot
Jamie Beaufort-Stuart, Julia's brother and a pilot
SS-Hauptsturmführer Amadeus von Linden, Julia's German interrogator
Anna Engel, von Linden's assistant

The Story

Imprisoned by the Nazis occupying Ormaie, France, in 1943, Julia "Queenie" Beaufort-Stuart has agreed to reveal Allied wireless transmitter codes and other classified information in exchange for paper, ink, and time to write the story of how she was captured. Queenie begins by relating her friendship back in England with Margaret "Maddie" Brodatt, who also worked in the Women's Auxiliary Air Force (WAAF). Shortly thereafter, Queenie was recruited by the secret Special Operations Executive (SOE) while Maddie became a civilian ferry pilot for the Air Transport Auxiliary (ATA) and also flew special missions to transport SOE operatives.

While Queenie writes about these events, she continues to undergo interrogations and is forced to watch her jailors torture other prisoners. Queenie is punished when her account strays from factual information into personal narrative, but Hauptsturmführer von Linden, the man in charge of the Gestapo headquarters where Queenie is imprisoned, intervenes because he appreciates her storytelling flair.

Continuing her account, Queenie notes that Maddie began to suspect that her friend was now an interrogator, spy, or both. Because she was on hand just as Queenie was scheduled to leave for France on an undercover assignment, Maddie took over when the scheduled pilot was injured, even though women pilots were not authorized for such missions. When their plane was damaged by antiaircraft guns, Maddie made Queenie parachute out before attempting to land the plane at the designated location.

Throughout this tale, Queenie interrupts herself frequently to express grief over the photos she has been shown of Maddie's crashed plane and burned body. As Queenie finishes her story, detailing not only the events leading to her capture but also her current treatment by the Nazis, she knows she will be sent to a concentration camp and subjected to medical experimentation until she dies.

The second half of the book is told from Maddie's perspective, beginning with her crash landing that is actually successful, although the plane cannot take off again. Stranded and lacking fluency in French, Maddie is hidden by Resistance fighters, who blow up the plane after placing a dead German sentry's body in the pilot seat. Maddie hides in a barn for weeks, desperately hoping to learn what happened to "Verity," which is Queenie's code name.

After several weeks, the Resistance receives a message from von Linden's assistant, Anna Engel, whom they have recruited. They learn that several prisoners, including Queenie, are about to be transported to a concentration camp. They successfully ambush the bus, but are forced into a stand-off when the Germans begin killing some prisoners and shooting others in such a way as to torture them. Just before they turn their weapons on Queenie, Maddie begins sobbing from her hiding place. Queenie hears her, and shouts "Kiss me, Hardy!" to her friend. Recognizing Queenie's reference to Admiral Horatio Nelson's dying words, Maddie deliberately shoots and kills Queenie to spare her additional torture before her inevitable death.

After barely escaping with their lives, Maddie and the surviving Resistance fighters receive a sheaf of papers; it is Queenie's written story, which Engel smuggled out of von Linden's quarters. Maddie quickly realizes that Queenie filled the entire account with cleverly disguised but precise logistical information about the Gestapo headquarters. The fighters use the information to free the remaining prisoners and destroy the building. Maddie finally returns to England and confesses to Queenie's family that she deliberately shot Queenie, and they find comfort in the fact that Queenie's suffering was not without purpose.

Critical Evaluation

In this novel that consists of stories within stories, author Elizabeth Wein skillfully utilizes the unreliable narrator technique to lead both Queenie's captors and the reader to believe that Queenie is giving away critical information when she is actually attempting to communicate with her allies. At the same time, the author softens the harsh and often graphic depiction of Queenie's torture with accounts of the young women's friendship, which Queenie notes likely would not have happened in peacetime due to their widely divergent backgrounds.

This novel is also noteworthy in its portrayal of the often overlooked contributions made by women during World War II. Although women were officially precluded from certain types of wartime activities, many of them risked their lives in unofficial operations or extraordinary circumstances when necessary, and Wein highlights this fact. In addition, she empowers her female characters by making them integral to the eventual success of the mission, rather than relegating them to supporting roles.

Finally, *Code Name Verity* presents realistic, carefully researched details about England and France during World War II, using those details to create an engaging and suspenseful story. In an afterword, the author describes the origins of several of the plot elements and also provides a bibliography of sources. This seamless integration of fact and fiction makes *Code Name Verity* a noteworthy example of young adult historical fiction, and the novel was named as an honored book for the Printz Award in 2013. Although it was not marketed as a mystery novel, it also won the Mystery Writers of America's Edgar Award for best young adult novel that same year.

Amy Sisson, MS, MLS

Further Reading

Baker, Deirdre F. Rev. of *Code Name Verity*, by Elizabeth Wein. *Horn Book Magazine* May/June 2012: 101–2. *Literary Reference Center*. Web. 21 Apr. 2015. <http://search.ebscohost.com/login.aspx?direct=true&db=lfh&AN=74608528&site=lrc-live>.

Ingall, Marjorie. "The Pilot and the Spy." *New York Times*. New York Times, 11 May 2012. Web. 21 Apr. 2015. <http://www.nytimes.com/2012/05/13/books/review/code-name-verity-by-elizabeth-wein.html?_r=0>.

Wein, Elizabeth. "Interview with Elizabeth Wein, Author of *Code Name Verity*." Interview by Monica Edinger. *Huffington Post*. HuffingtonPost.com, 22 May 2012. Web. 21 Apr. 2015. <http://www.huffingtonpost.com/monica-edinger/interview-with-elizabeth-_b_1535203.html>.

A Curse Dark as Gold

Author: Elizabeth C. Bunce
First published: 2008
Type of work: Novel
Type of plot: Fantasy
Time of plot: 1700s
Locale: Europe

Principal characters

Charlotte Miller, the eldest Miller daughter and operator of Stirwaters mill

Rosie Miller, Charlotte's younger sister

James Miller, Charlotte's father and previous owner of Stirwaters mill

Uncle Wheeler, Charlotte's uncle and legal guardian after Charlotte's father's death; caretaker of the mill

Randall Woodstone, Charlotte's husband, a city bank mortgage officer

Jack Spinner, a man who offers supernatural aid to the Millers whenever they are in danger of losing Stirwaters mill

The Story

Charlotte and Rosie, the daughters of James Miller, have just inherited the family mill, Stirwaters, after their father's passing. The other local mill owners, the Pinchfields, want to buy the mill to put it out of business, but Stirwaters has been owned by the Millers ever since anyone can remember. Faced with no money and no one else to run the mill, Charlotte steps up and assumes control of operations until their distant Uncle Wheeler comes from the city to fulfill his dead brother's wish that he take charge. Unfortunately for Charlotte and Rosie, Uncle Wheeler's only substantial plans for a sound future are to sell the mill and marry the daughters off, so to protect their inheritance, the sisters must take matters into their own hands in an era and society where women have little to no power.

The sisters soon find that there is a substantial mortgage on Stirwaters that their father took out and that they must pay back. Fortunately, the mortgage man from the bank, Randall Woodstone, is a generous man and sees potential within the mill to make money. He convinces the bank to continue the mortgage, but insists that the sisters make a large payment on the loan by the end of the summer. With no money to pay workers to make product, all seems lost for the mill until a strange man calling himself Jack Spinner shows up. Jack tells Charlotte that he will take a room full of straw and spin it into a room full of golden thread in exchange for a cheap ring that belonged to Charlotte's late mother. Charlotte accepts the offer, and everything seems fine again, for a while.

There is also another problem: many people in the village believe that there is a curse on Stirwaters. Rumors circulate: the mill cannot be fixed up; no dyes other than a certain blue can be used in any fabric made at the mill; and no son born in the Miller family can inherit the property. Charlotte does not believe these rumors, but they seem to hold true as the season continues. Meanwhile, she marries Randall Woodstone and becomes pregnant.

When the river freezes in the winter and snaps the main rod of the water wheel at the mill, everything seems to be lost again. The sisters once again cannot afford to pay workers, and they run dangerously low on fabric. Again any hopes of keeping the mill seem lost, especially after a local man burns down the millhouse. Once again, Jack Spinner comes and rescues the mill by doing what seems impossible. Again, he asks only for a small token in exchange—this time a brooch given to Charlotte by Randall. But as soon as the sisters seem out of each predicament, they are thrust back in by something else, either fate or bad decisions by the men around them.

Finally, as Charlotte is about to have her baby, she finds out that she is held responsible for a number of debts that her uncle, who has forged her signature, has incurred. The mill seems lost for sure, and again Jack Spinner appears, this time with a very different offer. When Charlotte's son is born, Jack presents her with the biggest decision of her life: she can save the mill and her family, but to do so she must give her newborn son to Jack Spinner. Charlotte must look within herself and to her family and its legacy and make a decision that will affect everyone. Of course, as in the original fairy tale, Charlotte finds another option, learning Jack Spinner's true identity as the vengeful spirit of a man wronged by Charlotte's ancestors and using this knowledge to break the hold he has long had over her family.

Critical Evaluation

As a retelling of the fairytale "Rumplestiltskin," *A Curse Dark as Gold* adds a new perspective and depth to the centuries-old narrative. While the role of the miller's daughter is integral to the original plot, the character herself is flat, almost without an identity except as a daughter and a woman who can bear children. It is the strange visitor who has the power within the story, and that power rests within his name. Bunce's retelling puts the power of the story back into the hands of the female protagonist. Although Charlotte still finds herself caught within the patriarchal culture of eighteenth-century Europe, she finds a way to express herself and retain her own identity and autonomy as the men in her life try to take control.

From her uncle who wants to marry her away quickly to her eventual husband who wants nothing more than for her to give up her family mill and live with him in the city, Charlotte's life can be likened to an adolescent's in modern society. When her father dies, she is left on her own without any substantial guidance or training and she is stuck between two worlds: she knows she does not want someone else controlling her life, but she does not know exactly how to run her own. To this point, Charlotte has essentially been a child, and she must find her own identity and voice through the difficulties that she faces running the mill. With this depth, Bunce not only adds a feminist twist to the traditional fairytale by empowering Charlotte, but also one of the most important conventions of the young adult genre, the coming-of-age theme. In so doing, Bunce creates a very new and modern perspective on a traditional tale.

Aaron Horton, MA

Further Reading

Clark, Ruth Cox. "Teen Savvy. Web Literate and Multi-Talented: New Authors and Their Debut Novels for Young Adults." *Library Media Connection* Oct. 2009: 10–13. *Literary Reference Center*. Web. 21 Dec. 2015.

Gross, Claire E. Rev. of *A Curse Dark as Gold*, by Elizabeth C. Bunce. *Horn Book* Mar.–Apr. 2008: 213. *Literary Reference Center*. Web. 21 Dec. 2015.

Dinky Hocker Shoots Smack!

Author: M. E. Kerr (b. 1927)
First published: 1972
Type of work: Novel
Type of plot: Realism
Time of plot: Present
Locale: Brooklyn, New York

Principal characters

Tucker Woolf, a reserved teenager
Susan "Dinky" Hocker, Tucker's overweight friend
Natalia Line, the troubled girl Tucker likes, Dinky's cousin
P. John Knight, Tucker's opinionated classmate, Dinky's love interest
Helen Hocker, Dinky's liberal mother

The Story

After Tucker Woolf's family moves to Brooklyn, Tucker's father loses his job and becomes allergic to cats, forcing Tucker to give up his new pet, Nader. Tucker puts signs up, and an overweight girl named Susan "Dinky" Hocker takes Nader in. Tucker visits Nader and meets the newest addition to Dinky's house, her cousin Natalia Line. Dinky also lives with her father and her mother, Helen, who helps young people struggling with drug addictions.

When Natalia leaves for a week, Tucker and Dinky spend an afternoon together, becoming friends. When he returns home, his father and uncle announce they are starting a health-food business. When Natalia returns, she, Tucker, and Dinky go to the Brooklyn Botanic Gardens and talk about the strangest things they have ever heard. Natalia tells Tucker that she went to a school for people with mental problems, and Dinky says that Natalia rhymes when she is nervous.

Tucker invites Natalia to a school dance, and she agrees if he will find Dinky a date, too. He decides on a large, conservative boy in his class, P. John Knight. At the dance, P. John and Dinky have a fantastic time, while Tucker and Natalia feel awkward around each other. Despite this, Natalia eventually invites Tucker over to the Hocker house one evening while Mrs. Hocker is treating addicts, and Tucker watches as P. John and Mrs. Hocker argue over Dinky eating cake. Eventually, Mrs. Hocker kicks P. John out of the home, and Dinky fails to show up to meet him at the next Weight Watchers meeting, which he has convinced her to join. Tucker agrees to bring Dinky a Christmas present from P. John and, while at P. John's house, meets his very liberal father.

Tucker's mother cautions him to not become too attached to Natalia because she has had a difficult life, revealing that her father killed himself. Dinky then sneaks away to see P. John, and when the police arrive to find her, they arrest Dewey, a friend of P. John's father who is an undocumented immigrant. At Christmas dinner, Dinky says something that makes her mother think Tucker and Natalia are sexually active. When Tucker gets home, he learns that his uncle fell asleep with a lit cigarette and burned down the health business. P. John is sent away to his aunt's school in Maine, and when Tucker gives Dinky a letter from him, she is dismissive.

Helen Hocker meets Tucker by chance and invites him to join her in helping poor children paint, saying that she has decided to give Tucker another chance and that Natalia will be there. While there, Dinky is hyper on diet pills and tells Tucker that he should take Nader back, as otherwise the cat might be put to sleep for relieving herself everywhere. Tucker and Natalia talk about how they feel as though they never have real conversations with people. The next time he sees Natalia, they manage to have a conversation, and they kiss and she invites him to the Valentine's dance.

P. John returns to the neighborhood, having lost weight. Dinky begins to act out, in part because of her diet pills. P. John visits her, and she is cruel to him. When her mother receives a community award for her work with addicts, Dinky paints the sentence "Dinky Hocker Shoots Smack" all over buildings and sidewalks and car doors outside. When Tucker and Natalia go to find Dinky, she is packing her bags to run away, and they realize she painted the slogan herself. Dinky's family begin to understand how unkind they have been to her, about her weight and in general. Natalia leaves for the summer, and she and Tucker write letters, excited to reunite in the fall.

Critical Evaluation

Dinky Hocker Shoots Smack! is a novel filled with social outcasts, whether because of their beliefs, their bodies, or their histories. While the main character, Tucker, is hardly the most popular boy in school, he is perhaps one of the least marginalized characters.

The choice to use Tucker rather than Dinky, Natalia, or P. John as the narrative focus is an important one. Rather than directly experiencing the cruelty Dinky faces because of her weight or the mental illness and family stigma that drives Natalia to silence, for example, readers learn about these realities from outside of their scenario. Tucker is not objective, and the narrative limits readers' information to what he knows (his prejudice about Dinky's weight being regularly apparent), but he is better able to observe the complex way that his peers are ignored and mistreated by their parents. Because of this, Dinky's ultimate betrayal of her family (graffitiing the titular slogan) comes after many chapters in which readers see Dinky's behavior, the way that P. John manipulates her, the unintentionally cruel and controlling behavior of her parents, and all the other factors that lead to the rebellious act. It is not a moment of irrational anger, but one that Tucker and readers instinctively understand without Dinky needing to explain it.

Ultimately, then, the novel becomes less about Dinky, Tucker, or any other individual character, and more about the broader ways that the hypocrisies of the adult world affect the ability of the adolescents to form relations with anyone, peers or parents. This makes Tucker an ideal central character. While, in his own words, he claims, "I don't think I even have any relationships," he is still present and observant, slowly learning to understand everyone as individuals who are also part of a complex social fabric.

T. Fleischmann, MFA

Further Reading

Chaston, Joel D. "Dinky Hocker Shoots Smack!." *Masterplots II: Juvenile & Young Adult Literature Series, Supplement* (1997): 1–2. *Literary Reference Center.* Web. 23 Feb. 2015. <http://search.ebscohost.com/login.aspx?direct=true&db=lfh&AN=103331JYS10879720000150&site=ehost-live>.

Sisson, Amy. "M. E. Kerr." *Magill's Survey of American Literature, Revised Edition* (2006): 1–5. *Literary Reference Center.* Web. 23 Feb. 2015. <http://search.ebscohost.com/login.aspx?direct=true&db=lfh&AN=103331MSA11639830000162&site=ehost-live>.

The Disreputable History of Frankie Landau-Banks

Author: E. Lockhart (b. 1967)
First published: 2008
Type of work: Novel
Type of plot: Coming-of-Age
Time of plot: 2007
Locale: the Jersey Shore; northern Massachusetts

Principal characters

Frankie Landau-Banks, a fifteen-year-old boarding-school student
Zada Landau-Banks, Frankie's self-assured older sister
Matthew Livingston, Frankie's boyfriend
Trish, Frankie's roommate
Alpha, Matthew's friend

The Story

In a written confession, Frankie Landau-Banks takes full responsibility for the mayhem that took place on campus during her sophomore year.

Several months earlier, during the summer between Frankie's freshman and sophomore years, Frankie develops physically into a very noticeable young woman. The change takes her by as much surprise as it does her older sister, Zada, and the rest of her family.

The day after Zada leaves for her freshman year at the University of California, Berkeley, Frankie's mother decides to take Frankie for a short vacation to the Jersey Shore. Frankie has finally earned the privilege of walking up the boardwalk by herself, so she heads off in her bikini, but she soon starts feeling cold and conspicuous.

When she encounters an attractive boy who asks for her unfinished chocolate frozen custard, she is interested in him but does not pursue him, assuming she will never see him again. Frankie's mother interrupts their conversation with a phone call that leaves Frankie feeling embarrassed, and the boy tells her he will see her soon.

On the drive to Alabaster Preparatory Academy in Massachusetts to begin her sophomore year, Frankie and her mother pick up Frankie's father, who talks to Frankie about these years being the best of her life. He expounds on the importance of the connections she will make at school, reminding her that she could be educated elsewhere for far less money, and he is paying for the connections she will make. Frankie feels sorry that his best days took place when he was fifteen, but she can see that his business and social connections all go back to his time at Alabaster. She would like to go on to Harvard University, as he did, and she would also like to have connections that last a lifetime.

Soon after arriving at school, Frankie bumps into Matthew Livingston, a boy two grades ahead of Frankie whom she has had a crush on for quite a while. The two begin to date, and she is introduced to his world of old-boy friendships in the making. Frankie soon learns that the boy she met at the beach also goes to Alabaster and is called Alpha because he is the head of the secret, male-only society on campus. She secretly follows Matthew when he cancels plans with her at the last minute and finds out who the other members are.

It becomes obvious that there is no way a girl can gain true access to the bonds shared by these boys. When one of them breaks up with his girlfriend, the rest of the group shuns her, and Frankie realizes that she is only in their lives and only shares their friendships because she is Matthew's girlfriend. When Alpha is away on a weekend retreat with his mother and cannot be contacted, Frankie decides to do something that she believes will earn her the lasting respect of Alpha and the other boys.

Frankie creates a fake e-mail account in Alpha's name and sends instructions to each of the boys, detailing the parts they are to play in a prank. Frankie's prank is far more sophisticated than the original plan Alpha and the group had planned, so when Alpha returns, rather than admit he had nothing to do with it, he takes the credit so as not to risk losing the respect of the group. Frankie continues to lead the boys in pranks while maintaining her anonymity, and she and Alpha being an e-mail correspondence in which she gains a grudging respect for him. Through it all, Frankie is frustrated to realize that she will never be completely accepted as part of the old-boy network simply because she is a girl.

When Alpha is caught is the school's underground tunnels and is accused of masterminding the pranks, Frankie steps forward to confess her part and save Alpha's prospects for the future. She is not punished severely, in part because she is a girl. When she sees Matthew again, she realizes that she wants more than to be an appendage to a good-looking, successful guy. She concludes that "it is better to lead than to follow. It is better to speak up than stay silent. It is better to open doors than to shut them on people."

Critical Evaluation

The Disreputable History of Frankie Landau-Banks, first published in 2008, is a coming-of-age story with a twist. Frankie's struggles with the old-boy network is brought to life with well-chosen scenes that bring Frankie's feelings of longing and alienation to life. Her older sister and roommate are well-drawn characters who provide outside interpretations of the events as Frankie works to understand her own reactions. Her questioning of the status quo is perfectly in line with her overall questioning of societal expectations and her place in the world.

Alabaster is depicted in ways that bring both the physical aspect of the school and the students' relationships with it and its traditions to life. The different groups and they ways they interrelate are well described.

Frankie's parents are drawn as one-dimensional characters. Her mother still perceives her as a little girl, and her father expresses his love for her, yet views her as ineffectual and the next-best thing to having a son.

Frankie's growing self-awareness is believable. She is not a girl who is content to merely accept things at face value, even things that make her happy. Just as believable is the conclusion she draws about the type of person she wants to be.

Gina Hagler, MBA

Further Reading

Bucher, Katherine T., and KaaVonia Hinton. *Young Adult Literature: Exploration, Evaluation, and Appreciation*. 3rd ed. New York: Pearson, 2014. Print.

Hill, Crag, ed. *The Critical Merits of Young Adult Literature: Coming of Age*. New York: Routledge, 2014. Print.

Wethern, Sarah. "31 Days of Teens' Top Ten—Legacy of Frankie Landau- Banks." *The Yalsa Hub*. ALA, 12

May 2011. Web. 29 Apr. 2015. <http://www.yalsa.ala.org/thehub/2011/05/12/31-days-of-teens-top-ten-legacy-of-frankie-landau-banks/>.

Divergent (Series)

First published: *Divergent* (2011)
   Insurgent (2012)
   Allegiant (2013)
   Four: A Divergent Collection (2014)
Type of work: Novel
Type of plot: Science fiction; Dystopian fiction
Time of plot: Future
Locales: In and around post-apocalyptic Chicago

Principal Characters

Beatrice "Tris" Prior: sixteen-year-old new initiate of the Dauntless faction who is secretly "Divergent"

Tobias "Four" Eaton: nearly fearless eighteen-year-old instructor of initiates to the Dauntless faction; his nickname, "Four," refers to the four fears he has yet to conquer

Caleb Prior: Tris's seventeen-year-old brother, a new initiate of the Erudite faction

Marcus Eaton: Tobias' abusive father and leader of the Abnegation faction

Jeanine Matthews: ruthlessly intelligent leader of the Erudite faction

The Story

The Divergent series is made up of three novels and a book of related short stories told, in the case of *Divergent* and *Insurgent*, from the first person perspective of series heroine Beatrice "Tris" Prior; from the first person perspectives of both Tris and Tobias "Four" Eaton in *Allegiant*; and from the first person perspective of Four in *Four: A Divergent Collection*. The novels are set in and around post-apocalyptic Chicago within a society that has organized its people into factions based on their dispositions and essential beliefs: Abnegation, who value selflessness; Amity, who value peace; Candor, who value honesty; Dauntless, who value bravery; and Erudite, who value intelligence. While young people are raised in the faction of their birth, each year, those who have turned sixteen complete an aptitude test that indicates the faction for which they are optimally suited. Once they receive the results of this test, each sixteen-year-old may choose to remain in the faction in which they were raised or be initiated into another faction of their choosing.

Divergent, the first novel in the series, begins on the day of the aptitude tests. Beatrice Prior, a sixteen-year-old member of Abnegation, worries about the test and the choice she must make about which faction to join. While Beatrice has never felt fully comfortable in Abnegation, she agonizes over whether to remain with her family or leave them to join another faction. When the results of her aptitude test reveal that she has an affinity for three factions—Abnegation, Dauntless, and Erudite—Beatrice is warned that these results identify her as "Divergent" and therefore threatening.

On Choosing Day, Beatrice selects Dauntless as her faction and her brother, Caleb, who is older than she but in the same class at school, chooses Erudite. When she arrives at Dauntless headquarters, Beatrice learns that only ten initiates will be allowed to join the faction; the remainder will become "factionless," a dangerous position in a society structured around strict divisions.

Training for initiation into Dauntless challenges Beatrice and, during the competitive process, she decides to rename herself "Tris." Training involves both physical and psychological exercises; initiates learn to fight and handle weapons and also work to overcome their fears in a simulated fear landscape they enter by consuming a serum. Tris's instructor, Four, is revered for his comparative lack of fear, as his fear landscape features only four obstacles.

As Tris undergoes training, she begins to develop feelings for Four, who seems to return her affection; however, soon after the two express their interest in one another, members of their faction enter a forcibly induced simulation that causes them to attack Abnegation headquarters. Tris realizes that a shot of "tracking" serum given to them by the Erudite under false pretenses is, in actuality, a simulation serum that, when activated, will force them all to act under the direction of a villainous third party. Tris's Divergent status makes her immune to the simulation serum and she works with Four, who is also Divergent, to release the Dauntless from the serum's spell and gain proof of Erudite's involvement in the attack.

Insurgent begins immediately following Dauntless' unwitting attack on Abnegation. Following numerous casualties—including the deaths of Tris's father and mother—Tris, Four, Caleb, Peter (a fellow Dauntless member), and Marcus, Four's estranged father, travel to the headquarters of Amity to search for survivors of the attack. The Amity faction issues a statement indicating that they will welcome and house survivors from any faction, as long as they uphold the peace the faction values.

When members of Erudite arrive at Amity with members of Dauntless who have joined their cause, Tris and her group flee and Tris and Four travel to Candor headquarters where they are arrested and subjected to a truth serum. While at Candor, the faction is attacked by a group of Dauntless traitors working with the Erudite and numerous people receive shots of a new simulation serum that, unlike the first, doesn't wear off.

Although members of Candor try to broker a peace agreement with Erudite, meetings between an Erudite spokesperson and members of Candor erupt into violence. Before this violence begins, however, Erudite issues its demands: Jeanine, the Erudite leader, wants the Dauntless to turn over their Divergent members to Erudite for study. When Dauntless refuses to surrender the Divergent, Jeanine triggers her simulation serum, forcing members of Dauntless to commit suicide every two days. Jeanine warns Dauntless that these deaths will continue until the Divergent are surrendered.

Against the wishes of Four, Tris surrenders herself to Erudite, and is subjected to numerous tests, the results of which frustrate Jeanine as she is unable to find a simulation that can fully control the Divergent Tris. After Jeanine announces her plans to execute Tris, Tris is saved by her fellow Dauntless.

Working with members of Dauntless as well as those who are factionless, Tris and Four attempt to infiltrate Erudite so that they can steal and disseminate their data. During the battle that follows, Jeanine is killed, and Evelyn, Four's mother and the leader of the increasingly powerful factionless, announces the triumph of a factionless society. On the heels of her announcement, the group uncovers and shares a historical video that suggests that the society to which they belong was created as an experiment.

Allegiant begins following the revelation that the society of factions is not only the result of experimentation but also that those members of the society deemed Divergent are now considered extremely valuable. When she travels outside the boundaries of her city, now being led by Evelyn as a factionless society, Tris encounters a rebel group known as the Allegiant. The Allegiant reveal that Tris's divided city is the result of government

genetic experimentation undertaken with the goal of ridding humanity of the genes believed to cause human error and conflict. Attempts to "correct" genetics resulted in the establishment of two classes of people: the Genetically Pure (GP)—those whose genes had not been "corrected"—and the Genetically Damaged (GD)—those who had been subject to government experimentation. These classes fought what became known as the Purity War, which resulted in the death of half the population.

In an attempt to rectify the damage resulting from both government experimentation and the Purity War, a Bureau of Genetic Welfare organized experimental and divided cities like those in which Tris was born. The goal of this experiment was to produce a critical mass of GP—known in the factioned societies as Divergent— who would then be led to repopulate the nation. Tris's newly factionless society is a threat to this experiment, and Tris learns that the Bureau was behind the Erudite's attack on Abnegation that begun her city's conflict.

Critical Evaluation

The Divergent series is characterized by a number of themes related to institutional power, identity, and personal strength.

Like Suzanne Collins's Hunger Games series, the Divergent series describes, as Michelle Dean, writing for the *New York Times* magazine, observes, "totalitarianism reducible to the lies of adults." Throughout the series, young rebels—typically led by Tris and Four— reveal that the adults in power are corrupt. These dishonest leaders are typically megalomaniacs: they are interested not only in maintaining absolute control over the members of their factions, but also in ensuring that the members of their factions represent the strongest and purest forms of their factions' values. The faction leadership depicted in *Divergent* and *Insurgent* are the most obvious examples of the series' critique of despotism. However, when an uprising of the factionless leads to the establishment of a factionless society, even its leadership is revealed as fascist.

Tris' Divergent status is a challenge to the divided society in which she lives and operates as a powerful symbol in the series. As the Divergent series depicts the downfall of a society divided into strictly defined categories or classes, it suggests that a society dependent on such rigid distinctions between its citizens is doomed to fail. Furthermore, as *Allegiant* demonstrates, attempts to program or naturalize these distinctions will always result in disaster. Humans, the series asserts, are not and cannot be reducible to a single trait.

As the series depicts Tris' adventures with Dauntless, it also depicts the development of her selflessness, a trait associated with the Abnegation faction to which she was born. Veronica Roth has written that much of *Divergent* addresses Tris' struggle to integrate her Abnegation and Dauntless identities. Roth writes: "It's just before her mother gives up her life that Tris figures out how those identities fit together, combining selflessness and bravery and love for her family and love for her faction all together under one umbrella: Divergent." The death of her parents leads to further confusion, and Tris mistakes acts of self-destruction for acts of selflessness throughout *Insurgent*. By *Allegiant*, however, Tris has fully realized her identity as Divergent and, when she makes the ultimate sacrifice at the end of the third novel, it comes from what Roth has described as a place of "love, strength, and necessity."

Amy Pattee

Bibliography

Dean, Michelle. "Our young adult dystopia." *New York Times Magazine*. The New York Times Company, 31 January 2014. Web. 8 February 2016. <http://www.nytimes.com/2014/02/02/magazine/our-young-adult-dystopia.html?_r=1>

Roth, Veronica. "About the End of Allegiant (Spoilers)." *Veronica Roth*. 28 October, 2013. Web. 22 February 2016.

Further Reading

Roth, Veronica. *Veronica Roth* [Veronica Roth's Tumblr blog]. <http://theartofnotwriting.tumblr.com/>

The Earth, My Butt, and Other Big Round Things

Author: Carolyn Mackler (b. 1973)
First published: 2003
Type of work: Novel
Type of plot: Bildungsroman
Time of plot: Around 2000
Locales: New York City; Seattle, Washington

Principal characters

Virginia Shreves, an insecure fifteen-year-old
Byron Shreves, Virginia's popular, well-liked older brother
Froggy Welsh the Fourth, Virginia's romantic interest
Dr. Phyllis Shreves, Virginia's psychologist mother
Shannon Iris Malloy-Newman, Virginia's best friend
Anaïs Shreves, Virginia's older sister
Annie Mills, a junior at Virginia's brother's university

The Story

Fifteen-year-old Virginia Shreves is making out with Froggy Welsh the Fourth, the boy with whom she makes out after school most Mondays. When he starts to reach up her shirt, however, she stops him, not because she does not want to be more physical (and maybe even be his girlfriend), but because she is insecure about her weight.

Virginia's wealthy family lives in Manhattan, and everyone but her is thin. Her mother, Phyllis, is a psychologist for adolescents, but she is so obsessed with other people that she does not give her own children attention, a character trait that drove Virginia's successful older sister, Anaïs, to flee and join the Peace Corps after college. Her older brother, Byron, is also gorgeous and successful, and at school one day Virginia hears the popular girls talking about him, then saying they would kill themselves if they looked like Virginia. She hears this because she hides in the bathroom stall to eat lunch alone, her only friend, Shannon, having moved to Washington State.

Virginia goes to visit Byron at Columbia University one weekend, but he is distant to her and does not invite her to the "Virgins and Sluts" party he is attending that evening. The following Monday, Virginia's mother comes home while she is making out with Froggy. Froggy has to hide under her bed and overhears her mother remind Virginia of her appointment with a weight loss doctor, which feels humiliating. Although they never compliment her, Virginia's parents begin to tell her they are proud when she starts her new diet. Virginia, however, feels worse and starts to avoid Froggy even though he is obviously interested in her.

Virginia breaks her diet when she finds out that Byron is moving back home because he date-raped a young woman at college. Virginia tries to avoid him by hiding in her room and sometimes e-mailing Shannon, who has made new friends. Shannon then invites Virginia to visit Seattle over Thanksgiving, but Virginia's parents insist she needs to stay for the family holiday. Virginia is upset both that she cannot travel and that her parents are in denial about Byron. She decides to buy her own plane ticket and go regardless.

In Seattle, Shannon helps Virginia admit that her brother was never perfect, and the friends get facial piercings to celebrate their vacation. When Virginia returns home, her mother tries to control the way she dresses and says disparaging things about her body, and Virginia kicks a wall out of frustration, breaking her toe. Knowing something has to give, she decides to go to Columbia and talk to the girl her brother raped. After a huge argument with Byron during which he calls her fat, she meets the girl, Annie Mills. Annie says that she is strong and not going to let Byron ruin her life, and Virginia feels empowered to write Anaïs a letter telling her the truth of what happened with their brother.

Virginia buys a dress she actually likes for the family friends' holiday party and dyes her hair purple. After getting drunk while talking with Shannon one night, she finally tells Byron that he is no longer her hero. At school, she starts a webzine, and Froggy joins the new club. Virginia even writes a piece for it about learning to love her body and tells her father that he should stop talking about her weight. As she develops new friends with the webzine crew and feels more independent, Froggy asks her for a kiss in Central Park, and she is confident enough to kiss him back.

Critical Evaluation

A bildungsroman is a coming-of-age story in which a young protagonist experiences a transformation, growing into his or her adult self. Virginia's transformation becomes particularly clear when one looks at the first and last scenes of the novel, parallel scenes in which she and Froggy kiss.

There is very little difference in Froggy's behavior between these scenes. In both, he is clearly smitten with Virginia and forthright and respectful about his attraction to her. In the first, however, Virginia is unable to let herself be fully present. Instead, her mind is preoccupied with other people's perceptions, even though she and Froggy are the only two in the room. By the closing scene, however, surrounded by peers, she is able to truly focus on Froggy and allow herself to take pleasure in her body and their relationship.

A great deal happens to cause this transformation, and little of it has to do with the shape of Virginia's body. Instead, Virginia changes because she comes to understand the complex power dynamics at play in her social world and family. Her brother, while thin and attractive, reveals himself to be a bad person. Annie, in contrast, shows Virginia that no matter how horribly other people treat you because of your body, it is still possible to retain power over yourself. These realizations allow Virginia to take control over her body image, dyeing her hair and piercing her eyebrow while also telling her father in no uncertain terms that he is not allowed to comment on her size.

When she finally kisses Froggy at school, then, it is not because her body has changed (even though she has started kickboxing and acquired an eyebrow ring), but because her perspective has changed. Like so many other popular characters from modern bildungsroman novels, from the gangs in S. E. Hinton's *The Outsiders* (1967) to the main characters of the Harry Potter series (1997–2007), changes in the outside world result in changes in the interior, emotional worlds of the characters. That Virginia expresses her own transformation with such humor and honesty makes her story one of the most successful contemporary entries in the subgenre.

T. Fleischmann, MFA

Further Reading

Colson, Diane. "Jukebooks: The Earth, My Butt, and Other Big Round Things by Carolyn Mackler." *YALSA: The Hub*. Amer. Lib. Assn., 24 Sept. 2014. Web. 4 Mar. 2014. <http://www.yalsa.ala.org/thehub/2014/09/24/jukebooks-the-earth-my-butt-and-other-big-round-things-by-carolyn-mackler/>.

Gray, B. Allison. Rev. of *The Earth, My Butt, and Other Big Round Things*, by Carolyn Mackler. *School Library Journal* Dec. 2004: 76–78. *Literary Reference Center*. Web. 4 Mar. 2015. <http://search.ebscohost.com/login.aspx?direct=true&db=lfh&AN=15396715&site=ehost-live>.

Eleanor & Park

Author: Rainbow Rowell (b. 1973)
First published: 2013
Type of work: Novel
Type of plot: Realism; Romance
Time of plot: 1986
Locale: Omaha, Nebraska

Principal characters

Park Sheridan, a sixteen-year-old loner

Eleanor Douglas, the new girl on Park's bus

Min-Dae "Mindy" Sheridan, Park's mother

Richie Trout, Eleanor's abusive stepfather

Steve Murphy, a bully at Park and Eleanor's school

The Story

Park Sheridan, a high school sophomore whose mother is a first-generation Korean immigrant, is one of few kids of Asian heritage in Omaha, Nebraska. Though he has grown up in the city and enjoys a fairly normal home life, he is still an outcast in school, where he has few friends. Park often retreats into his own world, listening to contemporary music on his Walkman while reading superhero comic books, particularly on the half-hour bus rides to and from school.

One day, a new student boards the bus: Eleanor Douglas, a chubby girl with flaming red hair, who dresses in unconventional fashion. Because nobody else on the bus will allow the new girl to sit down, and Steve Murphy and his friends loudly make fun of her, Park takes pity and offers to share his seat. Day after day, they ride together, never talking—though they share several honors classes at school—until Park notices Eleanor reading his comics over his shoulder. Making a concession to a common interest, he opens the comic book wider and turns the pages slowly enough so she can read along. After a time, he lends her comics to read at home.

So begins a budding, often awkward, sometimes painful romance between two social outcasts of vastly different backgrounds. While Park is open about his middle-class family, Eleanor is reticent, because her living situation is embarrassing: she shares a bedroom with four younger siblings in a tiny, squalid apartment where Richie, her drunken, drug-dealing, abusive stepfather dominates. Her family is dirt-poor; their food is bought at discount groceries and Eleanor's odd clothing comes from second-hand stores. To avoid talking about her home life, Eleanor discusses comic-book characters and music with Park. They hesitantly touch and draw closer together, and eventually their relationship deepens.

Because Eleanor is the target of school bullying—her textbooks are scribbled with nasty phrases, her clothes are dumped into a toilet so she has to walk home in her gym outfit—Park becomes protective of his girlfriend. One day, when Steve insults Eleanor yet again, calling her "Big Red," Park snaps. He attacks Steve with a move learned in taekwondo class, injuring the larger boy before Steve blacks Park's eyes and breaks his nose. Both boys are suspended from school for fighting.

Park and Eleanor spend as much time together as possible; Eleanor often crawls out of her bedroom window at night to meet him. Park invites Eleanor over to his house, and she begins spending considerable time there with him. While his parents are at first unimpressed with Eleanor, they are aware of her family situation and, over time, come to like her.

Ultimately, Eleanor's home life becomes intolerable as Richie concentrates his abuse on her. When she expresses a desire to escape to the house of an uncle in St. Paul, Minnesota, Park offers to drive her there in the second-hand Impala he acquired after obtaining his driver's license. Park's father, Jamie, catches him leaving on his mission and, rather than discouraging him, gives his son money and his truck to make the journey. Park safely delivers Eleanor. Afterward, missing her desperately, he writes her often and sends her mixtapes of his favorite bands. For months, she does not reply, then one day sends him a postcard containing just three little words.

Critical Evaluation

As the author has noted in interviews, the core of *Eleanor & Park* is largely autobiographical. Rainbow Rowell grew up in Omaha, Nebraska, was a teenager during the 1980s and had an abusive stepfather. While many writers use episodes from their past in fictional works, it takes real skill to transcend the mere recording of history in the process of creating art. Rowell has managed to take the painful memories of her youth and build them into a young adult novel that tenderly captures all the uncertainties and wonders of first love as experienced by two misfits. The halting growth and increasing intensity of the relationship between Eleanor and Park—with all its doubts, self-examinations, and setbacks—feels real. The structure of the novel, which begins with chapters labeled solely "Park" or "Eleanor," then shifts to chapters with multiple Park/Eleanor viewpoint divisions, reflects the changing emotions of the characters. Park's sacrifice at the end illustrates a maturity beyond the character's years: sometimes, true love means letting go.

Keeping the setting of the novel in the 1980s rather than updating it to a more modern era is an inspired choice. The less sophisticated time period gives the two main characters the opportunity to begin bonding over nonthreatening topics like comics, music, and television shows without such distractions as the Internet or cell phones.

The contrasts between the families of the protagonists adds conflict to the story by placing believable obstacles in the path of the romance. Though she is tall and beautiful, Eleanor's mother, Sabrina, is in an abusive relationship with her mean-spirited second husband. She does not stand up for her daughter against him or do anything to improve the family's circumstances. Meanwhile, Park's mother, known as Mindy, has fully adapted to an ambitious American lifestyle; she sells Avon products and runs a successful hair and nail salon in a converted garage at the Sheridan home. It is Mindy's growing affection for Eleanor—she gives her son's girlfriend a makeover—that drives the final wedge between the teenager and her stepfather, and forces her to flee to Minnesota for her own safety.

Jack Ewing

Further Reading

Green, John. "Two against the World." Rev. of *Eleanor & Park*, by Rainbow Rowell. *New York Times*. New York Times, 8 Mar. 2013. Web. 17 Oct. 2015. <http://www.nytimes.com/2013/03/10/books/review/eleanor-park-by-rainbow-rowell.html?_r=0>.

Ritter, Cynthia K. Rev. of *Eleanor & Park*, by Rainbow Rowell. *Horn Book Magazine* 89.3 (2013): 93–94. *Literary Reference Center*. Web. 2 Nov. 2015. <http://search.ebscohost.com/login.aspx?direct=true&db=lfh&AN=87024840&site=lrc-live>.

Rowell, Rainbow. "One Thing Leads to Another." Interview by Julie Bartel. *Hub*. YALSA, 27 Feb. 2014. Web. 17 Oct. 2015. <http://www.yalsa.ala.org/the-hub/2014/02/27/one-thing-leads-to-another-an-interview-with-rainbow-rowell>.

Elsewhere

Author: Gabrielle Zevin (b. 1977)
First published: 2005
Type of work: Novel
Type of plot: Fantasy
Time of plot: Unspecified
Locale: Otherworld

Principal characters

Elizabeth "Liz" Hall, a fifteen-year-old girl who has just died

Betty Bloom, Liz's deceased grandmother
Owen Welles, Liz's new friend and love interest
Thandiwe "Thandi" Washington, Liz's new friend
Alvy Hall, Liz's still-living younger brother
Zooey Brandon, Liz's still-living best friend
Curtis Jest, a deceased British musician

The Story

When Liz Hall unexpectedly wakes up aboard a ship, she thinks she is dreaming, but she soon discovers that the ship is ferrying the dead to the afterlife. Her cabinmate, Thandi, matter-of-factly mentions being shot in the head, while a famous British rock star named Curtis Jest also seems unfazed by his death from a drug overdose. Liz cannot understand how Thandi and Curtis can let go of their lives so easily. She is further disconcerted when a young version of her grandmother Betty, who died before she was born, meets her at the dock of a place called Elsewhere. Liz soon learns that everyone in Elsewhere ages in reverse until babyhood, when they are sent back to Earth to start new lives.

At first, Liz spends most of her time using coin-operated binoculars on Elsewhere's observation decks to watch her family and friends back on Earth. She even identifies the taxi driver who killed her in a hit-and-run accident and considers trying to bring him to justice, but she realizes he is a kind man desperately trying to care for his sick son. Somewhat reassured, Liz becomes a counselor for newly arrived dogs in Elsewhere and is thrilled to discover that she has a natural ability to speak Canine.

In spite of her progress, Liz takes a forbidden trip to the Well, a portal on the ocean floor where the deceased can speak through water to people on Earth. While trying to contact her younger brother, Alvy, Liz is arrested by Owen Welles, a young man who also had trouble adjusting to the afterlife ten years earlier. Liz realizes that her bungled encounter with Alvy has brought pain and confusion rather than closure, so she decides to move on. Her friendship with Owen is cemented when he comes to her for help adopting a dog, and although Liz struggles with the idea that the now-seventeen-year-old Owen was once married, she eventually accepts that love can work even under such strange circumstances.

Just when Liz finally feels comfortable in her backwards life, Owen's widow, Emily, arrives in Elsewhere. Conflicted, Owen believes that he owes his loyalty to Emily. The heartbroken Liz decides to invoke the Sneaker Clause, which allows those who died before the age of sixteen to go back to Earth immediately instead of waiting to revert to babyhood. Halfway through the journey, however, Liz realizes that she does not want to give up her life in Elsewhere any more than she had wanted to give up her life on Earth. She becomes stranded in the ocean between Earth and Elsewhere, but Owen, who now realizes that he and Emily cannot simply pick up where they left off, rescues Liz and brings her back.

Liz and Owen resume their relationship, and Curtis Jest unexpectedly falls in love with and marries Betty. Liz continues to grow younger, finding that the reverse-aging process is actually very liberating. She gains additional closure when she and Owen manage to talk to Alvy one last time to say goodbye, and she even has the opportunity to tell the taxi driver who hit her that she has long since forgiven him. The years pass, and when it is finally time, Betty, Curtis, and the now two-year-old Owen see the infant Liz off when she is wrapped in swaddling clothes and released down the River that leads back to Earth. There, a baby who is both Liz and not Liz is born, ready to start a new life.

Critical Evaluation

A debut novel written in a straightforward, simple style, *Elsewhere* tells the story of Liz's emotional journey as she grieves for the things she will never get to experience due to her early death, such as going to college and having children of her own. Although the book is set in what might be called Heaven, it does not dwell on theological questions, but rather on finding value in life no matter what form that life takes. The author uses humor to great effect, particularly in the wry conversations that dogs have about humans' inability to accept love as easily as dogs do. Similarly, life in Elsewhere entails a certain level of harmless but silly bureaucracy, such as the requirement that everyone visit the Department of Last Words to confirm their last utterances on Earth, no matter how undignified they may be.

Another theme the novel explores is the potential for unexpectedly fulfilling relationships, as opposed to the idea of every person having only one true love. Because those who arrive in Elsewhere immediately begin aging backwards, by the time their earthly spouses arrive, they may be completely out of sync with one another, as evidenced by Owen and Emily. However, new possibilities are introduced, such as when Curtis, the recently deceased young rock star, falls in love with Betty, who died in her fifties but has progressed back to her thirties by the time Liz arrives in Elsewhere. Witnessing these

relationships allows Liz to accept that even though she will not experience the traditional course of love and marriage as Liz, she still can have a satisfying, loving relationship before she goes back to Earth to become someone who both is and is not Liz. In addition, through the reversal of the aging process, *Elsewhere* emphasizes how railing against growing older is as futile as railing against growing younger would be and that people are responsible for finding happiness in the world around them no matter what their age.

Amy Sisson, MS, MLS

Further Reading

Flynn, Kitty. Rev. of *Elsewhere*, by Gabrielle Zevin. *Horn Book Magazine* Sept.–Oct. 2005: 591. *Literary Reference Center*. Web. 9 Apr. 2015. <http://search.ebscohost.com/login.aspx?direct=true&db=lfh&AN=18387280&site=lrc-live>

Mattson, Jennifer. "A Death Well Lived." Rev. of *Elsewhere*, by Gabrielle Zevin. *Booklist* Aug. 2005: 2017. *Literary Reference Center*. Web. 9 Apr. 2015. <http://search.ebscohost.com/login.aspx?direct=true&db=lfh&AN=17966598&site=lrc-live>.

Spires, Elizabeth. Rev. of *Elsewhere*, by Gabrielle Zevin. New York Times. New York Times, 4 Dec. 2005. Web. 9 Apr. 2015. <http://www.nytimes.com/2005/12/04/books/review/04spires.html?_r=>.

Ender's Game

Author: Orson Scott Card (b. 1951)
First published: 1985
Type of work: Novel
Type of plot: Science Fiction
Time of plot: An unspecified future
Locale: Earth; Outer space

Principal characters

Andrew "Ender" Wiggin, a young recruit being trained in interplanetary warfare
Peter, Ender's diabolical older brother
Valentine, Ender's kind older sister
Colonel Hyrum Graff, the director of Primary Training at the Battle School
Bonzo Madrid, Ender's fierce rival, another student at Battle School

Mazer Rackham, the most famous military commander of the human race

Plot Summary

In *Ender's Game*, Earth is at war with an extraterrestrial race called the buggers. The buggers are a sophisticated insect-like species that almost destroyed Earth decades before the present in what was called the Second Invasion. The human race was saved thanks to an admiral named Mazer Rackham.

It is into this world that Andrew "Ender" Wiggin, the youngest of three children, is born. His birth as a socially maligned "Third" is remarkable because the military government allows most parents to have only two children. Ender owes his existence to his genius older siblings—his evil brother, Peter, and his sister, Valentine, his only confidant. After allowing his conception, the military follows Ender's every move through an implanted monitor, just as they did with Peter and Valentine. When he is six years old, the monitor is removed. Ender violently beats his schoolyard bully and is subsequently recruited by Colonel Hyrum Graff to train to become an officer at the Battle School, located on a ship in Earth's orbit. New recruits at the Battle School are called Launchies, and Ender immediately distinguishes himself from his classmates by exhibiting a complex understanding of how bodies can orient themselves in zero gravity. This knowledge comes in handy when Ender first encounters the most important of the Battle School's activities—the Battle Room. The Battle Room is a zero-gravity space in which students simulate battle. Competition is cutthroat but Ender thrives in the Battle Room, as well as in a computer game called the Mind Game. Just as he begins to make friends, Ender is promoted to an army of older fighters. He learns new techniques—making a few enemies, including a student army commander named Bonzo, along the way—and begins teaching these techniques to his old group of Launchies. Ender felt emotionally isolated from his classmates from the beginning, but as his talent becomes more obvious to the school's leaders, that isolation is enforced. For example, when Ender gets into a violent fight with four older students, the teachers decide not to intervene.

Back on Earth, Peter and Valentine begin writing influential articles (under pseudonyms) on "the nets," their version of the Internet. Their writings make them major figures in world events. When Ender is nine, he is made commander of his own army. To test his mettle, the leaders of the school schedule Ender's army for more battles than any other army in the school's history. The school goes to incredible lengths to stack these battles against Ender, but he still wins every one. After beating his old commander and nemesis Bonzo, Ender accidentally kills him in a fight—though he does not immediately realize that he has killed the boy. After the encounter with Bonzo, Ender is sent to Command School, where he trains under the legendary Mazer Rackham. Rackham teaches him about the buggers and makes him lead elaborate simulated missions against them. He wins one mission at a tremendous cost. When the mission is completed, Ender discovers that all of his simulated missions at the Command School were real and that he has single-handedly wiped out the entire bugger race. This knowledge shapes the rest of his life.

On Earth, Peter has become a supreme ruler. Valentine and Ender seek out the bugger world and recolonize it. Years later, Ender, who had once communicated with the queen of the buggers through his thoughts, finds a landscape that he had encountered in the simulated Mind Game at Battle School. It was constructed by the buggers to lead him to a pupa, the last of the buggers. Ender makes it his life's mission to find a world where the buggers can live again.

Critical Evaluation

The novel *Ender's Game*, based on a short story that Orson Scott Card wrote in 1977, was published in 1985. It remains one of the best-loved young adult books in the science-fiction genre. Like many science fiction stories, Ender's Game explores real-world questions by placing them in a new context. In many ways, Ender's Game is about the "ethics of warfare," Laura Miller wrote for *Salon*. She cited a 2013 book called *Ender's Game and Philosophy*, which discusses a number of topics through the lens of the novel, among them genocide, drone technology, the concept of free will, and the "double effect," a thirteenth-century theory from Thomas Aquinas, which provides the basic moral argument for killing in self-defense. According to Aquinas, one is not responsible for the unintended consequences of one's actions. The double effect provides the moral basis of Ender's killing of his childhood bully, Bonzo, and the buggers, though Ender has difficulty coming to peace with these actions. Still, Miller argues that the "emotional charge" of *Ender's Game* lies in its depiction of tortured adolescence. According to Miller, Ender is both a hero and a victim. He struggles to give and receive love, all the while brooding over those times in which he had to fight to kill and did not want to. The violence in *Ender's Game*, Miller wrote, is an internal violence; ultimately, the most important battle that Ender must fight is with himself.

Molly Hagan

Further Reading

Card, Orson Scott, ed. *Ender's World: Fresh Perspectives on the SF Classic Ender's Game*. New York: Scholastic, 2013. Print.

Miller, Laura. "The Twisted Mind of 'Ender's Game.'" *Salon*. Salon Media Group, 30 Oct. 2013. Web. 23 Mar. 2015. <http://www.salon.com/2013/10/30/the_twisted_mind_of_enders_game>.

Wittkower, D. E., and Lucinda Rush. *Ender's Game and Philosophy: Genocide Is Child's Play*. Chicago: Open Court, 2013. Print.

Every Day

Author: David Levithan (b. 1972)
First published: 2012
Type of work: Novel
Type of plot: Science Fiction
Time of plot: Twenty-first century
Locale: United States

Principal characters

A, a sixteen-year-old boy who wakes up each day in another person's body

Rhiannon, A's love interest

Justin, Rhiannon's boyfriend

Nathan, a religious, studious sixteen-year-old possessed by A

Reverend Poole, Nathan's confidant and friend

Andrew, an average sixteen-year-old possessed by A

The Story

The narrative of *Every Day* begins under the heading "Day 5994." A, the main character and narrator, has been born beginning each day in someone else's body, which he lives in for only that day before moving on to another body of the same age. At the beginning of *Every Day*, A is sixteen and finds himself in the body of a boy named Justin.

A thinks this particular day will be no more remarkable than the ones before until he meets Rhiannon,

Courtesy of Penguin Young Readers

Justin's girlfriend. Justin is an angry, selfish sixteen-year-old who communicates with his girlfriend even less than he does with his mother and father. What he lacks in self-confidence, he makes up for in belittling the people around him, especially Rhiannon. A finds himself attracted to Rhiannon, so he decides to take her to the beach while he has Justin's body in order to provide her with a happy memory. However, A finds himself falling in love with Rhiannon, and before he switches to the next body, he creates an e-mail account with Rhiannon's e-mail and phone number so that he can contact her again.

For the next few days, A continues to contact Rhiannon, meeting her while he is in the bodies of different teenagers from around the same area. After a few meetings, he finally decides to tell her the truth about himself. However, because he is so focused on seeing Rhiannon as much as possible, he becomes reckless and leaves one of the bodies he has inhabited asleep in a car on the side of the road. The body belongs to a boy named Nathan, who is very intelligent and very religious.

Nathan becomes convinced that he has been possessed by the devil, a perspective that is championed by the leader of his church, a man by the name of Reverend Poole. Together, Poole and Nathan continue to e-mail A, demanding to know what has happened and how he has managed to do what he does. A avoids these traps for as long as he can while he begins a relationship with Rhiannon, who believes A and finds herself drawn to him in every body he possesses. At the end, A must face many decisions regarding his life, his feelings, his connection to Rhiannon, and who he really is.

Critical Evaluation

Every Day does not follow traditional narrative structure, character arcs, or other conventional storytelling conventions. It is in breaking free of tradition, however, that it also follows many of the conventions associated with young adult literature. In fact, it is by utilizing untraditional storytelling that *Every Day* is able to approach important young adult themes in new ways. The simple structure of A's rather unique life brings the theme of identity to the forefront of the novel, and it is through this theme that all other major ideas and conventions are explored. Although A does not have his own body, he still finds himself dealing with conventional issues of adolescence in the bodies he inhabits, such as personal relationships, drinking and drugs, social structures, and perhaps most importantly, love.

The novel begins with A talking about that despite having jumped from one body to another, he still knows that there is something about him that is distinctly "A" and has nothing to do with the body he inhabits. The idea of a mind-body dualism was made famous by philosopher René Descartes and is universal in the human experience. It is highlighted by the fact that A has no original body to call his own. His basic struggle with identity is something every human being must face, but he must also face other kinds of problems with identity while he inhabits different bodies. Much like the personae that people may create and maintain, and which are often an important part of life within the social structures of high school students, A must work behind a type of mask every day as he works to fulfill his own goals. Mirroring what many adolescents feel, A must keep up the projection and image of the person whose body he has taken over that day while still pursuing what is important to him at his core and in his soul.

While dealing with these issues of identity, A also finds himself in a number of situations in which he must make personal choices. In this respect, Levithan constructs A with what some might deem an ideal adolescent mind. Even though A is only sixteen years old, he has had the experiences that have taught him to distance himself from the emotions and desires of the bodies he inhabits. Therefore, while some might make reckless

decisions about drug use and drinking, sex, or personal relationships, A has the emotional maturity and intelligence to mostly make the ideal choices. For example, when A goes to the beach with Rhiannon for the first time, the body of Justin keeps pushing him to be cruel to her, but A overcomes these impulses and is able to create a strong bond with her.

By the end of the novel, Levithan presents a thorough study of the subgenre of science fiction and how it can highlight and approach various conventions from different perspectives within the young adult genre. His unconventional approach gives new meaning to often very conventional ideas.

Aaron Horton, MA

Further Reading

"David Levithan." *Baker & Taylor Author Biographies* (2000): 1. *Literary Reference Center*. Web. 16 Dec. 2015. <http://search.ebscohost.com/login.aspx?direct=true&db=lfh&AN=49646995&site=lrc-live>.

Deahl, Rachel. "David Levithan: The Happy Editor-Writer." *Publishers Weekly* 255.7 (2008): 16. *Literary Reference Center*. Web. 16 Dec. 2015. <http://search.ebscohost.com/login.aspx?direct=true&db=lfh&AN=30096364&site=lrc-live>.

"Don't Be Afraid to Write a Bad Book: David Levithan on *Every Day*." *Guardian*. Guardian News and Media, 7 Oct. 2013. Web. 9 Dec. 2015. <http://www.theguardian.com/books/2013/oct/07/david-levithan-every-day-interview>.

Everybody Sees the Ants

Author: A. S. King (b. 1970)
First published: 2011
Type of work: Novel
Type of plot: Psychological Fiction
Time of plot: 2011
Locale: Fredericksburg, Pennsylvania; Tempe, Arizona; Laos

Principal characters

Lucky Linderman, a high school student
Lori and Victor Linderman, Lucky's parents
Nader McMillan, bully
Virginia "Ginny" Clemens, Lucky's friend

Charlotte Dent, Lucky's classmate
Lara Jones, Lucky's classmate and friend
Uncle Dave and Aunt Jodi, Lucky's uncle and aunt
Harry Linderman, Lucky's grandfather

The Story

In his freshman year at Fredericksburg "Freddy" High School in Pennsylvania, fifteen-year-old Lucky Linderman receives the unwanted attention of school authorities when he distributes a survey to his fellow students as part of a social studies project. The survey asks, *"If you were going to commit suicide, what method would you choose?"* (3).

Lucky spends most of the next summer at the community swimming pool with his mother, Lori, who is a compulsive swimmer and calls herself a "reincarnated squid" (7). Lucky likes to play cards with his classmate Lara Jones. Victor, Lucky's father and a chef at a French restaurant, apparently can relate to his son and wife only by cooking for them. Lucky calls him a turtle, hiding in his shell.

Lucky's tormentor at school, Nader McMillan, works as lifeguard at the pool and viciously teases Lucky. When Nader tries to embarrass Charlotte Dent, who has lost her bikini top in the pool, Lucky dives in to recover it and return it to Charlotte. This earns Lucky more of Nader's hatred and abuse.

Lucky remembers when he was seven years old and his grandmother, Janice, died from cancer. She had lost her husband, Harry, almost forty years before in 1972. Despite being given the nickname "Lucky," Harry never returned from a mission during the Vietnam War. His grandson was given the name Lucky in his memory. Lucky and his parents go out to eat after Janice's death, and when Lucky goes to the restroom, Nader bullies Lucky for the first time, deliberately urinating on his feet.

Before she dies, Janice asks Lucky to rescue Harry, whom she irrationally believes is being held captive in postwar Laos. This triggers Lucky's fantasies of conducting a rescue mission to free his grandfather from a Laotian jungle prison. These different fantasies are described in many of the novel's chapters.

Lucky's father advises his son to ignore Nader, saying "'Fighting is for sissies'" (29). This advice doesn't help since Nader humiliates a much weaker student in the locker room with the help of a banana dipped in toilet water as a way to punish Lucky.

At the pool, Nader ambushes Lucky and grinds one side of Lucky's face on the concrete. Lucky sees imaginary ants mocking him for being a victim. Although

Lucky names his assailant to the pool manager, she is reluctant to act. Lori is outraged and decides to take Lucky to her brother Dave in Tempe, Arizona.

Dave's wife Jodi is worried that Lucky is suicidal and wants Lucky to take Prozac. Lucky and Lori reject this idea, and Dave introduces Lucky to lifting weights. Lucky admires Dave and takes up the sport. On an evening walk, Lucky sees the shadow of a girl moving stealthily, and the following Sunday, Lucky sees her singing in the church choir. While benchpressing weights, Dave confesses to Lucky he was a bully at school. The next night, Lucky is approached by the girl. Her name is Virginia "Ginny" Clemson, and she is a hair model and secret member of an all-girl amateur drama group that is about to stage the *Vagina Monologues*. She takes Lucky to her rehearsal.

Ginny tells Lucky that his uncle is a notorious adulterer and slept with Ginny's overbearing mother. She shows him a huge billboard that features her advertising a shampoo brand. Lucky's view of Dave has changed. The next night Lucky tells Ginny about his father and how Victor never got over the fact that his father died in the war before he knew him. Lucky also tells Ginny about being bullied. He does not tell her about being tormented with the banana. Ginny kisses Lucky to cheer him up.

On Lucky's last day in Arizona, Ginny appears at Dave's home. She has shaved her hair in protest of being hit in the eye by her mother. She and Lucky go to the play before Lori picks up Lucky for the flight home.

Back in Fredericksburg, Lucky asks his father for a weight set. Victor agrees. At the pool, Lucky has a nice time with Lara even though Nader is still there. The next day, Lucky confronts Nader, who has just been fired. He tells Nader to leave him alone or he will report him to the police. In his final jungle fantasy, Lucky buries his grandfather in Laos. Lucky and his father then bond over an early breakfast.

Critical Evaluation

The key theme of *Everybody Sees the Ants* is bullying. The novel shows bullying primarily through the experience of its victims: the narrator Lucky, his schoolmate Charlotte Dent, and even Ginny, who is bullied by her mother. Bullying can be verbal, as when Nader ridicules Lucky and debases Charlotte by calling them names. It can be physical, as when Nader assaults Lucky and gropes Charlotte or when Ginny's mother hits her. Bullying can also be psychological, as when Nader urinates on Lucky's feet or makes him eat a banana dipped in toilet water or tries to force Charlotte to exit the pool without her bikini top. Nader's bullying is always done with the intent of humiliating Lucky or Charlotte in front of their peers.

The novel shows the difficulty in standing up to bullies. Lucky's father preaches nonviolence, and Uncle Dave encourages weight training. Fighting a physically stronger opponent, however, is not always an option either.

The novel uses the image of the ants Lucky sees as a symbol of the inferiority felt by victims of bullying. Only when Lucky imagines his grandfather telling him that everybody has fears does Lucky decide to confront the bully and tell him to stop or he will go to the police.

In addition, the novel explores parent-child relationships (by juxtaposing the Linderman and Clemens families), teenage romance and sexuality (through Lucky, Ginny, Lara, and Charlotte), and the loss felt by family members for soldiers who are lost to war and declared missing in action.

R. C. Lutz, PhD

Further Reading

Rev. of *Everybody Sees the Ants*, by A. S. King. *Kirkus Reviews*. Kirkus Media, 3 Oct. 2011. Web. 26 March 2015. <https://www.kirkusreviews.com/book-reviews/as-king/everybody-sees-ants/>.

Rev. of *Everybody Sees the Ants*, by A. S. King. *Publishers Weekly*. PWxyz, 19 Sept. 2011. Web. 26 March 2015. <http://www.publishersweekly.com/pw/search/index.html?q=king+ants+everybody&submit.x=0&submit.y=0>.

Far, Far Away

Author: Tom McNeal (b. 1947)
First published: 2014
Type of work: Novel
Type of plot: Paranormal Fantasy
Time of plot: Present day
Locale: United States

Principal characters

Jeremy Johnson Johnson, fifteen-year-old boy who hears ghosts
Ginger Boultinghouse, Jeremy's classmate and love interest
Mr. Johnson, Jeremy's reclusive father
Jacob Grimm, a ghost who speaks to Jeremy

Sten Blix, town baker
Frank Bailey, baker's apprentice
Jenny Applegarth, town waitress and love interest for Mr. Johnson

The Story

Jeremy Johnson Johnson is an outcast. At fifteen years old, he knows he does not fit into his community. His dysfunctional family and his intelligence are two reasons; however, his most unusual talent, the ability to talk to ghosts, is what really sets him apart. The ghost in his life is the narrator of the story, and his identity, Jacob Grimm, sets readers up for the contemporary fairy tale of Jeremy's life.

The story starts with a typical school day. On his way home from school, Jeremy is stopped by Ginger Boultinghouse and two of her friends. Ginger, a pretty, popular girl, is interested in Jeremy because of his differences; he is a puzzle. She invites him to the bakery for Prince Cakes. Jacob, who has appointed himself as Jeremy's guardian, sees no harm in the trip, so he does not discourage his charge. This trip sets up conflicts as Conk Crinklaw, the local jock, and a group of his friends drive past and mock Jeremy. The other boys' comments show how separate Jeremy is from his schoolmates. It also marks the beginning of a friendship between Jeremy and Ginger.

Jacob is rightfully concerned about Ginger's influence on Jeremy as the story progresses. While Jacob has encouraged Jeremy's studies, Ginger wants Jeremy to experience normal teenage activities. One night she talks him into playing a trick on Sten Blix. The trick becomes a problem when Jeremy is identified as the culprit after Blix calls the police. Sten Blix covers for him, and seems to be a positive role model by providing Jeremy and Ginger with several jobs after the rest of the community turns their back on Jeremy's lawn-mowing business because of the trick. The teens begin to trust the baker.

Meanwhile, Jeremy receives a foreclosure statement from the bank for his home. The teen has been caretaker for himself and his father since his grandfather died, but his inability to earn money has led to the financial disaster. Ginger, however, has a brilliant idea to save his home. Jeremy will audition for a game show. The producers are thrilled with his knowledge of fairy tales, so they arrange for his appearance. As he answers questions on the show, he begins to think his financial woes are over. Then, the final query is a pop culture question that neither Jeremy nor Jacob can answer. Jeremy proves his integrity by refusing to answer even when an anonymous voice whispers it to him. His financial hopes are dashed.

Before Jeremy has to deal with the fallout from the bank's foreclosure, he and Ginger take another job with Sten Blix. It is a job from which neither teen returns. It turns out that Sten Blix has been kidnapping children from around the area for years, and the pair become his latest victims. They find themselves held prisoner in the basement of Sten's home, along with Frank Bailey, a former employee of the bakery. Sten, it seems, has been looking for a friend, but no one is capable of filling that role, so he has been trying to make friends. Since the kidnapped youngsters cannot do what he wants, he tortures them, and in most cases, he kills them. His previous victims, however, had not had the help of a ghost. After over a month of captivity, Jacob desperately reaches out to a family friend, leading her and Jeremy's father to the teens. They are rescued, but Sten Blix commits suicide before he can be punished for his crimes.

Critical Evaluation

The novel's most obvious feature is its relation to fairy tales. This connection is partially shown through the choice of Jacob Grimm as the ghostly narrator and partially through the plot connection to the tale of Hansel and Gretel. Jeremy and Ginger are a modern-day version of Hansel and Gretel with a budding romantic relationship replacing the sibling link. The witch is replaced with grandfatherly Sten Blix, and her gingerbread house becomes his bakery. His kidnapping and eventual burning of children in the bakery's oven is reminiscent of the witch's desire to bake children for food.

Another central theme is the importance of relationships. While prisoners, Jeremy and Ginger discover strength in each other and reach out to Frank Bailey, another outcast held by Blix. Frank understands the desire for a friend and shares Sten's motivation.

Outside of the teens' prison cell, other relationships grow. Jeremy's father takes control of his life. Along with an old friend, he starts to change his life. Conk Crinklaw, who has been romantically interested in Ginger, continues to show his attachment by helping in the search and continuing to believe in her. The town's deputy also shows a strange devotion to Ginger by searching tirelessly. Finally, Jacob Grimm learns that he must do things with which he is not comfortable if he is to save the boy he has come to love.

A final literary element important to the novel is symbolism. Sten Blix's specialty Prince Cakes represent several things. When they are introduced, Ginger reminds Jeremy of a town saying, "'Green smoke at midnight; Prince Cakes at first light.'" Prince cakes are a special treat that show up a few times a year; ironically, the treats hail the death of one of Blix's victims, a fact that is only discovered at the end. However, for Jeremy, the treat itself is also a reminder of his mother's abandonment. Jeremy's mother had always told him that "whatever living thing was looked upon during the first bite of *Prinsesstårta* would steal one's heart. It was said that this enchantment was so steadfast, it could be reversed only by the touch of a salted tear upon the lips of the spellbound." The legend became her excuse for leaving. Later, when Ginger looks at Jeremy while taking her first bite, a bond is formed. This bond holds throughout the story but is threatened after their rescue when a crying Jeremy leans down to kiss Ginger and a tear falls toward her mouth; a quick action on Jacob's part sends the tear in another direction, and the bond remains.

Theresa L. Stowell, PhD

Further Reading

Hand, Elizabeth. "Happily Never After." Rev. of *Far Far Away*, by Tom McNeal. *Magazine of Fantasy and Science Fiction* Jan.–Feb. 2014: 40+. Print.

Pavao, Kate. "Q/A Tom McNeal." *Publishers Weekly.* PWxyz, 29 May 2013. Web. 27 Sept. 2015. <http://www.publishersweekly.com/pw/by-topic/authors/interviews/article/57497-q-a-with-tom-mcneal.html>

Schall, Lucy. *Genre Talks for Teens: Booktalks and More for Every Teen Reading Interest.* Westport: Libraries Unlimited, 2009. Print.

The Fault in Our Stars

Author: John Green (b. 1977)
First published: 2012
Type of work: Novel
Type of plot: Romance; Realism
Time of plot: Early 2010s
Locales: Indianapolis, Indiana; Amsterdam, the Netherlands

Principal characters

Hazel Grace Lancaster, a sixteen-year-old cancer patient
Kaitlyn, Hazel's friend, also sixteen
Augustus "Gus" Waters, a tall, dark-haired, blue-eyed young man with a prosthetic leg

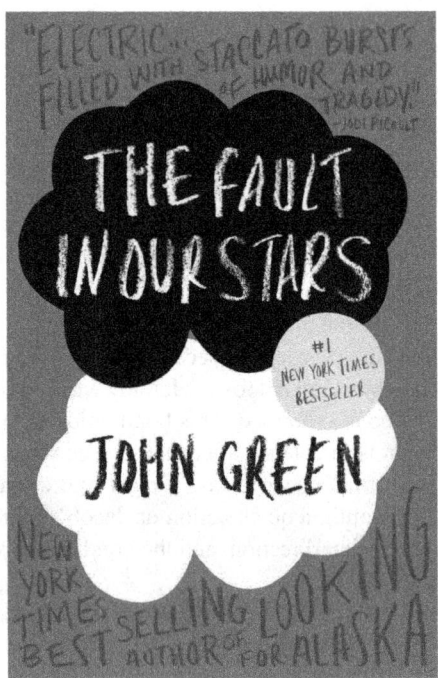

Courtesy of Penguin Young Readers

Isaac, a boy with eye cancer who is going blind
Peter Van Houten, a recluse who is Hazel's favorite author
Lidewij Vliegenthart, Van Houten's red-haired female
assistant in the Netherlands

The Story

Hazel Lancaster seldom leaves her house any more. No
wonder: several years before, she contracted thyroid cancer that has since spread to her lungs, her face is swollen
from an experimental tumor-shrinking drug, and she has
to use an oxygen tank. Depressed, she constantly rereads
An Imperial Affliction, a novel by Peter Van Houten about
the inevitability of death, and is obsessed about the fate
of a leukemia-stricken character. Hazel has written many
times to the reclusive author but has never received a reply.

In an effort to improve her mood and attitude, the
family doctor recommends that Hazel join a cancer support group, and she reluctantly agrees to attend. At the
group's first meeting, Hazel is attracted to the handsome
Augustus "Gus" Waters, who has lost a leg to osteosarcoma, a form of bone cancer, but is now apparently
cancer-free. Gus is accompanying his friend Isaac, who
has eye cancer and will soon be totally blind. Augustus
is similarly interested in Hazel, and the two teenagers,
who are both the only child in their respective families,
start to become better acquainted. As they learn more

about each other—Hazel has not attended school for
three years but earned a GED certificate, while Gus, a
former outstanding athlete and a fan of violent science-
fiction books and video games, who is still adjusting to
his prosthetic leg—the two teens draw closer together.

Hoping to please Hazel, Gus writes author Van Houten,
and he receives a long reply from the author's assistant
Lidewij Vliegenthart. Hazel writes a follow-up note to
the author, and she too receives a reply: Van Houten will
only answer questions about his work if asked in person,
and he invites her to visit if she is ever in Amsterdam,
the Netherlands. Because her parents cannot afford such
a trip, Gus uses his saved Make-a-Wish-type grant to arrange a four-day vacation for him and Hazel.

Upon arrival in the Netherlands, Hazel and Gus, as
Mr. and Mrs. Waters, enjoy a memorable meal at a fine
restaurant, compliments of Peter Van Houten. The following day, they meet with the author and his assistant
at Van Houten's house. He is a major disappointment:
balding, saggy, abrasive, and drunk. Lidewij, embarrassed at her employer's rude behavior, resigns her position. She escorts Gus and Hazel to the house where Anne
Frank and her family hid from the Nazis during World
War II, and the teens are profoundly affected. After returning to their hotel, Hazel and Gus make love for the
first and only time. Gus confesses that before they left
the United States, he had been experiencing pain, went
in for tests, and learned that he is riddled with cancer.

After returning home, Gus undergoes intensive chemotherapy but continues to deteriorate, until he is permanently confined to bed and fading fast. Hazel visits
frequently, meeting many members of Gus's family who
have gathered for his decline and his inevitable death. At
Gus's funeral, Van Houten shows up drunk, and Hazel
calls him pathetic. She suddenly realizes Van Houten
must have lost someone close to him to write so realistically about leukemia, and he confirms that his eight-
year-old daughter succumbed to the disease. Hazel subsequently learns Gus wrote something for her. She tracks
the missing message to Van Houten's home and persuades
Lidewij to find and send her Gus's final written words.

Critical Evaluation

Written in first-person from Hazel's point of view, *The
Fault in Our Stars*, despite its downbeat subject matter—the erosion of health of young people disabled by
cancer—is surprisingly positive and often humorous.
Much of the uplifting tone is due to the author's skill in
creating characters who are not just statistics or merely

stereotypical faceless victims of a debilitating disease, but are uniquely human, genuine-seeming individuals, often with deep reservoirs of courage. All of the youthful cancer patients depicted cope with their condition the best way they can and attempt to live their lives to the fullest for whatever span of time they are granted, in order to leave a mark on the world of their existence, however brief. In the throes of pain, in the midst of loss, under the shadow of death, Hazel, Isaac, Gus, and other cancer patients are able to make wisecracks, philosophize, relate to one another, and plan ahead.

A major theme of the novel (which has drawn inevitable comparisons to *Romeo and Juliet* because of its doomed young lovers) is sacrifice, particularly as embodied in the character of Gus. He allows his friend Isaac, angered because his longtime girlfriend Monica could not handle his blindness, to vent his fury by smashing the sports trophies Gus earned when he was healthy. Gus also sacrifices his own dying wish for Hazel's sake, so she can meet the author she admired from afar, and even his own life by foregoing needed therapy to travel with Hazel to Europe.

A critical and commercial success, *The Fault in Our Stars* was a *New York Times* best seller and has been translated into Hebrew, Dutch, German, Spanish, French, Chinese, Portuguese, and other languages. The novel served as basis of a well-received and highly profitable film adaptation released in 2014.

Jack Ewing

Further Reading

Dickinson, Kelly. "The Waiting Game: Teens React to *The Fault in Our Stars* Movie Trailer." *Hub*. YALSA, 24 Feb. 2014. Web. 7 Dec. 2015. <http://www.yalsa.ala.org/thehub/2014/02/24/the-waiting-game-teens-react-to-the-tfios-trailer>.

Green, John. "Teen's Top Ten: An Interview with John Green." Interview by Dena Little. *Hub*. YALSA, 23, Oct. 2012. Web. 7 Dec. 2015. <http://www.yalsa.ala.org/thehub/2012/10/23/teens-top-ten-an-interview-with-john-green>.

Feed

Author: M. T. Anderson (b. 1968)
First published: 2002
Type of work: Novel

Type of plot: Dystopian Fiction
Time of plot: An unspecified time in the future
Locale: United States

Principal characters

Titus, the teenaged narrator
Link Arwaker, Titus's friend, a partial clone of Abraham Lincoln
Marty, another friend, an expert game-player
Calista, Titus's former love interest
Quendy, another friend, a trendsetter
Violet Durn, a girl Titus meets on the moon

The Story

In *Feed*, Titus and his friends, like most future citizens, are part of an integrated network. They have been implanted from infancy with chips that make them virtual computers. Via the feed, an Internet-like system that derives precise demographic information from their activities for profit-oriented corporations, they stream live or recorded information, entertainment, and ads that tell them how to think and act and what to buy. Young adults, jaded and easily bored, are marked with red, raw, acne-like lesions, perhaps as a result of the feed. They mostly communicate electronically and their speech, severely limited in vocabulary, is peppered with slang.

While vacationing on the moon with friends Link, Marty, Calista, Loga, and Quendy, Titus meets attractive Violet Durn, who is quite different from girls he knows. The two teenagers hit it off as a couple. During a visit to a dance club, they involuntarily join an old man in shouting a revolutionary, antifeed slogan, causing the police to shut everyone down by disconnecting them from the feednet.

Titus and the others are kept offline while they are checked for viruses and evidence of hacking. They are barely able to function without the feed. In recovery, Titus and Violet visit various places on the moon, and he actually has to express himself without electronic assistance.

Eventually, all the friends are rebooted and the flow of information begins anew. They return to Earth. Titus thinks he may be in love with Violet. She tells Titus she did not get the feed until she was seven and admits her feedware may have been damaged by the hacking incident. She involves Titus in a project to resist the system by creating a false customer profile through shopping for bizarre products she has no intention of buying.

Titus's parents buy him a flying vehicle, and the young couple zip off on excursions to a steak farm, a mountain resort, and the beach. At a party, Titus's friends tease Violet for being different and untrendy. Violet demands Titus take her home, and during the trip they discuss the difference between real and simulated feelings. Violet admits the interface in her brain is deteriorating. Titus witnesses the beginning of her breakdown at another party.

Titus visits Violet in the hospital, where she is undergoing tests. Because of her efforts to undermine the system, she is not eligible for free repair, and her father cannot afford to pay for treatment. Violet loses memory during a seizure and wants to download everything she remembers to Titus, the most important person in her life, so afterward he can return memories she will have forgotten. But all the information gives Titus a headache, and he deletes everything. As Titus resumes his carefree life with his friends, he drifts away from Violet.

Violet slowly shuts down. Titus, who has already hooked up with Quendy, visits his former girlfriend at the request of her father. Violet lies in a vegetative state, unable to move or talk, think or react, at the brink of going permanently offline. Titus promises Violet he will remember her, but is immediately distracted by an ad for a close-out sale.

Critical Evaluation

Part science fiction, part satire, part tragedy, *Feed* presents a logical extrapolation of where early twenty-first century society is headed. Author M. T. (Matthew Tobin) Anderson posits that future external devices such as music players, smart phones and personal computers will be reduced to tiny electronic chips for implantation. Humans will, in essence, become the gadgets they use. Worse, they will increasingly become slaves, rather than masters, of new technology, and as a result will come more under the influence of profit-oriented corporations assuming the roles of national governments.

To enhance the portrayal of what might lie ahead, the author introduces a traditional narrative line from the viewpoint of protagonist Titus, a paradigm of future society. Titus attends SCHOOL™, where methods of education have changed. Instead of dry facts, he is taught "how to work technology and how to find bargains and what's the best way to get a job and how to decorate our bedrooms" (110).

Readers eavesdrop on Titus's shallow thoughts, his bare descriptions of what he sees and hears, and receive regular snippets from the feed: advertisements, promos for TV shows, fashion tips, and popular song lyrics. Feed excerpts help tell the story: humans are constantly mined for information about their habits, so they can be better persuaded to buy items for the benefit of

corporations bent on maintaining and increasing power and control. Occasional news sound bites advance a subplot: there is a growing underground antifeed movement, of which Titus's new love interest, Violet, is an active part.

The contrast between the haves, as represented by Titus, made dull and witless by the feed, and the have-nots, as represented by expressive, feeling Violet, consumes much of the story. Without the feed, the two young adults can briefly connect on the same level as normal humans. With the feed, there is no chance for romance, because they are too different and heading in opposite directions. Titus returns to his vapid existence. Sensitive Violet, symbol of the constant and not always beneficial sacrifice of old technology to new, begins her terminal, Alzheimer's-like descent toward oblivion. Titus may not feel her loss, but readers certainly will.

Jack Ewing

Further Reading

Hickey, Kris. "M. T. Anderson Reflects on Where We Are, Years After His Iconic Book, *Feed*." *YALSA*. YALSA, 20 Nov. 2013. Web. 3 Mar. 2015. <www.yalsa.ala.org/thehub/2013/11/20/m-t-anderson-reflects-on-where-we-are-years-after-his-iconic-book-feed/>.

Kolderup, Gretchen. "31 Days of Authors: M. T. Anderson." *YALSA*. YALSA, 10 Oct. 2011. Web. 3 Mar. 2015. <www.yalsa.ala.org/thehub.2011/10/10/31-days-of-authors-m-t-anderson/>.

The First Part Last

Author: Angela Johnson (b. 1961)
First published: 2003
Type of work: Novel
Type of plot: Realism
Time of plot: Undetermined present
Locale: New York City; Heaven, Ohio (fictional)

Principal characters

Bobby, a high school student who becomes a father at sixteen

Nia Wilkins, Bobby's girlfriend, who becomes a mother at sixteen

Feather, Nia and Bobby's baby girl

K-Boy, one of Bobby's two best friends
J. L., the second of Bobby's best friends
Mary, Bobby's mother
Fred, Bobby's father

The Story

The First Part Last is told through alternating short chapters entitled either "now" or "then." Chapters under the heading "now" take place after the baby girl Feather is born to her teenage parents, Nia and Bobby. "Then" covers the period when Nia discovers her pregnancy and the months preceding the birth. All but one of the chapters are told from Bobby's point of view.

As the novel opens, Bobby, who turned sixteen only months before, is holding his eleven-day-old daughter Feather tight to his body. As he considers Feather's innocence, Bobby muses that this innocent first part of life should actually come last, just before one's death.

Next, Bobby remembers his sixteenth birthday. After spending time with his two best friends, K-Boy and J. L., Bobby's father, Fred, made him his favorite meal. Going home to the apartment where he lived with his mother, Mary, who was separated from Fred, Bobby was surprised by Nia on his doorstep. She had big news for him.

Back in the present, Bobby tells K-Boy and J. L. that he will keep and raise Feather despite being a sixteen-year-old boy in high school. When he tells his parents about Nia's pregnancy, Bobby's father cries while his mother keeps silent.

Bobby struggles hard to take care of Feather. His mother is unwilling to help him except in emergencies. He remembers how Nia's wealthy parents were shocked by her unplanned teenage pregnancy.

At school, Bobby has trouble staying awake. Jackie, Feather's babysitter, lives relatively far away. This forces Bobby and Feather to traverse New York City on public transportation before and after Bobby goes to school.

One morning, Bobby drops Feather off with his downstairs neighbor, the kindly bluegrass musician Coco Fernandez. But instead of going to school, he sprays graffiti on a wall. He is arrested by a female police officer. In the past, Nia and Bobby appeared to let themselves be persuaded by Nia's parents and social workers to give up the baby for adoption. Now, Fred takes Bobby home from the police station.

One day, Bobby and Feather are visited by Bobby's older brother, Paul, and his children, Nick and Nora. Bobby tells Paul he and Feather will move in with Fred

as he seems to be the more caring of Bobby's parents. Instead of college, Bobby wants to spend time with Feather while holding a menial job. Bobby remembers how he, Nia, her mother, and Fred went to a social worker's office where it was seemingly decided that the baby would be given up for adoption.

Bobby and Feather move in with Fred. Bobby, K-Boy, and J. L. visit Nia, who has been absent in the present time so far. In the only chapter told from Nia's point of view, she relates giving birth. Due to eclampsia, Nia has slipped into a vegetative coma and is now being cared for in a nursing home. After this tragedy, Bobby recalls his decision to raise Feather and not give her up for adoption.

Bobby and Feather move in with his brother. Paul lives in the fictional small town of Heaven, Ohio. There, Bobby wants to raise Feather while living in an apartment by a car repair shop.

Critical Evaluation

The central theme of *The First Part Last*, winner of the Coretta Scott King Award, is the social issue of teen pregnancies in contemporary America, particularly the role of teenage fathers. This key theme is introduced right away when Nia tells Bobby on his sixteenth birthday that she is pregnant with their child.

By choosing the structure of alternating chapters relating the situation "now" after Feather's birth and "then" before, author Angela Johnson shows how Bobby and Nia's lives change through the prospect and experience of parenthood. Bobby, in particular, has to give up many of the things a regular sixteen-year-old boy enjoys, such as spending time hanging out with his friends, going to the movies, or staying up late. Now, Bobby is responsible for a new life, a baby who is almost totally dependent on him. He has to rise to this occasion, which he does.

Structurally, there are two plot lines in the novel. In the chapters of "then," things move to a climax with Nia giving birth and becoming comatose as a result of a relatively rare condition. In the "now" chapters, Bobby learns that he needs endurance and commitment to live up to his decision to raise his daughter. He has a crisis in the middle of the story when he leaves Feather with his neighbor, spray paints a wall, and is arrested. But he ultimately learns from this incident and exhibits an increasing level of maturity.

The issue of Bobby and Nia's ethnicity is never explicitly handled in the novel itself. There is just one reference that at least one of Feather's parents is African American upon the description of her skin color. This idea is suggested as well by the cover of the book featuring an African American man holding a baby in his arms. The fact that this aspect of race is alluded to and confirmed by the author but not directly dealt with in the text underscores the universality of this situation concerning unplanned parenthood that some young adults must face.

The First Part Last is a prequel to Johnson's earlier novel *Heaven* (1998). In *Heaven*, the young African American man Bobby Morris, who lives in Heaven, hires the novel's central character, Marley, as a babysitter for his daughter, Feather. *The First Part Last*, which gives neither Bobby's last name nor his ethnicity, tells how Bobby came to live there. Overall, *The First Part Last* is a solid literary achievement that speaks to an authentic, important situation that forces many young adults to grapple with concepts such as the meaning of family, responsibility, maturity, and identity.

R. C. Lutz, PhD

Further Reading

Engberg, Gillian. "The Booklist Interview: Angela Johnson." *Booklist* 100.12 (2004): 1074. Print.

Hinton-Johnson, Kaavonia. "Angela Johnson: Award–Winning Novels and the Search for Self." *ALAN Review* 34.1 (2006): 63–65. Web. 27 Mar. 2015. Digital file. <http://scholar.lib.vt.edu/ejournals/ALAN/v34n1/kaavonia.pdf>.

The Forest of Hands and Teeth

Author: Carrie Ryan
First published: 2010
Type of work: Novel
Type of plot: Dystopian Fiction
Time of plot: Undetermined future
Locale: Coastal United States

Principal characters

Mary, young woman who wants more from life than her small village can provide
Jed, Mary's brother
Harry, one of Mary's best friends; Mary's betrothed
Travis, Mary's real romantic interest; Harry's brother

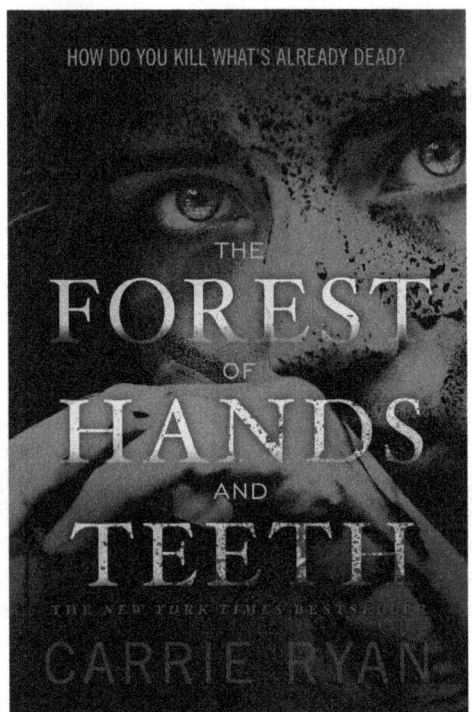

Courtesy of Ember, an imprint of Penguin Random House

Cassandra, Mary's best friend; Travis's betrothed
Jacob, young child orphaned by attack on Mary's village
Sister Tabitha, leader of the Sisterhood, the ruling group in Mary's village

The Story

Mary's village is surrounded by fences. The fences keep the villagers in, but more importantly, they keep the Unconsecrated out. The Unconsecrated hunger for flesh and attack anyone who comes close to the fence. Unfortunately, Mary's father disappeared months ago while performing guard duties; though Mary and her brother have faced his loss, her mother waits. One day while she is waiting, she gets too close to the fence and is bitten, which seals her fate. Mary is left to watch her mother die.

"So beautiful, the ocean. . . . It consumes me." These are the final words Mary hears from her dying mother, and this idea also "consumes" Mary, leaving her discontent. At the verge of adulthood, Mary should be getting married soon, and her friend Harry has asked her to commit to courtship that will lead to marriage. With her mother's death, plans change.

Angry at Mary for allowing their mother to choose to join the Unconsecrated rather than allowing the village leaders to give her true death, Jed refuses to let Mary return home. Even worse, Harry remains silent regarding courtship, so her only choice is to join the Sisterhood, a group of religious women who lead the village. Upon entering the Cathedral where the sisters live, Mary is terrorized by Sister Tabitha.

Banished in silence to a small cell, Mary grieves for her parents and the potential of a different life. Months later, she hears the sisters bring a screaming man into the Cathedral, and she is initiated into her duties as a member. The caretaking duties are for Travis, Harry's brother, the boy whom Mary has always loved. He has broken his leg and needs tending. The months of caring for Travis deepen her love for him, so when Cassandra, Mary's best friend and Travis' fiancée, finally comes to see him, Mary is torn with guilt over her feelings for Travis and with despair over the reminder that Travis cannot be hers.

Another strange event happens while Mary is at the Cathedral. One night a girl who is not from their village shows up. Since Mary did not know that living people existed outside of her village, she is intrigued. Almost as soon as the girl appears, she disappears. Life moves on for Mary; she knows life as a sister will never work, so when Harry asks Sister Tabitha to let Mary leave the sisterhood to become his wife, she accepts.

Within days, the village sirens sound again, signaling attack. The strange girl has returned as Unconsecrated and along with all of the zombie-like creatures who survive in the woods surrounding the village, she overtakes the town. Most of the townspeople have retreated to platforms built into trees, but Mary, Harry, Travis, Cassandra, a child named Jacob, Jed and his wife cannot make it to the platforms and must flee the village.

The group follows miles of fenced paths. As if the loss of everything they know is not enough, Mary discovers that Jed's wife has been infected, and he is forced to give her true death. Grief, compounded with hunger, leaves the group struggling until they find another village, but this new village has been breached. Mary and Travis are separated from the others. Time together reunites Mary's love for Travis and ignites his feelings for her. Cass and Harry grow close as well.

The Unconsecrated break down the door of the fortress where Mary and Travis have been staying. They make it to the tree platforms with the others, but Travis is infected. Jacob accidentally sets a fire, and they are again forced to flee. Unable to deal with Travis's death and the continued unknown, Mary runs, followed by Jed. Another attack sends Jed plummeting down a waterfall, leaving Mary alone again. She attempts to save him but is pulled into the water as well. When she awakes, she is on a beach. She has found the ocean, but the cost has been too high.

Critical Evaluation

The story takes place at some undetermined time in the future. All that readers know is an apocalyptic event has taken place and is referred to as The Return. Only a small number of people have survived and they live in comparatively primitive fenced villages. Though Mary's storyline is chronological, moving from the point of her mother's death to her own escape to the ocean, the author includes a variety of flashbacks into Mary's world. These glimpses into the past reinforce the problem with deciphering the skewed history that Mary has been taught and the lack of knowledge all the characters have about their past and their world. This frustrates Mary, who wants to understand how her world has become such a horrible place.

Threaded throughout the narrative is a theme of discontent. Mary is unhappy with her life. She wants more than the village can offer. She desires a love story like her parents shared, but Harry is not the partner she has envisioned. She is unsuited for the Sisterhood, and she is angry about the events that cause her little group to flee. Even when she experiences a snapshot of her dream life with Travis, she is dissatisfied. The repeated losses leave Mary reeling from an absence of hope. Her story ends with a reflection on the meaning of it all. She thinks, "And then I remember Travis pulling me against him and telling me about hope. His voice in my mind is soft, just out of reach like a spent echo. I wonder if these memories are worth holding on to. Are worth the burden. I wonder what purpose they serve." The dystopia of her world has failed her; even the discovery of the ocean comes too late and is not enough to feed her restlessness.

Theresa L. Stowell, PhD

Further Information

Balaka, Basu, Katherine R. Broad, and Carrie Hintz. *Contemporary Dystopian Fiction for Young Adults: Brave New Teenagers*. New York: Routledge, 2013. Print.

Jenson, Karen. "Art Inspired by YA Lit." *Voice of Youth Advocates* 36.3 (2013): 26. Print.

Kraus, Daniel. Rev. of *The Forest of Hands and Teeth*, by Carrie Ryan. *Booklist* 1 Jan. 2009: 66. *Literary Reference Center*. Web. 29 May 2015. <http://search.ebscohost.com/login.aspx?direct=true&db=lfh&AN =36295865&site=lrc-live>.

47

Author: Walter Mosley (b. 1952)
First published: 2005
Type of work: Novel
Type of plot: Historical Fiction; Science Fiction
Time of plot: 1832 and early twenty-first century
Locale: Georgia

Principal characters

Number 47, a fourteen-year-old African American slave
Master Tobias Turner, the white plantation owner
Mr. Stewart, the cruel white plantation overseer
Big Mama Flore, a slave who protects 47
Miss Eloise, Tobias's red-haired eleven-year-old daughter
Tall John (Lemuel; 12; N'Clect), a bronze-skinned runaway searching for 47
Andrew Pike (Wall), plantation owner

The Story

On Corinthian Plantation in Georgia in 1832 enslaved people are considered little different than animals. Most of the everyday workers have numbers rather than names. Those slaves who have survived for a long time, or who hold elevated positions, have nicknames, such as Big Mama Flore, elderly Mud Albert, muscular Champ Noland, and Fred Chocolate, the house manservant. The narrator, a fourteen-year-old boy known only as number 47, has just grown old enough to switch from grooming horses to picking cotton. Consequently, he is branded with his number and chained nightly in the slave quarters with other field-workers.

One day, a rival plantation owner, mustachioed Andrew Pike, appears at Corinthian in search of a teenage runaway slave named Lemuel. Soon afterward, Lemuel, calling himself Tall John, shows up to tell 47 he has been looking for him. John tells Tobias Turner, the plantation owner, that 47 caught him but denies he is Pike's runaway slave. He claims he formerly lived on a plantation

that burned down, that his old master died, and that he has been wandering ever since. John is given the number of a deceased slave, 12, and put among the other workers in the slave quarters, where he entertains them with tales of High John, a trickster from Africa who intends to free slaves and take them home. He admonishes the others to be neither master nor slave. As time passes, it becomes obvious Tall John is not of this earth. He has a handheld device that puts people to sleep, medicines that heal wounds, and the powers of invisibility and instant transportation.

John privately admits to 47 that he comes from a planet far away, that he has been traveling for three thousand years, and that he was sent to help 47—who has the proper blood code—to save the universe from an entity named Wall, who occupies the body of Andrew Pike. In a vision, John shows 47 his home planet, Elle, where his people, the Talam, are in conflict with the Calash, who seek to disrupt the universe. John encourages 47 to flee to the North, where there is no slavery. John tells 47 what Wall/Pike really wants: a green powdery metal to be mined on Earth, which can rip apart the universe.

Sensing his impending death, John transplants into 47 all his knowledge so he will be able to save the world. Meanwhile, the men of Pike's plantation, under control of the evil Wall, fight against the men of Tobias's plantation in an attempt to capture Tall John and to convert his spacecraft (called a Sun Ship) into a machine to mine the universe-destroying green metal. In the melee, many of the slaves escape, heading north to freedom. In an exciting conclusion, John and 47 engage Wall/Pike and his minions in battle in an effort to save the world.

Critical Evaluation

An unusual blend of historical fiction and science fiction, *47* begins as a traditional slave narrative, modeled perhaps after such exemplars of captivity literature as *A Narrative of the Life of Frederick Douglass, an American Slave* (1845); *Twelve Years a Slave* (1853) by Solomon Northup; or *Up from Slavery* (1901) by Booker T. Washington. The first-person narrator, however, indicates from the start that this will not be a typical story. In a preface he mentions that the events described unfolded more than 170 years before and involve a character, Tall John from beyond Africa, with the ability to fly between galaxies.

Having already asked readers not only to suspend disbelief but also to abandon it altogether, the narrator grounds the story in reality to provide a firm foundation before the plot slips the bonds of gravity and soars into the realm of speculative fiction and fantasy. Number 47 gives familiar details of what it was like to grow up in slavery in 1832: the casual cruelty of white people toward black people (who are considered property), the severe punishments for seemingly minor transgressions to keep the captives subdued, and the low-level expectations of those born in chains, who pass through four well-defined stages in their miserable, usually brief lives: infant, youth, old age, and death.

Black characters—Big Mama Flore, Mud Albert, Fred Chocolate, and number 84, a sullen female slave—are particularly well-drawn by Mosley, while most white characters (with the exception of young, kind-hearted Eloise) are two-dimensional stereotypes. The most interesting character is Tall John, the millennia-old alien from another galaxy who has taken the guise of a bronze-skinned slave. In addition to his other supernatural abilities and his bag of scientifically advanced gimmicks that seem magical to the uneducated people of the time, Tall John is capable of speaking in various styles depending upon the audience he is addressing. As is suggested in the narrative, Tall John is the extraterrestrial embodiment of the mythological High John of Africa, who has come to teach the slaves, under the leadership of the chosen one, 47, the meaning of freedom, so they can pursue it successfully.

Jack Ewing

Further Reading

Barnes, Steven. "Mosley's Intergalactic Coming-of-Age Tale: *47.*" *NPR Books*. National Public Radio, 6 July 2006. Web. 7 Oct. 2015. <http://www.npr.org/templates/story/story.php?storyId=5531667>.

Hong, Terry. "*47* by Walter Mosley." *Book Dragon*. Smithsonian Asian Pacific American Center, 12 Feb. 2015. Web. 28 Sept. 2015. <http://smithsonianapa.org/bookdragon/47-by-walter-mosley/>.

Gabi, a Girl in Pieces

Author: Isabel Quintero
First published: 2014
Type of work: Novel
Type of plot: Bildungsroman
Time of plot: The 2000s
Locale: California

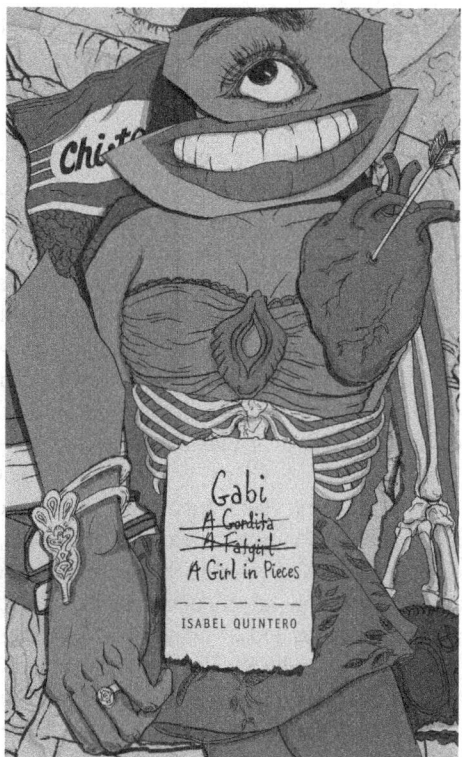

Courtesy of Cinco Punto Press

Principal characters

Gabriela "Gabi" Hernandez, a seventeen-year-old Mexican American girl who loves to read and to write poetry

Cindy, Gabi's classmate and best friend

Sebastian, Gabi's other best friend who comes out as gay

Martin Espada, Gabi's boyfriend and fellow poet

Bertha, Gabi's aunt, who speaks in tongues and is allegedly possessed by demons

The Story

Gabriela "Gabi" Hernandez is a senior at Santa Maria de Los Rosales High School, located in California. Her final year of high school is one of many firsts and struggles, all of which she records in her diary. The novel is organized according to Gabi's diary entries. Gabi is an enthusiastic student with an excellent grade point average and dreams of going to the University of California, Berkeley to study English. She struggles with her weight and forming her own identity against her mother's expectations and those of her Mexican American culture. Unfortunately, Gabi does not just have her own problems to deal with. Not only is her homelife troubling (her father is a methamphetamine addict, her mother is controlling, and her family has money troubles), but her two closest friends have major troubles of their own that Gabi must help them face.

Gabi uses binge eating as a means of coping. She eats in secret when she is alone in her room, and snacks in public when she is happy and in the company of acquaintances. Gabi is confident that the problem of her weight, and her own self-image, will work itself out in time.

At the beginning of the book, Gabi's best friend Cindy thinks she might be pregnant after having sex with a handsome boy named German. Gabi goes with Cindy to buy a home pregnancy test kit, after which the drugstore sales clerk Georgina, their classmate, spreads the news throughout the school. Cindy is indeed pregnant and wants to have the baby; Gabi supports her friend throughout her pregnancy. Months after becoming pregnant, Cindy reveals to Gabi and Sebastian that German raped her. Gabi and Sebastian are horrified and urge her to contact the police, which she chooses not to do. When she gives birth, she names the baby Sabi after Sebastian and Gabi.

Meanwhile, Gabi must also help other best friend, Sebastian, who is gay. Against Gabi's advice, he reveals his sexual identity to his parents and is thrown out of his house. He ends up sleeping on the couch at Gabi's house until he can find a permanent home. He goes to live with his aunt, who seems accepting until she catches Sebastian with a boy and sends him to both a psychologist and a priest.

While Gabi's friends struggle with the fallouts of their sexual explorations, Gabi makes her own endeavors at romance. She has a crush on a good-looking white boy, Joshua Moore, who says he dislikes fat girls. She is attracted to long-haired, weed-smoking Eric Ramirez, and becomes his girlfriend until he insults Sebastian. She makes out with a boy named Ian from a wealthy family, but ultimately rejects him in favor of nice, poetry-writing Martin Espada, whom she dates for the majority of the book.

Gabi's own poverty-stricken family presents the biggest roadblock to her success. Her younger brother Beto is somewhat wild: he drinks and gets into fights, and was even arrested defacing public property with graffiti. Their mother works in the kitchen of a hospital and sometimes has to collect aluminum cans to make the rent. Their fraternal aunt, Bertha, who belongs to a cult-like religious denomination, is often present, making judgments and scolding Gabi for wearing makeup and Beto for listening to secular music. Worse, Gabi's father

is a long-time meth addict who is absent from home for long periods. Gabi finds him one day in the garage, dead from an overdose.

Gabi deals with the many problems by writing about them, and creates a zine based on the female body. Her dream comes true and she is accepted to Berkeley. She attends the prom with Martin, and afterward they have sex for the first time—only after Martin gets Gabi's explicit consent. She confronts German about what he did to Cindy, slaps and shames him, and is suspended from school. Though she is not allowed at her graduation ceremony, Gabi feels that everything will nevertheless work out for the best as she and Martin are bound for Berkeley in the fall.

Critical Evaluation

The Morris Award–winning *Gabi, a Girl in Pieces* introduces a bold, no-nonsense, humorous, and thoughtful protagonist. Throughout the novel Gabi demonstrates her practical, optimistic nature by resolving a series of situations that would be too much for many people to handle. Gabi is flawed, but she confronts her problems and is not bogged down by them.

The novel focuses on the nature and consequences of sexuality and gender roles. While Gabi is able to make her own path with her sexuality and ambition, she witnesses her friends and family struggling in their own ways against the Catholicism and machismo characteristic of Latino culture. In her Mexican American family, Gabi is expected to be a good girl who will remain a virgin and stay at home with her family until marriage. Her own desires to go to college and explore her sexuality clash with her mother's traditional desires for her daughter. By contrast, Gabi's mother got pregnant out of wedlock and, though twenty-five, and was beaten by Gabi's grandmother for becoming pregnant. Sebastian is an outcast, a gay youth in a macho environment and in a family that considers homosexuality a sin. Cindy falls victim to a forceful rapist and becomes, as Gabi refers to it, another Hispanic teen mom. Georgina, who denigrated Cindy for becoming pregnant, later becomes pregnant herself, and has to solicit Gabi's help to secure an abortion—a taboo in a heavily Catholic community. At the book's end, Gabi is empowered and ready to start her collegiate life on her own terms, and is able to break free of the typical female roles in which her friends and mother are trapped.

Jack Ewing

Further Reading

Quintero, Isabel. "Constructing a Life: A Conversation with Isabel Quintero." Interview by Daryl Grabarek. *School Library Journal*. School Library Journal, 12 Aug. 2014. Web 10 Dec. 2015. <http://www.slj.com/2014/08/reviews/books/constructing-a-life-a-conversation-with-isabel-quintero/>.

Quintero, Isabel. "2015 Morris Award: An Interview with Finalist Isabel Quintero." Interview by Faythe Arredondo. *Hub*. YALSA, 26 Jan. 2015. Web. 10 Dec. 2015. <http://www.yalsa.ala.org/thehub/2015/01/26/morris-award-finalist-interview-isabel-quintero/>.

Gemma Doyle Trilogy (Series)

Author: Libba Bray (b. 1964)
First published: 2003–2007
A Great and Terrible Beauty (2003)
Rebel Angels (2005)
The Sweet, Far Thing (2007)
Type of work: Novel
Type of plot: Fantasy; Historical Fiction
Time of plot: 1895–96
Locales: London, England; India; the realms

Principal characters

Gemma Doyle, a nineteenth-century British girl with magical powers

Kartik, Gemma's romantic interest, a member of the Rakshana brotherhood

Ann Bradshaw, Gemma's roommate, a poor, unpopular student at Spence Academy

Felicity Worthington, a popular schoolgirl

Pippa Cross, another popular student, Felicity's close friend

Claire McCleethy, Gemma's teacher and a member of the order

Hester Moore, Gemma's teacher and an enemy of the order

Tom Doyle, Gemma's brother

Lillian Nightwing, the headmistress of Spence Academy

Nell Hawkins, a patient in Bedlam, a mental institution

The Story

Libba Bray's Gemma Doyle trilogy follows the adventures of a young British woman at the end of the

Courtesy of Penguin Random House

nineteenth century who learns that her deceased mother was part of an ancient order of sorceresses who once controlled access to the otherworldly realms. Gemma gradually realizes that she herself has inherited the ability to enter the realms, and she is torn between the various factions, in both the real world and the realms, that want to control the magic for themselves.

The first book, *A Great and Terrible Beauty* (2003), begins the day Gemma turns sixteen while living in India with her parents. Gemma is eager to experience life back in England for the first time, but her life is turned upside down when a mysterious man approaches her mother in the marketplace, telling her that Circe is near. Shortly thereafter, Gemma has a vision of a horrific creature attacking her mother, who in turn takes her own life in order to keep the creature from enslaving her soul.

Two months later Gemma and her father have arrived in England, where her father's grief has resulted in an addiction to laudanum, her stern grandmother continually finds fault with her, and her brother, Tom, insists that they pretend their mother died from cholera to avoid scandal. Gemma is sent to the Spence Academy for young ladies, where she initially feels out of place due to her unconventional upbringing. Before long, however, she forms close friendships with Ann Bradshaw,

Felicity Worthington, and Pippa Cross. While Ann is an unpopular scholarship student destined to work as a governess for her wealthy relatives, Felicity and Pippa are the two most beloved girls at the school, and Gemma is astonished that they, too, have more complex problems than are immediately apparent.

In the meantime, Gemma forms an uneasy relationship with Kartik, a young man from India who belongs to the Rakshana, a group that opposes the order to which Gemma's mother belonged. Kartik reveals that his brother Amar was killed trying to defend Gemma's mother from Circe's creature, and he warns Gemma to stay away from the realms. Gemma discovers the diary of Mary Dowd, a Spence student from years before who took part in sacrificing a gypsy child in order to gain entry to the realms. Gemma learns that Mary and another student named Sarah Rees-Toome, believed killed in a tragic fire, did not actually die; rather, Mary eventually became Gemma's mother and Sarah became the enemy called Circe.

Unsettled by these events and longing for her mother, Gemma finds herself bonding with Miss Moore, a beloved new art teacher at Spence who shows her students some nearby caves with ancient symbols painted on the walls. Gemma and her friends form a secret club they call the Order, and before long Gemma is able to conjure a portal to the realms, where the girls play with magic and enjoy an unaccustomed freedom during their nightly visits. Reality intrudes, however, when Miss Moore is dismissed from the school for being a bad influence on the students, and when Pippa's parents force her to accept a marriage proposal from a man old enough to be her father. Desperate, Pippa eats forbidden berries in the realms, trapping herself there and causing her earthly body to die in the real world. In her attempts to save Pippa, Gemma destroys the runes that bind the magic's power, releasing it within the realms and risking chaos.

In the second book, *Rebel Angels* (2005), a short section from Kartik's point of view reveals that his brotherhood expects him to trick Gemma into binding the magic to the Rakshana and then to kill her. The story then returns to Gemma's perspective as a stern new teacher, Miss McCleethy, arrives at Spence. When the girls revisit the realms, Ann and Felicity are delighted to find Pippa there, although Gemma remains wary lest Pippa's soul has become corrupted by not crossing from the realms to what lies beyond. The girls leave Spence for the Christmas holidays, with Ann accompanying Felicity to her parents' home, but they make plans to continue searching for the Temple, the source of magic within the realms.

Between holiday festivities in London, the girls visit their former teacher, Miss Moore, and Gemma tries to befriend Nell Hawkins, a mental patient in Bedlam, the hospital where her brother works. Gemma learns that Nell attended a school very similar to Spence where a Miss McCleethy worked and becomes convinced that her new teacher is Circe. Miss McCleethy turns out to be a current member of the order, however, while the beloved Miss Moore is instead revealed as Circe. Gemma kills Nell Hawkins in an act of mercy before Miss Moore can sacrifice the girl and binds the magic within her own body as the Temple. In so doing, she imprisons Miss Moore in the realms.

In the third book, *The Sweet Far Thing* (2007), Gemma has lost her ability to enter the realms at will, leaving Felicity and Ann anxious as they contemplate the restrictive futures they face without the magic. Gemma finally finds another route into the realms and is disturbed to find a changed Pippa leading a group of working-class girls who died in a factory fire. Relieved to have access to magic again, Ann uses it to make herself beautiful and audition for a theater company and Gemma uses it to help Felicity, who is in danger of losing her sponsorship for her society debut, upon which her inheritance depends.

Within the realms, Gemma is increasingly pressured by the creatures who live there to share the magic with them as she had previously promised. She finally takes Kartik into the realms, where they surrender to their growing attraction to one another and make love in a dream vision. Gemma then leads her friends to the Tree of All Souls, which is located in the forbidden Winterlands. When the girls visit the tree, they must confront their greatest fears and then are shown visions of their hearts' greatest desires, tempting them to stay there forever.

Once the seal between the realms and the real world is broken, Gemma and her allies must fight the dark forces, including Pippa, but they find surprising support from a former member of the Rakshana as well as Circe herself. Gemma finally gives up the magic, gifting it to the land of the realms so that all the creatures there will have a share of it. She is stabbed by Amar, Kartik's dead brother who has been corrupted by his stay in the Winterlands, but Kartik saves her by allowing himself to be absorbed into the Tree of All Souls. Back in the real world, the girls finally find the courage to change their own lives without magic. Felicity, having secured her inheritance, decides to move to Paris and live freely, in the hope that she may find love after Pippa. Ann pursues her theatrical ambitions but as herself, instead of the beautiful illusion within which she had previously hidden. Gemma persuades her father and brother, who now know the truth about her mother and Gemma's recent actions in the realms, to allow her to attend a university in New York. There, Gemma sees Kartik in her dreams and looks forward to meeting him in the realms again someday.

Critical Evaluation

A best-selling and award-winning series, the Gemma Doyle trilogy succeeds because it combines an engaging viewpoint character, a plot in which the players take action to change their own destinies, and an intriguing setting that combines both historical and fantastical elements. The trilogy's emphasis on personal choice, or the lack thereof, particularly resonates with young adult readers, who can sympathize with the way in which Gemma and her friends are all bound, in different ways, by social conventions and the specific circumstances to which they were born. Felicity, for instance, is the daughter of a respected admiral, but her mother's scandalous behavior has threatened Felicity's own reputation, upon which her inheritance literally depends. Furthermore, Felicity has not one but two secrets: the fact that her father has molested her and is beginning to do the same to Felicity's half-sister, who is presented to the world as the admiral's "ward," and Felicity's love for Pippa, which goes far beyond mere friendship.

Similarly, while all of the students at Spence envy Pippa's beauty, it brings its own burden in that her parents want to use it to improve their own situation. Gemma, too, is expected to make her debut at court before the queen, so that she may attract a suitable husband. Ann, who is not only intelligent but also a talented singer and actor, does not have the means to educate herself and so will be forced to work for her relatives for little or no wages because they are paying for her schooling. While the reader shares the girls' delight when they use the realms' magic to address some of their problems, the real satisfaction comes when the girls realize that they can come up with nonmagical solutions as well.

In addition to sexism, this trilogy also makes note of economic, ethnic, and other prejudices. Gemma is attracted to Kartik from the beginning, but they both know it is unthinkable for a young British lady to have a relationship with a young, working-class Indian man. Similarly, Felicity keeps a tight rein on her true feelings for Pippa, knowing that their society would consider such affections to be unnatural. The author also sprinkles references to other social injustices throughout these books, such as the fact that Pippa's new friends in the realms died in a tragic and preventable factory fire, and that the suffragists have to fight against social opinion in their attempts to get women the vote.

In terms of the writing, one of the author's greatest strengths lies in her ability to imbue so many characters with complex, unique personalities. In particular, Gemma and Felicity are alternately fierce and vulnerable and have to learn to identify their fears so they can face them. Felicity dreads being powerless due to her father's abusive treatment and to the fact that something as simple as malicious gossip may prevent her from receiving her inheritance. Gemma struggles to pinpoint what frightens her the most but finally understand that she fears not fitting in anywhere, particularly since her mother's death has left her family so fractured.

Another strong feature in these books is Gemma's unique and consistent voice, which displays a slightly sarcastic wit as Gemma observes some of the more absurd aspects of polite society. In addition, although Gemma makes foolish choices at times, she grows significantly throughout the trilogy, learning that she will sometimes have to make decisions that she finds painful, as part of the responsibility she has inherited along with her magical powers.

Amy Sisson, MS, MLS

Further Reading

"About Libba." *Libba Bray*. Libba Bray, n.d. Web. 14 Dec. 2015. <http://libbabray.com/about-libba>.

Corbett, Sue. "It Takes a Village to Finish a Trilogy." *Publishers Weekly* 254.45 (2007): 24. *Literary Reference Center*. Web. 14 Dec. 2015. <http://search.ebscohost.com/login.aspx?direct=true&db=lfh&AN=28026558&site=lrc-live>.

Rev. of *The Sweet Far Thing*, by Libba Bray. *Publishers Weekly* 254.43 (2007): 57–58. *Literary Reference Center*. Web. 14 Dec. 2015. <http://search.ebscohost.com/login.aspx?direct=true&db=lfh&AN=27351535&site=lrc-live>.

Gifts

Author: Ursula K. Le Guin (b. 1929)
First published: 2004
Type of work: Novel
Type of plot: Fantasy
Time of plot: Unknown
Locale: The Uplands

Courtesy of Penguin Young Readers

Principal characters

Orrec, a teenage boy
Gry, Orrec's best friend, a teenage girl who can call animals
Canoc, Orrec's father, who has the gift of undoing
Melle, Orrec's mother, a Lowlander with no gift
Parn, Gry's mother, who calls animals to be hunted
Ternoc, Gry's father, who has the gift of the knife
Ogge, the leader of a rival domain

The Story

Orrec lives in the Uplands, a region populated by families gifted with special powers. His father, Canoc, is the brantor, or master, of their domain, Caspromant. Brantor Canoc has the power to "undo" or "unmake": he can destroy things by looking at them and willing their collapse. Though he is thirteen, Orrec has shown no evidence of such a gift. This concerns him, because his best friend, Gry, manifested her gift of animal calling at age four. If Orrec does not inherit his father's gift, he cannot inherit his role as brantor.

While Orrec is out riding with Canoc, he saves his father from a snakebite by unmaking the snake, though he does not know how. After this event, Canoc relentlessly requests that his son demonstrate his gift, but Orrec refuses. Then another accidental unmaking occurs; Orrec kills his unmanageable dog, who was spooking his horse. Orrec fears he has the worst type of power: a wild gift, which cannot be controlled.

Orrec's father brings him to a wide-open space, determined to see what he can achieve. Filled with fear, doubt, and anger, Orrec unleashes his gift, and the two witness what he has unmade: a large hilltop and its animal denizens, an anthill, and an ash tree. For a moment, Orrec fears that Canoc was standing in the place of the tree and believes that he has destroyed his father. Orrec cannot control his power, so he asks to be blinded. His father places pads and a blindfold over his eyes. Orrec will now walk with the staff of Blind Caddard, an ancestor of his who also had the uncontrollable wild gift.

Rumors spread throughout the domain. Everyone fears Orrec, believing that he must be incredibly menacing and that his father blinded him for their protection. Amid this gossip, Canoc brings his son and his wife, Melle, to the home of Ogge, the brantor of the nearby domain of Drummant. Canoc wants to settle a marriage match for Orrec that the fearsome Ogge has proposed. While traveling there, Canoc spots his heifers that previously went missing.

Reluctantly, Orrec, who loves Gry, is introduced to Ogge's granddaughter. She is revealed to be "an idiot" who babbles. The girl suffers from seizures, and Melle is asked to help nurse her. When Melle comes back from tending the girl, she herself is sick. Her health declines, and she suffers a miscarriage.

During Melle's long illness, people whisper that Ogge cursed her with his gift of slow wasting. Honoring his mother's last request, Orrec removes his blindfold so she can see his eyes once more. He sees her face, and he also sees that his gaze does not harm her. That night, a year and a day after going to Ogge's home, she dies.

Orrec is enraged that his father has not sought vengeance on Ogge. To feel connected to his mother, he furtively removes his blindfold and reads her handmade books. He also reads a book called *Transformations*; its black print reminds him of ants, and the ants remind him of the hilltop. He feels distressed by the memory and closes his eyes. When he opens them, the book is still there. He has destroyed nothing. He looks into the eyes of his beloved guide dog, Coaly, whom Gry specially trained for him, and does not destroy her, either.

Orrec confronts his father with his conviction. He has no power, and this was a ploy his father masterminded to turn him into a bogeyman, to keep people afraid. Orrec says he has no gift because his mother was without magic and accuses his father of devastating the hilltop. Canoc is shocked by Orrec's tirade and denies that he has the ability to rain down such devastation.

Brantor Ogge invades the land where Orrec's family lives and says he is there to reclaim the heifers, which Canoc brought back home. Not blindfolded, armed with the staff as his only weapon, Orrec rides out with the men, though he stays above the melee. He sees his comrades below; he sees the invaders behind the trees. He blinks and calls out for his father. Canoc turns his horse to the woods. His arm is raised and there is joy and rage on his father's face. Then, before Orrec's eyes, Canoc is killed by a crossbow bolt.

The men of Orrec's domain find Ogge and his son among the dead, having been undone. Orrec believes that Canoc killed them before dying heroically.

After mourning for his father, Orrec marries Gry, and they leave the Uplands. They will go to the Lowlands, where Orrec's mother hailed from. Using her gift, Gry will work as an animal trainer. Orrec will tell stories and recite poems. They have been given the Silver Cow from his family's herd as a wedding gift, which they plan to sell for a good price. Together, they hope to build a new life together among the Lowland strangers.

Critical Evaluation

Adolescence is a time of uncertainty and anxiety. For Orrec and Gry, their coming of age is especially worrisome, as they are expected to control, cultivate, and utilize their gifts. Ursula K. Le Guin builds a world where people have powers to varying degrees, and teenagers are expected to restrain their self-interest and act for the greater good. At first, Orrec is convinced that he has no power. The undoing is a brutal gift to have, stripping creatures of their bones and shapes. Readers are never quite sure whether he truly does not have the ability or whether he is simply refusing to acknowledge and embrace it.

Orrec is a literary young man, and his love for stories is celebrated throughout *Gifts*. His mother, who was taken by Uplands people during a marauding of her town, has no magical powers; however, her ability to read and to spin tales is a gift that she bestows upon Orrec. Regardless of whether Orrec has the ability to unmake, he already has the gifts of reading, memorizing, learning, and sharing what he can imagine. He is able to make up stories and enchant listeners with his words. When Orrec's mother is dying and he requests that she share more tales with him, he likens her to "a well" from which he can draw a "bucket . . . full of stories." This is a brilliant metaphor that encapsulates the relationship between Le Guin's power as a premier fantasy author and her eager, enchanted readership.

Early on in the book, Orrec says he is "in the world of the never-ending stories." As such, it is fitting that *Gifts* is the first book in a trilogy, known as the Annals of the Western Shore. While the other two books follow different main characters, they both ultimately tie in with the first, further illuminating Orrec and Gry's life together.

Stephanie Finnegan

Further Reading

Le Guin, Ursula K. "Ursula K. Le Guin Steers Her Craft into a New Century." Interview by Scott Simon. *NPR*. NPR, 31 Aug. 2015. Web. 30 Nov. 2015. <http://www.npr.org/2015/08/29/435549081/ursula-k-le-guin-steers-her-craft-into-a-new-century>.

Le Guin, Ursula K. "Ursula K. Le Guin: Still Battling the Powers That Be." Interview by John Joseph Adams and David Barr Kirtley. *Wired*. Condé Nast, 25 July 2012. Web. 30 Nov. 2015. <http://www.wired.com/2012/07/geeks-guide-ursula-k-le-guin>.

The Girl of Fire and Thorns (Series)

Author: Rae Carson (b. 1973)
First published: *The Girl of Fire and Thorns* (2011)
The Crown of Embers (2012)
The Bitter Kingdom (2013)
Type of work: Novel
Type of plot: Fantasy
Time of plot: Indeterminate
Locale: Mythical kingdoms of Orovalle, Joya d'Arena, Basajuan, and Invierne.

Principal characters

Lucero-Elisa, the protagonist and narrator; Princess of Orovalle, then Queen Regnant of Joya d'Arena

Lord Hector, captain of Lucero-Elisa's Royal Guards

Ximena, Lucero-Elisa's nurse and guardian

Mara, Lucero-Elisa's maid

Alejandro de Vega, Lucero-Elisa's husband, King of Joya d'Arena

Rosario de Vega, Lucero-Elisa's stepson, heir to the throne of Joya d'Arena

Father Alentin, Lucero-Elisa's spiritual advisor, a priest and later ambassador to Joya d'Arena from Basajuan.

Conde Eduardo, noble on Lucero-Elisa's council and leader of a rebellion against her

The Story

Lucero-Elisa de Riqueza, princess of the Kingdom of Orovalle and second daughter to King Hitzedar de Riqueza of Orovalle has, up to the age of sixteen, led a sheltered, if bizarre life. Swarthy, dark-haired, and, by her own account, plump and self-indulgent, she is set apart by the presence of a huge blue gem in her navel, the Godstone, which is inextricably embedded there by divine will. This identifies her as "the Bearer" who, in the narrative's mythology, is especially destined to fulfill a great, though only vaguely specified, mission. Lucero-Elisa (who is mainly addressed as "Elisa" by her friends) never knew her mother, who died shortly after giving birth to her, and has been overshadowed by her assertive, slim, and beautiful older sister, Juana-Alodia. Her father is distant, and showers nearly all his attention and such scant affection as he possesses on Juana-Alodia, who, as his designated successor to the throne, has the political and courtly acumen that Elisa lacks. There is some jealousy and rivalry between the two that often masks a deep-set bond between the sisters. Elisa is carefully (sometimes fiercely) pampered, cossetted, and protected by her old nurse, the scholarly, pious, and secretive Ximena, and by a younger, equally devoted maidservant, Aneaxi.

Then her carefully cultivated world is shattered by a traumatic series of events. She is, at the start of the novel, about to be married to the widower king of Joya d'Arena. Like most royal marriages, it is a political union to cement an alliance between the two kingdoms. Both realms are threatened by the powerful nation of Invierne, but Joya d'Arena is in more immediate danger. However, she is swept up by the attractive King Alejandro de Vega, and eagerly anticipates the journey with her new husband to Brisadulce, capital of Joya d'Arena.

A series of events destroys much of her childhood innocence. The traveling entourage is attacked by wild jungle people called Perditos; Elisa has to kill one of them in order to save Alejandro, and Aneaxi is so gravely wounded that she later dies. Reaching Brisadulce provides no relief: Alejandro distances himself from her and for what he makes out as political and security reasons refuses to announce their marriage, instead passing off Elisa as a guest. Elisa is then plunged into the world of court intrigue made more intense by the treat of Invierne attack. She is disillusioned by the king's indecisiveness and the fact that he has an alluring mistress, Condesa Arina, daughter of the influential Conde Trevino—but she is most upset by the knowledge, acquired gradually, that the nature of her true destiny as a Bearer has been hidden from her and that she is in mortal danger because of her status. The Invierne, led by sorcerer-lords called animagi, are seeking out the Bearer in order to be able to harness the power of her Godstone, and other Godstones of part Bearers, to realize their schemes for world conquest. For Elisa, her Godstone is a mixed blessing because it seems to possess a life of its own and to either warm and comfort her in reaction to her prayers or to generate an icy cold sensation whenever danger is near. It does not help that she and her new maidservant, Cosme, mutually despise each other. At Alejandro's court, however, she impresses the formidable Lord Hector, captain of the Royal Guard, and finds in him a staunch friend and protector. She also earns the respect of six-year-old Prince Rosario, King Alejandro's only child by his first wife, Queen Rosaura.

After Cosme accidentally discovers that Elisa is the Bearer of the Godstone, Cosme, her brother Humberto and others, drug and kidnap Elisa. It turns out that Cosme and her companions are from Basajuan, the part of Joya d'Arena that has been hardest hit by Invierne raids, and they hope that Elisa's presence as the Bearer might work magic to counteract these attacks. After initial hostility, Elisa develops sympathy for her captors and their people; she befriends Father Alentin, one-armed priest from one of the villages ravaged by the Inviernos, and Mara, a badly injured girl from the same village. She also falls in love with Humberto. She and Cosme even form a friendship of sorts. Elisa forms the villagers into a guerrilla army dubbed the Malficio, which effectively harasses and hampers the invading Invierne armies.

The denouement sees the deaths of Humberto, Condesa Arina, and King Alejandro at the hands of the animagi. A fierce battle culminates in Elisa finally unleashing the power of the Godstone to destroy the animagi attacking Brisadulce. Elisa becomes Queen Regnant of Joya d'Arena, with Prince Rosario as her heir and Mara as her new maid. Conde Trevino is exposed as a traitor and his lands given to his illegitimate daughter, none other than Cosme, who is allowed to rule as an independent queen of Basajuan.

But Elisa soon finds that ultimate victory is far from assured and that the surviving animagi are determined to seize her and harness the power of the Godstone. There are also intrigues at her court and a great deal of pressure for her to marry. Unfortunately the suitors all fall short. By this time she has fallen in love again, with Lord Hector. She survives assassination attempts and now comes to the realization that she must undertake a dangerous quest across the ocean to reach the mysterious *zafira*, the legendary source of the earth's energy. Pursued by a relentless Invierne assassin known as Franco, Elisa and her party embark from the port of Puerto Verde, on board the ship *Aracely*, captained by Lord Hector's brother, Felix. On board ship, the Godstone pulsates, telling her of the direction to the zafira. As the ship nears the island of the zafira, the animagus protecting it unleashes a huge storm, but Elisa uses the Godstone's power to overcome it. Accompanied by a renegade Invierne prince named Storm, Elisa successfully confronts the gatekeeper and attains the zafira. Upon her return to Puerto Verde, however, she is confronted by the nefarious Franco, who can counteract her magic. He takes Lord Hector back to Invierne as a hostage and threatens to kill him unless Elisa comes there herself as a willing sacrifice to the animagi within two months.

In a desperate gambit, Elisa decides to risk all by leading a commando force to Invierne to free Hector before the two-month deadline expires. Going with her are Mara, Storm, and scout-assassin Belén, and along the way they are joined by a half-Joyan, half-Invierno waif named Mula, whom they rescue from enslavement. They catch up with Franco's party, which is taking the captive Hector to Invierne. In a night time ambush Elisa and her compatriots surprise their antagonists and free Hector. In the ensuing battle, Franco's men are killed, Mula saves Elisa's life, and Hector breaks Franco's neck. Elisa makes the decision that, instead of going to Basajuan as originally planned, the party would proceed into Invierne, to the enemy capital of Umbra de Deus to negotiate for peace with the Deciregi, Invierne's ruling council. There, they learn of a powerful Invierne

army marching towards Basajuan, and succeed in making their escape from Umbra de Deus in hopes of intervening in time. At Basajuan, Elisa is reunited with Queen Cosme, and with her sister Juana-Alodia, who reveals that their father has recently died and that she is now the queen regnant of Orovalle. Led by the Deciregi, the Invierne army is about to break into the city. As the three queens plot their strategy, Elisa compels the other two to swear fealty to her as new empress of the Joyan Empire in return for her facing the Deciregi with the power of the Godstone. Elisa defeats and captures the Deciregi and negotiates a peace settlement. Empress Elisa returns to Joya d'Arena but during her journey the Godstone falls from her body and cracks, leaving her bereft of her former power. Nonetheless, after returning to Joya d'Arena, she overcomes the rebellion fomented by Conde Eduardo and General Luz-Manuel, and finally marries Hector.

Critical Evaluation

The Girl of Fire and Thorns (2011) is the first volume of the Girl of Fire and Thorns trilogy and is followed by *The Crown of Embers* (2012) and *The Bitter Kingdom* (2013). The alternative world, the sense of the power of magic, the epic good-versus-evil struggle, and the trilogy vehicle are standard features of the genre. The Tolkienian influence is quite apparent, but in the case of Carson, she deviates from that in her emphasis on religion and in refraining from the use of nonhuman characters. While there are no dwarves, elves, or orcs, the ideas of mysticism, sorcery, prophecy, and destiny resound strongly. Carson's alternative world is unabashedly modeled on medieval Spain during the Reconquista—the names of the characters (Franco, Belén, Eduardo, Luz-Manuel, Alejandro, Ximena, etc.) and geographic locations (Puerto Verde, Invierne, Ventierra) continuously bear this out. Instead of Castile, Aragon, and Leon we have Orovalle, Joya d'Arena, and Basajuan. The "others" in this instance are the easterly Inviernes who are depicted as tall, fair-haired, pale, and inhabiting a land with a cold, rainy climate. The religious aspect is very strong, replete with sacred scriptural texts, scholar-priests in monasteries, and sacred ceremonies centering on bloodletting through the prick of a holy thorn from rosebushes.

The characterization is very strong; the only flaw might be in the depiction of Elisa as old and wise beyond her years—she behaves more like an older adult than a sixteen- or seventeen-year-old, and her acceptance as a superior by the more obviously veteran characters may be difficult to believe. Despite this anomaly, the character development and growing maturity acquired by Elisa is so skillfully handled by the author that, in the final analysis, one is totally convinced by this transformation

The propensity for suspense is another aspect masterfully handled by the author, and the ending of the trilogy only kindles a desire for more such adventures.

Raymond Pierre Hylton, PhD

Further Reading

Corbett, Sue. "Ending a Trilogy." *Publishers Weekly* 15 July 2013: 14–18. *Literary Reference Center*. Web. 21 Dec. 2015. <http://search.ebscohost.com/login.aspx?direct=true&db=lfh&AN=89060840&site=lrc-live>.

Lear, Elizabeth. "Rae Carson." *Publishers Weekly* 19 Dec. 2011: 16–17. *Literary Reference Center*. Web. 17 Dec. 2015. <http://search.ebscohost.com/login.aspx?direct=true&db=lfh&AN=71874778&site=lrc-live>.

Going Bovine

Author: Libba Bray (b. 1964)
First published: 2009
Type of work: Novel
Type of plot: Realism; Fantasy; Humorous
Time of plot: Early twenty-first century
Locale: United States

Principal characters

Cameron "Cam" John Smith, the sixteen-year-old narrator, who has mad cow disease
Jenna Smith, Cam's twin sister
Paul Ignacio "Gonzo" Gonzales, a dwarf with an attitude
Balder, a lawn gnome who is really a Norse god
Dulcie, a pink-haired messenger with wings
Dr. X, an Asian scientist whom Cam, Gonzo, and Dulcie seek

The Story

Going Bovine concerns Cameron "Cam" Smith, a typical high school student. Cam is tall, thin, unmotivated, and not athletic. He smokes marijuana, likes odd music, and hangs on the fringes of high school society in a small Texas town. He feuds with his popular twin sister, Jenna. His stuffy father is a university physics professor, and his flighty mother is a community college English teacher. His friends are nerds and outcasts, including Paul "Gonzo" Gonzales, a dwarf.

Cam's familiar world changes when he begins losing control of his body. He hallucinates strange sights, sounds, and smells. He has visions of fire and a knight in black armor. Cam's behavior troubles his parents, who have him subjected to medical tests. The findings are horrific. He has contracted—possibly through tainted beef from his part-time fast-food job—Creutzfeldt-Jakob disease, also known as bovine spongiform encephalopathy or mad cow disease. The neurological disorder is incurable and invariably fatal. Cam does not have long to live.

In the hospital, roommate to hypochondriac Gonzo, Cam is visited by a punkish, pink-haired, winged young woman named Dulcie, who gives him a mission. To save both himself and the world, he must find Dr. X, who brought back destabilizing dark energy while traveling through space and time. She gives him an e-ticket to Walt Disney World, final destination in the search for the mysterious scientist.

Cam recruits the reluctant Gonzo for the quest. They journey to New Orleans, where Cam again encounters the black knight, known as the Wizard of Reckoning, from whom he escapes. Dulcie, making another of her frequent appearances, provides a clue that leads the adventurers into Mississippi. There, for a time, they become involved with a cult, the Church of Everlasting Satisfaction and Snack 'N' Bowl, before fomenting a revolution that destroys the cult.

Their next stop, at a keg party, leads to an encounter with Balder, the Norse god of wisdom, who has been cursed and given the form of a lawn gnome destined to be photographed at tourist spots worldwide. After Cam and Gonzo rescue Balder from his ignominious fate, he joins their mission. The companions purchase a Cadillac and continue heading south.

In Florida, they come across a field of wind turbines, which power an underground supercollider run by doctors A, M, T, and O. The doctors are former colleagues of Dr. X, who may be trapped in an alternate universe. Cam volunteers for a time-travel experiment and successfully returns from another dimension.

The adventurers resume their journey, picking up three hitchhikers bound for Daytona, Florida, and uncover a nefarious plot to which Dulcie falls victim: she is miniaturized and trapped inside a snow globe. In battling employees of United Snow Globe Wholesalers, Balder is wounded by a sprig of mistletoe—the only substance that can harm him—and dies.

Cam and Gonzo follow the Snow Globe truck containing Dulcie to Disney World, where, in Tomorrowland, they encounter Dr. X. Cam obtains Dulcie's snow globe, but Dr. X refuses to release her. The Wizard of Reckoning materializes, reveals himself as Cam's alter ego, and tells Cam everything he has experienced is a dream and that he never left the hospital. When Cam fights his alternate self, the Wizard crumbles and the snow globes shatter, freeing Dulcie and others who were trapped.

In the hospital, his mother, father, sister, and a nurse are in attendance as Cam dies and the world disappears—then begins again on a different plane for Cam and Dulcie.

Critical Evaluation

Told in first person by the highly unreliable narrator Cam Smith, *Going Bovine* is a sustained speculation centered on a singular concept. How would a fictional young adult react if afflicted with a genuinely fatal, brain-killing disease while experiencing short-circuited bodily functions and warped perceptions, judgment, imagination, and memory?

To give the story structure and provide readers with additional layers of meaning, Bray modeled *Going Bovine* on Miguel de Cervantes Saavedra's *Don Quixote* (1605), considered the first modern novel. Both works follow the picaresque exploits of mentally flawed protagonists as they pursue quests of high importance to the main characters but of dubious worth in the real world. Allusions to Quixote abound throughout *Going Bovine*, as in the humorous explanatory chapter headings reminiscent of those found in Cervantes' novel. Like Quixote, Cam is tall and thin and has a short (or very short, in the case of Cam's companion, Gonzo), grumpy sidekick similar to Sancho Panza. Cam's muse, the angelic Dulcie, mirrors Quixote's true love, Dulcinea. The Cadillac purchased for transportation is named Rocinante, after Quixote's horse. Even the famous episode in which Quixote jousts with windmills, believing them giants, is echoed in a scene with wind turbines.

Like its earlier inspiration, *Going Bovine* also works as a satire. The novel offers a multitude of targets: medical reliance on prescriptions as cure-alls, the gullibility of religious cult followers, consumerism as represented by souvenir shops and theme parks, the language of arcane science, television as an opiate of the masses, and American rituals such as the annual spring break student orgy at Daytona Beach.

Going Bovine touches on many themes—friendship, loyalty, the blurred line between the real and the imaginary—but one of the more subtle and consistent threads is the notion of change, something all the major characters experience throughout.

Jack Ewing

Further Reading
Bray, Libba. "The Booklist Printz Interview: Libba Bray." Interview by Gillian Engberg. *Booklist* 1 Mar. 2010: 62. *Literary Reference Center*. Web. 23 Mar. 2015. <http://search.ebscohost.com/login.aspx?direct=true&db=lfh&AN=48639584&site=lrc-live>.

Von Drasek, Lisa. "Morbidity and Hilarity." Rev. of *Going Bovine*, by Libba Bray. *New York Times*. New York Times, 12 Feb. 2010. Web. 23 Mar. 2015. <http://www.nytimes.com/2010/02/14/books/review/VonDrasek-t.html?_r=0>.

Graceling (Series)

Author: Kristin Cashore (b. 1976)
First published: *Graceling* (2008)
   Fire (2009)
   Bitterblue (2012)
Type of work: Novel
Type of plot: Fantasy
Time of plot: Medieval era
Locale: Land of the Seven Kingdoms; the Dells

Principal characters

Katsa, a young woman who is graced with the power of survival and used by her uncle, King Randa, to torture and kill those who disagree with him

Po, a prince of a neighboring realm, a talented fighter who is graced with the ability to sense all thoughts directed toward him

Bitterblue, a child princess of another realm who is trying to escape the cruel intentions of her father

King Leck, Bitterblue's father, a cruel king who can manipulate anyone who hears his voice

Fire, a human "monster" who can manipulate the minds of those in her presence

Brigan, the war commander and prince of the Dells

Saf, a thief and Bitterblue's love interest

The Story

Graceling takes place in a land comprising seven neighboring kingdoms, which are neither friendly nor at war. In the land of the seven kingdoms, children whose eyes become different colors as they age are known as Gracelings. Each Graceling develops a unique and powerful gift. Katsa's gift is initially thought to be killing, when, at the age of eight, she accidentally kills someone in self-defense. Her uncle, the king, uses Katsa as his personal assassin until she decides to live her own life and only commit violence as she chooses.

While Katsa does the king's work she forms the Committee, which helps common people defend themselves against bandits and corrupt rulers. One of Katsa's missions involves rescuing a royal grandfather who has been kidnapped for unknown reasons. It is during this mission that Katsa meets Prince Po and is shocked to discover he is the only person to ever hold his own against her fighting skills. She soon learns Po is related to the old man she just rescued. The two work together to hone each other's combat skills and form a plan to escape the king and search for the truth behind the grandfather's kidnapping.

Katsa and Po travel to the land of King Leck and are suspicious of the seemingly benevolent king after questioning a group of men along the way. The men inform Katsa and Po of the king's animal shelter, where he keeps children to help him tend to the animals' bizarre wounds. Unfortunately, the men explain, some of the children have died due to mysterious illness.

Katsa and Po sense something is wrong and question why there would be so many animals with strange cuts and why the children have died. Po speculates that the king is graced with the power of manipulation and may be the only person in the world able to best Katsa.

Katsa and Po arrive in Leck's kingdom just in time to witness Leck murder his wife as she attempts to escape with her daughter, Bitterblue. The queen lives long enough to tell Po that her daughter is hiding in the forest and that she must be rescued before Leck's army can find her. Katsa and Po narrowly escape Leck and his soldiers and succeed in locating the frightened Bitterblue.

Bitterblue explains that her and her mother's fear that Leck would harm the princess protected them from his manipulation. Katsa and Po decide their only option is to kill Leck and instate Bitterblue as queen. Po becomes seriously wounded while trying to sneak past Leck's guards in the forest. Katsa is forced to leave him in order to escape the kingdom with Bitterblue.

After a dangerous journey, they make it to Po's kingdom only to discover that Leck is already there. In a moment of clarity from Leck's manipulative fog, Katsa kills Leck and returns to the forest where Po is hiding. She is glad to find him alive but saddened to discover his injuries have blinded him. The two decide to stay together and continue the Committee's work while Bitterblue must learn to rule a kingdom.

Fire is a prequel to *Graceling* and tells the story of Leck's past. In the Dells, a land outside the seven kingdoms, there are creatures called monsters. Monsters look just like their animal counterparts but are incredibly beautiful and even more dangerous. Monsters have the ability to manipulate others whose minds are not strong and guarded.

Fire is the last human monster and needs to be guarded at all times, as her monster nature brings out the worst qualities in others. Fire is constantly either fawned over or violently attacked for her "unnatural" beauty. Fire's deceased father was infamous for his cruelty and led the kingdom to ruin as the king's adviser. Fire strives to be nothing like her father and refuses to use her mental powers of manipulation for anything but self-defense.

Prince Brigan decides to ask Fire to travel with him to the city to use her powers for the good of the kingdom. During her stay in the city, Fire meets the child Leck. The young Leck has two different colored eyes and seems to manipulate minds despite not being a monster. Leck manipulates a group of soldiers into kidnapping Fire in the hope that he could convince her to help him control the king and rule the land together. Leck desires Fire as an equal and values her as she is the only person he has not been able to control. Fire's powers prove more powerful than Leck's, and she escapes into the wild. Leck follows her and ends up falling down a crevice, which presumably leads him back to the seven kingdoms. Fire returns to find the Dell kingdom at war.

Brigan defeats the rebel armies and brings peace to the land, and Fire discovers that she can use her abilities to ease the minds of the sick and wounded in hospitals.

Bitterblue acts as the sequel to Graceling and takes place eight years after the events of *Graceling*.

Bitterblue is eighteen years old and has acted as queen since she was ten. Bitterblue becomes bored by the monotony of signing endless decrees and yearns to be more than a figurehead. She sneaks out of the palace at night and experiences her city as a regular person for the first time. She soon sees that much of the city still suffers from her father's cruel reign.

Bitterblue befriends two thieves, Saf and Teddy, outside a pub and tells them she works in the queen's kitchens. Bitterblue develops feelings for Saf, a Graceling, who is charged unjustly with murder. Bitterblue convinces Po to help Saf and succeeds in proving him innocent.

Saf discovers Bitterblue is queen. He becomes angry and steals her crown. Throughout the rest of the book, Bitterblue deals with deception, betrayal, and court intrigue when she learns her advisers are plotting to kill her. While seeking the truth of Leck's influence on the kingdom, Bitterblue discovers the existence of the Dells and monsters.

Katsa, who appears with Po to help Bitterblue, leaves to find the Dells and returns with Fire. Bitterblue's goal is to continue making reparations for the sins of her father.

Critical Evaluation

Each protagonist in the Graceling series has an uncommon power over others and agonizes over how this power should be used. Katsa is graced with the power of killing, and no person or thing can stand against her physical prowess in regard to fighting and weaponry. While Katsa's power is physical, Fire has the extraordinary ability to control others mentally. Few can withstand Fire's powers of persuasion, and just the sight of her can bring out the worst qualities in any creature. Bitterblue is different from Katsa and Fire in that she does not have any physical or mental powers but is born a ruler and becomes queen at the age of ten. Each young woman is aware that her powers can be used for cruelty and strives to use her gifts only for self-defense or the good of others.

Katsa is raised to believe that she was born to kill. Her "Grace" appeared at the age of eight when she accidentally killed a man who molested young girls. From then on she was used by the king as a tool to incite fear in all his subjects and rivals. She was forced to torture and kill whomever the king wished, despite her internal reservations for causing others undeserved harm. Eventually Katsa realizes that she does not have to work for

the king nor do anything that she does not wish to do. She takes control of her power and vows only to use it for the defense of herself and others.

Katsa attempts to make up for past wrongs by forming a committee to protect innocent people from corrupt rulers. She discovers her grace is not limited to killing but is actually a grace of survival. Katsa uses her ability to rescue Princess Bitterblue, almost sacrificing herself to bring the child to safety. By the end of the book, Katsa decides to teach self-defense to girls and women.

While Fire can hold her own in a fight, her true abilities lie with her appearance and mental abilities. Fire feels her entire existence must be to make up for the sins of her father, Cansel. While Fire hides away and refuses to use her mental capabilities for anything but self-defense, Cansel revels in manipulating those around him. He uses his powers to manipulate the king, rape women, and lead the kingdom to ruin. Fire must prove to herself and others that she is nothing like her father and only wants to live a quiet life.

Fire must overcome her guilt in manipulating her father into committing suicide so he could no longer harm others with his monstrous powers. Like Katsa, she decides to use her powers for the good of the realm and seeks to uncover secret plots against it. Fire also finds a calling and spends her time in hospitals easing the minds of the wounded and dying.

Despite having no powers, Bitterblue feels the need to help her kingdom heal from the evils committed by her father, King Leck. Leck's sociopathic desire to gain power, control others, and harm animals and children appears in all three novels. Leck is the opposing force to all Cashore's protagonists in that he uses his grace to lie to and manipulate all those around him into believing him to be benevolent rather than immensely cruel. While Fire believed to have killed him as a child, and Katsa finished the job years later, Bitterblue must continue to fight against the lasting effects Leck had on the kingdom's people and do her best to allow her people to heal.

Cashore's strong female characters can hold their own next to other fantasy female protagonists such as Alanna in Tamora Pierce's four-part series the Song of the Lioness (1983–8), among others. Despite having fantastical powers, Cashore's protagonists are easy to relate to in that they are flawed. No character is a perfect hero without guilt or temptations. The series gives the message that women can be strong, can rescue themselves, and can make mistakes. Even fictional characters in a land of fantasy have to learn, grow, and negotiate through feelings of defeat and guilt in order to keep doing good and live satisfied lives.

The books of the Graceling series were well received by critics and readers alike. *Graceling* and *Fire* were named to *Publishers Weekly*'s list of the best children's fiction books of 2008 and 2009, respectively. *Fire* was also selected by the American Library Association as one of the best books for young adults in 2010 and received a 2009 Cybils Award for best young adult fantasy.

Alexandra McBride, MA

Further Reading

Quart, Alissa. "Dangerous Beauty." Rev. of *Fire*, by Kristin Cashore. *New York Times*. New York Times, 4 Dec. 2009. Web. 14 Mar. 2015. <http://www.nytimes.com/2009/12/06/books/review/Quart-t.html>.

Roiphe, Katie. "Lady Killer." Rev. of *Graceling*, by Kristin Cashore. *New York Times*. New York Times, 7 Nov. 2008. Web. 14 Mar. 2015. <http://www.nytimes.com/2008/11/09/books/review/Roiphe-t.html>.

Rubin, Gretchen. "By Her Majesty's Grace." Rev. of *Bitterblue*, by Kristin Cashore. *New York Times*. New York Times, 11 May 2012. Web. 14 Mar. 2015. <http://www.nytimes.com/2012/05/13/books/review/bitterblue-by-kristin-cashore.html?_r=1>.

Grasshopper Jungle

Author: Andrew Smith (b. 1959)
First published: 2014
Type of work: Novel
Type of plot: Science fiction
Time of plot: 2010s
Locale: Ealing, Iowa

Principal characters

Austin "Porcupine" Szerba, a fifteen-year-old recorder of history

Robert "Robby" Brees, Austin's best friend

Shannon "Shann" Collins, Austin's girlfriend

Johnny McKeon, the proprietor of local liquor and secondhand stores

Grant Wallace, a high school senior who undergoes a startling transformation

Charles R. "Hungry Jack" Hoofard, a homeless veteran and expert Dumpster diver

The Story

The sleepy town of Ealing, Iowa, has fallen on hard times. The main business—McKeon Industries, where half the townspeople were once employed—has shut down. The local strip mall is mostly abandoned, so it is a perfect place for tenth-grade classmates and best friends Austin Szerba and Robby Brees to practice skateboard techniques. One day, while engaged in their favorite pastime, they are confronted by four twelfth-graders from a rival high school, led by Grant Wallace. Grant and his cohorts beat up Austin and Robby, then toss their skateboards and shoes onto the roof of the mall.

Late that night, the boys return to the mall with Shann, Austin's girlfriend, to retrieve their belongings. While Shann waits in the car, they climb up on the roof and find, in addition to their skateboards and shoes, a number of other intriguing items: a lawn flamingo, a lemur mask, and two film canisters. An unlocked trapdoor on the roof leads into the consignment store run by Johnny McKeon, Shann's stepfather, where Austin works part-time. The boys climb down to explore. In Johnny's private office, where Austin has never been, they find shelves full of odd items in glass jars, salvaged from the defunct research laboratories of McKeon Industries: human body parts, a two-headed fetus, specimens of giant insects, and a globe full of goop that pulses with blue light, labeled "Contained MI Plague Strain 412E." As they are examining the objects, the boys hear noises. They hide just before Grant and his buddies arrive, having broken in to rob the liquor store next door. The drunken thieves, in addition to a case of gin, take the glowing globe. On their way out, they drop the globe, which breaks, splashing them with the blue substance. By the next morning, several other innocent people, including mall cleaners Travis and Eileen Pope and homeless vagrant Hungry Jack, have also inadvertently come into contact with the blue stuff.

Meanwhile, alerted by an old teletype machine hidden in the wall of her bedroom that activated upon the release of the plague, Shann has discovered the existence of a silo. She finds the concrete foundation of the silo behind her historical home, which formerly belonged to Johnny's late brother, Dr. Grady McKeon, an eccentric scientist and the founder of McKeon Industries. Austin, Robby, and Shann climb through a hatch in the foundation and find a huge, well-stocked 1960s-era underground bunker called Eden. While exploring the bunker, they learn about the effects of the plague strain and how to combat it.

Ealing townsfolk who are infected quickly become ill. After several days, they all undergo an amazing metamorphosis: they hatch into voracious, nearly indestructible six-feet-tall praying mantises who are only interested in eating and mating. The female of the species, the former Eileen Pope, is impregnated multiple times and eventually lays millions of eggs, which soon hatch to overrun Ealing and the rest of the world. The only human survivors are Austin; Robby; Shann; Shann's mother and stepfather; Robby's mother, Connie; and Connie's lover, Ah Wong Sing, who all live together in the underground bunker and start having children. Though they know how to kill the insects one at a time, there are simply too many to eradicate, and beyond their isolated outpost, humanity is doomed.

Critical Evaluation

Grasshopper Jungle is a rewarding, multilayered read. On the surface, it is a typical tale about unstoppable bug-eyed monsters, reminiscent of science-fiction movies from the 1950s such as *Them!* (1954), *Tarantula* (1955), *The Black Scorpion* (1957), *The Beginning of the End* (1957), and *The Deadly Mantis* (1957). As in these earlier examples, the outsized mantises of Smith's novel are the result of human handiwork. However, while the giant ants, spiders, and grasshoppers of the past were the accidental consequence of atomic testing, the creatures in *Grasshopper Jungle* were purposely created. While experimenting with crossbreeding genetic materials to create hybrid high-yield corn resistant to grasshoppers, McKeon Industries attracted the interest of the Department of Defense, which contracted Grady McKeon to work on a project to clone invincible soldiers. The enormous man-eating insects were the unfortunate result.

Unusually for end-of-the-world scenarios that focus primarily on a standard problem-complication-solution plot structure, the novel features several qualities that lift it above similar stories. The character of protagonist and narrator Austin Szerba is particularly well developed. His compulsively written daily journal entries, filled with sardonic humor, keen observations, and social commentary, reveal much of his family history as well as his own sexual confusion about his relationship with both his girlfriend, Shann, and his best friend, Robby, who is gay. Many secondary characters—a four-hundred-pound store clerk, a self-righteous pastor who haunts a gay bar, a tattooed state trooper, Austin's absent older brother who was horribly wounded in Afghanistan—are memorably sketched.

Though the situation presented in the novel is dire and the descriptions of mantis-human interactions are fairly graphic, *Grasshopper Jungle* is peppered throughout with comedic scenes and humorous asides that soften the serious thrust of the story. The lawn flamingo found on the roof of the mall, for example, is actually part of an early-warning system. Devices used to spot people infected with the plague strain are incongruously shaped like leering masks of lemurs.

In 2014 Sony Pictures acquired the rights to the film adaptation of *Grasshopper Jungle*. Edgar Wright, best known for his collaborations with Simon Pegg and Nick Frost on films such as *Shaun of the Dead* (2004), was attached to the project as director.

Jack Ewing

Further Reading

Smith, Andrew. "One Thing Leads to Another: An Interview with Andrew Smith." Interview by Julie Bartel. *Hub*. Young Adult Lib. Services Assn., 9 Oct. 2014. Web. 27 Oct. 2015. <http://www.yalsa.ala.org/the-hub/2014/10/09/one-thing-leads-to-another-an-interview-with-andrew-smith/>.

Thompson, Clive. "Being Green." Rev. of *Grasshopper Jungle*, by Andrew Smith. *New York Times*. New York Times, 14 Feb. 2014. Web. 27 Oct. 2015. <http://www.nytimes.com/2014/02/16/books/review/grasshopper-jungle-by-andrew-smith.html>.

Hard Love

Author: Ellen Wittlinger (b. 1948)
First published: 1999
Type of work: Novel
Type of plot: Romance, Realism
Time of plot: 1990s
Locale: Boston, Massachusetts

Principal characters

John Galardi Jr., teenage boy who has difficulty showing emotions
Marisol Guzman, John's outspoken friend and a self-described Puerto Rican Cuban Yankee lesbian

Brian Cookson, John's friend who is constantly falling in love

Anne Van Esterhausen, John's mother

John Galardi Sr., John's father

Al, John's future stepfather

Diana Crabtree/Diana Tree, a writer of self-published magazines, or zines

The Story

In Ellen Wittlinger's *Hard Love*, John F. Galardi Jr. is a teenager living at home with his emotionally distant mother. John's mother became depressed after she and John's father divorced six years earlier, and one of the side effects was her refusal to touch her son. His father sees him on the weekends, but his time is always limited due to pressing social events.

John's outlet is his fascination with self-published magazines, or "zines." One of his favorites is *Escape Velocity*, which is written by a high school student named Marisol Guzman. Guzman is very candid in her stories and boldly describes herself as a "Puerto Rican Cuban Yankee Cambridge, Massachusetts, rich spoiled lesbian private-school gifted-and-talented writer virgin looking for love."

Hoping to meet her, John goes to Tower Records on the day Marisol drops off her zines. John has his own zine, called *Bananafish*, and he has given himself the pen name Giovanni in order to sound more exotic. John meets Marisol, and the two not only have a shared interest in writing, they also share unconventional family situations. Marisol is adopted and often lampoons her culturally sensitive white mother and her Hispanic father.

John's friend Brian encourages him to invite Marisol to the prom. She accepts John's invitation and arrives at his house looking like Audrey Hepburn. He has been living without physical contact for so long that when he and Marisol are dancing, he is overwhelmed by her nearness. When he kisses her hair, Marisol stiffens. She pushes him away and angrily exits the dance. John pursues her out onto the street.

During their heated exchange, Marisol slaps him across the face. She emphasizes that they had a deep connection but a platonic one. John confesses that he loves her, but Marisol refuses to believe that. They end the night by going home early and not speaking to one another.

The next day, Marisol calls John and mentions that they should still go to the zine convention. It is a forum that is receptive to gay people, and a friend suggested it would offer her a chance to be openly "out." Marisol and John make plans to take a bus and travel together.

John lies to his mother and says he is taking the commuter train into Boston to see his dad. Before he leaves, he writes letters to his parents, pouring out the negative feelings that he has toward them. He states that he could have told the truth to his mother and father about the convention, but by being secretive he is feeding into a fantasy about running away with Marisol.

At the convention, Marisol meets a girl named June, and John becomes jealous. He spends time with Diana Tree, a zine writer whom he has admired. Diana is very intuitive and reads John's attitude toward Marisol. She understands that he has unrequited feelings for her.

Marisol tells John that she will not be returning to Boston. Instead, she and June and two other women will be traveling to New York City. She tells him that she is not romantically interested in June, but she wants to be herself without her parents' hovering. She reveals that she is at "escape velocity" and has to follow her gut.

During a gathering, Diana performs a song called "Hard Love." Moved by the lyric "The love that heals our lives," John slips away and phones his mother. He apologizes for giving her such a snide letter. The two communicate more than they have for the past several years.

The next morning John gets up early to say good-bye to Marisol. She says she was flattered when he invited her to prom, and besides her mother, he was the first person to call her beautiful. John thanks her for touching him. Before she walks away, she gives him one last gift: "Hey, I love you too, Gio. As much as I can."

Left alone, John's life has changed. He is anxious and slightly afraid, but he is "susceptible now to anything that might happen."

Critical Evaluation

The characters John and Marisol are not the typical romantic leads of a young adult novel. John has shut down emotionally and admits that he has no romantic feelings for girls or boys. He "can't imagine being in love with somebody, letting her touch me and tell me things I wouldn't know whether to believe." Marisol, who is his "dream girl," is truth-telling and astoundingly talented. She is also a lesbian. The romantic convention of "opposites attract" is turned upside down in this book, yet Marisol remains true to who she is and makes clear that she is not experimenting with being gay. John, who is worried about being hurt and misled in love, tells the volley of lies: he gives himself a phony first name and does not share information with his family and friend about Marisol's sexual orientation. What is fascinating about John's unrequited love for Marisol is that its basis is in her *Escape Velocity* zine. John has been infatuated with Marisol since before he ever met her.

Many authors will create characters who are writers, but their works are simply referenced. In *Hard Love*, readers get the chance to experience the articles, the poems, and the letters that define the characters. By reading what Marisol and John each create for their zines, readers are able to understand each character's attraction to the other. Regardless of any romantic or physical attraction between the two, they are more soul mates than boyfriend and girlfriend. Their connection has nothing to do with the physical attributes John's peers find appealing in their love interests, but rather they speak to one another from the deepest recesses of their heart.

Stephanie Finnegan

Further Reading

Matos, Angel Daniel. "On Asexuality and Kinship: Ellen Wittlinger's *Hard Love*." *The Ever and Ever That Fiction Allows*. Angel Matos, 10 Oct. 2013. Web. 24 Nov. 2015. <http://angelmatos.net/2013/10/10/ellen-wittlingers-hard-love>.

Wittlinger, Ellen. "ZigZag to 'Zines: A Conversation with Ellen Wittlinger." Interview by Toby Emert. *ALAN Review*. Digital Library and Archives, Virginia Tech, Fall 2005. PDF file.

Holes

Author: Louis Sachar (b. 1954)
First published: 1998
Type of work: Novel
Type of plot: Humorous
Time of plot: Present
Locale: Camp Green Lake, Texas

Principal characters

Stanley "Caveman" Yelnats IV, a teenager falsely accused of theft and sent to Camp Green Lake
Elya Yelnats, Stanley's ancestor
Stanley Yelnats I, Stanley's ancestor and Elya's son
Hector "Zero" Zeroni, an inmate at Camp Green Lake

Mr. Sir, a camp official
The Warden, the head of Camp Green Lake
Katherine "Kissin' Kate" Barlow, a nineteenth-century outlaw

The Story

In Louis Sachar's *Holes*, teenager Stanley Yelnats IV is sent to a correctional facility known as Camp Green Lake after he is falsely accused of stealing a valuable pair of sneakers. Stanley blames the bad luck that has led him to this point on his "no-good-dirty-rotten-pig-stealing-great-great-grandfather," Elya Yelnats. While a teenager living in Latvia, Elya promised an elderly woman named Madame Zeroni that he would carry her up a mountain. He broke the promise, and his family was cursed.

Upon arriving at the camp, Stanley learns that there is no lake, just miles of dried lakebed. The inmates are required to dig a circular hole, measuring five feet deep and five feet in diameter, every day of the week. The camp belongs to a woman known as the Warden, who runs it with the aid of second-in-command Mr. Sir and several camp counselors. Mr. Sir informs Stanley that he must alert camp officials if he finds something interesting while digging; when Stanley asks if they are searching for something in particular, however, Mr. Sir claims they are not.

As Stanley, known to the other campers as Caveman, acclimates to life at Camp Green Lake, he befriends a young camper known as Zero, whom he teaches to read. While digging one day, he finds half of a lipstick tube etched with the letters *KB*, which he gives to campmate X-Ray instead of showing to his counselor. When X-Ray turns it in to camp officials, they direct the boys to begin digging near where X-Ray claims to have found it rather than near the hole from which it actually came, confirming Stanley's suspicion that they are looking for something.

The novel reveals that more than a century before, a thriving town had existed near Green Lake, then an actual lake. Town schoolteacher Katherine Barlow, who was known for making the best canned peaches, was in love with an African American onion salesman named Sam and rejected the advances of wealthy landowner Trout Walker. After Katherine and Sam were spotted kissing, they tried to escape by boat, but Trout caught up with them and killed Sam. Thereafter, Katherine became an outlaw and gained the name Kissin' Kate Barlow for the lipstick marks she left on her victims. One of the men she robbed but did not kill was the first Stanley Yelnats, Elya's son, who attributed the loss of his fortune to the family curse. Walker, who still owned the dried-out and worthless land by the former lake, searched for Katherine's buried treasure for the rest of his life, but she died without revealing its location.

One day, refusing to dig any more holes, Zero runs off into the desert without any water or food. The Warden and the other adults decide to erase all records of his presence at the camp and let him die in the desert. Stanley searches for him, eventually finding Zero hiding under the remains of Sam's boat, where he has survived by eating the century-old canned peaches he found there. Hoping to find water, Stanley and Zero head for a mountain on the far edge of the lake bed; however, when they get there, Zero collapses, and Stanley must carry him up the mountain. There they find water and a patch of onions, and Stanley learns that Zero was responsible for the theft of the sneakers.

After recuperating, they decide to dig near where Stanley had found the lipstick tube. They find a suitcase but are immediately caught by the Warden and her helpers. The boys remain in the hole until authorities arrive. Stanley's lawyer also arrives, declaring that Stanley has been found innocent and is free to go home. The Warden, who is revealed to be a descendent of Walker, claims that Stanley stole the suitcase from her. However, Zero notices that the suitcase bears the name Stanley Yelnats and therefore must have belonged to Stanley's ancestor. Stanley and Zero leave the camp, which is soon shut down by law enforcement. Although Stanley did not realize when he carried him up the mountain that Zero, whose real name is Hector Zeroni, was Madame Zeroni's descendent, the curse is broken nonetheless, and the lives of both the Yelnats and the Zeroni families are changed forever.

Critical Evaluation

In the final chapter of *Holes*, the narrator notes that the book's readers will have to "fill in the holes" in the story, putting its many pieces together themselves in order to draw their own conclusions. In many ways, this statement is representative of the novel itself. *Holes* contains many mysteries, and solving such mysteries is an important part of the reading experience. The structure of the novel provides ample opportunity for dramatic irony, as readers may at times recognize the significance of people and events long before the characters do.

Much of the novel's effectiveness is the result of its nonlinear narrative. The novel is made up of fifty relatively short chapters that jump between time periods, revealing certain past events bit by bit. Scenes of Stanley's time at Camp Green Lake alternate with short chapters focusing on Elya Yelnats, demonstrating the roots of the Yelnats family's notorious bad luck and lending credence to Stanley's belief that external forces are at work. Additional chapters tell the story of Katherine Barlow, explaining how Green Lake came to be a desert and the reason for the camp's existence. Some pieces of the puzzle require additional thought. The Warden, for example, is not explicitly stated to be Trout Walker's descendent; however, the information provided in the chapters set in nineteenth-century Green Lake, combined with the Warden's desperate search for the treasure and her revealed last name of Walker, make the fact apparent. *Holes* is full of such details, waiting to be discovered by a careful reader.

Joy Crelin

Further Reading

Bodart, Joni Richards. *Radical Reads: 101 YA Novels on the Edge*. Lanham: Scarecrow, 2002. Print.

Greene, Meg. *Louis Sachar*. New York: Rosen, 2004. Print.

Møllegaard, Kirsten. "Haunting and History in Louis Sachar's *Holes*." *Western American Literature* 45.2 (2010): 138–61. *Literary Reference Center*. Web. 3 Mar. 2015. <http://search.ebscohost.com/login.aspx?direct=true&db=lfh&AN=52248202&site=lrc-live>.

Vescia, Monique. *Scholastic Bookfiles: A Guide to* Holes *by Louis Sachar*. New York: Scholastic, 2003. Print.

Zampino, Belinda, et al. *A Guide for Using* Holes *in the Classroom: Based on the Book Written by Louis Sachar*. 2000. Westminster: Teacher Created Resources, 2011. Print.

The House of the Scorpion

Author: Nancy Farmer (b. 1941)
First published: 2002
Type of work: Novel
Type of plot: Dystopian Fiction
Time of plot: An unspecified time in the future
Locale: Aztlán (formerly Mexico); Opium; United States

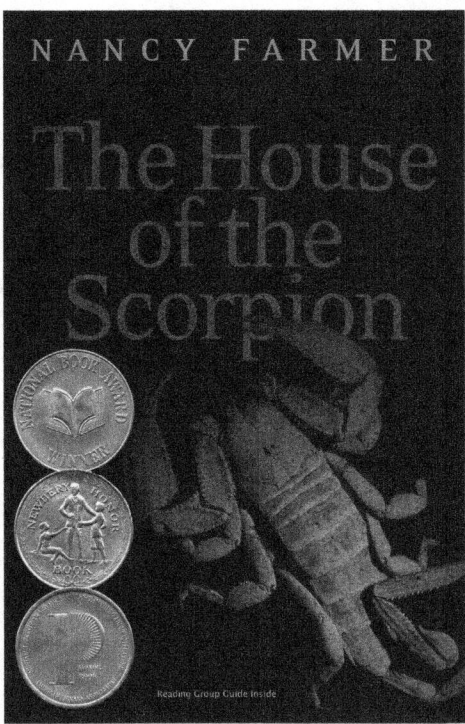

Courtesy of Simon & Schuster

Principal characters

Matteo Alacrán (Matthew Scorpion), known as *El Patrón (the Boss)*, a 140-year-old drug lord

Matteo "Matt" Alacrán, a clone of El Patrón

María Mendoza, daughter of a US senator and Matt's beloved

Celia, chief cook at El Patrón's compound and Matt's caregiver

Tam Lin, a muscular bodyguard first for El Patrón and later for Matt

Chacho, a Lost Boy at a plankton factory

The Story

For a century, Mexican-born El Patrón has reigned supreme in Opium, a vast territory between what used to be the southwestern United States and Aztlán, formerly Mexico. El Patrón and lesser drug lords are allowed to grow narcotic plants as long as they halt illegal immigrants. Farm Patrol mercenaries guard the land; those who are caught crossing are pressed into service as slaves called "eejits" to be worked to death.

El Patrón has survived so long thanks to a series of organ replacements harvested from clones rendered medically mindless. The last surviving clone is Matt, who has been permitted to develop normally and has been raised from birth by Celia, a cook who loves him.

One day, children visiting El Patrón's Big House discover Matt, and one of them, María, bonds with him. After the children leave, another servant, Rosa, keeps Matt prisoner under appalling conditions, until El Patrón learns of it, rescues Matt, and punishes Rosa by electronically lobotomizing her. To protect his investment, El Patrón brings Matt into his house and hires teachers to educate him. He also gives him a personal bodyguard, Tam Lin, a terrorist who once accidentally blew up a bus, killing twenty children.

Tam Lin shows Matt a secret desert oasis, teaches him survival skills, and leaves him a history of the land of Opium. Tam Lin also tells Matt about the huge fortune El Patrón has stashed underground and his intention to be buried with his wealth like a pharaoh. At the Big House, Matt, a multitalented student, explores and finds a hidden passage that allows him to spy on other residents. As Matt grows, he draws closer to Tam Lin and his relationship with María deepens.

After Matt reaches puberty, El Patrón suffers a heart attack. Matt is readied to become donor of the drug lord's new heart, but Celia reveals that she had fed Matt small doses of poison when he was a child, which has made his heart unsuitable for transplant. Angered by the news, El Patrón experiences another attack and dies. Justin Alacrán, El Patrón's great-grandson, who despises clones, orders Tam Lin to kill Matt. Tam Lin, however, helps Matt escape to the oasis, gives him a map, money, and other items, and suggests he head to Aztlán, where María resides at a convent in San Luis.

After great hardship, Matt arrives in Aztlán. As parentless Matt Ortega, he is put to work at a factory where plankton is produced for food by ill-fed young orphans called the Lost Boys and Girls, who are supervised and indoctrinated by guards known as Keepers. Matt ultimately foments a revolution at the factory and escapes with Lost Boys Chacho, Ton-Ton, and Fidelito. With Keepers in hot pursuit, the boys make their way to the convent, where the sisters join them in resisting the Keepers, who are arrested. Matt has a joyous reunion with María.

As Matt recovers from his ordeals, he learns something is wrong at Opium. Since his DNA is identical to El Patrón's, he is able to fool identification devices and use the late drug lord's hovercraft to return to the compound. There, Celia informs him that nearly everyone is dead, including Justin and Tam Lin, poisoned by liquor intended for El Patrón's 150th-birthday celebration, and the entrance to El Patrón's vault has been dynamited. Matt, newly master of Opium, finds another passage to the treasure, which he will use to dissolve the drug empire and work to restore Aztlán and the United States.

Critical Evaluation

The House of the Scorpion introduces a large cast of characters and sets them into motion in a tale covering a fourteen-year period. The novel incorporates a number of futuristic concepts, including hovercraft and the farming of plankton for food.

Primary among speculative advancements is an expansion upon controversial stem-cell technology. Author Nancy Farmer envisions a time when cloned cells will be nurtured routinely and implanted into cows as surrogate mothers. After birth, the clones—maintained as virtual vegetables—will be harvested for their organs. In the time of the novel, the procedure is illegal, but El Patrón, a powerful person above the law to whom even US senators are beholden, undergoes regular transplants of failing body parts with impunity.

The story of *Scorpion* revolves around Matt's struggle for identity through his gradual realization that he is a clone (even physically branded as property), his understanding that he is also a human being, and his eventual resistance to his artificially imposed destiny as an organ donor. A sequel, *The Lord of Opium* (2013), chronicles Matt's continued efforts to achieve his rightful place as an individual.

Other contemporary issues foreseen as major problems of the future are also woven into the fabric of the novel. In *Scorpion*, environmental concerns persist as pollution has decimated the whale population. Illegal immigration, heading north from Aztlán and south from a failing United States, is represented by many running the deadly gauntlet across the land of Opium at risk of being turned into zombie-like workers. The latter thread provides the opportunity for the author to create a sharply drawn contrast between the new, as represented by modern technology, and the old, as characterized by such traditions as El Día de los Muertos (the Day of the Dead), a pre-Columbian ritual celebration that is underway when Matt arrives in Aztlán. It can be inferred that Matt, a product of the new age who holds a heritage from old Mexico, will always be a nexus of conflict due to these two divergent contributing factors.

Jack Ewing

Further Reading

Farmer, Nancy. "The House of Farmer." Interview by Kathleen T. Horning. *School Library Journal* Feb. 2003: 48. *Literary Reference Center*. Web. 25 Mar. 2015. <http://search.ebscohost.com/login.aspx?direct=true&db=lfh&AN=9018348&site=lrc-live>.

Maughan, Shannon. "Nancy Farmer Returns with 'Scorpion' Sequel." *Publishers Weekly*. PWxyz, 10 Jan. 2013. Web. 25 Mar. 2015. <http://publishersweekly.com/pw/by-topic/childrens/childrens-book-news/article/55442-nancy-farmer-returns-with-scorpion-sequel.html>.

How I Live Now

Author: Meg Rosoff (b. 1956)
First published: 2004
Type of work: Novel
Type of plot: Apocalyptic Dystopian Fiction
Time of plot: Twenty-first century
Locale: England

Principal characters

Daisy, an American teenager visiting relatives in England

Edmond, Daisy's cousin

Piper, Daisy's cousin

Isaac, Daisy's cousin

Osbert, Daisy's cousin

Aunt Penn, Daisy's aunt

The Story

Suffering from an eating disorder and unable to get along with her stepmother, fifteen-year-old Daisy travels to England to stay at her Aunt Penn's farm. She immediately bonds with her cousins, particularly nine-year-old Piper and fourteen-year-old twins Edmond and Isaac. Daisy quickly realizes that her cousins have empathic and telepathic abilities that make them particularly close to one another and to nature, and Edmond in particular seems able to read Daisy's mind. Shortly after Daisy's arrival, Aunt Penn flies to Oslo for a peace conference, and Daisy is astonished at the lack of supervision she and her cousins enjoy. She and Edmond fall in love and begin a sexual relationship, even though Daisy recognizes that it is inappropriate.

While Aunt Penn is away, terrorists instigate several coordinated attacks against England and occupy it, prompting the closure of British borders and preventing Aunt Penn from returning. Because the farm is so isolated, Daisy and her cousins feel as though the war is very far away, and they initially believe they are quite safe. However, as the occupation continues and people begin to die due to lack of electricity, medicine, and adequate food, British soldiers arrive and commandeer the family's farm. Daisy's cousin Osbert is old enough to accept a job with the soldiers, but Daisy and Piper are taken to live with a military family some distance away, while Edmond and Isaac are sent to a different farm.

Devastated by this separation, Daisy spends her time taking care of Piper, plotting to find Edmond and Isaac, and picking crops with other civilians. Every night, Daisy finds some measure of peace by mentally connecting with Edmond in spite of the distance between them. When a confrontation at an occupation checkpoint turns deadly, however, Daisy and Piper must flee with a group of British soldiers. Knowing that they are still not safe, the girls set out alone, tramping across the countryside to look for Edmond and Isaac. With little food, their trek becomes a terrifying feat of endurance.

Disturbed because her connection with Edmond seems to be failing, Daisy is horrified to discover that a brutal massacre has taken place at the farm where Edmond and Isaac were sequestered. She examines the bodies and is relieved when the twins are not among them, and she and Piper continue on to their own farm, now deserted by the soldiers who took it over. They sleep in a secluded barn to stay out of sight, returning to the house only to bathe and look for supplies. They are caught completely off guard when the telephone rings and it is Daisy's father, who uses his connections to have Daisy sent back to New York against her will.

Six years later, Daisy notes that her only goal during this time was to return to Edmond. Although the occupation of Britain ended after nine months, there has still been little communication between England and the rest of the world, so Daisy has no idea how her cousins have fared. She is finally allowed to return and is relieved to find Piper and Isaac working the family farm. Aunt Penn has died, however, and Edmond is almost completely unresponsive, spending his days silently tending a garden that grows unnaturally fast and wild as an expression of Edmond's suppressed rage. Daisy realizes that Edmond personally witnessed the massacre that she and Piper discovered after the fact, and that his empathic abilities magnified the horror that he experienced. She works with Edmond in the garden, gradually regaining his trust and hoping to help him heal.

Critical Evaluation

How I Live Now was published in 2004, the debut novel of author Meg Rosoff. It has been widely praised for Daisy's unique narrative voice and for its original, compelling storyline about the possible nature of future wars. Although mildly fantastical in nature, the family's unique mental abilities are seamlessly absorbed into the larger story and do not detract from the book's realism. In addition, just as Daisy and her cousins do not immediately recognize their own dire circumstances, so is the reader taken by surprise when events escalate and the true horror of the situation is revealed.

Another compelling element lies in the characters' many-faceted relationships with one another. Because Daisy's mother died while giving birth to her, Daisy has grown up among people who are uncomfortable talking about her mother. In contrast, her Aunt Penn is willing to discuss the traits that Daisy and her mother have in common, giving Daisy much-needed perspective. In addition, Daisy's close relationship with Piper is touching, particularly because Daisy learns for the first time that taking responsibility for a loved one is not just an obligation but also a privilege.

How I Live Now won the 2005 Michael L. Printz Award and was included on that year's ALA Best Books for Young Adults list. It was also shortlisted for both the Orange Prize and the Whitbread Children's Book of the Year award. The novel was adapted into a 2013 feature film starring Saoirse Ronan.

Amy Sisson, MS, MLS

Further Reading

Rosoff, Meg. Interview by Ilene Cooper. *Booklist* 15 Mar. 2005: 1289. *Literary Reference Center*. Web. 25 Apr. 2015. <http://search.ebscohost.com/login.aspx?direct=true&db=lfh&AN=16668764&site=ehost-live>.

Mattson, Jennifer. Rev. of *How I Live Now*, by Meg Rosoff. *Booklist* 1 Sept. 2004: 123. *Literary Reference Center*. Web. 25 Apr. 2015. <http://search.ebscohost.com/login.aspx?direct=true&db=lfh&AN=14411849&site=ehost-live>.

Page, Benedicte. "Living through Wartime." *Bookseller* 4 June 2004: 28. *Literary Reference Center*. Web. 30 Apr. 2015. <http://search.ebscohost.com/login.aspx?direct=true&db=lfh&AN=14111486&site=ehost-live>.

I Know What You Did Last Summer

Author: Lois Duncan (b. 1934)
First Published: 1973
Type of Work: Novel
Type of Plot: Thriller
Time of Plot: 1970s
Locales: Unnamed town in the U.S.

Principal Characters

Julie James: high school senior planning to attend Smith College in the fall; she is the first to receive the threatening letter reading "I Know What You Did Last Summer"

Helen Rivers: former classmate of Julie's who dropped out of high school to become a local weather forecaster

Ray Bronson: Julie's former boyfriend who left town after high school graduation to hitchhike up the California coast

Barry Cox: Helen's boyfriend who graduated high school with Ray and attends the local university

The Story

After working to bury the memory of a tragedy in which she played a role, seventeen-year-old Julie James receives an anonymous letter reading, simply, "I Know What You Did Last Summer," and is forced to confront her past. One year earlier, after celebrating at a high school graduation party for her boyfriend Ray and his best friend, Barry, Julie and Helen, Barry's girlfriend, Barry, and Ray are involved in a car accident. Barry, who is driving Ray's car, accidentally hits and kills a young boy on a bicycle. Fearing criminal prosecution, especially as they had all been drinking and smoking pot at the party, the four friends flee the scene and vow to never speak of the event again.

Following the accident, the four friends go separate ways: Julie breaks up with Ray, withdraws socially, and focuses on her studies; Helen drops out of school to take a job as a local weathergirl; Ray departs for California, where he plans to hitchhike up and down the coast; and Barry attends college and continues to date Helen casually. After Julie receives the anonymous note, she contacts Helen, who calls Barry, and the three agree that it must be a prank. Soon after, however, the friends revise their theory when Ray returns to town and receives a newspaper clipping describing the accident in the mail and Helen finds a picture of a boy on a bicycle taped to the door of her apartment.

After Barry is shot following a mysterious telephone call arranging a meeting with the friends' anonymous pen pal, Julie and Ray work together to determine who is stalking them. The two feign car trouble to visit the home of the boy they had killed and discover that the boy's death had led to his mother's nervous breakdown and hospitalization. After a conversation with the boy's sister, Ray and Julie determine that their stalker is not a member of the boy's family. They then consider Helen's sister Elsa, as she has always been jealous of Helen.

The friends' stalker ultimately unmasks himself, and is revealed to be a person who has recently insinuated himself into their lives. After an attempt on both Helen's life and Julie's life, the letter-writer is exposed and the truth about the past comes to light.

Critical Evaluation

Lois Duncan's writing for young adults falls firmly within the suspense thriller genre and *I Know What You Did Last Summer* is no exception. Published after early thrillers *Ransom* (1966) and *They Never Came Home* (1969) and right before her later and more supernaturally tinged novels of suspense *Down a Dark Hall* (1974) and *Summer of Fear* (1976), *I Know What You Did Last Summer* addresses, as Duncan's other YA novels do, two themes Duncan has asserted are present in all of her works for teens: "the importance of resisting peer pressure and taking responsibility for your actions" (Kaywell).

Duncan's young adult thrillers arguably paved the way for R.L. Stine's "Fear Street" series and Christopher Pike's stand-alone horror novels, works that achieved significant popularity in the 1990s. Like Stine's and Pike's books, Duncan's novels feature "protagonists [who] are high school students—usually young women—who find themselves suddenly confronted with a sinister threat to their 'normal' existence" ("Duncan, Lois"). This characteristic, as well as some of the "core elements" librarian and critic Patrick Jones associates with the YA thrillers of the 90s—the appearance or suggestion of the supernatural and the threat to expose a secret—are certainly present in *I Know What You Did Last Summer*. In fact, Pike's 1986 novel, *Chain Letter*, features a premise strikingly similar to that of *I Know What You Did Last Summer*.

Reviews of *I Know What You Did Last Summer* note the chilling effectiveness of Duncan's novel. While the threatening notes and the mystery they create are at the center of the story and provide the most obvious "scares," Duncan's book, like many of her other thrillers, brings the themes of "trust, loyalty, and betrayal" common in the YA thriller genre to the fore (Campbell). The novel also offers commentary specific to the period in which it was written. As it introduces a character who has recently returned from fighting in the Vietnam War, the novel "suggest[s] … the long term effects of the Vietnam involvement on a generation of American young." (Churchill).

I Know What You Did Last Summer was made into a movie starring Jennifer Love Hewitt (as Julie) and Sarah Michelle Gellar (as Helen) in 1997. Duncan had little involvement with the creation of the movie and expressed dissatisfaction with the production. As she told Joan Kaywell in an interview published in the *Journal of Adolescent and Adult Literacy*: "I was kept so far out of the loop that I had no idea what was being done. Once I saw the movie, I understood why."

In 2010, Duncan's publisher announced plans to publish a new edition of *I Know What You Did Last Summer* as well as other YA titles from her backlist. The revised version of *I Know What You Did Last Summer* features new cover art, an interview with the author, and updated text. In an interview with *Publishers Weekly*, Duncan explained that she found surprisingly little of her original text needed revision; "just little fringe things … had to be reworked, mostly due to today's technology," she said (Lodge). She added technological accessories, updated descriptions of her characters' wardrobes, and modernized dialogue, maintaining the core and essence of each novel while re-situating her stories in a more contemporary milieu.

Amy Pattee

Further Reading

Duncan, Lois. *Lois Duncan*. Web. <http://loisduncan.arquettes.com/>

Stelloh, Tim. "Who Killed Lois Duncan's Daughter?" *BuzzFeed News*. BuzzFeed, Inc., 30 May 2014. Web. 27 February 2016.

Bibliography

Campbell, Patty. "The Sand in the Oyster." *Horn Book* 70.2 (March/April 1994): 234 – 240. *Library and Information Science Source*. Web. 27 February 2016.

Churchill, David. Rev. of *I Know What You Did Last Summer*. *The School Librarian* 30.1 (June 1982): 151-152. In *Children's Literature Review*. Ed. Gerard J. Senick. Vol. 29. Detroit: Gale, 1993. *Children's Literature Review Online*. Web. 26 February 2016.

"Duncan, Lois (1934-)." *Major 21st-Century Writers*. Ed. Tracey Matthews and Tracey Watson. Vol. 2. Detroit: Gale, 2005. *Gale Virtual Reference Library*. Web. 27 February 2016.

Jones, Patrick. "Nothing to Fear." *Collection Management* 25.4 (2001): 3 – 23.

Kaywell, Joan. "An Interview with Lois Duncan." *Journal of Adolescent and Adult Literacy* 56.2 (March 2009): 545. *Literature Resource Center*. Web. 26 February 2016.

Lodge, Sally. "Lois Duncan Thrillers Get an Update." *Publishers Weekly*. PWxyc, LLC., 23 September 2010. Web. 26 February 2016.

I'll Give You the Sun

Author: Jandy Nelson (b. 1965)
First published: 2014
Type of work: Novel
Type of plot: Realism
Time of plot: Early 2010s
Locale: Lost Cove, Northern California

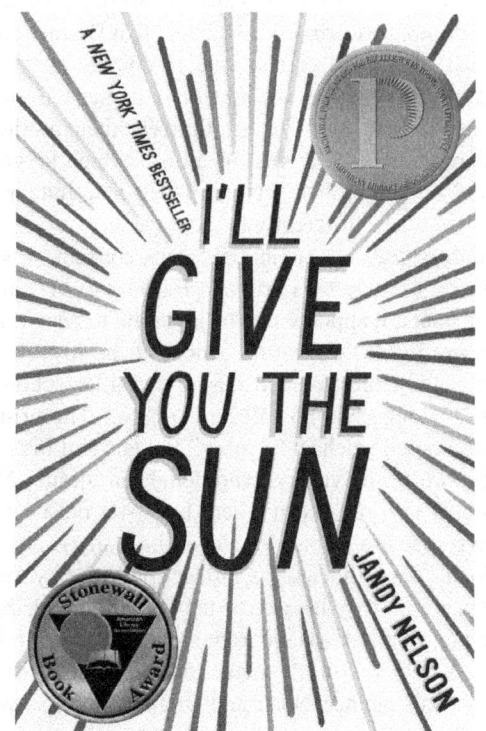

Courtesy of Penguin Young Readers

Principal characters

Noah Sweetwine, a sensitive, artistic teenage boy

Jude Sweetwine, Noah's athletic, extroverted fraternal twin sister

Dianna Sweetwine, the twins's mother

Benjamin Sweetwine, the twins's father

Brian Connelly, a teenage athlete and the twins's new neighbor

Guillermo Garcia, a sculptor

Oscar Ralph, Jude's boyfriend

Michael "Zephyr" Ravens, an older bully

The Story

The Sweetwine family—Dianna, Benjamin, and their twins, Jude and Noah—live in apparent contentment in the fictional setting of Lost Coast, California, an underpopulated area of steep mountains, deep woods, and untrammeled beaches along the state's northern coast. Appearances, however, are deceiving. Popular extrovert Jude and her twin brother, Noah, were once inseparable and thought of themselves as a single unit, "Noahand-Jude," and communicated as if by telepathy when they often finished each other's sentences. They have become highly competitive as they enter their teens, and their parents are also drifting apart. The couple's marital problems are exacerbated by the fact that Dianna clings to Noah, the sensitive son who resembles her, while Benjamin favors Jude, the athletic daughter who looks like him. When the twins are thirteen, their mother is killed when her car drives off a cliff, which serves to drive a wedge further between Noah and Jude when each twin reacts differently to the tragedy.

Noah is very artistic and sketches constantly while imagining even grander artwork. Because of his natural artistic talent, it appears as if he is certain to be admitted to the prestigious California School of the Arts (CSA). Noah is frequently bullied during and after school by older local surfers who call him "homo." The primary tormenters are Michael "Zephyr" Ravens and his hulking cohort, Franklyn Fry, who delight in tossing Noah off a cliff into the ocean where his sister occasionally has to rescue him. Noah wonders if he really is gay.

Noah's sexual identity is further conflicted by the arrival of a new boy his age to the neighborhood. Brian Connelly, an East Coast boarding school student visiting for the summer, collects meteorites and is an outstanding baseball pitcher. Noah and Brian become constant companions. Each boy is attracted physically, intellectually, and emotionally to the other. They meet in secret, where conversation leads to kisses and caresses. Though Brian eagerly participates in the increasingly intense relationship, he worries he will lose his athletic scholarship if he is exposed as gay. The two potential lovers are eventually split up through misunderstanding and jealousy.

Jude, meanwhile, has her own secrets. At fourteen, she was sexually assaulted by Zephyr. Later, through subterfuge, she lands what should have been Noah's spot at CSA. There she is nicknamed CJ, short for "Calamity Jude," because through bad luck or some other force everything she makes gets broken. Jude, who sometimes communes with her deceased, platitude-spouting grandmother Cassandra, thinks the ghost of her dead mother is destroying her artwork out of revenge for stealing her brother's place art school. To prevent further breakage, Jude decides to work in stone and is connected with the famous but reclusive sculptor Guillermo Garcia, who is obsessed with creating images of lovers. Through Garcia, she meets nineteen-year-old English figure model Oscar Ralph, a motorcycle-riding risk-taker who connects emotionally with the teenaged girl. Jude eventually learns her late mother and Garcia were romantically linked and that Dianna was killed when she was on her way to see Benjamin to ask him for a divorce in order to marry Guillermo.

With many secrets finally exposed, reconciliation begins. Jude confesses her betrayal about CSA to Noah and assists him in applying to art school, and the twins become friends again. Noah confesses to Jude he is gay, and she helps him reconnect with Brian. Benjamin, who was devastated by the separation from and the subsequent death of his unfaithful wife, recovers enough to start over in a fresh, less memory-tainted environment by moving with his children onto a houseboat.

Critical Evaluation

One of the strengths of the Printz Award–winning *I'll Give You the Sun* is the novel's structure, which is told alternately in first-person present by the twins. Noah's story is spun prior to and immediately after his mother's accidental death when he is thirteen and fourteen years old. His segments are headlined "The Invisible Museum," which relates to his animated mental processes, wherein he dreams up colorful artistic tableaux. Jude's story unfolds when she is sixteen and several years after her mother's death. Her chapters are labeled "The History of Luck," which relates both to her belief that her dead mother is sabotaging her artistic efforts and to her late grandmother's "bible," which contains advice on how to improve personal luck by taking superstitious actions and carrying talismans like four-leaf clovers and onions.

I'll Give You the Sun—the title refers to the twins' past habit of facetiously bartering elements from the natural world (the sun, moon, trees, or flowers) for special favors—follows a multitude of threads. Communication is a key theme: early unspoken conversations between the siblings degenerate into testy verbal exchanges leading to misunderstandings that cause unfortunate consequences and contribute to Noah's inability to fully express his feelings except through his artwork. Likewise, lack of communication between the twins and their parents results in many difficulties throughout the novel. There are numerous secrets and deceits, honesty that hurts and lies that heal. Many convoluted detours are taken before characters arrive at the truth.

Another theme in the novel is the impossibility of living up to assigned or expected roles. Early in the narrative, Benjamin wades with the two toddlers into the ocean. While Noah, who has been marked as a mama's boy and a weakling, is afraid to let go of his father, Jude is a fearless tomboy and a daddy's girl who eagerly plunges into the waves. The dissimilar reactions forever affect the book's character development and family relationships.

Jack Ewing

Further Reading

Brenner, Robin. "Jukebooks: *I'll Give You the Sun* by Jandy Nelson." *YALSA*. Amer. Lib. Assn., 4 Feb. 2015. Web. 9 Dec. 2015. <http://www.yalsa.ala.org/thehub/2015/02/04/jukebooks-ill-give-you-the-sun-by-jandy-nelson-2>.

Oliver, Lauren. Rev. of *I'll Give You the Sun*, by Jandy Nelson. *New York Times*. New York Times, 6 Nov. 2014. Web. 9 Dec. 2015. <http://www.nytimes.com/2014/11/09/books/review/ill-give-you-the-sun-by-jandy-nelson.html?_r=0>.

If I Stay

Author: Gayle Forman (b. 1970)
First published: 2009
Type of work: Novel

Courtesy of Penguin Young Readers

Type of plot: Fantasy; Realism
Time of plot: Early 2000s
Locale: Oregon

Principal characters

Mia Hall, a musically talented seventeen-year-old
Teddy, Mia's eight-year-old brother
Adam Wilde, Mia's boyfriend
Kim Schein, Mia's best friend
Gran, Mia's grandmother
Brooke Vega, the female lead singer in a popular local rock group

The Story

Early on a snow day in February, the Hall family—Denny, a teacher; Kat, a travel agent; and their children, Mia and Teddy—set out for a short drive to visit Denny and Kat's friends Henry and Willow. Soon after the family piles into their old, rusted Buick to begin the journey, the car is hit broadside by a pickup truck. Denny and Kat are thrown from the car on impact and are immediately killed, while Mia and Teddy are critically injured. The accident puts Mia in a coma from which she observes her present and past lives during periodic out-of-body experiences. As from a distance and in no pain, she observes her mother and father being zipped into body bags and watches her own mangled body being loaded into an ambulance. Mia then flashes back to a better time when she decided she was going to play the cello and remembers happy days taking lessons and giving recitals.

At the hospital, Mia's physical body is taken into surgery while her consciousness roams. As she is operated on for a collapsed lung, ruptured spleen, brain contusions, broken ribs, and multiple abrasions, she sees her grandparents in the hospital waiting room. Mia recalls her grandmother encouraging her to apply to Juilliard and all the effort she expended to be accepted at the renowned performance arts conservatory: collecting letters of recommendation, practicing, making recordings of her cello playing, and an audition.

As Mia is moved into the postoperative intensive-care unit (ICU) and in very grave condition, she thinks of her boyfriend, Adam, and recalls highlights of their relationship. Meanwhile, friends and family members have gathered at the hospital to keep vigil. Among those assembled is her best friend, Kim Schein, which causes Mia to reminisce about how they first met. While doctors and nurses come and go monitoring her condition, Mia's mind continues to wander. Her grandparents are allowed to visit and talk soothingly to her. When Mia overhears her grandparents discussing whether her dead parents want her to join them, she remembers something an attending nurse had said: whether she lives or dies, it is up to Mia. Her spirit spends time at the maternity ward where there is new life, joy, and promise for the future rather than with her family, where sadness reigns.

Adam arrives at the hospital but is not allowed to see Mia because he is not a family member. She observes Adam and Kim's failed attempt to disguise themselves as doctors or orderlies in order to gain access to the ICU. Adam then recruits Brooke Vega and members of her band to play and sing in the hallway in order to cause a distraction so Adam can sneak in to the ICU and see Mia. But security guards are called, and they prevent Adam from getting near Mia's bed. As Adam and Kim are being led away, her parents' friend Willow, who is also a nurse and works at the hospital where Teddy was taken, appears and convinces the guards to release the two teenagers. Mia concludes that Willow's presence means Teddy has died, and she thinks it unfair that he died so young. She remembers other people she knew who died before they were able to fully experience life.

Willow arranges for Adam to see Mia. He sits holding her hand and begs her to stay. She responds to his touch and squeezes his hand.

Critical Evaluation

If I Stay deals with a difficult subject matter for a young adult novel: the violent and sudden destruction of an entire family as the result of a car accident. It is a valid topic of consideration, however, because each year in the United States, there are tens of thousands of deaths and catastrophic injuries from automobile accidents, which in turn create far-ranging disruptions among the survivors and their relatives, coworkers, or acquaintances.

At the core of the story are Mia's near-death and out-of-body experiences. Near-death and out-of-body experiences are frequently reported on and are often studied by psychologists, physiologists, and occultists but are not fully understood or accepted as true. Caused by brain injuries, certain drugs, or sleep or sensory deprivation, the phenomena make subjects feel as though their mental awareness is separated from their physical being so that they can see themselves as outside observers would. In the novel, Forman also uses time distortion to structure the story, which is told exclusively in the first person for both current and past events. Forman titles the chapters in the novel with specific times of day, compressing Mia's four-day coma into a single day from Mia's perspective.

The major theme of the novel, which is reflected in the book's title, is whether to stay or to go. This key consideration is important in several ways and has several meanings. On its most basic, physical level, Mia has to decide if she should stay in Oregon with her boyfriend or leave for the East Coast and Juilliard and run the risk of losing him. On another level, there is the more general choice of whether to continue with what is familiar, known, and comfortable or to opt for the unknown. Finally, the theme of choosing to leave or stay relates directly to the test of Mia's will: should she decide to live and therefore stay with the people who love her and are still alive to share that love, or instead choose to die?

If I Stay found a receptive audience. Forman published a sequel to the novel in 2011 titled *Where She Went*, which continues Mia's story and is told from the viewpoint of her boyfriend, Adam. A film adaptation, also called *If I Stayed*, was released in 2014.

Jack Ewing

Further Reading

Driscoll, Molly. "'If I Stay' Author Gayle Forman Discusses the Movie Adaptation of Her YA Book." *Christian Science Monitor*. Christian Science Monitor, 15 Aug. 2014. Web. 30 Nov. 2015. <http://www.csmonitor.com/Books/chapter-and-verse/2014/0815/If-I-Stay-author-Gayle-Forman-discusses-the-movie-adaptation-of-her-YA-book>.

Rev. of *If I Stay*, by Gayle Forman. *Kirkus Reviews* 77.7 (2009): 382. *Literary Reference Center Plus*. Web. 11 Dec. 2015. <http://search.ebscohost.com/login.aspx?direct=true&db=lkh&AN=38120999&site=lrc-plus>.

Nation, Kaleb. "'If I Stay': Trapped Between Life and Death." Rev. of *If I Stayed*, by Gayle Forman. *All Things Considered*. NPR, 15 July 2011. Web. 11 Dec. 2015. <http://www.npr.org/2011/01/03/128800556/if-i-stay-trapped-between-life-and-death>.

The Impossible Knife of Memory

Author: Laurie Halse Anderson (b. 1961)
First published: 2014
Type of work: Novel
Type of plot: Realism
Time of plot: Present day
Locale: Belmont, New York

Principal characters

Hayley Kincain, a seventeen-year-old high school student
Andrew "Andy" Kincain, Hayley's veteran father
Finnegan "Finn" Ramos, Hayley's boyfriend
Gracie Rappaport, Hayley's friend
Trish, Hayley's father's ex-girlfriend

The Story

At the start of Laurie Halse Anderson's novel *The Impossible Knife of Memory*, seventeen-year-old Hayley Kincain has recently enrolled in high school for the first time, not as a freshman but as a senior. The daughter of US Army veteran Andrew "Andy" Kincain, Hayley had spent the previous five years on the road with her father, who worked as a truck driver and homeschooled his daughter as they traveled throughout the United States. Hoping to give Hayley a "normal" high school experience, he has now settled the family in his hometown of Belmont, New York.

Although Hayley is unhappy about her father's decision, she agrees to settle in Belmont in the hope that staying in one place will bring her father a measure of stability. Andy struggles with post-traumatic stress disorder (PTSD), including flashbacks that have intensified in recent months, and he seems unable to accept the assistance available to him as a veteran. Instead, he self-medicates with drugs and alcohol and consequently is unable to keep a job in town. With her mother long dead and Andy's ex-girlfriend Trish out of the picture, Hayley is her father's only true means of support, and the responsibility of caring for him falls heavily on her.

Hayley dislikes high school, deeming many of her classmates "zombies," but she quickly becomes friends with Gracie Rappaport, a girl with whom she was friends as a child, and Finnegan "Finn" Ramos, the editor of the school newspaper. With Finn's encouragement, Hayley agrees to write for the school paper in exchange for tutoring in precalculus. She grows closer to Finn and eventually agrees to date him; however, she is not open about her father's struggles or their effects on her.

Unbeknownst to Hayley, Andy reopens contact with Trish and invites her to Belmont. Trish had been Andy's serious girlfriend and for many years was a surrogate mother to Hayley; however, she struggled with alcohol abuse and eventually ended her relationship with Andy, leaving Hayley feeling abandoned and betrayed. Haley continues to feel that way when Trish, now sober and pursuing a career in nursing, arrives in Belmont, but she eventually grows accustomed to Trish's presence. Andy's mental state continues to deteriorate, however, and after unsuccessful attempts to convince him to seek help, Trish leaves again, returning only after Hayley is forced to call her for help.

Hayley's relationship with Finn suffers as she struggles with her father's illness, and she breaks up with him for a time, although they get back together after they agree to be more open with each other. During a snow storm several days after Christmas, the two decide to play a video game at Hayley's house, but when they arrive, they find the house empty and two wrapped boxes under the tree. After opening the boxes and finding Andy's wedding rings and military medals inside, Hayley immediately realizes that her father intends to commit suicide. She calls Trish and the police, but both are unable to help: Trish is out of state and unable to travel because of the snow, and the police cannot officially report Andy missing as he has been gone for only a few hours.

Fearing for Andy's life, Hayley and Finn go in search of him, eventually locating him at the edge of a deep, water-filled quarry. Hayley climbs over the fence and goes to him, trying to convince him not to jump, while Finn calls the police. The wind and snow have created an overhang that Hayley inadvertently stands on, but Andy is able to grab hold of her when it crumbles, preventing her from falling to her likely death. In the aftermath of this incident, Andy agrees to receive formal treatment, while Hayley completes high school and enrolls in college. Father and daughter have a long way to go, and the novel's final chapter suggests that recovery will be an extensive process. Nevertheless, as Hayley points out, she and her father may not have found their "Happily Ever After," but they have certainly found their "Good Enough for Today."

Critical Evaluation

Like many of Anderson's young adult novels, *The Impossible Knife of Memory* provides a complex look at a difficult subject. Although relatively common among active and veteran members of the military in the early twenty-first century, PTSD remains underrepresented in popular discourse, as do the devastating effects it can have on those struggling with it and the people who care for them. In many ways, Andy's trauma is mirrored in Hayley, whose experiences with fear and death occur not on the battlefield but in her own home. Hayley's first-person narration, transmitted through numerous short chapters, gives the reader a vivid sense of the anxiety and panic she feels in relation to her father as well as the intrusive nature of her traumatic memories and thoughts. The knife mentioned in the novel's title is not the literal object but an apt metaphor for such intrusion: the knife seems to cut holes in the fabric between the present and the past, allowing painful memories to travel and encroach upon the present.

In addition to its sensitive and thought-provoking depiction of PTSD, *The Impossible Knife of Memory* is also important because of its discussion of why individuals dealing with PTSD, unemployment, and the commonly concurrent substance use disorder may often refuse to seek help. Andy has a variety of resources at his disposal, but he is so deeply mired in traumatic memories and self-hatred that all sources of help seem beyond his reach. Similarly, although Hayley has a willing and compassionate confidant in Finn, she is reluctant to open up to him about her difficult family life and even lashes out at him rather than allow herself to be vulnerable. Through her depiction of Andy and Hayley's parallel struggles, Anderson points out that what appears to be a refusal of help may be more a result of inner self-loathing and a belief that such improvements are not possible or deserved.

Joy Crelin

Further Reading

Anderson, Laurie Halse. *The Impossible Knife of Memory*. New York: Penguin, 2014. Print.

"Healing the Wounds of Memory's 'Impossible Knife.'" *NPR Books*. NPR, 11 Jan. 2014. Web. 31 Mar. 2015. <http://www.npr.org/2014/01/11/261414341/healing-the-wounds-of-memorys-impossible-knife>.

Knowles, Jo. "Line of Fire: Laurie Halse Anderson's 'Impossible Knife of Memory.'" *New York Times*. New York Times, 10 Jan. 2014. Web. 31 Mar. 2015. <http://www.nytimes.com/2014/01/12/books/review/laurie-halse-andersons-impossible-knife-of-memory.html?_r=0>.

In Darkness

Author: Nick Lake (b. 1979)
First published: 2012
Type of work: Novel
Type of plot: Historical Fiction; Realism
Time of plot: 2010; 1791–1804
Locale: Port-au-Prince, Haiti, and environs

Principal characters

Shorty, also known as the Mechanic, a black teenaged slum-dweller and gang member
Marguerite, Shorty's angelic twin sister
Toussaint l'Ouverture, leader of a slave revolt in Haiti in the late eighteenth and early nineteenth century
Dread Wilmè, a gang leader, drug dealer, and slum benefactor
Biggie, Dread's lieutenant
Stéphanie, a twenty-five-year-old white French UN worker who is in love with Biggie
Tintin, a gang member and graffiti artist

The Story

On January 12, 2010, Haiti, one of the world's poorest nations, was devastated by an earthquake that leveled buildings and killed thousands of people. The plot of *In Darkness* (2012) begins during the earthquake. Shorty, a teenaged gangster who lives in a violent, poverty-stricken slum of Haiti's capital, Port-au-Prince, is in the hospital recovering from a gunshot wound when the earthquake strikes. The hospital collapses, crushing most patients and staff in falling debris. Shorty lives through the disaster but is trapped in a prisonlike air pocket without food or water. He can see nothing but faintly hears rescue workers burrowing into the rubble in search of survivors. While waiting for succor that may never arrive, Shorty reviews the events of his brief but volatile life. As time passes and he weakens, he begins to hallucinate, imagining the period when the nation of Haiti was born, following a successful revolt of slaves more than two hundred years earlier under the leadership of Toussaint l'Ouverture, a former slave.

Sections headed "Now" detail Shorty's experiences. He has grown up with his pretty, sweet-natured twin sister Marguerite in a slum where cakes made of mud are eaten and unwanted infants are thrown out with the trash. Shorty's family lives between the territories of two major groups competing for control of the slum, Route 9 and Boston. The gangs sell drugs, temporary respite from daily misery for the residents, and routinely engage in lethal shootouts among themselves or with well-armed United Nations Stabilization forces (MINUSTAH). Victims of the gang war include Shorty's own father, hacked to death with machetes, and his sister, kidnapped at age seven. Even before he reaches his teens, Shorty becomes affiliated with the Route 9 gang, under the leadership of Dread Wilmè, who dies protecting Shorty. After Dread's death, Biggie, who has aspirations of becoming a rapper, leads the gang and turns Shorty into a cold-blooded killer before he himself is murdered.

Alternating sections labeled "Then" focus on the slave revolt of two centuries before under the leadership of Toussaint l'Ouverture. Toussaint, like Shorty, also had a twin sister who was lost at a young age. Though illiterate, he is an outstanding military commander and, through various stratagems, triumphs over local white rulers, armies of soldiers sent from France by Napoleon Bonaparte, and English troops who invade in an attempt to take over the island's profitable sugar-producing industry. Though a former slave, Toussaint is compassionate toward his former master, who treated him fairly, and honorable in dealing with enemies. Ultimately betrayed, Toussaint is arrested for treason, transported to France, and imprisoned. When he refuses to reveal the location of a supposed (but nonexistent) hidden treasure in exchange for his freedom, he is confined in a windowless cell without food or water and allowed to die.

The two story lines ultimately merge. In the present, Shorty, after breaking his leg while attempting to clear his confined space and apparently doomed to starve, hears voices and dreams of Toussaint. In the past, Toussaint has visions of the future while nearing death in his prison. He sees strange machines—helicopters and cars—and views earthquake-shattered Port-au-Prince. His spirit settles into the destroyed hospital, occupying the body of his descendent, Shorty, just in time for the young gangster to be rescued and reunited with his mother, who has survived the earthquake.

Critical Evaluation

In Darkness won the 2013 Michael L. Printz Award, sponsored by the American Library Association's publication, *Booklist*. The artistry of *In Darkness* lies in the author's skill in using two distinctly different voices, one based on the historical record and one imagined, to recount Haiti's history. A nation born in a bloody slave revolt, modern Haiti remains a place of violence—geologically (the island of Hispaniola is in a tectonic fault zone), geographically (frequent hurricanes and tropical storms sweep through), and socially (continued ethnic tensions and great income disparity help perpetuate poverty, a contemporary form of oppression). The novel captures the brutality past and present through depictions of shocking incidents full of horrifically memorable images.

The fictional Shorty is portrayed through his first-person voice, peppered with slang, curses, and street patois, with matter-of-fact references to crimes committed or witnessed. In Shorty's narration, there is an underlying tone of fatalism. He has seen much in his young life and does not expect to reach adulthood. The semi-realistic, semi-fantastic flavor of *In Darkness* is suggested at the beginning, when Shorty notes: "I am a killer and I have been killed, too, over and over; I am constantly being born" (1).

Sections dealing with the historical figure Toussaint l'Ouverture are in third-person, with a corresponding contrast in tone: grammatically correct, polite, and well-expressed. Toussaint's passages demonstrate his ability to inspire, his reluctance to resort to cruelty, and his dignity in pursuing his destiny.

The two narrators are linked through their awareness of vodoun, an African-based religion that still influences the inhabitants of Haiti. Though neither protagonist is a true believer, each is conscious that vodoun powerfully affects their respective associates, and neither Shorty nor Toussaint does anything to show a skepticism that would fracture fragile alliances. Woven throughout the novel are numerous references to *lwa* (ancient gods), the conjuring of gods and ghosts by *houngans* (priests), belief in zombis (zombies), *veves* (written symbols), simples (natural curing remedies), and *pwen*, or protective charms. The vodoun theme reinforces the gulf between the powerful *blancs* (whites) and largely powerless *noirs* (blacks) of Haiti and prepares the reader to suspend disbelief when encountering the supernatural elements that make the story possible.

Jack Ewing

Further Reading

Hunt, Jonathan. Rev. of *In Darkness*, by Nick Lake. *Horn Book Magazine* 88.2 (2012): 111–12. *Literary Reference Center*. Web. 13 Apr. 2015. <http://search.ebscohost.com/login.aspx?direct=true&db=lfh&AN=71797924&site=lrc-live>.

Lake, Nick. "The Booklist Printz Interview: Nick Lake." By Daniel Kraus. *Booklist* 15 Mar. 2013: 80. *Literary Reference Center*. Web. 13 Apr. 2015. <http://search.ebscohost.com/login.aspx?direct=true&db=lfh&AN=86163416&site=lrc-live>.

Lake, Nick. "2013 Printz Speech." *Young Adult Library Services Association*. Young Adult Lib. Services Assn., 3 July 2013. PDF file. <http://www.ala.org/yalsa/sites/ala.org.yalsa/files/content/booklistsawards/bookawards/speeches/LakePrintzSpeech.pdf>.

Inexcusable

Author: Chris Lynch (b. 1962)
First published: 2007
Type of work: Novel
Type of plot: Realism
Time of plot: Early twenty-first century
Locale: United States

Principal characters

Keir Sarafian, a teen athlete getting ready to graduate high school
Gigi Boudakian, the classmate who accuses Keir of rape
Rollo, Keir's uncle who runs a limousine service
Fran and Mary, Keir's sisters, both in college
Ray Sarafian, Keir's father, an alcoholic

The Story

Inexcusable alternates between the present and the past. The narrator is Keir, a boy accused of rape by his crush, Gigi; the true story of the incident unfolds throughout the novel. Gigi is upset and feels trapped, while Keir is confused and frustrated by the very fact that Gigi is distraught. Keir repeatedly states that there must have been some miscommunication: he could not have done anything bad because he loves Gigi and is a good guy.

Now that his sisters, Fran and Mary, have moved out, Keir and his father behave more like roommates than like parent and child, often playing Risk and drinking alcohol together. They seem close and tease each other frequently. Keir worries that his father will be lonely when he joins his sisters at college.

Keir is nicknamed "Killer" by his classmates after an incident in which he seriously injures an opposing player in a football game during a tackle. The incident is investigated and deemed an unfortunate accident. Keir feels he has done nothing wrong and does not protest the new nickname. Fran and Mary believe Keir is not taking responsibility for the situation; Keir becomes defensive, arguing that the boy he wounded was not upset with him. Despite the incident, he receives an athletic scholarship to college, and thus decides that he no longer has to put in any effort at school.

His memories of attending goodbye parties begin to show the reader how Keir and Gigi could come to such a gross misunderstanding later in the novel. Keir describes a video that was taken of some football players harassing soccer players by a lake. Keir notices that the person forcing the boys to drink and then dunking them looks suspiciously like him, but is confused because he is convinced that he is a good person who would not do such a thing. In fact he harms and harasses others with some regularity, especially when drunk, but is so ashamed of his actions that he cannot admit them even to himself.

Keir's crush on Gigi becomes clear when he takes her to prom in place of her boyfriend. He repeatedly states that he is allowed to take her because he is trustworthy, but soon proves the opposite as he consumes too much alcohol and repeatedly touches Gigi without her consent. However, Keir apologizes for his actions and the two stay friends.

The story concludes the night of graduation. As a present, Keir asks to use his uncle's limousine. Rollo takes Keir to a party to meet up with Gigi, who kisses him when he arrives; the two drink before going into the party. When Gigi separates from Keir to call her boyfriend, Keir ends up in a room with other football players. They convince him to do some lines of cocaine and other drugs on top of drinking.

Keir soon discovers Gigi and her boyfriend are fighting, and convinces Gigi and Rollo to drive to his sisters' college to surprise them. He discovers that his sisters are out, and when Keir's sister Fran returns, the two argue. Keir tells Rollo to go back without them and tells Gigi that Rollo left them. He then leads Gigi to a dorm that can be used by prospective football players and sexually assaults Gigi in her sleep. Gigi repeatedly states that Keir raped her and that good guys do not commit rape. Keir begins to understand that what he did was not consensual and waits for the authorities to arrive.

Critical Evaluation

Inexcusable by Chris Lynch tells the story of a date rape from the perspective of the accused. Keir Sarafian is a teenage athlete and an all-around good guy, in his own estimation. He believes himself to be incapable of committing an atrocity such as rape. He describes the situation as being completely wrong and the result of a small misunderstanding.

Inexcusable stands apart from other young adult fiction dealing with rape and abuse, such as Sarah Dessen's *Dreamland* (2004) and Daisy Whitney's *The Mockingbirds* (2010), in that it is told from the first-person perspective of a deeply flawed protagonist and an unreliable narrator. Most authors write about date rape from the victim's perspective, or that of someone who sympathizes with them. By telling the story from the point of view of the aggressor, *Inexcusable* recognizes his humanity while holding him accountable.

At first Keir seems to make a good case for himself. He is a good guy, loves his family, and "does things by the book." However, the reader soon sees that Keir is in denial and refuses to take responsibility for his actions. He says letting down a loved one is inexcusable without realizing that he often does it himself. He does drugs, binge drinks, vandalizes, hazes, and eventually commits rape.

This novel deals with difficult, but relevant, issues for young adults. *Inexcusable* demonstrates that no one is all good or all bad. Real life is difficult and every decision has consequences. What is important is self-awareness and improvement, rather than masking or denying flaws.

Alexandra McBride, MA

Further Reading

Cooper, Ilene. "'Me, Dead Dad, & Alcatraz' and 'Inexcusable': How the Boys Are." Rev. of *Inexcusable*, by Chris Lynch. *New York Times*. New York Times, 13 Nov. 2005. Web. 19 Mar. 2015. <http://www.nytimes.com/2005/11/13/books/review/13cooper.html>.

Rev. of *Inexcusable*, by Chris Lynch. *Kirkus Reviews*. Kirkus Reviews, 20 May 2010. Web. 19 Mar. 2015. <https://www.kirkusreviews.com/book-reviews/chris-lynch/inexcusable/>.

The Inheritance Cycle (Series)

Author: Christopher Paolini (b. 1983)
First published: *Eragon* (2003)
   Eldest (2005)
   Brisingr (2008)
   Inheritance (2011)
Type of work: Novel
Type of plot: Fantasy
Time of plot: Medieval era
Locale: Alagaësia

Principal characters

Eragon, a teenage boy who finds a dragon egg in the forest and becomes a Dragon Rider

Saphira, Eragon's dragon and lifetime companion

Arya, elven princess whom Eragon rescues and who fights with him to defeat Galbatorix

Brom, Eragon's mentor and previous Dragon Rider

Galbatorix, king of the Empire who had all the Riders and dragons killed

Murtagh, Eragon's half-brother who is captured by Galbatorix and forced to fight for the Empire with his dragon Thorn

Oromis and Glaedr, an elven Rider and dragon, who train Eragon and Saphira to use magic and to fight

CHRISTOPHER PAOLINI
ERAGON · ELDEST
BRISINGR · INHERITANCE

The #1 NEW YORK TIMES Bestselling series
THE INHERITANCE CYCLE · Complete Collection
Alfred A. Knopf

Courtesy of Alfred A. Knopf

The Story

In *Eragon*, the fifteen-year-old protagonist Eragon finds a mysterious blue stone while hunting in the mountains. He brings the stone home to the farm where he lives, outside the village of Carvahall, with his cousin and uncle. In the village, an old man named Brom tells the tale of the Dragon Riders who acted as peace-keepers before Galbatorix rebelled, and killed all the Riders and dragons who stood against him.

Eragon's blue stone is a dragon egg. The egg hatches a female dragon named Saphira. She grows quickly and soon monstrous creatures called the Ra'zac are sent to reclaim her for Galbatorix. Eragon and Saphira manage to escape the Ra'zac, but they return to find the farm burned and his uncle killed. Eragon's cousin Roran escaped harm because he had left home to begin an apprenticeship. Brom, the old man from the village, states that Eragon and Saphira must leave at once to join the group of rebels called the Varden. Brom teaches Eragon sword fighting and magic on their journey.

One day the Ra'zac ambush the companions, and although they are rescued by a boy named Murtagh, Brom dies of his injuries. As Eragon and Saphira continue on to the Varden with Murtagh, Eragon sees visions of the elven princess, Arya. She was captured by Galbatorix's minions and is being tortured for the location of Saphira (whom she is responsible for hiding.) Eragon enters a trap trying to save her and is rescued by Murtagh and Saphira. The group flees to the Varden's location at Tronjheim. Murtagh is revealed to be the son of Galbatorix's right hand man and is imprisoned.

The Varden are soon attacked by an army of Urgals and an epic battle ensues. Eragon defeats the Shade named Durza (an evil and powerful creature) with Saphira and Arya's help. The Varden win the battle, although Eragon is gravely wounded. He recovers from his injuries and plans to depart to study with the elves.

In *Eldest*, the second book in the series, we learn that the leader of the Varden has been murdered and his daughter, Nasuada, is elected to take his place. Eragon and Saphira travel to the home of the elves called Du Weldenvarden. They meet Oromis and Glaedr, the only other Dragon Riders still alive, who had been thought to be dead. They have been in hiding due to their permanent injuries and train Eragon and Saphira to defeat Galbatorix. The teachers take up where Brom left off, and Eragon and Saphira continue to learn combat and magic skills, as well as to strengthen their bonds with each other.

As Eragon trains, the story moves to Eragon's cousin Roran who is now living in the village. The Ra'zac do not stop at just killing Eragon's uncle (Roran's father), but continue to attack the villagers. Roran leads the defense, but the Ra'zac end up kidnapping his fiancé, Katrina.

Nasuada leads the Varden to a neighboring country called Surda with the goal of attacking the Empire. Nasuada deals with political intrigue while attempting to gain the assistance from the Surdan government. A small girl whom Eragon blessed in the first book, saves Nasuada from an assassination attempt.

The story has now come back around to Eragon and Saphira, and we see them struggling both physically and emotionally. Eragon suffers from crippling seizures caused by the back injury he obtained in *Eragon*, and both Eragon and Saphira ache from unrequited love. Arya and Glaedr view Eragon and Saphira as children and help them to understand that they have more important responsibilities than love.

During the elven Blood-oath ceremony Eragon is transformed by an ethereal dragon. Eragon emerges with elven features, heightened senses, superior abilities, and free of any injury or scar. Eragon continues his training with renewed vigor until learning of the upcoming battle between the Varden and the Empire. After saying farewell to the elves and gaining invaluable gifts, Eragon and Saphira travel to Surda.

Back in the village, Roran decides to also travel to Surda with the survivors of the Ra'zac's latest attack, as he believes that will be his best chance of rescuing Katrina. Along the way, Roran learns from a friend of Brom that Eragon is a Dragon Rider.

A large scale battle ensues as Eragon, the Varden, and dwarven reinforcements battle Galbatorix's soldiers and monsters. To everyone's surprise, another Dragon Rider appears and kills the dwarf king. The Dragon Rider and Eragon fight until Eragon realizes it is the missing Murtagh. Murtagh has been enslaved by magic and forced to fight for the Empire. Despite having superior fighting skills, Murtagh allows Eragon to live and discloses that the two are actually half-brothers. Murtagh takes Eragon's sword (which belonged to Murtagh's father) and Galbatorix's army is forced to retreat. Roran and Eragon reunite and Eragon decides to help Roran rescue Katrina.

Brisingr, the third book in the Inheritance Cycle, begins with Eragon, Roran, and Saphira rescuing Katrina from the Ra'zac. Katrina is pregnant with Roran's child and the couple decide to get married, but the Varden is attacked prior to the wedding by Galbatorix. Galbatorix has created new soldiers who do not feel pain and the only way to stop them is to cut off their heads. Eragon and Saphira are aided by Varden spellcasters and force Murtagh and his dragon to retreat. Once the battle is over, Roran and Katrina are able to finish their wedding.

Nasuada orders Eragon to attend the new dwarf king election to prove the Varden support Eragon's friend Orik. While there, Eragon survives an assassination attempt, and Orik is crowned king. After the coronation, Eragon and Saphira return to the elves for more training. Eragon learns that Brom was his birth father and discovers the source behind Galbatorix's power. The evil emperor used the power of deceased dragon hearts to fuel his magic. Eragon also creates a new sword that burns with fire when he says "Brisingr," the magical word for fire.

Oromis and Glaedr decide to come out of seclusion and join the elven army against the Empire. Glaedr gifts Eragon with his heart in case he is killed. Eragon and Saphira fly to rejoin the Varden while they are laying siege to a city still under the Empire's hold. While Eragon and Arya are attempting to prevent the creation of another Shade, Eragon sees a possessed Murtagh kill Oromis and Glaedr in a vision. Meanwhile the Shade has been formed, and Eragon and Arya work together to defeat it. The Varden win the battle and now plan to invade the Empire.

Inheritance wraps up the epic cycle by telling the story in which Eragon and his companions finally overthrow Galbatorix. Murtagh finally breaks free of Galbatorix's control by changing his true self. Eragon discovers a secret cache of dragon hearts and uses the hearts to put him on a level playing field with Galbatorix. Inside Galbatorix's castle, Murtagh and Eragon work together to bring down Galbatorix's shields and Eragon defeats him with an improvised spell. Galbatorix's dragon is killed by Arya.

Murtagh and his dragon disappear on their own. Nasuada becomes queen of Alagaësia and Arya becomes queen of the elves. A green dragon egg hatches for Arya and she too becomes a Rider. Eragon officially reinstates the Dragon Riders and leaves with Saphira to find a safe space to train new Dragon Riders.

Critical Evaluation

The Inheritance Cycle is a swords and sorcery series about the struggle between good and evil. Paolini uses the Joseph Campbell hero's-journey formula, focusing on its themes of friendship and ableism of the chosen-one trope. A Western audience is most likely to compare the Inheritance Cycle to J. R. R. Tolkien's *The Lord of the Rings* (1954), or the Star Wars films (1977–), as both come from academic study of classic texts such as *Beowulf*.

The Inheritance Cycle is a structural work more than a formal work, because its prose is straightforward. Using the hero's journey allows the reader the comfort of knowing where the plot is going, having a sense of which story beats go where, and frees them to focus on the touches the author brings to the formula. Paolini's novels play to the formula and indulge in fan-fiction tropes.

Eragon is a chosen one, a last of his kind, much like J. K. Rowling's Harry Potter character in *Harry Potter and the Sorcerer's Stone* (1997). He comes from humble beginnings, but forges a relationship with an animal companion, as in Anne McCaffrey's *Dragonflight* (1968). Eragon shares a psychic link with the dragon Saphira, the totem guiding him on his quest to defeat evil. In this case, evil is the Empire led by a corrupt Dragon Rider.

The series moves toward escaping the might-makes-right problem of the genre when Eragon suffers a crippling back injury, similar to the disfigurement suffered by the protagonist in the movie *How to Train Your Dragon* (2010). But while that story is about adapting to different-ableness, Eragon's body is transformed into that of an elf so that he no longer suffers from a weak human body. For the chosen half-elf, violence has no consequences besides victory.

The Inheritance Cycle relies on its script of the call to action, the point of no return, and the cave to carry it to its conclusion, as opposed to using characters' personalities to resolve their stories. It is possible that Eragon would have been a stronger character if he had been forced to work around his disability to reach victory, like Luke Skywalker did after he lost his hand in *The Empire Strikes Back* (1980).

Alexandra McBride, MA

Further Reading

Campbell, Joseph. *The Hero with a Thousand Faces*. Princeton: Princeton UP, 1972. Print.

"Eldest." Rev. of *Eldest*, by Christopher Paolini. *Kirkus*. Kirkus Media, 20 May 2010. Web. 24 Mar. 2015. <https://www.kirkusreviews.com/book-reviews/christopher-paolini/eldest/>.

Rosenberg, Liz. "Children's Books; The Egg and Him." Rev. of *Eragon*, by Christopher Paolini. *New York Times*. New York Times, 16 Nov. 2003. Web. 24 Mar. 2015. <http://www.nytimes.com/2003/11/16/books/children-s-books-the-egg-and-him.html>.

Invisible

Author: Pete Hautman (b. 1952)
First published: 2005
Type of work: Novel
Type of plot: Psychological Fiction
Time of plot: Early 2000s
Locale: United States

Principal characters

Dougie Hanson, a troubled teenager
Andy Morrow, Dougie's best friend
Henry Clay Hanson, Dougie's father
Dr. Eleanor Ahlstrom, Dougie's counselor
Melissa Haverman, a popular girl

The Story

Troubled teen Dougie Hanson lives next door to his best friend Andy Morrow. Andy is much more popular than Dougie but still considers Dougie his best friend. In the morning, they talk through their windows: Andy describes the play he is in, while Dougie describes the progress he's making on his model train set, which he calls the Madham Line. He is building a new bridge—like the rest of the model town, it is constructed of matches with the phosphorous scraped off.

Andy and Dougie once broke into the Tuttle place, an abandoned house in their neighborhood, although Dougie does not like to talk about it anymore. After school, Dougie skips his appointment with his counselor to hang out with Andy, who tries to persuade him to ask out a girl named Melissa Haverman; Dougie thinks she would never agree to that. At night, he goes to a football game to watch Andy. Sitting alone in the bleachers, he lights matches.

The text reveals that Andy and Dougie once built a tree house, but it was destroyed when Dougie decided they should build a fire in it one Christmas, right after Andy gave him a knife as a present. Dougie goes to visit his counselor and avoids mentioning Andy to her, as she thinks Andy is the root of his problems. He does, however, show her the sigil (or seal) he designed based off his and Andy's initials, although he does not tell her what it means. He also does not tell her that he has stopped taking the pills she prescribed him.

At night, Dougie sometimes spies on Melissa as she gets ready for bed. One night Dougie almost gets caught peeking at Melissa through her bedroom window, but he lies his way out of it. Rumor spreads at school, however, and some jocks beat him up because of it. He spends a night in the hospital and then stays home from school for a week, working on his bridge. When he goes back to school, he is revealed to be an outcast. Andy persuades him to sneak out and call in a bomb threat. They get caught, and after Dougie is threatened with jail, he tells the police that it was Andy who made the call.

Dougie meets again with his counselor, who tells him that Andy died three years ago at the Tuttle house. At that time, the two friends had made a fire in the house to stay warm, and when it spread from the fireplace, they fled. Dougie forgot the knife that Andy had given him for a present, so Andy went back in to get it. Dougie insists that Andy escaped, but the counselor asserts firmly that Andy died inside. At this point, the reader is aware that Andy has become a figment of Dougie's imagination. The counselor gives Dougie new pills so he will not experience hallucinations of Andy anymore. Dougie only pretends to take them.

Dougie's parents decide he should attend St. Stephen's, a private school for students with mental health issues. Thinking he will be locked up forever, Dougie finishes the bridge and then sets fire to the set. When the train begins to move across the bridge, Madham begins to burn. The smoke is thick enough that Dougie cannot get out of the basement. He then goes to the Madham hospital burn unit, where he is reunited with Andy.

Critical Evaluation

From early on, *Invisible* gives hints that the main character is an unreliable narrator. Dougie states that he struggles with mental health and that there are aspects of his relationship with Andy that he will not discuss, while his parents and peers regularly allude to the fact that he speaks to himself. The book does not build up to the revelation that Andy is dead for its shock value but to allow readers to inhabit Dougie's troubled interior world.

Because of the care with which Hautman constructs Dougie's emotional state, readers develop a great deal of sympathy for him, even though many of his activities (particularly spying on Melissa) can be read as disturbing. The narrative makes clear that Dougie is lying to himself not because he wants to but because he is unable to face the truth of Andy's death. Similarly, the less insidious aspects of his mental illness, such as his obsessions with counting and bridges, fill the narrative while driving wedges between him and his peers. As his disease isolates him further and indirectly results in the jocks bullying and beating him, the narrative reinforces the lack of control that Dougie can exercise. Were the story told from an outside perspective, Dougie might seem like an instigator or a villain. But because the story is told from Dougie's perspective, readers can more easily summon sympathy.

Mental illness is heavily stigmatized in contemporary culture, and people often avoid talking about it. However, Hautman's use of an unreliable narrator means the issue of mental illness in brought to the surface in a sympathetic way. Readers come to understand that, even if they cannot trust Dougie, it is not because he is lying or intends to do harm. Rather, Dougie cannot trust himself, and as the world punishes him for his condition, he—and by extension, the reader—slips further into confusion, fear, and loneliness.

T. Fleischmann, MFA

Further Reading
B. C. "Invisible." Rev. of *Invisible*, by Pete Hautman. *Horn Book Magazine* 81.3 (2005): 325–26. *Literary Reference Center*. Web. 28 Feb. 2015. <http://search.ebscohost.com/login.aspx?direct=true&db=lfh&AN=16882877&site=ehost-live>.

Goldsmith, Francisca. "Invisible." Rev. of *Invisible*, by Pete Hautman. *School Library Journal* 52.6 (2006): 86. *Literary Reference Center*. Web. 3 Mar. 2015. <http://search.ebscohost.com/login.aspx?direct=true&db=lfh&AN=21088744&site=lrc-live>.

Hautman, Pete. Interview by Eileen Beha. *Water Stone Review* 8 (2005). Web. 28 Feb. 2015. <http://maryrockcastle.tripod.com/pdf/2005_excerpts8/petehautmaninterview.pdf>.

Jellicoe Road

Author: Melina Marchetta (b. 1965)
First published: *On the Jellicoe Road*, 2006 (*Jellicoe Road*, 2008)
Type of work: Novel
Type of plot: Mystery
Time of plot: Late 1980s and early 2000s
Locale: Jellicoe, New South Wales, Australia

Principal characters

Taylor Lily Markham, a seventeen-year-old girl at an Australian boarding school
Hannah Schroeder, a thirty-three-year-old house guardian and writer
Jonah Griggs, a military school student who killed his abusive father
Jude Scanlon, known as the Brigadier, the leader of the Cadets
Raffaela, also known as Raffy, a classmate and friend of Taylor's
Chaz Santangelo, a handsome leader of the Townies

The Story

The plot of *Jellicoe Road* hinges on two storylines—one set in the present day of the early 2000s and one in the late 1980s. The story is made suspenseful by the presence of a serial child kidnapper and murderer operating in the area.

In the present, events are described from the viewpoint of Taylor Markham, who was abandoned at age eleven by her drug-addicted mother. Taylor was rescued by a woman named Hannah and placed at Jellicoe School. Hannah lives nearby, works as house guardian, and remains close to Taylor. A government-funded boarding institution, the school is located in Jellicoe, a rural Australian town. Plagued by fragmented dreams and fractured memories, Taylor is the leader of Lachlan House, a school dormitory, and in charge of fifty younger girls. The school is preparing for the annual territory wars against the Townies, who attend a school in the neighboring town, and the Cadets, students at the local military school. The territory wars involve strategic maneuvers and negotiations carried out under strict rules to gain advantage of particular landmarks, such as favorite trees or water sources. The Townies are led by handsome Chaz Santangelo, and the Cadets are under command of the Brigadier. The wars are muddled for Taylor by her history with Cadet Jonah Griggs: they separately ran away at age fourteen, met on a train, and made a romantic connection. A further complication is the growing relationship between Raffy, a conflicted town girl attending the school, and Chaz, the son of a Jellicoe police officer.

The past is represented by nonsequential excerpts from a manuscript Hannah is writing, which Taylor is allowed to read and which are included at key points throughout *Jellicoe Road*. Allegedly a novel, the manuscript tells of a tragedy. Twenty-two years before, cars containing two families collided in a horrific crash. The adults were killed, and three children—a boy named Webb, his sister Narnie, and a girl named Tate—were trapped in the burning vehicles on Jellicoe Road. A local boy, Fitz, riding on a stolen bike, rescued the three children from the wreckage before the cars exploded, and the survivors were made wards of the state at Jellicoe School. Fitz and the children draw together because of the shared experience, and later accept a fifth member, Jude, a sympathetic young Cadet who plants poppies as a memorial where the accident occurred.

The two story lines merge as Taylor begins to understand the meaning of Hannah's writings, which help explain Taylor's dreams and memories. The five inseparable companions from the 1980s invented the territory wars. Hannah is the "Narnie" of the written story, and she is in love with the Cadet, Jude Scanlon, who became the Brigadier. Hannah's brother was Xavier Webster "Webb" Schroeder, who impregnated Tate, Taylor's

mother. Fitz, the rescuer, accidentally shot and killed Webb, after which he committed suicide.

Though there are further difficulties to endure—including a sudden fire at the school and several individuals suspected of being the serial killer—the novel concludes on a rising note of hope. Taylor is reunited with her dying mother, with whom she reconciles. Because of budding relationships between various members of the three warring factions—including Taylor and Jonah, Raffy and Chaz, and several school members and Townies who form a rock band—the territory wars may be drawing to a close. Finally, the serial killer is caught.

Critical Evaluation

Though set in Australia, *Jellicoe Road* demonstrates that the concerns of young adults are universal. Teenagers in every era, in any location, suffer from angst related to such issues as self-image, shifting relationships and alliances, and the separation of truth from falsehood—themes interwoven throughout the novel—that must be resolved to complete the difficult passage from adolescence to maturity.

Protagonist Taylor Markham has more to worry about than most young women her age. Through no fault of her own she is haunted by images in dreams she cannot initially understand, until Hannah's manuscript reveals their meaning. Only Taylor's innate strength of character, a gift passed down from her estranged mother and her barely remembered father, allows her to survive a situation that might destroy a weaker individual. Despite her myriad troubles, she remains an idealist.

The structure of *Jellicoe Road*—in which the present-tense, first-person narration in Taylor's unique voice is supplemented by passages from Hannah's manuscript—lends mystery and suspense to the story. Readers are given the opportunity to piece together clues to solve the puzzle at the same pace as the young heroine.

One of the more interesting aspects of the novel is the creation, by Narnie, Webb, Tate, and Fitz, of the territory wars. Though ostensibly invented out of boredom, the wars are actually a coping mechanism to deal with the sudden, violent death of their parents. As the origin of the wars becomes forgotten over time, the territorial struggle, initially a game, turns more serious and, as in William Golding's *Lord of the Flies* (1954), the children become more cruel to their opponents. A key piece of the puzzle relating to the wars is a tunnel that is discussed in Hannah's writings: "'I'm all for the tunnel. It could save our life one day,' Tate said. 'We could be chased by evil and have to hide down there'" (232). This foreshadows an event in the present when the tunnel, almost forgotten over time, serves as a refuge from a fire.

Jellicoe Road received widespread critical and popular acclaim when it was first published in 2006 in Australia and in 2008 in the United States. The novel received the 2008 West Australia Young Readers Book Award for older readers and the 2009 Michael L. Printz Award from the American Library Association.

Jack Ewing

Further Reading

Marchetta, Melina. "2009 Michael L. Printz Award Acceptance Speech." *YALSA*. Young Adult Lib. Services Assoc., 13 July 2009. Web. 20 Mar. 2015. <http://www.ala.org/yalsa/sites/ala.org.yalsa/files/content/booklistsawards/bookawards/printzaward/marchetta.pdf>.

Rev. of *Jellicoe Road,* by Melina Marchetta. Kirkus. Kirkus, 1 Sept. 2008. Web. 20 Mar. 2015. <https://www.kirkusreviews.com/book-reviews/melina-marchetta/jellicoe-road/>.

Killing Mr. Griffin

Author: Lois Duncan (b. 1934)
First published: 1978
Type of work: Novel
Type of plot: Thriller
Time of plot: Spring, late 1970s
Locale: Albuquerque, New Mexico

Principal characters:

Brian Griffin, a high school teacher of English literature and composition
Susan McConnell, a studious high school junior
Mark Kinney, a manipulative high school senior
David Ruggles, president of the high school's senior class
Jeff Garrett, a tall high school basketball star
Betsy Cline, a vivacious head cheerleader

The Story

High school English teacher Brian Griffin refuses to accept excuses for late or missing homework. Students Mark Kinney, Jeff Garrett, and Betsy Cline, who did not complete a recent assignment, hate Griffin for his inflexibility. Mark suggests they kidnap Mr. Griffin to teach him a lesson; since they are minors, the consequences of their prank would be insignificant. Jeff and Betsy agree to participate. As part of the plan, Mark wants to include David Ruggles, a boy above suspicion, to recruit mousy Susan McConnell, who has a crush on David.

David agrees to participate. He invites Susan to a picnic at a remote location and she eagerly attends. During the picnic, the kidnapping is discussed. The boys will grab the teacher, Betsy will provide alibis, and Susan will serve as decoy.

The day of the kidnapping David drugs his grandmother so he can slip away from home. Betsy fakes evidence to provide alibis. David, Jeff, and Mark jump Mr. Griffin in the parking lot where Susan has led him. They subdue, blindfold, and tie the teacher, then drive him in his own car into the mountains. They taunt him, threatening murder, but he refuses to beg for his life. Betsy arrives in a separate car after receiving a speeding ticket. Mr. Griffin's bottle of nitroglycerin pills falls from his pocket, and Jeff smashes the pills. They leave the teacher bound where they picnicked, hoping that being left alone overnight will change Mr. Griffin's attitude.

Later, David tells Susan, who went home after playing her part, what transpired. Remorseful, Susan persuades David to free Mr. Griffin. When they return, however, they find that Mr. Griffin has succumbed to an apparent heart attack.

Mark insists they cover up their crime. Mark, Jeff, and David bury Mr. Griffin where he died; David removes the teacher's college ring. Betsy drives the teacher's car to the airport, but she is witnessed, so it is decided to paint the auto and abandon it on an Indian reservation. Cathy, Griffin's pregnant wife, meets with police detective James Baca to report her husband missing.

Baca questions Susan, the last known person to see Mr. Griffin alive. She has been coached by Mark to suggest the teacher was seeing another woman. Cathy confronts Susan about inconsistencies in her story. David's grandmother shreds his alibi and finds the ring David removed from Mr. Griffin's body.

Mark's ex-girlfriend, Lana Turnbolt, meanwhile, finds Mr. Griffin's empty pill bottle at the picnic spot, and reports to the police that she noticed a place where someone had been digging. The police quickly excavate Mr. Griffin's body.

Susan, after informing Mark that David has Mr. Griffin's ring, tries to convince David to go with her to the police and confess, but he refuses. Jeff and Betsy, ready to dump Mr. Griffin's disguised car, notice activity at David's house. They stop to tell Susan, alone while her family is at a church function, that David's grandmother has been found dead. A neighbor saw her with a man fitting Mark's description shortly beforehand. Susan vows to tell the police, but Jeff overpowers her. Mark arrives and Jeff and Betsy leave. Mark decides to drive Mr. Griffin's car to the Indian reservation and return with Jeff and Betsy. He ties up Susan, sets her house on fire, and climbs out a window—straight into the arms of Detective Baca, who has come with Cathy to question Susan again.

Susan, rescued, receives immunity to turn state's evidence against the coconspirators. Widowed Mrs. Griffin gives Susan her late husband's notes, in which he praises Susan's final assignment.

Critical Evaluation

Author Lois Duncan is well known for her many young adult suspense novels, some of which have been adapted for the screen. Prior to *Killing Mr. Griffin*, she wrote such teen thrillers as *The Middle Sister* (1960), *Game of Danger* (1962), *Ransom* (1966), *They Never Came Home* (1968), and perhaps her best recognized work, *I Know What You Did Last Summer* (1973). Her later novels in the genre include *Daughters of Eve* (1979), *Locked in Time* (1989), *The Twisted Window* (1987), and *Don't Look Behind You* (1989). Duncan also has personal experience of crime involving teens: in 1989, her own fifteen-year-old daughter Kaitlyn was murdered, an incident she detailed in the nonfiction book *Who Killed My Daughter?* (1992).

Killing Mr. Griffin presents a plausible scenario: a malicious high school prank that backfires. The participants in the scheme each have an opportunity to strut and fret upon the stage from a third-person point of view. Fresher characters when sketched in 1978, they have since become stereotypes in young adult fiction: nerd, handsome class president, popular cheerleader, slow-witted jock, and psychopathic loner. Their flaws—neediness, pride, stupidity, carelessness, venality—in combination with Mr. Griffin's own misplaced dedication to teaching high school English to the undeserving—lead to their collective downfall.

Irony plays a strong role in the novel via Shakespearean-tinged allusions demonstrating that, as much as they despise him, they nevertheless managed to learn something from Mr. Griffin. Even as they are struggling with the teacher, David remembers a line from *Macbeth*. When Jeff is digging Mr. Griffin's grave, he says he feels like one of the gravedigger characters in *Hamlet*. Even Cathy, Griffin's wife, quotes Shakespeare in pointing out a falsehood in Susan's story: "Neither a borrower nor a lender be." While the events of *Killing Mr. Griffin* do not quite rise to the level of Shakespeare, they do define a tragedy: lives have been destroyed and the survivors will never be the same again.

Jack Ewing

Further Reading

Lodge, Sally. "Lois Duncan Thrillers Get an Update." *Publishers Weekly*. PWxyz, 23 Sept. 2010. Web. 9 Mar. 2015. <http://www.publishersweekly.com/pw/by-topic/childrens/childrens-book-news/article/44553-lois-duncan-thrillers-get-an-update.html>.

Scales, Pat. "15 Young Adult Classics." *Book Links* July 2006: 54–55. Web. *Literary Reference Center*. 31 Mar. 2015. <http://search.ebscohost.com/login.aspx?direct=true&db=lfh&AN=21276657&site=lrc-live>.

Legend (Series)

Author: Marie Lu (b. 1984)
First published: *Legend* (2011)
   Prodigy (2012)
   Champion (2013)
Type of work: Novel
Type of plot: Dystopian Fiction
Time of plot: Near future
Locale: Republic of America

Principal characters

June Iparis, a wealthy fifteen-year old girl who attained a perfect score on the Trial
Metias Iparis, June's older brother and mentor
Thomas Alexander Bryant, Metias's best friend
Daniel "Day" Altan Wing, a fifteen-year old boy who is the Republic's most wanted fugitive
Eden Bataar Wing, Day's younger brother
John Suren Wing, Day's older brother

"DOESN'T MERELY SURVIVE THE HYPE,
IT DESERVES IT."
—THE NEW YORK TIMES

MARIE LU

LEGEND

NEW YORK TIMES BESTSELLER

Courtesy of Penguin Young Readers

Kaede, a disillusioned freedom fighter

Anden Stavropoulos, the person slated to become the next Elector Primo, leader of the Republic

The Story

June Iparis is accustomed to a life of financial ease in the Republic of America, a successor state in the western half of what used to be the United States, which fell into anarchy after most of the East Coast was submerged by a global flood. Her older brother, Metias, has cared for her since their parents were killed in a car accident when she was very young. Metias is a respected member of the military. June is the only one in the Republic who has ever earned a perfect score on the Trial, the test that is used to decide the future path of every child at the age of ten. Because of her perfect score, June attends a school with students who are much older than she is, where she is being trained for a spot in the military. She is proud to serve the Republic and looks forward to a very bright future.

Day Wing has grown up in an impoverished family in Los Angeles. He is angry at the inequality in the Republic and his actions against the Republic have earned him a place as the most wanted criminal in the country.

People know only what he has done and not his name or what he looks like. As a result, his family is unaware that he is the infamous fugitive. Only his older brother knows that he is still alive since Day works in the background to bring his family the things they need to survive. He passes these items to his older brother without his younger brother or mother knowing. Those who are unhappy with the Republic consider him a hero.

One day Metias tells June he has something he must discuss with her, but he is murdered that night before they have a chance to speak. All evidence indicates that Day is the one who murdered him. June finds that hard to believe, since Day has never killed anyone, but everything she sees supports that claim. She vows to avenge her brother and is supported in this by the fanatical commander who puts her on the case. June is soon able to make contact with Day, but the more time she spends with him, the more uncertain she is that he is the one who killed her brother.

Despite her doubts, June helps to capture Day. In the process, Day's mother is shot dead and his younger brother, Eden, is taken captive. June interrogates Day while he is in prison and he admits to everything except killing Metias, insisting that he is nearly certain his knife only hit Metias in the shoulder. Day tells June he did not throw the knife to kill Metias but only to give himself time to escape. When June takes another look at the photos from the crime scene, she realizes that all of the photos are taken at an angle that makes it nearly impossible to see her brother's shoulder clearly. She comes to believe that Day was not the one who drove the knife through Metias's heart. Through her research into sites that Metias taught her about, as well as a secret site that Metias created for her, June learns that Day actually had a perfect score on his Trial; that low scorers are not sent to labor camps but are instead killed or used for medical research; and that the plague that kills those in the poorer sections of the Republic each year are actually introduced by the Republic as a form of population control. She also suspects that it was Metias's best friend Thomas who killed him. She realizes if Day is telling the truth about Metias, he may be right about many of the other things he has said.

June pays Kaede and the freedom fighters to help her free Day from prison. In the process, his older brother, John, chooses to die in his place. In the ensuing chaos that ends the first volume of the trilogy, *Legend*, and opens the second volume, *Prodigy*, June and Day make their way to Las Vegas to locate Kaede and the Patriots for additional help. June and Day are becoming more than friends, but they can never erase the fact that it is because of June that Day has lost his mother and older brother and had his younger brother captured and held.

When June and Day reach Vegas, they are able to meet with the Patriots. The Patriots are well funded in Vegas and have a Republican officer working with them. They agree to help to rescue Eden. The only thing Day and June must do in return is help to assassinate Anden, who is about to become the Elector Primo following his father's death. In keeping with the plan, June returns to Los Angeles and is captured. She pledges her loyalty to the Republic and works to get close to Anden so that she can deliver him into the assassination plot. As June, now sick with a mysterious illness, becomes more familiar with Anden, she becomes convinced that he is sincere in his desire to make the Republic a better place. At the last minute, she leaps from the car as the ambush is about to take place. Day follows her lead, and the two must make their escape through a tunnel that leads to the Colonies of America, in the eastern half of what used to be the United States.

Kaede tracks them through the tunnel and is in time to save them as the Colonists prepare to arrest June. She flies them back to the Republic because she has come to believe that the best future for the Republic lies in working with Anden. Kaede is killed when the plane crashes, but Day makes it up to a balcony as Anden is making a speech to a restless crowd. They want Day to be their leader, but Day urges the people to support Anden. Anden arranges for Eden to live with Day. They are given everything they need.

Anden wants June to train to be his partner, the Princeps, with no strings attached. June seeks Day's approval, and Day, who has just learned he does not have long to live, tells her to pursue her future with Anden. June, realizing they can never overcome their shared past, reluctantly agrees. Day says he wishes they had just met in a way that began with "Hi. I'm Daniel."

In *Champion*, the third volume of the trilogy, the Colonies attack the Republic because they believe the Republic has released a plague in their territory. Anden and his entourage visit Iceland, home to the most sophisticated technologies, to help them in their battle. The only way they will support the Republic is if the Republic can prove they did not release the virus. After much trial and error, they realize that the illness June contracted was an earlier version of the virus. They find a cure and are supported by Iceland. Day, sickening, goes to Iceland

for medical help for Eden and is also treated. He is much better but has a sort of amnesia that makes it difficult for him to remember some things from the past. Most notably, he does not remember June.

Eden is accepted to an engineering school in Iceland, and Day goes with him. June decides that a life of politics is not for her. She misses Day and wishes there had been a way for them to be together. One day they pass each other on the street. Day feels he has known her. He approaches her and says, "Hi. I'm Daniel," to which June replies, "Hi. I'm June."

Critical Evaluation

The Legend trilogy is an example of a well-crafted dystopian novel for young adults. The future world is described with details chosen to bring to life the feeling of pervasive hopelessness felt by those who are not members of the elite. The relationships between those who live in squalor and need are experienced through the actions of the characters. The reader sees firsthand that characters like Day and his associates have bonded through their difficulties and will not turn their backs on one another. As a result of the care taken to describe this world, Day's actions throughout the novel are consistent with who readers know him to be—a teen who values his relationships with others and who has little tolerance for injustice. The fact that his driving force is the rescue of his younger brother is not only believable; it has the reader on his side from the start.

The portrayal of June is just as well drawn. She has grown up with service to the Republic as a given. Her growing disillusionment with the Republic, her disgust at the idea that duty should trump truth, and her realization that most of what she has always believed is a lie make her growth into an independent young woman who trusts her own instincts essential to the story. It is also believable that she is moved to take action, given her portrayal from the start as someone who is not content to sit on the sidelines. Likewise, Kaede, once a street-fighting rebel, comes to decide that hoping for a brighter future and putting her trust in someone else is not a doomed or stupid decision.

The themes of trust, loyalty, and duty occur in each book of the trilogy. At first it is easier for the characters to trust without knowing much about the person they are trusting. This is certainly the case when June is forced to rely upon the boy who saves her before she realizes that boy is Day. Day is similarly drawn to her before he learns that she is June Iparis. The difficulty they have in reconciling what they have experienced of each other with what they "know" of each other causes each to re-examine what it means to "know" anything about another person.

The soldiers of the Republic are loyal to the Republic, as are the Colonists loyal to the Colonies, and the Rebels to their cause. Blind loyalty is shown to be flawed throughout the trilogy. Loyalty without judgment leads to missed opportunities for understanding, which in turn lead to situations where lives are lost. This is especially true when the Colonists attack because they are sure the Republic has set out to harm them. There is no middle ground allowed in the loyalty they must show their cause. They are uninterested in explanations and do not believe the Republic is ignorant of the plague.

The folly of blind duty also appears as a theme when Thomas carries out his commander's order to murder Metias. Thomas explains to June that it was a direct order, as if this makes it beyond reproach. June cannot understand how he could kill someone who had done so much for him and was always trustworthy. Thomas explains that he turned a blind eye when he learned Metias was investigating forbidden things but that following a direct order was part of his duty and duty must be obeyed or there would be chaos. In the world of the Legend trilogy, however, it is such unthinking duty that leads to chaos, just as surely as misplaced trust and blind loyalty do. The message conveyed by these books is that trust must be based upon experience, while loyalty and duty must be tempered by that same experience.

Gina Hagler, MBA

Further Reading

Corbett, Sue. "Trilogies: Marie Lu." *Publishers Weekly*. PWxyz, 12 July 2013. Web. 14 Nov. 2015. <http://www.publishersweekly.com/pw/by-topic/childrens/childrens-authors/article/58229-trilogies-marie-lu.html>.

Hunt, Jonathan. Rev. of *Prodigy: A Legend Novel*, by Marie Lu. *Horn Book Magazine* Mar.–Apr. 2013: 110. *Literary Reference Center*. Web. 1 Dec. 2015. <http://search.ebscohost.com/login.aspx?direct=true&db=lfh&AN=85726427&site=lrc-live>. Pearson, Ridley. "Post-Apocalyptic Teenagers in Love." *New York Times Sunday Book Review*. New York Times, 3 Dec. 2011. Web. 28 Nov. 2015. <http://www.nytimes.com/2011/12/04/books/review/legend-by-marie-lu-book-review.html?_r=0>.

Liar

Author: Justine Larbalestier (b. 1967)
First published: 2009
Type of work: Novel
Type of plot: Psychological Fiction
Time of plot: Early 2000s
Locales: New York City; upstate New York

Principal characters

Micah Wilkins, a seventeen-year-old mixed-race high schooler
Zachary "Zach" Rubin, Micah's boyfriend
Yayeko Shoji, Micah's biology teacher
Hope, Micah's grandmother

Courtesy of Bloomsbury USA

The Story

When Micah Wilkins was in her first year at a small, progressive high school in New York City she pretended to be a boy because of her androgynous name, appearance, and mannerisms. She was soon exposed as a girl, however, and instantly gained a reputation as a liar.

Rather than work to improve her image, Micah continues to tell more lies to fellow students and teachers. For instance, she mentions to one student that she was born a hermaphrodite. She tells another student that her black father is an arms dealer and that she takes birth-control pills to control acne. She claims her family is plagued with a hereditary disease.

Eventually, it becomes almost impossible for anyone to separate what Micah says as fact or fiction. Micah's lies not only alienate the school's administrators, who lecture her several times about how lying erodes trust, but also distances her from the other students. Not surprisingly, Micah does not have many friends.

In Micah's junior year, one of the most popular students, handsome Zachary Rubin, approaches her off campus, talks sweetly to her, touches her tenderly, and kisses her. Zach initiates an intense clandestine relationship with Micah that she eagerly embraces, although she continues to lie to him about her personal life. At school, Micah and Zack never look at one another or speak and never acknowledge each other's presence in any way. After school, however, they continue their passionate romance.

They jog together in Central Park—Micah can run faster than athletic Zach, and she has an uncanny ability to find wild animals living in the city (or her secret boyfriend) simply by tracking their scents. At night she often climbs a fire escape to his family's seventh-floor apartment and crawls through a window he leaves open for her in order to spend time with him. Sometimes, when Micah is running by herself on the streets of New York before or after her lovemaking sessions with Zach, she encounters a skinny white street kid who, like her, is capable of moving quickly through crowds of people without touching them.

One day during their senior year and a few days after Micah last saw him, Zach goes missing and does not show up for school. A few days later it is announced that Zach has been found dead and most likely has been murdered. The police investigate and question everyone at the school. When a student named Brandon Duncan tells the police that he witnessed Micah and Zach kissing, they interrogate Micah again at her home and accuse her of being a liar. The tension surrounding the death of Zach heightens when another student from the school, a freshman girl, also disappears.

Critical Evaluation

Liar presents two intriguing, interwoven, and related story lines that are developed in three parts over the course of a complex, multifaceted novel. The first strand concerns Micah Wilkins—who, because of her

proclivity for lying, could be considered an unreliable narrator—and the reason she constantly lies. The second thread concerns the mystery surrounding who killed Zach Rubin and why. The novel answers these questions in a suspenseful fashion by doling out small, seemingly insignificant clues. The story maintains tension by moving backward to provide brief, labeled sections of the distant past, forward to the recent past, and forward again to the present, which is set after Zach has died.

Micah is a fascinating protagonist on several levels. In "Part One: Telling the Truth," she introduces herself as a liar who is from a family of liars, and she promises to never lie again. Micah is also presented as a divided individual since she has several noticeable and juxtaposing characteristics: she is born a girl, but her mannerisms and outward appearance are masculine; she is of mixed-race heritage yet does not belong firmly to either race nor is she content to be of two races; and she is strong physically and an accomplished athlete, yet displays and enjoys the softer aspects of romance.

This division of Micah's personality and personal qualities is explained to the reader in "Part Two: Telling the True Truth" when she travels to upstate New York to visit family and the reader learns she is considerably more than she appears—she is half-human and half-werewolf. Her confession explains her need to lie and cover up her family's secret. As Micah introduces various family members, the reader becomes aware that some are like her and are shape-shifters. Others are only carriers of the werewolf gene, and one relative in particular, Great-Uncle Hilliard, is permanently a wolf. Micah's unique viewpoint of her dual nature allows readers to vicariously experience the painful process of changing from human to beast as well as the excitement and thrill of the hunt for prey.

In "Part Three: The Actual Real Truth," Micah confronts and explains ten specific lies that she has told. Her dialogue not only reveals to the reader who killed Zach Rubin, but also provides details into Micah's life as well as any key surviving acquaintances—who may or may not exist in reality—after graduation from high school. Ultimately, Micah insists that everything she has admitted is true, but it is up to the reader to determine whether or how well she has kept her promise to tell the truth. Is her story all true, half true, or a complete fabrication that was created and fueled by a serious mental illness?

Jack Ewing

Further Reading

Carter, Regina Sierra. "YA Literature: The Inside and Cover Story." *YALSA*. ALA, 18 Apr. 2013. Web. 6 Oct. 2015. <http://www.yalsa.ala.org/jrlya/2013/04/ya-literature-the-inside-and-cover-story>.

Chappell, Shelley. "Contemporary Werewolf Schemata: Shifting Representations of Racial and Ethnic Difference." *International Research in Children's Literature* 2.1 (2009): 21–35. *Literary Reference Center Plus*. Web. 24 Nov. 2015. <http://search.ebscohost.com/login.aspx?direct=true&db=lkh&AN=43441181&site=lrc-plus>.

Schutte, Annie. "It Matters If You're Black or White: The Racism of YA Book Covers." *YALSA*. ALA, 10 Dec. 2012. Web. 6 Oct. 2015. <http://www.yalsa.ala.org/thehub/2012/12/10/it-matters-if-youre-black-or-white-the-racism-of-ya-book-covers>.

Life as We Knew It (Series)

Author: Susan Beth Pfeffer (b. 1948)
First published: *Life as We Knew It* (2006)
   The Dead and the Gone (2008)
   This World We Live In (2010)
   The Shade of the Moon (2013)
Type of work: Novel
Type of plot: Apocalyptic Dystopian Fiction
Time of plot: Present and near future
Locales: Pennsylvania; New York City; Sexton Tennessee,

Principal characters

Miranda Evans, a sixteen-year-old who lives in a small town and keeps a diary
Laura Evans, Miranda's mother
Matt Evans, Miranda's older brother, a college student
Jonny Evans, Miranda's thirteen-year-old brother, a star athlete
Hal Evans, Miranda's father
Lisa Evans, Miranda's stepmother, who is expecting a baby
Alex Morales, a seventeen-year-old New Yorker who must keep his sisters alive
Briana "Bri" Morales, Alex's fourteen-year-old sister
Julie Morales, Alex's twelve-year-old sister

The Story

In *Life as We Knew It*, the first book in the series, Miranda Evans is a sixteen-year-old who lives in Pennsylvania and keeps a diary about her largely uneventful life. She lives with her mother, Laura, and younger brother, Jonny, and has an older brother, Matt, who is away at college as the story begins. The entire country is looking forward to watching an asteroid strike the moon. Miranda writes that nothing bad is anticipated as a result of the collision, and everyone is outside with a block-party atmosphere as the asteroid makes contact with the moon. In the next instant, it is clear that the moon has been knocked closer to the earth. Although they are not experiencing the tsunamis and wildly gyrating tides, Miranda and her family quickly realize that the life they knew has ended.

Laura makes sure her family has ample supplies to last until things return to normal, although it quickly becomes apparent that she is not expecting this to happen any time soon. As the family learns more about the devastation that has occurred on both coasts, they also learn of the deaths of people they know. The offshore oilrigs and tankers have been destroyed by storms, leaving doubt about the ability to provide power in the future. Sporadic blackouts make day-to-day life difficult. There are soon shortages of food, and the schools close early for the year because they have no food to feed the students at lunch. Miranda wonders if it is truly a case of not enough food, or rather a case of not wanting to share food.

Laura begins to eat less to leave more for Jonny. Once Jonny leaves for a two-week-long baseball camp where he will be well fed in return for working on a nearby farm, Laura begins to ration food. This makes Miranda anxious and angry. Her father, Hal, and his pregnant stepmother, Lisa, bring Jonny home from camp. Hal leaves more food with Laura before heading for Colorado to be nearer to his new wife's family.

Other problems become apparent. Most notably, as a result of volcanic activity around the world, a huge cloud of dust makes it impossible to grow food and causes frigid temperatures; at the same time there is no other way than wood to heat a home. Miranda and her family ultimately live in the sunroom of their home, heating it with a wood-burning stove. They have a happy Christmas with their survival so far to celebrate. Not long afterward, a flu pandemic sweeps through their town and Miranda must nurse her family back to health. When they have recovered, Miranda realizes the only way for Jonny to survive is if he has more to eat. She decides to walk into town, an excursion she believes will kill her and allow her brother to survive, but upon arriving, she finds there are men handing out bags of food. They promise to bring her family more food each week. Miranda returns home, knowing her family is through the worst of the crisis.

The Dead and the Gone tells the story of seventeen-year-old Alex Morales and his two sisters, Bri and Julie. The story takes place in the same time frame as *Life as We Knew It*, depicting events that occurred in New York City. The Morales parents are not home at the time of the collision and remain missing throughout the book. They are eventually presumed dead, casualties of the tsunami and ensuing flooding. Carlos, the eldest Morales child, is also away, serving in the military.

Bri, a very religious teen, is certain her parents will come back for her. Julie is only twelve and has to leave childhood behind quickly, with little warning. Alex soon learns to take valuables from dead bodies in order to trade those things for what he needs to meet his family's needs. Alex's good friend Kevin, who has helped him to provide for his family, dies, and Bri is trapped and dies after her elevator loses power. This leaves Alex with little to hold on to but his faith. As the novel ends, the school headmaster, Father Mulrooney, and Sister Rita have come up with a way to get him and Julie to safety.

This World We Live In begins one year after the asteroid collision. It takes up the story of Miranda and her family again and introduces Alex and Julie into her life when they arrive with her father and Lisa. Food remains scarce. Miranda learns of "safe towns" set up by the government to house important or essential people. Alex has three passes to a safe town but does not know where to find one. Miranda discovers one in Sexton, Tennessee, and Alex plans to give the passes to Lisa, baby Gabe, and Julie while he, Hal, and Miranda will live near the town. They are about to leave when a tornado hits. Days after, Julie dies of injuries she sustained during the storm and the rest must leave because there is neither food nor a safe place to live.

The Shade of the Moon is the last book in the series. In the dystopia that has arisen since the asteroid collision, the clavers (haves) and the grubs (have-nots) lead very different lives. Jon, Lisa, and Gabe are living the relative "good life" as clavers. Hal has died, and Miranda, Alex, and Laura are living as grubs in a nearby town. Life in the claver enclave is not ideal. There is much class-based sexual violence and inequity. Jon, now a spoiled and unpleasant person, recalls his attempt to rape Julie, which happened just before she died. Miranda and Alex have a baby, and Miranda is told, but

does not believe, that the baby died soon after birth. She also does not believe Jon when he tells her that their mother has died, although it later is seen that that is true.

Jon soon learns that a grubber girl had a baby girl at the hospital but became hysterical when told it was a girl. According to the person telling the story, the grubber said her husband would beat her if the baby were not a boy. The new mother left the baby behind at the hospital, to be adopted by a claver family. Jon knows at once that the grubber was Miranda and that it is not true that she refused her baby. Lisa helps him plan to kidnap the baby and return her to Miranda and Alex. The plan works, and Jon returns to the enclave to stand by Lisa in the aftermath of what they have done. He finds Lisa dead, with a note saying that she, Alex, and Miranda are responsible for the kidnapping. Jon helps a friend escape and is then reunited with his love, Sarah. The remaining family will live near one another in an egalitarian community, New Harmony, Kentucky, as they work for a better future.

Critical Evaluation

The Life as We Knew It series begins as a postapocalyptic tale and ends with a dystopian novel. The story itself is deeply disturbing, with the slight alteration of the moon's course resulting in the death of billions of people around the world and the advent of a perpetual winter in which it is impossible to grow food in open fields. Everything is changed in the aftermath of the asteroid collision: even the tides become unpredictable, yet life continues as those who are hardy and resilient enough find their way. Themes of loyalty, resilience, happiness, religious faith, and love are explored over the course of the four books, with the ultimate message that the members of a family, in whatever configuration it may take, stand strong and work together for their common good.

The first two books of the series, *Life as We Knew It* and *The Dead and the Gone*, are equally compelling and well-written novels in which the characters are fully realized and the scene is set for the later titles. Miranda, the protagonist-narrator of *Life as We Knew It*, matures from a carefree high school teen into a young woman who will never again take anything for granted. This growth is believable because readers are privy to her journal, in which she shares her most personal feelings. Similarly, in *The Dead and the Gone*, Alex Morales begins as a high school boy with a bright future. Within a few minutes, his world is just as shattered as the world in *Life as We Knew It*. The greatest difference is that

Alex is living in New York City, where conditions are already cramped and resources scarce. In the absence of their parents and older brother, Alex must step into the role of caretaker to his younger sisters. Once he has undertaken this responsibility, he must do whatever it takes to ensure his survival and his struggles with the decisions he must make are brought fully to life.

The story in *The Dead and the Gone* also has greater thematic depth than that of *Life as We Knew It*. Alex's sister, Bri, is deeply religious. Her faith sustains her and convinces her to leave Alex and Julie to live in a convent. When she becomes ill, she returns and is once again Alex's responsibility. Julie becomes increasingly religious as well. The role of religion and the ways in which religion can carry a person through difficult times is explored as part of the storyline. Alex and Julie are ultimately "saved by the church," leading to the conclusion that their faith has been rewarded. It is also made clear that people we love are not truly lost when Julie assures her brother that she will always have Bri with her.

This World We Live In examines the ties of family as well as just what constitutes family. Miranda's father arrives with his wife, new baby, and several others. Those others become family in the sense that they will all do what it takes to ensure one another's survival. Miranda's brother Matt marries someone he has not known long, who must earn a spot in the family as well. Over the course of this work, Miranda realizes that happiness in the way she once knew it no longer exists but she decides to take her happiness where she finds it.

The Shade of the Moon is the grimmest of the books in this series. It tells of life after the collision with the moon and its aftermath is complete. The society that has grown up around the two classes of survivors is not one that is informed by the best in humankind. There is a great deal of unjustified violence. The grubs receive poor treatment not only from the clavers but also often from their fellow grubs. Among the clavers, things are not much better. It takes only a small misstep to lose one's place within the enclave that is designed for those who are deemed important to society. Ultimately, Pfeffer reaffirms the importance of family by having Jonny, Sarah, and Lisa—the most spoiled of the original family, the newest addition to their number, and the second wife of their father—earn enduring places in the family by sacrificing everything to save Miranda's baby.

Gina Hagler, MBA

Further Reading

Bucher, Katherine T., and KaaVonia Hinton. *Young Adult Literature: Exploration, Evaluation, and Appreciation*. 3rd ed. Boston: Pearson, 2014. Print.

Green, John. "Scary New World." *New York Times*. New York Times, 7 Nov. 2008. Web. 15 Nov. 2015. <http://www.nytimes.com/2008/11/09/books/review/Green-t.html?pagewanted=all>.

Pfeffer, Susan Beth. "How I Came to Write 'Life as We Knew It.'" *Susan Beth Pfeffer Blog*. Blogspot.com, 28 Nov. 2012. Web. 15 Nov. 2015. <http://susanbethpfeffer.blogspot.com/2012/11/how-i-came-to-write-life-as-we-knew-it.html>.

Looking for Alaska

Author: John Green (b. 1977)
First published: 2005
Type of work: Novel
Type of plot: Realism
Time of plot: Early twenty-first century
Locale: Alabama

Principal characters

Miles "Pudge" Halter, a high school junior
Alaska Young, Pudge's friend and love interest
Chip "The Colonel" Martin, Alaska's friend and Pudge's roommate
Lara Buterskaya, their friend
Takumi Hikohito, their friend

The Story

Divided into sections with countdown headings starting at "one hundred and thirty-six days before," the first half of *Looking for Alaska* begins when high school junior Miles Halter transfers to Culver Creek Preparatory School, a boarding school outside of Birmingham, Alabama, in order to shake up his heretofore dull life. His new roommate, Chip "the Colonel" Martin, gives the slender Miles the nickname "Pudge," and introduces him to his closest friends, Alaska and Takumi. Pudge is immediately drawn to the attractive, vibrant Alaska, who smokes constantly in violation of school rules and spends her time dreaming up elaborate pranks.

Within his first week, a group of students "kidnap" Pudge during the night, bind him with duct tape, and throw him in a lake. The Colonel is outraged and vows revenge against these "Weekend Warriors," or wealthy local students who go home every weekend. Thrilled to have close friends for the first time, Pudge begins hanging out and smoking with Alaska, the Colonel, and Takumi on a regular basis. Alaska also introduces Pudge to Lara, a Romanian immigrant and fellow student whom Pudge tentatively begins to date.

As Pudge settles into school, his narrative continues to count down to the unspecified event. He learns that Alaska is often inconsiderate and moody, and has a boyfriend named Jake who is not at the school, but Pudge still hopes that Alaska will eventually become romantically interested in him. He is thrilled when Alaska urges him to spend Thanksgiving vacation at the school instead of going home, and the pair pass the time drinking cheap bottled wine and snooping through their classmates' dorm rooms. Their shared isolation and camaraderie makes Pudge feel he knows Alaska more intimately than anyone else.

Shortly after Christmas vacation, the friends spend the night in the woods during an elaborate prank, sharing personal stories of the best and worst days of their lives. Pudge learns that Alaska's mother died when Alaska was eight years old, and that Alaska blames herself for not realizing she should call 911. Two days later, Pudge and Alaska end up kissing after they and the Colonel get very drunk. They fall asleep before anything else happens, but Alaska is awakened by a phone call. She becomes hysterical and insists that Pudge and the Colonel help her sneak off campus, although she will not tell them why.

In the second half of the book, which is titled "After" and has section headings that are now counting away from the pivotal event instead of toward it, the reader learns that Alaska died that night when she drove her car at high speed into a police car. Pudge and the Colonel are consumed with guilt for not only letting Alaska drive in a highly impaired state but also helping her sneak off campus in the first place. The guilt increases when they realize that Alaska may have committed suicide by deliberately not swerving to avoid the police car.

Alternating between grief and anger, Pudge and the Colonel are determined to reconstruct Alaska's state of mind that night. Over time, they learn that Alaska was hysterical because she suddenly remembered that she had forgotten to put flowers on her mother's grave that day, which was the anniversary of her death. Even so, Pudge and the Colonel cannot definitively conclude whether Alaska's death was accidental or deliberate,

and Pudge realizes that he will have to find closure regardless.

Critical Evaluation

Much of this debut novel's success lies in Pudge's thoughtful introspection. Unlike most of his classmates, he particularly enjoys a comparative religion class because the teacher poses interesting questions that make Pudge reflect on what is happening in his own life. Similarly, Pudge has a hobby of memorizing the last words of famous people throughout history. Both the religion class and Pudge's fondness for last words direct his feelings as he first tries to analyze Alaska's motives and then concludes that a lack of definitive answers does not have to define his memories of her.

Another noteworthy aspect of this novel is its authentic portrayal of the characters, due in part to the fact that they are loosely based on Green himself and on people he knew at the Alabama boarding school he attended, where a similar tragedy occurred during the time Green was there. The characters' sometimes swaggering bravado and their tendency to place disproportionate significance on the success or failure of their pranks feel very true to life.

Finally, the "before" and "after" structure of the novel is particularly effective in building suspense and engaging the reader, who does not know the nature of the impending event for the entire first half of the book. Because Pudge tells the story in retrospect, he knows but does not reveal to the reader what is to happen, and the author manages to make this structure seem natural rather than contrived. Similarly, the development of events in the second half of the book mirror the natural process of grief that Pudge experiences. Combined, these elements create a memorable and moving narrative, and the book was awarded the 2006 Michael L. Printz Award by the American Library Association.

Amy Sisson, MS, MLS

Further Reading

"Last Words from a First Novelist." *Booklist* 101.13 (2005): 1181. *Literary Reference Center*. Web. 25 Apr. 2015.
<http://search.ebscohost.com/login.aspx?direct=true&db=lfh&AN=16472894&site=lrc-live>.

Lewis, Johanna, et al. Rev. of *Looking for Alaska*, by John Green. *School Library Journal* 51.2 (2005): 136. *Literary Reference Center*. Web. 25 Apr. 2015.

<http://search.ebscohost.com/login.aspx?direct=true&db=lfh&AN=16010621&site=lrc-live>.

Sieruta, Peter D. Rev. of *Looking for Alaska*, by John Green. *Horn Book Magazine* 81.2 (2005): 201–202. *Literary Reference Center*. Web. 24 Apr. 2015. <http://search.ebscohost.com/login.aspx?direct=true&db=lfh&AN=16096071&site=lrc-live>.

Love and Other Perishable Items

Author: Laura Buzo
First published: *Good Oil*, 2010 (*Love and Other Perishable Items*, 2012)
Type of work: Novel
Type of plot: Romance
Time of plot: Early 2000s
Locale: Australia

Principal characters

Amelia Hayes, an intelligent, slightly overweight, socially naive fifteen-year-old

Christopher John "Chris" Harvey, Amelia's friendly, twenty-one-year-old coworker

Bianca, the twenty-three-year-old supervisor at the store where Amelia works

The Story

Amelia Hayes, to help her poverty-stricken family, lands a part-time job at a Coles supermarket in Australia, where night and weekend staff are high school or university students or other young adults. Amelia is trained in her duties by good-natured Chris Harvey, an English and sociology student at the University of New South Wales. Chris, who calls Amelia "Youngster," shows her how to pack groceries, teaches her about produce sold at the store, and lets her read his school papers. During slack periods, they exchange information about their respective, somewhat dysfunctional families and talk about favorite movies and books. Amelia soon develops a romantic interest in her older coworker, which she realizes is unrealistic because of the difference in their ages and experience. Several other better-looking girls are also after Chris, who is in a long, painful recovery from the breakup of a passionate relationship with a young woman who has moved across the continent to be with her true love, Brad. Amelia has hope, however, because other unlikely attachments have formed: Bianca,

twenty-three, is dating Andy from Canned Goods, five years her junior. Several younger female employees have a crush on good-looking eighteen-year-old Ed, but he is oblivious to their attentions because he is usually high on pot. Unbeknownst to Amelia, Chris has noticed her as a person rather than merely as a fellow employee. He increasingly writes in his notebook about how interesting, funny, and articulate she is and how they share many of the same tastes in literature and other subjects.

At an employee party in the house of Bianca's absent wealthy parents, Amelia gets tipsy and makes out with a checkout boy, earning a reprimand from a protective Chris for her behavior. He later apologizes to Amelia for his intrusion. Chris, conflicted about his feelings, continues to mention Amelia in his notebook, writing that unlike most of the other girls he is interested in, she is real, not artificial, and that he thinks she would be the woman of his dreams once she comes of age. At another employee party, Amelia and Chris drink tequila together, and he confesses that if she were older he would eagerly date her, a declaration that makes her heart soar. They kiss in chaste fashion and Amelia impulsively declares her love, blurting out that she would do anything for him.

Afterward, a troubled and confused Chris seems to purposely avoid her at work. He finally calls to tell her he is moving to Japan for a year to teach English, and invites her to a going-away party. He gives her a box containing all the diaries he has kept since his teens, knowing—and not minding—that she will not be able to resist reading them. He promises to write her from Japan, and during the time he is gone, Chris and Amelia carry on an animated long-distance correspondence, keeping possibilities alive.

Critical Evaluation

Though outwardly a simple coming-of-age tale of longing and romance that unfolds over the course of a year, beneath the surface *Love and Other Perishable Items* seethes with repressed emotions, especially frustration with the present, hunger for the future, and uncertainty about how to advance from one stage to the next.

The environment where Amelia and Chris work is a hotbed of pettiness, rivalries, desire, and jealousy among the employees. Off the job, there is little respite from tension for either protagonist. High school, with its various cliques, is mostly torture for Amelia, except for English class, which allows her the chance to express herself and brings her into contact with new reading material that she eagerly devours. Chris is likewise uneasy at the university he attends: he is falling behind in his work, concerned about mounting debt from student loans, and envious of a wealthy friend who has already finished his degree and is working at a highly paid job. Nor is there relief to be found at home, a common refuge from worry for the young. Amelia's parents smoke, aggravating her asthma and tainting her clothes and hair; her father, a theatrical director, is away for long periods of time, and when he is present does little to help around the house. Chris, still living at home, also resents his parents and wants to move out, but for most of the novel is incapable of taking action to rectify his situation.

Told from the first-person point of view by Amelia and Chris in turn, *Love and Other Perishable Items* touches upon the multitude of everyday difficulties encountered in the process of moving from adolescence toward adulthood (in Amelia's case) and in accepting the responsibilities of maturity (in Chris's case). Except for a few references—the major high-school sport is rugby, and during the Christmas shopping season the weather is sweltering—little occurs in the story that could not happen in the United States. Perhaps that is the main point of the novel: whether in Australia or elsewhere, the feelings associated with falling in love for the first time are universal.

Jack Ewing

Further Reading

Arredondo, Faythe. "Morris Award Finalist: Love and Other Perishable Items by Laura Buzo." Rev. of *Love and Other Perishable Items*, by Laura Buzo. *Hub*. YALSA, 4 Jan. 2013. Web. 7 Dec. 2015. <http://www.yalsa.ala.org/thehub/2013/01/04/morris-award-finalist-love-and-other-perishable-items-by-laura-buzo>.

Rev. of *Love and Other Perishable Items*, by Laura Buzo. *Kirkus Reviews*. Kirkus Reviews, 24 Oct. 2012. Web. 7 Dec., 2015. <https://www.kirkusreviews.com/book-reviews/laura-buzo/love-and-other-perishable-items>.

Luna

Author: Julie Anne Peters (b. 1952)
First published: 2004
Type of work: Novel

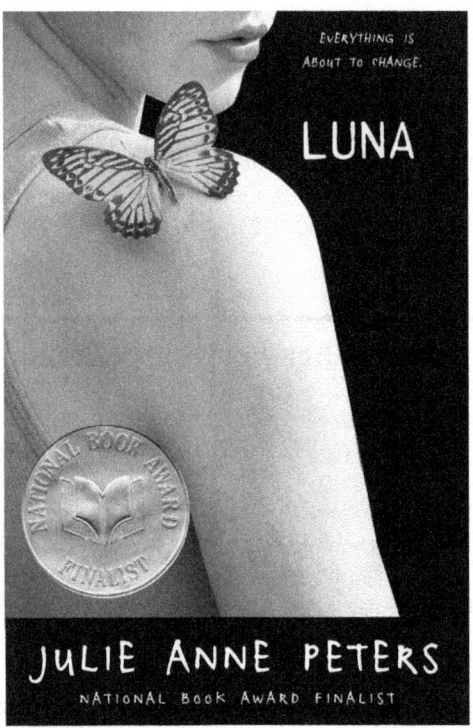

Courtesy of Little, Brown Books for Young Readers

Type of plot: Realism
Time of plot: Early twenty-first century
Locale: United States

Principal characters

Regan, the narrator, a teen girl
Liam, Regan's sister, a transgender teen who prefers to go by Luna
Chris, Regan's classmate and love interest
Alyson, Liam's best friend since childhood
Mr. and Mrs. O'Neill, Regan and Liam's parents
Elise and David Matera, the couple who employs Regan as their babysitter

The Story

Luna is the coming-out story of a transgender teen, focusing on her relationship with her sister. Liam is a girl born in a boy's body and prefers to go by Luna. The only person who knows the truth about Luna is her sister Regan. Regan struggles to be supportive but feels that she cannot have her own life and also be there for Luna.

Regan wakes up in the middle of the night to find Luna dancing in her room. Luna uses Regan's room as a safe space to wear women's clothing, wigs, and makeup.

Luna confesses that she cannot stand to pretend to be a boy any longer and that she must begin to transition. At first this involves presenting as female in public, but Luna also expresses her desire to have a sex change.

Regan remembers when Liam and his best friend Alyson shared a birthday party and Liam announced that he wanted a bra and some dolls. He became upset by his mother's refusal to buy these things and was punished by his father.

Regan keeps to herself at school and does not have many friends because she is scared that she might accidentally reveal Liam's secret if she opens up to someone. Things become more difficult when she meets Chris in her chemistry class. Regan is surprised and thrilled when Chris asks her to go to a rave Saturday night even though she is supposed to babysit for Elise and David Matera. In order to make it work out, Liam offers to cover for her while Regan is out with Chris.

On their way back Regan realizes she is late and needs to get back to the house before the Materas get home and discover Liam there in her place. Unfortunately Chris is pulled over while speeding and gets a ticket.

Regan walks into a nightmarish scene where David Matera is threatening Luna, who is dressed in Elise's nightgown, with a knife. Regan explains that Luna is her brother and did not mean any harm. Regan is fired and the two go home.

Regan is furious that Liam dressed as Luna while babysitting. She realizes that she should not have allowed Liam to cover for her in the first place.

Regan tries to be supportive and goes out into public with Luna. It is hard for Regan to see people's reactions to Luna and it hurts her to see Luna snickered at and made fun of. Regan wishes Liam could be normal for Liam's sake.

One day Liam goes to school dressed up as Luna and Regan watches as a bully starts to beat her up, calling her a pervert. Regan is mortified because she and Chris were there to witness it and rather than help Luna she runs out with Chris. Regan becomes overwhelmed by guilt because she failed to protect Luna.

Liam dresses as Luna on her eighteenth birthday and presents herself for the first time to her parents. Her mom refuses to deal with the situation and walks out. Her father yells and states that if Luna leaves the house dressed as a girl she is never to return.

The novel ends with Luna driving to the airport with Regan. Luna says that she is going to fly to California and begin transitioning into a woman. Regan feels that Luna is leaving because Regan failed to be there for her. Luna says that this is what she needs to do to be happy and tells Regan that she will keep in touch. As Regan says goodbye to Liam, Luna says hello.

Critical Evaluation

Luna is a novel in the vein of lesbian-gay-bisexual-transgender-questioning (LGBTQ) coming-out stories for young adults. This subgenre builds on young adult novels such as Judy Blume's work, as well as S. E. Hinton's *The Outsiders* (1967), and Robert Cormier's *The Chocolate War* (1974), which deal with teenagers' feelings of not fitting in, and focuses on this sense of otherness as it applies to sexual orientation or gender identity.

Unlike Jenny Wood's *A Boy Like Me* (2014), *Luna*'s narrator is not the transgender character herself, but her sister, Regan. Regan is cisgender, and identifies as female, the sex she was assigned at birth. By using Regan as the narrator, Peters invites cis readers into the trans experience, allowing them to project onto Regan, who messes up the same way any teenager might (such as when she decides to go out with Chris instead of babysitting.)

It also shows the reader what Regan suffers as she supports, or fails to support, Luna. If the story were from Luna's perspective, any failure on Regan's part could only be understood as an obstacle to the protagonist, prompting the reader to forgive her only as much as Luna could. Instead, Peters helps the reader understand how painful it is to watch a loved one suffer because of his or her identity.

As is typical of LGBTQ YA novels, the setting takes place in a hostile community and home environment. Liam's transition into Luna shows some of the things transgender teenagers have to fear upon coming out, such as emotional violence in the home and physical violence in school. While it would be good to see more novels written from the perspective of the LGBTQ character (as in Wood's *A Boy Like Me*), *Luna* is step in the right direction and its plot and themes are standard for a queer identity story.

Alexandra McBride, MA

Further Reading

Gross, Claire. "What Makes a Good YA Coming-Out Novel?" *Horn Book*. Horn Book, 26 Mar. 2013. Web.

22 Mar. 2015. <http://www.hbook.com/2013/03/choosing-books/what-makes-a-good-ya-coming-out-novel/>.

Rev. of *Luna* by Julie Anne Peters. *Kirkus Reviews*. Kirkus Reviews, 20 May 2010. Web. 22 Mar. 2015. <https://www.kirkusreviews.com/book-reviews/julie-anne-peters/luna/>.

Midwinterblood

Author: Marcus Sedgwick (b. 1968)
First published: 2011
Type of work: Novel
Type of plot: Paranormal Fantasy
Time of plot: Various, from prehistorical times to 2073
Locale: Blessed Island, a.k.a. Blest Island, a.k.a. Bloed Isle, a small island off the coast of Scandinavia

Principal characters

Eric Seven, a.k.a. *Erik*, *Erika*, *Eirik*, and *Eirikr*, a journalist who has lived many lives

Merle, a.k.a. *Melle*, the woman Eric loves

Tor, a.k.a. *Thorolf*, an antagonist

Edward, an archaeologist

David Thompson, an Air Force flight lieutenant in World War II

The Story

In June 2073, journalist Eric Seven travels to Blessed Island, a remote Scandinavian island about which little is known. Rumors about the island abound; some claim that the residents have become immortal. When he arrives, Eric is met by a group of five islanders who identify themselves as "wards." He immediately falls in love with Merle, the youngest of the wards, and is disturbed by Tor, their leader, although Tor has done nothing to make him feel unwelcome.

Strange things happen to Eric on the island. He loses time and starts to forget why he came. At one point, he notices that there are no children there. Reading some notes he made earlier, about a rare flower called the blessed dragon orchid, Eric finally recalls the rumors he came to investigate; the orchid is said to be the source of the islanders' immortality. Eric begins searching the island for the flower, with no luck. He tries to follow a path to the western side of the island, but the journey is inexplicably difficult, and he turns back. As days pass,

he loses interest and forgets that he has fallen in love with Merle. Eventually he even forgets who he is.

One night, Eric wakes from a nightmare and finds a note telling him to remember, and to try the path again. The next day, he forces himself to the end of the path, where he finds fields full of the orchids. He also finds Tor and the other wards, who capture him, intending to sacrifice him in an ancient ritual to appease the gods. Eric has the sudden sense that he has lived this before.

In July 2011, an archaeological dig on the island reveals the skeletal remains of two intertwined figures. Edward, the professor in charge of the dig, was led to the grave by a mentally challenged teenage boy. The teenager, Eric, lives nearby with his mother, Merle. After Eric saves one of Edward's students from the unexploded shell of a bomb left over from a decades-old war, he and his mother invite Edward and his students to their home for a celebratory dinner. When Eric is scolded by his mother for his rash rescue of the student, he replies, "No. I couldn't die. I'm not quite the last."

An airman plummets to earth in August 1944. Erik, the farmer who rescues him, is angry that David's arrival also brings enemy soldiers. As David heals, he learns that Erik lost a daughter when a bomb fell from the sky. Later, it is revealed that David, too, has a daughter: Merle. When enemy soldiers come seeking David, Erik helps him escape. David gets away, but Erik is killed. Years later, when David is 101 years old, he reads a newspaper story about an archaeological find on an unnamed island. He thinks he remembers the island, but he is not sure. He dies later that day.

In 1902, for her seventh birthday, a young girl named Merle is taken on a trip to the western side of Blest Island. There, she sees a big house that looks like a church. Her mother tells her a dragon lives there. Curious, Merle sneaks away the next day to meet the dragon, who turns out to be a painter. She finds the old man injured and brings her mother to help. Mother and daughter discover that the man is Eric Carlsson, a once-famous artist whose studio holds an unfinished painting depicting the sacrifice of King Eirikr in a blood ritual meant to heal the island's crops. Eric reveals that it is the first painting he has worked on in twenty-five years. Eric and Merle forge an unlikely but heartfelt friendship, inspiring Eric to finish his painting. The Swedish National Museum is considering purchasing the painting, but the representatives who come to see it are unimpressed. One of them, Tor Bearvald, sends Eric a scathing rejection letter. Crushed by disappointment, Eric is found by Bridget and Merle the next day, dead in front of his painting. Before he died, he added one last detail: a young girl with Merle's face, standing next to the sacrificial king.

In October 1848, two children are told a ghost story by Laura, their nanny. The tale reveals a forbidden love between Merle, a woman from a rich family, and Erik, a poor fisherman. When their secret romance is found out, Merle's father threatens Erik. Knowing that they will never be together, Erik takes his own life. Merle lies on his grave every night for a year and a day. Her sanity gone, she sees a hare near the grave and starts to believe that it is actually Erik. She seeks a witch's help to turn her into a hare, too, so that she can reunite with her lover. Her transformation is successful, but when she returns to Erik's grave as a hare, she is killed by a huntsman. Later, the children learn that Merle's lover was not Erik, a poor fisherman, but rather Erika, another woman from a rich family, and realize that "Laura" was in fact Erika's ghost.

During the tenth century, Blest Island is occupied by Vikings. Brothers Tor and Wulf quarrel over the paternity of Wulf's children, twins Eirik and Melle, with Tor claiming that Wulf is infertile and that he is their real father. After Wulf kills Tor, Tor returns as a vampire and terrorizes the community, demanding his children. Eirik realizes that nothing will stop him, so he offers himself to Tor in order to save Melle and his community. Tor returns to his grave with Eirik, and the two lie there, entwined.

In a time unknown, King Eirikr offers himself as a sacrifice to save his people, who have suffered from famine and disease for the past three years. Among those in attendance at the ritual are Thorolf, a sage, and Gunnar, who will succeed Eirikr as king. Eirikr is stoic about the sacrifice until Melle, his young wife, tries to save him. Then he tells her, "I will live seven times, and I will look for you in each one. We will always be together." He asks her to follow him. After Eirikr is killed, Melle disappears from the village. She returns seven years later and lives at the edge of the village for many years, outlasting Gunnar, Thorolf, and even the temple in which Eirikr was sacrificed. Just before she dies of old age, she answer's Eirikr's question: "Yes, I will follow you."

Back in 2073, Eric Seven is about to be sacrificed. He remembers now that this has happened before, and that Merle has lived his other lives with him. Tor reveals that nobody on the island can have children—Merle was the last islander to be born. He believes that if they recreate Eirikr's sacrifice, the seeming curse of infertility will be lifted. Merle convinces Tor to let her make the sacrifice. Instead of killing Eric, however, she turns the knife on the other wards, cutting Tor's throat, and frees Eric. Merle and Eric flee, but just when it seems that they will finally have a chance, some other islanders find them and drag them back. In the end, they die together, remembering their love for one another.

Critical Evaluation

Marcus Sedgwick's inspiration for *Midwinterblood* was a real painting called *Midvinterblot*, or "midwinter sacrifice," completed by Swedish artist Carl Larsson in 1915. Much like Eric Carlsson's painting in the story, *Midvinterblot* depicts the legendary sacrifice of a Swedish king and was initially rejected by Sweden's Nationalmuseum. Based on this, Sedgwick created an epic story following two souls through a span of centuries. Told as a sequence of seven short tales, *Midwinterblood* offers a seemingly disconnected series of incidents that are inexplicably tied together by the painting, the characters, the island where the stories take place, and the bonds of love.

The structure is innovative, with each incarnation written as a stand-alone multichaptered story. Sedgwick organizes the tales in reverse chronological order, starting sixty-odd years in the future and going back so far in the past that the setting is described as "time unknown." The novel starts at the end of the couple's story and builds to their beginning, before looping back to the end again. Details about the souls that have been torn apart are revealed in snapshots of their varied incarnations. Woven throughout the various stories is the motif of the dragon orchid, which, when brewed into an elixir and consumed, seems to have the ability to extend life at the expense of fertility. The story about the painting is given central placement, with three tales appearing before it and three following. Once the painting is described in that fourth tale, the pieces of the puzzle fall into place, orienting the readers to the unifying themes of love, sacrifice, and immortality in Eric and Merle's story.

That unifying theme is showcased in the various ways that love ties lives together. Sedgwick begins with traditional romance: Eric Seven falls in love with Merle at first sight, and they are drawn together, making Eric forget his life before Blessed Island and reminding Merle of her past. The second story finds Merle and Eric as mother and son. The bond between parent and child is explored again in the third story, where Eric is a grief-stricken father and Merle is the child of the man he saves. The central story in the series finds Eric as an old man who is befriended by young Merle, thus exploring issues of age and companionship. Families and forbidden love are explored in the next two stories. Sibling love is first seen between the two children who hear a love story from a ghostly Erika, who lost her first her life and then her lover because of the forbidden nature of their relationship. In the second horror-themed story, brothers compete for the hand of a woman and argue over the paternity of her children. When one brother kills the other, the dead man returns as a vampire to claim his children. One of those twin children, Eirik, sacrifices himself to save his community while his sister, Melle, is left behind. The novel's final story returns to romantic love, revealing a king sacrificing himself for the betterment of his realm and a wife unwilling to let go. Their love forms the bedrock of all the other relationships in the novel.

Theresa L. Stowell, PhD

Further Reading

Colfer, Eoin. "Seven Stories." Rev. of *Midwinterblood*, by Marcus Sedgwick. *New York Times*. New York Times, 8 Feb. 2013. Web. 5 May 2015. <http://www.nytimes.com/2013/02/10/books/review/midwinterblood-by-marcus-sedgwick.html>.

Sedgwick, Marcus. Interview by Ilene Cooper. *Booklist* 15 Mar. 2014: 76. *Literary Reference Center*. Web. 4 May 2015. <http://search.ebscohost.com/login.aspx?direct=true&db=lfh&AN=94947102&site=ehost-live>.

Rev. of *Midwinterblood*, by Marcus Sedgwick. *Kirkus Reviews* 15 Dec. 2012: 144. *Literary Reference Center*. Web. 4 May 2015. <http://search.ebscohost.com/login.aspx?direct=true&db=lfh&AN=84330133&site=ehost-live>.

Miss Peregrine's Home for Peculiar Children

Author: Ransom Riggs (b. 1980)
First published: 2011
Type of work: Novel
Type of plot: Horror Fantasy

Courtesy of Quirk Publishing

Time of plot: Early 2010s; September 3, 1940
Locale: Englewood, Florida; Cairnholm Island, Wales

Principal characters

Jacob Magellan "Jake" Portman, a sixteen-year-old boy with untapped skills
Abraham "Abe" Portman, Jacob's grandfather
Alma LeFay Peregrine, the headmistress of a Welsh orphanage
Emma Bloom, a teenager with the ability to control fire
Millard Nullings, an invisible boy
Bronwyn Bruntley, a girl with incredible strength

The Story

From the time he was a toddler, Jacob Portman's grandfather Abraham entertained him with stories supplemented by photographs. Born in Poland, Abraham escaped the Holocaust that claimed his family. He took refuge with other Jewish children of special abilities at an orphanage on an island off the coast of Wales.

As he ages, Jacob doubts the veracity of his grandfather's tales. One day, however, when visiting his grandfather, he finds Abraham seriously injured. The old man whispers a few cryptic words about a bird, a loop, a grave, and a date before dying in Jacob's arms. Jacob glimpses a nightmarish figure running away: a face with tentacles dangling from its mouth. Though Jacob tells the police what he saw, Abraham's death is attributed to feral dogs.

Jacob's parents put him into therapy with a psychiatrist, Dr. Golan. Later, when going through his late grandfather's belongings, Jacob finds evidence that the island and the orphanage Abraham spoke of really do exist. He wants to travel to Wales to find out what his grandfather's final words meant. His father, Frank, an amateur ornithologist, is excited by the idea because there is a bird sanctuary on the island, so Jacob and his father plan a three-week sojourn. Once on the island, Jacob finds the orphanage deserted and falling into ruin. Disappointed, he visits the village museum, where the curator talks about a prized display: an ancient man preserved in a nearby peat bog. The curator introduces Jacob to an elderly resident who tells him the orphanage was bombed in an air raid on September 3, 1940—the very date his dying grandfather whispered.

Jacob returns to explore the derelict orphanage. He thinks he hears voices and believes he sees visions of children. He follows the footprints of one illusion to a Neolithic cairn, crawls through, and exits into the world of 1940. He encounters two orphans: pretty, fire-creating Emma Bloom and invisible boy Millard Nullings. They take Jacob to the orphanage, where he meets headmistress Miss Peregrine, a woman who can manipulate time and shape-shift into a bird. He meets other peculiar children, including Olive, who can levitate; Enoch O'Connor, who creates homunculi; and Bronwyn Bruntley, who has incredible strength. Miss Peregrine recognizes Jacob as Abe's grandson and tells him he has a special skill, too: he can see monsters called hollowgasts. She tells him that she and the children are living in a temporal loop, one of many in different times and places, which protected them from being killed in the German bombing. The loop must be reset daily by crossing through the cairn-portal.

Over the next several days, Jacob passes back and forth between past and present. In the twenty-first century, he learns that sheep have been slaughtered and that a strange, bearded bird fancier has shown up. He reports these happenings to the orphanage. Miss Peregrine says the events herald the arrival of the enemies of the hollowgast and their companions, the wights, who look human but have no pupils in their eyes.

Soon, Jacob and the children are engaged in combat against the hollowgasts and wights. In the course of the battle, the loop is disrupted, and Miss Peregrine, in the shape of a bird, is injured and trapped in her animal form. Jacob decides to remain and help the children in their war for survival rather than return to the present world, which offers little for him. Together, the children abandon the orphanage, leave the island, and begin their search for safety in a different time loop.

Critical Evaluation

A charming, if sometimes disturbing, fairy tale for mature young adults, *Miss Peregrine's Home for Peculiar Children* posits alternative worlds—so-called temporal loops in different historical ages, maintained by bird-women called ymbrynes—where the eternal battle between good and evil is waged between opponents with formidable special skills. The novel combines figures from European legend and folklore (wights, which are zombie-like imps, are mentioned in Geoffrey Chaucer's *The Canterbury Tales*, first published in 1475) with made-up creatures (ymbrynes and hollowgasts) to create a universe where neither the everyday laws of physics nor the rules of normal behavior always apply.

The end result, while a unique concoction narrated from the first-person viewpoint of reluctant but likeable hero Jacob, contains elements reminiscent of earlier works. The orphanage of 1940 seems like the idyllic Shangri-La of English author James Hilton's 1933 novel *Lost Horizon*; the idea of the same day repeating over and over strongly recalls the central plot point of the 1993 comedy film *Groundhog Day*; and the children with special, peculiar abilities who are feared or misunderstood by ordinary, if xenophobic, people are quite similar to the mutants in the X-Men stories. The story is greatly enhanced by the periodic inclusion of genuine, unsettling period photographs gathered from private collections and rummage sales, which underscore the creepy atmosphere and help advance the fantasy-laden plotline.

Riggs's debut novel and a *New York Times* best seller, *Miss Peregrine's Home for Peculiar Children* struck a responsive chord with readers. It also spawned two sequels, *Hollow City* (2014) and *Library of Souls* (2015), as well as an original English-language manga-style graphic novel adaptation. A film adaptation of the first book of the trilogy, directed by Tim Burton, is scheduled for release in 2016.

Jack Ewing

Further Reading

Driscoll, Molly. "*Miss Peregrine's Home for Peculiar Children* Author Ransom Riggs Discusses His Sequel." *Christian Science Monitor*. Christian Science Monitor, 10 Dec. 2013. Web. 22 Oct. 2015. <http://www.csmonitor.com/Books/chapter-and-verse/2013/1210/Miss-Peregrine-s-Home-for-Peculiar-Children-author-Ransom-Riggs-discusses-his-sequel>.

Russo, Maria. "A Book That Started with Its Pictures." *New York Times*. New York Times, 30 Dec. 2013. Web. 22 Oct. 2015. <http://www.nytimes.com/2013/12/31/books/ransom-riggs-is-inspired-by-vintage-snapshots.html>.

A Moment Comes

Author: Jennifer Bradbury (b. 1975)
First published: 2013
Type of work: Novel
Type of plot: Historical Fiction
Time of plot: 1947
Locales: Pakistan, India

Principal characters

Margaret Darnsley, a British teenager forced to move to India with her parents
Mr. Darnsley, Margaret's father, a British surveyor
Anupreet, a fifteen-year-old Sikh who works in the Darnsley house to support her family
Tariq, an eighteen-year-old Muslim who works as a translator and courier for Mr. Darnsley
Sameer, a violent Muslim activist and childhood classmate of Tariq

The Story

The first four chapters of the novel open with narratives told from the perspectives of the three main characters living in India after World War II. In the summer of 1947, Tariq, Anupreet, and Margaret find themselves at the height of violent riots and fights between Muslims and Sikhs. Margaret has been forced to come to India because of her father's job. Tariq only wants to continue his education and study at Oxford University, and hopes that his job working for Margaret's father will offer an opportunity. Anupreet, whose face is healing after an attack, also begins work for Margaret's family as her family struggles to keep safe.

Headed by the British government, the partition of India, which took place August 15, 1947, created the two independent states of Pakistan and India. Margaret's father is one of the cartographers charged with drawing the boundary, and the disturbance and violence that have gripped so much of their society and now dictate most of Tariq and Anupreet's everyday lives is the consequence of this decision. At the beginning of the novel, Margaret is self-centered and focused mostly on her failed relationship with a twenty-five-year-old American soldier and the fact that she now finds herself in a completely foreign land away from everything and everyone she knew. She notices Tariq from the first moment she gets out of her car, taking interest in his tall and handsome features. Tariq also shows interest in Margaret, but he knows that getting involved to any degree could be very dangerous for him.

Meanwhile, Anupreet, nicknamed Anu, also helps Margaret, accompanying her around town and working generally as her personal translator. Margaret truly cares about what Anu thinks and values her input on Indian society. Slowly, the two girls become friends, while Margaret continues to have a crush on Tariq. But for Tariq, his plans for life seem to keep moving farther away. He learns from his family that there is not enough money for him to pay for Oxford, or even to get to England, and his hopes to travel with the Darnsleys is similarly stymied when Mr. Darnsley refuses to take him to England, telling him that his place is in the new Pakistan.

As angry as Tariq is, he is not a violent person, and when he follows Sameer with a package to the Darnsley compound, he realizes that the package contains a bomb meant for his employer. He diverts the dangerous package, placing it against a back alley wall. When the bomb goes off, a beggar child is gravely injured, and Tariq rescues him but remains racked with guilt.

As the three teenagers navigate their separate lives through the violence and unrest of the summer of 1947, they learn more about each other and become closer. Tariq finds himself having feelings for Anu, but he knows that a Sikh and a Muslim cannot be together now, no matter what he feels deep down and no matter that such a romance could have been in the past. He redeems himself, however, near the end, saving Anu from Sameer and his gang when they corner Anu and Tariq on the street. In the end, while these three teenagers live incredibly different lives, they find themselves coming together in the violence of the summer to protect each other and find out about themselves at the same time.

Critical Evaluation

When what is known today as young adult literature began in the late 1960s in the United States, realistic fiction was the dominant subgenre of the literary form. The stories were defined by the focus on young adult lives and the issues and dilemmas associated with growing up, generally in the typical American high school. While the 1990s ushered in a plethora of young adult subgenres, including fantasy, science fiction, and horror, authors tended to pick contemporary time periods. As young adult literature has continued to thrive in the twenty-first century, period pieces like *A Moment Comes* are becoming more popular.

As a period piece, Bradbury's novel is not necessarily unique, but the specific events and the location on which she focuses make *A Moment Comes* stand out among other young adult novels written by American authors. Very few authors choose to write about characters living in India and Asia, and particularly during a time that was significant to the formation of what is now modern Pakistan and the Republic of India. By then creating a narrative that weaves together three separate perspectives and story lines, Bradbury has created a work of fiction that has been well received by readers, critics, and scholars.

This story creates not just a coming-of-age story of three young protagonists, but it reveals a moment in world history that largely goes unstudied in mainstream history studies in the United States. It thus opens up new worldviews to adolescent American audiences. For this, this novel has won several honors, including the American Library Association/Young Adult Library Services Association award in 2014 for best young adult fiction.

Aaron Horton, MA

Further Reading

Bates, Crispin. "The Hidden Story of Partition and Its Legacies." *BBC History*. BBC, 3 Mar. 2011. Web. 11 Dec. 2015. <http://www.bbc.co.uk/history/british/modern/partition1947_01.shtml>.

Bradbury, Jennifer. "A Moment Comes." Interview by Hemlata Vasavada. *India Currents: The Complete Indian American Magazine*. India Currents, 6 Mar. 2015. Web. 18 Dec. 2015. <https://www.indiacurrents.com/articles/2015/03/06/moment-comes>.

Rev. of *A Moment Comes*, by Jennifer Bradbury. *Kirkus Reviews* 81.9 (2013): 72–73. *Literary Reference Center*. Web. 18 Dec. 2015. <http://search.ebscohost.com/login.aspx?direct=true&db=lfh&AN=87455872&site=lrc-live>.

Monster

Author: Walter Dean Myers (1937–2014)
First published: 1999
Type of work: Novel
Type of plot: Realism
Time of plot: Late 1990s
Locale: New York City

Principal characters

Steve Harmon, a skinny sixteen-year-old African American boy

Kathy O'Brien, Steve's freckled, red-haired defense attorney

James King, a twenty-three-year-old thug

Richard "Bobo" Evans, a twenty-two-year-old felon

Osvaldo Cruz, a fourteen-year-old Hispanic boy bearing tattoos of the Diablos gang

Asa Briggs, the blue-eyed, white-haired defense attorney for James King

The Story

Young Steve Harmon is in big trouble. He languishes in Cell Block D of the Manhattan Detention Center awaiting trial. Though he has consistently protested his innocence, Steve has been implicated as one of several people who participated in the robbery of a Harlem drugstore just before last Christmas. The crime went horribly wrong when the store owner, Mr. Nesbitt, a middle-aged man from the West Indies, pulled out a gun to defend his property and was fatally shot during a struggle for the gun.

Now it is July of the following year. Two of the individuals involved in the robbery—Richard "Bobo" Evans and Osvaldo Cruz—have both confessed and made plea bargain deals for lesser sentences in exchange for naming the others who were involved in the crime. Steve and James King, though they have separate defense counsels, are to be tried simultaneously for felony murder. They both face potential death sentences or lengthy prison terms without the possibility of parole if found guilty.

As the trial progresses over the course of two weeks, the prosecution, under the direction of Sandra Petrocelli, presents a parade of witnesses who detail the crime and its aftermath. A store employee recounts finding Nesbitt's body after returning from lunch. A man incarcerated at Riker's Island tells of a conversation he had with another prisoner who had bought cartons of cigarettes taken during the robbery. A store customer recalls seeing James King arguing with Mr. Nesbitt. Police detectives recall their investigation of the crime. Osvaldo Cruz and Richard "Bobo" Evans testify against Harmon and King. Though their respective attorneys mount a vigorous defense that demonstrates Cruz is a liar and not as meek as he appears on the stand and that Evans is a callous, habitual criminal who would do anything to help himself, the outcome seems bleak for the two defendants when the prosecution rests. Steve feels certain they are losing the case, and his attorney confirms she is worried about what the final result will be.

Desperate to separate her client from the fate of King, who appears certain to be convicted despite the fact that most evidence presented has been circumstantial and hearsay, attorney O'Brien puts Steve on the stand. Steve denies acting as lookout for the store robbery—the role Cruz and Evans claimed he played—or having any involvement whatsoever in the crime. Under cross-examination by the prosecutor, Steve maintains that he barely knew King, Evans, or Cruz and that he was only in the vicinity of the store because he was scouting locations for a film about the neighborhood for a school project. To reinforce the impression that Steve is an innocent victim of the judicial system, O'Brien calls as a character witness Mr. Sawicki, Steve's film teacher, who testifies that his student is bright, talented, and honest.

After closing arguments and jury instructions, James and Steve are kept in a holding cell with guards; it is the first time they have spoken to one another since a casual conversation on a neighborhood stoop many months earlier. James, who has been through the court system before, is fatalistic, while Steve is scared out of his wits about what will happen to him.

Critical Evaluation

The structure of *Monster* adds to the reading enjoyment. Protagonist Steve Harmon, self-described from the beginning as an aspiring filmmaker, presents his experience as though it were a script, with Steve as the screenwriter, producer, director, and star. The bulk of the story advances in straightforward, linear fashion. The script realistically depicts a typical felony trial, in which there are no "Perry Mason moments" of sudden, surprising revelations or forced confessions. Readers are forced to serve as surrogate jurors, to weigh the testimony and evidence, and to judge for themselves what is true or false and who is innocent or guilty. The script is periodically enhanced with cinematic techniques—montages, cuts, dissolves, and other prospective camera movements—for dramatic impact. Flashbacks show Steve's brief encounters with the other characters and moments spent in the past with family members, demonstrating the love of Steve's caring parents and his admiring younger brother Jerry, who will all be changed by the traumatic experience of Steve's arrest and trial. Scenes are capped with Steve's notes detailing his impressions, feelings, doubts, and fears concerning the particular day's events.

In addition to delineating a crime, its aftereffects, and the course of meting out punishment, *Monster* also deals with a number of larger social issues. The plight of young inner-city men of color—plagued by high rates of unemployment and few prospects for the future—is starkly portrayed. The perpetrators purposely chose Mr. Nesbitt as their target because he was an immigrant and they knew the authorities would be less zealous in their investigation than if the victim had been white. The penal system is shown as jungle-like, where the weak are brutalized. The inequality of the judicial system is especially taken to task. There is considerable truth in what O'Brien tells Steve during a conference: despite the admonition that suspects are innocent until proven guilty, half of the jury members believe from the start that Steve committed the crime simply because he is young, black, and on trial.

Because of the novel's multiple strengths in storytelling, *Monster* won the inaugural Michael L. Printz Award for excellence in young adult literature and was named a Coretta Scott King honor book in 2000.

Jack Ewing

Further Reading

Gómez, Hannah. "On Walter Dean Myers." *Hub*. YALSA, 13 July 2014. Web. 16 Oct. 2015. <http://www.yalsa.ala.org/thehub/2014/07/13/on-walter-dean-myers/>.

Rev. of *Monster*, by Walter Dean Myers. *Kirkus*. Kirkus, 1 May 1999. Web. 16 Oct. 2015. <https://www.

kirkusreviews.com/book-reviews/walter-dean-my-ers/monster-myers/>.

Rev. of *Monster*, by Walter Dean Myers. *Publishers Weekly*. PWxyz, n.d. Web. 16 Oct. 2015.

The Mortal Instruments (Series)

Author: Cassandra Clare (pen name of Judith Rumelt, b. 1973)
First published: *City of Bones* (2007)
   City of Ashes (2008)
   City of Glass (2009)
   City of Fallen Angels (2011)
   City of Lost Souls (2012)
   City of Heavenly Fire (2014)
Type of work: Novel
Type of plot: Paranormal Romance
Time of plot: 2007
Locale: New York City; the fictional city of Idris

Principal characters

Clary Fray, young woman whose life is changed after learning of the Shadowhunter world
Jace Wayland, Clary's romantic interest and a Shadowhunter
Simon Lewis, Clary's best friend
Sebastian Morgenstern, Clary's long-lost brother
Valentine Morgenstern, Clary's father
Isabelle Lightwood, the fiery and strong middle Lightwood child, a Shadowhunter
Alec Lightwood, the protective oldest of the Lightwood children, a Shadowhunter

The Story

In the first book of The Mortal Instruments series, *City of Bones* (2007), Clary Fray is introduced to a world that she could not have even dreamed into existence. Out for the night with her best friend Simon Lewis, Clary sees a boy being attacked. Despite hearing a discussion of demons that is beyond her understanding, Clary is disturbed that no one else seems to have seen either the attackers or the murder itself. When Clary learns the next day that her mother, Jocelyn, is moving them to the country, the incident momentarily loses importance. Then, out again with Simon, Clary sees one of the boys who led the previous night's attack.

Jace Wayland is a Shadowhunter, a protector of the human race. It is his duty to hunt and destroy demons.

Mundanes (normal humans) cannot see either Shadowhunters or demons, so he knows Clary must have Shadowhunter blood. When Clary's mother contacts her with a mysterious message telling her to stay away from home and to warn their family friend Luke that she has been found, Clary is thrust into a different reality, one that will change her life.

Nothing is the same once she discovers this new world. She finds out that demons, werewolves, and vampires exist. Worse yet, her whole life has been a lie. Her mother, who is now missing, was a Shadowhunter who hired a warlock to repress Clary's memories of life in their world. Further, the man who has been her father figure is a werewolf. Even worse, her biological father, named Valentine and a former Shadowhunter, is not dead; he is a villain who has kidnapped her mother. He is demanding the return of a Shadowhunter relic known as the Mortal Cup, which Jocelyn took with her when she fled Valentine.

The novel becomes a quest to find this relic. Clary works with Jace and two of his friends, Isabel and Alec Lightwood, to find the cup before it is too late for not only Jocelyn but also for peace within the whole Shadowhunter world. In the process, Clary and Jace develop a romance. Though the novel ends with the rescue of Jocelyn, who is in a comatose state, Valentine has obtained the Mortal Cup; the budding romance between Clary and Jace is derailed when the novel ends with the revelation that the two are siblings.

The second book in the series, *City of Ashes* (2008), begins with Jace being accused of working alongside Valentine to undermine the Shadowhunter regime. He is imprisoned in the Silent City, an underground monastery for the Silent Brothers. While he is locked up, he hears a disturbance that turns out to be Valentine killing all of the Silent Brothers who guard the Mortal Sword. This situation aggravates his case with the Inquisitor who had planned to use the sword to make Jace reveal Valentine's plans.

The group of friends returns to New York, with Jace under Magnus Bane's guardianship. Clary's ability to create angelic runes develops, and Alec reveals his feelings for Magnus during this time. Jace continues to be torn about his relationship with Valentine, still believing the older man is his father, so he agrees to meet Valentine aboard an old ship in the harbor. The Inquisitor finds out about the meeting and places Jace back in prison as she plans revenge on Valentine, who was responsible for her son's death years before.

Meanwhile, Valentine has kidnapped one of the female werewolves to use as bait. The teens rescue her, but Valentine kills Simon during the fight. Simon is brought back when Jace feeds him his own blood, turning him into a vampire who can walk in daylight.

The novel ends with Clary and Jace once again confused about their relationship. Clary is ready to commit to Jace, despite the rumors that they are siblings, but Jace tells her he plans to be like a brother to her before she has a chance to share her heart. The end of the novel introduces a new character who claims to be an old friend of Jocelyn. This new woman says she knows how to wake Clary's mother, distracting the girl from her heartbreak.

The third book, *City of Glass* (2009), deals with the final mortal instrument: the Mortal Mirror (which is also called the Mortal Glass). The Mortal Mirror is a portal created by the Angel Raziel, who created the Shadowhunters centuries earlier. When used for its intended purpose, the mirror provides transport to Alicante (the Shadowhunters' home country) from the outside; however, if used for evil, it becomes a portal for demons. Luke and Clary land in the lake after Clary creates a transportation rune in order to follow Jace and Simon, who have gone to Idris. The lake, however, is dangerous to Shadowhunters, causing illness and hallucinations. Thus, Clary is affected by its poisons while Luke is safe since he is a werewolf. Attempting to save Clary, Luke takes her to his sister's home.

During the time in Idris, the conflict over Jace's loyalty to Valentine continues. Simon has been imprisoned because of his connection to Jace, so once again the teens must free someone from the Shadowhunter leadership. They do so with the help of the Lightwoods' cousin, Sebastian, a young man who ends up killing Simon's cellmate. When they return to the house where the Lightwoods are staying, the group discovers that Sebastian is working with Valentine and has killed Max Lightwood, Alec, and Isabelle's younger brother. The death is necessary for a ritual Valentine will use to call Raziel.

This installment ends with Raziel killing Valentine, but not before Valentine has stabbed Jace. The angel resurrects Jace at Clary's request, and she thinks all will work out well with her world.

Though the series could have ended with *City of Glass*, Clare responded to its popularity by creating what feels like a second trilogy rather than a coherent continuance of the first three books. The fourth book, *City of Fallen Angels* (2011), has a dual focus, split between Simon as a vampire and Clary and Jace. Vampires

are featured as the main villains, with Lilith (a vampire who has been around since the beginning of time) gaining control over Jace and attempting to kill Clary. The novel ends with Lilith's death and the rescue of Simon and Jace from her clutches.

City of Lost Souls (2012) reintroduces the Seelie Queen while complicating the relationship between Clary, Jace, and Sebastian. Sebastian is Clary's true brother, and Jace has been possessed by him. Sebastian is planning to continue Valentine's plans by using the Mortal Cup to create a group of dark Shadowhunters.

Simon, Isabelle, and Alec summon Raziel for help, and Simon is presented with another angelic sword, but he returns to mortality as a result. Clary uses the sword in an attempt to save Jace, leading to what seems to be his death; he is later discovered to be alive and possessing a new power.

Clary and her friends battle Sebastian in the final book in the series, *City of Heavenly Fire* (2014). Returning to the sanctuary of Idris, the group finds that Sebastian has begun to take over the souls of Shadowhunters, turning once good fighters into evil ones. In an effort to win the battle, the teens enter the demon realm to gain a final victory over Sebastian. New characters are introduced, new conflicts are created, and the old war is ended. The group seems to be reunited with Clary and Jace together, Simon and Isabelle developing a relationship, and Alec and Magnus once again a couple.

Critical Evaluation

The Mortal Instruments series follows a fairly straightforward chronological pattern beginning with the moments when Clary Fray first discovers the world of the Shadowhunters. There are occasional flashbacks throughout the novels to establish background stories or develop characterization, but these are informative scenes that do not confuse readers. For example, there are occasional flashbacks to Jace's youth when he was living with Valentine, which are used to establish the confusion that often interferes with the young man's personality and choices. There are also flashbacks into the lives of Clary's parents to establish when Valentine chose a path toward power despite the dangers that direction posed to his wife and children. These snapshots into the past also establish Jocelyn and Luke's relationship before and after her marriage to Valentine.

The novels follow a quest format in many cases with the search for three "mortal instruments" as the primary goal of the stories. As the first novel explains, the Mortal Cup was created by the Angel Raziel to help Jonathan Shadowhunter build an army of soldiers who could fight demons. Centuries later, the cup was stolen by Valentine, but Jocelyn took it with her when she left Valentine to protect her daughter. She hid the cup in the painting on a set of tarot cards she entrusted to her neighbor. As the first novel progresses and Clary learns her own power with art, she figures out the location of the cup and brings it back into the world, where it is stolen once again by Valentine. In searching for the cup, Clary learns about the world from which she came and she grows in confidence.

In the second novel, the Mortal Sword is sought. The main gift of this weapon is to force the Nephilim (Shadowhunters—humans who are born with angel blood) to tell the truth. It is meant to be wielded only by a neutral party, such as a monk of the Silent Brotherhood. However, it can be used for evil, as when Valentine steals it and kills a group of children in a ritual meant to warp the sword's purpose. Its new purpose, to draw an army of demons, begins a Shadowhunter war. The quest for the sword is mostly Valentine's journey. In his mission to destroy the Shadowhunters, readers learn about Clary's parentage and the powers that will help her in the battles throughout the rest of the series.

The final mortal instrument is the Mortal Mirror. The mirror turns out to be Lake Lyn, a portal into and out of Idris, the refuge city of the Shadowhunters. The water of the lake is dangerous to the Nephilim but harmless to Mundanes. The lake is where Raziel rose to give Jonathan Shadowhunter the other two mortal instruments. Valentine searches for the Mortal Mirror because he can summon Raziel or demons if he has all three mortal instruments. Clary and her friends pursue these instruments to keep Valentine from gaining that power.

The worlds that Cassandra Clare builds in the novels is significant to their popularity. The transition from New York City to Idris, from the institute where Jace and the Lightfoots live and the city where their kind are sheltered, is worked carefully into the story, so readers can easily understand the locations of the events within each of the stories. In addition, the paranormal groups, especially the Shadowhunters, are well-developed and consistent. The interaction between the groups is complex, but the author establishes the history of each group with enough detail to make the conflicts believable. The fact that readers learn about the

Shadowhunter world as Clary does further simplifies the connections.

Young adult literature is inundated with predictable romance, and this series is no different. Though one might expect the romantic relationships to be straightforward and obvious, Clare provides enough plot twists to create conflicts and keep readers wondering whether their favorite pairs will end up together. The two most obvious complications are between Clary and Jace, especially early on when the two are told they are siblings, and Alec and the warlock Magnus Bane. The homosexual relationship between the latter two characters introduces a sympathetic consideration of the difficulties young people, regardless of sexual orientation, may experience when choosing to fall in love.

Theresa L. Stowell, PhD

Further Reading
Clare, Cassandra, ed. *Shadowhunters and Downworlders: A Mortal Instruments Reader*. Dallas: SmartPop, 2013. Print.

Clare, Cassandra, and Joshua Lewis. *The Shadowhunter's Codex: Being a Record of the Ways and Laws of the Nephilim, the Chosen of the Angel Raziel*. New York: McElderry, 2013. Print.

Gresh, Lois H. *The Mortal Instruments Companion: City of Bones, Shadowhunters, and The Sight: The Unauthorized Guide*. New York: St. Martin's Griffin, 2013. Print.

Nick & Norah's Infinite Playlist

Author: Rachel Cohn (b. 1968) and David Levithan (b. 1972)
First published: 2006
Type of work: Novel
Type of plot: Romance
Time of plot: 2000s
Locale: New York City, New York

Principal characters
Nick, a teenage bassist
Norah, a teenage music fan
Tal, Norah's ex-boyfriend
Tris, Nick's ex-girlfriend
Caroline, Norah's drunk friend

The Story

Nick is the only straight musician in a queercore band. As he plays bass at a crowded show, he notices his ex-girlfriend, Tris, in the crowd. When Tris and her date approach Nick later, he turns to the girl standing beside him, a stranger, and asks if she will be his girlfriend for the next five minutes.

The girl is Norah, and because Tris happens to be a friend that Norah is avoiding, she agrees and starts kissing Nick. Norah's friend, Caroline, is already drunk and flirting with guys, and Norah feels responsible for bringing her home safely. She tells Nick that she will be his girlfriend for two additional minutes if he drives her and Caroline home to New Jersey.

Nick agrees, but his car will not start, and he and Norah banter and flirt. Thom, a member of Nick's band, comes over and offers to jump the car. He takes Norah aside and offers her fifty dollars if she will take Nick out on a date, saying he and his boyfriend can drive Caroline home. Norah agrees, but before she and Nick leave, her ex-boyfriend Tal approaches. She is angered when Tal tells Nick that she has no heart, and she and Nick drive off.

Nick and Norah go to a burlesque club to watch drag queen nuns perform. They slow dance inside and feel closer, and Norah learns that her favorite band, Where's Fluffy, is performing a late-night show there. Friends from the other club start to show up, and as Where's Fluffy plays, Nick and Norah dance in the mosh pit. Norah then pulls Nick into a side room to make out, but it feels wrong to Nick and he stops. Norah finds Tris in the crowd and leaves with her to go a nearby Korean grocery store. Tris tells Norah that Nick is a great guy who loved her, but because she could not love him back, she broke up with him. Norah decides she should also end this date with Nick and says a quick good-bye to him, leaving wearing the jacket he loaned her.

Norah takes a cab to a Ukrainian restaurant she and Tris like. Nick sits on a curb outside of the club, where his friend Dev comforts him before he realizes that his cell phone was in his jacket and calls it from a payphone. Norah tells him where she is and he joins her at the Ukrainian restaurant, where their date resumes. Tris goes to the restaurant also and pulls Norah into the bathroom, demanding money to get a cab home. Norah then tells Tris she is nervous about kissing Nick, so they kiss each other to practice.

When Norah rejoins Nick and Tris leaves, she is energized about the date again. They decide to go to Midtown, where they talk about song titles, spirituality, and love. When it begins to rain around sunrise, Nick dances in the downpour and kisses Norah. They take cover in a hotel and fool around in an ice room before an old man and woman walk in on them. Finally, they decide to return to Nick's car, which will not start again. When they try to take the train back to New Jersey, they realize they only have enough money to pay for one person. Norah then jumps the turnstile with Nick's help, feeling like she is jumping into something much bigger, something scary but exhilarating, too.

Critical Evaluation

Nick & Norah's Infinite Playlist is structured through chapters that alternate between each title character's perspective (Nick's chapters are written by Levithan and Norah's chapters by Cohn). This structure limits what readers can know in any given scene, as they receive the interior thoughts and observations from only one character. However, it also allows readers to contrast Nick and Norah's individual understandings of their shared experiences, revealing that even in seemingly straightforward moments, complexities and contradictions run beneath the surface.

One of the most complicated moments of understanding and misunderstanding comes when Norah pulls Nick into the side room of the burlesque club, trying to initiate sex, which Nick declines, sensing that Norah is not truly into it. They are both overwhelmed and confused, illustrated by the lengthy, almost circular streams of consciousness that dominate their narratives, such as when Nick describes getting close to Norah at the club: "Dev's elbow hits my back and I press forward and she's right there . . . it becomes my heartbeat and her heartbeat and I know it and she knows it and this is the point where we could break apart and that would be it, totally it."

When Norah asks Nick if he saw his ex-girlfriend, he in turn asks her if she saw her ex-boyfriend, with her answering in the affirmative, leading Nick to believe that the entire scene had been motivated by Tal. However, when the narrative switches to Norah's perspective, we find her in an even more conflicted, confused emotional state than Nick. We learn that she did not see Tal (although she did see Tris) after all, and that she only lied about this in order to give Nick an explanation for her irrational behavior. Norah and Nick are not only perplexed by each other's actions, then—they are perhaps even more perplexed by their own actions.

Ultimately, these tensions between knowing and not knowing, between understanding and misunderstanding, drive the book. The simple moment in which Norah tries to seduce Nick at the club becomes the catalyst for chapters of confusion, each character running from the other even as they hope to connect. As a portrait of young romance, the structure of *Nick & Norah's Infinite Playlist* successfully conveys that growing up and growing into love is never a private activity, but rather a collaborative process of shared, hard-earned truth, with plenty of beauty and mistakes along the way.

T. Fleischmann, MFA

Further Reading

Baldwin, Evelyn. "What's Going On Inside of Me? Emergent Female Sexuality and Identity Formation in Young Adult Literature." *ALAN Review* 39.2 (2012): 6–12. Print.

Levithan, Dan, and Rachel Cohn. "The Real Couple behind the 'Infinite Playlist.'" Interview by Alex Cohen. *Day to Day*. NPR, 3 Oct. 2008. Web. 23 Feb. 2015. Transcript.

Noggin

Author: John Corey Whaley (b. 1984)
First published: 2014
Type of work: Novel
Type of plot: Science fiction
Time of plot: Near future
Locale: Colorado

Principal characters

Travis Coates, a sixteen-year-old boy
Kyle, Travis's former best friend
Cate, Travis's former girlfriend
Hatton, Travis's new best friend
Lawrence, a body transplant recipient
Mr. and Mrs. Coates, Travis's parents

The Story

The novel begins as Travis awakens in a hospital five years after having agreed to an experimental procedure to remove his head, freeze it, and then reattach it to another person's body once technology and scientific advances allowed it. Travis's former body had been riddled with cancer and he was dying. Despite his parents' objections, he agreed to the procedure, and his head is now attached to the body of Jeremy Pratt, who was a sixteen-year-old skateboarder and athlete when he died of brain cancer. The story then proceeds to Travis's homecoming and his readjustment to life.

While at home, Travis finds the urn with the ashes of his old body, and he is not quite sure how to respond and drops it in shock. He returns to school and finds that everything has changed. He is bombarded by mail and the media, as well as reactions from others that range from condemnation to worship, but what disturbs him the most is that he feels detached from everyone he once knew. He tries to reconnect with his former best friend and girlfriend, but too many things have changed. Kyle and Cate are both twenty-one. Kyle says he is now no longer gay, and Cate is engaged to be married. With Kyle, Travis soon adapts and the two develop a new friendship that is now more distant due to the passage of time and the changes that each has undergone. Despite this, Travis fears that Kyle is lying to himself. Simultaneously, Travis tries to rekindle things with Cate. However, Cate avoids him.

Travis meanwhile reintegrates to life at school and talks to the guidance counselor. He develops a friendship with a boy named Hatton. He also speaks to Lawrence, the only other person to have undergone a body transplant. Travis hopes to get guidance from Lawrence and tries to use Lawrence's experiences to help him deal with his own. After spending time with Kyle and getting to know each other again, Travis convinces Kyle to acknowledge the truth and tell his girlfriend and his parents that he is gay. Travis interprets this as a sign to resurrect the lost past and decides that perhaps Cate still does care for him and wants to commit to him. They eventually meet at karaoke and she tells him that she understands why he still has feelings for her, but she has moved on and he must as well. Travis, however, cannot, and he tries repeatedly to get her to acknowledge her feelings for him. He also begins to notice that his father often sneaks off, so with the help of his friends, he does some detective work and confronts his father.

Travis's parents tell him that with the stress of his "death," they could not stay together but remain good friends. This helps Travis understand Cate, who agrees to meet him for coffee but brings her fiancé to drive the point home. Though Travis at first intends to propose to Cate and even buys an engagement ring, Hatton and Kyle convince him that he is being foolish. Having reconciled to the new world around him, Travis and his friends go to scatter his ashes on Jeremy's grave. In the process they bump into Jeremy's family and come to an acceptance and understanding.

Critical Evaluation

Noggin is touching and moving, but the story also manages to surprise the reader with offbeat humor. Travis is likeable, despite his obsession with Cate, as are the rest of the characters. Part of this is due to Whaley's remarkable prose. The story has a unique premise, but *Noggin* is at its core an emotionally driven coming-of-age story. The novel was a finalist for the 2014 National Book Award.

Despite the original storyline and the likeability of the characters, the book can appear flat and the characterization one-dimensional. Travis is so much the everyman that there is little to mark him as unique. In many ways, the only difference between Travis's old best friend Kyle and his new best friend Hatton is that Kyle is gay. Likewise, Travis's emotional responses are often superficial—he judges kids at school by their hair—and his most emotional reaction is when he has trouble playing video games. After Travis's initial shock and uncertainty in how to deal with a world that has moved on, he continues to remain numb. Additionally, Travis's unwavering quest for Cate turns from a normal desire to reclaim what once was to a slightly disturbing and unsettling obsession.

Whaley does not dwell on the larger moral and ethical implications of body transplants and cryogenics. The subjects are there in the background, but Travis tunes them out and Whaley does not address them in any meaningful way. Equally, there is little consideration of Travis's coming to terms with his new body or with the notion that it once was somebody else's body. Instead, Travis works to regain normalcy through a relationship with Cate, but this instead feels more like the elephant in the room that is rarely acknowledged.

The characters in *Noggin* are vivid, yet they are crafted simply. The premise is unique, but the storyline evolves through Travis's cycle of numerous attempts to win back Cate, and in doing so, it feels repetitive. However, Whaley's prose carries the story and provides a different spin on the well-trod genre of the bildungsroman.

Gina Hagler, MBA

Further Reading

Hill, Crag. *The Critical Merits of Young Adult Literature: Coming of Age*. New York: Routledge, 2014. Print.

Jacobs, A. J. "Out-of-Body Experience." *New York Times*. New York Times, 9 May 2014. Web. 31 May 2015.

Kaplan, Jeffrey S. "The Changing Face of Young Adult Literature." *Teaching Young Adult Literature Today: Insights, Considerations, and Perspectives for the Classroom Teacher* (2012): 19. Print.

The Perks of Being a Wallflower

Author: Stephen Chbosky (b. 1970)
First published: 1999
Type of Work: Novel
Type of Plot: Epistolary Realism
Time of Plot: 1991–2
Locale: Suburban Pittsburgh

#1 *new york times* bestseller
the perks of being a wallflower

stephen chbosky

Courtesy of Gallery Books, an imprint of Simon & Schuster

Principal Characters

Charlie, an earnest, socially awkward high school freshman

Sam, a pretty, punkish high school senior

Patrick, Sam's stepbrother; a kind-hearted, gay high school senior

Aunt Helen, Charlie's beloved, deceased aunt

The Story

The Perks of Being a Wallflower is told from the perspective of Charlie, a high school freshman, in the form of letters addressed to an unknown pen pal. Charlie is shy—later, his friends will dub him a "wallflower"—and often painfully awkward in social situations. He is extremely intelligent, but he views the world with a childlike earnestness that leaves him all too exposed to the emotions of love and loss. When the book begins, Charlie's only friend, Michael, has committed suicide a year before. The prospect of beginning high school without Michael has Charlie despondent. After a week of being ignored (aside from a fight after he captures the attention of a senior bully) Charlie meets a gregarious senior nicknamed Patrick and Patrick's beautiful stepsister, Sam. Patrick and Sam are not like the other kids at school; they like Charlie, and they are not interested in being popular. They listen to cool music, smoke cigarettes (and cannabis), wear vintage clothes, and run a monthly showing of the cult movie *The Rocky Horror Picture Show*.

At first, Charlie's friendship with Sam and Patrick seems a little one-sided. They let him tag along with them, and Sam is delighted (but discouraging) when Charlie develops what she terms a very "Charlie-esque" crush on her, but they seem less attached to him than he is to them. Over a short amount of time, however, they grow to genuinely love Charlie, though that love is of a very different character than the ardent love Charlie feels for Sam.

Meanwhile, in school, Charlie is singled out as a gifted student by a young English teacher named Bill. Throughout the book, Bill introduces Charlie to classic and formative novels such as *The Catcher in the Rye* (1951), *Peter Pan* (1904), *The Great Gatsby* (1925), and *The Stranger* (1942). The books give Charlie a lens through which he can understand his own life.

At home, he is secretly tormented by the sporadic affection of his family. He craves the kind of unabashed love he feels for others but rarely gets it—particularly from his father or older brother. Both are good men, but they disdain public displays of emotion in themselves or others males, which is unfortunate for Charlie because he is quick to cry (both happy and sad tears). The only family member who ever truly understood Charlie, he believes, was his aunt Helen, who died in a car accident on his seventh birthday.

Charlie falls in with Sam and Patrick's friends, including an opinionated and artsy girl named Mary Elizabeth, whom he begins to date. Charlie is bewildered by intimacy with Mary Elizabeth, in no small part because he really loves Sam. Sam, however, is dating a college boy who moonlights as a male model. Meanwhile, Patrick is secretly dating the school's popular quarterback, Brad. Charlie's relationship with Mary Elizabeth is telling because, as Sam later explains to him, he lets his wallflower tendencies get the best of him. He lets Mary Elizabeth steamroll over him, becomes unhappy, and, unable to express his desire to end the relationship, ends up hurting her. For a short time after the Mary Elizabeth debacle, he falls out with his tight-knit group and picks up smoking, but he also bonds with his older sister, a popular high school senior with an abusive boyfriend. He earns back his friends (in a roundabout way) after standing up for Patrick in a lunchroom brawl with Brad's friends. (Patrick's relationship with Brad met a devastating end after Brad's father caught the two boys together.)

Charlie gets melancholy as graduation draws nearer; soon all of his friends will be gone. He has suffered bouts of panic and depression throughout the book and even begun seeing a psychiatrist, but despite the sadness of parting, Charlie seems to be doing well. On his last night with Sam (who has, by this point, broken up with the unfaithful model), he kisses her. She kisses back. As she begins to undress him, Charlie has a panic attack and stops her, though he is unable to understand why. Later, the reader discovers that Charlie suffered a breakdown the next day. He reveals his own discovery, that his aunt Helen molested him when he was a child. Despite the heavy turning point, Charlie writes as though a weight has been lifted, and he closes his last letter a year from his first, looking forward to his sophomore year.

Critical Evaluation

The Perks of Being a Wallflower has become one of the most popular young adult novels of the late twentieth and early twenty-first centuries. Almost ten years after it was published, in 2007, a reporter for the *New York Times* wrote that the book is still "passed from adolescent to adolescent like a hot potato." However, early reviews of the novel were very poor. *Publishers Weekly* described it as "trite," and criticized the book's "droning insistence on Charlie's supersensitive disposition." *Kirkus* deemed it a bad "rip-off" of J. D. Salinger's *The Catcher in the Rye*. Both reviewers reserved special disdain for the book's connection with MTV (it was published by MTV Books). Adults have not grown any fonder of the book, as it remains one of the most frequently challenged and banned books in the United States, but the book's popularity exists, and endures, independent of reviews and school reading lists. Readers respond to Charlie's "supersensitive disposition" as a nuanced exploration of empathy. Charlie is clear about one thing: he desperately wants everyone (even the reader) to be happy. In *Perks* he must grapple with the realization that happiness is relative, and that not everyone gets the lot they deserve. Even before Charlie unearths his repressed memories of his aunt, he muses about how his family has shaped him (and how his parents were shaped by their parents, and so on down the line), and how, like his parents, he could grow both because of and in spite of them. The characters in *Perks* have been criticized as self-absorbed, but this seems particularly unfair in Charlie's case, given that he must learn to love himself before he can truly love others.

Molly Hagan

Further Reading

"The Island; Reluctant Readers? Try Resistant Parents." *New York Times*. New York Times, 8 July 2007. Web. 27 May 2015. <http://query.nytimes.com/gst/full-page.html?res=9D01E0DC153EF93BA35754C0A9619C8B63>.

Rev. of *The Perks of Being a Wallflower*, by Stephen Chbosky. *Kirkus Reviews*. Kirkus Media, 4 Feb. 1999. Web. 27 May 2015. <https://www.kirkusreviews.com/book-reviews/stephen-chbosky/the-perks-of-being-a-wallflower/#review>.

Rev. of *The Perks of Being a Wallflower*, by Stephen Chbosky. *Publishers Weekly*. PWxyz, 1 Feb. 1999. Web. 27 May 2015. <http://www.publishersweekly.com/978-0-671-02734-6>.

Postcards from No Man's Land

Author: Aidan Chambers (b. 1934)
First published: 1999
Type of work: Novel
Type of plot: Historical Fiction
Time of plot: World War II; mid-1990s
Locale: Amsterdam, Netherlands; Oosterbeek and vicinity, Netherlands

Principal characters

Jacob Todd, a seventeen-year-old English boy visiting Amsterdam in 1995
Jacob Todd, his grandfather, a British paratrooper wounded at the Battle of Arnhem in 1944
Geertrui Marije "Maria" Wesseling, a Dutch woman who was nineteen years old in 1944
Daan van Riet, Geertrui's grandson, a twenty-four-year-old student
Ton, Daan's boyfriend
Hille Babbe, an outspoken seventeen-year-old Dutch schoolgirl
Alma, a kindly, elderly Dutch woman

The Story

On September 15, 1995, English teenager Jacob Todd visits a café in Amsterdam. While there, he is approached by a young, attractive girl who introduces herself as Ton. She writes down her telephone number, and then she guides Jacob's hand to her crotch, where Jacob feels a penis. Shocked at his error and distracted from his surroundings, Jacob is robbed.

Half a century earlier, on September 17, 1944, British soldiers parachute into Holland to liberate the Dutch from the German occupation during World War II. Two of the soldiers arrive at a house in Oosterbeek, near Arnhem, where nineteen-year-old Geertrui lives with her parents. Geertrui's family and their neighbors cheer the landing British paratroopers.

In 1995 Jacob is befriended by a kind, elderly woman named Alma. She takes him to a café and asks about his story. Jacob has come to visit the grave of his grandfather, Jacob Todd, who is buried in a soldiers' cemetery at Oosterbeek. The younger Jacob, who was named after his grandfather, has been living with his widowed grandmother, Sarah Todd. Sarah has kept in touch with Geertrui Wesseling, who nursed Sarah's wounded husband after the Battle of Arnhem in September 1944. An injury prevented Sarah from visiting herself, so Jacob traveled in her stead. He is staying with Geertrui's family. Alma contacts Geertrui's grandson Daan van Riet and gives Jacob directions to their home.

In 1944 the two soldiers bring a third, a wounded man named Jacob Todd, into Geertrui's home. She cares for him. He calls her Maria, for her second name, Marije, as he cannot pronounce her first name.

Jacob finds Daan living in the loft of his grandmother's home. Jacob tells Daan about his life, including his close relationship with Sarah. Daan hints that his mother—Geertrui's daughter, Tessel van Riet—is unhappy about Jacob's visit.

It is September 1944, and the Germans are starting to take hold of the city again. Geertrui is still caring for Jacob Todd, but it is not safe to remain in the city. Geertrui, her brother Henk, and his friend Dirk Wesseling leave the city, taking the still-wounded Jacob with them, and escape the German lines encircling the defeated British paratroopers.

Daan and Jacob have dinner at a café, where Daan reveals that Geertrui is in pain from terminal stomach cancer. She has decided on euthanasia, or physician-assisted suicide, which is legal in the Netherlands. Her family is upset but accepting. The procedure will be performed soon.

In 1944 Geertrui's party makes it to relative safety at Dirk's parents' farm. Geertrui is happy there with Jacob until the end.

Jacob sees Ton again and discovers that he is Daan's boyfriend. The next day, Jacob meets Geertrui at the hospice. Geertrui has Jacob read aloud her favorite British Renaissance poem.

In 1944, German soldiers search the farm but do not find Jacob. He is hiding in bed under Geertrui's body while she pretends to have tuberculosis.

On Sunday, September 17, 1995, Jacob joins Daan's mother in the annual ceremony honoring the Allied soldiers who fought in the Battle of Arnhem. It is the fifty-first anniversary of the battle. The ceremony moves Jacob. While there, he befriends Hille Babbe, an outspoken seventeen-year-old Dutch girl. Hille's younger brother, Wilfred, lays flowers on Jacob's grandfather's grave, as Dutch children do annually for the fallen Allied soldiers.

After Henk and Dirk leave to join the Dutch resistance in late 1944, Geertrui remains with Jacob Todd as he recovers. She falls in love with him and gives herself to him, even though she knows he is married.

Hille and Jacob talk alone, first in a restaurant and then in a park. Hille kisses Jacob, and they agree to see each other again.

Geertrui and Jacob spend six weeks together at the farm, which Geertrui will later recall as the happiest time of her life. Suddenly, Jacob, who is still recovering, has a heart attack and dies. Geertrui holds a vigil. Jacob is secretly buried on the Wesseling farm.

The day after Jacob meets Hille, he wakes up to find Daan gone. In a note, Daan explains that he has gone to visit Geertrui and suggests that Jacob call Ton. Jacob wants to send his grandmother a postcard, so he asks Ton to help him find a post office. The two explore Amsterdam together.

Late in 1944, Geertrui finds out that she is pregnant. When Dirk Wesseling returns in March 1945, she agrees to his marriage proposal after confessing her affair with Jacob. Tessel is born in August.

Geertrui's narrative is revealed to be a memoir she has dictated to Daan while on her deathbed. She wanted to confess the truth to Sarah, but because Sarah could not come, she decided to tell Jacob instead. The next time Jacob visits her, she gives him Daan's transcript of her story.

Jacob is unsure if he should tell Sarah of Geertrui's confession. Daan and Tessel advise against it. Alma, whom Jacob visits, suggests telling the truth. Jacob calls Hille. She visits him before his plane leaves. He tells Hille his grandmother has sent him a postcard every week since Jacob was six. He hates to hurt her with Geertrui's confession. Jacob remains undecided as he and Hille make love.

Critical Evaluation

In 1999, the UK Library Association awarded *Postcards from No Man's Land* the prestigious Carnegie Medal for the best new young adult novel of the year. After Chambers's novel was published in the United States in 2002, it won the Young Adult Library Services Association's Michael L. Printz Award for the year's best book for teenagers in 2003.

The novel's key themes of family legacy, heroism, young love, and growing into adulthood are explored by juxtaposing the experiences of two different generations. The story effects this examination of similarities and differences by using two plotlines, which alternate throughout before converging at the end. By setting the two plots in almost the same location, near the Battle of Arnhem, the novel illuminates how some things have changed in the intervening years, while others have remained constant.

Through his experiences, the younger Jason Todd learns that his grandfather's wartime romance has given him not only a Dutch grandmother but also a new cousin, Daan. Jacob, like his namesake before him, has fallen in love with a young Dutch woman. As Hille does not want an absent boyfriend, Jacob decides to study Dutch and go to university in the Netherlands, acting on Alma's advice to never give up. At least he and Hille live in peace, unlike his grandfather and Geertrui.

The novel leaves open the question of whether Jacob will tell his grandmother of her late husband's wartime romance, potentially breaking her heart. His closeness to her is symbolized by the weekly postcards she sends to him, even when he lives with her. The theme of becoming an adult by learning to make hard choices is exemplified by this unresolved moral dilemma.

R. C. Lutz, PhD

Further Reading

Rev. of *Postcards from No Man's Land*, by Aidan Chambers. *Kirkus Reviews* 15 Apr. 2002: 564. *Literary Reference Center*. Web. 20 May 2015. <http://search.ebscohost.com/login.aspx?direct=true&db=lfh&AN=6578107&site=ehost-live>.

Rev. of *Postcards from No Man's Land*, by Aidan Chambers. *Publishers Weekly* 29 Apr. 2002: 72. *Literary Reference Center*. Web. 20 May 2015. <http://search.ebscohost.com/login.aspx?direct=true&db=lfh&AN=6596911&site=ehost-live>.

Princess Diaries (Series)

Author: Meg Cabot (b. 1967)
First published: *The Princess Diaries, Vol. I* (2000)
The Princess Diaries, Vol. II: Princess in the Spotlight (2001)
The Princess Diaries, Vol. III: Princess in Love (2002)
The Princess Diaries, Vol. IV: Princess in Waiting (2003)
The Princess Diaries, Vol. IV and a Half: Project Princess (2003)
Princess Lessons: A Princess Diaries Book (2003)
The Princess Diaries, Vol. V: Princess in Pink (2004)

Perfect Princess: A Princess Diaries Book (2004)
The Princess Diaries, Vol. VI: Princess in Training (2005)
Holiday Princess: A Princess Diaries Book (2005)
The Princess Diaries, Vol. VI and a Half: The Princess Present (2004)
The Princess Diaries, Vol. VII: Party Princess (2006)
The Princess Diaries, Vol. VII and a Half: Sweet Sixteen Princess (2006)
Valentine Princess: A Princess Diaries Book (2006)
The Princess Diaries, Vol. VIII: Princess on the Brink (2006)
The Princess Diaries, Vol. IX: Princess Mia (2007)
The Princess Diaries, Vol. X: Forever Princess (2009)
Ransom My Heart, by Mia Thermopolis (2009)
The Princess Diaries, Vol. XI: Royal Wedding (2015)
Type of work: Novel
Type of plot: Humorous Romance
Time of plot: 2000s-2010s
Locales: Manhattan; Genovia (a fictional European country situated between France and Italy)

Principal Characters

Princess Amelia "Mia" Mignonette Grimaldi Thermopolis Renaldo: the series' heroine, Mia is a Manhattan high school student and the crown princess of the fictional European country of Genovia

Lilly Moscovitz: Mia's best friend and the fiercely smart and social-justice minded daughter of psychoanalysts, in the early volumes of the series Lilly is also the host of a public access cable television show called "Lilly Tells it Like it Is"

Michael Moscovitz: Lilly's older brother and Mia's longtime crush and eventual boyfriend, Michael is highly intelligent and talented and once authored a webzine called Crackhead

Dowager Princess Clarisse Renaldo (aka "Grandmère"): Mia's paternal grandmother, Grandmère has put herself in charge of training Mia in the art of royal comportment

The Story

In the first installment of Meg Cabot's Princess Diaries series, *The Princess Diaries*, fourteen-year-old Mia Thermopolis makes two shocking discoveries. The first is only locally awkward and embarrassing: her mother is dating her algebra teacher, Mr. Gianini. The second has international repercussions: Mia's father reveals that he is not merely a European politician as he has led Mia to believe; he is the prince of Genovia, a European principality situated between Italy and France, and Mia, his only heir, is the country's crown princess. Though her father tries to convince Mia that she must move from Manhattan, where she lives with her mother, to Genovia to assume her royal duties, he and Mia finally agree that she can remain in New York and finish high school. Though she attempts to keep her princess status a secret, an article in the newspaper reveals the truth, forcing Mia to employ a bodyguard and introducing conflict between her and her best friend.

While *The Princess Diaries* focuses mainly on Mia's discovery of her royal bloodline, the sequels feature Mia's attempts to maintain a "normal life" in spite of her royal status. In *Princess in the Spotlight*, Mia announces to the world during a televised interview that her mother and Mr. Gianini are expecting a child, leading Mia's Grandmère to begin planning an elaborate society wedding neither Mia nor her mother consider their style. *Princess in Love* finds Mia in a half-hearted romantic relationship with a classmate and pining for Michael Moscovitz, her best friend Lilly's older brother. Though this third volume in the series concludes with Mia and Michael sharing their first kiss, the romantic relationship born of this kiss is tested throughout the remainder of the series when Michael goes to college and, eventually, abroad, and Mia must balance her royal duties against her studies and social life.

The Princess Diaries and its sequels are told from the first person perspective of Mia, in the form of her journal or diary. While the novels primarily feature Mia's musings and immediate internal responses to the events in her life, they also include shopping and "to do" lists, descriptions of homework assignments and attempts at solving algebra problems. Mia writes of "self-actualization" as a consistent goal in her diaries, and the "princess lessons" she must endure with her cigarette-smoking and sidecar-drinking Grandmère challenge her progress towards this goal. As Grandmère works to shape Mia into a fashionable member of the royal class, Mia makes clumsy but good-hearted attempts to advance the social justice causes she holds close to her heart on a local and international scale.

The Princess Diaries series follows Mia through her senior year of high school, when she completes and publishes a bodice-ripping romance (*Ransom My Heart*) as her senior project, attends the prom, and consummates

her relationship with Michael, with whom she has, after numerous challenges, recently reunited.

Six years after the publication of final young adult installment of the series (*Forever Princess*), Meg Cabot published an adult novel that offers an extended conclusion to the series: *The Princess Diaries Vol. XI: Royal Wedding*. Featuring a 26-year-old Mia, *Royal Wedding* describes Mia's and Michael's attempts to plan their wedding around Mia's royal and professional obligations. When asked about what motivated her to write the adult novel, Cabot told *Cosmopolitan* magazine: "When I started the series, I really only intended it to go until she graduated from high school, and I had no ideas after that. And then I kept hearing from readers who were like, 'Keep it going!'" (Thompson).

Critical Evaluation

The Princess Diaries series falls firmly within what Christine Meloni, writing for *School Media Connection*, calls the "humorous chick lit" genre. Unlike the more sophisticated and cynical "privileged" chick lit (examples of which include the Gossip Girl and Clique series), humorous chick lit "features real girls teens can relate to. The characters are flat-chested (or too curvy), struggle to fit in at school, and are embarrassed by their families" (Meloni 16). Mia, who laments her 5'9" height and flat chest and who finds her mother's relationship with her algebra teacher incredibly embarrassing, fits well within Meloni's model. Meloni continues: "These amusing, light-hearted books also tell the story of first romance, including all the embarrassing details. In some of these novels, the typical girl-next-door is thrust into the spotlight" (16). Here, again, Princess Diaries fits the bill, as the novels depict Mia struggling with her romantic decisions, especially after she is "thrust into the spotlight" as the princess of Genovia.

The Princess Diaries series has been both lauded and criticized as an example of young adult chick lit. Reviews of individual installments of the series have praised Cabot's "fine grasp of teen dialect" (Sherman) and "Mia's bubbly, chatty voice" (Stewart). Mia's first person narrative, which has been compared to Helen Fielding's classic adult chick lit novel, *Bridget Jones' Diary* (Penguin, 2001), very much reflects the confessional and humorously self-deprecating style associated with chick lit. That Mia's narrative is also peppered with popular culture references, including brand names and references to contemporary movies and stars, is a source of criticism, particularly among those who would argue that such brand name-dropping encourages overly emphasizes consumption.

Critic Patty Campbell characterizes chick lit as "dramas of social class" (489) and The Princess Diaries series plays up the social and political elements of this "drama" to effect. Dierdre Baker points out the "high level of political awareness and concern for social justice that is consistently, and humorously, evident in the teenaged cast," and argues that "Cabot both parodies and champions this liberal bent ... making sure that her readers, while succumbing to the seduction of royalty, also revel in the fantasy of a democratic, equitable society" (682). Cabot's novels underscore the tension between Mia's recognition of the status her unearned royal privilege has afforded her and her genuine desire to affect social change. By casting Grandmère as Mia's foil and describing Mia's "princess lessons" as comically torturous, rather than as wish-fulfilling makeover fantasies, Cabot ensures that readers learn that the real work of rule happens on the ground and not in the dressing room.

Amy Pattee

Bibliography

Baker, Dierdre F. "Airheads." *Horn Book Magazine* 80.6 (Nov./Dec. 2004): 681 – 692.

Cabot, Meg. "The Princess Diaries Vol. 1." *Meg Cabot.* Meggin Cabot, n.d. Web. 28 February 2016.

Campbell, Patty. "The Lit of Chick Lit." *Horn Book Magazine* 82.4 (July/August 2006): 487 – 491.

"Interview with Meg Cabot." *Scholastic Book Club Kids.* Scholastic Ltd., n.d. Web. 28 February 2016.

"Meg Cabot." Contemporary Authors Online. Detroit: Gale, 2010. *Literature Resource Center.* Web. 27 February 2016.

Meloni, Christine. "Teen Chick Lit." *School Media Connection* 25.2 (October 2006): 16 – 19.

Sherman, Chris. Rev. of *The Princess Diaries. Booklist* 97.2 (15 September 2000): 233.

Stewart, Debbie. Rev. of *The Princess Diaries. School Library Journal* 46.10 (October 2000): 155.

Thompson, Eliza. "The New 'Princess Diaries" Book May or May Not Include Sex in the Throne Room." *Cosmopolitan.* Hearst Communications, Inc., 13 May 2015. Web. 28 February 2016.

Further Reading

Cabot, Meg. *Meg Cabot.* Meggin Cabot, n.d. Web. 27 February 2016. <http://www.megcabot.com/>

Cabot, Meg. The Princess Diaries. Meggin Cabot, n.d. Web. 27 February 2016. <http://www.megcabot.com/princessdiaries/>

Thermopolis, Mia (Meg Cabot). *Princess of Genovia Mia Thermopolis.* Meggin Cabot, n.d. Web. 27 February 2016. <http://www.miathermopolis.com/>

Punkzilla

Author: Adam Rapp (b. 1968)
First published: 2009
Type of work: Novel
Type of plot: Epistolary Literature
Time of plot: 2007–8
Locale: Portland, Oregon; Memphis, Tennessee; various locations in between

Principal characters

Jamie, also known as Punkzilla, a runaway teen
Peter, also known as P, Jamie's older brother
The Major, Jamie's strict father
Branson, Jamie's best friend
Lewis, a friendly stranger
Jorge, his brother's boyfriend

The Story

Jamie, who goes by the nickname Punkzilla, writes his brother Peter, whom he addresses as P, from a Greyhound bus, saying that he is jittery from having done methamphetamine the night before. He has been living in Portland, Oregon, and stealing iPods for a man named Fat Larkin to make money. As he tells his brother about the schemes he pulls with his best friend, Branson, he occasionally references their strict, conservative father, whom they call the Major.

In an earlier letter, Peter told Jamie about life with his boyfriend, Jorge, and his mildly successful career as a performer and actor. He also revealed that he has cancer and is likely to die soon. Along with the letter, Peter sent enough money for Jamie to buy a Greyhound ticket to visit him in Memphis, Tennessee, which is what Jamie is doing.

While on the bus, Jamie continues to write to Peter in a notebook he carries with him, narrating both his past experiences and the events of his ongoing journey. He never sends the letters, hoping to give them to Peter in person instead. Jamie describes his life at Buckner Military Academy in Missouri, where the Major sent him after he got into trouble the previous summer. He was miserable at Buckner and kept getting demerits and failing tests. Eventually he ran away in the middle of the night and hitchhiked to Portland. He met some kind people while hitchhiking, although he also met a man who wanted to use him for sex. Jamie tells Peter about meeting Branson at Washington House, a home for street youth in Portland. Like a lot of other people, Branson assumed that Jamie was a girl at first.

At a rest stop in Idaho, Jamie is mugged and left unconscious, and his bus leaves him behind. He meets a boy named Sam, who also mistakes him for a girl, and Sam's mother offers to host Jamie for a couple of days. On the way to their house, however, Jamie steals Sam's backpack and runs away. After hitchhiking some more, he meets a man named Lewis, who reveals to Jamie that he is transgender and has just spent all his money on surgery to have his breasts removed. Lewis feeds and shelters Jamie, after which Jamie starts heading east again, hitchhiking once more. He runs into a man who offers to pay him one hundred dollars to model for photographs. Although Jamie is worried that the man will harm him, he decides that the money is worth the risk.

Next, Jamie is picked up by a friendly man named Kent, who drives him across several states, paying for hotel rooms and even buying him a haircut. Jamie is skeptical at first, but Kent seems to be nonjudgmental, and they soon feel like friends, especially when Kent lets Jamie drive the car. They stop to meet Kent's ex-wife, with whom Jamie gets in a fight, and later meet his daughter, with whom Jamie loses his virginity. The next day, however, Kent leaves before Jamie wakes up. Abandoned, he gets on another Greyhound bus.

By the time Jamie arrives in Memphis, Peter is comatose and under hospice care. Jamie sits beside him and reads all the letters he has written. Peter dies soon after. At the funeral, Jamie hides behind some trees so his family will not take him back. Afterward, Jorge offers to let him stay with him. In the book's final letter, Jamie tells Peter that he is excited to stay with Jorge for a while and that he will continue to write to his brother, even though he is gone.

Critical Evaluation

As an epistolary novel, *Punkzilla* alternates among the voices and narrative styles of its main characters. The majority, of course, is taken up by the informal, stream-of-consciousness writing of its protagonist, a character whose forceful personality makes up for his lack of skills in grammar and narrative construction.

Jamie's time as a teenage runaway sees him delving deeply into the gritty realities of urban and rural poverty—from the theft and drug abuse that were common during his time in Portland to the sexual exploitation and the mugging that he encounters while hitchhiking across the country. The narrative voice that Rapp develops for Jamie reflects these realities; Jamie constantly spells words incorrectly, constructs run-on sentences, drops off subjects abruptly, and fails to adequately explain basic details such as setting and character. However, these qualities are also what allow him to confront the realities of his journey head-on in his letters. When describing the moment when an older man coerces him into receiving oral sex, for instance, he slips into a run-on sentence that continues for almost an entire paragraph, including such lines as "I was feeling mad disgusted and I kept looking at myself in the motel room mirror and sort of hating what I was seeing like my eyes and my mouth and the way my nose sort of turns up a little at the end like a f——g rabbit . . ." (67). The scene is unpleasant and complicated, and Jamie's understanding of what has happened is likewise jumbled, his emotions fast moving rather than clearly formed. The run-on sentence captures this energy, allowing the experience the stand as it is rather than forcing it to be something cleaner or more logical, as a standard narrative and grammar might entail.

This writing style is reminiscent of many other stream-of-consciousness narratives, including Jack Kerouac's classic beat novel *On the Road* (1957), which also heavily features hitchhiking and drug use. By applying these literary tools to the very contemporary cast of characters, Rapp has crafted a unique protagonist in Jamie: standoffish yet compassionate, lost yet purposeful, and able to supply the consistent insights and surprising humor that turn an often-bleak narrative into a story of hope, uncensored and raw as it is.

T. Fleischmann, MFA

Further Reading

Ng, David. "Cutting Loose with Adam Rapp." *American Theatre* Oct. 2007: 38–41. *Literary Reference Center*. Web. 6 Mar. 2015. <http://search.ebscohost.com/login.aspx?direct=true&db=lfh&AN=26902225&site=lrc-live>.

Rapp, Adam. Interview by Marsha Norman. *Bomb Magazine*. New Art, Spring 2006. Web. 6 Mar. 2015. <http://bombmagazine.org/article/2819/adam-rapp>.

Rose Under Fire

Author: Elizabeth Wein (b. 1964)
First published: 2013
Type of work: Novel
Type of plot: Historical Fiction
Time of plot: 1944–46
Locale: Ravensbrück, Germany

Principal characters

Rose Justice, an American civilian pilot and concentration-camp prisoner
Róża Czajkowska, a Polish prisoner
Irina Korsakova, a Russian pilot and prisoner
Lisette Romilly, a French prisoner
Karolina Salska, a Polish prisoner
Anna Engel, a German prisoner
Maddie Beaufort-Stuart, a British civilian pilot

The Story

Divided into sections titled "Southampton," "Ravensbrück," and "Nuremberg," *Rose Under Fire* is the story of a young American woman working as a civilian ferry pilot for Britain's Air Transport Auxiliary (ATA) during World War II. Rose Justice is particularly excited when her uncle arranges an assignment to fly to Paris, which has just been liberated from Nazi occupation. While ferrying a Spitfire plane back to England, however, Rose vanishes, and her friends and family exchange letters lamenting her disappearance. Even though they have little hope that Rose has survived, they leave money and temporary papers for her at the American embassy in Paris.

The section titled Ravensbrück begins in April 1945 as Rose arrives back in Paris after six months as a prisoner in the Ravensbrück concentration camp. Rose is devastated at having lost track of two fellow prisoners, Róża and Irina. To distract herself, she writes down her account of events, beginning with her last ferry flight. While returning to England in September 1944, Rose encountered a pilotless plane, or "doodlebug" as the self-flying German bombs were called. Having heard combat pilots discuss the maneuver, Rose chases down the bomb and tips it so it falls harmlessly out of the sky, but in doing so flies significantly off course. Detected by German pilots, she is forced to land near Mannheim, Germany, and is ultimately sent to Ravensbrück.

Assigned to factory work, Rose refuses to continue when she realizes she is making fuses for doodlebugs. She is sentenced to savage lashings, and she later wakes up in a new cell block with Russian and Polish prisoners, including a Polish Rabbit named Róża. Róża promises Rose bread and protection if Rose will teach her the poems she recited while she was delirious after the beating. Rose is quickly accepted by Lisette, who is referred to as the camp mother to the Rabbits. They are named this because they have been subjected to disfiguring medical experiments by Nazi doctors. Because the Rabbits have already been officially sentenced to death, they have no expectations of survival, but they want the world to know what has happened to them.

As the Germans realize that defeat is inevitable, they begin executing the prisoners more quickly; Rose is forced to help build a gas chamber and move dead bodies. The Rabbits are particularly targeted because they constitute evidence of Nazi war crimes, but Lisette and a German prisoner named Anna Engel work to hide the Rabbits when they are selected for execution. Rose, Róża, and a Russian pilot named Irina manage to escape when they realize there is an unguarded plane outside the hangar that they have been locked in temporarily. Later when they are being transported out of Germany by a Red Cross convoy, Rose loses track of Irina and Róża.

In the section titled Nuremburg, Rose has been living in Scotland for eighteen months after her escape from Germany. Unable to bring herself to testify, Rose is ashamed because she has not told the Rabbits' story as she promised, but she decides to attend the tribunal as a journalist. There, Rose reconnects with Róża, which gives her the courage to finally tell the story. She does this in the form of an extended article that intersperses flying metaphors with factual information. Rose learns that in spite of Róża's bravado, her friend is struggling to find a place for herself in postwar Europe, so Rose decides to take Róża back to Scotland with her where they can continue to tell their story together.

Critical Evaluation

Although technically a sequel to Elizabeth Wein's award-winning novel *Code Name Verity* (2012), *Rose*

Under Fire can also be read as a stand-alone book. Carefully researched, this novel draws attention to the fact that German concentration camps housed not only Jewish prisoners but also political and criminal prisoners of many nationalities. In many cases, these individuals banded together to try and make the constant fear and miserable conditions more bearable. In the book's afterword, Wein draws attention to the seventy-four real-life Polish women who were experimented on in Ravensbrück; their names, included in the story as a mnemonic rhyme composed by Rose, also appear on the novel's endpapers as a tribute. In addition, Wein highlights the contribution made by female pilots of many nationalities during World War II, many of whom risked their lives on a daily basis.

As in *Code Name Verity*, Wein emphasizes the power of storytelling in terms of recording history and surviving adversity. Even at a time and under conditions in which paper was scarce, her characters find places and ways to write things down. Rose in particular uses poetry, including excerpts from work by Edna St. Vincent Millay, to both escape from and relate to the horrors she had heard about before her imprisonment but did not actually believe could be true. Knowing that she likely would have died without the protection of Lisette and the Rabbits, Rose believes that poetry saved her life, because that is what led Róża to befriend her.

Amy Sisson, MS, MLS

Further Information

"Rose Under Fire." *Publishers Weekly* 15 July 2013: 1. *Literary Reference Center*. Web. 8 June 2015. <http://search.ebscohost.com/login.aspx?direct=true&db=lfh&AN=89060806&site=lrc-live>.

Wein, Elizabeth. Interview by Deirdre F Baker. "An Interview with Elizabeth Wein." *Horn Book* 90.3 (2014): 23–29. *Literary Reference Center*. Web. 8 June 2015. <http://search.ebscohost.com/login.aspx?direct=true&db=lfh&AN=95651370&site=lrc-live>.

Wein, Elizabeth. Interview by Julie Bartel. "One Thing Leads to Another: An Interview with Elizabeth Wein." *YALSA*. American Library Association, 3 Oct. 2013. Web. 26 June 2015. <http://www.yalsa.ala.org/the-hub/2013/10/03/one-thing-leads-to-another-an-interview-with-elizabeth-wein/>.

The Scorpio Races

Author: Maggie Stiefvater (b. 1982)
First published: 2011
Type of work: Novel
Type of plot: Fantasy
Time of plot: Present or near past
Locale: Island of Thisby

Principal characters

Kate "Puck" Connolly, an orphan who loves horses
Sean Kendrick, an orphan and local water horse–riding champion
Benjamin Malvern, a wealthy stable-owner and Sean Kendrick's boss
Matthew "Mutt" Malvern, Benjamin's conniving and deadly only son

The Story

Sean Kendrick's father died in the Scorpio Races when Sean was only ten years old. The Scorpio Races are an ancient tradition on Thisby, a fictional island on the Scorpio Sea. Thisby is the only island in the world where the water horses known as *capaill uisce* crawl from the depths of the sea every October to hunt on land. Though capaill uisce look like enormous horses, but they are far deadlier: they eat meat and have haunting, serpentine eyes. While capaill uisce can be ridden, they can hardly be tamed; the ocean calls them to return to it every moment they are on the land. This is what makes the annual Scorpio Races so dangerous. Each November, tourists flock to Thisby to watch the men of the island race the capaill uisce along the shore, and each year, at least one man dies trying to reach the finish line. This is what happened to Sean's father. He was pulled from his water horse by another and trampled to death in the sand. In some respects, he was lucky. Some capaill uisce eat their riders. Only Sean, now a teenager, truly understands the dangerous beauty of the creatures, which is why he is a highly sought-after trainer on the small island and a Scorpio Race champion, with his red stallion, Corr, for four years running.

Puck Connolly's relationship to the water horses is characterized by fear. Her parents were both killed by capaill uisce while at sea, leaving Puck, her older brother, Gabe, and her younger brother, Finn, to fend for themselves. Puck is fierce and resourceful—and a stellar hand on her mare, Dove—but she and her brothers live in grinding poverty. When Gabe announces that he must go to the mainland to find work, Puck is horrified. She is so shaken that she says something rash: if he is going to leave, she is going to enter the Scorpio Races. Gabe agrees to stay until the race is over, though he does not believe she will really go through with it. No woman has ever ridden in the races. Puck hardly believes herself until the wealthy Benjamin Malvern, the island's villain and Sean Kendrick's slave-driving employer, informs her that she must come up with enough money to save her parents' house or he will evict her. Puck realizes that not only must she enter the race now, but she must win to save the house.

Sean Kendrick, champion though he is, is facing a similar situation. He has worked for the ungrateful Malvern for years and put up with Malvern's horrible son, Mutt, who torments Sean at every opportunity. This year he makes a deal: if he wins, he will buy his beloved water horse, Corr, and break out on his own. As the race day nears, Sean is drawn to the audacious Puck, who is constantly harassed by the men of the town who believe that her gender and her horse (who is not a water horse) will besmirch the tradition of the Scorpio Races. The two begin to train together, and soon, Sean discovers Puck and Dove to be formidable opponents. Their growing love for one another is informed by their mutual respect. Together they devise a racing strategy, though each one hopes to be the sole winner. Meanwhile, Sean must contend with Mutt. Mutt, jealous that his father takes more pride in Sean than himself, slashes the hamstrings of his own water horse, Edana, before the race, mistaking it for Corr. Then, during the race, Mutt tries to set his new water horse, Skata, on Dove to kill Puck. Sean comes between them but is thrown when Mutt slashes his own water horse's throat in an attempt to kill Sean along with himself. Thanks to Corr's unshakeable loyalty, Sean survives the fall, and thanks to Dove's imperviousness to the siren song of the ocean, Puck wins the race. But Corr has suffered a broken leg in shielding Sean from the stampede; she will never race again. With her winnings, Puck buys her house, and with the earnings of her little brother's gamble (he bet on her with forty-five-to odds) she buys Corr for Sean. Sean tries to send Corr back to the sea, but instead of diving into the ocean, she walks right back to him.

Critical Evaluation

Maggie Stiefvater is best known as the author of the Werewolves of Mercy Falls series, a modern-day take on the werewolf myth. While *The Scorpio Races*, a

standalone novel, is not a part of that series, it was born of a similar seed. Stiefvater drew inspiration for her capaill uisce from Celtic myths in which dangerous horse-like creatures come out of the sea to lure maidens into the waves and eat them. The novel, which is set in the present day, explores the ancient connection between humans and animals, the sacredness of ritual (Puck and her brothers are Catholic, though the pagan practices of the island are given equal weight), and the complications that can arise from a true partnership. Puck and Sean are equals, but as the race dictates, only one can win.

The Scorpio Races was published to overwhelmingly positive reviews in 2011 and was named a Michael L. Printz Honor Book in 2012. The book was praised for its depictions of both the fictional capaill uisce and life in a small town island, populated with nosy neighbors, mother figures fretful for Puck's safety, and backward-looking men. *The Scorpio Races* has its own mythology and history. From the Malvern stables, made long ago from carved stones and stained with ancient blood, to the cave paintings of humans with horses' heads, Stiefvater's fictional Celtic people, Jennifer Hubert Swan wrote for the *New York Times*, feel "entirely real."

Molly Hagan

Further Reading

Rev. of *The Scorpio Races*, by Maggie Stiefvater. *Kirkus*. Kirkus, 17 Aug. 2011. Web. 19 Nov. 2015. <https://www.kirkusreviews.com/book-reviews/maggie-stiefvater/scorpio-races>.

Swan, Jennifer Hubert. "The Ride of Their Lives." Rev. of *The Scorpio Races*, by Maggie Stiefvater. *New York Times*. New York Times, 10 Nov. 2011. Web. 19 Nov. 2015. <http://www.nytimes.com/2011/11/13/books/review/the-scorpio-races-by-maggie-stiefvater-book-review.html>.

Ship Breaker

Author: Paolo Bacigalupi (b. 1972)
First published: 2010
Type of work: Novel
Type of plot: Dystopian Fiction
Time of plot: Near Future
Locale: American Gulf Coast region

Courtesy of Little, Brown Books for Young Readers

Principal characters

Nailer Lopez, a poor adolescent boy who works as a ship breaker

Nita "Lucky Girl" Chaudhury, a wealthy girl whom Nailer rescues

Richard Lopez, Nailer's abusive father

Tool, a genetically engineered half man

Pima, Nailer's best friend and head of his crew

Sadna, Pima's mother

The Story

As *Ship Breaker* (2010) opens, Nailer Lopez is crawling through a service duct, scavenging valuable copper wire from one of many abandoned ocean tankers that litter what is left of the Gulf Coast region. Nailer is fortunate that he is still physically small, but his future is uncertain because he will inevitably outgrow his usefulness as a light crew "ship breaker." Nailer is accustomed to surviving day to day, however, due to his dangerous work environment and his unstable, poverty-stricken life with his alcoholic and drug-addicted father.

When a category 6 hurricane—no longer an uncommon occurrence—races through Nailer's beach slum

community, he has the opportunity to let his abusive father die, but he saves him out of a sense of familial obligation. After the storm, Nailer and Pima, his best friend and light crew boss, scavenge the beaches and stumble upon a half-sunken clipper ship. Awed by the vessel's luxury, Nailer and Pima are strategizing about how to keep this "lucky strike" for themselves when they find Nita, the wreck's lone survivor and daughter of an unimaginably wealthy shipping magnate. Pima advocates killing Nita for her jewelry and the ship's salvage rights. Nailer, however, decides to help Nita, whom he nicknames "Lucky Girl," in the hope of earning a reward. Unfortunately, Nailer's father, Richard, discovers the wreck and decides to ransom Nita. When her people do not come looking for her, Richard grows impatient and threatens to sell her to organ harvesters. Desperate, Nailer and Nita manage to escape. Accompanied by a genetically engineered half man named Tool, they stow away on a train heading inland past the remains of New Orleans and Orleans II, which are now mostly submerged under the risen sea levels.

Once the trio arrives in the latest incarnation of Orleans, they scrounge what daily work they can while squatting with other homeless people and trying to locate a ship from Nita's father's fleet. Because Nita's clipper sank while being pursued by a traitorous faction within the family's company, Nita is unsure which ship captains she can trust. The situation worsens when Nailer's father tracks the trio down, captures Nita, and delivers her to one of her father's enemies. Once again, Nailer must decide whether to risk his life trying to help the "swank" whom he barely knows; her grim determination to survive and her willingness to work alongside Nailer have affected him. Tool decides to go his own way, but Nailer joins forces with a clipper captain loyal to Nita's father. Although Nailer feels out of place among the educated and comparatively wealthy sailors, he proves his worth by guiding the ship safely through the Teeth (submerged buildings from the drowned cities). As planned, the larger enemy ship pursuing them is skewered on the Teeth and begins to sink, allowing Nailer's crew to board and search for Nita. Nailer goes below deck and finds his bound and gagged friend, unfortunately guarded by Nailer's own father, who now intends to kill Nailer as revenge for his "betrayal." Nailer manages to trick his father into chasing him through the ship's internal engine room and turns on the machinery so that his father is mangled by it. Once this personal fight and the larger battle between the two ships are over, Nita is finally able to contact her family. Nailer now has the means to escape the brutal ship-breaking life, taking Pima and her mother, Sadna, away from it as well.

Critical Evaluation

Widely praised as an environmental action thriller with broad appeal for young adult readers, *Ship Breaker* won the 2011 Michael L. Printz Award and was also a 2010 National Book Award finalist. The book particularly excels in its world-building, which depicts an environmentally devastated Gulf Coast region divided sharply into haves and have-nots. The author does not explicitly reveal all the details of how this future has come about, but instead weaves subtle details into the narrative, particularly as they relate to the ship-breaking community in which Nailer and Pima live.

The book also thoughtfully examines the meaning of family and the nature of loyalty. Early in the story, Nailer finds himself stuck and in danger of drowning in a tanker hold full of oil. Even though every member of his light crew has sworn a blood oath of loyalty, one of his crewmates leaves him for dead, wanting to claim the lucky oil strike for herself. In spite of this betrayal, Nailer still believes in abiding by his oaths. Once he and Pima agree to help Nita, they swear an oath with her, in part to remove the temptation to exploit her for her wealth, which would allow them to escape the miserable conditions of their lives.

Similarly, Nailer has wildly conflicted feelings about his father, who invokes their family connection when he needs help from Nailer but sees nothing wrong with beating his son while drunk. Nailer reflects that Pima's mother, Sadna, has always been more of a parent to him than his own father and concludes that behavior rather than genetics creates a true family. The character of Tool provides yet another perspective on the concept of loyalty; as a half man, he is supposed to be irrevocably bonded to a single human master, but he makes his own choices, helping Sadna, Nailer, and Nita. Tool also appears in *The Drowned Cities* (2012), a novel set in the same world as *Ship Breaker*.

Amy Sisson, MS, MLS

Further Reading

Bacigalupi, Paolo. "The *Booklist* Printz Interview: Paolo Bacigalupi." Interview by Gillian Engberg. *Booklist* 15 Feb. 2011: 71. *Literary Reference Center.* Web. 8 June 2015. <http://search.ebscohost.com/log-in.aspx?direct=true&db=lfh&AN=58784250&site=1 rc-live>.

Bacigalupi, Paolo. "Q&A with Paolo Bacigalupi." Interview by Carolyn Juris. *Publishers Weekly.* PWxyz, 26 Apr. 2012. Web. 8 June 2015. <http://www.publishersweekly.com/pw/by-topic/authors/interviews/article/51699-q-a-with-paolo-bacigalupi.html>.

Rev. of *Ship Breaker*, by Paolo Bacigalupi. *Publishers Weekly* 19 Apr. 2010: 54. *Literary Reference Center.* Web. 8 June 2015. <http://search.ebscohost.com/login.aspx?direct=true&db=lfh&AN=49786131&site=lrc-live>.

The Sin-Eater's Confession

Author: Ilsa J. Bick
First published: 2013
Type of work: Novel
Type of plot: Bildungsroman; Psychological Fiction
Time of plot: 2010s
Locale: Merit, Wisconsin

Principal Characters

Ben, a Navy medic who witnessed a murder while still in high school

Jimmy Lange, the fifteen-year-old victim, Ben's friend

Harlan Lange, Jimmy's father

Angela Thorne, an FBI agent investigating Jimmy's murder

Brooke, Ben's friend

The Story

Ben is serving as a Navy medic in Afghanistan and is about to volunteer for a dangerous mission, but is still consumed with guilt and fear over a terrible crime that he witnessed a few years before. Over the span of about twenty-two hours, Ben writes down his memories of the events in order to work out his feelings and confess that he hid his knowledge of the crime, out of fear of being accused himself.

Ben begins his story during fall of his senior year, when he is busy maintaining his grades, working at the local hospital, and perfecting his application to Yale University, where his mother desperately wants him to go. When a classmate is killed in a car accident, Ben begins helping the boy's family, the Langes, on their dairy farm. It soon becomes apparent that Jimmy, the deceased boy's younger brother, is becoming dependent upon Ben for friendship and advice, particularly because Mr. Lange does not approve of Jimmy's ambition to become a photographer. Ben's life is thrown into turmoil when Jimmy wins second place in a national photography contest by entering sensual photos of Ben and Mr. Lange, taken without their knowledge.

Before long, rumors begin circulating that Jimmy is homosexual, and Mr. Lange angrily tells Ben to stay away from his son. Ben realizes that he too is suspected of being gay, and although he tries to distance himself from Jimmy, he cannot refuse when Jimmy asks to meet with him. Since Mr. Lange is closely monitoring Jimmy's actions, Jimmy asks Ben to mail an application for a photography scholarship on his behalf. When Ben arrives for their rendezvous, still unsure whether he should help Jimmy, he sees Jimmy kissing someone wearing a black hoodie and then getting into a car. Wondering whether Jimmy is in danger, Ben follows the car to a remote location and witnesses Jimmy being savagely attacked by two additional people with a stone and a hatchet. Ben panics and runs but cannot bring himself to call the police, because he realizes it could appear as though he had deliberately lured Jimmy to his death.

Overcome with paranoia, Ben takes extraordinary steps to cover up his presence at the crime scene, even going back to Jimmy's body to remove an envelope addressed to Ben as well as the memory card in Jimmy's cell phone. Ben also rekindles his friendship with a girl named Brooke, in order to give the appearance of normalcy. The situation worsens, however, when Special Agent Angela Thorne from the FBI is called in because the murder appears to be a hate crime and begins interviewing students who knew Jimmy.

Ben muddles through the next several months, wondering all the while whether Agent Thorne will reappear to arrest him. He also continues wracking his brain, trying to determine whether the person he saw kissing Jimmy was a girl or a boy and whether he might be able to identify that person. He finally confronts a young girl whose family plays live music at the Christian coffeehouse where Jimmy had worked and confronts the girl's father for killing Jimmy. The man denies it while insinuating Ben's guilt in not stopping the attack or reporting it if he indeed witnessed it, and Ben begins to seriously doubt not only his memory but his sanity.

Ultimately, nothing is resolved. Ben finds he cannot go back to a normal, unquestioning life and tells his parents that he has been rejected by Yale when he actually was accepted. He joins the Navy, but after months of witnessing violence and death in Afghanistan, he writes down his story and debates whether to send it to either Brooke or Agent Thorne.

Critical Evaluation

As in her other young adult novels, Bick tackles complex and difficult themes in this work, including guilt, fear, societal expectations, and the unreliability of memory. The main theme of guilt is reflected in the novel's title; in researching anonymous confessions online, Ben learns about sin-eaters, who in old times would sit next to dying or dead people and eat bread they had touched in order to absorb their sins. Ben finds it ironic that sin-eaters were then shunned as unclean, when in fact they were performing a selfless act. He realizes that to send his confession to Brooke would be to burden her, but he also hopes it will help her learn to choose her own path, rather than let adults choose it for her.

In addition, Bick addresses the expectations teenagers face from society, their parents, and even themselves. Before Jimmy's murder, Ben was working so hard that he did not realize he had been letting his mother define his ambitions to attend Yale and eventually become a doctor. Once Jimmy's photographs are published, Ben realizes that everyone in his rural Wisconsin hometown assumes that a sensual photo of a male taken by another male must be indicative of a homosexual relationship. Ben suddenly becomes aware that because he has been too busy to consider dating, he does not even know whether he is straight or gay, and he no longer trusts his instincts and motivations about anything, let alone his own identity.

Finally, this book portrays the inconclusive nature of life in a way that most novels do not, in that Jimmy's murder remains unresolved and Ben's future is uncertain. He may not survive his upcoming mission, and even if he does, he may face criminal charges for obstruction of justice, depending on whether he mails his confession, to whom he mails it, and what that person does with the information. In that regard, *The Sin-Eater's Confession* bravely acknowledges that real life is often far untidier than most people would like it to be.

Amy Sisson, MS, MLS

Further Reading

Kraus, Daniel. Rev. of *The Sin-Eater's Confession*, by Ilsa Bick. *Booklist* 109.13 (2013): 64. *Literary Reference Center*. Web. 17 Nov. 2015. <http://search.eb-scohost.com/login.aspx?direct=true&db=lfh&AN=8 5826164&site=lrc-live>.

Rev. of *The Sin-Eater's Confession*, by Ilsa Bick. *Kirkus Reviews* 81.1 (2013): 69. *Literary Reference Center*. Web. 17 Nov. 2015. <http://search.ebscohost.com/login.aspx?direct=true&db=lfh&AN=84545110&site=lrc-live>.

The Sisterhood of the Traveling Pants (Series)

Author: Ann Brashares (b. 1967)
First published: *The Sisterhood of the Traveling Pants* (2001)
The Second Summer of the Sisterhood (2003)
Girls in Pants (2005)
Forever in Blue (2007)
Sisterhood Everlasting (2011)
Type of work: Novel
Type of plot: Coming-of-Age
Time of plot: Twenty-first century
Locales: Bethesda, Maryland; Baja California, Mexico; Santorini, Greece; South Carolina; Alabama; Rhode Island; New York; Turkey; Australia

Principal characters

Lena Kaligaris, an artist
Carmen Lowell, an aspiring actor
Tabitha "Tibby" Tomko-Rollins, a budding filmmaker
Bridget "Bee" Vreeland, an athlete

The Story

Ann Brashares's Sisterhood of the Traveling Pants series follows the summer adventures of four teenage girls—Lena Kaligaris, Carmen Lowell, Tabitha "Tibby" Tomko-Rollins, and Bridget "Bee" Vreeland—who have been friends since their pregnant mothers met in an aerobics class and all gave birth daughters in the month of September. Bound together by a pair of jeans that takes on an almost mystical quality, the girls' lives remain entwined each summer, despite the physical distance between each of the four protagonists. The series, which began with the publication of *The Sisterhood of the Traveling Pants* (2001), also includes the books *The Second Summer of the Sisterhood* (2003), *Girls in Pants* (2005), *Forever in Blue* (2007), and *Sisterhood Everlasting* (2011), the last of which is set ten years after the previous installment.

The first book in the series, *The Sisterhood of the Traveling Pants*, begins at the start of the summer before the protagonists' junior year of high school, the first summer in many years that the four girls will not spend together. Lena will be visiting grandparents in Greece; Bridget plans to attend soccer camp in Baja California, Mexico; and Carmen is headed to South Carolina to see her divorced father. Tibby, on the other hand, will remain in their hometown of Bethesda, Maryland. Shortly before they go their separate ways, Carmen purchases a pair of jeans at a thrift store. Each girl tries them on, and the friends find that despite their physical differences, the jeans fit each of them. The girls decided that they will share the jeans—the titular traveling pants—all summer, passing them from friend to friend along with the letters they promise to write.

While on the Greek island of Santorini, Lena, who is staying with her grandparents, meets a young man named Kostos. Kostos, though interested in Lena, begins to avoid her after a misunderstanding causes her grandparents to believe something inappropriate had occurred between Lena and Kostos. His distance hurts Lena, who has fallen in love with him, but by the end of the summer she is finally able to tell him how she feels. Meanwhile, Carmen arrives in South Carolina and learns that her father has gotten engaged without telling her. She feels disconnected from her father's new family, and her emotions cause her to act out. She flees back to Maryland for a time, but eventually returns to South Carolina to reconcile with her father and attend his wedding.

Tibby spends the summer working at the store Wallman's, a job she hates, and begins to make a mocking documentary about her lackluster summer. While working at Wallman's she meets a younger girl named Bailey, whom she befriends. Bailey has leukemia, and her death late in the summer has a profound effect on Tibby. Bridget, meanwhile, attends soccer camp in Mexico, where she meets an attractive young coach named Eric. She succeeds in seducing him but falls into a depression afterward, recovering only with the help of Lena, who travels to Mexico after returning from Greece. The four friends reunite at the end of the summer and share their stories.

In *The Second Summer of the Sisterhood*, Lena and Carmen remain primarily in Maryland, while Tibby attends a summer film program at Williamston College in Virginia, and Bridget travels to Alabama to visit Greta, a grandmother she has not seen in years. At home in Maryland, Lena reunites with the visiting Kostos, but is hurt when he unexpectedly returns to Greece. After the death of her grandfather, Lena attends his funeral on Santorini and learns that Kostos has married a young woman whom he believes he has gotten pregnant. Carmen spends the summer upset that her mother is dating a new man, but her life is sent into further upheaval when her stepsister, Krista, arrives in Bethesda, having run away from home after a fight with her own mother. Carmen eventually comes to terms with her own mother's new relationship and helps reunite Krista with the rest of the family.

While studying film at Williamston College, Tibby befriends several fellow students who are revealed to be somewhat cruel. Although she initially mimics her classmates' cynicism, she eventually decides to make a film about her friendship with Bailey, a friendship more real and loving than any she has made in the program, and the experience helps her process her grief about Bailey's death. In Alabama, Bridget meets her maternal grandmother for the first time in years, showing up at her home unannounced, but decides not to tell her grandmother who she is, and instead dyes her hair brown and uses a fake name and backstory. While helping her grandmother out around the house, she learns more about her family, particularly her mother, who committed suicide when Bridget was a child. Through her time with her grandmother, Bridget finally begins to emerge from the depression that had set in the previous summer.

Girls in Pants is set the summer before the girls' first year of college and continues to follow their separate adventures, although most of the friends remain in Maryland for the summer. Lena deals with family conflict related in part to her Greek grandmother's presence in her parents' home. She takes an art class while preparing to attend art school in the fall, but a disagreement with her father forces Lena to attempt to raise the money to pay for college herself. Both family disputes are resolved by the end of the novel, and Lena prepares to attend art school as planned. Carmen spends much of the summer helping take care of Lena's grandmother as well as dealing with her own mother, who is pregnant. She struggles with her perception of herself and ultimately opens up

not only to her family, but also to her new prospective love interest, a hospital volunteer.

Tibby likewise spends the summer in Maryland, where she struggles with her romantic feelings for her friend Brian, with whom she first became close two summers before. Although she loves Brian, she attempts to put her feeling aside, especially after her younger sister is injured due to what Tibby perceives as her own negligence. She later helps Carmen's mother give birth, an experience that causes her to reevaluate her choices. Meanwhile, Bridget travels to a soccer camp in Pennsylvania, where she works as a coach. There she encounters Eric, an older coach with whom she fell in love two summers prior. Although their encounter two years before was a negative experience for Bridget, the two remain attracted to each other, and they end the summer as a couple.

In *Forever in Blue*, the four friends have completed their first year of college and now embark on a new summer of adventures. Carmen struggled during her freshman year, and she spends the summer attending a theater program with her one college friend, Julia. As Carmen thrives and begins to regain her self-confidence, earning a major role in one of the program's plays, she comes to realize that Julia has been feeding off of her unhappiness. Refusing to allow her supposed friend to bring her down, Carmen ends the friendship. Lena likewise dedicates her summer to artistic pursuits, taking a painting class at her college. She is mutually attracted to a fellow painter named Leo, but their budding relationship is complicated when Kostos arrives in Rhode Island, telling Lena that he has divorced his wife because she lied about being pregnant when they first married. Although they are unable to make a relationship work, both Lena and Kostos hope that they may be able to be together in the future.

Daunted by the idea of spending the summer in Maryland without her friends or Eric, Bridget decides to participate in an archaeological dig in Turkey. Her experience with a professor there prompts her to attempt to grow closer to her father and brother when she returns to the United States. She reunites with Eric, and their relationship is strengthened. Tibby spends the summer in New York City, where she takes a screenwriting class. Following a pregnancy scare, she breaks up with Brian, a decision she regrets when he begins dating Lena's younger sister, Effie. The two reunite late in the summer, which prompts Effie to steal the traveling pants and take them with her to Greece. At the end of the book, the pants are lost in Greece, but the friendships among

Lena, Carmen, Tibby, and Bridget remain as strong as ever.

Sisterhood Everlasting is set ten years after the events of *Forever in Blue*. In the novel, Tibby, who is living in Australia and facing a fatal genetic disease, invites her three friends on a trip to Greece. After her accidental death, her friends process their grief, reconsider their romantic relationships, and rekindle their friendships.

Critical Evaluation

Like many young adult series, the Sisterhood of the Traveling Pants series documents the coming of age of its four young protagonists, focusing in particular on various life changes that many teens and young adults experience. Such life events include being separated from one's core social group for the first time, falling in love, experimenting with sexual activity, experiencing changes to family structures, losing loved ones, dealing with grief, beginning college, and reevaluating oneself in a new environment. As each book focuses on four characters rather than one, the series provides ample opportunities to compare and contrast each individual character's experiences as they mature and discover, through various realistic hardships and challenges, who they truly are. Relationships with friends, relatives, and romantic partners are of great importance to each of the maturing protagonists, but most important of all are the friendships among the four girls, which endure despite their frequent physical separation and their unique individual experiences. The titular traveling pants, which the girls share while they are separated, in many ways are a tangible manifestation of those bonds of friendship.

Each of the four main characters has a journey that is set up in the first novel and continues through the subsequent installments of the series. Lena's journey is marked by her tumultuous relationship with Kostos as well as conflicts between her own desires in life and those of her more traditional family members. Romance is likewise particularly important in Bridget's ongoing story, as she progresses from her initial involvement with Eric, which occurred before she was emotionally prepared, to her later, more mature and emotionally stable relationship with him. For Carmen, the need to feel that she is a member of her family pervades the series; in several of the novels she initially reacts poorly to changes in her family, only to accept those changes as she grows as an individual. Tibby's cynicism, one of her defining characteristics at the beginning of the first novel, is replaced by grief

that continues to affect her decisions throughout the remaining novels.

The ongoing stories told in the series create a strong sense of continuity between the novels and enhance their realism, demonstrating that past events can continue to influence those who experienced them for years after their occurrence. For example, the depression that overtakes Bridget near the end of *The Sisterhood of the Traveling Pants* does not dissipate during the time between that novel and *The Second Summer of the Sisterhood*; instead, much of Bridget's portion of the second novel focuses on her escape from her negative mindset. Similarly, Tibby remains strongly affected by Bailey's death through all of the novels, and in *Sisterhood Everlasting*, it is revealed that she has named her young daughter after her deceased friend. In this way, the later novels in the series are shaped by the events of the earlier installments, mimicking the way in which the lives of young adults are often shaped by their earlier experiences.

Joy Crelin

Further Reading

Brashares, Ann. *Sisterhood Everlasting*. New York: Random, 2011. Print.

Brashares, Ann. *The Sisterhood of the Traveling Pants: Complete Collection*. New York: Delacorte, 2008. Print.

Hill, Craig. *The Critical Merits of Young Adult Literature: Coming of Age*. New York: Routledge, 2014. Print.

Skinny

Author: Donna Cooner (b. 1959)
First published: 2012
Type of work: Novel
Type of plot: Realism
Time of plot: Early 2010s
Locale: Huntsville, Texas

Principal characters

Ever Davies, a severely overweight fifteen-year-old girl with a terrific singing voice
Briella, Ever's fifteen-year-old stepsister
Theodore Simon "Rat" Wilson, Ever's longtime friend and neighbor, a sixteen-year-old computer geek

Jackson Barnett, a tall, handsome teen who was Ever's best friend before she began gaining weight

Whitney Stone, a beautiful, slim, popular high school student and style specialist

The Story

Despite her writing talent and a secret (but amazing) singing voice, Ever Davies is a high school outcast. She began eating compulsively at age ten after her mother died of cancer, and now, at age fifteen, she is five feet six and weighs 302 pounds. Worse, she is plagued by an inner voice, which Ever has nicknamed Skinny, that constantly and cruelly taunts her about her weight and eating habits (in public, Ever consumes salads and fruits, in private she wolfs down candy). Ever's father, a county sheriff, tries to be supportive, but his work keeps him away from home much of the time. Her stepmother, Charlotte, and her stepsisters Lindsey, sixteen, and Briella, fifteen, have never really connected with Ever and remain distant. She gets teased at school for her size. Her only true friend is Theodore Simon Wilson, a bespectacled science nerd whom everybody calls Rat because of his long nose.

Ever's misery reaches a new low during an award ceremony at school. She wins a writing honor, but the folding chair she is seated in onstage collapses under her weight. At this point, knowing she cannot change on her own, Ever decides to undergo gastric bypass surgery. With support from Rat and her father, she attends pre-surgery education sessions and support group meetings to learn the pros and cons of the procedure.

After surgery, though Ever begins to lose weight—Rat meticulously charts her progress—the voice of Skinny is still there to undermine her confidence. As the pounds drop away, Ever begins to draw more attention. Popular Whitney Stone, hoping to establish a career as a professional stylist, decides to use Ever as her pet project and takes Ever under her wing. Whitney helps her shop for fashionable new clothes and accessories, and takes Ever to a salon for a complete makeover.

By the time she begins her junior year in high school, Ever has lost more than sixty pounds. She is determined to try out for the lead part in the fall musical, *Rodgers and Hammerstein's Cinderella*, a favorite that she knows by heart. To prepare for the audition, she takes drama workshops and classes. Meanwhile, Whitney prepares Ever for the Fall Ball, choosing a flattering gown and providing an escort for her protégé: Jackson

Barnett, Ever's crush and former best friend. Rat, who had assumed he would be taking Ever to the ball, is greatly disappointed, and shows up at the ball with his date, Ever's stepsister Briella.

At the dance, Jackson quickly deserts Ever; she later finds him kissing another girl. Miserable, Ever returns home early. Briella also left the ball to go home, and the two girls have a long-delayed heart-to-heart talk, after which Briella pledges to become Ever's biggest fan. Briella not only lends Ever support in successfully preparing for the musical audition, she also acts as go-between for Ever and Rat, who ultimately declare their love for one another. While Ever amends her relationships with friends and family, she also confronts Skinny and realizes that the self-loathing that Skinny enabled cut her off from those around her.

Critical Evaluation

According to numerous author interviews, *Skinny* was inspired by the author's own experiences. Like her protagonist Ever, Donna Cooner suffered many of the same humiliations before she underwent gastric bypass surgery, and has remained vigilant about her diet ever since. Cooner does a service for obese adolescents who might be considering the drastic weight-reduction method by providing a wealth of information detailing advantages and drawbacks of the surgical procedure. While obesity is an issue many teens face, it is not one that is dealt with as frequently in young adult literature, and weight loss surgery is certainly an underrepresented topic. Cooner has been applauded by reviewers for the detail and accuracy of its portrayal of the gastric bypass experience. Some reviewers, however, have expressed a wish for more depth on the topic, particularly counseling for Ever, especially because it is one of so few young adult novels that portrays weight-loss surgery.

To give the story immediacy, the novel is told in present tense. The Cinderella theme is present throughout *Skinny,* and some of the characters and plot points run parallel to the famous fairy tale. The stepmother and stepsisters who seem indifferent to Ever's plight, the plain heroine whose hidden qualities are brought out via physical transformation, the formal ball the protagonist flees before midnight, and a semi-supernatural element, in the form of omnipresent whisperings from her disparaging alter ego—have all been borrowed from the tale of Cinderella.

The novel is structured in six parts that work together like a classical five-act play. Part 1, "Ashes," introduces main characters, the setting and the protagonist's major problems: her extreme weight and her self-deprecating inner voice. Part 2, "Prince Charming," deepens the conflict: the physical manifestation of Ever's obesity—the breaking of a chair under her weight—at what should be a moment of triumph, culminates in her decision to make a radical break with the past by undergoing surgery. Part 3, "Abracadabra," presents the climax of the story: the preliminaries leading to her operation, the actual surgery, and its aftermath. In parts 4 and 5, "The Ball" and "Midnight," the action falls off, as previously hidden details are revealed: Whitney is really only helping Ever to advance her own potential career; Ever realizes Jackson does not actually care about her, and that Rat should be the true object of her affection. Also, Briella always wanted to be friends with her stepsister but Ever never gave her the chance. Part 6, "Ever After," provides the resolution: though she may never become as slender as she dreams, Ever continues to successfully lose weight, finally silencing the voice of Skinny. She also lands the lead role in the fall musical, becomes fast friends with her stepsister Briella, and winds up with a dedicated boyfriend, Rat, with whom she might live happily ever after.

Jack Ewing

Further Reading

Cooner, Donna. "Author Interview: Donna Cooner, Author of the YA Novel SKINNY." Interview by Chuck Sambuchino. *Writer's Digest.* F+W, 14 Oct. 2015. Web. 8 Nov. 2015. <http://www.writersdigest.com/editor-blogs/guide-to-literary-agents/author-interviews-author-donna-cooner>.

Valdez, Katherine. "Author Donna Cooner Shows Why Readers 'Can't Look Away.'" *Coloradoan.* Gannett, 31 Oct. 2014. Web. 8 Nov. 2015. <http://www.coloradoan.com/story/life/2014/11/01/author-donna-cooner-shows-readers-look-away/18276367/>.

Speak

Author: Laurie Halse Anderson (b. 1961)
First published: 1999
Type of work: Novel

Type of plot: Psychological Fiction
Time of plot: The late 1990s
Locale: Syracuse, New York

Principal characters

Melinda Sordino, a fourteen-year-old high school freshman
Heather, Melinda's new friend
Rachel Bruin, Melinda's former best friend
Andy Evans, a popular senior student
Mr. Freeman, the art teacher

The Story

Laurie Halse Anderson's debut novel, *Speak* (1999), begins on protagonist Melinda Sordino's first day at Merryweather High School in Syracuse, New York. She begins her high school career utterly friendless, as her middle school friends have turned their backs on her because of an incident that occurred during the summer. At ninth-grade orientation, Melinda sits next to Heather, a new student who has moved to Syracuse from Ohio and is desperate to make friends. The first day of school goes as badly as Melinda seems to expect: she is given a demerit for being in the halls without a pass when she cannot find her first class, gets on the bad side of her social studies teacher almost immediately, and is hit with flying mashed potatoes during lunch. The one bright spot is art class, taught by Mr. Freeman, who becomes Melinda's favorite teacher.

Over the next weeks, Melinda remains largely silent in her classes and often neglects her homework assignments. She spends much of her free time with Heather, who, seeking acceptance at her new school and having difficulty making plans, tries to convince Melinda to participate in various extracurricular activities. At a pep rally held for homecoming, Melinda is harassed by other students who reveal that she had called the police during a party late in the summer, causing the party to be broken up and some attendees to be arrested. This event is what led Melinda to be ostracized at school, and although she does not yet state her reason for calling the police that night, it soon becomes clear that something serious had occurred. Not long afterward, Melinda sees something or someone she refers to as "IT" in the hallway; IT, she explains, is her nightmare, and when she sees IT, she wants to throw up. In search of safety and privacy in a school that offers little of either, Melinda spends much of her time hiding in an unused janitor's closet, which she transforms into her private sanctuary.

In the winter, Melinda reveals that IT is Andy Evans, a senior student at her school. She encounters Andy on several occasions, including while spending time with Heather as she attempts to win over her new clique of Martha Stewart wannabes. Heather soon tells Melinda that she does not want to be friends anymore, as Melinda is too negative and supposedly has a reputation at school. Already on shaky ground with both the school and her parents, Melinda gets into trouble when the adults learn that she has been skipping classes and, at times, the school day altogether. Both her parents and the school administrators are frustrated by Melinda's seeming refusal to speak; however, it becomes clear to the reader by this point that she is not remaining silent out of stubbornness or defiance. Eventually, Melinda reveals to the reader that Andy raped her at the party the previous summer. She had called the police to report the rape but found herself unable to articulate what had happened, and she has found speaking in public difficult ever since.

When Rachel starts dating Andy, Melinda feels compelled to save her former friend. She tells Rachel the truth about Andy, and although Rachel initially accuses her of lying, she later breaks up with Andy at prom. Angry that Melinda told Rachel about him, Andy corners Melinda in the janitor's closet and attempts to rape her again, but she screams and fights him off. News of this incident spreads throughout the school, revealing Andy for what he is. Having conquered her fear and shame, Melinda ends the school year hopeful for the future and finally truly able to speak.

Critical Evaluation

Anderson's novels often tackle difficult topics—*Wintergirls* (2009), for example, deals with eating disorders, while *The Impossible Knife of Memory* (2014) depicts the effects of posttraumatic stress disorder—and *Speak*, her first novel, is no exception. In telling Melinda's story, the novel presents a powerful portrayal of trauma and its effects on the psyche of a young woman. Unable to tell those closest to her about her rape, Melinda retreats into silence during her everyday life, demonstrating the unfortunate fact that many survivors of trauma remain silent not because they want to but because they simply cannot express what they have gone through.

In addition to its strong themes of trauma and recovery, *Speak* also serves as an intriguing look at the pressures facing teenagers, particularly in regard to popularity and acceptance by peers. Heather's obsessive quest for popularity and social acceptance—which ultimately ruins her friendship with Melinda and leaves her overworked and taken advantage of—is perhaps the most blatant example of this. However, the insidious power and lure of popularity is present throughout the novel. Andy, for instance, is able to get away with what seems to be a long history of predatory behavior because he is attractive and popular; his social acceptance at school becomes a protective barrier that shields him from the accusations of the women he has harmed.

Speak is often included in high school English curricula and used not only as a complex piece of literature but also as a teaching tool that allows teachers to start discussions about topics that are otherwise difficult to bring up. Some individuals and organizations have challenged its use in schools, deeming its subject matter inappropriate; opponents have gone so far as to deem the novel pornographic, despite the nongraphic nature of its one sex scene and the overall horror associated with it. However, most educators have seen the novel's value as an educational tool, particularly in sparking conversations about the importance of consent and in encouraging teens who have experienced similarly traumatic events to speak out without fear or shame.

Joy Crelin

Further Reading

Glenn, Wendy J. *Laurie Halse Anderson: Speaking in Tongues*. Lanham: Scarecrow, 2010. Print.

Snider, Jessi. "'Be the Tree': Classical Literature, Art Therapy, And Transcending Trauma in *Speak*." *Children's Literature in Education* 45.4 (2014): 298–309. *Literary Reference Center*. Web. 2 Apr. 2015. <http://search.ebscohost.com/login.aspx?direct=true&db=lfh&AN=99045318&site=lrc-live>.

Town, Caren J. *"Unsuitable" Books: Young Adult Fiction and Censorship*. Jefferson: McFarland, 2014. Print.

Story of a Girl

Author: Sara Zarr (b. 1970)
First published: 2007
Type of work: Novel
Type of plot: Coming-of-Age
Time of plot: 2007
Locale: Pacifica, California

Principal Characters

Deanna Lambert, a sixteen-year-old girl who has not lived down the mistake she made at thirteen

Darren Lambert, Deanna's older brother and staunch supporter

Stacy Lambert, Darren's girlfriend and mother of their infant daughter

Jason, Deanna's best male friend since childhood and Lee's boyfriend

Lee, Deanna's best friend since the start of sophomore year

Tommy Webber, the boy with whom Deanna made the mistake that haunts her

Michael, Deanna's boss and owner of the pizza place

The Story

Story of a Girl is the story of sixteen-year-old Deanna Lambert, a lonely teenager in the small, dead-end town of Pacifica, California. When she was thirteen, her father caught her in mid-act in the back seat of Tommy Webber's car. Tommy, her older brother's so-called best friend, was seventeen at the time. Her father dragged Deanna out of the car, and Tommy spread the story of Deanna's eager participation and her father's reaction at school the next day. Deanna's father has not looked her in the eye since that night. The kids at school and people in town still talk about it, and Deanna is sure they always will. She dreams of getting out of Pacifica and moving somewhere where not everyone knows her business.

Deanna has one truly good friend, Jason, who defends her and sticks by her. They have been friends for years. When a new girl starts in sophomore year and does not immediately befriend the popular girls, Deanna takes the opportunity to get to know her before anyone else has the chance to tell her Deanna's promiscuous reputation. She tells the new girl, Lee, the story of Tommy in her own words. Lee is not bothered by this admission. Through Deanna's efforts, Jason and Lee begin to date. Deanna is initially happy about this but begins to feel like a third wheel when they display affection.

Deanna's home has never been the most comfortable place. Now her father has been laid off and works at a job he hates. Her mother also must work long hours. Her brother, Darren, and his girlfriend, Stacy, are living in the basement with their baby, April, an arrangement of which Deanna's father does not approve. Darren and Deanna are very close and look out for one another—Darren beat Tommy up when he learned about Tommy's relationship with Deanna. Deanna daydreams about moving out with Darren and Stacy, so she decides to get a job for the summer and give all her money to her brother to help him rent an apartment.

Deanna finds a job at the local pizza place, where, she soon discovers, Tommy Webber also works. He begins to flirt with her immediately, calling her Dee Dee, as he used to when they were together. The restaurant's owner, Michael, is a decent person who realizes something has happened between Deanna and Tommy in the past. He acts as a buffer when needed and makes it clear to Deanna that he is there to help her out or talk with her if she wants.

Everything seems to be going well until Stacy takes off without telling Darren, throwing a wrench in Deanna's escape plans, which she still has not told Darren about. When he finds out, he tells her that he does not believe it to be a good idea, given the instability of his and Stacy's relationship; Deanna will have to find her own way out of her parents' house, and Pacifica as a whole. Later, Lee tells Deanna that she is thinking about having sex with Jason. Deanna reacts by being nasty to Lee, making out with Tommy—though she quickly realizes that that is not what she wants—and kissing Jason. Then things get even worse: in quick succession, one of the school bullies molests Deanna by putting his hand between her legs in public, a sleazy customer hits on her at the pizza place, and Deanna's father becomes suspicious and angry when Michael gives her a ride home. Finally pushed to her limits, Deanna confronts her father—which leads to the two beginning the slow process of reconciliation.

After a few further attempts to offer Darren her savings, she realizes that he is right that the money she has earned should go to her own future, not Darren's. She and Darren also realize that they do not have to be like their father and can instead offer the people in their lives forgiveness and second chances. Darren and Stacy reconcile and begin making plans to move out in earnest, while Deanna sends a note to Lee, asking her to meet at the tree before school starts on the first day of junior year. The story ends with Darren driving Deanna to school, where she sees Jason and Lee waiting for her at their tree.

Critical Evaluation

Story of a Girl is a strong narrative told in a compelling voice. Deanna is a high school girl who relates her story in first person, without self-pity or drama, making the story all the more effective. The use of first-person present tense brings a sense of immediacy and intimacy to the tale she has to tell.

The protagonist's journal is put to effective use in *Story of a Girl*. It is not a journal that is used to convey essential parts of the story. Instead, it serves as a window into Deanna's emotions, as she uses her journal to write stories of a surfer girl to whom Deanna attributes the "personal feelings [she] didn't want to feel." Thus, Deanna's inner turmoil and desire to repair her relationship with her father are reflected in the excerpts of her journal that serve as interludes to the novel's main story.

The parents in this novel are fully formed characters. They do not appear frequently, but their presence and opinions are felt throughout. When they are described, it is with enough detail to give a good sense of who they are and how they have changed during the time of Deanna's difficulties. The relationships between Deanna and her brother and between Deanna and her friends are believable both as relationships and as sources of support for Deanna.

Gina Hagler, MBA

Further Reading

Bucher, Katherine, and KaaVonia Hinton. "Exploring Contemporary Realistic Fiction." *Young Adult Literature: Exploration, Evaluation, and Appreciation.* 3rd ed. New York: Pearson, 2014. 125–58. Print.

Cole, Pam B. "Realistic Fiction." *Young Adult Literature in the 21st Century.* New York: McGraw, 2009. 98–162. Print.

Cole, Pam B. "Romance, Humor, and Sports." *Young Adult Literature in the 21st Century.* New York: McGraw, 2009. 163–81. Print.

Surrender

Author: Sonya Hartnett (b. 1968)
First published: 2006
Type of work: Psychological Fiction
Time of plot: Present day
Local: Rural Australia

Principal characters

Gabriel (a.k.a. Anwell), boy who lives with emotionally and physically abusive parents

Evangeline, Gabriel's high school crush
Vernon, Gabriel's intellectually disabled older brother
Surrender, Gabriel's dog
Henry and Beth, Gabriel's parents
Finnigan, boy who lives in the wild and forms a dysfunctional friendship with Anwell

The Story

Twenty-year-old Gabriel (a.k.a. Anwell) lies on his deathbed, skeleton thin, racked with pain, aware he does not have much longer to live. Gabriel mentions that "the bones" have been found and that this has something to do with him. Finnigan, a boy of Gabriel's age who lives in the wild, is also aware the bones have been discovered and knows Gabriel will need his help.

Anwell meets Finnigan for the first time as a young boy. Anwell is abused by his parents and isolated from the small, rural town near their home. He desperately wishes that Finnigan will be his friend. The text reveals that Finnigan stole money from Anwell's mother; he asks Anwell to hide it. Anwell agrees but is soon caught by his mother and beaten by his father.

Later, Finnigan asks Anwell to make a pact stating that Finnigan will protect Gabriel and do all the "bad things that need to be done." In return Anwell will be an angel henceforth known as Gabriel.

Gabriel learns that Finnigan has been setting fires all over town in order to punish the people who have made fun of Gabriel. The town bands together to catch the arsonist. In the meantime, nothing is safe from the arsonist. Gabriel begs Finnigan to stop his destructive rampage.

Gabriel tells Finnigan the details of his brother Vernon's death. Their parents were ashamed of their disabled son and kept him isolated in his bedroom. Gabriel, who claims he loved his brother, became Vernon's caretaker. In a moment of frustration and fear because of his inability to keep Vernon quiet, Gabriel gags Vernon to keep him from screaming and shuts him in a refrigerator to hide him from their mother. Vernon dies; Gabriel tells his parents he was only trying to comfort him.

After Finnigan burns Gabriel's father's car, the fires cease. The family gets a wild and violent dog named Surrender. Eventually Surrender is caught killing a neighbor's goats and must be put down. In order to save him, Gabriel runs away to bring Surrender to Finnigan. Finnigan states that he will take Surrender if Gabriel promises to stop spending time with Evangeline, Gabriel's crush. Gabriel refuses and becomes frightened that Finnigan will kill Evangeline.

At this point, the order of the book's events is unclear. Gabriel begs Evangeline to leave town for her own safety. Gabriel fears Finnigan is at the house, but it is only his mother, who drags him home.

Gabriel then tells of his father forcing him to shoot Surrender. Gabriel says it is okay because Surrender's soul is with Finnigan and that the dog he shot was just a "shell."

When Gabriel gets home after warning Evangeline, his father plans to whip him, which has not occurred since Gabriel was a boy. Instead of allowing himself to be beaten, Gabriel returns with a hatchet and murders both of his parents. He cries as he buries the dog but sheds no tears over his parents.

The reader learns that both the discovered bones were probably his parents' and Finnigan was a figment of Gabriel's imagination. Gabriel's impending death is one that he has forced upon his body so his dark side, Finnigan, will die also.

At the end, there is only Anwell and an apparition of Vernon. Anwell and Vernon are transported to a place in which they experience bits of the idyllic childhood they never had before they are separated forever. Vernon remains with fiery beasts while Anwell is raised up by angel wings.

Critical Evaluation

Surrender is a psychological thriller told by an unreliable narrator. Anwell/Gabriel masks reality to portray himself as innocent and good.

Anwell was abused as a child, but he also commits acts of destruction and violence. To deal with his guilt from essentially killing his disabled brother, Vernon, Anwell creates other personas. Anwell constructs Gabriel and Finnigan as opposing forces that mirror and balance each other. Gabriel is angelic, while Finnigan does all the bad that needs doing in order to protect Anwell.

Through the conflation of three characters into one, readers see the depth of Anwell's conflicted emotions. Finnigan terrorizes the town and lights fires to take revenge on all those who have mocked Anwell. Gabriel argues with Finnigan, begging him to stop. Anwell uses Gabriel and Finnigan as tools to forgive himself. Finnigan states that he has every right to do the things he does because Gabriel

will be there to provide balance. Eventually, Gabriel taints his purity by killing his parents and decides that forcing his body to die is the only way to stop Finnigan.

The dog Surrender acts as a catalyst for Anwell. Anwell envies Surrender's connection with his alter ego Finnigan, but he relinquishes ownership of the dog in order to keep him safe. The act of losing Surrender triggers Gabriel's downward spiral, resulting in the murder of his parents.

Alexandra McBride, MA

Further Reading

Carter, Felicity. "Know the Author Sonya Hartnett." *Magpies* 20.2 (2005): 14. *MasterFILE Premier*. Web. 16 Apr. 2015. <http://search.ebscohost.com/login.asp x?direct=true&db=f5h&AN=17090949&site= eds-live>.

Goldsmith, Francisca. "Surrender." Rev. of *Surrender*, by Sonya Hartnett. *School Library Journal* Mar. 2006: 222. *Literary Reference Center Plus*. Web. 16 Apr. 2015. <http://search.ebscohost.com/login.aspx? direct=true&db=lkh&AN=20090019&site=lrc-plus>.

"Surrender." Rev. of *Surrender*, by Sonya Hartnett. *Kirkus Reviews*. Kirkus Media, 20 May 2010. Web. 23 Mar. 2015. <https://www.kirkusreviews.com/ book-reviews/sonya-hartnett/surrender/>.

13 Little Blue Envelopes

Author: Maureen Johnson (b. 1973)
First published: 2005
Type of work: Novel
Type of plot: Adventure
Time of plot: The 2000s
Locale: New York City, London, and several European cities

Principal characters

Virginia "Ginny" Blackstone, a shy seventeen-year-old
Aunt Peg, Ginny's late eccentric aunt
Keith Dobson, a London theater artist
Richard, Aunt Peg's friend
Beppe, a twenty-year-old Italian with whom Ginny has a romantic encounter

The Story

The summer she is seventeen, Virginia "Ginny" Blackstone receives an envelope from her aunt Peg with a set of mysterious instructions and a thousand dollars. Ginny is to head to New York City, and then fly to London on a one-way ticket with no extra money or electronic devices. The letter claims that Ginny will be gone for several weeks and that Aunt Peg will take care of everything. Aunt Peg was the free-spirited eccentric of the family. A few months earlier, she had disappeared, traveling across Europe and dying there of cancer at age thirty-five.

Ginny acquires more envelopes from Aunt Peg's former home and flies to London. The second envelope instructs that Ginny must complete the task in every envelope before opening the next, then gives directions to an apartment. There, she meets her aunt's friend Richard, who takes her to Harrods department store. The next morning, Richard helps her complete her first task and access money with Aunt Peg's bank card.

The third envelope tells Ginny to give a large sum of money to an artist of her choice, which leads Ginny to attend *Starbucks: The Musical*. She buys out the remaining run of the unpopular show and attracts the attention of its star and writer, Keith Dobson. Keith invites her out for a drink, and she helps him pack up the musical to take it to the Fringe Festival in Edinburgh. Luckily, the next envelope also sends her to Edinburgh to meet Mari Adams, a painter who was Aunt Peg's idol. Ginny and Keith bond there.

The next envelopes send Ginny to Rome, where she pays tribute to ancient statues of the vestal virgins and is instructed to ask a Roman boy on a date. The letters then send her to Paris, where she visits the Louvre and is set the task of finding a café Aunt Peg decorated. She quickly e-mails Keith to say hello. The café is filled with collaged pictures of dogs on the wall, and when Ginny returns to her hostel, she finds Keith waiting. They spend an evening in Paris, kissing in a cemetery, before he departs and she heads to Amsterdam.

In Amsterdam, Ginny gets swept up into the vacation of an American family, the Knapps. While they take her along on heavily scheduled sightseeing trips, their friendliness makes it difficult for her to complete her task from Aunt Peg. The Knapps give her a bill for nearly five hundred euros on the last day, meant to cover her expenses during the family trip. Opening the next envelope, she is glad to leave for Copenhagen.

There, she meets an artist friend of Aunt Peg's who takes her out on a boat to watch the "midnight sun" of the region. After Ginny makes some Australian friends and wins a karaoke competition in a packed bar (much to her surprise), the next envelope sends her to Greece.

While swimming on the beach in Corfu, Greece, Ginny has her bag stolen (including the final envelope), and when she heads to an ATM, realizes she is out of money. Richard flies her back to London, and there tells her that he and Aunt Peg had married before she died. She reunites with Keith and tries to process all that has happened before finding a hidden key in Aunt Peg's former home, which Richard identifies as opening a storage box in Harrods. There, she finds Aunt Peg's paintings with instructions, which lead her to an art dealer. The dealer sells the paintings for a large amount of money, giving the proceeds to Ginny. Before she decides what to do next, Ginny tells Keith how she feels about him and sits down to write a letter to her aunt.

Critical Evaluation

A lot happens to Ginny over the course of *13 Little Blue Envelopes*, but perhaps the biggest change comes through how she views herself. At the start of the novel, Ginny is an insecure and quiet teenager who does not believe she can ever be as interesting as her Aunt Peg. By the end, however, she begins to come into her confidence, realizing that she can also be engaging, unique, and independent.

One of the ways the novel accomplishes this progression is through its epistolary structure. Third-person-narrative sections follow Ginny closely, refraining from revealing any information that is not from her perspective. The letters from Aunt Peg, in contrast, provide that precious outside information, both illuminating Aunt Peg's life (making it less mysterious) and inviting Ginny to form her own adventures. As readers who are given as much mystery as Ginny is, wondering the same questions that preoccupy her, the letters become a source of authority.

For Ginny to become independent and interesting, however, she cannot rely entirely on the authority of any other person, even Aunt Peg. For this reason, as the novel progresses, she begins to rebel against the envelopes a bit, recognizing Aunt Peg's own imperfections when several envelopes fail to deliver on their expected promises. This progression allows Ginny to understand her aunt not as a magical, charmed person, always flying through life joyfully, but as someone who could at times be as insecure or misguided as Ginny. It also gives Ginny permission to break away from the rules of the letters from time to time, asserting her individuality by doing so.

This progression concludes with the novel's last chapter, when Ginny writes her own letter to her aunt. Explaining that the final letter was stolen, she writes, "Anyway, I figured I'd take over." Although when Ginny writes the letter it may seem that she is symbolically becoming Aunt Peg, in actuality, she is becoming her own person, "taking over" her own life once and for all. There is much more for her to learn on these adventures, much more mystery ahead, but navigating the envelopes has helped her to understand that it is not Aunt Peg and not her parents, but in fact only she herself who will decide what that life will be.

T. Fleischmann, MFA

Further Reading

Corbett, Sue. "The Queen of Teen." *Publishers Weekly* 25 Feb. 2013: 26. *Literary Reference Center*. Web. 23 Feb. 2015. <http://search.ebscohost.com/login.aspx?direct=true&db=lfh&AN=85761413&site=lrc-live>.

McCann, Erin. "Status Update with Maureen Johnson: Writer and Ideal Dinner-Party Guest." *Guardian*. Guardian News and Media, 27 Sept. 2013. Web. 23 Feb. 2015. <http://www.theguardian.com/culture/2013/sep/27/maureen-johnson-status-update-books>.

Thirteen Reasons Why

Author: Jay Asher (b. 1975)
First published: 2007
Type of work: Novel
Type of plot: Realism
Time of plot: Early twenty-first century
Locale: United States

Principal characters

Hannah Baker, a high school student who recently committed suicide
Clay Jensen, a classmate of Hannah's
Justin Foley, a blabbermouth high school senior
Skye Miller, Clay's classmate, an outcast

Jessica Davis, a newcomer to the school
Marcus Cooley, a school goof-off
Courtney Crimsen, a pretty, popular poser

Courtesy of Razorbill, an imprint of Penguin Random House

The Story

Thirteen Reasons Why opens with Clay Jensen mailing a package to Jenny Kurtz, a high school cheerleader. The package contains seven audiocassette tapes. Thirteen half-hour sides have been recorded by Hannah Baker, a high school junior who committed suicide with an overdose of pills two weeks earlier. Each side describes incidents—along with significant locations marked on a map she also distributed—involving a specific person who interacted with Hannah and who contributed to her decision to kill herself. Through these recorded messages, Hannah orders each recipient to listen to the stories, rewind them, and send them to the next person mentioned. She warns that she has made copies of the tapes that will be made public if her demands are not followed.

Clay is shocked and confused to be included. He was Hannah's acquaintance and had a crush on her but was too shy and uncertain to act on his feelings. Clay nonetheless dutifully carries out Hannah's last wishes, borrowing a Walkman from his casual high school friend Tony to listen while on the go. As he follows the map to each destination, Clay learns distasteful details about his classmates' behavior that collectively drove Hannah over the edge. Along the way, he also pieces together clues revealing a series of acts that resulted in another death.

The first named offender is Justin Foley, a senior who gave Hannah her first kiss, then spread rumors that ruined Hannah's reputation. Newcomer Alex Standall aided and abetted this tarnishing by publishing a list that named Hannah "Best Ass in Freshman Class," causing her to be viewed as a sexual object. Jessica Davis, who regularly met and chatted with Hannah at a local café, later hit and scarred Hannah in a fit of jealousy.

Other contributors to Hannah's downfall include Tyler Down, a photographer who peeped through Hannah's bedroom window. Courtney Crimsen used Hannah to enhance her own image. Marcus Cooley invited Hannah on a date but stood her up, subjecting her to vicious innuendo. Zach Dempsey undermined her self-confidence out of spite. Ryan Shaver, editor of the school newspaper, stole and published one of Hannah's poems without her permission. At a party, Bryce Walker raped drunken, unconscious Jessica while horrified Hannah observed, hidden in a closet, powerless to do anything. Even Mr. Porter, an English teacher and counselor, is on the list, because of his incompetence as an adviser.

The sins continue to pile up, relentlessly detailed by Hannah. Cheerleader Jenny Kurtz, tipsy from the same party, drove Hannah home, but on the way knocked down a stop sign. The missing sign caused a collision between cars driven by an elderly man and a teenage pizza delivery boy who was fatally injured. Hannah, unhinged by the tragic chain of events, later permitted Bryce to have his way with her; Bryce's girlfriend, Courtney, walked away, allowing it to happen.

Clay, number 9 among those Hannah names, learns that she entrusted Tony with the duplicate tapes. Tony has followed each recipient in turn, and he drives his old Mustang while Clay, a passenger, listens to his role in Hannah's demise. His is a crime of omission: Hannah muses that Clay could have been her soul mate, but the opportunity was lost through misunderstanding. Both attended the big party and made out, but Clay, scared he was not worthy of Hannah, ran away, which she interpreted as his reaction to her falsely besmirched reputation.

Feeling guilty for having judged Hannah on the basis of rumor, and for being fearful of his own reputation, Clay approaches Skye Miller, a school outcast, in the end. He will become involved this time and help with whatever is troubling her, in hopes of preventing another tragedy.

Critical Evaluation

A *New York Times* best seller and winner of numerous honors, including the California Book Award, *Thirteen Reasons Why* presents a realistic explanation for the specific causes behind a particular young adult's choice to take her own life.

The gradual popularity and critical reception of the novel are understandable, due to the suspenseful way the story unfolds and the subtle way it suggests what to look for in potential suicide cases without becoming didactic. Told in present tense for immediacy and broken into sections marked with symbols for "play," "pause," "fast forward," and "rewind" that further bring the reader into the tape-recorded experience of the tale, the storytelling technique of *Thirteen Reasons Why* allows the reader to discover the causes and effects of Hannah's pain alongside co-narrator and protagonist Clay Jensen. Alternating between Clay's living thoughts, words, emotions, and deeds as he retraces incidents via the map and the late Hannah's recordings—though dead, she now has the power to force recipients both to find out who she really was and to be confronted by the flaws of the surviving offenders—creates a dynamic, moving story arc. By the end of the book, debut author Jay Asher has produced fully rounded portraits of two intelligent, sensitive, likeable, and unique individuals who are modern-day figures as tragic as Romeo and Juliet.

One major thread that prevails throughout the novel is the concept that people are so self-centered, so concerned with their own images, that they do not notice important details about others. People often miss obvious signs that someone is seriously troubled, such as a drastically changing appearance—as when Hannah cut off most of her hair or gave away her possessions. Another theme is that seemingly small slights can add up to large injuries, particularly among impressionable people in volatile environments such as high schools. As Hannah sadly concludes to those she holds responsible, "A lot of you cared, just not enough."

Jack Ewing

Further Reading

Asher, Jay. Interview by Bryan Gillis. *Journal of Adolescent & Adult Literacy* 54.7 (2011): 543–45. Literary Reference Center. Web. 16 Mar. 2015. <http://search.ebscohost.com/login.aspx?direct=true&db=lfh&AN=59897036&site=lrc-live>.

Asher, Jay. "Why Teen-Suicide Novel 'Thirteen Reasons Why' Is Saving Lives." Interview by Rob Brunner. *Entertainment Weekly*. Entertainment Weekly, 13 June 2011. Web. 16 Mar. 2015. <http://www.ew.com/article/2011/06/13/jay-asher-thirteen-reasons-why>.

Bucher, Katherine T., and KaaVonia Hinton. "Exploring Contemporary Realistic Fiction." *Young Adult Literature: Exploration, Evaluation, and Appreciation*. 3rd ed. New York: Pearson, 2014. 125–58. Print.

Tyrell

Author: Coe Booth
First published: 2007
Type of work: Novel
Type of plot: Realism
Time of plot: 2007
Locale: Bronx, New York

Principal characters

Tyrell Green, a fifteen-year-old African American boy
Troy Green, Tyrell's seven-year-old brother
Lisa Green, Tyrell's mother
Novisha Jenkins, Tyrell's girlfriend
Cal, his friend
Jasmine, a Hispanic girl who lives in transitional housing
Mrs. Jenkins, Novisha's mother

The Story

Fifteen-year-old Tyrell Green carries the world on his shoulders. His dad is in prison, again, and his mom is irresponsible. Tyrell holds the family together, but his life becomes even harder when his homeless family is sent to the Bennett Motel until shelter space becomes available. Bennett is the worst of the worst; it "look[s] like a bombed-out building from the outside," and the inside smells of old sneakers.

The Green family's life is difficult. The mother, Lisa Green, is incapable of working let alone taking care of Troy, her seven-year-old son. Tyrell makes sure Troy's physical and educational needs are met, and as the novel progresses, Tyrell deals with his mother's inability to act like an adult when she leaves Troy alone for long periods of time and wants to keep him in special education programs just for the state check. His greatest fear is being placed in foster care, which happened the last time his father was in prison.

Romance is also complicated for Tyrell. One of the most important plot directions in the novel is the development of his romantic relationships. He and Novisha Jenkins have been a couple for several years, and he has his life with her planned. He will follow her to college, taking care of her while she is in school, and they will eventually marry. In his eyes, Novisha is perfect; she has loving and supporting parents and does not know the abject poverty that is Tyrell's life. She lives in a decent apartment in the projects, goes to a parochial school, and has plenty of food to eat. However, she seems to be growing away from Tyrell: she plants notes about Tyrell in her diary, knowing he will read them. Fearing that she is embarrassed by him, Tyrell struggles emotionally, and when she tells him that a boy has been bothering her at school, he becomes violently jealous.

His friendship with Jasmine is newer and less complicated; it starts when he and his family are waiting to be moved from the Bennett Motel to the homeless shelter. When Tyrell and Jasmine begin to talk, he notices how attractive she is and how the two of them understand each other. While they are in the motel, Jasmine's sister abandons her, and Tyrell steps up to take care of her along with his family. He spends the nights in Jasmine's room because she is afraid to be alone. This leads to a one-time sexual encounter for which he feels guilty because he is faithful to and loves Novisha and because he does not want to be disrespectful of Jasmine. As Tyrell and Jasmine grow closer, however, he realizes she is the kind of girl who is worthy of his friendship and possibly even his love.

When Tyrell's mother tells him it is his job to support the family, he devises a plan to host a teen party with his father's DJ equipment. For financial backing, he contacts his friend Cal, who deals drugs, and arranges the party with some of his father's old colleagues. The novel culminates with the party, which is a financial success, but it brings problems as well. Tyrell learns that the boy bothering Novisha is an old boyfriend with whom Novisha had been sexually active, and Tyrell is even less secure in their relationship.

After the party, Tyrell returns to the Bennett with news that he has money for an apartment. He is met, however, with a letter from New York's Administration for Children's Services (ACS) stating that Troy has been taken to foster care. Lisa expects Tyrell to tell the judge that he was babysitting and left Troy alone, and Tyrell realizes that his mother will never change if he continues to cover and lie for her, so he sets off on his own. He will remain friends with Jasmine, and his relationship with Novisha will figure itself out. He is torn, but he finally feels some semblance of freedom.

Critical Evaluation

Coe Booth's novel is unashamedly graphic in its language, sexual situations, and presentation of life. Gritty reality slaps readers in the face early in the novel and never lets up. External and internal character dialogues bring these situations to life.

Thematic concerns of poverty and skewed morality further enhance the reality of the novel. Vivid description is used to showcase the poverty experienced by Tyrell's family. When the family goes to the Bennett Motel, for instance, Tyrell recalls being told that "the roaches was getting paid to run Bennett, that the roaches signed you in and took you to your room, and that Bennett even hired roaches that would come to your room to kill other roaches." Morality is another issue confronted in the novel. Tyrell is clear that he does not want to break the law because he does not want to go to jail like his father, but he is willing to bend it. He refuses to sell drugs for Cal and Cal's brothers, but he will host a party that trespasses on and damages private property, sell alcohol at the party, and drink beer and smoke marijuana. These themes further illustrate the confusion of life for this young man.

The novel's organization and point of view work together effectively. The novel's structure is primarily chronological, but there is some use of flashback when Tyrell recalls life before his father's imprisonment. The emphasis is, however, on the present and how Tyrell will overcome difficulties. First-person narration in the form of Tyrell's thoughts, dialogue, and experiences further draws readers into his internal struggles over his family, his relationships with the girls, and his desire to stay out of legal trouble. Although first-person narration limits readers' understanding of other characters' viewpoints and motivation, it allows Tyrell to be the unifying element in the chaos of his life.

Theresa L. Stowell, PhD

Further Information

Booth, Coe. "Keeping It Real: An Interview with Coe Booth." Interview by Julie Prince. *Teacher Librarian* 36.4 (2009): 62. Print.

Margolis, Rick. "A Bronx Tale: First-Time Author Coe Booth Follows a Teen's Struggle to Stay Alive." *School Library Jour.* 53.2 (2007): 32. Print.

Rountree, Wendy. *Just Us Girls: Essays on the Contemporary African American Young Adult Novel.* New York: Lang, 2008. Print.

Uglies (Series)

Author: Scott Westerfeld (b. 1963)
First published: *Uglies* (2005)
 Pretties (2005)
 Specials (2006)
 Extras (2007)
Type of work: Novel
Type of plot: Dystopian Fiction
Time of plot: About three hundred years in the future
Locale: United States, Japan

Principal characters

Tally, a teenage Ugly on the verge of becoming a surgically modified Pretty

Peris, Tally's childhood friend and new Pretty

Shay, Tally's new friend who questions the need to be pretty

David, a young man who was born in the wild and guides Uglies to the Smoke

Dr. Cable, the leader of Special Circumstances

Zane, the Pretty leader of the Crims

Aya Fuse, the protagonist of the fourth book in the series

The Story

Uglies begins with Tally sneaking into New Pretty Town from Uglyville. The Uglies live together in dorms until their sixteenth birthday, when they have an operation to become a Pretty. Tally's childhood friend Peris has recently become a Pretty and lives in New Pretty Town. Instead of finding her old friend, she finds a perfectly handsome boy who is more concerned with appearance and parties than their friendship. While sneaking back into Uglyville, Tally meets Shay, who is of the same age and is impressed with Tally's risk taking. The two grow close as Shay teaches Tally how to hoverboard, and they begin to sneak outside of the city limits to the ruins that lie beyond. Eventually, Shay confesses she does not want to become pretty and tells Tally there are people in the wild who have chosen to stay ugly. Tally does not understand why anyone would do so and begs Shay to turn pretty together on their shared birthday. Shay says the procedure takes away everything that makes a person interesting and that she plans to run away to a place called the Smoke with a boy named David.

David recruits Uglies and leads them to a hidden society of people who refuse to undergo the operation. When Tally refuses to leave, Shay gives Tally an encoded set of directions so that Tally can follow if she changes her mind. Even though Tally misses Shay, she is excited for her operation and yearns to see Peris again. Instead of becoming a Pretty on her sixteenth birthday, she is taken to Special Circumstances and is questioned about Shay's location. Tally is given the ultimatum that she can choose to lead Special Circumstances to the Smoke or live her entire life as an Ugly. Soon Peris convinces her to do as she is asked so that she can be pretty. Tally goes to the Smoke with her hoverboard, survival pack, and Shay's directions to guide her. Instead of alerting Special Circumstances immediately upon arrival, Tally stays and works to improve the Smoke. Tally grows to think of the Smoke as her home and is ashamed she came to them as a spy. Tally and David develop feelings for each other, which makes Shay jealous. Tally learns from David's parents, Az and Maddy, that they discovered that the operation also causes lesions in the brain that make people pliant and easily controlled. Tally inadvertently alerts Special Circumstances of their location when she throws her tracking necklace into a fire in an attempt to destroy it. Special Circumstances appears the next day and captures all of the Smokies except for David. The leader of Special Circumstances believes that Tally knowingly activated her tracking device to help them locate the Smoke. Tally ultimately escapes from Special Circumstances and returns to the wild, where she finds David.

Upon sneaking into the Special Circumstances facility to rescue their friends and family, Tally and David find Shay, newly made pretty, and convince her to join them. They rescue the others but learn Special Circumstances murdered David's father. They escape to the ruins, and David's mother finds a possible cure for the lesions with technology stolen from Special Circumstances. Shay refuses to take the cure, so Tally volunteers to go back with Shay, get the operation, and take the cure upon rescue as a test subject. David finds out that Tally had been sent to the Smoke as a spy and leaves feeling betrayed. *Uglies* ends with Tally turning herself in to Special Circumstances.

The second book, *Pretties*, begins with Tally living a picturesque life in New Pretty Town with Shay, Peris, and a clique called the Crims. While at a costume party, Tally notices a person dressed up as a member of Special Circumstances is following her. She recognizes him as Croy, an Ugly she worked with in the Smoke. Pretty Tally does not want half-remembered memories of her time in the wild to ruin her happiness. Croy tells Tally that he has a package for her but she has to find it. Zane, leader of the Crims, helps her find the package in which Tally reads a letter written by her past self, telling her to take the two experimental pills that she hopes will cure her lesions. Zane and Tally both take a pill and their heads begin to clear. As Tally remembers why she chose to live in the Smoke in the first place, she and Zane plan to escape the city with other Crims. Unfortunately, the dose was not meant to be shared, and Zane begins to have headaches due to brain damage caused by nanobots in the second pill. The New Smoke is soon discovered because of a tracker implanted in Zane's mouth. Tally decides to stay with Zane while the rest escape. They discover that Special Circumstances have drafted Shay and plan to do the same to Tally.

In *Specials*, Tally is transformed into a member of Special Circumstances and joins Shay's new group, the Cutters. Zane is recovering from brain damage in the hospital. Shay and Tally disguise themselves as Uglies in order to identify and capture Smokies at an Ugly party. They find a Smokie girl handing out pills, and in their pursuit, Shay and Tally run into David. After a hoverboard chase and fight between the Smokies and Cutters, Tally is left injured. Tally recovers and resumes following the Smokies. When Tally finds Shay and other Cutters, they learn the Smokies are handing off the pills to Zane in New Pretty Town. Tally is surprised to find that Zane is still in league with the Smokies and convinces him to help the Cutters, and in return, they will make Zane a Special. Tally and Shay track Zane and the Crims to Diego, a runaway city where everyone is free to look how they please and cure their brain lesions.

Tally is caught and almost forced to undergo surgery to cure her "special" brain. A cured Shay helps her to escape right before the surgery begins so that she can help to defend the city against Special Circumstances and its leader, Dr. Cable. Zane dies during the hospital evacuation. David intercepts Tally on her way to speak to Dr. Cable and gives her the cure for her "special" surgery, asking her to take it. Tally chooses to remain a Special and ends up imprisoned and again forced to be "despecialized." Tally instead gets Dr. Cable to inject herself with the cure. The cure spreads, and more people begin to live without surgical enhancements or brain lesions. Tally remains a Special, and she and David decide to form the New Special Circumstances, which will protect the environment from humanity.

In *Extras*, which takes place three years after the events in *Specials*, a new protagonist, Aya Fuse, lives in a futuristic Japan where people classify themselves by face rank and strive to become famous. Aya wants to be a "kicker" (an amateur journalist) and become famous (increasing her face rank) until she discovers a group called the Sly Girls who hate fame. They use Aya to show the world weapons found underground. Aya becomes instantly famous and soon receives a message from Tally telling her that she is in danger and to hide. After Aya meets up with Tally and Tally's friends, they are captured by creatures called Extras. They discover these creatures want to build space colonies to lessen the impact humans have on the environment. Tally views them as a threat, but Aya prevents Tally from destroying the Extras' ships. The series wraps up at a party where characters go their separate ways.

Critical Evaluation

The Uglies series is composed of four dystopian science-fiction novels in the tradition of Lois Lowry's *The Giver* (1993) and reminiscent of such works as the Hunger Games series (2008–10) by Suzanne Collins, *The Maze Runner* (2009) by James Dashner, and *Divergent* (2011) by Veronica Roth. Its main plot follows a resistance movement fighting an oppressive, if well-intentioned, government. Its subplots deal with teenage romance (and accompanying angst), self-image, and environmentalism. As is often the case with young adult novels, the Uglies series leverages these themes to appeal to a sense of outsiderness, a tradition going back to S. E. Hinton's *The Outsiders* (1967) and Robert Cormier's *The Chocolate War* (1974). That feeling of being an outlier is tempered with an inner feeling of superiority to the conventional.

In the Uglies series, everyone is forced to undergo surgery to become a Pretty on their sixteenth birthday. Compulsory beautification is assumed to have done away with racism, classism, and other forms of discrimination, leading to a utopia in which everyone leads a happy existence free of hard questions. This manifests when protagonist Tally discovers her best friend Peris has been transformed into a vapid party boy. Tally decides not to become pretty herself, striking out of civilization to live among everyone else who has decided to maintain their individuality. The novels link superficial beauty with shallowness by explaining that a side effect of the surgery produces lesions on the brain, turning a metaphor into an aspect of the plot.

As Tally discovers compulsory beautification is a means of keeping the populace stupid and complacent, the Uglies series takes its place among contemporary fascist dystopian literature. Young adult novels such as Lowry's *The Giver* parallel the plots of George Orwell's *Nineteen Eighty-Four* (1949) and Aldous Huxley's *Brave New World* (1932), in which systems of violent punishment are unnecessary as people have willingly handed over their freedom for comfort and safety. It is cynical but reasonable, especially in a genre aimed at teenagers. In the case of the Uglies series, the population is brought to heel with the promise of popularity.

This creates a villainous force (given face by Dr. Cable and the Special Circumstances) against which Tally can justifiably use violence, at least in self-defense. This positions her as an action hero in the mold of Katniss of *The Hunger Games*, despite Tally being less capable than Katniss with weaponry. Many of the heroes' solutions to problems in the Uglies series lie not in violence but in science.

While, as in *The Giver*, the government wants to use homogenization to pacify its citizens, the Uglies series blends this with the ostracized feeling that is explored in *The Outsiders* and Stephen Chbosky's *The Perks of Being a Wallflower* (1999). It is to Scott Westerfeld's credit that he found a way to turn the dystopian "civilizing" force into one that makes the protagonist (and, cathartically, the reader) superior by virtue of uniqueness. Tally's desire to hold onto her identity (the most appealing concept for an adolescent of any age) not only fuels her struggle against the villains of the main plot but also sustains her in her character arc.

Tally's character arc is also a romantic one. While this is the same device used in *The Perks of Being a Wallflower*, especially as the protagonist's Otherness is both supported and ameliorated by a love interest, the Uglies series takes a more realistic approach to teenage relationships. That is, they rarely last. Tally's crushes become friends, enemies, and switch again. The relationships are tempestuous, and relationships affect the characters' allegiances.

Those edifying relationships, both to oneself and to the environment, are the strongest themes of the Uglies series. The characters' desire to ameliorate humans' impact on the environment (while heavy handed) serves as a metaphor for their acceptance of their own bodies by choosing to stay "ugly."

Alexandra McBride, MA

Further Reading

Hynes, James. "Looks Aren't Everything." Rev. of *Extras*, by Scott Westerfeld. *New York Times*. New York Times, 11 Nov. 2007. Web. 5 Mar. 2015. <http://www.nytimes.com/2007/11/11/books/review/Hynes-t.html>.

Rev. of *Uglies*, by Scott Westerfeld. *Guardian*. Guardian News and Media, 23 June 2012. Web. 9 Mar. 2015. <http://www.theguardian.com/books/2012/jun/23/review-uglies-scott-westerfield>.

The Vampire Diaries (Series)

Author: L. J. Smith (b. 1965)
First published: *The Vampire Diaries: The Awakening* (1991)
The Vampire Diaries: The Struggle (1991)
The Vampire Diaries: The Fury (1991)
The Vampire Diaries: Dark Reunion (1992)
Type of work: Novel
Type of plot: Paranormal; Romance
Time of plot: 1990s
Locale: Fell's Church, Virginia

Principal characters

Elena Gilbert, a high school senior and the main diarist
Stefan Salvatore, a vampire who is in love with Elena's
Damon Salvatore, a vampire and Stefan's brother
Bonnie McCullough, Elena's friend and a diarist in the fourth volume
Meredith Sulez, Elena's friend
Caroline Forbes, Elena's former friend and now archrival
Matt Honeycutt, Elena's former boyfriend and Stefan's friend

The Story

Elena Gilbert, a senior at Robert E. Lee High School in the fictional northern Virginia town of Fell's Church, has returned from a summer vacation in Paris. For some inexplicable reason, she is gripped with an unusual sense of foreboding. Elena's parents had been killed in an automobile accident three years prior, and she and Margaret, her four-year-old sister, now live with their aunt Judith and Robert Maxwell, Aunt Judith's fiancé. The first entry of Elena's diary is dated September 4, 1991, and the first line consists of the crossed-out sentence, "Something awful is going to happen today." Then she states that she has no idea why she wrote this and attributes it to an irrational fear. At school, she is the most popular girl and has been voted homecoming queen. The boys are drawn to her, and the girls either emulate or envy her. She has a small circle of friends: Meredith Sulez, who is dark, proper, level-headed, and protective; Bonnie McCullough, who is high strung and very interested in the occult; and her boyfriend, Matt Honeycutt. One former friend named Caroline Forbes has become her enemy over some unspecified wrong.

The reader also learns that Elena has decided to break up with Matt because she feels their relationship can never go beyond the point of friendship. Matt, though saddened, accepts it calmly. Two things also happen this day that unsettle Elena. First is an encounter with a huge crow sitting on a tree branch peering at her in a strange way. She is so unnerved by this that she throws stones to drive the bird away. Second, there is the unexpected arrival at school of a new student who intrigues and disturbs her.

Stefan Salvatore is from Italy, and he is dark complexioned, handsome, and mysterious. Elena is immediately taken by him, but he resists her attempts at conversation, something that Elena is not accustomed to and that hurts and humiliates her. She develops a longing that evolves into an obsession with winning him over. Through the use of flashbacks the reader learns that Stefan is a vampire who was born in Florence, Italy, during the fifteenth century. He and his equally swarthy and handsome older brother Damon were sons of a count. When the very lovely Katherine, daughter of a German baron, stays with the Salvatore family to regain her health in the warmer Italian climate, the two brothers are smitten and develop a murderously intense rivalry over her. Katherine, however, is a vampire, and when she is unable to choose between Stefan and Damon, she visits each one on the same night and bites their necks, mingling their blood with hers to possess them. Her plan is that all three will live together harmoniously as undead beings. When she realizes that she has underestimated the intensity of the hatred between the siblings, she leaves to kill herself by removing the ring that protected her from the sun's rays. The brothers blame each other for Katherine's death and duel with swords, killing each other. The circumstances of their deaths condemned them to be reborn as vampires, endowed with extraordinary strength and powers but living a furtive existence and doomed to survive on animal and human blood.

Damon embraces his new nature with much more zeal than Stefan, drinking mainly human blood and becoming more powerful. Stefan, however, is riddled with guilt over Katherine's death and tries to be as unobtrusive as possible. He enrolls as a student at Robert E. Lee in order to blend in. He sees Elena, who bears an uncanny resemblance to Katherine, and although he longs for her, he assumes a cold and indifferent attitude around her in order to protect her from himself. Damon, who has arrived in Fell's Church in the form of a crow, watches Elena, recognizes her resemblance to Katherine, and determines to have her. Elena has several frightening encounters with Damon, and Stefan confesses the truth that he and Damon are vampires and tells Elena the story of Katherine. Regardless, Elena declares her love for Stefan and yields herself to him in order to be bitten on the neck.

Strange and disturbing things happen: an old man is found bitten on the neck and nearly dies from the loss of blood; an unpopular history teacher is stabbed to death at a Halloween haunted house event; and Stefan disappears. Although Stefan is suspected, Damon is the reason for the teacher's death. Stefan is nearly killed by Damon, who then traps Stefan in a well. Elena discovers where Stefan is and rescues him.

Meanwhile, the vengeful Caroline has stolen Elena's diary and plans to publicly embarrass Elena at the Founder's Day ceremony. Elena learns this, but all attempts to retrieve the diary fail. She is especially concerned about the diary's intimate passages that pledge her love for Stefan. When Caroline steps up to the podium, she discovers that the diary has been switched with another. She is so embarrassed that she runs away in tears. Elena then has an argument with her aunt over Stefan, and she angrily leaves in Matt's car. She feels a sinister force pursuing her and drives recklessly over a bridge and into the river. Her body is retrieved by Stefan

and her friends, and the enraged Stefan assumes the shape of a falcon and engages in a death struggle with Damon.

During the time that Elena's body is unattended, she is reborn as a vampire and intervenes to stop the fight between Stefan and Damon and then declares her love for Damon. Damon and Stefan (who suspects brainwashing on Damon's part) grudgingly call a temporary truce in order to help Elena adjust to her new existence. A short while later Damon's mind control wears off and she is reconciled with Stefan.

Because Elena's body is never found, she is assumed to be dead. She secretively attends her own memorial service and then witnesses neighborhood dogs turning against the humans. She learns that Damon was not responsible for pursuing her on the night she died or for many of the other sinister events that took place. She and the brothers then decide that a malevolent force is at work. Elena reveals herself to Bonnie, Meredith, and Matt, and with the assistance of a psychologist and amateur vampire hunter named Alaric Saltzman, they discover that the "Other Force" is none other than Katherine, who never killed herself and has acquired incredible powers. She planned to control Elena, Stefan, and Damon and then kill them while unleashing the dogs that she controlled in order to annihilate the town. Elena defeats Katherine by throwing her into the sunlight, but also sacrifices her own life in doing so.

The focus of the story then switches in the fourth book with the narrative revolving around Bonnie, who begins a diary of her own. In its first entry, which is dated December 16, 1991, Bonnie is contacted by the deceased Elena, who warns her of a great danger lurking in the town. Two of their friends are murdered by this new menace, and Bonnie, Meredith, Matt, Stefan, and Damon, who are also joined by a repentant Caroline, endeavor to solve the mystery. They learn that a very powerful vampire known as Klaus has come to Fell's Church to avenge Katherine's death. Klaus helps a local student named Tyler Smallwood transform into a werewolf, and they are trying to destroy the teens. The conflict culminates in the cemetery on the night of the summer solstice. Meredith and Bonnie fight and temporarily defeat Tyler. Meanwhile, Klaus is about to kill Stefan. Damon tries to save his brother; Klaus retreats but returns to kill Stefan. Bonnie calls out Elena's name three times, which makes Klaus recoil and conjures up the hundreds of unquiet spirits of Civil War soldiers who had fought and died there. They are led by the spirit of

Elena. The spectral soldiers swarm Klaus and apparently destroy him. Elena heals all the combatants and is transformed from the spirit form and walks off with Stefan. Readers are left to wonder whether she is human or vampire.

Critical Evaluation

Although the narrative of *The Vampire Diaries* is compelling with enough romance, suspense, mystery, and violence to appeal to a wide range of tastes, the story also has a melodramatic feel to it that is akin to the 1960s daytime television soap opera *Dark Shadows*. There are certain integral elements of the murder-mystery genre as the protagonists, their friends, and allies work to peel back the layers of events and circumstance to reveal various truths, which seem to change based on a character's status and motives. Older adult characters, such as Aunt Judith, Robert Maxwell, and Mr. Tanner, come across as stilted, ineffectual, and even irrelevant to the narrative.

The overriding themes are the familiar ones of good triumphing over evil and love prevailing over all obstacles. What makes this approach interesting and fresh, however, is the blurred line between good and evil both in the spirit and the material human realm. A constant refrain, referred to by more than one character is that "everything is not what it seems." Damon, who comes across initially as cold-hearted and cynical, becomes a valuable, though sometimes grudging, ally who is capable of kind and selfless actions. Katherine, depicted as a sweet and delicate but rather weak girl, is in the final analysis revealed as a vengeful and calculating entity bent on having her own way at the expense of others. Emotions are tangled: Elena fluctuates from Stefan to Damon and back again before becoming firm in her love for Stefan; Caroline's spiteful hostility gives way in the end to a strongly hinted, though not quite arrived-at, reconciliation with her erstwhile friend Elena; Bonnie's timid personality develops into a pivotal leadership role in the last volume, where she takes over as diarist and conduit of the narrative.

Suspense, characterization, and duality that forestalls any possible banality are strengths that the author has adroitly juxtaposed through highly differing personalities. She deftly plays these personalities against each other in both their conversations and their actions and creates an unusually convincing series of scenarios. These diverse internal and external character conflicts give rise to many of the story's most fascinating qualities. An exemplary instance of the tension and clash between personalities are Damon's jaundiced view of the world, where any means justifies a strictly self-interested end, against Stefan's oppositely exaggerated sense of honor and loyalty. Also noteworthy is Bonnie's escape from low self-esteem into the occult spirituality inspired by druidism, which is countered by Meredith's cool, unflappably assured posture of pragmatic common sense and logic.

Of all the characters, Elena, even when she is not present, commands the center stage and the triangular interchange between her and the Salvatore brothers maintains its hold to the very end. It is Elena that is the author's most compelling creation, with such a strong and enthralling characterization that she—not unlike the character of Sherlock Holmes—could not remain dead for long.

Raymond Pierre Hylton, PhD

Further Reading

Alter, Alexandra. "'Vampire Diaries' Writer Bites Back." *Wall Street Journal*. Dow Jones, 17 Apr. 2014. Web. 28 Dec. 2015. <http://www.wsj.com/articles/SB 10001424052702304058204579495491652398358>.

Clements, Susannah M. *The Vampire Defanged: How the Embodiment of Evil Became a Romantic Hero.* Grand Rapids: Brazos, 2011. Print.

McCoy, Karen. "What Teens Are Really Reading." *School Library Journal* 58.1 (2014): 32–34. *Academic Search Complete*. Web. 28 Dec. 2015. <http://search.ebscohost.com/login.aspx?direct=true&db=a9h&AN=70247909>.

Weetzie Bat

Author: Francesca Lia Block (b. 1962)
First published: 1989
Type of Work: Novel
Type of Plot: Fantasy; Realism
Time of Plot: 1980s
Locale: Los Angeles, California

Principal Characters

Weetzie Bat, a skinny, punkish Angelino navigating life after high school in a changing city

Charlie Bat, Weetzie's melancholy, playwright father who lives in New York City

My Secret Agent Lover Man, Weetzie's filmmaker lover and partner

Dirk, Weetzie's gay, Mohawk-sporting best friend

Duck, Dirk's surfer partner

Fifi, Dirk's nurturing grandmother with a prodigious wardrobe

The Story

Weetzie Bat, a teenager so named by her father, Charlie Bat, lives in a Los Angeles that to most Angelinos would be passingly familiar. Weetzie loves finding plastic palm tree wallets at the farmers' market, fitting her tiny hands into Marilyn Monroe's handprints in front of Grauman's Chinese Theater, watching the roller-skating servers at Tiny Naylor's, eating pastrami burritos at Oki Dogs, and eating strawberry sundaes at Schwab's Pharmacy. The places she inhabits are real (or were real at one time), but the world in which Weetzie moves is a punkish fairy tale. Her experiences are rich in color but vague in detail; her life is always fantastical, if not always a fantasy. Her parents, who met in Hollywood in the 1950s, are divorced and do not speak. Animosity for the other, along with booze and pills, infuses each, and both could be described, in their attitudes toward Weetzie, as loving but absent. No one understands Weetzie—or her love of the actress Jayne Mansfield, or her elaborate American Indian–inspired feathered headdress—until she meets a fellow student named Dirk. All the girls are in love with Dirk; he wears his hair in a black Mohawk and drives a 1955 red Pontiac named Jerry.

The two teenagers become inseparable, going to movies and concerts together. Eventually Dirk confesses that he is gay, and the two embark on a number of misguided trysts with terrible men. They refer to men as "ducks," and Weetzie names her imaginary dream duck My Secret Agent Lover Man. A bright spot in their already fairly sunny life is their relationship with Dirk's grandmother, Fifi. Fifi lives in a cottage full of beautiful old dresses and strange objects—including a golden lamp with a genie inside, which she gives to Weetzie. Weetzie wishes for "a duck for Dirk, and My Secret Agent Lover Man for me," as well as a nice little house where they all can live "happily ever after." Almost immediately, Fifi dies and leaves Dirk and Weetzie her cottage. Dirk meets a surfer named Duck. Time passes, and just when Weetzie thinks that the genie forgot about her, she meets a mysterious man named, of course, My Secret Agent Lover Man. He moves in. The foursome is happy until Weetzie decides that she wants to have a baby. My Secret Agent Lover

Man is not ready to be a father, so Weetzie conspires to sleep with Dirk and Duck to conceive a child. She becomes pregnant, and My Secret Agent Lover Man, feeling betrayed, leaves her. After she gives birth—to a baby named Cherokee—My Secret Agent Lover Man comes back, but Weetzie soon discovers that he has a secret. While he was gone, he slept with a witch. The witch had a baby, which she leaves on Weetzie's doorstep. The baby is named Lily, though they mostly call her Witch Baby because she is so strange. They make for a large and loving family; however, "happily ever after" eludes them—Weetzie's father dies and Duck runs away when his friend dies of AIDS. Dirk must travel to San Francisco to retrieve him. The final image of the book is the family, together again, sharing a meal and Weetzie realizes that great pain walks hand in hand with great love. "I don't know about happily ever after . . . but I know about happily," Weetzie thinks.

Critical Evaluation

Weetzie Bat, Francesca Lia Block's first book, was published in 1989. Betsy Hearne for the *New York Times* described the book as a "punk, young adult fairy tale" about family. Hearne praised Block's vivid imagery (for instance, "He reminded [Weetzie] of a cigarette") and inventive language, but Block's skill with words is only a part of the book's enduring appeal. When *Weetzie Bat* was published it was criticized by readers for its portrayal of sexual relationships between both gay and heterosexual partners. The response to Hearne's praise in the *New York Times* was met with some readers questioning if the book provided a good role model for American teenagers. This response may have been prompted by the AIDS epidemic reaching its height in July of 1988; in June of 1989, the *Orlando Sentinel* posted a report from the US Centers for Disease Control and Prevention reporting that researchers were disturbed by the epidemic proportions of American teenagers becoming infected with the virus. Yet, it was Block's unorthodox view of love during this time, and her embrace of adult themes like death, disease, and parenthood that captured the imaginations of two generations of teenagers. Weetzie lives out a child's fantasy of adulthood; she is Cinderella with a bleached blond flat top wearing "old fifties' taffeta dresses covered with poetry written in glitter." She is reassurance that though there are bad things in the world, the world itself is not bad. And for all of its specificity, the book bears a universal theme: love conquers all—and then everyone drinks champagne on a beach.

Francesca Lia Block wrote several sequels to *Weetzie Bat*. The books are called the Dangerous Angels series after a quote from *Weetzie Bat*.

Molly Hagan

Further Reading

Block, Francesca Lia. "Danger Angels." Interview by Autumn De Wilde. *Paper Magazine*. Paper Pub., 3 Mar. 2011. Web. 30 Apr. 2015. <http://www.paper-mag.com/2011/03/danger_angels.php>.

Hearne, Betsy. "Children's Books: Pretty in Punk." Rev. of *Weetzie Bat*, by Francesca Lia Block. *New York Times*. New York Times, 21 May 1989. Web. 30 Apr. 2015. <http://www.nytimes.com/1989/05/21/books/children-s-books-pretty-in-punk.html>.

Madison, Bennett. "Weetzie Bat Meets the Genie." Rev. of *Weetzie Bat*, by Francesca Lia Block. *Los Angeles Review of Books*. Los Angeles Rev. of Books, 23 Apr. 2012. Web. 30 Apr. 2015. <http://lareviewofbooks.org/essay/weetzie-bat-meets-the-genie>.

Where Things Come Back

Author: John Corey Whaley
First published: 2011
Type of work: Novel
Type of plot: Realism
Time of plot: Early twenty-first century
Locale: Arkansas; Atlanta; Georgia; Ethiopia

Principal characters:

Cullen Witter, an existentially troubled seventeen-year-old high school student

Gabriel Witter, Cullen's younger brother, disappears at fifteen

Lucas Cader, Cullen's best friend

Cabot Searcy, a philosophy graduate turned religious fanatic

Alma Ember, Cabot's estranged wife, becomes attracted to Cullen

Ada Taylor, a high school graduate on whom Cullen has a crush

Sarah and Samuel Witter, a hairdresser and a truck driver, parents of Cullen and Gabriel

The Story

One day in late spring of the novel's present, seventeen-year-old high school junior Cullen Witter must identify his cousin Oslo Fouke in a morgue in Little Rock, Arkansas. Oslo has died at the age of nineteen from a heroin overdose. Because Cullen's father, Samuel, has a hauling job, Cullen drives his mother, Sarah, and his fifteen-year-old brother, Gabriel, to the morgue and back to their home in the small town of Lily, Arkansas, where his mother runs a hair salon.

Cullen's best friend, Lucas Cader, protects Gabriel from bullies at school, which Cullen appreciates. However, Cullen feels ambivalent about Lucas's obnoxiously perky girlfriend, Mena Prescott. Cullen has a crush on senior Ada Taylor, who is dating the bully Russell Quitman. Two of Ada's previous boyfriends have died, one in a car crash and one in a boating accident.

The second chapter introduces the second plotline. The two plots are told in alternating chapters until they convene at the end. In Ethiopia, five years earlier, eighteen-year-old American Benton Sage is performing missionary work, aided by a shrewd local convert. However, he feels overwhelmed and out of his depth. Benton has a vision of God sending the angel Gabriel to help him.

At Oslo's funeral Cullen reflects on his complicated relationship with his father, who cannot attend because of another haul. Cullen then has a daydream about people around him turning into zombies. Excitement builds in town about the sighting of a supposedly extinct bird, soon called the Lazarus woodpecker, by an out-of-town professor, John Barling.

Lucas arranges a double date for Cullen with nineteen-year-old Alma Ember, who has returned to her native town after separating from her husband in Savannah, Georgia. They begin an affair, though Cullen is less enthusiastic about it than Alma. When Cullen returns home, Gabriel is missing, and before long the family has begun a frantic search. The excitement about the Lazarus woodpecker continues, and Cullen is angry that the town seems to consider this more newsworthy than Gabriel's disappearance.

Benton gives up missionary work and flies back to Atlanta, Georgia. His parents are so disappointed in his failure that they will not speak to him. Benton enrolls at the University of Atlanta, where he rooms with Cabot Searcy, but commits suicide several months later, on Christmas Eve.

The weeks-long wait for news about Gabriel has the Witters in despair. Cullen learns that Ada has broken up with Russell, who then got into a car accident due to drunk driving and is now paralyzed from the waist down. Cullen breaks up with Alma. Ada visits the convenience store where Cullen works to console him about his brother's disappearance.

Cullen's father hires a psychic, Vilonia Kline, but Kline's search for Gabriel proves futile. Ada and Cullen make love. Not long after, however, he learns Russell is back in town and that Ada still cares for him; when Cullen confronts Ada about this, she dumps him. Lucas attacks Barling on stage on Cullen's behalf.

After going through Benton's notebooks, Cabot becomes fascinated with the apocryphal biblical Book of Enoch, where the angel Gabriel acts as God's avenger. Cabot graduates college and moves to Savannah; there he meets Alma and the two begin a relationship. She gets pregnant and Cabot proposes to her. However, after Alma miscarries, their marriage quickly sours. Cabot becomes a religious fanatic.

Alma files for divorce from Cabot and moves back to Lily, where she has a date with Cullen. Cabot comes to Lily to confront Alma, who tells him of her date. This brings the two plotlines together on the day Gabriel disappears. Cabot drives to the Witters' and mistakes Gabriel for Cullen. He knocks Gabriel unconscious, locks him in his car trunk, and drives into a garage. He lets Gabriel out and learns he is Cullen's brother. The name Gabriel sends Cabot over the edge. He locks Gabriel back in the trunk and drives away.

After ten weeks of being imprisoned by Cabot in a locked room, Gabriel has a final conversation with his captor in which he says Cabot was not chosen by God. Cabot tells Gabriel: "It's time to say good-bye." Cullen has a vision of Gabriel returning alive.

Critical Evaluation

In 2012, *Where Things Come Back* won both the Michael L. Printz Award for best young adult book of 2011 and the William C. Morris YA Debut Award from the Young Adult Library Services Association (YALSA) for outstanding young adult first novel. The two awards recognized Whaley as a new author of literary merit.

The novel's key theme is how people deal with the loss, or potential loss, of a loved one. Beginning with Oslo's death from an overdose, there are many teenagers dying, seriously injured, or possibly dead in the story. Two of Ada's previous boyfriends died in accidents, Benton commits suicide, Lucas's older brother died in a drunken car crash, Russell is paralyzed for the same

reason, and Gabriel is abducted. The surviving characters—Cullen as well as Lucas, Oslo's mother, and Gabriel's parents—are shown to each cope differently with this loss. This gives Whaley's book a strong focus.

The question of whether Gabriel survives or is killed by Cabot is the final mystery that the novel refuses to answer directly. Cullen tells his story from a future point in time, yet he never says if Gabriel is alive or dead by then. The kindly psychologist Dr. Webb tells Cullen that when people "find it hard to cope," as Cabot does when Gabriel tells him Cabot was not chosen by God, it "leads to people throwing themselves in front of trains." The question is if Cabot killed Gabriel before committing suicide. Cabot's last words to Gabriel are deliberately ambiguous. The reader must decide if they mean suicide or murder-suicide. Cullen's final description of Gabriel returning home alive, however, is portrayed as a vision.

R. C. Lutz, PhD

Further Reading

Roper, Ingrid. "Spring 2011 Flying Stars: John Corey Whaley." *Publishers Weekly*. PWxyz, 20 June 2011. Web. 25 Mar. 2015. <http://www.publishersweekly.com/pw/by-topic/authors/interviews/article/47656-spring-2011-flying-starts-john-corey-whaley.html>.

Spicer, Ed. "Flying High: The Improbable True Tale of Debut Novelist John Corey Whaley." *School Library Journal*. School Library Journal, 1 May 2012. Web. 25 Mar. 2015. <http://www.slj.com/2012/05/authors-illustrators/flying-high-the-improbable-true-tale-of-debut-novelist-john-corey-whaley/>.

A Year Down Yonder

Author: Richard Peck (b. 1934)
First published: 2000
Type of work: Novel
Type of plot: Historical fiction; Humorous fiction
Time of plot: 1937–38
Locale: Rural Illinois

Principal characters

Mary Alice Dowdel, a fifteen-year-old girl from Chicago
Bootsie, Mary Alice's white-pawed cat

Grandma Dowdel, Mary Alice's white-haired, eccentric grandmother

Mildred Burdick, a tough local teen

Royce McNabb, a handsome teenager who recently arrived in town

The Story

In the fall of 1937, the Great Depression is in full swing. There is no room for Mary Alice Dowdel in the small Chicago apartment where her cash-strapped parents have been forced to move. Mary Alice is put aboard a train with a trunk full of clothes, her portable radio, and her cat Bootsie to travel to downstate Illinois to stay with her grandmother. Mary Alice and her older brother Joe, who is currently working out west for the Civilian Conservation Corps, often visited their grandmother during past summers. Now Mary Alice will attend school there. Grandma Dowdel, a tall, large-figured, and intimidating woman, greets her granddaughter at the station and immediately marches her to the local school, as she has already missed two weeks of classes.

The school features a water pump and privies, and a principal, Mr. Fluke, who is also the janitor, shop teacher, and sports coach. The twenty-five students—with a ratio of two girls to each boy—ride horses or mules to school. Newcomer Mary Alice is treated as a rich city girl and an outcast, in what promises to be a difficult year for the teenager.

Luckily, feisty Grandma Dowdel, a font of country wisdom who knows everything about everybody locally and has the boldness of a burglar, makes life interesting for Mary Alice. Grandma at once comes to her granddaughter's aid by putting school bully Mildred Burdick in her place, pointing out the less savory aspects of her family's history: Mildred's father is in prison for stealing sheep, and the horse she rides is likewise stolen.

Grandma, the mischievous instigator, involves Mary Alice in a number of rollicking adventures throughout the school year. Around Halloween, they foil a group of vandalizing pranksters. They also use a tractor to ram a pecan tree to collect nuts and steal pumpkins to make pies for a school party. During November's charitable turkey shoot, Grandma uses her wiles, threats, and blackmail to collect additional money from wealthy residents to assist disabled World War I veterans. At Christmas time, Grandma traps foxes and sells the skins in order to buy round-trip tickets so Mary Alice and her brother can go home for the holidays. For Washington's Birthday, Grandma talks the snooty women of the Daughters of the American Revolution into holding their annual tea at her house, where she defuses the banker's wife by revealing she was born into a low-class family and then adopted. Mary Alice dutifully (and gleefully) reports such facts in a gossipy column she is anonymously writing for a local newspaper.

One of the highlights of Mary Alice's experiences at Grandma's is the arrival at school of a newcomer, the handsome, Royce McNabb. Because they are both outsiders, Mary Alice and Royce naturally gravitate to one another. By the end of the school year it has become obvious that although Mary Alice will return to Chicago, she has not seen the last of Royce—or Grandma Dowdel.

Critical Evaluation

A Year Down Yonder is the sequel to the author's *A Long Way from Chicago* (1998), both of which won the Newbery Medal for children's literature. *A Year Down Yonder* continues the exploits of two major characters from the first novel (which, presented from Joey Dowdel's point of view, was accurately subtitled "a novel in stories"), Mary Alice and Grandma Dowdel.

As in the first book, the young woman and the old lady are depicted in episodic fashion in a series of humorous, almost slapstick incidents keyed to seasonal celebrations. The novel is essentially a dual character study. Elderly Grandma Dowdel is viewed from the wide-eyed, first-person perspective of the impressionable Mary Alice, who at the same time reveals aspects of herself as she evolves from childish homesickness and resentment through a grudging acceptance of her situation to an enthusiastic admiration of her grandmother's special qualities. The novel's individual chapters are self-contained, and each could stand alone as a complete short story, with a setup, development, and conclusion. However, the separate stories are linked by time, place, and character into a cohesive narrative that collectively illustrate young Mary Alice's growth and maturity during the year she spends in the company of her dynamic elderly relative.

Both main and secondary characters are well drawn in *A Year Down Yonder*, with small, telling details—personality quirks, speaking habits, unconscious gestures—that make it possible for readers to visualize them. Haughty Mrs. Weidenbach, cross-eyed and bucktoothed Effie Wilcox, man-hungry postmistress Maxine Patch, and itinerant Works Progress Administration artist Arnold Green all come to life on the page. Though events described in *Down Yonder* are supposed to have occurred in an innocent, less technologically sophisticated age, they are nonetheless understandable to contemporary readers. The narrative is spiced with items of country lore (such as buttering a cat's paws to help it adapt to a new environment; by the time the feline licks its paws clean, it will feel right at home) to maintain interest. Most readers may never have heard of the radio programs Mary Alice listens to on her radio at night (such as *The Baby Snooks Show*, *Fibber McGee and Molly*, and the *Edgar Bergen–Charlie McCarthy Show*), but they can appreciate the similarity to the contentment provided by modern programming. Adolescents can likewise easily relate to the difficulties of adapting to an unfamiliar environment, the uncertainty of how to act among strangers, the shame of being associated with an embarrassing older relative, or the thrill of fresh romance as highlighted in the novel.

Jack Ewing

Further Reading

Burnet, Matia. "Great Expectations: An Interactive Workshop with Richard Peck." *Publishers Weekly*. PWxyz, 17 June 2014. Web. 28 Sept. 2015. <http://www.publishersweekly.com/pw/by-topic/childrens/childrens-authors/article/62904-great-expectations-an-interactive-workshop-with-richard-peck.html>.

Peck, Richard. Interview by Lori Tracy. *Macklin Educational Resources*. Macklin Educational Resources, n.d. Web. 28 Sept. 2015. <https://www.mackin.com/LIBRARY/AUTHOR_INTERVIEWS-PECK.aspx>.

FILM ADAPTATIONS OF
YOUNG ADULT
LITERATURE

Alex Rider: Operation Stormbreaker

The Book

Author: Anthony Horowitz (b. 1955)
First published: 2000

The Film

Director: Geoffrey Sax
Screenplay by: Anthony Horowitz
Starring: Alex Pettyfer, Ewan McGregor, Damian Lewis, Mickey Rourke, Bill Nighy, Sophie Okonedo

Context

During the first decade of the twenty-first century, young adult literature experienced a meteoric rise in popularity as many teens became avid readers of books about characters their own age within all genres, from science fiction and fantasy to mystery to realistic fiction. In light of the popularity of young adult fiction, film studios adapted many popular novels for the screen in an attempt to capture such books' devoted young audiences. The success of the Harry Potter film series, based on the novels by British author J. K. Rowling, demonstrated unequivocally that young adult series had the potential to inspire profitable and long-running film franchises. At the same time, the genre of spy and secret agent narratives was experiencing a resurgence in popularity in film; the decade brought two new films in the Mission: Impossible film series, as well as the first three Jason Bourne films, adapted from the novels of American writer Robert Ludlum. Perhaps the most famous of cinema's spies, James Bond, appeared in three films during the decade, portrayed by two different actors. Even spy films for children were popular during the decade; the 2001 film *Spy Kids* was not only a critical and financial success but also launched a multifilm franchise. A spy film for teens adapted from a popular novel, then, was in line with trends in genre as well as viewership.

Alex Rider: Operation Stormbreaker, known in the United Kingdom as *Alex Rider: Stormbreaker*, was based on the novel *Stormbreaker* by British writer Anthony Horowitz. The author of numerous books for children as well as a television writer, Horowitz would later be tapped to write novels about established characters such as Sherlock Holmes and James Bond, in part because of his success as a writer of mystery and spy

novels for young readers. Published in 2000, *Stormbreaker* tells the story of fourteen-year-old Alex Rider, who, upon learning that his uncle and sole guardian has been killed while secretly working for the British intelligence agency MI6, is recruited into the high-stakes world of international espionage. In *Stormbreaker*, Alex investigates and must stop the devious supercomputer scheme of billionaire Darius Sayle. The novel proved popular in the United Kingdom and the United States and inspired the writing of numerous other novels in the Alex Rider series, including *Point Blanc* (2001), *Ark Angel* (2005), and *Russian Roulette* (2013), as well as various graphic novels and tie-in books.

The film adaptation of the novel was directed by Geoffrey Sax, a British director who had primarily worked in television. Unlike many adaptations of popular books, *Alex Rider: Operation Stormbreaker* was written by the author of the original novels rather than an unrelated screenwriter. Horowitz was a good fit for the job, considering his two decades of work as a screenwriter; he had previously written for a variety of television series and also penned *Just Ask for Diamond* (1988; released in the United States as *Diamond's Edge*), the film adaptation of his 1986 novel *The Falcon's Malteser*. Starring relative newcomer Alex Pettyfer as its protagonist and Mickey Rourke as its antagonist, *Alex Rider: Operation Stormbreaker* premiered in US and UK theaters in 2006.

Film Analysis

As the screenplay for *Alex Rider: Operation Stormbreaker* was written by Horowitz, the author of the original novel, the adaptation is a relatively straightforward one; a number of key scenes and conversations adhere very closely to those in the original work. Although relatively faithful to the original, the narrative was altered in several respects while being adapted for the screen, for a variety of purposes. Some changes were made simply for the purpose of modernizing elements of the novel, which was published six years before the premiere of the film; for example, the Nintendo Game Boy Color portable game console featured in the book is replaced with the more modern Nintendo DS in the film. Others, however, concerned the need to render the narrative more suitable for the medium of film, which tends to demand more action sequences and visually entertaining scenes.

A scene at the beginning of the film exemplifies this sort of change. While Alex Rider (Alex Pettyfer) tells his class at school about his family, his secret agent uncle, Ian (Ewan McGregor), is seen riding a motorcycle, with enemies in pursuit. A chase ensues, with Ian switching his mode of transportation to a flashy BMW after seemingly evading his pursuers. After he briefly speaks to Alex on the phone, a helicopter descends on Ian, and the assassin Yassen Gregorovich (Damian Lewis) shoots and kills him. Ian's death is not seen in the novel, which begins with Alex learning that his uncle has died, supposedly in a car accident. The true circumstances of his death are not immediately revealed, and the reader learns the pertinent details along with Alex. By including this scene in the film, however, the filmmakers accomplish several things. First, it enables the film to begin with an exciting action sequence that sets the stage for the action-focused narrative. Second, through this depiction of Ian, the film establishes him as a character reminiscent of the famous cinematic spy James Bond, who is often depicted evading pursuit via automobile in his films. Unlike Bond, Ian does not emerge from the car chase unscathed. Indeed, including the death of Ian Rider in the film allows the filmmakers to make a strong statement: the film is not about him. The suave adult spy is killed before the title of the film even appears on screen; the film, then, will be devoted not to adults but to the teenage Alex.

The remainder of the film further demonstrates the ways in which written narratives are often made more action-focused when adapted for the screen. In one scene, Alex spots a moving van in front of his uncle's house. Suspecting that the van has something to do with his uncle's mysterious demise, Alex chases the van across London on his bicycle, weaving between cars, narrowly avoiding multiple collisions, and even jumping over a car that blocks his path. He follows the van to a junkyard, where he discovers his uncle's car and its telltale bullet holes. He hides in the car to avoid detection but is nearly crushed when the car is placed into a compactor. Struggling to escape from certain death, he manages to activate the car's ejector seat, which launches him out of the car in the nick of time. He flees the scene but, spotted by the scrapyard's workers, is forced to use his martial arts skills to defeat several grown men. One man attempts to shoot him, but Alex evades the bullets and speeds away on his bicycle. This scene differs significantly from the scene in the novel, which provides a more restrained take on Alex's discovery of his uncle's bullet-riddled car. Rather than chasing the suspicious van through London, he browses the phonebook in search of junkyards—a far less visually interesting means of determining where his uncle's car was taken. While he is nearly crushed by the car compactor, he escapes by clambering through a small opening rather than with the aid of an ejector seat. Alex

has the opportunity to put his martial arts skills to use when escaping the junkyard, but he faces only one opponent rather than several. The version of this scene presented in the film, then, provides a more exaggerated take on its events, featuring additional action sequences that demonstrate Alex's physical skills.

The inclusion of the ejector seat, a device strongly associated with spy films in general and the Bond films in particular, in the scene at the junkyard provides a tangible connection between *Alex Rider: Operation Stormbreaker* and earlier films in its genre. In many ways, the film engages with the narrative tropes of the genre throughout, including numerous elements common in spy films. There is a long history of the use of inventive and at-times absurd gadgets in spy media, and *Alex Rider* is no exception. After being recruited by MI6 agents Alan Blunt (Bill Nighy) and Mrs. Jones (Sophie Okonedo), Alex visits a man named Smithers (Stephen Fry) to obtain the necessary gadgets for his mission. Smithers, who fills a role similar to that of the James Bond films' Q, provides him with a variety of age-appropriate devices that will assist him in his mission. Some, such as a container of pimple cream that can burn its way through metal, are mentioned in the book, while others, such as a fountain pen that dispenses a mind-control drug, are original to the film. The inclusion of the entirely unrealistic fountain pen, much like the ejector seat, enhances the overall tone of the film, rendering it more escapist and lighthearted than many more realistic films in the genre. Similarly, the film's inclusion of action sequences not present in the novel enables it to meet the expectations of moviegoers familiar with the film tradition at hand.

Significance

Upon its release in 2006, *Alex Rider: Operation Stormbreaker* performed poorly in the United States, grossing less than $700,000. The film fared better internationally, grossing $23 million, more than half of that in the United Kingdom, its country of origin. Because of those relatively low revenues, the film was considered a financial disappointment by its studio. *Alex Rider: Operation Stormbreaker* likewise fared poorly with critics, earning largely negative reviews. While some critics found the film entertaining and praised the performances of its supporting cast in particular, the majority of reviewers deemed it a lackluster attempt at making a James Bond film for teens. The video game based on the film, released for the Nintendo DS—a device featured in the film—was likewise poorly received.

As the first book in a lengthy series of novels (ten as of 2015), *Stormbreaker* provided a strong potential jumping-off point for a film franchise, a greatly sought-after quality after the international success of the Harry Potter franchise. Horowitz stated in interviews at the time of the film's release that he had already completed two drafts of an adaptation of the second Alex Rider novel, *Point Blanc*, the fate of which depended on the success of the first film. Despite the series' franchise potential, however, the poor critical and financial performance of *Alex Rider: Operation Stormbreaker* rendered the possibility of future sequels highly unlikely.

Joy Crelin

Further Reading

Horowitz, Anthony. "Exclusive Interview with Writer Anthony Horowitz." Interview by Rebecca Murray. *About Entertainment*. About.com, 2006. Web. 30 Nov. 2015. <http://movies.about.com/od/stormbreaker/a/stormah100106.htm>.

Horowitz, Anthony. *Stormbreaker*. New York: Penguin, 2006. Print.

Bibliography

Bradshaw, Peter. "Stormbreaker." Rev. of *Alex Rider: Stormbreaker*, dir. Geoffrey Sax. *Guardian*. Guardian News and Media, 20 July 2006. Web. 30 Nov. 2015. <http://www.theguardian.com/film/2006/jul/21/family.comedy>.

Hartlaub, Peter. "Ho-Hum Spy Caper Would Be Barely Worth TiVo-ing." Rev. of *Alex Rider: Operation Stormbreaker*, dir. Geoffrey Sax. *SFGate*. Hearst Communications, 13 Oct. 2006. Web. 8 Dec. 2015. <http://www.sfgate.com/movies/article/Ho-hum-spy-caper-would-be-barely-worth-TiVo-ing-2550081.php>.

Lee, Nathan. "Alex Rider: Operation Stormbreaker (2006)." Rev. of *Alex Rider: Operation Stormbreaker*, dir. Geoffrey Sax. *New York Times*. New York Times, 13 Oct. 2006. Web. 30 Nov. 2015. <http://www.nytimes.com/2006/10/13/movies/13stor.html?_r=0>.

Phipps, Keith. "Alex Rider: Operation Stormbreaker." Rev. of *Alex Rider: Operation Stormbreaker*, dir. Geoffrey Sax. *A.V. Club*. Onion, 12 Oct. 2006. Web. 30 Nov. 2015. <http://www.avclub.com/review/alex-rider-operation-stormbreaker-3756>.

Angus, Thongs and Perfect Snogging

The Books

Author: Louise Rennison (b. 1951)
First published: *Angus, Thongs and Full-Frontal Snogging* (1999)
It's OK, I'm Wearing Really Big Knickers (2000; *On the Bright Side, I'm Now the Girlfriend of a Sex God*, 2001)

The Film

Director: Gurinder Chadha (b. 1960)
Screenplay by: Gurinder Chadha, Paul Mayeda Berges, Will McRobb, Chris Viscardi
Starring: Georgia Groome, Aaron Taylor-Johnson, Karen Taylor, Alan Davies

Context

Amid the increasing popularity of young adult literature in the late twentieth and early twenty-first centuries, countless novels have explored the teenage experience of growing up and coming of age in contemporary times and have done so from the teenager's point of view. While many books often take a serious approach to such issues, a significant number of authors of young adult fiction have recognized that humor can likewise shed light on the worries, failures, and triumphs of the teenage years. The Confessions of Georgia Nicolson series, published between 1999 and 2009 by British writer and comedian Louise Rennison, provides a humorous take on teenage life, friendships, and romance from the point of view of Georgia Nicolson, an often self-absorbed but nevertheless kindhearted young teen growing up in England. Written in diary format, the Confessions of Georgia Nicolson series could in many ways be considered a young adult successor to Helen Fielding's Bridget Jones series (1996–2013), which documents the misadventures of an adult British woman through her comical diary entries. However, Rennison, a former comic and performer, was primarily inspired not by existing works but by her own experiences as a teenager as well as her interactions with teens both before and after the inception of the series. A number of the events and characters in the novels are drawn directly from Rennison's own life, lending her books an additional degree of realism despite their often outlandish humor.

The 2008 film *Angus, Thongs and Perfect Snogging* incorporates elements from the first two books in Rennison's series, *Angus, Thongs and Full-Frontal Snogging* (1999) and *It's OK, I'm Wearing Really Big Knickers* (2000), the latter of which was published in the United States under the title *On the Bright Side, I'm Now the Girlfriend of a Sex God* in 2001. American film executives felt the phrase "full-frontal" would discourage parents from letting their teens see the film, so they requested the name change. The film was directed and cowritten by Gurinder Chadha, who is perhaps best known for the 2002 film *Bend It Like Beckham*. Although focusing on older teens and dealing with issues of race, tradition, and family that are not considered in *Angus, Thongs and Perfect Snogging*, *Bend It Like Beckham* displays a similar emphasis on humor and friendships among young women. In adapting the Georgia Nicolson books, Chadha intended to present a somewhat different take on the narrative than that of the source material; in an interview with David Gritten for the *Telegraph* published shortly before the film's release, Chadha explained that while Rennison's novels are marketed almost exclusively to preteen and teenage girls, she intended for the film to appeal to a wider audience, in a manner similar to that of 1980s teen comedies such as *Sixteen Candles*, which was directed and written by American filmmaker John Hughes. Chadha likewise noted that she hoped to give the film a somewhat more serious tone while still retaining the spirit of the original novels, which became best sellers and were widely popular in the United Kingdom as well as the United States.

Film Analysis

Angus, Thongs and Perfect Snogging begins with a memorable scene that sets the tone for much of the remainder of the film. Fourteen-year-old Georgia (Georgia Groome), dressed as a stuffed olive, walks down the street as her father drives alongside her, attempting to persuade her to get into the car and allow him to drive her to her destination, a costume party. She refuses, considering being driven places by her father to be childish and embarrassing. Upon her arrival at the party, Georgia realizes that her friends, who had planned to dress as various hors d'oeuvres as well, have instead dressed in more socially acceptable devil, angel, and fairy costumes. Embarrassed by her fellow partygoers' reactions to her costume, Georgia flees the party and runs all the way home.

The opening establishes the overall drive for social acceptance that motivates Georgia throughout the film,

which combines events from the novels and also introduces several new events that do not take place in the novels.

Over the course of the film, Georgia meets and attempts to win over a handsome older boy named Robbie (played by Aaron Taylor-Johnson), feuds with Robbie's girlfriend, takes kissing lessons from a would-be teenage Casanova, dates another boy in order to make Robbie jealous, and ultimately wins her crush's affections at her fifteenth birthday party. While many of Georgia's actions seem solely intended to win Robbie's attention, her true needs are more well-rounded. Just as Georgia seeks Robbie's acknowledgement, she also desires the acceptance of her female friends and peers as well as her parents' recognition of her as a young woman rather than as a child. Though often misguided in her methods, Georgia ultimately craves unconditional love and understanding, a need shared by most people regardless of age.

Georgia's pursuit of Robbie is an ongoing story line in the Confessions of Georgia Nicolson series. For the film, however, it was necessary to construct a narrative with a defined endpoint and resolution. As such, much of the action of the film leads up to Georgia's climactic birthday party. Early on in the film, Georgia attempts to persuade her parents, Bob (played by Alan Davies) and Connie (played by Karen Taylor), to let her rent a dance club for her party, believing that holding a party at such a venue would express her maturity and sophistication. She continues in that vein for much of the film. However, by the time her mother is ready to talk about party plans, Georgia, feeling hopeless about her social life and worried about her family, tells her that she no longer wants a party and wants the family to join her father in New Zealand, where he is working for a time. On the night of Georgia's birthday, her mother takes her to a dance club, where she and Georgia's friends have thrown a surprise party. Georgia's father attends as well, having returned from New Zealand without her knowledge. Finally, Robbie publicly chooses Georgia over the cruel and stuck-up Lindsay (played by Kimberley Nixon), rendering her party an especially triumphant moment. The birthday party subplot does not exist in either of the novels on which the film is based, and Georgia's relationship with Robbie is portrayed as greatly in flux in the books. The film, however, crystalizes many of Georgia's worries, hopes, and aspirations through the party subplot.

In addition to these changes to the narrative, one of the most major differences between the novels and the film is the noticeable shift in tone. This was a conscious choice on the part of director Chadha, who explained in her interview with Gritten that the film has "more at stake" than the novels, which are heavily comedic and rarely touch on serious topics more than briefly. Perhaps the most obvious example of the film's more serious treatment of Georgia's life is the subplot concerning her worries about the stability of her family. Midway through the film, Bob leaves for New Zealand to take a new position in his company there. Georgia initially seems not to mind that her father, whom she perceives as tragically embarrassing, is gone. However, she grows concerned when Connie hires an attractive interior decorator named Jem (played by Steve Jones) to redecorate one of the rooms of their house while Bob is gone. Georgia believes her mother is blatantly flirting with Jem and is upset when Jem seems to reciprocate, cooking for Connie and accompanying her to a salsa-dancing class. Fearing that her parents will divorce, Georgia visits her father's former office and tearfully confides in the receptionist; soon afterward, she puts her own desires aside and tells her mother that she wants the family to move to New Zealand. Ultimately her father is able to return to England, and Jem is revealed to be gay, alleviating Georgia's worries.

This subplot is dramatically different from similar plots in the series' first two novels. In *Angus, Thongs and Full-Frontal Snogging*, Connie hires Jem as in the film, and Georgia takes note of her mother's tendency to flirt with him. However, she demonstrates little true concern, writing in her diary,

> What next? My mum goes off with a builder while my vati is trying to build a new life for her in the Antipodes?
> Actually, when put like that, it seems fair enough.
> (161)

She later writes that she will talk to her mother about Jem, but in an entry written an hour later she writes, "Can't be bothered" (162). A somewhat similar situation occurs in the second novel in the series, *It's OK, I'm Wearing Really Big Knickers!*, in which Connie seems to flirt with an attractive doctor and repeatedly makes excuses to see him. Though embarrassed by her mother's behavior, Georgia is not very upset and at one point notes that if her mother had an affair with the doctor, he could potentially get Georgia "a good deal on [a] nose job" (198). As these reactions demonstrate, the Georgia who is featured in the novels is not seriously concerned about her parents' relationship; rather, she is merely embarrassed by the idea of adults as sexual beings, and any true concern that her mother is having an affair is eclipsed by her own social and relationship concerns. Hoping to make the tone of the film more serious as well as present Georgia's parents as three-dimensional characters in their own right, Chadha and her cowriters transformed some of the novels' comical moments into a serious subplot with clear emotional stakes.

Significance

Angus, Thongs and Perfect Snogging premiered in UK movie theaters in July of 2008. Although distributed by the American film company Paramount, the film did not receive a theatrical release in the United States, perhaps in part because of its uniquely British characters. However, the film did air on American television as part of the channel Nickelodeon's teen-oriented evening programming, and it was also released on DVD. The film ultimately grossed nearly 15 million dollars worldwide.

The film met with mixed critical response following its release, with some critics finding it to be awkward and somewhat frivolous. Other critics familiar with the original novels felt that the film failed to capture the spirit of its source material and lacked much of the humor that made the books so entertaining. Prior to the film's release, Rennison herself remarked to Gritten that she believed the film should have contained more jokes. However, a number of other film reviewers praised *Angus, Thongs and Perfect Snogging*, calling attention to its charming depiction of realistic teenage worries as well as friendships, romances, and family relationships.

Joy Crelin

Further Reading

Chadha, Gurinder. "Gurinder Chadha on 'Angus, Thongs and Perfect Snogging.'" Interview by Wally Hammond. *Time Out London*. Time Out, 2008. Web. 31 Mar. 2015. <http://www.timeout.com/london/film/gurinder-chadha-on-angus-thongs-and-perfect-snogging>.

Gritten, David. "Gurinder Chadha Talks about *Angus, Thongs and Perfect Snogging*." *Telegraph*. Telegraph Media Group, 12 July 2008. Web. 31 Mar. 2015. <http://www.telegraph.co.uk/culture/film/3556336/Gurinder-Chadha-talks-about-Angus-Thongs-and-Perfect-Snogging.html>.

Official Georgia Nicolson Website. HarperCollins, 2013. Web. 31 Mar. 2015. <http://www.georgianicolson.com/index.html>.

Bibliography

Bradshaw, Peter. Rev. of *Angus, Thongs, and Perfect Snogging. Guardian*. Guardian News and Media, 24 July 2008. Web. 31 Mar. 2015. <http://www.theguardian.com/film/2008/jul/25/comedy>.

Hall, Sandra. Rev. of *Angus, Thongs and Perfect Snogging. Sydney Morning Herald*. Fairfax Digital, 18 Sept. 2008. Web. 31 Mar. 2015. <http://www.smh.com.au/news/entertainment/film/film-reviews/angus-thongs-and-perfect-snogging/2008/09/18/1221330985991.html>.

Johnson, Joanna Webb. "Chick Lit Jr.: More Than Glitz and Glamour for Teens and Tweens." *Chick Lit: The New Woman's Fiction*. Ed. Suzanne Ferriss and Mallory Young. New York: Routledge, 2006. 141–58. Print.

Kermode, Jennie. Rev. of *Angus, Thongs and Perfect Snogging. Eye for Film*. Eye for Film, 21 July 2008. Web. 31 Mar. 2015. <http://www.eyeforfilm.co.uk/review/angus-thongs-and-perfect-snogging-film-review-by-jennie-kermode>.

Robey, Tim. Rev. of *Angus, Thongs and Perfect Snogging. Telegraph*. Telegraph Media Group, 25 July 2008. Web. 31 Mar. 2015. <http://www.telegraph.co.uk/culture/film/filmreviews/3557094/Film-reviews-Angus-Thongs-and-Perfect-Snogging-and-Baby-Mama.html>.

Aquamarine

The Book

Author: Alice Hoffman (b. 1952)
First published: 2001

The Film

Director: Elizabeth Allen Rosenbaum
Screenplay by: John Quaintance, Jessica Bendinger
Starring: Emma Roberts, Joanna Levesque, Sara Paxton, Jake McDorman

Context

Alice Hoffman's *Aquamarine* is a mermaid tale and the first of two preteen novels comprising the Water Tales series. The magical tone of the *Aquamarine* novel is also part of the film version, although the film and novel differ greatly in several ways. The film features the niece of actor Julia Roberts, Emma Roberts, who later starred in *Nancy Drew* (2007) and *Hotel for Dogs* (2009). *Aquamarine* also includes performances by Joanna Levesque and Sara Paxton. Elizabeth Allen Rosenbaum directed the film before directing such films as *Beezus and Ramona* (2010) and *Careful What You Wish For* (2015).

Aquamarine is a film that employs aspects of the coming-of-age, romance, and fantasy genres. The coming-of-age tale is told through the conflict between the main characters' wishes and the choices they must make to help a friend. The romance story is an integral part of the story line: it is the vehicle that drives the tale, as Aquamarine must attain love for the desired outcome to be realized. The fact that the film involves a mermaid makes it instantly recognizable as a fairy tale. Another important theme in the film version of *Aquamarine* is that of the "mean girl."

Film Analysis

Aquamarine has a great deal of visual appeal. In the opening scenes of the beach, viewers are immediately drawn to the bustle of activity. This includes people in the water, on the beach, and watching the other people on the beach. The two main characters, Claire and Hailey, are introduced, and viewers realize the beach is seen through their eyes. In fact, their perceptions are integral to the film from beginning to end.

The film differs markedly from the novel from the start. Most strikingly, in the film, Hailey is about to move, while in the book Claire is about to. Hailey is moving for her mother's job. Also, she is not leaving a dying beach community, as is the case in the novel. She is leaving a vibrant, thriving community where Claire will likely have many adventures without her best friend.

The interest the girls have in Raymond, a local boy, is also an important part of this film. The girls scour teen magazines for information on love and relationships. They also study Raymond, having cataloged his actions so that they can instantly tell whether or not he is interested in a girl. However, Raymond is not interested in either Hailey or Claire except as friends.

The camera technique using the point of view of the main characters is employed with success throughout the film. Scenes with mean girl Cecelia Banks are viewed from the perspective of Hailey and Claire. Whether in scenes in which Cecelia is being nasty while sitting in her car with her posse or protesting to her father at the water tower, there is no intimacy in shots with this character. As an overall effect, the camera's point of view helps convey the message that Cecelia is someone to watch from afar and to avoid. Even when she is most upset, Cecelia is portrayed as a character that few would want to be around.

Cecelia's minions are almost caricatures. They follow her lead, no matter what, and are unflinching in their devotion. It becomes increasingly clear that their allegiance to Cecelia is misplaced as Cecelia grows more and more angry and obnoxious. There is a growing expectation that her followers will revolt and pursue their own best interests.

The primary cinematographic technique of the film helps underscore the relationship between Hailey and Claire: each seems to know what the other is thinking. Each often correctly anticipates the action the other will take. The girls are supportive of one another throughout, with Hailey being careful not to push Claire to do things that are beyond her. When Claire finally dives into the water, Hailey is just as proud as the audience to see Claire moving past the fears brought about by the death of her parents.

By using many "two shots" that include Hailey and Claire, the director shows the closeness of their relationship, as the two of them fill the frame as they brainstorm. Throughout the film, they are often physically closer to each other than they are to the other characters in the scene.

One scene that shows the girls at their best, as well as how readily they take the mermaid Aquamarine into their friendship, is in the bedroom where they look through magazines. The scene indicates the passage of time and the sheer number of magazines the girls have been reading. Clearly, they have garnered all their knowledge from these magazines. As Aquamarine tries to make sense of these "rules to live by," the audience understands the humor brought about by Aquamarine's displacement: the magazines may not work as indicated in real life.

The mall scene, in which the girls try on outfits for Aquamarine's date, reveals lot of about Aquamarine. She does not want to dress like everyone else. She wants to be recognized as her own person. She decides to wear vintage clothing. The other girls follow her, but still each has a look of her own. This is an effective moment because so much is covered in a short time, with the girls supporting one another in ways that Cecilia and her posse do not.

In *Aquamarine*, the effective use of camera technique brings the audience into the friendship between Claire and Hailey, then the open friendship of the girls with Aquamarine and ultimately Raymond. It also makes clear that Cecilia and her friends have a relationship that does not approach the sincerity and support of the relationship forged by Hailey and Claire with one another, or the relationships they create with those around them.

Director Elizabeth Allen Rosenbaum also makes excellent use of the weather in this film. When Aquamarine angers her father, the waves crash, lightning flashes, and the wind blows. During such weather Aquamarine is deposited in the swimming pool at the beach Hailey and Claire frequent.

Significance

Aquamarine fits nicely with other mermaid films such as *The Little Mermaid* (1989) and *Splash* (1984), but it does not have the YA appeal of such films as the Twilight series. Essentially, it is a lighthearted beach movie.

The message of the book version, however, runs deeper. Hoffman's book explores the nature and limits of friendship. The magic of the film is in the way the girls try to stop Hailey's impending move, resulting in the violent storm that deposits Aquamarine in the swimming pool. However, the book's magic is in its tone and not so much in the events it relates. The book has the engaging feel of a fairy tale, but one for a teen, not a "tween." The narrative voice is engaging and comforting as it addresses the difficult issue of making peace with the loss of parents through death and divorce. The message of the book is that things will work out, even if not as anticipated, both because of the magic in interpersonal relationships and through the journey of self-discovery.

The film plays with these themes through the interactions between Hailey and Claire. For example, when Claire refuses to enter the water, Hailey anticipates this and supports her. Their connection is clear through their ability to communicate seemingly without effort. In the book, Hoffman writes, "best friends don't need to be told when something extraordinary has happened, and this was the case with Hailey and Claire."

The film is an excellent example of the mermaid genre, employing the conventions of mermaid life to good effect. There is also some mermaid lore, unknown to the main characters at the start, that plays a vital role in bringing the action to a satisfactory conclusion.

Aquamarine is a significant film because it tries to adapt a preteen novel to a YA film. It preserves the fantasy aspects of the book and the innocence of the main characters, and it elevates the importance of true love above the importance of enduring friendship. Fundamentally, the tale is one of friendship and growing independence.

Gina Hagler, MBA

Further Reading

Spotswood, Jessica. "Positive Girl Friendships in YA." *Stacked*. Stacked, 11 Mar. 2014. Web. 10 May 2015. <http://www.stackedbooks.org/2014/03/positive-girl-friendships-in-ya-guest.html>.

Zaleski, Jeff, et al. "Aquamarine (Book Review)." Rev. of *Aquamarine*, by Alice Hoffman. *Publishers Weekly* 248.8 (2001): 92. *Literary Reference Center*. Web. 19 June 2015. <http://search.ebscohost.com/login.aspx?direct=true&db=lfh&AN=4126232&site=lrc-live>.

Zieger, Gay Pitman. "Alice Hoffman." *Critical Survey of Long Fiction, Fourth Edition* (2010): 1–3. *Literary Reference Center*. Web. 19 June 2015. <http://search.ebscohost.com/login.aspx?direct=true&db=lfh&AN=103331CSLF13110141000051&site=lrc-live>.

Bibliography

Bucher, Katherine, and KaaVonia Hinton. *Young Adult Literature: Exploration, Evaluation, and Appreciation*. 3rd ed. New York: Pearson, 2014. 125–58. Print.

Cole, Pam B. "Romance, Humor, and Sports." *Young Adult Literature in the Twenty-First Century*. New York: McGraw, 2009. 163–81. Print.

De Lint, Charles. "Aquamarine (Book)." Rev. of *Aquamarine*, by Alice Hoffman. *Fantasy & Science Fiction* 102.2 (2002): 37. *Literary Reference Center*. Web. 19 June 2015. <http://search.ebscohost.com/login.aspx?direct=true&db=lfh&AN=5769058&site=lrc-live>.

Avalon High

The Book

Author: Meg Cabot (b. 1967)
First published: 2005

The Film

Director: Stuart Gillard (b. 1950)
Screenplay by: Julie Sherman Wolfe, Amy Talkington
Starring: Britt Robertson, Gregg Sulkin, Joey Pollari, Devon Graye, Chris Tavarez, Molly Quinn

Context

Avalon High, a made-for-television movie produced for the Disney Channel, is inspired by, but not faithful to, Meg Cabot's original young adult novel of the same name. First published in 2005, the novel centers on the possible reincarnation of the legendary King Arthur, who, according to prophecy, will reappear along with his knights of the Round Table. *Avalon High* is situated in an Arthurian tradition that seeks to bring the legend of King Arthur and his court to life for modern readers.

The playful reimagining of traditional legends in a modern setting allows for clever recrafting of ancient figures while also profiting from a great deal of freedom from the restrictions of those traditions. For example, the main character's name, Ellie Harrison, is a reference to the tragic figure of Elaine of Astolat, a young woman in Arthurian legend who dies after her love for Sir Lancelot is rebuffed. In Cabot's version, Ellie is a strong young woman who rejects this legacy.

The film of *Avalon High* preserves the core of the novel's plot but alters the characters' roles and their final destinies. Ellie is renamed Allie Pennington, a change that is symbolic of the greater liberties taken with the tale. While it pays homage to Arthurian legend, Disney's remake also focuses more closely on an uplifting, feminist message for its audience.

Cabot is a prolific author, having published more than seventy books since 1998. Her contributions to young adult fiction include the numerous volumes of the Princess Diaries series (2000–2009) and the shorter Allie Finkle's Rules for Girls series (2008–10). Although *Avalon High* was published as a stand-alone volume, Cabot has subsequently released three graphic novels under the title *Avalon High: Coronation* (2007–9). Cabot's larger oeuvre also includes a number of novels for adults, among them the Heather Wells murder mystery series (2005–13), and she has recently begun to connect her young adult and adult publications through synchronous publication of related materials. *Avalon High* is the most historically rooted of her projects, but she has displayed an interest in historicized fantasy in several other of her young adult works.

In addition to *Avalon High*, Stuart Gillard directed the film *Teenage Mutant Ninja Turtles III* (1993) as well as several episodes of television series aimed at young adults, including *Charmed* (1998–2006) and *One Tree Hill* (2003–12). Between 2009 and 2013, he was the primary director for the *90210* television series (2008–13), with twenty episodes to his name.

Film Analysis

Avalon High opens as Allie Pennington (Britt Robertson) and her parents (Don Lake, Ingrid Park) begin to settle into their new residence. As the stacks of books mount up on every surface in the house, the viewer quickly learns that Allie is the daughter of two scholars, both of whose research focuses on Arthurian legend. Their work has moved the family frequently from one location to another. To Allie's delight, her parents announce that they will be staying in the vicinity of Avalon High for at least three years, allowing Allie to complete her high school career there. They omit the information that they have selected this area because of their belief that it may be the site of the prophesied reincarnation of King Arthur.

As the school year opens, unexpected excitements begin to trouble Allie. She starts to have odd dreams involving the stories of King Arthur on which her parents raised her. Further, she and her classmates are assigned by their literature teacher, Mr. Moore (Steve Valentine), to complete research projects related to Arthurian legend. In collaboration with her research partner and eventual sidekick, Miles (Joey Pollari), Allie is assigned to research the "Order of the Bear." The two discover an ancient prophecy about the reincarnation of King Arthur and eventually come to believe that it will be realized in Avalon High within a few days. The prophecy seems to hang on the fate of Will Wagner (Gregg Sulkin), high school quarterback and honors student. Eventually Allie, Miles, Mr. Moore, and Allie's parents all come to believe that Will is the reincarnation of King Arthur and that he will come into his own on the same Friday night that he will lead his football team in the state championship games.

If doe-eyed Will is the beacon of shining goodness, his surly stepbrother Marco (Devon Graye) is his antithesis. Marco perpetually bullies the other students, and his negative presence casts a dark cloud over the otherwise sunny Avalon High. Another dark side beneath the glowing surface is the illicit romance between Lance (Chris Tavarez), Will's best friend, and Jen (Molly Quinn), Will's longtime girlfriend. As all of the plot twists surge toward a climax, Allie and Miles attempt to sustain Will's future while also warding off what they see as threats from Lance, Jen, and Marco. After seeming perfectly predictable throughout, though, the movie ends with a surprising reversal in the roles of hero and villain: Marco, who seemed to be such a negative figure, turns out to be a hero instead, while the seemingly affable Mr. Moore is revealed as Mordred, King Arthur's nemesis. Meanwhile, Will is not King Arthur at all; instead, it is Allie herself who holds this honor, and she is transformed in the final scenes into the ancient hero.

The Disney film has many deviations from the original novel, which change the nuance and tensions of the plot. For example, Miles, whose character is associated with Merlin, did not exist in the novel; instead, Merlin was represented by English teacher Mr. Morton, who became Mr. Moore in the film, and Mordred was represented by Marco, as hinted at in the film before the role reversal at the end. This switch is perhaps due to a desire to heighten audience engagement by thwarting viewer expectations.

The most important difference, though, is the decision to make Allie, not Will, the reincarnation (or, as in the novel, representation) of King Arthur. This transposition of Arthur's character and heroic future from the young, idealized male character to his female counterpart makes an assertive, feel-good, feminist statement. At the same time, though, it significantly reduces the intellectual connections between Cabot's novel and its literary precedents. The original character of Ellie had close ties to the historical figure of Elaine of Astolat, also known as the Lady of Shalott. The association was woven throughout the novel, which incorporated quotations from Alfred Lord Tennyson's famous poem "The Lady of Shalott" (1833, 1842) as tone-setting passages for each chapter. The changes made to the character of Ellie are not justified within the film by any equivalent intellectual investment in the Arthurian tradition or any alternative routes by which to develop the character.

Instead, Allie is celebrated in the film as a somewhat anti-intellectual young woman (she rejects the academic knowledge of her parents until it is absolutely necessary for her success) who is focused on her efforts for the track team and her developing interest in Will. Ultimately, the character loses a potential for richness, and the final remaking of Allie into a female King Arthur is so brief that it fails to offer any further sense of how the character would develop after this transformation.

What *Avalon High* lacks in terms of character and plot development, it partially makes up for with the beauty of its cinematography. The setting of the film is left unspecified—unlike the novel, which took place in Annapolis, Maryland—but it was filmed in New Zealand, and the rich flora contributes greatly to the aesthetic beauty of the film. A tidy visual symbolism is established across the film in order to set the scene for the larger strokes of the plot. When Allie's parents share an old tome about the Order of the Bear with her, for example, she finds a rendering of King Arthur's castle in the book that is identical to the façade of her new high school, alerting the viewer to the likely associations between the two places. While none of this is subtle, or particularly accurate to the historical themes, the visual qualities add to the fairy-tale or fantasy sensibility of the film, which is consistent with Disney's previous offerings.

Significance

Avalon High was made for television, a fact that makes ascertaining its success or viewership challenging. If the impact of a film is judged based on the movie reviews and media attention received, then *Avalon High* completely failed to register. Based on the number of citations in articles and online, the original novel seems to have garnered significantly more interest than its adaptation.

Despite the lack of public engagement, *Avalon High* surely has a great deal to offer young viewers. The film puts forward a positive, heroic female role model in the figure of Allie. Although her ties to traditional Arthurian figures are tentative, her re-creation into a modern-day King Arthur replaces an old, male hero with a younger, more dynamic female successor. Considering that Allie's promotion comes at the cost of Will, who had previously been considered Arthur's likely heir, this reflects a conscious decision to promote Allie's future and potential at the expense of her young, male peer. Such a move by a corporation that has often been criticized for presenting a negative or unrealistic self-image to

young women seems like a conscious reversal of previous priorities. Further, while the movie pays little consideration to the actual legends of King Arthur and his court, it at least perpetuates the relevance of such figures in modern society. The young target audience of the film also allows a new generation to be exposed to the romance, mystery, and enduring appeal of the legend of the knights of the Round Table, while at the same time suggesting that certain elements of their stories—love, rivalry, jealousy, betrayal—remain constant across the long span of human civilization.

Julia A. Sienkewicz

Further Reading

Lacy, Norris J. "Arthurian Film and the Tyranny of Tradition." *Arthurian Interpretations* 4.1 (1989): 75–85. JSTOR. Web. 28 Oct. 2015. <http://www.jstor.org/stable/27868674>.

Lupack, Alan, and Barbara Tepa Lupack. *King Arthur in America*. Cambridge: Brewer, 1999. *eBook Collection*. Web. 28 Oct. 2015. <http://search.ebscohost.com/login.aspx?direct=true&db=nlebk&AN=16608&site=ehost-live>.

Tichelaar, Tyler R. "Creating King Arthur's Children: A Trend in Modern Fiction." *Arthuriana* 9.1 (1999): 39–56. *Project Muse*. Web. 27 Oct. 2015. <http://muse.jhu.edu/journals/arthuriana/v009/9.1.tichelaar.pdf>.

Bibliography

Castleberry, Kristi Janelle. "Elaine of Astolat / The Lady of Shalott." *The Camelot Project*. Rossell Hope Robbins Lib., U of Rochester, n.d. Web. 27 Oct. 2015. <http://d.lib.rochester.edu/camelot/theme/elaine-of-astalot>.

Harty, Kevin J. "Cinema Arthuriana." *A History of Arthurian Scholarship*. Ed. Norris J. Lacy. Cambridge: Brewer, 2006. 252–60. Print.

Snyder, Christopher A. "The Use of History and Archaeology in Contemporary Arthurian Fiction." *Arthuriana* 19.3 (2009): 114–22. *Literary Reference Center*. Web. 27 Oct. 2015. <http://search.ebscohost.com/login.aspx?direct=true&db=lfh&AN=46812780&site=lrc-live>.

Thompson, Raymond H., and Norris J. Lacy, eds. "The Arthurian Legend in Literature, Popular Culture and the Performing Arts, 2004–2008." *Arthurian Literature*. Vol. 26. Ed. Elizabeth Archibald and David F.

Johnson. Cambridge: Brewer, 2009. 171–214. *eBook Collection*. Web. 27 Oct. 2015. <http://search.ebsco-host.com/login.aspx?direct=true&db=nlebk&AN=35 4359&site=ehost-live>.

Vasquez, Felix, Jr. Rev. of *Avalon High*, dir. Stuart Gillard. *Cinema Crazed*. Author, 17 Nov. 2010. Web. 28 Oct. 2015. <http://cinema-crazed.com/blog/2010/11/17/avalon-high-2010/>.

Beastly

The Book

Author: Alex Flinn
First published: 2007

The Film

Director: Daniel Barnz
Screenplay by: Daniel Barnz
Starring: Vanessa Hudgens, Alex Pettyfer, Neil Patrick Harris, Mary-Kate Olsen

Context

Stories featuring the archetypes of the beauty and the beast have long existed, and they continue to be popular today. In fact, Alex Flinn's 2007 novel *Beastly* discusses such tales in an afterword, mentioning such examples as *Cupid and Psyche*, *The Dragon Prince*, *The Rose and the Beast*, and, of course, both the written and filmed versions of *Beauty and the Beast*. Within the novel itself, she alludes to other examples, including *The Hunchback of Notre Dame* and *The Phantom of the Opera*. All these works show that a beastly appearance may not necessarily reflect a person's genuine character.

No wonder such stories remain popular. They appeal to very basic emotions (both of vanity and insecurity) felt by almost everyone. Young adults are particularly likely to find those emotions relevant, especially if they are high school students. High schools are notorious sites of peer pressure and competitions for popularity. Good-looking, wealthy, or athletic students are often more popular than students whose best traits are not as immediately obvious. People in high school often emphasize a person's least important, least enduring features, especially when romantic attraction is involved.

For this reason books and films like *Beastly* are likely to appeal especially to young people. Both works emphasize that superficial beauty is only skin-deep. Both works teach that the traits most important in the long run have very little to do with physical appearance.

Alex Flinn's fiction often focuses on the lives of teens, their troubled relations with their parents, and their difficulties with fitting in. They also often (like *Beastly*) feature characters with supernatural powers and draw on plots derived from fairy tales.

Film Analysis

Flinn's novel differs significantly from its film adaptation, which appeared in 2011. The book's tone is more whimsical: it opens with (and is punctuated by) humorous online chats among a group of young people facing "Unexpected Changes." This group includes a mermaid who wants to become human, a young-man-turned-frog, and the novel's main character, whose chat name is "BeastNYC." The film also has some humorous touches but is generally more somber.

Unlike the film, the novel is narrated by the main character, a young man named Kyle (Alex Pettyfer). He has been transformed from an exceptionally handsome (and exceptionally vain) high school sophomore into a hairy beast. This transformation is designed by Kendra, a witch he has insulted (Mary-Kate Olsen), to teach him that looks are less important than genuine love. He has two years to earn such love or remain a beast forever.

By describing these experiences from Kyle's perspective, the novel inevitably provides fuller insights into his thoughts and feelings than the film can offer. The film depicts Kyle from the outside in, and the young man's voice, in every sense, is less present in the film than in the book.

In the film, the transformed Kyle is far less physically unattractive than in the book. The novel's Kyle resembles the werewolves popular in numerous young adult novels and films. The film's Kyle mainly goes bald (losing his thick blond hair), and his face is partially obscured by thin tattoos and some odd metallic growths. He retains, however, most of his original good looks and is as athletically fit as ever. He has enviable abs and is often shown shirtless. Viewers are never allowed to forget that he had (and still has) an unusually attractive physique.

Paradoxically, then, a film designed to emphasize that looks do not really matter is populated with main characters who are never truly ugly. The witch, in particular, is far more attractive in the film than in the novel.

Kyle, with his interesting tattoos, might easily appeal to many viewers, even in his transformed state. It is as if the filmmakers avoided the risk of featuring obviously unattractive persons.

Two especially interesting aspects of the film are its symbolism and its structure. Flowers are emphasized throughout both the novel and the film. In the film the transformed Kyle builds a greenhouse to impress Lindy (Vanessa Hudgens), a young woman whose love he hopes to win within a year if he is to regain his good looks. The greenhouse symbolizes his growing appreciation for genuine beauty, his intense commitment to winning Lindy's love, and their growing closeness. At one point, for instance, they sit in the greenhouse, facing each other and reading a poem together. A bridging shot suggests the passage of time and seasons, and, as the seasons pass, Kyle and Lindy move literally and symbolically closer together.

Later, we see further examples of such symbolism: first Lindy takes Kyle's hand, then she puts her head on his shoulder, and finally she rests her head in his lap. The symbolism is clear: as they spend time in the greenhouse, they are growing closer both physically and emotionally. Later, when their relationship is temporarily in tatters, we see the greenhouse wrecked.

In addition to symbolism, the film also employs foreshadowing and echoes. Thus, at the very beginning Kyle is surrounded by admirers at school and addresses them confidently. Near the end, back at the same school, he is an outcast who speaks hesitantly and shyly. Similarly, Kyle at first is witty and self-assured; near the very end, he is practically tongue-tied. In the movie's first half, his transformation from stud to beast seems almost hallucinogenic, and hallucinogenic overtones reappear when he eventually changes back from a beast to a stud. In short, in a film that emphasizes opposites, the contrastive structure mirrors the film's key theme.

Perhaps the most important way the filmmakers altered the story for the big screen involves the motivation of Lindy's father in allowing his young teenage daughter to move into the home of a rich teenage "freak" (as Kyle often calls himself). In her afterword, Flinn notes

> As a writer, I write about what disturbs me, and what disturbed me about many versions of Beauty and the Beast was that as beloved as Beauty is said to be, in each case, her father gives her over willingly to the Beast, in order to save his own life (the Disney movie version is a much gentler version of the tale, in which Belle's father has no choice in the matter).

The film version of *Beastly* follows this Disney lead: Kyle forces Lindy's father to send Lindy to live with the youthful beast. Indeed, the plan even makes good sense, because Lindy's life has been threatened by a criminal who knows where her father lives.

In the book, however, the father's decision seems positively immoral. Kyle catches the father stealing from him. Kyle physically restrains the father, who is so desperate to escape that he offers his daughter to Kyle as a girlfriend if Kyle will just let him go. The father will even bring his daughter to Kyle, if only Kyle will release him.

The novel makes absolutely no excuses for the father's repulsive self-interest. The filmmakers concluded (probably wisely) that few audience members would find such behavior credible or palatable. In this way as in many others, the film presents a much tamer version of the novel's basic plot.

Significance

Reactions to the film version of *Beastly* were decidedly mixed. Critics tended to pan it, while broader audiences tended to enjoy it. The film cost roughly $17 million to make and grossed roughly $43 million worldwide. Thus, while neither a critical favorite nor a box office smash hit, it earned its investors a reasonable profit.

Whether or not it remains widely watched, surely the issues it explores will continue to be important, especially to young adults. Teenagers are highly vulnerable to peer pressure, particularly the pressures to conform to shallow standards of appearance, fashion, and behavior. They are the individuals most likely to be judged by others (and to judge themselves) by essentially superficial criteria.

Beastly deals most prominently with the perceived need to look good, but the same pressures can affect other aspects of a young person's life. These include the felt need to act (or not act) in various ways the peer group determines. Everyone is familiar with tragic news stories of teens killing themselves because they do not fit in, and everyone is equally familiar with stories in which teens lash out violently against others if they feel unaccepted or bullied. Peer pressure often leads young people to take drugs, abuse alcohol, and commit (or submit to) unethical or unwise sexual behavior. *Beastly*, in the film version but especially as a novel, reminds young adults that true worth is not defined by others' superficial judgments. It implies that the best reasons to be respected have nothing to do with appearance and everything to do with how morally one treats other people.

This lesson never ceases to be relevant, and it is one that both the novel and the film memorably convey.

Robert C. Evans, PhD

Further Reading

Anderson, Amanda L. "Beastly." *Marvels & Tales* 26.1 (2012): 131–33. *Literary Reference Center*. Web. 16 Mar. 2015. <http://search.ebscohost.com/login.aspx?direct=true&db=lfh&AN=74388905&site=lrc-live>

Griswold, Jerry. *The Meanings of "Beauty and the Beast": A Handbook*. Peterborough: Broadview, 2004. Print.

Hearne, Betsy. *Beauties and Beasts*. Phoenix: Oryx, 1993. Print.

Bibliography

"*Beastly*." *IMDb*. IMDb.com. 4 Mar. 2011. Web. 13 Mar. 2015. <http://www.imdb.com/title/tt1152398/?ref_=fn_al_tt_1>

Honeycutt, Kirk. Rev. of *Beastly*, dir. Daniel Barnz. *Hollywood Reporter*. Hollywoodreporter.com. 2 Mar. 2011. Web. 13 March 2015. <http://www.hollywood-reporter.com/review/beastly-film-review-163468>.

Mattson, Jennifer. Rev. of *Beastly*, by Alex Flinn. *Booklist* Feb. 2008. *Literary Reference Center*. 30 Mar. 2015. <http://search.ebscohost.com/login.aspx?direct=true&db=lfh&AN=29988968&site=lrc-live>.

Olsen, Mark. Rev. of Beastly, dir. Daniel Barnz. *Los Angeles Times*. Los Angeles Times, 4 Mar. 2011. Web. 30 Mar. 2015.

Beautiful Creatures

The Book

Authors: Kami Garcia (b. 1972), Margaret Stohl (b. 1967)
First published: 2009

The Film

Director: Richard LaGravenese (b. 1959)
Screenplay by: Richard LaGravenese
Starring: Alden Ehrenreich, Alice Englert, Jeremy Irons, Viola Davis, Emmy Rossum, Emma Thompson

Context

In the early twenty-first century, the success of Stephanie Meyer's runaway best seller, *Twilight* (2005), popularized the inclusion of the supernatural in young adult romantic fiction. *Twilight*'s story of the romance between a mortal teenage girl and a century-old vampire in the body of a handsome teenage boy captured a million-strong readership. While *Twilight* had struggled to find a publisher, its success opened up a ready market for similar works.

Kami Garcia and Margaret Stohl, neither of whom had ever published a book before, got together to write the young adult supernatural romance *Beautiful Creatures* (2009). Kami Garcia worked on the novel's Southern setting in the fictional small town of Gatlin, South Carolina. Margaret Stohl created the supernatural elements, centering on a family of American witchcraft masters, called casters.

In *Beautiful Creatures*, it is the teenage girl, Lena Duchannes, who has supernatural powers, while an ordinary human boy, Ethan Lawson Wate, falls for her. The novel is narrated by Ethan, taking the reader along as he enters Lena's world, driven by his undying love for Lena. The novel quickly became a best seller, and was particularly popular with young female readers.

As Meyer did with *Twilight*, Garcia and Stohl wrote three sequels to *Beautiful Creatures*. They closed their tetralogy with *Beautiful Redemption* (2012).

When the movie adaptation of *Twilight*, directed by Catherine Hardwicke, was released on November 21, 2008, it was a resounding success. Globally, it grossed $392 million, more than twelve times its budget of about $32 million. This success continued throughout the Twilight Saga film series, with a total of five movies released between 2008 and 2012.

Trying to reproduce the Twilight Saga's popularity, a Hollywood film production company, Alcon Entertainment, bought the film rights to *Beautiful Creatures* in 2009. Richard LaGravenese, an Academy Award–winning screenwriter, was chosen as director and screenwriter. Before committing to *Beautiful Creatures*, LaGravenese wrote and directed the romantic drama *PS I Love You* (2007) for Alcon Entertainment.

Though many critics condemned it as overly sentimental, *PS I Love You* was a commercial success, earning five times its $30 million budget worldwide. Based on this success, LaGravenese appeared a good choice to write and direct *Beautiful Creatures*. The producers hoped for a commercially rewarding movie aimed at the young adult audience that had loved the novel.

Film Analysis

The film condenses some of the novel's characters into one and leaves out many minor characters. Ethan's father, for example, plays a role in the climax of the novel, but in the film he never appears and is mentioned only once. The Wate's housekeeper and town librarian from the novel are combined into one character, Amarie "Amma" Tredeau (Viola Davis), who supports Ethan and Lena in the film.

Like Garcia and Stohl's novel, LaGravenese's film has the male lead, Ethan Lawson Wate (Alden Ehrenreich), narrating the story, sharing his inner monologue in voice-over form. Like all characters in the film, Ethan speaks with a heavy Southern accent.

Ethan says he has been dreaming of a girl for some nights. In the dream sequence which opens the movie, she is shown standing on a meadow near the town's Civil War monument. Suddenly, there are superimposed images of Ethan and the girl meeting, and a close-up showing their lips engaging in a kiss. Ethan's voice states, "I want her, no matter what happens." Ethan says "Then I die," just as lightning strikes and a sound like a gunshot is heard. Next cut is to Ethan waking up in his bed, stating that he is about to begin his junior year of high school.

As the camera tracks Ethan jogging through the fictional town of Gatlin, South Carolina, his voice-over gives more introductory information. He mentions the recent death of his mother, whose gravestone he passes. Another long shot shows Ethan running along the meadow the viewer recognizes from his dream before. He pauses in front of the ruins of the antebellum Duchannes mansion. He hears a woman shouting "Ethan!" and hears a gunshot. On the ground, he finds a Civil War era locket.

After his breakfast, the film follows Ethan as he jumps over a wall and observes through an open porch door, all captured in a medium distance shot, how Mrs. Lincoln (Emma Thompson) readies her son, Wesley Jefferson "Link" Lincoln (Thomas Mann), for school.

At high school, first Ethan fends off his former cheerleader girlfriend, Emily Asher (Zoey Deutch). When the new student, Lena (Alice Englert), enters history class, Ethan is intrigued. Lena is pale and dark-haired, wears no makeup, and wears a conservative ankle-length dress.

Accelerating the time used in the novel to bring Ethan and Lena together, Ethan stops after class on a road where Lena's car (a vintage Mercedes, rather than the hearse she drives in the novel) has broken down in the rain. After Ethan drives Lena to Ravenwood Mansion, she closes its black cast-iron driveway gates on him.

Through special effects, the film shows Lena's supernatural powers. In school, Emily and a friend accuse Lena and her family of being Satanists. Suddenly, the glass of the classroom windows shatters.

Next, Ethan is driving to Lena's mansion. Eerie music sounds as the gate creaks open. Once inside, Ethan gives Lena the locket he found. Lena's well-dressed uncle, Macon Ravenwood (Jeremy Irons), warns Lena to stay away from mortals like Ethan.

In a series of cross-cuts, Lena and Ethan's relationship is developed further. A close-up shows the locket, with the date December 21, 1863, engraved on it. Lena tells Ethan that December 21 is her sixteenth birthday. The film uses the special effect of a double exposure to show Ethan, in period costume, falling dead on the ground and a woman, Genevieve Katherine Duchannes (Rachel Brosnahan), crying over him. The scene cuts straight to Ethan back at home, asking Amma, "How did I get here?"

When Ethan returns to Lena's place, he sees himself in a double exposure walking toward the mansion. Tree roots rope him up and transport him to Lena's room. He asks her if she is a witch. She replies that she and her family prefer to be called casters, as in casters of spells. They share their first kiss in a medium close-up.

Lena reveals more of her fate. On her sixteenth birthday, supernatural powers will claim her to become either good or evil. She does not know which one it will be.

The film shows that Lena's evil caster mother Sarafine Duchannes (Emma Thompson) has taken over the body of Link's mother. Macon and Sarafine argue over what Lena's fate will be once she turns sixteen.

With Ridley Duchannes (Emmy Rossum), *Beautiful Creatures* brings Lena's vampy cousin onto the screen. She takes a spellbound Ethan to Ravenwood Mansion. There, Lena's family members, including Macon, Sarafine, and Lena's grandmother (Eileen Atkins), gather for a family meal. Lena and Ridley use their supernatural powers to fight over mental control of Ethan.

Lena wins, Ethan collapses, and Lena tells Ridley to "get away from my boyfriend."

Ridley is revealed to be a siren with the power to enchant men, and makes Link fall in love with her. Ethan and Lena find out that during the Civil War, Ethan's ancestor was shot dead and revived by a forbidden spell cast by Lena's ancestor, Genevieve. This cast a curse on Genevieve's descendants, making them far more likely to be claimed by the dark side than the light.

Ethan and Lena go to the town library run by Amma. Amma lets them into the secret caster's library hidden there so that Lena can search for a spell to save herself from the dark side.

Lena learns how the curse can be broken: someone she loves must die. In a series of cross-cuts between Ethan and Lena on opposite sides of a locked library door, Lena tells Ethan she will remove the curse on her own. Outside, they kiss and laugh, and Lena makes it snow. After a white-out, Ethan finds himself on his bed, robbed of all his memories of his relationship with Lena.

The climax and ending of the film version of *Beautiful Creatures* differ substantially from the novel. In the film, Lena's birthday coincides with Gatlin reenacting a Civil War battle. Ethan and Link are dressed as Union and Confederate soldiers. They decide to "shoot" each other at the Duchannes ruins so they can go home. Unfortunately, Link uses a real bullet provided by the jealous Ridley instead of a blank, fatally shooting Ethan. Lena rushes to the body, which changes into that of Macon, who had magically disguised himself as Ethan. Mortally wounded, Macon tells Lena, "The curse had to be paid . . . somebody you loved had to die." After Macon dies, Lena confronts her mother and Ridley. Lena lets Ridley go and attacks her mother, casting her spirit out of Mrs. Lincoln's body and into the ruins of the mansion.

Six months later Ethan, still not remembering his relationship with Lena, says good-bye to her at the library as he and Link take off for college. Just as he passes the town's exit sign, Ethan regains his memory. He gets out of the car, shouting "Lena!" The camera cuts to her face as the movie ends.

Significance

Beautiful Creatures failed at the box office. After its general release on February 14, 2013, it earned just $10 million in its first week, and doubled this amount by the end of its US theatrical run. This hardly recouped the $60 million production costs, however. Eventually, the film earned about $40 million worldwide and some $10 million in DVD and Blu-ray sales, making back its budget but falling well below anticipated earnings.

Beautiful Creatures received mixed reviews. In the *New York Times*, Manohla Dargis gave the movie an overall positive evaluation, but noted the slow pace and relatively thin subject material. Writing for the *New Yorker*, David Denby found the movie unsatisfactory for both young adults and general audiences looking for an enjoyable film, calling it a "classic example of the confusions and the outright blunders that can overtake talented people who commit themselves to a concept driven purely by the movie marketplace." Owen Gleiberman gave it a B- in *Entertainment Weekly*, praising the acting and cinematography but writing that the film "lacks danger and momentum."

Perhaps most significantly, US audiences never warmed to *Beautiful Creatures*. Young adults stayed away, never accepting the film as the next Twilight Saga. The factors in its lack of appeal may have included the relative length of the film spent without much action or drama and the film's lack of glamour.

Because of the film's commercial failure, Alcorn Entertainment dropped its plan to develop *Beautiful Creatures* into a series and a franchise. The fate of the film *Beautiful Creatures* testifies to the difficulties, and unpredictability of success, when adapting a popular young adult novel for the screen.

R. C. Lutz, PhD

Further Reading

Perez, Lidia. Rev. of *Beautiful Creatures*, by Kami Garcia and Margaret Stohl. *Journal of Adolescent & Adult Literacy* 54.2 (2010): 154. Print.

Puig, Claudia. "Humor Makes *Beautiful Creatures* Attractive." Rev. of *Beautiful Creatures*, dir. Richard LaGravenese. *USA Today* 14 Feb. 2013: 3. Print.

Reklis, Kathryn. "Supernatural Romance." Rev. of *Beautiful Creatures*, dir. Richard LaGravenese. *Christian Century* 130.6 (2013): 42–43. Print.

Smith, Anna. Rev. of *Beautiful Creatures*, dir. Richard LaGravenese. *Sight and Sound* 23.4 (2013): 89. Print.

Bibliography

Dargis, Manohla. "Ding Dong! The Witch Is Cute." Rev. of *Beautiful Creatures*, dir. Richard LaGravenese. *New York Times*. New York Times, 13 Feb. 2013. Web. 20 Mar. 2015. <http://www.nytimes.com/2013/02/14/

movies/richard-lagraveneses-beautiful-creatures.html>

Denby, David. "Dangerous Liaisons." Rev. of *Beautiful Creatures*, dir. Richard LaGravenese. *New Yorker*. Condé Nast, 4 Mar. 2013. Web. 19 Mar. 2015. <http://www.newyorker.com/magazine/2013/03/04/dangerous-liaisons-3>.

Gleiberman, Owen. Rev. of *Beautiful Creatures*, dir. Richard LaGravenese. *Entertainment Weekly*. Entertainment Weekly, 28 Feb. 2013. Web. 19 Mar. 2013. <http://www.ew.com/article/2013/02/28/beautiful-creatures>.

Blood and Chocolate

The Book

Author: Annette Curtis Klause (b. 1953)
First published: 1997

The Film

Director: Katja von Garnier (b. 1966)
Screenplay by: Ehren Kruger, Christopher Landon
Starring: Agnes Bruckner, Hugh Dancy, Olivier Martinez, Bryan Dick

Context

During the 1980s, popular themes in young adult literature included many social topics, such as prejudice, homelessness, and underage drinking. The 1990s saw an upswing in young adult fiction with a supernatural twist. Fantasy became increasingly integrated into stories about teens dealing with relatable issues. There were also more hard-fantasy novels such as *The Giver* (1993) and *The Golden Compass* (1996). Supernatural young adult fiction really took off with the publication of the first of author L. J. Smith's Vampire Diaries series, *The Awakening* (1991). This series found an audience in young adults and general readers alike.

A different kind of supernatural being was the center of author Annette Curtis Klause's *Blood and Chocolate* (1997). Her story of forbidden love and loyalty revolves around a secret society of werewolves blending in with society in Maryland. This was Klause's third book. Her first two works were also aimed at young adults and contained supernatural elements like vampires and aliens. *Blood and Chocolate* was well received by critics and named among the 1998 Young Adult Library Services Association's list of the best books for young adults. After *Blood and Chocolate*, Klause did not publish another novel until *Freaks: Alive, on the Inside* (2006).

In her novel, Klause explores many themes prevalent in young adult fiction for females, particularly the *Romeo and Juliet* form of forbidden love. However, she does take a unique perspective on this theme, as the main character finds that in the end it is better to love your own kind than an outsider. This is in great contrast to the common portrayal of love in young adult fiction, wherein love typically supersedes all boundaries and prejudices. This distinctive conclusion reached by the main character is drastically changed in the film, as are several other aspects of Klause's original story.

Shortly after *Blood and Chocolate* was published, studio Metro Goldwyn Mayer (MGM) purchased the rights to create a film adaptation. Development of the film took nearly a decade, with a total of five directors attached to the project. Christopher Landon, whose father starred in the film *I Was a Teenage Werewolf* (1957), wrote the first draft of the screenplay, which was then revised by Ehren Kruger. Director Katja von Garnier signed on as director in January 2005. Von Garnier, born in Germany, was selected to direct since her two previous films, *Bandits* (1997) and *Iron Jawed Angels* (2004), both had strong female leads. The film was released to theaters in 2007.

Film Analysis

The film opens with a flashback to the tragedy that befell the family of the main character, Vivian Gandillon (Agnes Bruckner), when she was nine years old. She comes from a family of werewolves (referred also as *loup-garoux* from the French) who relocated from Bucharest, Romania, to the United States. During the flashback, a group of hunters set fire to their Colorado house, then proceed to shoot her fleeing parents and siblings. Vivian is then sent to live with her aunt Astrid (Katja Riemann) back in Bucharest. The film then jumps forward a decade, with nineteen-year-old Vivian living in Bucharest. The murder of her family is shot with very quick cuts, implying more violence than is shown on screen. The use of these cuts, as well as slow motion, gives the scene a dreamlike quality.

This opening scene is very different from the book, as are numerous other aspects. The book's setting remains in the United States, and all of the characters are American. Vivian, who turns sixteen years old in the book, did lose her father a year prior to the story's action due to a fire set by suspicious townspeople in West Virginia, but only after he killed a member of their pack who murdered a human girl. Her mother, Esmé, is still alive. Vivian and the remaining members of the pack then relocate to Maryland, where she attends high school.

The location for the film was changed from Maryland to Romania since werewolf lore is intrinsic to that country's culture. Klause disagreed with the change of setting, arguing that the reason her book was set in Maryland was to convey the idea that werewolves could be living among us without our knowledge. Moving the film's setting to Romania does work in the cinematic sense by providing a backdrop rich with history and mythology. Much of the film takes place at night, and Bucharest's buildings, with its tall church spires and winding streets, cast long shadows, creating a feeling of danger onscreen. The city's architecture adds palpable tension especially when Vivian is walking alone at night.

Much of the werewolf mythology and lore of Romania and other Indo-European countries is explained in the film through the character Aiden (Hugh Dancy), a comic-book artist doing research in Bucharest. He is Vivian's romantic interest, and during one of their dates, he delivers several pieces of information concerning werewolf lore. This form of exposition is one of the weak points of the script, as it delivers information to the audience in an uninteresting manner. Aiden's character in the book is also Vivian's romantic interest, although he is one of her classmates. He writes poetry about werewolves, which sparks Vivian's interest in him. Love between humans and werewolves is forbidden in her culture, which sets up much of the story's conflict in both versions.

While her illicit relationship with Aiden is the main conflict in the film, the book centers on the fights within Vivian's pack. After her father dies, there is a power struggle to see who will be the next alpha male. The title eventually goes to Gabriel (Olivier Martinez) and then the female members of the pack vow to be his mate. In the film, Gabriel is already the leader and there is no question of his authority.

Many other elements of the book's plot were removed from the film, including a mystery concerning whether Vivian is murdering humans at night. The film strips these elements away so that the core of the story revolves around the forbidden romance between Vivian and Aiden. This choice was made to streamline the plot so that the love story could be the focus, making the film more appealing to a young female audience. Perhaps the most glaring difference between the two versions comes out of this romance. In the film, there is a happily-ever-after ending, with Vivian and Aiden driving off to a new life together, having defeated Gabriel. In the book, however, Vivian takes a silver bullet fired by Aiden, and in the end, she stays with Gabriel, deciding that it is better for her to be with her own kind. She also sees it as a way to make up for her father's death, stating, "This is what I owe him. This is how I make it up to him." This ending polarized readers, which is most likely why the filmmakers decided to go with a more traditional happy ending. The film's ambiguous ending also sets up the story for a sequel.

There are many action sequences in the film, including several chases in the city and its surrounding forests. During these chases, while the loup-garoux are in their human form, von Garnier utilizes stunt doubles that perform parkour, a combination of gymnastics and climbing that is typically performed in urban areas. The use of parkour in cinematic action scenes became popular in the United States thanks to the film *Casino Royale* (2006), part of the James Bond series of films. Parkour can also be seen in the films *The Bourne Ultimatum* (2007) and *Brick Mansions* (2014), which is a remake of a French film, *District B13* (2004), that helped popularize parkour. In *Blood and Chocolate*, many of the loup-garoux use parkour when pursuing their prey.

As Vivian and Aiden are falling in love, von Garnier employs traditional cinematic techniques in the romantic traditions, such as a montage showing them falling further in love. The more time she spends with Aiden, the more Vivian's confidence in herself grows. She blames herself for the death of her parents and Aiden's love helps her let go of the guilt and gain strength.

The computer-generated special effects in the film are mainly used to show the werewolf transformations. Traditionally, werewolf transformations in films are gruesome in nature, showing the human skin ripping apart to reveal the wolf beneath. In *Blood and Chocolate*, the transformations are simple and without blood and gore. The loup-garoux take a running leap, light surrounds them, and when they hit the ground they are in their wolf form. This shows that they are taking a leap of faith (both figuratively and literally) when they transform.

Von Garnier wished to how that being a werewolf was a blessing, not a curse. This take on the supernatural genre is a unique one, though by focusing the narrative on Vivian and Aiden's romance, many of Klause's ideas were left out, resulting in an adaptation that barely resembles its source material.

Significance

When *Blood and Chocolate* was published in 1997, it was frequently challenged by parents and was even banned in some areas. Its critics cited it as sexually explicit (although no sexual intercourse occurs in its pages) and inappropriate for the age group it targets. In 2001, it was one of the top ten most frequently banned books in the United States, with Vivian's sexual agency being one of the core reasons.

The film contains one scene that suggests a sexual relationship with Aiden, but it is toned down for the young audience. This, in turn, toned down Klause's characters and themes, resulting in a fairly straightforward love story in the vein of *Romeo and Juliet*, only between a werewolf and a human. Due to the stripped down story line focusing on a forbidden romance (a theme that has been done copious times before), the film offered little originality and was panned by critics. Some of the negative criticism regarding the film targets the screenplay and particularly the dialogue, and some critics thought the film took itself too seriously.

Blood and Chocolate did not perform well at the box office. Against its $15 million budget, it only earned $6.3 million worldwide. Its opening weekend brought in just under $2.1 million, and during its second week, it fell from the top twenty grossing movies in the United States. The book's fan base was upset over the direction the film went in, and Klause herself has stated that she did not like the changes made to her original ending.

While the film was a failure both critically and financially, the book still has a strong fan base and remains a popular piece of young adult fiction. It contains many themes that young girls can relate to that were left out of the movie, which in turn alienated its main audience. The choice to go with a happy, love-conquers-all ending may have been the film's downfall.

Patrick G. Cooper

Further Reading

Koss, Melanie D., and William H. Teale. "What's Happening in YA Literature? Trends in Books for Adoles-

cents." *Journal of Adolescent & Adult Literacy* 52.7 (2009): 563–72. *Literary Reference Center*. Web. 5 Mar. 2015. <http://search.ebscohost.com/login.aspx?direct=true&db=lfh&AN=37294811&site=lrc-live>.

Von Garnier, Katja. Interview by Jennifer Merin. *Alliance of Women Film Journalists*. Alliance of Women Film Journalists, 26 Jan. 2007. Web. 28 Feb. 2015. <http://awfj.org/blog/2007/01/26/jennifer-merin-interviews-katja-von-garnier-blood-and-chocolate-director/>.

Reid, Calvin. "Fat Vampires, Sexy Werewolves, and the Future of Teen Reading." *Publishers Weekly*. PWxyz, 7 Apr. 2010. Web. 28 Feb. 2015. <http://www.publishersweekly.com/pw/by-topic/childrens/childrens-book-news/article/42743-fat-vampires-sexy-werewolves-and-the-future-of-teen-reading.html>.

Bibliography

Catsoulis, Jeannette. "Yes, She Has a Sweet Tooth, But She's a Major Carnivore." Rev. of *Blood and Chocolate*, dir. Katja von Garnier. *New York Times*. New York Times, 27 Jan. 2007. Web.5 Mar. 2015. <http://www.nytimes.com/2007/01/27/movies/27bloo.html?_r=0>.

Klause, Annette Curtis. "What Did This YA Author Do to Get Banned from School Libraries?" Interview by Brenna Ehrlich. *MTVNews*. Viacom International, 26 Sept. 2014. Web. 6 Mar. 2015. <http://www.mtv.com/news/1944296/banned-books-week-annette-curtis-klause>.

McCurdy, Eric C. *The Pop Culture Effect: Trends in Young Adult Literature*. Diss. U of Central Missouri, 2013. Digital file.

The Book Thief

The Book

Author: Markus Zusak (b. 1975)
First published: 2005

The Film

Director: Brian Percival (b. 1962)
Screenplay by: Michael Petroni
Starring: Roger Allam, Sophie Nélisse, Geoffrey Rush, Emily Watson, Nico Liersch, Ben Schnetzer

Context

The Book Thief is both a coming-of-age story and a story of the Holocaust. Coming-of-age novels have long been a staple of young adult literature. *The Book Thief* adds an intelligent and caring female protagonist in the form of Liesel Meminger to this genre. *The Book Thief* is also one of the newest additions to the genre of Holocaust literature. This type of literature is not new to young adults, but it is only recently gaining in popularity because the subject matter had been previously perceived as very dark for a young adult audience.

One of the first Holocaust novels with an intended audience of teens was *Number the Stars* by Lois Lowry, published in 1989. Until that point, *The Diary of a Young* Girl by Anne Frank, published in 1947, had a Jewish teenage girl recounting her life while hiding from the Nazis during World War II. *Night* by Elie Wiesel, published in Yiddish in 1955 and translated into French three years later, was told from the point of view of an older Wiesel and his earlier life under Nazi rule. Any of these books could be pointed to as having teenage protagonists, but among them only *Number the Stars* was clearly intended for a young adult audience.

Themes of personal responsibility and identity figure prominently in Holocaust literature. A close look at both those who perpetuated the acts and those who stood silently by is also an inherent theme in this genre. Some of the literature includes accounts of those who tried to help the Jews, along with accounts of Jews who escaped. The tangled process of being divested of "German-ness" and thrust into "Jewish-ness" for the Jews of the Holocaust period is another recurring theme.

The Book Thief, published in 2005, combines several themes into one work. The theme of survivor guilt is explored through Max Vandenburg, the Jewish man who hides with the Hubermanns and feels guilty that he took the one chance to escape and left his mother behind. The guilt is compounded by his realization that he would do it again if given the opportunity. The theme of trust is explored through the experience of Liesel, the young Christian girl who joins the Hubermanns after her mother gives custody of her children to them as she hurries to escape the consequences of her political beliefs. Over the course of the novel, Liesel loses whatever innocence she still possesses when she comes to realize that it is the Nazis who are after her mother and who are responsible for her mother's absence from her life.

The question of culpability in the face of wrongdoing is exemplified by Hans Hubermann, who, because of his act of kindness to Max, is forced to walk to his death at the Dachau concentration camp. Hans regrets his action, but not because it was the wrong thing to do. Rather, he regrets it because it will likely cause the downfall of his family.

In Holocaust literature, survival is the overriding consideration that drives everything else. That fact leaves the characters involved with agonizing decisions that do not lend themselves to many, if any, positive outcomes. This reality is expressed beautifully in both the film and novel versions of *The Book Thief*.

Film Analysis

Both the film and the novel versions of *The Book Thief* have Death as the narrator. In the book and the film, his is the first voice we hear. The novel begins with a prologue in which Death tells us that we are all going to die. He then describes the colors he sees as he goes about his work. In the film, there is only a brief sort of prologue as Death narrows in on the train where the first scene will take place. During this moment of moving through the sky and down to the train, Death introduces himself in the film as he does in the novel. In the film he tells us that once in a great while a living human catches his attention. He tells us that Liesel Meminger catches his attention, and that he cares.

The first scene in the novel and the first scene in the film centers on the death of Liesel's younger brother, Werner. In the film, Death walks us through the rail car and we see Liesel's eyes open wide as she realizes he has died. In the novel, Death gives the reader a look at Liesel's thoughts before and during her realization, as well as the actions of Liesel's mother.

Perspective is one of the most powerful filmic tools used throughout *The Book Thief*, with the camera angle regularly giving us Death's perspective on events as they unfold. From the first moments that we soar above the clouds, then drop down to follow the train, and finally walk through the car with Death, the viewer is aware that Death will lead the way, explaining as he goes.

The high angle shot is used throughout the film. It serves to keep Death in the viewer's consciousness even when Death is silent. It also makes it so that the viewer is never sure when Death is actively watching and when the action is taking place outside of Death's purview. When Liesel is found alive beneath the rubble of Himmel Street, for instance, the shot switches from the high angle at her discovery to a straight-on shot as the viewer experiences her disorientation and grief.

The high angle shot is also used when Liesel is fighting with one of her schoolmates who taunts her within a ring of taunting children after they learn that she cannot read. It is the switch from a conventional shot of Liesel within the ring to a high angle shot of Liesel fighting that reminds the viewer that Death has taken an interest in Liesel and will be observing her at times.

The panning shot is also used to good effect in this film, especially when Liesel is in the classroom. The sense that she is one of many students, as well as her intense discomfort at being summoned to the front of the room, are well portrayed through the use of this technique. The mood of the film is also true to that of the novel. Death sees the world as a snow globe. He doesn't focus on the horror of what he watches even as he makes reference to being aware of the horror. To him, humans are confusing and they don't make sense. He can't reconcile the ways in which they can be at both heroic and despicable. The viewer sees the action in the film through Death's eyes, and when it all seems a bit too neat, a bit too white, it is clear these are not human eyes.

The film follows the novel in the most important ways. It tells the tale of Liesel, her friendship with Rudy Steiner, the love she feels for Hans Hubermann, and the way his spirit lights the room for her. It also reveals Rosa Hubermann to be warmer than the novel does, although she is not a totally cold person in the novel. Liesel's love of Werner and her desperate attempt to hold on to him by holding onto the book that dropped at the grave is also clear in the film. Her love of books and words is marvelously captured in the scene when the mayor's wife takes her into the library and Liesel is surrounded by more books than she has ever seen. As she runs her fingers across the spines of the books, her excitement is portrayed fully in the film.

One major difference between the novel and the film is that the film portrays the relationship between Max and Liesel as a brother and sister relationship. In the novel it is less clear, leaving the reader to wonder how exactly Liesel feels about Max. He shares far more of himself in the novel, too, even leaving a book with his thoughts and drawings behind for her. When she sees him in the street on the way to Dachau—a scene that is not in the movie—she recites what he has written as a way to affirm to him that he does still matter as a human being.

Another difference between the novel and the film is that in the novel, Rudy does not learn of Max's existence until after the danger is past. In the film, he guesses early on that something is going on and Liesel is forced to trust him, bringing them closer in the film and changing their relationship slightly from what it is in the novel. Rudy's personality, however, is the same in both the novel and the film; he is a churlish and charming boy with an eye for Liesel and the wish above all else for a kiss. He will do anything for her, be it helping her through the window to steal a book or jumping into a frigid river to retrieve a book that is being swept along. He will never understand how it is that she can enter a house with a full pantry and emerge with nothing more than a book, but his loyalty to her is staunch from the moment he lays eyes on her.

Significance

The critics generally felt that the film version of *The Book Thief* was a bit too safe in the way it handled the setting and characterization of Nazi Germany. However, with a PG-13 rating, it was not possible to portray much of the horrible truth of the time. The scene of the prisoners walking to their deaths at Dachau, as well as the moment when Hans Hubermann stands up for his Jewish neighbor only to be left in a panic about what it will mean to his family, is well done and effective. It vividly expresses the danger everyday people found themselves in, whether or not they considered themselves political or involved.

Considered an adult novel when first published in Australia, *The Book Thief* quickly gained a young adult audience in the United States. It received a 2006 Printz Honor, which is awarded annually by the American Library Association for the best book for teenagers. Reviews for the book were far more positive than those for the film.

Markus Zusak, author of *The Book Thief*, was not involved in writing the screenplay. In interviews, he has said that he considers the novel and the movie two different works. The novel included far more than could be incorporated into the movie. He expressed his view that each needed to be appreciated for its own merit.

About the suitability of *The Book Thief* for a young adult audience, John Green writes in his review for the *New York Times* that "it's the kind of book that can be life-changing, because without ever denying the essential amorality and randomness of the natural order, *The Book Thief* offers us a believable, hard-won hope. . . . The hope we see in Liesel is unassailable, the kind you can hang onto in the midst of poverty and war and violence."

Gina Hagler, MBA

Further Reading

Harvey, Dennis. "Film Review: 'The Book Thief.'" *Variety.* Variety Media, 4 Oct 2013. Web. 10 May 2015. <http://variety.com/2013/film/markets-festivals/the-book-thief-review-1200694271/>.

Kaplan, Jeffrey S. "The Changing Face of Young Adult Literature." *Teaching Young Adult Literature Today: Insights, Considerations, and Perspectives for the Classroom Teacher.* Ed. Judith A. Hayn and Jeffrey S. Kaplan. Lanham: Rowman, 2012. 19–40. Print.

Pearce, Sharyn, Vivienne Muller, and Lesley Hawkes. *Popular Appeal: Books and Films in Contemporary Youth Culture.* Newcastle upon Tyne: Cambridge Scholars, 2013. Print.

Bibliography

"'Book Thief' Hits Two Million in US Sales." *Publishers Weekly.* PWxyz, 15 Dec. 2011. Web. 10 May 2015. <http://www.publishersweekly.com/pw/by-topic/childrens/childrens-book-news/article/49886-book-thief-hits-two-million-in-u-s-sales.html>.

Green, John. "Fighting for Their Lives." *New York Times.* New York Times, 14 May, 2006. Web. 10 May 2015. <http://www.nytimes.com/2006/05/14/books/review/14greenj.html>.

Vineyard, Jennifer. "Geoffrey Rush on *The Book Thief*, Magic Tricks, and Nazi Movies." *Vulture.* New York Media, 5 Nov. 2013. Web. 10 May 2015. <http://www.vulture.com/2013/11/geoffrey-rush-the-book-thief-interview.html>.

The Boy in the Striped Pajamas

The Book

Author: John Boyne (b. 1971)
First published: 2006

The Film

Director: Mark Herman (b. 1954)
Screenplay by: Mark Herman
Starring: Asa Butterfield, Vera Farmiga, David Thewlis, Amber Beattie

Context

Within the context of both young adult literature and film, *The Boy in the Striped Pajamas* is situated in a robust tradition of Holocaust literature intended for a youth audience. It makes its mark within books and movies about the Holocaust through its approach of telling the narrative from a German perspective. *The Boy in the Striped Pajamas* gives its audience a privileged look into the family of a high-ranking Nazi officer, presenting each member of the family as a complex individual with redeemable aspects of the human spirit. By following a narrative sequence through which the Nazi machine eventually has devastating consequences on the innocence of a young German boy, the story explores the human tragedy of the Holocaust not solely as a Jewish concern, but rather as a burden for all of humanity.

In book form, the text is introduced as a fable, thus emphasizing its fictional nature and allowing its content to be somewhat distanced from historical reality. This act of occupying the space of youthful imagination allows the narrative to have a degree of emotional and intellectual freedom that a fact-based text could not achieve. When adapting the novel to film, director Mark Herman utilized techniques in lighting, film perspective, and dialogue in order to invite the viewer into the innocence and imagination of Bruno's mind. While some may recognize a child's innocence as temporary, others could easily be drawn in, only to have the perspective shattered at the conclusion of the film.

Within the work of John Boyne, *The Boy in the Striped Pajamas* is one of several young adult fiction books he has published. Among these however, *The Boy in the Striped Pajamas* is his most successful, having won a number of awards, including the Irish Book Award for Children, the Que Leer Award for Best International-al Novel of the Year, and the Iowa Teen Book Award. Boyne has also published several novels, two nonfiction books, and numerous short stories for adults. *The Boy in the Striped Pajamas* (2008) is Herman's second film intended for a young adult audience. His first, *Purely Better* (2000), was adapted from the novel *The Season Ticket* (2000) by Jonathan Tulloch. He has worked on a range of other films, including both comedy and dramas, though his earliest career was in animation.

Film Analysis

The Boy in the Striped Pajamas unfolds around the ex-periences of Bruno (Asa Butterfield), a nine-year-old German boy. Opening in Berlin during World War II, the movie provides a privileged view into an elite fam-ily within the Nazi regime. The first minutes of the film take the viewer far away from the ugly and intimidating machines of war into the fantasy world of young boys at play. Bruno and his group of friends run through the streets of their neighborhood. Hands held straight out to simulate the wings of airplanes, they circulate like a swarm of bees mimicking the noises of airplanes in flight. The city around them seems healthy, with abound-ing wealth and resources. Bruno flies himself into a luxurious mansion that proves to be his own home. The beautiful environment, lovely people, and pleasant in-teractions seem to contradict the wartime context and characterizations of wartime Berlin. From this moment the storyline begins to unfold that will eventually lead Bruno out of his protected bubble. That evening, Bru-no's parents host a posh gala at which the assembled guests celebrate the promotion of Bruno's father (David Thewlis) to a high official post in Hitler's military. Al-though the night is celebratory, Bruno's paternal grand-parents (Richard Johnson and Sheila Hancock) attend the party and his grandmother, in particular, chastises her son's decision to take on the post and, especially, his continued willingness to serve the desires of a man like Hitler, whom she quietly criticizes, which causes her son to become anxious. Bruno is clearly very close to his grandmother and her disapproval is the first fore-shadowing of evil to come for a viewer insufficiently familiar with Nazi atrocities.

As it turns out, the promotion moves Bruno and his family far from the luxurious Berlin life and deep into the countryside to live in an isolated, though still sub-stantial, home. Bruno and his older sister Gretel (Amber Beattie) begin a lonely existence in which their principal

companionship is with their mother (Vera Farmiga). Their father, who is shown to be a loving and devoted family man, becomes increasingly distanced from his family as he attends to his military duties. A hired tutor fills the children's heads with Nazi propaganda, which Gretel eagerly absorbs but to which Bruno is resistant. Gretel finds further intrigue in the attentions of a sol-dier named Karl (Henry Kingsmill). Lonely and largely unsupervised, Bruno spends most of his time swinging in the barren front yard and chaffing at the restrictions that keep him from adventuring beyond it. In particu-lar, Bruno is curious about a farm that he has spotted through his bedroom window and his curiosity is further piqued when his parents evade his inquiries about it and the people who live there.

Eventually, Bruno finds an opportunity to sneak out of the yard, and he heads off to play in the surround-ing woods. It is not long before he stumbles onto the farm that he had seen in the distance from his window. The farm now reveals itself to be a large, barren tract of dusty land, enclosed within imposing barbed wire. Inside the barbed wire are rudimentary dwellings and a whole community of people dressed in a distinctive striped uniform. Just on the other side of the barbed wire fence, and hiding from the other inhabitants of the en-closure, is a young boy of approximately the same age as Bruno. Delighted to see a potential companion, Bru-no begins talking to the boy, whose name turns out to be Shmuel. The script attempts to bridge the insuperable gaps between the two boys by placing them in context with one another. Yet, if Bruno exemplifies youthful in-nocence, Shmuel is old beyond his years, having already seen much and suffered greatly. Bruno seeks a playmate while Shmuel lives in fear and desperately seeks suf-ficient food to survive. Although the movie (at variance with the book) never specifically states the location, Bruno has now come face to face with a prisoner in the death camp at Auschwitz.

From the moment in which the boys begin their il-licit friendship, the movie begins to cascade out into various tragic plot lines. For example, the marriage be-tween Bruno's parents begins to fall apart as Bruno's mother gradually realizes that her husband's promotion means that he is to supervise a Nazi death camp. A Jew-ish house-servant, who is also a resident of the prison camp and has shown exceptional kindness to Bruno, is beaten to death by Karl the Nazi soldier after wine is spilled on the family's tablecloth. The movie grows in-creasingly darker, with the early scenes involving flights of childlike innocence being juxtaposed to the culminating scenes within the restrictive confines of a Nazi gas chamber.

Although many aspects of *The Boy in the Striped Pajamas* are predictable, others are surprising. The movie offers a Holocaust narrative from the perspective of a privileged and contented young German boy. It presents his parents as human and affectionate rather than as violent and animalistic servants of the Reich—though, particularly in this later point, the story also takes risks that have caused it to receive mixed critical appraisals. The film's conclusion is devastating and effective, if contrived.

Significance

Critical response to the movie *The Boy in the Striped Pajamas* was mixed, largely due to its narrative and the artistic approach to its topic. *New York Times* film critic Manohla Dargis panned the film in her review, concluding that it would make its audience "see the Holocaust trivialized, glossed over, kitsched up, commercially exploited, and hijacked for a tragedy about a Nazi family." Tim Robey for the *Telegraph* expressed concerns about the movie's message based on its cinematography, commenting "the production lacks the personal touch that might allow this story to resonate as parable—it's too conventionally classy and Miramaxed, with its swooping, prestige-picture camerawork and lachrymose score." By contrast, Peter Rainer for the *Christian Science Monitor* concluded that *The Boy in the Striped Pajamas* is rare in its success at studying the Holocaust as an act of horror "perpetrated by human beings, not monsters." The extreme divergence of views concerning the quality of the movie and its message speaks to the significant and emotional nature of addressing the Holocaust. In approaching this topic, *The Boy in the Striped Pajamas* is bold in its decision to focus on a German family and to show the events through their eyes, but this same focus leaves it subject to critics' concerns and the approach risks a perceived trivializing of such an intensely emotional and tragic topic by attempting to elicit sympathy for those who committed the acts of atrocity. While criticisms of the film are well founded, such deep disparagement of its social enterprise fails to take into account that a young adult film might not be the medium through which to convey the harsh, ugly depths of the Holocaust. In its perspective and format, *The Boy in the Striped Pajamas* has been designed to draw the viewer in visually and emotionally, and its conclusion contains a surprising and devastating twist that flies in the face of any expectations of the happy ending a viewer might anticipate from a film for young audiences. Thus, although the film may soften some of the hard edges of the Holocaust by humanizing individual members of the Nazi forces, it effectively uses its emotional and artistic tools to convey a meaningful lesson about the evil of the Holocaust. It does so by informing the viewer of the principles of a common human spirit and the importance of respecting that spirit across historical time periods and geographical boundaries.

As a film intended for youth audiences, *The Boy in the Striped Pajamas* takes additional risks with the emotional well-being and innocence of its audience. The film is certainly not for very young audiences or those with little exposure to violent or challenging topics. There is some degree of violence and emotionally challenging material throughout the film, once the family moves to the countryside. The ending of the movie, in particular, is wrenching even for an adult, and the film should certainly not be shown to younger audiences without taking individual character and sensitivity into account.

Julia A. Sienkewicz

Further Reading

Hunter, Anna. "Tales from Over There: The Uses and Meaning of Fairy Tales in Contemporary Holocaust Narrative." *Modernism/Modernity* 20.1 (2013): 59–75. Print.

Niens, Ulrike, and Jacqueline Reilly. "Education for Global Citizenship in a Divided Society? Young People's Views and Experiences." *Comparative Education* 48.1 (2012): 103–18. Print.

Pearce, Sharyn. "Writing the Barbaric Recent Past: Holocaust Fiction for Young Adults." *Popular Appeal: Books and Films in Contemporary Youth Culture* (2013): 13–42. Print

Bibliography

Dargis, Manohla A. "Horror through a Child's Eyes." *New York Times*. New York Times, 6 Nov. 2008. Web. 1 May 2015. <http://www.nytimes.com/2008/11/07/movies/07paja.html?_r=0>.

Rainer, Peter. *Christian Science Monitor*. Christian Science Monitor, 8 Nov. 2008. Web. 1 May 2015. <http://www.csmonitor.com/The-Culture/Movies/2008/1108/p25s02-almo.html>.

Robey, Tim. *Telegraph*. Telegraph Media Group, 12 Sept. 2008. (Web) 1 May 2015. <http://www.telegraph.co.uk/journalists/tim-robey/3560318/Film-review-The-Boy-in-the-Striped-Pyjamas.html>.

The Chocolate War

The Book

Author: Robert Cormier (1925–2000)
First published: 1974

The Film

Director: Keith Gordon (b. 1961)
Screenplay by: Keith Gordon
Starring: Ilan Mitchell-Smith, John Glover, Wallace Langham

Context

In the early twenty-first century, film adaptations of young adult novels were often major blockbusters that established long-running series and grossed millions, or even billions, of dollars in income from ticket sales and merchandise. Even many of the films that ultimately did not become blockbusters were initially positioned as such, with film studios choosing which works to adapt based in large part on their potential to launch profitable franchises. However, not all films are major Hollywood affairs, and this was especially true in the decades prior to the twenty-first-century boom in young adult films. The 1988 independent film *The Chocolate War*, though based on a novel for teenagers, serves as an intriguing counterpoint to the flashy young adult films of later decades. Made for only $700,000, the film is a quieter and more intimate production than many of its later counterparts; nevertheless, the story it tells about society and human nature is at least as significant in meaning as that in any of the popular young adult films of the early twenty-first century.

The Chocolate War is based on the Robert Cormier novel of the same name, published in 1974. The author of numerous novels for young adults, Cormier is known for works such as *I Am the Cheese* (1977), *The Bumblebee Flies Anyway* (1983), and *In the Middle of the Night* (1995). *The Chocolate War* tells the story of teenager Jerry Renault, a freshman at an all-male Catholic school who comes into conflict with the Vigils, a manipulative secret society, and Brother Leon, the school's assistant headmaster. When the annual school chocolate-selling fundraiser begins, the Vigils give Jerry the assignment of refusing to sell the chocolates for ten days, after which he is expected to relent and participate in the fundraiser. However, Jerry continues to refuse to sell the chocolates after his assignment is finished, a decision that threatens the school's harshly enforced hierarchy. Though frequently challenged and even banned from schools and libraries by concerned organizations and individuals, the novel gained critical acclaim and received many awards in the decades after its publication, becoming known as a classic of young adult literature. Cormier followed the novel with the sequel *Beyond the Chocolate War* (1985), which features many of the same characters as well as some new ones.

The film adaptation of *The Chocolate War* was the directorial debut of Keith Gordon, who also wrote the screenplay. Originally an actor, having appeared in films such as *Dressed to Kill* (1980), Gordon received his first screenwriting credit in 1985, for the film *Static*. After moving into directing with *The Chocolate War*, he primarily pursued a career in that arena; during the first decades of the twenty-first century, he directed numerous episodes of television shows, including *Dexter*, *Homeland*, and *Fargo*. Starring Ilan Mitchell-Smith as Jerry and John Glover as the cruel Brother Leon, *The Chocolate War* received a limited release in US theaters beginning in November of 1988. The film was later released on DVD.

Film Analysis

The Chocolate War is in many ways a straightforward adaptation of Cormier's original novel. The film's narrative follows the plot of the novel closely, and numerous scenes and conversations between characters are drawn directly from the text. The beginning of the film, for instance, features a scene in which Archie (Wallace Langham) and Obie (Doug Hutchison), members of a secret society known as the Vigils, are sitting on the bleachers by the football field, watching their schoolmates practice. Archie, the "assigner" of the Vigils, chooses the students to whom he will assign bizarre and often humiliating tasks; the last name added to his list is that of Jerry Renault (Ilan Mitchell-Smith), a freshman whom he spots on the football field. Archie and Obie's conversation concerning Jerry follows the conversation depicted in the novel closely, diverging from it primarily to tighten the dialogue. Other pivotal scenes in the film likewise adhere closely to their novel counterparts; the scene in which Jerry, in accordance with his assignment, refuses to sell chocolates during a school fundraiser similarly follows along with the novel, although some of the dialogue is condensed.

As is often the case with film adaptations of novels, *The Chocolate War* demonstrates some of the notable challenges and benefits associated with adapting a written work for the screen. First is the challenge of conveying characters' thoughts and motivations. The novel is written in the third-person limited point of view, with the focal character changing from chapter to chapter. This enables the reader to see events through the eyes of various characters: the scene on the bleachers, for instance, is seen from Obie's point of view, and his mingled disgust at and admiration for Archie is palpable, while Jerry's first refusal to sell the chocolates is seen from the point of view of his friend Roland Goubert, known as the Goober, who is shocked by Jerry's defiance. This shifting point of view makes the thoughts and motivations of many of the characters apparent to the reader, even as the other characters are unaware of them, creating a certain degree of dramatic irony. While this is an effective narrative technique in written form, however, it presents some difficulty when it comes to film adaptations, as viewers are no longer privy to the inner workings of the characters. In large part, screenwriter and director Keith Gordon was able to convey the characters' thoughts and feelings through dialogue and the actors' body language. Jerry is in some ways a cipher, but this is perhaps a reflection of his inner turmoil and unclear motivations in the novel. The film likewise demonstrates the ways in which use of the visual medium of film can benefit a narrative. In one memorable scene, the students in one classroom have been tasked by Archie with jumping out of their seats and dancing wildly every time the teacher says the word "environment." In the novel, this event is described by Obie, who is one of the students in the classroom. In the film, however, this is depicted visually, and the wild flailing of the students is an entertaining and comical image. However, the scene, in all its absurdity, also serves to underscore the power of Archie and the Vigils; students are willing to do anything the group commands, no matter how ridiculous it may make them look.

The bulk of the plot of *The Chocolate War* follows the events of the book closely, eliminating select scenes for the sake of time but nevertheless telling essentially the same story. The film's ending, however, diverges from that of the novel significantly. In the novel, as punishment for Jerry's ongoing defiance, Archie arranges for Jerry to fight bully Emile Janza in front of the other students. Prior to the fight, Archie is presented with a box of marbles and draws two white ones; had he drawn a black marble, he would have had to fight Jerry in Emile's place. The fight commences, and Jerry and Emile's moves are decided by the boys around them. Unable to defend himself, Jerry is pummeled into unconsciousness. He awakens utterly defeated and attempts to express that fact to the Goober: "He had to tell Goober to play ball, to play football, to run, to make the team, to sell the chocolates, to do whatever they wanted you to do. . . . Don't disturb the universe" (258–89). In the film, however, events take what initially seems to be a more positive turn, leading to a more upbeat conclusion to Jerry's story. When Archie draws from the box of marbles, he draws a black one and is thus required to take Emile's place. Jerry therefore faces off against the boy who was the cause of his pain rather than a proxy. The two fight, and Jerry emerges triumphant. However, as he hears his audience cheering for him and sees their approving expressions and gestures, his own smile fades. He has not truly triumphed; rather, he has merely fallen into the role expected of him. In the decades since the film's theatrical release, this altered ending has been interpreted by some, particularly fans of the original novel, as an attempt at a clichéd positive "Hollywood ending." That interpretation relies generally on Jerry's apparent defeat of Archie and Archie's subsequent downfall. However, the interpretation of the film's ending as a positive one ignores Jerry's physical response to the cheers of the crowd as well as his final lines in the film: "I should have just sold the chocolates. I played their game, anyway." With those lines, Jerry makes essentially the same point as his novel counterpart: resistance to the status quo is futile. In a discussion board post on the website IMDb, Gordon supports this interpretation, noting that he used the cliché of the protagonist defeating his enemy to demonstrate that Jerry cannot truly defeat the corrupt system around him. The film's ending, then, is neither the bleak ending of the novel nor the upbeat ending expected of most films.

Significance

As an independent production, *The Chocolate War* received a very limited US release beginning on November

18, 1988, playing in only eleven theaters, according to the website Box Office Mojo. The film grossed a total of just over $300,000, falling short of its $700,000 budget. Nevertheless, the film was remembered as a strong independent effort and was released on DVD in 2007.

The Chocolate War was received well by critics upon its theatrical release, with reviewers praising the performances of its actors, particularly Glover's menacing performance as Brother Leon, and the film's overall adherence to the events of the novel. A number of critics found the film too slowly paced and disliked its overall tone, while some fans of original novel objected to the few changes Gordon made to the narrative in adapting the film, particularly in regard to the ending. However, the critical response to the film was largely positive in both contemporary and retrospective reviews, a factor that likely contributed to its release on DVD nearly twenty years after its original debut in theaters.

Joy Crelin

Further Reading

Flowers, Mark. "Defending the 'Hollywood Ending': Robert Cormier on Film." *Hub.* Amer. Lib. Assn., 8 Mar. 2012. Web. 30 Nov. 2015. <http://www.yalsa.ala.org/thehub/2012/03/08/defending-the-hollywood-ending-robert-cormier-on-film/>.

Macpherson, Heather J. "The Story of 'What If?'" *Worcester Rev.* 29.1/2 (2008): 36–42. *Literary Reference Center.* Web. 7 Dec. 2015. <http://search.ebscohost.com/login.aspx?direct=true&db=lfh&AN=36400971&site=lrc-live>.

Bibliography

Benson, Sheila. "Movie Review: Probing the Darkness in 'The Chocolate War.'" *Los Angeles Times.* Los Angeles Times, 23 Nov. 1988. Web. 30 Nov. 2015. <http://articles.latimes.com/1988-11-23/entertainment/ca-242_1_chocolate-war>.

"The Chocolate War." *Box Office Mojo.* IMDB.com, 2015. Web. 30 Nov. 2015. <http://www.boxofficemojo.com/movies/?id=chocolatewar.htm>.

Goldstein, Patrick. "Dark 'Chocolate War' Sweet Debut for Director Gordon." *Los Angeles Times.* Los Angeles Times, 29 Nov. 1988. Web. 7 Dec. 2015. <http://articles.latimes.com/1988-11-29/entertainment/ca-528_1_chocolate-war>.

Gordon, Keith. "DVD Finally on the Way!/Comment on Ending." *IMDb.* IMDB.com, 6 Feb. 2006. Web. 30 Nov. 2015. <http://www.imdb.com/title/tt0094869/board/nest/35326871?p=1>.

Kipp, Jeremiah. "The Chocolate War." *Slant.* Slant, 15 Apr. 2007. Web. 30 Nov. 2015. <http://www.slant-magazine.com/film/review/the-chocolate-war>.

Maslin, Janet. "The Chocolate War (1988)." *New York Times.* New York Times, 27 Jan. 1989. Web. 30 Nov. 2015. <http://www.nytimes.com/movie/review?res=950DE2D91E3DF934A15752C0A96F948260>.

Cirque du Freak: The Vampire's Assistant

The Book

Author: Darren Shan (b. 1972)
First published: 2000

The Film

Director: Paul Weitz (b. 1965)
Screenplay by: Paul Weitz, Brian Helgeland
Starring: Chris Massoglia, John C. Reilly, Ken Watanabe, Josh Hutcherson, Salma Hayek, Patrick Fugit, Willem Dafoe

Context

Horror fiction geared toward young adults has been a staple of literature for some time, and in the 2000s, it saw a sharp increase in popularity. Much of this was due to the Twilight book series (2005–8), by Stephenie Meyer, featuring a vampire and a human who fall in love. Other popular books such as Richelle Mead's Vampire Academy series (2007–10) and Annette Curtis Klause's *Blood and Chocolate* (1997) also featured supernatural beings involved in romantic relationships with humans. These examples were geared toward a female readership and amassed devoted followings consisting largely of female readers.

Irish author Darren O'Shaughnessy, writing under the pen name Darren Shan, found success targeting a male audience with the Saga of Darren Shan (2000–2004), a twelve-book series divided into four trilogies. The first book in the series, *Cirque du Freak*, also known as *Cirque du Freak: A Living Nightmare*, was first published in the United Kingdom in 2000 and in the United States in 2002. O'Shaughnessy became a full-time writer at age twenty-three, though his first two novels, *Ayuamarca* (1999) and *Hell's Horizon* (2000), sold poorly. *Cirque du Freak* was published between those two books, in January 2000. He was inspired to write the novel after skimming through a book in R. L. Stine's original Goosebumps series (1992–97) series; O'Shaughnessy disliked Stine's writing but understood how young adults could enjoy the supernatural aspects and frequent cliffhangers. He began writing *Cirque du Freak*, which he conceived of as a fun read incorporating some of the darkness of renowned horror author Stephen King.

Cirque du Freak was a success, and Warner Bros. film studio purchased the adaptation rights prior to its US publication. The studio never developed the film, however, and after three years the rights reverted to O'Shaughnessy. Meanwhile, O'Shaughnessy continued the saga, following up the success of *Cirque du Freak* with *The Vampire's Assistant* and *Tunnels of Blood*, published in June 2000 and November 2000, respectively. These three novels make up *Vampire Blood*, the first trilogy of the Saga of Darren Shan, later followed by *Vampire Rites* (2001–2), *Vampire War* (2002–3), and *Vampire Destiny* (2003–4).

After O'Shaughnessy regained the film rights, they were purchased again, this time by Universal Pictures. By then, the books had sold more than 4.4 million copies worldwide. To direct, the studio selected seasoned comedy filmmaker Paul Weitz, whose previous credits included the teen sex comedy *American Pie* (1999), the dramedy *About a Boy* (2002), and the political satire *American Dreamz* (2006). The resulting film, *Cirque du Freak: The Vampire's Assistant*, is an adaptation of all three books in the *Vampire Blood* trilogy. It was released in October 2009.

Film Analysis

Cirque du Freak: The Vampire's Assistant opens with protagonist Darren Shan (Chris Massoglia) narrating his own funeral as his family and friends mourn. The camera pans to Darren's casket and reveals he is alive inside, playing a handheld video game. The humorous narration and the special effects used to move the camera down into the casket work together to establish the playful nature of the film's universe, where horror is mixed with comedy. From here, the animated opening credits play over composer Steven Trask's quirky orchestral score, both further signifiers of the offbeat quality of the film.

This opening scene differs from the book, which is told from Darren's perspective and begins with him talking about his obsession with spiders. This personality trait is maintained in the film, though it is expanded on further.

Following the credits, the film flashes back to several days before the funeral and introduces Darren's best friend, Steve Leonard (Josh Hutcherson), who has a reputation as a troublemaker. Steve's delinquency stems from him feeling like an outsider—or, as the title suggests, a "freak." This is a typical theme in teenage movies, as are many of the other themes in the film. After Steve argues with his parents over his friendship with Darren, the two teens sneak away to the titular *Cirque du Freak*, a freak show that has rolled into town against the wishes of local parents. In the book, Darren has two other good friends who wish to go to the show, but these characters were removed from the film version in order to streamline the plot.

At the freak show, the teens witness a series of grotesqueries, including Madame Truska (Salma Hayek), the bearded lady, and Evra Von (Patrick Fugit), the snake boy. Some gruesome effects are computer generated, including a man with two bulging stomachs who swallows various large objects. The camera shots in the freak show are framed in darkness, suggesting danger all around Darren and Steve. One of the performers is Larten Crepsley (John C. Reilly), whose act involves a highly poisonous spider named Madam Octa. Reilly is mainly known for his comedic acting, and he contributes to the humorous tone of the film. Darren, being obsessed with spiders, is mesmerized by Madam Octa and sneaks into Crepsley's dressing room for a closer look.

Steve, on the other hand, is obsessed with vampires and recognizes Crepsley from one of his books. He too sneaks into the dressing room, where he begs for Crepsley and one of his vampiric compatriots, Gavner Purl (Willem Dafoe), to turn him into a vampire. When he is declined, his wish to become a vampire causes a rift in his friendship with Darren. Falling out with one's best friend is another recurring theme in teen films, and it is only through various tribulations that the two friends rekindle their bond in the end.

Darren steals Madam Octa from Crepsley's dressing room and takes her to school the next day. When the spider escapes, Steve is bitten trying to recapture her, and the only way to save his life is with an antidote Crepsley possesses. Crepsley agrees to save Steve only if Darren will become a half vampire and act as his assistant.

Steve approves of this arrangement, which forces Darren to fake his own death, leave his family and his old life behind, and live with Crepsley at the freak show's campground. The production design at the campground is reminiscent of Victorian times with an eerie twist. The costumes are also influenced by Victorian dress and feature top hats and frocks. This aesthetic creates an otherworldly atmosphere that complements the offbeat tone of the film. Weitz maintains this tone even during the larger action sequences toward the end of the film.

In many instances during the film, as Darren is assimilating to his new life as a half human, half vampire, there is an unusual amount of camera movement. This technique adds to the sense of wonder and fantasy, as well as Darren's sense of disorientation, especially when he is exploring the freak show's campground and it is revealed to the audience through these movements.

Despite the pervasive humor of the film, there are many dark elements as well. The vampires, including Crepsley, choose not to kill humans when they feed, only drinking a small amount of blood and leaving the human dazed but still alive; they are at war with the "vampaneze," a rival faction who drain humans of their blood completely, killing them. The fight scenes between the two factions are filled with stunts and use extensive wirework to throw the characters over long distances, implying that the vampires possess great strength. The fights are sometimes unusually graphic for a PG-13 film, featuring spilled blood and even a severed limb. Since the target audience is male teens, however, these bouts of violence are less of a surprise.

The themes in the film are reinforced mainly through Darren, who, before becoming a vampire, is a model student. He is unsure of what he wants from life and who he is as a person. Early in the film, while he is being berated by his parents for getting in trouble at school, Darren envisions his future if he follows the path of his father. His vision makes it clear that the idea of living a quaint, suburban life scares him. When he joins Crepsley at the campground, he becomes more of his own person. While *Cirque du Freak* contains none of the teenage angst that is found in movies such as *Twilight* (2008) and its sequels, there is a small romantic subplot between Darren and one of the "freaks," a monkey girl named Rebecca (Jessica Carlson). The subplot is not deeply explored, but it supports the story's coming-of-age elements.

The approaches taken in *Cirque du Freak* make it a unique young adult adaptation. The angst found in many films of the teen supernatural genre is absent, and the vampires are shown in a new light. Casting John C. Reilly as a vampire was an inspired choice; while modern popular culture has tended to portray vampires as highly sexual beings, Reilly plays Crepsley more like a tired, working-class man. The themes addressed by the film are common, but Weitz's film makes them feel fresh.

Significance

The Saga of Darren Shan books were well received by critics and readers alike, though some of their darker aspects made parents and school librarians wary. Given the series' success worldwide and the popularity of film adaptations of young adult novels with supernatural elements, it was only a matter of time before an adaptation was made. The film failed to spawn a franchise, but the book series remains popular and O'Shaughnessy followed it up several years later with a four-book prequel series called the Saga of Larten Crepsley (2010–12).

Cirque du Freak: The Vampire's Assistant retains many of the first trilogy's elements and core themes. Still, it failed to perform as well as Universal Pictures had hoped, making more than $14 million in the United States and $25 million internationally—falling just short of the film's $39.2 million budget, meaning the studio took a loss. Critically, the film received mixed reviews. Some critics felt that while the film serves up exciting chills and humor, there is nothing happening at an emotional level, and the integration between the real world and the world of the "freaks" is not cohesive. Positive reviews tended to highlight the film's humor and the overall tone that binds the horror and comedy elements together.

Cirque du Freak: The Vampire's Assistant is unique in that it is a young adult adaptation targeted at teenage boys, while the majority of supernatural-themed young adult novels are those centered on young women and the trials they experience in high school and at home. *Cirque du Freak* addresses the same themes from a male perspective, with an emphasis on the fantastical elements and adventure.

Patrick G. Cooper

Further Reading

Koss, Melanie D., and William H. Teale. "What's Happening in YA Literature? Trends in Books for Adolescents." *Journal of Adolescent & Adult Literacy*

52.7 (2009): 563–72. *Literary Reference Center.* Web. 10 Mar. 2015. <http://search.ebscohost.com/login.aspx?direct=true&db=lfh&AN=37294811&site=lrc-live>.

McCurdy, Erin C. "The Pop Culture Effect: Trends in Young Adult Literature." MS thesis. U of Central Missouri, 2013. *CENTRALspace.* Web. 10 Mar. 2015. <https://centralspace.ucmo.edu:8443/xmlui/handle/123456789/310>.

Bibliography

"About Darren." *Darren Shan.* Darren Shan, 2014. Web. 10 Mar. 2015. <http://www.darrenshan.com/about>.

Scott, A. O. "Amid Vampires, Boy Meets Girl, Complete with Monkey's Tail." Rev. of *Cirque du Freak: The Vampire's Assistant*, dir. Paul Weitz. *New York Times.* New York Times, 22 Oct. 2009. Web. 10 Mar. 2015. <http://www.nytimes.com/2009/10/23/movies/23cirque.html>.

Shan, Darren. Interview by Lisa Morton. *Nightmare* Apr. 2014: n. pag. Web. 30 Mar. 2015. <http://www.nightmare-magazine.com/nonfiction/interview-darren-shan>.

Shan, Darren. "The Master of Horror." Interview by Michael Mullooly. *University Times.* Trinity Coll. Dublin, 11 Feb. 2015. Web. 10 Mar. 2015. <http://www.universitytimes.ie/?p=32981>.

Sharkey, Betsy. Rev. of *Cirque du Freak: The Vampire's Assistant*, dir. Paul Weitz. *Los Angeles Times.* Los Angeles Times, 23 Oct. 2009. Web. 10 Mar. 2015. <http://articles.latimes.com/2009/oct/23/entertainment/et-cirque23>.

City of Ember

The Book

Author: Jeanne DuPrau (b. 1944)
First published: 2003

The Film

Director: Gil Kenan (b. 1976)
Screenplay by: Caroline Thompson
Starring: Saoirse Ronan, Harry Treadaway, Bill Murray, Tim Robbins, Mary Kay Place

Context

The City of Ember is the first in a series of four books by Jeanne DuPrau, known as the Books of Ember. Moving forward and backward in time, the series explores human civilization immediately preceding and in the centuries following an apocalypse.

The Books of Ember fit within contemporary trends toward dystopian narratives in young adult fiction. Although the series would best fit under the heading of science fiction, it is not focused on the triumphs of technology or the exploration of unknown worlds. Rather, its protagonists live in a world where technology is failing and their civilization is focused on maintaining the status quo and extant infrastructure rather than devising new and better systems. Indeed, most technological knowledge seems to have been lost. Further, the strange, dark environment surrounding Ember proves to be the inner recesses of the planet Earth, and the residents of the city have lost all knowledge of the planet's surface and human history.

Both the dystopian nature of the book and its seemingly antitechnology stance fit within larger literary trends in young adult literature, focusing on discontent with modern society and emphasizing the corrosive or unappealing nature of technology—themes that are faithfully preserved in the movie adaptation. At the same time, *The City of Ember* is centered on two protagonists who seek to alter the social system and have the courage to envision the possibility that the future could be better than the present. Lina Mayfleet and Doon Harrow collaborate in order to discover the escape route from Ember. *The City of Ember* participates in a trend toward developing children's social imagination, a concept defined by Maxine Greene as "the capacity to invent visions of what should be and what might be in our deficient society" (5). Both book and movie focus on helping their young audience imagine their own ability to help shape a better world.

Author Jeanne DuPrau is best known for writing the Books of Ember, of which *The City of Ember* received the most critical and popular acclaim. Among other honors, it was included in *Kirkus Reviews*' Editor's Choice list *ld* magazine's Best Children's Books list n 2003 and was named one of the American Library Association's Notable Children's Books for 2004.

In addition to *City of Ember*, Gil Kenan has directed two other feature films, *Monster House* (2006) and *Poltergeist* (2015). *Monster House* was intended for a young adult audience, while the horror-film remake *Poltergeist* is aimed at adults.

Film Analysis

City of Ember follows two central protagonists, Lina Mayfleet (Saoirse Ronan) and Doon Harrow (Harry Treadaway), as they transition from childhood to adult life. The movie opens with the teenagers attending their final school day, during which they receive their work assignments, which are chosen by lot and are permanent life positions. Doon is designated a "Messenger," and Lina is assigned to labor in the "Pipeworks." Dissatisfied, the teenagers secretly swap job assignments. Young and visionary, Doon already has dreams of helping to reverse Ember's degeneration by repairing the city's failing electrical generator, and working in the subterranean pipe system gets him closer to this goal. For Lina, the job of messenger is a perfect fit with her active lifestyle and curious nature. The movie unfolds over their first days of work, which coincide with the rapid deterioration of the city's generator, ineffectual pronouncements by Ember's mayor, and general anxiety among the city's population.

While the receipt of their work assignments represents their official coming of age, both Lina and Doon have long relied on their own premature maturity. Lina is an orphan who is responsible for her much-younger sister, Poppy (Amy Quinn; Catherine Quinn), and her ailing grandmother (Liz Smith). The death of Lina's grandmother midway through the movie only exacerbates the young heroine's struggles. Having to move in with a well-meaning neighbor (Mary Kay Place), Lina finds her freedoms suddenly curtailed. Her new guardian maintains a deep religious faith in the Builders and fails to respect or even acknowledge Lina's quest and questioning, even as she maintains a tight hold over Poppy and, ultimately, betrays Lina to the authorities. Doon, meanwhile, is the son of a largely reclusive inventor who, although apathetic and downhearted, is skeptical about Ember's infrastructure and social system. As an only child, Doon has a close relationship with his father, and he has been raised to chafe at Ember's social strictures. Eventually, the teenagers discover that Lina's deceased parents and Doon's father were once close friends and that they had plotted to escape from Ember together, an attempt that ended in Lina's father's death. With this revelation, Lina and Doon realize that their own quest follows in the footsteps of their parents, which gives them even greater passion for their mission.

A key theme in the movie is the corruption of society, with Lina and Doon's actions modeling the individual's power to break free from an unhealthy and oppressive system. In *City of Ember*, both religion and patriotism are questioned, portrayed as leading forces in a society that relies on blind faith in order to bolster social constraints. Lina's neighbor models a futile form of religion, instructing Lina to passively trust in her faith in the Builders even as the city falls to pieces around them. As Ember reaches a point of crisis, its citizens gather in a public plaza for a day of singing led by the corrupt mayor (Bill Murray), and this performance of unthinking patriotism provides the opportunity for Lina and Doon to slip under the radar and make their final escape—an example for the audience of the rewards of independent thinking over blind obedience. These lessons, in keeping with the literary trope of the social imagination, work collectively to emphasize the forward-thinking conceptualization of a more ideal society that can be realized through the visionary and decisive actions of free-thinking individuals.

The mayor and his administration offer the most blatant lessons in mistrust of civic structure. In her position as a messenger, Lina delivers privileged, if cryptic, messages to the mayor, which she eventually learns indicate that he is corrupt. Indeed, the situation is dire, for the mayor is hoarding large quantities of food for himself as supplies are dwindling for the city's population. Yet when Lina attempts to blow the whistle on his behavior, she and Doon become fugitives from the law, with the full strength of law enforcement pitted against them.

With all these negative forces mounted against its protagonists, *City of Ember* would be a dark tale for its young target audience if it did not center on a combined treasure hunt and mystery, as Lina and Doon strive to decode the instructions conveyed to them through a mysterious box that has passed several generations stashed in a corner of Lina's family home. As it transpires, this box is a significant talisman for the city, because it contained the founders' instructions for how to return to earth's surface. Its significance had been forgotten because of the untimely death of an early mayor of the city (who happened to be Lina's distant ancestor).

The short movie seems to rush through many of the significant reveals of information yielded by the box. The plot rises to a dramatic peak in the subterranean caverns of Ember as Lina and Doon rush against time to dislodge a small boat, adjust the water levels of the rivers, and be carried off to safety. The actions taken during this escape sequence differ significantly from those in the book. Further, certain details of the book that increase the robustness of its plot, such as Lina finding and reading a journal from the elders during her journey up the shaft, are completely omitted from the movie. After a relatively slow buildup to the escape sequence, the movie catapults rapidly through to the teenagers' escape from the underground cavern in which Ember is housed. Given the speed at which the scene moves forward, multiple aspects of the sequence are insufficiently explained or portrayed, and there is no room left for reflection on the part of the movie's protagonists.

Significance

City of Ember received poor critical reviews and fared poorly at the box office. Its short run time of ninety-five minutes was perhaps designed to appeal to a youthful audience, but it led to the justified criticism that, as Stephen Holden wrote for the *New York Times*, "the movie feels as though it had been shredded in the editing room." Like many movies drawn from books of a substantial length, *City of Ember* contains many unexplained details that appear as gaps in narrative or logic, likely also a result of the editing process. As Roger Ebert wrote in his scathing review of the movie, "It is hopeless to try to understand everything that's thrown at us." The film has also been criticized as unsuccessful in its intellectual aspirations. Holden observed glimmers of critical satire that were barely realized, noting that certain points in the film "suggest a mild satire of end-of-days ideology, especially when Mary Kay Place appears as a prating, singsongy proselytizer for the status quo." Ebert characterized the movie's adoption of the book's antitechnology stance as humorous rather than thoughtful, commenting, "There are no computers in this future world. Therefore, no e-mail. They have messengers wearing red vests who run around and tell people things. So you never accidentally copy your boss." Further, he noted that the city's population is almost completely void of racial diversity, offering a dangerous social model for its young audience. Viewed in the context of movies intended for a broader audience, *City of Ember* disappoints in its uncritical approach, but critic Elizabeth Weitzman noted that in the context of family films, its "grim" tone is bold and true to the original book, an observation that she summed up in the following terms: "The city is a bleak dystopia; the grownups can't all be counted on, and the children have to rely on their own intelligence and strength, rather than luck. And yet there is

an undimmed light at the center of this story, thanks to the resourcefulness of its young protagonists."

Still, critics acknowledged that the movie would likely appeal to a young audience, though Ebert further qualified that it would only satisfy an audience that "ha[s]n't already been hopelessly corrupted by high-powered sci-fi on TV and video." The relative naiveté of the people of Ember, who live in a post-technological society and experience only a small and protected community, is paralleled by the innocent feel of the movie's fantasies and its light tone, which allow the audience to go along for a joyride without focusing on its intellectual outcomes. Holden concluded that the significance of the film lies precisely in its capacity for youthful entertainment, stating, "It's a whiz-bang kid's film with neat gadgets and sound effects and an extended chase and escape sequence through underground rivers and tunnels."

Julia A. Sienkewicz

Further Reading

DuPrau, Jeanne, Dallas Middaugh, and Niklas Asker. *The City of Ember: The Graphic Novel*. New York: Random, 2012. Print.

Wolk, Stephen. "Reading for a Better World: Teaching for Social Responsibility with Young Adult Literature." *Journal of Adolescent and Adult Literacy* 52:8 (2009): 664–73. Print.

Bibliography

Ebert, Roger. Rev. of *City of Ember*, dir. Gil Kenan. *RogerEbert.com*. al, 8 Oct. 2008. Web. 6 May. 2015. <http://www.rogerebert.com/reviews/city-of-ember-2008>.

Greene, Maxine. *Releasing the Imagination: Essays on Education, the Arts, and Social Change*. San Francisco: Jossey, 1995. Print.

Holden, Stephen. "Fleeing a Dying Civilization, toward Hope and Sunlight." Rev. of *City of Ember*, dir. Gil Kenan. *New York Times*. New York Times, 9 Oct. 2008. Web. 6 Apr. 2015. <http://www.nytimes.com/2008/10/10/movies/10embe.html>.

Weitzman, Elizabeth. "*ity of Ember* oes Underground." Rev. of *City of Ember*, dir. Gil Kenan. *New York Daily News*. NYDailyNews.com, 9 Oct. 2008. Web. 30 Apr. 2015. <http://www.nydailynews.com/entertainment/tv-movies/city-ember-underground-article-1.301549>.

Confessions of a Teenage Drama Queen

The Book

Author: Dyan Sheldon
First published: 1999

The Film

Director: Sara Sugarman (b. 1962)
Screenplay by: Gail Parent
Starring: Lindsay Lohan, Glenne Headley, Megan Fox, Adam Garcia, Alison Pill

Context

Beginning in the 1980s, young adult fiction started to delve into topics that addressed tough topics that adolescents were facing, including depression and suicide, sexual assault, and the death of a parent. The boundaries continued to be pushed in the 1990s, when topics such as drug use, sexuality, teen pregnancy, and other difficult subjects became prevalent in young adult fiction. Not all young adult fiction explored these tough topics, however. There were also many lighthearted and amusing books that still addressed topics relevant to adolescents but did so in a more humorous manner. Books such as Joan Bauer's *Squashed* (1994), M. T. Anderson's *Burger Wuss* (1999), and Meg Cabot's *The Princess Diaries* (2000) all looked at issues such as identity, familial struggles, and romance from a comedic angle.

Another example is American author Dyan Sheldon's *Confessions of a Teenage Drama Queen* (1999), which has been categorized as "teen chick lit." This genre typically entails a young girl dreaming of a more glamorous life than her present reality. Sheldon was already an established author when the book was published, having previously written numerous novels for adults, teenagers, and children, including some picture books. She was inspired to write *Confessions of a Teenage Drama Queen* after hearing her younger daughter complain about her teenage sister, stating that if she were to ever write a book about it she would call it *Confessions of a Teenage Drama Queen*. Sheldon enjoyed the title and built the story around that, using her experiences in high school with her best friend for further influence.

Several themes addressed in *Confessions of a Teenage Drama Queen* are common to young adult fiction aimed at adolescent girls. These themes include feelings of being an outsider, a rift between best friends, and disillusionment when meeting an idol. The overarching theme that the book explores is the struggle to accept oneself. The main character, Mary Elizabeth Cep, constantly lies to herself and her classmates about many things, even demanding to be called by the name Lola, because she feels that is what she should have been named. Throughout the book, Mary learns the toll her lies have taken on her family and best friend.

The book was well received by critics, and it became a *New York Times* best seller. Walt Disney Pictures produced the film adaptation, which was distributed by Buena Vista Pictures. Welsh director Sara Sugarman directed the film. Sugarman had previously directed only two feature films, the comedy *Mad Cows* (1999) and the coming-of-age film *Very Annie Mary* (2001). Both of those films contain strong female leads, which is most likely why she was chosen to direct *Confessions of a Teenage Drama Queen*.

Film Analysis

Like the book, the film is told through the eyes of New York City native Mary Elizabeth Cep (Lindsay Lohan). Her single mother, Karen (Glenne Headley), moves Mary and her younger sister from the city to the fictional suburb of Dellwood, New Jersey, much to Mary's chagrin. In the book, Mary explains that her parents are divorced and her father lives in the city's East Village neighborhood, the "coolest place in Manhattan." This information is left out of Mary's opening narration in the film so it can serve a dramatic purpose later. What the audience does learn early on from Mary's narration is her penchant for self-aggrandizement, as she explains how her destiny lies on Broadway as a famous actor. Since the film's narration is typically given in a voice-over of a scene in which the audience can see the truth, Mary is not exactly an unreliable narrator as much as she simply has an unchecked ego.

Sugarman establishes early in the film that *Confessions of a Teenage Drama Queen* has a light element of the fantastical. When Mary tells her new friend Ella Gerard (Alison Pill) at Dellwood High School about how her father died in a motorcycle accident, for example, the flashback is shown using animation. This is a false flashback, since it is revealed later that her father is alive. These animation sequences occur when Mary is romanticizing her life. As she tells Ella later in the film, she lied about her father being dead to make her life seem more interesting.

Mary goes into her new school with confidence. As she says in both the book and the film, "A legend is about to be born." While she is not exactly condescending to the Dellwood natives, she does talk to them in a way that suggests she is more cultured and knowledgeable about the world because she is from New York City. During her first class, she comes into conflict with Carla Santini (Megan Fox), the popular girl in school. Their initial conflict boils over when both girls try out for the lead in the school play, a modernized musical version of the 1913 play *Pygmalion* by George Bernard Shaw. The lead role of Eliza winds up going to Mary after she impresses the play's director with her rendition of "Don't Move On," a song by her favorite band Sidarthur. Lohan did the actual singing for this scene, and while it is a short moment, it serves to set the stage for the big musical number that closes the film.

The fictional band Sidarthur causes further strife between Mary and Carla as Carla's father is the band's lawyer, allowing Carla to possess VIP tickets to the band's farewell concert and the exclusive after-party. Not wanting to seem like a pedestrian fan, Mary says that she and Ella both have tickets as well. To actually go the concert and after-party, Mary and Ella come up with a scheme that gets them to the venue but not inside. The two girls quarrel along the way, which is the beginning of their rift. The tearing apart of a friendship only to reconcile in the end is a common theme in young adult fiction and film.

As the girls wander around New York City deciding what to do next, they come across Mary's father. Here Sugarman utilizes a film technique known as diopter, or split-focus, which is when an object is in focus closeup to the camera lens and another object is farther away but still in focus. This technique can be seen in such movies as *Jaws* (1975) and *Reservoir Dogs* (1992). Sugarman uses it to show Ella's confusion as Mary converses quietly with her father. The audience can clearly see Mary perpetuate her lie as Ella becomes increasingly perplexed.

The girls wind up finding the lead singer of Sidarthur, Stuart Wolff (Adam Garcia), drunk in an alley. They are picked up by the police, and Mary's father has to come and get them at the station. Ella learns the complete truth about her father and forgives Mary. The singer thanks them and lets them into the after-party, where the film cuts to a montage of Mary and Ella trying on his clothes.

There are three montages in the film. All of them are set over pop music and show the passage of time. During the final montage at the after-party, which is shot in the fashion of a music video, Mary "breaks the fourth wall" and looks into the camera. This is a further example of Sugarman having fun and adding a fantastical element to the film.

At the party, Mary finds out that Stuart, whom she has idolized, is an alcoholic and that the lyrics he has written for Sidarthur do not mean anything, he just wanted to make money. This moment has a significant impact on Mary, and it helps her realize that she should try to be more like herself rather than a romanticized version to get people to like her. She does not fully learn her lesson until everyone at school refuses to believe she attended Stuart's party. Ella helps her realize that she should not care what others think, yet another common theme running through many stories for young adults.

The film culminates with the school musical, which is shot like a music video with quick cuts and lots of camera movement. In the end, Mary makes amends with Carla, and the two learn to accept each other. Carla does not need to brag or put people down anymore, and Mary does not need to lie to make people like her. These are classic themes of young adult fiction, and the clear way they are presented in *Confessions of a Teenage Drama Queen* makes it an appealing film for young viewers.

Significance

Sheldon's book was a big success for the author. Positive reviews of the book noted its humor, charm, and supporting characters. The American Library Association selected it as one of their book picks in 2006, and Sheldon followed up with the sequel *My Perfect Life* (2002), which centers on the character of Ella running in a school election against Carla, and *Confessions of a Teenage Hollywood Star* (2006), in which Mary attempts to be cast in a film.

The film version, although it retained many of the book's plot points, did not fare as well with critics. Some reviewers called the film a vehicle for Lindsay Lohan, whose previous film, *Freaky Friday* (2003), found mild success. Other critics found the film inconsequential, self-absorbed, and insipid. Some of the positive criticism it did receive remarked on the film's spirit, quirkiness, and the enthusiasm of Lohan. Despite the negative criticism, the film earned $9.3 million at the box office during its opening weekend. In total, it took in $33 million worldwide, earning more than double its $15 million budget. The soundtrack featured the song "Drama Queen," performed by Lohan. It was released as a single and played regularly on the radio network Radio Disney.

Both versions of *Confessions of a Teenage Drama Queen* offer classic themes in young adult fiction, ranging from self-image to reconciling with a rival. The humor and charisma of the main character, Mary, make it an appealing story for young adults who do not wish to delve into a story with grimmer topics that are prevalent in young adult fiction.

Patrick G. Cooper

Further Reading

Rev. of *Confessions of a Teenage Drama Queen*, by Dyan Sheldon. *Publisher's Weekly*. PWxyz, n.d. Web. 19 Mar. 2015. <http://www.publishersweekly.com/978-0-7636-0822-4>.

Ferriss, Suzanne, and Mallory Young. *Chick Lit: The New Woman's Fiction*. New York: Routledge, 2006. Print.

Kim, Ellen A. "Too Much *Drama Queen*." Rev. of *Confessions of a Teenage Drama Queen*, dir. Sara Sugarman. *Seattle Post Intelligencer*. Hearst Seattle Media, 19 Feb. 2004. Web. 19 Mar. 2015. <http://www.seattlepi.com/ae/movies/article/Too-much-Drama-Queen-1137406.php>.

Bibliography

Kehr, Dave. "A Teenager Struggles to Star in Her New Town." Rev. of *Confessions of a Teenage Drama Queen*, dir. Sara Sugarman. *New York Times*. New York Times, 20 Feb. 2004. Web. 19 Mar. 2015. <http://www.nytimes.com/movie/review?res=9906E6DA103DF933A15751C0A9629C8B63>.

McCurdy, Eric C. "The Pop Culture Effect: Trends in Young Adult Literature." Diss. University of Central Missouri, 2013. Web. 19 Mar. 2015. <https://centralspace.ucmo.edu:8443/xmlui/bitstream/handle/123456789/310/McCurdy_LIBRARY.pdf?sequence=1>.

Sheldon, Dyan. Interview. *LitPick*. LitPick, n.d. Web. 19 Mar. 2015. <http://www.litpick.com/author/dyan-sheldon>.

Divergent

The Book

Author: Veronica Roth (b. 1988)
First published: 2011

The Film

Director: Neil Burger
Screenplay by: Evan Daugherty, Vanessa Taylor
Starring: Shailene Woodley, Theo James, Jai Courtney, Kate Winslet

Context

Divergent falls firmly into the established trend of dystopian fantasies for young adult audiences. Both the novel and the film present a society that purports to be ideal, but in reality is founded on flawed and dangerous principles. All citizens must join one of five factions, each of which is charged with a particular task to serve humanity, and each of which is centered on a desirable character trait. Amity are peace-loving farmers. Abnegation are selfless, devote themselves to acts of charity and kindness, and are also the city's governing class. Candor are the truth-tellers who uphold the justice system. Dauntless are the city's military protectors. Erudite are the wise rule makers. Faced with a broken social compact that limits freedom of development and excludes many despite its idealism, young people in this society must seek to conform in order to survive, often altering their inborn characteristics in order to better fit into the system. Driven by a mixture of self-preservation, family loyalty, a sense of justice, and a desire to protect the innocent, the two principal protagonists of the story, Tris (Shailene Woodley), who is named Beatrice Prior by her family in Abnegation, and Four (Theo James), find themselves embattled in a fight to save their fellow citizens and upset a dysfunctional world order.

For Tris this battle is an extended coming-of-age ritual in which she seeks to establish her own identity independent of her childhood family unit. Born into Abnegation, Tris had been taught to value and practice selfless acts of service to society. Yet selflessness will not serve her well as she steps up and selects Dauntless, the faction to which she must vow lifelong allegiance. Now, instead of thinking about others and practicing selfless acts, she must focus on thinking about herself. Faced with decisions for which her training in Abnegation has not prepared her, Tris must trust her instinct and spend the rest of the movie proving she made the correct decision choosing Dauntless through a combination of grit, hard work, and determination. In following Tris along her journey of self-discovery, *Divergent* fits within a long tradition of young adult literature that is primarily concerned with identity. Similarly, in its focus on Tris, the story fits with other narratives centered on an assertive, young female heroine.

Divergent, the first book in the trilogy known as the Divergent Series, was written by Veronica Roth, an undergraduate student at Northwestern at the time of its publication. The Divergent books have met with great popular interest, some awards, and mixed critical acclaim.

Film Analysis

In the film, Beatrice Prior learns she is a Divergent at age sixteen, when she takes a required aptitude test that helps citizens of her society determine which faction best suits their personality. Beatrice soon learns that being a Divergent has negative ramifications. In a society that values strict adherence to character expectations, her personality does not fit within the civilization's rigid structure. Of the five factions into which humankind is divided, she has elements of each characteristic and thus, fits perfectly into none. More concerning, Divergents are considered deviant figures for their inborn failure to conform. They are systematically persecuted and eradicated, often by the factions into which they have been adopted. During Beatrice's aptitude test, the terrified supervisor in the testing center helps Beatrice to slip out a back door and tells her to conceal this secret from everyone. As Beatrice prepares to attend her Choosing Ceremony the following day in order to select the faction to which she will belong for the rest of her life, she knows that she cannot make the perfect choice for her character, since no acceptable option exists. Though she is not aware, her course has already been set for her, living as an outcast in between the accepted categories of society.

Still, in addition to her concealed identity Beatrice has the freedom of choice to select the identity to which she would most like to conform. The factional system in *Divergent*'s postapocalyptic society follows the motto "faction before blood." Her decision will mean that she will never be allowed to visit with her family, who are members of Abnegation, if she chooses to enter a different faction. Should she prove a misfit in her chosen faction, she will not be permitted to select again. Instead, she will be forced to join the ranks of society's lowest outcasts, the factionless. Much to her parents' disappointment, at the appointed moment, Beatrice hesitates before selecting Dauntless to be her new faction. Thus begins a series of trials and training that she and the other initiates must pass in order to join the ranks of their chosen faction. The training is rigorous and it is led by a cruel overseer named Eric (Jai Courtney), who assures the initiates that many in their group will not succeed, and that the lowest ranking initiates will be thrown out to fend for themselves in the ruined city. The first hazing rituals of the group include jumping on and off a moving subway train and taking a leap into the shaft of a ruined skyscraper. Standing at the bottom of the shaft after her fall, Beatrice is asked what her Dauntless name will be, and she takes the first step to reformulating her identity by answering simply, "Tris."

Much of the drama of the film unfolds along the course of Tris's training. She struggles through the physical trials and might not have survived were it not for some advice from Four, the assigned trainer for her group of initiates. The film reaches a triumphant climax when Tris helps lead Four's team of initiates to victory over Eric's initiates in the final war games trial of training. The euphoria Tris feels from her victory deflates as she enters the next phase of training, in which a drug cocktail is administered and triggers a dream sequence of her worst nightmares. Each initiate must battle his or her fears, while his or her brain waves are monitored by the trainer. Although Tris excels at these trials, she soon learns her speed and skill are a liability rather than a boon. Indeed, her skills have the potential to reveal her secret Divergent identity if not properly hidden. Four again comes to the rescue, and predictably, romance starts to kindle between the two.

The real dramatic action of the movie reveals itself in the final segment of the plot. The Dauntless world implodes on the exact same day in which the initiates' training is completed. The masterminds of Erudite, led by Jeanine (Kate Winslet), have banded together with a selection of Dauntless leaders, including Eric, in order to plot a coup of government. Erudite intends to unseat the governing Abnegation and to do so by using Dauntless warriors (turned into mindless fighting drones through the administration of a mind-controlling serum) to massacre the entire Abnegation faction. However, the serum does not work on Divergents, and has the effect of enabling Erudite and Dauntless leaders to further seek out and eradicate the threat of these outliers. In the quickly moving scenes that follow, Tris and Four battle to stop the massacre and save their Dauntless faction. Even as they fight to save humankind, they inevitably will become outcasts from the civilization that they have rescued. In the final scene, Tris says that she now has absolutely no idea what her identity is, but Four replies: "I know exactly who you are." Tris's identity has been remade again, this time in the role of life companion.

Divergent ends with the expectant tone of a movie awaiting its sequel. Across the scope of this first movie in the Divergent series, Tris has come into her own as an adult woman and found a life partner. Though beautifully shot, the movie throughout has a dark and foreboding tone, which is apt both for the gloomy struggles of adolescence and the nature of life in a postapocalyptic city. Fitting with the dystopian tradition, Tris and Four seek out their own Divergent identities along the fringes of society's expectations. Their struggles and successes model the possibilities of individual achievement, while their personalities suggest the value of balance in the human character.

Significance

Divergent was a box office success, though it met with mixed critical reviews. Christy Lemire for RogerEbert.com called the movie "mostly" a success in its remaking of the book and pinned its failings on the fact that the book itself can easily be seen as "derivative and inferior." Michael O'Sullivan for the *Washington Post* wrote that the movie was a much greater success than the book, citing improvements to the plot, pace, and characters. He asserted that Tris, as played by Woodley, is "appealingly complex,"; she achieves a level of character independence in the movie that she does not in the book, which defines her more by her relationship with Four than by her own actions. Other reviewers found the movie's treatment of its female protagonist concerning. On the one hand, Tris is a hard-hitting and successful young woman who manages to fight effectively for her cause. On the other hand, the visible persona of her character is often somewhat withdrawn or passive, and as Manohla Dargis for the *New York Times* observed, "there's a tentative, awkward quality to her physical performance that at times registers as a lack of confidence." While these aspects of Tris's character could be attributed to acting, choreography, or screenwriting, Dargis argued that they are indicative of a larger problem of the struggles of female heroines. Whether or not one agrees with the depth of Dargis's concerns, gender balance seems to be one of the central strings of *Divergent* that bubbles beneath the surface of the story. Both the lead protagonist and the chief villain are female. Tris's mother plays a much more defined and fierce role than her father. Most of the combat training scenes focus on women fighting women. If empowerment is found in visibility, then the women of *Divergent*, certainly offer a new model for the future. However, looking below the surface, the power and agency of this dystopic society still seem to lie in male hands. Four's closing comment to Tris, "I know exactly who you are," exemplifies this imbalance. Tris is incapable of pinpointing her own identity, and needs instead, to be informed of it by her male partner. Though they fight, aspire, and speak, the women of *Divergent* have yet to find their authentic assertive voices.

Julia A. Sienkewicz

Further Reading

Dominus, Susan. "In this Dystopia, Teens Must Choose Wisely." Rev. of *Divergent*, by Veronica Roth. *New York Times*. New York Times, 12 May 2011. Web. 2 May 2015. <http://www.nytimes.com/2011/05/15/books/review/young-adult-books-divergent-by-veronica-roth.html?_r=1>.

Gomez, Luis. "'Divergent' Sequel Will Film in Atlanta, but What about Chicago?" *Chicago Tribune*. Chicago Tribune, 6 Mar. 2014. Web. 2 May 2015. <http://articles.chicagotribune.com/2014-03-06/entertainment/chi-insurgent-filming-atlanta-divergent-chicago-20140306_1_dystopian-chicago-film-incentive-veronica-roth>.

Roth, Veronica. "'Divergent' Author Veronica Roth on Her Film Adaptation." Interview by Michelle Kung. *Wall Street Journal*. Dow Jones, 23 July 2011. Web. 2 May 2015. <http://blogs.wsj.com/speakeasy/2011/07/23/divergent-author-veronica-roth-on-her-film-adaptation/>.

Bibliography

Dargis, Manohla. "In *Divergent*, Jolted Awake by Fear and Romance." Rev. of *Divergent*, dir. Neil Burger. *New York Times*. New York Times, 20 Mar. 2014. Web. 2 May 2015. <http://www.nytimes.com/2014/03/21/movies/in-divergent-jolted-awake-by-fear-and-romance.html?_r=0&module=ArrowsN

av&contentCollection=Movies&action=keypress&region=FixedLeft&pgtype=article>.

Lemire, Christy. Rev. of *Divergent*, dir. Neil Burger. *RogerEbert.com*. Ebert Digital, 21 Mar. 2014. Web. 2 May 2015. <http://www.rogerebert.com/reviews/divergent-2014>.

Linshi, Jack. "*Insurgent* Tops Weekly Box Office but Misses *Divergent* Mark." Rev. of *Insurgent*, dir. Robert Schwentke. *Time*. Time, Mar. 22, 2015. Web. 2 May 2015. <http://time.com/3753522/insurgent-box-office/>.

O'Sullivan, Michael. "*Divergent* Movie Review: Better Than the Book? Believe It." Rev. of *Divergent*, dir. Neil Burger. *Washington Post*. Washington Post, 20 Mar. 2014. Web. 2 May 2015. <http://www.washingtonpost.com/goingoutguide/movies/divergent-movie-review-better-than-the-book-believe-it/2014/03/19/03b9bfe2-af75-11e3-96dc-d6ea14c099f9_story.html>.

Drive Me Crazy

The Book

Author: Todd Strasser (b. 1950)
First published: 1999 (*How I Created My Perfect Prom Date,* 1996)

The Film

Director: John Schultz
Screenplay by: Rob Thomas
Starring: Melissa Joan Hart, Adrian Grenier, Stephen Collins, Keri Lynn Pratt

Context

While books written primarily for younger audiences have been a part of literature since the popularization of the novel, the term "young adult" was not coined until the late 1960s. The definition of this genre has stayed essentially the same since its inception, referring to a text written for adolescents and with more mature themes. From the start, with novels such as *The Outsiders* by S.E. Hinton, realistic depictions of adolescent life dealing with the environment and relationships surrounding high school life were a major aspect of the genre. Today, the subgenre of realistic literature is still an important element of the YA genre, although it does not hold quite as strong a position as it once did.

The 1990s were an important decade in the development in YA literature, as this decade was marked by the expansion of YA themes into new areas of adolescent life. While previous eras of the genre included themes surrounding high school social structure, peer pressure, death, violence, and romantic relationships (particularly in the 1980s), the 1990s focused heavily on the consequences of giving into social pressures. The major themes of this period revolve around drinking, sexuality, identity, and characters' thoughts on these issues, including profane language, entered into the mainstream of the genre. *How I Created My Perfect Prom Date* is no exception to this trend, with a particular focus on social structure and pressure, drinking, drugs, and sexuality.

The novel *How I Created My Perfect Prom Date* and the film adaptation *Drive Me Crazy* (1999) find a place in the YA realistic genre next to best sellers such as *The Perks of Being a Wallflower* (1999) by Stephen Chbosky and *Someone Like You* (1998) by Sara Dessen. However, realistic young adult fiction during this decade was relatively unpopular. While many authors were writing short novels dealing with contemporary adolescent life, fantasy and other genres of speculative fiction saw a huge increase in popularity. Books like *The Giver* (1993) by Lois Lowry and the Harry Potter series (1997–2007) by J. K. Rowling gained a huge following for the young adult genre. Yet beyond the fantastic, readers still showed a strong interest in powerful real-world issues. One example of this focus on real-life issues is the 1999 novel *Speak* by Laurie Halse Anderson, which details the emotional and social consequences for a female high school student who is raped at a party.

While Strasser's YA works do not deal with issues as intense as some other novels of this time period, they do focus on issues important to teenagers engaging in the world of high school social structures. *How I Created My Perfect Prom Date* (initially titled *Girl Gives Birth to Own Prom Date* and later renamed to distance the book from a real-life news story) is the second in the *Time Zone High* trilogy, (named for the students' fictional high school, Timothy Zonin High), following the somewhat successful first book, *How I Changed My Life* (1995). This follow-on novel deals with similar themes, such as high school social structure, adolescent relationships, and social image, as it focuses on how one student works to reinvent herself. The trilogy ends with *How I Spent My Last Night on Earth* (1998), which adds a fantasy/science-fiction element that threatens the entire social structure. Neither the first nor the last book in the trilogy reached the same popularity as the second book.

Film Analysis

The structure of the beginning of the film mirrors the start of the novel. Rather than divide the story into chapters, the novel is divided into many sections that alternate between the points of view of the main characters, Chase Hammond and Nicole Maris. Each section of the book is written in first person and follows the style of a personal journal entry. The film begins with an introduction to Nicole and follows her on the start of a normal day, giving the audience details of her life and her personality.

In both the novel and the film, the break between the two protagonists' perspectives does not coincide with the conclusion of any smaller story within the narrative. Each "entry" is incomplete, and this device of not neatly wrapping up each character's perspective before switching to the other gives the reader and audience a sense that neither narrative is complete without the other. In short, this technique conveys to the reader that the full story can only be found through the combination of both characters. Once Chase (Adrian Grenier) and Nicole (Melissa Joan Hart) come together under their guise as a couple in the film, the changes between character perspectives become less frequent except to show scenes that imply they may be falling in love with each other. However, the structure and perspective of the book (especially because it is written in first person), does not similarly change to reflect the feelings of the characters.

The focus on romance between Chase and Nicole is a departure that the film undertakes, working to align the narrative more closely with film genres and conventions. At the end of the book, Chase and Nicole find each other and the possibility of having a romantic relationship appears just before it is cut short by the surprise ending. However, the film follows much more closely the conventions of the romantic comedy genre. Although each character initially enters into their agreement with selfish motivations, various scenes in the film focus on one character watching the other from afar as a way to imply the blossoming of emotional attachment.

Although their fake relationship falls apart because they have refused to accept their true feelings, at the end Chase makes a grand romantic gesture and they realize that they have feelings for one another. For good or ill, the novel never reaches the same fulfillment of romantic plot conventions. Adhering to the idea of the vagueness and volatility of teenage emotion, the language of the book is much more ambivalent toward the start of their new relationship.

Perhaps because director John Schultz's vision was of a romantic comedy film, many of the novel's other main themes are relatively ignored. In both the book and the film, Chase is portrayed as a freethinking, relatively rebellious teenager. Yet where the book details this rebellion and refusal to be common, the film tends to paint a more two-dimensional portrayal, having characters say Chase is not willing to be a part of the popular crowd rather than presenting his own personal philosophy. A central theme of the book is the idea of Darwin's theory of natural selection. During a discussion, Chase's best friend Ray says, "Cars, man . . . Darwinism everywhere you look," later adding, "That's why you hung up your board. Faster wheels came along" (101–2). This is a key component to Strasser's novel as the social structure at Timothy Zonin High relies largely on a notion of social Darwinism. The film lacks the depth of this critique, relying on more generalized stereotypes and genre conventions to convey the idea of Chase's climb up the social ladder.

Another major theme developed in the novel is the idea that every person is a deep, complex individual. While the nature of the story dictates that not every character will be developed completely, Strasser does look to certain characters that represent stereotypes and works to give them more complex motivations. For example, Brad, the handsome basketball player who is the focus of Nicole's attentions initially, confesses to her, "I *hate* basketball. I really do. . . . I mean, how can you like something you're lousy at?" (156). Brad's identity is as the basketball team's center, and yet he confesses to Nicole that it is only a persona he has adopted. Similarly, Ray plays the anarchic, loner stereotype, someone whom everyone thinks is taking drugs and refusing any sort of order or authority. Ray does not do drugs, and it is his philosophies that drive Chase's own rebellion against the system and keep him from becoming another of the "sheep" at Time Zone High. It is only when Ray loses hope that he falls into the stereotype that he teeters on and then does LSD and drives the wrong way on the freeway. In the film, each of these characters is simply changed, and so neither undergoes any real development as an individual. Brad is a good basketball player who is a bit vacuous yet good-hearted, while Ray is portrayed as a much more wholesome character whose antics only ever get him into small amounts of trouble.

The one character that is more developed in the film is that of Dee Vine (Keri Lynn Pratt). Perhaps Schultz gives Dee, formerly known as Bo, a larger role as a reference to the first novel in the *Time Zone High* trilogy, in which an overweight Bo sheds her low social status and reinvents herself as Dee, a new, attractive member of the popular crowd. Schultz focuses on the theme of identity in *Drive Me Crazy* through Dee, who at one point talks to Chase and asks him if giving up his former self is worth it to be a part of the in-crowd. Neither character can say for certain at the time, but in the end, both shed the expectations of the traditional social structure in order to be with the people they like and have the life they are most happy with.

Significance

Just as many of Todd Strasser's numerous novels have met with some success but have not reached the height of popularity that many novels in the realistic YA genre have found, *Drive Me Crazy* met with limited success in theaters. Having grossed just $22.6 million worldwide, it reached nowhere near the success of the film adaptations of *Harry Potter and the Sorcerer's Stone* (2001; $974.7 million worldwide) or of realistic YA novels such as *The Fault in Our Stars* (2014; $307.2 million worldwide). The film did relatively well compared to adaptations of similar books initially published in the 1990s, such as *The Perks of Being a Wallflower* (2012; $33.4 million worldwide). Moreover, *Drive Me Crazy* made more double than its $8.5 million production budget—in short, the film was a commercial success.

It is difficult to tell the exact reason for the film's success. Perhaps it was the film's reliance on the conventions of the romantic comedy genre that got people to see the film, despite less than ecstatic reviews. Or maybe the popularity of the themes, plot, and vision of *How I Created My Perfect Prom Date* was enough to get audiences to see the film in theaters. Although both the book and the film have been popular to a certain degree, there has been little critical attention paid to either narrative. This speaks to the caliber of YA books written by Todd Strasser: while they are entertaining, there is not a great deal about them that scholars, critics, and readers have found worth talking about.

One of the most important aspects of the success of *Drive Me Crazy* may simply be the popularity of the YA genre as a whole and particularly of major themes within the film. The story is about finding an identity in the often-confusing world of adolescence and high school, which has a certain universality. Similarly, the portrayal of the complexities of society and social structure and the critique of them are ideas that nearly anyone can relate to. Together, these themes make *Drive Me Crazy* a story that is easily relatable for audiences of any age.

Aaron Horton, MA

Further Reading

Bily, Cynthia A. "Todd Strasser." *Guide to Literary Masters & Their Works* (2007): 1. *Literary Reference Center*. Web. 6 Apr. 2015. <http://search.ebscohost.com/login.aspx?direct=true&db=lfh&AN=103331LM72319790307138&site=lrc-live>.

Strasser, Todd. *Drive Me Crazy Film Tie In*. New York: Simon Pulse, 1999. Print.

"Time Zone High." *Help! You're Trapped in Todd Strasser's Body*. N.p., 12 Nov. 2008. Web. 6 Apr. 2015. <http://toddstrasser.blogspot.com/2008/11/time-zone-high.html>.

Bibliography

Cart, Michael. "The Renaissance Continues: Young Adult Literature for the 21st Century." *Catholic Library World* June 2009: 279–85. *Poetry & Short Story Reference Center*. Web. 19 Mar. 2015. <http://search.ebscohost.com/login.aspx?direct=true&db=prf&AN=41423480&site=ehost-live&scope=site>.

Lubar, David. "Everything." *ALAN Review* Spring/Summer 2003: n. pag. *Virginia Tech Digital Library and Archives*. Web. 6 Apr. 2015. <http://scholar.lib.vt.edu/ejournals/ALAN/v30n3/lubar.html>.

Strickland, Ashley. "A Brief History of Young Adult Literature." *CNN*. Cable News Network, 17 Oct 2013. Web. 15 Mar. 2015. <http://www.cnn.com/2013/10/15/living/young-adult-fiction-evolution>.

The DUFF

The Book

Author: Kody Keplinger (b. 1991)
First published: 2010

The Film

Director: Ari Sandel
Screenplay by: Josh A. Cagan
Starring: Mae Whitman, Robbie Amell, Bella Thorne

Context

The teen comedy has long been a popular genre of film, from the teen beach films of the 1950s to the raunchy teen comedies of the 1990s and early 2000s. During the first two decades of the twenty-first century, some films adhered strongly to the tropes set in place by their predecessors, featuring definable character types such as the jock or the nerd and falling into typical patterns of romance and humor. Other teen films, such as 2004's *Mean Girls* and 2010's *Easy A*, engaged with such tropes while calling attention to and subverting them, creating insightful narratives within established cinematic frameworks. The 2015 film *The DUFF* in many ways follows the examples set by the latter category of films, knowingly using the structures and patterns of teen films to express a deeper message about self-acceptance.

The DUFF is based on the 2010 young adult book of the same name, the debut novel by Kody Keplinger, who was herself in her late teens when the work was published. The novel follows teenager Bianca Piper's journey after she learns from womanizing classmate Wesley Rush, whom she loathes, that she is considered the DUFF ("the designated ugly fat friend") of her group of friends. Experiencing a crisis of identity and also dealing with stressful family situations, including her parents' divorce and her father's alcoholism, she begins a sexual relationship with Wesley as a means of distracting herself from her problems. The two eventually fall for each other and begin dating, and Bianca embraces her status as a DUFF, having come to realize that there is no one who does not fall into that category at one time or another.

Like many adaptations of young adult novels, the film incarnation of *The DUFF* is not completely faithful to the novel's plot and characterization; rather, the filmmakers sought to capture the spirit of the story while also making changes to the narrative in order to render it more appropriate for the screen and for its teenage audience. The novel was adapted for the screen by Josh A. Cagan, who had previously written for the MTV animated series *Undergrads* (2001). In directing the adaptation, Ari Sandel, the Academy Award–winning director of the short film *West Bank Story* (2005), made his feature-length debut. *The DUFF* premiered in US theaters in February of 2015 and was released internationally over the following months.

Film Analysis

As is the case with many film adaptations of popular novels, *The DUFF* is strongly inspired by the novel of the same name but takes the narrative in a somewhat different direction. The event that sets the plot in motion is very similar to the catalyst of the novel: while at a party with her friends Jess (Skyler Samuels) and Casey (Bianca A. Santos), Bianca (Mae Whitman) has a conversation with Wesley (Robbie Amell)—who, in the film, is her neighbor and childhood friend rather than an enemy—in which he informs her that she is considered a DUFF, or "designated ugly fat friend." As Wesley explains, this term does not literally mean that the person in question is ugly or fat. Rather, in any given friendship the DUFF, in Wesley's words, is "the one who doesn't look as good, thus making their friends look better. The one who's easy to talk to, because no one's trying to get with them." Now aware of her perceived role in her group of friends, Bianca ends her friendships with Jess and Casey and enlists Wesley's help in "reverse-DUFF-ing" herself, hoping to become seen as her own person and also to catch the eye of Toby (Nick Eversman), a boy she likes. All the while, she endures bullying at the hands of Wesley's sometime girlfriend, Madison (Bella Thorne), a cruel popular girl. Bianca succeeds in asking Toby on a date but eventually realizes that he is using her to gain access to Jess and Casey. Having made up with her friends, Bianca attends homecoming, where she tells Wesley that she has feelings for him and explains to Madison that labels are meaningless. Wesley rejects the title of homecoming king and goes to Bianca, with whom he begins a relationship. At the end of the film, Bianca clearly states the lesson she has learned: "It's not about popularity or even getting the guy. It's about understanding that no matter what label is thrown your way, only you can define yourself."

As part of the modern wave of teen comedies, *The DUFF* builds upon the films that came before, engaging with a wide variety of tropes and stereotypes typically found within the genre. The film acknowledges that cinematic history directly: for example, Bianca explains through voiceover at the beginning of the film that "for generations of high-schoolers, you could only be a jock, a geek, a princess, a bully, or a basket case." This assortment of stereotypes reflects the character types featured in the classic teen film *The Breakfast Club* (1985), in which teenagers from separate cliques are brought together during Saturday detention. Although Bianca explains that she believed she was living in a society that had risen above such labels, the film goes on to introduce a new label: that of the DUFF. This category exists alongside the others, as Wesley notes to Bianca when explaining the term; DUFFs exist in every clique and even among the popular students. In introducing that term as a label to be initially rejected but eventually embraced, the film acknowledges the history of clique-based labels in teen films while also rejecting them as ultimately meaningless.

In addition to engaging with such teen film tropes, *The DUFF* falls within the subgenre of teen makeover films. In such films, a (typically female) teenager undergoes a physical and social transformation, often with the goal of gaining the attention of a love interest as well as social acceptance. Such transformations are an established characteristic of many teen films: in *The Breakfast Club*, for instance, the "basket case" character undergoes an impromptu makeover that results in her catching the eye of the jock. In the 1990s, makeovers of quirky, unfashionable girls were a memorable component of films such as *Clueless* (1995) and *She's All That* (1999), and this trend was later parodied in 2001's *Not Another Teen Movie*. In the early twenty-first century, some teen films addressed such transformations in more nuanced ways; in *Mean Girls*, the protagonist undergoes a gradual transformation that gains her both popularity and the attention of her love interest but has a corresponding detrimental effect on her personality and true friendships. While *The DUFF* is generally more nuanced than many of its predecessors, the film features a relatively straightforward makeover narrative, in which Bianca enlists Wesley to, in his words, "reverse-DUFF" her. This transformation is primarily physical and social: Wesley helps Bianca dress differently, instructs her in how to behave on a date, and teaches her to kiss. Although Bianca eventually decides that she is happiest just being herself, her makeover does succeed in gaining her romantic attention, the typical goal of most films in the teen makeover subgenre. This entire plot is a departure from the original novel, which does not

feature a makeover narrative. In making this change, the filmmakers reshaped the plot of the original novel, conforming it to a standard film narrative while retaining elements of the original story.

In addition to altering the novel's plot for the film, the filmmakers made a number of changes in order to make the film suitable for its target audience of teens. The novel's at-times coarse language was significantly softened for the film: at the end of the novel, for example, Bianca tells Wesley, "The fact is, I am the Duff. But so is everyone else in the world, We're all f——ing Duffs" (276). In the film, on the other hand, Bianca tells Madison, "Yeah, I'm somebody's DUFF. Guess what, so are you. So is everybody." While those two statements express the same idea, the tone and feel are quite different. Bianca's relationship with Wesley, which in the novel becomes sexual very quickly, is presented differently in the film, in which they only kiss. Such changes were likely made in order to render the film eligible for the PG-13 rating, which allows for limited swearing and sexual content. While the practical reasoning behind such changes is clear, they have a significant effect on the characterization of Bianca and the other teenage characters.

Significance

Following its release in the United States in February of 2015, *The DUFF* grossed $34 million domestically, according to the website Box Office Mojo. The film was also later released in the United Kingdom, Australia, and Germany, among other countries, ultimately grossing an additional $9.5 million internationally. As the film's total budget was $8.5 million, it proved to be a relative financial success.

Reviews of the film were generally positive, with critics praising its humor, depiction of contemporary technology and social media, and references to previous teen films. Critics who disliked the film largely deemed its plot clichéd and argued that the film undermines its message of self-acceptance through its emphasis on romance and Bianca's makeover. Regardless of whether they enjoyed the film as a whole, however, the majority of critics praised the performances of the main cast, particularly Whitman as Bianca. While some fans of the original novel were displeased that the film differed significantly from the book, Keplinger herself was pleased with the final product, stating in interviews that she believed the film remained true to the novel's overall message.

Joy Crelin

Further Reading

Keplinger, Kody. "Interview: Kody Keplinger, Author of *The DUFF*." Interview by Joyce Lamb. *Happy Ever After*. USA Today, 20 Feb. 2015. Web. 31 Oct. 2015. <http://happyeverafter.usatoday.com/2015/02/20/kody-keplinger-interview-the-duff>.

Keplinger, Kody. "Newsmaker: Kody Keplinger." Interview. *American Libraries* 46.5 (2015): 23. *Academic Search Complete*. Web. 10 Nov. 2015. <http://search.ebscohost.com/login.aspx?direct=true&db=a9h&AN=102654424>.

Bibliography

Ebiri, Bilge. "The DUFF Is a New High-School Comedy Classic." *Vulture*. New York Media, 20 Feb. 2015. Web. 31 Oct. 2015. <http://www.vulture.com/2015/02/movie-review-the-duff-is-a-new-classic.html>.

Lemire, Christy. Rev. of *The DUFF*, dir. Ari Sandel. *RogerEbert.com*. Ebert Digital, 20 Feb. 2015. Web. 31 Oct. 2015. <http://www.rogerebert.com/reviews/the-duff-2015>.

Schager, Nick. "Film Review: 'The Duff.'" *Variety*. Variety Media, 20 Feb. 2015. Web. 31 Oct. 2015. <http://variety.com/2015/film/reviews/film-review-the-duff-1201438357>.

Sharkey, Betsy. "Strong Acting Can't Right Topsy-Turvy Priorities in 'The DUFF.'" *Los Angeles Times*. Los Angeles Times, 19 Feb. 2015. Web. 31 Oct. 2015. <http://www.latimes.com/entertainment/movies/la-et-mn-the-duff-review-whitman-amell-thorne-20150220-column.html>.

Ender's Game

The Book

Author: Orson Scott Card (b. 1951)
First published: 1985

The Film

Director: Gavin Hood (b. 1963)
Screenplay by: Gavin Hood
Starring: Harrison Ford, Asa Butterfield, Viola Davis, Hailee Steinfeld, Ben Kingsley

Context

In 1977 science-fiction writer Orson Scott Card published a novella called "Ender's Game" in *Analog* magazine. It was Card's first published piece of writing. He got the idea for the story, which was based around the concept of the Battle Room, when he was sixteen years old after reading Isaac Asimov's 1963 Foundation trilogy (including *Foundation*, 1951; *Foundation and Empire*, 1952; and *Second Foundation*, 1953), which in turn was based on Edward Gibbon's classic *History of the Decline and Fall of the Roman Empire*, published in the late eighteenth century. Card was struck by Asimov's depiction of empathy; Asimov's characters, who exist in a distant future, learned (not evolved) to fundamentally understand and help others. At the time, he was also devouring biographies and books about the Civil War, and he began to see his passion for science fiction and his concerns about war and the cyclical nature of history converge. In his introduction to the 1991 edition of *Ender's Game* the novel, Card describes how he speculated about how armies of the future would be trained for space warfare, and in 1975—the year of the fall of Saigon in Vietnam—considered the absurd youth of most of the soldiers who had ever gone to battle in an American war. The result of these early musings was "Ender's Game," a story about a place called the Battle Room, where absurdly young recruits (in this case, sometimes six and seven years old) practice war games in a zero-gravity chamber. He adapted the story, which was a finalist for some of the science-fiction genre's top prizes, into a novel in 1985.

Ender's Game (1985) is one of the best loved young adult stories in the science-fiction genre. In it, six-year-old Andrew "Ender" Wiggin is chosen by the military government as a recruit for the highly selective Battle School, located on an orbiting space station. In Ender's world, humans are terrified of reprising a conflict with an alien race known as the buggers (or Formics, in the film adaptation). The buggers are highly developed person-sized insects. Decades before Ender was born, the buggers were defeated in a decisive battle led by a man named Mazer Rackham. In the battle's aftermath, the humans of Earth have organized their lives around war, training the smartest and most cunning of their offspring in battle should the buggers ever return to Earth. Ender is quickly singled out as the most promising recruit and is fast-tracked to Command School, where he leads elaborate simulated battles in order to graduate. In one last decisive battle, against all odds and at an extraordinary price, Ender wins by committing what in the real world would be considered a war crime. After his victory, he finds out that all of the simulated battles were real and that he has single-handedly exterminated the bugger race. *Ender's Game* won both the Nebula Award and Hugo Award for best science-fiction novel. Card wrote three sequels to the book as well as a number of books that involve Ender or his world. The film adaptation of *Ender's Game* was released in November 2013.

Film Analysis

About a month before the film was released, D. E. Wittkower and Lucinda Rush of Old Dominion University edited and published a book of essays about *Ender's Game* called *Ender's Game and Philosophy: Genocide Is Child's Play.* The book explores a few of the ethical questions raised in the novel about genocide, drone warfare, the Internet, and child soldiers. Given the complexity of his source material and the time constraints of a movie, screenwriter and director Gavin Hood was forced to narrow the thematic focus of the story in its film adaptation. Hood envisioned a film in which Ender is constantly fighting to balance his predisposition for violence with his predisposition for love and empathy—traits that are personified in his aggressive brother, Peter, and his gentle sister, Valentine. Peter and Valentine, who enjoy their own subplot in the book, exist in the film largely for the paths they represent. Valentine is good and Peter is bad, the film suggests; which will Ender choose to be? Of course, Ender's task is far more complicated. How can one who has been chosen to be a killer, also be good? The movie begins with a title card flashing a quote from Ender, which also appears in the novel. It says: "In the moment when I truly understand my enemy, understand him well enough to defeat him, then in that very moment I also love him."

The thematic streamlining of the film allowed Hood more time to focus on the action sequences—Ender's fights with his bullies, the simulated Mind Game, and most importantly, the Battle Room—that are so integral to the plot of *Ender's Game*. In the book, there is little physical description of the Battle Room, but Hood renders it as a terrific, glass-paneled orb that looks curiously like a hamster wheel located in the middle of the Battle School's ship. While visual depictions of Earth in the film indistinctly suggest "the future," with gracefully sloping skyscrapers that look they are made of stainless steel set against an incongruously lush landscape, the film's vision of the Battle School is cold, with that same steely gray. Spaces like the Battle Room, which offers a stunning view of Earth, physically dwarf the characters, as if to reinforce the enormity of the task set before them. War games are central to Hood's, as well as Card's, story; Ender's relationship to simulated killing changes and matures over time. As Hood explained to Clark, Ender views the games in the Battle Room—and later in the visually similar game room at Command School—as a closed system. For him, games are separate in themselves, without effect on games in the past or in the future, and certainly (at least for now, he believes) without effect in the real world where people live and die. Thus, he develops a meaningful phrase, forged in the Battle Room with his second-in-command, Bean: "The enemy's gate is down," meaning that sometimes, it is necessary to win by breaking the rules.

Ender's Game is one of several dystopian science-fiction films in the 2010s to employ the concept of game-as-metaphor. As Nick Schager points out in an article for *New York Magazine*, movie adaptations like *The Hunger Games* (2012) and *The Maze Runner* (2014) feature young adult protagonists caught in the mechanism of "games" constructed by authority figures. (In the film, Ender is twelve, though in the book, he enters Battle School when he is six.) The power structure is visually enforced by casting: adult authority figures in these worlds are lent the gravitas of celebrity in ours. Ender's mentors—who are also, Hood suggests, his enemies—are played by Harrison Ford, Viola Davis, and Ben Kingsley. By contrast, Asa Butterfield, the young actor who plays Ender, appeared in the 2011 film *Hugo*, but after a serious growth-spurt, is almost unrecognizable. One significant difference between *Ender's Game* and similar films is Ender's lack of awareness as to the extent of the game in which he finds himself. Ender is groomed as a leader, but he is also a pawn. For all his youthful wisdom, he has no idea that he is being had.

It was necessary for Hood to compress the time line of the book, and this decision makes Ender's revulsion to his own triumph over the Formics all the more unsettling. Instead of brooding on his own actions of thirty years—as he does in the book—Ender barely makes it through a night's sleep. He is drawn to the real ruins of the castle he saw in the Mind Game (for compression's sake, those ruins are visible out his window at Command School), where he finds a pupa—the last of the Formics race. The film's last scene shows Ender as he is hurtling through space, in search of suitable planet for the Formics to repopulate. In the book, this action is taken by an adult Ender who, crucially, has the support of an adult Valentine and a thriving commune, in which he is loved and respected. In the movie, Ender is still a child, Valentine still lives on Earth, and the final image of the film is a lot like its first: Ender, metaphorically at least, is alone.

Significance

The premiere of *Ender's Game*, so long anticipated by fans, was marred after it was discovered that Card routinely aired his vitriolic views about homosexuality on his blog. (Card's views had not been public knowledge when he sold the movie rights to the book nearly ten years before the film was made.) Card wrote that homosexuality was a crime and, in another post, compared President Barack Obama to Hitler. It was a strange turn of events for a movie based on a book about tolerance, empathy, and respect for the differences of others. A number of groups encouraged moviegoers to boycott the movie, prompting Card, Lionsgate, and star Harrison Ford to release statements separating Card's views from the film itself. Reportedly, Card did not make any profits from ticket sales. *Ender's Game* premiered in early November 2013. The film opened number one at the US box office that weekend, though the $27 million it earned then was not enough to deem the opening an unqualified success. Many predicted that its lukewarm audience reception killed any talk of a sequel, much less any hope for a larger franchise like the Hunger Games films.

Critical reception was mixed, skewing toward cold. "I suspect," Chris Nashawaty wrote for *Entertainment Weekly*, "that diehard fans [of the book] might walk out of Gavin Hood's lavish, eye-candy adaptation [feeling like] they've spent more than two decades waiting for what ends up being an oddly lifeless and emotionally unaffecting film." Manohla Dargis of the *New York Times* praised Hood's depiction of the Battle Room and the Mind Game but was disturbed by the film's "creepy" adults and the "appealing" yet overly "intense" Ender, who "can't help feeling like a pint-sized psycho." The *Guardian*'s Peter Bradshaw was a fan of the film but wrote that, despite Hood's best efforts to distill the book's complexities, its "apocalyptic finale indicates that it's bitten off considerably more than it can chew in terms of ideas."

Molly Hagan

Further Reading

Corliss, Richard. "*Ender's Game*: Is This Boy 'The One?'" Rev. of Ender's Game, dir. by Gavin Hood. *Time*. Time, 1 Nov. 2013. Web. 1 Apr. 2015. <http://entertainment.time.com/2013/11/01/enders-game-is-this-boy-the-one>.

Dargis, Manohla. "And a Child Shall Lead Them into Space Battle." Rev. of *Ender's Game*, dir. by Gavin Hood. *New York Times*. New York Times, 31 Oct. 2013. Web. 1 Apr. 2015. <http://www.nytimes.com/2013/11/01/movies/enders-game-with-harrison-ford-and-asa-butterfield.html>.

Wittkower, D. E., and Lucinda Rush, eds. *Ender's Game and Philosophy: Genocide Is Child's Play*. Chicago: Open Court, 2013. Print.

Bibliography

Bradshaw, Peter. Rev. of *Ender's Game*, dir. by Gavin Hood. *Guardian*. Guardian News and Media, 24 Oct. 2013. Web. 2 Apr. 2015. <http://www.theguardian.com/film/2013/oct/24/enders-game-review>.

Card, Orson Scott. Introduction. *Ender's Game*. New York: Tor, 1991. Print.

Child, Ben. "Ender's Game Sequel No Longer Likely after Unspectacular US Box Office." *Guardian*. Guardian News and Media, 5 Nov. 2013. Web. 2 Apr. 2015. <http://www.theguardian.com/film/2013/nov/05/enders-game-sequel-harrison-ford-not-likely>.

Clark, Noelene. "'Ender's Game' Director Gavin Hood on Why He Changed Ender's Age." *Hero Complex*. Los Angeles Times, 31 Oct. 2013. Web. 2 Apr. 2015. <http://herocomplex.latimes.com/movies/enders-game-gavin-hood-changed-age/#/0>.

Lapidos, Juliet. "The 'Ender's Game' Boycott." *New York Times*. New York Times, 20 July 2013. Web. 1 Apr. 2015. <http://www.nytimes.com/2013/07/21/opinion/sunday/the-enders-game-boycott.html?_r=0>.

Nashawaty, Chris. Rev. of *Ender's Game*, dir. by Gavin Hood. *Entertainment Weekly*. Entertainment Weekly, 17 Jan. 2015. Web. 2 Apr. 2015. <http://www.ew.com/article/2013/11/20/enders-game-movie>.

Schager, Nick. "YA Dystopian Films Have Become What They Hate." *New York Magazine*. New York Media, 21 Nov. 2014. Web. 2 Apr. 2015. <http://www.vulture.com/2014/11/ya-dystopian-films-have-become-what-they-hate.html>.

Eragon

The Book

Author: Christopher Paolini (b. 1983)
First published: 2002

The Film

Director: Stefen Fangmeier (b. 1960)
Screenplay by: Peter Buchman
Starring: Edward Speleers, Jeremy Irons, Sienna Guillory, Robert Carlyle, John Malkovich, and Djimon Hounsou

Context

Ever since the release of the first of the Star Wars films in the late 1970s, fantasy films about young men learning wisdom from older men as they join forces to fight tyranny have been enormously popular. The film adaptations of J. R. R. Tolkien's *Lord of the Rings* trilogy, as well as the books that inspired them, have only increased the popularity of the heroic fantasy genre. *Eragon* the book and *Eragon* the film are both indebted to the influence of Star Wars and Tolkien. They are also indebted to many similar stories (such as the ancient legend of Beowulf) about heroic youths battling oppressive evil—stories that are almost as old as literature itself.

The filmed version of *Eragon* celebrates many traditional values. The idea that the young can learn important lessons from the old is just one of these ideals. Another is the concept of a clear opposition between good and evil and the need to oppose evil even at great personal risk. Masculine bravery, the need for self-discipline, the value of friendship, and the belief that evil can and must be crushed through physical combat are just a few more of the themes celebrated not only in *Eragon* but in much of the traditional literature of Western civilization. In all these respects, *Eragon* is a film that uses the modern cinematic technology to teach classic lessons.

Other traditional values also undergird this film. These include the beliefs that one individual can make a key difference, that good sense is as important as physical strength and bravery, that virtue is worth cultivating and fighting for, and that good ultimately will triumph over evil. Many of these ideas have been challenged in much contemporary literature and other media, but the popularity of *Eragon* the novel (if not of *Eragon* the film) suggests that they are still widely appealing.

Film Analysis

Eragon the novel is too long and complex to have been adapted with complete fidelity in a film that lasts only an hour and a half. Initially the plot of the film follows the plot of the book reasonably closely—a beautiful female (in the book she is an elf) named Arya (Sienna Guillory) is being pursued through a dark forest by the ugly henchmen of an evil "shade," or wizard, named Durza (Robert Carlyle). He, in turn, is acting at the behest of an even more evil king, Galbatorix (John Malkovich). The king is desperate to recover a magical blue stone Arya has stolen, but just before she is captured, she manages to magically transport the stone into the midst of a dark forest.

There it is found by a handsome teenager named Eragon (Ed Speleers). He is, stereotypically, blond-haired and blue-eyed (in the book his eyes and hair are brown), and he eventually discovers that the stone is actually an egg from which a dragon, Saphira, ultimately hatches. Under the tutelage of a wise older man, Brom (Jeremy Irons), Eragon learns, through various trials and many errors, to become a heroic dragon rider. He and Saphira use their combined powers to destroy Durza and frustrate Galbatorix, although the ending of the film suggests that Galbatorix's evil is far from finally defeated.

Inevitably, many characters, places, and pieces of plot found in the novel are cut or collapsed in the film—a fact that frustrated many viewers of the film who were purist fans of the book. Some of the major deviations that prompted such disappointment involved perceived losses in character and relationship development. Since the novel serves as a coming-of-age story, some audiences were dissatisfied with the short time allowed in the film version for Brom's character to interact with Eragon as his crucial mentor; he seems to die much sooner onscreen than in the book. Others similarly despaired that they could not witness Saphira's parallel growth and bonding with Eragon; instead, she grows to maturity almost instantly at first flight. Viewers unfamiliar with the novel have tended to be more charitable when reviewing the film, although not entirely.

The film version of *Eragon* uses a number of techniques repeatedly to emphasize its key themes. The most obvious of these is a pervasive opposition between light and darkness. The well-lit scenes are almost always set outdoors and are frequently used to emphasize the beauty of the natural environment. The film brims with panoramic overhead shots of mountains, forests, fields, and lakes. These shots are rarely static; instead, they are sweeping and soaring, as if viewers were seeing Earth from the perspective of Saphira, the free-flying dragon who is Eragon's friend, ally, and protector. Scenes such as these remind viewers of the beauty of the world—a beauty under dangerous threat by such evil characters as Durza and Galbatorix.

Appropriately enough, the places associated with the latter two characters and their underlings are almost always dark, dank, and dreary. They are usually located inside massive castles, barely illuminated by burning torches. One outside shot of Durza's castle is particularly revealing. The castle is massive, square, and architecturally uninteresting. It looks like a giant black box sitting atop a treeless mountain. As Eragon views it from behind nearby boulders, many viewers will be reminded of the scene in *The Wizard of Oz* when Dorothy's three friends come to rescue her from the evil witch who has imprisoned the girl in her own dark castle. Indeed, the similarities between this episode in *Eragon* and that episode in *The Wizard of Oz* are so numerous that the parallels must be deliberate. It is as if the director of *Eragon* is paying homage to one of the greatest fantasy films of all time. Yet both films, of course, are drawing on some of the most ancient literary symbols and archetypes. *Eragon*— both the film and the book—helps illustrate the common claim that few stories are truly original or ever really could be. What matters is less the tale than the telling.

One narrative method frequently used in *Eragon* the film involves constant, sudden cross-cutting from darkness to light and back to darkness. Rarely do the filmmakers present gradual transitions from one kind of setting to another. Instead, the movie usually jumps abruptly from one kind of scene or setting to its opposite. Thus, very early in the film, just as viewers are caught up in the suspense of whether Arya will be captured and perhaps killed in the dark forest, the film suddenly jumps to a scene of the handsome young Eragon awakening from a night's rest. Then, just as abruptly, viewers find themselves back in the dark forest again. This kind of cross-cutting pervades the film and helps highlight the movie's emphasis on stark differences between light and darkness, good and evil.

Rarely are there shades of gray or moral ambiguities in this film. This is not a philosophical meditation on ethical complexities. It is, instead, a heroic action-and-adventure drama, in which the good characters are almost entirely good and the evil characters are thoroughly evil. In the novel, the complex origins of Galbatorix's evil make him almost sound pitiable (at least for a page or so). In the movie, he is simply evil from start to finish.

Significance

Despite receiving generally poor reviews from both professional and amateur critics, *Eragon* made a profit for its investors. It cost roughly $100 million to make but grossed nearly $250 million worldwide. The absence of both a major female lead and a real romantic subplot may have hurt the film with young female viewers, but such viewers may also have been attracted by the presence of the handsome young hero. The film's poor performance with reviewers ultimately raised questions as to whether any of the subsequent books in the Inheritance Cycle series would be made into films as well.

Eragon is probably most significant as one more piece of evidence of the continuing appeal of time-tested legends of heroic youth learning from wise elders to combat oppressive evil. Many viewers of *Eragon* were disappointed with the film, but they were dissatisfied not with the premises of the plot but with the way the plot was presented. Most critics of the film faulted it for not doing justice to the novel, for being too imitative of other, better films, or for both alleged flaws at once. Few critics attacked the film for promoting traditional values such as virtue and selfless heroism. In a time, then, when the young are often depicted in the media and in popular culture as self-indulgent narcissists focused on superficial pleasures, both the novel and the film of *Eragon* suggest that many young adults still appreciate virtue and noble aspirations. *Eragon* the film may have fallen short of the lofty hopes many viewers had for it, but the mere existence of those hopes suggests the continuing existence of high standards—both ethically and aesthetically—among numerous young adults.

Robert C. Evans, PhD

Further Reading

Gresh, Lois H. *The Ultimate Unauthorized* Eragon *Guide: The Hidden Facts behind the World of Alagaësia*. New York: St. Martin's, 2006. Print.

Lissauer, Gabrielle. *The Tropes of Fantasy Fiction*. Jefferson: McFarland, 2015. Print.

Macauley, Michael. *The Inheritance Almanac: An A–Z Guide to the World of* Eragon. New York: Knopf, 2010. Print.

Bibliography

Cahill, Bryon. "Magic and Dragons and Writing . . . Oh, My!" *Writing* Jan. 2007: 18–20. *Literary Reference Center*. Web. 25 Mar. 2015. <http://search.ebscohost.com/login.aspx?direct=true&db=lfh&AN=23465169&site=lrc-live>.

Gopnik, Adam. "The Dragon's Egg." *New Yorker* 5 Dec. 2011: 86–89. *Literary Reference Center*. Web. 25 Mar. 2015. <http://search.ebscohost.com/login.aspx?direct=true&db=lfh&AN=67767351&site=lrc-live>.

Paolini, Christopher. "Christopher Paolini's Amazing Success: For the Bestselling Author of the Inheritance Cycle, It All Came Together Thanks to Discipline and Learning How to Structure and Pre-Plot a Story." Interview by Philip Martin. *Writer* May 2012: 24–26. *Literary Reference Center*. Web. 30 Mar. 2015. <http://search.ebscohost.com/login.aspx?direct=true&db=lfh&AN=74158784&site=lrc-live>.

Paolini, Christopher. "Christopher Paolini: Inspiration Strikes about Once Every Blue Moon." Interview. *Guardian*. Guardian News and Media, 16 Nov. 2011. Web. 25 Mar. 2015. <http://www.theguardian.com/childrens-books-site/2011/nov/16/christopher-paolini-interview>.

Fat Kid Rules the World

The Book

Author: K. L. Going (b. 1973)
First published: 2003

The Film

Director: Matthew Lillard (b. 1970)
Screenplay by: Michael M. B. Galvin and Peter Speakman
Starring: Jacob Wysocki, Matt O'Leary, and Billy Campbell

Context

The publication of the novel *Fat Kid Rules the World* (2003) coincides with the resurgence of realistic young adult fiction during the early and mid-2000s. The realistic subgenre has always been a major part of young adult (YA) literature since its beginnings in the late 1960s. The literary form that is recognized today as YA literature, meaning texts that are written for and marketed to an audience between the ages of twelve to eighteen, can be said to begin with the publication of the American novel *The Outsiders* (1967) by S. E. Hinton. In the 1970s, this new literary genre gained huge popularity and became an important part of the literature market not only in the United States but internationally as well. The realistic genre was largely the only genre of YA fiction for over a decade, even into the 1980s, when YA literature saw a sharp decline in popularity, writers like Judy Blume continued to produce realistic fiction for a teenage audience.

In the 1990s, a renewal of the popularity of YA literature took place, although this time a plethora of subgenres arose and took the forefront of the genre. Fantasy, horror, dystopian, science-fiction, and other speculative genres dominated the market. It was not until the 2000s that realistic fiction found a firm footing again, although it differed from the realistic fiction of three decades before. YA writers began to deal with issues that in the past had often been considered too mature for a younger audience, including more graphic issues such as the effects of addiction, violence, mental illness, and other emotional trauma. The film and novel version of *Fat Kid Rules the World* are a part of the latter perspective on teenage lives. They both focus primarily on issues related to suicide, drug addiction, and fitting in (or not) into the social order of high school.

The film was actor Matthew Lillard's directorial debut after he optioned the rights to the novel shortly after its release. Similarly, the novel was writer K. L. Going's first published work. She has continued to publish YA and children's literature since, but this book stands as her most popular work and has gained the most critical praise, being named an honor book for the Michael L. Printz Award in 2004.

Film Analysis

The film adaptation of *Fat Kid Rules the World* remains very loyal to the original plot of the novel. While there are some differences between the two versions, the relationship between the two main characters, the issues that they must face, and the obstacles and assistance they receive from the people in their lives are nearly identical. For example, the novel is placed in New York City and opens with a scene where Troy Billings stands dangerously close to the tracks at a metro station, contemplating jumping in front of the train when it comes. He is tired of being ridiculed at school and thinks to himself, "And that's the one thing that can't happen. People can't laugh. Even I deserve a decent suicide." He is pulled away by Curt Mac-Crae, a local school legend, who talks to him and gets him away from the edge. The movie is set in Seattle, Washington, and begins with a scene of Troy (Jacob Wysocki) waiting on a steep hill for his bus. He steps into the street just before the bus comes but is pushed out of the way by Marcus (Matt O'Leary), a dropout and star of a popular local band. He demands twenty dollars from Troy for saving his life, and Troy gives him everything he has in his wallet.

In the movie, the relationship between these two characters continues largely through Marcus's initiation. He shows up at Troy's school and charismatically demands the rest of the money Troy owes him, and convinces Troy that they need to start a band together with Troy on drums and Marcus on guitar and vocals. Troy having no particular talent in any area other than playing video games online, is reluctant, but Marcus continues to find and pester Troy, even setting him up with an acquaintance of his for drum lessons. While this is going on, Troy's father (Billy Campbell), a law enforcement officer, is not entirely happy that his son is hanging out with a person like Marcus, who is homeless and seems like a drug addict. However, he sees that Marcus stirs something in Troy, something that was lost after the death of his mother. Troy's issue with weight started after his mother died, and since then, he has had very little personal motivation in his life. So, hesitatingly, Mr. Billings allows the friendship between the two to continue.

Marcus, on the other hand, has his own problems. He has had constant issues with drugs, to the point that his mother and stepfather refuse to have anything to do with him. He was kicked out of Troy's school the year before, and to this point only had his place in his band as a positive influence. However, the members of his band, like his parents, no longer want to deal with Marcus's addiction issues, so they kick him out. Throughout the movie, Marcus is mostly drifting, finding food, drugs, and a place to stay wherever he can. He has been rejected by every person in his life and falls deeper into drugs because "feel good" is the only thing he thinks he has. Troy represents the one person in his life who cares about his well-being. The climax of the story comes when Marcus is hospitalized after an overdose. Again,

no one seems to care that this has happened to Marcus but Troy, and in a turn of events, the generally cold Mr. Billings realizes that Marcus needs his support. Troy and Marcus's band, the Tectonics, has played only one disastrous show, but Troy hatches a plan to break Marcus out of the hospital for one gig to remind him that he has something to live for.

Because the novel is narrated from Troy's perspective, the reader gains access to more intimate details of his thought process and emotional state than in the film adaptation. For example, Troy is under a constant barrage of criticism and denigration from his schoolmates and younger brother about his weight, and he passively accepts this harassment because he feels that he deserves it. There are constant references to Troy's weight from others and himself. On the other hand, the film makes infrequent references to Troy's weight, and while the audience does get the sense that Troy has little self-confidence or self-respect, the use of repetition is not an important device. In one of the first scenes when Troy is forced to play basketball with his dad and brother, it is apparent that he simply has few skills related to things such as sports—it is not his weight that is necessarily holding him back. Lillard himself said in an interview at the time of the film's release that it is not a movie about fatness or being fat and that he was almost sorry that "fat" was even in the title because the story is really not about weight.

Other differences between the film and the novel surround details in plot and the focus placed on certain aspects. In the novel, for example, Curt is not only abandoned by his mother and stepfather, but by his father as well. The emotional state that this abandonment puts him in seems much more intense, and so when he is hospitalized for pneumonia after doing too many drugs, the response by Troy and this father is that much more powerful. Troy's desire to be in a band is also displayed differently in each version. In the novel, Troy is very uninterested in forming a band until he is invited backstage at a show by Curt. When he sees the energy and excitement that comes from being in a band, he finds a personal motivation to keep practicing drums. In the film, Marcus seems to be mostly cutoff from the music scene and it is partly Troy's fantasies of fame, Marcus's constant pressure, and Mr. Billings' decision to buy Troy a drum kit that keep Troy motivated.

While the film adaptation is not shot from Troy's point of view, it does give the audience access to Troy's inner world through the inclusion of Troy's fantasies. For example, when Troy is contemplating suicide at the beginning of the movie, a clip of him walking into the street, getting hit, and blood splattering all over the bus's windshield is juxtaposed with the shot of him waiting at the bus stop. There is a certain suddenness to these fantasies as there is no warning before they take place, compared to the same fantasies in the novel that are generally introduced with phrases such as "I imagine." Other than this device, the movie employs few unusual cinematic devices.

Significance

The film adaptation of *Fat Kid Rules the World* was released in 2012 to generally good reviews from critics and audiences around the world. Critics did cite problems with the movie, such as the general character introduction and development at the start of the movie. There is a sense as though the audience is supposed to connect with Troy more through empathy with his isolation and lack of skills than as a fully developed character. Similarly, Marcus comes across as a generally unlikeable character until he finally begins to bond with Troy near the end of the movie. However, at the end, these characters are not only very likeable but also well developed. The story was praised for its originality and refusal to follow genre standards such as making everything work out in the end. In the end, the title clearly appears to have to do with Troy's own mindset more than his particular fame or any traditionally measured achievements. Neither has everything worked out for Marcus nor between Troy and his brother, but there is hope that everything might.

The novel and film adaptation have been praised for delivering a direct look at the life of a teenager who does not fit in and the difficulties he must face every day. Nothing is glossed over, and this is perhaps one of the reasons the film was praised highly. However, the untraditional scope and perspective of the tale may also be why, while the movie was considered a commercial success, it did not reach box office numbers close to those achieved by other realistic YA novel adaptations such as Josh Boone's 2014 film version of John Green's *The Fault in Our Stars* (2011). Nevertheless, in the end, the novel and film prove to be strong additions to the realistic YA genre.

Aaron Horton, MA

Further Reading

Lillard, Matthew. "Director Matthew Lillard on *Fat Kid Rules the World*." Interview by Billy Brennan. *Filmmaker Magazine*. Filmmaker Magazine, 25 Oct. 2012. Web. 1 Nov. 2015. <http://filmmakermagazine.com/56905-matthew-lillard-on-fat-kid-rules-the-world/#.VkkxVN-rTUo>.

Rapold, Nicolas. "An Outsider Trying to Get Out of the Doldrums." Rev. of *Fat Kid Rules the World*, dir. Matthew Lillard. *New York Times*. New York Times, 4 Oct. 2012. Web. 1 Nov. 2015. <http://www.nytimes.com/2012/10/05/movies/fat-kid-rules-the-world-directed-by-matthew-lillard.html>.

Roback, Diane, et al. "*Fat Kid Rules the World* (Book." Rev. of *Fat Kid Rules the World*, by K. L. Going. *Publishers Weekly* 23 June 2003: 69. *Literary Reference Center*. Web. 15 Nov. 2015. <http://search.ebscohost.com/login.aspx?direct=true&db=lfh&AN=10090507&site=lrc-live>.

Bibliography

Carlson, Daniel. "*Fat Kid Rules the World* Review: Don't Call It a Comeback, I Been Here for Years." Rev. of *Fat Kid Rules the World*, dir. Matthew Lillard. *Pajiba*. Pajiba, 5 Oct. 2012. Web. 1 Nov. 2015. <http://www.pajiba.com/film_reviews/fat-kid-rules-the-world-review-dont-call-it-a-comeback-i-been-here-for-years.php>.

Going, K. L. "Michael L. Printz Honor Speech." *Young Adult Library Services* 3.1 (2004): 28–41. *Education Source*. Web. 17 Nov. 2015. <http://search.ebscohost.com/login.aspx?direct=true&db=eue&AN=502937186&site=eds-live>.

Going, K. L. "Q&A with K. L. Going." Interview by Sue Corbett. *Publishers Weekly*. PWxyz, 12 Feb. 2009. Web. 1 Nov. 2015. <http://www.publishersweekly.com/pw/by-topic/authors/interviews/article/970-q-a-with-k-l-going.html>.

Going, K. L. *K. L. Going*. K. L. Going, n.d. Web. 1 Nov. 2015. <http://klgoing.com>

Lillard, Matthew. "Matthew Lillard on Why *Fat Kid Rules the World* Isn't about Being Fat." Interview by Rebecca Ford. *Hollywood Reporter*. Hollywood Reporter, 12 Oct. 2015. Web. 1 Nov. 2015. <http://www.hollywoodreporter.com/news/matthew-lillard-fat-kid-rules-378457>.

The Fault in Our Stars

The Book

Author: John Green (b. 1977)
First published: 2012

The Film

Director: Josh Boone (b. 1979)
Screenplay by: Scott Neustadter, Michael H. Weber
Starring: Shailene Woodley, Ansel Elgort, Laura Dern, Willem Dafoe

Context

In 2012, the young adult author John Green published his fifth novel, *The Fault in Our Stars*, about two teenagers with terminal cancer who fall in love. The book takes its title from a line from Shakespeare's *Julius Caesar* in which Cassius says, "The fault, dear Brutus, is not in our stars / But in ourselves" (act 1, sc. 2). Unfortunately for Green's tragic heroes, the fault really is in their stars, the "cruel fate," Emma Brockes wrote for the May 2014 issue of *Intelligent Life* magazine, "which brings them together only to rip them asunder." The premise of the book might seem saccharine, but Natalie Standiford, in her January 13, 2012, review of the book for the *New York Times*, praised Green's refusal to sugarcoat descriptions of pain, illness, and death. "These unpleasant details do nothing to diminish the romance; in Green's hands, they only make it more moving," Standiford wrote. "He shows us true love—two teenagers helping and accepting each other through the most humiliating physical and emotional ordeals—and it is far more romantic than any sunset on the beach." *The Fault in Our Stars* was a best seller before it was even published and became a cultural phenomenon that sparked a surprisingly heated debate about adult enthusiasm for young adult fiction—a debate that continued in 2014, when *Fault* was adapted for the screen.

As Margaret Talbot reported in a June 2014 *New Yorker* profile of Green, the enormous success of the book was thanks in part to Green's massive Internet following, a group affectionately self-styled the Nerdfighters. In 2006, Green and his brother Hank began making a series of YouTube videos. The videos were meant to be semiprivate and irreverent, a simple means for two tech-savvy siblings (these were the early days of Internet videos, after all) to stay in touch. But the videos developed a much larger audience than the Green family, and by 2007, their numbers were in the thousands. They called themselves the Nerdfighters, a term Green coined himself in a riff about a misread word. *Fault* is Green's fifth novel—his first, *Looking for Alaska*, won the Michael L. Printz Award in 2006—but his built-in fan base gave the book the heft of a highly anticipated debut. Just before the film adaptation was released, the book had spent 124 consecutive weeks on the *New York Times* best seller list and had been the number one YA book for 43 weeks.

Through the Nerdfighters, Green was introduced to a young girl named Esther Grace Earl, a sixteen-year-old suffering from thyroid cancer. She died in 2010. The character Hazel Grace Lancaster, who is also dependent on an oxygen tank, is loosely based on Esther. The story also draws on Green's own brief experience as a chaplain working with kids with terminal diseases. "The truth is, or at least the argument of the book is, I think, that a short life can also be a good life," Green told Rebecca J. Rosen for the February 2013 issue of the *Atlantic*.

Film Analysis

The Fault in Our Stars joins a long tradition of romantic films that deal with terminal illness. The subgenre is derisively known as the "sick flick." The archetypal sick flick is the 1970 film *Love Story*, based on the Erich Segal novel of the same name. According to Talbot, Green "loved and hated" the book when he read it in high school. When he wrote *Fault*, he was cautious not to fall into the same sentimental traps. The story, told in flashback, recounts the love between the son of a millionaire named Oliver (Ryan O'Neal) and the blue-collar daughter of an Italian baker named Jenny (Ali MacGraw). Jenny suffers from a rare and unidentified blood disease that ultimately kills her. Twenty-first-century sick flicks include *A Walk to Remember* (2002), based on the Nicholas Sparks novel of the same name, in which a high school bad boy, Landon (Shane West), falls for a quiet girl in the drama club named Jamie (Mandy Moore). Jamie eventually dies of leukemia. In the film *Sweet November* (2001), based on a 1968 film of the same name, an advertising executive named Nelson (Keanu Reeves) falls for a quirky woman named Sara (Charlize Theron) who has terminal cancer in the form of non-Hodgkin lymphoma.

According to Eliza Berman's June 5, 2014, *Slate* article, the sick flick has four distinct tropes. First, the man is the protagonist; though the woman is physically dying, he is spiritually dying and relies on her disease-wrought wisdom to save him. Second, the woman tries to end their relationship, afraid that her death will hurt her partner. Third, in death, the woman is "elevated to near-sainthood," and lastly, the man's life is improved for having known his dead lover. Of the aforementioned films, *Sweet November* is the most flagrant offender in terms of the first trope. In the movie, Theron's character Sara seeks out men for the express purpose of entering their lives for one month and imbuing them with her quirky worldview. She is most persistent with Reeves's conceited ad man, but of course, her plans are spoiled when they fall in love. *A Walk to Remember*, meanwhile, provides a fairly straightforward example of the fourth trope. West's character is an aimless troublemaker, but after his life-changing relationship with Jamie, he is inspired to go to medical school—making Jamie's death merely a plot point (albeit a necessary one) in the larger success story of Landon's life.

The Fault in Our Stars upends the first trope of the sick flick by making the sarcastic sixteen-year-old Hazel Grace (Shailene Woodley) the story's protagonist. Her life is little more than reading the same book over and over again and hanging out with her parents. When her mother forces her to go a group therapy session for teenagers with cancer, she meets Augustus "Gus" Waters (Ansel Elgort). Gus is a former basketball star who lost part of his leg to osteosarcoma and pursues with Hazel with zeal, eventually charming her with his sincerity and zest for life. While Gus convinces Hazel to embrace life while she has it (a little like Sara in *Sweet November*), Hazel helps the superhero-obsessed Gus see that it is equally important to embrace darker feelings; she quotes her favorite book, telling him, "That's the thing about pain. It demands to be felt." The relationship between Hazel and Gus is a nuanced give-and-take, though it is also one aspect in which the film struggles to capture the breadth of the novel fully. Gus often comes across as one-dimensionally charming, whereas in the book, as Green has stressed, Gus takes a perverse pleasure in his performance of himself. It takes Hazel to help him drop the act and learn to be content with himself as he is.

Despite the gender swapping of the main character, *Fault* actually follows the second trope of the classic sick flick. As the two begin to fall for one another, Hazel warns Gus that she is a "grenade," just waiting to "blow up" and "obliterate everything in my wake." Of course, Gus ignores her plea to end their friendship altogether. They eventually decide to enjoy their time together, however short, though this decision is never presented as a "you-only-live-once" platitude. In fact, both characters abhor platitudes of any kind, enduring them or accepting them only when they must and secretly laughing at their inanity. Hazel and Gus's dark humor and stark observations prevent the film from becoming sentimental, though here too the book is able to portray this duality much more fully, allowing Hazel to smile politely at a framed inspirational quote while thinking that "its stupidity and lack of sophistication could be plumbed for centuries."

As *Fault*'s reversal of the first trope might suggest, the death depicted in the film is not Hazel's death but Gus's—and his passing could not be more human. In *Love Story*, Jenny dies the death of a saint. As *New York Times* critic Vincent Canby wrote (18 Dec. 1970), she is practically iridescent in death, "as if she were suffering from some kind of vaguely unpleasant Elizabeth Arden treatment," he wrote. "Jenny doesn't die. She just slips away in beauty." Though Elgort and Woodley—who, at Green's instance, wears an oxygen tube on her face throughout the entire film—are beautiful actors, director Josh Boone does his best to show the characters' humiliating reality, vomit and all. (Though, again, the book gets more graphic.) Hazel even says in a voiceover, that she wishes she could report that Gus died with dignity but that he did not; in capturing the agony of his death, the movie also captures one of the fundamental truths about dying from cancer: it is not inspirational or pretty. As for the fourth trope of the sick flick, Berman argues that Hazel and Gus are both enriched by their relationship. And given Hazel's limited future, she will have little chance to use any "lessons" she learned from Gus. The movie is in part about coming to terms with endings as real endings and not, as they are so often sold to the grieving, new beginnings.

Significance

The Fault in Our Stars premiered on June 6, 2014. By the end of the month, it had grossed nearly $200 million worldwide, making it one of the most profitable films of the year. It was popular with most critics as well, though many struggled over its distinction as a "young adult" film. A. O. Scott, the film critic for the *New York Times* gave *Fault* a positive review, but also called it a "celebration of adolescent narcissism." His critique was echoed by Ruth Graham of *Slate*, who, inspired by the release of the film, wrote that adults should be embarrassed to enjoy books for young adults because YA books are "maudlin" and "present the teenage perspective in a fundamentally uncritical way." Graham's article in particular provoked a heated debate in which no teenager participated, just as, Green has noted in interviews, no teenager has ever commented that Hazel and Gus are "wise beyond their years"—a common adult observation. Laura Miller, a book critic at *Salon*, responded to Graham and Scott's articles, writing, "Green may offer a more accessible treatment of the same themes [as adult novels that feature teenage characters], but it's not a less honest one. A work of art is only sentimental to the extent that it lies to its audience, and I just don't see lies in Green's novel."

Though Green did not work on the screenplay for the film, he worked closely with the production team while it was being made. He is working with the writer, actor, and filmmaker Sarah Polley to adapt his first novel, *Looking for Alaska* (2005), for the screen, while the same crew from *The Fault in Our Stars* is looking to adapt Green's 2008 novel *Paper Towns*. No casting or release dates have been announced for either film.

Molly Hagan

Further Reading

Berman, Eliza. "How *The Fault in Our Stars* Dramatically Improves the 'Sick Flick.'" *Slate*. Slate, 5 June 2014. Web. 5 Mar. 2015. <http://www.slate.com/blogs/browbeat/2014/06/05/the_fault_in_our_stars_review_the_sick_flick_reinvented_with_shailene_woodley.html>.

Robinson, Tasha. Rev. of *The Fault in Our Stars*, dir. by Josh Boone. *Dissolve*. Pitchfork Media, 5 June 2014. Web. 5 Mar. 2015. <https://thedissolve.com/reviews/848-the-fault-in-our-stars>.

Scott, A.O. "Young Love, Complicated by Cancer." Rev. of *The Fault in Our Stars*, dir. by Josh Boone. *New York Times*. New York Times, 5 June 2014. Web. 4 Mar. 2015. <http://www.nytimes.com/2014/06/06/movies/the-fault-in-our-stars-sets-out-to-make-you-cry.html>.

Standiford, Natalie. "The Tenacity of Hope." Rev. of *The Fault in Our Stars*, by John Green. *New York Times*. New York Times, 13 Jan. 2012. Web. 5 Mar. 2015. <http://www.nytimes.com/2012/01/15/books/review/the-tenacity-of-hope.html?pagewanted=all>.

Bibliography

Brockes, Emma. "John Green: Teenager, Aged 36." *Intelligent Life*. Economist, 1 May 2014. Web. 5 Mar. 2015. <http://moreintelligentlife.com/content/features/emma-brockes/john-green?page=full>.

Canby, Vincent. "Perfection and a 'Love Story': Erich Segal's Romantic Tale Begins Run." Rev. of *Love Story*, dir. by Arthur Hiller. *New York Times*. New York Times, 18 Dec. 1970. Web. 5 Mar. 2015. <http://www.nytimes.com/movie/review?res=9E07E5DA1E30E337A2575BC1A9649D946190D6CF>.

Miller, Laura. "'The Fault in Our Stars' Has Been Unfairly Bashed by Critics Who Don't Understand It." *Salon*. Salon Media, 6 June 2014. Web. 5 Mar. 2015. <http://www.salon.com/2014/06/06/the_fault_in_our_stars_has_been_unfairly_bashed_by_critics_who_dont_understand_it>.

Green, John. Interview by Rebecca J. Rosen. *Atlantic* Feb. 2013: n. pag. Print.

Talbot, Margaret. "The Teen Whisperer." *New Yorker*. Condé Nast, 9 June 2014. Web. 4 Mar. 2015. <http://www.newyorker.com/magazine/2014/06/09/the-teen-whisperer>.

Williams, Mary Elizabeth. "It's John Green's World Now—and That's a Good Thing." *Salon*. Salon Media, 2 June 2014. Web. 5 Mar. 2015. <http://www.salon.com/2014/06/02/its_john_greens_world_now_and_thats_a_good_thing>.

The Geography Club

The Book

Author: Brent Hartinger (b. 1964)
First published: 2003

The Film

Director: Gary Entin
Screenplay by: Edmund Entin
Starring: Cameron Deane Stewart, Justin Deeley, Meaghan Martin, Andrew Caldwell, and Ally Maki

Context

The publication of the novel *The Geography Club* (2003) by American author Brent Hartinger came during the resurgence in young adult literature that took place starting in the 1990s with incredibly popular titles such as Harry Potter. While many subgenres of YA literature increased in popularity during the 1990s, it was not really until the early 2000s that realistic fiction began a resurgence and reasserted itself as the cornerstone subgenre of YA literature. The twenty-first century saw a variety of YA titles produced across the globe, with authors from countries like Australia, the United Kingdom, and the United States writing works that tested the traditional conventions of the modern teenage genre that first began in the late 1960s. YA poetry and experimental forms like the verse novel rose in popularity around this time as well.

In the late 1990s and early 2000s, awareness of LGBTQ rights in the United States was increasing and federal and state governments began to address issues such as hate crimes and same-sex marriage. The novel, Hartinger's first, was published in the spring of 2003, the same year that the Massachusetts Supreme Court became the first in the nation to rule that a ban on same-sex civil marriage was unconstitutional. By the time the film was released in 2013, acceptance of gay rights had progressed even further: The Matthew Shepard and James Byrd Jr. Hate Crimes Prevention Act was signed into law in 2009; "Don't Ask, Don't Tell," which banned lesbians and gay men from serving openly in the US military, was repealed in 2011; and President Barack Obama became the first sitting president to support same-sex marriage in 2012. In 2013, the Boy Scouts of America lifted the ban against gay scouts, the US Supreme Court ruled that the 1996 Defense of Marriage Act, which defined marriage as being between one man and one woman, was unconstitutional, and an increasing number of states were legalizing same-sex marriage. Thus the novel and the film, director Gary Entin's first major motion picture, reflect important contemporary social and cultural attitudes toward LGBTQ rights in the United States, showing growing acceptance while also acknowledging the intolerance that remains.

Film Analysis

The film opens similarly to the novel with a scene of the main character, Russell Middlebrook (Cameron Deane Stewart), making an appointment to meet up with another teen he has met on the Internet. Although he does not know the identity of the person he has been chatting with, they decide to meet in a park and are equally nervous about anyone finding out about their sexuality. The meeting fails to happen because Russell runs into a boy from his high school, football star Kevin Land (Justin Deeley). The next day, the class takes an overnight field trip to a camp outside of town, and under the guise of Kevin needing help with his science report, the two start talking. They grow closer and, on the last night at the camp, kiss while standing outside and Russell learns that it was Kevin whom he was supposed to meet in the park. However, the kiss is interrupted when Min (Ally Maki), another student walks by.

There are a couple key points where the film and novel differ at the beginning. Russell and Kevin meet and find out about each other in a similar way, but Russell's motivations are a bit different. In the film, Gary Entin focuses on teenagers' general lack of knowledge of self, casting Russell as someone who is not sure about sexuality in general, let alone if he is unequivocally gay. However, if he is, he still wants anonymity because he is not interested in being labeled. In the novel, Russell is sure of his own sexuality from the very first page. However, he is equally worried about anyone finding out that he is gay because he wants to fit into the social structure at Goodkind High. He explains that he is neither highest on the social order nor lowest, but that if his sexuality were revealed, he would probably become like Brian, a nerdy outcast who is picked on frequently by the jocks at the school.

In the film, Min leaves notes in Kevin and Russell's lockers, asking them to meet her afterschool. Both are afraid she is going to out them or try to blackmail them, and Kevin refuses to go. However, when Russell arrives at the room mentioned in Min's note, he sees a sign for "Geography Club." When he enters, he finds three students sitting on the far side of the room. Min approaches him and explains that "Geography Club" was created so that gay students could have a safe place to come and talk with one another. Feeling hurt that Min has outed him, Russell leaves quickly but returns back the next week. Meanwhile, Kevin is worried about what people will think about him hanging out with Russell all of a sudden, so he signs Russell up for the football team. Russell is incredibly nervous about this, but he quickly finds a place on the team as a running back and among the jock crowd. Kevin and Russell's relationship begins to grow slowly, but Russell's best friend, Gunnar (Andrew Caldwell), creates more problems when he asks Russell to double date with him so that he can go out with Kimberly (Allie Gonino), one of the most popular girls in school.

As Russell experiences new things with Kevin and runs into problems with Kimberly's friend Trish (Meaghan Martin) on their double dates with Gunnar and Kimberly, he finds that the Geography Club is a place where he can talk about anything he wants to, without judgment. Yet despite the safety of this newfound place, Russell's life starts to become more complicated as he tries to navigate the social situations of Goodkind High and keep his sexuality a secret. Although he is not interested in Trish, he continues to go out with her to help Gunnar win over Kimberly; as Trish throws herself at Russell, he must find a different reason each time to explain why he does not want to have sex with her. Similarly, he believes he must fit into the jock crowd in order to be close to Kevin, which means pulling often mean-spirited pranks. Near the climax of the novel, the social outcast Brian comes to the Geography Club. Although he is not gay, he wants to join because he needs a safe place to express himself as well, and the club accepts him as a new member. However, during lunch one day the jocks force Brian into a closet, take off his shirt, and put a bra on him. They pull Russell in and tell him that if he wants to fit in, he needs to put lipstick on Brian and help them force him into the lunchroom. Russell helps but feels awful, and this guilt becomes one of the factors that make keeping his sexuality a secret such a burden. The decision, however, is made for him when Kimberly outs him and he decides to embrace his sexuality publicly.

The film and novel are similar in showing how multiple issues compound Russell's stress to the point where he is tired of remaining in the closet. It is not just at the climax of the story that Russell feels anxious about his sexuality. From the beginning of the novel, Hartinger uses internal monologues to depict Russell's constant state of anxiety that his sexuality will be discovered by others. At every moment, Russell is worried about the legibility of his body, making sure he acts in such a way that demonstrates to everyone around him that he is straight. For example, when Kevin makes a simple remark in the locker room to Russell (before they find out about each other), Russell worries to himself, "Everything now depended on my reaction. Would I pass this, Kevin Land's latest test of my manhood?"

The film adaptations mirrors moments like this when Russell does not know how to respond to questions that have double meanings related to sexuality. For example, when Kevin's dad asks Russell where he has been hiding for so long, he is unsure how to respond and does not realize that Kevin's dad is referring to Russell as a football player rather than as Kevin's romantic partner.

The film focuses on different intersections of sexuality, adolescent development, and high school social order, but in the end comes to the same conclusions and perspective as the book. The relationships between the main characters are initially different, and in the book Russell is a part of the founding of the Geography Club, but the mostly upbeat ending is clear in both versions. While Russell finds a new place and a new identity, he does not get everything he wanted at the end. Kevin, whose main passion in life is football, refuses to acknowledge his sexuality because he knows he will not be able to play again. And through this detail, Entin acknowledges that homophobia, though slowly receding, remains in American culture.

Significance

The Geography Club opened to overall positive reviews from critics and audiences. Many found the central theme of learning to embrace difference, especially when it relates to your own identity, to be powerful and engaging. Critics applauded the onscreen depiction of the relationship between Kevin and Russell, but also found that it was often not focused enough for a movie with a romantic relationship at its core. While Russell's relationship with Kevin never goes too far because it must be kept a secret, their romance and its ramifications had less screen time than Gunnar and Russell's friendship. Critics generally agreed that, as a coming-out story, the film spent too much time on superfluous heterosexual relationships. Equally, audiences felt that more time could have been spent on the potentially much more interesting members of the Geography Club. In the end, while the film contained many moving moments, it was not pieced together well enough to make it a top young adult film.

The film did relatively well commercially and won two awards, and reviewers felt that, like the novel, the film presents an accurate reflection of American society and culture. Yet some reviewers also felt that the film's scope is so specific that it might become outdated quickly. The landscape of American attitudes toward sexuality is changing so rapidly that while a story of this kind might reflect a period in history, it runs the risk that its central lesson may be become less relevant to teens within a few years of its release.

Aaron Horton, MA

Further Reading

Hartinger, Brent. Interview. *NCAC: National Coalition against Censorship.* NCAC, 19 June 2009. Web. 9 Nov. 2015. <http://ncac.org/update/interview-with-brent-hartinger>.

Hartinger, Brent. "The Freedom of DIY." Interview by Kate Pavao. *Publishers Weekly* 8 July 2013: 31. *Literary Reference Center.* Web. 16 Nov. 2015. <http://search.ebscohost.com/login.aspx?direct=true&db=lfh&AN=88937590&site=lrc-live>.

Kneen, Bonnie. "Neither Very Bi nor Particularly Sexual: The Essence of the Bisexual in Young Adult Literature." *Children's Literature in Education* 46.4 (2015): 359–77. *Literary Reference Center.* Web. 16 Nov. 2015. <http://search.ebscohost.com/login.aspx?direct=true&db=lfh&AN=110652964&site=lrc-live>.

Bibliography

Brown, Michael. "A Geographer Reads *Geography Club*: Spatial Metaphor and Metonym in Textual/Sexual Space." *Cultural Geographies* 13.3 (2006): 313–39. *Literary Reference Center.* Web. 16 Nov. 2015. <http://search.ebscohost.com/login.aspx?direct=true&db=lfh&AN=21117138&site=lrc-live>.

Debruge, Peter. "Film Review: 'Geography Club.'" Rev. of *The Geography Club,* dir. Gary Entin. *Variety.* Variety Media, 25 Mar. 2014. Web. 18 Nov. 2015. <http://variety.com/2014/film/reviews/film-review-geography-club-1201146564>.

"Film Review: The Geography Club." Rev. of *The Geography Club,* dir. Gary Entin. *FilmJournal Intl.* FilmJournal Intl., 15 Nov. 2013. Web. 18 Nov. 2015. <http://www.filmjournal.com/content/film-review-geography-club>.

Genzlinger, Neil. "Closeted High School Romances." Rev. of *The Geography Club,* dir. Gary Entin. *New York Times.* New York Times, 14 Nov. 2013. Web. 18 Nov. 2015. <http://www.nytimes.com/2013/11/15/movies/gay-students-find-support-in-geography-club.html?_r=0>.

Goldstein, Gary. Rev. of *Geography Club,* dir. Gary Entin. *Los Angeles Times.* Los Angeles Times, 21 Nov. 2013. Web. 9 Nov. 2015. <http://articles.latimes.com/2013/nov/21/entertainment/la-et-mn-geography-club-review-20131122>.

"LGBT Rights Milestones Fast Facts." *CNN.* Cable News Network, 30 Oct. 2015. Web. 18 Nov. 2015. <http://www.cnn.com/2015/06/19/us/lgbt-rights-milestones-fast-facts>.

The Golden Compass

The Book

Author: Philip Pullman (b. 1946)
First published: 1995

The Film

Director: Chris Weitz (b. 1969)
Screenplay by: Chris Weitz
Starring: Dakota Blue Richards, Nicole Kidman, Daniel Craig

Context

During the first decade of the twenty-first century, the fantasy genre experienced a surge in popularity in film. The success of the *Lord of the Rings* films (2001–3), the adaptations of the classic fantasy trilogy by J. R. R. Tolkien, was particularly influential and signaled the willingness of both fantasy fans and the general public to watch film adaptations of beloved novels. Fantasy novels for young adult readers proved especially profitable sources of inspiration for filmmakers; the Harry Potter film series (2001–11), based on the seven-novel series by British author J. K. Rowling, grossed billions of dollars and led to the creation of a wide variety of merchandise, museum exhibits, and even theme-park venues. Seeking to replicate the success of the Harry Potter films, studios adapted numerous works of young adult fantasy for the screen during the decade, with varying degrees of success.

One of the many adaptations during this period was of *The Golden Compass,* the first book in British author Philip Pullman's His Dark Materials trilogy. Pullman, already an established writer of various books for young adults, including the Sally Lockhart historical mystery series, gained significant notice and acclaim with the publication of the His Dark Materials trilogy, which also includes *The Subtle Knife* (1997) and *The Amber Spyglass* (2000).

Originally published in the United Kingdom in 1995 as *Northern Lights*, the novel *The Golden Compass* tells the story of a girl named Lyra who gains the ability to read a device known as an "alethiometer," which provides a truthful answer to any question. After becoming embroiled in a conspiracy that involves both her world's oppressive Church and the adults closest to her, Lyra embarks on an adventure that culminates in a devastating betrayal and a multiverse-altering opportunity.

The film adaptation of *The Golden Compass* was produced by New Line Cinema, the studio that had previously experienced great success with the *Lord of the Rings* trilogy. In many ways, the novel represented an ideal property to adapt: it not only featured a cast of colorful characters, intriguing magic, and the potential for visually stunning set pieces but also, as the first novel in a trilogy, could serve to establish a profitable franchise. Despite the adaptation's potential, however, the film remained in development for several years as the studio struggled to find the ideal screenwriter and director. The film was ultimately written and directed by Chris Weitz, who had previously been nominated for an Academy Award for best adapted screenplay for the 2002 film *About a Boy*; he would later direct *New Moon* (2009), the second installment in the *Twilight* film franchise.

Among the issues raised during the film's development was that of the novel's take on religion. The His Dark Materials trilogy is intensely critical of organized religion, and the Church of Lyra's world, also referred to as the Magisterium, resembles the Catholic Church in many ways. Various religious organizations spoke out against the novel's adaptation, while many fans of the book objected to the filmmakers' ultimate decision to eliminate or lessen many of the religious aspects of the novel. This change, along with a substantial alteration to the narrative's conclusion, had a significant effect on the film's overall tone and message, despite the general faithfulness of the adaptation.

Film Analysis

The film adaptation of *The Golden Compass* begins with an opening voiceover by the witch Serafina Pekkala (Eva Green). In this voiceover, Serafina explains

that the film takes place in an alternate world parallel to that of the audience, one of many worlds in a multiverse. Setting the stage for the events to come, she defines three core concepts that will prove crucial to the film's plot: dæmons, the animal companions that represent their human counterparts' souls; Dust, a mysterious substance that connects all things, discussion of which has been banned by the ruling power known as the Magisterium; and the alethiometer, or titular "golden compass," a device capable of answering any question if one knows how to read it. Only one such device still exists, Serafina notes, and there is only one person in her world capable of deciphering its messages. This voiceover provides the essential information to understand the remainder of the film, which follows a girl named Lyra (Dakota Blue Richards), who is also the only person who is able to read the alethiometer.

In explaining those core concepts, the opening takes a different strategy than the original novel, which does not initially explain concepts such as dæmons or Dust. Written in the third-person limited perspective, the novel drops its readers directly into the action, allowing them to learn the secrets of dæmons, Dust, the alethiometer, and the multiverse along with Lyra. At times, Lyra and the readers do not immediately understand the significance of such concepts; they discover secrets and unravel mysteries together over the course of the book. In beginning the film adaptation with an expository voiceover, the filmmakers ensure that the audience will understand the story's complex yet essential concepts from the beginning and thus be able to enjoy the action without becoming confused. At the same time, explaining those concepts rather than allowing members of the audience to come to their own understanding of them renders the film somewhat less thought-provoking than the original novel.

Following the opening voiceover, the film adheres to the novel's plot relatively faithfully. Lyra, a young orphan, is living at Jordan College when her uncle, Lord Asriel (Daniel Craig), visits in preparation for a journey to the far north, where he hopes to investigate the mysteries of Dust and the possibility of parallel worlds. Seeking to prevent Lord Asriel from embarking on his journey, a representative of the Magisterium attempts to poison him, but Lyra warns him in time and he is able to carry out his expedition as planned. After receiving the alethiometer from the Master of the college, Lyra and her dæmon, Pantalaimon (voiced by Freddie

Highmore), leave the college to live with Mrs. Coulter (Nicole Kidman), a charismatic woman whom Lyra soon learns is head of a mysterious organization that is affiliated with the Magisterium and has been kidnapping children. When two of her friends are kidnapped, she joins a group of nomadic Gyptians on their journey to the north, where the missing children are being held. Over the course of her journey, she meets and befriends the witch Serafina Pekkala, the aeronaut Lee Scoresby (Sam Elliott), and the sentient armored polar bear Iorek Byrnison (voiced by Ian McKellan). Upon arriving at the northern facility, Lyra learns that Mrs. Coulter and the other members of her organization have been forcibly separating children from their dæmons in an attempt to rid them of the influence of Dust, to which the Magisterium attributes all evil in the world. Lyra herself is nearly separated from Pantalaimon but is rescued by Mrs. Coulter, who reveals that she and Lord Asriel are Lyra's true parents. After escaping and destroying the facility, Lyra and her friend Roger (Ben Walker), along with their dæmons and several of their allies, fly away, intent to locate Lord Asriel and assist him in his mission.

Although relatively faithful to the novel in terms of plot, *The Golden Compass* ultimately differs from the novel in tone and message due to a series of changes made in adapting the work. First is the minimizing of the novel's critique of organized religion. In the novel, the Magisterium, also referred to as the Church, is clearly presented as a religious organization that seeks to uphold the will of the Authority, or god. The organization views Dust as the root of original sin and hopes that by severing the bond between child and dæmon, it can prevent children from falling prey to that sin. While the presentation of the Magisterium is still suggestive of a religious organization, it is generally presented as a secular authoritarian government rather than a theocratic one. This change, and others made to minimize the novel's critique, costs the film a bit of its potential depth, although the plot of the film proceeds largely unaltered.

Much more significant, however, is the modification made to the film's ending. *The Golden Compass* concludes with Lyra and her friends flying to meet Lord Asriel. What will happen when they find him is left unclear. The novel's conclusion is quite different: Lyra, Roger, and Iorek travel to meet Lord Asriel, who has established a laboratory in the north and seeks to discover the source of Dust. After they find

him, he severs the bond between Roger and his dæmon, which kills the boy. Lord Asriel uses the energy that is released during the process to open a portal to another universe, which he enters. Devastated by this betrayal yet determined to discover the source of Dust before Lord Asriel can, Lyra and Pantalaimon follow him through the rift in the fabric of their world and into another. This ending both emphasizes the serious stakes of the narrative and sets the stage for the next two books in the trilogy, which feature significant travel between worlds. The film, on the other hand, eliminates this bittersweet ending, replacing it with one that is happier yet less satisfying. In interviews, Weitz noted that this change was made at the behest of the studio, which wanted a more upbeat ending. The original ending, portions of which had been filmed, would be included in the film adaptation of the sequel: *The Subtle Knife*. Because that film and the next in the trilogy, *The Amber Spyglass*, were not made, the ending of *The Golden Compass* has remained an upbeat yet inconclusive cliffhanger.

Significance

Released in the United States and internationally in early December 2007, *The Golden Compass* was a modest financial success that ultimately grossed approximately $70 million domestically and an additional $300 million internationally, according to the website Box Office Mojo. The film performed especially well in the United Kingdom, where the original novel had been first published, grossing more than $50 million in UK theaters alone. However, the film was generally considered one in a string of disappointments for New Line Cinema, which underwent corporate restructuring shortly after the release of *The Golden Compass*.

As one might expect from the potentially controversial nature of the original novel, the film adaptation of *The Golden Compass* was met with negative responses. Several Christian activist groups and conservative commentators who opposed the novel's message perceived the work as anti-Christian despite the filmmakers' attempts to decrease the film's religious references. Likewise, some fans objected to the changes made to the narrative, which were generally perceived as having been made in an attempt to render it more palatable to American audiences. While neither boycotts nor negative fan responses were conclusively determined to have affected the film's performance, numerous commentators, including some of the film's actors, argued that such responses effectively eliminated the possibility of adapting the sequels.

Reviews of *The Golden Compass* were mixed, with some reviewers praising the film's overall faithfulness to the novel and others arguing that the filmmakers' attempt to condense the novel's plot into a runtime of less than two hours made it feel rushed and its characters underdeveloped. The cast, however, was generally well received, and most reviewers deemed the film's visuals exceptional. *The Golden Compass* was nominated for numerous awards for its visual effects and won the award for best achievement in visual effects at the 2008 Academy Awards.

Joy Crelin

Further Reading

Ebert, Roger. Rev. of *The Golden Compass*, dir. Chris Weitz. *RogerEbert*. Ebert Digital, 6 Dec. 2007. Web. 31 Oct. 2015. <http://www.rogerebert.com/reviews/the-golden-compass-2007>.

McGrath, Charles. "Unholy Production with a Fairy-Tale Ending." *New York Times*. New York Times, 2 Dec. 2007. Web. 31 Oct. 2015. <http://www.nytimes.com/2007/12/02/movies/02mcgr.html?_r=2&oref=slogin&>.

Bibliography

Heritage, Stuart. "Who Killed Off *The Golden Compass*?" *Guardian*. Guardian News and Media, 15 Dec. 2009. Web. 31 Oct. 2015. <http://www.theguardian.com/film/filmblog/2009/dec/15/golden-compass-sam-elliot-catholic-church>.

"New Line Merged with Warner Bros Pictures." *Guardian*. Guardian News and Media, 29 Feb. 2008. Web. 31 Oct. 2015. <http://www.theguardian.com/film/2008/feb/29/news>.

Pullman, Philip. *The Golden Compass*. New York: Knopf, 1996. Print.

Rosin, Hanna. "How Hollywood Saved God." *Atlantic* 300.5 (2007): 68–79. *Literary Reference Center*. Web. 24 Nov. 2015. <http://search.ebscohost.com/login.aspx?direct=true&db=lfh&AN=27462961&site=lrc-live>.

Sibley, Brian. *The Golden Compass: The Official Illustrated Movie Companion*. New York: Scholastic, 2007. Print.

Harry Potter (Series)

The Books

Author: J. K. Rowling (b. 1965)
First published: *Harry Potter and the Philosopher's Stone* (1997; *Harry Potter and the Sorcerer's Stone*, 1998)
Harry Potter and the Sorcerer's Stone (1998)
Harry Potter and the Chamber of Secrets (1999)
Harry Potter and the Prisoner of Azkaban (1999)
Harry Potter and the Goblet of Fire (2000)
Harry Potter and the Order of the Phoenix (2003)
Harry Potter and the Half-Blood Prince (2005)
Harry Potter and the Deathly Hallows (2007)

The Films

Directors: Chris Columbus (b. 1958), *Harry Potter and the Sorcerer's Stone; Harry Potter and the Chamber of Secrets*
Alfonso Cuaron (b. 1961), *Harry Potter and the Prince of Azkaban*
Mike Newell (b. 1942), *Harry Potter and the Goblet of Fire*
David Yates (b. 1963), *Harry Potter and the Order of the Phoenix; Harry Potter and the Half-Blood Prince; Harry Potter and the Deathly Hallows*, Parts 1 and 2
Screenplay by: Steve Kloves, Michael Goldenberg
Starring: Daniel Radcliffe, Rupert Grint, Emma Watson

Context

In the first years of the twenty-first century, the moviegoing public in the United States seemed particularly drawn to fantasy films. Following the events of September 11, 2001, the United States was at war, and the stresses of the real world were felt heavily by many. During that era, a number of films captured the imaginations of moviegoers with their magic, unfamiliar worlds, and battles between good and evil that bore little resemblance to events occurring in the United States or overseas. At the same time, such films often featured subtext and themes of trauma that some scholars argue allowed audiences to work through their feelings in an indirect manner. Films such as the *Lord of the Rings* trilogy, which began in December of 2001 with *The Fellowship of the Ring* and concluded two years later with *The Return of the King*, performed well at the box office and earned critical accolades during that period, ushering in a new age in fantasy filmmaking.

More popular than even those films, however, were the films in the Harry Potter series, based on the best-selling novels by British author J. K. Rowling. The novels, intended to be read by children and young adults, attracted a devoted adult fan base as well, and by 2001 anticipation for the first installment of the film adaptation was high. Known as *Harry Potter and the Philosopher's Stone* in the United Kingdom and *Harry Potter and the Sorcerer's Stone* in the United States, the film premiered in November of 2001 to a positive critical and fan response. Following the success of that film, the remaining six books in the Harry Potter series were adapted into films over the course of the next decade.

The success of the Harry Potter film franchise inspired the adaptation of many other children's and young adult fantasy books, which remained wildly popular until late in the decade, when trends began to shift more toward paranormal romance and urban fantasy following the blockbuster success of *Twilight* in 2008. Even as the Twilight series and later films sparked new trends in publishing and filmmaking, the Harry Potter series remained as popular as ever through the release of the final film in the series, *Harry Potter and the Deathly Hallows: Part 2*, in 2011.

Film Analysis

Largely adhering to the events of the Harry Potter novels, the Harry Potter film series follows the adventures of the titular Harry Potter (Daniel Radcliffe), an orphan who, on his eleventh birthday, learns that he is truly a wizard. Over the course of the series, he progresses through his schooling at Hogwarts School of Witchcraft and Wizardry under the guidance of the school's headmaster, Albus Dumbledore (Richard Harris; Michael Gambon). With the help of his friends Ron Weasley (Rupert Grint) and Hermione Granger (Emma Watson), Harry repeatedly battles the agents of Lord Voldemort (Ralph Fiennes), the evil wizard who murdered his parents, and eventually comes into direct conflict with Voldemort himself. By the end of the series, Voldemort's dark magic and ceaseless pursuit of power threaten both the wizarding world and the mundane (or Muggle) one, and Harry must make terrible sacrifices to save everyone he loves. As a long-running series with numerous characters and plot lines, the Harry Potter franchise presented a set of unique challenges to filmmakers, many having to do with the difficult process of adapting a much-loved

series of books for the screen. While it would be impossible to translate the books completely and directly into films, the stylistic and directorial choices made by the filmmakers nevertheless made the Harry Potter series a successful and enduring part of popular culture.

Between 2001 and 2011, the seven Harry Potter novels were adapted into eight films: *Harry Potter and the Sorcerer's Stone* (2001; *Harry Potter and the Philosopher's Stone* in the United Kingdom), *Harry Potter and the Chamber of Secrets* (2002), *Harry Potter and the Prisoner of Azkaban* (2004), *Harry Potter and the Goblet of Fire* (2005), *Harry Potter and the Order of the Phoenix* (2007), *Harry Potter and the Half-Blood Prince* (2009), *Harry Potter and the Deathly Hallows: Part 1* (2010), and *Harry Potter and the Deathly Hallows: Part 2* (2011). As the eight films in the series were directed by four different directors, each of whom brought a unique take to the series, there is no one definite directorial and aesthetic vision to the series. However, as all but one of the films were written by screenwriter Steve Kloves—the screenplay for *Harry Potter and the Order of the Phoenix* having been written by Michael Goldenberg—there is a sense of internal consistency to the films' events. In addition, Rowling retained a degree of control over the adaptation process; as Kloves noted in an interview with the *Los Angeles Times* blog *Hero Complex*, Rowling provided additional details about character backgrounds and motivations when needed and at times warned the filmmakers against including new dialogue or events that would contradict events in the not-yet-released books.

The first two films in the series, *Harry Potter and the Sorcerer's Stone* and *Harry Potter and the Chamber of Secrets*, were directed by Chris Columbus, who at the time was best known for directing films such as *Home Alone* (1990) and *Mrs. Doubtfire* (1993). Columbus's two films were relatively straightforward adaptations of the novels and had the difficult task of introducing viewers to a secret wizarding world that all of the subsequent films would build on. Like its source material, the first film features a degree of danger in the form of the final conflict between Harry and Professor Quirrell (Ian Hart), whose evil actions signal the approaching threats that Harry and his newfound world will soon face; however, both the film and the novel only hint at the true scope of danger to come. In an interview with *Empire* magazine, Columbus noted that while the first film was relatively light in tone, the books themselves grow progressively darker as Harry ages; as such, the film of *Chamber of Secrets* takes on a somewhat darker tone, introducing the strong possibility of mortal peril into the series.

A significant stylistic shift takes place in *Harry Potter and the Prisoner of Azkaban*. Directed by Alfonso Cuarón, the film significantly expands upon the world of the first two films, taking on a darker tone than its predecessors, introducing new locations in Hogwarts, and providing a more detailed glimpse at the emotions and mindsets of Harry, Ron, and Hermione. One particularly interesting aesthetic choice that is readily apparent in the film concerns the cast's wardrobe. In the previous two films, Hogwarts students were generally seen in school uniforms or wizards' robes; in the third film, however, Harry and his friends wear more ordinary styles of clothing during their free time. This decision carried on to the later films, giving a greater visual sense that the characters are in many ways ordinary teenagers. Much like the source novel, *Harry Potter and the Goblet of Fire*, directed by Mike Newell, serves as a turning point in the series. The darkest film in the series to that point, it features the first onscreen deaths in the series, most notably that of Cedric Diggory (Robert Pattinson), whose murder by Voldemort signals to both the viewers and the parts of the wizarding world willing to listen that a dark new era is beginning.

The remainder of the series was directed by David Yates, and thus those films have a somewhat more cohesive directorial vision. The films continue to take on a darker tone, which is reflected visually, and both *Harry Potter and the Order of the Phoenix* and *Harry Potter and the Half-Blood Prince* have interesting psychological and political notes. The length of the films had long been a subject of concern, as Rowling's novels grew progressively longer as the series went on and thus presented a challenge to the filmmakers. Typically, the need to meet certain time constraints was dealt with by cutting scenes, characters, locations, or plot points. For the final book, however, the filmmakers opted to split the film in two, ultimately releasing *Harry Potter and the Deathly Hallows* in two parts, in 2010 and 2011. This decision would start a trend in Hollywood; the final films in both the Twilight series and the dystopian Hunger Games series would later follow suit. By splitting *Deathly Hallows* in two, Yates and Kloves were able to devote more time to various aspects of the plot as well as to delve more deeply into the complex dynamics among Harry, Ron, and Hermione, whose friendship is tested as the three attempt to locate and destroy Voldemort's Horcruxes, magical items that contain pieces of the dark wizard's soul.

In adapting the Harry Potter series for the screen, the series' screenwriters and directors faced a number of major challenges. First and foremost was the need to meet the expectations of the series' devoted fans. By the time *Harry Potter and the Sorcerer's Stone* began production in 2000, the first four books in the series had already been published, and the series had garnered numerous fans in the United Kingdom, the United States, and elsewhere, with high expectations. Another major concern was the length of the books and the amount of characters and extensive world building they feature. In order to adapt the books into films of a standard length, it was necessary to change and omit various sections of the ongoing narrative, sometimes major ones. Finally, the filmmakers had to consider the differences between written and visual media when adapting the novels, at times adding new scenes to shed light on events only mentioned or alluded to in the books.

Many of the changes made for the film adaptations involve the omission of scenes and plot points or changes to minor details. One change that generated significant controversy among fans of the novels concerned Harry's eye color; in the novels, Harry has green eyes, while in the film, they are Radcliffe's natural blue color. Although this change attracted significant attention, it was ultimately merely a cosmetic one. Another change that was quite apparent to fans of the novels but largely did not affect the overarching plot was the omission of most scenes in which Harry plays the wizarding sport Quidditch. The books devote a good deal of time to Quidditch, as Harry's success in the sport is one of the major components to his feeling at home at Hogwarts and in the wizarding world in general. In the films, however, most Quidditch scenes are omitted. Even the Quidditch World Cup, a major event at the beginning of *Harry Potter and the Goblet of Fire*, is largely omitted, as the film focuses instead on the events leading up to it and its immediate aftermath. This omission was likely necessitated both by time constraints—indeed, there are enough vital plot points in *Goblet of Fire* that the World Cup may be considered a trifle in comparison—and the fact that Quidditch scenes require extensive special effects. Ultimately, the omission of many of the series' Quidditch scenes was a disappointment to some viewers but did little harm to the films as a whole.

At times, however, the omissions made in the attempt to condense the narrative prove detrimental to the storytelling. In *Harry Potter and the Prisoner of Azkaban*, vital information that characters provide in the novel, including enlightening insights about Harry's father and his school friends, is not mentioned in the film. This has the effect of rendering the plot confusing for readers unfamiliar with the book. In his review of the film, critic Roger Ebert deemed the plotting "a little murky" and noted that the film "needs to explain more than it should." Similarly, a change made in adapting *Harry Potter and the Order of the Phoenix* for film had far-reaching consequences, as the fifth book in fact laid the groundwork for a vital plot point in *Harry Potter and the Deathly Hallows*. In the novel, a locket found in the ancestral home of Harry's godfather, Sirius Black (Gary Oldman), proves in the seventh book to be one of the Horcruxes Harry and his friends seek to destroy. Having left the locket out of the fifth film, the filmmakers were instead forced to introduce it in part 1 of *Deathly Hallows*. While Harry and friends ultimately destroy the Horcrux, the locket's omission from the fifth film removes a degree of the foreshadowing that is a characteristic aspect of Rowling's series.

Despite such issues, a number of changes made during the adaptation process made valuable contributions to the film. One such change occurs in *Harry Potter and the Half-Blood Prince*, to which the filmmakers added a scene in which Voldemort's followers, known as Death Eaters, attack London's Millennium Bridge, a footbridge over the Thames. An attack on a bridge called the Brockdale Bridge is mentioned in the first chapter of the novel, but the incident is not shown as it occurs. In the scene added to the film, several Death Eaters emerge out of the storm clouds above London, flying through the air in streaks of what appears to be black smoke. (This too is an addition to the film, as the Death Eaters generally ride brooms or Apparate—a process akin to teleportation—in the novels.) As the Death Eaters fly through the streets of London, the camera takes their perspective, rendering the scene dizzying and frenetic. After the Death Eaters reach the wizarding enclave of Diagon Alley and complete their business there, the camera returns to an external perspective and follows the smoke-shrouded dark wizards as they attack the bridge, snapping the cables. The bridge twists and begins to fall, Muggle pedestrians run for their lives, and the camera pulls back and watches from above as the bridge sinks into the river. The Death Eaters fly toward the camera and past it, leaving their incredible destruction behind them. Although not in the book, this scene provides a powerful depiction of the intrusion of dark magic into the Muggle world, giving the already-dark film an increased sense of menace. In many ways, this scene underscores the increasing darkness of the series: both of Harry's worlds are no longer safe—if they ever truly were.

Significance

As the massive global popularity of the Harry Potter novels predicted, the film adaptations were incredibly popular, earning billions of dollars in box-office revenue and transforming its three young leads from unknowns into international celebrities. In addition to sparking the production of toys, companion books, costumes, and other licensed merchandise, the films inspired the creation of a theme park, the Wizarding World of Harry Potter, at the Universal Resort in Orlando, Florida. The theme park, which includes attractions based on Diagon Alley, the wizarding village of Hogsmeade, and the Hogwarts Express train, features rides, shops, and themed restaurants. Even more significant than the series' financial success is the extent of fan involvement with the novels and films. Inspired by the source materials, fans have devoted themselves not only to in-depth discussions of the works but also to the creation of stories, songs, and even full-length musicals based Rowling's characters and world.

The success of the Harry Potter films was widely recognized by the film industry, and in an attempt to duplicate that success, film executives greenlit numerous film adaptations of other children's and young adult fantasy books that they believed would appeal to Harry Potter fans. Films in this wave included *The Chronicles of Narnia: The Lion, the Witch and the Wardrobe* (2005), based on C. S. Lewis's 1950 novel, and *The Golden Compass* (2007), based on the 1996 Philip Pullman novel of the same name (published in the United Kingdom in 1995 as *Northern Lights*). Less successful attempts to recapture to Harry Potter zeitgeist included *Eragon* (2006), based on the 2002 Christopher Paolini novel, and *The Seeker: The Dark Is Rising* (2007), loosely based on the 1973 Susan Cooper novel *The Dark Is Rising*. Although some of the young adult fantasy films released during the first decade of the twenty-first century proved popular with audiences, none matched the popularity of the Harry Potter films, nor did they develop as enduring a following among fans, critics, and academics worldwide.

Joy Crelin

Further Reading
Heilman, Elizabeth E., ed. *Critical Perspectives on Harry Potter*. New York: Routledge, 2009. Print.

Thomas, Scott. *The Making of the Potterverse: A Month-by-Month Look at Harry's First 10 Years*. Toronto: ECW, 2007. Print.

Bibliography

Brown, Noel. *The Hollywood Family Film: A History, from Shirley Temple to Harry Potter*. London: Tauris, 2012. Print.

Columbus, Chris. "Christopher Columbus Remembers Harry Potter." Interview with Helen O'Hara. *Empire*. Bauer Consumer Media, n. d. Web. 28 Feb. 2015 <http://www.empireonline.com/interviews/interview.asp?IID=1310>.

Ebert, Roger. Rev. of *Harry Potter and the Prisoner of Azkaban*. *RogerEbert.com*. Ebert Digital, 3 June 2004. Web. 28 Feb. 2015. <http://www.rogerebert.com/reviews/harry-potter-and-the-prisoner-of-azkaban-2004>.

Fowkes, Katherine A. *The Fantasy Film*. Malden: Wiley, 2013. Print.

Kloves, Steve. "'Harry Potter' Countdown: Steve Kloves on a 'Haunting Moment' in 'Half-Blood Prince.'" Interview with Denise Martin. *Hero Complex*. Los Angeles Times, 17 June 2009. Web. 28 Feb. 2015. <http://herocomplex.latimes.com/uncategorized/countdown-to-harry-potter-and-the-half-blood-prince-steve-kloves-talks-up-the-final-moments-between>.

Pheasant-Kelly, Frances. *Fantasy Films Post 9/11*. New York: Palgrave, 2013. Print.

Holes

The Book

Author: Louis Sachar (b. 1954)
First published: 1998

The Film

Director: Andrew Davis (b. 1946)
Screenplay by: Louis Sachar
Starring: Shia LaBeouf, Khleo Thomas, Sigourney Weaver, Jon Voight, Patricia Arquette

Context

Young adult fiction has long dealt with the conflict between teenagers and authority figures, including parents, teachers, and at times even governments. In Louis Sachar's bestselling novel *Holes* (1998), the conflict is between teenager Stanley Yelnats and the cruel adults in charge of a harsh youth prison camp known as Camp Green Lake, at which each inmate is required to dig a deep whole each day and to which Stanley has been sent after being falsely convicted of theft. Protagonists of young adult novels often feel as if their lives are being shaped by forces beyond their control, but for Stanley, it appears this is literal: his bad luck, and that of his father and grandfather before him, seems to be the result of a century-old family curse. Over the course of the novel, Stanley not only overcomes the hardships he faces at the camp but also manages to reverse the curse, unwittingly changing the course of his life forever.

Written by veteran children's novelist Louis Sachar, who had previously gained a following for works such as the humorous Wayside School series, *Holes* became very popular among readers, educators, and critics soon after its release, and it won the 1998 National Book Award for young people's literature as well as the 1999 Boston Globe–Horn Book Award for fiction and the 1999 Newbery Medal. Director Andrew Davis, who had previously directed such films as *The Fugitive* (1993), bought the rights to the book and approached Sachar about writing the screenplay. Although concerned that a film adaptation of his novel could become overly simplified or "fluffy," particularly in light of Walt Disney Pictures' involvement in the film's production, Sachar was reassured by the fact that he would write the screenplay himself and as well as by Davis's history of directing gritty action films.

The issue of faithfulness to source material is often of great concern in regard to the adaptation of beloved children's and young adult novels, as viewers and critics often object to films that are either too faithful to their written counterparts or not faithful enough. The first two installments in the popular Harry Potter film series, for instance, were released in the two years prior to *Holes*' 2003 premiere and faced criticisms for both adhering too closely to the original novels and leaving out certain plot points and characters. In adapting *Holes*, Sachar and the film's team had to find a balance between meeting the expectations of readers and taking into account the needs of the film medium. The novel's complex and somewhat nonlinear narrative requires the reader to play close attention and, as the narrator notes in the book's final chapter, to "fill in the holes" themselves. To convey the novel's plot and strong themes of friendship, fate, and overcoming adversity in an effective and faithful manner, the film would have to adhere closely to its source material while at the same time striking the balance necessary when bringing any literary work to the screen.

Film Analysis

The opening scenes of *Holes* provide an informative illustration of the ways in which the novel was adapted for the screen. The film opens with shots of the unrelenting sun and the dry, cracked desert earth before panning over to show teenage inmates digging deep holes under the supervision of a rifle-toting adult. A shot of the area from above gives the viewer the first glimpse of the scale of the digging operation, as the pockmarked landscape stretches to every edge of the picture. While various inmates chatter in the background, the camera focuses on an exhausted camper whose labeled canteen reveals his nickname to be Barfbag (Zane Holtz). Spotting a rattlesnake near his hole, Barfbag removes his shoes and socks and steps close to the snake, allowing it to bite his bare foot. The camera follows his screaming face in slow motion before returning its focus to the hot sun above him.

This opening scene is effective for several reasons. First, the lingering shots of the sun and the dry ground provide a palpable sense of heat and drought, suggesting a vast desert while showing only a relatively small area. Barfbag's intentional injury, which is witnessed but not prevented by his fellow campers, aptly demonstrates the misery and desperation the camp inflicts on its inmates; Barfbag is willing to endure severe pain in order to have a chance to leave. Most of all, the opening scene demonstrates the various ways in which the film's creators altered the narrative to better meet the needs of the film medium. The novel opens with a chapter in which the third-person narrator describes Camp Green Lake and explains the dangers of the various creatures that live in the desert around the camp, particularly the rattlesnakes, scorpions, and deadly yellow-spotted lizards. "Sometimes," the narrator notes, "a camper will try to be bitten by a scorpion, or even a small rattlesnake" in order to get out of digging. This chapter is an effective opening to the novel, as it sets the scene and makes the unpleasantness of Camp Green Lake clear. The third-person narrator who tells the reader this information in the novel is absent from the film, however, largely because the inherent differences between the two media. Instead, the film shows the audience the bleak landscape through both aerial and ground-level shots and demonstrates the misery of the campers through Barfbag, whose encounter with the rattlesnake is mentioned but never seen in the novel.

The introduction of the film's protagonist, Stanley Yelnats (Shia LaBeouf), is similarly adapted to the narrative's new medium. The shot of the sun above Barfbag and his fellow campers transforms into the sun above Stanley, which is partially eclipsed by a pair of sneakers falling from above in slow motion. This transition ushers Stanley abruptly into the plot as the sneakers land on his head while he is walking home from school. Taking a cue from the novel's often nonlinear narrative, the film cuts from Stanley's encounter with the sneakers to Stanley riding in a bus as it passes through the parched desert landscape. It next shows Stanley being escorted to his home by the police, who incorrectly believe that Stanley stole the shoes, which belonged to an athlete and were being auctioned off for charity. After he is sentenced to eighteen months at Camp Green Lake in a brief trial scene, the scene shifts to a shot of the bus from above as it drives deeper into the scarred desert landscape, the lackluster oasis of the camp the sole spot of green in the distance. Stanley's voice-over replaces the book narrator's voice, further differentiating the film from the novel. The changes made to these opening scenes exemplify the sorts of edits made to the narrative and structure of the novel in adapting it to the medium of film. Where the novel's third-person narrator tells, the film shows, giving viewers a tangible sense of the film's setting and characters.

One of the novel's defining features is its extensive use of flashbacks. Throughout the book, chapters about Stanley's life at Camp Green Lake alternate with chapters that take place more than one hundred years in the past, explaining the origin of the Yelnats family curse as well as the history of the area around Camp Green Lake. In the film, the inclusion of such historical flashbacks is first hinted at when Stanley seems to see a ghostly figure outside the bus when he is first approaching the camp. The ghostly figure is that of Sam (Dulé Hill), an African American onion salesman who was murdered for his romance with schoolteacher-turned-outlaw Katherine "Kissin' Kate" Barlow (Patricia Arquette) more than a century before, in the years when the area around the lake was a thriving town. Flashbacks telling the story of Katherine and Sam are scattered throughout the film and often appear following a present-day event that ties in to them. For example, after Stanley asks his camp counselor about whether the dry lakebed was once a lake, the lake appears, beginning a flashback about the town that once thrived there. In another instance, a shot of Stanley using the camp's outdoor shower transitions into a shot of rain falling on Katherine's schoolhouse.

The flashbacks that reveal the origins of the Yelnats family curse are presented in a similar manner to their presentation in the book: while digging his hole, Stanley reflects on the bad luck and fabled curse that brought him to that point. In a series of flashbacks intercut with short scenes of Stanley digging and interacting with his campmates and camp officials, Latvian peasant Elya Yelnats (Damien Luvara) promises elderly fortuneteller Madame Zeroni (Eartha Kitt) that he will carry her up a mountain and sing to her while she drinks from a stream. In exchange, she will help him win the hand of a beautiful local girl. When his attempt to win the young woman over fails, Elya immigrates to the United States, neglecting to keep his promise to Madame Zeroni and thus inflicting her curse on his family. The scenes from Camp Green Lake that appear alongside these flashbacks aptly illustrate the ill effects of the curse, as Stanley struggles with digging under the hot sun and develops painful blisters. Through the use of such flashbacks, the film ties the past and present together, making the strong connections between the periods abundantly clear.

Significance

Much like its source material, the film *Holes* was received well by most critics, who praised its depiction of teenage male friendships and its exploration of fate and free will. Critics also commented on the film's sensitive depiction of race relations and racism, which play a key role in the flashbacks to nineteenth-century Green Lake, as well as immigrant identity. Those two themes of the original novel resonated deeply with director Andrew Davis, and critics generally agreed that they lent additional depth to the film's already complex narrative.

Holes performed well at the box office, bringing in more than 70 million dollars worldwide. The film was one of the top ten highest grossing PG-rated films of the year, demonstrating its success among young audiences. *Holes* was nominated for numerous awards, including the Broadcast Film Critics Association Award for best live-action family film. Three of the film's young actors, Shia LaBeouf (Stanley), Noah Poletiek (Twitch), and Khleo Thomas (Zero), were nominated for Young Artist Awards for their performances; LaBeouf was also nominated for the MTV Movie Award for breakthrough male performance in 2004.

As a largely faithful adaptation of the novel, *Holes* is often screened in schools in which the novel is part of the curriculum. The novel itself has been challenged in school systems and libraries on various occasions, and parents have sometimes challenged the screening of the film as well. However, educators and librarians have been ardent defenders of both the novel and the film, praising the strong message about overcoming adversity and powerful overarching themes.

Joy Crelin

Further Reading

Armitstead, Claire. "The *Holes* Phenomenon." *Guardian*. Guardian News and Media, 16 Oct. 2003. Web. 28 Feb. 2015. <http://www.theguardian.com/film/2003/oct/17/booksforchildrenandteenagers>.

Kovacs, Deborah, and Karin LeMaire. *Holes: The Official Movie Scrapbook*. New York: Barnes & Noble, 2003. Print.

Bibliography

Ebert, Roger. Rev. of *Holes*. *RogerEbert.com*. Ebert Digital, 18 Apr. 2003. Web. 28 Feb. 2015. <http://www.rogerebert.com/reviews/holes-2003>.

LaSalle, Mick. "It's Easy to Dig 'Holes.'" *SFGate*. SFGate, 18 Apr. 2003. Web. 28 Feb. 2015. <http://www.sfgate.com/movies/article/It-s-easy-to-dig-Holes-Fugitive-director-2654284.php>.

Scott, A. O. "*Holes* (2003) Film Review; Not Just for Children, a Suspenseful Allegory of Greed, Fate, and Racism." *New York Times*. New York Times, 18 Apr. 2003. Web. 28 Feb. 2015. <http://www.nytimes.com/movie/review?res=9B0CEFD7163AF93BA25757C0A9659C8B63>.

Hoot

The Book

Author: Carl Hiaasen (b. 1953)
First published: 2002

The Film

Director: Wil Shriner (b. 1953)
Screenplay by: Wil Shriner
Starring: Logan Lerman, Brie Larson, Cody Linley, and Luke Wilson

Context

Film and fiction about environmental issues have become increasingly popular in the midst of growing concerns about pollution, climate change, and destruction of wildlife and their natural habitats. Such concerns are at the heart of many of Carl Hiaasen's writings for young adults, including *Hoot*. The publication in 2013 of Alice Curry's book *Environmental Crisis in Young Adult Fiction: A Poetics of Earth* is another sign of growing interest in this topic, not only by scholars but especially by filmmakers and creative writers. *Hoot* is just one of numerous books and films from the last several decades that highlight the potentially important roles young people can play in trying to preserve the environment.

Even contemporary fiction and films that do not advocate explicitly for environmental protection often do so indirectly. Dystopian writings and movies—works that depict dark, corrupt, dysfunctional societies—often present destruction of the environment as a background issue, if not as a central theme. The worlds of dystopian fiction are often both morally and environmentally ugly. Works featuring such worlds usually imply that the ethical corruption of human beings can lead to the environmental destruction of the planet. Rarely is evil associated with imagery of natural beauty. Far more often than not, moral, political, and spiritual failings are set within ugly, unnatural environments. Neither the film, released in 2006, nor the book version of *Hoot* presents much dark, revolting ugliness, either ethically or environmentally. Instead, both works highlight threatened natural beauty rather than showing the aftermath of its actual destruction. This is especially true of the film.

Another important issue dealt with both in the book and in the film is the issue of bullying. This problem has become far more visible in the years since Hiaasen composed his novel. Bullying, both in person and online, has become such a serious concern that the treatment of it in both the movie and the book can seem a bit comic or whimsical. The bullying presented in *Hoot* does not lead—as it often leads in real life—to real physical injury, severe psychological damage, deep depression, suicide, or violent revenge. While the novel and film are comedies, not serious examinations of the torment many young people suffer at school, the bullying depicted (especially in the film) is often jarring, and the narrow escapes and happy outcomes presented can make both the movie and the book appear unrealistic to the point of seeming naive.

Film Analysis

Except for omissions of some peripheral characters and major changes near the end, the film version of *Hoot* follows the novel fairly faithfully. Middle schooler Roy Eberhardt (Logan Lerman) and his parents (Neil Flynn and Kiersten Warren) have moved from the mountains of Montana to their latest new home, this time in Florida. They move frequently because of Roy's father's job. Roy, as the new kid at school, is immediately picked on by a thuggish bully named Dana (Eric Phillips), who makes Roy's life increasingly miserable. Dana's opposite, in many ways, is a mysterious youth whom Roy sees running one day. He runs at enormous speed and without wearing shoes. Increasingly intrigued by this almost phantom figure, Roy eventually discovers that the boy (Cody Linley), nicknamed Mullet Fingers, is the stepbrother of one of Roy's schoolmates, the imposing, athletic Beatrice (Brie Larson).

Mullet Fingers is trying, in increasingly bold ways, to sabotage construction of a new pancake restaurant on a site populated by rare burrowing owls. A policeman, Officer Delinko (Luke Wilson), ineptly investigates the damage the property is suffering. He is urged on by the construction site foreman (Tim Blake Nelson), who in turn is under pressure from his boss, Mr. Muckle (Clark Gregg). Ultimately, thanks to the combined efforts of Roy, Mullet Fingers, and Beatrice, construction is stopped, the owls are saved, and everyone (except Muckle) is happy. The film adheres well to the basic plot and characterization of the novel, although Officer Delinko is a far more obviously comic figure in the film than in the book.

One distinct advantage of the film over the novel is the film's ability to *show* the beauty of nature. The film opens, for instance, with a panoramic overhead shot of the splendors of Montana, with its stunning mountains, enormous fields, and abundant wildlife. Roy narrates the film (he is presented more objectively in the third person in the novel), and so the audience literally hears, from time to time, in Roy's own voice, what he is feeling and thinking. The overhead shots of Montana are immediately followed by similarly beautiful overhead panoramas of the beauties of Florida. The film thus subtly emphasizes, from the very beginning, the theme of natural beauty—a theme crucial to the plots of both the film and the book.

Instantly after the film features these magnificent shots of nature, it shows Roy, on a school bus, being tormented by the bully. The bus is thus associated with oppression and humiliation, in contrast to the freedom and openness of the great outdoors. Paradoxically, while Roy's face is crammed against a window by the bully, he first sees Mullet Fingers running alongside the bus, barefoot, and at amazing speed. The mysterious boy's hair is long, blonde, and free flowing; young and handsome, he is symbolically associated with liberty and is literally in close contact with the environment.

Equally attractive is blond Beatrice, Mullet Fingers's stepsister, but she is tough and can easily handle Dana. In the film, far more obviously than in the book, the three young heroic figures are all physically attractive, while the clear villain (Dana) is anything but. The film thus buys into standard stereotypes that associate good looks with good character. Mullet Fingers, the handsome young blond, is assisted by Beatrice, his attractive blond stepsister, and Roy, a good-looking young brunet. Roy seems the personification of wide-eyed innocence. These good-looking characters are selfless in their determination to save the cute burrowing owls, while Dana, the ugly bully, seems to care about no one and nothing but himself. His abuse of Roy makes him resemble, in some ways, the environmentally abusive Mr. Muckle. Both characters are enormously self-centered, and the film seems to imply that Muckle is the result when a bully like Dana becomes an adult. Dana's malevolent abuse of poor Roy resembles Muckle's calculated, deliberate abuse of the environment.

Among the most effective scenes in the film are some that show the developing friendship between Roy and Mullet Fingers. As the latter escorts Roy on tours of Florida's rivers, swamps, and ocean coasts, the filmmakers take full advantage of aerial shots and close-ups of natural beauty and intriguing wildlife. The growing bond between Roy and his new friend develops against background shots of stunning natural beauty. While happy, upbeat music plays in the background, the characters are silent—viewers *see* their growing connection rather than hear Roy explain it or comment on it.

The film reveals, much sooner than the novel, that Mullet Fingers is behind the sabotage of the construction site and that his motive is to protect the owls. The film also emphasizes slapstick comedy more than the book does, although the book is full of satiric wit. Both the book and the film lack much character development or diversity and are generally very straightforward and conventional in the ways they tell their stories. Mostly playing by very traditional cinematic rules, the film even uses fade-outs to black to indicate a transition from one day to the next.

Significance

The film version of *Hoot* is estimated to have cost about $15 million to make. It grossed roughly $8 million initially, although later sales via DVDs and other media brought in more money. Therefore, the film was anything but a great financial success, and its critical reception was not spectacular either. Most critics found it well intended but uninspired; a few praised it for encouraging young people to think about preserving the environment. One environmentalist, Larry J. Schweiger, called *Hoot* "a great film for the whole family and a reminder that we can make a difference for wildlife if we are willing to take a stand." The movie failed, however, to win much praise as a cinematic feature in itself.

Films about young people and the environment are likely to become more and more important in coming years as environmental degradation becomes an increasingly important political and cultural issue. If predictions of the dire consequences of climate change prove true (as many scientists believe is already happening), it is hard to see how environmental issues can fail to become the subject of widespread concern, debate, and fear. Hollywood will undoubtedly see potential profit in these developments, and so *Hoot* may eventually be seen as an early forerunner of a genre of films that is likely to grow in importance.

The fact that *Hoot* targeted a particularly young audience (youths in their early rather than later teens) may also set a precedent for later films. Kate Kelly, writing for the *Wall Street Journal*, noted that *Hoot* premiered in the same year as *Happy Feet* and *Ice Age: The Meltdown*, two successful family films with similar environmental motifs. Young people, in particular, have the most to lose if the environment is severely damaged or destroyed. They will also have the greatest incentives to try to repair or reverse some of the damage that has already been done—if repairs and reversals are even possible.

Robert C. Evans, PhD

Further Reading

Hiaasen, Carl. "We Interview." Interview by Ron Charles. *Washington Post*. Washington Post, 21 May 2006. Web. 19 Mar. 2015. <http://www.washington-

post.com/wp-dyn/content/article/2006/05/19/ AR2006051901408.html>.

Magrs, Paul. "Owl Trouble." Rev. of *Hoot*, by Carl Hiaasen. *Guardian*. Guardian News and Media, 22 Feb. 2003. Web. 19 Mar. 2015. <http://www.theguardian. com/books/2003/feb/22/featuresreviews.guardianreview28>.

Bibliography

Curry, Alice. *Environmental Crisis in Young Adult Fiction: A Poetics of Earth*. New York: Palgrave, 2013. Print.

Kelly, Kate. "The New Animated Film 'Happy Feet' Doesn't Dance Around Serious Issues." *Wall Street Journal*. Dow Jones, 17 Nov. 2006. Web. 19 Mar. 2015. <http://www.wsj.com/articles/ SB116373257478225933>.

Schweiger, Larry J. "Kids and Wildlife—A Perfect Big Screen Combination." *National Wildlife Federation*. Natl. Wildlife Federation, 10 Apr. 2006. Web. 19 Mar. 2015. <http://blog.nwf.org/2006/04/kids-and-wildlife-%E280%93-a-perfect-big-screen-combination>.

How I Live Now

The Book

Author: Meg Rosoff (b. 1956)
First published: 2004

The Film

Director: Kevin Macdonald (b. 1967)
Screenplay by: Jeremy Brock, Tony Grisoni, and Penelope Skinner
Starring: Saoirse Ronan, Tom Holland, and George MacKay

Context

When young adult (YA) literature took form in the late 1960s and around the publication of *The Outsiders* (1967), the literary genre was made up almost entirely of realistic fiction, which became the dominant subgenre through the 1970s and the reason for the decline in popularity of the genre in the 1980s. In the following decade, however, YA literature exploded with a new variety of subgenres, such as fantasy, with books like the Harry Potter series becoming international best sellers. While realistic fiction has always been a key component of YA stories, it did not see a major resurgence until the 2000s.

How I Live Now (2004) was first published in the United Kingdom about same time as the new wave of realistic authors were finding international popularity. While both the novel and film fall into the realistic genre, there is also a speculative aspect that drives much of the plot: the setting is England during a time of invasion from an unidentified country. Like much realistic fiction in the twenty-first century, Rosoff's story contains graphic subject matter suitable for more mature audiences. This adds a grittiness to the story that many reviewers of both the book and film found to be appealing.

How I Live Now is the first major publication for author Meg Rosoff, and it has become her most popular and best-reviewed title to date. Her other novels also fall into the realistic fiction subgenre, and a few include speculative elements as well. *Just in Case* (2006), for example, focuses on a young boy who is convinced that Fate is stalking him.

The film adaptation of *How I Live Now* was released in 2013 in the United Kingdom and was directed by Kevin Macdonald, a veteran Scottish filmmaker known primarily for documentaries and suspenseful dramas. Before directing the adaptation of Rosoff's novel, Macdonald had gained fame for realistic fictional dramas, such as *The Last King of Scotland* (2006), a fictional account of the last days of Ugandan dictator Idi Amin's reign, and *State of Play* (2009), a political thriller set in the United States.

Film Analysis

The film and novel begin with the same scene of the main character Daisy (Saoirse Ronan), arriving at the airport in England. She has been sent to live with her aunt and cousins by her father and his girlfriend. Although the plot at the beginning of the novel and film is the same, a difference in perspective gives the film a dramatically different tone. The novel is narrated entirely by Daisy. Rosoff utilizes a stream-of-consciousness style that resembles diary entries, and the novel reads like a direct transcription of Daisy's thoughts and includes many long, grammatically incorrect sentences and idiosyncratic turns of phrase and interjections. With this very personal and intimate style, it is easy to connect with Daisy's character almost immediately in the novel. However, since the perspective of the movie is the camera's eye, creating a sense of a third-person kind of narration, there is little for the audience to connect with Daisy on a personal level. Moreover, Daisy is portrayed in the film as a very caustic, rude young woman who does not care whether she offends others.

The main focus of both stories is the relationship between Daisy and her older cousin Edmond (George MacKay). In the novel, Edmond picks Daisy up from the airport, and from the start, even though he is smoking a cigarette and is generally unkempt, Daisy is attracted to him. Although Edmond's younger brother Isaac (Tom Holland) is the one in the film who meets Daisy at the airport, the element of love at first sight is equally captured when Daisy sees Edmond at the house.

Although everything in England is foreign to Daisy, she is intrigued by her new surroundings and the people around her. There are four children at the house: Isaac, Edmond, Piper (Harley Bird), and Osbert, who appears in the novel but is replaced by the neighbor Joe (Danny McEvoy) in the film. Piper is the youngest and the only girl, and in both the film and novel she is described as acting beyond her years, talking in a slightly affected way like an overeducated adult. Edmond is the oldest, and Joe, a teenage neighbor who is always over at the house, is like another member of the family. In the novel, Daisy is fifteen years old and Edmond is fourteen. They develop a sexual relationship that continues for many weeks while the children live together without parents after the United Kingdom is invaded and Daisy's aunt (who was away on business) is unable to return home. In the novel, when an adult finally arrives at the home, Daisy explains, "So there we are carrying on our happy little life of underage sex, child labor and espionage when someone came to visit us, which . . . kind of took us by surprise."

The lack of any substantial adult figures in both the novel and film is not unique for a YA story; parents and adults often play a secondary role to the relationships between teenage main characters. Rosoff's novel takes this motif one step further by creating a mother figure who is absent because of her demanding work as a peace negotiator. Since she was called away to just before the invasion begins and is not able to return, Daisy and her cousins live without supervision. In the book, the cousins all live together in their own world while the war rages on around them, but the film shortens this time to only one day. When British soldiers come to the farm looking for insurgents, they split up the family, sending the boys to one farm and the girls another to live and work with an army family that supplies fresh food to the local area.

Before the cousins were separated, Daisy promised Edmond she would return to the house as soon as possible and they would all be together again, but Piper and Daisy stay in their new home and work longer than hoped for. It is not until a traumatic incident on the way home from the farm that Daisy finds the impetus to escape and get back to the house. As the truck carrying the farm workers nears a military checkpoint, they realize it has been taken over by the enemy. A boy that Daisy worked with on the farm stands up in the truck and begins yelling at the girls for killing his dog, and in a scene that captures the graphic violence in this story, he is shot dead. In the novel, Daisy describes the scene in detail, "and there was a loud crack and part of [his] face exploded and there was blood everywhere and he fell out of the truck into the road." That night Piper and Daisy escape as the fighting gets dangerously close to the house where they are staying. Once they escape, they eventually make it back to the house.

The final chapters of the book depict Daisy and Piper returning to the house to find Edmond, Isaac, and Osbert alive and well. Daisy's father soon finds her and brings her back to the United States. Because the war continues in England, she is not able to return for six years. When she does, Edmond is angry and will not talk to her, but she stays and is determined to be with him. The film ends with Daisy and Piper finding Edmond badly beaten in the woods near their house. They take care of his physical injuries, but he has witnessed so much horror and has endured so much trauma since being relocated to the farm, he refuses to speak. Daisy remains and is determined to take care of him.

Without direct access into Daisy's mind, the film employs a number of cinematic effects that are meant to show the more intense emotions that affect Daisy. The novel hints that Daisy might be overly focused on rules and ensuring she acts the right way. In the film when Daisy is most nervous or uncomfortable with her surroundings, her thoughts are conveyed as angry whispering voices that seem to be fighting with each other. Edmond quiets her inner self-judgment and overthinking, and Daisy's thoughts remain relatively quiet for the rest of the film. Similarly, after she and Edmond begin their romantic relationship and are then separated, she dreams of him and sees him in different scenarios that reflect her anxiety toward his well-being. For instance, in her final dream in the film and after witnessing a massacre, she imagines Edmond lying underground covered by dirt and tree roots.

The movie and film both conclude with narration by Daisy, who explains her life: It is not what she expected it to be in any way, but she loves Edmond and is determined to stay with him.

Significance

How I Live Now was first screened at the Toronto International Film Festival in 2013 and quickly spread to movie theaters around the world that year. It was generally well received by critics, who praised it for not following the typical conventions of a YA story line. There are graphic elements in the film, and it does not try to force itself into traditional standards. While the setting is apocalyptic, it is not a dystopian story like many of the YA films that came out around the same time. *How I Live Now* follows many conventions of the YA genre, such as teenage protagonists figuring out the world without strong adults and romance as a theme, but it also embraces its differences, which critics and audiences applauded. Despite the movie being a commercial success, earning about sixty thousand dollars in domestic revenues, critics and audiences found the characters to be uneven. Many scenes of the film were exciting and entertaining, but in an equal number of moments, neither the acting nor the story line were inspired. Thus, however interesting Rosoff's voice and perspective may be in *How I Live Now*, it failed to translate into an equally compelling film narrative.

Aaron Horton, MA

Further Reading

Crawford, Philip Charles. "Literary Awards and the Enigma of *How I Live Now*." *Knowledge Quest* 34.2 (2005): 56–58. *Literary Reference Center*. Web. 10 Nov. 2015. <http://search.ebscohost.com/login.aspx?direct=true&db=lfh&AN=19157043&site=lrc-live>.

Hsin-Chun (Jamie), Tsai. "The Girls Who Do Not Eat: Food, Hunger, and Thinness in Meg Rosoff's *How I Live Now* and Laurie Halse Anderson's *Wintergirls*." *Jeunesse: Young People, Texts, Cultures* 6.1 (2014): 36–55. *Literary Reference Center*. Web. 16 Nov. 2015. <http://search.ebscohost.com/login.aspx?direct=true&db=lfh&AN=98488715&site=lrc-live>.

Lockney, Karen. "Progressive Presentations of Place-Based Identities in Meg Rosoff's *How I Live Now*." *Children's Literature in Education* 44.4 (2013): 311–25. *Literary Reference Center*. Web. 10 Nov. 2015. <http://search.ebscohost.com/login.aspx?direct=true&db=lfh&AN=90672452&site=lrc-live>.

Bibliography

Baker, Deirdre F. Rev. of *How I Live Now*, by Meg Rosoff. *Horn Book Magazine* 80.5 (2004): 597–80. *Literary Reference Center*. Web. 24 Nov. 2015. <http://search.ebscohost.com/login.aspx?direct=true&db=lfh&AN=14198209&site=lrc-live>.

"How I Live Now: When Love Means Survival." *Mag Pictures*. Magnolia Pictures, n.d. Web. 10 Nov. 2015. <http://www.magpictures.com/howilivenow>.

"Meg Rosoff." *Baker & Taylor Author Biographies* (2000): 1. *Literary Reference Center*. Web. 16 Nov. 2015. <http://search.ebscohost.com/login.aspx?direct=true&db=lfh&AN=49347823&site=lrc-live>.

"Meg Rosoff." *British Council: Literature*. British Council, 2015. Web. 10 Nov. 2015. <http://literature.britishcouncil.org/writer/meg-rosoff>.

Kenny, Glenn. Rev. of *How I Live Now*." *RogerEbert*. Ebert Digital, 8 Nov. 2013. Web. 10 Nov. 2015. <http://www.rogerebert.com/reviews/how-i-live-now-2013>.

How to Deal

The Books

Author: Sarah Dessen (b. 1970)
First published: *That Summer* (1996)
Someone Like You (1998)

The Film

Director: Clare Kilner
Screenplay by: Neena Beber
Starring: Mandy Moore, Allison Janney, Trent Ford, Alexandra Holden, and Mary Catherine Garrison

Context

In the 1990s, the term "chick lit" became a popular way to refer to fiction that explored issues of contemporary women, both adolescent and adult. A major staple of this subgenre of fiction is a lead female protagonist whose womanhood and its definition go through changes through the course of the story. Examples of chick-lit books published around the time the trend began to rise in popularity are Terry McMillan's *Waiting to Exhale* (1992), Helen Fielding's *Bridget Jones's Diary* (1996), and Candace Bushnell's *Sex and the City* (1997). While these books were aimed toward adult women, chick lit is also prevalent in young adult fiction for adolescent girls. Popular examples are Meg Cabot's *The Princess Diaries* (2000), Ann Brashares's *The Sisterhood of the Traveling Pants* (2001), and Cecily von Ziegesar's *Gossip Girl* (2002).

Author Sarah Dessen has written several chick-lit novels for young adults as well, including her first book *That Summer* (1996) and her follow-up *Someone Like You* (1998). Both books address numerous issues of adolescence, such as self-identity, the concept of love, teen pregnancy, divorce, loss of virginity, and abortion. They were well received by critics from major publications like the *New York Times* and *Publishers Weekly*. Dessen has stated that out of all of the books she has written, *Someone Like You* has the largest fan base.

The rights to both of the books were purchased by film studio New Line Cinema. Screenwriter Neena Beber, who had previously worked on teen comedies for television like *Clarissa Explains It All* (1992–94), was tasked with combining the books into one script. She took many of the familial elements from *That Summer* and merged them with the characters and plot points from *Someone Like You*. The result was the film *How to Deal* (2003), directed by Clare Kilner, a British filmmaker previously known for the television comedy *EastEnders* (1997) and the comedy *Janice Beard* (1999), a film that drew comparisons to *Bridget Jones's Diary*. The producers had seen *Janice Beard* and thought that Kilner was the right fit for *How to Deal*. For the lead role, pop-music artist Mandy Moore was cast. Moore had previously starred in the popular teen coming-of-age film *A Walk to Remember* (2002).

Film Analysis
How to Deal takes the character names and the familial situation present in *That Summer* and combines them with many of the plot points from *Someone Like You*. The result is a film that addresses numerous issues prevalent in young adult fiction for teenage girls. The beginning of the film shows home videos of sixteen-year-old

Halley Martin (Mandy Moore) at the beach when she was a small child. Through her narration, the audience learns that due to the turmoil within her family, Halley finds herself thinking back on the happier times in her life and how as a child there were many trite uncertainties in the world. Now that she is older, her childhood has given way to more stressing uncertainties. This opening flashback and narration establishes that Halley is nostalgic for simpler times and stubborn about facing life's difficult situations.

Halley is a high school student from a dysfunctional family. On the same day her parents Lydia (Allison Janney) and Len Martin (Peter Gallagher) divorce, her sister Ashley (Mary Catherine Garrison) announces that she is engaged. Distressed and disillusioned, Halley goes to the house of her friend Scarlett Smith (Alexandra Holden), where she walks in on Scarlett having sex with her boyfriend, Michael (John White). Halley did not know Scarlett and Michael had such a serious relationship, which further distresses her. Eventually Halley begins to fall in love with Michael's best friend, Macon Forrester (Trent Ford). These relationships in Halley's life and the strife within them form the crux of *How to Deal*.

The sheer number of plot devices the protagonist has to deal with leads to a hectic, relentless plotline of teenage frustration and tragedy. Michael suffers a heart attack and dies, Scarlett only realizes after Michael's death that she is pregnant with his child, Halley's father remarries a much younger woman, and Halley gets into a car accident with Macon after refusing to have sex with him at a New Year's Eve party. Just one of these plot devices would be sufficient for a single melodrama, but *How to Deal* includes them all, and more; consequently the film plays out like a gauntlet of turmoil. Negative criticism of the film pointed out the cumbersomeness of the screenplay that combined two of Dessen's novels into one film, which made many of the plot devices feel contrived.

The film is not all downbeat, however. There are some lighthearted moments of comedy and romance. Kilner includes a montage set to pop music that features Halley and Macon falling in love with each other over time. This approach is typical in romantic films that need to show a great deal of time passing in order to propel the movie and the relationship forward. The couple also share their first kiss in a romantic scene at a dam, which Kilner dramatically shoots with a long shot. The sight of the two lovers kissing beneath this massive dam is symbolic of the feelings they are both holding back for one another. Halley is afraid to get into a serious relationship because she sees the pain it has brought her mother, while Macon is simply unsure what he wants. The dam serves as a strong symbol of this. Right before they kiss, water is released from the dam, symbolizing both characters letting go of their fears, at least for the time being.

Scarlett's pregnancy and its ramifications are explored more deeply in the novel than they are in the film. In the book, Scarlett's mother decides for her that she must have an abortion. Scarlett actually goes to an abortion appointment at a clinic in Dessen's version, but she decides against it and has Halley drive her home. In the film, Scarlett's mother implies that she would like her to get an abortion, but the topic is not discussed any further and Scarlett goes into labor during the wedding of Halley's sister. At the hospital, Halley and Macon resolve their problems and share a dance in the hallway while pop music plays. This segment is shot like a music video with quick cuts and off-kilter camera angles.

How to Deal is rated PG-13 but includes some moments that may push the boundary of that rating in order to deal honestly with the problems its young audience may face in real life. Halley's mother says a harsh expletive, and her grandmother smokes marijuana and frequently refers to being under its influence. Also, Halley, in a moment of extreme stress, smokes a cigarette. While some parents may object to these moments of the film, it does make *How to Deal* feel more authentic and palpable to its young audience.

Aside from the montage and the quickly cut dance scene in the hospital hallway, *How to Deal* is shot in a very conventional manner for a teenage comedy. Since she is the audience's point of reference for everything else in the film, Moore is in nearly every shot. Kilner clearly frames her expressions as they display her reactions to the characters around her. Perhaps her most expressive moment takes place after Michael's funeral. It begins to rain and Kilner shoots Halley from a bird's-eye view directly from above as she tilts her head up toward the storm and spreads her arms. This shot in the rain is frequently used in cinema to show a moment of clarity or emotional cleansing. With that in mind, it is odd for this particular shot to come around the halfway point of the film, when Halley has a slew of troubles still to come.

Significance

Dessen's young adult novels found a strong audience of adolescent girls due to their honest look at real life and the tribulations it brings. Her novels *That Summer* and *Someone Like You* addressed several issues, and Dessen would continue to do so in her subsequent books. One of them, *Just Listen* (2006), concerns a young girl dealing with a sexual assault. This book was banned in some high schools because it was deemed too intense for young readers.

How to Deal also covered numerous issues, but the large number of them was one of the major reasons it received mixed reviews. Critics frequently brought up the volume of plot devices, remarking that it makes the whole narrative feel artificial and the plot contrived. There was some positive review of the film, mostly focusing on its honest portrayal of issues facing teenagers and the ensemble cast and how the amateurish production and, in some cases, acting, actually complemented this authenticity. Despite some negative criticism, *How to Deal* performed well at the box office. It came just short of making back its nearly $16 million budget, with a total gross of $14.3 million worldwide.

While Dessen's two novels and their film adaptation both address numerous issues relevant to teenage girls, critics tended to concede that condensing both stories into one film made the narrative too cluttered and contrived. The film is unique in that manner, however, as it presents several relevant young adult topics during its running time. Its honesty and willingness to push its PG-13 rating to the limit also make it stand out amid other teenage dramas.

Patrick G. Cooper

Further Reading

Dessen, Sarah. Interview by Regina Hayes. *Slate*. Slate Media, 7 June 2013. Web. 9 Mar. 2015. <http://www.slate.com/articles/arts/books/2013/06/ya_author_sarah_dessen_and_her_book_editor_regina_hayes_of_viking_in_conversation.html>.

Glenn, Wendy J. *Sarah Dessen: From Burritos to Box Office*. Lanham: Scarecrow, 2005. Print.

Bibliography

Hornaday, Ann. "'How to Deal': Angst in Spades." Rev. of *How to Deal*, dir. Clare Kilner. *Washington Post*. Washington Post, 18 July 2003. Web. 9 Mar. 2015.

<http://www.washingtonpost.com/wp-dyn/content/article/2003/07/18/AR2005033117046.html>.

Kilner, Clare. Interview by Danny Manus. *Script*. F+W, 23 Apr. 2013. Web. 9 Mar. 2015. <http://www.scriptmag.com/news/an-interview-with-writerdirector-clare-kilner>.

Scott, A. O. "Pimples Are the Least of This Girl's Worries." Rev. of *How to Deal*, dir. Clare Kilner. *New York Times*. New York Times, 18 July 2003. Web. 9 Mar. 2015. <http://www.nytimes.com/movie/review?res=9C0CE5DA133CF93BA25754C0A9659C8B63>.

Howl's Moving Castle

The Book

Author: Diana Wynne Jones (1934–2011)
First published: 1986

The Film

Director: Hayao Miyazaki (b. 1941)
Screenplay by: Hayao Miyazaki
Starring: Emily Mortimer, Jean Simmons, Christian Bale, Billy Crystal (English version)

Context

Young adult novels adapted for the screen and based on young adult fantasy novels were particularly popular during the first decade of the twenty-first century. In most cases, young adult film adaptations were live-action films, often featuring computer-generated characters—such as Dobby the Elf in the Harry Potter film franchise—and numerous computer-generated special effects. There were, however, a few exceptions to that trend during the decade. One major exception was the film *Howl's Moving Castle*, which, unlike many of its contemporaries, presents its narrative entirely through animation.

The film, which premiered in Japan in late 2004 and in the United States in mid-2005, is based on English writer Diana Wynne Jones's 1986 novel, *Howl's Moving Castle*. *Howl's Moving Castle* is the first installment in a trilogy that also includes the novels *Castle in the Air* (1990) and *House of Many Ways* (2008). Set in the magical kingdom of Ingary, the novel follows an eighteen-year-old shopkeeper named Sophie who, after being transformed into an elderly woman by the evil Witch of the Waste, begins working for the wizard Howl. As Sophie attempts to reverse her transformation, she comes to learn that Howl has likewise been cursed by the witch, but is also bound by a magical contract with the fire-demon Calcifer. Howl agrees to help Sophie only if she determines how to break his contract with Calcifer.

The film adaptation of *Howl's Moving Castle* (known in Japan as *Hauru no ugoku shiro*) was produced by the Japanese film company Studio Ghibli and directed by one of the studio's founders, veteran filmmaker, Hayao Miyazaki. Studio Ghibli specializes in producing feature-length animated films and is best known for films such as *My Neighbor Totoro* (1988), *Princess Mononoke* (1997), and *Spirited Away* (2001), all of which were written and directed by Miyazaki himself. Many of the studio's films have been dubbed into languages other than Japanese and released worldwide, and *Howl's Moving Castle* was no exception; an English-language version of the film, featuring the voices of a number of well-known American and British actors, was released in the United States by Walt Disney Pictures, which had previously distributed several of Studio Ghibli's earlier films.

Film Analysis

As a novel being adapted into a film, *Howl's Moving Castle* presented a number of unique challenges to the filmmakers. First and foremost was the challenge of translating the story from the written medium into a visual one. As Studio Ghibli is dedicated to animation, it is no surprise that Miyazaki, the film's director and writer, chose to work in that medium. In many ways, the novel is far more suited to animation than to live action, as is the case with many works of fantasy. Fantasy novels often feature visible use of magic, magical creatures, transformations, and other fantastical elements that in live-action films would require significant use of special effects; such effects mesh well with the film as a whole, but often computer-generated characters and images age poorly as special-effects technology improves over the years, and can appear jarring in later viewings. The novel incarnation of *Howl's Moving Castle* features a number of elements that would present significant challenges to any filmmakers hoping to work in live action. The fire demon Calcifer for instance, would likely be difficult to depict on screen in a live-action film, while the transformation of eighteen-year-old Sophie into an elderly woman would require either the casting of two actors to play the young and old versions of the character, or the use of extensive old-age makeup or computer-generated imagery. Animation, however, allows creatures such as Calcifer (Billy Crystal), and magical events such as Sophie's (Emily Mortimer, Jean Simmons) transformation to blend seamlessly with the overall look and feel of the film.

The titular moving castle would likewise be difficult to portray on screen, even if its depiction was limited to the description provided in the novel. In the book, the castle is a sinister-looking dwelling made of dark, coal-like blocks that spouts clouds of smoke as it rumbles across the countryside. By rendering the castle in animation, Miyazaki and his team were able not only to depict its movement against the backdrops of rural Ingary, but also to expand upon Wynne Jones's description, creating an imposing yet whimsical version of the castle that many critics cited as the film's most iconic image. The castle of the film is a misshapen building seemingly composed of mismatching parts that jut out in every direction, and it walks over the hills and fields outside of Sophie's town on skinny, chicken-like legs. The castle's movement makes it seem like a living creature, an impression one may not gain from the description of the building in the novel, and gives the building an increased sense of strangeness.

Miyazaki has been counted among Japan's most influential filmmakers, and he is known for his signature visual style and frequent use of a number of recurring themes. Most of his films are based on concepts he developed or his own short comics, and as such, he had full control over each narrative and how it was rendered through animation. A few of Miyazaki's previous films for Studio Ghibli, including *Kiki's Delivery Service* (1989) and *Whisper of the Heart* (1995), were based on Japanese books or comics that Miyazaki did not create. *Howl's Moving Castle* is particularly interesting because it is one of very few films by Miyazaki that was based on European rather than Japanese source material. Although not based on one of Miyazaki's own narratives, the film takes on a number of his commonly used themes, including some that are not present in the original novel.

Perhaps the most obvious change made to the narrative is Miyazaki's introduction of a war plot. In the film, the wizard Howl (Christian Bale), is involved in a war that begins when, in a nearby country, a member of the royal family goes missing. Although reluctant to become involved, he is forced to join the fight by the magical adviser to the king, Madame Suliman (Blythe Danner). This war plot does not exist in the novel; the Howl presented in the book is far more concerned with charming the various women he meets. War is a common theme in Miyazaki's films, and the director, a noted pacifist who was born during World War II and grew up during the war's aftermath, demonstrates the damaging effects of war on peaceful realms in many of his works. In an interview with *Newsweek* published shortly after the film's US premiere, Miyazaki explained that the development of *Howl's Moving Castle* was influenced in part by the then-ongoing Iraq War, which he strongly opposed.

In addition to their frequent use of war themes, Miyazaki's films also often feature themes of physical transformation. The novel *Howl's Moving Castle* thus seems an especially appropriate choice of source material, as Sophie's transformation shapes the narrative as a whole. The film presents Sophie's initial transformation and also shows her wavering back and forth between her young and old selves, thus calling further attention to the physical changes she has experienced. In addition, the film includes another pertinent plot point not featured in the original novel: Howl's transformation into a large bird-man during the war as a means of fighting the invading military. The frequent transformations are not without risk, however, and Howl is in danger of losing his humanity altogether. Animal transformations feature in several Miyazaki films, at times in relation to war or violence; in *Porco Rosso* (1992), for example, a World War I fighter pilot is transformed into a pig following the war, perhaps suggesting the damaging effects of combat on those participating in it. In *Howl's Moving Castle*, physical transformation can be both enlightening, in the case of Sophie, and damaging, in the case of Howl. By the end of the film, however, both transformations are resolved, and Sophie and Howl are able to carry out their lives as their true selves, having learned much from their experiences.

Significance

Like many Studio Ghibli films, *Howl's Moving Castle* proved immensely popular with Japanese audiences, grossing nearly $200 million at the box office. Following its Japanese debut on November 20, 2004, the film was released in numerous other countries, including

South Korea, France, and New Zealand. For the US release, the film was dubbed into English by a large voice cast that featured the voices of prominent live-action actors rather than career voice actors in the major roles.

Howl's Moving Castle had a relatively limited release in the United States, appearing in significantly fewer theaters than Studio Ghibli's previous US theatrical release, *Spirited Away*. The film grossed nearly $5 million dollars in the United States and received acclaim from both fans of Japanese animation and American moviegoers in general. In addition to receiving numerous awards from film festivals and critics' associations, *Howl's Moving Castle* was nominated for the Academy Award for best animated film in 2006. Although it ultimately lost the award to *Wallace and Gromit: The Curse of the Were-Rabbit* (2005), *Howl's Moving Castle*'s nomination gained the film additional name recognition among American film enthusiasts.

The film was well received by most critics, many of whom praised the film's lush and whimsical animation as well as Sophie's powerful and emotional journey following her transformation. Some critics argued that the film was weaker than many of Miyazaki's previous offerings, but even those reviewers were captivated by its visual beauty. Miyazaki undoubtedly made numerous changes to the narrative during the adaptation process, a fact that irked some fans of the novel, but Wynne Jones herself deemed the film "wonderful" in a 2005 interview with the *Telegraph*. A fan of Miyazaki's work for decades, she explained in the interview that he had seen and understood the novel "from the inside out"—a crucial step in the adaptation of any book.

Joy Crelin

Further Reading

Brown, Noel, and Bruce Babington. *Family Films in Global Cinema: The World beyond Disney*. London: Tauris, 2015. Print.

Cavallaro, Dani. *The Animé Art of Hayao Miyazaki*. Jefferson: McFarland, 2006. Print.

Cavallaro, Dani. *Hayao Miyazaki's World Picture*. Jefferson: McFarland, 2015. Print.

Bibliography

Ebert, Roger. Rev. of *Howl's Moving Castle*, dir. Hayao Miyazaki. *RogerEbert.com*. Ebert Digital, 9 June 2005. Web. 30 Apr. 2015. <http://www.rogerebert.com/reviews/howls-moving-castle-2005>.

"Howl's Moving Castle." *Box Office Mojo*. IMDb.com, n.d. Web. 30 Apr. 2015. <http://www.boxofficemojo.com/movies/?page=main&id=howlsmovingcastle.htm>.

Jones, Diana Wynne. "He Saw My Books from the Inside Out." Interview by Nick Bradshaw. *Telegraph*. Telegraph Media, 23 Sept. 2005. Web. 30 Apr. 2015. <http://www.telegraph.co.uk/culture/film/3646735/He-saw-my-books-from-the-inside-out.html>.

Miyazaki, Hayao. "A 'Positive Pessimist.'" Interview by Devin Gordon. *Newsweek*. Newsweek, 19 June 2005. Web. 30 Apr. 2015. <http://www.newsweek.com/positive-pessimist-119801>.

Scott, A. O. "A Cursed Teenager Turns 90. Let the Adventures Begin." Rev. of *Howl's Moving Castle*, dir. Hayao Miyazaki. *New York Times*. New York Times, 10 June 2005. Web. 30 Apr. 2015. <http://www.nytimes.com/2005/06/10/movies/10howl.html?_r=0>.

Hugo

The Book

Author: Brian Selznick (b. 1966)
First published: *The Invention of Hugo Cabret* (2007)

The Film

Director: Martin Scorsese (b. 1942)
Screenplay by: John Logan
Starring: Asa Butterfield, Chloë Grace Moretz, Ben Kingsley, Sacha Baron Cohen, and Emily Mortimer

Context

In 2007, author and illustrator Brian Selznick published a unique illustrated novel for children called *The Invention of Hugo Cabret*. "This is much more than a graphic novel," John Schwartz wrote in his review of the book for the *New York Times*. "It is more like a silent film on paper." Indeed, this appears to have been Selznick's intention. From the introduction on, the book establishes a cinematic atmosphere though language, drawings, and plot elements. Hugo, who is twelve, lives in a train station, Paris's famous Gare Montparnasse, in 1931. His father, a clockmaker, died in a fire at a museum, and Hugo's only remaining connection to him is a strange, broken automaton that his father found in the museum's storage. Hugo is taken in by his alcoholic uncle, who winds the clocks at the train station, but with Hugo available to do the job for him, he quickly disappears. Hugo is left to fend for himself, thieving bits of food as well as bits of machinery to fix the automaton. Hugo believes that when it is in working order, it will convey a message to him.

Selznick was inspired by the true story of the early French filmmaker Georges Méliès. Méliès was a magician who began making short fantasy and science-fiction films in the late 1890s. He was a special effects pioneer and an artist of illusion. One of his most famous films, *A Trip to the Moon* (1902), depicts a rocket being shot into the eye of the man in the moon. Méliès's studio fell on hard times after the outbreak of World War I, and he eventually lost his film equipment and career. Méliès worked at a toy booth building trinkets at Gare Montparnasse before being rediscovered by film buffs and enjoying one last moment in the spotlight before his death in 1938.

Many of these details are woven into Selznick's story, which becomes deeply engaged with the history of filmmaking. Similarly, the film adaptation is a meeting place for cinema's past and present, and serves as an homage to the work of Méliès as well as other landmarks of film history. Director Martin Scorsese, one of the most influential filmmakers of his own generation, lovingly presents the history of film while telling a story using cinema's newest 3-D technology. And not only does he invoke the magic of early films, with their revolutionary special effects, but he draws on the illustrations from Selznick's book, creating a complex series of intertwined inspirations and styles.

Film Analysis

It is a curious task to adapt a graphic novel for film, much less one that is itself significantly about filmmaking. *The Invention of Hugo Cabret* tests the boundaries of the two mediums by essentially providing a storyboard for its adaptation in the form of extensive illustrations. Director Martin Scorsese takes care to follow Selznick's blueprint—many of the drawn scenes are recreated almost verbatim throughout *Hugo*. Examples include the opening aerial shot of the streets of 1930s Paris, Hugo's eyes peeking out from within the station's clocks, the view of the labyrinthine passages behind the station's walls, and the solid mass of commuters rushing to make their train. Although the film is largely faithful

to the novel, as Jennifer Clement and Christian B. Long point out in their essay about the film for *Senses of Cinema* (1 July 2012), *Hugo* is not merely an adaptation of the book but an ongoing dialogue with it.

Selznick's novel is partly visual and about a filmmaker; Scorsese's film is certainly visual—visceral, even, in the way storybook exaggerations are brought to life—but it also celebrates books. Hugo's friend Isabelle (Chloë Grace Moretz) loves books and takes Hugo (Asa Butterfield) to visit the bookseller at Gare Montparnasse. Her conversations are rife with literary references, among them an allusion to *David Copperfield* by Charles Dickens—a book about an orphan like Hugo. In the film, Isabelle has read widely but never seen a movie, so Hugo, using his superior lock-picking skills, sneaks her into a movie house. Isabelle's introduction to film establishes a link between literature and cinema without denigrating the former—in fact, as Scorsese and screenwriter John Logan seem to suggest, the magic of cinema lies not in the technology that makes it possible but the use of that technology in service of telling a story.

Scorsese wastes no time beginning Hugo's story. The film opens on the ticking cogs of a machine, which dissolve into an aerial view of Paris. The camera swings into the train station, where the steam from the locomotives dissipates into the ebbing crowd of commuters—an eerie metaphor, particularly in a nostalgic film in which clocks are central image, about the mists of time and people (like Méliès and Hugo's father, for instance) fading into the past. The briefest of cameos from actors playing guitarist Django Reinhardt and author James Joyce moments later reinforce the theme and the film's overall tribute to a past age. The sweeping shot continues until it lands on Hugo eyeing the Gare Montparnasse through the numbers of a clock. The introduction to time and place—lasting for a full fifteen minutes before the title card (there are no opening credits) is lush richly textured. Scorsese and cinematographer Robert Richardson work to place the camera at a child's eye level as Hugo winds his way through the station. Compounded by the 3-D effects, this gives the viewer a new perspective on the otherwise familiar scene of a train station, paralleling the wonder generated by early film technology.

In Hugo's world, everything—from the machines, to the courtyard statues, to the costume of the station guard—is stylized. Hard surfaces are smoother; color is more intense, and there is sharp contrast between aesthetics of different characters and places. Like the

Méliès films that are eventually wound into the plot, the world is a storybook version of reality. Scorsese deliberately creates a romanticized version of Paris, with the Eiffel Tower visible in nearly every shot of the city. It was no coincidence that Méliès found his way to filmmaking through a career as a magician— the two professions share many goals. *Hugo* celebrates this connection by making a modern film according to Méliès's vision: movies as illusion, magic—the stuff of dreams. "If you've ever wondered where your dreams come from, you look around . . . ," a young Méliès (Ben Kingsley) tells a boy (who will later become a film historian) on the set of one of his films. "This is where they're made."

Scorsese, a scholar of cinema himself, endeavors to teach his audience about classic films through references both direct and indirect. The movie is indeed filled with various types of references to films and filmmakers throughout history. Scorsese includes clips from *A Trip to the Moon* and the Harold Lloyd comedy *Safety Last* (1923), in which Lloyd hangs from the hand of a giant clock. Hugo, being chased by the station guard (Sacha Baron Cohen) mimics the feat near the end of the film. Other direct references include the work of early filmmakers such as W. K. L. Dickson (1860–1935), Edwin S. Porter (1870–1941), D. W. Griffith (1875–1948), Robert Wiene (1873–1938), and the Lumière brothers.

The Lumières' *Arrival of a Train at La Ciotat* (1896), which inspired Méliès to make his own films, is given particular attention within *Hugo*, as it is shown being screened. Scorsese's depiction follows the popular story that the original short film terrified audiences unfamiliar with the film medium, who thought that the train was going to emerge from the screen and run them over, and *Hugo* draws further connections through its own use of trains. By including a representation of the historic impact of cinema's storytelling power, the film builds multiple layers of symbolism, homage, and adaptation. This is also apparent in ways other than direct incorporation of historic films in Hugo's world: for example, in the use of stock characters. Scorsese's affection for physical comedians like Chaplin and Buster Keaton is referenced outright, but also more obliquely in Sacha Baron Cohen's character, the lonely station guard with a malfunctioning metal leg brace who trolls the Gare Montparnasse for boys like Hugo so that he can ship them off to the orphanage.

Significance

Hugo premiered in November 2011. Critical reception of the film was strong, with reviewers almost universally praising the visuals and most finding the story admirable as well. Still, *Hugo* failed to draw a large enough audience to cover its estimated $180 million budget. The movie earned $181 million worldwide, causing a significant loss for Scorsese's producer, Graham King. It was, however, nominated for eleven Academy Awards—the most of any film that year—and won five, including trophies for cinematography and visual effects and for art direction. Scorsese also won a Golden Globe for best director for the film in 2012.

Why exactly the film performed so poorly at the box office is unclear. *Hugo* remains highly rated on film review aggregator sites like Rotten Tomatoes. In addition to the film's spectacle, audiences seemed to respond to its themes of love and belonging using machines as a metaphor. Hugo tells Isabelle that he knows he was put on earth for a reason because "machines don't come with extra parts," meaning that every person exists for a purpose. At its heart, Hugo is not only about filmmaking but about family and friendship. Even bit characters like the station guard and the florist (Emily Mortimer) all find some measure of happiness at the end of the film, realized through a new relationship formed in the great meeting place of the Gare Montparnasse.

Molly Hagan

Further Reading

Clement, Jennifer, and Christian B. Long. "*Hugo*, Remediation, and the Cinema of Attractions, or, the Adaptation of Hugo Cabret." *Senses of Cinema*. Senses of Cinema, Jul. 2012. Web. 2 Apr. 2015. <http://sensesofcinema.com/2012/feature-articles/hugo-remediation-and-the-cinema-of-attractions-or-the-adaptation-of-hugo-cabret>.

Denby, David. "Fantastic Voyages." Rev. of *Hugo*, dir. Martin Scorsese. *New Yorker*. Condé Nast, 28 Nov. 2011. Web. 2 Apr. 2015. <http://www.newyorker.com/magazine/2011/11/28/fantastic-voyages>.

Murty, Govindini. "From Méliès to Montparnasse, a Cultural Cheat Sheet for 'Hugo.'" *Atlantic*. Atlantic Monthly, 22 Feb. 2012. Web. 3 Apr. 2015. <http://www.theatlantic.com/entertainment/archive/2012/02/from-m-li-s-to-montparnasse-a-cultural-cheat-sheet-for-hugo/253409/#slide1>.

Bibliography

Bradshaw, Peter. Rev. of *Hugo*, dir. Martin Scorsese. *Guardian*. Guardian News and Media, 1 Dec. 2011. Web. 3 Apr. 2015. <http://www.theguardian.com/film/2011/dec/01/hugo-scorsese-film-review>.

Scorsese, Martin. "Martin Scorsese's Magical 'Hugo.'" Interview by John Bowe. *New York Times Magazine*. New York Times, 2 Nov. 2011. Web. 6 Apr. 2015. <http://www.nytimes.com/2011/11/06/magazine/martin-scorseses-magical-hugo.html>.

Dargis, Manohla. "Inventing a World, Just Like Clockwork." Rev. of *Hugo*, dir. Martin Scorsese. *New York Times*. New York Times, 22 Nov. 2011. Web. 6 Apr. 2015. <http://www.nytimes.com/2011/11/23/movies/martin-scorseses-hugo-with-ben-kingsley-and-sacha-baron-cohen-review.html>.

Masters, Kim. "How 'Hugo's' Massive Losses Are Straining Producer Graham King's Partnerships." *Hollywood Reporter*. Hollywood Reporter, 25 Apr. 2012. Web. 6 Apr. 2015. <http://www.hollywoodreporter.com/news/hugo-martin-scorsese-graham-king-losses-315798>.

Schwartz, John. Rev. of *The Invention of Hugo Cabret: A Novel in Words and Pictures*, by Brian Selznick. *New York Times*. New York Times, 11 Mar. 2007. Web. 3 Apr. 2015. <http://www.nytimes.com/2007/03/11/books/review/Schwartz.t.html>.

The Hunger Games (Series)

The Books

Author: Suzanne Collins (b. 1962)
First published: *The Hunger Games* (2008)
Catching Fire (2009)
Mockingjay (2010)

The Films

Directors: *Gary Ross* (b. 1956), *The Hunger Games*; *Francis Lawrence* (b. 1971), *Catching Fire, Mockingjay:* Part 1, and *Mockingjay:* Part 2
Screenplay by: Gary Ross, Suzanne Collins, and Billy Ray, The Hunger Games; Simon Beaufoy and Michael Arndt, Catching Fire; Danny Strong and Peter Craig, Mockingjay: Part 1 and Mockingjay: Part 2

Starring: Jennifer Lawrence, Josh Hutcherson, Liam Hemsworth, Woody Harrelson, Donald Sutherland

Context

The emergence of the Hunger Games series comes in tandem with widespread interest in young adult dystopias and science fiction narratives among general audiences—with the Hunger Games being one of the earliest and most successful entries in this subgenre of film and literature, it is difficult to distinguish the degree to which the films owe their success to the genre, or the genre to the films. Critics generally agree, however, that one factor in the series's popularity is the ability of dystopian narratives to explore themes relevant to twenty-first century culture and global politics. As corporations and states become increasingly powerful, technology advances at a startling rate, and threats ranging from environmental collapse and nuclear terrorism to total surveillance confront us, the sense of fear and distrust that resonates through dystopian realities does not seem as far removed from our own world as it might have ten or twenty years ago. While recent popular teen film franchises (among them Harry Potter and the Twilight, both also based on books) had captured teen psyches quite well, the dystopian genre infuses those psyches with a political awareness.

The Hunger Games franchise also, of course, has succeeded due to the skill of its creators. Author Suzanne Collins had already honed her skills as a writer on successful children's television shows and as the author of the young adult fantasy series the Underland Chronicles. The director of the first film, Gary Ross, had an established directorial career, including *Seabiscuit*, which was nominated for an Academy Award for best picture. The director of the following films, Francis Lawrence, had achieved popularity with action films such as *I Am Legend* and *Constantine* as well as a score of stylish music videos. Together with the hugely successful actors, producers, writers, and remaining cast, the films were poised from the start to be box office successes.

Looking more broadly at science fiction and young adult literature, Hunger Games is not as entirely revolutionary as it might seem in the present day. Author Suzanne Collins notes that she drew some inspiration from the ancient Greek tale of Theseus and the Minotaur, a myth in which seven Athenian boys and seven Athenian girls are sacrificed every seven years by being placed in a maze where the monster will devour them. There have also been a number of books and movies in which children are forced to fight one another to the death, most notably the Japanese writer Koushun Takami's *Battle Royale*, published in 1999. What differentiates the Hunger Games series, then, is the particular way the narrative applies these tropes to its near-future dystopia. Its strong and determined protagonist and the accompanying commentary on wealth and war all speak clearly to a generation of young people encountering an uncertain and sometimes terrifying future, just as the characters in the film themselves express uncertainty about what role hope might play in their lives even as they fight to survive.

Film Analysis

The Hunger Games series is as much about its main character, Katniss Everdeen (Jennifer Lawrence), as it is about the world she inhabits. In what appears to be a near-future, postapocalyptic version of North America, now known as Panem, a tyrannical government rules over a strictly segmented society. The ruling class lives in the Capitol, a place of obscene wealth and decadence, and the remaining citizens are divided among twelve districts, with each successive district experiencing greater extremes of poverty and oppression. As punishment for a rebellion against the Capitol in the past, there is a yearly Reaping, an event in which one boy and one girl are randomly selected from each district, then sent to fight to their deaths, with only one survivor escaping from each year's Hunger Games.

In order to introduce this world, the first film in the series, *The Hunger Games*, elects to explicitly explain the history and parameters of its dystopian reality. It opens with text that describes the historical facts of Panem and the Reaping, moves into a brief scene set in the Capitol where two people discuss the Games, then cuts abruptly to District 12, the home of Katniss. While the information provided here is almost identical to the information eventually provided in the book, there is one very noticeable difference: while the book is told in first person from the perspective of Katniss, the film is told in third person, able to focus on any aspect of Panem that is appropriate for the plot at that moment. The opening line of the novel, "When I wake up, the other side of the bed is cold," thrusts readers directly into the mind of Katniss, leaving a good deal of information about the world mysterious, unveiling it piece by piece. The film, however, provides audiences with that information at the very start in order to help viewers navigate this complex reality, and in turn places even

greater emphasis on the politics and culture of Panem as they exist independent of Katniss.

These opening moments also introduce audiences to the use of color and lighting, which become some of the most consistent stylistic techniques throughout the films. The first glimpse of the Capitol is of a world of glitz and bright colors, with moving lights glistening in the background and the two characters with ornate clothing and hair—dyed bright blue, in the case of television host Caesar Flickerman (Stanley Tucci). They are also lit brightly, barely a shadow cast across them—a style of cinematic lighting that is common in optimistic, happy scenes, as well as broadcast talk shows. Abruptly, however, the camera cuts away from this glamorous reality and redirects us to Katniss's home in District 12. Here, all the colors are pale, the scene saturated with gray. The lighting further mutes the colors, washing out the actors and making the landscape itself appear dull. In similar contrast to the Capitol, the camera no longer stays still to present a clear, direct shot of the scene, but instead becomes a handheld camera, a name for the effect in which the camera bounces around and shakes. In the first moments of District 12, the viewer can never get a full picture of what occurs, can never stay focused long enough to gain his or her bearings—but what the viewer can do is sense the confusion, fear, and depression of this place.

The shaky, handheld camera effect becomes a prime tool as the film progresses along the same basic plot as the novel. As Katniss volunteers for the Reaping in place of her younger sister and leaves District 12 for the brilliantly colored opulence of the Capitol and the threat of the Hunger Games, the handheld camera is often used to create a sense of immediacy and to place the audience in Katniss's perspective. The effect recreates the dire, intense mood that the book is able to form through first-person narrative. When Katniss is overwhelmed by nervousness and confusion during her interview with Caesar, for instance, the book narrates "What? What did he say? It's as if the words make no sense. My mouth has gone as dry as sawdust." In the film, it is the camera that creates this sense of Katniss's confusion and panic at the most dramatic and unfamiliar moments: the Reaping itself, her introduction to Capitol life, and the first minutes of the Games. It also serves to remind us that, even if we might have some of the basic information about Panem given to us, this is still a place of confusion and mystery, and the audience should remain as skeptical and on-guard as Katniss does.

Within the Games, the difference between the third-person view of the film and the first-person view of the book becomes more obvious. In the novel, readers remain unaware that Katniss has sparked riots and revolution in District 11; as Katniss only knows what she can see, this information is not revealed until the second book. In the film, however, audiences can see the direct correlation between her actions and the uprising in District 11, the camera cutting back and forth between the two locations. Similarly, audiences are privy to sinister conversations between President Snow (Donald Sutherland) and his advisors, as well as the manipulations and scheming of the Games' controllers. In the novel it is clear from the organization of the larger world and government that Panem is an oppressive and unjust society (that Katniss must face the Games at all proves it to be so). In the film, however, this point is made explicit, the scenes outside the Arena revealing that President Snow and his ruling class are intentionally and maliciously oppressing the Districts.

In *Catching Fire*, these political dimensions become a greater focus, and it is evident from the opening scenes that the violence and horror of the world are not limited to the Arena. Katniss begins to have direct interactions with President Snow, signs of the rebellion rise up continually, and audiences see violence against citizens in the Districts, a violence that is presented even more graphically than the violence in the Arena from the first film. Visually, *Catching Fire* remains consistent with its prequel—District 12 is pale gray and harshly lit, implying the desolation and despair that resides there, while the Capitol is a world of garish outfits and brilliant colors. Notably, however, the handheld camera effect is used markedly less often. While the first film was infused with the sense of uncertainty and fear, this film is more confident and steady, a reflection of Katniss's own maturation. She is no longer encountering the Games for the first time, unaccustomed to the machinations and cruelty of this world. Instead, she is increasingly confident and ready to fight for her people—the camera captures this bravery with direct, steady shots, lingering over the determined and unblinking face of the actress.

As *Catching Fire* also does away with the strict first-person point of view present in the novels, audiences continue to see more of the backstage strategizing that prepares for the coming revolution, in particular through game designer Plutarch Heavensbee (Philip Seymour Hoffman) subtly manipulating President Snow. The novel provides several hints that Heavensbee might be

on the side of the revolution, but the film, with its ability to give the audience information Katniss does not know, provides much clearer hints that this is the case. When the film ends and Katniss is finally told about the conspiracy and the ongoing rebellion, audiences are in on the ploy. The film's Katniss goes relatively quickly from anger at being kept in ignorance to fury at the Capitol, having learned that they destroyed District 12; the Katniss of the books takes much longer in comprehending this reality, and the first part of *Mockingjay* is spent with Katniss processing the emotional and intellectual ramifications of this destruction. As Katniss describes it in the novel, "The memories swirl as I try to sort out what is true and what is false. What series of events led me to be standing in the ruins of my city?" The film, however, moves almost immediately to an empowered Katniss, ready for justice.

Mockingjay: Part 1 (the final book being split into two films) marks a further shift away from the visual style and focus of the first film. Panem now more closely resembles an apocalyptic landscape then a dystopian one, and the thrills of trying to survive in the violent Arena are replaced instead with the horror of a war-torn landscape. The color palette of the film, which has been one of the clearest indications of mood and meaning in previous installments, is now almost entirely consumed by the pale grays and browns of District 12—even Effie Trinket (Elizabeth Banks), previously the most colorful character, is largely denied any color. Taken in concert with the previous films, this is not a departure stylistically, but rather an intensification for a very particular effect. The war is underway, the movie darker and more violent than any of its predecessors, and the time for bright glamour has come to a definitive end.

In this darker landscape, the film also places greater emphasis on the power of images and propaganda. While the Games have always been a media event intended to manipulate the Panem public, in the war-torn world of *Mockingjay*, the rebels engage in their own propaganda battle, creating films that star Katniss in order to stir revolt. The Capitol responds with films starring their prisoner, Peeta (Josh Hutcherson). The bombed out landscapes and sweeping rubble of the film are even more powerful than the book's descriptions, which render the world with lines such as "The summer's been scorching hot and dry as a bone. There's been next to no rain to disturb the piles of ash left by the attack." More importantly, however, as Katniss eventually accepts her iconic status and the camera frames her in heroic shots (far removed from the shaky camera of the first film), it becomes clear how easily images and media can be manipulated, a core theme of the series.

As warships and bombs replace knives and arrows, *Mockingjay: Part 1* displays a markedly different style and mood than the first film, yet still one that is cohesive with the Hunger Games series as a whole. What started primarily from the perspective of Katniss, driven by her bewilderment and desperate hope to survive in the unfair games, ends as an outward problem, implicating every single person in Panem. The shaky camera that showed us only a sliver of Katniss's face as she entered the Reaping is now a wide, encompassing shot of the young hero, defiant in the rubble of a former city. This progression, from interior turmoil to political struggle, is a progression of maturation, of youth coming to not only live in the world, but take charge of its future. As a young adult dystopia, this is the ultimate theme of *The Hunger Games*—the story is not about Katniss or Panem, but rather about what happens when one person realizes she has a responsibility to her world and the people that surround her, whether she wishes to or not.

Significance

Both the film and book versions of the Hunger Games series have been extraordinary successes, commercially as well as critically, and their stories and characters have become touchstones of popular culture in the twenty-first century. In the United States, over 65 million copies of the books were sold by 2014, while the film series by 2014 had grossed more than $2 billion across the world (a number that does not include the final installment, set for release in 2015). The films have also set numerous records for opening night film sales.

Similar young adult dystopian novels-turned-film-series such as *The Maze Runner* and *Divergent* have found large audiences as well, while studios and publishing houses have a significant number of works in the genre planned for the coming years. The Hunger Games, however, remains the critical and commercial apex of the dystopian resurgence in popular culture. Critics and academic papers have explored the film's relationship to teenage distrust of authority (especially in relation to protest movements such as the Occupy movement), while Katniss has emerged as a sort of feminist icon, one of the most powerful and dangerous forces in a frightening world. What some critics at first dismissed as an exploitive film, reveling in teenagers killing other teenagers, has

instead become a sophisticated political allegory. Protesters against the military government in Thailand were even arrested in 2014 for using the three-finger salute that originated as a sign of rebellion in the Hunger Games. With the final film yet to be released and books and movies continuing to sell at a startling rate, it seems certain that both the commercial success and cultural importance of the Hunger Games will evolve further over time.

T. Fleischmann, MFA

Further Reading

Beck, Bernard. "Baby's Gone A-Hunting: The Hunger Games, Bully, and Struggling to Grow Up." *Multicultural Perspectives* 15.1 (2013): 27–30. *Academic Search Premier*. Web. 31 Jan. 2015. <http://search.ebscohost.com/login.aspx?direct=true&db=aph&AN=85408051&site=ehost-live&scope=site>.

Moore, Suzanne. "Why The Hunger Games' Katniss Everdeen Is a Role Model for Our Times." *Guardian*. Guardian News and Media, 27 Nov. 2013. Web. 26 Feb. 2015. <http://www.theguardian.com/commentisfree/2013/nov/27/why-hunger-games-katniss-everdeen-role-model-jennifer-lawrence>.

Rosen, Sarah Maya, and David M. Rosen. "Representing Child Soldiers in Fiction and Film." *Peace Review* 24.3 (2012): 305–12. *Academic Search Premier*. Web. 31 Jan. 2015. <http://search.ebscohost.com/login.aspx?direct=true&db=aph&AN=79195290&site=ehost-live&scope=site>.

Bibliography

Collins, Suzanne. "An Interview with Suzanne Collins." Interview by James Blasingame. *Jour. of Adolescent & Adult Literacy* 52.8 (2009): 726–27. *Literary Reference Center*. Web. 31 Jan. 2015. <http://search.ebscohost.com/login.aspx?direct=true&db=lfh&AN=39260027&site=lrc-live>.

Mydans, Seth. "Thai Protestors Are Detained after Using 'Hunger Games' Salute." *New York Times*. New York Times, 20 Nov. 2014. Web. 26 Feb. 2015. <http://www.nytimes.com/2014/11/21/world/asia/thailand-protesters-hunger-games-salute.html>.

Pondiscio, Robert. "The Hunger Games Is a Civics Lesson." *Wall Street Journal*. Dow Jones, 4 Dec. 2013. Web. 26 Feb. 2015. <http://www.wsj.com/articles/SB10001424052702303367080457923445136 2849142>

I Am Number Four

The Book

Author: Pittacus Lore, pseudonym of James Frey (b. 1969) and Jobie Hughes (b. 1980)
First published: 2010

The Film

Director: D. J. Caruso (b. 1965)
Screenplay by: Alfred Gough, Miles Millar, and Marti Noxon
Starring: Alex Pettyfer, Timothy Olyphant, Teresa Palmer, Dianna Agron, and Callan McAuliffe

Context

Books and films about aliens on Earth have been popular since at least the 1950s (and even earlier, as in H. G. Wells's 1898 novel *The War of the Worlds*). The 1950s and '60s saw a growing interest in outer space, and they also produced numerous alleged sightings of unidentified flying objects (UFOs). Sometimes extraterrestrials were imagined as having friendly intentions, but far more often their plans were depicted as hostile.

Both versions of *I Am Number Four* present both friendly and hostile aliens. John (Alex Pettyfer) and Henri (Timothy Olyphant), the two main characters, have fled Lorien, their home planet, seeking to escape vicious creatures that have pillaged and decimated it. These creatures, the Mogadorians, not only plan to hunt down and kill John and a few other refugees like him; they also intend to conquer Earth and destroy its inhabitants. The Lorien refugees are eventually aided by a few friends on Earth. Both the book and film suggest that one's worth—whether good or bad—is not determined by one's origins but rather by one's values, motives, and conduct.

In some respects, then, the novel and the movie embrace the kind of multiculturalism increasingly influential in twenty-first-century America, especially in education and in popular culture. Superficial distinctions (including whether or not one is human or nonhuman) seem less important than shared values. Both the book and movie suggest that true friendship, rooted in real virtue, can transcend unimportant differences, including place of origin. Interestingly enough, however, neither version of *I Am Number Four* includes a diversity of characters in terms of ethnicity and sexual orientation; all the main characters are white and heterosexual.

Both the novel and film deal with bullying at school, an issue of importance to young adults that has been increasingly covered in the media and discussed in public in recent years. In some ways, the Mogadorians are evil bullies writ large.

Film Analysis

As a novel, *I Am Number Four* is straightforward both in story and in style. It is told effectively in simple, unadorned first-person prose by protagonist John Smith. John and other special youth, accompanied by single, wise guardians, have been sent from Lorien to Earth. There, in time, they can nurture their special powers and, ideally, one day free Lorien. In the meantime, Mogadorian thugs are trying to track down and kill these special youth. Three have already been murdered. John is Number Four and is thus next in line for destruction. Therefore he and Henri have been moving all over the United States, keeping a low profile to escape detection.

The most obvious difference between the book and the film is the relative absence of John's first-person narrative voice in the movie. It is heard occasionally, but for the most part the filmmakers tell the story objectively. Viewers of the film thus gain less detailed insight into John's feelings, thoughts, and character than do readers of the book. Moreover, the film's John seems far more mature and independent than he is in the novel. In print, he is merely fifteen years old. In the movie, he is played by Alex Pettyfer, who was twenty-one when he was offered the role and who often looks even older.

One especially appealing aspect of the book is its emphasis on the close relationship between young John and Henri, his middle-aged (or even older) tutor and guardian. The book's Henri is a loving, beloved father figure. He and John obviously care deeply for one another. Henri provides John not only with wisdom but also with factual, practical information about Lorien's history. In contrast, in the film the relationship between Pettyfer and the youthful-looking Timothy Olyphant (who plays Henri) seems immediately testy. John and Henri in the movie could easily be younger and older brothers. Their relationship seems strained throughout, and the fact that Henri dies much earlier in the film than in the book gives them less time to bond than in the novel, where their relationship had already seemed strong right from the start. Henri's death in the book is more powerfully affecting than in the film.

Another key difference between the book and film involves the absence, in the movie, of flashbacks depicting the destruction of Lorien. These are prominently featured in the book. They help readers understand various matters, including how beautiful Lorien once was, how much the Loriens damaged their own planet through short-sighted, misguided behavior, how fierce the fight was between the Loriens and Mogadorians, and how viciously the Mogadorians overcame nearly all resistance. The book lets readers know, well in advance of the climax, how much John, Henri, and all Earthlings have to fear if the Mogadorians ever achieve their plans to conquer the planet. In the film, the Mogadorians seem much less overwhelmingly terrifying than in the book. In fact, one Mogadorian is even presented as a snide jokester who delights in toying with unintelligent Earthlings. The Mogadorians shop in supermarkets, intimidate passing motorists, and are in general played for laughs in ways that never happen in the novel.

Sam (Callan McAuliffe), John's teenaged friend, seems much pluckier and more active in the movie than in the novel. In the book, he is more obviously a bullied "nerd"; in the movie, he is very much a main player, especially in the final battle. The movie also includes a new character, Sam's mean-spirited stepfather, who does not appear in the novel.

Another difference between versions involves Mark (Jake Abel), the high school jock who torments both John and Sam. Ultimately he becomes a kind of hero in the book. In the movie, Mark remains a bully and is bullied himself by a particularly sadistic Mogadorian. Finally, Number Six (Teresa Palmer)—who shows up just in time to help John and his friends battle the evil creatures—is more obviously a sexy vixen in the film than in the book. She rides a big red motorcycle, sports skin-tight leather pants, and makes suggestive, wise-cracking comments to John. In this way as well as in many others, the film seems designed for an older audience than the book.

Like most fantasy sci-fi films, especially any involving conflict between good and evil, *I Am Number Four* strongly emphasizes contrasts between light and darkness. Most of the ominous, frightening scenes take place at night, when it is difficult both for the characters and the audience to see clearly. This contrast is especially emphasized at the very end of the film, when viewers see the charred, smoking remains of the football field where the climactic battle has just taken place. The field, filmed at first up close and then from overhead, is now a dark, gaping pit, illuminated mostly by embers. And then, suddenly, viewers find themselves near a lush green field of crops, right outside an old church, with the sun shining brightly and tall trees both close by and in the distance. The switch from one field to its opposite is fairly obvious, as are many techniques in this film, including the final drive off into the west, toward the setting sun. Such imagery, however, is also archetypal, rooted deep in human psychology. With its handsome young hero, beautiful young love interest, loyal sidekick, dangerous villains, and even its faithful dog, both versions of *I Am Number Four* exploit motifs, symbolism, and narrative elements that are as old as story-telling itself. If the book does so more successfully than the movie, that, too, is not at all unusual.

Significance

I Am Number Four cost roughly $50 million to make and grossed, in various forms (including home media), roughly $166 million. Although some critics admired the movie, most were negative or indifferent in their reviews and the sequel or sequels obviously prepared for at the close of the film have not materialized. In general, the movie was less successful than its creators, backers, and intended audiences had hoped.

I Am Number Four is probably most significant for the ways it helps perpetuate many standard features of young adult films. Male heroism, a tender love interest, protest against bullies, and friendship between apparent opposites (such as the nerd and the superhero) are long likely to remain popular with young adult audiences. More broadly, the film appeals to many common human fantasies, especially that of a small band of outnumbered, ill-equipped, but virtuous allies triumphing over seemingly unstoppable evil.

Both the film and book, however, are also typical of contemporary narratives in their emphasis on heroic females. Without the help of Number Six, Number Four might never have survived, let alone triumphed. Heroism in the early twenty-first century is just as often a trait of women as of men, and the film version of *I Am Number Four* is particularly notable for the agility, strength, sauciness, and even sarcasm displayed by its daring biker-heroine. In this sense, the film provides vivid evidence of the ways women's roles have changed, both on screen and in real life, since the mid-to-late twentieth century. In older sci-fi films, it would have been unusual to see any crucial heroine, let alone one as prominent and talented as Number Six. This movie shows men and women cooperatively fighting and defeating evil and saving each other's lives. If anything, Number Six seems much more stereotypically masculine than Number Four. He seems more passive and sensitive than she, especially as the film concludes. It is Number Six, after all, who takes the lead, on her bright red motorcycle, with her hair blowing in the wind, as the young heroes head off, in the final frames, toward their next adventure.

Robert C. Evans, PhD

Further Reading

Aldiss, Brian W. "Outside Practical Perspectives." *Science Fiction Studies* 36.2 (2009): 193–94. *Literary Reference Center*. Web. 13 Apr. 2015. <http://search.ebscohost.com/login.aspx?direct=true&db=lfh&AN=43386925&site=lrc-live>.

Flynn, John L. *War of the Worlds: From Wells to Spielberg*. Owings Mills: Galactic, 2005. Print.

Johnston, Keith M. *Science Fiction Film: A Critical Introduction*. New York: Berg, 2011. Print.

Bibliography

Bowles, Scott. "Concept for 'I Am Number Four' Is Anything but Alien." *USA Today* 17 Feb. 2011: n. pag. *NewsBank*. Web. 16 Apr. 2015. <http://search.ebscohost.com/login.aspx?direct=true&db=edsnbk&AN=1357BA81D8F3A260&site=eds-live>.

Rev. of *I Am Number Four*, by Pittacus Lore. *Publishers Weekly* 257.28 (2010): 131. *Literary Reference Center*. Web. 13 Apr. 2015. <http://search.ebscohost.com/login.aspx?direct=true&db=lfh&AN=52570229&site=lrc-live>.

Kraus, Daniel. Rev. of *I Am Number Four*, by Pittacus Lore. Booklist 106.19/20 (2010): 53. *Literary Reference Center*. Web. 13 Apr. 2015. <http://search.ebscohost.com/login.aspx?direct=true&db=lfh&AN=51809424&site=lrc-live>.

Ritter, Cynthia K. Rev. of *I Am Number Four*, by Pittacus Lore. *Horn Book Magazine*. 86.5 (2010): 82–83. *Literary Reference Center*. Web. 16 Apr. 2015. <http://search.ebscohost.com/login.aspx?direct=true&db=lfh&AN=53883660&site=lrc-live.>

I Know What You Did Last Summer

The Book

Author: Lois Duncan (b. 1934)
First published: 1973

The Film

Director: Jim Gillespie
Screenplay by: Kevin Williamson
Starring: Jennifer Love Hewitt, Sarah Michelle Gellar, Freddie Prinze Jr., Ryan Phillippe, and Anne Heche

Context

The novelist Lois Duncan—whose real name is Lois Arquette—got her start writing lurid "true" confessions for pulp magazines. A single mother of three, Duncan's most successful "confession" was titled "I Wanted to Have an Affair with a Teenage Boy." She began writing popular suspense novels in the late 1960s and became an early master of the genre for young adults. One of her novels—popular with teenage readers but otherwise unrecognized at the time—was titled *I Know What You Did Last Summer*, about a group of teenagers, bound for adult success, who hit a little boy on his bicycle with their car. Afraid of punishment, they leave him in the road and he dies. A year later, the book's protagonist receives an ominous message that reads, "I know what you did last summer." The note sparks a terrifying game of cat and mouse in which a mysterious stalker seeks revenge for the boy's death. The novel was published in 1973. Duncan continued to publish suspense novels by the dozens until the death of her daughter in 1989, and returned to the genre in the late 1990s. The rights for *I Know What You Did Last Summer* were optioned around the same time. It was the first major motion picture adaptation of one of Duncan's books, though she was not involved in the making of the film and her name was never used in its marketing.

When Duncan watched the film for the first time upon its premier in 1997, she was horrified—and not in a good way. Not only was the film's plot markedly different from the plot of her book, it was, unlike the novel, a bloodbath. "It's not just like I'm real picky," Duncan told Laura Lippman for the *Baltimore Sun*. "This [film] simply made statements that were upsetting to me, by trivializing violence and making murder seem like a game, which was not true to the spirit of my book." She acknowledged that the studio had the legal right to tell the story the way it did, but her reaction was unsurprising. Her own daughter, Kaitlyn Arquette, had been brutally murdered in what Duncan still suspects was a contract killing less than ten years before. The studio claimed not to have known about the murder, though Duncan wrote a book about the case titled *Who Killed My Daughter?* in 1992. Though she did not approve of the film, she used its box office success to draw public attention to her daughter's case. The murder remains unsolved.

Film Analysis

Though the film version of *I Know What You Did Last Summer* makes several deviations from the novel, the most crucial difference between the book and the film lies in the fact that Duncan wrote a suspense novel, while screenwriter Kevin Williamson wrote a horror film. Both writers employed classic tropes to tell the tale, but those tropes are of two very different genres. For instance, in Duncan's version, there is no serial killer. After the event in question, the book's four teenage characters—Julie, Ray, Helen, and, Barry—report the accident anonymously and make a pact to keep their guilt a secret. They only find out later that the boy died in the road. After a year passes, each character begins receiving strange messages from someone who knows what they have done. Barry is shot, but recovers. They struggle under the tremendous pressure of living a lie—though, like the film, the protagonist Julie feels that guilt the most strongly—until it is discovered that Julie's new beau, Bud, is the little boy's half-brother. Bud is foiled in his attempt to kill the teenagers, but in the end, their crime is revealed.

Duncan's revenge plot is bloodless (with the exception of Barry) but horrifying in its thematic gravity. It explores the guilt of taking another human being's life. Williamson's version raises some of the questions associated with the teens' guilt only to neatly resolve them through an incredible—and highly implausible—twist at the end of the film. But the teen slasher genre is not interested in complex emotions. The film adaptation of *I Know What You Did Last Summer* owes more of a debt to classic teen slasher films like *Halloween* (1978) and *A Nightmare on Elm Street* (1984) than the book on which it is based. These films established tropes—including the serial killer with a calling card, the final confrontation, the "final girl"—that would be repeated

again and again, and even satirized in Williamson and Wes Craven's 1996 film *Scream*. Williamson lifted Duncan's characters—and a very rough semblance of her plot—and rearranged them to fit the demands of the teen slasher genre.

The film opens with an aerial shot of the North Carolina coast (Duncan's book takes place in New Mexico) and focuses in on a teenager sitting on a cliff. It is the Fourth of July in a small fishing village, and Julie (Jennifer Love Hewitt), Ray (Freddie Prinze Jr.), and Barry (Ryan Phillippe) are celebrating Helen's (Sarah Michelle Gellar) beauty pageant win. She has been crowned Croaker Queen, after a local fish, but as Roger Ebert wrote in a review, the pun is clearly intended. Like *Scream*, *I Know What You Did Last Summer* has moments of self-awareness, though it is, on the whole, a straightforward genre film. Drinking on the beach, the foursome discuss an urban legend in which a teenage couple—engaging in premarital sex—hear a scratching noise, only to find a giant fishing hook embedded in their car door. Julie and Helen joke that they know the story is not true because such stories are made up to discourage women from having sex. A few beats later, Julie loses her virginity to her boyfriend, Ray. The scene is important because Julie, played by a fresh-faced Hewitt, is the film's "final girl." The trope, epitomized by Julie and Helen, was coined by feminist scholar Carol J. Clover. A horror film's "final girl," the one who survives, often does so by dint of her virginity. Williamson half-heartedly subverts this trope by having Julie lose her virginity, but the sex itself is immaterial. Her character is smart and otherwise virtuous unlike (the film suggests) her vain friend Helen, who wears short skirts and oozes sexual confidence.

Driving home from the beach—with Ray at the wheel, not the drunk and belligerent Barry as in the book—their car hits something. They stop the car and find a man's body. Williamson softens the emotional blow of the killing by making the victim an adult, but raises the stakes by having the characters dispose of the body in the lake. The plot chugs along as in the book, except instead of a faceless stalker, the teens are terrorized by a serial killer wearing a fisherman's slicker who has a hook for a hand. The frightful image fulfills the slasher genre's most important trope: killers must have a calling card. Thanks to the earlier reference to the urban legend, this killer has a fishing hook, just as Freddie Krueger, of *A Nightmare on Elm Street*, had knives for fingers. As the teens desperately try to find out who he is, the fisherman continues to kill, his methods escalating in brutality. The first of the main characters to die is Barry (the jock) followed by Helen (the beauty queen). With Ray a suspect, that leaves only Julie, who unwittingly climbs aboard the killer's boat to face him, alone, in the film's heart-thumping "final confrontation."

In the end, Julie and Ray survive and the killer is thought to be dead, but actually escapes—providing another teen slasher trope, the possibility of a sequel. But the film ends on a starkly different note than the book. Through an elaborate twist, Julie discovers that she and her friends did not actually kill anyone that night the summer before. The body belonged to the serial killer who was "not quite dead," another trope. Williamson lets his characters off the hook (literally and figuratively) and thus undercuts the single moral take-away from Duncan's book—that one must take responsibility for one's actions. While Duncan warns readers about the perils of living a lie, Williamson's script says lie harder; the film's marketing tagline was "If you're going to bury the truth, make sure it stays buried."

But as Duncan herself said, this was all fair game, both legally and in terms of genre. Teen slasher films inhabit a crude moral universe. Like the trope of the "final girl," character traits are deemed either good or bad—there is no in-between—and crucially, those traits exist only to foreshadow whether that character will live or die. Barry was mean and unrepentant—he died. Helen was too sexual—she died. Ray wanted to report the crime—he lived. Julie tried, on several occasions, to repent for the crime—she lived. In the film, the teenagers' guilt is merely a mechanism to introduce the real point of the film, which is survival.

Significance

Coming on the heels of the wildly popular horror film *Scream*, *I Know What You Did Last Summer* grossed over $125 million worldwide. The inevitable sequel, *I Still Know What You Did Last Summer*, came out the next year, in 1998. It starred Hewitt and Prinze Jr., as well as Mekhi Phifer and Brandy Norwood. The story is similar—the group is terrorized by the same killer, played by Ben Willis—but it takes place at a resort in the Bahamas. A third, direct-to-video installment titled *I'll Always Know What You Did Last Summer* was released in 2006. The original and its sequel were both financially successful but panned by critics, including Ebert. However, the franchise remains popular because of its predictability, not in spite of it. In 2015 Sony

announced that it planned to remake the original film, setting a tentative release date for 2016.

I Know What You Did Last Summer was the first of Duncan's novels to be made into a big-screen production. Earlier that year, however, her 1978 novel *Killing Mr. Griffin* was adapted as a made-for-television film that aired on a major network channel. In 2009, her more lighthearted book *Hotel for Dogs* (1971) was made into a film starring Emma Roberts and Lisa Kudrow, and in 2014, the author of the Twilight series, Stephenie Meyer, signed on to produce a film adaptation of Duncan's 1974 thriller *Down a Dark Hall*, about a boarding-school student with supernatural abilities.

Molly Hagan

Further Reading
Lippman, Laura. "The Story behind 'Last Summer' Writer: Lois Duncan Will Use the Film Version of Her Book, 'I Know What You Did Last Summer,' To Draw Attention to the Murder of Her Daughter." *Baltimore Sun*. Tribune Interactive, 19 Nov. 1997. Web. 6 Mar. 2015. <http://articles.baltimoresun.com/1997-11-19/features/1997323052_1_lois-duncan-kait-duncan-wrote>.

Gettel, Oliver. "'Oculus' Writers to Reboot 'I Know What You Did Last Summer.'" *Los Angeles Times*. Los Angeles Times, 15 Sept. 2014. Web. 6 Mar. 2015.

Van Gelder, Lawrence. "Creepy Guys, Ghost Stories, Teen-Age Sex: Uh-Oh." Rev. of *I Know What You Did Last Summer*, dir. by Jim Gillespie. *New York Times*. New York Times, 17 Oct. 1997. Web. 6 Mar. 2015. <http://www.nytimes.com/movie/review?res=9F0CE3D7123FF934A25753C1A961958260>.

Bibliography
Duncan, Lois. "An Interview with Lois Duncan." Interview by Joan Kaywell. *Journal of Adolescent & Adult Literacy* 52.6 (2009): 545–7. *Literary Reference Center*. Web. 6 Mar. 2015. <http://search.ebscohost.com/login.aspx?direct=true&db=lfh&AN=37012205&site=lrc-live>.

Kenny, Glenn. "The Rise and Fall (and Rise?) of Teen Horror Movies." *Salon*. Salon Media, 3 May 2010. Web. 6 Mar. 2015. <http://www.salon.com/2010/05/03/teen_horror_films/>.

Lodge, Sally. "Lois Duncan Thrillers Get an Update." *Publishers Weekly*. PWxyz, 23 Sept. 2010. Web. 6

Mar. 2015. <http://www.publishersweekly.com/pw/by-topic/childrens/childrens-book-news/article/44553-lois-duncan-thrillers-get-an-update.html>.

Stelloh, Tim. "Who Killed Lois Duncan's Daughter?" *BuzzFeed News*. BuzzFeed, 30 May 2014. Web. 6 Mar. 2015. <http://www.buzzfeed.com/timstelloh/who-killed-lois-duncan-s-daughter#.odYJQewvJ>.

If I Stay

The Book

Author: Gayle Forman (b. 1970)
First published: 2009

The Film

Director: R. J. Cutler (b. 1962)
Screenplay by: Shauna Cross
Starring: Chloë Grace Moretz, Jamie Blackley, Mireille Enos, Joshua Leonard, and Stacy Keach

Context

Frank Capra's 1946 classic *It's a Wonderful Life* encourages viewers to appreciate the simple joys of being alive, especially the joys of close family relationships. These joys, Capra suggests, are too often taken for granted. Much the same message is communicated in both the novel and film versions of *If I Stay*. Mia (Chloë Grace Moretz in the film), the teenage narrator of both versions, is on the brink of enjoying an even more wonderful life than the one she has already experienced. She is part of an immensely loving family, has good friends, and has recently fallen in love with Adam, whom she finds attractive as much for his genuine, thoughtful personality as for his musical talent and popularity with his peers. Significantly, the novel mentions that one of the only two times Mia has seen Adam cry occurred when they watched *It's a Wonderful Life* together. The film version of *If I Stay* (2014), even more strongly than the book, communicates the joys of Mia's family life, and the film also stresses that it is precisely this kind of close connection with a family that Adam (Jamie Blackley) misses and yearns for.

The emphasis on the importance of family and friends in both versions of *If I Stay* is not surprising, nor is the appeal of that emphasis. Over the past fifty years, divorce rates in the United States have increased. More and more children are born out of wedlock and are raised in single-parent households. The kind of traditional homelife enjoyed by Mia, which is presented in especially attractive ways in the film, is increasingly rare. Adam, who is depicted in the film as the child of a broken home and an uncaring father who has essentially abandoned his son, is the kind of character to whom many contemporary young people will be able to relate.

In these ways, *If I Stay* resembles other recent, popular films adapted from young adult novels, such as *Eragon* (2006), *Hoot* (2006), *Beastly* (2011)*, and *City of Bones* (2013). In these works as well as in a remarkable number of other literature and films aimed at young adult audiences, teenagers are often on their own, with parents who are distant either literally, figuratively, or both. Mia is unusual among recent protagonists in young adult fiction and film in having a loving, intact family. But that family is essentially destroyed in a horrific auto accident shortly after the book and film begin. Suddenly Mia finds herself in much the same situation as Adam: alone, cut off from loved ones, and yearning for the kind of family life she once was able to take for granted but that is now lost to her forever.

Film Analysis

Perhaps the most striking structural feature of both the novel and the film versions of *If I Stay* is the use of constant cross-cutting between Mia's life before and after the terrible accident—an accident that claims the lives of everyone in her family except Mia herself. Both the book and the film gain richness, resonance, and irony as readers and viewers alternate back and forth between Mia's life as it once was and her current tenuous grip on existence. Throughout both versions of the story, suspense grows: neither the book nor the film reveals, until the very end, whether Mia will live or die. Even at the very end her ultimate fate remains unclear. The film and novel help reveal how rich her life has been, how much talent and potential she possesses, and how much will be lost (even more than has been lost already) if she also loses the will or the struggle to live.

One advantage the film has over the book is that the film relies less than the novel on Mia's first-person narration. The film dramatizes events that the novel more often simply describes from Mia's limited perspective. The film also contains much more dialogue than the book, and the film's point of view is more objective and distanced than that of the novel. The other characters in the film seem more three-dimensional on screen than they often seem in the book. They come alive as independent people rather than as figures Mia merely remembers and talks about. This is especially true of Adam. He comes across as a much more intriguing, fleshed-out individual in the film than in the novel. The film helps viewers better understand his attraction both to Mia as well as to the kind of family Mia comes from.

In moments from the film, such as when Adam first spends time with Mia's family and when he rejects the idea of a long-distance relationship conducted via Skype, viewers sense the void at the center of Adam's existence. He tries to fill that void, in part, through his commitment to his music. In the novel, his devotion to his career as a rock musician can seem merely formulaic or even frivolous—the sort of thing typical of many teenage boys. In the film, however, Adam emerges as an even more sensitive, more caring, more mature, and more loving character than he had already seemed in the book. He yearns for real, enduring love, and he also likes the idea of being part of a loving, committed, and supportive family.

This is the sort of romantic young man who might especially appeal to the target audience of both the book and the film, which consists largely of young women. But Adam is also the sort of young man with whom large numbers of young people in general—male or female—might be able to identify. He, far more than Mia, is missing something important in his life. He is missing a real family. In Mia, he sees the opportunity for the kind of meaningful relationship absent from his current existence. This hope is part of the reason he seems to want so desperately for Mia to survive.

Love—and especially love within families—is a key theme of the book and particularly of the film. One way the film underscores this theme quite effectively involves the use of occasional scenes that resemble compilations of home videos. These are interspersed at various points in the film. Each time a member of Mia's family dies, the screen is filled with a fast-moving montage of grainy-looking flashbacks featuring that person and his or her interactions with Mia and other family members. By making these scenes look as if they were shot with a home video recorder—and thus distinguishing them sharply from the vivid professional photography of the film as a whole—the director subtly reinforces the importance of family life and family love as key themes of this film.

The film, with its soundtrack, has another advantage over the book because music is an important motif in both versions of *If I Stay*. Adam is as devoted to rock music as Mia is devoted to classical cello music. Each appreciates the other's music and especially the passion and commitment that a true devotion to music involves. Both the film and the book suggest that genuine love and respect transcend superficial differences. Adam and Mia are both open-minded in their ability to appreciate each other's music as well as each other as people. The film devotes much time to actual musical performances, including Adam's singing and playing at rock concerts and Mia's performances on the cello, adding another dimension of beauty to its presentation of the lives of these energetic, talented young people. Viewers get to see and hear, rather than simply read about, the musical gifts of the two key characters. The potential death of Mia in the film will lead not merely to her own nonexistence but to the silencing of the beauty she creates with her cello—a beauty memorably audible at many points throughout the film.

Significance

If I Stay was made with an estimated budget of $11 million; it grossed more than $78 million and has earned even more income since being released on home media. Yet critical reaction to the film was mostly negative, focusing on its formulaic tendencies. At the same time, positive amateur reviews suggested that the production reached its target audience successfully; regular filmgoers admired the film more than most critics did.

If I Stay is a significant young adult film because of its strong emphasis on the thoughts, feelings, and perspective of an intelligent, talented young woman. In a time when many films made for young audiences feature supernatural heroes, otherworldly villains, and fantastic adventures and events, *If I Stay* is relatively unusual in presenting credible young people facing an utterly believable crisis. While film adaptations of dystopian novels have become increasingly popular, this film is instead set in the real, everyday world. Both the film and the book depict the lives of young people in thoroughly convincing terms, and indeed the film may have an advantage over the book because less of the film is filtered through Mia's limited first-person point of view.

The film, with its striking locations, effective acting, subtle use of background music, and depiction of various credible social scenes, sometimes has an almost documentary feel to it. This effect is not surprising given the fact that the film's director began as a documentary filmmaker. *If I Stay* is a basically realistic film about a young woman, her family, her friends, and a crisis she faces. The film does not depend on werewolves, vampires, car chases, or battles with aliens to make its appeal. While it does have a supernatural element in the form of Mia's comatose limbo, it mainly deals with issues anyone might someday face, and offers a sense of the preciousness of life to which anyone can relate.

Robert C. Evans, PhD

Further Reading

Cutler, R. J., and Gayle Forman. "Director RJ Cutler and Author Gayle Forman Talk *If I Stay*, the Emotional Response, and the Potential Sequel *Where She Went*." Interview by Christina Radish. *Collider*. Complex Media, 19 Aug. 2014. Web. 15 Apr. 2015. <http://collider.com/rj-cutler-gayle-forman-if-i-stay-interview/>.

Moretz, Chloë Grace. "*If I Stay*'s Chloë Grace Moretz: 'I Have Literally No Idea' What's Cool with Teenagers." Interview by Nolan Feeney. *Time*. Time, 22 Aug. 2014. Web. 15 Aug. 2015. <http://time.com/3155172/chloe-grace-moretz-if-i-stay-interview/>.

Bibliography

Burnett, Matia. "'Stay'-ing Power." *Publishers Weekly* 28 July 2014: 15. *Literary Reference Center*. Web. 15 Apr. 2015. <http://search.ebscohost.com/login.aspx?direct=true&db=lfh&AN=97306889&site=lrc-live>.

Chang, Justin. "Film Review: 'If I Stay.'" Rev. of If I Stay, dir. R. J. Cutler. *Variety*. Variety Media, 19 Aug. 2014. Web. 15 Apr. 2015. <http://variety.com/2014/film/reviews/film-review-if-i-stay-1201283269/>.

Hornaday, Ann. 'If I Stay' Movie Review: An End-of-Summer Tear-Jerker." Rev. of *If I Stay*, dir. R. J. Cutler. *Washington Post*. Washington Post, 21 Aug. 2014. Web. 15 Apr. 2015. <http://www.washingtonpost.com/goingoutguide/if-i-stay-movie-review-an-end-of-summer-tear-jerker/2014/08/20/17248686-27a5-11e4-8593-da634b334390_story.html>.

Inkheart

The Book

Author: Cornelia Funke (b. 1958)
First published: 2003

The Film

Director: Iain Softley (b. 1956)
Screenplay by: David Lindsay-Abaire
Starring: Brendan Fraser, Eliza Bennett, Paul Bettany, Helen Mirren, Andy Serkis

Context

Fantasy in young adult literature has been one of the most popular genres throughout the twentieth and twenty-first centuries. In the early to mid-twentieth century, novels such as *The Wonderful Wizard of Oz* (1900) by L. Frank Baum, the Chronicles of Narnia series (1950–56) by C. S. Lewis, and the Chronicles of Prydain series (1964–73) by Lloyd Alexander became popular. *Inkheart*, which references *Oz* and other such works, was originally written in German but published in 2003 in German and English. The story was adapted for film in 2008–9, placing the release of the novel and the film in the midst of the publication (1997–2007) and film releases (2001–11) of the most popular young adult fantasy series of the early twenty-first century, Harry Potter.

Inkheart is the first in a series of novels known as the Inkheart trilogy, written by German writer Cornelia Funke. It was the second young adult book written by Funke, following the success of her first fantasy novel, *The Thief Lord* (2002). For director Iain Softley, the film marked his first young adult adaptation, although he had earned success for his vision in such speculative-fiction adaptations as the science-fiction film *K-Pax* (2001) and the gothic thriller *The Skeleton Key* (2005).

Taking its place as a notable addition to the young adult fantasy genre, *Inkheart* shares key elements of young adult fiction. For instance, it puts its young protagonist in an imaginative yet very dangerous world, much as Lewis Carroll does in the still-popular *Alice's Adventures in Wonderland* (1866). Another of the conventions of the young adult fantasy genre is the presence of an evil antagonist who creates obstacles and danger for the protagonist, but how much danger the hero faces has changed since the late nineteenth century. At the start of the twentieth century, even in the face of danger, most protagonists of young adult literature found themselves protected in some way or another from serious harm. They faced danger, but generally, it was too fantastic to be seriously threatening (as in *Alice's Adventures in Wonderland*) or there was an adult intermediary who was able to protect the protagonist. However, as children's literature scholar Melody Green notes, at the end of World War II, a shift took place in which child protagonists found themselves facing (and resolving) real danger on their own. This shift came to define speculative young adult fiction and the fantasy genre, and this element has arguably become an important element in its success. The dangers are real and often life threatening, and for young adult readers trying to navigate and make sense of their own lives, these books may present a way for them to deal with their own real-life issues and inner struggles by associating themselves with the problems and inner struggles of a character in an imaginary world, as scholar Sharon Black argues.

Inkheart is no exception to this rule as both the novel and the film focus on the young protagonist, Meggie, who is often put in life-threatening danger by the villain Capricorn and his minions. While Capricorn is a character that has been brought into the "real world" from a children's book (titled *Inkheart*), he is still a very serious threat to the heroes of the story. While he robs, plunders, and burns buildings to the ground in the style of a fairy-tale villain, he also commits cold-blooded murder without hesitation or regret. Although the book and film differ in the degree to which Meggie herself solves key problems or takes charge, the series as a whole provides Meggie opportunities in which to prove her mettle.

Film Analysis

The opening scene of the film differs from the first chapter of the novel as it begins with Mortimer "Mo" Folchart (Brendan Fraser) reading aloud to his infant daughter, Meggie. A voice-over narration explains a gift a few people called readers have, wherein the events, people, and things found in a book that they read aloud from appear in the real world. After this initial narration, the film then jumps ahead twelve years to a scene of Mo driving with the now-teenaged Meggie (Eliza Bennett).

The perspective of these initial scenes and the film in general are more objective than the novel, as the audience is given more information about the foundation of the story. In the novel, readers are dropped into the middle of the story and only learn about Mo's ability when

Meggie does. The first chapter, titled "A Stranger in the Night," immediately introduces a tone of mystery and suspense as Meggie wakes up to find a stranger in her yard staring up at her window in the middle of the night. Still sleepy, she looks out the window, and "the rain cast a kind of pallor on the darkness, and the stranger was little more than a shadow. Only his face gleamed white" (2). While the film does not attempt to create the same atmosphere of suspense, it does continue with the *in medias res* technique, as it does not explain why Meggie's mother is no longer present.

In the film, the stranger, Dustfinger (Paul Bettany), is introduced near the start of the narrative when Meggie and Mo visit a small mountain town in Europe. Immediately, Dustfinger warns Mo and Meggie of some unknown danger they are in as Capricorn (Andy Serkis) is close to finding them. Continuing the atmosphere of mystery, Capricorn's identity and why he is looking for them are not explained initially, nor is the relationship between Dustfinger and Mo, whom he calls Silvertongue. Mo and Meggie then quickly escape and drive to Italy to see Meggie's affluent great-aunt Elinor (Helen Mirren). The lack of information provided in both the book and the film are perhaps the most important storytelling devices, as they increase the suspense and thrill of the story. However, the choice of location for the film in the mountains of Italy works to provide an atmosphere of fantasy and magic in an otherwise ordinary world.

As the plot progresses and the characters start on different paths, the film, like the book, follows each story line, following the traditional third-person omniscient perspective, although staying mostly with Meggie.

One difference between the film and the book is the addition of animals, monsters, and other things brought into the real world through the readings of Mo, Meggie, or the misfortunate Darius (another reader with a stammer whom Capricorn captured and imprisoned). These new additions to the plot add a stronger magical atmosphere to the film. For example, when Mo and Meggie escape from Capricorn's jails for the first time, Mo reads the twister scene from *The Wonderful Wizard of Oz* in order to bring the tornado into the real world and distract the guards.

Similarly, the figure of the Shadow is taken to a much greater proportion in the film than in the novel. When Meggie reads the Shadow out of *Inkheart*, it stands tall before her made of burning ash without a face, "but it had eyes, terrible eyes, red as the embers of a hidden fire." Softley's vision is grander, taking the size of the Shadow to new heights, making him taller than the buildings of Capricorn's small village. These additions, combined with the use of special effects, give the film a more dramatic and intense atmosphere, looking to thrill audiences visually along with the storytelling.

The major theme of both book and film is the importance of literature and of reading to the world. With the exception of the characters read from *Inkheart*, literature and books themselves are very important to every major character. Yet while the major themes of the film remain relatively the same as the novel, there are a few slight differences in tone. The book focuses intensely on not just the power of literature, but of books themselves, seeming to mirror the author's, or at least the narrator's, strong affinity for the printed word. The physical features, including the covers, bindings, pages, and the words on them hold power in the world of *Inkheart*. At one point in the book, as Elinor, Mo, and Meggie are caught by Capricorn's men, who then burn all of Elinor's extensive book collection, Elinor says, "You know what they say: when people start burning books they'll soon burn human beings."

The film, however, is more interested in the literature, story, and indeed words themselves. While both novel and film empower the young adult protagonist, it is the film that gives Meggie the power not only to read, but also to write and create her own story. In the novel, it is the author of *Inkheart*, Fenoglio, who writes the new ending to the story that foils Capricorn's plot and Mo who reads aloud the final lines that finish off the malevolent Capricorn. In the film, Meggie must write the ending herself with a pen on her arm. This power over not only the reading of words but their creation as well might be seen to align Meggie more with the traditional protagonists of the young adult fantasy genre. Rather than rely on Mo to read the final paragraph, Meggie takes full control of the situation, needing no parental help or protection.

Significance

While the novel was received by readers and literary critics with generally high praise and good sales, the film met with mixed reception. The book was an international best seller and gained much critical attention as a great work of literature for younger readers. However, the film made a modest $62.4 million worldwide, barely making back its $60 million production budget. Its release in January 2009 was more than halfway through the run of films based on the Harry Potter series, which, in comparison, grossed between $250 and $400 million

for each of its eight films. It is difficult for any contemporary young adult fantasy book to escape from the shadow of Harry Potter, although *Inkheart* could have met with more success.

An area of success in the novel is the way that Funke brings the world of literature, fantasy, and imagination into reality. The world of Meggie and Mo is as unremorseful and raw as the real world, and the world of books adds something magical that both softens the harshness of reality and brings out the inherent creativity and imagination in the otherwise ordinary. While the film does achieve a good deal of success in mirroring these contrasts, it is possible to find fault with the "real" world of the film. It is still softened, not as gritty as it could be. Moreover, the departure of the plot of the film could be faulted similarly. Yet these departures are rather small in the scheme of film adaptation of novels in general. Ultimately, the major themes of the novel are generally held to and adopted by the film. Nevertheless, the adaptations of the other two internationally best-selling novels in the series, *Inkspell* (2005) and *Inkdeath* (2008), had not been put into production even five years after the release of *Inkheart*. Some reviewers, such as Claire E. Gross for the *Horn Book Magazine*, speculated that the film's more conclusive ending, which returned Dustfinger to his family in Inkworld, might have precluded the possibility of further film adaptations for the series; that interpretation may be sound, as *Inkspell* deals with Dustfinger's desperate quest to be read back into *Inkheart*.

Perhaps one of the elements most important to the success of the *Inkheart* film is the general popularity of the young adult fantasy genre. Funke's creativity is certainly another major factor in the success of the book, and the world that is created in both the film and the novel is both a frightening and yet comforting one. More importantly, the empowerment of a young protagonist and the appeal of the power available to young people in this book and young adult fantasy in general is one that drives this story just as many stories before.

Aaron Horton, MA

Further Reading

"Books at Heart of Film Releases This Winter." *Bookseller* 5362 (2008): 9. *Literary Reference Center.* Web. 6 Apr. 2015. <http://search.ebscohost.com/login.aspx?direct=true&db=lfh&AN=36125524&site=lrc-live>.

"Bringing Characters to Life." *Bookseller* 5082 (2003): 32. *Literary Reference Center*. Web. 6 Apr. 2015. <http://search.ebscohost.com/login.aspx?direct=true&db=lfh&AN=10202830&site=lrc-live>.

Bibliography

Black, Sharon. "The Magic of Harry Potter: Symbols and Heroes of Fantasy." *Children's Literature in Education* 34.3 (2003): 237–47. *Literary Reference Center*. Web. 6 Apr. 2015. <http://search.ebscohost.com/login.aspx?direct=true&db=lfh&AN=10665850&site=lrc-live>.

Green, Melody. "Jesus, Girard, and Twentieth-Century Fantasy for Young Adults." *Studies in the Literary Imagination* 46.2 (2013): 19–33. *Literary Reference Center*. Web. 6 Apr. 2015. <http://search.ebscohost.com/login.aspx?direct=true&db=lfh&AN=101079990&site=lrc-live>.

Gross, Claire E. "From Page to Screen: *Inkheart* the Movie." Rev. of *Inkheart*, dir. Iain Softley. *Horn Book Magazine*. Horn Book, n.d. Web. 6 Apr. 2015. <http://archive.hbook.com/resources/films/inkheart.asp>.

Jones, Diana Wynne. "Leaping Off the Page." Rev. of *Inkheart*, by Cornelia Funke. *Guardian*. Guardian News and Media, 21 Nov. 2003. Web. 6 Apr. 2015. <http://www.theguardian.com/books/2003/nov/22/featuresreviews.guardianreview31>.

Island of the Blue Dolphins

The Book

Author: Scott O'Dell (1898–1989)
First published: 1960

The Film

Director: James B. Clark (1908–2000)
Screenplay by: Jane Klove, Ted Sherdeman
Starring: Celia Kaye, Larry Domasin, Ann Daniel, Carlos Romero

Context

As a work of historical fiction, Scott O'Dell's *Island of the Blue Dolphins* was intended both to offer an interpretation of a unique life story from the nineteenth century and to inspire in its readers admiration for the romanticized version of the indigenous hunter-gatherer lifestyle it portrays. *Island of the Blue Dolphins* centers on the life of a young indigenous woman, based on a real-life historical figure: the last surviving member of the Nicoleño tribe of San Nicolas Island, off the southern coast of California. Following her discovery in 1853, this woman came to be known as the Lone Woman of San Nicolas Island; her real name was unknown, and she was later dubbed Juana Maria by Spanish missionaries. However, O'Dell was inspired to write the book out of an interest in naturalism more than anthropology. Specifically, he wrote it as a protest against the hunters who would decimate wild animal populations in the name of trade and profit.

The primary protagonist of both book and movie is a woman named Karana. At the opening of the story, she lives with her father, Chowig, and her younger brother, Ramo, in a small island village, of which Chowig is the chief. The villagers live close to nature, in domed huts of wood and bark, and they gather food from the abundant flora and fauna of the island and cook it in earthenware pots over a campfire. Their life on an isolated Pacific island is soon interrupted by a boat full of Aleut hunters (in the novel; in the film, the hunters are white) who, ultimately, break the terms of a trade deal they have made with the island's leaders, resulting in a battle that kills many of the men in the village. Through a series of further misfortunes, Karana and Ramo end up stranded on the island after the remaining villagers leave. When Ramo is subsequently killed by wild dogs, Karana becomes the sole human inhabitant of the island.

Although both book and movie were conceived as educational in nature, they must now be understood as products of their time, particularly with reference to their romanticized and somewhat paternalistic portrayal of the islanders. With the passage of time, the educational value of *Island of the Blue Dolphins* has moved beyond the realm of the historical tale it purports to convey and now also provides the opportunity to historicize and deconstruct the lens through which it assesses indigenous American history and culture.

Island of the Blue Dolphins was O'Dell's first work of young adult literature. Prior to its publication in 1960, he had published three novels and a historical travel guide for adults. Though each of O'Dell's books deals with a different topic, they are generally were set in or near California, which was both his native landscape and his inspiration.

James B. Clark was a prolific director who focused on films for young audiences, many of which had an animal-centered theme. Among the most renowned of his productions were the film *Flipper* (1963) and several episodes of the television shows *Lassie* (1954–73) and *My Friend Flicka* (1956–57).

Film Analysis

From its opening scenes, the film of *Island of the Blue Dolphins* works to convey O'Dell's message of the importance of treating nature with delicacy. Karana (Celia Kaye), Ramo (Larry Domasin), and Chowig (Carlos Romero) move through the rocky island, gathering food and maintaining a steady banter concerning traditional lifestyle practices. The two children are actively learning their tribe's approach to gender divisions, hunting, and spirituality. Shortly after the start of the film, a large sailing vessel is spotted in the distance. When the vessel lands on the island, the crew, a group of European hunters, announce their desire to hunt sea otters and offer to remunerate the tribe with various trade goods. This change from O'Dell's novel, in which the hunters were Aleuts (though led by a Russian captain), serves to simplify the ensuing cultural conflict for the audience. The film sidesteps the topic of clashes between different indigenous cultures, instead casting the white hunters as European colonizers overtaking a generic, if not monolithic, native population.

Chowig, who is the local chief, bargains with the hunters in order to receive the promise of a knife for every male inhabitant of the island. The tribe closely observes the hunters' behavior, allowing the movie to critically highlight the Europeans' thoughtless slaughter of the local animal population. Karana is horrified at the large numbers of sea otters that are killed for their skins. The situation becomes even worse when the tribe realizes that the hunters are preparing to leave without fulfilling their trade promises. The warriors of the tribe run to the beach to confront the hunters, and in the resulting interaction, many of them are killed, including Karana's father. From this point, the situation deteriorates rapidly. Having lost all the able-bodied men, the tribe must turn for leadership to an elderly man, who realizes that their only hope lies in leaving the island. He travels off in search of a mission or another tribe that will offer them a new home and eventually returns with Spanish priests who have agreed to transport them from the island. Through an unfortunate series of events, Karana and Ramo are left behind. Shortly thereafter, Ramo is killed by a pack of dogs who run wild on the island. Karana is now alone.

The remainder of the movie, which moves much more slowly than the beginning, is the story of Karana's solitary existence on the island. It is not made clear how much time passes, and Karana does not visibly age as the movie progresses, in contrast to both the novel and the real historical events on which it is based. Still, it is clear that Karana is alone for several years. During this time, she tames a wild dog from the pack and names him Rontu. The violence involved in the taming process will likely disturb many young viewers. When Rontu eventually dies of old age, Karana then befriends a puppy in the pack, which is presented as likely the child of her former canine companion. She also domesticates several birds and befriends a sea otter.

At one point, another group of white hunters arrives on the island, again taking the place of the Aleut hunters in the book. Though Karana hides from them, she does end up befriending a native woman named Tutok (Ann Daniel) who is traveling with them. This friendship affords the opportunity for the film to focus on the two scantily clad young women as they embrace, cavort in the fields, and groom each other. Herein lies the movie's intended appeal for an adult audience, as it emphasizes what is evident throughout but is made most apparent here: Karana and Tutok are offered as objects of desire to the viewer, though in a tame manner that remains mindful of the primarily youthful audience.

Tutok eventually leaves the island along with her hunter companions, much to Karana's distress. Finally, the movie comes to its conclusion with a mission priest and a few companions arriving on the island in search of Karana. She decides to make her presence known to them, bids farewell to the graves of Ramo and Rontu, and sets sail from her island.

Although its basic outline is grounded in history, much of the movie is pure fantasy. This is also true of the book, but it becomes even more problematic in movie form. As framed in the film, Karana's story is that of an innocent, sensuous, beautiful young woman who represents a past, primitive type of humanity. She offers the occasional statement or exclamation, but conversation with the audience, and thus any expression of interior life, is minimal; this is in sharp contrast to the novel, in which Karana's emotions, ideas, and experiences are immediate and fully realized for the reader. The viewer is encouraged to enjoy Karana's quaint observations, study her primitive technologies, and assess her faith as foreign but vaguely alluring for its connection to nature. As noted above, she does not age as the movie progresses, leaving her youth and beauty unmarred, and although she mourns the extreme losses that she endures, her grief does not seem to alter her personality or her appearance. The movie version of Karana is presented as truly a child of nature, over whom trouble can wash without changing her essentially carefree nature. Such a portrayal of an indigenous character is both simplistic and troubling, recalling the "noble savage" stereotype commonly associated with American Indians as well as casting her in a subordinate, childlike role in relation to her eventual rescuers. The mission priests are, ultimately, posited as the future salvation for Karana and those like her, clearly presenting indigenous ways as a thing of the past and the European colonists' lifestyle as the direction of progress.

Throughout the movie, the camera focuses on impressive views of nature, including rocky coasts, the ocean, and the island's flora and fauna. Through the use of lighting and panning of the camera across long vistas, the film encourages the viewer to enjoy the beauty of nature and, as a result, to sympathize with the goal of preserving the natural environment.

Significance

When the film adaptation of *Island of the Blue Dolphins* was first released, Howard Thompson observed in his *New York Times* review that it "is a children's movie that is pretty and harmless, if not especially meaningful." Dan Bates noted more critically that the movie is representative of many of the issues apparent in young adult film, commenting that it is "as stilted, boring, and amateur as it is antiseptic." Further, he highlighted that its essential premise was concerning, noting, "What frightens me is that Radnitz . . . thinks he is making something revolutionary, timeless, even 'intellectual,' that parents will gain from as well as children. The gargantuan naïveté of it all is dumfounding."

These comments are useful in thinking about the film within the context in which it was made. If it failed to achieve much in terms of critical argument or meaning, as Thompson observed, through its luxuriant focus on the beauty of nature and the bodies of native women and its lack of intelligent or engaging dialogue, it did serve to further an assessment of indigenous peoples as lesser cultural counterparts to those of European descent. Bates further emphasized that such a saccharine production would have little ability to build children intellectually,

a fact that is still true today unless the film is interpreted from a historicized and postcolonial perspective. While O'Dell's book is a significant and acclaimed children's book, the movie offers only a pale reinterpretation of the text. Nevertheless, both film and novel can be of use in today's classrooms as an opportunity to evaluate historical truth and to consider the appropriate lenses through which different cultures can be interpreted.

Julia A. Sienkewicz

Further Reading

Lorenzi, Rossella. "*Island of Blue Dolphins* Cave Possibly Found." *Discovery News*. Discovery Communications, 1 Nov. 2012. Web. 27 Oct. 2015. <http://news.discovery.com/history/archaeology/juana-maria-cave-121101.htm>.

Rycik, Mary Taylor, and Brenda Rosler. "The Return of Historical Fiction." *Reading Teacher* 63.2 (2009): 163–66. *Literary Reference Center*. Web. 27 Oct. 2015. <http://search.ebscohost.com/login.aspx?direct=true&db=1fh&AN=44618157&site=lrc-live>.

Schwebel, Sara L. "Doubly Historical: Consider This Layer of Historical Novels." Interview by Jenny Wei. *O Say Can You See?* Natl. Museum of Amer. Hist., 31 Jan. 2013. Web. 27 Oct. 2015. <http://americanhistory.si.edu/blog/2013/01/doubly-historical-consider-this-layer-of-historical-novels.html>.

Bibliography

Bates, Dan. Rev. of *Island of the Blue Dolphins*, dir. James B. Clark. *Film Quarterly* 18.1 (1964): 61. Print.

Beardwood, Valerie. "Scott O'Dell and *Island of the Blue Dolphins*." *Elementary English* 38.6 (1961): 373–76. Print.

Noffsinger, John, et al. "Still Good Reading: Adolescent Novels Written before 1967." *English Journal* 81.4 (1992): 87–90. Print.

Stott, Jon C. "Narrative Technique and Meaning in *Island of the Blue Dolphins*." *Elementary English* 52.4 (1975): 442–46. Print.

Thompson, Howard. "*Island of Blue Dolphins* Has Premiere." Rev. of *Island of the Blue Dolphins*, dir. James B. Clark. *New York Times*. New York Times, 4 July 1964. Web. 27 Oct. 2015. <http://www.nytimes.com/movie/review?res=9403E6DC123CEE3ABC4C53DFB166838F679EDE/>.

It's Kind of a Funny Story

The Book

Author: Ned Vizzini (1981–2013)
First published: 2006

The Film

Director: Ryan Fleck (b. 1976), Anna Boden (b. 1976)
Screenplay by: Ryan Fleck, Anna Boden
Starring: Keir Gilchrist, Zach Galifianakis, Emma Roberts, Zoë Kravitz, Viola Davis

Context

Author Ned Vizzini wrote *It's Kind of a Funny Story* (2006) based on his own experience of a brief stay in a psychological ward in 2004. The book was both popular and received critical praise, including being selected as one of the American Library Association's best books for young adults in 2007. Though the movie deviates from the plot of the original novel in places, it is close enough to maintain the autobiographical core of the story. The essential elements of the 2010 movie—an overworked teenager who experiences suicidal thoughts and spends a week in a psychological ward—are all essential components of Vizzini's life story. Like the central character, Craig, Vizzini also grew up in New York City and attended a high-pressure high school. Unfortunately, Vizzini was unable to overcome his battle with depression in the long run and committed suicide in 2013. Vizzini's story adds a poignancy and dark reality to Craig's ultimately hopeful story about teenage depression and suicide.

The film *It's Kind of a Funny Story* is the third collaboration of directors Ryan Fleck and Anna Boden. Unlike with the independent films *Sugar* (2008) and *Half Nelson* (2006), *It's Kind of a Funny Story* was the first time the pair worked with a somewhat major studio and their first film adaptation of a book.

Film Analysis

Despite the suggestion of humor in its title, *It's Kind of a Funny Story* is a study of depression, centered on a sixteen-year-old high school student named Craig (Keir Gilchrist). The film, like the novel on which it is based, is set in New York City. Although he lives with his well-intentioned parents and attends an elite public school where he is a solid student, Craig caves under the pressures of the high-powered expectations of his father, the demanding curriculum of his school, the discomfort of living in his best friend's shadow, and his crush on his best friend's girlfriend, Nia (Zoë Kravitz). He is also struggling with depression and is having dreams about committing suicide. The tipping point for Craig is an application he has to complete for an exclusive summer school program; he has been told much of his future success depends on his acceptance to the program. Craig just cannot persuade himself to fill out the application. His self-doubt and anxieties snowball, and depression takes over.

The movie opens with a dramatic scene in which Craig has ridden his bicycle to the Brooklyn Bridge. As he prepares to jump from the bridge, his parents and younger sister suddenly appear by his side. Craig wakes up from his dream and calls a suicide hotline. Following the call, he decides to check himself into a hospital to seek treatment for his depression. This particular incident might have been triggered by his decision to stop taking the Zoloft prescribed by his psychologist—a decision he did not tell his parents about.

At the local hospital, Craig struggles to explain the compounded significance of these triggers for his depression to the emergency room doctor. He worries that his concerns sound silly or insufficient and has difficulty answering the doctor's questions. Craig is eventually checked into the overcrowded adult psychological ward (the juvenile ward is closed for renovations) for a week-long stay. As Craig gains some perspective from the other patients, he is able to see ways to rearrange his priorities and start to cope. During the course of his week in the hospital, Craig rediscovers his passion for art, finds a new girlfriend, Noelle, and abandons his plans for a high-powered future in favor of a life passed in the pursuit of passion.

In the interest of lighthearted humor and appeal to a youthful audience, the film *It's Kind of a Funny Story* downplays the harsh realities of such a hospital environment and does not go in-depth with the darker side of mental illness, a criticism voiced by many. Chief among Craig's companions in the ward is a man named Bobby (Zach Galifianakis), who has attempted suicide six times. Bobby shows an immediate interest in Craig, showing him around the ward and introducing him to the other residents and their habits. Though Craig has two visits with the ward's doctor, Eden Minerva (Viola Davis), it is really Bobby who offers him the day-to-day contact that helps him to heal. Bobby is a doting father, but his condition has made him feel that his daughter might just be better off without him (an idea that her mother supports with poisonous invectives thrown at him during her visit to the ward). As Bobby prepares to leave on the same day as Craig, he faces the challenge of exiting the protected life in the hospital and attempting to right himself on the outside. In one of the turning points of the film, Craig helps Bobby to practice interviewing for a slot in a group home. The pressure is intense, as Bobby's alternative will be homelessness. For Craig, this process highlights both his own resources and greater preparation for life, as well as the relative ease of his own situation. Also significant is Craig's budding interest in Noelle (Emma Roberts), a beautiful teenage girl who was admitted to the ward after attempting suicide by wrist-cutting. The viewer never learns what has caused Noelle's own grief, but Craig senses a kindred spirit in her, and the two begin to plan their own futures outside of the hospital together.

An interesting attribute of this movie is its setting. It exploits the architectural drama of New York City in the opening scene on the Brooklyn Bridge, as well as in the final scenes atop the roof of the hospital, looking out at the skyline. In between these two bookends, though, the movie takes place deep within the bowels of a hospital that is cut off from the world. No windows share soaring views with their inhabitants; no scenes focus on the glass and lights of Manhattan. The claustrophobic nature of the hospital is highlighted in certain scenes, including those shot in Craig's shared room in the ward, and also during the visit from his parents, as his father twitches for the relative safety and comfort of the high-powered world outside of the hospital's doors. Craig has benefitted from the best that the city has to offer, but he has also fallen victim to its pressures. While his story could have been set anywhere in the country, it is significant that it takes place in New York City, because it makes the viewer realize that the issues Craig faces are, in some sense quintessentially American. Indeed, as the movie proceeds, Craig is relieved, or perhaps bemused, to discover that his closest companions at his elite high school are similarly suffering from depression.

Craig leaves the hospital after this relatively short five-day stay feeling hopeful but realistic. In the book, he states that "I'm not better, you know. The weight hasn't left my head. I feel how easily I could fall back into it. . . All of that is still there. The only thing is, it's not an option now. It's just . . . a possibility . . . not

a very likely possibility." The movie ends on a similar note—Craig's life and relationships have benefited from his hospital stay, and he feels better equipped to cope with his life.

Significance

It's Kind of a Funny Story is courageous and rare in its focus on teenage depression and suicide. Simply choosing to address the topic makes this film significant, since beginning to talk about issues is the first step toward addressing them. Indeed, it is the freedom to talk, to express his feelings without judgment, and to seek a new direction true to his own spirit that promises to set Craig on a new and more positive path. The film makes a goal of getting people to talk about depression and the very real threat of teenage suicide. The challenge, though, is that this subject matter clashes on occasion with the humorous approach of the film. While critical reception for Vizzini's book generally praised how funny the story was, the film was less successful in this sense. In his *New York Times* review, A. O. Scott noted that the film is "missing is the sometimes awkward, occasionally self-conscious but unmistakably authentic energy that characterizes Mr. Vizzini's prose and also, more important, the zest and irreverence with which he approaches difficult themes . . . the brazenness and flair of the original have been diminished." Some critics appreciated the film's emphasis on comedy. Mark Jenkins, writing for *NPR*, said that the movie's highlights were its funnier moments, but that its light-handed approach to solving mental problems would likely irk viewers who had experienced struggles of their own. Others, such as the *Guardian's* Peter Bradshaw, found the movie's premise to be problematic and condemned the film for romanticizing mental illness. The film is ultimately a black comedy, but Bradshaw and others found fault with the film's occasional sweetness and moments of lighter comedy.

Ultimately, *It's Kind of a Funny Story* might open some eyes to the pervasive and severe issues of youth depression. It is praiseworthy in its intention to raise awareness of mental illness, but the film is also dangerous in its suggestion that these issues can be ameliorated in a brief period or made rosy through humor. As the first step toward having a serious conversation about mental illness, this film could be a valuable educational tool. Viewers must be careful, though, not to take it too seriously.

Julia A. Sienkewicz

Further Reading

Marsico, Katie. *Depression and Stress*. New York: Cavendish, 2012. Print.

Vizzini, Ned. "Interview with Ned Vizzini." Interview by James Blasingame. *Journal of Adolescent and Adult Literacy* 50.7 (2007): 607–8. *Literary Reference Center*. Web. 8 Dec. 2015. <http://search.ebscohost.com/login.aspx?direct=true&db=lfh&AN=24572516&site=lrc-live>.

Bibliography

Bradshaw, Peter. Rev. of *It's Kind of a Funny Story*, dir. Ryan Fleck and Anna Boden. *Guardian*. Guardian News and Media, 6 Jan. 2011. Web. 26 Nov. 2015. <http://www.theguardian.com/film/2011/jan/06/its-kind-of-a-funny-story-review>.

Jenkins, Mark. "A 'Funny Story' of Just the Right Kind." Rev. of *It's Kind of a Funny Story*, dir. Ryan Fleck and Anna Boden. *NPR*. NPR, 8 Oct. 2010. Web. 26 Nov. 2015. <http://www.npr.org/templates/story/story.php?storyId=130195398>.

Phillips, Michael. "Filmmaking Duo Good Even Not at Their Best." Rev. of *It's Kind of a Funny Story*, dir. Ryan Fleck and Anna Boden. *Chicago Tribune*. Chicago Tribune, 7 Oct. 2010. Web. 26 Nov. 2015. <http://articles.chicagotribune.com/2010-10-07/entertainment/sc-mov-1005-its-kind-of-a-funny-story20101007_1_fleck-and-boden-filmmaking-duo-ned-vizzini>.

Scott, A. O. "A Coming-of-Age Tale, Set among the Sad." Rev. of *It's Kind of a Funny Story*, dir. Ryan Fleck and Anna Boden. *New York Times*. New York Times, 7 Oct. 2010. Web. 27 Nov. 2015. <http://www.nytimes.com/2010/10/08/movies/08funny.html?_r=0>.

Sharkey, Betsy. Rev. of *It's Kind of a Funny Story*, dir. Ryan Fleck and Anna Boden. *Los Angeles Times*. Tribune, 8 Oct. 2010 Web. 26 Nov. 2015. <http://articles.latimes.com/2010/oct/08/entertainment/la-et-funny-story-20101008>.

Strauss, Valerie. "A Farewell to 'It's Kind of a Funny Story' Author." *Washington Post*. Washington Post, 25 Dec. 2013. Web. 26 Nov. 2015. <https://www.washingtonpost.com/news/answer-sheet/wp/2013/12/25/a-farewell-to-its-kind-of-a-funny-story-author>.

Life, Above All

The Book

Author: Allan Stratton (b. 1951)
First published: *Chanda's Secrets* (2004)

The Film

Director: Oliver Schmitz (b. 1960)
Screenplay by: Dennis Foon
Starring: Khomotso Manyaka, Keobaka Makanyane, Harriet Manamela, Lerato Mvelase, Aubrey Poolo

Context

Life, Above All (2011) and *Chanda's Secrets* (2004), the book on which it is based, are responses to the dire epidemic of AIDS in South Africa. Approximately 25 percent of the adult population was HIV-positive when the book was published, yet the national government had largely ignored the epidemic, worsening the crisis by turning a blind eye to modern medicine and promoting fear, stigmas, and traditional remedies. Such a widespread public health crisis has severe implications beyond the sickness and death of these adults—including national development, economic crisis and child welfare. This story addresses primarily the latter concern, focusing on the tragic story of Chanda, a young girl growing up in the Johannesburg area. Her father has already succumbed to the disease (though this reality has been hidden from her), and over the course of the story, both her mother and her stepfather die directly or indirectly of AIDS. Chanda's valiant efforts to live in the shadow of this disease are conveyed in shocking parallel with those of her best friend, Esther, who has been ostracized because she is the orphan of two AIDS victims, help to shed light on the dire extent of the situation.

Canadian author Allan Stratton is the author of a large number of books for a young adult audience, of which *Chanda's Secrets* was one of the first. This novel was followed by *Chanda's Wars* (2008), grappling with the phenomenon of children being kidnapped and forced into armed fighting in parts of Africa. After these serious books, Stratton primarily focused on psychological thrillers and suspense novels for a young adult audience. *Chanda's Secrets* was published in more than a dozen countries, including South Africa; was named a Michael L. Printz Honor Book by the American Library

Association; and received a Children's Africana Book Award from the African Studies Association.

Born in Cape Town, South Africa, director Oliver Schmitz here returns to the concerns of his home country. *Mapantsula* (1989) and *Hijack Stories* (2000), written and directed by Schmitz, address South African social issues through dramas that focus on an individual's experiences, the former dealing with the harsh apartheid-era imprisonment of a black man and the latter with a wannabe actor turned gangster.

Film Analysis

Like the novel on which it is based, *Life, Above All*, opens with a weighty scene. The young protagonist, Chanda (Khomotso Manyaka), pays a visit to a local undertaker. As the limited family resources are made clear, the man signals to an array of diminutive coffins. He promises that the infant Sara will look beautiful, though in the shabby surroundings it is clear that this is an empty and, in the face of such tragedy, perhaps an irrelevant promise. This wrenching sequence is followed by a series of events that are just as bad and that rapidly introduce the viewer to the dire situation in which twelve-year-old Chanda finds herself (she is sixteen in the novel). Having returned home to her family's tiny cottage, she finds her mother reclined in the darkness, mourning over her dead sister's body. Lillian (Lerato Mvelase), her mother, says that the agreement with the undertaker will have to be canceled because all the family's savings are gone. Angry but stoic, Chanda heads out to confront her stepfather, Jonah (Aubrey Poolo), whom she finds drunk in a bar with another woman. She succeeds, through a combination of righteous indignation and wiles, in stealing back enough money for her infant sister's funeral. Thus, Chanda must take on the adult and caretaker role for her family. In the process, she encounters hatred, mob violence, and superstition.

At first after Sara's funeral it seems like there may be healing and a positive move forward for Chanda. Friends gather together to collect a large monetary gift for Lillian. They promise to help her get back on her feet. Chanda struggles to return to school. In the film, big exams are approaching, but her teacher is supportive. The family's neighbor, Mrs. Tafa (Harriet Manamela), who mourns the loss of her own only son, is supportive, though also nosy and domineering over Lillian; director Oliver Schmitz said in an interview that Mrs. Tafa provides comic relief in the novel but that the film

version is more serious, an authority figure in the neighborhood. Through these positive turns, troubles persist. Lillian, who at first appears understandably depressed, does not make progress, and eventually starts to seem unwell. She only has the energy to complete her sewing in short spurts, yet her family depends on her high-quality handiwork for survival. Meanwhile, Chanda's two younger half siblings cannot understand where Sara has gone nor where their father is. The truth has been hidden from them, and they get angry and rebel under their older sister's care.

Things get worse, even though that seems impossible. Chanda's mother's health continues to worsen. Suddenly, her stepfather makes a dramatic return. He is discarded, like a pile of rubbish, on their doorstep by his own relatives. They leave him so sick he can barely move, but still poisonous in disposition, in a cart that they have pulled behind their car. In a dramatic scene that brings all the neighbors to stare in a threatening crowd, he loudly denounces Lillian, claiming that she has poisoned him as well as their infant daughter. Nevertheless, Lillian promises to give him water and care for him. He refuses to enter the house, and they leave him outside. He mysteriously disappears only to appear dead later in the film—clearly murdered due to fear of his illness. It is when her stepfather returns that Chanda first verbalizes her realization that "the bug" has infected her family. She seeks help from the local hospital. After an impossibly long wait, she meets a kindly doctor who, unfortunately, says help can only be offered if the patient comes in to the hospital. This is another place where the film diverges from the book, where Chanda encounters a sympathetic nurse who arranges for home visit from a health care worker and an AIDS test for Jonah and instructs Chanda how to protect herself while caring for Jonah in the meantime.

With the secret "out of the bag," at least to the viewer, Chanda's story proceeds around her mother's decline due to AIDS. Mrs. Tafa takes Lillian and Chanda to see a locally renowned doctor, who tries to sell them astronomically expensive herbal medicines. He would have succeeded, had Chanda not read the so-called diplomas on his wall that were bogus. They get a bargain on the medicines, but, of course, they do not work. Eventually, after a witch doctor prescribes that Lillian must return to her family village and confront her sister if she hopes to get well, Lillian leaves Chanda in charge of her siblings and heads off. By the time that Chanda realizes her mother has been sent away to die and heads out on a mission to save Lillian, her mother has already reached the final stages of illness and Chanda only succeeds in giving her the dignity of death under loving care. Given the complete devastation experienced throughout the film, even the positive turns at the end of the film seem improbable, even if they are hardly happy or miraculous.

Chanda's misfortunes pale alongside those of her best friend, Esther (Keobaka Makanyane). At the beginning of the film, Esther is already an ostracized figure in their town. She is an AIDS orphan and has been relegated to living in a hovel. Lillian and Mrs. Tafa berate Chanda for her friendship with Esther, and they do their best to separate the two girls. But they have sworn to be there for each other forever, which they manage to achieve despite some periods of argument and misunderstanding. Without any supportive adults, Esther has rapidly fallen into a destitute situation. She eventually makes the decision to turn to prostitution in order to earn enough money to reunite her siblings. She drifts out of sight only to eventually reappear on Chanda's doorstep after having been gang-raped and brutalized. One of the rapists also brags that he has now infected her with AIDS. Chanda saves her friend's life, and from that point, the two work together to offer each other support, forming an alternative family structure for Chanda's younger siblings.

The movie's dialogue is in Sotho with English subtitles, which gives the film an air of authenticity that might arguably support its accessibility to a South African audience for whom the film's message is surely most urgent. That being said, the dialogue is minimal, with much of the feeling of the film is conveyed through the body language of its actors rather than their words. For international audiences, the film creates an intimate relationship between its actors and its audience through shots that focus on faces and emotions. The powerful effect of the movie is, therefore, a special tribute to the cast of mostly novice actors.

Significance

At its premier at the 2010 Cannes Film Festival, *Life, Above All* received a rare standing ovation, a tribute to its emotion and beauty. Subsequent reviews have generally been very positive, though some critics, such as NPR's Ella Taylor, have found the treatment of Chanda's fellow townspeople to be demeaning and the ultimate message of the movie to be insufficiently political.

Indeed, Stratton and Schmitz have chosen to confront the local and individual effects of governmental policies, without explicitly laying blame on the political leadership. Schmitz's identity as a white South African by birth, further complicates the implications of the film and led Taylor, while recognizing its good intentions, to be cautious of the film's connections to the long histories of imperialism and racism in the nation. Despite these criticisms, the film has overall been highly acclaimed, and particular praise has gone to the cast, whose performances are noteworthy and give the film both power and authenticity.

Although it deals with the life of a child and is based on a young adult novel, this movie is not intended for a young adult audience. Rather, it addresses itself to activists, leaders, and others with the power to make some difference in the ongoing AIDS epidemic in Africa. It is an important film, with the emotional and psychological power to convey this message assertively to its audience. Though the film deals with subjects of sexual violence and death, these take place offscreen, allowing the viewer to focus on the devastating emotional consequences on the movie's protagonists.

Julia A. Sienkewicz

Further Reading

Brower, Jennifer, and Peter Chalk. "AIDS in South Africa: Extent, Implications, and Response." *The Global Threat of New and Reemerging Infectious Diseases: Reconciling U.S. National Security and Public Health Policy.* By Brower and Chalk. Santa Monica: RAND, 2003. 31–60. Print.

Schmitz, Oliver. "Mighty Movie Podcast: Oliver Schmitz on *Life, Above All.*" Interview by Dan Persons. *Huffington Post.* TheHuffingtonPost.com, 15 July 2011. Web. 3 Dec. 2015. <http://www.huffingtonpost.com/dan-persons/mighty-movie-podcast-oliv_b_900388.html>.

Bibliography

Burr, Ty. "Life, Above All: Close-Up View of a Courageous Preteen." Rev. of *Life, Above All*, dir. Oliver Schmitz. *Boston Globe.* Globe Newspaper Company, 4 Aug. 2011 Web. 3 Dec. 2015. <http://www.boston.com/ae/movies/articles/2011/08/05/life_above_all_offers_a_close_up_view_of_a_courageous_preteen>.

Dargis, Manohla. "Burdened in a Ravaged South Africa." *New York Times*. New York Times, 14 July 2011. Web. 3 Dec. 2015. <http://www.nytimes.com/2011/07/15/movies/life-above-all-aids-and-bias-in-south-africa-review.html?_r=0>.

Ebert, Roger. Rev. of *Life, Above All*, dir. Oliver Schmitz. *RogerEbert.com*. 31 Aug. 2011. Web. 3 Dec. 2015. <http://www.rogerebert.com/reviews/life-above-all-2011>.

Fine, Marshall. Rev. of *Life, Above All*, dir. Oliver Schmitz. *HuffPost Entertainment*. TheHuffingtonPost.com, 13 July 2011. Web. 3 Dec. 2015. <http://www.huffingtonpost.com/marshall-fine/huff-post-review-ilife-abo_b_896954.html>.

Lederman, Marsha. "In *Life, Above All* Canadians Tell the Story of AIDS in Africa." *Globe and Mail*. Globe and Mail, 12 July 2011. Web. 3 Dec. 2015. <http://www.theglobeandmail.com/arts/film/in-life-above-all-canadians-tell-the-story-of-aids-in-africa/article586906>.

Taylor, Ella. "A 'Life' Where HIV and Ignorance Are Twin Epidemics." *National Public Radio*. NPR, 22 July 2011. Web. 3 Dec. 2015. <http://www.npr.org/2011/07/22/137797106/a-life-where-hiv-and-ignorance-are-twin-epidemics>.

Looking for Alibrandi

The Book

Author: Melina Marchetta (b. 1965)
First published: 1992

The Film

Director: Kate Woods
Screenplay by: Melina Marchetta
Starring: Pia Miranda, Greta Scacchi, Anthony LaPaglia, Elena Cotta, Kick Gurry, and Matthew Newton

Context

The appeal of *Looking for Alibrandi*, as both a book and film, to young adults is easy to understand. Like many other stories for young adults, it deals with many of the most typical issues teenagers confront, and it seems especially relevant to the lives of teenagers in the late twentieth and early twenty-first century. Tensions between young people and their parents are nothing new and have probably existed since the beginnings of human life. But *Looking for Alibrandi* also deals with the rise of single-parent families, especially when those single parents are mothers trying to cope on their own, with little to no help from the fathers of their children. The movie, like the book, deals with the close—if very complicated—bonds that can develop between such mothers and their children, and it also explores the longing such children often have for fuller, more satisfying contacts with their fathers.

Tensions involving adolescents and their peers are also prominent in this film, and these again are tensions relevant to most teenagers' lives. Feelings of inferiority and inadequacy—whether rooted in differences of class, ethnicity, race, or personal appearance—are also issues to which most teenagers can relate. So, too, are the support and consolations provided by close friends, as well as the desire for genuine love, preferably from someone whom other people also find attractive. Yearnings for independence, confidence, and satisfying accomplishments are further themes dealt with in this movie that are also relevant to the lives of most young people. The film additionally explores the ways schools function as microcosms of society at large: rather than providing an escape from social pressures, life at school often magnifies and intensifies such stresses.

The mere fact that *Looking for Alibrandi* examines the life of a young woman is significant. The further fact that that young woman is spirited, feisty, outspoken, and assertive reflects the rise of feminism during the last quarter of the twentieth century. Yet *Looking for Alibrandi* is ultimately fairly conservative, implying the importance of family (including an extended family), parental love, and the love of a good, genuine, respectful, and self-respecting partner. The film ends happily, emphasizing reconciliation and community. It shows how its young heroine has matured during the course of a year. In all the ways just mentioned, then, *Looking for Alibrandi* treats themes common in many novels and movies aimed at young adults, such as the significance of life at school, the importance of friendship, tensions with parents, conflicts with age peers, the attractions of independence and nonconformity, the dangers of pressures to conform, and the tragedy that can result when those pressures seem overwhelming.

Film Analysis

Both the book and film versions of *Looking for Alibrandi* are narrated by Josie Alibrandi (Pia Miranda), who bluntly but humorously describes her loving but tense relations with her spirited mother (Greta Scacchi) and her eventual reconnection with her estranged father (Anthony LaPaglia). While attending a Catholic girls' school on an academic scholarship, the lower-middle-class Josie is attracted to the handsome, intelligent, sensitive John Barton (Matthew Newton). From a wealthy, prominent family, John feels pressured by his father to conform to demanding expectations, with results that ultimately prove tragic. Eventually, however, Josie finds herself becoming more and more involved with, and attracted to, the handsome, scruffy, devil-may-care Jacob Cootes (Kick Gurry). By the time the film ends, most tensions in Josie's life have been resolved, especially those involving her immediate and extended family.

For the most part, the movie and book versions of *Looking for Alibrandi* are realistic, straightforward, slice-of-life productions, although the movie includes some amusing whimsy. Both works mirror the kinds of lives actually lived by believable, if somewhat stereotypical, characters residing in Australia in the late 1980s or early 1990s. Yet both the film and the novel hold up well because they deal with archetypal issues and enduring kinds of personalities.

In the film, for instance, the episode in which Josie and Jacob both address an audience at a Have Your Say Day event typifies how skillfully the director manages to sketch the distinct natures of various main characters by depicting the ways they dress, speak, behave, and even sit or stand. The scene opens with two of Josie's friends arriving late at the event, which is being held in the lobby of the famous Sydney Opera House. This setting exemplifies the ways the director employs significant Australian locations throughout the movie.

When the friends arrive, Josie, with a large audience of teachers and other students listening, is already in the middle of her speech. She is appropriately dressed in a dark blue school uniform, with her hair tied in a neat ponytail, and her speech as is tidy and proper as her appearance. Her speech deals with death but lacks any passion; Josie offers the kinds of trite clichés one often hears in formal speeches. When she ends, people genuinely applaud, and her prim, aging, gray-haired teacher smiles with pride.

Returning to her seat, Josie is positioned between John Barton (on her right) and Jacob Cootes (immediately behind her). Both young men seem pleased with her performance, but the differences in their appearances could hardly be more striking. John's blond hair is thick but neatly combed and trimmed. He is clean-shaven, boyish looking, and dressed in the conventional uniform of an upper-class Australian schoolboy: a blue suit jacket prominently trimmed in gold, a clean white dress shirt, and a thin striped tie. Both he and Jacob clap enthusiastically as Josie begins to sit down. John is obviously Josie's genuine friend (he immediately leans over to whisper in her ear), but he is just as obviously a young man who plays by the rules.

Jacob, on the other hand, starkly contrasts with John. His dark brown hair hangs down freely to his shoulder. He sports a tiny goatee, and he wears a casual white short-sleeved polo shirt, open at the neck, that reveals his tanned, muscular arms. He then leans forward (speaking right into Josie's ear) and confesses that thanks to her speech about death, he realizes he should have worn condoms much sooner than he did. (The film was released when the AIDS crisis was at its height.) Josie sarcastically thanks him for sharing that bit of information. Jacob then pulls a packaged condom out of his pocket and tells Josie he plans to show the audience how to put a condom on properly. He then struts to the podium.

In little more than a minute, then, the director of *Looking for Alibrandi* manages to reinforce many aspects of the film's themes and characterization. Josie is literally flanked by the young men who represent two of her main but conflicting desires in life: the desire to succeed conventionally and the desire to achieve independence. John represents everything that is safe, conventional, sensible, and traditionally Australian. Jacob symbolizes everything that seems risky and unconventional. To its great credit, *Looking for Alibrandi* makes each young man attractive in his own way. Both, it turns out, are good and decent people. Viewers can easily see why Josie finds each appealing. Neither John nor Jacob is reduced to a caricature, and Josie's conflicting feelings for both of them typify the complex situations in which she often finds herself.

As it turns out, Jacob is less of a "bad boy" than he seems to be. His speech does not in fact deal with properly fitting on a condom; instead, it ultimately builds (after an exceedingly relaxed beginning) into a spirited plea for young persons' involvement in politics. By the same token, John turns out to be far less conventional and conformist than his neat appearance might imply. The Have Your Say Day episode thus effectively reinforces many of the film's key thematic concerns and details of characterization. And it does so in ways that seem realistic, straightforward, and credible. In all these ways, this episode epitomizes the movie as a whole. The film generally treats its characters with real respect, showing genuine appreciation for their distinctive personal traits and not reducing them to stereotypes. Nearly every major character in the movie seems a recognizably complex human being.

Significance

Despite winning wide acclaim and various prizes in Australia, *Looking for Alibrandi* does not seem to have been distributed on a large scale in the United States, and American reviews are therefore difficult to trace. The film was high grossing in Australian when it was released in 2000, but it is not currently available for American audiences. The film would probably seem far more significant to audiences outside Australia if it were simply more broadly available to non-Australian viewers.

In 2000, *Looking for Alibrandi* won five Australian Academy of Cinema and Television Arts awards, including best picture, best adapted screenplay, best editing, best actress, and best supporting actress. The few available reviews praise the film almost without reservation. For instance, David Stratton, writing for *Variety*, called the movie "beautifully written" and also extolled the "skill and precision" of its director. He especially admired Miranda's performance as Josie, and he asserted that "production values are all on the button, with excellent use made of prime Sydney locations." Stratton also suggested that "the inevitable music track filled with songs by local groups can only enhance the film's appeal to the youth audience."

In an especially thoughtful review at efilmcritic.com, Andrew Howe praised the movie by asserting that "there are few who can fail to be touched" by such matters as: "its meditations upon the way in which family ties can be simultaneously comforting, stifling, and exasperating . . . [and] the moments when we realize that what we want and what we need are two very different things." Meanwhile, Rich Cline, in a much briefer assessment, concluded that "there's a natural humor running through this film that makes it utterly disarming . . . But [its] also not afraid to turn the tone around 180 degrees at times, dipping into some wrenching emotion without losing the film's momentum at all."

Given this kind of enthusiastic praise, it seems especially unfortunate that the film is so difficult for so many viewers to watch because of its limited distribution. Young Americans might especially enjoy this intriguing glimpse of teenaged life in Australia. It shows, in a winning, winsome, sometimes disturbing way, that life for young adults is pretty much the same everywhere.

Robert C. Evans, PhD

Further Reading

Adams, Lauren. "Looking for Alibrandi." *Horn Book* 75.3 (1999): 334–35. Literary Reference Center. Web. 10 May 2015. <http://search.ebscohost.com/login.aspx?direct=true&db=lfh&AN=1849733&site=ehost-live&scope=site>.

Hynes, Louise. "Looking for Identity: Food, Generation, and Hybridity in Looking for Alibrandi." *Australian Screen Education* 24 (2000): 30. Communication & Mass Media Complete. Web. 10 May 2015. <http://search.ebscohost.com/login.aspx?direct=true&db=ufh&AN=3838607&site=ehost-live&scope=site>.

McInally, Kathryn. "Not Quite White (Enough): Intersecting Ethnic and Gendered Identities in Looking for Alibrandi." *Papers: Explorations into Children's Literature* 17.2 (2007): 59–66. MLA International Bibliography. Web. 10 May 2015. <http://search.ebscohost.com/login.aspx?direct=true&db=mzh&AN=2009041193&site=ehost-live&scope=site>.

Bibliography

Adams, Lauren. "Looking for Alibrandi." *Horn Book* 75.3 (1999): 334–35. *Literary Reference Center.* Web. 15 June 2015. <http://search.ebscohost.com/login.aspx?direct=true&db=lfh&AN=1849733&site=lrc-live>.

Andronik, Catherine M. "Author Profile: Melina Marchetta." *Library Media Connection* 29.5 (2011): 30–32. *Literary Reference Center.* Web. 15 June 2015. <http://search.ebscohost.com/login.aspx?direct=true&db=lfh&AN=59620471&site=lrc-live>.

Cline, Rich. "*Looking for Alibrandi.*" Shadowsonthewall.co.uk. Shadows on the Wall, 2000. Web. 15 May 2015. <http://www.shadowsonthewall.co.uk/swlooali.htm>

Howe, Andrew. "*Looking for Alibrandi.*" Efilmcritic.com. Efilmcritic, 14 May 2000. Web. 10 May 2015. <http://www.efilmcritic.com/review.php?movie=4339&reviewer=193>.

Mason-Jones, Hugh, and Augusta Zeeng. "Looking for Alibrandi, Kate Woods, 2000." *Media Reloaded.* Melbourne: Cambridge UP, 2012. 41–45. Print.

Pung, Alice. Rev. of *Looking for Alibrandi*, by Melina Marchetta. Reading Australia. Copyright Agency, 2013. Web. 18 June 2015. <http://readingaustralia.com.au/Secondary/LookingforAlibrandi/Essay.aspx>.

The Lovely Bones

The Book

Author: Alice Sebold (b. 1963)
First published: 2002

The Film

Director: Peter Jackson (b. 1961)
Screenplay by: Fran Walsh, Philippa Boyens, Peter Jackson
Starring: Mark Wahlberg, Rachel Weisz, Saoirse Ronan, Susan Sarandon, Stanley Tucci

Context

After the revival of young adult literature in the 1990s, the genre has grown more popular and lucrative in the twenty-first century. Alice Sebold's *The Lovely Bones* was published in 2002, at the beginning of the booming decade in young adult literature when the Harry Potter books and film series were at their height, fantasy was becoming the best-selling genre for young adults, and realist authors like John Green were also rising in popularity. The novel and film versions of *The Lovely Bones* are difficult to place within a single subgenre, as there are elements of many different subgenres present in the story line, from realism to romance, mystery, thriller, and fantasy.

For Sebold, *The Lovely Bones* was her second novel, following *Lucky* (1999), a critically and commercially successful memoir recounting the author's experiences after being raped in her first year of college. Perhaps because of the personal proximity of these themes, rape and violence hold a high importance in Sebold's writing. *The Lovely Bones* is narrated by Susie Salmon, a fourteen-year-old girl who is raped and murdered. However, the story is not so much about the events themselves as it is about overcoming and moving past them.

The themes of trauma and dealing with emotional distress became popular in the 1990s through works such as *Junk* (1996) by Melvin Burgess, *Dear Miffy* (1997) by John Marsden, and *Care Factor Zero* (1997) by Margaret Clark, which deal with confronting and overcoming issues such as anorexia, depression, and addiction. The popularity of the theme has continued with works such as Jay Asher's *Thirteen Reasons Why* (2007), a novel about one student coming to understand why another classmate committed suicide, and Green's *The Fault in Our Stars* (2012), about teens dealing with the diagnosis of terminal cancer.

The Lovely Bones stands out because it is narrated by a girl who has died and observes life continuing on after her death from her own personal heaven. This fantasy element of the plot is an angle that fits well into director Peter Jackson's body of work. Jackson began his career with films such as *The Frighteners* (1996) and *Dead Alive* (1992), imaginative and creative works meant to be funny and scary; they were considered highly creative. His reputation for cinematic vision was secured by the time he started working on *The Lovely Bones* due to his work on such international fantasy blockbusters as the *Lord of the Rings* trilogy (2001–3) and *King Kong* (2005).

Film Analysis

The film and the novel begin with the same scene. Susie Salmon (Saoirse Ronan) describes a snow globe she remembers from her youth. In the snow globe is a small penguin, which she was worried was trapped inside, but her father (Mark Wahlberg) told her the penguin was safe because it was "trapped in a perfect world," foreshadowing Susie's stay in her personal heaven while dealing with her own death. Susie then introduces herself, explaining what she was like when she was alive and when she died. From this point, the narrative arcs of the novel and film begin to separate. While they address much of the same basic subject matter, the film tells the story in chronological order, while the novel jumps back and forth between Susie's heaven, her memories of the past, and events unfolding after her death.

The film recounts major events from Susie's childhood, piecing together the story of who she is until she reaches the age of fourteen. While the effect of nostalgia is present in both the novel and film from the start, the emotion is presented on two different levels. In the novel, Susie's tone is nostalgic because she misses being alive. On the other hand, since the narrative of the film is chronological, the nostalgia is presented more as a general mood of the 1970s and childhood in general than from the perspective of the narrator.

The technique of telling the story as an almost singularly chronological narration creates a very different effect for the film audience than the book does for the reader. While there is mystery and suspense, drawing both the readers and the audience in immediately to find out why Susie was murdered, the film also utilizes cinematic techniques related to mystery and suspense genres. Susie does not refer to her murderer by name, nor does the camera show the face of George Harvey (Stanley Tucci) until the scene in which she is murdered. In this way, the film follows more traditional suspense film techniques in order to create tension for the audience. Even after the murder, the film continues chronologically and keeps information from the audience in order to increase the sense of anticipation. The location of Susie's body, for example, is not revealed until the end, although clues are given throughout the film. By presenting the story line in this fashion, the film does ultimately focus less on the theme of overcoming trauma until the final scenes.

The reasoning behind emphasizing more popular cinematic genre conventions may be the same reason that the film never mentions Susie's rape, while the book refers to the event directly many times. With a budget of $65 million, the film needed to be marketed toward a very large audience. By pushing some of the less conventional aspects of the book into the background, Peter Jackson was hoping for reception by a larger audience. This may also be the reason for the tighter chronological narrative. While the book continues on, stretching out nearly ten years after the murder, the perspective of the film goes little beyond two years into the future, with the exception of the very end, as it shows how everyone's life has continued after Susie's death. In the portrayal of all of the main characters' lives years later, the film realigns with the book. After observing the lives of everyone important in her life, Susie is able to deal with her own death, perhaps fully coming to a climax when her murderer is killed in an accidental fall.

Similar in spirit and theme, under the direction of Peter Jackson, the film departs radically from the novel in the depiction of Susie's personal heaven. Sebold refers to the perfection of the world that Susie lives in throughout the novel but does not go into detailed descriptions of the heaven, with the exception of key objects like Susie's gazebo or the olive tree shown to Susie by her companion, Franny. On the other hand, Jackson creates a world of computer-generated imagery that is both wonderful and terrifying. In the film, Susie's heaven is not simply an idealized version of Earth. It comes alive with visually stunning scenes that sometimes heighten the natural beauty found on Earth and at other times take the imagery to surreal heights of imagination. For example, in a scene in which Susie's father destroys all the ships in a bottle that he built with Susie, smashing them against the walls, desk, and floor of his study, Susie's world transforms into a beach where enormous ships in bottles drift in from the sea and dash themselves against the rocks of the shore around her. In another scene, the leaves of the olive tree fly off the branches like a swarm of insects, flying briefly in the air before returning and settling back upon the branches.

Jackson does not allow Susie's heaven to just be perfect either. To convey the psychological impact of the horrible death that she had to endure, the film includes moments of terror. For example, after Susie dies, she finds herself at Harvey's house. She walks through a door and must endure the scene of her killer resting in a bathtub after the event, while mud, dried corn husks, and blood are smeared on the tiles. Similarly, near the end of the film, Harvey's safe begins to appear in different places in her heaven. Like many things in Susie's world, it is a symbol of something more. It is significant to both Susie and the audience because it is where (the audience discovers) Harvey put Susie's remains. When he finally dumps the safe into a sinkhole, the two worlds join for one last time, and Susie is able to see and do what she needs to on Earth in order to finally move beyond her heaven.

Significance

Commercially, the novel was a complete success, remaining on the *New York Times* best seller list for over a year and selling over one million copies in that time. The novel was also praised by critics in general, although it did garner some mixed reception due to its realistic and sensitive subject matter. Critics generally gave the film mixed reviews, usually noting the disjunction between the subject matter and the fantastic world of Susie's heaven. The film ultimately did not achieve the same commercial success as the novel. For some, the translation of Susie's nostalgic tone toward her own life into the nostalgic mood of the film was seen as a major flaw. Critics praised Jackson's beautiful vision of Susie's heaven, confirming his reputation as a director adept in visually stunning cinematography but condemned his failure to treat the subject matter with the appropriate tone.

The novel and the film marked the introduction of an untraditional mix of child and adult themes in the young adult genre. The inclusion of serious subjects, such as death, addiction, sex and sexuality, and even murder, were nothing new to the genre when the book was published in 2002. However, the genre traditionally focused on dealing with these issues. The focus was on young adults struggling with adult issues, but Sebold took her story one step further, and this step has not always been looked upon favorably by readers. By twisting traditional storytelling and making her protagonist both the victim of violence and the "survivor" having to work it through it, Sebold created a story for young adults that includes fantastic elements while overwhelmingly highlighting a very real trauma.

Aaron Horton, MA

Further Reading

Bliss, Ann V. "'Share Moments, Share Life': The Domestic Photograph as a Symbol of Disruption and Trauma in *The Lovely Bones*." *Women's Studies* 37.7 (2008): 861–84. *Literary Reference Center*. Web. 12 May 2015. <http://search.ebscohost.com/login.aspx?direct=true&db=lfh&AN=34146250&site=lrc-live>.

Gurdon, Meghan Cox. "Darkness Too Visible." *Wall Street Journal*. Dow Jones, 4 June 2011. Web. 12 May 2015. <http://www.wsj.com/articles/SB10001424052702303657404576357622592697038>.

Bibliography

Alleva, Richard. "Restless Spirits." Rev. of *The Lovely Bones*, dir. Peter Jackson, and *A Single Man*, dir. Tom Ford. *Commonweal* 12 Feb. 2010: 18–19. *Literary Reference Center*. Web. 12 May 2015. <http://search.ebscohost.com/login.aspx?direct=true&db=lfh&AN=48042430&site=lrc-live>.

Belluci, Elizabeth. "Alice Sebold's 'The Lovely Bones.'" *Literary Contexts in Novels* (2012): 1. *Literary Reference Center*. Web. 13 May 2015. <http://search.ebscohost.com/login.aspx?direct=true&db=lfh&AN=84667514&site=lrc-live>.

Hodge, Diana. "Young Adult Fiction's Dark Themes Give the Hope to Cope." *Conversation*. Conversation, 12 June 2014. Web. 12 May 2015. <http://theconversation.com/young adult-fictions-dark-themes-give-the-hope-to-cope-27335>.

Jackson, Peter. "Peter Jackson: 'Lovely Bones' Was Lovely to Make." Interview by Scott Bowles. *USA Today*. USA Today, 19 Apr. 2009. Web. 12 May 2015. <http://usatoday30.usatoday.com/life/movies/news/2009-04-19-bones-jackson_N.htm>.

The Maze Runner

The Book

Author: James Dashner (b. 1972)
First published: 2009

The Film

Director: Wes Ball (b. 1985)
Screenplay by: Noah Oppenheim, Grant Pierce Myers, T. S. Nowlin
Starring: Dylan O'Brien, Kaya Scodelario, Will Poulter

Context

Around the start of the twenty-first century, the phrase "dystopian young adult novel" might not have sparked much recognition in the average reader. While popular twentieth-century works such as Lois Lowry's *The Giver* (1993) had explored dystopian worlds—that is, worlds shaped by disaster and the common loss of humanity—it was not until the extraordinary success of Suzanne Collins's *Hunger Games* books (2008–10) and film adaptations (2012–15) that dystopias became one of the most popular subgenres of film and novels for both young adults and general audiences. It was following this success that *The Maze Runner* was released, first as a book in 2009 and then as a film in 2014.

The first in a series of novels that includes prequels and sequels, *The Maze Runner* was both the first national release for author James Dashner and the major directorial debut for film director Wes Ball. Dashner had enjoyed some regional success for his young adult series prior to *The Maze Runner*, while Ball earned his spot based on a short film that showcased his skill with imagery and moody graphics.

In addition to presenting a dystopia, *The Maze Runner* shares with its contemporaries a distinct sense of distrust for larger systems of power. These dystopias are defined not simply by disaster and destruction but also by the massive corporations and governments that oppress the common people, particularly the teenaged protagonists. While the evil government of Panem in the Hunger Games series and the faction leaders of the Divergent series are somewhat clearly defined, the systems of power in *The Maze Runner* remain hidden at first, their motivations and identity a mystery to the main characters. It is with this uncertainty and lack of knowledge that the characters must navigate their world, uniting in the common dystopian task of challenging older rulers while transitioning from children to adults.

Film Analysis

Both the film and the novel versions of *The Maze Runner* open with the main character, Thomas (Dylan O'Brien), entering the Glade at the center at the maze. This entrance is a moment of unknowing and confusion; Thomas is completely deprived of all memory (in the novel he retains his name, while in the movie he does not recall it for several days), and the setting is deeply mysterious. The novel is able to emphasize this lack of knowledge by entering Thomas's mind, exploring the confusion and fear that arise as he first meets the boys who will, in time, become his allies.

The book's first scene describes the opening of the box that delivers Thomas: "He heard noises above—voices—and fear squeezed his chest." In the film, this effect is accomplished instead by a few carefully timed point-of-view shots in which the camera shows the audience exactly what Thomas is looking at. The viewer enters his perspective as the elevator rises into the Glade, light flashing occasionally in to provide brief hints of what the world might be, and again when Thomas first sees the other boys, who stand above him and look down. This second shot emphasizes the power that the boys hold—they know this world and its rules—as well as the fear that has overtaken Thomas, as the perspective makes the boys appear to be larger and stronger in comparison to him than they actually are.

Perspective is one of the most powerful filmic tools used throughout *The Maze Runner*, with the camera angle regularly providing a glimpse into Thomas's interior emotional world. While the science-fiction landscape and dystopian elements are unreal seeming, the emotional battles that Thomas faces are in fact incredibly human, and common to many teenagers. He must challenge an existing structure of power that remains mysterious to him, for instance, while learning to build trust and work collaboratively with his group of peers, a description that will sound familiar to many people who have attended high school. Perspective-wise, the film summarizes this emotional world with one powerful shot: the first time Thomas sees the maze doors close in the evening. While the camera has favored close, head-on shots of the boys up to this point, the closing of the maze doors is suddenly presented in an extreme wide shot. As the boys stand together in front of the massive walls, the audience can both see the seeming impossibility of their task (the maze dwarfing the boys, its true magnitude still not entirely visible even from this extreme angle) while also noting their collective reliance on one another, unified in a straight line by the camera. Notably, Thomas is now one of them, equal in this line rather than peering up from below.

This extreme wide shot is echoed several times throughout the film, employed whenever the group from the Glade faces the maze directly to challenge the power that lies secretly behind it. Within the maze, however, different techniques are used to present the characters' chaotic fear. It is there that the movie employs the technique called "handheld camera" or "free camera." Instead of using the digital and physical tools that stabilize a film image, free camera instead uses a camera that is held in the hand of the cameraperson, resulting in a shaky, unsteady shot. These types of shots suggest the point of view of the characters, throwing the audience into Thomas's panicked perspective. At the same time, their instability and motion create a heightened level of immediacy, as though the film itself does not know what is coming next and must adjust in the moment. This technique mirrors the book's similarly panicked, jerky movement the first time Thomas enters the maze and sees a biomechanical creature called a Griever:

Please go the other way, Thomas pleaded silently.
Turn.
Go.
That way.
Please!
The Griever's spikes popped out; its body rolled toward Thomas and Alby.
whirrrrrrrrrrrrrr
click-click-click

The short paragraphs of the prose mirror the quick movement from Thomas's mind to the physical realities of the outside world, while the emphasis on actions and sounds makes the danger of the Griever hyper-present, just as in the film. In both novel and film, these moments seem to stand in stark contrast to what else has been revealed about the Glade. Although still a frightening and unknown world, the Glade represents relative safety, its stable shots and lengthier prose used to explore the group bonding of the prisoners, and is nowhere near as frightening as the immediate danger of the maze itself.

These film techniques do a great deal to increase the suspense and thrill of *The Maze Runner* and are employed along with dramatic lighting in order to do justice to the heavy action of the novel. Just as importantly, they always turn the audience's attention back to Thomas and his relationships with the other prisoners of the Glade, which are the "real" experiences of the narrative. In fact, one of the most significant changes made in the film version is the removal of plot devices that fall into the realm of fantasy instead of science fiction, most specifically the telepathic link between Thomas and Teresa (Kaya Scodelario). While the plot is still outside the possibilities of the world we live in, by only allowing in elements that could theoretically be present in a near-future dystopian reality, the film makes the characters seem more believable and relatable, and the threats more ominous. It is this tendency on the part of the film that makes a large, sweeping shot of the maze as much about the boys standing in front of it as it is about the implications and the danger of the structure itself, just as the first shot of the maze from above, taken from a helicopter as the survivors escape, is more about their position of power over the structure at that moment than it is about viewing the actual landscape. Thomas is but one adolescent, attempting to survive on his own, as the camera constantly reminds the viewer; however, even when one is most alone or most independent, one can still be stronger by turning to allies in one's community.

Significance

Similarly to how the novel, from a relatively unknown author, quickly became a *New York Times* best seller, the film of *The Maze Runner* grossed more than $300 million while also earning praise from many critics. While not as popular as the wildly successful Hunger Games series, *The Maze Runner* established itself as one of the major players in the subgenre of dystopias and apocalypses featuring teenage lead characters.

In large part, the success of *The Maze Runner* rests on how well the plot, visuals, and characterization are executed. The themes it explores are presented a bit more darkly than is typical of young adult dystopian films, with a large number of gruesome character deaths and the central power seeming to have total control and unending resources at its disposal. On the whole, however, rather than departing wildly from the genre elements that distinguish science-fiction dystopias, *The Maze Runner* performs these themes with technical grace. The actors are engaging and honest, the special are effects convincing, and the metaphoric elements are clear without being too heavy handed.

One of the most significant aspects of the *Maze Runner* film has less to do with the specifics of the movie than with the general popularity of the themes it explores. The world it inhabits is an incredibly dark one, where absolutely no person in charge can be trusted with power and where, even within the group spirit of survival and camaraderie, betrayal is still a common risk. As teenagers enter an era of massive global powers, surveillance states, wars on and of terrorism, and the threat of environmental collapse, the massive popularity of films such as *The Maze Runner* provides some hint as to what effects this modern world has had on the psyches of those who are about to inherit it.

T. Fleischmann, MFA

Further Reading

"Dystopian Novels: Have You Read One Lately?" *Library Media Connection* 31.1 (2012): 28–29. *Literary Reference Center*. Web. 10 Feb. 2015. <http://search.ebscohost.com/login.aspx?direct=true&db=lkh&AN=79243483&site=lrc-plus>.

Mendelson, Scott. "Review: *The Maze Runner* Breaks from the Pack." Rev. of *The Maze Runner*, dir. Wes Ball. *Forbes*. Forbes.com, 18 Sept. 2014. Web. 2 Feb. 2015. <http://www.forbes.com/sites/scottmendelson/2014/09/18/review-the-maze-runner-seperates-itself-from-the-pack/>.

Robertson, Barbara. "Amazing." *Computer Graphics World* Sept.–Oct. 2014: 20–26. *Academic Search Complete*. Web. 10 Feb. 2015. <http://search.ebscohost.com/login.aspx?direct=true&db=a9h&AN=99398009&site=ehost-live>.

Bibliography

Abrams, Sara. Rev. of *The Maze Runner*, by James Dashner. *Journal of Adolescent & Adult Literacy* 54.2 (2010): 158–59. *Literary Reference Center*. Web. 10 Feb. 2015. <http://search.ebscohost.com/login.aspx?direct=true&db=lfh&AN=54303712&site=lrc-live>.

Dickison, Cynthia. "While Not Innovative, *Maze Runner* Themes Deftly Mined." Rev. of *The Maze Runner*, dir. Wes Ball. *Star Tribune* [Minneapolis] 17 Sept. 2014: n. pag. *Points of View Reference Center*. Web. 10 Feb. 2015. <http://search.ebscohost.com/login.aspx?direct=true&db=pwh&AN=2W63164752830&site=pov-live>.

Spisak, April. "Dystopian Novel?" *Horn Book Magazine* May–June 2012: 55–60. *Literary Reference Center*. Web. 10 Feb. 2015. <http://search.ebscohost.com/login.aspx?direct=true&db=lfh&AN=74608467&site=lrc-live>.

Me and Earl and the Dying Girl

The Book

Author: Jesse Andrews (b. 1982)
First published: 2012

The Film

Director: Alfonso Gomez-Rejon (b. 1972)
Screenplay by: Jesse Andrews
Starring: Thomas Mann, RJ Cyler, Olivia Cooke, Nick Offerman, and Molly Shannon

Context

Me and Earl and the Dying Girl was Jesse Andrews's debut novel. It was a critically acclaimed best seller, was named one of the best books of 2012 by *Kirkus Reviews*, and won the Cybils Award for Young Adult Fiction in 2012. The book was optioned for film rights before it was even published. Andrews wrote the book after watching his grandfather battle with terminal illness and his family's efforts to cope with that loss. In response, he decided to write a book about illness that was both funny and heartfelt. The book's humor and the self-deprecating tone of the main character distinguished it from other young adult literature with terminal illness as a central theme. The book was released the same year as another wildly popular young adult book about cancer, John Green's emotional *The Fault in Our Stars* (2012). Likewise, the film *Me and Earl and the Dying Girl* was released within a year of the film adaptation of *The Fault in Our Stars*, as well as *If I Stay* (2014), the cinematic interpretation of Gayle Forman's 2009 novel about a girl in a coma following a fatal car crash.

Me and Earl and the Dying Girl fits into the young adult genre that Julie Passanante Elman, a professor at the University of Missouri-Columbia, named "teen sick-lit" in 2012. This category, which became popular in the 1980s, typically features a character with some kind of illness and focuses on that character's romances and friendships. Lurlene McDaniel, who wrote over fifty young adult sick-lit novels, is one of the most well-known writers of the genre, known for the popular *Six Months to Live* (1985) and the other novels in her Dawn Rochelle series. These stories are related to the illness narrative that dates back to the Victorian era of literature. *Me and Earl and the Dying Girl* is unique, however, for its focus on friendship and lack of romance. Though most early illness narratives ended happily, many contemporary pieces, like *Me and Earl and the Dying Girl*, have broken away from that kind of ending.

Critics and readers alike were drawn to *Me and Earl and the Dying Girl* for protagonist Greg Gaines's narrative voice and relatability. It was the character of Greg that drew director Alfonso Gomez-Rejon to the project. He came across the script shortly after the death of his father and found that he understood the story's struggle with grief and felt a deep connection with Greg. Gomez-Rejon had directed episodes of *Glee* and *American Horror Story* and served as second-unit director on several acclaimed films, but had only helmed one feature before signing on to direct *Me and Earl and the Dying Girl*.

Film Analysis

Viewers are introduced to the story with a shot of Greg Gaines (Thomas Mann) sitting in front of his computer. In a voice over Greg draws viewers into the plot as he says, "I have no idea how to tell this story. I don't even know how to start it. . . . This is the story of my senior year of high school, and how it destroyed my life." The actual story starts when high school senior Greg Gaines's mother asks him to spend time with Rachel Kushner (Olivia Cooke), a classmate who has been diagnosed with leukemia. Greg goes to Rachel's house only because his mother nags him, but the teens' friendship is quickly established. He and his lifelong best friend, Earl (RJ Cyler), make parody films of classic films together, which he shares with Rachel. Eventually, they decide to make a film for Rachel at the suggestion of their friend Madison. In the time spent together, Greg learns what it means to be a friend, something that Earl understands is difficult for Greg, who fears rejection. Greg finds it difficult even to call Earl his friend, referring to him instead as his coworker. Greg must learn to put others first before he loses the two relationships that matter the most.

In addition to the theme of friendship, the film shows how both Greg and Rachel must learn when it is time to hold on and when it is time to let go. Greg feels like his life is falling apart after he and Rachel argue about giving up on life. Each thinks the other is giving up after Rachel chooses to stop treatments. Rachel challenges Greg to do something with his life and stop avoiding relationships, while Greg is angry that Rachel seems to be accepting death without fighting. He struggles to make sense of his life. After Earl confronts Greg about his selfishness, he ditches his prom date, Madison, and goes to the hospital to see Rachel. He gifts her with a wrist corsage and her film, which he has finally finished. This trip turns out to be the teens' final visit. Rachel falls into a coma after watching the film and dies ten hours later. Greg realizes that Rachel's film was too hard to make because it meant something, like Rachel herself.

The film ends with Rachel's wake. Before Greg can leave, Rachel's mother gives him a letter Rachel had written before she died. She shares a final legacy through artwork: a 3-D sculpture in a book she leaves for him, hand-drawn squirrels on her wallpaper, and a letter to the university he wants to attend. These little details show Greg that it is time to move forward with his life, and he turns their story into his college application.

Another layer of depth is added to the film with the integration of the filmmaking element. Greg's and Earl's favorite pastime is creating mock foreign films. The naïve animation, bad plots, and corny dialogue in these films is seen throughout the movie as cuts of their work are integrated to add to the storyline. Greg's internal monologue is often illustrated through a version of one of these little pieces. For example, at the beginning of the film when Greg is wondering how to start his work, he plays with the now cliché line "It was the best of times; it was the worst of times," which then leads to an animated glimpse at how one person may experience a wonderful day including Vietnamese food and a harp player while another might have the worst day ever with alligators and a vat of acid. The clips add humor throughout, lightening the tone of the sad story. Greg's and Earl's filmmaking talent is challenged when they make their film for Rachel. The boys find that making a film that matters is much harder than it seems, and their struggle to do it right almost destroys their friendship.

The director's incorporation of these pieces breaks the film up in a similar way as his use of varied camera shots does. Though much of the film uses medium shots to show viewers the context of the setting and details of the characters' nonverbal actions, there are numerous places where long shots add to the perspective. In one instance there is a long shot of Rachel walking down the road from Greg's house. The camera work foreshadows the end of the film, a visual complement to Greg's comment that he likes Rachel and will not be happy if she dies at the end of the film. Camera angles also reveal more about the characters' feelings throughout the film. In many cases, Greg approaches Rachel's house and looks up at her window; this reflects the first scene between Rachel and Greg when he goes to her house at his mother's urging. Rachel stands at the top of the stairs looking down at Greg, and viewers see her from below. It is as if Greg is always gazing up at her, beneath her in some way. Another memorable camera technique that is found in the film is in a Dutch angle where the camera is turned on its side. The technique is used in scenes that are disorienting in tone to impress upon the viewers the sense of bewilderment that the characters are experiencing.

Significance

Me and Earl and the Dying Girl premiered on the film festival circuit, where it was successful. The film won the prestigious Grand Jury Prize and the Audience Award at the 2015 Sundance Film Festival. The film won an additional twelve awards at film festivals in 2015, including the Golden Space Needle Award for best director and the third place Golden Space Needle Award for best film at the Seattle International Film Festival, among many others. In addition to film festival success, the film was nominated for five additional prizes, including the Teen Choice Award nominations for choice summer movie, choice movie: chemistry, and choice movie: breakout star for Thomas Mann.

The film did receive both positive and negative criticism. Among the positives, the film was lauded for its intelligent dialogue and realism. The less than perfect characters whose lives reflected the real world also drew audiences. The thematic focus on friendship over romance was also praised. Though many critics appreciated the film, there were some who found it cliché, and one critic even argued that it encourages stereotypes. The harshest criticism claimed a lack of reality in the development of Greg and Rachel's friendship, citing the fact that the two were not likely to have been spent time together without the encouragement of Greg's mother. Though the movie was largely a critical success, it was not a commercial success and made close to a million dollars less in the theaters than the eight million dollars it took to make the film.

Theresa L. Stowell, PhD

Further Reading

Alter, Ethan. "Friends 4Ever." *Film Journal International* 118.7 (2015): n.pag. Print.

Elman, Julie Passanante. "'Nothing Feels as Real': Teen Sick-Lit, Sadness, and the Condition of Adolescence." *Journal of Literacy & Cultural Disability Studies* 6.2 (2012): 175–91. Print.

Bibliography

Anderson, John. "Jesse Andrews Learns on the Fly to Write *Me and Earl and the Dying Girl*." *New York Times*. New York Times, 5 June 2015. Web. 15 Dec. 2015. <http://www.nytimes.com/2015/06/07/movies/jesse-andrews-learns-on-the-fly-to-write-me-and-earl-and-the-dying-girl.html?_r=0>.

Jacobs, Matthew. "The Quirky Heartbreaker *Me and Earl and the Dying Girl* Is Summer's Signature Teen Movie." *Huffington Post*. TheHuffingtonPost.com, 14 June 2015. Web. 24 Nov. 2015. <http://www.huffingtonpost.com/2015/06/14/me-and-earl-and-the-dying-girl_n_7573230.html>.

O'Malley, Sheila. Rev. of *Me and Earl and the Dying Girl*, dir. Alfonso Gomez-Rejon. *RogerEbert.com*. Ebert Digital, 12 June 2015. Web. 24 Nov. 2015. <http://www.rogerebert.com/reviews/me-and-earl-and-the-dying-girl-2015>.

Scott, A. O. "Review: In *Me and Earl and the Dying Girl*, a Comfort Zone That Cannot Last." Rev. of *Me and Earl and the Dying Girl*, dir. Alfonso Gomez-Rejon. *New York Times*. New York Times, 11 June 2015. Web. 24 Nov. 2015. <http://www.nytimes.com/2015/06/12/movies/review-in-me-and-earl-and-the-dying-girl-a-comfort-zone-that-cannot-last.html?_r=0>.

Mermaids

The Book

Author: Patty Dann (b. 1953)
First published: 1986

The Film

Director: Richard Benjamin (b. 1938)
Screenplay by: June Roberts
Starring: Cher, Bob Hoskins, Winona Ryder, and Christina Ricci

Context

Young adult literature is a relatively modern genre. The publication of S. E. Hinton's novel *The Outsiders* in 1967 is generally considered to be the beginning of the genre. Young adult literature is written for and marketed to readers between the ages of twelve and eighteen, with a central protagonist of the same age. Young adult fiction is often composed of coming-of-age stories that focus on teenagers as they attempt to make sense of their own lives and developing new identities as adults. The central conflicts generally revolve around important obstacles the average adolescent faces in life including identity, love, social status, school, family, and personal relationships.

During the 1980s, young adult literature titles were not selling as well in the previous decades, in part because the recession in the United States led to many libraries cutting their book-buying budget. At this time, libraries and schools were the main purchasers of young adult titles, and so with less buying power, fewer publishers were interested in releasing young adult books. Despite this, the 1980s did see the continued popularity of some major young adult authors such as Judy Blume and Christopher Pike and the release of many now-classic young adult novels. Dann published *Mermaids* in 1986. Dann's style is similar to Blume's and the female protagonist of *Mermaids*, Charlotte Flax, has much in common with Blume's more popular teenage narrators. The release of a movie version of *Mermaids* four years later in 1990 stands out for being one of the few film adaptations of a young adult novel to be made before the resurgence of the young adult genre in the early 1990s.

Film Analysis

The film opens in 1963 on a swimming pool, as Charlotte's younger sister, Kate (Christina Ricci), is taking part in a swim meet. Kate is an essential part of the family, Charlotte (Winona Ryder) explains in voice-over, because she is the only thing that she and her mother (whom she calls Mrs. Flax) can agree upon. They both think she is the best person in the world. The scene quickly transitions to the Flax home in Oklahoma, where Charlotte and Kate are watching a television show about nuns. Charlotte is a very religious young woman. Although her mother does not observe any religion, Charlotte has been obsessed with Catholicism since the first time she saw a girl cross herself and say the Hail Mary before a spelling bee. This obsession is perhaps in response to her mother's frenetic lifestyle, which includes many failed relationships with men. Neither Charlotte nor Kate knows their father, and no one has been in their life long enough because Mrs. Flax (Cher) moves every time her relationship with a man in one city does not work out. Immediately after her relationship with a married man in Oklahoma falls apart, the Flax family moves for the eighteenth time, to Massachusetts. In the book, they live in the fictional town of Grove, while in the movie, they move to Eastport.

The novel starts in a similar fashion and in the same year. It too is narrated by Charlotte, and the first two chapters are reserved for a description of her family, particularly of her mother. The film adaptation remains remarkably faithful to the novel, even using dialogue directly from the text, such as when Charlotte describes her mother's view of religion, "Mrs. Flax doesn't believe in ritual or tradition." A few details are changed at the beginning of the movie. First, Charlotte is fifteen years old instead of fourteen, and the movie suggests that she has never really been in love before she meets Joe (Michael Schoeffling), a local twenty-six-year-old who is a caretaker at the abbey down the road from the new Flax house. In the book, Charlotte is very specific about her feelings. She explains before she meets Joe that she has been in love exactly ninety-two times in her life. She wants nothing more than to settle down in a town, finish school at one high school, and find someone that she can fall in love with. However, she is very worried when she truly falls in love with Joe because she does not want to "fall in love and want to do disgusting things." While she does not castigate her mother for the lascivious life she leads, Charlotte is overly judgmental of her own emotions and private thoughts. One of her rituals is to write down all the impure thoughts she has each week so that she can confess them. In the book, she goes as far as to flagellate herself following a more extreme religious purification. These details are toned down in the movie. Charlotte wears almost exclusively black and always wears a crucifix around her neck.

However Charlotte cannot help herself around Joe. Not only does he work down the road from where she lives, he also drives the school bus. Her mother approves of her getting into a relationship (and may even have an interest in Joe for herself), despite the fact that Joe is almost twice Charlotte's age and an adult. But even though Charlotte makes many of the first moves to be around Joe, she is still in control of herself and does not allow much anything to happen. It is not until President John F. Kennedy is assassinated that she becomes so overwhelmed that she allows herself to kiss Joe. Despite the fact that sex is a constant issue in Mrs. Flax's life, Charlotte knows very little about it. After the kiss, she convinces herself that she is pregnant, partly due to her lack of knowledge, and partly due to a number of stories about saints she has read. She believes that the kiss was a sin, and so her punishment from God is a miraculous conception.

Both the novel and the movie are more driven by characters than plot, focusing on major points in the lives of the Flax family members through Charlotte's perspective. While they stay in Massachusetts, Mrs. Flax begins to see a local man, Lou Landsky (Bob Hoskins), who tries to bring some normality into the lives of the family. Lou is a rough but lovable townie who wants to have a life with the Flax family, but Mrs. Flax's inability to get emotionally close to men keeps their relationship from fully developing during the course of the story. After a particularly angry argument with her mother, Charlotte finally decides that she is ready to have sex. While Charlotte is babysitting Kate, she drives to the bell tower of the abbey to have sex with Joe and leaves Kate in the car. But Kate does not stay in the car and decides instead to try to swim in the lake near the abbey and nearly drowns. She is rescued by nuns from the abbey. Mrs. Flax and Charlotte have a blowout fight over what happened, but by the film's end, they have forgiven one another and life continues as normal.

The details of Mrs. Flax's relationship represent a change in perspective between the novel and the film. The novel is told entirely from Charlotte's perspective, the movie is also filmed around the limited perspective of Charlotte. Generally, the film mimics the first-person narration of the book and perspective limited to just Charlotte by showing scenes in which she is present. However, there are some scenes in the movie in which the camera takes a more omniscient perspective, following other characters around to develop them more fully. This takes place in the scene where Kate nearly drowns in the lake and in other scenes that develop the relationship between Mrs. Flax and Lou. Aside from the voice-over narration, it is the only notable technique that the film uses.

Significance

Dann's *Mermaids* became successful for its characters. Readers and critics found the entire Flax family quirky and interesting. Dann loads her characters with idiosyncrasies: from Mrs. Flax's penchant for hors d'oeuvres (she never makes a full meal and serves everything on a toothpick), to Charlotte's religious zeal, and to Kate's determination to break the world record for holding breath underwater and swim the English Channel.

Though the film depicts the same characters, it did not receive particularly positive reviews from critics or audiences, though it met some commercial success. Critics like Roger Ebert particularly were uninterested in Cher's performance of Mrs. Flax and found the character herself to be largely implausible. Winona Ryder was widely praised for her performance as Charlotte; Vincent Canby suggested in his *New York Times* review that the film might have gone darker to push Ryder further. Although Cher was billed first, many critics noted that *Mermaids* was really Ryder's film. And although they did like the performances of Bob Hoskins and Christina Ricci, they found nothing dynamic about the movie as a whole. After the initial release, however, the movie has continued to be a favorite of audiences and gone on to become a cult classic.

Aaron Horton, MA

Further Reading

Dann, Patty. Interview by Derek Alger. *Pif Magazine*. Pif Magazine, 1 Oct. 2013. Web. 10 Nov. 2015. <http://www.pifmagazine.com/2013/10/patty-dann>.

Dann, Patty. "Telling Stories." *Writer* 113.4 (2000): 5. *Literary Reference Center.* Web. 10 Nov. 2015. <http://search.ebscohost.com/login.aspx?direct=true&db=lfh&AN=2860346&site=lrc-live>.

Hudson, Kathy. "There's a Bittersweet Love Story behind Author Patty Dann's Sequel to *Mermaids*." *Baltimore Sun*. Tribune, 4 Mar. 2014. Web. 10 Nov. 2015. <http://www.baltimoresun.com/news/maryland/baltimore-city/north-baltimore/ph-ms-hudsons-corner-0306-20140304-story.html>.

Bibliography

Canby, Vincent. "Cher's the Mother (Don't Eat the Snacks)." Rev. of *Mermaids*, dir. Richard Benjamin. *New York Times*. New York Times, 14 Dec. 1990. Web. 23 Nov. 2015. <http://www.nytimes.com/movie/review?res=9C0CE7D6123AF937A25751C1A966958260>.

Ebert, Roger. Rev. of *Mermaids*, dir. Richard Benjamin. *RogerEbert.com*. Ebert Digital, 14 Dec. 1990. Web. 10 Nov. 2015. <http://www.rogerebert.com/reviews/mermaids-1990>.

Kennedy, Marina. "Mermaids, Starfish, and Goldfish: Patty Dann's Real Life Inspires Her Books." *Woman around Town*. Woman around Town, 16 June 2014. Web. 10 Nov. 2015. <http://www.womanaroundtown.com/sections/woman-around-town/mermaids-starfish-and-goldfish-patty-danns-real-life-inspires-her-books>.

"Patty Dann." *PattyDann.com*. Patty Dan, n.d. Web. 10 Nov. 2015. <http://www.pattydann.com>.

Mortal Instruments: The City of Bones

The Book

Author: Cassandra Clare (b. 1973)
First published: *City of Bones* (2007)

The Film

Director: Harald Zwart (b. 1965)
Screenplay by: Jessica Postigo Paquette
Starring: Lily Collins, Jamie Campbell Bower, Robert Sheehan, Kevin Zegers, Jemima West, Godfrey Gao, Lena Headey, Jonathan Rhys Meyers, Aidan Turner

Context

Books and films about dark supernatural phenomena and bizarre beings have long been popular. *Beowulf* and *Sir Gawain and the Green Knight* are two early examples in English literature of such writings. Homer's *Odyssey* is an even earlier source of such legends. Of course, the rise of gothic literature in England, especially in the nineteenth century, set a precedent for many mysterious stories and novels, all the way up to the present day. Gothic movies, meanwhile, have been especially popular in the early twenty-first century. The Twilight series of novels and movies, with their combinations of werewolves and vampires, are perhaps the most famous (or infamous) examples of how broadly such material appeals to readers and viewers.

The Mortal Instruments: City of Bones, a 2013 film based on the 2007 novel *City of Bones* (the first book in the six-volume Mortal Instruments series), is clearly indebted to all these traditions. The influence of the Twilight series seems especially obvious. The film appeals to elements rooted deeply in the human psyche, such as the fear of evil, the fear of death, and the fear of monsters. The film also appeals to fundamental human desires, such as love, friendship, heroism, safety, adventure, discovery, and excitement. The movie (far more than the book) is full of gripping suspense, terrifying shocks, and all manner of plot developments that get a viewer's adrenaline pumping.

Film Analysis

The film version of *City of Bones* features a highly complicated backstory that is much easier to follow than in the book. Much of the book is given over to lengthy historical exposition involving numerous, endlessly proliferating characters. Plot twists abound, and sometimes it is difficult to keep the stories straight. The film has been criticized for some of these same reasons, but a case can be made that the film is far more effective in engaging viewers' imaginations and emotions than the book. After all, the filmmakers had all the tricks of the modern cinematic trade at their disposal. These cinematic tricks include stunning photography, sometimes tender but often gripping music, and a whole range of computer-generated special effects designed to fascinate and terrify.

The film is also brimming with young, good-looking actors, whose outfits are sometimes a matter of explicit humor. At one point, for instance, the film's teenaged heroine, Clary (Lily Collins), gets instructions about how to dress from the nearly always scantily dressed Isabelle (Jemima West). Frustrated with her new, and nearly nonexistent black outfit, Clary asks, "How is being dressed like a hooker going to help me find my mom?" To which Isabelle responds, "Easy now, those are my clothes." Isabelle's brother, Alec (Kevin Zegers) is even more skeptical about the outfit Clary is wearing, "She looks like somebody whose phone number should be on a bathroom wall." Such dialogue is typical of the often witty humor that makes the film so appealing. The movie's ability to combine wit with terror makes it especially effective (at least to some viewers).

The terror in the film, in fact, seems far more gripping than the terror in the book. This is not surprising, because the film can actually show terrifying creatures, events, and scenes, while the book can merely describe them. The prose created by novelist Cassandra Clare has impressed many book buyers, but it is arguably little match for the real-life special effects Hollywood can now produce.

Barely twelve minutes into the film, but several chapters into the book, the real horror begins; and from that point on, consistently escalates. Clary is at a coffee shop with her friend Simon (Robert Sheehan) when she receives a phone call from her mother. Her mother sounds panicked on the other end of the phone as she tells Clary, "Don't come home! Do you understand me, Clary? Don't you dare come home! Tell Luke (Aidan Turner), tell him he's found me." Clary then hears the sound of shattering and something hitting the floor, and her phone goes dead. Clary races home, but when Clary reaches her apartment she is confronted with what seems to be a huge and vicious Doberman pinscher. The dog soon morphs quite convincingly into a creature far more hideous and dangerous. Here and throughout the film, Clary holds her own while battling monsters and evil villains. This movie taps into a strong feminist consciousness and surely part of the film's appeal results from its focus on a brave, heroic young woman.

Other particularly memorable and terrifying special effects involved the transformation of a warm-hearted, aging woman into an evil beast with a nasty attitude; the transformation of ravens into menacing creatures that are seemingly composed of fiery ash; and the spectacular moment when an ugly little girl seems about to transform into something far uglier and more vicious, only to be whisked off the screen, out of the blue, by a heroic werewolf. No expenses seem to have been spared on the film's special effects, and what the movie may (allegedly) lack in a convincing, comprehensible plot is more than made up for by the sheer shock value of the sights it offers.

Visually, in fact, the film is stunning. Especially impressive is the scene when Clary and the brooding young hero, Jace (Jamie Campbell Bower), first visit the Institute—a refuge, smack in the heart of New York City, for supernatural beings. What first appears to be an old church is soon magnificently transformed into an imposing, almost castle-like structure. Only supernatural beings can see this building and its extra dimensions, but the filmmakers render this building visible to anyone viewing the movie. Here, and throughout the film, the technicians charged with creating computer-generated images have definitely earned their pay. So, too, have the persons in charge of choreographing the highly believable fight scenes. The movie is brimming with battles, often involving hand-to-hand (or hand-to-claw) combat. Most of the major characters seem to have had extensive martial arts training (or maybe their skills are innate). In any case, the film is full of impressive moves, and the battles are never less than stirring. Again, the film seems to have an intrinsic advantage over the book. Whereas some readers may feel that the book drags (and drags, and drags), the movie is full of kinetic energy.

Fight scenes have, of course, always appealed to moviegoers, but the fight scenes here are never so overwhelming and apocalyptic (as they are, for instance, in the conclusion of the film *I Am Number Four*) that they seem overdone. In *Mortal Instruments: The City of Bones*, the fights usually involve just two combatants, as in the final fight between Jace and the movie's evil mastermind, Valentine (Jonathan Rhys Meyers). Thus the fights often contribute effectively to characterization, especially since the characters usually talk while trying to kill each other. The combat scenes in this film differ from those in some other movies, where often the main emphasis seems to be on creating as many explosions as possible.

Finally, one other appealing feature that makes the film memorable is its emphasis on witty banter. Such wit is also prominent in the book, but there it often seems almost too clever, as if the author is trying to display her own cleverness rather than letting the characters speak convincingly for themselves. In the movie, the acting is almost entirely superb, so the witty exchanges sound credible. The film visually quite impressive, as is its dialogue.

Significance

The Mortal Instruments: City of Bones cost an estimated $60 million to make and grossed a little over $90 million worldwide. Perhaps this relatively disappointing figure resulted from the fact that critics almost universally trashed the movie. Regular audiences seem to have been more easily impressed, but they did not appreciate the film enough to give it the kind of word-of-mouth praise that would have made it a hit.

The film was harshly criticized for many different reasons. Critics attacked the movie as derivative, incoherent, superficial, overly long, and convoluted. Most negative criticism focused on the film's obvious debts to earlier movies (including *Star Wars*) and literary franchises (including the Harry Potter books and movies). One senses that if this film had somehow come before those earlier works, it would have been more positively received. History—both literary and cinematic—cannot be undone, and so *The Mortal Instruments: City of Bones* will go down in history for having arrived too late in an already overcrowded field. When seen on its own terms by someone unfamiliar with the books, it arguably works just fine.

Despite mostly negative reviews, a few critics were kind. Colin Covert for the *Star Tribune* praised the film's "dark, grandiose interiors, cobwebby catacombs and several varieties of demons," concluding that with "its spectacle, morbid sense of humor and hustling pace, *The Mortal Instruments* encourages you to shrug and just go with it."

Robert C. Evans, PhD

Further Reading

Bethune, Brian. "The Hunger Games and Then Some: Mortal Instruments Pushes Even More Boundaries Than Its Girl-Powered Predecessors." *Maclean's* 26 Aug. 2013: 74. Print.

Bryan Miller, Sarah. "'Mortal Instruments' Has Big Fights, Small Wit." *St. Louis Post-Dispatch*. Stltoday. com, 20 Aug. 2013. Web. 9 May 2015. <http://www.stltoday.com/entertainment/movies/reviews/mortal-instruments-has-big-fights-small-wit/article_369aa9d2-f870-55bf-80b6-b877d783c7b7.html>.

Rev. of *Mortal Instruments: City of Bones*, dir. Harald Zwart. *Tribute* 30.2 (2013): 2. *MasterFILE Premier*. Web. 29 May 2015. <http://search.ebscohost.com/login.aspx?direct=true&db=f5h&AN=88314859&site=eds-live>.

Bibliography

Covert, Colin. "Paranormal Heart Beats in *Mortal Instruments*." *Star Tribune*. StarTribune, 23 Aug. 2013. Web. 9 May 2015. <http://www.startribune.com/paranormal-heart-beats-in-mortal-instruments/220392711/>.

Hawker, Phillipa. "DVD Review: *The Mortal Instruments City of Bones*." *Newcastle Herald*. Fairfax Media, 22 Aug. 2013. Web. 9 May 2015. <http://www.theherald.com.au/story/1724431/dvd-review-the-mortal-instruments-city-of-bones/>.

Pambid, Diadem. "*The Mortal Instruments Movie*: Five Reasons Why It Isn't a Twilight Rip Off.'" *International Business Times*. IBT Media, 26 Aug. 2013. Web. 9 May 2015. <http://www.ibtimes.com.au/mortal-instruments-movie-five-reasons-why-it-isnt-twilight-rip-photos-1267747>.

Mrs. Doubtfire

The Book

Author: Anne Fine (b. 1947)
First published: *Madame Doubtfire* (1987; *Alias Madame Doubtfire*, 1988)

Film

Director: Chris Columbus (b. 1958)
Screenplay by: Randi Mayem Singer and Leslie Dixon
Starring: Robin Williams, Sally Field, Pierce Brosnan, and Harvey Fierstein

Context

Madame Doubtfire (1987) was first published in the United Kingdom and was one of many works by British young adult writer Anne Fine. It was first published in the United States in 1988 as *Alias Madame Doubtfire*. Fine, who had been writing children's and young adult novels since the late 1970s, wrote the novel to show the effect that divorce can have on every member of a family. The book was seen as a unique addition to young adult fiction, for its unique portrayal of a cross-dressing father doing anything to spend time with his children after a particularly ugly divorce, and its detailed and uncompromising look at the impact of divorce on adolescents. During the 1980s, the young adult genre was a firmly established literary genre around the world. Young adult literature came into its own as a genre in the 1960s and flourished in the following decade, and although it saw some decline in the 1980s, it continued to be an important genre in literature of the twentieth century. Fine had already established herself as a young adult writer by the time *Madame Doubtfire*, her eighth book, was published. It received high praise and was shortlisted for three children's book awards in the same year. Although the novel focuses on the funny adventures of Daniel Hilliard and his alias, it also looks closely and unflinchingly at the effect that warring parents can have on their children when those children are stuck in the middle of a bitter divorce. For this reason, the novel is considered an important addition to the realistic subgenre of British young adult literature.

The film *Mrs. Doubtfire* was optioned by 20th Century Fox Studios and released in 1993, six years after the initial publication of the novel. With a cast including highly acclaimed comedian Robin Williams and accomplished actor Sally Field, the film is considered a commercial and critical success. The film was directed by American director Chris Columbus, who was making his name writing and directing films aimed at young adult audiences as well as other major Hollywood titles. He directed other commercially and critically successful movies such as 1990's *Home Alone*, two films in the Harry Potter series in 2001 and 2002, and the first installment of the film adaptations of the Percy Jackson and the Olympians series in 2010. The novel *Madame Doubtfire* and its film adaptation stand as important and beloved additions to the young adult genre.

Film Analysis

The novel and its film adaptation share the central conceit of a father disguising himself as a woman in order to spend more time with his children after divorcing their mother. They also share a character list with essentially the same characteristics. The father, Daniel Hilliard (Robin Williams), is an actor who cannot find work and has few visitation rights for his children because he has not proven to the courts or his ex-wife, Miranda (Sally Field), that he is responsible enough to take care of his children on his own for an extended period of time. The children love both of their parents and want to spend time equally with them, but the parents' relationship and personal issues keep them from being happy. Both the film and novel are humorous and rely on the wit and comedy of Daniel and his alter ego. However, past these similarities, the film largely diverges from the book.

While Daniel's character was always meant to be humorous, the role in the film was adapted for American comedian and actor Robin Williams's personal talents and became more focused on the cross-dressing nanny than the family as a whole. In the film, Daniel is an actor who loses his job because he believes in certain standards for children's programming. His talent, mirroring Williams's own, is performing different humorous voices and impersonations, so when he decides to take the job as his ex-wife's housekeeper, pretending to be an older Scottish woman both conceals his identity and plays to his strengths. In the novel, Daniel is not shown as having any particular acting strengths, and Madame Doubtfire is more of an eccentric, overly rouged, outrageous middle-aged woman who wears a turban everywhere she goes. Because the novel is set in England, the fact that she speaks with a bit of a posh accent has less of a comedic impact than Williams's Scottish accent in the movie, which is set in California.

While there is a certain didactic element to the novel around the idea of divorce as it focuses on the emotional reactions of the Hilliard children: Lydia, Natalie, and Christopher. This element is largely missing from the film. While Daniel and Miranda's characters do check themselves occasionally to stop from criticizing each other in front of the children, their divorce is much more civil than in the book. The film opens with the couple still together until Daniel throws an out-of-control birthday party for Christopher. While he is angry that he must move out, the interactions between Daniel and Miranda are generally quite amicable. The novel, on the other hand, begins after the two have already divorced and

was so bitter that Daniel and Miranda cannot help but harshly criticize each other, even in front of their children. They harbor a true disdain for each other, while in the movie Daniel wants to get back together with Miranda, and there remains the possibility of this happening at some point. In the end, the film seems to have been created more as an entertaining comedy suitable for the entire family than as a specifically young adult story. It was meant to showcase the acting talent of Robin Williams and place him and his alter ego in humorous situations as he attempts to live as both Daniel and Mrs. Doubtfire.

In this same vein, the film also tones down the real-world concerns that motivate the characters of the novel. While the onscreen Daniel does not take life very seriously and has difficulty holding down a job or cleaning up after himself, he is always a great father to his children. The novel, however, depicts Daniel as a more complicated character. While his love for his children is never questioned, the emotional strain that he is put under dealing with Miranda, his low-paying job as a nude model for an art school, and taking care of his children sometimes leads him to say hurtful things to his own children. He also continues to place his children between himself and Miranda, asking them to stand up for him in situations that they should not be a part of. For example, when Christopher blames his father for not putting up with more from Miranda while they were married, Daniel loses his temper and pushes his son against a wall, yelling at Christopher for not understanding how hard life can be. At no point in the movie does Robin Williams's character come remotely close to any physical violence, nor does he take out his frustrations on his children.

In the climax of both the film and the novel, Daniel's two worlds are thrown together when he must appear at the same place at the same time as both Mrs. Doubtfire and himself. This situational comedy plays out to the same effect in both media. In the novel, Daniel must model for an art class at Miranda's house while taking care of the children as Doubtfire. After one too many changes back and forth between the two personas, he is caught. Miranda is furious but, in the end, realizes that she needs to allow him more time with the children. Similarly in the film, Daniel meets with a television studio executive about a job at the same restaurant where his wife is having her birthday dinner with the entire family. In the end, the latex mask of Mrs. Doubtfire comes off as he is performing the Heimlich maneuver to save the life of Miranda's new boyfriend, and Miranda can only express anger when she finds out the woman she has become so close with is her ex-husband. Both the film and novel end rather uncharacteristically for the young adult genre with the parents, not adolescent protagonists, learning a lesson about themselves.

Significance

Mrs. Doubtfire was considered to be a very big commercial success. It was filmed on a budget of $25 million and, during its run in theaters in 1993, earned nearly ten times that amount of money. It was the second-highest-grossing movie in 1993, only earning less than *Jurassic Park*. Audiences clearly loved the film, and critics also generally praised it, although it was not nearly as much of a critical success as it was a commercial one. Critics applauded Robin Williams's acting ability and the performances of the entire cast, but found that the plot was at times clichéd and overly emotional. They noted a general lack of depth in the characters and found that the film glossed over the emotionally complex consequences of divorce. The decision to focus the film on comedy at the expense of other themes kept it from achieving a stronger critical reception.

As an addition to young adult literature, the novel stands on the fringe of the genre. While it was marketed to teenage readers and was written for a younger audience, it does not keep the adolescent protagonists at the heart of its narrative. Rather, it focuses more on Daniel's life than his children's lives. While considered a young adult novel, it does not necessarily follow all the major conventions of the literary genre. The film, while appropriate for a young adult audience, it was marketed to the family as a whole, with elements for both children and adults. In the end, the novel and film mirror their cross-dressing protagonist by not following the expectations of those around them. For this reason, they stand out as unique additions to the world of young adult storytelling.

Aaron Horton, MA

Further Reading

Jones, Jim. "Chapter 12: Anne Fine's Stories for Life." *Teaching through Texts*. New York: Taylor & Francis, 1999. 150–61.*Literary Reference Center*. Web. 10 Nov. 2015. <http://search.ebscohost.com/login.aspx?direct=true&db=lkh&AN=16888744&site=lrc-plus>.

Tucker, Nicholas. "The United Kingdom Children's Laureate: The Story So Far." *Children's Literature in Education* 45.1 (2014): 47–59. *Literary Reference Center*. Web. 16 Nov. 2015. <http://search.ebscohost.com/login.aspx?direct=true&db=lkh&AN=94081211&site=lrc-plus>.

Bibliography

"Chris Columbus Biography." *Biography.com*. A&E Television Networks, n.d. Web. 10 Nov. 2015. <http://www.biography.com/people/chris-columbus-14424605#film-career>.

Ebert, Roger. Rev. of *Mrs. Doubtfire*, dir. Chris Columbus. *RogerEbert.com*. Ebert Digital, 24 Nov. 1993. Web. 23 Nov. 2015. <http://www.rogerebert.com/reviews/mrs-doubtfire-1993>.

Ewing, Jack. "Anne Fine." *Guide to Literary Masters & Their Works (*2007): 1. *Literary Reference Center*. Web. 16 Nov. 2015. <http://search.ebscohost.com/login.aspx?direct=true&db=lfh&AN=103331LM29579790302541&site=lrc-live>.

Fine, Anne. "Major Awards." *AnneFine.com*. Anne Fine, n.d. Web. 10 Nov. 2015. <http://www.annefine.co.uk/awards.php>.

Maslin, Jane. Rev. of *Mrs. Doubtfire*, dir. Chris Columbus. *New York Times*. New York Times, 24 Nov. 1993. Web. 10 Nov. 2015. <http://www.nytimes.com/movie/review?res=9F0CE4DE1638F937A15752C1A965958260>.

Nick and Norah's Infinite Playlist

The Book

Authors: Rachel Cohn (b. 1968), David Levithan (b. 1972)
First published: 2006

The Film

Director: Peter Sollett (b. 1976)
Screenplay by: Lorene Scafaria
Starring: Michael Cera and Kat Dennings

Context

The novel *Nick and Norah's Infinite Playlist* was published in 2006. Author Rachel Cohn, who wrote the award-winning novel *Gingerbread* (2002) about a California punk girl, contacted David Levithan, author of the small town love story *Boy Meets Boy* (2003), to help her write *Nick and Norah's Infinite Playlist*, after an epiphany she had while strolling through New York's Central Park. "I was just thinking about the *Thin Man* movies," Cohn recalled in 2008 to Madeleine Brand for National Public Radio (NPR). Cohn was referring to a series of 1930s-era films that feature the sharp and boozy couple, Nick and Nora Charles. "I was thinking oh, it would really be fun to write a book about two characters named Nick and Norah and just kind of make them straight edge kids from New Jersey." Cohn felt that there was one problem: she did not trust herself to write the character of Nick. "She had tried writing from a guy's perspective before and felt she hadn't quite gotten it right," Levithan told Brand. Cohn contacted Levithan, who agreed to write the book's first chapter from Nick's perspective. Cohn's idea turned into an entire novel, written chapter by chapter, switching between the perspective of Norah, a tough-on-the-outside, soft-on-the-inside daughter of a famous record producer, and Nick, a heterosexual, lovelorn bassist for a band of gay men.

The book was a playful riff on Cohn and Levithan's shared love of music. The novel's playlist includes songs from the Ramones, Johnny Cash, Green Day, the Cure, Ani DiFranco, the Beatles (the song, "I Want to Hold Your Hand," is important in the plot), Patsy Cline, Lucinda Williams, Merle Haggard, and Belle and Sebastian, to name a few. *Nick and Norah's Infinite Playlist* was well received by readers and critics and earned a handful of regional awards. In 2006 a reviewer for *Publishers Weekly* praised the novel for its scrapbook quality, which Cohn told Brand made it so "fun" for them to write. It "has that pumped-up feeling of a story passed among friends who each add a section, spontaneously incorporating unforeseen elements," the reviewer wrote.

Film Analysis

In adapting the novel for film, director Lorene Scafaria was inspired by classic teen movies from the 1980s, which were directed by John Hughes (*The Breakfast Club*, 1985; *Ferris Bueller's Day Off*, 1986) and Cameron Crowe, who wrote *Fast Times at Ridgemont High* (1982). *Nick and Nora's Infinite Playlist* fit easily into the teen-romantic-comedy genre, but Scafaria knew she

would have to make some important changes to make the story more "cinematic," she told Kevin Kelly for *Indiewire*, in 2008. The plot of the film is propelled by two main devices: the hunt for Norah's inebriated best friend, Caroline, and a wild goose chase across New York City to find the venue at which Nick and Norah's favorite band, Where's Fluffy?, will play at the end of the night. The Where's Fluffy? concert is only one plot point on a larger, metaphorical quest for connection between Nick (Michael Cera) and Nora (Kat Dennings). In the film, Norah sidles up to Nick at the bar after his band finished playing a set and asks him to pretend to be her boyfriend "for five minutes" to make her frenemy, Tris, jealous. Only then does she realize that Nick is Tris's ex-boyfriend and the maestro behind the mixed CDs that she has been swooning over, after Tris tossed them in the trash. In the book, Nick makes the same overture to Norah (a stranger) when he sees Tris with another guy.

At its heart, the film is still about finding meaningful connections with people who respect you for who you are; Tris seems to be interested in Nick only when someone else is, and Norah's on-again, off-again boyfriend, Tal, is more interested in her father's fame than in her. But Scafaria and director, Peter Sollett, made other, more cosmetic decisions that affected the aesthetic of the film. Most importantly, they changed the playlist to include bands that were popular around 2006, like the National, Vampire Weekend, Band of Horses and the Shout Out Louds. Contemporary music has long been an important part of teen movies, beginning with director John Hughes's 1985 movie *The Breakfast Club*, about a socially stratified group of teens serving Saturday detention together. That movie has an iconic ending sequence that rests on the particular bittersweet quality of the 1985 song "Don't You (Forget about Me)" by Simple Minds. The song was considered cutting edge that year, and Hughes's movie was able to define it for audiences as sexy, nostalgic, triumphant and—played under Anthony Michael Hall's flippant voice-over—rebellious.

Music is far more important to Nick and Norah than a cinematic device; their love story argues that music does not merely define moments in one's life, but is a force that brings people together. This argument rings particularly true for teenagers, who form emotional attachments to songs that last a lifetime. According to an article in 2014 for *Slate*, neuroscientists have found evidence that the affection one feels for the music one listened to as a teenager is biological, and "doesn't weaken as we age." Nick and Norah are also true audiophiles; for them, defining their own musical tastes is akin to defining, in concrete terms, the most difficult thing for any teen to define: themselves. It is notable, in this respect, that the first thing Norah falls in love with about Nick, via Tris's discarded gifts, is his music collection. Other teen movies have used a shared love of music as romantic fodder. Notable among them is the movie *Juno* (2007), a gleefully subversive comedy (also starring Michael Cera) about an obscure music-loving, pregnant teen. Juno (Ellen Page) plans to give her baby to a yuppyish, adult couple. While she waits to give birth, she befriends the husband, Mark (Jason Bateman), a former musician. In one scene, they slow dance to Mott the Hoople's 1972 song, "All the Young Dudes," before screenwriter Diablo Cody (a close friend of *Nick and Norah* screenwriter Scafaria), subverts the mood of the scene—and audience expectations—by having Juno realize that Mark is not all he is cracked up to be.

Music is an important component in movies about teenagers not only because it brings people together, but because it has a long history as a symbol of both freedom and escape. Most characters in teen movies stand at the brink of adulthood, looking for one last big hurrah. In *Nick and Norah*, Norah has to decide whether or not she will accept her slot at Brown University. There are no adults, or more accurately, no parents, in *Nick and Norah*. Nick is in a band and has his own car, and Norah, utilizing the special privileges afforded to her as the daughter of a famous producer, has the run of all of New York City. Having escaped the bounds of their home lives, they are free to spend an entire night—without any nagging phone calls from parents—pursuing an elusive band all over one of the world's most beguiling cities. Norah's friend Caroline captures the euphoria of this adventure at the "Where's Fluffy?" concert on a rooftop in Manhattan at 4 a.m., "I love you, New York!" she shouts into the night. The shot of the Empire State Building behind her is a powerful symbol; these kids are on top of the world. Another teen movie contains a similar musical ode to freedom. In Hughes's 1986 film *Ferris Bueller's Day Off*, Ferris's best friend, and girlfriend, are regretting their decision to play hooky from school, and are desperately afraid of getting caught. So is Ferris, on some level, but he is far too cool to be played by fear.

Significance

Nick and Norah's Infinite Playlist opened at the Toronto Film Festival in 2008. It was the sophomore film of director Peter Sollett, whose *Raising Victor Vargas* was critically acclaimed in 2002. He was attracted to the *Nick and Norah* script, he told Nick Dawson for *Filmmaker* in 2008, because as a Brooklyn native it felt almost autobiographical. (Scafaria, who grew up in New Jersey, had the same thought when she read the book.) "It's about people who are passionate about music, especially new music, and most importantly because it's about falling in love in the East Village, which is something that I've experienced," he said. "I read the script and I said, 'My God, I feel expert in many of these areas! I have to do this because I think I could do this pretty well.'" The resulting film was popular with audiences, and largely successful with critics. Michael Ordona for the *Los Angeles Times* praised it as both goofy and sophisticated writing, "[I]t's an example of how art can be the mortar for two people who feel deeply and often lack the words or courage. It's a common language, a sympathetic frequency." Like other reviewers, Ordona used the word "charming" to describe the film, highlighting his biggest criticism: that it lacks any of the defining characteristics of similar films, like the bite of *Juno* or the crudeness of another Cera comedy, *Superbad* (2007). The late film critic Roger Ebert gave the film a poor review, writing that it "didn't bring much to the party." *New York Times* critic A. O. Scott was more evenhanded in his review, but he reserved special praise for music as the film's most emotive character, writing, "The tunes that play alongside [Nick and Norah's] nocturnal adventure express longing, sadness, anxiety, and joy with more intensity than they can muster themselves."

Molly Hagan

Further Reading

Cohn, Rachel, and David Levithan. "The Real Couple behind the 'Infinite Playlist.'" Interview by Alex Cohen. *NPR*. NPR, 3 Oct. 2008. Web. 21 May 2015. <http://www.npr.org/templates/transcript/transcript.php?storyId=95335682>.

Rev. of *Nick and Norah's Infinite Playlist*, by Rachel Cohn and David Levithan. *Publisher's Weekly*. PWxyz, 1 May 2006. Web. 21 May 2015. <http://www.publishersweekly.com/978-0-375-83531-5>.

Sollett, Peter. "Peter Sollett, *Nick and Norah's Infinite Playlist*." Interview by Nick Dawson. *Filmmaker Magazine*. Filmmaker Magazine, 3 Oct. 2008. Web. 21 May 2015. <http://filmmakermagazine.com/1336-peter-sollett-nick-and-norahs-infinite-playlist/#. VV58HCT4vFI>.

Bibliography

Bartyzel, Monika. "Girls on Film: How *The Thin Man*'s Nora Charles became Hollywood's 'Perfect Wife.'" *The Week*. The Week, 30 May 2014. Web. 21 May 2015. <http://theweek.com/articles/446570/girls-film-how-thin-mans-nora-charles-became-hollywoods-perfect-wife>.

Ebert, Roger. Rev. of *Nick and Norah's Infinite Playlist*, dir. Peter Sollett. *RogerEbert.com*. RogerEbert.com, 2 Oct. 2008. Web. 21 May 2015. <http://www.rogerebert.com/reviews/nick-and-norahs-infinite-playlist-2008>.

Scafaria, Lorene. "Lorene Scafaria Interview, *Nick and Norah's Infinite Playlist*, Toronto 2008." Interview by Kevin Kelly. *Indiewire*. Indiewire.com, 2008. Web. 21 May 2015. <http://web.archive.org/web/20091126170634/http://blog.spout.com/2008/09/19/lorene-scafaria-interview-nick-and-norahs-infinite-playlist-toronto-2008/>.

Ordona, Michael. "Romance Charms with a Teen Beat." *Los Angeles Times*. Los Angeles Times, 3 Oct. 2008. Web. 21 May 2015. <http://articles.latimes.com/2008/oct/03/entertainment/et-playlist3>.

Rev. of *Nick and Norah's Infinite Playlist*, by Rachel Cohn and David Levithan. *Kirkus*. Kirkus Media, 23 May 2006. Web. 21 May 2015. <https://www.kirkusreviews.com/book-reviews/rachel-cohn/nick-and-norahs-infinite-playlist/>.

Scott, A. O. "For Muddled Youth, Music to Live By." Rev. of *Nick and Norah's Infinite Playlist*, dir. Peter Sollett. *New York Times*. New York Times, 2 Oct. 2008. Web. 21 May 2015. <http://www.nytimes.com/2008/10/03/movies/03play.html?_r=0>.

Spitz, Marc. "John Hughes and the Soundtrack to Our Lives." *SPIN*. SPIN Media, 7 Aug. 2009. Web. 21 May 2015. <http://www.spin.com/2009/08/john-hughes-and-soundtracks-our-lives/>.

Stern, Mark Joseph. "Neural Nostalgia." *Slate*. Slate, 12 Aug. 2014. Web. 21 May 2015. <http://www.slate.com/articles/health_and_science/science/2014/08/musical_nostalgia_the_psychology_and_neuroscience_for_song_preference_and.html>.

Now Is Good

The Book

Author: Jenny Downham (b. 1964)
First published: *Before I Die* (2007)

The Film

Director: Ol Parker (b. 1969)
Screenplay by: Ol Parker
Starring: Dakota Fanning, Jeremy Irvine, Paddy Considine, Olivia Williams, and Kaya Scodelario

Context

Death has been an important theme and subject matter in YA fiction since the modern genre first began in the late 1960s. YA literature, literary texts written for readers between the ages of twelve to eighteen and containing at least one protagonist of the same age, naturally treats death as it is concerned with issues that teenagers face in real life. Historically, the most popular themes of YA literature have revolved around identity, social status, romance, and personal relationships, among other coming-of-age issues that young people face in that transitional stage between childhood and adulthood. Death is an inescapable a part of any person's life, and for adolescents who are still struggling with understanding the world, the death of a loved one can be a particularly challenging obstacle to face. It can change a person's life and often takes a long time for individuals of all ages to be able to deal with fully. For this reason, many stories in the YA genre deal with adolescent protagonists who must overcome the death of a parental figure and struggle to deal with the loss, or sometimes are unable to fully carry on with their life.

The novel *Before I Die* (2007) and the 2012 film adaptation *Now Is Good* are rare in the YA genre because the basic story line is narrated from the point of view of Tessa, a teenager dying of leukemia. Death is central to the story, but it is the main character's own death that she must learn to deal with as the story progresses. This addition to the realistic subgenre of YA literature is not wholly unique, although few novels have been written from this perspective. Popular American book-to-film adaptations within that subgenre include *The Fault in Our Stars* (2012) by John Green and *If I Stay* (2009) by

Gayle Forman, which also deal with protagonists who must face death rather than coming of age. *Before I Die* met with positive critical reviews and was translated into nearly a dozen languages.

Film Analysis

The novel begins as Tessa is lying in bed wishing for a boyfriend as she smells dinner cooking downstairs and listens to her father and brother talking. Later, her best friend Zoey comes into the room to get her to go dancing. The reader is not initially given details about Tessa's condition, but as Tessa and Zoey talk, Zoey asks whether she is in pain, implying something may be wrong with her. Finally, Zoey gets Tessa to go out to a club for the night. At the end of the night, they both go home with boys they met at the club, and Tessa has sex for the first time, although it is such an unpleasant experience that she cries and leaves the boy's house directly. It is not for a few chapters that the reader is told that Tessa has terminal leukemia and will die in a relatively short time.

The film adaptation of the novel follows the original story line very closely, but the first scene is designed to convey more uncertainty. The scene opens in media res as Tessa (Dakota Fanning) wipes fog away from the mirror in a bathroom as she talks to Zoey (Kaya Scodelario). She asks if having sex with someone she does not know will make her a "slag," to which Zoey replies that it simply means she is alive. When the girls leave the bathroom and meet up with the boys in the living room, Tessa tells the boy she is with that she was sick once but she is not any longer. As they begin to make out, Tessa does not like the boy or the atmosphere of the night and so she leaves the apartment as quickly as she can. At this point, the chronology of the film follows the plot line set out in the novel. Foregoing flashbacks or voiceover narration, the film's audience learns from Tessa while she does an interview for a local radio station that after four years of chemotherapy, she has decided the best quality of life she can have now is to stop treatment. Although the therapy does help, she explains that the amount of time it will give her is not worth the terrible effect it has on her body and on her mind. The film works to portray Tessa's character, for the most part, as someone beyond her years. She is very adult about her decision and has no regrets, being interested now in only enjoying life and doing everything she has ever wanted to do or will miss out on not being able to do as an adult. With this in mind, she creates a list for herself of everything she will

do before she dies, and from here, the plot relies on her completion of each item on the list.

One important difference in plot between the novel and the film is the reliance of the novel upon the list. The novel puts the completion of the list at the center of the plot. While the story line involves many other things happening in her life, it is the achievement of each item that drives the story and pushes her on to the next thing. For example, in the novel one of the first things on the list is for Tessa to spend a day saying "yes" to every question that is posed to her. This sets off a chain of events throughout the day that lead to outcomes she never could have imagined. This list is also the main reason why she goes out to the club to have sex (as it is one of the most important items). On the other hand, while Tessa's list is important in the movie, it plays a less central role in the presentation of the relationships in Tessa's life, particularly with her divorced parents and in her romance with her new neighbor, Adam (Jeremy Irvine).

Adam's father has recently died, and he lives at home with his mother. When Tessa and a withdrawn Adam meet in his back yard, they make an instant connection. However, when Adam learns that Tessa is dying, he pulls away from her because he is unwilling to get involved in a relationship where he will be alone in the end again. Eventually though, he realizes that Tessa is the one thing making him want to live again, and he chooses to embrace what they have at the time and live his life as much as he can after she is gone. The character of Adam in the film is represented as nearly the same as in the novel.

Similarly, there are no significant differences between Tessa's parents in the novel and the film. They offer support but also serve as storytelling devices to provide different perspectives on death. Tessa's mother and father take two very different roles in their daughter's life. Her father, played by Paddy Considine in the film, refuses to leave her alone and cannot accept the fact that she has essentially given up. He cannot live his life without the hope that she will get better and so proves to be a complicated foil to Tessa's last wishes because he pushes too hard to keep her safe, compensation for his failure to keep her safe from leukemia. Her mother (Olivia Williams), on the other hand, has completely withdrawn from Tessa's life and constantly forgets major appointments and other significant events. As two extremes of the spectrum, Tessa finds herself in constant battle with both because she is looking for both autonomy and some understanding in her last days. Tessa's younger brother, Cal, is the only family member she gets along with. Cal is unapologetically honest in his jokes and conversations with Tessa, says that he will miss her when she is gone, and just before she dies, whispers that she can haunt him if she would like. With respect to characters, the film also follows the novel quite closely. It is only in the details of the story that the film departs from the novel.

The novel's positive depiction of drinking, drug use, and underage sex posed some challenges for adaptation. While the film does include a scene in which Tessa and Zoey take psychedelic mushrooms and Adam takes them to the woods so they can play in nature, its shies away from the more controversial details of the book and makes Tessa seventeen, not sixteen. For example, the book goes into a good deal of detail when Tessa and Adam have sex for the first time. On the other hand, this event is completely left out of the movie. Only the fact that both are lying in bed without shirts on suggests the fact that something just happened. Similarly, the book spends a good deal of time in the last stages of Tessa's cancer as she loses the ability to see, walk, and talk. While the movie shows her inability to start to know what is real and what is imaginary, she is able to see and even walk until the last scene. In the end though, neither story concludes the relationship between Adam and Tessa, only that he stays by her side until the end.

Significance

When the film adaptation of *Before I Die* was released under a name that focused less on the last months of a teenage girl's life, it was met with relatively tepid reviews from critics. It did well given its production budget, but commercially, audiences were not overly interested to see the movie either. One of the major problems that the film faced was simply that it was immediately pegged as a "weepie" or "tear-jerker," and criticism of the film tended to focus on the emotionally manipulative nature of this film genre. With respect to the quality of the film, the main characters were generally seen as flat and, in the end, not entirely likeable. While moviegoers appreciated Dakota Fanning's role and acting ability, the Zoey character, and Considine's performance as Tessa's father, they reacted negatively to Fanning's healthful, stylish appearance and clichéd scenes between Tessa and Adam, as when they take a motorbike ride at sunset alongside wild horses. Laura Peneric, in her review for the Young Adult Library Services Association, commented that because the film adaptation lacked the extensive interior monologue that made the novel emotionally compelling, it could not convey Tessa's motivations as completely and thus failed to engage viewers the same way.

In short, the novel and film present a narrative that few writers in the YA genre choose to follow. However, breaking some of the more major conventions of the genre does not necessarily guarantee a place of major recognition within the genre. Readers and audiences enjoyed both the novel and film, but did not hold up the story as a cornerstone of the YA genre.

Aaron Horton, MA

Further Reading

Burling, Alexis. "Jenny Downham." *Publishers Weekly* 254.51 (2007): 16. *Literary Reference Center*. Web. 10 Nov. 2015. <http://search.ebscohost.com/login.aspx?direct=true&db=lfh&AN=28812898&site=lrc-live>.

Downham, Jenny. Interview. *New York Times*. New York Times, 14 Oct. 2007. Web. 7 Nov. 2015. <http://www.nytimes.com/2007/10/14/books/review/interview-downham.html>.

Julian, Janet. Rev. of *Before I Die*, by Jenny Downham. Narr. Charlotte Parry. *Kliatt* Nov. 2008: 50–52. *Literary Reference Center*. Web. 10 Nov. 2015. <http://search.ebscohost.com/login.aspx?direct=true&db=lfh&AN=35376746&site=lrc-live>.

Bibliography

Johanson, MaryAnn. Rev. of *Now Is Good*, dir. Ol Parker. *FlickFilosopher.com*. MaryAnn Johanson, 21 Sept. 2012. Web. 6 Nov. 2015. <http://www.flickfilosopher.com/2012/09/now-is-good-review.html>.

Lodge, Guy. Rev. of *Now Is Good*, dir. Ol Parker. *Variety*. Variety Media, 17 Sept. 2012. Web. 20 Nov. 2015. <http://variety.com/2012/film/reviews/now-is-good-1117948351>.

O'Neill, Phelim. Rev. of *Now Is Good*, dir. Ol Parker. *Guardian*. Guardian News and Media, 20 Sept. 2012. Web. 6 Nov. 2015. <http://www.theguardian.com/film/2012/sep/20/now-is-good-review>.

Perenic, Laura. "Book to Movie: Before I Die and Now Is Good." *Hub.com*. YALSA, 17 July 2013. Web. 6 Nov. 2015. <http://www.yalsa.ala.org/the-

hub/2013/07/17/book-to-movie-before-i-die-and-now-is-good>.

Robshaw, Brandon. Rev. of *Before I Die*, by Jenny Downham. *Independent.co.uk*. Independent, 22 Oct. 2011. Web. 20 Nov. 2015.

The Outsiders

The Book

Author: S. E. Hinton (b. 1948)
First published: 1967

The Film

Director: Francis Ford Coppola (b. 1939)
Screenplay by: Kathleen Rowell
Starring: C. Thomas Howell, Matt Dillon, Ralph Macchio, Patrick Swayze, Rob Lowe, Emilio Estevez, Tom Cruise, and Diane Lane

Context

The author Susan Eloise "S. E." Hinton began writing a short story about rival gangs in Oklahoma when she was in high school. Her novel based on that story, *The Outsiders*, was published when she was seventeen. In October 2014, Hinton told Jon Michaud for the *New Yorker* that she wrote the book because she was disappointed by the lack of familiar characters in books about teenagers. Hinton herself was more interested in adult books like *Gone with the Wind* (which figures heavily into the plot of *The Outsiders*) and Shirley Jackson's *The Haunting of Hill House* (1959). Books that featured teenage characters, she said, were about girls finding a date for the prom and high school football stars. "That didn't ring true to my life," she told Michaud. "I was surrounded by teens and I couldn't see anything going on in those books that had anything to do with real life." *The Outsiders*, marketed as a pulpy, drugstore paperback, sold poorly when it was published in 1967. Adults were not reading the book, but surprisingly, Hinton's publisher found, teachers were buying it to teach in their classrooms. With that realization—the idea that teenagers craved books that were true to their experience—the young adult (YA) genre was born.

Given the number of stories in literature that feature young protagonists—among them Shakespeare's *Romeo and Juliet* (ca. 1594), Mark Twain's *Huckleberry Finn* (1884), William Golding's *Lord of the Flies* (1954), and Harper Lee's *To Kill a Mockingbird* (1960)—it is surprising that Hinton's *Outsiders* gave birth to the same rich and varied genre that produced the Harry Potter series. Though *The Outsiders* has little thematic relation to the popular fantasy series, its success paved the commercial way for writers like J. K. Rowling by connecting books about teenagers to teenagers themselves. Though the appeal of *The Outsiders* is far-reaching in terms of age, Hinton's young readers devoured her novel. About a close-knit gang of poor boys in Hinton's own hometown of Tulsa, Oklahoma, *The Outsiders* is, at its heart, about holding on to goodness—and finding goodness in others—in a cruel world. Ponyboy, the novel's fourteen-year-old narrator and protagonist, lost both of his parents in a car accident. His friend Johnny is unloved by his drunken, brawling parents and frequently beaten to a pulp by the neighborhood's gang of rich kids, the Socs (short for Socials), but Dallas, the ultimate loner who was first arrested when he was ten years old, is the most hardened in the group. There are two murders, one prolonged and painful death, and a scene in which the characters must run into a church on fire to save a group of small children. The book is violent, dramatic, and at times heavy-handed, but its faults only enhance its appeal. Like teenagers themselves, *The Outsiders* burns with the particular intensity of discovery of first death or first love; it is emotional, immediate, and ultimately, strikes at the heart of what it means to find one's way in the world.

Film Analysis

The film adaptation of *The Outsiders* was released in March 1983. It was directed by the lauded director of *The Godfather* (1972), Francis Ford Coppola, and starred a veritable who's who of young male actors of the era, including Matt Dillon, Patrick Swayze, Ralph Macchio (*The Karate Kid*), Emilio Estevez, Rob Lowe, and Tom Cruise. Diane Lane played the film's diminished female role, and C. Thomas Howell, the least well-known actor in the cast, played Ponyboy. The film was well-received among audiences, but for the most part, critics hated it. Many wrote that it sounded the death knell of Coppola's illustrious career. Vincent Canby, the late film critic of the *New York Times*, gave the movie a scathing review, writing that *The Outsiders* was a "melodramatic kidfilm" that was "spectacularly out of touch" and "laughably earnest."

The film opens with Ponyboy sitting at his desk, penning the opening line of book, which begins, "When I stepped out into the bright sunlight . . ." The opening is in keeping with the conceit of the novel itself—it is the memoir of Ponyboy Curtis—but the words also sets a visual conceit from the heart of the story. In the book, the characters recite the Robert Frost poem "Nothing Gold Can Stay," leading Johnny, just before he dies, to tell Ponyboy, to "stay gold." The color gold and the appreciation of the natural beauty of the sunset (another image from the book) inform the painterly cinematography of the film. Sunsets and the color gold—everything bright and shining—is good. By contrast, everything bad—the murder of the Soc that puts Johnny and Ponyboy on the run, the climactic rumble, the shooting death of Dallas—happens in the darkness of night. In several scenes, Coppola creates a vivid landscape in which characters appear in shadow against a brilliant sunrise or sunset. The stage picture is reminiscent of the famous scene in the film adaptation of Johnny's beloved *Gone with the Wind,* in which a starving Scarlet raises her fist against the sky and vows to start over, declaring, "As God is my witness . . . I'll never be hungry again." The shot is most certainly an homage; when the film was released, Coppola described it as "a 'Gone with the Wind' for teenage girls."

The movie also owes obvious debt to films like *Rebel without a Cause* (1955), a classic tale of teenage alienation starring James Dean, and the musical *West Side Story* (1961). But Coppola's direct references to *Gone with the Wind*—the splashy colors, the swelling music—are where the film actually falters. The content of the story was drastically cut to satisfy the time restraints of the movie (as, of course, most books are), but the nuance of the boys' relationships to each other and their female counterpart, Cherry, are all but completely lost in service of the book's melodramatic plot. Canby said as much when he wrote in his review, "Try to imagine a 'West Side Story' that is set in Tulsa, Oklahoma, in the 1960s, with no dancing or singing, but with a lot of not-super Carmine Coppola [the director's father] soundtrack music replacing the Leonard Bernstein score. Or, think of a remake of 'Rebel without a Cause' directed by someone under the delusion he's D. W. Griffith shooting 'The Birth of a Nation.'"

In the book, Ponyboy's idiosyncratic and beguiling interior voice tempered the excesses of the story, but despite its absence, several of the novel's more complex secondary themes are apparent in the film. The Socs, clad in candy-colored polos, swagger their way from the drive-in movie theater to the gas station to their purring Mustangs. They troll the desolate thoroughfares and dusty back roads of Tulsa, clutching silver flasks and itching for a fight. By contrast, the Greasers wear black, gray, and denim. Their elaborately coiffed hair makes up for the rattiness of their clothes. Their neighborhood is characterized by chain-link fences and the rusty hull of an automobile in the front lawn. When they drive a car, it needs a push to get started. At the beginning of film, Pony literally crosses the train tracks on his way home from the movie theater—he does not come from the respectable part of town. The visual differences between the two groups are stark and their meaning is immediate; the Socs and their kin are oil-money wealthy, the nouveau riche of the plains. Ponyboy and his brothers will spend their lives toiling, like Sodapop, at the gas station. The film is so thoroughly specific, so thoroughly Tulsa—Coppola shot on location, rendering the town in gorgeously wrought cinematography—that it has achieved a kind of universality, a classic tale of the "outsiders" versus the in-crowd, the haves versus the have-nots.

In Hinton's world, the Socs are ever trying to demonstrate their power, keeping the Greasers on the defensive as they go to the movies and walk home alone. Most, like Johnny, do not feel much more secure on their own turf, though Johnny and Ponyboy are the only ones sensitive enough to admit it. The boys' braggadocio masks desperation and hints at a deeper longing that goes beyond popularity, money, or getting the girl. They desire safety and solace, love and protection—comforts that they can only elicit from one another. Coppola captures the camaraderie among the boys as they jostle and wrestle with one another, but deleted scenes suggest that more powerful and intimate moments of their friendship—the real love story in *The Outsiders*—were left on the cutting room floor in 1983.

Significance

Like the book on which it is based, *The Outsiders* was a labor of love. The novel had been popular for over a decade when a librarian named Jo Ellen Misakian and a group of seventh- and eighth-grade students at Lone Star Junior High School in Fresno, California, sent a petition to Coppola, asking him to make a film adaptation of the book, in 1980. Shockingly, Coppola, one of the most famous directors of the era, agreed. His producer, Frank Roos, even included the students in the film's development. In a May, 4, 2012, interview with Kurt Anderson for *Studio 360*, Misakian recalled telling him that she disliked an early draft of the script. It was rewritten. Coppola also developed Hinton's novel *Rumble Fish* (1975). The film adaptation, starring Matt Dillon and Diane Lane, was released in 1983, the same year as *The Outsiders*. In 2005, almost twenty-five years after its initial release, Coppola revisited *The Outsiders* at the behest of fans. He added twenty-two minutes of deleted footage, including a scene in which Sodapop and Ponyboy cuddle in their shared bed. Dargis praised the scene, writing, "There is sweetness in the brothers' embrace and innocence, too. But there is also a palpable sense of desire in their grappling—a vague longing, if not necessarily for each other, then for something or someone." The scene was initially cut because audiences found the idea of two straight male characters sharing a bed too funny to be meaningful. The revised cut, called *The Outsiders: The Complete Novel*, also replaces a bulk of Coppola's father's melodramatic score, though it retains his song "Stay Gold," based on the Frost poem and performed by Stevie Wonder.

Molly Hagan

Further Reading

Canby, Vincent. "'Outsiders,' Teen-Age Violence." Rev. of *The Outsiders*, dir. by Francis Ford Coppola. *New York Times*. New York Times, 25 Mar. 1983. Web. 17 Feb. 2015. <http://www.nytimes.com/1983/03/25/movies/outsiders-teen-age-violence.html>.

Dargis, Manohla. "Coppola Pays a Return Visit to His 'Gone With the Wind' for Teenagers." *New York Times*. New York Times, 9 Sep. 2005. Web. 17 Feb. 2015. <http://www.nytimes.com/2005/09/09/movies/09choi.html>.

Hinton, S. E. "An Outsider, Out of the Shadows." Interview by Dinitia Smith. *New York Times*. New York Times, 7 Sept. 2005. Web. 17 Feb. 2015. <http://www.nytimes.com/2005/09/07/movies/MoviesFeatures/07hint.html?pagewanted=all>.

Bibliography

Dickerson, Justin. "An Inside Look at 'The Outsiders.'" *USA Today*. USA Today, 19 Sept. 2005. Web. 4 Mar. 2015. <http://usatoday30.usatoday.com/life/movies/news/2005-09-19-dvd-outsiders_x.htm>.

Hinton, S. E. "American Icons: The Outsiders." Interview by Kurt Anderson. *Studio 360*. Studio 360, 4 May 2012. Web. 17 Feb. 2015. <http://www.studio360.org/story/205279-american-icons-outsiders>.

Michaud, Jon. "S. E. Hinton and the Y. A. Debate." *New Yorker*. Condé Nast, 14 Oct. 2014. Web. 17 Feb. 2015. <http://www.newyorker.com/culture/cultural-comment/hinton-outsiders-young adult-literature>.

Peck, Dale. "'The Outsiders': 40 Years Later." *New York Times*. New York Times, 23 Sept. 2007. Web. 17 Feb. 2015. <http://www.nytimes.com/2007/09/23/books/review/Peck-t.html?pagewanted=1&_r=1&>.

Paper Towns

The Book

Author: John Green (b. 1977)
First published: 2008

The Film

Director: Jake Schreier (b. 1981)
Screenplay by: Scott Neustadter and Michael H. Weber
Starring: Nat Wolff, Cara Delevingne, Halston Sage, Austin Abrams, Justice Smith, Jaz Sinclair

Context

Paper Towns is an Edgar Award–winning young adult mystery novel whose plot seems tailor-made for a movie. The main protagonist, Q, is smart, verbal, and observant, with the right disposition to solve a mystery. His two best friends, Radar and Ben, are also intelligent. The three teens have been outcasts in their school, but having the chance to track down the most talked-about girl in the school broadens their social circle and their social standing. The plot utilizes the classic "fish out of water" trope by taking the characters and placing them in unfamiliar, daunting circumstances.

The film version of *Paper Towns* is directed by Jake Schreier, who has had great success in advertising and music videos. Prior to this movie, he had directed only one full-length film, *Robot & Frank* (2012). Screenwriting partners Scott Neustadter and Michael H. Weber previously wrote the screenplay for *The Fault in Our Stars* (2014), another adaptation of a John Green novel, as well as *(500) Days of Summer* (2009) and *The Spectacular Now* (2013), so they were well versed in material dealing with unresolved crushes, unrequited love, teen angst, sexual desire, and witty banter.

John Green is a "rock star" in the YA genre. His sixth novel, *The Fault in Our Stars* (2012), debuted as a number one New York Times best seller and was made into a highly successful film starring Shailene Woodley and Ansel Elgort as the romantic leads. The movie's high box-office gross (more than $300 million worldwide) and its positive reviews have made John Green's works sought after for filming. *Paper Towns* was published four years earlier to wide acclaim, with many critics hailing it for presenting a look at life in an ordinary suburb. Green's raw depictions of teenagers in their "natural habitat" have earned him both fans and detractors; his work has been applauded for showing teenagers who drink alcohol, have sex, and talk candidly, and it has been condemned for those very same reasons.

For Green, *Paper Towns* had one very important, significant purpose: to deconstruct the character type known as the "manic pixie dream girl," a phrase coined by film critic Nathan Rabin in a review of the 2005 film *Elizabethtown* to describe a female character who "exists solely in the fevered imaginations of sensitive writer-directors to teach broodingly soulful young men to embrace life and its infinite mysteries and adventures" (Rabin, "Bataan"). Though the manic pixie dream girl is typically quirky and free spirited, her main defining feature is her lack of independent goals beyond improving the life of the protagonist. As such, it is a "fundamentally sexist" trope, according to Rabin, one that relegates a female character—usually the primary romantic lead—to nothing more than a "[prop] to help mopey, sad white men self-actualize" ("I'm Sorry"). Green intended *Paper Towns* to be a thorough rebuttal of this trope. On his Tumblr account, he wrote, "*Paper Towns* is devoted IN ITS ENTIRETY to destroying the lie of the manic pixie dream girl; the novel ends (this is not really a spoiler) with a young woman essentially saying, 'Do you really still live in this fantasy land where boys can save girls by being romantically interested in them?' I do not know how I could have been less ambiguous about this without calling the novel *The Patriarchal Lie of the Manic Pixie Dream Girl Must Be Stabbed in the Heart and Killed.*"

Film Analysis

At the heart of the movie *Paper Towns* is a question: After Margo Roth Spiegelman (Cara Delevingne) vanishes, will she be found or not? A better question to ask is, how can someone be found if they were never there in the first place? In a voice-over that helps advance the plot and fill in necessary details, Quentin "Q" Jacobsen (Nat Wolff) muses, "She always loved mysteries. Maybe with all the things that happened afterward, she became one."

Throughout the movie, following the novel's example, the screenwriters and the director emphasize the role of windows in advancing the plot points. Symbolically, the windows represent the way Q has been looking through, rather than at, Margo. He has been her neighbor for nearly a decade, but how well does he really know her? Has he ever really seen into her—the real Margo—as opposed to just looking at her and through her, fabricating what he wants to see?

At the film's very beginning, after childhood friends Margo and Q part ways, the passage of time is depicted via glimpses of Margo through her bedroom window. Margo grows incrementally older as the audience watches her evolve through the window into her room. Q's voice-over tells the viewers that the pair drifted apart over the ensuing years, so that "by the end of school," he "barely thought of her at all." Though his words claim that he is no longer interested in her, he is shown eyeing her at the exact moment that this statement is made. She, obviously, has never left his consciousness. He cannot forget that the "miracle of Margo" ever happened.

One night, weeks before graduation, Margo reenters Q's life by crawling through his bedroom window. Her unannounced arrival draws him into her orbit once again, and she persuades him to take part in nine acts of vengeance during the night. "We are righting wrongs," she tells him. The movie shows four of the pranks, all of which end with a large *M* spray-painted on a wall or a door and a carefully worded pun handwritten by Margo and left on a note. After finishing the final act, the two get in Q's car to drive away.

With her head resting against the car window and the lights of traffic glowing behind her, Margo looks radiant. Gazing at his dream girl beside him, Q has never felt more alive. Rather than just going home, Margo says they need to "reflect and think of our great achievements." They go to the SunTrust office building, where the guard lets them in after hours. Standing in front of floor-to-ceiling windows, the two look out at downtown Orlando, sprawled beneath them. Q notes how the city and the developments all look "beautiful at a distance." Margo turns to him and states, "Everything is uglier up close." He quickly says, "Not you."

During this office interlude, Margo shares a major theme of the film and the book: "It's a paper town, full of paper houses and paper streets. All the people, too. I've lived here eleven years and I've never come across anyone who cares about anything that matters." At the end of the night, when they return to their houses, Q asks if things will be different tomorrow. She replies that she hopes so and then embraces him tightly. Margo encourages Q to always feel this way—his newfound confidence and boldness should be his regular manner. She then exits his vision, returning to her house by way of her bedroom window.

When it is obvious to everyone at home and at school that Margo has once again disappeared—she has a habit of running away—Q feels the need to locate her. Because he felt so liberated during their night of the "great adventure," he begins to look for clues about where she has gone. However, Q is smart enough to recognize, as he acknowledges in his voice-over, that "if she's gone, she won't be found until she wants to be."

Windows factor in once again when Q discovers a poster of musician Woody Guthrie taped to the back of Margo's window shade. He immediately sees that as a sign, a clue as to where Margo might be, and persuades his friends Radar (Justice Smith) and Ben (Austin Abrams) to go across the way and investigate.

The "clues" that are left behind for Q to decode involve the music of Woody Guthrie and the poems of Walt Whitman. Because of time constraints and the attention span of the audience, the unraveling of the messages is faster and simpler than in the book. One of the clues leads to a note that is left in Q's doorjamb. It is the address of an old, forgotten souvenir shop. On the walls of the shop, there is graffiti about "paper towns," warning that if one goes there, one may never come back. Q looks up what a "paper town" is and discovers that it is a fake town placed on a map to guard against copyright infringement.

The next day, while he is in English class, his teacher lectures about "the pursuit of the white whale"—a reference to Herman Melville's novel *Moby-Dick* (1851). It is clear that Q is becoming Ahab, and the missing Margo is his white whale. Q, Ben, and Radar agree to go on a 1,200-mile road trip to find Margo, whom they believe is holed up in a paper town called Agloe, New York. They are joined by Ben's new love interest, Lacey (Halston Sage), and Radar's girlfriend, Angela (Jaz Sinclair). The addition of Angela to the road trip is a distinct departure from the original novel. While driving, Q proclaims proudly that he is Captain Ahab, and Angela wisely points out that Ahab is not the hero of that book.

As with Ahab, Don Quixote, and other literary crusaders who go off tilting at windmills, Q's mission seems to be doomed to failure. When they arrive in Agloe, Margo is nowhere to be found. Q's friends desert him and head back to Orlando. He waits for Margo to reveal herself, but she does not show. Eventually, he hitchhikes to the bus depot so he can buy a ticket home. While he is in a convenience store, he looks out the window and sees Margo casually strolling by.

When he catches up to her, Q and the audience discover that there never were any clues. None of the messages that he uncovered were intended to guide him to her; they were just notes to let him know that she was all right. At that moment, an observation from the beginning voice-over resonates: as Q noted that Margo would always leave messages for her little sister, Ruthie, letting her know that she was all right, the scene showed a note written in a bowl of alphabet soup.

The final conversation between Q and Margo is steeped in unspoken truths finally given voice. Margo dismisses the notion that Q loves her and reveals, "People have always looked at me and seen what they want to see. It's a myth." She has chosen to hide out in Agloe because it is a "paper town for a paper girl. Not a lot to do, but a great place to think and read." She involved Q in this because he was her first partner in crime, and she wanted him to be her last. Q bids her good-bye and gets on the bus bound for Orlando. As the bus pulls away, Margo is left standing on the street. She watches it drive away, and the audience sees Q through the bus window as he heads for his brand-new life. Q's closing voice-over tells the audience that Margo was not a miracle; she was not something special; she was just a girl.

Significance

When the book *Paper Towns* debuted, it received primarily positive reviews. *Orlando Sentinel* reviewer Rebecca Swain noted that the book "convinced [her] that jaded adult readers need to start raiding the Teens section at the bookstore." In his review for *Booklist*, critic Michael Cart praised Green for his use of symbolism that fused reality with a heightened, stylized imagination: "Green ponders the interconnectedness of imagination and perception, of mirrors and windows, of illusion and reality."

The film adaptation of *Paper Towns* is faithful to the spirit of the book, even though certain events have been streamlined or eliminated from the script. In a video posted on YouTube in April 2015, Green stated, as reported by Ashley Ross for *Time* magazine, "Yes, the *Paper Towns* movie is like the book but also, you know, it isn't. What I really want from an adaptation is to feel the feelings I felt while reading the book, right? But the *Paper Towns* script that Weber and Neustadter wrote . . . is just brilliant because it finds a way to capture both the story and the ideas."

The novel has had its share of controversy. In June 2014 it was removed from the summer reading list of a middle school in Pasco County, Florida, after a parent had objected to its sexual content; it was returned to the list the following month after the National Coalition Against Censorship wrote a letter to the school district superintendent challenging the removal. The movie has not had any such complaints lodged against it, due to its rating of PG-13. Though there are some references to sexually transmitted diseases, a few profanities, and a glimpse of a boy streaking naked from a house—his genitals are not seen—the movie is devoid of full nudity and overt acts of sexuality.

The movie opened in July 2015 and had grossed $85.5 million worldwide by December of that year. Its reviews were mixed, with some critics stating that it had a talented cast of young performers but that it somehow failed to forge an emotional bond with its viewers.

Stephanie Finnegan

Further Reading

Alter, Alexandra. "John Green and His Nerdfighters Are Upending the Summer Blockbuster Model." *Wall Street Journal*. Dow Jones, 14 May 2014. Web. 30 Nov. 2015. <http://www.wsj.com/articles/john-green-and-his-nerdfighters-are-upending-the-summer-blockbuster-model-1400088712>.

Barragan, James. "John Green Rocks 'Bookchella' and Reveals His Favorite Written Words." *Los Angeles Times*. Tribune, 13 Apr. 2014. Web. 30 Nov. 2015. <http://articles.latimes.com/2014/apr/13/entertainment/la-et-jc-john-green-favorite-lines-20140413>.

Talbot, Margaret. "The Teen Whisperer." *New Yorker*. Condé Nast, 9 June 2014. Web. 30 Nov. 2015. <http://www.newyorker.com/magazine/2014/06/09/the-teen-whisperer/>.

Bibliography

Cart, Michael. Rev. of *Paper Towns*, by John Green. *Booklist* 1 June 2008: 79. *Literary Reference Center*. Web. 17 Dec. 2015. <http://search.ebscohost.com/login.aspx?direct=true&db=lfh&AN=32821005&site=lrc-live>.

Green, John. Online posting. *John Green's Tumblr*. Tumblr, 9 Aug. 2013. Web. 30 Nov. 2015. <http://fishingboatproceeds.tumblr.com/post/57820644828/hey-john-i-was-just-wondering-what-your>.

"Paper Towns." *Box Office Mojo*. IMDb.com, 2015. Web. 17 Dec. 2015. <http://www.boxofficemojo.com/movies/?id=papertowns.htm>.

Rabin, Nathan. "The Bataan Death March of Whimsy Case File #1: *Elizabethtown*." Rev. of *Elizabethtown*, dir. Cameron Crowe. *AV Club*. Onion, 25 Jan. 2007. Web. 17 Dec. 2015. <http://www.avclub.com/article/the-bataan-death-march-of-whimsy-case-file-1-emeli-15577>.

Rabin, Nathan. "I'm Sorry for Coining the Phrase 'Manic Pixie Dream Girl.'" *Salon*. Salon Media Group, 15 July 2014. Web. 17 Dec. 2015. <http://www.salon.com/2014/07/15/im_sorry_for_coining_the_phrase_manic_pixie_dream_girl/>.

Ross, Ashley. "These Are the Biggest Differences between the *Paper Towns* Movie and Book." *Time*. Time, 24 July 2015. Web. 30 Nov. 2015. <http://time.com/3969840/paper-towns-movie-and-book/>.

Swain, Rebecca. Rev. of *Paper Towns*, by John Green. *Shakespeare's Coffee*. Orlando Sentinel, 11 Oct. 2008. *Internet Archive: Wayback Machine*. Web. 17 Dec. 2015. <http://web.archive.org/web/20090421073443/http://blogs.orlandosentinel.com/entertainment_books_blog/2008/10/review-paper-to.html>.

Percy Jackson & the Olympians (Series)

The Books

Author: Rick Riordan (b. 1964)
First published: *The Lightening Thief* (2005)
The Sea of Monsters (2006)
The Titan's Curse (2007)
The Battle of the Labyrinth (2008)
The Last Olympian (2009)

The Films

Directors: Chris Columbus (b. 1958), *Percy Jackson & the Olympians: the Lightning Thief*
Thor Freudenthal (b. 1972), *Percy Jackson: Sea of Monsters*
Screenplays by: Craig Titley; Marc Guggenheim
Starring: Logan Lerman, Alexandra Daddario, Brandon T. Jackson, Douglas Smith, Leven Rambin, Jake Abel

Context

The Percy Jackson & The Olympians series tells the story of a boy who becomes aware that his legacy is not of the human kind: he is the son of the Greek god Poseidon and a human mother. Percy must grapple with questions of identity while in the face of danger. He must decide who is a trustworthy and loyal friend and who is out to harm him. In many ways, his dilemmas echo those of Harry Potter series as well as other works produced for the growing genre of young adult fantasy/action adventure.

The Percy Jackson series is true to the conventions of the genre in that it introduces a naïve, apparently average, and unsettled adolescent who is unwittingly thrust into other-worldly dangers that converge around him, dangers that threaten his life because of previously unknown information about himself. Percy discovers the information through his adventures, which resemble quests in nature and design, and from other characters as the story progresses. There is a race-against-time pressure to discover the pieces of his past and put them together in a coherent picture that gives him not only a fighting chance to survive as well as a chance for the possibility of a balanced future, but also a deeper understanding of who he is.

Percy's true friends stand by him, no matter the level of danger or mystery and often at great personal peril to themselves. Then again, peril and danger often find the friends for no other reason other than that they are in the vicinity of Percy at the moment that one of his many enemies strikes.

Camp Half-Blood is the place where other children and adolescents who are like Percy spend their summer vacation. They are all demigods: children of a Greek god or goddess and a human. They are born with gifts, both physical and mental, that reflect the strengths of their god or goddess parent, and they are taught the skills they need in order to use their gifts for good and not evil.

However, because demigods are able to be harmed or even killed by either human or celestial weapons and individuals, the demigods of Camp Half-Blood are also taught ways to defend themselves.

Similar to the Hogwarts School of Witchcraft and Wizardry in the Harry Potter series, the campers are grouped together and live in units, called cabins in the Percy Jackson series, and are safe while on the grounds. Magical borders assure their safety. Dionysus is the camp director and the centaur (half man, half horse) Chiron is the activities director at the camp.

Camp Half-Blood is described in great detail. The magic of the place, as well as of the demigods, is an essential part of the story. In keeping with the characteristics of the fantasy genre, once that magic is defined, it is consistent throughout and becomes an integral part of the story. It is often the vehicle through which the author allows the story to progress. Percy, his friends, and several of the campers and camp personnel are involved in battles that pit traditionally "good" characters against traditionally "bad" characters. The internal struggle against good and evil, as it is portrayed in physical altercations often involving potential and real life-or-death situations, is characteristic of the action/adventure genre of young adult literature.

Author Rick Riordan has created more than one fantasy series, and they have similar themes and characterization to the Percy Jackson series. One series, which features the character Magnus Chase, tells the story of a troubled boy who has always been a loner and has difficulty fitting in. After the death of his mother, an uncle comes to tell him that his father is a Norse god. The Kane Chronicles series features two siblings, Carter and Sadie Kane, and their adventures that ensue after the Egyptian gods are accidentally unleashed into the modern world. As with the character Percy Jackson, Riordan's other series protagonists are in search of identity and a sense of belonging to one world or another as they battle for their lives.

Coming-of-age tales for young adults have been a significant facet of young adult literature for generations. The precursors to the Percy Jackson series can be found not only in the Harry Potter series, but also in movies such as the Star Wars franchise, where Luke Skywalker battles against evil, often at great risk to his own life, only to discover that he is the son of his enemy, a powerful Jedi warrior who was once worthy of respect but in his quest to attain absolute power and omniscience became corrupt and malevolent. Luke, like Percy Jackson, embarks on a hero's journey with the intent to save his world from destruction, and over the course of events travels a path of self-discovery as well. In Mark Twain's novel *Adventures of Huckleberry Finn* (1884), Huck must decide whether he will be defined as the son of the town drunk and a person who mistreats the runaway slave named Jim because of the color of Jim's skin or whether he will become a person in his own right and one who follows his own conscience. The battle between good and evil is more covert and is a subplot to the journey of self-discovery that Huck embarks upon.

Film Analysis

As of 2015, the first two films in the *Percy Jackson & the Olympians* series have been released. The first, *The Lightning Thief*, based on the first novel in the series, was released in 2010. The second film, *Sea of Monsters*, based on the second novel, was released in 2013. The fate of the third film, *The Titan's Curse*, based on the third novel, has not been officially stated, but there are persistent and conflicting reports that it will not be made.

Movie goers' reactions to *The Lightning Thief* were largely negative, especially among fans of the print series. The primary reason for this was because the film veered so sharply away from the plot and characterization of the first novel. Entire sections from the book were omitted in the film; significant characters, who many felt were integral to the plot, were not included in the movie; and plot lines considered important to the feel and popularity of the book were either changed completely or glossed over in the film. Many who went to see the movie because they loved the book felt they saw a film that diverged in large ways from the story Riordan created, making many movie-goers feel as if the cinematic version of a *Percy Jackson* experience had been ruined for them. Many reported that they would not pay to see a second movie if it were made.

Fans also questioned Riordan's lack of involvement in the movie, pointing out that J. K. Rowling was retained as a script consultant and had final script approval for all of the Harry Potter films. She was also present at much of the filming of the movies to ensure that her vision of her series was translated to the screen. Stephenie Meyer, author of the best-selling Twilight series, also had final script approval for the film adaptations, was consulted during the casting of the main characters, and was asked to provide notes and suggestions to the director during the filming. Riordan, on the other hand, sold the film rights to *The Lightning Thief* before the novel was published, giving the studio, Fox 2000, and the film's director complete creative control of the movie. On his webpage, Riordan explains that he did this to improve the appeal of the book and help the Percy Jackson series "catch on." Riordan went on to state that he had not seen the movies because he did not want them to alter the way he envisioned the characters he created.

Both the Harry Potter and Twilight movies and their sequels did significantly better at the box office than did the Percy Jackson films: *Harry Potter and the Sorcerer's Stone* (the first film in the eight-film series), for example, grossed over $90 million its first weekend in theaters. The final film, *Harry Potter and the Deathly Hallows: Part 2*, grossed over $169 million its first weekend. *Twilight*, the first film in the five-film series, grossed over $70 million its first weekend, while the last film in the series, *The Twilight Sage: Breaking Dawn—Part 2*, grossed over $141 million. *Percy Jackson & the Olympians: The Lightening Thief* grossed just over $31 million its first weekend. The second film, *Sea of Monsters*, grossed only $14.4 million. The poor box office numbers for these films, especially with the second film in the proposed series grossing over 45 percent less in its first weekend than did the first film, is a possible reason for the uncertainty surrounding whether a third film will be released. Furthermore, *The Lightning Thief* and *The Sea of Monsters* were panned by critics as having awkward camera angles and lacking in believable special effects.

Despite being hailed by some critics and the public as having excellent cinematic quality and technique, the Percy Jackson movies were also criticized for the way in which the films addressed the passage of time. For instance, Percy's mother seemed to labor too long about explaining his parentage to him and that the god Poseidon was his father. In another scene the walk Percy and his friends took from Coney Island, New York, to midtown Manhattan (a distance of almost twenty miles), was compressed in the film to appear as an easy stroll.

Overall, the Percy Jackson movies were relatively strong enough to stand on their own, but not strong enough to satisfy diehard fans of the print series. Despite the action and adventure that were included in the films, it was not enough to retain interest to bring in the necessary and desired gross box office numbers that are required to make making the third movie a sure thing.

Significance
Rick Riordan taught middle school English and history for fifteen years. He received a Master Teacher Award from Saint Mary's Hall in San Antonio, Texas. He was not known as a children's or young adult's author when *The Lightning Thief* was published. Today, more than forty million copies of his books for young adults are in print, and he has received numerous awards for his various series.

Riordan's works bring mythology to life for his readers. When asked if he feels compelled to stay true to the stories behind each god or other entity, he explains that he brings them into the modern world. As a result, he may have one riding a motorbike because that is the modern corollary to his ancient past. He also explains that his goal is not to encourage every child to read *Homer*, although he believes that would a good thing too. Instead, the goal of his books, Riordan explains, is to engage his readers, young or old, in a fantasy world that is peopled with mythological beings. While in those worlds, adventures occur as his characters move toward greater self-understanding.

While Stephenie Meyer's work is significant because it brought attention to the market for teen romance, Riordan's work is significant because it reinforces the role of action/adventure for both male and female teenagers while simultaneously teaching the reader aspects of Greek mythology. Percy Jackson is not necessarily seen as an exclusively male series. The young adults attending the films are not exclusively male, and Riordan has incorporated strong female protagonists in both the Percy Jackson and the Olympians and the Kane Chronicle series. His books are not filled with weak females who require being rescued by the boys. His books are populated with teens who are facing obstacles and working hard to solve them on their own.

The Lightning Thief and *The Sea of Monsters*, which have already been released, as well as the novels in the series, have had a significant impact on the popularity of young adult literature. They have blended well-drawn characters with a fantasy based

in mythology and have been bundled into a wholly satisfying series that has young adults reading and discussing the action and characters long after reading the books.

Gina Hagler, MBA

Further Reading
Farley, Christopher John. "'Lightning Thief' Author Rick Riordan Doesn't Plan to See the Movie." *Wall Street Journal*. Dow Jones, 15 Mar. 2010. Web. 10 May 2015. <http://blogs.wsj.com/speakeasy/2010/03/15/lightning-thief-author-rick-riordan-doesnt-plan-to-see-the-movie/>.

Thorpe, Vanessa. "Rick Riordan: 'Myths Are Universal and Are Totally Ingrained in Our Culture." *Guardian*. Guardian News and Media, 8 Dec. 2012. Web. Retrieved 10 May 2015. <http://www.theguardian.com/books/2012/dec/09/rick-riordan-interview-heroes-olympus>.

Turitz, Neil. "Books to Film: The Young Adult (YA) Lit Phenomenon." *SSN Insider*. TSS News, 4 Oct. 2014. Web. 2 July 2015. <http://www.ssninsider.com/books-to-film-the-young adult-ya-lit-phenomenon/>.

Bibliography
Cole, Pam B. *Young Adult Literature in the 21st Century*. Boston: McGraw, 2009. Print.

Leighton, Alexander. "Re-Discovering Mythology: Adaptation and Appropriation in the Percy Jackson and the Olympians Saga." Spec. issue of *Mousaion* 32.2 (2014): 60–73. Print.

Lynch-Brown, Carol G, Kathy G. Short, and Carl M. Tomlinson. *Essentials of Children's Literature*. 7th ed. Harlow: Pearson, 2014. Print.

"Percy Jackson's World." *Rick Riordan*. Rick Riordan, n.d. Web. 10 May 2015. <http://www.rickriordan.com/books/percy-jacksons-world/percy-jackson-and-the-olympians>.

Sanchez, Matt. "Fantasy." *Genre Fiction as Literature*. Matt Sanchez, 2005. Web. 5 May 2015. <http://iml.jou.ufl.edu/projects/Spring05/Sanchez/fantasy.htm>.

Strickland, Ashley. "A Brief History of Young Adult Literature." CNN. Cable News Network, Turner Broadcasting System, 15 Feb. 2015. Web. 10 May 2015. <http://www.cnn.com/2013/10/15/living/young adult-fiction-evolution/>.

The Perks of Being a Wallflower

The Book

Author: Stephen Chbosky (b. 1970)
First published: 1999

The Film

Director: Stephen Chbosky
Screenplay by: Stephen Chbosky
Starring: Logan Lerman, Emma Watson, Ezra Miller

Context

Stephen Chbosky published the young adult (YA) novel *The Perks of Being a Wallflower* in 1999. Set in suburban Pittsburgh, Pennsylvania, in the early 1990s, it chronicles a year in the life of a socially awkward teenager named Charlie. Charlie's best (and only) friend, Michael, killed himself when he and Charlie were in the eighth grade. Now, as a prospective high school freshman, Charlie is having trouble imagining going through school alone. To cope with his anxieties, he chronicles his experiences in letters addressed to an unknown pen pal. The device is similar to writing a novel in diary entries, but the letters make Charlie's story immediate. They are charged with Charlie's desperate desire to find someone who might understand him. Chbosky's use of the epistolary format added another dimension to the YA genre as it proved to be an effective method for directly conveying the inner turmoil that the protagonist experiences. The book became an instant hit with teenage readers at a time when the genre began its rise, appealing to the universal and very real issues with which young adults often struggle as they go through high school.

Chbosky's story is unique in Hollywood. The list of authors who have directed feature films based on their own work is very small, and the list of authors who have done so successfully is nonexistent. According to Chbosky, however, he had always planned to take on a film version of *Perks* himself. Trained as a screenwriter at the film school at the University of Southern California, Chbosky was initially known for a small, independent comedy called *The Four Corners of Nowhere*, which played at the Sundance Film Festival in 1995. After publishing *Perks* in 1999, he wrote the screenplay for the Broadway musical *Rent* in 2005 and created the popular, though short-lived, network television drama *Jericho* in 2006.

The amount of work Chbosky has had in Hollywood makes his novel seem like the anomaly in his career. However, despite his familiarity with the cinematic terrain, his adaptation remains particularly masterful, both technically and metaphorically. He was able to translate the inner workings of one teenage brain into scenes, with credible emotional stakes, that play out in real time. He also successfully imbued his screenplay with a measure of restraint and adult perspective that the novel, written when he was in his twenties, lacked.

Film Analysis

Chbosky's success in adapting *Perks* for the screen lay in his ability to accurately translate literary moments into emotionally resonant images. He took liberties with the story that only an author would feel comfortable taking, cutting certain story lines and adding others, tweaking subplots and character traits, and relying on evocative visuals rather than voice-over narration—a tempting idea when adapting a novel—to tell his story. Those liberties, in addition to Chbosky's distance from his source material (he shot the film more than a decade after he wrote the book), yielded a new and fruitful dimension to the story. At the same time, the film version of *Perks* is faithful to the overall spirit of its source material.

Among the story lines Chbosky chose to cut is the subplot involving Charlie's deepening relationship with his sister who, unnamed in the novel, is referred to as Candace (Nina Dobrev) in the film. Still environmentally conscious, she dates a loser named Derek—or Ponytail Derek (Nicholas Braun), as he is known in the film. Ponytail Derek makes Candace mixtapes, which she regifts to Charlie (Logan Lerman), and he unexpectedly punches her in the face after she berates him for not standing up for himself. The scene in the film is just as disturbing and ambiguous as it is in the book, but her subsequent forced separation from Derek and her abortion have all been dropped from the story. In the film, Charlie does not tell anyone about the abuse, and Candace decides on her own that Ponytail Derek is an awful boyfriend. The omission is notable because, in the book, Candace's situation is presented in the context of a larger story line involving oppressive gender roles and the history of physical abuse in Charlie's family. In the film, these stories fall away in service of the major turning point for Charlie's character: the moment he realizes that he was sexually abused by his beloved Aunt Helen (Melanie Lynskey).

Along with other moments that Chbosky decided to cut for the film, there are a handful of new and reconfigured scenes. In the book, Charlie chronicles his exploits after they happen, intellectualizing how each new experience makes him think and feel. In the film, when Chbosky wants to show that Charlie is experimenting with new substances, for example, he intercuts a scene of Charlie taking a communion wafer with a shot of him using drugs at a party. There are three scenes that best demonstrate Chbosky's strategy in this particular regard: a scene in which Charlie, Sam (Emma Watson), and Patrick (Ezra Miller) find each other on the dance floor at a school dance, a scene between Patrick and Charlie on a golf course, and a scene in which Charlie suffers a mental breakdown. These three moments, which exist only in the film, capture Chbosky's ability to elegantly dispense information from Charlie's letters in real time as well as his ability to translate words into potent images.

In the novel, Charlie's initiation into Sam and Patrick's group of friends is gradual, consisting of many moments in the school hallway, outside smoking cigarettes, and in the bleachers at school football games. The true-to-life pace of building a friendship typically does not work well in films, however—particularly in films where most of the plot takes place after the characters have become friends. In the film version of *Perks*, Chbosky chose to write a scene in which all three main characters are at a high school dance. This happens (fleetingly) in the book, but the characters' actions are contingent on another absent story line. In the film, viewers see Charlie at the dance, crouched in the shadows like a true wallflower. (Lerman's Charlie is less outwardly emotional than the Charlie in the book, who breaks into tears easily; he conveys Charlie's vulnerability with more nuance.) He watches the dancers passively as "Come On, Eileen," a 1982 song from Dexys Midnight Runners starts to play. Sam and Patrick, elated by the song, break into a fully choreographed dance routine in the middle of the dance floor, while Charlie, likely for the first time that night, breaks from the wall to join them. The scene is evocative because it establishes Charlie's love for Sam and Patrick (they are the only ones he wants to dance with) as well as a tacit understanding among the three that they are the same.

In the novel, Patrick and his secret boyfriend, Brad, the popular quarterback of the football team, are discovered by Brad's homophobic father. In both versions, the relationship is put to a brutal end when Brad's cronies beat Patrick in the lunchroom and Brad (Johnny Simmons) insults his Patrick. Patrick looks to Charlie for solace, and one night, the two are sitting on a golf course, drinking wine. They discuss stories of students long since graduated. In the book, this scene is meandering and part of a larger sequence about Patrick's relationship woes. In the film, on the other hand, Chbosky uses the template of the scene to draw an affecting monologue from Patrick about how he felt when Brad's father started beating him. The same information is related to Charlie second hand in the book, but Chbosky's cinematic treatment of Patrick's pain is more direct and arguably more devastating coming from Patrick himself.

Finally, shooting the film allowed Chbosky to visually portray Charlie's mental breakdown near the end of the story. In the novel, this event is described in retrospect. In the film, however, instead of fading out, Chbosky effectively chops and shuffles images from previous scenes with evocative flashbacks to Charlie's Aunt Helen and the night she died. Viewers see Charlie stumble home from Sam and Patrick's house and when he opens the door to his own house, everything is topsy-turvy. The shot is off-kilter, making the ceiling look like the floor. The images escalate—his fight with Brad's cronies, his sister being punched in the face—and speed up until Charlie calls his sister, and she calls the police. Chbosky's portrayal of Charlie's breakdown relies totally on images (and perhaps the plaintive violin in the underscore) to convey the dissonance Charlie feels with the world around him.

Significance

The Perks of Being a Wallflower premiered in September 2012. It opened in limited release its first week and was expanded in its second. More surprising than how well the film performed were exit polls revealing that most of the people going to see it were over the age of twenty-five. *Perks* also impressed critics. Commentators typically lauded Chbosky's ability to successfully master the challenge of directing the film version of his own book and his effective casting choices. The late Roger Ebert reviewed the film on his website, giving it three and a half stars out of four.

Chbosky was pleased that adults as well as teenagers responded to the film. "I wanted to straddle both worlds," he told Bruce Handy in an October 5, 2012, interview for *Vanity Fair*. This is evident at the end of the film in Charlie's voice-over monologue (pieces of which are found in the book) that says, in part, "I know we'll all become somebody—we'll all become old photographs and we'll all become somebody's mom and dad. Right now these moments are not stories, this is happening. I'm here and I'm looking at her. And she is so beautiful." The nostalgia that Chbosky describes comes from the life he lived in between writing *Perks* the book and *Perks* the film. He got married, had a child, and began to look at his younger years a bit differently than he had when he was twenty-six. "I think that Charlie had that perspective in the book, but me myself, as an adult, I know so well that the pictures *will* become old photographs," he told Handy, "and I just wanted to encourage any young person seeing the movie to embrace those moments and celebrate their lives."

Molly Hagan

Further Reading

Dargis, Manohla. "An Introvert Finds His Way through Teenage Terrain." Rev. of *The Perks of Being a Wallflower*, by Stephen Chbosky. *New York Times*. New York Times, 20 Sept. 2012. Web. 3 June 2015. <http://www.nytimes.com/2012/09/21/movies/the-perks-of-being-a-wallflower-directed-by-stephen-chbosky.html?_r=1>.

Vancheri, Barbara. "The Perks of Being Stephen Chbosky: Upper St. Clair Native Talks about His Novel and New Film." *Pittsburgh Post-Gazette*. PG, 26 Sept. 2012. Web. 3 June 2015. <http://www.post-gazette.com/ae/movies/2012/09/26/The-perks-of-being-Stephen-Chbosky-Upper-St-Clair-native-talks-about-his-novel-and-new-film/stories/201209260184>.

Bibliography

Buckwalter, Ian. "How *Perks of Being a Wallflower* Breaks an Old Filmmaking Curse." *Atlantic*. Atlantic Media Group, 21 Sept. 2012. Web. 3 June 2015. <http://www.theatlantic.com/entertainment/archive/2012/09/how-perks-of-being-a-wallflower-breaks-an-old-filmmaking-curse/262671/>.

Chbosky, Stephen. "Interview: *The Perks of Being a Wallflower* Director Stephen Chbosky Talks Finding the Perfect Cast and Changing Teens' Lives." Interview by Tara Aquino. *Complex*. Complex Media, 22 Sept. 2012. Web. 3 June 2015. <http://www.complex.com/pop-culture/2012/09/interview-the-perks-of-being-a-wallflower-director-stephen-chbosky>.

Chbosky, Stephen. "Q&A: *Perks of Being a Wallflower*'s Stephen Chbosky on Emma Watson's Casting, High School Yearning, and 'Heroes.'" Interview by Bruce Handy. *Vanity Fair*. Condé Nast, 5 Oct. 2012. Web. 3 June 2015. <http://www.vanityfair.com/culture/2012/10/qa-stephen-chbosky-perks-of-being-a-wallflower>.

Ebert, Roger. Rev. of *The Perks of Being a Wallflower*, dir. Stephen Chbosky. *RogerEbert.com*. Ebert Digital, 26 Sept. 2012. Web. 3 June 2015. <http://www.rogerebert.com/reviews/the-perks-of-being-a-wallflower-2012>.

The Princess Bride

The Book

Author: William Goldman (b. 1931)
First published: 1973

The Film

Director: Rob Reiner (b. 1947)
Screenplay by: William Goldman
Starring: Robin Wright, Cary Elwes, Chris Sarandon, Peter Falk, Fred Savage

Context

During the 1980s, fantasy films experienced a boom in popularity among moviegoers, and films in that genre were common in American movie theaters. Some of these films, such as *Legend* (1985) and *Willow* (1988), were set entirely in fantasy worlds, while others, such as *The NeverEnding Story* (1984) and *Labyrinth* (1986), bridged the gap between the real world and a fantasy realm. The 1987 film *The Princess Bride* is unique in that it does not truly fall into either category; rather, the film features a fantasy narrative nested within a real-world frame narrative that grounds the comedic yet high-stakes fantasy action in reality.

Much like the film, the 1973 novel *The Princess Bride* blurs the line between fantasy and reality. Although written entirely by novelist and screenwriter

William Goldman, the novel is ostensibly the creation of S. Morgenstern, a writer from the fictional European country of Florin. Goldman presents himself as the abridger of what the title page describes as "S. Morgenstern's classic tale of true love and high adventure," claiming that he has retained only the "good parts" of the narrative while eliminating various long digressions on subjects such as Florin's history and politics. By excising such sections, Goldman supposedly transformed the novel from a lengthy political satire into a romantic, adventure-filled tale about a beautiful young woman named Buttercup, who agrees to marry the scheming Prince Humperdinck after her true love, Westley, is presumed killed by the Dread Pirate Roberts. When Prince Humperdinck hires three men to abduct and kill Buttercup and frame the rival country of Guilder, Westley—who, rather than being killed by the Dread Pirate Roberts, has instead taken on his mantle—makes it his mission to save her. He ultimately allies himself with two of the abductors, Inigo Montoya and Fezzik, to defeat Prince Humperdinck and his right-hand man, Count Rugen. Goldman periodically interrupts the narrative to prove brief glosses of excised sections and other editorial comments. The abridgement conceit extends even to Goldman's introduction, in which he not only presents a fictionalized tale of the book's development but also includes a completely fictional depiction of his family life.

When it came time to adapt *The Princess Bride* for the screen, Goldman was an ideal candidate for the job, having previously won two Academy Awards for his screenplays, one for *Butch Cassidy and the Sundance Kid* (1969) and the other for his adaptation of *All the President's Men* (1976). *The Princess Bride* was directed by Rob Reiner, a filmmaker and actor who had previously directed the critically acclaimed film *Stand by Me* (1986) as well as the cult comedy *This Is Spinal Tap* (1984). Although he was well known for his dramas, Reiner would become equally known for his comedies, of which *The Princess Bride* is a particularly notable example.

Film Analysis

As both a novelist and a screenwriter, Goldman was uniquely suited to adapting *The Princess Bride*, a novel with a distinctive spirit and brand of humor that could easily have been lost had the task of adapting the book fallen into the wrong hands. Remaining faithful to the original work was of great importance. At the same time, however, some elements of the book that were effective in the context of a literary work were essentially unfilmable. In adapting the novel, Goldman had to strike a careful balance, retaining elements of the novel's unique character while reshaping the narrative to one better suited to the screen.

The film begins in the real world, as a young boy (Fred Savage) is recovering from an illness. His grandfather (Peter Falk) visits and begins to read him the book *The Princess Bride*. The main narrative of the film continues on from this point, with occasional interruptions by the boy or the grandfather. For example, during a romantic scene between Buttercup (Robin Wright) and Westley (Cary Elwes) early in the film, the boy interrupts his grandfather and asks suspiciously, "Is this a kissing book?" Later, when Buttercup is in danger of being attacked by shrieking eels, the grandfather pauses his story and reassures the boy, "She doesn't get eaten by the eels at this time." Such brief interruptions both remind the viewer of the underlying conceit and add comedic or touching moments in keeping with the original novel's tone.

The scenes featuring the boy and his grandfather form a frame narrative that surrounds the main plot of the film. A number of 1980s fantasy films mixed fantasy scenes with scenes set in the real world, and *The Princess Bride* is a prime example of this trend. However, the film's frame narrative serves a significantly more important purpose than merely conforming to trends in the genre. Among the most notable potential challenges in adapting *The Princess Bride* was capturing the conceit that the novel is an existing work that was abridged by Goldman. In adapting the novel for the screen, Goldman could have opted to eliminate that conceit altogether and instead written a straightforward fantasy screenplay. However, doing so would have eliminated much of the novel's unique character, and the film's overall adherence to the novel indicates that doing so would be counter to Goldman's goal. At the same time, interspersing the fantasy narrative with interruptions by the writer abridging the story would be a strange choice for a film.

Thus, rather than reproducing this conceit completely in the film, Goldman instead incorporates a portion of the novel's introduction into the film, adapting it to form the frame narrative. In his heavily fictionalized introduction to the novel, Goldman claims that he was first introduced to the novel *The Princess Bride* as a child, when his father, an immigrant from Florin, read the book to him while he was recovering from pneumonia. As the novel contained numerous parts not of interest to a young boy, the father abridged the novel as he read, eliminating the political satire and historical digressions and retaining the adventure and romance. Goldman explains that he followed his father's example in abridging the novel, keeping his own son in mind as the potential reader. As such, the novel features various interjections by Goldman. At the beginning of the second chapter, "The Groom," for example, Goldman includes a note stating that he has chosen to cut most of the chapter, as it dealt not with the titular groom, Prince Humperdinck, but with "sixty-six pages of Florinese history" (67). In fact, Goldman's entire story about his childhood experience with *The Princess Bride* and his later efforts to abridge the novel is fictitious; the country of Florin does not exist, Goldman has two daughters rather than a son, and the entire novel was written by Goldman himself. However, Goldman's fictionalized childhood provided the inspiration for the frame narrative, with the grandfather taking on the role of Goldman's father and the boy representing Goldman himself.

In addition to featuring a frame narrative that echoes the fictionalized origin of the novel, Goldman's screenplay captures the heart of the novel's main plot while streamlining it for the film. The novel features a number of segments that provide information about certain characters' motivations and backstories through flashbacks or other digressions. For example, the book's fifth chapter features two lengthy sections detailing the origins of Inigo and Fezzik, chronicling through flashbacks the former's quest for revenge against the man who murdered his father and the latter's career as a professional fighter. The film, however, does not feature such flashbacks and devotes minimal time to providing backstory for Fezzik (André the Giant). A bit more attention is given to Inigo (Mandy Patinkin), who provides a brief explanation of his quest to Westley prior to their fight at the Cliffs of Insanity. Although it concerns a secondary character rather than the protagonists, this particular bit of backstory is essential to the main narrative, as the murderer Inigo seeks is revealed to be Count Rugen (Christopher Guest), crony of the villainous Prince Humperdinck (Chris Sarandon). While including only the essential details about Inigo and Fezzik's lives in the film does render them somewhat less developed than their novel counterparts, doing so also eliminates the need for lengthy flashbacks that could potentially distract from the core plot.

At the end of the film, Buttercup and Westley flee Prince Humperdinck's palace on white horses and, their escape successful, ultimately share a passionate kiss.

The novel's conclusion, however, is quite different: although Buttercup, Westley, and their allies escape the palace successfully, Humperdinck and his men give chase, "and the night behind them [i]s filled with the crescendoing sound of pursuit" (327). In a note just before that ending, Goldman explains that he long believed that the book had a more traditional ending in which Buttercup and Westley lived happily ever after, as that is how his father told the story when he first read the novel to the young Goldman. In ending the film in such a fashion, Goldman not only provides the sort of ending expected of such a narrative but also echoes his original work, demonstrating once again that a film adaptation can differ significantly from the original work while still capturing its spirit.

Significance

As a unique film mixing elements of fantasy, comedy, and romance, *The Princess Bride* was a difficult film to market. In his 2014 book *As You Wish: Inconceivable Tales from the Making of* The Princess Bride, written with Joe Layden, Cary Elwes notes that the poster for the film depicted Savage and Falk as the grandson and grandfather and did not give any indication that it was a fantasy film. Despite such marketing difficulties, *The Princess Bride* proved to be a modest financial success following its US release in the fall of 1987, grossing nearly US$31 million domestically. Critical response to the film was mixed, with some reviewers expressing confusion regarding the film's mix of genres and its offbeat sensibility. Nevertheless, a number of critics praised the film's mixture of comedy and fantasy action, deeming it suitable for both adults and children. While *The Princess Bride* was only modestly successful when it was first released, it found a significant cult following over the subsequent decades, becoming widely considered one of the most significant comedies of the 1980s.

Joy Crelin

Further Reading

Ebert, Roger. Rev. of *The Princess Bride*, dir. Rob Reiner. *RogerEbert.com*. Ebert Digital, 9 Oct. 1987. Web. 31 Oct. 2015. <http://www.rogerebert.com/reviews/the-princess-bride-1987>.

Greene, Richard, and Rachel Robison-Greene, eds. *The Princess Bride and Philosophy: Inconceivable!* Chicago: Open Court, 2016. Print. Popular Culture and Philosophy 98.

Maslin, Janet. Rev. of *The Princess Bride*, dir. Rob Reiner. *New York Times*. New York Times, 25 Sept. 1987. Web. 31 Oct. 2015. <http://www.nytimes.com/movie/review?res=9B0DE2D8133DF936A1575AC0A961948260>.

Bibliography

Elwes, Cary, and Joe Layden. *As You Wish: Inconceivable Tales from the Making of* The Princess Bride. New York: Touchstone, 2014. Print.

Goldman, William. *The Princess Bride: S. Morgenstern's Classic Tale of True Love and High Adventure; The "Good Parts" Version, Abridged*. 1973. Orlando: Harcourt, 2007. Print.

"The Princess Bride." *Box Office Mojo*. IMDB.com, n.d. Web. 31 Oct. 2015. <http://www.boxofficemojo.com/movies/?id=princessbride.htm>.

The Princess Diaries (Series)

The Books

Author: Meg Cabot (b. 1967)
First published: *The Princess Diaries* (2000)
Princess in the Spotlight (2001)
Princess in Love (2002)
Princess in Waiting (2003)
Project Princess (2003)
Princess in Pink (2004)
Princess in Training (2005)
The Princess Present (2004)
Party Princess (2006)
Sweet Sixteen Princess (2006)
Valentine Princess (2006)
Princess on the Brink (2007)
Princess Mia (2007)
Forever Princess (2008)
Royal Wedding (2015)

The Films

Director: Garry Marshall (b. 1934)
Screenplay by: Gina Wendkos, Shonda Rhimes
Starring: Anne Hathaway, Julie Andrews, Heather Matarazzo

Context

Young adult literature of the early twenty-first century was marked by a number of major trends, including the prominence of the fantasy and romance genres as well as an emphasis on books detailing the sometimes outlandish adventures of high school students. One of the most popular young adult subgenres during the first decade of the twenty-first century was the epistolary novel, that is, a novel made up of letters, diaries, emails, or similar forms of communication. These novels provide an intimate look into the mindsets of their protagonists, allowing the characters to share, in their own words and at their own pace, their feelings about friends, family, and enemies as well as the events taking place around them. Epistolary series such as Louise Rennison's Confessions of Georgia Nicolson and Megan McCafferty's Jessica Darling series proved popular among young adult readers, particularly teenage girls.

In the first decade of the twenty-first century, one of the most popular series in the epistolary novel subgenre was the Princess Diaries series, written by Meg Cabot. The main series was published between 2000 and 2009, beginning with *The Princess Diaries* and ending with *Forever Princess*. An additional novel intended for adult readers, *Royal Wedding*, was published in 2015. The series chronicles the life of teenager Mia Thermopolis, who learns that her father, whom she sees rarely, is in fact the ruler of a small European principality known as Genovia. Over the course of the series, Mia undergoes princess training at the hands of her cruel yet somewhat absurd grandmother while also dealing with typical teenage problems such as popularity, unrequited love, and conflicts with friends, all of which are documented in Mia's humorous and relatable diary.

The first book in the series, *The Princess Diaries*, was adapted into the 2001 film of the same name. *The Princess Diaries* was written by Gina Wendkos and directed by Garry Marshall, a veteran filmmaker known for popular films such as *Pretty Woman* (1990) and *Runaway Bride* (1999). Marshall returned for the sequel, *The Princess Diaries 2: Royal Engagement* (2004), which was based on a story by Wendkos and screenplay by future television mogul Shonda Rhimes. Unlike its predecessor, *The Princess Diaries 2* is not based on one or more of Cabot's novels; rather, it continues Mia's story into adulthood, dealing with issues of romance, politics, and royal succession. Some of the most popular adaptations of young adult epistolary novels, the Princess Diaries films demonstrate many of the benefits and challenges of adapting such works for the screen.

Film Analysis

The film *The Princess Diaries* is an adaptation of the 2000 novel of the same name, and as such, it shares many of the novel's general themes and plot points. In the film, teenager Amelia Mignonette Thermopolis Renaldi (Anne Hathaway), known to her friends and immediate family as Mia Thermopolis, learns that her paternal grandmother, Clarisse (Julie Andrews), is the queen of a small, fictional European country known as Genovia. With her father deceased, Mia is next in line for the Genovian throne. Despite her lineage, however, Mia hardly resembles the stereotypical princess: she is an awkward and unpopular young woman who is often frumpily dressed, nervous in front of crowds and terrible at sports, and demonstrates typical teenage mannerisms and behavior that her grandmother deems inappropriate for a princess. Clarisse embarks on a mission to transform Mia into a proper princess, giving her a physical makeover while also working to improve her manners, knowledge of Genovian culture, and understanding of the responsibility she faces. Although Mia faces a number of conflicts during her journey to becoming a princess, including the judgment of her friend Lilly (Heather Matarazzo), ridicule and exploitation at the hands of popular teens Lana (Mandy Moore) and Josh (Erik von Detten), and distressing encounters with the press, she eventually succeeds in both claiming her rightful place as Genovia's princess and winning the heart of Lilly's older brother, Michael (Robert Schwartzman).

As a film based on an epistolary novel, *The Princess Diaries* presented a number of challenges to the filmmakers, who had to translate the narrative from a diary narrated in Mia's distinctive personal voice to a film with a somewhat more distant, external viewpoint. The film largely avoids voiceover but does reference Mia's diary at the end of the film, when a voiceover narrating one her diary entries informs the audience of her plans following the events of the film. Another cinematic technique used to express Mia's personal viewpoint is the inclusion of imagined sequences that demonstrate her desires and way of thinking. Those sequences are typically brief and shed light on the scenes into which they are incorporated. In one such scene near the beginning of the film, Mia sees the popular and handsome Josh while at school. In one moment, Josh is a significant distance away, being affectionate

toward his girlfriend, Lana; in the next, he is kissing Mia where she stands by her locker. The camera next cuts from Mia's smiling face back to a shot of Josh with Lana, demonstrating that the kiss was entirely in Mia's head. This imagined sequence thus conveys not only Mia's attraction to Josh but also her tendency to romanticize situations such as having a boyfriend. In a later scene, Mia explains to her mother (Caroline Goodall) her hope that when she receives her first kiss from Josh, her foot will "pop" like a romantic heroine's. The following imagined sequence shows the lower legs of a man and a woman—presumably Josh and Mia—as they kiss. The woman's leg does begin to pop upward, but she has stepped on a piece of chewed gum, which stretches yet ultimately tethers her foot to the ground. As she struggles to free herself, the man walks away. This sequence provides a humorous and self-deprecating counterpoint to Mia's romantic notions and also serves to foreshadow her later attempted first kiss with Josh, which is awkward and has been orchestrated by him as a publicity stunt. Just as the gum traps the woman's foot in the imagined sequence, a net traps Mia's foot when she is with Josh, and ultimately his invitation to be his date to a beach party is revealed to be a trap as well. When Josh finally succeeds in kissing her in front of the paparazzi, Mia raises her foot only so she can remove her shoe and hit him with it.

As a whole, *The Princess Diaries* could be described as a makeover film, as it focuses heavily on Mia's physical, behavioral, and emotional transformation under her grandmother's tutelage. Elizabeth A. Ford and Deborah C. Mitchell, authors of *The Makeover in Movies: Before and After in Hollywood Films, 1941–2002* (2004), argue that the film is in fact part of a long tradition of makeover films that began with the 1942 Bette Davis vehicle *Now, Voyager*, which, although likely not the first film to feature a makeover, introduced many of the conventions of the genre. One of the conventions Ford and Mitchell particularly note is the tradition of costuming the protagonists of makeover films so that they initially appear frumpy and unattractive in order to make the later transformation, which tends to reveal the actors as they actually are, more dramatic. In the case of Mia, Hathaway is initially dressed in ill-fitting school uniforms and clunky shoes as well as given a frizzy hairpiece that transforms her usually straight hair into a mass of unruly curls and additional hairs glued to her face to give the impression of thick, ungroomed eyebrows. Transformed, her appearance resembles less the description of post-makeover Mia from the novel and more Hathaway's typical appearance in real life.

Early on in the film, Clarisse makes her mission clear, telling Mia, "I can teach you to walk, talk, sit, stand, eat, dress like a princess." Although Clarisse's mission has the ostensible goal of transforming Mia into a well-rounded, poised young woman capable of ruling a small country, the film's emphasis is more on Mia's physical changes, in terms of both her looks and her comportment and presentation. In the novel, Mia's physical makeover is balanced by vocabulary lessons, etiquette quizzes, and instructions in how to behave in difficult situations. The film, however, largely omits such lessons. As Ford and Mitchell note, the film's primary makeover scene takes on a different significance than the scene in the book in large part because of the film's shift away from diary format. In the book, Mia comments humorously on all aspects of her makeover, sharing her impressions of her stylist, Paolo, and comparing her new look unfavorably to a "human Q-tip" (129). Her personality is readily apparent from her commentary, and her mingled discomfort and ambivalence about her newfound status shed further light on her character. In the film, as Ford and Mitchell point out, the lack of voiceover or similar commentary means that Mia is unable to express her opinions about the changes being made to her physical appearance. Rather, she is essentially rendered a passive participant in her own transformation.

As with many film adaptations of young adult novels, *The Princess Diaries* makes a variety of changes to the narrative and its characters, some minor and some very significant. Many of the changes seem calculated to simplify the narrative and prevent confusion among the film's young viewers: for example, Mia's full name is changed from Amelia Mignonette Grimaldi Thermopolis Renaldo to the shorter Amelia Mignonette Thermopolis Renaldi. This change also has the effect of removing any association with the Grimaldi family, the royal family of Monaco.

Another change concerns the political status of Genovia itself. In the novel, Genovia is a principality rather than a traditional monarchy, and it is ruled by Mia's father, the prince, rather than by Clarisse, who is not the queen but the dowager princess. As American tweens and teens would likely be more familiar with traditional monarchies than with principalities, this change likely prevented some confusion among viewers.

A number of other changes were likely intended to remove the novel's small amount of potentially controversial subject matter. In the book, Mia is the product of a college fling, and her parents never married; in the film, her divorced parents likewise met in college but did not have Mia until after their marriage. Similarly, Mia's father is alive in the novel, and he has been forced to acknowledge his illegitimate daughter as his heir only because a bout with testicular cancer left him unable to have any more children. The film explains that Mia's father has been dead for some time, thus sidestepping the cancer issue and avoiding possible questions about the mechanics of human reproduction among its young viewers.

Several additional changes to the narrative seem designed to acknowledge the strengths of the film's actors. The novel's version of Clarisse is often cruel, demanding, and somewhat ridiculous; the film's incarnation of the character is strict but generally kind and well intentioned. As Clarisse is played by Andrews, who remains best known for playing aggressively kind characters such as Mary Poppins and Maria von Trapp, this change accommodates both her acting style and the expectations of viewers familiar with her previous work. Similarly, a brief musical performance by Lana partway through the film acknowledges the actress's real-life status as a popular recording artist whom audience members would likely expect to hear sing at some point in the film.

Unlike the previous film, *The Princess Diaries 2: Royal Engagement* is not based on one of Cabot's novels; as such, it is able to explore new aspects of Mia's life without adhering to existing source material. The beginning of the film ties this sequel to its predecessor through the use of a variety of cinematic techniques. After a brief scene set at Mia's college graduation, the film features a voiceover in which Mia narrates one of her diary entries, mirroring the conclusion of the previous film. As Mia reminds the audience of the events that have led her to this point, the film cuts between footage of her writing in her diary and flashbacks to the previous films, showing several of the characters she mentions. Several of those characters, including Lilly and Mia's mother, later appear in the film, further connecting it to the previous installment.

Whereas *The Princess Diaries* focuses primarily on Mia's overall transformation, *The Princess Diaries 2* has no need for a makeover plot: although demonstrating in several scenes that she is still clumsy and bad at athletic activities, Mia is much more comfortable in her skin and looks every part the princess. Instead, the film focuses on Mia's need to find a husband within thirty days, as conservative members of the Genovian parliament plan to enforce an archaic law stating that an unmarried woman may not rule as queen. Mia chooses a British duke, Andrew (Callum Blue), as her fiancé and encounters roadblocks in the form of the scheming Viscount Mabrey (John Rhys-Davies) and his nephew Nicholas (Chris Pine) before ultimately rebelling against the patriarchal law. With the help of her grandmother and the sympathetic Genovian prime minister (Joel McCrary), Mia overturns the law and, following Clarisse's abdication, is crowned queen of Genovia.

Despite their very different plots, the two Princess Diaries films in many ways have parallel structures. Both films begin with a symbolic entrance into a particular world; the first begins with Mia getting ready for and traveling to the strange and often-unfriendly realm of high school, while the second begins with Mia's college graduation, signaling her entrance into adulthood. In each film Mia faces the betrayal or seeming betrayal of the young men to which she is attracted (Josh and Nicholas), which in both cases features the intrusive involvement of the press. The resulting media circus causes Mia emotional distress and also causes authority figures to doubt her suitability as a future Genovian leader. Both films conclude with the resolution of the romance subplot and some sort of event demonstrating both Mia's commitment to Genovia and her personal growth as a princess and a woman. Finally, a brief sequence hints at Mia's plans for the future; in the first film, her voiceover explains that she will be moving to Genovia, while the second film features a montage showing some of Mia's accomplishments as queen. Although *The Princess Diaries 2* is not based on any of the novels in Cabot's series, the parallel structures of the two films create a sense of continuity and reinforce that they are part of an ongoing story line.

Significance

The Princess Diaries novels were incredibly popular during the first decade of the twenty-first century, and the films were similarly received by young audiences, grossing hundreds of millions of dollars worldwide. In addition to the popularity of the source material, the success of the films was likely boosted by their association with Walt Disney Pictures, which promoted the films heavily and marketed the films as family fare appropriate for young viewers. The casting of well-known entertainment figures such as Andrews and Moore likely also proved helpful, raising the film's profile among viewers familiar with their previous work.

In addition to being popular young adult films of the early twenty-first century, the Princess Diaries films are significant for their introduction of various actors and filmmakers to international audiences. *The Princess Diaries* marked the film debut of Hathaway, who would go on to star not only in the film's sequel but also in well-regarded films such as *Les Misérables* (2012), for which she received the Academy Award for best supporting actress. *The Princess Diaries 2* was likewise the feature film debut of Pine, who would go on to star in the blockbuster *Star Trek* film reboot (2009), as well as only the second feature film penned by Rhimes, who would later become famous as the creator of television shows such as *Grey's Anatomy*, which debuted in 2005, and *Scandal* in 2012. In the years since the films' debuts, they have become especially interesting as early examples of those entertainers' work.

Although popular among preteen and teen audiences, the Princess Diaries films received mixed reviews that trended toward the negative from many critics, who largely found the first film to be a lackluster adaptation of the novel. *The Princess Diaries 2* was even more poorly received, and many critics called attention to its rather predictable plot. However, some critics devoted to reviewing children's films praised the films for their age-appropriate plots and morals, and many reviewers, regardless of their opinions of the film as a whole, praised Hathaway's portrayal of Mia. Following the release of the two films, a number of scholars referenced them, along with the Princess Diaries novels, in books and papers dealing with a broad range of subjects. In addition to Ford and Mitchell's study of *The Princess Diaries* as a makeover film, other scholarly works that examine the Princess Diaries series consider the discovery of unknown royal heritage in literature and film, the influence of the Cinderella story on modern works, the emphasis on appearance in American society, and the use of humor in young adult fiction.

Joy Crelin

Further Reading

Ebert, Roger. Rev. of *The Princess Diaries*. *RogerEbert. com*. Ebert Digital, 3 Aug. 2001. Web. 31 Mar. 2015. <http://www.rogerebert.com/reviews/the-princess-diaries-2001>.

Gebhardt, Sara. "Predictable 'Princess.'" Rev. of *The Princess Diaries 2: Royal Engagement. Washington Post.* Washington Post, 13 Aug. 2004. Web. 31 Mar. 2015. <http://www.washingtonpost.com/wp-dyn/articles/A59693-2004Aug12.html>.

"The Princess Diaries." *MegCabot.com.* Cabot, 2014. Web. 31 Mar. 2015. <http://www.megcabot.com/princessdiaries/>.

Bibliography

Cabot, Meg. *The Princess Diaries.* New York: Harper-Collins, 2000. Print.

Ford, Elizabeth A., and Deborah C. Mitchell. *The Makeover in Movies: Before and After in Hollywood Films, 1941–2002.* Jefferson: McFarland, 2004. Print.

Gruner, Elizabeth Rose. "Telling Old Tales Newly: Intertextuality in Young Adult Fiction for Girls." *Telling Children's Stories: Narrative Theory and Children's Literature.* Ed. Mike Cadden. Lincoln: U of Nebraska P, 2011. 3–21. Print.

Johnson, Joanna Webb. "Chick Lit Jr.: More Than Glitz and Glamour for Teens and Tweens." *Chick Lit: The New Woman's Fiction.* Ed. Suzanne Ferriss and Mallory Young. New York: Routledge, 2006. 141–58. Print.

Mitchell, Elvis. "*The Princess Diaries* (2001) Film Review: Pygmalion for Another Fair Lady." *New York Times.* New York Times, 3 Aug. 2001. Web. 31 Mar. 2015. <http://www.nytimes.com/movie/review?res=9E04E4D9143CF930A3575BC0A9679C8B63>.

Rumble Fish

The Book

Author: S. E. Hinton (b. 1948)
First published: 1975

The Film

Director: Francis Ford Coppola (b. 1939)
Screenplay by: S. E. Hinton, Francis Coppola
Starring: Nicolas Cage, Matt Dillon, Diane Lane, Dennis Hopper, Mickey Rourke

Context

Rumble Fish presents a stark opposition to the glitter and commercialism of the 1980s, focusing on a teenage hero struggling to find himself in the modern, urban United States. Rusty James (Matt Dillon) is the central protagonist of *Rumble Fish*, but he cannot be said to be its hero; that title is reserved for his older brother, known by everyone in the anonymous city in which the brothers live as the Motorcycle Boy (Mickey Rourke). The two brothers are nearly opposite from one another: Rusty James (Rusty-James in the novel) talks too much, while the Motorcycle Boy rarely speaks; Rusty James is always being outsmarted, while his brother is of uncommon intelligence; Rusty James loses every fight in which he participates, while the Motorcycle Boy seems to win without even trying. Because of his own failures and his brother's successes, Rusty James idolizes his older brother and hopes to mature into a person much more like the Motorcycle Boy. As the saga of the movie unfolds, it follows Rusty James's attempts to make an adult name for himself in the neighborhood, while also exploring the disaffected life he lives in the struggling, amoral squalor of urban America. In its exploration of the tragic male hero, who is disconnected and disaffected by the American city, *Rumble Fish* pursues a line of inquiry that is particularly appropriate in the years that saw the depopulation of the American city and the disintegration of its urban form.

Rumble Fish is a relatively little-known film in the career of the director Francis Ford Coppola. His fame as a director was firmly established by *The Godfather* (1972), when he chose to work on *Rumble Fish*, which he envisioned as an art film for young adults. Coppola shot *Rumble Fish* back-to-back with *The Outsiders* (1983), developed from another book by S. E. Hinton, *How We Made It*. Hinton is the author of nine young adult and children's books. Four of these books have been made into movies.

Film Analysis

Rumble Fish opens with Rusty James and his small posse of grungy teenage boys in a tussle with another gang in a dark underpass. As a policeman approaches, both gangs agree to a more serious fight on the following day, mano a mano, in which Rusty James will be one of the combatants. In the hours that intervene between the first and second fight, Rusty James cajoles his friends to go with him to the second appointed encounter. He then meets up with his girlfriend and proceeds to have a romantic interlude that nearly makes him late for his evening fight. Rusty James purports to be fighting in the name of the Motorcycle Boy, who had left the city for parts unknown with the injunction that no more street fights should happen in his city. As Rusty James throws himself into the fight, the revving of a motorcycle sounds, and the Motorcycle Boy himself breaks through the darkness. The fight is broken up, but not before Rusty James is sliced in the chest by a knife-wielding opponent. A policeman who had warned the Motorcycle Boy away from the city, appears and now threatens him on his return. The foundation for the movie's doomsday plot is now set.

After the reappearance of the Motorcycle Boy, much of the movie is spent with the two brothers wandering around the city, launching into various idle activities, and attempting to reconnect with one another. Although Rusty James idolizes his brother, he does not really understand him. Rusty James just knows that one day he will become just like the Motorcycle Boy. The pitiful heroism of the two brothers within the disaffected urban sphere becomes especially apparent when they retreat to their family apartment in order to dress Rusty James's wound. The family lives in squalor in a shoddy tenement. Their father, an alcoholic, staggers in on the second day after the Motorcycle Boy's return and cannot even remember seeing his older son the night before. In one of Rusty James's teenage jibes against his father, the viewer learns that the father supports the family through welfare checks.

The reunion with his older brother does not stop Rusty James's misfortunes. He is mugged and severely beaten in an alley and his girlfriend leaves him for one of his closest friends. All signs seem to indicate that his life is spiraling out of control, heading in the opposite direction from the heroic ideal he held in his mind. At the same time, the Motorcycle Boy enters a cycle of high-keyed tension that is threatening. The local policeman pursues the brothers mercilessly, even when they are merely chatting on a street corner. There are the signs that the Motorcycle Boy may be mentally unstable. Rusty James inquires with his father about whether or not his brother is crazy. The most telling sign of the mental instability of the Motorcycle Boy are the hours that he spends examining the piranhas, which he calls rumble fish, in small tanks at a pet store. While all the rest of the film is shot in black and white, these fish appear in vibrant hues, highlighting their symbolic

significance for the story. The Motorcycle Boy resolves to free the fish. Having heard that the fish will fight one another to the death if placed in the same tank, he believes that setting them free into the river will allow them able to share the same space peacefully. On a late summer's night, to Rusty James's dismay, the Motorcycle Boy breaks into the store and begins to free the animals. Then, with Rusty James in pursuit, the Motorcycle Boy sets off with the rumble fish, running to get them quickly to the river. In the sequence of events that unfolds rapidly from this moment, the Motorcycle Boy is killed and Rusty James completes his brother's mission to rescue the fish. In the last shots of the movie, Rusty James appears on a motorcycle, facing the Pacific Ocean. He has indeed fulfilled his desire to become his brother, and has perhaps even supplanted his brother's achievements by actually arriving in California.

The plot of *Rumble Fish* is not particularly deep or subtle, but the movie's mythic tone and sense of pressing significance is crafted through highly keyed lighting, music, and symbolism. Stewart Copeland composed the musical score for the film, and in an interview with the *Guardian* said that it is a "90-minute story, not a three-minute song," which builds tension through "a sense of time ticking down to a confrontation with destiny." Similarly, the stark contrasts of light and shadow build a threatening ambiance while also setting a tone of heightened emotion. Other visual tricks leave the viewer wondering about higher levels of symbolism, such as a scene wherein Rusty James's intoxicated father runs into what he believes is a wild dog, which he pauses to greet. As the intoxicated father stumbles off, the viewer sees clearly that the dog is nothing more than a shadow—no live animal is present and the source of the shadow is nowhere to be seen. Moments of dialogue also indicate that these instances of seeming symbolism are fully self-conscious. For instance, Rusty James encounters an old flame of his brother's, Cassandra. When he reports to his brother and father that Cassandra now claims to be off drugs, a dialogue occurs in which the Motorcycle Boy and his father laughingly make reference to the dangerous consequences of not believing Cassandra. Viewers might wonder if all characters and symbols throughout the film have such deeply contemplated meaning, whether the movie's mythic tone and aspiring heroic drama add up to something intellectually worthy of such a timeless reference, or, by contrast, whether it is all some form of a large-scale joke or puzzle through which a viewer might contemplate symbolism and never identify a greater meaning. This ambiguity and general refusal to openly embrace grand-scale significance is a testament to the film's postmodern nature.

Significance

Rumble Fish did poorly at the box office overall and initially received mixed reviews, though it has come to be more highly regarded with the distance of time. Roger Ebert wrote that while teenagers might appreciate the movie despite its "gaps in narrative and character," a general audience might not be as forgiving: "This is a movie you are likely to hate, unless you can love it for its crazy, feverish charm. It's all style and flash, all emotion and impact." The film's symbolic structure and intellectual complexity do not offer a tidy package to viewers, and moreover, remain inscrutable to critics.

A central contradiction of the film is its attempt to combine an art film with a young adult target audience. As Janet Maslin wrote in her review of the film for the *New York Times*, Coppola attempted to take a young adult narrative and permeate it "with the rhapsodic passion of opera, the sharp contrasts of German Expressionism, the angst of existentialism and the imagery of Dada." Yet, there is no apparent explanation as to why Coppola would have selected this story as worthy, or what he hoped to achieve through mythologizing such a basic plot. Ultimately, Maslin concluded, this movie was "a sign of how very paradoxical, even aimless, Mr. Coppola's work has become." Concerning the film's legacy and subsequent reception, in *Whom God Wishes to Destroy: Francis Coppola and the New Hollywood*, Jon Lewis has written:

> "The picture is dedicated to Coppola's elder brother, August, a college professor, and, ironically, it is on college campuses today (in film courses) that *Rumble Fish* is finally being seen and appreciated. But in its initial release, on virtually every front that matters to the industry, the film was a failure." (108)

Likely, *Rumble Fish* will continue to garner critical attention, if only as an interesting sidebar within the career of its renowned director.

Julia A. Sienkewicz

Further Reading

Benjamin, Richard. "The Sense of an Ending: Youth Apocalypse Films." *Journal of Film and Video* 56.4 (2004): 34–49. Print.

Goodwin, Michael, and Naomi Wise. *On the Edge: The Life & Times of Francis Coppola.* New York: Morrow, 1989. Print.

Phillips, Gene D. *Godfather: The Intimate Francis Ford Coppola.* Lexington: U of Kentucky P, 2004. Print.

Bibliography

Coppola, Francis Ford, and Stewart Copeland. "How We Made . . . Francis Ford Coppola and Stewart Copeland on Rumble Fish." Interview by Jack Watkins. *Guardian.* Guardian News and Media, 13 Aug. 2012. Web. 3 May 2015. <http://www.theguardian.com/film/2012/aug/13/how-we-made-rumble-fish>.

Ebert, Robert. Rev. of *Rumble Fish*, dir. Francis Ford Coppola. *RogerEbert.com.* Ebert Digital, 26 Aug. 1983. Web. 3 May 2015. <http://www.rogerebert.com/reviews/rumble-fish>.

Lewis, Jon. *Whom God Wishes to Destroy: Francis Coppola and the New Hollywood.* Durham: Duke UP, 2012. Print.

Maslin, Janet. "Matt Dillon Is Coppola's *Rumble Fish*." Rev. of *Rumble Fish*, dir. Francis Ford Coppola. *New York Times.* New York Times, 7 Oct. 1983. Web. 3 May 2015. <http://www.nytimes.com/movie/review?_r=1&res=9A05E1D7123BF934A35753C1A965948260&partner=Rotten%2520Tomatoes>.

Seventh Son

The Book

Author: Joseph Delaney (b. 1945)
First published: *The Spook's Apprentice* (2004; *Revenge of the Witch,* 2005)

The Film

Director: Sergey Bodrov (b. 1948)
Screenplay by: Charles Leavitt, Steven Knight, Matt Greenberg
Starring: Ben Barnes, Jeff Bridges, Julianne Moore

Context

During the first decade of the twenty-first century, fantasy was a popular genre in film and literature for young adults, and film adaptations of young adult fantasy novels proved both appealing to audiences and financially successful. Among the most popular adaptations were the eight films in the Harry Potter series (2001–11), based on the seven-novel series by British author J. K. Rowling. Inspired by the success of the Harry Potter films and hoping to capture a similarly large and profitable audience, film studios adapted numerous fantasy books for children and young adults into films. Some such adaptations, such as *The Chronicles of Narnia: The Lion, the Witch, and the Wardrobe* (2005) and its sequels, based on the classic novels by C. S. Lewis, were financial and critical successes. Other films in that wave were less successful; the 2006 film *Eragon* and the 2007 film *The Seeker*, both adaptations of popular books, disappointed both critics and their respective studios. By the second decade of the twenty-first century, tastes in young adult adaptations had begun to shift toward paranormal romance, as exemplified by the Twilight films (2008–12), and dystopian stories, as in the Hunger Games (2012–15) and Divergent (2014–) series. Despite that shift, the 2015 film *Seventh Son* falls more within the earlier trend in film, featuring a magical conflict between good and evil in a high-fantasy setting.

Seventh Son was based on the novel *The Spook's Apprentice* (2004), published in the United States in 2005 under the title *Revenge of the Witch*. The first novel in Joseph Delaney's Wardstone Chronicles, known in the United States as the Last Apprentice series, *The Spook's Apprentice* tells the story of twelve-year-old Tom Ward, who is apprenticed to Mr. Gregory, known as the Spook. The Spook is responsible for protecting the County, a region based on northern England, from witches, ghosts, and other dangerous beings. Because Tom is the seventh son of a seventh son, he is uniquely suited to the position of the Spook's apprentice. When Tom inadvertently frees the witch Mother Malkin from the prison in which she had been placed by the Spook, he must work with his new friend Alice to defeat the dangerous witch. His adventures as the Spook's apprentice continue after the conclusion of the book, with more than fifteen additional novels and spin-off books set in the world of the novel.

The film was written by Charles Leavitt and Steven Knight, with a screen story by Matt Greenberg, and directed by Russian-born filmmaker Sergey Bodrov, who is perhaps best known for the Academy Award–nominated films *Prisoner of the Mountains* (1996) and *Mongol: The Rise of Genghis Khan* (2007). Although originally scheduled for release in early 2013, *Seventh Son* was ultimately released in the United States in February of 2015.

Film Analysis

As is often the case in films adapted from novels, *Seventh Son* bears relatively little resemblance to the novel on which it is based. The film's departure from the novel's plot is clear from the beginning of the film and is especially evident in an early scene that sets the stage for the events to come. The Spook, John Gregory (Jeff Bridges), and his apprentice, William Bradley (Kit Harington), have been called upon to help a young girl who has been possessed by a malevolent entity. When they attempt to help the girl, they learn that the being possessing her is Mother Malkin (Julianne Moore), a powerful witch who had previously escaped from the prison in which Gregory had trapped her. Gregory succeeds in forcing Mother Malkin to leave the girl's body, but when he and William attempt to capture her, she transforms into a dragon and escapes, killing William in the process. This scene serves several purposes, not only establishing the conflict between Gregory and Mother Malkin but also emphasizing the deadly stakes of the conflict, rendering the danger of the film's world palpable.

In addition to setting the plot in motion, the scene features two clear deviations from the novel, changes that have a significant effect on the remainder of the narrative. First, the scene explains what happened to the apprentice who studied under Gregory prior to the film's protagonist, Tom Ward (Ben Barnes), in a manner significantly different from that in the book. The question of what happened to William, known in the book as Billy, plagues Tom for much of the novel, and he eventually learns that his predecessor died after being bitten by a boggart. William's death in the film, however, is far more dramatic, underscoring the danger that faces any of Gregory's apprentices. In addition, the film ties William's death to the film's primary conflict, providing additional motivation for Gregory to defeat Mother Malkin. Second, this scene eliminates Tom's role in setting the main conflict in motion. In the novel, Tom accidentally frees Mother Malkin from her prison after being tricked by Alice. This action clearly demonstrates young Tom's naiveté and inexperience when it comes to witches, suggesting that he has a long way to go before he will be ready to take on the role of the Spook himself. In light of his role in her escape, his attempt to defeat Mother Malkin similarly becomes an attempt to take responsibility for his mistake. In the film, however, Mother Malkin escapes prior to Tom and Gregory's first meeting. While Tom does make some mistakes early in his apprenticeship, and he is tricked by Alice (Alicia Vikander) at one point, those events do not have the same impact as the inadvertent freeing of Mother Malkin would have. Because of this, the film incarnation of Tom seems worldlier and somewhat better equipped to handle the responsibilities of the Spook.

From that point the film loosely follows the plot of the novel, presenting a narrative that is somewhat more mature and high-stakes than its source material. After William's death, Gregory approaches Tom about becoming an apprentice. As the seventh son of a seventh son, Tom has abilities that make him well suited for the job, including visions of potential future events. While Mother Malkin plots to kill Gregory when her powers are bolstered by the approaching Blood Moon, Tom trains with Gregory and meets Alice, who is later revealed to be a half-witch and Mother Malkin's niece and with whom Tom begins a romance. After a series of confrontations with Mother Malkin and her minions, Tom and Gregory defeat the witch once and for all, with Tom striking the killing blow. After the battle has concluded, Gregory leaves town, passing the role of the Spook on to Tom.

Much like the beginning of the film, its ending differs significantly from the source material. The novel, as the first installment in a series, depicts only a portion of Tom's apprenticeship, which continues after the defeat of Mother Malkin. He remains an apprentice throughout the Wardstone Chronicles and does not become the new Spook until *A New Darkness* (2014), the first installment in a new series following his adventures in that role. The film, on the other end, concludes with Gregory passing his title on to Tom, who has completed his training and demonstrated through his defeat of Mother Malkin that he is ready to take on that responsibility. The decision to end the film in this way was likely in part a practical one, in light of the age of the actor. In the novel, Tom is twelve years old; however, the character is significantly older in the film, and Barnes was in his early thirties when *Seventh Son* began filming in early 2012. In addition, while this ending differs from that of the novel, it suits the narrative presented in the film, providing a satisfying conclusion to Tom's coming-of-age story rather than a cliffhanger suggesting further adventures: having come into his own over the course of the film, Tom has proven his capabilities and no longer has any need for a mentor's guidance.

Significance

Although the filming of *Seventh Son* proceeded largely as planned, the project experienced some difficulties beginning during postproduction. Initially scheduled for release in February of 2013, the film was first pushed back to October of that year, a delay that some industry observers attributed to the need to complete the film's numerous special effects. The release date was pushed back again, this time to early 2014, before finally settling in early 2015. Commentators speculated that the latter delays may have been the result of the termination of a distribution partnership between Legendary Pictures, which coproduced the film, and Warner Bros. *Seventh Son* ultimately debuted in US theaters in February of 2015, two years after its original scheduled release date.

Perhaps in part because of its significantly delayed release and ultimate premiere in February, a notoriously difficult month for films, *Seventh Son* was largely a financial disappointment, grossing only 17 million dollars domestically, according to the website Box Office Mojo. The film went on to gross more than 90 million dollars internationally and performed particularly well in China, where it grossed more than 27 million dollars. However, the film's relatively large budget rendered its box-office performance particularly poor in comparison.

The critical response to the film was largely negative, with many reviewers arguing that it lacked a coherent vision and deeming its script and acting subpar. While some critics praised *Seventh Son*'s visual design and effects, others found the film overdesigned and the frequent computer-generated transformations undergone by Mother Malkin and her minions distracting. Many fans of the original novels were likewise disappointed by the numerous changes made to the plot, characters, and overall tone. While *The Spook's Apprentice* is the first novel in a long series, the possibility of a sequel film is unlikely, given *Seventh Son*'s poor financial and critical performance.

Joy Crelin

Further Reading

"Seventh Son." *Box Office Mojo*. Box Office Mojo, 2015. Web. 31 Oct. 2015. <http://www.boxofficemojo.com/movies/?id=seventhson.htm>.

Shaw-Williams, H. "'Seventh Son' Release Delayed Again; Warner Bros. Passes Movie to Universal." *Screen Rant*. Screen Rant, 16 Aug. 2013. Web. 31 Oct. 2015. <http://screenrant.com/seventh-son-movie-release-date-delay-warner-bros-universal/>.

Bibliography

Child, Ben. "Will *Seventh Son* Bear Only a Faint Family Resemblance to the Books?" *Guardian*. Guardian News and Media, 12 July 2013. Web. 31 Oct. 2015. <http://www.theguardian.com/film/filmblog/2013/jul/12/seventh-son-books-joseph-delaney-spooks-apprentice>.

Dargis, Manohla. "What Oscar Nominees Do to Pass the Time." Rev. of *Seventh Son*, dir. Sergey Bodrov. *New York Times*. New York Times, 5 Feb. 2015. Web. 31 Oct. 2015. <http://www.nytimes.com/2015/02/06/movies/seventh-son-stars-jeff-bridges-julianne-moore-and-kit-harington.html?_r=0>.

Debruge, Peter. Rev. of *Seventh Son*, dir. Sergey Bodrov. *Variety*. Variety Media, 17 Dec. 2014. Web. 31 Oct. 2015. <http://variety.com/2014/film/reviews/film-review-seventh-son-1201381740/>.

Kenny, Glenn. Rev. of *Seventh Son*, dir. Sergey Bodrov. *RogerEbert.com*. Ebert Digital, 6 Feb. 2015. Web. 31 Oct. 2015. <http://www.rogerebert.com/reviews/seventh-son-2015>.

The Sisterhood of the Traveling Pants (Series)

The Books

Author: Ann Brashares (b. 1967)
First published: *The Sisterhood of the Traveling Pants* (2001)
The Second Summer of the Sisterhood (2003)
Girls in Pants (2005)
Forever in Blue (2007)
Sisterhood Everlasting (2011)

The Films

Directors: Ken Kwapis (b. 1957), *The Sisterhood of the Traveling Pants*
Sanaa Hamri, *The Sisterhood of the Traveling Pants, 2*
Screenplay by: Delia Ephron, Elizabeth Chandler
Starring: Alexis Bledel, America Ferrera, Blake Lively, Amber Tamblyn

Context

With the increasing popularity and visibility of young adult literature in the twenty-first century came a corresponding trend in film. Feature adaptations of young adult novels were numerous during the first decade, based on both fantasy and paranormal novels as well as more realistic works grounded in the challenges of everyday life. Released between 2001 and 2011, the novels in the Sisterhood of the Traveling Pants series fall into the latter category, detailing realistic adventures of four young women as they come of age during their summers.

The Sisterhood of the Traveling Pants series consists of two films. The first, *The Sisterhood of the Traveling Pants* (2005), a straightforward adaptation of the novel of the same title, and the first in the series. The screenplay, written by Delia Ephron and Elizabeth Chandler was directed by Ken Kwapis. The second film, *The Sisterhood of the Traveling Pants 2*, premiered in 2008 and was written by Chandler and directed by Sanaa Hamri. That film combines elements from the next three books in the series, *The Second Summer of the Sisterhood* (2003), *Girls in Pants* (2005), and *Forever in Blue* (2007), though it is based primarily on the lattermost.

The novels on which the films are based were written by Ann Brashares, a longtime publishing professional, who began writing the series while working for book packager Alloy Entertainment, a company known for producing young adult series aimed at teenage girls. In the series, four teenage girls who have been close friends since childhood must spend their summer vacations largely apart. Their friendships, however, remain strong and are reinforced by sharing a pair of jeans that miraculously fits all four of their very different bodies. Over the course of their summers, the girls learn important lessons about life, love, family, and friendship—lessons deeply relevant to many young women. With an emphasis on female friendship, diverse settings, and compelling cast of characters, the *Sisterhood of the Traveling Pants* novels were well suited to film adaptation.

Film Analysis

The novel *Sisterhood of the Traveling Pants* takes place during the summer, as four teenage friends from Bethesda, Maryland, who have been inseparable during previous summers, must take their first steps out into the world without each other's constant support. The film is a relatively straightforward adaptation that adheres closely to the plot of the book, including a number of small details that give the characters and situations found in the novel their unique color. At times, however, director Kwapis and screenwriters Ephron and Chandler opted to make changes to the novel's narrative and structure in order to provide the viewer with necessary information, create a sense of connection and continuity between the film's separate story lines, and bring certain subplots to a satisfactory conclusion. In so doing, the filmmakers created a faithful adaptation that remains true to both the spirit of the novel and its overall narrative but also meets the needs of the visual medium.

Like the novel on which it is based, *The Sisterhood of the Traveling Pants* follows four unique story lines: those of Carmen (America Ferrera), Lena (Alexis Bledel), Tibby (Amber Tamblyn), and Bridget (Blake Lively). In the novel, each character's story is presented in the third-person limited perspective, allowing Brashares to show the reader what the character is thinking and feeling while also providing the opportunity for mysteries, misunderstandings, and instances of dramatic irony. To convey all of the necessary information in the film while maintaining the spirit of the characters' individual perspectives, the filmmakers used a number of popular and effective cinematic techniques, including flashbacks and voice-overs.

The novel begins with a prologue detailing the origin of the girls' friendship and the discovery of the pants and continues in the third person focusing on one girl at a time throughout the book. The film, however, is narrated from Carmen's first-person perspective, and begins with a voice-over by her while she provides similar information on the discovery of the pants. This opening section includes a flashback to the prenatal aerobics class at which the girls' mothers met, as well as flashbacks to pivotal moments in their childhood. Each of those flashbacks provides crucial information about each girl's backstory. Carmen's parents divorced when she was young, Lena was in need of her friends' protection, Tibby was angry about her parents' decision to have more children, and Bridget lost her mother to suicide. Working such information into the film's dialogue would have been difficult and potentially clumsy, but allowing the viewers to see a bit of the essential backstory for themselves is a far more effective tactic. The film also shows the introduction of the titular jeans and follows the girls as they each try on the pants, realizing that the pants somehow miraculously fit each of them. Finally, this opening section follows the girls as they break into the room where their mothers' aerobics class was once held, light candles, and draft a manifesto that will guide their use of the pants and ultimately their entire summer. As they brainstorm their rules, the film cuts between the candlelit room and scenes of the girls

packing and otherwise preparing for their summer, with their voices continuing over the scenes. Voice-overs are used to great effect throughout the film, as the girls write letters to each other in which they discuss their experiences and their emotional states. The film ultimately ends with a voice-over in which all four girls acknowledge the pants' role as witness to that summer and affirm their lasting friendship.

In any film with multiple unconnected plots, it is often necessary for the filmmaker to take extra care in tying the plots together. In *The Sisterhood of the Traveling Pants*, the filmmakers establish a sense of continuity between the various plots and settings in a number of ways. The most obvious means of doing that is through the pants themselves, which travel from Lena to Tibby to Carmen, and to Bridget over the course of the film. Rather than simply letting the pants appear without fanfare in each of the film's main locations, the filmmakers opted to include a brief sequence showing the jeans being packaged and shipped to each girl. The circumstances change each time, calling attention to the geographical distance between the four friends; for example, when the pants travel from Lena to Tibby, they are seen aboard a ship traveling from Greece to the United States, while the pants journey from Carmen to Bridget takes them on a Mexican cargo plane. At times, events or elements of the scenery are used to provide transitions between the different story lines. At one point in the film, Bridget is playing soccer at her soccer camp in Mexico, and seemingly at the same time, Carmen's stepbrother-to-be, Paul (Kyle Schmid), is playing soccer in South Carolina. The film cuts between the two soccer games and shows Bridget's moment of triumph as she shows off for attractive coach Eric (Mike Vogel), and Carmen's moment of disappointment as her father (Bradley Whitford) backs out of his plan to play tennis with her. Later in the film, several emotional scenes that take place at night are presented in quick succession: Tibby and her young friend Bailey (Jenna Boyd), who has leukemia, discuss mortality; Lena kisses the handsome Greek fisherman Kostas (played by Michael Rady; spelled Kostos in the book); and Carmen leaves her father on bad terms and travels home to Maryland. By presenting those scenes in that way, the film underscores the deep connections between the friends despite their physical separation.

The Sisterhood of the Traveling Pants is a remarkably faithful adaptation of its source material, and in most cases, changes made to the narrative seem intended to prevent confusion and simplify some aspects of the story. For example, Effie (Lucy Hale), Lena's younger sister accompanies her to their grandparents' home in Greece in the novel, but she does not in the film. Other changes, namely those made to the film's romance subplots, seem designed to provide a more definite conclusion, which in the novel are left somewhat open ended. Lena's plot shows the most evidence of such changes. In the novel, Lena's grandparents introduce her to Kostos, the grandson of family friends, and succeed in setting Lena up on a date with him. Lena's grandparents change their opinion of the young man only after a misunderstanding, Lena believes Kostos has spied on her while she was skinny dipping, and when she returns to her grandparents' house upset and with her clothes askew, they assume that something untoward took place. In the film, Lena meets Kostas on her own, and a conflict exists between her grandfather and Kostas's grandfather from the beginning. Her grandparents forbid her from seeing him, but after Lena confronts her grandfather about the situation, she is able to reunite with Kostas just before he plans to leave town. Although Lena and Kostos do resolve their various misunderstandings in the novel, their tumultuous relationship remains a major part of Lena's narrative throughout the subsequent books. The film, however, provides a more conclusively happy ending, in part, perhaps, because the status of any sequel films was then unclear.

A similar change is made to Bridget's narrative. In both the book and the film, Bridget meets a handsome coach named Eric while at soccer camp in Mexico and seduces him. Afterward, she sinks into a depression, having been emotionally unprepared for the aftermath of their affair. In the novel, Lena travels to Mexico to help Bridget after returning from Greece; however, Bridget's depression continues into *The Second Summer of the Sisterhood*. In the film, Lena, who is still in Greece, alerts Tibby and Carmen of Bridget's unhappiness, and they make cheering her up their mission after her return to Maryland. When Bridget's dog steals the pants and runs down the street with them, she chases after the dog only to encounter Eric, who has come to apologize to her. They agree to be friends, and Bridget's emotional state is dramatically improved, thus bringing that particular story line to a close.

Unlike the first film in the series, *The Sisterhood of the Traveling Pants 2* is based not on one book, but on three books, taking much of its narrative from *Forever in Blue*, the fourth book in the series, but incorporating elements from *The Second Summer of the Sisterhood*

and *Girls in Pants* as well. In the film, the four young women spend the summer after their first year of college largely apart: Lena takes summer classes at the Rhode Island School of Design, Tibby works at a video store in New York, Carmen attends a theater program in Vermont, and Bridget participates in an archaeological dig in Turkey and later travels to Alabama to meet her estranged grandmother, Greta (Blythe Danner). The former three plot lines and Bridget's time in Turkey are based on *Forever in Blue*, while Bridget's time with her grandmother is drawn from *The Second Summer of the Sisterhood*.

Many of the cinematic techniques used to link the four story lines together in the previous film are not present in *The Sisterhood of the Traveling Pants 2*. This change can likely be attributed to the film's change in director. However, the geographical settings in which the four young women find themselves are somewhat less diverse than in the previous film; aside from Bridget's time in Turkey, Lena's trip to Greece at the beginning of the film, and all four friends' time in Greece at the end, the film is set in the United States, and primarily in New England and New York. As such, the transitions between the story lines are perhaps inherently less jarring, and the girls' geographical proximity to each other allows them to spend more time together and thus share more screen time than in the previous films; Lena travels from Rhode Island to New York to visit Tibby at one point, and Tibby later travels to Vermont to see Carmen. As such, the girls themselves, as well as several secondary characters, create a sense of continuity between story lines.

Although the change in directors renders *The Sisterhood of the Traveling Pants 2* structurally quite different from its predecessor, the use of voice-overs and flashbacks in the film is largely consistent with that in the first. The beginning of the second film in many ways mirrors the start of the previous one. A voice-over by Carmen explains the origin of the pants and their importance to her circle of friends, providing necessary backstory to viewers who may not have seen the first installment. The camera pans over the pants, which have been decorated with markers and embroidery over the years, documenting the girls' many adventures. As Carmen's narration continues, the film cuts to various flashbacks of previous summers, showing the girls receiving and wearing the pants during their important moments. This section also gives the viewer some information about what took place during the years between the first and second films; for example, Lena and Kostas are shown to have reunited in Greece, Carmen is shown at her mother's wedding, and all four girls are shown at their high school graduation. Carmen concludes her voice-over by sharing some of her own feelings, noting that while her friends seem to have found their place at their various colleges, she feels isolated and lost in her new world. The film likewise ends with a voice-over that, much like the ending voice-over of the first film, explains that the pants are ultimately far less important than the friendships they represent. This point is especially important in *The Sisterhood of the Traveling Pants 2*, as the pants themselves are lost toward the end of the film. The series' strong theme of friendship, however, remains very present.

Significance

Following its release in June of 2005, *The Sisterhood of the Traveling Pants* proved quite popular among American moviegoers, grossing more than $39 million at the US box office. The film also experienced international success, performing particularly well in Australia. Its sequel, *The Sisterhood of the Traveling Pants 2*, exceeded the first film's box office grosses, earning more than $44 million in the United States, however, the second film did not experience as much success outside of the United States. Among possible reasons for the second film's United States success are its status as a sequel to an established film as well as the increased popularity and name recognition of Ferrera, who was then starring in the series *Ugly Betty* (2006–10). Lively had been an unknown prior to the first film, but by the time of the second film, was starring in the Alloy Entertainment–produced television series *Gossip Girl* (2007–12). The popular and critical success of the two films led many industry publications to speculate about whether another sequel would be released, and in mid-2014, Alloy Entertainment announced plans to develop a third film in the series, based on the 2011 novel *Sisterhood Everlasting*.

Critical response to *The Sisterhood of the Traveling Pants* film was overall quite positive. Many critics praised the film's faithfulness to the original novel, contrasting it with contemporary film adaptations that failed to capture the spirit of their source material. Brashares herself was pleased with the adaptation and noted in an interview with *Writer's Digest* that although she did not have much say over the film's development, she enjoyed the filmmakers' take on her novel. Although some reviewers found that not all four main performances were equally good, they particularly praised Bledel and

Ferrera for the emotional depth they brought to their characters' respective story lines. *The Sisterhood of the Traveling Pants 2* received a similar level of critical praise, although since its narrative was compiled from three of Brashares's novels, the faithfulness of the adaptation did not receive quite as much acclaim as that of its predecessor. In reviews of both films, critics called attention to their positive messages and refreshing focus on female friendship that is not marked by the jealousy and competition that fuels many other female-oriented teen films.

Joy Crelin

Further Reading

Brashares, Ann. "The WD Interview: Ann Brashares; One Leg at a Time." Interview by Kara Gebhart Uhl. *Writer's Digest*. F+W, 11 Mar. 2008. Web. 30 Apr. 2015. <http://www.writersdigest.com/writing-articles/by-writing-genre/young-adult-childrens/the_wd_interview_ann_brashares_one_leg_at_a_time>.

Ebert, Roger. Rev. of *The Sisterhood of the Traveling Pants*, dir. Ken Kwapis. *RogerEbert.com*. Ebert Digital, 31 May 2005. Web. 30 Apr. 2015. <http://www.rogerebert.com/reviews/the-sisterhood-of-the-traveling-pants-2005>.

Holden, Stephen. "Four Jills in Jeans (One Pair) Go to College, Find Romance (or Not), Stay Connected." Rev. of *The Sisterhood of the Traveling Pants 2*, dir. Sanaa Hamri. *New York Times*. New York Times, 5 Aug. 2008. Web. 30 Apr. 2015. <http://www.nytimes.com/2008/08/06/movies/06pant.html?_r=0>.

Bibliography

Johns, Nikara. "Third 'The Sisterhood of the Traveling Pants' Film in Development." *Variety*. Variety Media, 23 Apr. 2014. Web. 30 Apr. 2015. <http://variety.com/2014/film/news/third-the-sisterhood-of-the-traveling-pants-film-in-development-1201162187>.

"The Sisterhood of the Traveling Pants." *Box Office Mojo*. IMDb.com, n. d. Web. 30 Apr. 2015. <http://www.boxofficemojo.com/movies/?id=travelingpants.htm>.

"The Sisterhood of the Traveling Pants 2." *Box Office Mojo*. IMDb.com, n. d. Web. 30 Apr. 2015. <http://www.boxofficemojo.com/movies/?id=travelingpants2.htm>.

Stein, Ruthe. "Review: 'Sisterhood of the Traveling Pants 2.'" Rev. of *Sisterhood of the Traveling Pants 2*, dir. Sanaa Hamri. *SFGate*. Hearst Communications, 6 Aug. 2008. Web. 30 Apr. 2015. <http://www.sfgate.com/movies/article/Review-Sisterhood-of-the-Traveling-Pants-2-3274574.php>.

Tucker, Ken. "Movie Review: Worldwide Pants." Rev. of *Sisterhood of the Traveling Pants*, dir. Ken Kwapis. *NYMag.com*. New York, 2005. Web. 30 Apr. 2015. <http://nymag.com/nymetro/movies/reviews/11891>.

Something Wicked This Way Comes

The Book

Author: Ray Bradbury (1920–2012)
First published: 1962

The Film

Director: Jack Clayton (1921–95)
Screenplay by: Ray Bradbury
Starring: Jason Robards, Jonathan Pryce, Diane Ladd, Vidal Peterson, Shawn Carson

Context

Something Wicked This Way Comes is hailed as an influential precursor in the young adult horror and fantasy genres. Though Bradbury wrote a screenplay of the story in the early 1950s, he could not find financial backers for the project. The screenplay was later adapted as a novel, which was first published in 1962. Bradbury's novel was the second in his Green Town series which also included *Dandelion Wine* (1957) and *Farewell Summer* (2006). *Something Wicked This Way Comes* was published the same year as Bradbury's science-fiction collection of short stories titled *R Is for Rocket*, and both targeted a young adult audience.

The novel and film are both important in the ability to cross genre categories. Though clearly a horror story in nature, *Something Wicked This Way Comes* has also been called dark fantasy for its sideshow themes. Its universal audience appeal is also important as it can be called either a young adult novel or an adult one. Horror literature from the earlier part of the twentieth century was more gothic in format, with works by authors such as H. P. Lovecraft creating recognizable monsters, but Bradbury's horror is more insidious with its inclusion of psychological aspects that emphasize the darker emotional undertones found in the kinds of horror that continue to be popular today.

According to Bradbury, his writing career blossomed when he was a child. Returning home from a family funeral, he begged his father to allow him to go to a roadside carnival where he met a magician calling himself Mr. Electrico. The magician reportedly told the young Bradbury "Live forever!" which inspired Bradbury to do just that through the written word. Bradbury's writing career was extremely prolific, starting in the early 1940s and spanning until his death in 2012. His body of work includes fifty books, as well as numerous short stories, screenplays, poems, essays, and plays. His best known work, *Fahrenheit 451*, a dystopia written in 1953, is often compared to Aldous Huxley's *Brave New World*. He is also well known for *The Martian Chronicles* (1950).

Bradbury won several awards for his work, including the National Book Foundation Medal for distinguished contributions to American letters in 2000, the National Medal of Arts in 2004, and the Pulitzer Prize Special Citation in 2007. His work is particularly important for the influence it had on later writers, such as R. L. Stine, Stephen King, and Neil Gaiman, as well as filmmakers such as Steven Spielberg and James Cameron.

Film Analysis

The film tells the story of Will Halloway and Jim Nightshade, two boys coming to age in the early part of the twentieth century. They live in a small town where life is simple. Best friends and neighbors, the boys seem to share everything, even a birthday though one was born just before midnight and the second was born just after the witching hour. During the fall of their thirteenth year, the boys are exposed to a series of events that will change them forever.

The tale starts with a shot of a ragged man walking down a country road. The arrival of this man, a lightning-rod salesman, combined with the train rushing into town in the dark of night, ushers in a spooky atmosphere as it foreshadows the coming storm. Despite this coming doom, the scene changes to show the boys sitting in detention, punished for whispering during Miss Foley's class. The narrative voice, Will Halloway from a later point in his life, shares the old woman's despair over her lost beauty, and when Jim hides an unflattering pencil drawing he has done of her, viewers are unsurprised at her desire to see the artwork and at her anguish over the image presented. Bradbury uses foreshadowing as a way to continue suggesting a darker note as the boys run through town, meeting with a variety of adults who struggle with unfulfilled dreams. In addition to Miss Foley, these characters include Mr. Tetley, the newspaper and cigar salesman who wants riches; Ed, the bartender whose injuries ended a promising career in football; and Mr. Crosetti, the town barber whose desire for "far away ladies" limits his ability to relate to women. The lightning-rod salesman catches the boys outside of their homes after they leave town and talks Jim into purchasing a rod with Egyptian symbols that will serve as a protection measure. This purchase further promises that an attack on Jim and his home is pending.

As the night progresses, the boys hear the trumpet of the arriving steam engine that carries Mr. Dark's Pandemonium Carnival into town. This carnival will bring temptation and destruction to the town's citizens with its charismatic leader, Mr. Dark, his partner Mr. Cooger, and a mysterious witch feeding on the pain of those they entice. While Miss Foley quickly caves into the desire to be young and beautiful again but loses her sight in payment, Mr. Tetley rejoices over the boon of a thousand-dollar game win but becomes a wooden Indian, Mr. Crosetti is overwhelmed by exotic dancers but is turned into the bearded lady, and Ed returns to health but as a child. These people fail to fight temptation, a challenge that is presented to Jim, Will, and Will's father, Charlie, as well. The film centers on the battle of good over evil in these choices. Jim is tempted with adulthood; he wants to grow up too fast. In contrast, Will understands the value of youth. Charlie, who became a father late in life, is tempted with good health and youth. Though Jim's willpower is weaker than Will's and Charlie's, the three triumph in the end, destroying Mr. Dark in their refusal to give in to his enticement.

The horror in the film comes as the boys realize Mr. Dark's intentions. In one scene, they see Dark torturing the lightning-rod salesman. After fleeing to the safety of their homes, they are beset by spiders sent by the witch. In another scene, Dark torments Charlie over his perceived failures, age, and health. The horror can only be overcome by a strength of mind that allows Charlie and Will to choose their relationship over the pain.

Clayton uses music and light as effective tools in the film. The musical score and lighting change with the tone of the scenes. Dark, frightening notes and the sound of a train's whistle accompany a black background and the outline of a dark train whose bright headlight seemingly speeds toward the audience. The heavy music emphasizes the danger of whatever the train carries. However, when the scene changes to the small town in autumn, the music becomes upbeat and cheerful, creating a nostalgic view of a small town where two young boys are safe and loved. The musical score becomes discordant to highlight the jarring horror of the carnival whenever the circus or performers are present. The closing scene of the film returns to a lighter note with gentle tones reminiscent of the beginning of the film. Like the music, the lighting adapts to the atmosphere, with sunlight stressing the innocence of not only the town but specifically of the two young boys around whom the story revolves. Once the carnival arrives in town, however, the scenes become primarily dark with the main action sequences being nocturnal. Though there are glimpses of light throughout—the train's headlight, lightning flashes, a bright flash that accompanies the mirror maze and carousel, an eerie green fog that announces the presence of the witch—the focus on the darkness as a way to establish tone is clear. A return to daylight at the end showcases the triumph of good over the evil with the death of Mr. Dark and the rebirth of Charlie Halloway.

Significance

Something Wicked This Way Comes is the second novel in Bradbury's Green Town series, set in a fictional version of his hometown, Waukegan, Illinois. The novel itself is one of Bradbury's most popular works.

Although Paramount Studios purchased film rights to the novel in 1977, Paramount did not do anything with the project. Six years later, Disney produced the film version of *Something Wicked This Way Comes* in an attempt to break free of their traditional image. Despite Disney's desire to do something different, the company's perception of the way the film should be presented caused problems in the production process. Though the studio clearly knew the horror themes of the film, they were reluctant to focus too much on that horror since the genre was new for them, and executives were interested in creating a story that felt real despite the novel's clear fantasy/horror themes. As a result, many of the special effects that had been created for the film were changed or dropped. A second filming of some scenes took place after the first cut was finished, and at least two scenes (the spider scene with Will and Jim and the mirror scene with Will and Charlie) show obviously older child actors. The original musical score was thrown out in favor of something lighter, and the original editor was replaced by his assistant in an effort to save money.

Though the film grossed less than half of its production costs, it is important as one of Disney's first films with a more mature theme. The film was praised for its similarity to the book's tone, mood, and style as well as the lyrical dialogue. The novel itself received accolades for characterization, description, and depth of theme and meaning. The ongoing popularity of the story is evidenced in the fact that it has been remade as a stage play and a radio play.

The film was noted as award worthy. In 1984 it won two Saturn Awards, one for best fantasy film and one for best writing, and was nominated for several others. It was also nominated for the Hugo Award for best dramatic presentation and the Grand Jury Prize at the 1984 Avoriaz Fantastic Film Festival (for directing).

Theresa L. Stowell, PhD

Further Reading

Reid, Robin Anne. *Ray Bradbury: A Critical Companion*. Westport: Greenwood, 2000. Print.

Weller, Sam. *The Bradbury Chronicles: The Life of Ray Bradbury*. New York: Morrow, 2005. Print.

Weller, Sam. *Ray Bradbury: The Last Interview and Other Conversations*. Brooklyn: Melville, 2014. *eBook Collection (EBSCOhost)*. Web. 3 Nov. 2015. <http://search.ebscohost.com/login.aspx?direct=true&db=nlebk&AN=799830&site=ehost-live>.

Bibliography

Bernardo, Anthony. "Something Wicked This Way Comes." *Masterplots II: American Fiction Series, Revised Edition* (2000): 1–3. *Literary Reference Center*. Web. 3 Nov. 2015. <http://search.ebscohost.com/login.aspx?direct=true&db=lfh&AN=103331AMF14480011000448&site=lrc-live>.

Brown, Eric C. "Popularizing Pandaemonium: Milton and the Horror Film." *Milton in Popular Culture*. Eds. Laura Lunger Knoppers and Gregory M. Colon Semenza. New York: Palgrave, 2006. 85–97. *eBook Collection (EBSCOhost)*. Web. 3 Nov. 2015. <http://search.ebscohost.com/login.aspx?direct=true&db=nlebk&AN=202199&site=ehost-live>.

Ebert, Roger. "Something Wicked This Way Comes." Rev. of *Something Wicked This Way* Comes, dir. by Jack Clayton. *RogerEbert.com*. Ebert Digital, 29 Apr. 1983. Web. 23 Oct. 2015. <www.rogerebert.com/reviews/something-wicked-this-way-comes-1983>.

Kakutani, Michiko. "Up from the Depths of Pulp and into the Mainstream." *New York Times*. New York Times, 6 June 2012. Web. 23 Oct. 2015. <http://www.nytimes.com/2012/06/07/books/ray-bradbury-who-made-science-fiction-respectable.html?_r=0>.

Maslin, Janet. "Something Wicked This Way Comes (1983): Disney's Bradbury." Rev. of *Something Wicked This Way Comes*, dir. by Jack Clayton. *New York Times*. New York Times, 29 Apr. 1983. Web. 3 Nov. 2015.

Seed, David. *Ray Bradbury*. Urbana: U of Illinois P, 2015. *eBook Collection (EBSCOhost)*. Web. 3 Nov. 2015. <http://search.ebscohost.com/login.aspx?direct=true&db=nlebk&AN=944462&site=ehost-live>.

Speak

The Book

Author: Laurie Halse Anderson (b. 1961)
First published: 1999

The Film

Director: Jessica Sharzer (b. 1972)
Screenplay by: Jessica Sharzer, Annie Young-Frisbie
Starring: Kristen Stewart, Elizabeth Perkins, Steve Zahn

Context

In 1999, debut novelist Laurie Halse Anderson published a young adult book called *Speak*, about a thirteen-year-old girl who is raped at a party. The protagonist, Melinda Sordino, calls the police after the assault, but the truth gets lost in the melee as kids scatter to avoid arrest for underage drinking. When she starts high school in the fall, she is socially ostracized because everyone thinks she called the cops to get them in trouble. For the duration of the novel, Melinda struggles to put her pain into words—thus the book's title. Anderson told Thomas J. Brady for the *Philadelphia Inquirer* that the idea for the book came from a nightmare. "I wrote [it] down and the character who became Melinda started to talk to me," she recalled. "For the first many, many, many pages, I was just taking notes." Melinda may have had a lot to say to Anderson, but at fictional Merryweather High, her trauma and added social anxieties render her nearly mute. At home, her mother is absorbed in her own problems, as is her recently unemployed father. They interpret her silence as teenage sullenness. Only Melinda's art teacher, an eccentric older man, senses something amiss behind Melinda's somber mien; he never explicitly asks her what the trouble is, but he gives her the tools to express it herself through art.

Speak was a finalist for the National Book Award in 1999 and was a Michael L. Printz Honor Book in 2000. Though it was banned by a number of schools for its frank depiction of sexual assault, it went on to become a *New York Times* best seller and remains popular with teenagers today. Nancy Matson, for CNN, found that Melinda's inner monologue perfectly captures the timeless brutality of high school. "Readers will appreciate [Anderson's] honesty," Matson wrote. In 2004, filmmaker Jessica Sharzer wrote and directed a movie adaptation of the book starring Kristen Stewart, who was thirteen years old when filming began. The film played at the Sundance Film Festival and aired on the Showtime and Lifetime television networks.

Film Analysis

The film opens with a meandering shot of Melinda's bedroom. The room is pink and purple, with stuffed animals and other childish knickknacks that stand in stark contrast to the sullen girl sitting on the floor. Melinda looks into a mirror, carefully drawing lines over her lips, making them look as if they were sewn together. (The image of sewing one's lips shut is a potent one, often used as a form of protest. In 1989, the late artist and AIDS activist David Wojnarowicz used a needle and thread to sew his mouth shut for a performance piece.) Melinda's mother (Elizabeth Perkins) comes into the room; seeing Melinda's artwork, she says, "I don't want to know." After she leaves, Melinda looks in the mirror again and, after a moment, wipes the lines off of her mouth. With this introductory scene, screenwriter and director Jessica Sharzer effectively sums up the arc of the entire film: Melinda is alone and out of place; the adults in her life do not see, or fail to understand, the pain clearly written on her face; and ultimately, Melinda makes the decision to speak about her trauma on her own—she wipes away the lines herself. Throughout the film, Sharzer finds similar ways to make Melinda's inner life visible. Rather than rely

too heavily on voice-over narration, she renders the unspeakable through an intricate series of images. Sometimes these images come in flashbacks to the night Melinda was raped; other times, the symbols (trees, apples, leaves) are more obscure. Sharzer also accurately captures the world depicted in the novel thanks to her decision to shoot the film at an actual high school, with real teenagers as extras. Finally, star Kristen Stewart adds necessary depth to film; the complexity of her performance contrasts with the broad-stroke characters that surround her.

On the first day of high school, students in Melinda's art class must pick a slip of paper to find the object or concept on which they are required to focus throughout the entire school year. On Melinda's paper is the word "tree." At first, she is disappointed by her assignment. But art class—thanks to the kindness of her art teacher (Steve Zahn)—soon becomes her most absorbing endeavor. Trees become the image through which Melinda can comfortably express herself and one of the central images of the film. Trees in the film are, by turns, frightening, nostalgic (a memory of reaching up and plucking an apple from a branch is so strong that she takes a bite of the one that was supposed to be used for an experiment in science class), and comforting. As Melinda's mental health improves, Sharzer inserts a shot of Melinda's father, sawing the dead branches off a tree in the yard. In addition to the trees, Melinda's inner life is explicitly depicted in the form of a small, hidden room attached to a janitor's closet at school. This is Melinda's "safe space," her emotional interior made physical. She found the room when she was looking for a place to hide from her history teacher, an overzealous disciplinarian, and it becomes her sanctuary. The sanctity of the space is violated at the end of the film—when her rapist tries to attack her there—but by then, her secret is out, and the room has served its purpose.

Sharzer shot the film in Columbus, Ohio, at a real high school with real students—"which is definitely not how most Hollywood films are made," she told John Crook for the New York *Buffalo News*. "You can smell the cafeteria in our movie." The age-appropriate cast is strikingly young compared to those of most movies about teenagers, which feature actors in their twenties. Their youth, coupled with their cruelty, is disturbingly realistic. Sharzer heightens this dynamic with a few well-chosen shots from Melinda's point of view. In one, viewers see Melinda's former best friend talking about her through a field of seats on the school bus. Sharzer also includes a handful of flashbacks and other evocative suggestions that Melinda and her friends have crossed the wide maturity gulf separating middle school and high school. Melinda recalls how her pack of girlfriends dressed up as witches for Halloween the previous year, before telling her art teacher that she is far too old to go trick or treating.

But Sharzer's filmic choices would be inert without the nuanced performance of Kristen Stewart as Melinda. Given the circumstances of her character, Stewart relies on facial expressions and physicality to convey a host of emotions. The audience must understand what the adults around her do not—that Melinda is not being silent because she is going through a phase but (perversely) because she has something to say. The supporting characters in *Speak* are not drawn with the same care as Melinda: her parents often seem implausibly self-involved, as do her teachers, who keep finding ways to actively ignore their students. But, just as the book was told from Melinda's wry perspective, so is the movie. For a teenager like Melinda, who feels alone for reasons that she believes adults would never understand, the world can seem like a very uncaring place.

Significance

Speak never appeared in theaters but was broadcast on the cable networks Showtime and Lifetime in a partnership with the Rape, Abuse & Incest National Network (RAINN) in 2005. Neil Genzlinger, for the *New York Times*, gave the film an even-handed review, writing, "It comes nowhere near capturing the wise, subtle tone of the book it's based on, but 'Speak,' the story of a teenage girl trying to cope with having been date-raped, is still an effective treatment of a difficult subject, thanks almost entirely to the performance of Kristen Stewart as the young victim." The film remains popular largely because of its educational value; both novel and film are taught in schools, mostly to students around Melinda's age. Author Laurie Halse Anderson does not shy away from using her book as an educational tool and has spoken at schools about rape and sexual assault many times since the book's publication. She also knows firsthand the trauma of teenagers in Melinda's situation: *Speak* is partially drawn from Anderson's own experience of having been raped as a teenager. Her message to teens in this situation is simple: speak up. *Speak*, the film, is a bit didactic in this regard, but when it comes to sexual assault, it does not hurt to emphasize the point. "When I speak to kids, I often say none of us would ever be embarrassed or ashamed if we got mugged in the parking lot," Anderson told Rachel Simon for *Bustle*. "The older I get, the more convinced I get that you have to speak up about these hard things if anything is going to get better for anybody."

Molly Hagan

Further Reading

Gross, Sarah, and Katherine Schulten. "Text to Text: 'Speak' and 'Waking Up to the Enduring Memory of Rape.'" *New York Times*. New York Times, 19 Mar. 2015. Web. 10 June 2015. <http://learning.blogs.nytimes.com/2015/03/19/text-to-text-speak-and-waking-up-to-the-enduring-memory-of-rape>.

Smith, Sally. Rev. of *Speak*, by Laurie Halse Anderson. *Journal of Adolescent and Adult Literacy* 43.6 (2000): 585–87. Print.

Rev. of *Speak*, by Laurie Halse Anderson. *Publishers Weekly*. PWxyz, 25 Oct. 1999. Web. 10 June 2015. <http://www.publishersweekly.com/978-0-374-37152-4>.

Bibliography

Brady, Thomas J. "Mute Character Said a Lot to Her Creator." *Philadelphia Inquirer* 16 Apr. 2000: K02. Print.

Crook, John. "Young Rape Victim Fights to Reclaim Her Life in 'Speak.'" *Buffalo News* [New York] 4 Sept. 2005: TV37. Print.

Genzlinger, Neil. "For One Teenager, the Party's Over." *New York Times*. New York Times, 5 Sept. 2005. Web. 10 June 2015. <http://www.nytimes.com/2005/09/05/arts/television/for-one-teenager-the-partys-over.html>.

Grinberg, Emanuella. "'Speak' Author: 'We as Adults Struggle to Talk to Kids Honestly about Sex.'" *CNN*. CNN, 12 Apr. 2014. Web. 10 June 2015. <http://www.cnn.com/2014/04/12/living/laurie-halse-anderson-speak>.

Matson, Nancy. "Review: Book Recalls the Tumult of the Teen Years." Rev. of *Speak*, by Laurie Halse Anderson. *CNN*. CNN, 29 Nov. 1999. Web. 10 June 2015. <http://www.cnn.com/books/reviews/9911/29/speak>.

Simon, Rachel. "Laurie Halse Anderson on 'Speak,' Censorship, and 'The Impossible Knife of Memory.'" *Bustle*. Bustle.com, 6 Jan. 2014. Web. 10 June 2015.

<http://www.bustle.com/articles/11009-laurie-halse-anderson-on-speak-censorship-and-the-impossible-knife-of-memory>.

The Spectacular Now

The Book

Author: Tim Tharp (b. 1957)
First published: 2008

The Film

Director: James Ponsoldt
Screenplay by: Scott Neustadter, Michael H. Weber
Starring: Miles Teller, Shailene Woodley, Kyle Chandler, Brie Larson

Context

The Spectacular Now fits into the popular genre of high-school movies. Yet, unlike many such films that present saccharine love stories, overblown angst, and shallow characters, this film offers a deep look at profound adolescent challenges. At its core is a teenage love story, but one that is psychologically and emotionally intense. The central characters, Sutter Keely (Miles Teller) and Aimee Finecky (Shailene Woodley), meet one another in the film and gradually fall for each other, but their relationship faces real-world challenges that give it dimension and interest. While the central love story draws the audience in, the film focuses on two themes that are of greater critical importance: alcoholism and college enrollment. Its treatment of both these topics is complex and thoughtful.

Novelist and college professor Tim Tharp wrote *The Spectacular Now* after developing a serious interest in young adult literature. His first young adult novel, *Knights of the Hill Country* (2006), focuses on high-school football but, similar to *The Spectacular Now*, deals with a troubled central male protagonist. His latest contributions to the genre are *Badd* (2012), which deals with post-traumatic stress disorder, and *Mojo* (2013), which is a teenage crime mystery.

James Ponsoldt directed *The Spectacular Now*, which followed his work on another movie that also focused on alcohol abuse. *Smashed* (2012) puts alcoholism as the central theme of the film, while *The Spectacular Now* engages with this subject matter a bit more subtly. Ponsoldt's film *The End of the Tour* (2015) is very different in its story of an interview with the novelist David Foster Wallace.

Film Analysis

Sutter Keely, who narrates *The Spectacular Now* and is the central protagonist of the film, is at once a lovable and an infuriating character. He is funny, charming, and the center of social life at his high school. When the film opens, he and his girlfriend Cassidy (Brie Larson), are at the height of teenage society and their relationship centers on excesses of all kinds. This fits closely with the mantra that Sutter has developed for himself of living in the moment—the "spectacular now" to which the title refers. While his enjoyment of life is not in and of itself bad, Sutter's particular model of it, which involves such imminent self-indulgence that he neglects to mature and build toward the future, is profoundly problematic. This is amplified by his overindulgence in alcohol. At first his drinking seems relatively harmless, albeit illegal, but as the film develops it becomes an increasingly threatening aspect of his life.

Everything changes in the film when Cassidy breaks up with Sutter. Since Cassidy is a distinctly unlikeable character, this seems like a happy turn of events. Still, Sutter, whose single mother is a nurse and works long hours, does not have the emotional maturity to help himself get through this in a healthy way. He therefore parties and drinks to excess in order to numb the negative feelings he has. Eventually, he winds up drunk and passed out on the lawn of a stranger's house where he is found in the early morning by Aimee Finecky. At first she thinks he is dead, so it is a relief when she is able to rouse him. The two begin to talk, despite Sutter's foggy hangover, and thus they begin the start of a friendship and a cautious romance. The two are classmates at the local high school, but they have never really met before because they are part of two different and distinct social worlds. Aimee is a quiet, diligent student and an avid reader. She is also being raised by a single mother, but her economic circumstances are much more constrained than Sutter's—so much so that her family depends on Aimee's paper route in order to make ends meet. Sutter has a job in retail, but it is portrayed as merely another venue in which he can show off his charming and irresponsible personality rather than as a means of putting food on the family's table.

Sutter and Aimee initially agree to meet again because she agrees to tutor him.

A concern that both Sutter and Aimee share is the question of what life will be like after high school. The film opens with Sutter attempting to work on a college application essay. He just cannot seem to put it together, though, likely because his heart is not in it. He loves his youth, his philosophy of living in the now, and he cannot imagine an older and adult life in the future. By contrast, Aimee aches to go to college, but she is convinced that this is an unrealistic dream for her. Her mother depends on her to make ends meet for the family, discourages her from going away to any of the dream schools on her list, and generally makes it clear that college is for people of greater social privilege. For both teens the question of if, where, and how they will go to college is a central emotional stressor. It is also, perhaps, the only point on which a viewer can be absolutely certain that knowing Sutter actually does quantifiable good for Aimee.

Being raised by a single mother is a point of particular angst for Sutter that leads to another watershed encounter in the film. Although he barely remembers his father, he does recall a fun-loving man and devoted dad, and he faults his strained and overworked mother with pushing his father out of the family's life. Sutter's older sister, who clearly knows more about the circumstances between their parents, will not provide him with any information about their estranged father. Eventually, Aimee and Sutter head out on a quest to find his father. The scenes that result from this journey are some of the most powerful and heartrending of the film. Sutter winds up shattered a second time by his encounter with his father, and while the events are certainly upsetting, Sutter is even more shaken because he must come to terms with the reality of what he will become if his life continues on a similar track. Sutter must decide whether he is able to change his life or whether his path is destined to progress in a predetermined way. At the heart of these musings is his relationship with alcohol. As he drives home drunk with Aimee in the car, the dark hold of addiction seems intensely present.

Alongside these heady themes, *The Spectacular Now* is a film with great sensitivity to realism, emotion, and the bonds of love. Though the relationship between Aimee and Sutter is central in the film, the viewer gets a chance to consider other types of love such as that of mothers and siblings. Missing in Sutter's life, however, is any form of paternal love, though he does have a few would-be male role models. As the film's drama unfolds,

The Spectacular Now allows the viewer also to explore the challenges of teenage life in the United States and the particular pressures that modern society puts on its youth. Watching Sutter and Aimee struggle for survival and seek to identify what valuable and meaningful future might look like, presents a sympathetic narrative for a youth audience while allowing adult viewers to understand particularly important issues on the mind's and in the lives of today's youth.

Significance

The Spectacular Now has received extensive critical acclaim, which has been largely focused on its thoughtful treatment of teenage alcoholism. Sutter's abuse of alcohol begins as a familiar theme from film and popular culture. Youth binge drinking is a scarcely hidden reality of high school and college life. Yet, it becomes rapidly clear that for Sutter this habit has become an addiction. A small flask accompanies his daily activities and it is not long before he introduces Aimee to the thrill of a semi-continuous daily high. Gradually his offenses mount and climax in drunk driving, which transforms the affable partier into a dangerous and threatening figure. As more of the pieces of his life puzzle fit together, the viewer understands that Sutter is the son of an alcoholic and that he is therefore predisposed to addiction. Ponsoldt ends the film without a clear narrative into the future, and the viewer is given hints as to how both Aimee and Sutter's relationship will move forward and of the decisions Sutter must make to address his addiction. Rather than offering a tidy, happy Hollywood ending, this film asks the viewer to think critically about the issues that have been raised.

More subtle, yet likewise of value, is the film's focus on the struggles that Aimee faces as the first member of her family to want to go to college. Her passion to build a future for herself is at odds with the needs and emotional pressures of her family. Although she is smart and accomplished at school, she seems ready to give up her dream in order to continue to bring a modest income to her family. While the viewer knows from the outset what Aimee's decision should be, it is important to see the struggles and setbacks of her college application and admission process in this film. First-generation college students often struggle to succeed without family support and deal with the guilt of defying parental expectations as they seek to build their own futures. Too often these issues are represented in film as only pertaining to minorities, so it is particularly useful to see Aimee, a

Caucasian girl from a family with limited means, grappling with these same issues, which transcend ethnic and racial boundaries.

While this film addresses serious issues, it has also been praised for its natural dialogue and its balanced and realistic treatment of its characters. *The Spectacular Now* sets an emotional and psychological tone that seems to engage viewers in a thoughtful and constructive way, while neither preaching about the issues it raises nor belittling its characters through shallow representations. Both Teller and Woodley offer strong performances, which make the viewer sympathetic toward these two young individuals, and which present these teenagers as multidimensional, interesting, and fallible personalities.

Julia A. Sienkewicz

Further Reading

Cole, Timothy. "'Old Enough to Live': Age, Alcohol, and Adulthood in the United States, 1970–1994." *Age in America: The Colonial Era to the Present.* Ed. Corinne T. Field and Nicholas L. Syrett. New York: New York UP, 2015. 237–58. Print.

Denzin, Norman K. *Hollywood Shot by Shot: Alcoholism in American Cinema.* New York: Aldine, 1991. Print.

Shippee, Nathan D., and Timothy J. Owens. "GPA, Depression, and Drinking: A Longitudinal Comparison of High School Boys and Girls." *Sociological Perspectives* 54.3 (2011): 351–76. Print.

Bibliography

Ebert, Roger. Rev. of *The Spectacular Now*, dir. James Ponsoldt. *RogerEbert.* Ebert Digital, 2 Aug. 2013. Web. 30 Dec. 2015. <http://www.rogerebert.com/reviews/the-spectacular-now-2013>.

Mathieson, Craig. "The Spectacular Now Review: Love Changes Everything." Rev. of *The Spectacular Now*, dir. James Ponsoldt. *SMH.* Fairfax Media, 1 Dec. 2013. Web. 30 Dec. 2015. <http://www.smh.com.au/entertainment/movies/the-spectacular-now-review-love-changes-everything-20131129-2ygrw.html>.

Merry, Stephanie. "'The Spectacular Now' Movie Review." Rev. of *The Spectacular Now*, dir. James Ponsoldt. *Washington Post.* Washington Post, 8 Aug. 2013. Web. 30 Dec. 2015. <https://www.washingtonpost.com/goingoutguide/movies/the-spectacular-now-movie-review/2013/08/07/cccaeea2-fade-11e2-8752-b41d7ed1f685_story.html>.

Rapold, Nicolas. "The Spectacular Now." Rev. of *The Spectacular Now*, dir. James Ponsoldt. *New York Times.* New York Times, 1 Aug. 2013. Web. 30 Dec. 2015. <http://www.nytimes.com/2013/08/02/movies/in-the-spectacular-now-growing-pains-precede-graduation.html?mtrref=www.nytimes.com&gwh=F92F1D19DCAB67877CBBD02FA2B2F8A8&gwt=pay>.

Stardust

The Book

Author: Neil Gaiman (b. 1960)
First published: 1998

The Film

Director: Matthew Vaughn (b. 1971)
Screenplay by: Jane Goldman, Matthew Vaughn
Starring: Charlie Cox, Claire Danes, Michelle Pfeiffer

Context

In the first decade of the twenty-first century, a surge in popularity of film adaptations of fantasy novels brought numerous works to the screen. This trend was spurred on by the success of films such as the *Lord of the Rings* trilogy (2001–3), based on the classic novels by J. R. R. Tolkien. Adaptations of fantasy novels for young adult readers were especially common, in large part due the success of the Harry Potter series, based on the young adult novels by British writer J. K. Rowling. In an attempt to duplicate that success, film studios adapted numerous novels for the screen, among them the novel *Stardust*.

Written by noted fantasy and comic book writer Neil Gaiman, *Stardust* was originally designed as an illustrated novel featuring text by Gaiman and illustrations by Charles Vess. The novel was initially released in 1997 in a four-part format similar to that of comic books and was collected in book form the following year. In 1999 Gaiman published a more traditional edition of the novel that consisted of the text without the illustrations. *Stardust* tells the story of a young man named Tristran who, in an attempt to win the heart of a young woman in his village, vows to bring her a star that has fallen from the sky. He crosses the wall at the edge of his village and enters the realm of Faerie to find the fallen star, which, to his surprise, has taken the form of a young woman, Yvaine. The two gradually fall in love as they travel across the magical realm, pursued by the sons of the ruler of the country of Stormhold, who seek a gem Yvaine carries, as well as an evil witch-queen who hopes to capture Yvaine and eat her heart.

Gaiman first sold the film rights to *Stardust* in 1998, shortly after its publication. However, initial attempts at finding a writer, director, and stars for the film were unsuccessful, and the film did not truly begin production until 2006. The adaptation of the novel was ultimately directed by British filmmaker Matthew Vaughn, who had previously produced a short film written and directed by Gaiman, *A Short Film about John Bolton* (2003). The director of the 2004 crime film *Layer Cake*, Vaughn would go on to direct several film adaptations of comic book properties, including *X-Men: First Class* (2011) and *Kingsman: The Secret Service* (2015). Cowritten by Vaughn and frequent collaborator Jane Goldman, *Stardust* debuted in US theaters in the summer of 2007.

Film Analysis

The film adaptation of *Stardust* begins with an opening voice-over by a narrator (Ian McKellen) that sets the stage for the story to come. The narrator initially delves into philosophy, asking whether stars gaze back at the humans who look up at them, but quickly switches to the topic at hand, the events leading up to the film's core story. "Our story really begins here," the narrator explains, "150 years ago at the Royal Academy of Science in London, England." The camera lingers on a shot of the night sky before moving down the tube of a telescope and into a room at the academy, in which men in nineteenth-century dress conduct various scientific pursuits. One of the men is writing a letter in response to young Dunstan Thorn (Ben Barnes; played as an adult by Nathaniel Parker), who had sent a letter asking a question that the scientist found quite peculiar; in his response, the man explains that the existence of a separate world beyond the wall at the edge of Dunstan's village is just "rural folklore." To the members of the Royal Academy of Science, firmly rooted in the real world, that answer seems to be the only possible one. To the people of the village of Wall, however, reality and the world of Faerie are not mutually exclusive.

This opening scene not only sets in motion the events of the film's plot and introduces the central concept of the world beyond the wall but also establishes that despite the existence of that magical realm, the world of the film is essentially the real world, rather than the sort of secondary world featured in many fantasy narratives. While the novel does not begin with a scene in the Royal Academy of Science, it likewise calls attention to the narrative's connection to the real world through a series of historical references. Early in the book, Gaiman writes,

> Queen Victoria was on the throne of England, but she was not yet the black-clad widow of Windsor. . . . Mr. Charles Dickens was serializing his novel *Oliver Twist*; Mr. Draper had just taken his first photograph of the moon, freezing her pale face on cold paper; Mr. Morse had recently announced a way of transmitting messages down metal wires. (5)

These references firmly locate the beginning of the narrative in the England of the 1830s. In interviews, Gaiman has explained that he wanted to write a novel reminiscent of the fantasy works that were prevalent prior to the surge in popularity of secondary world stories, which was in large part brought about by the publication of J. R. R. Tolkien's *Lord of the Rings* trilogy in the mid-twentieth century. Rather than take place in a secondary world populated by beings such as elves and dwarves, such novels frequently took place in the real world and dealt with the intrusion of magic into it. As Gaiman intended, his original novel falls within that narrative tradition, and the film adaptation reinforces this intent as well.

From there, the film generally follows the basic plot of the novel, with some differences. Despite the Royal Academy of Science's official ruling that the realm beyond the wall is mere folklore, Dunstan crosses through a gap in the wall and finds himself in a world of magic. There, before returning to Wall he encounters a young woman (Kate Magowan) who has been enslaved by a witch. After nine months pass, a baby named Tristan (Tristran in the novel), the son of Dunstan and the slave woman, is delivered to the village. Eighteen years later, Tristan (Charlie Cox), now a young man, is in love with Victoria (Sienna Miller), a beautiful young woman who does not see him as a potential suitor. When the two see a shooting star that seems to land in the realm beyond the wall, Tristan tells Victoria that he will find the star and bring it back to her in exchange for her hand in marriage. Using a magical candle left to him by his mother, Tristan travels instantly to where the star has fallen, but upon arriving there, he finds that the star has taken the form of a young woman named Yvaine (Claire Danes). Accompanied by a highly reluctant Yvaine, Tristan sets out for home on foot, a journey far more difficult than his initial journey into the realm beyond the wall. In this way, the film presents an intriguing inversion of the typical quest narrative, in which the protagonist faces numerous challenges throughout his or her journey toward a particular objective. In *Stardust*, the return portion of the journey is far more difficult than the initial quest.

As Tristan and Yvaine travel toward the wall, they are pursued by various individuals with their own objectives: the sons of the king of Stormhold (Peter O'Toole) seek a gem Yvaine carries that will determine who will succeed their father as king, while the witch Lamia (Michelle Pfeiffer) hopes to capture Yvaine and eat her heart, as a star's heart will grant her strong magical power as well as youth and beauty. After various adventures, in which they are assisted by the airship pirate Captain Shakespeare (Robert De Niro), they defeat the witch in a climactic confrontation. Tristan is reunited with his mother, the missing princess of Stormhold, and, with all his uncles now dead, learns that he is heir to the throne. He and Yvaine rule the land for many years and at the end of their reign travel into the sky, where they live forever as stars. This ending differs significantly from the conclusion of the novel, being both more upbeat in tone and more suited to the medium of film. In the novel, the conflict with the witch ends not with a battle but with a peaceful conversation: Yvaine tells her that she has given her heart to Tristran, and the witch is thus unable to claim it. In the film, however, Lamia captures Yvaine and attempts to kill Tristan when he tries to rescue her. In keeping with the visual nature of film, the conflict resolves with a visually engaging action sequence, and Lamia is eventually defeated by a blast of blinding starlight that emanates from Yvaine and ultimately fills the entire frame. Similarly, the novel's epilogue differs somewhat from the film in plot and tone: Tristran and Yvaine reign together for many years, but in a melancholy yet more realistic ending, he eventually dies, leaving her to rule over her land alone. The ending of the film, in which Tristan and Yvaine live happily ever after in the sky, seems designed to meet moviegoers' expectations of an upbeat ending and aptly demonstrates one of the major ways in which narratives are often adapted to suit the medium of film.

Significance

Stardust proved to be a modest financial success after debuting in theaters in August of 2007, ultimately grossing more than $38 million in the United States and nearly $97 million internationally, according to the website Box Office Mojo. Nearly one-third of its international earnings came from the United Kingdom alone; this is unsurprising, as the film is set in England and based on the writing of Gaiman, a respected British novelist. As the film's production budget was estimated at $70 million, *Stardust* was generally considered moderately profitable.

Critical response to the film was mixed but trended toward the positive. Many critics found it entertaining and enjoyed the performances of the film's ensemble cast, particularly Pfeiffer's scene-stealing performance as Lamia and De Niro's campy appearance as Captain Shakespeare. However, some reviewers found the film cluttered and unfocused, with the more comedic and action-focused moments overshadowing the love story and the coming-of-age journey of its protagonist. As is often the case with film adaptations of novels, some fans of the original book were dissatisfied with the changes the filmmakers made in adapting the novel. Gaiman, however, was pleased with the final product despite its differences from his original work; in a question-and-answer session on the website Reddit, he likened the film incarnation of *Stardust* to an alternate-universe version of the original novel. Generally well received within the speculative fiction community, *Stardust* was nominated for various awards and in 2008 won the Hugo Award for best dramatic presentation, long form.

Joy Crelin

Further Reading

Gaiman, Neil. "Happily Ever After." *Guardian*. Guardian News and Media, 12 Oct. 2007. Web. 30 Nov. 2015. <http://www.theguardian.com/books/2007/oct/13/film.fiction>.

Maio, Kathi. "Films: How I Wonder What You Are." Rev. of *Stardust*, dir. Matthew Vaughn. *Fantasy & Science Fiction* 114.1 (2008): 110–15. *Academic Search Complete*. Web. 3 Dec. 2015. <http://search.ebscohost.com/login.aspx?direct=true&db=a9h&AN=27746911&site=eds-live>.

Bibliography

Ebert, Roger. Rev. of *Stardust*, dir. Matthew Vaughn. *RogerEbert.com*. Ebert Digital, 9 Aug. 2007. Web. 30 Nov. 2015. <http://www.rogerebert.com/reviews/stardust-2007>.

Gaiman, Neil. "Quint Has a Long Chat with Neil Gaiman about *Stardust, Beowulf, Coraline, Sandman, Death*, and Comic-Con!!!" Interview by Eric Vespe. *Ain't It Cool News*. Ain't It Cool News, 14 June 2007. Web. 30 Nov. 2015. <http://www.aintitcool.com/node/33002>.

Gaiman, Neil, and Amanda Palmer. "An Evening with Neil Gaiman and Amanda Palmer: Ask Us Anything. Go On. You Know You Want To." *Reddit*. Reddit, 19 Nov. 2013. Web. 3 Dec. 2015. <https://www.reddit.com/r/IAmA/comments/1qzpe3/an_evening_with_neil_gaiman_and_amanda_palmer_ask>.

Holden, Stephen. "When Stars (Celestial) Fall, and Stars (Hollywood) Fly." Rev. of *Stardust*, dir. Matthew Vaughn. *New York Times*. New York Times, 10 Aug. 2007. Web. 30 Nov. 2015. <http://www.nytimes.com/2007/08/10/movies/10star.html?_r=2&>.

Robinson, Tasha. Rev. of *Stardust*, dir. Matthew Vaughn. *A. V. Club*. Onion, 10 Aug. 2007. Web. 30 Nov. 2015. <http://www.avclub.com/review/stardust-3346>.

"Stardust." *Box Office Mojo*. IMDB.com, 2015. Web. 30 Nov. 2015. <http://www.boxofficemojo.com/movies/?page=main&id=stardust.htm>.

The Seeker

The Book

Author: Susan Cooper (b. 1935)
First published: *The Dark is Rising* (1973)

The Film

Director: David L. Cunningham (b. 1971)
Screenplay by: John Hodge
Starring: Alexander Ludwig, Ian McShane, Christopher Eccleston, Frances Conroy, Amelia Warner

Context

Susan Cooper's The Dark Is Rising sequence debuted in 1965 with *Over Sea, Under Stone*. This novel features siblings Simon, Jane, and Barney Drew as protagonists. The three children, along with their granduncle Merriman Lyon, are on a quest to find an ancient grail—one of the artifacts of the Old Ones, a group of guardians who protect the world from the Dark.

The second novel, *The Dark Is Rising* (1973), moves away from the Drew siblings to focus on eleven-year-old Will Stanton. On the morning of Will's birthday, he wakes to find himself in an alternate time, where he encounters Merriman Lyon and an elderly woman. They inform him that he is the Sign-Seeker, the last of the Old Ones to be born, and that it is his destiny to find and protect the Signs—six medallions that, once united, form one of the four Things of Power that will help the Old Ones defeat the Dark. The novel follows Will on his quest to find the signs, guided by a short poem told to him by Merriman:

When the Dark comes rising, six shall turn it back,
Three from the circle, three from the track;
Wood, bronze, iron; water, fire, stone;
Five will return, and one go alone. (44)

The series has three additional volumes. The third novel, *Greenwitch* (1974), brings together the characters from the first two novels in a dreamy fantasy story that focuses on Jane's innocence and passion. *The Grey King* (1975) introduces Bran Davies, a young albino boy around Will's age who helps Will in his new quest: waking the Sleepers, a group of ancient knights, so that they can help in the fight against the Dark. The last book in the series, *Silver on the Tree* (1977), intertwines the present-day fight against the Dark with King Arthur's fight against the same power.

Cooper's deft incorporation of her background knowledge of British literary tradition makes this series one of the most memorable fantasy series for children. Cooper's efforts were well recognized, and she received a variety of awards for the series. *The Dark Is Rising* received a Newbery Honor in 1974, while *The Grey King* won the Newbery Medal and the Welsh Books Council's Tir na n-Og Award for children's literature in 1976, and *Silver on the Tree* earned Cooper another Tir na n-Og Award in 1978. In 2012, Cooper won the American Library Association's Margaret A. Edwards Award for the series as a whole.

In the early 2000s, in order to capitalize on the popularity of the Harry Potter films, Cooper's books were suggested as the basis for a new film series. The film adaptation of the second book was announced in 2005, two years before its release. The similarities between the Dark Is Rising sequence and J. K. Rowling's Harry Potter series—both feature an eleven-year-old boy with magical powers who is destined to save the world—suggested that this classic series could perform well with a new audience of readers whom Rowling had introduced to the joys of children's fantasy.

Film Analysis

The film adaptation of *The Dark Is Rising*, released in the United States under the title *The Seeker*, failed in several areas, due largely to the changes made to the setting, characters, and plot. The change in setting is immediately evident in the opening scenes of the film. While the novel begins with Will and his brother James traveling from their rural farmhouse to the neighboring farm to fetch hay for their animals, the film starts with a school scene. The excited chatter of students preparing for Christmas break and a rush of teens down a crowded hallway bring the film solidly into the twenty-first century, far removed from the innocence of the novel's characters and the isolation of its setting. Pushing his way through the other students, Will (Alexander Ludwig) catches the eye of a pretty girl at the end of the hall. Director David L. Cunningham stresses the importance of this potential relationship with a series of slow-motion close-up shots of their faces and the girl's red scarf. Though this girl, Maggie Barnes, plays an important role in the novel, Cooper never suggests a romantic link between Will and Maggie; rather, Cooper's Maggie is interested in Will's older brother Max.

The character of Will has undergone major changes as well. The novel introduces Will on the morning before his eleventh birthday—the same age as Harry Potter in the first book of Rowling's series. Will is the youngest son in a large, active family that includes sisters Mary, Gwen, and Barbara and brothers Stephen, Max, Robin, Paul, and James. At Christmas, while the family is decorating their tree, Will discovers that he is in fact his parents' seventh son rather than their sixth; his parents' first child, a boy named Tom, died in infancy. The film, in contrast, introduces Will as a thirteen-year-old on the verge of his fourteenth birthday and changes his family's nationality from English to American, explaining that they recently moved to England from the United States. As Will is now a teenager, his romantic awakening plays a part in the story, as his attraction to Maggie (Amelia Warner) strains his relationship with his brother Max (Gregory Smith) and threatens to derail him from his quest. Further, though Will is still the seventh son, the film turns Tom from the firstborn child into Will's twin brother who was stolen away when he was two weeks old. Though one of Will's siblings is kidnapped by the Dark in the novel, this twin connection makes the kidnapping more seem more frightening and serious in the film.

Other character complications arise from the altered personalities of the other Old Ones and the rest of Will's family. Simple changes include different names for two of Will's brothers, the dismissal of two of his sisters, and the Dark's use of Max as a potential weapon against him. Merriman Lyon (Ian McShane), who serves as a kind and patient mentor throughout the novels, becomes harsh, impatient, and disconnected in the film. Without Merriman's positive mentoring, Will is forced to find his own way through his quest, making him a potentially more mature character.

The plot changes are numerous as well. While Will is still sent on a quest to find the six Signs, he is not given much guidance in his journey. Rather than having any established historical significance or connection to the Old Ones, as they do in the novel, the Signs merely show themselves sporadically to Will, and he travels through time in an instant to the places where they can be found.

One of the most significant plot changes comes at the end of the story. The novel ends with a battle between the Light, led by Herne the Hunter, and the Dark. Herne the Hunter, a legendary ghost in English folklore, never even appears in the film; instead, the film ends with a fight between Will and the Rider (Christopher Eccleston), who represents the side of Dark. This change again suggests that Will is undertaking a journey to mental maturity. In the novel, Will's journey occurs on a more psychological plane, which would be difficult to indicate in the visual medium.

Cunningham uses lighting and camerawork to establish theme and tone in the film. As viewers know from other adaptations of novels to film, it is difficult to transfer interior monologue and narration from a textual work to a visual one, so lighting is often used to provide subtextual clues. In *The Seeker*, three different types of lighting—dark lighting, twilight lighting, and bright lighting—are used to indicate when the world is struggling, when the Dark is approaching, and when the Light is winning, respectively. The darkest scenes in the film are those in which Will is besieged with emotional distress or confusion. The most obvious examples are the scenes in the Great Hall when Will is told who he is and what he must do. In another scene, when Will goes to the manor to talk to Merriman, darkness is used to indicate Will's puzzlement over his assignment. Though the scene does show a spot of brightness, with the characters standing next to a roaring fire, darkness covers the room all around the fireplace, and Will exits into that darkness, suggesting that he has not achieved the enlightenment he had sought.

The twilight scenes are the ones ruled by the Rider. Whenever he appears, daylight disappears, and the hour before true darkness descends. This twilight signals the approach of true midnight, which will fall if the Dark is triumphant. The one exception to this is when the Rider seems to be winning and sweeps across the countryside, followed by a dark, smoky fog; at this point, the lighting becomes much darker.

Bright lighting is used to indicate when Will is traveling through time and to emphasize the triumph of the Light. In all but one of the instances when Will is sent to another time, the camera shows a swirling of the scenery and a movement into a bright, sunlit day. The sunlight allows Will to quickly find the sign he has been sent to locate. The final scenes of the film make careful use of backlighting to depict Will as the triumphant hero; as he moves forward to conquer the Rider, a fan of light follows him, marking his as the winning side. The last setting change brings Will and Tom back to the village, where blue skies and bright sunlight further showcase the theme of good's victory over evil.

Significance

Attempts to differentiate *The Seeker* from the popular Harry Potter movies resulted in a less-than-satisfying experience for viewers of the film. Many adult audiences who had grown up with the novels were devastated by the changes in setting, plot, and characterization. When interviewed, Cooper herself revealed that she was unhappy with the alterations and was disappointed that her opinions were not taken into account.

Critical reception of the film was lukewarm at best. In an essay for NPR's website, longtime series fan Alison Macadam feared that the film was so poorly done that children would not seek out the books. Most reviews ranged from lukewarm to harshly critical. Some critics such as Stephen Farber and Kyle Smith suggested that while younger viewers unfamiliar with the conventions of the fantasy genre "might" enjoy the film, most were likely to find it dull and predictable. Others were more diplomatic, such as reviewer Ruthe Stein, who called it "a mostly entertaining movie with built-in appeal to young audiences." Positive comments on the film cited its special effects, some of the dialogue, and the acting, while negative notes include the hurried story line and what Ty Burr called "choppy editing and

Ritalin camerawork." Reviews of the acting lauded performances by established cast members, such as Christopher Eccleston, Frances Conroy, and Ian McShane, but suggested that Alexander Ludwig, who played Will, had a harder time holding the film together. Overall, critics generally agreed that the book was disserved by the film.

The box-office statistics further illustrate the failure of the film. *The Seeker* opened in fifth place and earned just $3.7 million in its first weekend. It grossed around $8.8 million domestically and another $22.6 million overseas, or $31.4 million altogether.

Theresa L. Stowell, PhD

Further Reading

Cooper, Susan. "But Myth Has No Prototype." *Horn Book Magazine* May–June 2015: 22–23. *Literary Reference Center*. Web. 2 June 2015. <http://search.ebscohost.com/login.aspx?direct=true&db=lfh&AN=102479978&site=ehost-live>.

Pepetone, Gregory G. *Hogwarts and All: Gothic Perspectives on Children's Literature*. New York: Lang, 2012. Print.

Perry, Phyllis J. *Teaching Fantasy Novels: From* The Hobbit *to* Harry Potter and the Goblet of Fire. Portsmouth: Teacher Ideas, 2003. Print.

Bibliography

Adler, Margot. "Author Uncertain about *Dark* Leap to Big Screen." *NPR*. NPR, 1 Oct. 2007. Web. 2 June 2015. <http://www.npr.org/templates/story/story.php?storyId=14783609>.

Burr, Ty. "Hide from *The Seeker*." Rev. of *The Seeker*, dir. David L. Cunningham. *Boston.com*. New York Times, 5 Oct. 2007. Web. 2 June 2015. <http://www.boston.com/ae/movies/articles/2007/10/05/hide_from_the_seeker>.

Cooper, Susan. *The Dark Is Rising*. 1973. New York: Aladdin, 1999. Print.

Farber, Stephen. Rev. of *The Seeker*, dir. David L. Cunningham. *Hollywood Reporter*. Hollywood Reporter, 4 Oct. 2007. Web. 2 June 2015. <http://www.hollywoodreporter.com/review/seeker-dark-is-rising-159473>.

Harvey, Dennis. "*Seeker* Hides Cooper's Fantasy in a Flurry of F/X." Rev. of *The Seeker*, dir. David L. Cunningham. *Variety* 8–14 Oct. 2007: 54+. *Biography Reference Bank*. Web. 2 June 2015. <http://search.

ebscohost.com/login.aspx?direct=true&db=brb&AN
=510698570&site=ehost-live>.

Macadam, Alison. "Fear of the Dark: A Favorite Novel Goes Hollywood." *NPR*. NPR, 1 Oct. 2007. Web. 2 June 2015. <http://www.npr.org/templates/story/story.php?storyId=14861567>.

"The Seeker: The Dark Is Rising." Box Office Mojo. IMDB.com, 2007. Web. 2 June 2015. <http://www.boxofficemojo.com/movies/?id=darkisrising.htm>.

Smith, Kyle. "Bad Harry Day." Rev. of *The Seeker*, dir. David L. Cunningham. *New York Post*. NYP Holdings, 5 Oct. 2007. Web. 2 June 2015. <http://nypost.com/2007/10/05/bad-harry-day>.

Stein, Ruthe. "Review: Teen on Mission to Save Universe in *The Seeker*." Rev. of *The Seeker*, dir. David L. Cunningham. *SFGate*. Hearst Communications, 4 Oct. 2007. Web. 2 June 2015. <http://www.sfgate.com/movies/article/Review-Teen-on-mission-to-save-universe-in-The-2499132.php>.

Tiger Eyes

The Book

Author: Judy Blume (b. 1938)
First published: 1981

The Film

Director: Lawrence Blume (b. 1963)
Screenplay by: Lawrence Blume, Judy Blume
Starring: Willa Holland, Amy Jo Johnson, Tatanka Means, Russell Means, Cynthia Stevenson

Context

The origins of contemporary young adult literature date back to the 1960s with the publication of S. E. Hinton's novel *The Outsiders* (1967). Authors appealed to teens by writing honestly about realistic issues and events that often affect them. The genre, marketed toward readers between the ages of twelve and eighteen, rose quickly in popularity during the following decade. Judy Blume first began writing at that time, which has been considered the first real golden age of young adult literature. While the early 1990s saw a decline in the popularity of the genre, by 2000 it had started to peak once more.

Publishers had begun to market directly to their target audiences, and the next decade included best-selling books such as the Harry Potter (1997–2007) and Twilight (2005–8) series that brought attention to further subgenres.

Blume is an example of a young adult author whose work has been consistently successful and popular regardless of the decade. She has been praised as an author who can reach young adult audiences of any generation, creating realistic story lines that endure. Starting with the success of *Are You There God? It's Me, Margaret* (1970), Blume has defined herself as an author capable of writing from the perspective of a teenage protagonist. *Tiger Eyes* (1981) is an example of the timelessness of Blume's work. Although it was written over thirty years before the film was released, the script underwent very few changes in order to appeal to a more modern audience.

While the young female protagonist encountering problems during her teenage years is not a very big departure from Blume's traditional oeuvre, *Tiger Eyes* does contain themes of violence, trauma, and sexuality that could be considered more adult—which was perhaps one of the reasons that an adaptation was not attempted before 2012. The main focus of the story is how the protagonist, Davey, deals with the death of her father after he is shot in his own convenience store.

Tiger Eyes was the first cinematic adaptation of one of Blume's novels. The director, Lawrence Blume, had a very limited directing résumé when he began writing, producing, and directing the film with the help of Judy Blume, his mother. In this respect, a young adult story line, particularly involving violence and trauma, was a very different type of work for him. However, the timing of the film's release in 2012 coincided with Hollywood's increased interest in adapting realistic young adult novels, particularly those focused on recovery, loss, and trauma. John Green's *The Fault in Our Stars* (2012), about two teens facing diagnoses of terminal cancer, was published in the same year, and novels about young women dealing with traumatic situations, such as Alice Sebold's *The Lovely Bones* (2002), had proven popular in both literature and film.

Film Analysis

The film begins in a slightly different way from the novel but otherwise essentially honors the plot and dialogue. It opens with a close-up of Davey's face and a voiceover narration as she ponders the nature of death—whether it is quick and energetic or slow and peaceful.

As Davey (Willa Holland) speaks, the camera moves in slow motion over her face and then quickly transitions to her bedroom, where she is looking for shoes to wear to her father's funeral. This is the scene where the novel begins, told from the first-person perspective of Davey. To achieve this same perspective in the film, the director included Davey in every scene.

In short, simple sentences with very basic, straightforward language, she narrates the events of her father's funeral. The lack of detail in the narration sets a tone of removal and distance from the events taking place around her. Davey cannot accept the death of her father, and so she can only deal with the things happening around her in a very superficial way. When her best friend, Lenaya (Nephele Jackson), comes over, Davey is in bed. Rather than hold a conversation, she rummages through the articles about her father's murder she has collected and shows them to Lenaya. The film also captures this mood, using similarly sparse and distracted dialogue and incorporating shots where the camera is far off to help convey the disjunction from reality that Davey is feeling.

Rather quickly, the film moves from the dangerous neighborhood where Davey and her family live in Atlantic City to the wide open, bare landscape of New Mexico. Unable to cope with the death of her husband, Davey's mother (Amy Jo Johnson) decides to move the family for a short period to live with her sister (Cynthia Stevenson) and her husband (Forrest Fyre) in Los Alamos. Immediately, the landscape becomes an important device in the film, echoing Davey's own mindset. The camera spends a significant amount of time surveying the terrain, scanning over arid dirt, dried streambeds, and canyons running deep and wide. There is generally no music accompanying these shots at first, creating a mood of isolation.

As the story progresses, the symbolism of the landscape changes as well. Before Davey starts school, she becomes overwhelmed with her new living situation with her aunt and uncle and rides her bike to a canyon in order to be alone. Connecting with the desolate land around her, she tries to make sense of her loss but is then quickly interrupted by Martin Ortiz (Tatanka Means), an American Indian boy who lives in town and is an experienced outdoorsman. From this point, the landscape becomes less alien and isolating. As Davey's relationship with Martin continues, she learns to connect more and more to the natural world. She hikes with Martin and learns about how his ancestors made their homes within the high canyon walls that she initially found so formidable. In the end, Davey's acceptance of the loss of her father is symbolized when she goes to the canyon and buries the clothes she was wearing the day her father died in the ruins of the American Indian buildings.

The themes of the film stay very true to those of the novel. First and foremost is the theme of trauma and learning to move beyond a terrible life event. However, as Davey is forced to go to school in Los Alamos because her mother cannot cope with the murder, more traditional young adult genre themes come into play. While *Tiger Eyes* could be seen as untraditional for its inclusion of violence and murder, particularly for the time period in which it was written, it takes a very traditional turn during Davey's time at the Los Alamos high school. On the first day, Davey becomes friends with Jane (Elise Eberle), a girl who deals with her own troubled life by drinking alcohol. She must also deal with relationships with boys and the conflict she confronts regarding the strict rules of her aunt and uncle, two people who have lived most of their lives safely and afraid to take any risks.

But what weighs more heavily on Davey throughout the book are not these traditional issues of adolescence. She cannot even approach the death of her father because she is primarily wracked with guilt over his death. When he was shot to death in the convenience store, she was behind the store, making out with her boyfriend in a car. When she heard the shots, she ran inside and could only hold her father as he died in her arms. This guilt cripples her both socially and emotionally, and it is not until her relationship with Martin develops that she can finally start to move past it and be able to touch upon the loss of her father.

Death and loss then become perhaps the most important themes, which Davey deals with when she is working at a hospital as a candy striper. Here, she meets an older American Indian man, Willie Ortiz (Russell Means), who is dying of cancer. As they talk, she learns his perspective on death, that life is simply one great adventure and death is just another part of that adventure. Death does not have to be the end of anything. When he dies, Davey is finally able to accept death as something natural, and she is able to translate the experience to the loss of her father. At the end of the school year, Davey comes to be at peace with herself. She has found a place at school, a relationship with Martin, and her own place in the story of her life. She is able to let her father go, and at the same time her mother is able to deal with the loss as well. As a whole family again, they move back to Atlantic City to continue their lives.

Significance

Judy Blume has been highly regarded for her novels that directly reference taboo subjects and focus on adolescent girls working through difficult moments in their lives. *Tiger Eyes* is seen as a successful addition to her body of work, though it is by no means her most popular or highly regarded novel. The book itself earned no particular recognition and was published over ten years into her writing career. However, the film was the first adaptation of any of Blume's books to be released in theaters.

The film version of *Tiger Eyes*, which many believed appropriately reflected the author's characteristically honest material, was generally met with critical and commercial success at the box office. However, as an independent film, it did not come close to earning the revenue of films such as those in the Harry Potter series. The success of the film came not only from Blume's name and recognition, but also from its place within the realism subgenre of the young adult genre. The late 1990s and the start of the twenty-first century were marked by the wild success of the fantasy subgenre for young adult literature, but those years also saw audiences take a renewed interest in realistic young adult story lines.

Critics generally commended Lawrence Blume's directing talent, casting choices, and connection to the main character's struggles for the cinematic representation of *Tiger Eyes*. While the film itself might not have made much of a cultural impact, it is an example of the rising popularity of characters dealing with real-life issues in the young adult genre.

Aaron Horton, MA

Further Reading

Busis, Hillary. "Here's to You, Judy Blume: A Toast to 'Tiger Eyes' and 'Regular Kid' Lit." *Entertainment Weekly*. Entertainment Weekly, 8 June 2013. Web. 15 May 2015. <http://www.ew.com/article/2013/06/08/tiger-eyes-judy-blume-movie>.

Scales, Pat. "What Makes a Good Banned Book?" *Horn Book Magazine* Sept.–Oct. 2009: 533–36. *Literary Reference Center*. Web. 15 May 2015. <http://search.ebscohost.com/login.aspx?direct=true&db=lfh&AN=43777088&site=lrc-live>.

Bibliography

Blume, Judy. "Judy Blume on the *Tiger Eyes* Film, What She's Reading, and Why Moms Can't Get Their Daughters to Read Her Books." Interview by Andrea Cuttler. *Vanity Fair*. Condé Nast, 6 June 2013. Web. 15 May 2015. <http://www.vanityfair.com/culture/2013/06/judy-blume-tiger-eyes-film>.

Corbett, Sue. "'Tiger Eyes': A Family Film." *Publishers Weekly* 6 May 2013: 17. *Literary Reference Center*. Web. 15 May 2015. <http://search.ebscohost.com/login.aspx?direct=true&db=lfh&AN=87499936&site=lrc-live>.

Hodge, Diana. "Young Adult Fiction's Dark Themes Give the Hope to Cope." *Conversation*. Conversation, 12 June 2014. Web. 15 May 2015. <http://theconversation.com/young adult-fictions-dark-themes-give-the-hope-to-cope-27335>.

Strickland, Ashley. "A Brief History of Young Adult Literature." *CNN*. Cable News Network, 15 Apr. 2015. Web. 15 May 2015. <http://www.cnn.com/2013/10/15/living/young adult-fiction-evolution/>.

Tomorrow, When the War Began

The Book

Author: John Marsden (b. 1950)
First published: 1993

The Film

Director: Stuart Beattie (b. 1972)
Screenplay by: Stuart Beattie
Starring: Caitlin Stasey, Rachel Hurd-Wood, Lincoln Lewis, Deniz Akdeniz, Phoebe Tonkin, Chris Pang, Ashleigh Cummings, Andy Ryan

Context

One of the most enduring themes in young adult fiction is the passage of young, innocent protagonists into older, wiser version of themselves. Very often, the characters discover unknown facets of their own personalities, other people, and the world around them by being thrust into unusual, difficult circumstances. John Marsden's novel *Tomorrow, When the War Began* follows that theme by introducing seven Australian teenagers who are normal, everyday kids worried about parents, popularity, and school. During their camping trip in a remote, rugged region of the Australian Alps, an invading army conquers and controls the teens' hometown. The seven schoolmates, plus an eighth who joins later, must band together to face the soldiers, try to free their families, and attempt to restore the order and normality of their lives.

With so much critical acclaim, commercial success, and worldwide interest, the movie version of *Tomorrow, When the War Began* was produced with high hopes. In 2009, the movie began its production, helmed by writer-director Stuart Beattie. Beattie faced a special challenge in adapting the beloved novel. The series was written in the 1990s, before the September 11, 2001, terrorist attacks on the United States. After 2001, moviegoers were more jaded about such attacks, having had more exposure to them in the news. Beattie had to adapt the book to allow a contemporary audience to believe that a nation's communication infrastructure, cell phone towers, and technological advancements of 2010 could be expertly and totally dismantled by an invading army in a short span of time.

Another challenge that Beattie faced was balancing the big-screen pyrotechnics of an action movie with the introspection of teenage characters who are coming into their own. The cast looked considerably older than high-school students and might have been a departure from how the readers envisioned the characters. The film also received an R rating in the United States, preventing the majority of the teenage target audience from seeing it in theaters.

Film Analysis

The movie *Tomorrow, When the War Began*, like the novel, begins with Ellie Linton (Caitlin Stasey) explaining how the world seemed to change overnight. Unlike the book, where she keeps a written journal to record the events, the film updates Ellie's method of chronicling to a handheld video camera. She talks into the camera about how best to tell her tale. She decides "to go back to where it all began."

The movie then immediately switches to a flashback. From this point on, the entire film's narrative is told in linear direction, starting at the events preceding the invasion of Australia. The movie introduces viewers to Ellie and her best friend, Corrie (Rachel Hurd-Wood). The two girls decide to plan a camping getaway and

draw up the invitation list. It is an expansive one, involving both good friends and people whom they never really got the chance to know within the confines of school. Their trip coincides with a large fair at the Wirrawee Showground, but the kids are excited about their upcoming adventure.

In an example of foreshadowing, which is a device prominently used in this movie, only Kevin (Lincoln Lewis), Corrie's boyfriend, expresses any preference for staying home and attending the fairground goings-on. One by one, the other campers are introduced. There is Homer (Deniz Akdeniz), a prankster who is often in trouble with the law. His penchant for mayhem will serve him well in the new world. Robyn Mathers (Ashleigh Cummings), the daughter of a stern, religious man, is first seen explaining to her father how "nature will bring them closer to God." Fiona "Fi" Maxwell (Phoebe Tonkin), who is beautiful but insecure, is introduced at a hair salon, being pampered and reliant on her mother. Lee Takkam (Chris Pang), the son of Asian restaurant owners and a "mystery" to most members of the group, is hard at work when he is given the invitation. Their backstories will either be the roots of their success or will be shattered when they are forced to deal with life-and-death decisions.

Again, foreshadowing is used to reveal that this camping trip will evolve into something much more. Since the group has never really socialized together, there is an initial awkwardness among them. When the other teens help to unload Fi's heavy belongings, they are astounded that she has brought along an arsenal of cosmetics. She explains, "You never know who you'll meet." Without realizing it, Fi has encapsulated exactly what they will stumble upon by the end of their trip. Likewise, when she stares wide-eyed at their camping grub—types of food she has never seen before—Homer playfully says: "It's an awesome feeling knowing you're going to change someone's life forever."

One night while they are sleeping, Ellie hears the sound of aircraft overhead. She looks up and sees a phalanx of planes. She dismisses it as a "bunch of army planes going somewhere." Her friend Corrie jokes: "Maybe it's the start of World War III!"

The book creates a fictional landscape, steeped in Australia's actual terrain. In both the movie and the novel, the region that they are camping in is called Hell, but despite its terrifying name, Ellie is impressed by it. In a conversation with Lee, she wonders if Hell is named that because it is so wild. In his response, which suggests what the characters are about to face, Lee says: "Wild is difficult and wonderful and fascinating, but it's not hell. People stick labels on things, until people can't see them for who and what they are anymore." In the novel, Ellie comes to a similar realization, but the film gives the insight to Lee.

The film chronicles the group of seven traveling together as their true natures—strengths and weaknesses—become obvious. Ellie emerges as the group leader. She is strong and decisive. Robyn is the friends' moral compass. Lee is the strategist and planner. Homer is brave and fearless. Even Fi, who was the group's "princess," discovers that she has strength and courage. When they return to their hometown, it is evident that the airplanes flying overhead were not just a drill. Their homes are vacant; many of their dogs and animals have been killed; their parents are missing. The electricity and phone service has been cut off. Every home they travel to is the same, except for Kevin's. At his house, his dog is still alive and he insists on bringing it along. The other group members disagree with his decision, but he is insistent, demonstrating his need to mature.

When the film begins, the scenes of the fairgrounds are bright and colorful. It looks pretty and welcoming. Now at night, while doing reconnaissance, Ellie, Corrie, and Kevin discover that the fairgrounds have been transformed into an internment center. Their fellow citizens are being lined up and processed there. They hear a loudspeaker issuing orders, and when one of the Wirrawee citizens objects to what is happening, he is executed. The trio is stunned by what they have seen, and Ellie is spotted and is shot at. In the melee, Kevin races away, abandoning his girlfriend and Ellie. He claims he thought they were ahead of him, so he ran to find them. Right after that, terror and confusion leads him to run once more, again leaving the girls behind. His character is called into question.

The movie contains many action sequences that showcase Ellie's driving abilities and physical stamina. When the movie begins, there is a montage of Ellie working on her family farm, showing that she is physically adept and capable, and her emergence as a risk-taking driver should not come as a surprise given her confession that her driving instructor always said she was a "danger."

A new member is added to the core group of seven when they arrive at their schoolmate Chris's house. Chris (Andy Ryan) is a stoner and did not even realize that his hometown was under attack. Chris is a "genius," according to Ellie, but also irresponsible. When he first joins the other teens, he puts their lives in jeopardy with his careless behavior and falls asleep during guard duty. However, after Ellie reads him the riot act, he sobers up and uses his intellect to hatch a plan for destroying a bridge held by the enemy.

The movie ends with Corrie being severely injured and Kevin volunteering to bring her to a hospital for medical attention—possibly risking internment himself and thus redeeming himself after his earlier selfish, cowardly behavior. The other six teens are now acclimating to the new way of life. Ellie tells her video recorder: "A month ago we were typical teens, studying for school and complaining about our parents. Now we're soldiers trapped behind enemy lines. We will fight and keep on fighting. We will never give up until this war is finally won."

Significance

Written by John Marsden, *Tomorrow, When the War Began* struck an immediate chord with Australian readers. Between 1993 and 1998, over three million copies of the novel were sold. It has been translated into several languages and continually tops Australian polls of favorite books for young readers. Its success has not been limited to Australia alone. In 1996, the American Library Association named it as one of the best young adult books published in the United States for that year, and in 2000, the Swedish government recognized the volume as one of the best books to inspire within young people an enthusiasm for reading.

The success of *Tomorrow, When the War Began* is not a stand-alone triumph. The book is the first in Marsden's Tomorrow series, which continues to trace the aftermath of the invasion. The series consists of seven titles, and each one further explores how the young band of guerrilla fighters is forced to deal with their country's occupation. The Tomorrow books have also spawned a spin-off series called the Ellie Chronicles, named after the Tomorrow series' most popular character.

The film was released in Australia in September 2010 and set box-office records, ending up as Australia's highest-grossing domestic film of that year. It similarly did well in New Zealand but failed to find an audience in other nations.

One of the reasons cited for the film's failure to connect with international audiences might be its similarity to the 1984 American invasion movie *Red Dawn*, which led some critics to view it as derivative. In addition, *Red Dawn* was widely criticized for xenophobia, which many reviewers also saw in *Tomorrow*, arguing that the film's Asian invaders evoke white Australians' racist fears of their Asian neighbors. Other critics lay the blame on writer-director Beattie. Though Beattie had a high-profile track record as a screenwriter, having penned *Pirates of the Caribbean: The Curse of the Black Pearl* (2003) and *Collateral* (2004), among other projects, he had never directed a motion picture before. Many reviews questioned the wisdom of matching a first-time director with a cast of mainly unknown actors. Despite the film's poor reception abroad, there has been talk about producing a sequel or adapting it into a weekly television series.

Stephanie Finnegan

Further Reading

Knoth, Maeve Visser. Rev. of *Tomorrow, When the War Began*, by John Marsden. *Horn Book Magazine* 71.4 (1995): 467. Print.

"Tomorrow, When the War Began." *Film Education*. Film Education, n.d. Web. 2 Dec. 2015. <http://www.filmeducation.org/tomorrowwhenthewarbegan>.

Bibliography

Caldwell, Thomas. Rev. of *Tomorrow, When the War Began*, dir. Stuart Beattie. *Cinema Autopsy*. Cinema Autopsy, 30 Aug. 2010. Web. 2 Dec. 2015. <blog.cinemaautopsy.com/2010/08/30/film-review-tomorrow-when-the-war-began-2010>.

Lehmann, Megan. Rev. of *Tomorrow, When the War Began*, dir. Stuart Beattie. *Hollywood Reporter*. Hollywood Reporter, 14 Oct. 2015. Web. 2 Dec. 2015. <http://www.hollywoodreporter.com/review/tomorrow-when-war-began-film-29931>.

Marsh, Calum. Rev. of *Tomorrow, When the War Began*, dir. Stuart Beattie. *Slant Magazine*. Slant Magazine, 21 Feb. 2012. Web. 2 Dec. 2015. <www.slantmagazine.com/film/review/tomorrow-when-the-war-began>.

Twilight (Series)

The Books

Author: Stephenie Meyer (b. 1973)
First published: *Twilight* (2005)
    New Moon (2006)
    Eclipse (2007)
    Breaking Dawn (2008)

The Films

Directors: Catherine Hardwicke (b. 1955), *Twilight*
    Chris Weitz. (b. 1969), *New Moon*
    David Slade (b. 1969), *Eclipse*
    Bill Condon (b. 1955), *Breaking Dawn,* Parts 1 and 2
Screenplays by: Melissa Rosenberg
Starring: Kristen Stewart, Robert Pattinson, Billy Burke, Taylor Lautner, Ashley Greene

Context

The films in the Twilight series are, at their heart, about teen love and vampires. Teen love is a widely accepted part of young adult literature and has been a part of teen and young adult literature since the Victoria Holt romance novels of the 1940s. Vampire literature also has an established place in literature, most notably in since Bram Stoker's *Dracula* was published in 1897. Stephen King added to the genre with *Salem's Lot* in 1975; Anne Rice contributed *The Vampire Chronicles*, the first of which was published in 1976. The popularity of the vampire novel carried over to some earlier works, with *I Am Legend*, published in 1954 and adapted to film in 2007.

Vampire television shows have been popular since the daytime soap opera *Dark Shadows* debuted in 1966. *Buffy the Vampire Slayer* began in 1997, and *The Vampire Diaries* made their debut in 2009. *Vampire Academy*, a vampire movie marketed toward teenage girls that blends the popular films *Mean Girls* and *Heathers*, was released in 2014.

Stephenie Meyer introduced the characters Edward Cullen and Bella Swan in *Twilight*, the first book in the five-book gothic series about star-crossed lovers. The book was hugely popular worldwide, especially among teenaged girls. With human Bella wanting nothing more than to join vampire Edward in immortality and Edward wanting Bella to instead to spend her human lifetime with him without becoming a vampire herself, the book soon became a best seller.

Meyer developed her vampire characters in unique ways. Edward Cullen's family, for instance, is a group of vampires who all live as "foster children" under the direction of Dr. Carlisle Cullen. They choose not to drink human blood and instead live off animal blood and therefore consider themselves vegetarians. To keep the tension high throughout the novels, there are also werewolves who are the enemies of the vampires—until Bella, a friend to both factions, is in danger.

The Twilight series explores the young adult themes of identity, belonging, loyalty, and idealism. Can a vampire love a human without succumbing to his passion and taking her life? Can sworn enemies work together to save an innocent who becomes involved in their struggles? Is it truly possible to join an affinity group through simple force of will?

By bringing these conflicts to life, Meyer uses the love story of a vampire and a human to touch on the lives and concerns of her young adult readers. Her works fit well within the conventions of vampire literature. Meyer's vampire characters have some slight variations on conventional vampire lore despite explaining that the *Twilight* vampires are able to turn a human into a vampire by biting them. The *Twilight* vampires do not sleep in coffins and do not require any sleep at all. They also do not eat food in the traditional sense. They can be seen in mirrors and they appear in photographs. They are not affected by garlic or religious items and cannot by killed only by a wooden stake through the heart. They are not damaged by sunlight, but their skin "sparkles" when direct sunlight hits it. They have the ability to foresee the future, to influence human emotions, and to read human thoughts.

Meyer's vampires bring a new dimension to vampire literature with their ethical stance on who they will attack and their moral belief that all human life is valuable. They choose to live unobtrusive lives among humans in the small fictional town of Forks, a town where it rains more than anyplace else in the United States, making it easy for them to avoid the bright light of day.

Film Analysis

The films in the Twilight series stay very close to the novels because their intended audience is not interested in a different interpretation of the books. They want to see the novels and beloved characters come to life on the screen. As a result, the setting, character development, and storylines in the films are largely what the readers expect. Even when the films make slight departures from their respective print versions, these facilitate an overall adherence to the story as it is set forth in the books.

For instance, in the first film, *Twilight*, which was released in 2008, it is necessary to establish that the Cullens are atypical vampires. The fact that they feed on animal rather than human blood is essential to the character of the family. To make it clear that they are ethical and live by a code of their own, the "other" vampires who come to the town ravage their victims, teasing them first and then viewing their deaths with sadistic pleasure. In the movie, three vampires are seen interacting with and later killing the character Waylon Forge, who does not appear in the book. It is essential in the film, however, to set the stage for the other vampires to later viciously kill the character and to contrast this group with the Cullens in this and subsequent films in the series.

The camera techniques used in the first film continue to be used in subsequent films of the series. Some of these techniques include people morphing into animals. Another is to show Edward Cullen moving at super-human speed. The scenes of Edward as he climbs a tree with Bella on his back allow the audience to witness his strength, agility, and stamina. They also allow the audience to appreciate Bella's complete willingness to trust Edward. Other scenes highlight the Cullens' abilities by filming in rapid stop-action as the actors move from place to place. A similar method is used for the "other" vampires as well.

In the opening scene, the audience watches as a deer is stalked and hunted by a vampire. The lush background of the Pacific Northwest is part of that experience. The film's first few moments showing tremendous natural beauty with the feeling that something treacherous is lurking just out of the field of vision and sets the tone for this and all the movies in the saga.

The family baseball game occurs in both the first book and the first movie. Edward is excited because a thunderstorm is approaching, and for him that is the perfect time to play. Bella accepts the invitation to attend the game despite not understanding the importance or excitement surrounding it and the weather. She soon witnesses the Cullens' incredible speed and agility and understands that the crack of a baseball bat in the hand of a vampire is what has been causing the sound of thunder all her life. When the other vampires come along by chance, they soon realize Bella is human, and assume she is a snack. When it becomes clear that she is not and Edward insults one of them, Bella is in even more danger. The Cullens draw together to protect her only because she is so important to Edward.

Special effects continue to play an important role throughout the film series. In *New Moon* (2009), the second film in the series, Bella suffers from depression at what she believes to be Edward's abandonment. She then realizes she can hear his voice whenever she is in danger. To keep him in her life in at least this way, she pushes the limits in every conceivable way. Edward's voice speaks to her and that effect, as well as the daredevil risks she takes, are accomplished effectively through multiple cameras utilizing varied angles.

The more time Bella spends with the werewolf Jacob in Edward's absence, the more Jacob grows to care about her. Bella develops feelings for Jacob, as well, but her feelings for Edward are stronger. Meanwhile, in the film as in the novel, Jacob is undergoing a change. It is both physical and emotional, as he becomes more and more influenced by the wolf pack's leader, the alpha male. As he matures, Jacob becomes increasingly wolf-like.

The cinematography in this second film is as stunning as in the first. The lushness of the forests and the beauty of the coast are part of the background for this love story. As in the first film, all of this can quickly become ominous through the use of half-formed images and camera angles that give a sense of watching from a point of view other than the viewer's.

By the time Bella and Edward marry and Bella becomes pregnant, nearly dies, and has a half-human, half-vampire child in *Breaking Dawn I* (2011) and *Breaking Dawn II* (2012), the climax of the series is at hand. The werewolves, all vampires from around the world, and the ruling vampire powers converge on the town of Forks. The life of Bella and Edward's child is at stake, and since Jacob has imprinted on the child, the werewolves are prepared to defend her to the death as well. This is especially true once they realize that Bella was transformed into a vampire when she was on the verge of death due to complications of her pregnancy and delivery.

An epic battle ensues and unfolds utilizing complex camera work. It is very well done, with the transformation between teens and beasts occurring in expected ways and timeframes throughout the battle. The various abilities of the many characters in the final films are also well represented, much as the Cullen family's abilities have been represented throughout. All of the rules pertaining to vampire physical characteristics and behavior that Meyer laid down for viewers in earlier films are

carried into the final films, such as having Edward's skin sparkle when the sunlight hits it. It is this level of consistency and trueness to the details and characterization of the books that helps to ensure the popularity of the Twilight films.

One unifying factor in the Twilight series is that all the screenplays were written by one writer, Melissa Rosenberg. Rosenberg's unified vision for the series ensured that the character development from the novels was successfully translated to the screen. Because Rosenberg was the screenwriter for all for the films, Bella and the other main and supporting characters are consistently portrayed across all of the films. Being the only screenwriter also gave Rosenberg an emotional investment in the films' outcomes.

Rosenberg's rapport with Stephenie Meyer and the various directors on the project gave her a voice in shaping the series. She was also committed to successfully bringing the print series to the screen rather than using the books as a springboard for the films. Because of this, the material in the films is very close to the material in the novels in the most important details.

Rosenberg is said to have been guided in her adaptation of the Twilight novels by a document from Stephenie Meyer that outlined for her what could and could not be changed in the movie versions. Meyer has said that she did not discourage changes simply to keep the novels and films alike but that she resisted changes that would alter the depiction of the characters. For instance, when it was suggested that Bella's mother could be eliminated from the storyline, Meyer objected. She felt it was crucial to establishing Bella's character that she move to the town of Forks as a gift to her mother.

Rosenberg based her twenty-five-page outline for the film on Meyer's document, the short story "Brokeback Mountain" (from which the 2005 film was based), and Shakespeare's *Romeo and Juliet*. She is quoted as saying that she chose "Brokeback Mountain" and *Romeo and Juliet* because both were great models of forbidden love. When she needed another view on Bella's motivation to decide not to terminate her pregnancy and to keep her child despite putting her own life and well-being in jeopardy, Rosenberg sought inspiration and input from people she respected who also had children.

Rosenberg is an advocate of creating strong female characters who have a confidence in their emotional intensity and possess a clear vision for where and who they want to be. She did not view Bella as a boy-crazy teenager, willing to blindly hand over her identity and power for the sake of a relationship with a boy. Instead, she envisioned Bella as someone who was determined to attain what she wanted for herself in life, regardless of whether Edward was entirely comfortable with her decisions.

The use of special effects to represent the superhuman abilities of the main characters combined with a consistent, humanizing view of the characters and their motivations led to a screen version of the novels that resonated deeply with audiences. The natural beauty of the setting of the films provide a firm sense of place and time. Without the use of these conventions, the films would not have been so visually lush or effective. Without the expression of the Cullen family's ethical concerns and the photography that allowed their eye color to be conspicuous to those looking to see their state of thirst, they would not have been as fully realized as characters. They are a long way from early vampires portrayed in films and television shows, and the Twilight film series brought to life characters that audiences connected with from film to film as readily as readers connected with them throughout each of Meyer's books.

Significance

Stephenie Meyer was completely unknown when *Twilight* was published. By the time the series ended, more than 100 million copies of the books had been sold worldwide. The films have made more than $3.3 billion at the box office. The books and movies were megahits among women of all ages.

The success of *Twilight* and the books and movies that followed was due primarily to the love story between Bella and Edward. The fact that there were vampires and other creatures involved certainly piqued the interest of the intended audience, but at its core, the story is a teen romance involving two people facing obstacles to their love and happiness but whose love is stronger than any hardship they encounter. Rosenberg saw this in the books and brought it into the screenplays and onto the screen.

Meyer's work is significant because it brought the buying power of young adult females to the attention of Hollywood and the marketers of the world. The message was clear that when there was something worth reading, plenty of young adult women would be willing to read books, no matter their length. It was also apparent that when there was something worth seeing, young adult women would go out of their way to watch the movie in the theater, often seeing it more than once, and would then purchase the digital or online versions once released.

Gina Hagler, MBA

Further Reading

Berlatsky, Noah. "How Could Someone Who Writes about Lovesick Teen Girls Be a Feminist?" *Atlantic.* Atlantic Monthly Group, 12 Mar 2013. Web. 10 May 2015. <http://www.theatlantic.com/sexes/archive/2013/03/how-could-someone-who-writes-about-lovesick-teen-girls-be-a-feminist/273955/>.

McNary, Dave. "Stephenie Meyer on 'Twilight': 'I Am So Over It." *Variety.* Variety Media, 13 Aug. 2014. Web. 10 May 2015. <http://variety.com/2013/film/news/stephenie-meyer-on-twilight-i-am-so-over-it-1200577245/>.

"The 20 Best Modern Vampire Movies, 1979 to the Present." *Village Voice.* Village Voice, 9 Oct. 2014. Web. 10 May 2015. <http://blogs.villagevoice.com/runninscared/2014/10/the_best_vampire_movies_1979_to_the_present.php?page=2>.

Bibliography

Ebert, Roger. "Twilight." Roger Ebert. Ebert Digital, 19 Nov. 2008. Web. 10 May 2015. <http://www.rogerebert.com/reviews/twilight-2008>.

Flood, Alison. "Twilight Author Stephenie Meyer 'Can't Write Worth a Darn,' says Stephen King." *Guardian.* Guardian News and Media, 5 Feb. 2009. Web. 10 May 2015 <http://www.theguardian.com/books/2009/feb/05/stephenking-fiction>.

Rosenberg, Melissa. "Interview: 'Twilight' Scribe Melissa Rosenberg on 'Breaking Dawn' & Feminism." By Roth Cornet. *ScreenRant.* Screen Rant, 18 Nov 2011. Web. 10 May 2015. <http://screenrant.com/twilight-breaking-dawn-interview-melissa-rosenberg-rothc-140261/>.

Schillinger, Liesl. "Children's Books/Young Adult: Eclipse." *New York Times.* New York Times, 12 Aug. 2007. Web. 10 May 2015. http://www.nytimes.com/2007/08/12/books/review/Schillinger7-t.html>.

Vampire Academy

The Book

Author: Richelle Mead (b. 1976)
First published: 2007

The Film

Director: Mark Waters (b. 1964)
Screenplay by: Daniel Waters
Starring: Zoey Deutch, Lucy Fry, Danila Kozlovsky, Gabriel Byrne

Context

The immense popularity of author Stephenie Meyer's Twilight books (2005–8) helped bring about a sharp increase in interest in young adult literature combining romance and supernatural elements. The series even spawned a highly popular and lucrative film series, the Twilight Saga (2008–12). Previously there had been other vampire-related young adult series, such as L. J. Smith's Vampire Diaries series (1991–2014) and Christopher Pike's Last Vampire series (1994–2013). The tremendous popularity of Meyer's series, however, brought about a wave of new vampire-related young adult fiction, including Melissa de la Cruz's Blue Bloods series (2006–13), Heather Brewer's Chronicles of Vladimir Tod (2007–10), and, one of the most popular of the post-Twilight series, Richelle Mead's Vampire Academy series (2007–10).

The first book in Mead's series, *Vampire Academy*, was published in August 2007—just six months after the release of *Succubus Blues*, her first published novel and the first in her Georgina Kincaid urban fantasy series for adults. *Vampire Academy* received mainly positive reviews and went on to become a *New York Times* best seller. The film adaptation started production in 2010, and in 2012 it was announced that veteran filmmaker Mark Waters would be directing from a screenplay by his brother, Daniel Waters. The film was released in February 2014.

Waters was chosen as director based on his success with the teen comedies *Freaky Friday* (2003) and *Mean Girls* (2004), as well as another young adult fantasy fiction adaptation, *The Spiderwick Chronicles* (2008). His experience directing teenagers was important because in addition to its fantasy elements, *Vampire Academy* also includes numerous elements of high school drama and comedy. Before *Vampire Academy*, Daniel Waters had written a variety of screenplays, including for action films such as *Batman Returns* (1992) and *Demolition Man* (1993), though he was probably best known for writing the dark high school comedy *Heathers* (1988).

Alongside popular elements such as romance and teen drama, the film explores various class and gender themes through its portrayal of the academy's different cliques. While these themes are also evident in the Twilight series, *Vampire Academy* plays out more like a high school drama, focusing on themes a high school student could relate to more than the themes of forbidden love and sacrifice explored in the Twilight books and films. The film has a much lighter tone than other popular young adult adaptations, such the Hunger Games series. The humor is more at the forefront, and many of the main characters deliver witty quips to break up more serious conversations.

Film Analysis

Both the film and the novel versions of *Vampire Academy* are told from the point of view of high school student Rosemarie "Rose" Hathaway (Zoey Deutch). The book is told from her first-person perspective, and her narration drives the film and provides much of its exposition. At the beginning of both, Rose wakes because she senses that her best friend, Vasilisa "Lissa" Dragomir (Lucy Fry), is having a nightmare.

In the book, the details of Lissa's nightmare are sparse and are not revealed until later. In the film, Waters shows the audience the extent of the dream, in which Lissa and Rose are riding in the backseat of Lissa's family's car at night. A drunk driver slams into them, killing everyone but Rose and Lissa. The scene is grim in both mood and subject matter, establishing a dark undertone to the film's lighter high school movie sensibilities.

After waking from the nightmare, Lissa sucks some of Rose's blood to refresh herself. It is an established aspect of their friendship that Rose allows Lissa to feed on her. In the film, this feeding scene happens casually, with Lissa commenting how weird it is and Rose making a joke of it. However, the novel reveals that the experience gives Rose a feeling of euphoria, which she describes as "better than any of the times I'd been drunk or high." Although she has never had sex before, she imagines that being fed on is even better than that.

The theme of sexual awakening is prevalent in both the film and book, though it is discussed more extensively in the latter. The loss of virginity, the damage that sexual rumors can cause, and the confusion of lust with love are all frequent issues raised in the book. They are present in the film as well but are typically glossed over in favor of action sequences and confrontations between the cliques at school.

The first of these action scenes occurs directly after Lissa feeds on Rose. As Rose looks down out of their apartment window, she sees a shadowy figure looming on the street below. Here the reader learns that the girls are on the run, having fled from St. Vladimir's Academy, a school for young vampires (or moroi, of which Lissa is one) and their half-human, half-vampire guardians (dhampirs, of which Rose is one). Rose and Lissa escaped two years ago and have been hunted ever since. In both the novel and the film, their shared history is revealed through Rose's narration.

During the action scene that ensues, a fight takes place between Rose and other guardians. Waters makes heavy use of stunt work in the film's many fight scenes, including the use of wirework to create the illusion of people being thrown or hit great distances. Accordingly, this initial fight is much more elaborate in the film than in the book, with Rose fighting off several guardians and even blowing up a motorcycle as a distraction. The sequence uses numerous quick cuts, a popular editing technique in contemporary action cinema; however, Waters also uses some long shots so the full scope of the fight can be seen. Speed ramping, in which the frame rate is changed to shift between slow motion and real time, is also used. This is also a popular form of editing manipulation to give the scene a more cinematic feel. Many of the fight scenes in the *Vampire Academy* film use this in combination with a Dutch angle shot, which is a tilted camera angle meant to convey tension.

The fight scenes in the book are much more toned down. During this initial fight, for instance, Rose only battles one opponent, Dimitri Belikov (Danila Kozlovsky), one of the academy's most skilled guardians. Mead keeps the tone light for her teenage audience, having Rose comment on Dimitri's attractiveness even during the fight.

To maintain the swift pace of the film's action elements, a new action scene inserted, one that does not occur in the book. When Dimitri and the other guardians bring Lissa and Rose back to the academy, they are attacked at the gates by a group of strigoi, the evil vampires who possess great speed and strength. Rose briefly talks about the strigoi in her narration, but the book features a more in-depth look at the vampire mythology Mead has created. This is another example of Waters favoring action over exposition.

The rest of the film and book take place at the academy, which resembles an early English university more than a high school. Waters uses many standard medium shots when characters are talking. It is shot very much like a typical high school film, with no particularly expressive angles or shots. Many of the interior shots of the academy are filled with deep shadows and contrasting lighting to give an atmosphere of mystery and to suggest the presence of danger.

The film increases the mystery elements of the story not just with these shadowy interior shots but also through a major change in Rose's knowledge about former teacher Ms. Karp (Claire Foy). In the book, Rose has flashbacks of why Ms. Karp left the academy, but in the movie it is a mystery for her to solve. Rose is a much more contemplative character in the book, at one point wishing that she "could have a normal life and a normal best friend." In the movie, this is played down, and she is overtly witty and offers much comic relief to lighten the film's tone.

The film version of Lissa differs greatly from the book as well, downplaying her sense of being an outcast due to her royal heritage. In the book, her emotional difficulties are severe enough that she cuts her wrists, not to kill herself but as a coping mechanism. In the film, the same cuts are inflicted through supernatural means, trading psychological insight into Lissa's character for a heightened fantasy element.

While *Vampire Academy* depicts a world of fantasy, the teenage protagonists go through many coming-of-age conflicts based in reality, making them more relatable to the story's target audience of young adults. The ideas of friendship and compassion are clearly conveyed, particularly through the bond of Rose and Lissa, two characters who remain close companions despite their differences.

Significance

When the film adaptation of *Vampire Academy* was released in 2014, it followed on the heels of several other financially successful adaptations of young adult books, in addition to the Twilight series. The first two films of the Hunger Games film series (2012–15), based on the novels by Suzanne Collins (2008–10), had already been released and had grossed billions at the box office. *Vampire Academy* did not fare as well, grossing only $15 million worldwide against its $30 million budget and opening in seventh place at the box office. Many believed that the film failed to resonate with a larger audience who had not read the books, which was a crucial component of the success of more lucrative young adult film adaptations.

Critical reception was also poor, with many critics citing the script, the action sequences, the special effects, or the acting as particular weak points. The computer-generated effects used to animate the psi-hounds (wolves that guard the academy grounds) were also panned by critics. The end of the film sets up a sequel, which is what the distributor, the Weinstein Company, was hoping for when they initially signed on to release the film. Due to its financial and critical failure, plans to continue the film series were put on hold.

By the time the film premiered, Daniel Waters already had a screenplay draft written for the sequel, *Frostbite*, but the producers said that they would only pursue the film if there was enough support from fans. An online fundraising website was established with the goal of raising $1.5 million toward the sequel within a month, and costumes and other props from the film were auctioned off, but ultimately only $272,882 was raised. The production company canceled the sequel.

Mead's Vampire Academy series found a strong following with female readers, thanks to her exploration of many of the issues any normal teenager would have to confront in high school. The themes grouped within a coming-of-age story are timelessly relatable, and Mead's unique spin on them helped make the books a success. The film, however, downplayed many of the girls' emotional struggles, choosing to highlight the action and fantasy elements instead, and ultimately suffered for it.

Patrick Cooper

Further Reading

Heos, Bridget. *Vampires in Literature*. New York: Rosen, 2012. *eBook Collection (EBSCOhost)*. Web. 2 Mar. 2015. <http://search.ebscohost.com/login.aspx?direct=true&db=nlebk&AN=617575&site=eds-live>.

Williams, Rebecca. "Unlocking the Vampire Diaries." *Gothic Studies*. 15.1 (2013): 88–99. *Humanities International Complete*. 2 Mar. 2015. <http://search.ebscohost.com/login.aspx?direct=true&db=hlh&AN=93917640&site=eds-live>.

Wloszcyna, Susan. Rev. of *Vampire Academy*, dir. Mark Waters. *RogerEbert.com*. Ebert Digital, 7 Feb. 2014. Web. 26 Feb. 2015. <http://www.rogerebert.com/reviews/vampire-academy-2014>.

Bibliography

Dargis, Manohla. "Bloody Trouble at School." Rev. of *Vampire Academy*, dir. Mark Waters. *New York Times*. New York Times, 9 Feb. 2014. Web. 25 Feb. 2015. <http://www.nytimes.com/2014/02/10/movies/vampire-academy-a-film-based-on-richelle-meads-series.html>.

Merry, Stephanie. "*Vampire Academy* Movie Review: A Lazy, Bloody Tale." Rev. of *Vampire Academy*, dir. Mark Waters. *Washington Post*. Washington Post, 7 Feb. 2014. Web. 26 Feb. 2015. <http://www.washingtonpost.com/goingoutguide/movies/vampire-academy-movie-review-a-lazy-bloody-tale/2014/02/07/aa5917ee-9026-11e3-b227-12a45d109e03_story.html>.

Rosenberg, Liz. "Where the Coolest Kids Are, Like, Undead." *Boston.com*. Boston Globe Media Partners, 28 June 2009. Web. 26 Feb. 2015. <http://www.boston.com/ae/books/articles/2009/06/28/young_adults_feel_affinity_with_supernatural_characters_in_books/>.

Warm Bodies

The Book

Author: Isaac Marion (b. 1981)
First published: 2011

The Film

Director: Jonathan Levine (b. 1976)
Screenplay by: Jonathan Levine, Isaac Marion
Starring: Nicholas Hoult, Teresa Palmer, Analeigh Tipton, Rob Corddry, John Malkovich

Context

From the start of the young adult (YA) literary genre in the late 1960s and 1970s to it resurgence in the 1990s, horror played a relatively small role. While horror was common in popular culture during these time periods, it remained relatively separate from YA literature until the beginning of the twenty-first century. At this point, traditional horror story lines, characters, monsters, and themes had been covered in a wide variety of media, and the genre had created its own place within the US cultural consciousness. Perhaps because readers, writers, and audiences were so familiar with the conventions of traditional horror, young adult novels in the horror genre took up a new perspective, working within the traditions of the genre, but giving the once two-dimensional monsters new depth. At this point, the creatures that were once feared became the protagonists, dealing instead with common adolescent issues. The

Twilight series by Stephenie Meyer is an example of this YA genre that was a great success with readers.

As the horror genre changed during this time, so did the boundaries of the genres themselves. As protagonists, particularly young adults, faced adolescent problems under the shadow of horror, they also faced themes once traditionally reserved for other popular genres. Themes of romance, mystery, thriller, action, and adventure genres figured prominently in novels such as *Beautiful Creatures* (2009) by Margaret Stohl and Kami Garcia and the Mortal Instruments series by Cassandra Clare. The boundary lines of genre began to dissolve and a new kind of horror subgenre appeared in the late 2000s and early 2010s. Published in 2011, *Warm Bodies* fits in the horror subgenre of YA literature, but it holds equal footing in the romance subgenre and can be considered a fantasy novel because of its unrealistic elements.

Warm Bodies was the first novel published by American writer Isaac Marion and was originally self-published. After a very small first printing, Marion's story found a small following and was eventually noticed by a major publisher, which bought the rights to the book and released an official first edition in 2011. The rights to the movie were bought quickly after publication of the book and the film by the same name, directed by Jonathan Levine, was released in 2013. Levine had worked with both YA and horror material before in films such as *All the Boys Love Mandy Lane* (2006), *The Wackness* (2008), and *50/50* (2011). The film and novel were very successful, although they did not become major mainstream hits like the Twilight series.

Film Analysis

Both the film and the novel versions of *Warm Bodies* begin with an introduction and narration by the main character, identified only by the first letter of what he thinks his name once was, "R." R (Nicholas Hoult) cannot remember anything from his past when he was living. He is dead, as he explains, "But it's not so bad." R introduces the world that he now lives in, detailing his daily routine, hobbies, and interests now that he is a zombie. He is happy that he still has all of his skin and limbs and dark circles around his eyes. However, zombies can be in any stage of decomposition, and the oldest are those called "Boneys," who have lost nearly every sense of their humanity. R still

keeps much of his. He has a friend named "M" (Rob Corddry), he enjoys riding the escalators of the airport in which he lives, and he still has regrets about eating the living, although he eats them anyway, with an acceptance that "this is the world now." Eating brains is one of the only things left connecting him to the living. M relishes this greatly because as he eats a person's brains, he absorbs and experiences their memories.

Narrated by R, the novel spends a great deal of time discussing details of the zombie "culture" of which he is now a part. This is a point where the movie departs directly from its source material, depicting the collection of zombies living at the airport more as a group of animals working together for survival than a human-like society. In the novel, R chafes under the expectations of a society not unlike American society at the time the novel was written, with the Boneys taking the role of the conservative older generation, encouraging young zombies to attend church, marry, and have children.

The movie departs from the YA convention of reluctance to follow societal rules by simplifying the lives of the zombies. With no society to rebel against, R differs from the other zombies simply because he does not wish to kill and eat all living humans. This slight change in theme and focus puts a stronger emphasis on the romantic aspects of the story, which develop during a hunt undertaken by R and a pack of fellow hungry zombies. Stumbling into the city, the pack finds a small group of teenagers and attacks them. During the melee, R sees a young woman named Julie (Teresa Palmer). After eating her boyfriend's brains, R falls in love with Julie and saves her from being eaten by the other zombies. With his limited vocabulary (he cannot string more than four syllables together at one time), he gets Julie to come back with him to the airport and keeps her safe in a plane that he has made into his home.

From this point, both the novel and the movie follow the general story line of star-crossed lovers. As Julie and R grow to know each other, the differences between humans and zombies become less distinct. The development of their romance also coincides with R's development of more human feelings and attributes. Little by little he regains parts of his humanity as he begins to love again. However, Julie's father (John Malkovich), the leader of the human survivors, is singularly obsessed with the survival of the human race through the destruction of all zombies. Aware of how her father would react to her burgeoning relationship with R, Julie finally sneaks away from R to rejoin the human survivors. Abandoned, R makes his way back to the airport, but finds that many of the other zombies are also beginning to change as he has. The Boneys hate this change and have expelled these zombies from the airport, and so the group decides to help R win back Julie.

In the end of both the novel and the film, the Boneys are defeated by the humans and the living zombies, and with a kiss, R becomes fully human again. The zombies are just humans who forgot how to live. As they relearn this, those without humanity simply wither away to nothing, leaving the world with the potential to become normal again. R and Julie face the world together.

The tone of the novel and movie are similar to one another. Both are narrated by an adolescent speaker with a certain distanced, sarcastic, and yet intelligent perspective of the world around him. Conventions of society and traditions are both mocked and upheld, following the conventions of a coming-of-age story. The novel is more of a bildungsroman than the movie, as R grows up and learns to become a member of society both physically and emotionally. Levine chose to direct the movie with a stronger emphasis on the romantic conventions. It ends with the lovers living happily ever after (a sentiment that is not necessarily shared in the novel).

Significance

The novel was first released through Marion's own efforts; he self-published only a few hundred copies. One of these copies found its way to a major publisher, and the first official publication took place several years after Marion wrote the novel. Through the work of both Marion and publisher Simon and Schuster, the book found its way to a wide audience and quickly became a commercial and critical success. Critics in general applauded the movie and enjoyed the fact that the plot was something of a modernized version of William Shakespeare's *Romeo and Juliet* and that it was one of the first zombie stories told from the perspective of the undead. The popularity of classic stories retold with the addition of supernatural beings, such as *Pride and Prejudice and Zombies* (2009) by Seth Grahame-Smith, has grown; therefore it's not surprising audiences embraced both the novel and the film *Warm Bodies*.

The film was also a commercial success upon its release. The box office gross worldwide, more than $116 million, far exceeded the film's $35 million budget. Since Levine decided to fashion his movie as more of a love story than a coming-of-age narrative, many of the YA themes of the novel are lost in the adaptation. Nevertheless, audiences still responded favorably to Levine's vision, perhaps because of the timelessness of the romantic aspects of the tale.

Aaron Horton, MA

Further Reading

Kee, Chera. "Good Girls Don't Date Dead Boys: Toying With Miscegenation in Zombie Films." *Journal of Popular Film & Television* 42.4 (2014): 176–85. *Literary Reference Center*. Web. 16 May 2015. <http://search.ebscohost.com/login.aspx?direct=true&db=lfh&AN=100015808&site=lrc-live>

Valby, Karen. "The Twilight Effect." *Entertainment Weekly* 23 Nov. 2012: 44–47. *Academic Search Premier*. Web. 16 May 2015. <http://search.ebscohost.com/login.aspx?direct=true&db=a9h&AN=83431613>.

Bibliography

Bogino, Jeanne. "Zombie Fiction." Rev. of *Warm Bodies*, by Isaac Marion. *Library Journal* 136.15 (2011): 70–71. *Literary Reference Center*. Web. 16 May 2015. <http://search.ebscohost.com/login.aspx?direct=true&db=lfh&AN=65806824&site=lrc-live>.

Deahl, Rachel. "Self-Pubbed Book Finds Homes in Hollywood, New York." *Publishers Weekly* 257.7 (2010): 8. *Literary Reference Center*. Web. 16 May 2015. <http://search.ebscohost.com/login.aspx?direct=true&db=lfh&AN=48312349&site=lrc-live>.

Rosenberg, Alyssa. "From 'Harry Potter' to 'Twilight,' the Enduring Draw of Young Adult Fiction." *Atlantic*. Atlantic Monthly Group, 31 May 2011. Web. 23 June 2015. <http://www.theatlantic.com/entertainment/archive/2011/05/from-harry-potter-to-twilight-the-enduring-draw-of-young adult-fiction/239639/>.

Thomson, David. "Bring Out Your Dead." Rev. of *Warm Bodies*, dir. Jonathan Levine. *New Republic* 244.3 (2013): 60–62. *Academic Search Premier*. Web. 16 May 2015. <http://search.ebscohost.com/login.aspx?direct=true&db=aph&AN=85728409&site=ehost-live&scope=site>.

Rev. of *Warm Bodies*, by Isaac Marion. *Kirkus Reviews* 79.5 (2011): 357–58. *Literary Reference Center*. Web. 16 May 2015. <http://search.ebscohost.com/login.aspx?direct=true&db=lfh&AN=59659622&site=lrc-live>.

A Wrinkle in Time

The Book

Author: Madeleine L'Engle (1918–2007)
First published: 1962

The Film

Director: John Kent Harrison
Screenplay by: Susan Shilliday
Starring: Katie Stuart, Gregory Smith, David Dorfman

Context

During the first decade of the twenty-first century, films in the fantasy and science-fiction genres proved incredibly popular with viewers, particularly children and young adults. Adaptations of popular literary works in those genres, particularly those intended for younger audiences, were especially successful. This success was perhaps exemplified by the Harry Potter film franchise, based on the novels by J. K. Rowling, and its legion of imitators. While many films released during this period adapted books published relatively recently, film studios also seized the opportunity to capitalize on some of the classics of fantasy and science-fiction literature; adaptations of several books in British author C. S. Lewis's Chronicles of Narnia, originally published in the 1950s, for instance, were financial successes and received well by audiences and critics. Among the classic works adapted during this period was Madeleine L'Engle's 1962 novel *A Wrinkle in Time*, a work that had, in the decades since its publication, established her as one of the premier writers of speculative fiction for children and young adults.

A Wrinkle in Time tells the story of Meg Murry, an intelligent and awkward twelve-year-old who, with the help of her younger brother Charles Wallace, her new friend Calvin O'Keefe, and a trio of mysterious women, travels across the universe to locate and rescue her missing father. Along the way, she learns of the importance of friendship and love in a narrative that blends L'Engle's lifelong interest in complex scientific concepts with her strong Christian faith. L'Engle was awarded the Newbery Medal, one of the United States' most prestigious awards for children's literature, in recognition of her work on the novel. The first book about the Murry family, *A Wrinkle in Time* was followed by the four subsequent novels in L'Engle's Time Quintet— *A Wind in the Door* (1973), *A Swiftly Tilting Planet* (1978), *Many Waters* (1986), and *An Acceptable Time* (1989)—as well as several books about the lives of Meg's children.

Intended to be broadcast on television rather than released in theaters, the film adaptation of *A Wrinkle in Time* was directed by John Kent Harrison, a filmmaker well versed in television movies, having directed numerous works in that medium. The film was written by Susan Shilliday, who had previously cowritten the Academy Award–winning 1994 film *Legends of the Fall*. Although initially set to air on television as a two-part miniseries in early 2002, *A Wrinkle in Time* was delayed significantly and edited into a single, 128-minute film during that time. It ultimately premiered on the US television network ABC in May of 2004, as part of the *Wonderful World of Disney* program. The film was later released on DVD.

Film Analysis

An adaptation of L'Engle's classic novel, the television film *A Wrinkle in Time* adheres closely to the original book in terms of plot. The film begins by showing a cloud of darkness expanding through space, absorbing everything in its path. A nearby star explodes, pushing the darkness back, and a small remnant of the star travels through space and eventually lands on Earth. This sequence of events, which is revisited later in the film during the protagonist's meeting with the crystal ball–gazing Happy Medium, sets the stage for the story at hand; the darkness is the film's ultimate villain, while the star is one of the protagonist's allies. With its science-fictional and fantastic influences, this opening sequence likewise reflects the multiple genres at play in the original novel, which is sometimes classified as a work of science fantasy.

From there, *A Wrinkle in Time* generally follows the plot of the novel, with some changes made for the sake of the medium. The film's protagonist, Meg Murry (Katie Stuart), watches the sky as the star from the opening sequence falls to Earth. The scene transitions into a flashback in which Meg and her father (Chris Potter), are stargazing in their yard. As Meg explains through voice-over narration, her father is missing, and this is a source of difficulty for her family; Meg acts out in school and comes into conflict with other children in part because of her sadness about her father's disappearance. These events are presented somewhat differently in the film than in the book, in large part because of the requirements of the film medium. The novel is written in the third-person limited perspective, and Meg's thoughts and emotions are a crucial part of the narrative. Her conflicts with teachers and fellow students are primarily presented through dialogue and Meg's memories. In a film, however, backstory provided solely through dialogue or narration could be perceived as overly expository. As such, the movie version depicts Meg's difficulties in school, for instance, through a scene in which she corrects and speaks disrespectfully to her teacher and is subsequently sent to speak with the principal. Later, the conflicts between the Murrys and others in their town are demonstrated through a scene in which Meg attempts to fight a group of boys who make fun of her younger brother, Charles Wallace (David Dorfman), and mock them for their father's disappearance. However, unlike in the novel, in which Meg is said to have emerged from this fight "with her blouse torn and a big bruise under one eye" (4), Meg and Charles Wallace are rescued by teenager Calvin O'Keefe (Gregory Smith) before the fight can progress past shoving. While this scene succeeds in introducing Calvin earlier than he initially appears in the books and eliminating the depiction of further violence, it gives the unfortunate implication that Meg is unable to defend herself without male assistance.

Much of the remainder of the film follows the novel closely. After meeting the strange and mysterious Mrs. Whatsit (Alfre Woodard), Meg, Charles Wallace, and Calvin travel first to the planet Uriel, where they learn of the terrible darkness that is engulfing planets, including their own. Joined by Mrs. Whatsit's associates, Mrs. Who (Alison Elliott) and Mrs. Which (Kate Nelligan), they pay a visit to the Happy Medium (Seán Cullen) before proceeding on to the planet of Camazotz, where Meg and Charles Wallace's father is being held captive. The depiction of Camazotz in the film is relatively faithful to that in the novel; however, the areas in which it diverges are indicative of a broader characteristic of the adaptation as a whole. When Meg and her companions arrive on the planet of Camazotz in the novel, they land on a wooded hill that reminds Meg of Earth, and the text notes that "there seemed to be nothing strange, or different, or frightening, in the landscape" (99). Upon entering the nearest town, however, Meg, Charles Wallace, and Calvin realize that something is very off about this world: all of the children are bouncing balls and skipping rope in unison, and

everyone seems afraid. They soon learn that Camazotz is under the control of an entity known as IT, which enforces its own brand of order on the world's people. The film reflects much of this description, depicting rows of identical houses and children playing in perfect rhythm. However, the creeping sense of wrongness evoked by the novel is not reflected in the film. Rather, it takes a far less subtle approach. When Meg and her companions are transported onto the planet, they land not on a wooded hill but in a desert, where they are pursued by a cloud of sand. The sky is dark, and bolts of lightning crackle constantly overhead. The town, which in the novel is said to resemble "any number of familiar towns" (99), is arranged in a rigid, spoke-like fashion around the ominous CENTRAL Central Intelligence building, which glows a sickly green against the storm clouds. Such visual markers identify Camazotz as obviously dangerous and frightening, removing any potential subtlety or ambiguity from L'Engle's thought-provoking take on totalitarianism. This change was likely made for the purpose of rendering the film easier for younger viewers to understand; however, it emphasizes the extent to which the novel's overall plot and tone were simplified during the adaptation process, to the detriment of much of the novel's subtlety and nuance.

Significance

A Wrinkle in Time aired on television in the United States on May 10, 2004, as part of the *Wonderful World of Disney* program. In a review of the DVD release of the film for the website DVDizzy, critic Luke Bonanno notes that the film performed relatively poorly in terms of viewership, a fact that he attributes to its assigned timeslot; the network's decision to air the film relatively late on a school night, Bonanno argues, significantly limited its ability to attract the young viewers who were its target audience. As a direct-to-television film, *A Wrinkle in Time* was never released in US theaters, but a DVD edition was made available for purchase several months after the film's television premiere.

Likely because of its status as a made-for-television film, *A Wrinkle in Time* received relatively little critical attention at the time of its premiere. In retrospective reviews, the film's reception was mixed and trended toward the negative. Various reviewers deemed the film a lackluster adaptation of a classic work, calling attention to its condensed story, simplified (and beautified) characters, and expanded focus on elements such as Meg and Calvin's romance. Among the film's harshest critics was L'Engle herself, who, when asked in a May 2004 interview with *Newsweek* whether the film met her expectations, replied, "I expected it to be bad, and it is." However, some critics found the film to be an enjoyable piece of family-friendly entertainment. While the 2004 adaptation was moderately successful at best, the original novel continued to appeal to filmmakers as a potential property to adapt. In 2014, Disney announced plans to adapt *A Wrinkle in Time* into a theatrical feature film, with Jennifer Lee, writer and codirector of the popular animated film *Frozen* (2013), penning the screenplay.

Joy Crelin

Further Reading

Bonanno, Luke. "A Wrinkle in Time DVD Review." Rev. of *A Wrinkle in Time*, dir. John Kent Harrison. *DVDizzy*. DVDizzy, 2004. Web. 30 Nov. 2015. <http://www.dvdizzy.com/awrinkleintime.html>.

Zarin, Cynthia. "The Storyteller." *New Yorker*. Condé Nast, 12 Apr. 2004. Web. 30 Nov. 2015. <http://www.newyorker.com/magazine/2004/04/12/the-storyteller-cynthia-zarin>.

Bibliography

Graser, Marc, and Dave McNary. "'Frozen' Director Jennifer Lee to Adapt 'A Wrinkle in Time' for Disney." *Variety*. Variety, 5 Aug. 2014. Web. 30 Nov. 2015. <http://variety.com/2014/film/news/frozen-director-jennifer-lee-to-adapt-a-wrinkle-in-time-for-disney-exclusive-1201275488>.

L'Engle, Madeleine. "I Dare You." *Newsweek*. Newsweek, 6 May 2004. Web. 30 Nov. 2015. <http://www.newsweek.com/i-dare-you-127959>.

L'Engle, Madeleine. *A Wrinkle in Time*. New York: Bantam, 1973. Print.

Munley, Kyle. "Challenged and Banned: *A Wrinkle in Time*." *Suvudu*. Random House, 2 Oct. 2008. Web. 30 Nov. 2015. <http://suvudu.com/2008/10/challenged-and-banned-a-wrinkle-in-time.html>.

Stone, Susan. "L'Engle's 'A Wrinkle in Time' to Make TV Debut." *All Things Considered*. NPR, 9 May 2004. Web. 30 Nov. 2015. <http://www.npr.org/templates/story/story.php?storyId=1890065>.

The Yearling

The Book

Author: Marjorie Kinnan Rawlings (1896–1953)
First published: 1938

The Film

Director: Clarence Brown (1890–1987)
Screenplay by: Paul Osborn
Starring: Gregory Peck, Jane Wyman, Claude Jarman Jr., Donn Gift

Context

The Yearling is a book in the time-honored tradition of a boy's coming of age. Like many other novels that center around a boy and his pet (though usually it is a canine friend), *The Yearling* explores the close bond that develops between young Jody and his fawn, Flag. The repercussions of owning an animal that cannot be tamed teaches Jody the meaning of maturity and sacrifice and solidifies his arrival into the world of adulthood.

The book sold more than 250,000 copies in its first year and won the 1939 Pulitzer Prize for the Novel (later the Pulitzer Prize for Fiction). Its author, Marjorie Kinnan Rawlings, was a protégé of renowned editor Maxwell Perkins, who was influential in guiding the careers of authors Ernest Hemingway and F. Scott Fitzgerald. The commercial success of *The Yearling*, combined with its literary pedigree, made it a sought-after title to be made into a film.

Metro-Goldwyn-Mayer (MGM) had bought the rights to film *The Yearling* and had intended to do so in 1941. However, personality clashes and artistic differences prevented the film from being made for five years. The original cast of *The Yearling* included Spencer Tracy, Anne Revere, and Gene Eckman, but they were ultimately replaced by Gregory Peck, Jane Wyman, and Claude Jarman Jr.

The book features long, in-depth passages describing the Florida setting, so much so that the natural landscape functions almost as another character in the plot. The creative team that was assembled for the film paid tribute to the otherworldly and almost primeval look of the place. The well-respected, award-winning director Clarence Brown was selected to direct the film, in part due to the excellent work he had done with 1944's *National Velvet*, the film adaptation of Enid Bagnold's 1935 novel about a young girl's coming of age and her dream of being a jockey. Studio executives knew Brown would be able to handle the emotions and the pathos that were central to the plot of *The Yearling*.

Due to the book's prestige and popularity, the filmmakers did not tinker too much when transferring it to the screen. The subplot of the family's bear hunt was abridged, and the cast was far more attractive than their rural counterparts were described to be in the novel. Other than that, the movie was an attempt to bring the author's words to the screen in a visual fashion that would honor her intentions and purpose. One of the novel's main strengths is how Rawlings brought the wildlife and terrain of Florida alive for her readers. The cinematic adaptation was ideal for translating Rawlings's vivid verbal descriptions into a striking visual context.

Film Analysis

The Yearling begins with Ezra "Penny" Baxter (Gregory Peck) explaining in voice-over how he discovered Lake George, Florida, as a soldier returning from the Civil War. Penny was infatuated with the lake's beauty and remoteness and decided to build a life there. The film opens in 1878, after Penny has established a difficult but satisfying life as a farmer on Lake George, tilling the land he owns, which he has named Baxter Island. When Penny's voice-over ends, the audience hears his wife, Orry (Jane Wyman), calling for their son, Jody (Claude Jarman Jr.). As Orry's exasperated voice yells for his whereabouts, the camera moves over a plot of land and a hoe left abandoned among the crops. This opening sequence demonstrates through dialogue and visual clues what will be the point of contention in the movie. Orry, often called Ma, is a realist; Penny, called Pa, is more soft-hearted and impressed with nature. Their son, Jody, is not suited for the hard work and sacrifice needed to survive on a farm. He does not toil alongside his parents, instead abandoning his work to go "rambling."

The first glimpse of Jody in the film captures the boy's deep ties to the flora and fauna of Baxter Island. He almost seems to be embedded in the glen where he is resting. As he lies there, dreaming and lounging, animals come out of their habitats and fearlessly walk before him, showing how Jody is one with nature. The cinematographer and set decorator have given Jody and his landscape an otherworldly, almost fairy-tale feel. With his silky yellow hair and pale skin, Jody does not appear to be mortal. He seems to be the embodiment of nature.

It is Jody's connection to nature—he feels more attuned to animals than to people—that sets the visual tone of the film. Growing up in this isolated part of the world, Jody does not have an abundance of friends. In fact, he only has three: his father, a seafaring townsman named Oliver, and a sickly boy named Fodder-wing (Donn Gift). Fodder-wing is said to have "hatch[ed] out peculiar." Once, convinced he could fly, he leapt off a roof and ended up crippling himself. Fodder-wing has a way with animals and is Jody's role model. Jody yearns to have pets like Fodder-wing's extensive, exotic menagerie: raccoons, eagles, rabbits, anything he can catch. During a heart-to-heart conversation, Fodder-wing explains his theory on clouds. He believes that clouds are "the backs of angels" and that they will be the only things left at the end of the world. They are "looking after things," he claims, and will look after Jody "until [he's] ready to fly."

Jody's identification with animals is visually underscored with the first appearance of the fawn he will adopt and love. The fawn is shown lounging amid the landscape, in almost the exact same pose and location as Jody when he first appeared on-screen, and shows no fear when Jody picks him up to bring him home. As Jody carries the fawn away from the glen to the farm, the huge blue sky behind him is filled with an abundance of puffy white clouds, bringing to mind both Fodder-wing's description of clouds as benign guardian angels and his warning that clouds will be the only thing left when the world ends.

The folly of bringing an untamed fawn onto the Baxter's property is immediately shown upon its arrival at the home. Because Pa killed the fawn's mother in order to use its heart and liver as a poison remedy, he feels an obligation to the orphaned creature. He puts his foot down and tells Ma that the fawn is as welcome in the house as his hunting hound, Julie. Though chastened by Pa's stern tone, Ma is not convinced that this is a workable arrangement. As the conversation about the fawn is played out inside the cabin, the camera moves to the exterior of the house, where the fawn is busy dipping its head into the family's milk supply, lapping away. Jody sees the fawn's mischief, picks it up quickly, and furtively looks around. The fawn has been there a matter of minutes and has already committed a transgression.

The affection and bonding between the boy and the fawn is shown most effectively and joyfully in a sequence in which the two race through the forest together. The fawn runs and leaps effortlessly, and Jody follows behind. Every hurdle and jump that the fawn makes, Jody makes too. He mirrors its every movement, showing once more that he identifies with nature above his family. As the two frolic together, other deer come out to watch. There is a long interlude in which the watchful deer begin to run alongside the boy and the fawn. The deer follow the playful duo, and soon the whole screen is filled with deer racing, leaping, and bounding everywhere. Jody, a boy with limited human contact, is one with these animals and their world. There is no dialogue or voiceover during this extended scene, and none is needed. The visuals convey Jody's jubilation and the deer's acceptance of him.

Yet nature, which attracted Pa in his youth and holds sway over eleven-year-old Jody, does not have a conscience, and it can be cruel and destructive. The way nature can change without warning is shown on the day of Fodder-wing's funeral. Young Fodder-wing has died, and Pa is asked to say some words at his burial. Pa eulogizes the boy, telling his family that in Heaven the boy's mind and legs will no longer be "crookedy" and that the Lord might see fit to give him some "redbirds and maybe a squirrel or a coon to keep him company." As the funeral winds down, the sky is bright blue, and the clouds above the burial site are enormous and plentiful, filling the frame. Hours later, those same clouds wreak havoc and destruction as a deluge washes away and destroys Baxter Island's crops. Nature is unreliable and inexplicable. Jody brings the young deer, Flag, into the house to protect him from the rain. Almost instantly, Flag begins to eat what he should not and is whacked hard by Ma. Time has passed, Flag has grown, and Ma has not lost her opposition to the foolishness of trying to tame a deer. When the near-biblical rain finally ends, there is a shot of the clouds with the glowing sun breaking through, looking almost like an oil painting. This shot emphasizes that the beauty of nature can be glorious, but its power cannot be diminished.

When Pa orders Jody to kill Flag because of his incessant eating of their crops, the movie takes on a darker tone, and so do the visuals. Jody leads Flag into the heart of the forest, but the surroundings are not as lushly photographed as they were during his playful encounters with the fawn. Unable to execute his pet, Jody tries to shoo the deer away, even resorting to throwing handfuls of dirt and pebbles at it. The deer, now a yearling on the verge of adulthood, follows Jody back home. The yearling is an animal, and he cannot behave contrary to his nature. Jody is a boy, on the verge of becoming a man, and he must act like a man and kill Flag. After Ma mortally wounds Flag, Jody must take the rifle and end the deer's life. He does so, but he cannot accept the action and runs away from home, back into nature. These scenes of the forest are dark and poorly lit. The crystal-clear river now appears brown and brackish. Jody is lying on the embankment, dirty and muddied, having lost his innocence and been soiled by the world.

Jody's return to his family and home—to the world of being a man—is accompanied by a shot of the sky, which is a deep purple, and the clouds, which are a sepia brown. His world has changed. He is no longer a nature boy; he is no longer a boy at all. Seeing the difference in his son, Pa tells Ma, "He's done come back different. . . . He ain't a yearling no longer."

Significance

The movie *The Yearling* received high praise from both critics and the public. Viewers were especially impressed by the performance of Claude Jarman Jr. as Jody. In his January 1947 review, *New York Times* critic Bosley Crowther wrote, "As Jody, the tow-headed farm boy, this youngster who had never acted before achieves a child characterization as haunting and appealing as any we've ever seen. Spindly, delicate of features and possessed of a melting Southern voice, he makes not a single sound or movement which does not seem completely genuine." Jarman was honored for his role with a special Academy Juvenile Award, previously awarded to such famous child stars as Shirley Temple and Judy Garland.

The Yearling also won Academy Awards for its cinematography and its art direction—the visuals that helped to define it as a classic movie for young and old—and was nominated for best motion picture, best actor (Gregory Peck), best actress (Jane Wyman), best directing, and best film editing. It was MGM's highest-grossing movie of the year and still delights audiences when it airs on Turner Classic Movies. *The Yearling* was remade as a television movie in 1994, starring Peter Strauss as Pa, Jean Smart as Ma, and Wil Horneff as Jody.

The Yearling continues to rank among one of the most discussed films of the 1940s. Because of its harsh ending, in which a young boy is forced to kill his pet and loses his innocence, contemporary parents often worry about showing the movie to their children. The same way that Pa wants to shield Jody from growing up—"A man's heart aches, seeing his young'uns face the world, knowing they got to get their insides tore out"—parents fret that the conclusion is too brutal and too callous for today's children. When the film of *The Yearling* was first released, the world was struggling with the horrific aftermath of World War II. Families had been touched by the deaths and injuries of loved ones. Children had suffered through the deaths, maimings, injuries, and prolonged absences of family members. Seen against that backdrop, the killing of Flag at Jody's hands, though certainly sad and tearful, was not a reason to prevent children from experiencing the movie and understanding its implications. The world was not always a nice, safe place, and children would need to know that to endure. *The Yearling* is often cited along with *Bambi* (1942) and *Old Yeller* (1957) as films that might worry children due to deaths of animals. More recently, *Marley & Me* (2008) joined that list of possibly upsetting animal films.

Stephanie Finnegan

Further Reading

Allen, Greg. "On Location: The Central Florida of *The Yearling*." *NPR*. NPR, 21 July 2011. Web. 25 Nov. 2015. <http://www.npr.org/2011/07/21/138561573/on-location-the-central-florida-of-the-yearling>.

Silverthorne, Elizabeth. *Marjorie Kinnan Rawlings: Sojourner at Cross Creek*. Woodstock: Overlook, 1988. Print.

Bibliography

Crowther, Bosley. Rev. of *The Yearling*, dir. Clarence Brown. *New York Times*. New York Times, 24 Jan. 1947. Web. 25 Nov. 2015. <http://www.nytimes.com/movie/review?res=9505E3DE123EEE3BBc4c51DFB766838C659EDE>.

Erickson, Hal. "*The Yearling* Synopsis." *Fandango*. Fandango, 2015. Web. 25 Nov. 2015. <http://www.fandango.com/theyearling_20048/plotsummary>.

"*The Yearling*." *Teach with Movies*. TeachWithMovies.com, 2 Aug. 2010. Web. 25 Nov. 2015. <http://www.teachwithmovies.org/guides/yearling.html>.

"*The Yearling* (1947)." *TCM.com*. Turner Entertainment Networks, 2015. Web. 25 Nov. 2015. <http://www.tcm.com/tcmdb/title/2523/The-Yearling/>.

Youth in Revolt

The Book

Author: C. D. Payne (b. 1949)
First published: 1993

The Film

Director: Miguel Arteta (b. 1965)
Screenplay by: Gustin Nash
Starring: Michael Cera, Portia Doubleday, Jean Smart, Zach Galifianakis, Ray Liotta, and Steve Buscemi

Context

Michael Cera, who stars in the 2010 film adaptation of the 1993 novel *Youth in Revolt*, signed on to play the role of Nick Twisp immediately after his star-making role in the Judd Apatow–produced comedy *Superbad* (2007). Cera would later star in similar roles in *Juno* (2007), *Nick and Norah's Infinite Playlist* (2008), and *Scott Pilgrim vs. the World* (2010), with the Canadian Press in 2010 calling him "the quintessential screen geek of the 2000s." Cera's association with *Youth in Revolt* tends to overshadow the uniqueness of the work itself, however, and while Cera's portrayal of the awkward teenager resembles his other onscreen characters, *Youth in Revolt* is much darker and more absurd than the other films in his oeuvre.

The film is based on the C. D. Payne novel *Youth in Revolt: The Journals of Nick Twisp*, which Payne self-published in 1993. The book became a cult hit when it was released, and among Payne's many fans was a sixteen-year-old Cera, who later described his signed copy of the novel as one of his most prized possessions. Director Miguel Arteta credits Cera as one of the film's co-creators because he weighed in on everything from the script to casting to editing the final cut.

Although Payne had a small acting part in the movie, Gustin Nash wrote was the screenwriter and Miguel Arteta directed. Nash had previously written the screenplay for the 2007 teen comedy *Charlie Bartlett*, and Arteta would go on to direct *Alexander and the Terrible, Horrible, No Good, Very Bad Day* in 2014. With *Youth in Revolt*, Nash and Arteta were able to condense Payne's nearly five-hundred-page novel into a ninety-minute script primarily by maintaining Payne's unusual voice rather than focusing on incorporating all of Nick's exploits. For example, by way of introduction, Nick explains, "I am a voracious reader of classic prose, an aspiring novelist, and feel the world would be a better place if every radio station played Frank Sinatra's 'My One and Only Love' at least once an hour. Needless to say, I'm still a virgin." Though Nick might seem a more artful version of Cera's character in *Superbad*, stylistically, Nick uses more heightened language and expresses himself through aspirational interests and allusions to obscure intellectual culture. For instance, in one scene Nick and his girlfriend debate the merits of the French film director Jean-Luc Godard's 1960 drama *Breathless* versus Japanese director and screenwriter Yasujiro Ozu's *Tokyo Story* (1953), allusions most of the *Youth in Revolt* audience would not understand.

Film Analysis

Youth in Revolt is not a realistic novel. Payne's Nick Twisp takes his love for Sheeni Saunders, a girl he meets during summer vacation, to absurd and hilarious ends. To maintain his relationship with Sheeni at any cost, the bashful, law-abiding Nick creates a dastardly alter ego named François Dillinger to wreak havoc as a "youth in revolt"—though all of his misdeeds are performed in Sheeni's name. While the film maintains the raucous spirit of Payne's novel, it necessarily pares down much of the plot to keep Nick careening into Sheeni's arms: a subplot in the novel in which Nick develops a crush on his friend Vijay's sister is omitted, the amount of time Nick spends masquerading as a girl named Carlotta is pared down, and most notably, the film takes place nearly twenty years after the book was originally set. Still, the bones of Payne's story remain. The film opens with Nick Twisp in a voice-over narration introducing himself as a lover of art, music, and poetry—and a virgin. His mother, Estelle (Jean Smart), is a chain-smoking, forty-something with terrible taste in men. Nick's father, George (Steve Buscemi), is present in Nick's life to the extent that he makes regular child-support payments, but for the most part he, like Estelle, is too involved in his own romantic exploits to take any interest in his lonely son. The film's plot is set in motion when Estelle's boyfriend Jerry (Zach Galifianakis) needs to leave town quickly to escape some angry customers, and Estelle and Nick join him for a week-long getaway at a trailer park.

Nick meets Sheeni (Portia Doubleday) at the park, and his world turns upside down. Despite the wrath of Sheeni's ultrareligious parents, their relationship blossoms over the course of a few days. They adopt a puppy and fall, at least from Nick's viewpoint, irrevocably in love. In order to stay together, they hatch an elaborate plan: Sheeni will finagle George a job in town, and Nick will behave so badly that his mother will have no choice but to send him to live with his father. In order to effectively become a "youth in revolt," Nick imagines a character inspired by French actor (and *Breathless* star) Jean-Paul Belmondo, the sexy, rakish leading man of French New Wave cinema. Nick's alter ego, François Dillinger, wears a sleek blue button-down shirt, slim white pants, and a thin mustache. Like Belmondo, François, also played by Cera, usually has a cigarette dangling from his mouth, and Arteta employs a classic film trick to allow both characters to exist on screen at the same time. François convinces Nick to perform increasingly illegal acts of rebellion—culminating in a spectacular explosion that consumes half the town of Berkeley—but he is also a physical representation of Nick's unexpressed resentment toward his parents and even Sheeni. In one scene, just after Nick sets the town ablaze by exploding his mother's prized Lincoln, he faces off with Estelle's newest boyfriend, Lance (Ray Liotta). With Estelle's blessing, Lance beats Nick with a whip, except that it appears to be François on the receiving end of the blows. The darkness of the scene is emphasized by the sound of the whip amid total silence before Nick says in voice-over, "I stepped away for a few minutes; François offered to take the thrashing." The fact that it appears to be François who is beaten and not Nick is symbolic of Nick's ability to dissociate from abuse. Here, François offers to take the brunt of the beating, but later in the film his intervention is not necessary. "François feels that a man can only take so much before his dignity demands he rise up against an absurd and unjust universe," Nick muses after he fails to get Sheeni expelled from her French private school and thus separate her from her ex-boyfriend Trent. Notably, it is Nick who performs the darkest deed of all by conspiring with a lonely classmate at Sheeni's school to slip her sleeping pills so that she fails all of her classes.

While the tension between François and Nick, the two sides of Nick's conflicted psyche, are at the heart of the film, Arteta employs other cinematic nuances to illustrate the "absurd and unjust" world that Nick sees all around him. Just as Nick speaks with heightened language, so too is his world visually heightened, most notably with animation by Peter Sluszka. The animation—which includes three-dimensional Claymation, two-dimensional illustration, and collage—is stylistically scattered and reminiscent of the original cover of the *Youth in Revolt* novel, which Payne designed and created using cut-outs, sketches, and tape. In the opening credits, clay figures representing Nick, his mother, and Jerry make their way to the trailer park with a three-headed monster hot in pursuit. Later, when Nick and his friend Vijay drive to Santa Cruz to visit Sheeni at school, their road trip is illustrated in an assortment of collaged photographs. Arteta also makes playful use of slow motion and a dramatic orchestral underscore—homages to the classic films Nick and Sheeni love. For example, after Nick first sees Sheeni while walking to the trailer park's communal showers, Arteta cuts to a close-up shot of Nick in the shower, his mouth hanging open, dumb with love. Water droplets runs down his face in slow motion. A burst of orchestral music signals his newfound devotion.

Significance

Youth in Revolt premiered in January 2010 and performed only moderately well at the box office though it was critically praised. Manohla Dargis of the *New York Times* wrote that while the film "treads [the] well-cultivated ground" of the "frustrated virgin," Cera's winsome portrayal, Arteta's creative eye, and a supporting cast of serious actors make *Youth in Revolt* both successful and sincere. Peter Bradshaw, of the *Guardian* newspaper, gave the film four out of five stars. Other reviewers, like Michael Phillips of the *Los Angeles Times*, criticized the script as episodic and wrote that the film suffered because of Cera's overexposure. (The film was shot in 2008 but sat on the shelf—reportedly due to the Hollywood writers' strike—for nearly two years. By the time it appeared in theaters, Cera had appeared in at least three films about lovesick teenagers.)

Despite its many deviations from the novel, Payne loved the adaptation. He even makes a cameo appearance as one of Nick's neighbors at the beginning of the film. Critics agree that whatever enduring appeal *Youth in Revolt* might have comes from the charm of its source material. While the film is not as popular with young adults as other movies with similar themes, it found a cult audience that shares the same aesthetic as those who found and loved Payne's 1993 novel, which he reportedly printed 3,000 copies of and left on library and bookstore shelves throughout Berkeley, California.

The absurdity of Nick's world speaks powerfully to a specific variety of teenage alienation; it is about sexual frustration but also about the frustration of feeling and thinking like an adult while still being treated like a child. "It's a very comforting book," Cera told Jesse McKinley for the *New York Times*, adding that he hoped to convey his connection to the material in his performance. "You feel like the world makes sense when you're reading it."

Molly Hagan

Further Reading

Cera, Michael. "Michael Cera Interview YOUTH IN REVOLT." Interview by Sarah Wayland. *Collider.* Complex Media, 3 Jan. 2010. Web. 7 Dec. 2015. <http://collider.com/michael-cera-interview-youth-in-revolt>.

Roston, Tom. "'Youth in Revolt' Tries to Be a Different Teen-Virginity Film." Rev. of *Youth in Revolt*, dir. Miguel Arteta. *Los Angeles Times.* Los Angeles Times, 3 Jan. 2010. Web. 8 Dec. 2015. <http://articles.latimes.com/2010/jan/03/entertainment/la-ca-losingit3-2010jan03>.

Bibliography

Bradshaw, Peter. Rev. of *Youth in Revolt*, dir. Miguel Arteta. *Guardian.* Guardian News and Media, 4 Feb. 2010. Web. 7 Dec. 2015. <http://www.theguardian.com/film/2010/feb/04/youth-in-revolt-film-review>.

Dargis, Manohla. "He's in Love; Excuse His French." Rev. of *Youth in Revolt*, dir. Miguel Arteta. *New York Times.* New York Times, 7 Jan. 2010. Web. 7 Dec. 2015. <http://www.nytimes.com/2010/01/08/movies/08youth.html>.

"King of the Geeks." Rev. of *Youth in Revolt*, dir. Miguel Arteta. *Alberta Local News.* Black Press, 5 Jan. 2010. Web. 10 Dec. 2015. <http://www.albertalocalnews.com/entertainment/King_of_the_geeks_80706912.html?mobile=true>.

McKinley, Jesse. "Keeping Options Open, Novelist Tows Museum on Road to Dream." Rev. of *Youth in Revolt*, dir. Miguel Arteta. *New York Times.* New York Times, 25 Jan. 2010. Web. 10 Dec. 2015. <http://www.nytimes.com/2010/01/26/books/26payne.html>.

Phillips, Michael. Rev. of *Youth in Revolt*, dir. Miguel Arteta. *Los Angeles Times.* Los Angeles Times, 8 Jan. 2010. Web. 8 Dec. 2015. <http://articles.latimes.com/2010/jan/08/entertainment/la-et-youth8-2010jan08>.

THEMES IN YOUNG ADULT LITERATURE

Alienation

Titles Discussed

All the Truth That's in Me by Julie Berry
Speak by Laurie Halse Anderson
33 Snowfish by Adam Rapp

Thematic Overview

For many young adults, their teenage years are spent developing a self-identity, shaping the ideas and beliefs that will guide them over the next decades. Along with this very personal task, however, comes the social task of finding a community outside of one's family or home life. While a person's childhood identity is deeply entwined with the role in the family, the young adult identity is newly developed in relation to others, and as such, the search for community and the search for self are often indistinguishable tasks.

While ideally this process of change would result in finding a loving and supporting community, in reality, many young adults instead experience alienation, feeling entirely alone and cut off from both the broader society they are trying to enter and the home life they may be trying to escape. Alienation is, in fact, at the core of the stereotypical teenager, a figure often portrayed in popular culture as being angst ridden, sullen, and withdrawn. Since the emergence of young adult literature as a distinct genre in the mid-twentieth century, it has likewise been populated by the alienated teenager. J. D. Salinger's *The Catcher in the Rye* (1951), a classic of both young adult literature and modern fiction, features Holden Caulfield, an alienated youth who thinks everyone he meets is a "phony." While Salinger's book has been met with ample controversy and censorship, the broad appeal of the "troubled teenager" as a sympathetic and relatable character, particularly to young adult readers, has solidified its place in the canon.

Following the popularity of problem novels in the 1970s, young adult literature in the 1980s and onward increasingly addressed political and cultural topics. While Holden Caulfield felt a general sort of angst about growing up and entering the adult world, protagonists in later novels often felt alienated due to specific cultural or identity-based positions. Any aspect of difference, such as lesbian, gay, bisexual, or transgender (LGBT) identities, immigration status, or physical disability, holds the potential to alienate youth from their peers and communities. As there is no true "normal teenager," every young adult reader experiences some aspect of difference, making the potential for alienation universal. The 1980s and 1990s also saw a rise in young adult literature addressing traumatic and violent events, including rape. Such literature explores further dimensions of alienation, with traumatized protagonists abruptly shifting from feeling included in peer groups to feeling alone and alienated because of the violence they experienced, about which they often feel unable to talk.

While alienation is a difficult topic for many young adults, it also holds great potential, especially when novels addressing this theme are presented in a classroom as part of the development of critical reading skills. Alienation places a protagonist at a remove from society and from peers, and this remove can often be an opportunity to critique and challenge cultural norms. Laurie Halse Anderson's *Speak* (1999), Adam Rapp's *33 Snowfish* (2003), and Julie Berry's *All the Truth That's in Me* (2013) all situate the traumas and oppressions faced by their characters in the context of greater societal problems, thus highlighting the tension between the young adult protagonists and the world they are about to inherit and possibly change.

Works

Alienation is presented through a particularly violent and graphic narrative in Adam Rapp's *33 Snowfish*, with characters encountering a society defined by exploitation and abuse. As the novel opens, protagonists Custis, Boobie, and Curl are flee on a road trip across Illinois, having stolen both a car and Boobie's baby brother. Through flashbacks, the characters' backstories are unveiled. Seventeen-year-old Boobie, whose real name is Darrin Flowers, is a pyromaniac who murdered his parents; ten-year-old Custis has escaped from a man who kept him prisoner and forced him to appear in pornographic films; and fourteen-year-old Curl has fled an aunt who forced her to work as a child prostitute in their small apartment. While Boobie rarely speaks, the group stays together, stealing to survive and planning to sell the baby, while Curl expresses a desire to marry both of her companions. They stay for a while in an abandoned van in the woods, but the midwestern winter takes its toll; first Curl dies of exposure, and then Boobie disappears, presumed dead. Custis and the baby are finally found by Seldom, a reclusive older man who takes them to his cabin, where they develop family-like bonds.

The three main characters must deal with two forms of simultaneous alienation: they are alienated from society (an alienation they embrace in both radical and sometimes destructive ways), and they are alienated from one another, having never learned how to form healthy or productive relationships with peers or family. The narratives switches from the perspective of one character to another, revealing how their histories have formed their senses of alienation. Boobie, for instance, is driven by his violent outbursts and pyromania, with his destructive tendencies replacing speech as his method of communication and human connection; we see this both in his sections of the narrative, which are filled with violent drawings rather than language, and through the perspectives of others, who integrate his muteness into their ersatz family structure.

Custis, by contrast, is verbose in his sections and in conversation with others, his language studded with profanities and inappropriate remarks. While he is able to communicate in one sense, his childhood trauma has left him with wildly skewed ideas of what it means to connect with another human, even one he might truly care for. Even Seldom, the man who welcomes Custis and shows him that a family is possible, is at first met with scorn, Custis describing him with a racial slur on their first meeting. Even when together, all of the characters experience alienation, being unable to see themselves as loved or accepted due to histories of traumatic abuse that prevented human connection and affinity. Despite the extremity of this violence, however, the novel does offer hope, with Custis, Seldom, and the baby forming something like a family—and, importantly, a family that exists outside of the strictures and norms of the society that caused Custis such harm in the first place.

While the violence at the heart of *33 Snowfish* is shown graphically and often, the violence in *Speak*, by Laurie Halse Anderson, is obscured for most of the text, leaving the focus instead on the emotional experience of alienation following a violent act. *Speak* is the story of Melinda, a girl who finds herself ostracized from her friends as she enters her first year of high school, with the entire school angry at her for calling the police on a party that summer. As she is openly mocked and tormented, she finds small solace in a few places—her friendship with a new girl named Heather, her work in art class, and a janitor's closet in which she often hides. Retreating further into herself, Melinda largely stops speaking, constantly chews her lips, and begins failing her classes. Her anxiety is further heightened whenever she encounters a boy she calls IT, who flirts with her aggressively. Once she begins skipping school, she finally reveals through the narration that IT (actually named Andy) raped her at the party, which led to the phone call to the police. When Andy begins dating her best friend Rachel, however, Melinda slowly begins to speak: first writing Rachel an anonymous note to warn her, then writing a warning about Andy on the bathroom wall, and finally telling Rachel about the rape. Rachel at first reacts with anger. However, when other girls share their own experiences with Andy on the bathroom wall, Melinda is empowered and begins to speak about her trauma with others.

Melinda's alienation is rendered in large part through her inability to communicate with others, which in many ways includes the readers and Melinda herself. The novel is written in the first person, and Melinda's thoughts are often brief and poetic, staying in the present tense with fairly few exceptions. While she obliquely references the rape in her narration, it is not until the novel is nearing its end that she directly acknowledges the violence she experienced. This narrative style mimics Melinda's inner monologue, and as such, the fact that she does not acknowledge the rape directly means that she is unable to state that reality even to herself. This creates a dilemma—Melinda is largely mute throughout the book, finding herself incapable of speaking to peers or family about even the most banal of topics; in order to speak to others, she must first acknowledge the rape to herself, yet in order to acknowledge the rape, she needs the support of others. Her alienation is a kind of cruel trap, especially considering that it only takes acknowledgment of the rape to explain her phone call to the police and end the ostracism and bullying she has been experiencing. *Speak*, however, does not keep Melinda trapped in the double bind of silence and alienation. Instead, she slowly finds ways to communicate: drawing inspiration from studying suffragettes in social studies class, embracing the anonymity of the bathroom graffiti, and learning to express herself metaphorically through her work in art class. As the novel ends and she first reveals the rape to her art teacher, it becomes evident that her alienation was in some ways also a tool, with Melinda retreating from the world in order to protect herself until she gathered the strength to challenge Andy and the culture that had treated her with such cruelty.

All the Truth That's in Me, by Julie Berry, likewise features an adolescent girl who has lost her voice and must learn to speak again. In this case, however, the silence is literal, as the protagonist, Judith, has had her tongue cut out. Set in an unspecified historical setting that resembles, but is not identified as, the colonial

United States, the novel opens when Judith is eighteen. At fourteen, she disappeared from her small town along with another girl; the other girl was found dead several days later, and Judith returned after two years, maimed and mute. Rather than warmly welcoming her back, the community believes that she lost her virginity while gone, making her a "fallen woman" and a social outcast, a situation worsened by her muteness. With even her own mother treating her cruelly, Judith takes small comfort in her growing friendship with Lucas, a boy she has loved for her entire life.

When a small army of men attack the town, Judith makes the brave choice to return to the man who held her captive, knowing he has a supply of ammunition and explosives. Her actions save the town, but a new series of violence and misunderstandings unfolds after the battle, as the kidnapper is found and identified as Lucas's father. Judith and Lucas are both put on trial for their perceived crimes—Judith under suspicion of having been involved in the murder of the other missing girl, and Lucas for, as the town believes, having known about his father all along. With the encouragement of an older woman and the love of Lucas, Judith finally manages to speak the truth of her experience: it was the missing girl's father who killed her, and Lucas's father had held Judith prisoner in order to protect her from this man. When he found himself sexually obsessed with Judith, he cut out her tongue and sent her home, hoping her forced silence would protect her from the real killer.

While Melinda's narrative in *Speak* is an internal monologue, Judith's first-person narration is addressed directly to Lucas, her lifelong love. This creates a narrative tension, with Judith revealing the truth of her experience to Lucas on every page, yet at the same time unable to actually speak those truths, even when Lucas acknowledges that he loves her too. Judith lives in an extreme of alienation, an outcast in a small village and the victim of constant physical and sexual violence, with even her supposed savior cutting out her tongue and threatening to sexually abuse her. Yet she also longs for the human connection that will undo that alienation. The prose constantly presents this struggle in plain, direct language: "To tell the truth will make me loathsome in your eyes. Even more than I already am," she declares. Yet she immediately continues, "I pledged to give you all the truth that's in me." Because this is rendered as direct address, the experience of longing is heightened, as readers are put in the position of Lucas while still having access to the thoughts that Lucas himself cannot hear. At the same time, those thoughts—and, by extension, Judith herself—are shown to be quite powerful. It is only Judith who has the knowledge to save the town when it is attacked by the outsiders, and likewise it is Judith alone who knows the real danger in the town, revealing the killer who lives among their small community. When she finally triumphs in the end by using her voice and sharing her story, it is evident that her alienation, and by extension alienation in general, is not simply the problem of the one who is alienated; rather, both the individual and the community suffer when any one person is alienated from the society.

Conclusions

Alienation has been a constant theme of young adult literature since the formation of the genre, yet the specifics of how and why teenagers feel alienated continue to change as societies evolve. While in the past teenagers found their lives fairly fixed in the realms of family and school, modern teenagers are more likely to find themselves in broadly public spaces, such as malls, parks, train stations, and highways. Even more significantly, teenagers are forming their identities in the virtual world of social media as much as in the physical world of peer interactions. As a result, teenage alienation has the potential to take place on a much broader scale than in the past, and likewise to carry with it broader social implications.

In many young adult novels, this means that protagonists are not simply encountering individualized experience of alienation, as with Holden Caulfield and his discontent, but rather are experiencing a politicized alienation that recognizes the societal and political roots of the problems the protagonists face. As young adult literature is also often concerned with teaching readers how to be engaged and thoughtful citizens of society, this often means that such alienation must be overcome not just to feel at home among peers but also to change the culture that created the alienation in the first place. This general trend can be seen across a wide range of subgenres, from young adult dystopian literature featuring protagonists who are fantastically and violently kicked out of their communities to romance novels in which LGBT youths must challenge the dominant society in order to win acceptance of their genders and sexualities. While alienation is still a problem in these novels, it is also importantly a source of potential change.

Even as teenagers are increasingly in constant technological communication with peers, their sense of alienation is generally as strong as it has ever been, and their desire for novels that reflect that alienation in nuanced and contemporary ways remains. Regardless of whether such novels are set in historical time periods or imagined dystopias, in small towns or major urban centers, teenagers still turn to them as remedies for their own alienation—the protagonists providing a sense of peer connection—and for the promise that they might one day emerge from their experiences of loneliness and dissatisfaction, sharing their own voices in order to better the broader world.

T. Fleischmann, MFA

Further Reading

Alsup, Janet. "Politicizing Young Adult Literature: Reading Anderson's *Speak* as a Critical Text." *Journal of Adolescent & Adult Literacy* 47.2 (2003): 158–66. *Literary Reference Center*. Web. 14 May 2015. <http://search.ebscohost.com/login.aspx?direct=true&db=lfh&AN=11455383&site=ehost-live>.

Bean, Thomas W., and Karen Moni. "Developing Students' Critical Literacy: Exploring Identity Construction in Young Adult Fiction." *Journal of Adolescent & Adult Literacy* 46.8 (2003): 638–48. *Literary Reference Center*. Web. 14 May 2015. <http://search.ebscohost.com/login.aspx?direct=true&db=lfh&AN=9539932&site=ehost-live>.

Bibliography

Barth, F. Diane. "Social Media and Adolescent Development: Hazards, Pitfalls and Opportunities for Growth." *Entering the Digital World: Cybertechnology and Clinical Social Work Practice*. Ed. Laura W. Groshong and Faye Mishna. Spec. issue of *Clinical Social Work Journal* 43.2 (2015): 201–8. Print.

Brown, Monica R., Kyle Higgins, and Kim Paulsen. "Adolescent Alienation: What Is It and What Can Educators Do about It?" *Intervention in School and Clinic* 39.1 (2003): 3–9. *Academic Search Premier*. Web. 14 May 2015. <http://search.ebscohost.com/login.aspx?direct=true&db=aph&AN=10598967&site=ehost-live>.

Cart, Michael. *Young Adult Literature: From Romance to Realism*. Chicago: ALA, 2011. Print.

Body Image

Titles Discussed
Deenie by Judy Blume
Life in the Fat Lane by Cherie Bennett
Wintergirls by Laurie Halse Anderson

Thematic Overview

"Body image" refers to the values, particularly the sexual and aesthetic values, a person attaches to his or her body, as well the values that are perceived to be attached to that person's body by his or her peers and by society in general. For young adults, body image is often a particularly fraught issue. As their bodies rapidly change, sexuality and the importance of looking sexually attractive become dramatically more important, and peer groups apply heightened pressure on individuals, leading at times to social ostracism and bullying. While body image is a recurrent theme across all genres of literature, it is an especially urgent theme in young adult novels.

Body-image issues affect young adults of all genders, but they are particularly pertinent to teenage girls, whose concerns about weight often manifest in diseases such as anorexia nervosa and bulimia. Since the 1930s, the rate of anorexia among teenage girls has increased every decade, with the occurrence of eating disorders roughly equal across racial categories. In part this is due to societal pressures around sexuality, as teenage girls receive the message that they should be ashamed of and hide their sexualities at the same time that society in general begins to sexualize them in extreme and sometimes violent ways. This prevalence also reflects issues of control in general; young girls and women have historically been given less agency than their male peers, and it is not uncommon for them to attempt to reclaim control of their lives by enacting it on their bodies instead.

Young adult literature has the potential to either uphold these norms and trends or challenge them. During the second half of the twentieth century, a good number of novels that addressed body image largely reinforced dominant ideas around weight and sexuality. The 1972 young adult classic *Dinky Hocker Shoots Smack*, by M. E. Kerr, features an intelligent and confident teenage girl who nonetheless is coerced into dieting and extreme weight-loss measures against her will, with no clear indication to readers that her body is acceptable or attractive as it is. Although the authors of such books might have good intentions, their novels tend to echo the damaging messages sent by television, movies, and popular music that extremely thin bodies are the only socially acceptable bodies and weight loss and painful dieting are necessary for young women to find happiness. Many young adult novels that explore body image even come with conflicting messages, as the covers of these novels, which serve as marketing tools, are likely to feature girls who weigh much less than the protagonists described in the text.

At the same time, a small number of young adult novels operate against these trends. Judy Blume's 1973 novel *Deenie*, for instance, features a girl who learns to accept her scoliosis and the back brace she must wear, while Cherie Bennett's *Life in the Fat Lane* (1998) follows a young girl who learns to find happiness regardless of her weight. Other novels, such as Laurie Halse Anderson's *Wintergirls* (2009), focus on the damaging and often deadly realities of anorexia and bulimia and their effects on the lives of the protagonists. Because negative messages about body image are so prevalent in young adult popular culture, novels that celebrate acceptance rather than change can be particularly powerful for young readers.

Works

Judy Blume's works were among the most widely read and critically praised young adult novels of the later twentieth century, due in large part to Blume's willingness to present honest and progressive depictions of teenage sexuality and other topics that were viewed as particularly controversial at the time. This honest engagement with teenagers' lives made Blume's novels frequent targets of censorship, with classics such as *Forever . . .* (1975), which deals frankly with teenage sex, facing regular bans in schools and libraries. *Deenie* likewise includes frank discussions of sexuality, although the focus of the book is instead on the protagonist's diagnosis of scoliosis and the back brace she must wear as a result. Thirteen-year-old Deenie is a beautiful girl, and her mother tells her constantly that her beauty gives her worth in the world, even encouraging her to become a model. The brace and Deenie's new insecurities about her appearance affect her in several ways. She finds herself newly jealous of her attractive best friend Janet, who is chosen to be a cheerleader, and she struggles to enjoy kissing a boy when her insecurity overwhelms her.

Deenie's body image is directly affected by her newly revealed medical condition, which allows her character to go through a somewhat dramatic change.

Rather than someone who has always felt dissatisfied with her body, she is a character who transitions from self-confident to suddenly insecure. While the novel's most obvious theme is Deenie's eventual acceptance of her body, it is equally as concerned with the ways in which her body image influences other aspects of her life. As a result, the novel largely explores Deenie's own perception of herself rather than the perceptions of her by others. There is increased social tension and competition among her group of friends, for instance, yet this is largely because Deenie herself feels sudden jealousy over the easy confidence the others exhibit; her friends themselves seem to want to support her through her troubles. Deenie also gains a new empathy for others, as is evidenced by her gradual acceptance of an ostracized new student who suffers from eczema and by her role in welcoming this student into her social world.

Similarly, the revelation of Deenie's scoliosis coincides with her burgeoning sexuality, and the two events deeply influence one another. While Deenie's body suddenly feels foreign and stressful to her, she discovers that masturbation, and by extension sexuality, is a tool that allows her to enjoy and celebrate that body. This tension becomes most heightened in the evenings, when the stress over her scoliosis prevents her from falling asleep, while masturbation releases that stress. She also finds herself unable to enjoy her first romantic relationship until she accepts her body. When a boy named Buddy kisses her and begins to feel her body, she at first finds herself unable to kiss him back, despite wanting to, which upsets Buddy. After she has worked to accept herself, she is finally able to both kiss Buddy and enjoy the experience, feeling hopeful about the possibility of future sexual pleasure. These overlapping experiences provide a complicated portrait of Deenie's body image. She is not defined by how she views her body, nor by how others understand it. Instead, her body image is one aspect of her rapidly changing personality and interests, and she can only learn to accept and celebrate herself by accepting her entire self, body and mind. As sexual pleasure has been linked to self-acceptance and stress relief throughout the novel, the implication is that her future romantic relationship with Buddy might lead to even greater happiness and greater release from the stress of the back brace.

Cherie Bennett's *Life in the Fat Lane* is similarly a story of transformation, with the thin and popular protagonist, Lara, developing a medical condition that results in sudden, drastic weight gain. Compared to Deenie, Lara's transformation is radically dramatic. The homecoming queen of her high school, Lara views herself as loved by everyone, including her idealized parents. She also understands her conventional attractiveness to be a result of her healthy habits, as she exercises every day and pays careful attention to what she eats. When she begins to gain weight, however, her mother and father stop supporting her, instead pressuring her into unhealthy eating habits, and her popularity at school quickly drops. The pressure from this change causes her parents to begin arguing frequently, and the family even relocates to a new state, hoping to give Lara a fresh start. Lara is ostracized in her new school, but she makes friends with some unpopular students and begins to date a blind boy. She also comes to realize that her home life was never perfect, she had just viewed it that way. She finally begins to lose some weight, which makes her happy, although she also appreciates what she learned by gaining weight.

This novel falls into a somewhat nebulous middle ground—while it attempts to challenge dominant ideas about body image and weight, and in some respects succeeds, it also reinforces many societal norms. The narrative splices excerpts from television shows and similar media into the main storyline, demonstrating the overwhelmingly destructive ideas about weight that young women hear on a daily basis and emphasizing that Lara, her family, and her friends did not organically develop their prejudices but rather learned them from a broader culture. Similarly, as Lara gains weight and finds her perspective on the world changing along with her body, she comes to realize both her family's deep-seated unhappiness and the importance of developing relationships based on emotional and intellectual connections, as well as the pleasure that can be gained when someone values her personality rather than her body. At the same time, however, the characters in the book who value Lara are those who are themselves socially outcast, and her new romantic interest after moving to Michigan is a blind a boy who does not "see" her weight. While the novel does present a protagonist who matures in relation to her body image, she exists in a world that is extremely hostile toward young women with larger bodies; her weight gain even seems to destroy her parents' marriage (although this is later revealed to not be the whole story). For young readers with normatively attractive bodies, Lara's story might provide some insight. For readers who themselves struggle with body-image

issues, however, it has the potential to simply reinforce the negative messages.

While *Life in the Fat Lane* is focused on societal ideas about weight and the ways that peers and family affect Lara's body image, *Wintergirls*, by Laurie Halse Anderson, is more concerned with the protagonist's interior world. Eighteen-year-old Lia lives with the mental disorder anorexia nervosa. As the novel opens, Lia's former best friend Cassie is found dead in a motel room, having succumbed to her own battle with bulimia. Cassie attempted to call Lia for a reconciliation during her final moments, but Lia ignored the calls, and her guilt and her grief trigger an escalation of her disorder. Over the course of the novel, Lia continues to starve herself while arguing with her distant parents, who are unable or unwilling to provide the love and understanding that she needs. Due in part to her starvation, she regularly hallucinates Cassie, who encourages her to end her life. As her condition worsens, so does her tendency for self-mutilation, and when her beloved younger stepsister walks in on her slicing her chest open, she is finally hospitalized. Fearing she will be institutionalized, Lia attempts to run away from home, but she realizes that she is about to die herself and finally reaches out for help, ending the novel on a note of hope and survival.

For Lia, her body image is shaped by the interior world of mental illness as well as the exterior world of family stress, cultural misogyny, and other, similarly destructive forces. Lia's first-person narration hints that Cassie's bulimia was triggered by being sexualized at a young age; it is implied that a neighbor boy molested her, for instance, and when she was the first girl in fifth grade to develop breasts, boys regularly snapped her bra while girls mocked and ostracized her. The first-person perspective also emphasizes the conflict between Lia's own mind and the world itself. Her thoughts are regularly crossed out on the page, especially thoughts about desiring food or fighting back against her uncaring family, demonstrating the self-negation that informs every moment of her life. The narrative is filled with details about food, including descriptions of the eating habits of everyone Lia meets and her obsessive tally of her own caloric intake. As is the case for anorexia sufferers in real life, it becomes impossible to separate the cultural reality in which Lia lives from the mental disorder from which she suffers; in the space of the novel, one could not exist without the other, as even Lia's visual hallucinations echo negative cultural ideas about weight, physical attractiveness, and misogyny. In this way, while

Wintergirls is concerned primarily with Lia's personal experience of body image, it also explores the nuanced ways in which body image exists not as a singular topic but rather as a suite reflecting psychological, cultural, and familial forces.

Conclusions

Young adult novels in the early twenty-first century are typically more willing to address sexuality and sexual development than they were decades prior. While body image is not exclusively concerned with sexuality, the two influence one another in complex and profound ways, and the increasing acceptance of sexuality has led to greater opportunities for forthright and complex portrayals of body image. In particular, while twentieth-century novels might present body image as a preoccupation of the protagonist, novels from the twenty-first century are more likely to examine the personal and cultural complexities that shape it.

From the 1990s onward, scholars have also started writing more about body image in young adult literature. Much of this is influenced by contemporary feminist theory, including Beth Younger's comprehensive and valuable *Learning Curves: Body Image and Female Sexuality in Young Adult Literature* (2009). These works have helped nuance the critical discussion around body image, challenging texts that advertently or inadvertently uphold cultural norms while also celebrating the uniquely powerful role that young adult literature plays in the lives of many young girls and women. This critical attention has further pushed the genre toward complex, candid portrayals of young adult bodies, continuing the legacy that began with Judy Blume's groundbreaking discussions of menstruation, sexuality, and masturbation.

On a broader cultural level, it is clear that the topic of body image is becoming more relevant to young readers with every passing year. Rates of anorexia and bulimia continue to rise, and popular culture finds new ways to sexualize young women and girls; a 1997 study showed, for instance, that advertisements sexualizing children featured girls rather than boys 85 percent of the time. Other recent studies have revealed that disorders such as anorexia and bulimia, and body-image issues in general, are not exclusive to young women but rather influence male adolescents as well. According to a study published in the *American Journal of Psychiatry* in 2001, the gender ratio for full anorexia nervosa is estimated to be 4.2:1, meaning that nearly 20 percent of anorexia sufferers are male. While body image was once considered a "girl's issue" by many, writers and scholars are working to shift that understanding, illuminating the insecurities and control issues adolescent boys feel about their own changing bodies.

Writers responding to these urgent realities are influenced by the possibilities opened up by feminist and literary studies. Since the early 2000s, a number of award-winning novels have been published that celebrate protagonists who identify as fat, embracing the term and their bodies rather than seeking change. Just as importantly, young adult readers can find novels that feature insecure or struggling protagonists, including those with mental disorders rooted in body image, who have the same complexities as other young adult characters, rather than being entirely defined by their body image. While the challenges associated with developing a positive body image as a young adult are unlikely to change, young adult literature increasingly offers readers a chance to understand themselves not as damaged but as full human beings, capable of navigating these challenges and emerging with a healthy perception of their bodies and sexualities.

T. Fleischmann, MFA

Further Reading

Glessner, Marci M., John H. Hoover, and Lisa A. Hazlett. "The Portrayal of Overweight in Adolescent Fiction." *Reclaiming Children and Youth* 15.2 (2006): 116–23. *Academic Search Premier*. Web. 13 May 2015. <http://search.ebscohost.com/login.aspx?direct=true&db=aph&AN=22065693&site=ehost-live>.

Younger, Beth. *Learning Curves: Body Image and Female Sexuality in Young Adult Literature*. Lanham: Scarecrow, 2009. Print.

Bibliography

"Eating Disorders Statistics." *National Association of Anorexia Nervosa and Associated Disorders*. ANAD, 2015. Web. 13 May 2015. <http://www.anad.org/get-information/about-eating-disorders/eating-disorders-statistics/>.

Mahood, Ramona Madson. "Deenie." *Masterplots II: Juvenile and Young Adult Literature Series Supplement*. Ed. Tracy Irons-Georges. Pasadena: Salem,

1997. *Literary Reference Center*. Web. 13 May 2015. <http://search.ebscohost.com/login.aspx?direct=true&db=lfh&AN=103331JYS10849720000147&site=lrc-live>.

Woodside, D. Blake, et al. "Comparisons of Men with Full or Partial Eating Disorders, Men without Eating Disorders, and Women with Eating Disorders in the Community." *American Journal of Psychiatry* 158.4 (2001): 570–74. Web. 29 May 2015. <http://ajp.psychiatryonline.org/doi/abs/10.1176/appi.ajp.158.4.570>.

Younger, Beth. "Pleasure, Pain, and the Power of Being Thin: Female Sexuality in Young Adult Literature." *NWSA Journal* 15.2 (2003): 45–56. *Literary Reference Center*. Web. 13 May 2015. <http://search.ebscohost.com/login.aspx?direct=true&db=lfh&AN=10252518&site=lrc-live>.

Bullying

Titles Discussed

Please Stop Laughing at Me . . . : One Woman's Inspirational Story by Jodee Blanco
Fade to Black by Alex Flinn
Thirteen Reasons Why by Jay Asher
Crossing Lines by Paul Volponi

Thematic Overview

Bullying is not a new phenomenon. The biblical Old Testament contains the story of Goliath (1 Samuel 17), a Philistine champion "six cubits and a span" (about nine feet, nine inches tall). A classic bully who relies upon enormous size to intimidate, Goliath taunts the Israelite armies. When puny shepherd David volunteers to confront him in single combat, Goliath, insulted, vows to feed his opponent's flesh "to the birds and the wild animals"—but he cannot make good his boast, since David kills him. The Israelites have their own bully: musclebound Samson (Judges 13–16). He torments Philistines by releasing burning foxes to destroy crops, kills a thousand soldiers with an animal's jawbone, and rips away the gates of a city before dying in the rubble of a temple he pulls down with his bare hands.

Such examples illustrate humanity's long tradition of violence while encapsulating the confrontational nature of civilization, a perennial struggle between opposing forces: the strong who seek to dominate and those less

powerful they target to subdue. History has been shaped by a succession of bullies (Alexander the Great, Roman emperor Nero, Attila the Hun, Ivan the Terrible, Napoleon Bonaparte, Joseph Stalin) who all gained their reputations partially by preying upon the weak.

Because it has played such a significant role throughout history, the subject of bullying has often figured in classical literature. Achilles and Hector are prominent bullies in Homer's *Iliad*, for the Greek and Trojan sides, respectively. Children's fairy tales—such as "The Three Little Pigs," "Cinderella," "Snow White," "Hansel and Gretel," and others collected by the Brothers Grimm—are rife with taunting and acts of spiteful cruelty perpetrated on the helpless by those in positions of power. Victorian authors likewise tackled the topic. Many of Charles Dickens's adult and youthful characters—Bob Cratchit in *A Christmas Carol*, Pip in *Great Expectations*, the hero of *Oliver Twist*—are victims of such fictional bullies as Mr. Scrooge, Estella, and Bill Sykes. Twentieth-century authors William Golding (*Lord of the Flies*), Harper Lee (*To Kill a Mockingbird*), E. B. White (*Charlotte's Web*), John Knowles (*A Separate Peace*), S. E. Hinton (*The Outsiders*), Stephen King (*Carrie*), Robert Cormier (*The Chocolate War*), J. K. Rowling (the Harry Potter series), and many others have dealt memorably with the motivations for and consequences of bullying, often focusing on young adult protagonists.

In modern literature, bullying remains a popular topic because it is still a popular pastime. Though methods of torment have grown more subtle in the electronic age, the purpose is still the same: to wound and control individuals through repeated physical force, threats, coercion, rumors, gossip, or lies. The four books discussed here—Jodee Blanco's *Please Stop Laughing at Me* (2003), Alex Flinn's *Fade to Black* (2005), Jay Asher's *Thirteen Reasons Why* (2007), and Paul Volponi's *Crossing Lines* (2011)—illustrate a wide range of bullying behavior.

Works

Please Stop Laughing at Me is a nonfiction memoir. In the introduction, author Jodee Blanco is in her hometown, Chicago, Illinois, attending her high school reunion. She fears she will run into the bullies who tormented her.

Straightforward, unembellished flashbacks make up the bulk of the book. Jodee recalls when the bullying started, while she was attending Catholic grammar school. Jodee becomes attached to Marianne, a five-year-old with a clubfoot, enrolled in a special program for the deaf. Jodee's best friend, Jo Ellen, warns that their friendship will be destroyed if she continues playing with "retard" Marianne, but after Jodee's mother tells her that "sometimes people are frightened by anyone who is different," Jodee sticks with Marianne and loses Jo Ellen. When other kids tease Marianne, Jodee tells the nuns, who punish the culprits; as a result, Jodee is shunned.

In sixth grade Jodee transfers to a private school for gifted children and regains her popularity. But after derailing a session of inappropriate sexual games, she again becomes an outcast, the victim of pranks and physical abuse. She suffers tension-related ailments, causing her parents to take her to a pediatric psychiatrist, who medicates her. She begins keeping a journal, recording her thoughts, and wonders why it is always victims, rather than bullies, who wind up in therapy.

Jodee's family moves to the suburbs, and she gets a fresh start among new acquaintances in the neighborhood and at school. But when she refuses to conform to the demands of the most popular students, her reputation and grades suffer, and she once again becomes a victim of bullying.

Many of Jodee's former classmates attend her new high school, and they poison potential friendships in advance. Her grades suffer. She descends into depression. Worse, her breasts are developing at different rates due to a congenital birth defect called tubular asymmetry, necessitating reconstructive surgery. Ultimately, Jodee falls in with tattooed loner Annie and her circle of other social misfits. She survives high school before launching a successful career as an entertainment publicist, publishing executive, and author.

In the ironic conclusion of her memoir, apprehensive Jodee attends the reunion. There, former classmates greet her warmly, having forgotten they were ever cruel to her; during high school they were preoccupied with their own fears and individual issues. Since the publication of *Please Stop Laughing at Me*, Blanco has been much in demand as a motivational speaker at high schools, lecturing about bullying. A sequel to her book, *Please Stop Laughing at Us*, was published in 2013.

In contrast to the highly personal nonfiction account related in *Please Stop Laughing*, the fictional *Fade to Black* is told in three distinct alternating voices. One voice, tough and slangy, is that of Clinton Cole, a muscular sixteen-year-old student at Pinedale High School in Pinedale, Florida, and the son of an alcoholic bigot

prejudiced against Latinos, whom he blames for his job loss. Another voice, consisting of short, almost poetic outbursts, belongs to Daria Bickell, a special-education student with Down syndrome who is called "retarded" and feels invisible. The third voice, natural and expressive, is Alejandro "Alex" Crusan's. He is a tall, skinny seventeen-year-old Hispanic boy, a recent transfer to Pinedale, who is HIV-positive, allegedly from a tainted transfusion.

The story opens with a report about an incident that affects the three narrators. Someone in a Pinedale Panthers jacket attacked and smashed the windows of Alex's vehicle with a baseball bat, cutting Alex with flying glass. Daria Cole witnessed the assault, and though she did not see the assailant's face, she testifies that she glimpsed Clinton near the scene. Clinton denies being the perpetrator. The police are investigating the incident as a possible hate crime. Over the course of a week the investigation slowly approaches the truth.

Fade to Black is complicated by the fact that all three narrators are unreliable for various reasons; the relationships among them are too complex to be easily compartmentalized. Clinton, a bully, is afraid of being infected by Alex, and fearful for his overweight, gifted younger sister Melody, whose only friend is Alex's younger sister Lina. Clinton tried to scare Alex away by throwing a rock through a window of the Crusan house while the family was at church. Daria, who has a childlike crush on Alex because he treats her like a normal person, was hanging out near Alex's house when Clinton threw the rock. Because of her mental disability, she has conflated the separate attacks directed at Alex. Recovering in the hospital, Alex encounters classmate Jennifer Atkinson, a candy striper, who is initially afraid of approaching Alex. The injured teen, afraid he will die and "fade to black," has his own secret: he did not acquire HIV from tainted blood but from unprotected sex with an anonymous woman during a party.

As the story progresses, the dynamics of the high school society change. Clinton's buddies shun him until the real criminal—a graduate from the previous year—is caught. Daria briefly enjoys the spotlight as an important witness to the assault, before her classmates revert to type and again ignore her. Alex, scarred, makes peace with a chagrined Clinton, returns to school, and establishes a friendship with Jennifer, to whom he decides to tell the truth about how he got HIV. Alex thinks, "Even hurting is good. Being hurt is at least being alive. Being real."

Unlike *Fade to Black*, which uses living viewpoint characters to tell the story, Jay Asher's suspenseful *Thirteen Reasons Why* takes a different approach. The novel examines the possible consequences of bullying through an unusual medium: the voice from beyond the grave. In a plausible, nonsupernatural fashion, a victim accuses her tormenters and exacts a form of revenge.

High school student Clay Jensen receives a package in the mail. He is astonished to discover it contains audiocassette tapes recorded by Hannah Baker, a pretty, sensitive classmate who recently committed suicide. The tapes hold Hannah's descriptions of thirteen incidents of subtle cruelty perpetrated against her by her classmates, and the names of the perpetrators that drove Hannah to take her own life. Under threat of exposure—copies of the tapes will be made public if her orders are not followed exactly—each of the thirteen recipients, similar to a chain letter, is supposed to listen to learn of the crimes committed, then forward the tapes to the next person named. Clay, ninth on Hannah's list, does not initially think he belongs among the offenders, since he was shy and lacked the confidence to interact with her, but ultimately realizes his inaction did indeed exacerbate her despair and lead to her eventual death.

Conscience-stricken, Clay faithfully carries out Hannah's instructions. He follows a provided map to the sites of the various offenses, meanwhile learning how shallow, petty, and mean-spirited his fellow students really are. One ruined Hannah's reputation. Another teased her unmercifully. A female student physically abused her. Another girl tore down Hannah to build up her own status. One student is a Peeping Tom, another student is a rapist, and a third is a potential alcoholic. In the process of discovery, Clay finds evidence of another death caused by the carelessness of several named participants.

Part cautionary tale about the cumulative effect of small deeds, part mystery for the way the plot comes together like pieces of a jigsaw puzzle, and part horror story for the unflinching way in which youthful depravity is depicted, *Thirteen Reasons Why* resonated with young adults. Since its publication, the award-winning novel has been translated into numerous languages and released in over thirty countries across Europe, the Americas, and Asia. Asher has also used the book as a jumping-off point to discuss the realities of bullying and teen suicide, traveling across the United States to speak at various high schools.

Despite the downbeat story, *Thirteen Reasons Why* nevertheless contains a positive message: teenagers who can transcend their self-absorption long enough to notice signs indicating someone is troubled—such as making major changes in appearance or giving away prized possessions—can make a difference in another person's life. At the end of the book, Clay does exactly that, coming out of his shell to approach another outcast at risk of self-destruction.

Paul Volponi's *Crossing Lines* employs a more traditional storytelling technique: a tale told from the viewpoint of a single conflicted character. The novel is dedicated to "those who are brave enough to set aside what they've been told and decide for themselves what is right." The lines referred to in the title relate both to the lines on a football field (the main character is a football player) and to lines drawn in culture regarding what constitutes masculinity.

The narrator of the story is Adonis, a six-foot-two senior varsity football lineman. He is in classes with several football teammates, who taunt a small, effeminate newcomer, Alan Harspring. Team quarterback Ethan, who used to tease Adonis when Adonis was overweight, demonstrates that he is also homophobic. While Adonis does not go along with taunting Alan, neither does he speak out against it.

Snide comments increase in frequency after Alan is elected president of the otherwise all-female Fashion Club. Members of the club include Adonis's younger sister Jeannie and Melody Singer, a pretty senior Adonis has dated, who asks him to protect Alan from the other jocks. The Fashion Club sometimes meets at Adonis's home, causing tension with his homophobic father, a firefighter. Adonis himself is conflicted about his own attitude toward Alan, and feels as if he is "balanced on a tightrope." His tension increases when Alan takes to wearing lipstick and dresses. Jeannie points out to her brother the hypocrisy of homophobia among "butt-slapping, crotch-grabbing football players who shower together."

In English class Adonis, Alan, and two girls become teammates for an assignment to research Cincinnati, Ohio, for the purpose of creating a potential new sports team. For inspiration, the ponytailed teacher hands out a Walt Whitman poem with suggestive implications: "Are you the new person drawn to me?" In gym class, where clumsy Adonis is trying to improve agility, Alan shows him the proper way to skip rope, and Adonis afterward also becomes the butt of jokes.

Eventually the situation comes to a head. A corps of football players plans to attack and humiliate Alan during a fashion show to be held at a local mall as part of a pep rally for a school football game. Though Adonis knows the plan in advance, he does nothing to prevent it. When the attack begins and Alan is knocked out, however, Adonis takes a stand: he fights against the football players, who are arrested and suspended. Though he appears a hero, Adonis feels ashamed. He visits the hospital to beg for forgiveness, and shakes hands with his friend, who reintroduces herself as Alana.

Conclusions

Collected scholarly explorations reveal that bullying is common throughout the world. At least 50 percent (ranging as high as 80 percent in some locations) of all children will be victims of some form of bullying at some point during their K–12 years; at least 10 percent will be chronic victims. Bullying often starts in kindergarten, intensifies during the middle grades, and becomes routine during high school.

Both girls and boys are equally likely to be perpetrators or targets for regular abuse. Male abusers usually operate alone, or in the company of hangers-on or sidekicks. Such accomplices encourage their destructive behavior, which typically involves intimidation via actual or threatened physical violence directed at targets of both sexes chosen for perceived differences (such as ethnicity, religion, physical appearance, or language). Female abusers often work in groups, preferring verbal and emotional weapons primarily against other girls of different social status. With the ready availability of modern electronic devices, both sexes employ the anonymity of cyberbullying to post text and photos intended to embarrass the victim and ruin his or her reputation. Regardless of who carries out bullying, and the methods used, the object is the same: to harm, demean, and humiliate. The results are fairly predictable: victims of peer abuse often demonstrate low self-esteem, feelings of isolation, difficulties in socializing, and symptoms of depression, all factors that can contribute to self-harm or suicide when there is no positive support in place. Because virtually all young adults have been exposed to bullying at some point in their lives—as perpetrator, victim, or observer—it has been, and will continue to be, a popular subject for fiction.

Bullying will also remain a topic of interest in literature as adolescents transition to adulthood. Though traditionally associated with school, bullying also commonly occurs in a variety of other environments. Blue-collar jobs and military installations where male populations dominate, for example, often experience a high incidence of physical bullying in combination with other tactics to neutralize competitors and curry favor with superiors. In white-collar (medical, legal, academic, corporate, and professional business) workplaces, bullying methods are usually more subtle and covert. Bullies in such occupations employ a variety of shrewd verbal and psychological tactics, such as rumor, suggestion, gossip, and manipulation of facts, to adversely affect the performance of perceived rivals. By causing enough discomfort to bring down someone else, the perpetrator creates an opportunity to rise within the organization. All such situations provide authors with fertile material for fiction.

Jack Ewing

Further Reading

Bond, Gwenda. "Books against Bullies." *Publishers Weekly*. PWxyz, 18 Oct. 2013. Web. 24 June 2015. <http://www.publishersweekly.com/pw/by-topic/childrens/childrens-book-news/article/59616-books-against-bullies-self-help-2013.html>.

Koehler, Elizabeth. "The Silent Message: Professional Journals' Failure to Address LGBTQ Issues." *Journal of Research on Libraries and Young Adults*. YALSA, Summer 2011. Web. 24 June 2015. <http://www.yalsa.ala.org/jrlya/2011/08/the-silent-message-professional-journals%E2%80%99-failure-to-address-lgbtq-issues/>.

Bibliography

Englander, Elizabeth Kandel. *Bullying and Cyberbullying: What Every Educator Needs to Know*. Cambridge: Harvard Education P, 2013. Print.

Hirsch, Lee, and Cynthia Lowen. *Bully: An Action Plan for Teachers, Parents, and Communities to Combat the Bullying Crisis*. New York: Weinstein, 2012. Print.

Martocci, Laura. *Bullying: The Social Destruction of Self*. Philadelphia: Temple UP, 2015. Print.

Olweus, Dan. *Bullying at School: What We Know and What We Can Do*. Hoboken: Wiley, 1993. Print.

Subramanian, Mathangi. *Bullying: The Ultimate Teen Guide*. Lanham: Rowman, 2014. Print. It Happened to Me.

Walton, Alice G. "The Psychological Effects of Bullying Last Well into Adulthood, Study Finds." *Forbes.* Forbes, 21 Feb. 2013. Web. 25 June 2015. <http://www.forbes.com/sites/alicegwalton/2013/02/21/the-psychological-effects-of-bullying-last-well-into-adulthood-study-finds/>.

Choices and Transitions

Titles Discussed

The Sin-Eater's Confession by Ilsa J. Bick
Please Ignore Vera Dietz by A. S. King
A Step from Heaven by An Na
Jumped by Rita Williams-Garcia

Thematic Overview

The theme of choices and transitions is central to young adult literature in America. Young adults are aware they may be required to make life-altering choices that could affect them as they transition from child to adult. Literature featuring a young adult protagonist who experiences change and transition can often resonate with certain key aspects in a reader's life, reinforcing the importance of the overall theme. It is the belief in the ability to make independent choices that has shaped the American national self-concept, starting in late childhood and moving into and through adulthood, allowing people to affect their own destiny.

Since the idea of choices and transitions is so central a theme in American culture and literature, it is no surprise that some of the first literary works that appealed to a young adult readership in America, like Mark Twain's *The Adventures of Tom Sawyer* (1876) and its sequel, *The Adventures of Huckleberry Finn* (1884), helped to give this theme a central place. Theme remains a critical factor in deciding whether books appeal to a young adult readership. In Betty Smith's *A Tree Grows in Brooklyn* (1943), the theme's centrality helped make the novel and its popular teenage protagonist, Francie Nolan, a runaway success with young adult readers.

Young adults continued to like and read books that featured young protagonists making difficult choices and transitions, even though these novels were not yet specifically marketed to them. J. D. Salinger's *The Catcher in the Rye* (1951) and S. E. Hinton's *The Outsiders* (1967), with troubled teenager Ponyboy Curtis, appealed to young readers.

In young adult fiction, its own literary category since the 1970s, social, cultural, and political events have shaped the kind of choices faced by teenage protagonists. In Rita Williams-Garcia's *Jumped* (2010), African American teenage protagonist Leticia Moore confronts the issue of female-on-female violence in American schools. An Na's *A Step from Heaven* (2001) looks at the choices faced by protagonist Young Ju Park as she transitions from a four-year-old Korean immigrant to a college-bound American high school graduate. Finally, Young Ju has to make a choice regarding domestic violence, which can be seen as a key contemporary social problem in American society. In Ilsa J. Bick's *The Sin-Eater's Confession* (2013), white protagonist Ben observes the hate-crime murder of his gay friend, Jimmy. The novel relates to such real-life hate crimes as the fatal assault in 1998 on Matthew Shepard, a gay college student, and the murder of Arthur "J. R." Warren, a gay man, by two male teenagers, in 2000. Ben, who is not gay, must decide if he will tell the authorities what he knows about the death of his friend, but the truth comes at a price to Ben, who fears being linked romantically to his deceased friend. Similarly, Vera Dietz, the protagonist in A. S. King's *Please Ignore Vera Dietz*, witnesses a disturbing scene, on the night her former friend, Charlie Kahn, dies. Charlie hurt and humiliated Vera while the two were in high school, and now Vera agonizes over telling the authorities the truth—which would restore Charlie's good name and punish the culprit who set a pet store ablaze.

In these four young adult novels discussed below, the protagonists must make painful choices as they transition from adolescence into adulthood. Each transition brings a different outcome. All together, these four novels illustrate the ongoing importance of the theme of choices and transitions in contemporary American young adult literature.

Works

In Rita Williams-Garcia's *Jumped* (2010), three teenage girls, Leticia, Dominique, and Trina, attend a New York City high school and make choices that in two cases effect a transition in their lives. Each has made her own choices leading up to the crucial decisions that form the narrative's turning point, and each tells the story from her perspective.

Leticia Moore is in the hallway at school when she overhears Dominique Duncan threaten to attack Trina.

Leticia must then decide either to warn Trina of the impending attack or to say nothing. Leticia has chosen to take high school and life as easy as possible, resulting in her assignment to a remedial morning geometry class, which she resents. One morning, Leticia sees the pretty, overconfident, and bouncy sophomore Trina, who loves creating art, walk through the middle of a group of sophomores that includes Dominique Duncan, a benched basketball player. As Trina sees it, "I ease through these girls." Dominique sees this as a personal affront. She mentally accuses Trina of moving "like she don't see I'm here and all the space around me is mines." To her two sidekicks, Dominique vows to beat up Trina after school is over. The conversation is overheard by Leticia but warning Trina would go against Leticia's previous choice of not getting involved at school.

Jumped makes it clear that Dominique is very angry about being unable to play in the high school basketball games because she is failing to maintain academic standards and playing on the basketball team is everything for this "all-ball girl." Dominique chooses to reject the clear-cut instructions of her coach: "Kick up your grades and I'll play you." Leticia decides not to warn Trina about the impending attack, and Dominique ends up hurting Trina so badly in the after-school fight that she is hospitalized and in need of "reconstructive surgeries." Trina has now transitioned from a carefree, spunky sophomore into a traumatized victim of violence. Dominique has become a juvenile delinquent. Six months after the attack on Trina, Leticia sees Dominique on TV, unrepentant, at a correctional facility. Only Leticia makes no transition, continuing to live her complacent life.

Williams-Garcia's characters in *Jumped* diverges from her characters in her earlier novels, who make the right choice, whereas both Dominique and Leticia make the wrong choice. In *Blue Tights* (1988), African American protagonist Joyce Collins is cut from ballet, much as Dominique is benched. Yet Collins finds artistic and personal fulfillment joining an African dance troupe. In *Like Sisters on the Homefront* (1995), Williams-Garcia gives her fourteen-year-old African American protagonist Gayle a great-grandmother who helps her to make positive choices.

In An Na's Michael L. Printz Award–winning novel *A Step from Heaven* (2001), Young Ju Park transitions from a four-year-old girl, unable to make decisions for herself, to a college-bound teenager, capable of making hard personal choices.

In the beginning of the novel, Young Ju's parents make the choice to emigrate from South Korea to the United States. Young Ju's mother, Uhmma, who is pregnant, tells four-year-old Young Ju that in America "you can grow up to be anything you want." Her brother, Joon Ho Park, is born in America and is favored by their father, Apa.

Initially, when Young Ju and her family come to America, Young Ju lies to please her family and to create a more pleasing fantasy world for herself. Young Ju's mother takes her to get a perm, and when her mother asks if she likes her new, curly hair, she lies and says, "Yes." Young Ju also lies to her friends about where she lives because she is embarrassed by her family's shabby apartment. She tells the parents of her white friend, Amanda, to drop her off in front of a nice home she claims is her family's and then has to walk a few miles back home. This lying gives moral ambiguity to her character.

Young Ju is forced to make her biggest choice when she must call the police after her alcoholic father, in a drunken stupor, violently beats her and her mother. Her choice changes the fate of the family. Uhmma declines to press charges against Apa, but Apa leaves and returns home to Korea. Uhmma buys a home after her husband leaves and Young Ju transitions to college, paying for school with a scholarship. Young Ju's choice to call for help shows her assumption of personal responsibility as she gets older. In the end, the choices Young Ju makes provide more opportunities and a better life for her mother, her brother, and herself.

Throughout Ilsa Bick's *The Sin-Eater's Confession* (2013), the twenty-year-old narrator, Ben, is a Marine Corps medic deployed in Afghanistan who is still agonizing over the wrong choices he made in his senior year at high school. While in high school, Ben decided not to intervene when a hate crime was committed against his gay friend, Jimmy, in a deserted Wisconsin state park. The night of Jimmy's death, Ben was to meet Jimmy in the parking lot of a coffee shop; however, when Ben arrived at the coffee shop parking lot, he saw Jimmy get into a car with an unidentified person in a hoodie. Ben decides to follow the car and witnesses a group of people beat Jimmy to death in the park. After the murder, Ben stays silent and does not share his observations with the police. He blames himself for Jimmy's death, thinking, "I had let Jimmy die alone." This choice makes Ben feel guilty, but he makes it nonetheless because he fears being linked romantically to Jimmy. Jimmy may have had sexual feelings for Ben, but Ben adamantly declares, "I'm not gay."

Ben tells the story of his choices and of the impact of those choices in an unaddressed letter. Bick uses long, confessional flashbacks to structure the plot of *The Sin-Eater's Confession*; this is the same structure she employed in her book *Drowning Instinct* (2012). In his letters, Ben writes that his choice to befriend Jimmy forced him to make difficult choices. Jimmy confesses his desire for Ben, but Ben does not reciprocate those feelings, and he decides to end their friendship.

The ending of Bick's novel is left open. Ben still has a choice to tell the truth but does not say whether, or to whom, he might send his confessional letter. Ben considers himself the eater of sins. He feels that by serving his country as a Marine he is atoning for his sins and those of his community.

A. S. King's *Please Ignore Vera Dietz* revolves around the central choice that Vera Dietz has to make as she transitions into her senior year at high school. In September, Vera attends the funeral of her former best friend, Charlie Kahn. Vera feels resentful that her "best friend [is] dying after he screws [her] over." Silently, Vera blames Charlie's new girlfriend, Jenny Flick, as "the reason he's dead." Vera has information about Charlie's death: he was unjustly blamed for setting a pet store on fire. Yet, because Charlie hurt her, Vera is unwilling to tell the truth and to clear Charlie's name.

As Vera ponders whether or not to share this knowledge, King tells the story of Vera's transition from a twelve-year-old girl to a high school senior through a series of flashbacks. These flashbacks are occasionally interrupted by chapters from the viewpoint of Vera's thirty-something-year-old father, Ken, and the ominous Pagoda, an abandoned restaurant. The voice of the Pagoda resembles a Greek chorus. This technique foreshadows that of King's later novel *Everybody Sees the Ants* (2011), where the ants provide a Pagoda-like commentary. The deceased Charlie also speaks in the novel, insisting, "I didn't have a choice" in the events leading to his death.

After agonizing for nine months, Vera finally decides to clear Charlie's name. Vera's father brings her to the local police to make her statement. Vera tells the police that Jenny torched the pet shop because Charlie decided to break up with her. After her statement, Vera feels she has transitioned from the coward "invisible Vera Dietz to invincible Vera Dietz."

Together, the four protagonists of the four novels mirror a large spectrum of what young adults may or may not do when faced with making a tough choice. At first, all four choose to stay silent in the face of some dark events. This reflects the pressure to keep silent, experienced by many young readers. Eventually, faced with making a choice, some of the four characters act differently. Their choices are embedded in a wide range of contemporary social and personal issues. In the end, Young Ju makes the courageous call to the police to report her abusive father, and similarly, Vera goes to the police with her father, Ken. Each has transitioned into a responsible young adult, a moral choice. In *The Sin-Eater's Confession,* Bick deliberately leaves the novel open-ended as to whether or not Ben decides to mail his letter and share his dark knowledge. Leticia is a weaker character than the rest. She chooses to remain silent and fails to accept responsibility. All four characters illustrate how powerful, central and appealing the theme of choices and transitions is for young adult literature in America.

Conclusions

Among American scholars, there is a general consensus that the themes of choices and transitions are central to young adult literature; it gives this fiction greater cultural relevance and helps to form a strong background for analysis. For instance, Crag Hill, in his essay "Dystopian Novels" sees this happening in the science-fiction genre, where the story is a "typical coming-of-age trope in young adult literature." Hill also says that teenagers are "making choices on their own terms with full awareness of the positive and negative consequences." These choices affect not only the literary characters themselves but their communities as well.

Michael Cart, senior editor and former president of the Young Adult Library Services Association, expresses a similarly positive conviction regarding the persistence of these themes. In his 2012 book *Young Adult Literature: From Romance to Realism*, Cart explains that in young adult literature the range of subject matter is becoming more daring, and the form in which young adult fiction is presented, including graphic novels or e-books, has and will change. Yet the themes of choices and transitions will remain a key defining element of young adult fiction, and it will keep its cultural significance in America.

Scholarly guides used for teaching young adult literature emphasize how important and useful the themes of choices and transitions can be. This view is expressed, both explicitly and implicitly, in such major guides as late Kenneth Donelson's *Literature for Today's Young Adults* (2012) and Carl Tomlinson's *Essentials of Young Adult Literature* (2014).

Scholars continue to discuss how the key themes of choices and transitions are at the cutting edge of new movements in American culture and literature. For example, in the essay "Out of the Closet and into the Open," Laura Renzi, Mark Letcher, and Kristen Miraglia praise young adult novels featuring alternative sexual transitions experienced by teenage characters. The three scholars suggest that American young adult literature will "continue to push the boundaries for possible transitions of their characters in the future."

R. C. Lutz, PhD

Further Reading

Hayn, Judith A., and Jeffrey S. Kaplan. *Teaching Young Adult Literature Today: Insights, Considerations, and Perspectives for the Classroom Teacher.* Lanham: Rowman, 2012. Print.

Tomlinson, Carl M., and Carol Lynch-Brown. *Essentials of Young Adult Literature.* Boston: Pearson, 2007. Print.

Trupe, Alice. *Thematic Guide to Young Adult Literature.* Westport: Greenwood, 2006. Print.

Bibliography

Cart, Michael. *Young Adult Literature: From Romance to Realism*, 2010. Chicago: ALA, 2011. Print.

Cole, Pam Burress. *Young Adult Literature in the Twenty-first Century.* Boston: McGraw, 2009. Print.

Donelson, Kenneth, and Alleen Pace Nilsen. *Literature for Today's Young Adults.* Glenview: Scott, 1980. Print.

Hill, Crag. *The Critical Merits of Young Adult Literature.* New York: Routledge, 2014. Print.

Tribunella, Eric. *Melancholia and Maturation: The Use of Trauma in American Children's Literature.* Knoxville: U of Tennessee P, 2010. Print.

Wolf, Shelby Anne. *Handbook of Research on Children's and Young Adult Literature.* New York: Routledge, 2011. Print.

Younger, Beth. *Learning Curves: Body Image and Female Sexuality in Young Adult Literature.* Lanham: Scarecrow P, 2009. Print.

Death, Illness, and Loss

Titles Discussed

Conversion by Katherine Howe
The Fault in Our Stars by John Green
Going Bovine by Libba Bray

Thematic Overview

Literature is rich with stories about what it feels like to lose a loved one. In Roman poet Ovid's *Metamorphoses* (8 CE), Niobe offends the gods and suffers the loss of her fourteen children and her husband as punishment. Overwhelmed by her grief, she turns to stone. In English poet and playwright William Shakespeare's *Hamlet* (1603), the title character wishes for the opposite after the death of his father. "O that this too too solid flesh would melt / Thaw and resolve itself into dew!" he says, when, after almost two months, his mother asks him why he cannot just move on already. Grief for the dead is a force that shapes the living, and people have developed a wide range of images to express it.

But what of the dying? Societal attitudes toward death and dying—particularly in regard to those who are dying not from old age but from illness—have evolved since the days of Shakespeare and Ovid, when superstition informed both the medical treatment of the dying person and how the dying person was treated by the healthy. Just as Niobe's actions brought about the death of her family, so too must there be a reason why people were stricken by disease, the thinking went. Even into the twentieth century in the United States, terminal diseases such as cancer, particularly breast cancer in women, were considered taboo. In the 1980s the AIDS epidemic ravaged the country, disproportionately killing gay men, and outdated ideas about human sexuality and ignorance about how the virus was spread exacerbated the spread of the human immunodeficiency virus that causes the disease. It was not until the media began publicizing the cases of "blameless" victims, such as those who had acquired the disease from a blood transfusion and heterosexual women who had gotten it from their husbands, that major efforts were made to study the treatment of AIDS and disseminate information on its prevention. In 2014 an outbreak of the deadly Ebola virus in West Africa caused panic in the United States, where only a few cases were reported and, ultimately, successfully treated.

Illness may be frightening, but for most, it is not unfamiliar. As Susan Sontag wrote in *Illness as Metaphor* (1978), "Illness is the night-side of life, a more onerous citizenship. Everyone who is born holds dual citizenship, in the kingdom of the well and in the kingdom of the sick. Although we all prefer to use only the good passport, sooner or later each of us is obliged, at least for a spell, to identify ourselves as citizens of that other place." In regards to cancer, the American Cancer Society estimated that more than 1.6 million new cases of cancer would be diagnosed in the United States in 2015—more people than live in the city of San Diego, California, which had a population of 1.3 million as of 2013. Given the number of people with a history of cancer—an estimated 13.7 million people in the United States in 2012—most people know someone who has had or has died from cancer. So many people are afflicted, in fact, that appropriate narratives have been fashioned about the treatment of the disease. Cancer is a battle to be won, as the popular narrative goes, and positivity and courage are the most effective weapons.

The novel *The Fault in Our Stars* (2012) by John Green challenges this narrative by focusing on what novelist Gayle Forman called, in an article for *Time* magazine in February 2015, "the messy stuff of human mortality." It also explores deeper philosophical questions, one of which provides the centerpiece of the novel *Going Bovine* (2009) by Libba Bray. Bray's surrealist tale, based on Miguel de Cervantes's *Don Quixote* (1605–15), explores the nature of reality and deals with the question of what happens to a person's mind when he or she dies. Meanwhile, the illness in Katherine Howe's novel *Conversion* (2014) is not terminal, but it does provide the opportunity to examine the interplay between illness and societal attitudes toward certain groups of people (in this case, teenaged girls).

Works

The mysterious affliction at the heart of Katherine Howe's novel *Conversion* is not terminal, but thanks to its unknown origins, it is arguably just as frightening as one that is. Howe based one of the novel's two intertwining plots on a 2012 case in which a number of teenage girls in Le Roy, New York, were stricken with a strange ailment that caused them to suffer from uncontrollable physical tics, such as twitching and flailing. According to an article by Susan Dominus in the

New York Times in March 2012, one girl could not stop hitting herself in the face with her cell phone. In real life, as in Howe's telling, the diagnosis is something called conversion disorder: the girls were converting mental and emotional stress, doctors argued, into actual physical symptoms. "And because so many students were afflicted with similar symptoms, it was also considered to be mass psychogenic illness, which is another way of saying mass hysteria," Dominus wrote. The conclusion seemed fishy to Howe. When she first heard the story, she immediately thought of a similar "affliction" from the past: the ailments suffered by a handful of young women in Salem, Massachusetts, in the late 1600s, who claimed to be possessed by witches. The fictionalized testimony of Ann Putnam, the only one of the girls to admit that the witch trials began with a ruse, provides the second thread of *Conversion*.

Howe's novel is less about the illness itself than what the illusion that illness affords the privileged high school students in her story, as well as the more unfortunate pilgrims of the Salem witch trials. Books dealing with serious physical illness also touch on the ways in which the protagonists are treated differently because they are ill. In *The Fault in Our Stars*, protagonist Hazel Grace Lancaster sardonically refers to certain gestures as "Cancer Perks." For example, a flight attendant happily pours Hazel and her boyfriend Gus a glass of champagne even though they are not of legal drinking age. In *Going Bovine*, the protagonist, Cameron, is reviled at his high school. When he is diagnosed with a terminal illness, the same students who taunted him throw him a pep rally.

In *Conversion*, the young girls of old Salem lead thankless lives of servitude. They are invisible, particularly to the town elders who use them physically (the girls hardly ever sleep for all their labor) and, as Howe suggests at one point, sexually. For these young women, "illness" was a remedy for their powerlessness. Their illness was a way of being seen. The modern girls of Salem (Howe sets her Le Roy–inspired tale in the town) are similarly damned and exalted, though their plight is vastly different from that of Ann and her ilk. Twenty-first-century teenage girls are crumbling under societal pressures to succeed, Howe argues, and when they stumble they are accused of being hysterical.

John Green's novel *The Fault in Our Stars* has been included in a subgenre known as "sick-lit," but to label his complex tale about two teenagers diagnosed with cancer as such does it a disservice. Green defies nearly all of the genre's tropes, taking particular aim at its most sacred: the one in which the dying person is a hero in the battle that is disease. Green prefers to focus on the essential humanness of his characters rather than create mythologies around them. "I think generally we have a habit of imagining the very sick or the dying as being kind of fundamentally other," he told Rebecca J. Rosen for the *Atlantic* magazine in February 2013. "I guess I wanted to argue for their humanity, their complete humanity." In doing so, Green builds a powerful picture of love and loss. Most people—over half of Americans—die in a hospital or another institution such as hospice. For many of those people, these settings leave much to be desired. In *Going Bovine*, an old woman complains of her sterile surroundings, saying, "This is not how I'm supposed to die." When the protagonist asks her how she is supposed to die, she replies, "In a house by the sea in an upstairs bedroom." Hospitals and bodily fluids are prevalent in *The Fault in Our Stars*—toward the end of his life, Gus has a tube inserted into his stomach—as are the mundaneness and disappointment inherent to living with a terminal disease.

For Hazel and Gus, every day is not a battle won; every day is another day. The tension between their desire to be "normal" teenagers and their extraordinary circumstances gives the story its texture and a layer of fundamental truth. Hazel's experience, buoyed by Green's honesty, does not jive with popular cancer narratives. While Gus is preoccupied with all of things he will never be, Hazel is happy, or at least content, to work with what she has. She has made her peace with the fact that most people do not die the way they would have wanted to die and may not even be remembered for the things they want to be remembered for, and she encourages Gus to adopt the same outlook.

However, Hazel's philosophical attitude toward her own death does not protect her from the pain of losing a loved one. Green applies as much realism to this experience as to that of the illness itself. Hazel watches the disingenuous Facebook condolences pour in when Gus dies and, at his funeral, kisses his "plasticized" face. But before all that, she dreads the phone call in the middle of the night, and when she finally gets it she feels an unbearable and suffocating pain. "Every second worse than the last," she says. Green uses iconic imagery to describe her indescribable pain, the only "ten" on the pain scale she has ever felt. "And here it was," she says, "the great and terrible ten, slamming me again and again as I lay still and alone in my bed staring at the ceiling, the waves tossing me against the rocks then pulling me back out to sea so they could launch me again into the jagged face of the cliff, leaving me floating faceup on the water, undrowned." For Hazel (as for Niobe and Hamlet before her) the death of a loved one feels like almost dying but not quite.

Libba Bray's *Going Bovine* takes a central theme of *The Fault in Our Stars* and pushes it to the outer limits of thought. In *Stars*, Hazel muses on her and Gus's big trip to Amsterdam that it will be the first and only time she sees the beautiful city. Hazel and Gus share a deep love for one another, and together, they get to share new and incredible experiences with their limited time. But Cameron, the protagonist of *Going Bovine*, does not even have a real friend. However, over the course of the book, he travels to distant places and forges romantic and friendly relationships without ever leaving his hospital bed. Cameron suffers from a rare disease called Creutzfeldt-Jakob disease, a transmissible spongiform encephalopathy similar to mad cow disease. The illness literally eats away at his brain, causing him to hallucinate giants made out of fire, a hooded knight wielding a sword, and an angel with torn fishnet stockings and pink hair. These illusions are very real to Cameron, and as his illness progresses, the line between reality and hallucination is blurred. Bray weaves together an impressive array of images from Cameron's real world to construct his fantasy, but some of the most notable additions are scientific concepts such as the theory of quantum physics, which says, in part, that you can be in two places at the same time. As Cameron builds the relationships he never did in life, Bray suggests that the adventures people take in their minds are just as significant as the ones they take with their bodies.

Going Bovine also employs a trope common to science fiction and fantasy and rooted in philosophy of Swiss psychologist Carl Jung, in which the thing a person fears is actually a version of him or herself. In *Bovine*, Cameron is chased by a specter he calls the Wizard of Reckoning. When the Wizard takes off his hood at the end of the book, Cameron sees that the Wizard has his (Cameron's) face. The same concept provides the backbone for the plot of *A Wizard of Earthsea* (1968) by Ursula K. Le Guin, in which the hero is trailed by a Shadow of his darker deeds. In *The Amber Spyglass* (2000), the third book of Philip Pullman's His Dark Materials trilogy, each character discovers that they are followed, throughout their entire life, by their own personal Death embodied in a haunted-looking person cowering just out of reach.

The "death-with-my-face" trope encompasses both intimacy (like a friend) and fear (like a murderer), which perhaps accurately describes people's relationship with their inevitable deaths. Like Bray, Pullman employs scientific concepts such as the multiverse to explain the mysterious nature of reality. Both authors imagine death as one among the infinite universes, wrought with classical imagery. Pullman's land of the dead is accessible by boat—harkening back the River Styx, the body of water that the ancient Greeks imagined separated Earth from the underworld. Bray's concept of death, too, features boats and a river, but with a modern twist: it looks, to Cameron, curiously like the It's a Small World river ride at Walt Disney World.

Conclusion

As evidenced by these three novels, modern young adult literature is moving toward a more honest portrayal of death, illness, and dying—though the theme itself is not new. The star-crossed lovers of Shakespeare's *Romeo and Juliet* (1597) commit suicide, as does an acquaintance of Holden Caulfield in J. D. Salinger's 1951 novel *Catcher in the Rye*, an event that sets the teenager on his existential drift through New York City. In Katherine Paterson's classic 1977 novel, *Bridge to Terabithia*, a young boy grapples with the sudden death by drowning of his best friend, and there is an entire subgenre of young adult literature, derisively termed "sick-lit," that deals with terminal illness. But for every book like Sylvia Plath's *The Bell Jar* (1963), a semiautobiographical narrative about mental illness, there are many more that avoid the subject or dealt with it less honestly. Most books about teenagers, until the late 1960s, favored plot over emotional truth. In early serial books featuring teens, such as Nancy Drew and the Hardy Boys, characters never aged, much less got sick or died, and if a peripheral character really did die, it was usually done offstage. When not ignored completely, death was usually treated melodramatically, as in Louisa May Alcott's *Little Women* (1868–69), where young Beth does not so much die as ascend to heaven in a haze of purity and goodness. In the 1980s and 1990s, young adult literature was largely educational. Characters died, but most often they did so as a warning or a lesson, having brought death on themselves by making mistakes such as drinking and driving or taking drugs.

In the twenty-first century, authors are pushing the boundaries of the genre by tackling more complicated subject matter. The novels discussed above are not merely about death and illness. They portray how the sick are both exalted and damned, how a departure from the familiar tropes of "sick-lit" can uncover deeper truths about the process of dying, and how questions regarding the physical bounds of reality can help people gain a better understanding of death. Like any adult reader, teenagers look to literature to apply meaning to seemingly meaningless events. Why do people fall ill? Why does society at large ostracize people who suffer? And why do people have to die? The three books discussed in this article—which could not, on the surface, be more different from one another—seek to address these questions in their own unique ways. The "dark" themes pervading young adult literature, Forman wrote, are really "about life," and how catharsis and a better of understanding of death can enhance the experience of being alive.

Molly Hagan

Further Reading

Wallis, Rupert. "Why Death Is So Important in YA Fiction." *Guardian*. Guardian News and Media, 18 Aug. 2014. Web. 13 May 2015. <http://www.theguardian.com/childrens-books-site/2014/aug/18/death-important-young adult-fiction-rupert-wallis>.

Wilson, Laura W. "Helping Adolescents Understand Death and Dying through Literature." *English Journal* 73.7 (1984): 78–82. Print.

Bibliography

Dominus, Susan. "What Happened to the Girls in Le Roy." *New York Times*. New York Times, 7 Mar. 2012. Web. 13 May 2015. <http://www.nytimes.com/2012/03/11/magazine/teenage-girls-twitching-le-roy.html>.

Green, John. "How John Green Wrote a Cancer Book but Not a 'Bullsh*t Cancer Book.'" Interview by Rebecca J. Rosen. *Atlantic*. Atlantic Monthly, 25 Feb.

2013. Web. 13 May 2015. <http://www.theatlantic.com/entertainment/archive/2013/02/how-john-green-wrote-a-cancer-book-but-not-a-bullshit-cancer-book/273441/>.

Forman, Gayle. "Teens Crave Young Adult Books on Really Dark Topics (And That's OK)." *Time*. Time, 6 Feb. 2015. Web. 13 May 2015. <http://time.com/3697845/if-i-stay-gayle-forman-young adult-i-was-here/>.

Depression, Mental Illness, and Suicide

Titles Discussed

Chinese Handcuffs by Chris Crutcher
Impulse by Ellen Hopkins
It's Kind of a Funny Story by Ned Vizzini

Thematic Overview

For many years, publishers and writers considered the topic of suicide to be taboo for young adult literature, fearing that open discussions of the subject would lead to suicidal ideation and imitations among young readers. Contributing to this belief was the lack of common knowledge about mental illness and depression, particularly among young adults. Established medical and psychiatric professionals experimented with new treatments on patients through the twentieth century, yet quite a few of the treatments were problematic, even damaging. While classic novels like Sylvia Plath's *The Bell Jar* (1963) and J. D. Salinger's *The Catcher in the Rye* (1951) featured teenage protagonists struggling with mental illness, it was not until the 1990s that the public began to have a better general understanding of mental health. This knowledge helped to create more diverse and mature young adult novels and also created a body of literature in which adolescent mental illness was regularly portrayed with nuance.

Mental illness often appears early in life, and half of the people who struggle with it first experience their illness by the age of fourteen. This means that for many people, the appearance of mental illness comes during adolescence and is complicated by confusion, rapid mental and physical changes, and increased social pressure from that time period in the person's life. One of the most common questions in all young adult literature asks what it means for an individual to form a self-identity. When mental illness enters the equation, however, a protagonist can encounter a major additional hurtle as their emerging self-identity suddenly becomes untrustworthy due to symptoms of depression and anxiety, particularly in social situations.

Of course, the definition of mental illness is incredibly broad and is regularly being updated and refined by mental health professionals. A teenager living with obsessive-compulsive disorder faces very different challenges than a teenager living with low-level depression or schizophrenia. Likewise, depression can be caused by a chemical imbalance in the brain or societal and personal factors, among them stress and trauma. Similarly, while suicide is often attributed to mental illness in teenagers, it can also be the result of physical or sexual abuse, or of societal exclusion.

Young adult literature that addresses themes of mental illness, depression, and suicide does its best when it addresses the condition on multiple levels—biological, cultural, personal, and medical. Chris Crutcher's *Chinese Handcuffs* (1989), for instance, explores the intersections of mental illness, suicide, and rape; while Ellen Hopkin's *Impulse* (2007) features three teenagers who have attempted suicide for different reasons, and must learn to live with one another in the context of a mental institution. Ned Vizzini's *It's Kind of a Funny Story* (2006) partially takes place in a psychiatric care facility, and his book uses the protagonist's mental illness to explore peer and academic pressure and mental illness. All three novels feature characters who experience their mental illness as one aspect of their complex lives, and who face questions of what it means to live with mental illness or depression (or the reality of the suicide of a loved one) as conditions that might well be present throughout their lives.

Works

Chinese Handcuffs features two main characters, Dillon and Jennifer. Both characters have mental health issues rooted in traumatic violence and abuse, and both are star athletes who throw themselves into physical activity as a way to escape their own problems. Dillon's older brother, Preston, has recently committed suicide, and throughout the novel, Dillon writes him a series of letters in an attempt to process the loss. Dillon is shocked by his brother's death, and while processing his grief over the loss of his brother, Dillon becomes close friends with Jennifer. Jennifer shares her own trauma with him, revealing that she was sexually abused by her father at a young age and is now continually abused and raped by her stepfather, who is a prominent and respected community figure. Jennifer plans to flee her family with her younger sister, but when Jennifer's mother announces that she is pregnant with a baby girl (a child who will inevitably experience the same trauma and abuse), Jennifer attempts suicide instead. Dillon, unwilling to lose another person to suicide, promises Jennifer a better future and captures photographic evidence of the stepfather abusing Jennifer, and uses the evidence to drive him out of town.

The novel alternates between the first-person narration of Dillon and the wandering and omniscient third-person narration, a technique that shows the difference between the interior worlds of the characters and the external worlds of the school and the family. While mental illness can presents itself in obvious ways to the outside observer, it is also possible that depression, anxiety, and suicidal thoughts (especially those caused by trauma) can remain invisible or obscured, even to close friends and family members. We see the first clear instance of this after a third-person scene in which Dillon writes a letter to his deceased brother, after completing a triathlon. The letter from Dillon to Preston reveals that Dillon feels he cannot share his story with anyone but his deceased brother. While people expect him to crumble under the sorrow and trauma of witnessing the suicide, he instead decides to present strength, saying that to share his story would only burden those he cares about further. This letter also references an incident with a cat, which Dillon attempts to brush off. Once the novel returns to third-person narration, the cat incident is portrayed in gruesome detail through a flashback, with Dillon and Preston violently killing the animal, and with brief glimpses into Dillon's mind showing how Dillon was traumatized by this event.

For Dillon to process his brother's death, he turns outward and engages with another teenager who lives with mental illness—in this case, Jennifer. Again, the alternating narratives are used to show that the reality of Jennifer's trauma-induced mental illness is discordant with the way others perceive her. For instance, after Jennifer's basketball team wins a game, her coach observes how incredibly tough she is, yet in Jennifer's own mind, she feels weak and recalls that the last time she felt safe was when she was five years old, before the sexual abuse began. Jennifer and Dillon are both like the titular metaphor of the Chinese handcuffs, trying so hard to survive and appear normal that they only fixate further on their traumas and fall deeper in their depression and anxiety. When Jennifer and Dillon connect and share their stories with each other, they perform the "relaxing" of the Chinese handcuffs, as they are finally able to release some of that pressure. In this way, each character has affirmed the importance of sharing and overcoming the effects of mental illness. Jennifer and Dillon find happiness only when they can share their stories with others.

Craig, the protagonist of *It's Kind of a Funny Story*, likewise experiences mental health issues that are inseparable from other factors in his life—in his case, the stress of a high-performance high school. After earning admission into the Executive Pre-Professional High School in Brooklyn, Craig feels socially alienated while struggling with extraordinarily high expectations and daily homework. He must also watch the girl he loves, Nia, begin a relationship with his best friend. Against the advice of his psychiatrist, Craig stops taking his antidepressant medicine and manages to get by for some time before he becomes suicidal; however, before attempting to end his life he has enough clarity to call a hotline for help. He is admitted to an adult psychiatric care facility, and he forms new friendships with other patients, discovers his love of art, and even turns down Nia when she visits and tries to seduce him. At the end of his short visit to the psychiatric care facility, he is excited to begin a new life and to once more experience the world.

As with the characters in *Chinese Handcuffs*, Craig's mental illness is presented not as a singular issue, but rather as a challenge exacerbated by external factors, among them the social and academic pressures that many teenagers face. Craig does not have a major trauma that he must overcome, but instead he must learn to live with the ongoing reality of his depression through smaller challenges. This is made clear at the start of the novel, when the overlap of academic pressure and his choice to cease taking his medicine initiates the suicide attempt. The fact that it is possible to overcome these challenges is further emphasized by Craig's narrative voice, which finds casual humor in even the darkest moments. After sharing with his therapist that he experiences life as a nightmare he goes on to note, "Cosmic moment, I guess. *Ooooh*, is life really a nightmare? We need to spend like ten seconds contemplating that." This constant levity is an obvious coping mechanism, similar to the letters Dillon writes to his deceased brother, in that both characters are able to acknowledge their deep depression without facing it directly. This humor also carries Craig through his brief stay at the psychiatric facility, where he connects with other residents and provides mutual support, often lightening other people's moods. When he emerges from his stay at the facility, it is clear that proper treatment has not only helped with his mental health, but has also improved other aspects of his life—he now has the confidence to pursue his goals of art school and to reject the shallow advances of Nia, in favor of more rewarding social and romantic connections. By facing his mental health challenges, Craig reshapes his entire life, starting himself on a healthier trajectory.

In contrast to the near-suicides in *Chinese Handcuffs* and *It's Kind of a Funny Story*, *Impulse*, a novel in verse, instead ends with the suicide of the main character, Conner. The novel begins when three teenagers meet in the Aspen Springs psychiatric institution, after they have all attempted suicide. Conner comes from a well-to-do family and faces constant pressure to excel in all aspects of his life; Tony spent years in juvenile detention, after killing the man who molested him as a child; and Vanessa has bipolar disorder and turns to self-mutilation when her family life starts to fall apart. Over the course of the novel, each character receives treatment and begins the long process of overcoming personal challenges, all while having flashbacks of trauma from earlier experiences. When the teens attend the final excursion of their program—a long hike up a mountain—there is both hope and further despair. Conner succumbs to his internal torment and jumps off a cliff to his death, and Tony and Vanessa turn to each other, with Tony wondering whether Vanessa would care if he, too, took his own life.

Impulse places much greater emphasis on the emotional landscape of the main characters, presenting their mental health challenges not as something that they will overcome with the help of medication, positive attitudes, and social support (as with *Chinese Handcuffs* and *It's Kind of a Funny Story*), but instead as difficulties that might overwhelm those characters, costing them their lives. The novel accomplishes this stylistically by alternating between the first-person perspectives of three main characters and by rendering their voices in verse rather than prose. The verse allows the characters' voices to linger on brief and sometimes fleeting thoughts, while also giving those thoughts heightened emphasis, with each chapter only a page or two long.

When Conner finally commits suicide, for instance, the moment itself is relatively ephemeral, with Conner's internal monologue leading him to a realization, as "Suddenly it comes to me, / toes tempted to test the ledge, / that there is a way out of this." While it might be surprising to some readers that Conner succumbs at this exact moment, it is also clear that the suicidal ideation, however fleeting, is also a recurrent and powerful aspect of his daily life.

The characters in these novels encounter a wide range of outcomes, from death and ongoing doubt in *Impulse*, to the optimistic, renewed conclusion of *It's Kind of a Funny Story*. This range of outcomes is appropriate to the range of experiences adolescents will have with mental illness. There is no singular story of mental illness or suicide—instead, there is an incredible diversity in every story. Each is shaped by social realities, personal traumas, brain chemistry, medical and therapeutic interventions, and countless other factors. What young adult readers need, and what these novels provide, are characters who encounter diverse experiences with honesty and candor, and refuse to shy away from tragedy, even as they hope for survival and happiness.

Conclusions

Medically and culturally, our understanding of mental illness continues to evolve at a rapid rate. The treatments for severe depression and anxiety change nearly every decade, while suicide is increasingly understood in the context of social problems (among them homophobia, racism, misogyny, poverty, and abuse) as well as biological health. Young adult literature is no exception, especially as the best writers are aware of and respondent to the most recent developments in the field of mental health. Novels from the 1970s, for instance, would likely feature characters who live with dissociative identity disorder. The characters would be forced to take medication with extremely adverse side effects and would likely struggle to function in society; however, by the late 1990s, advances in care meant that teenagers exhibiting signs of the disorder might instead take medicines with relatively minor side effects, and in turn, might expect to integrate into society.

In the twenty-first century, young adult novels must respond to rapidly changing social conditions. As novels are more likely to tackle mature subject matter, young adult literature is also more likely to feature mental illness and suicide that are linked to rape, sexual abuse, and other major traumas. Some critics take issue with this focus on a subject matter that they see as shocking or "gritty," and argue that such novels (including those listed here) are exploitive of real life tragedies.

Other critics, however, applaud these novels for shedding light on a topic that has long been ignored by society at large. Even established classics like Plath's *The Bell Jar*, for instance, face criticism for their portrayals of mental illness, with the very real topic of depression seen as melodramatic or over-wrought by some readers. The stigma around mental illness is fading, and more and more people are re-alizing that adolescents who exhibit signs of mental illness, depression, or suicidal ideation are not simply being "melodramatic teenagers," but rather are expe-riencing medical conditions and signs of trauma that might well inform the rest of their lives. Although some novels certainly fall into the unfortunate cat-egory of exploiting these complex issues in order to gain readers, the subject on whole deserves urgent and repeated attention, with the best novels evolving as quickly as the medical and cultural conditions that inform them.

T. Fleischmann, MFA

Further Reading

Campbell, Patty. "The Sand in the Oyster." *Horn Book Magazine* 71.1 (1995): 94–98. *Literary Reference Center*. Web. 3 May 2015. <http://search.ebscohost.com/login.aspx?direct=true&db=lfh&AN=9502034361&site=ehost-live>.

Scrofano, Diane. "Not as Crazy as It Seems: Discussing the New YA Literature of Mental Illness in Your Classroom or Library." *Young Adult Library Services* 13.2 (2015): 15–20. *Literary Reference Center*. Web. 3 May 2015. <http://search.ebscohost.com/login.aspx?direct=true&db=aph&AN=100503059&site=ehost-live>.

Bibliography

Hill, Crag. *The Critical Merits of Young Adult Litera-ture: Coming of Age*. New York: Routledge, 2014. Print.

Jones, Jami L. "Freak Out or Melt Down: Teen Re-sponses to Trauma and Depression." *Young Adult Li-brary Services* 7.1 (2008): 30–34. *Academic Search Premier*. Web. 3 May 2015. <http://search.ebscohost.com/login.aspx?direct=true&db=aph&AN=34919244&site=ehost-live>.

Porter, Roy. *Madness: A Brief History*. Oxford: Oxford UP, 2003. Print.

Diversity

Titles Discussed

A Hero Ain't Nothin' But a Sandwich by Alice Childress
Boy Meets Boy by David Levithan
Marcelo in the Real World by Francisco X. Stork

Thematic Overview

In 1965, educator, editor, and founder of the Inter-national Reading Association Nancy Larrick brought the issue of diversity in literature for young people to the attention of the public. In an essay for the *Satur-day Review*, Larrick described the "all-white world of children's books," noting that, of the over 5,000 books published from 1962 through 1964, only 6.7% fea-tured Black characters. The remainder—93.3%—told the stories of White characters exclusively. Over 50 years after Larrick published her observations, "we've made some progress," Kathleen T. Horning writes, "but children's literature still represents a mostly white world in a real one that's becoming increasingly diverse."

The growing racial and ethnic diversity to which Horning refers is not currently reflected in the ma-jority of books published for children and young adults. According to the ACT for Youth Center for Excellence, racial and ethnic diversity is increasing among young people in the United States. Currently, approximately one third of the population in the U.S. identifies as non-white. By 2018, "children and youth of color (under age 18) will be the majority youth population" (ACT for Youth). Since 1985, the Coop-erative Children's Book Center (CCBC) at the Uni-versity of Wisconsin, Madison has been document-ing children's and young adult literary diversity and, as Jason Low of Lee and Low Books, citing these statistics, concludes, "the number of diverse books published each year over the past twenty years has been stuck in neutral, never exceeding, on average, 10 percent." While the American population has be-come, as Horning writes, "increasingly diverse," the literature reflecting the youth of this population has failed to keep up.

The discussion of diversity in young adult literature is not limited to critiques of racial and ethnic representation; gender, sexuality, and ability status represent three additional aspects of diversity critics argue are not often explored in literature for young people. Young adult author Malindo Lo, writing for the "Diversity in YA" blog she created with fellow author Cindy Pon, examined the *New York Times*' lists of young adult best sellers and young adult series on the best-selling children's series lists compiled during 2013 to determine the diversity of racial, ethnic, and gender identities; sexualities; and abilities represented by the books on the list. Lo's conclusions echo and add to those reached by the CCBC: only15% of these best-selling novels featured primary characters of color; 12% included central characters who identified as LGBTQ; and 3% included protagonists with disabilities. In short, Lo found, popular young adult novels are overwhelmingly populated by White characters and reflect the experiences of straight and typically abled people almost exclusively.

Margaret A. Edwards Award winning YA author Walter Dean Myers, in an opinion piece written in 2014 and published in the *New York Times*, described the lack of diversity in young people's literature as a significant problem. "Books transmit values," wrote Myers. "They explore our common humanity. What is the message when some children are not represented in those books?" Sharon Flake, a children's and YA author, made a similar statement to the *New York Times* in 2012, pointing out that "In a world where youth of color are often told how much they are lacking, young adult novels about them and their communities tell the rest of the story."

Literary diversity isn't just about incorporating a diverse cast of characters into a book or story. Authors, readers, and critics argue that how a character is represented—how she speaks, lives, and exists in the world of the book—is of central importance. Stereotypical, racist, or incorrect portrayals of people who identify as LGBTQ, of people who identify as members of one or more racial or ethnic minorities, or of people with disabilities, are politically incorrect, at best, and harmful and even dangerous, at worst. Books featuring characters who challenge or exceed stereotype provide readers with new and expanded models of humanity that confront, correct or overturn

assumptions. Additionally, books featuring diversity can also become models and informants of new narratives that enlarge young adult literature's literary potential.

Works

Alice Childress's *A Hero Ain't Nothin' But a Sandwich*, David Levithan's *Boy Meets Boy*, and Francisco X. Stork's *Marcelo in the Real World* represent three notable novels that have broken boundaries related to the depiction of diversity in young adult literature. By complicating the depiction of racial inequality (*Hero*), imagining a world without prejudice (*Boy Meets Boy*), and giving voice to a person with a disability (*Marcelo*), all three novels challenged the literary status quo and opened the door for more diverse representation in young adult literature.

A prominent playwright and figure of the Harlem Left, Alice Childress was challenged by a friend to write a book for young adults that dealt with some of the social issues she had been addressing in her work for adults. *A Hero Ain't Nothin' But a Sandwich* emerged as the result of this challenge and, as Alleen Pace Nilsen has written, "helped shape the [then] new genre [of young adult literature] as well as bring it respect."

Published in 1973 and told from multiple perspectives in the form of chapter-long "monologues," Childress's novel centers around thirteen-year-old Benji, a young, Black heroin addict living with his mother in the Harlem ghetto. Childress gives voice to a diverse cast of characters including Benji, his mother, his best friend, two teachers and a principal at his school, and even the "pusher" who supplies the neighborhood with narcotics. Each of these characters has a unique voice characterized, in many cases, by their use of colloquialisms and what Sandra Y. Govan calls "urban Black folk speech." (73)

Childress's use of multiple voices to tell Benji's story reveals both commonalities and diversity of Black experience. As the novel works to challenge Benji's assertion that a hero "ain't nothin' but a sandwich," it depicts its characters with a complexity that reveals the influences of personal and national history, politics, and economics on each individual. With *A Hero Ain't Nothin' But a Sandwich*, as with her other novels for young adults, Childress "reject[s] the premise that the [Black] writer's duty was to compose inspirational tracts about Black high achievers."

(Govan 71) Instead, Childress focuses on the challenges and triumphs of people considered both ordinary and marginalized, creating whole characters that are not defined by solely by their social or racialized status.

A Hero Ain't Nothin' But a Sandwich was honored with an award from the Jane Addams Peace Association, received a National Book Award nomination, and was named an Outstanding Book of the Year by the *New York Times* and a Best Young Adult Book by the American Library Association. The novel was also the subject of numerous challenges and was one of eleven books removed from school library shelves by the Island Trees Union Free School District, a move that was challenged by student petitioners through the judicial system to the Supreme Court.

Childress's complex and varied depictions of the lives of urban Black people as well as her address of a social problem—drug use and abuse—from a nuanced perspective make *A Hero Ain't Nothin' But a Sandwich* a revolutionary book. Childress's novel represents one of the first—along with works by Walter Dean Myers, Mildred Taylor, and Sharon Bell Mathis—works of young adult realism that would not only, as critics have written, "shape the genre," but also serve as part of a foundation of African American children's and young adult literature for others to build upon.

Author and editor David Levithan's first novel, *Boy Meets Boy*, represents a breakthrough in LGBTQ literature for young people. Told from the first-person perspective of Paul, a high school sophomore, the novel describes Paul's rocky road to romantic relationship with Noah, a classmate.

Levithan's novel is notable for its utopian setting and vision. Paul lives in a town where the gay and the straight "scene[s] … got all mixed up a while back" (Levithan 1), where same-sex couples are free to love one another openly and publicly, where transgender people are celebrated (the school's homecoming queen, Infinite Darlene, is also its star quarterback), and where gender and sexual identity are understood and celebrated in their diversity. Michael Cart and Christine Jenkins have called *Boy Meets Boy* the "first authentically feel-good gay novel" (158) and, though moments of realism—in the form of Paul's friend Tony, who lives in a less enlightened town and must remain "closeted" at home—encroach on the novel's setting, the novel remains, at heart, an optimistic love story.

Early young adult novels featuring LGBTQ characters were characterized by heartbreak and tragedy (e.g., John Donovan's 1969 novel, *I'll Get There. It Better Be Worth the Trip*, which featured the death of the protagonist's dog following his first gay experience), while later novels (e.g., M.E. Kerr's 1995 novel, *Deliver Us From Evie*) depicted LGBTQ life in terms of struggle. *Boy Meets Boy* broke from these traditions. As David Levithan writes on his website, he "basically set out to write the book that [he] dreamed of getting as an editor—a book about gay teens that doesn't conform to the old norms about gay teens in literature (i.e. it has to be about a gay uncle, or a teen who gets beaten up for being gay, or about outcasts who come out and find they're still outcasts, albeit outcasts with their outcastedness in common.)."

While movements like the "It Gets Better" Project work to "communicate to lesbian, gay, bisexual and transgender youth around the world that it gets better," *Boy Meets Boy* envisioned a world where it was already better. As it did so, it challenged assumptions that books about LGBTQ youth had to prioritize strife and opened up a literary space where LGBTQ characters could celebrate their sexual identities.

The depiction of people with disabilities in children's and young adult literature has been both historically limited and historically questionable. As Emily Wopperer has noted, "in the past, literature often did not portray characters with disabilities in a positive or respective manner." (28) More recently, however, the depiction of characters with disabilities has shifted "from stereotypical representation to realistic and meaningful stories of human beings." (Wopperer 29) Francisco X. Stork's 2009 novel, *Marcelo in the Real World*, represents one notable example of such "meaningful stories."

Stork's novel is told from the first person perspective of Marcelo, a seventeen-year-old with an unnamed cognitive impairment that critics of the book have compared to Asperger's Syndrome. Marcelo attends a school for young people with special needs and his father, worried that Marcelo has been too shielded from the "real world," arranges for his son to work at his law firm for the summer.

Stork's novel represents one of the first attempts to depict a person with cognitive impairment in mainstream young adult literature. Mark Haddon's 2003 novel, *The Curious Incident of the Dog in the Night-time*, is considered an early mainstream work told from the perspective of a person with autism; however, this book is a "crossover" work of adult fiction. While other young adult works have depicted characters with autism through the lens of a sibling or other family member (e.g., Nancy Werlin's 1994 *Are You Alone on Purpose* and Gennifer Choldenko's 2003 *Al Capone Does My Shirts*), Stork's novel is notable for its first person perspective.

Marcelo in the Real World was honored with the Schneider Family Book Award, which is given annually to titles that "embody an artistic expression of the disability experience for child and adolescent audiences," and this accolade reflects the novel's success at accurately and respectfully depicting a disability experience. Writing for the blog "Disability in Kidlit," S. E. Smith praised Stork for capturing "an authentic depiction of one facet of the autistic experience."

Stork's novel seems to have paved the way for increased representation of people with disabilities of all kinds in mainstream young adult literature. Additionally, the critical success of Stork's novel has drawn teachers' and librarians' attention to literature featuring people with disabilities.

Conclusion

Young adult literature provides readers with what Rudine Sims Bishop has called "mirrors, windows and sliding glass doors" through which they can see their lives—and the lives of others—reflected. The diversity and nature of this reflection are important, Bishop writes; when readers "cannot find themselves reflected in the books they read, or when the images they see are distorted, negative, or laughable, they learn a powerful lesson about how they are devalued in the society of which they are part."

For over 50 years, readers, teachers, librarians, authors, and publishers have been lamenting the lack of diversity in the world of literature for young people and arguing, essentially, that the literary reflections Bishop describes remain sadly limited. In the first decade of the twenty-first century, however, voices of people advocating for greater representation in youth literature have become louder and more persuasive, drawing increased public attention to diversity in children's and young adult literature. "We Need Diverse Books" (WNDB), a grassroots campaign

established in 2014, represents one notable effort to draw attention to diversity in youth literature. WNDB spearheaded a social media campaign that drew great attention to the organization's cause and has since worked to develop internships, mentorships, and programming aimed at encouraging the publication of diverse material.

Campaigns like WNDB represent ongoing efforts to depict diversity in youth literature and, as they draw readers' attention to existing and forthcoming diverse literature, highlight the diversity of the human experience.

Amy Pattee

Further Reading

Keplinger, Kody, Corinne Duyvis, and Kayla Whaley. *Disability in Kidlit*. Web. 22 February 2016. <http://disabilityinkidlit.com/>

Lo, Malinda and Cindy Pon. *Diversity in YA*. Web. 26 February 2016. <http://www.diversityinya.com/>

We Need Diverse Books Official Campaign Site. 1 August 2014. Web. 22 February 2016. <http://weneeddiversebooks.tumblr.com/>

Bibliography

ACT for Youth Center for Excellence. "U.S. Teen Demographics." *ACT for Youth Center for Excellence.* ACT for Youth Center for Excellence, n.d. Web. 25 February 2016.

Bishop, Rudine Sims. "Mirrors, Windows, and Sliding Glass Doors." *Perspectives: Choosing and Using Books for the Classroom* 6.3 (Summer 1990). Web. 27 February 2016.

Cart, Michael and Christine A. Jenkins. *The Heart Has Its Reasons: Young Adult Literature with Gay/Lesbian/Queer Content, 1969–2004.* Lanham, MD: Scarecrow Press, 2006. Print.

Curwood, Jen Scott. "Redefining Normal: A Critical Analysis of (Dis)Ability in Young Adult Literature." *Children's Literature in Education* 44.1 (March 2013): 15–28.

Ehrlich, Hannah. "The Diversity Gap in Children's Publishing, 2015." *The Open Book.* Lee and Low Books, 5 March 2015. Web. 23 February 2016.

Flake, Sharon. "More Nonwhite Characters are Needed." *New York Times.* New York Times, 28 March 2012. Web. 22 February 2016.

Govan, Sandra Y. "Alice Childress's Rainbow Jordan: The Black Aesthetic Returns Dressed in Adolescent Fiction." *Children's Literature Association Quarterly* 13.2 (Summer 1988): 70 – 74.

Horning, Kathleen T. "Children's Books: Still an All-White World?" *School Library Journal*. Media Source, Inc, 1 May 2014. Web. 25 February 2016.

It Gets Better Project. "What Is the It Gets Better Project?" *It Gets Better Project*. n.d. Web. 26 February 2016.

Koppelman, Susan. "Alice Childress: An Appreciation." *Belles Lettres: A Review of Books by Women* 10.1 (Fall 1994): 6. Literature Resource Center. Web. 25 February 2016.

Larrick, Nancy. "The All-White World of Children's Books." *Saturday Review*. 11 September 1965. UNZ. org. Web. 24 February 2016.

Levithan, David. "About Me." *David Levithan*. n.d. Web. 26 February 2016.

Lo, Malinda. "Diversity in 2013 New York Times Young Adult Bestsellers." *Diversity in YA*. Malinda Lo and Cindy Pon, 21 April 2014. Web. 23 February 2016.

Low, Jason T. "Where is the Diversity in Publishing? The 2015 Diversity Baseline Survey Results." *The Open Book*. Lee and Low Books, 26 January 2016. Web. 22 February 2016.

Myers, Walter Dean. "Where are the People of Color in Children's Books?" *New York Times*. New York Times, 15 March 2014. Web. 23 February 2016.

Nilsen, Alleen Pace. "Alice Childress: Overview." *Twentieth-Century Young Adult Writers*. Ed. Laura Standley Berger. Detroit: St. James Press, 1994. Literature Resource Center. Web. 26 February 2016.

smith, s.e. "Review: *Marcelo in the Real World* by Francisco X. Stork." *Disability in Kidlit*. 1 July 2013. Web. 23 February 2016.

Wopperer, Emily. "Inclusive Literature in the Library and the Classroom: The Importance of Young Adult and Children's Books that Portray Characters with Disabilities." *Knowledge Quest* 39.3 (Jan./Feb. 2011): 26 – 35.

Divorce

Titles Discussed

That Summer by Sarah Dessen
How to Build a House by Dana Reinhardt
What Happened to Goodbye by Sarah Dessen

Thematic Overview

It was not until around 1970 that "no-fault" divorces became somewhat common across the United States. These divorces allowed couples to end their union without either person showing wrongdoing, such as cruelty or adultery. This general legalization indicated a greater acceptance of divorce in general, with the end of marriage seen less as a traumatic and shameful failure that must be avoided at all costs and more as an unfortunate but sometimes unavoidable reality. This evolving attitude toward marriage also reflects shifting gender norms—while marriage in the nineteenth century largely signaled a union in which a wife would be subservient to a bread-winning husband, by the end of the twentieth century, marriage was widely considered a romantic partnership, responsive to the needs and desires of both partners.

However, political and cultural debates around marriage and divorce did not often focus exclusively on adult partners but turned attention to the effects of divorce on the children of those adults. For many young adults, the teenage years involve both their first romantic relationships and the beginning of their separation from the childhood home and family. A parental divorce can both upset the idea that romantic unions should last for a lifetime and radically disrupt the stability of the home from which young adults are just beginning to establish their independence. Because of this, divorce has been an important and recurrent topic in YA literature since the 1970s. However, what divorce can or should mean has rapidly changed.

In 1970, the divorce rate jumped rapidly to 33 percent of the total number of marriages that year. YA literature in that decade featured a number of novels in which teenage protagonists find their world upset by the announcement of parental divorce. These novels, however, focused primarily on dealing with the divorce itself, as well as the social awkwardness and shame that many young adults might feel as their parents split. By 1985, however, divorce rates had reached 50 percent. With that increase, divorce no longer seemed as shameful or traumatic as a topic; instead, many teenagers experiencing parental divorce would find themselves with a number of peers who had already lived similar experiences. Reflecting this, YA literature more commonly shifted its focus to the reality of living after, rather than during, a divorce. Protagonists learned to live with (and sometimes love) stepfamilies, while concepts such as "family" and "home" were no longer homogenous, but rather ideas that could be revised by every individual.

While the commonality of divorce means that social pressure and shame are less common themes, the radical disruption of the childhood home still has varied repercussions for YA protagonists, making the theme a perennially common one for YA writers. Sarah Dessen's novels *That Summer* (2006) and *What Happened to Goodbye* (2011) both explore divorce in the same small city but feature protagonists with markedly different strategies for processing the changes in their lives. While still centered on a divorce, Dana Reinhardt's *How to Build a House* (2009) features a young woman who comes from a blended family and who, in turn, must rely on her previous experience while developing her identity in the face of radical change at home. In all cases, the divorce presents unique challenges to the protagonists; in turn, each character must chart her own path in emerging from the change with a strong sense of individuality and identity.

Works

While divorce is a catalyst of change in *That Summer*, it is only one change among many in the life of fifteen-year-old protagonist Haven. The novel is set during the summer of her father's remarriage and her older sister Ashley's first marriage, yet it regularly flashes back four years, to a summer that Haven has come to idealize. During the season of the flashbacks, her mother and father appear happy together, the father not yet having left the mother for a young woman with whom he works. Likewise, Ashley is dating Sumner, a boy who is warm and generous to the entire family, which helps Haven and Ashley bond. In contrast, the current summer is filled with change, including Haven's rapid growth (which makes her feel alienated from her own body) and the changes in her social world, with her closest friend dating older boys and getting herself into trouble. The changes begin to feel too rapid and too drastic to Haven, especially as she fails to bond with Ashley's fiancé. Eventually, she attempts to abandon her life before it can abandon her, running away from home and hiding in the woods. There, Ashley discovers her, revealing that she and Sumner broke up because he had cheated on her, just as their father had left their mother for another woman. This revelation causes Haven to grasp the degree to which she had been idealizing the past, which in turn allows her to better appreciate the present and the coming future.

In *That Summer*, the immediate moment of divorce is less important than the trajectory of change that it

initiates, a change that Haven experiences by comparing her present moment with the past narrative of "that summer" four years prior. The divorce is addressed early in the text and presented as a matter-of-fact reality—it is difficult on the family, but not excessively tragic. "My mother had read all the books about divorce and tried hard to make it smooth for me and my sister," Haven explains, revealing that the family viewed divorce as something that could be properly managed, worked through with the right resources. What Haven struggles with, then, is the encroaching reality that adult life (and particularly romantic relationships) are not as simple and joyful as she once believed. Regarding her father's new marriage, it is the uncomfortable knowledge of his bride's young age (only five years older than Ashley) that upsets Haven, in large part because of the implication that physical attraction to youth took precedence over family commitment in her father's life. Likewise, she views Sumner as a perfectly kind and gentle boy, stating, "Sumner was the kind of person that you wanted to sit with in the sun and spend the day," idealizing him as a figure of safety. Because Haven's first-person narration regularly shifts between these two summers, the novel is able to establish the emotional differences between these time periods while also making clear the ways that Haven deludes herself. When she eventually has her break and flees the family, she must reconcile these different perceptions, both acknowledging the imperfection of the past and the good of the present moment. Ultimately, this synthesis is a turn toward self-growth, with Haven realizing the ways she has been preventing others in her family from experiencing happiness, instead deciding to support Ashley's wedding and the future joy it promises.

How to Build a House is similarly structured between flashbacks and a present, first-person narrative, although in Reinhardt's novel, the disjuncture of the divorce propels the main character into positive change and personal growth rather than self-delusion. The novel alternates between sections labeled "Home" and "Here." In "Here," the protagonist, Harper, arrives in Tennessee after a tornado destroys a small town. Harper is volunteering for an organization that rebuilds houses, and while she is deeply invested in environmental politics, she also alludes to the fact that she is fleeing a difficult year back home in Los Angeles. In the "Home" section, the details of that year are slowly revealed. After her mother died when Harper was two, her father remarried, and Harper was raised in a blended family, becoming best friends with her stepsister, Tess, and even connecting with her stepmother's former husband. When Harper is a teenager, however, her father and stepmother announce their seemingly sudden divorce, and Tess makes out with Harper's on-again, off-again romantic partner at a party, causing a drastic rift between them. As Harper processes these changes while volunteering in Tennessee, she also slowly comes into her own, developing a new romance with a boy from the town and learning to focus her energy on the future rather than the past.

Harper's story is driven forward by an overriding metaphor of building homes (both literal and figurative), a site of meaning of which she is herself aware, stating early on that "I know a thing or two about people whose homes have been destroyed." This previous knowledge is important to how the novel progresses. Unlike Haven, who finds her world shattered by her parent's divorce and is forced to accept the messiness of romance and life, Harper has already learned how to form new families and develop affinity in nontraditional homes. She has thrived in a family defined as much by her father's atheism as by her stepmother's Judaism, has learned to count her stepsister's birth father as part of her family, and even ventured on her own sexual relationship with a close male friend who is not her boyfriend. Harper is not a character unprepared for the disruption of divorce, then, even as she does experience stress about the changing relationship with her family members. Her challenge instead is one of learning to build a future in order to maintain her past. She must build her own future by developing new skills, pursuing her political passion of environmental preservation and social activism, and engaging in a mutually respectful romantic and sexual relationship with a new boyfriend. She also must build a future for others, providing and nurturing compassion through the activism of the construction project. It is only once she has learned to take care of herself that she can engage once more with her family in Los Angeles, confident and strong enough to extend her compassion to a family that has made mistakes but still loves one another. The novel's closing scene emphasizes this change—the physical house constructed and Tess having arrived in Tennessee, the sisters drive across the country together, returning to Los Angeles. For the first time, a "Home" section exists not in California but rather in the open space of the road trip, with Harper sharing the knowledge that, while they might not know exactly what roads will lead them home, "One way or another, we'll find the road back."

While Harper has some familiarity with the disruption of divorce, the protagonist of *What Happened to Goodbye* embraces that disruption in order to avoid the difficult challenges of personal growth and young adulthood. Set in Lakeview (the same city as *That Summer*), *What Happened to Goodbye* focuses on Mclean, a teenager whose parents divorced two years prior. Following that divorce, Mclean has moved with her father roughly every six months, forcing her to adjust to new cities, new schools, and new social groups. Mclean deals with this constant change by embracing it, and with each new school, she selects a new name and personality, leaving behind whatever friends she makes when the next move comes. In Lakeview, however, she sticks with her old name and, in turn, begins to develop friends through her authentic personality, even developing a crush on a boy, Dave. When these new friends discover the social-media profiles of her old personalities, Mclean worries that the relationships will end. However, after an emotionally tumultuous weekend with her mother, she decides to reach out to Dave, and she slowly realizes that her friends simply want to support her, not judge her for her past. When the novel ends, Mclean has accepted Lakeview as a home, electing to stay there rather than move on with her father to a new city.

Divorce initiates a shift in identity for both Harper and Haven. But while they both resist this change at first, Mclean embraces it as a tool of self-preservation, with her false identities preventing anyone from experiencing (and in turn hurting or abandoning) the "real" Mclean. Through the first-person narration, she confesses the link between her identity and the divorce to the readers, declaring, "Since my parents' split, I hadn't had much faith in relationships and even less of an inclination to start any lasting ones of my own." The fact that Mclean can share this insight with the reader is indicative of a central tension in the novel—while her inner life is filled with sharp observations and intentionality, her social life is defined instead by anonymity and distance, preventing anyone else from truly experiencing the richness expressed through her narration. For Mclean, then, in order to process and move on from the disruption of the divorce and her constant relocations, she must reconcile the disparity between her interior life and her social life. Narratively, this occurs when she goes on vacation with her mother and, after mishearing a conversation, feels unwanted by her mother and in turn further alienated from both family and friends. In this moment, she reaches out to Dave (trusting her peers for the first time), who in turns reaches out to her parents. When the parents realize the pain that Mclean has been hiding, they are able to talk openly about the divorce, initiating a process of healing and growth. From that moment on, the novel presents a Mclean who still struggles at times but has learned that it is only through sharing her true self with both family and friends that she can find happiness.

Conclusions

From the start of the twenty-first century and onward, roughly 50 percent of marriages in the United States have ended in divorce, often while children still live at home. In reflection of this commonality, a large number of YA novels include divorced or blended families without making the divorce a central theme. Rather, divorced parents (of either the protagonists or peers) provide some contextual background. The divorce perhaps influences the actions of the characters but is not treated as the major preoccupation in the novels. Even when divorce is a major theme, it is rarely the only major theme—in the novels discussed above, for instance, divorce is only understood in the context of other significant events in the characters' lives, from Haven's changing body to Harper's environmental activism.

At the same time, while divorce is common, it is not easy, especially for teenagers who are likewise involved in the tumultuous emotions and radical change associated with developing their identities as young adults. For this reason, divorce remains a perennial topic for many writers, the most astute of whom address the specificity of divorce through a contemporary lens. This is the case with *What Happened to Goodbye*, in which identity is heavily influenced by social media, and in *How to Build a House*, in which it is a complex and loving blended family (rather than the original family of birth) that experiences divorce.

Divorce is rarely easy, even when it obviously presages a positive change in the life of a young adult or the family in general. However, modern teenagers live in a world in which they not only have seen many happy, thriving adults who have experienced divorces but also one in which they are likely to anticipate divorce as a possibility in their own lives, no matter how optimistic they might be at the moment. While the boom in novels that focused on divorce in the 1980s is unlikely to repeat itself, the number of novels in which divorce

plays some role has risen drastically since then. In turn, young adults have developed a heightened sophistication in understanding divorce and in reading literature that presents adult relationships with complexity and candor.

T. Fleischmann, MFA

Further Reading

Dessen, Sarah. Interview by Roger Sutton. *Horn Book* 85.3 (2009): 243–50. *Literary Reference Center.* Web. 31 May 2015. <http://search.ebscohost.com/login.aspx?direct=true&db=lfh&AN=37925708&site=ehost-live>.

Williams, Juan. "Analysis: Long-Term Effects of Divorce on Children." *Talk of the Nation (NPR)* 24 Oct. 2000. *Newspaper Source.* Web. 31 May 2015. <http://search.ebscohost.com/login.aspx?direct=true&db=nfh&AN=6XN200010241401&site=ehost-live&scope=site>.

Bibliography

Cart, Michael. Young Adult Literature: From Romance to Realism. Chicago: Amer. Lib. Assn., 2011. Print.

Issitt, Micah. "Divorce Rate: Overview." Points of View: Divorce Rate (2014): 1. Points of View Reference Center. Web. 31 May 2015. <http://search.ebscohost.com/login.aspx?direct=true&db=pwh&AN=93663182&site=ehost-live>.

Ming, Cui, and Frank D. Ficham. "The Differential Effects of Parental Divorce and Marital Conflict on Young Adult Romantic Relationships." Personal Relationships 17.3 (2010): 331–43. Academic Search Premier. Web. 31 May 2015. <http://search.ebscohost.com/login.aspx?direct=true&db=aph&AN=53323317&site=ehost-live>.

Faith and Religion

Titles Discussed

Godless by Pete Hautman
The Patron Saint of Butterflies by Cecilia Galante
The Gospel According to Larry by Janet Tashjian
Dark Sons by Nikki Grimes

Thematic Overview

Religious stories have been a part of the training of young people as long as there have been stories. With the precarious balance between a communities' faiths and their government, public schools avoid the topic altogether, however. Faith and religion in young adult literature help teenagers to deal with religious questions and doubts they have and feel uncomfortable asking their parents or religious leaders. These books also teach teens about other religions and how their belief system affects their behavior and worldview, and attempt to impart acceptance of diversity in religion.

Aaron Hartzler writes about the absence of religion in young adult literature in his article for Children's Book Council, "Diversity 101: Religion in YA." Hartzler states that he sees people write about the absence of religion in YA novels due to lack of interest, but he feels the opposite to be true. Religion is still important and relevant to many young adults, especially since they are at a stage of development when many beliefs come into question. Many teenagers reevaluate their religious beliefs in high school or as they head into their college years. It is helpful to read about characters going through similar situations, and it is important to know experiencing doubt does not indicate negative character flaws. It is natural to question beliefs and even to form new beliefs that may be separate from the beliefs of parents or other authority figures.

Hartzler discusses various stereotypes often found in young adult books that deal with faith and religion including hypocritical characters, religion as mass hysteria, a book marketed exclusively to religious people, and religion as being a "relic of the past." Hartzler uses Pete Hautman's *Godless* as an example of a book that many religious people would probably not like, but he feels these books should be more common because they show the struggles many teens have regarding their faith. Cecilia Galante's *The Patron Saint of Butterflies* would be a good example of a novel dealing with hypocritical characters and with a largely negative view of religion. Nikki Grimes's *Dark Sons* transforms religion as being a "relic of the past" and parallels the biblical story of Abraham and Sarah with similar contemporary characters. Janet Tashjian's *The Gospel According to Larry* is an example of a contemporary book that deals with the subjects of spirituality and faith apart from formal religion.

Works

The Gospel According to Larry by Janet Tashjian tells the life of a seventeen-year-old boy named Josh. Josh is intelligent and has a lot going for him, including getting early acceptance into Princeton University. What most people do not know about Josh is that he is the new Internet sensation. In Josh's free time he writes anti-consumerist "sermons" on a blog titled *The Gospel According to Larry*. Most of the sermons are opinion articles to spread awareness of how advertisements affect daily life. Josh encourages people to abandon brands, stop celebrity worship, and focus more on living rather than on accumulating "stuff."

While Larry is accomplishing Josh's goal of changing the world, there are those who stop at nothing to bring Larry's true identity to the world. When Larry/Josh is found out, Josh decides to fake his suicide to get away from the media and start a new life. At the end of the book Larry chooses to have someone write his "real" story, a gospel about him and his work.

While Josh does not talk about being religious in any sense, he refers to his blogs as sermons, and he mentions picking the name Larry because it was the least Christian name he could think of. The author also includes excerpts from the Bible between several chapters. Josh believes in an afterlife and often feels his dead mother's presence and speaks to her. He feels that she responds to his questions and gives advice based on the first words he hears someone else say. It is ironic that Josh is superstitious and makes important life choices, such as whether or not to fake his suicide, based on otherworldly signs despite being so driven by technology.

While this is not a novel about religion, it is about the desire to change the world for the good, to have a positive impact on society, and to have faith that change is possible despite one's age or life circumstances. With the help of technology Larry affects billions of people with his words. Those people then hold protests, stop wearing brand name clothes, and gather together at a festivals promoting love and sustainability. Josh's spirituality, faith, intelligence, and desire to do good influences readers into believing that they too can make a change in the world if they only try and believe they can.

The Patron Saint of Butterflies by Cecilia Galante shows the dangers of blind faith. The characters Hope and Agnes have spent their entire lives in a religious commune in New England. Mount Blessing is an isolated farm that is run by a charismatic man named Emmanuel. The people who live in Mount Blessing must obey strict commandments laid out by Emmanuel so they may aspire to become perfect. Agnes muses, "It's not always easy, especially the striving for perfection one . . . but like Emmanuel says: The only thing worse than not being perfect is not trying to be perfect. So I keep trying." She believes that God speaks through Emmanuel to lead the commune to holiness. Her goal in life is to become a saint. On the other hand, Hope sees past Emmanuel's holy mask and knows him to be a cruel man who enjoys manipulating others.

The book begins after Hope and Agnes are whipped and abused in the Regulation Room, where children and adults are sent to be "retrained" by Emmanuel. While Hope is aware that this is child abuse, Agnes believes it is only to help them achieve perfection. Although Agnes's parents are aware of what goes on in the Regulation Room, they do nothing to stop it. Soon Agnes's grandmother comes to visit and learns about the Regulation Room by accident. Hope persuades her to take them away from Mount Blessing as soon as possible. She agrees when Agnes's younger brother is gravely injured and Emmanuel prevents anyone from calling an ambulance.

Agnes eventually realizes that Emmanuel was not the man she thought, but it takes tragedy and hardship for her to believe this. If not for her brother's pleading, Agnes might have never told the police about the abuse at Mount Blessing. Hope explains that Agnes needed to be reprogrammed from Emmanuel's brainwashing. Agnes must learn to live away from Mount Blessing, make her own decisions, and form a new relationship with God. She states, "I don't want to be Saint Agnes anymore. I just want to be Agnes. Whoever she might be."

While *The Gospel According to Larry* inspires faith, *The Patron Saint of Butterflies* shows what happens when people place so much faith in a human leader that they become blind to the dangers and no longer think for themselves. It is important to note that Galante is not ridiculing or criticizing religion but instead is warning of the importance for all individuals to make informed decisions rather than become a mindless follower.

Jason Bock in *Godless* by Pete Hautman learns the dangers of being charismatic. As his father points out, Jason's friends listen to him. He is very creative and a self-described atheist, despite his father's serious belief in Catholicism. He often writes and draws comic books and imagines exciting adventures in order to endure everyday boredom.

During a church meeting his father makes him attend, Jason creates the religion of the Ten Legged God for shock value. The Ten Legged God is the town water tower. Rather than stopping there, Jason tells his closest friend about his idea for a new religion that worships the

tower and its life-giving water. To Jason's surprise, his friends latch on to the idea, form a religious hierarchy, and even create commandments. Most of the members, including Jason, are using this religion as a way to get together, pass the time, and have fun. Jason makes no secret that he is mocking religion in general.

Jason does make a point to tell the reader that just because he does not believe in his made-up religion does not mean he does not take it seriously, stating: "So you ask, how can Jason Bock be serious about a religion that worships a false god? Are you kidding?" Jason then gives the example of watching a football game. He says that people take the game seriously even though it is not a "real battle" but a made-up spectator sport. "Same thing about water towers and God. I don't have to be a believer to be serious about my religion."

Despite the seemingly harmless nature of Jason's religion, it all goes wrong when the group decides to hold a service on the water tower at midnight. They climb the tower and break it open in order to swim inside. One boy, Henry, slips and falls off the side and onto the catwalk. He survives but breaks his leg. The police are called, and Jason is blamed for influencing the others.

The situation worsens as Jason realizes his friend Shin is having a mental break and truly believes that the water tower is a god and that it speaks to him. Shin, trying to get closer to his god, climbs the tower in a lightning storm. Jason finds him, calls the police after being unable to get him down, and is again blamed as a negative influence Shin.

Jason has a difficult time understanding the power he has over his friends, but at the same time he feels it is unfair to receive most of the blame. In reality, both are true: Jason is exciting and charismatic, but for the most part, his friends are responsible for their own actions.

Jason still has a hard time believing in religion but admits that "you can't really understand what it means to be Catholic (or Muslim, or whatever) unless you have faith." Jason envies people who have faith but is resigned to the belief system he currently has. "Maybe one day I'll find a deity to believe in. Until then, my god is made of steel and dust."

Godless is much more light hearted than *The Patron Saint of Butterflies*, but they both discuss the dangers of following others blindly and respecting diverse beliefs about religion. Hope and Agnes must learn to respect each other's beliefs and understand there are many ways to worship God. Jason must learn that it is inappropriate to mock religions just because one believes differently and that charisma and power can be dangerous.

Dark Sons by Nikki Grimes is written almost entirely as a prose poem and tells the story of two boys from different times. Ishmael is the son of the biblical Abraham and talks about how he and his mother deal with the jealousy of Abraham's first wife, Sarah. With the birth of Isaac, Abraham's son by Sarah, Ishmael and his mother leave to fend for themselves in the desert.

Samuel is a modern-day teenager dealing with his parents' divorce and his father's remarriage. Samuel's father also has another son, and Samuel worries he is losing his father's love and attention.

Both boys foster a close connection with God and use that relationship to help them deal with their problems. Samuel asks his prayer group to help him pray for an "attitude adjustment" in order to help him deal with his new stepmother. Both boys feel close to their mothers and seek to protect and defend them from the hurt and pain the men in their lives caused them, while also learning to forgive their fathers for that hurt. Samuel asks God to help him forgive his father for leaving his mother and starting a new family. He mentions that he is finally tired of holding on to the anger and bitterness. He learns to let go of negative feelings, move on, and understand that although his father is not perfect, it does not mean that they cannot love each other.

At the end of the book Samuel reads the story of Abraham and realizes he is a lot like Ishmael, and if Ishmael survived, then so can he. In an interview with Grimes, she states her goal in writing *Dark Sons* was to show young adults that they can struggle with their relationship with their family and with God, but that having faith in God will always see them through.

Conclusions

Historically, questions of morality and ethics were answered through one's religion, and many religions claim that apart from their god there is no goodness. Philosophy and aesthetics in young adult novels can offer the scaffolding for young adults to engage in and improve their world.

Young adults' emerging civic mindedness and departure from traditional religion is no coincidence. Many young people consider history and myriad atrocities committed in the names of various gods, possibly while recognizing that much good has been done in those same names. As young people try to create identities that can function for them, they must decide whether injecting belief in a god into their sense of responsibility will benefit them. Young adult literature offers a safe place to ask how to relate to the world with or without a god.

With more people adopting postmodernist and relativist views, religion as it has traditionally been understood will often not be compatible with how readers see the world. Characters within young adult novels are given the freedom to approach their internal lives without a "right versus wrong," or correct/incorrect binary, and consider a "helpful/harmful" dichotomy.

Many people, including atheists and antitheists, want meaningful experiences, peace in ritual, and community in shared beliefs. Young adult literature can provide a place for readers to explore these processes without having to believe any particular thing and without needing a particular opinion. Literature creates a space to elevate discourse and enjoy life, and the only requirement for entry is reading it.

Alexandra McBride, MA

Further Reading

Hartzler, Aaron. "Diversity 101: Religion in YA." *CBC Diversity*. Children's Book Council, 2014. Web. 16 May 2015. <http://www.cbcdiversity.com/post/76251960183/diversity-101-religion-in-ya>.

Rawson, Casey H. "Are All Lists Created Equal? Diversity in Award-Winning and Bestselling Young Adult Fiction." *YALSA*. Journal of Research on Libraries and Young Adults, 14 June 2011. Web. 16 May 2015. <http://www.yalsa.ala.org/jrlya/2011/06/are-all-lists-created-equal-diversity-in-award-winning-and-best-selling-young adult-fiction>.

Bibliography

Rev. of *Dark Sons*, by Nikki Grimes. *Kirkus Reviews* 73.15 (2005): 848. *Academic Search Complete*. Web. 16 May 2015. <http://search.ebscohost.com/login.aspx?direct=true&db=a9h&AN=17945835>.

Rev. of *Godless*, by Pete Hautman. *Kirkus Reviews* 72.9 (2004): 442. *Academic Search Complete*. Web. 16 May 2015. <http://search.ebscohost.com/login.aspx?direct=true&db=a9h&AN=13155922>.

Jemtegaard, Kristi Elle. "The Gospel According to Larry/Vote for Larry (Book)." Rev. of *The Gospel according to Larry*, by Janet Tashjian. *Horn Book Magazine* 80.5 (2004): 610. *Academic Search Complete*. Web. 1 July 2015. <http://search.ebscohost.com/login.aspx?direct=true&db=a9h&AN=14198415>.

Rev. of *The Patron Saint of Butterflies*, by Cecilia Galante. *Kirkus Reviews* 76.8 (2008): 424. *Academic Search Complete*. Web. 16 May 2015. <http://search.ebscohost.com/login.aspx?direct=true&db=a9h&AN=31908026>.

Fate versus Free Will

Titles Discussed

Holes by Louis Sachar
Beatle Meets Destiny by Gabrielle Williams
Ender's Game by Orson Scott Card

Thematic Overview

Throughout history, people have debated the theme of fate versus free will. Is one's life predetermined, or do the choices one makes determine one's future? Is free will just a pretense to make people feel like they have the power to control their future? Many people want the freedom to choose their own paths, especially in Western culture. On the other hand, there are also people who like the idea of a future that is already determined.

Fate versus free will has long been a common theme among young adult (YA) fiction. Some popular titles that employ this theme include Christopher Paolini's *Eragon* (2002), Louis Lowry's *The Giver* (1993), J. K. Rowling's Harry Potter series (1997–2007), and Suzanne Collins's Hunger Games series (2008–10). Each protagonist in these novels must decide to take matters into his or her own hands. The protagonists in these novels choose to fight for what they believe in, which is, in many cases, freedom.

The rise in popularity of dystopian YA novels has complicated the fate-versus-free-will debate. In many cases, novels in this genre—including *The Hunger Games* (2008), *The Giver*, and even Veronica Roth's *Divergent* (2011)—portray a corrupt and cruel government posing as the epitome of peace and order. These governments want their citizens to believe fate exists and that the government is the arbiter of fate. For example in *Divergent*, people are born into certain factions and they are taught that the way their faction lives is the way things were meant to be. The protagonists in these books realize things are not what they seem; governments are made of people and therefore do not implement the laws of God or other sources of authority. Upon realizing this, the protagonists' lives get much more complicated, as they often lead rebellions against the state.

The theme of fate versus free will is important to YA literature because it teaches adolescents to question authority, to make their own decisions, and to prevent past mistakes such as genocide, slavery, or internment. YA novels personalize this abstraction of history by demonstrating that the situation into which one is born does not necessarily dictate the choices and actions characters may take to change their lives.

Works

This essay discusses the importance of fate versus free will in *Ender's Game* (1985) by Orson Scott Card, *Holes* by Louis Sachar (1997), and *Beatle Meets Destiny* (2010) by Gabrielle Williams. Stanley Yelnats, the protagonist of *Holes*, is literally cursed with bad luck. His family was cursed generations ago by a Gypsy, although "Stanley and his parents didn't believe in curses, of course, but whenever anything went wrong, it felt good to be able to blame someone." The novel begins as he heads to a juvenile detention center called Camp Green Lake for a crime he did not commit. Stanley's first act of free will is deciding to go to Camp Green Lake (actually a desert) instead of jail. He assumes camp will be better than jail, but soon realizes that his time at camp will be spent digging holes.

Stanley was arrested for stealing sneakers that had actually fallen on him from a highway overpass. Was it fate or just bad luck that he walked under the overpass at that exact time? Stanley states that the shoes fell on his head as if they were a sign from God. Rather than blame the family curse, Stanley chalks up the event to bad luck. The narrator states that a lot of people do not believe in curses just as some may not believe in other myths: "A lot of people don't believe in yellow-spotted lizards either, but if one bites you, it doesn't make a difference whether you believe in it or not."

A counselor at the camp lectures Stanley about how he is responsible for his own life and that he alone can set it straight. The counselor is clearly in favor of free will over destiny, which is ironic because some of the boys are at the camp as a result of circumstances rather than any wrongdoing. For example, Stanley's friend Zero is there because he had the misfortune of being homeless.

Stanley experiences other instances of bad luck, such as when a bag of stolen sunflower seeds falls into his hole. Even though Stanley is innocent, he receives punishment from the unstable and violent Warden. This incident also solidifies Stanley's relationship with Zero as they make a trade: reading lessons from Stanley for Zero's help digging.

Readers soon discover Stanley's ancestor is linked with the Warden's hunt for treasure. Stanley's great-grandfather was robbed by Kissin' Kate (who was rumored to have buried her treasure.) One wonders if it is fate or coincidence that Stanley and the Warden, whose ancestors were linked, should end up at camp together.

Reader also discover that Zero's ancestor was the Gypsy who cursed Stanley's family. Stanley unknowingly breaks the curse by saving Zero's life. Readers also learn that it was Zero who unintentionally stole the sneakers. He had taken them, realized he had stolen them, and then threw them off the overpass.

Now Stanley believes it was his destiny to be hit with the sneakers, "When the shoes first fell from the sky, he remembered thinking that destiny had struck him. Now, he thought so again. It was more than a coincidence. It had to be destiny." Stanley views the event as destiny because of the events that followed, allowing him to gain pride and confidence in himself.

Holes is not necessarily centered on the theme of fate versus free will; a more overarching theme is fate versus coincidence. The text is riddled with coincidences, including the fact that Stanley and Zero were forced to eat onions for days to prevent starvation, which then inadvertently saved them from the yellow-spotted lizards, which are repelled by onions. Another significant coincidence occurs when Stanley finds the treasure in luggage that has his name on it. (The luggage had belonged to his great-grandfather.)

In *Holes*, Sachar also asks whether or not an individual's perspective on destiny can change their approach to their future. Stanley's mother insists that the family is not cursed and reminds them to think of all the good luck they have. For instance, Stanley's great-grandfather could have been killed instead of just robbed. In fact, the events that follow the incident with the stolen shoes lead him and his family to great fortune. But then again, this outcome would not have happened if Stanley had chosen to go to jail rather than to Camp Green Lake. Stanley may have forces controlling his path, but he chooses to follow it.

In *Ender's Game*, it is almost impossible to believe that anyone or anything has control over Ender's future but himself. Ender is a manipulative tactician, always making and analyzing his own decisions. Everything he does has a purpose. Even though he is but a child, Ender appears to have great agency. After all, he is a born soldier.

The crux of being a soldier is trusting that commanders have superior knowledge. In any game, player agency can only be understood in relation to one's knowledge, so imperfect knowledge leads to imperfect agency.

Ender is told that the battles in which he fights are simulations, but they are actual sorties. Ender's basis for any decision he would make (which is the basic principle of free will) is denied him. Card offers the reader snippets of Ender's superiors to let the audience know that, in Ender's case, there can be no true free will because Ender has imperfect knowledge of situations in which he is involved.

Therefore, without free will, Ender seems bound by fate and destiny, especially given that he has been bred and nurtured to be the most brilliant military commander in history. Thus, Ender cannot make choices. If a game has an optimal strategy, then the player has no choice but to play that way. Ender was created to implement the best strategy, from a militaristic perspective, for any scenario. As the novel plays out, however, Ender rejects his destiny, revealing that he had at least some form of free will all along.

After Ender unwittingly commits genocide against the Buggers, he finds an egg with which he can repopulate the species. He takes the moniker "Speaker for the Dead," hoping to make humans realize both how awful and destructive they were toward the Buggers and how terrible the military was in forcing Ender to kill them. This is the pivotal moment in Ender's coming-of-age story, as he recognizes that the way he was designed is antithetical to his sense of self. He becomes a person able to make decisions, which endows him with free will. When Ender becomes self-aware, he kills his "destiny."

Almost everything in *Beatle Meets Destiny* revolves around fate and superstition. The book's main character is named John Lennon, and is nicknamed Beatle, while Destiny's last name is McCartney. Many would call their meeting fate. Beatle decides to go home early on a Friday the thirteenth, and Destiny also heads home because she cannot score a ticket to a show to which her friends went. The two characters meet by chance and hit it off (even though Beatle already had a girlfriend).

Beatle blames bad luck on things like black cats and walking under ladders. Despite these superstitions he is not interested in the horoscopes that obsess his mother. Coincidentally, Destiny also does not believe in astrology even though she writes a column on horoscopes. Furthermore, Destiny does not believe in fate, contrary to her name, "As far as Destiny was concerned, there were no such things as signs. Fate wasn't watching out for you every step of the way, dropping little clues like bread crumbs for you to pick up and examine. . . . Life was what you made of it."

The second time Beatle and Destiny meet by chance is on Valentine's Day. She walks into a random café, where Beatle happens to work. Lucky for Beatle, his girlfriend is busy that day, and he has the time for a spontaneous outing with Destiny after his shift.

Despite his superstitions, Beatle is aware he is responsible for his own actions. He could have met Destiny and chosen to stay loyal to his girlfriend, or he could have broken up with her to date Destiny. He worries that he is predisposed to cheating because his father cheated: "The question was, exactly what part of your parents is bred in you, and what isn't?" (74). Beatle's musings on genetic predisposition align him with Ender, who ponders the fact that he was created to master military tactics.

There are ridiculous and unrealistic coincidences throughout *Beatle Meets Destiny*, mostly showing how funny fate can be. For instance, at the end of the novel, Beatle is literally hit on the head with a Cupid sign. He and Destiny take this as a figurative sign that they should get back together. The novel does discuss responsibility for one's own actions and promotes overcoming superstitions.

By the end of the novel Beatle decides to overcome his fears of black cats and Friday the thirteenth. For this, he is rewarded with one more encounter with Destiny on the year's last Friday the thirteenth. This time he is single, and she is ready to forgive his past transgressions. The novel ends with, "And if you were even the slightly superstitious type, you might think to yourself that those two were made for each other" (336).

Conclusions
The question of fate/destiny and free will is prevalent in YA literature, as so many novels in the genre are coming-of-age stories. Another reason the theme is prevalent in YA novels is because many of them follow a rather formulaic structure, namely the hero's journey. In *Ender's Game*, *Holes*, and *Beatle*, protagonists are forced to come of age away from parents and other authority figures and therefore must shake off destiny and prophecy to become themselves.

Sachar's use of the theme of incarceration in *Holes* can provide readers with insight when determining what the text has to say about fate versus free will. The act of being incarcerated precludes one from free will. However, in the case of *Holes*, fate, or more appropriately coincidence, eventually allows Stanley to fulfill a sort of destiny.

Ender chooses not to fulfill the destiny assigned to him. Therefore, he exhibits free will by deciding not to follow orders anymore. Social demands have created a fate for Ender, but when he begins to understand the life laid out for him, he makes a conscious decision to become his own person. Ender, then, becomes a relatable hero to modern people.

Beatle Meets Destiny engages free will on a personal, instead of a cultural, level, and is played out through the tensions between rationalism and mysticism. While Beatle chooses to absolve himself of personal responsibility (as opposed to authority figures usurping his agency), his selectivity reveals cultural attitudes. Beatle has to learn to make the distinction between fate and free will as he wrestles with his own past actions, as well as his father's. In the end, these three novels seem to say that fate and free will depend on whether a person can take responsibility for him- or herself, which ultimately is a matter of crossing from adolescence to adulthood, a major component of YA novels.

Alexandra McBride, MA

Further Reading
Doyle, Christine. "Orson Scott Card's Ender and Bean: The Exceptional Child as Hero." *Children's Literature in Education* 35.4 (2004): 301–18. *Literary Reference Center*. Web. 16 Apr. 2015. <http://search.ebscohost.com/login.aspx?direct=true&db=lfh&AN=15226160&site=lrc-live>.

Gross, Melissa. "Prisoners of Childhood? Child Abuse and the Development of Heroes and Monsters in Ender's Game." *Children's Literature in Education* 38.2 (2007): 115–26. *Literary Reference Center*.

Web. 16 Apr. 2015. <http://search.ebscohost.com/login.aspx?direct=true&db=lfh&AN=24486922&site=lrc-live>.

Reynolds, Susan S. "Louis Sachar's Odyssey." *Los Angeles Times*. Los Angeles Times, 5 Jan. 2003. Web. 16 Apr. 2015. <http://articles.latimes.com/2003/jan/05/magazine/tm-sachar1>.

Bibliography

"Beatle Meets Destiny." Rev. of *Beatle Meets Destiny*, Gabrielle Williams. *Kirkus Reviews*. Kirkus Media, 31 Aug. 2010. Web. 16 Apr. 2015. <https://www.kirkusreviews.com/book-reviews/gabrielle-williams/beatle-meets-destiny/>.

"Ender's Game." Rev. of *Ender's Game*, by Orson Scott Card. *Kirkus Reviews*. Kirkus Media, 2 Nov. 2011. Web. 16 Apr. 2015. <https://www.kirkusreviews.com/book-reviews/orson-scott-card/enders-game/>.

"Holes." Rev of *Holes*, by Louis Sachar." *Kirkus Reviews*. Kirkus Media, 20 May 2010. Web. 16 Apr. 2015. <https://www.kirkusreviews.com/book-reviews/louis-sachar/holes/>.

Modenait, Mr. "Ender's Game by Orson Scott Card." Rev. of *Ender's Game*, by Orson Scott Card. *Guardian*. Guardian News and Media, 14 May 2012. Web. 16 Apr. 2015. <http://www.theguardian.com/books/2012/may/14/enders-game-scott-card-review>.

Friendship

Titles Discussed

The Perks of Being a Wallflower by Stephen Chbosky
The Sisterhood of the Traveling Pants by Ann Brashares
Will Grayson, Will Grayson by John Green and David Levithan

Thematic Overview

In the United States, the twentieth century saw the development of unique and thriving youth cultures. This development was credited to a number of different forces, including the popularity of the automobile and the introduction of compulsory schooling, which resulted in students spending a large amount of time in peer groups and away from adults. From the 1950s onward, a large number of adolescents spent most of their education and social time in the company of peers. They began to develop unique subcultures—often overlapping with musical genres, such as goth, hip-hop, and rock and roll—entwining personal and peer identities through fashion, politics, and other cultural markers. Youth cultures did not simply indicate fads; they also indicated the rising importance of friendship and social interactions for young adults.

This movement away from adult oversight and into peer social spaces is a major milestone in the establishment of YA identity. Young adults tend to develop friendships based on similarities, a fact that explains why many friendship circles are fairly homogenous in terms of factors such as race, gender, national origin, and economic class. At the same time, however, adolescents typically attempt to distance themselves from their families. In this way, peer groups may also develop around gay and lesbian identities, particular academic and cultural interests and goals, or similar factors that might distinguish the young adult from the home. As young adults enter into, and at times leave, a variety of peer groups, those friendships can have wide-ranging effects. Studies have shown that anything from grade point average to athletic performance and propensity for alcohol abuse may change when an individual enters a new close friendship. At the same time, factors such as bullying and social stratification place stress on many of these friendships, making them seem fraught and adding stress to teenagers who suddenly find themselves and their identities reliant on their friendships.

The importance of friendships is one of the most ubiquitous qualities across YA literature. As YA novels typically take place in social spheres outside the family, such as school or extracurricular activities, friendships and peer groups become the defining context of most interactions. In many classic YA novels, including S. E. Hinton's *The Outsiders* (1967) and John Knowles's *A Separate Peace* (1959), almost no action takes place outside the context of close friendships and peer groups, with the home life appearing more as an intruding factor than a defining setting. Even in novels where friendship and peer interactions are not a dominant theme, there is, almost without exception, at least one friend as a major or secondary character, vital to both the plot and the development of the protagonist. As youth culture continues to be a major force both in the lives of young adults and in popular culture as a whole, many of the most widely read YA novels of the early twenty-first century focus on the opportunities and challenges of close friendships and peer groups. Stephen Chbosky's *The Perks of Being a Wallflower* (1999) features a young protagonist learning to emerge from his self-protective social withdrawal and enter a dynamic and challenging group of outsider peers, while Ann Brashares's *The Sisterhood of the Traveling Pants* (2001) follows four longtime friends who maintain their important bond with one another while navigating their independence away from the protection of the peer group. In John Green and David Levithan's collaborative novel *Will Grayson, Will Grayson* (2010), complicated and sometimes vexed friendships serve as one important mode among many in the personal development of the two title characters.

Works

The Perks of Being a Wallflower, by Stephen Chbosky, is told from the point of view of Charlie, a freshman in high school who feels deeply alone after the suicide of his best friend the previous year. Charlie is notably shy and hesitant to participate in any social activities, but he is pulled out of his self-protective shell when he begins to interact with Patrick and his stepsister Sam, two senior students and social outsiders who use drugs and alcohol and love independent music and *The Rocky Horror Picture Show* (1975). Charlie also makes a connection with his English teacher, who provides Charlie with additional novels and nurtures his writing talent.

While Charlie becomes more deeply engaged in Patrick's and Sam's peer groups, he struggles with his home life, where he sees his sister being physically abused by her boyfriend, and begins to experience flashbacks of his Aunt Helen, who died in a car accident. Charlie revels in his new friendships, supporting Patrick when Patrick's closeted boyfriend, Brad, breaks up with him and nurturing a crush on Sam even as he dates an older girl named Mary Elizabeth. Eventually, despite some tumultuous arguments during which Charlie finds himself again alone and cut off from his peers, the year ends with renewed connections to his older friends. With the support of his friends, Charlie realizes that his Aunt Helen sexually abused him when he was young. As Charlie's friends graduate high school and move on to new lives, Charlie is sad to lose them, yet resolved to build new connections and stay socially engaged.

While Charlie's narrative takes him through a number of issues that are important in YA literature—suicide, drug use, alienation, physical abuse, sexuality—every aspect of his experience is deeply influenced by

his burgeoning friendships. As the novel is epistolary, with Charlie writing anonymously to an unnamed person whom he addresses only as "friend"—somebody he has heard "listens and understands and doesn't try to sleep with people even if they could have"—readers experience the influence of these friendships through Charlie's unreliable narration. In large part because of the trauma Charlie endured after his friend's suicide and the sexual abuse he experienced as a child, he actively detaches himself from human connection, often describing events as seeming unreal or dreamlike. This occurs both in joyous moments, such as when he first socializes with Patrick and Sam and they drive through a tunnel while listening to their favorite songs, and in moments of particular stress, such as when he witnesses Patrick getting in a fight with Brad and his friends and jumps in to defend Patrick. In the latter case, Charlie ends the fight with surprising brutality, though he glosses over the specifics, saying only: I don't really want to go into detail except to say that by the end of it, Brad and two of his buddies stopped fighting and just stared at me. His other two friends were lying on the ground. One was clutching the knee I bashed in with one of those metal cafeteria chairs. The other one was holding his face. I kind of swiped at his eyes, but not too bad. I didn't want to be too bad. (151)

Charlie does not fully understand himself in these moments, and readers are likewise given the task of moving forward with a narrator whose engagement with the outside world only gradually provides him with insight into himself. This is a multivalent process: the more time Charlie spends with friends who aid him in his path of self-discovery and reveal new aspects of the world to him (particularly their countercultural obsessions), the more the world is made real and the process of disassociation dissolved, which in turn reveals new challenges for Charlie and new opportunities to complicate and sometimes damage those friendships. This process reaches its apex when Charlie and Sam begin to engage in sexual activity, only for Charlie to experience a psychotic break and become catatonic, finally remembering his childhood molestation. Despite these challenges, the book's closing affirms Charlie's choice to pursue and develop friendships. As Sam and Patrick visit him and offer renewed support, he realizes that engagement with the world and with others is the best way for him to become the person he truly wants to be.

While Charlie must develop new friendships in order to assume his YA identity, the characters of *The*

Sisterhood of the Traveling Pants, by Ann Brashares, instead must rely on an established peer group while they explore their individuality. The novel tells the story of Carmen, Lena, Tibby, and Bridget, who date their friendship to before they were born, their mothers having met in an aerobics class while pregnant. The girls rely on one another for everything and have learned over time to view themselves in the context of this close peer group. The summer after their sophomore year of high school, however, the girls are apart from one another for the first time; while Tibby stays in their hometown, Carmen visits her father in South Carolina, Bridget goes to soccer camp in Mexico, and Lena goes to visit her grandparents in Greece. Strengthening their bond, the girls agree to send each other a pair of magical pants that fit all four of them perfectly despite their different body sizes. Each girl experiences life-altering changes over the summer: Bridget has sex with her soccer coach; Tibby forms a friendship with a younger girl who dies; Lena falls in love; and Carmen's relationship with her father and his fiancé turns so tumultuous that she runs away from their home. Throughout these events, the girls maintain contact through letters and through the pants, which affirm their connection to one another. When Lena prepares to leave Greece, for instance, it is the arrival of the pants that gives her the courage to confess her love to a boy, while also motivating her to fly to Mexico and support Bridget, who is emotionally damaged after her sexual encounter. Home together at the end of the novel, they share their stories and write them on the pants.

While all of the girls understand the value of their friendships from the start of the novel, their independence over the summer allows them to both deepen their appreciation of those friendships and experiment further with their individuality apart from the group. The narrative emphasizes this by including the letters they write to one another; while chapters typically tell the story of one girl at a time, the letters are featured throughout, acknowledging the importance of those friendships while revealing the distance between them. Carmen, for instance, finds herself without her trusted outlets to express her emotions, which leads to escalating frustration with her father, ultimately resulting in her smashing his front window and running away from home. The extreme nature of this action makes her appreciate the fact that she can share and process her emotions with her friends, causing her to reach out to her father and promise to be more honest with him in the future—in essence, extending that sense of trust to someone outside

of the core group of girls. Bridget, in contrast, finds a new freedom in her unfamiliar social setting, as none of her acquaintances know about the trauma of her mother's death. While this at first causes her to assume a new personality as an optimistic and fun-obsessed teenager, it also causes her to engage in actions she regrets and subsequently sink into a deep depression, and she realizes the importance of having people in her life who understand her troubled past. The letters emphasize the importance of the peer group as well as each girl's independence; for example, Bridget, after sleeping with her coach, writes to Carmen but does not reveal what actually happened, instead just stating that she feels confused. When they return home at the novel's end, all of the girls are finally able to share their stories and to understand what happened with the support of well-known friends. They also all find themselves changed by their independence, their sense of self-identity evolved. As in *The Perks of Being a Wallflower*, the concluding message of *The Sisterhood of the Traveling Pants* is not simply that friendships are important but that friendships and individuality must grow alongside one another. Even as the girls meet to tell their summer stories, they are already planning the next summer of independence, trusting that they will be able to share the pants then just as they do now.

The protagonists of *Will Grayson, Will Grayson*, by John Green and David Levithan, likewise find themselves influenced and affected by friendships while they assume their adult identities; unlike in the other novels, however, these friendships are fraught and often unreliable. *Will Grayson, Will Grayson* tells the story of two protagonists with the same name, with chapters alternating between their perspectives. The first Will Grayson is a straight teenage boy with only one close friend, a remarkably large football player named Tiny, who is also the flamboyantly gay, student director of the school musical. While Will prefers to avoid talking or interacting whenever possible, the outgoing Tiny pushes him into dating a girl named Jane. The other "will grayson," who never capitalizes his name, is a gay teenager at a nearby school who deeply hates everyone, including his few friends and a girl named Maura who has a crush on him. Maura invents a fake Internet profile for a boy named Isaac and, through that persona, begins online dating will grayson, eventually convincing him to meet for a date. With no Isaac to show, will grayson meets Will Grayson by coincidence, and through him begins to date Tiny. As Will Grayson suddenly feels alienated by his only friend, who is now obsessed with will grayson; will grayson finds his misanthropic worldview being shaken. When both Will Graysons manage to hurt Tiny, they conspire to show him an act of love at his musical opening. While the novel leaves the future romantic relationship between Tiny and will grayson, as well as that between Will Grayson and Jane, uncertain, all the characters are prepared to move forward with the risks and possible reward of friendship.

Neither of the title characters of *Will Grayson, Will Grayson* enter the novel with particularly good experiences of friendship to guide them, and as a result their journey is less about developing idealized friendships than about learning to navigate and nourish friendships despite significant interpersonal challenges. The first Will Grayson opens the novel by stating, "You cannot possibly pick your friends, or else I never would have ended up with Tiny Cooper." While Tiny has deep respect and love for Will, the major differences in their personalities, such as Tiny sharing his emotions and reaching out to others while Will follows his core rules of "Don't care too much" and "Shut up" at every moment, cause constant rifts between them. The second will grayson, likewise, has only Maura as a consistent friend in his life, yet describes their relationship early on by stating, "it's like those people who become friends in prison even thought they would never really talk to each other if they weren't in prison" (24). Neither character particularly desires friends, largely because being alone prevents them from being hurt, and will grayson's own struggles with mental illness make him distrustful of his ability to care for others. Yet as readers alternate between chapters and experience this distrust articulated again and again, both Will Graysons also stumble into genuine connections with the gregarious, if self-obsessed, Tiny. In the malaise of teenage moodiness and the poor decisions made in early romance, these friendships never become perfect. At the same time, however, both boys find themselves in a social space, connecting with others and surrounded by burgeoning friendships, newly aware that the imperfections of individuals make friendship necessary, not impossible.

Conclusions

In the twenty-first century, social media and digital communication have radically altered the possibilities of friendship for young adults. While novels in the 1970s and 1980s featured teenagers engaging in social activity through spaces such as school, the mall, or parks, the prevalence of digital communication technologies in the twenty-first century means that many teenagers are able to be in contact with their friends at every moment of the day. As these technologies offer one-to-one communication, such as texting and video chats, as well as more public forums, including social media applications, many twenty-first-century teenagers are able to conceive of their sociality and the availability of peer groups in a radically new way, with previous boundaries disintegrating. Even the home, which might in the past have been construed as a location away from peers and friends, is now a place from which teenagers can communicate and develop relationships.For YA novels, friendship remains one of the most recurrent and significant themes, regardless of subgenre or target audience. Instead of portraying digital communication as posing entirely new or unprecedented challenges to the friendships of twenty-first-century young adults, the best novels instead understand how familiar themes from the past—the dependence on close friends to develop an individual identity, the challenges of exclusion from peer groups, the evolving nature of friendship over time—present themselves in these new contexts. Particularly as some teenagers develop close friendships with strangers through their online personas, as is seen in the case of will grayson, the specifics of how friendships form have shifted. What has not shifted, however, is the importance of peer groups during these years. The oddly transitory space in which teenagers find themselves—living at home while developing independence at school and navigating new challenges with the support of established allies such as family members—means that friendship, or its lack, will remain a vital part of any YA experience, thus providing a perennially important theme for YA novels of all types.

T. Fleischmann, MFA

Further Reading

Ojanen, Tiina, Jelle J. Sijtsema, and Ashwin J. Rambaran. "Social Goals and Adolescent Friendships: Social Selection, Deselection, and Influence." *Journal of Research on Adolescence* 23.3 (2013): 550–62. *Academic Search Premier*. Web. 8 June 2015. <http://search.ebscohost.com/login.aspx?direct=true&db=aph&AN=89768895&site=ehost-live>.

Shuman, R. Baird. "Stephen Chbosky." *Guide to Literary Masters and Their Works*. Pasadena: Salem, 2007.

Literary Reference Center. Web. 8 June 2015. <http://search.ebscohost.com/login.aspx?direct=true&db=lfh&AN=103331LM90129790309103&site=ehost-live>.

Bibliography

Chbosky, Stephen. *The Perks of Being a Wallflower*. New York: MTV, 1999. Print.

Green, John, and David Levithan. *Will Grayson, Will Grayson*. New York: Dutton, 2010. Print.

Madden, Mary, et al. *Teens, Social Media, and Privacy*. Washington: Pew Research Center, 2013. *Pew Research Center: Internet, Science & Technology*. Web. 22 June 2015. <http://www.pewinternet.org/2013/05/21/teens-social-media-and-privacy/>.

McInally, Kate. "Who Wears the Pants? The (Multi)Cultural Politics of *The Sisterhood of the Traveling Pants*." *Children's Literature in Education* 39.3 (2008): 187–200. *Literary Reference Center*. Web. 8 June 2015. <http://search.ebscohost.com/login.aspx?direct=true&db=lfh&AN=32679773&site=ehost-live>.

Rubin, Kenneth, Bridget Fredstrom, and Julie Bowker. "Future Directions in . . . Friendship in Childhood and Early Adolescence." *Social Development* 17.4 (2008): 1085–96. *Academic Search Premier*. Web. 8 June 2015. <<http://search.ebscohost.com/login.aspx?direct=true&db=aph&AN=34728293&site=ehost-live>.

Way, Niobe. "Boys' Friendships during Adolescence: Intimacy, Desire, and Loss." *Journal of Research on Adolescence* 23.2 (2013): 201–13. *Academic Search Premier*. Web. 8 June 2015. <http://search.ebscohost.com/login.aspx?direct=true&db=aph&AN=87622526&site=ehost-live>.

Gender and Sexuality

Titles Discussed

Anyone but You by Lara M. Zeises
Fly on the Wall: How One Girl Saw Everything by E. Lockhart
Forever . . . by Judy Blume

Thematic Overview

The 1970s saw two concurrent developments in the United States. In national culture, a new wave of feminism advancing women's rights aligned with a sexual rights movement that prioritized the agency of individuals to make choices about their own bodies. Medical developments such as the birth-control pill further bolstered these movements, helping shift the national view of women's sexuality and ease some of the judgment put on women (and men) who viewed sex as a source of pleasure that could exist healthily outside of marriage. At the same time, young adult literature experienced a boom in the popularity of problem novels, books that attempt to present social problems such as alcoholism, pregnancy, and suicide with candor and sometimes explicit detail to young audiences. These young adult novels, influenced in part by the sexual revolution, featured more honest and straightforward depictions of teenage sexuality than had been the norm throughout the twentieth century.

The increased representations of sexuality within young adult novels, however, did not indicate a total acceptance of these trends. Instead, young adult novels that feature sexuality—especially instances of teenage sexuality without negative consequences, such as unwanted pregnancy or the transmission of disease—have regularly been the target of censorship, facing more challenges in general than novels that depict drug use, violence, or other sensitive and mature topics. The debates around these novels reflect another national trend: the growing ideological battle over whether students should receive abstinence-only education or comprehensive sex education that teaches proper use of contraceptives.

Throughout these debates, two facts have remained consistent: a large number of teenagers do become sexually active, and the rate of sexual activity among teenagers does not necessarily increase either over time or in alignment with societal acceptance of sexuality outside of marriage. Although the 1970s and 1980s did show sharp increases in the rate of sexual activity among teenagers in the United States, a 2011 study found evidence of a steady decline ever since. In 1988, 51 percent of never-married females and 60 percent of never-married males between the ages of fifteen and nineteen had had sexual intercourse; in 2006–10, those percentages had decreased to 43 percent of females and 42 percent of males.

Even so, these are significant percentages, highlighting why teenage sexuality is such an important theme in young adult novels. Not only are many teenagers having sex, they are doing so in the midst of a decades-long cultural and political debate about the appropriateness and safety of that sex. At the same time, as young adult bodies rapidly change and many teenagers engage in their first romantic relationships, their sexual choices and activities become an important part of their identity formation. This experience is further complicated by the disparate messages that male and female teenagers receive from society in general, which tends to encourage male sexuality while problematizing female sexuality.

Seminal young adult author Judy Blume wrote explicitly about young adult sexuality in her 1975 novel *Forever . . .* , making it one of the most frequently challenged and censored books for several decades. By the twenty-first century, the range of acceptable depictions of sexuality in mainstream young adult literature had broadened considerably, with novels such as Lara M. Zeises's *Anyone but You* (2005) featuring explicit descriptions of casual sex, while E. Lockhart's *Fly on the Wall: How One Girl Saw Everything* (2006) features a protagonist only tentatively exploring the world of sexualized relationships and male sociality. Despite regular censorship challenges, countless modern young adult novels of all genres focus extensively or even exclusively on gendered relations and sexuality, providing young readers with a diverse set of characters, experiences, and points of view.

Works

Judy Blume's classic young adult novel *Forever . . .* centers on the decision of its teenage protagonist to have sex, with her deliberations about the choice and the eventual outcome of her relationship taking up the majority of the text. The protagonist, Katherine, is a high school senior who falls in love with her boyfriend, Michael. While Michael has previously been sexually active, Katherine has not, yet she knows through conversations with sexually active friends and through her own self-knowledge that she is ready to take this step. Katherine and Michael date alongside their friends Erica and Artie, who themselves are navigating Artie's realization that he might be gay and Erica's belief that sexual pleasure should be disconnected from romance. Katherine is fortunate to receive honest advice from her parents and grandmother, as well as medical advice from Planned Parenthood, so that she is fully prepared when she enters into a sexual relationship with Michael. Deepening their commitment to one another, the couple promise to stay together forever, viewing their connection as true love. However, when separate summer plans take them

apart, Katherine begins to feel distant and finds herself attracted to her older, more sexually experienced tennis instructor. Eventually, she realizes that she must end her relationship with Michael, and while she mourns the end of that connection, she also realizes that it presages further, more emotionally mature romantic relationships in the future.

Forever . . . adopts an honest and emotionally complex point of view regarding sexuality and gender that was radical at the time of its publication and continues to be refreshing to many readers today. From the start of the novel, it is clear that the narrative will not shy away from the reality or the complexity of teen sexuality; this is made obvious in the opening line, which states, "Sybil Davison has a genius I.Q. and has been laid by at least six different guys" (1). At the same time that Sybil is explicitly said to be sexually active, she is praised for her intelligence rather than belittled or treated as unintelligent for the choices she has made, even as the main characters wonder about her motivations. Katherine's first sexual experience is handled with a similar matter-of-factness. As she and Michael confirm their love for another during an awkward series of encounters limited by Michael's premature ejaculation, the narrative is explicit with physical details, with lines such as "I could feel him halfway inside of me" (101). Sexual encounters in the novel are never singular experiences of pure love or of physical passion; instead, they are moments in which emotional intimacy, shifting self-identities, physical urges, and societal forces all present themselves. The sex is not perfect, and neither is the relationship, destined as it is to end a short while later. Blume, however, embraces these imperfections as aspects of an honest sexual relationship, and as such, she is able to craft compelling characters such as Katherine, who is educated, self-aware, and able to make choices about her own body. Even when those choices result in unhappiness or stress, Katherine still considers them positive experiences on her path to adulthood.

While Katherine makes many intelligent and careful choices regarding her sexuality, the characters of *Anyone but You*, by Lara M. Zeises, instead find themselves propelled forward by confused and sometimes irrational urges. The story focuses on Critter and Seattle, two stepsiblings who live with Critter's birth mother, Layla, after Seattle's father abandoned their combined family. Critter and Seattle are close friends and allies in their home environment, both struggling with school and both at times angry about the world that has left their mother overworked and their futures uncertain. When Critter begins flirting with an attractive girl at the local pool, Seattle reacts with jealousy and anger, emotions that drive her to shave her head and begin dating a skater boy who is visiting town for the summer. Critter, in turn, finds himself suddenly jealous and begins to experience sexual attraction toward his stepsister. When Seattle's father returns unexpectedly, both teenagers are sent into emotional spirals. While Seattle aggressively tries to convince her love interest to sleep with her, Critter falls for the girl from the pool despite her having a boyfriend. Eventually, Critter and Seattle kiss in a vulnerable moment, their summer romances having ended. While neither knows what to make of the moment of physical contact, they also know that they are close again, once more able to offer mutual support through the difficulties of their lives.

The characters in *Anyone but You* experience their sexualities and desires as aspects of their larger, more complex and wrought emotions. As a result, their experiences of sexuality appear normalized, even if their decisions are driven by unclear motives. Part of this is accomplished through the direct and uncensored narration, which switches between Critter and Seattle, both of whom talk frankly about each other's bodies as well as their own. Seattle describes wrestling with Critter while swimming together in the pool, only to realize that "Critter had this enormous hard-on" (15) and swim away. Critter, in turn, masturbates in the shower and cannot stop himself from thinking about "Sea's enormous boobs making direct contact with [his] chest" (88). The characters can speak clearly of their bodily desires, even as they feel shame about being attracted to a stepsibling, but they cannot always understand what those desires mean. Seattle, for instance, tries to initiate sex with her summer fling immediately after meeting him, removing her clothes and climbing onto his body. While her desire is clear, her narration makes no indication that she understands why she has this undeniable urge—that she saw Critter hitting on the lifeguard earlier that day and reacted with confused jealousy. In the end, *Anyone but You* offers a rendition of teenage sexuality that is stripped of the morality lessons on which young adult novels have historically relied. This not a story about learning to form mature relationships or growing from past sexual mistakes. Rather, it is one that lingers on the emotionally and physically charged moments of adolescence, asking readers to accept the characters and their choices with

the same frank honesty embodied in the characters' narrative voices.

In contrast to the raging desires of Critter and Seattle, Gretchen, the protagonist of E. Lockhart's *Fly on the Wall: How One Girl Saw Everything*, feels more alienated from than aligned with her sexuality. At the start of the novel, Gretchen is a reserved teenager at an arts school in New York. She discourages her best friend from spending time with a group of boys she calls the "Art Rats," and while she has had one short, barely physical relationship and now nurtures a crush on a boy named Titus, her experiences and fantasies remain mild and fairly innocent. After her parents announce their surprise divorce, however, Gretchen magically turns into a fly in the boy's locker room for several days, which gives her uncensored access to male bodies as well as male socialization and secrets. In addition to enjoying the prurient pleasure of viewing her naked peers, Gretchen also overhears a boy discuss having a crush on her, learns that her best friend is secretly dating a nice boy, witnesses homophobic bullying, and discovers that Titus is even kinder and more good-hearted than she first realized. When she turns back into a human, Gretchen engages with her classmates with a new openness and sense of understanding, the boys in her class having been demystified at the same time she discovered her own sexual desires.

Even though Gretchen is not a character navigating explicit sexual relationships, her life is still shaped by how she experiences gender and sexuality. At the start of the novel, she is sitting alone at school while her best friend, Katya, talks to the Art Rats, about whom Gretchen only says they "make [her] nervous" (3). She expresses her hesitance to engage with sexuality or explore the social world defined by the boys in several ways, including her tendency to shut down and refuse to talk when sexuality comes up in conversations and her regressive choice to hold onto her childhood toys and dolls, despite her mother asking her to part ways with them in preparation for their relocation to a smaller apartment. Gretchen's experience in the locker room, however, gives her an unmitigated view into the reality of the teenage male sexuality. While at first she is focused almost exclusively on bodies (having never seen a naked male before, and finding herself suddenly desirous of sexual contact in a way she had not previously been), the long conversations she overhears gradually reveal to her that the boys are as emotionally complex as she is. She witnesses them studying themselves self-consciously in the mirrors and sees the sometimes subtle ways that boys often stand up for their peers in the face of bullying. Gretchen's exploration of gender and sexuality is not defined by actual sexual contact, but it is nonetheless as significant to her as sexuality is to characters such as Critter, Seattle, and Katherine. The world of gendered relations and sexual attraction that she is entering is confusing, and her own desires are not always clear, but she still must honestly confront those differences in order to enter her own young adulthood.

Conclusions

In the popular media, sensational articles about teenage sexuality and "oversexed" teenagers became particularly popular in the early twenty-first century. Despite the rate of teen sexual activity having fallen since the 1990s and teen pregnancy being less common than in previous decades, an increase in explicit depictions of sexuality in mass media aimed at teenagers led many pundits to decry a teenage population that they saw as engaging with sexuality purely for pleasure rather than in the context of romantic love. These criticisms came from a variety of political and cultural positions, from those wishing to prevent teenagers from engaging in sexuality at all to those who feel that the heavily gendered nature of teenage relations, with boys receiving social rewards for sexual activity while girls receive criticism and shame, is itself an impediment to the development of healthy sexuality. At the same time, the growth of social media gave rise to sensational articles about teenagers sending naked photos to one another and accessing pornographic videos at young ages.

In truth, young adults' understanding of gender and sexuality does change over the decades, influenced by political and cultural forces that range from feminism and LGBT rights to conservative abstinence-only education systems. What does not change is that the young adult years are when the effects of puberty become evident, with bodily changes beginning between ages eight and thirteen for girls and between nine and fifteen for boys, and that it is during these years that roughly half of the population will experience their first sexual relationships. While a cultural debate continues around when and how discussion of sexuality and gendered differences might be appropriate, young adults continue to experience these changes, and young adult novels continue to feature complex characters who face their

own sexualities with honesty. These novels still face constant censorship challenges, just as Judy Blume's groundbreaking novels faced outcry in the 1970s. Yet the most popular novels with young adults are not the most explicit or the most instructional but rather those that avoid talking down to their audiences, instead presenting sexuality as one aspect of adolescents' rapidly changing lives with the confidence that young adult readers can understand the complexities of these relationships.

T. Fleischmann, MFA

Further Reading

Hubler, Angela E. "Beyond the Image: Adolescent Girls, Reading, and Social Reality." *NWSA Journal* 12.1 (2000): 84–99. *Literary Reference Center*. Web. 8 June 2015. <http://search.ebscohost.com/login.aspx?direct=true&db=1fh&AN=3158179&site=lrc-live>.

James, Kathryn. *Death, Gender, and Sexuality in Contemporary Adolescent Literature*. New York: Routledge, 2009. Print.

Sommers, Joseph Michael. "Judy Blume." *Magill's Survey of American Literature*. Ed. Steven G. Kellman. Rev. ed. Vol. 1. Pasadena: Salem, 2007. *Literary Reference Center*. Web. 8 June 2015. <http://search.ebscohost.com/login.aspx?direct=true&db=1fh&AN=103331MSA10349830000033&site=lrc-live>.

Bibliography

Blume, Judy. *Forever . . . .* Scarsdale: Bradbury, 1975. Print.

Bullen, Elizabeth, Kim Toffoletti, and Liz Parsons. "Doing What Your Big Sister Does: Sex, Postfeminism and the YA Chick Lit Series." *Gender and Education* 23.4 (2011): 497–511. *Academic Search Premier*. Web. 8 June 2015. <http://search.ebscohost.com/login.aspx?direct=true&db=sih&AN=63295061&site=eds-live>.

Martinez, Gladys, Casey E. Copen, and Joyce C. Abma. *Teenagers in the United States: Sexual Activity, Contraceptive Use, and Childbearing, 2006–2010 National Survey of Family Growth*. Washington, DC: GPO, 2011. *Centers for Disease Control and Prevention*. Web. 8 June 2015. <http://www.cdc.gov/nchs/data/series/sr_23/sr23_031.pdf>.

Zeises, Lara M. *Anyone but You*. 2005. New York: Laurel-Leaf, 2007. Print.

Heroism

Titles Discussed

The Bumblebee Flies Anyway by Robert Cormier
Code Name Verity by Elizabeth Wein
Staying Fat for Sarah Byrnes by Chris Crutcher

Thematic Overview

Throughout literary history, the character of the hero has passed through several stages of evolution. Ancient and prehistoric cultures created myths and legends to make the joys and sorrows of life understandable. Stories explaining tribal origins, beliefs, and customs were peopled with archetypal heroic figures whose feats and bravery engendered a sense of pride in the cultures that originated them. Such heroes as Gilgamesh (Sumerian), Odysseus (Greek), and Aeneas (Roman) helped establish the qualities of the classical archetype. He (most classical heroes were male; female examples such as Antigone, Electra, Hecuba, and Iphigenia did exist, but female heroism was of a different nature, characterized mainly by self-sacrifice and providing aid to men) was a person of high birth, possibly a demigod with supernatural abilities, who operated under the aegis of the gods. For personal honor, he embarked on a quest or goal: to find treasure, to found a new homeland, to explore unfamiliar territory in search of fresh wonders. Over the course of the quest, he performed risky physical deeds and triumphed through a combination of strength, boldness, determination, and cunning.

By the medieval period in Europe, which spanned from the fifth to the fifteenth century, the traditional hero had metamorphosed into a more human, more vulnerable figure. Now reflecting the high morality and complex codes of conduct innate to the concept of chivalry, the hero no longer had to be of noble birth, although he usually still was. His quests were for sacred objects or for victory against worthy opponents who posed a threat to well-being. He fought not so much for personal glory as from a sense of loyalty and obedience owed to his ruler. Beowulf (probably Germanic or Scandinavian), King Arthur (British), Roland (Frankish), and El Cid (Castilian) are all examples of heroes of the medieval period.

By the romantic period, from the mid-eighteenth to the late nineteenth century, the heroic ideal had changed once again, taking a turn toward the antihero in the wake of the revolutionary spirit that charged the age. Class or circumstance of birth no longer mattered; the hero was often an outcast, a brooding, flawed loner who operated beyond the boundaries of a society riddled with corruption. They waged their battles sometimes against the establishment and sometimes against internal demons. Quests were more personal, more passionate, and the journey was as important as the destination. Sidney Carton (Charles Dickens, *A Tale of Two Cities*, 1859), Jean Valjean (Victor Hugo, *Les Misérables*, 1862), Natty "Hawkeye" Bumppo (James Fenimore Cooper, the Leatherstocking Tales, 1827–41), and the title characters of Sir Walter Scott's *Rob Roy* (1817) and Alexandre Dumas's *Count of Monte Cristo* (1844) collectively demonstrate the various types of the romantic hero.

In the modern era, virtually anyone is capable of becoming a hero, regardless of class, ethnicity, physical appearance, gender, or sexual identity. Contemporary heroes often struggle with personal problems—physical or mental disabilities, substance abuse, sexuality, adherence to unconventional mores—in a chaotic, violent world dominated by faceless bureaucracies imposing arbitrary rules. The modern hero's quest is more modest than those of yore: to find personal meaning through self-discovery, to exist with individual principles intact. Robert Cormier's *The Bumblebee Flies Anyway* (1983), Chris Crutcher's *Staying Fat for Sarah Byrnes* (1993), and Elizabeth Wein's *Code Name Verity* (2012) all provide memorable examples of the wide range of modern heroes.

Works

Robert Cormier's *The Bumblebee Flies Anyway* unfolds at the Complex, a facility where experimental drug tests are conducted by Doctor Lakendorp, known as "the Handyman." The story is told mainly from the viewpoint of Barney Snow, an apparently normal sixteen-year-old who serves as a control among young terminal patients. Though Billy "the Kidney," preteen Allie Roon, and formerly handsome sports star Alberto "Mazzo" Mazzofono are all doomed, they have volunteered to undergo tests in hopes of contributing to future cures. The drugs affect each patient differently. Billy, unable to walk, is wheelchair bound. Allie becomes twitchy and stammers. Mazzo, his skin blotchy, is confined to bed. Barney has lost his senses of smell and taste, his memory is sketchy, and he is troubled by recurring nightmares of an impending automobile accident.

The only subject able to move freely about, Barney explores, inside and outside. The Complex is surrounded by a high wooden fence, which Barney scales. From the top, he sees a huge junkyard of wrecked vehicles and what looks like an undamaged red MG; when he examines the sports car more closely, he discovers it is made of balsa wood.

Mazzo, bitter about his disease, convinces Barney to be present when his "spooky" fraternal twin sister, Cassie, visits. Cassie is beautiful, and Barney wants to "be strong and brave for her." Privately, Cassie tells Barney about "the Thing": she has always felt the pains her brother experienced, and she wonders if she will die when Mazzo does. When Mazzo, who once enjoyed driving fast cars, expresses a desire to die "in a blaze of glory," Barney vows to make it happen.

To carry out his promise, Barney sneaks into the junkyard, deconstructs the wooden sports car—nicknamed "the Bumblebee"—and smuggles the pieces into the attic of the facility to reassemble. While doing so, Barney stumbles across a room with a television monitor displaying a scene from his nightmare. The Handyman discovers him and tells him the nightmare was created as a means to block the truth: Barney is also dying.

Barney does not dwell on the troubling news, working tirelessly to complete his task with Billy and Allie's assistance. He finishes the car, transports Mazzo via freight elevator to the attic, and poises the fake car outside a skylight for its final plunge. Though Mazzo dies before he can board, the car rolls down the steep roof and makes no sound when it crashes, creating the impression that it really did fly.

The Bumblebee Flies Anyway, though downbeat in tone, has a hopeful message as it explores the heroism of terminal volunteers who will never reap the benefits of the tests they undergo. Though the patients have no chance of surviving, they nonetheless unite in a selfless project to grant a fellow sufferer's last wish.

One of more than a dozen young adult novels written by Cormier, *Bumblebee* uses several symbols to underscore its themes. The fence between the Complex and junkyard, for example, represents a dividing line between the vibrancy of life and the decay of death. The wooden sports car and the image of the non-aerodynamic bumblebee, which flies despite its unwieldy build, symbolize the difference between appearance and reality.

In *Staying Fat for Sarah Byrnes*, Chris Crutcher explores themes of friendship and loyalty between two teenage outcasts who are both heroic figures. Narrator Eric Calhoune, a.k.a. "Moby" or "Fat Boy," is a smart, well-read high school senior with a good sense of humor. Obese as a child, he has become a skilled long-distance swimmer. Eric, whose father deserted Eric's mother before he was born, has been best friends for years with motherless Sarah Byrnes, a.k.a. "Scarface," whose face and hands were horribly disfigured when she was a toddler, allegedly because she accidentally overturned a pot of boiling water. Eric stays overweight to remain a misfit and maintain Sarah's friendship. Eric and Sarah brave the administration's wrath by publishing a satirical school paper, *Crispy Pork Rinds* ("crispy" for Sarah, "pork" for Eric's size, and "rinds" for the part "no one pays attention to"), aimed at those cruel to underdogs. Eric and Sarah have been through much together, particularly sessions with school bully Dale Thornton. Now there is a new hurdle: Sarah has stopped talking and is under observation at the psychiatric unit of the local hospital. Eric visits frequently, where he encounters Sarah's intimidating father, Virgil.

In school, Eric's favorite class is Contemporary American Thought, taught by his swimming coach, Ms. Lemry. He takes the class along with Sarah, his sacrilegious friend and fellow swimmer Steve Ellerby, pompous rival swimmer Mark Brittain, and Mark's pretty but submissive girlfriend Jody Mueller, on whom Eric has a secret crush. The class discusses controversial issues such as child abuse and racism. When they talk about abortion, battle lines form, with sanctimonious Mark and disciples on the pro-life side and Eric, Ellerby, and others pro-choice. Eric initiates contact with Jody, who privately admits that she underwent an abortion. The father was Mark, who feels people as committed to religion as he is should "get special leeway in the Lord's eyes." When Mark learns what Jody said, he calls her a liar in class and later attempts suicide via overdose.

At the hospital, Sarah surreptitiously communicates with Eric via coded hand signals. She finally tells him the truth: her father burned her on purpose on a wood stove during an argument with her mother. Her father is becoming more irrational, so she moves into a room at Ms. Lemry's house and returns to school. Ms. Lemry and Sarah travel to Reno in search of Sarah's mother, but when they find her, she is too frightened to testify against Virgil.

Meanwhile, Virgil Byrnes terrorizes Eric over the phone, trying to get him to reveal his daughter's whereabouts so he can ensure her continued silence. Virgil hides in the backseat of Eric's car and threatens him with a knife, but Eric refuses to give up his friend. Eric escapes, but Virgil chases him and stabs him in the back. Eric survives to tell the story to the police, who hunt for

Virgil. He is eventually found severely beaten by Eric's mother's latest boyfriend, a former Special Forces soldier who fought in Vietnam. Virgil is ultimately convicted and sentenced to prison, and the Lemrys formally adopt Sarah.

Like many of Crutcher's other young adult novels, including *Running Loose* (1983), *Chinese Handcuffs* (1989), and *Ironman* (1995), *Staying Fat* uses athletic competition as a framework for the story, focusing on dedication to practice and commitment to a cause. Crutcher's works have frequently been challenged or banned for language or controversial subject matter.

Elizabeth Wein's *Code Name Verity* opens with the written chronicle of a young, petite blond woman named Queenie, who begins with a lie: "I am a coward." Under the code name Verity, she was dropped into France as a spy in late 1943. Captured, she has been held in a former hotel in Ormaie and tortured by the Gestapo until she agreed to tell the Nazis what they want to know.

Given pen and paper, Queenie spins a story, similar to journal entries, over a three-month period. Most of the story concerns her friend Magraret "Maddie" Brodatt, a pilot of the Women's Auxiliary Air Force, but it also includes details of airfields, personnel, equipment, and radio codes. The pages are translated from English into German by Anna Engel, a reluctant secretary to Captain Amadeus von Linden of the SS. When the story is complete, Queenie, who ultimately reveals her true name to be Julie Beaufort-Stuart, will be sent to a concentration camp for medical experiments and ultimately, execution.

Part 2 belongs to dark-haired Maddie, code-named Kittyhawk, the pilot who delivered Julie to France, substituting for an injured man. Julie and Maddie's identity papers were inadvertently mixed up: Julie has Maddie's ID, and Maddie has Julie's papers in the name of Katharina Habicht. After Maddie's plane crashes, she is rescued by the French Resistance and hidden in a barn. Meanwhile, Georgia Penn, an American and seeming turncoat making propaganda broadcasts for the Germans, finds and interviews Julie, who gives her coded messages. Georgia passes along information to the Resistance indicating that Julie has given the Nazis obsolete information and invented codes; most of her elaborate story, except for her friendship with Maddie, is fiction. Maddie and the Resistance plan a rescue with the help of Anna Engel,

who has a "crisis of conscience" and gives Maddie Julie's writings.

With Maddie along, the Resistance blows up a bridge, stopping a German bus carrying Julie and other prisoners. But the plan goes wrong: Nazi guards begin shooting and maiming the prisoners in reprisal. Before they can harm Julie, she shouts Admiral Horatio Nelson's legendary dying words—"Kiss me, Hardy"—to Maddie, who knows what to do: she shoots and kills Julie. Later, the Resistance carries out a successful attack, blowing up Gestapo headquarters, and Maddie is rescued and returned to England.

The story of a close friendship between two vastly different individuals—the Scottish, wealthy, aristocratic Julie and the Jewish, working-class Maddie—*Code Name Verity* is a fictionalized account of the very real types of people who worked for the Allied cause during World War II. As the author notes at the end, women did serve as pilots and spies, and some of them died in action. Unlike *The Bumblebee Flies Anyway* and *Staying Fat for Sarah Byrnes*, which deal with heroism on a small, personal scale, *Code Name Verity* looks at individual heroism on a large scale at a time when the fate of the world was in the balance and millions of lives were at risk. Wein has since written a sequel, *Rose under Fire* (2013), which places a captured female pilot in peril at Ravensbrück concentration camp.

Conclusions

There is a remarkable uniformity of opinion among sociologists, psychologists, and academics that heroes are not only beneficial but necessary to the overall health of a society. This is particularly true in the United States, which, though a relatively young nation, is universally considered the current economic, military, and cultural leader of the world. Role models, whether historical entities (Nathan Hale, Daniel Boone, Sacajawea, Davy Crockett, Harriet Tubman, Susan B. Anthony, Rosa Parks, and Martin Luther King Jr.) or mythical creations (Paul Bunyan, John Henry, Superman, and Wonder Woman) help highlight important milestones of national existence. These are men and women, fashioned out of genuine human experience, whose real or imagined feats Americans can point to with pride. Their stories are used both to entertain and to inculcate respect for cultural values. Heroic principles, positive work ethics, and unyielding perseverance serve as motivational examples for subsequent generations to emulate.

Heroes are especially important for young adults as the contemporary world grows increasingly cynical and fraught with tension. Each day seems to bring new crises from which there is no escape, because every event is endlessly examined from all possible angles in print or broadcast. Controversial issues—abortion, same-sex marriage, income equality, climate change, religious freedom, racism, gun control, fracking, immigration, child abuse—are polarizing the nation into camps of angry adherents unwilling to countenance opposing views. Information overload from myriad media sources that often represent opinion as objective reportage confuses matters further in young minds, equating celebrity with excellence. It is not surprising that in polls teenagers typically name movie, sports, and music stars as their personal heroes. While there is nothing wrong in admiring such individuals for achieving fame and fortune, they do not always provide ideal examples of inspirational behavior worthy of imitation.

In the absence of readily identifiable true heroes, young adult literature does a service by filling the gap, providing characters and situations with which adolescents can identify. Believability is a key concept in such storytelling. Despite some protective and well-meaning adults' long-standing objections to colorfully blunt language, overt sexuality, substance abuse, and similarly controversial traits, fictional heroes must be flawed in the same way as real people. When placed in commonly confronted situations and dealing in realistic fashion with problems that might occur in real life, such heroes can lead by example, teaching without preaching about the difference between right and wrong and educating readers about desirable qualities and behaviors. Unlike in real life, which is often illogical, fictional heroism can bring a semblance of order to a chaotic world, providing a satisfying sense of justice and completeness where it is sorely lacking.

Jack Ewing

Further Reading

Campbell, Joseph. *The Hero's Journey: Joseph Campbell on His Life and Work*. Ed. Phil Cousineau. San Francisco: Harper, 1990. Print.

Carter, Regina Sierra. "YA Literature: The Inside and Cover Story." *Journal of Research on Libraries and Young Adults* 3 (2013): n. pag. Web. 13 May 2015.

<http://www.yalsa.ala.org/jrlya/2013/04/ya-literature-the-inside-and-cover-story/>.

Bibliography

Campbell, Joseph. *The Hero with a Thousand Faces*. 3rd ed. Novato: New World, 2008. Print.

Cowden, Tami D., Caro LaFever, and Sue Viders. *The Complete Writer's Guide to Heroes and Heroines: Sixteen Master Archetypes*. 2000. Las Vegas: Archetype, 2013. Print.

Fike, Matthew A. *The One Mind: C. G. Jung and the Future of Literary Criticism*. New York: Routledge, 2014. Print.

Knapp, Bettina. *Machine, Metaphor, and the Writer: A Jungian View*. University Park: Pennsylvania State UP, 1989. Print.

McLuhan, Marshall, and Wilfred Watson. *From Cliché to Archetype*. 1970. Ed. W. Terrence Gordon. Berkeley: Gingko, 2011. Print.

Raglan, FitzRoy Richard Somerset, Baron. *The Hero: A Study in Tradition, Myth, and Drama*. 1936. Mineola: Dover, 2011. Print.

Identity and Self-Discovery

Titles Discussed
Uglies by Scott Westerfield
The Meaning of Consuelo by Judith Ortiz Cofer
The Absolutely True Diary of a Part-Time Indian by Sherman Alexie

Thematic Overview
Questions of identity and self take on new urgency as students enter high school. So many life-shaping decisions loom large on the horizon. There are classes and specializations that must be chosen, clubs that will either look good on a college application or bring genuine enjoyment to decide among, and opportunities to volunteer or work at companies that will give the student a peek at a future career—if only the student knew what he or she wanted to be.

For the young adult reader, struggles with identity and the process of self-discovery touch at the heart of their experience. They stand at the edge of adulthood, and they want to know as much about what they can expect as possible before that take that next big step. The problem is that it is hard to know what you want to know when you are not even certain who you are.

Before the emergence of young adult literature as a genre, questions of adolescent identity were not often explored in literature. The first novel to gain a young adult audience for its exploration of these themes was *The Catcher in the Rye* by J. D. Salinger. Published in 1951 for an adult audience, it is now a staple of YA literature. In *The Catcher in the Rye*, Holden Caulfield's attempts to bring meaning to the losses he has experienced are futile. How can he bring meaning to events he does not understand? How can he understand the motives of others when he cannot even make sense of his own?

Holden Caulfield may have been one of the first questioning teenagers in literature, but he was hardly the last. Changes in American society and culture took place in the 1960s and 1970s, when Vietnam War protests, the black power movement, and the feminist movement brought a new intensity to questions of identity and self-discovery. Efforts to get in touch with the inner self spawned personal empowerment programs.

The introduction of the birth control pill in 1960 and the legalization of abortion in 1973 introduced additional possibilities for women. Their sexuality was suddenly perceived as something that was within their control. By the 1980s, the theme of identity and self-discovery had become a permanent fixture in American culture. It was inevitable that it would occupy a prominent place in young adult literature.

One especially notable exploration of identity and self-discovery in the teen years came in the form of a film. *The Breakfast Club* (1985), directed by John Hughes and starring a group of teens who would go on to fame as the "Brat Pack," packed years of angst into a one-day detention session in a single room. The film is an enduring classic, in part because of its searing look into the struggles of adolescents.

By the 1990s, J. K. Rowling would immortalize the search for identity and purpose of Harry Potter and his friends. Rick Riordan would follow suit with Percy Jackson and the Kanes—three more young adults in search for answers about the self.

Works

To know oneself can be a difficult proposition, especially for a teenager. It implies an ability to take an unflinching and dispassionate view of one's true motives, wants, and needs. *Uglies*, *The Meaning of Consuelo*, and *The Absolutely True Diary of a Part-Time Indian*, all published in the first decade of the twenty-first century, follow young people in their attempts to sort these things out and figure out their place in society.

Uglies (2005), by Scott Westerfield, explores the theme of identity and self-identity by juxtaposing a teen's need for autonomy with a societal desire for perfection in a dystopian society where every teen receives plastic surgery when he or she turns sixteen. Once the surgery is completed, the teen moves to an area that is home only to others who have achieved similar perfection.

On the surface, this practice takes a lot of pressure off the teens. All they have to do is have the surgery as anticipated. Then they can move on with their lives with others who are similarly perfect.

There is just one problem: the surgery that makes everyone perfect also damages the brain, making them unable to realize their full potential. The central question of *Uglies* is whether the trade-off is worth it. The answer is not as straightforward as it would seem. The surgery is mandatory, so to escape the surgery, one must escape the society. Of course, the authorities have a lot at stake. They are not about to allow anyone to truly have a choice in this matter. The ramifications of that cause conflict and bloodshed. At least one teenager in the book has the chance to make her own choice about the surgery, but the decision she makes is not necessarily the one that is best for her *self*.

The book leaves many questions unanswered. These include questions about the ethics of the surgery, the importance of the search for a cure to reverse the effects of the surgery, and the need for the surgery in the first place. It is a lot for a young adult reader to contemplate, but *Uglies*, and the rest of the series that follows, has been hugely popular since it first came out.

The Meaning of Consuelo (2003), by Judith Ortiz Cofer, tells the story of a Latino family living in Puerto Rico in the 1950s. American investment is changing the island. At the same time, the family is undergoing a series of mounting tragedies. As trouble grows and the younger sister in the family, Mili, shows increasing signs of being mentally ill, Consuelo, the older sister, must take on an increasingly adult role. Not only must she help to watch her sister night and day, she must serve as the one to console her mother during this difficult time.

Consuelo has her own problems, though. She is turning fifteen. She is ready to be more independent just at the time when her family is shrilly insisting that she put the family first. Consuelo resents this, but more than resenting it, she is aware of the ways in which these competing expectations are changing her. Stung by the fact that her fifteenth birthday—a significant birthday in her culture—is not acknowledged at all by her family, she not only spends the evening with the boy she likes but also has sex for the first time. Rather than bringing them closer, however, it ends up driving him away.

Consuelo has seen her older cousin and close friend Patricio leave Puerto Rico and create the life he wanted for himself in America, and begins wondering if she should do the same. She is reluctant to leave her family, but she is equally reluctant to stay where she is. "I had to find other ways to survive," she says. "And I had to leave La Casa de la Mama Isadora and start my story in a completely new place." This awareness on her part is part of her growing sense of identity and self-discovery. Consuelo recognizes that she could stay where she is. Her parents love her and will have space in their lives for her again after their grief has lessened. But she does not want that space any more. "I no longer wanted the part I'd been assigned," she says. She wants to construct her role in the world for herself rather than allow her parents to do so for her, even if this means "becoming the character always off-stage, the one who can be talked about and reinvented according to the demands of the tale or the motives of the teller."

When Consuelo both recognizes and accepts the price she will pay for an identity of her own, one that is separate from her family, she has completed an essential step in her quest for independence.

In *The Absolutely True Diary of a Part-Time Indian* (2007), the protagonist, Junior, is faced with a similar dilemma. Junior is an intelligent, creative teenager living on an impoverished American Indian reservation whose underfunded high school cannot give him the knowledge he hungers for. The adults on the reservation—including Junior's equally smart older sister, who is unemployed and living in their parents' basement—all seem to have been trapped by poverty into lives of broken dreams and wasted potential, a fate which Junior hopes to avoid. Given the chance to attend a school in a wealthier (and very white) suburb, he leaps at it but soon finds his situation more complicated than he expected. He has difficulty fitting in with the students at his new school, most of whom have never seen an Indian other than the school's cartoonish mascot. Yet he also no longer fits in with his former friends on the reservation, who now see him as a sell-out—a "part-time Indian."

His best friend, Rowdy, is not happy for him, nor are most of the other people he knows. It is not a matter of being jealous of Junior's good fortune as much as a matter of being angry that he makes them face up to their own wasted potential. Junior is smart enough to understand that but is not sure what to do about it. He is simply attempting to define his own identity and discover his place in both of the worlds he now inhabits.

By the end of the school year, Junior is far more self-aware than at the start. As he has settled into life at his new school, he has come to terms with straddling two worlds and belonging, as he thinks of it, to many different tribes. He manages to reconcile with his old friends as well; when they make up, Rowdy calls him an "old-time nomad," moving around in search of the best resources as Indians used to do before they were placed on reservations. Still, Junior has conflicted feelings about the prospect of leaving his family and friends behind: "I hoped and prayed that they would someday forgive me for leaving them. I hoped and prayed that I would someday forgive myself for leaving them." He has made considerable progress in his journey of self-discovery, but the journey is not over.

Conclusions

While *Uglies* tells a tale with a central theme of identity and self-discovery set in a dystopian society, both *The Meaning of Consuelo* and *The Absolutely True Story of a Part-Time Indian* set their stories in realistic settings. With *The Meaning of Consuelo*, it was set within a large and loving Puerto Rican family. As the family was faced with change to the island, change to their prospects, and change within the family, Consuelo was faced with the changes that go with becoming a young adult. Her journey was complicated by the mental illness of her younger sister, her father's infidelity, and the social mores of her culture. Consuelo's navigation of these obstacles and the part they play in making her the woman she is becoming add a layer of depth to the story, making it not simply a coming-of-age story, but also a richer examination of the sticky bonds of culture.

For Junior in *The Absolutely True Diary of a Part-Time Indian*, the journey is just as complex. He knows, as does Consuelo, that his path must lead him away from everything he knows. Yet Junior realizes the formation of his identity and quest for self-discovery cannot be completed within the narrow confines of the reservation. He also knows that his tribe is an integral part of who he will become. His task will be to reconcile these two opposites and to reach a place of peace.

All three of these works were well received. *The Absolutely True Diary of a Part-Time Indian* received the National Book Award, and top or best book of the year designations from *Publishers Weekly*, *School Library Journal*, Amazon.com, and *Kirkus Reviews*. Both *Uglies* and *The Meaning of Consuelo* also received multiple awards. In all three books, the themes of identity and self-discovery are played out against a conformist background. In *The Absolutely True Diary of a Part-Time Indian* and *The Meaning of Consuelo*, this conformist background is the harder to escape and leave behind because the protagonists' beloved families are part of this conformity. To leave that behind means walking away from everything familiar and facing new challenges that cannot be anticipated because they are not part of the character's experience. To take this step as a young adult is especially difficult. That difficulty is a key part of the draw of these novels.

Gina Hagler, MBA

Further Reading

Blasingame, Nilsen. *Literature for Today's Young Adults*. Boston: Pearson, 2014. Print.

Cart, Michael. *Young Adult Literature: From Romance to Realism*. Chicago: Amer. Library Assn., 2010. Print.

Chance, Rosemary. *Young Adult Literature in Action: A Librarian's Guide*. Santa Barbara: ABC-CLIO, 2014. Print.

Bibliography

Barcott, Bruce. "Off the Rez." *New York Times*. New York Times, 10 Nov. 2007. Web. 10 May 2015. <http://www.nytimes.com/2007/11/11/books/review/Barcott3-t.html?_r=0>.

Bucher, Katherine, and KaaVonia M. Hinton. "Exploring Contemporary Realistic Fiction." *Young Adult Literature: Exploration, Evaluation, and Appreciation*. 3rd ed. New York: Pearson, 2014. 125–58. Print.

Cole, Pam B. *Young Adult Literature in the 21st Century*. New York: McGraw, 2009. Print.

Rev. of *The Meaning of Consuelo*, by Judith Ortiz Cofer. *Publishers Weekly*. PWxyz, 1 Nov. 2003. Web. 15 May 2015. <http://www.publishersweekly.com/978-0-374-20509-6>.

Lynch-Brown, Carol G., Kathy G. Short, and Carl M. Tomlinson. *Essentials of Children's Literature*. Harlow: Pearson, 2014. Print.

Strickland, Ashley. "A Brief History of Young Adult Literature." *CNN*. CNN, 15 Feb. 2015. Web. 10 May 2015. <http://www.cnn.com/2013/10/15/living/young adult-fiction-evolution>.

Rev. of *Uglies*, by Scott Westerfield. *Guardian*. Guardian News and Media, 23 June 2012. Web. 14 May 2015. <http://www.theguardian.com/books/2012/jun/23/review-uglies-scott-westerfield>.

Jobs and Working

Titles Discussed
Love and Other Perishable Items by Laura Buzo
Dead-End Job by Vicki Grant
Ask the Passengers by A.S. King
Dairy Queen by Catherine Gilbert Murdock

Thematic Overview
In an article for the Young Adult Library Services Association (YALSA) on the history of young adult literature, Michael Cart said that it "is made valuable not only by its artistry but also by its relevance to the lives of its readers." Cart goes on to say it is also important that young adult novels are relevant to the intended target audience's interests. It is better to promote literacy among young adults by allowing them to choose what interests them rather than forcing them to value literature just for being literature.

Young adult literature about jobs and working is becoming more relevant as more teens hold jobs while in high school. As *NPR*'s Marcela Valdes wrote in 2013, more young adult books are focusing on dystopian societies fraught with "economic anxiety." Examples of economic anxiety are readily available in novels such as Veronica Roth's *Divergent* (2011), where people are placed in communities and jobs based on the kind of work for which they are best suited, and in Suzanne Collins's Hunger Games series, in which characters fight a government that starves its people in order to control them. The protagonist in each series takes responsibility for providing for her family. The need to provide for one's family mirrors the emerging awareness of young adult readers as they begin to notice the economics of their own families. Works following characters who have a sense of economic responsibility help readers to contextualize their own experiences of money and family.

Teens who have jobs while in high school have an interest in young adult novels that include protagonists with jobs—whether it is for supporting their families or for earning spending money. Either way, many teens need to reconcile their feelings about having to work instead of just having to worry about homework and their social lives. Working teens may react by saying "life is not fair" or envying those who seem to "have it easy." Reading about young adults who must work may help teens to realize that they are not alone, and that many young adults do not have families who can pay for luxuries like cars, computers, and phones. Even if young adult readers do not work, they can learn to value those who do.

Frances, in *Dead End Job,* works the late shift at a secluded convenience store to save money for art school; Amelia, in *Love and Other Perishable Items,* puts in long hours at a local grocery store to become financially independent; D. J., in *Dairy Queen,* works extremely hard to keep her family's dairy farm running while her dad is recovering from a hip injury; Astrid, in *Ask the Passengers,* works weekends for extra cash. Each protagonist has a personal reason for working that may resonate with young adult readers who work while in school. Frances wants a good future; Amelia hates having to ask her parents for money because she knows they cannot afford all the things she wants; D. J. feels responsible for keeping her family's farm going, even though it gets in the way of her schoolwork.

Works

Frances is a seventeen-year-old girl who works every day after school until midnight. The convenience store where she works is in a secluded location, and she often works alone until the overnight manager starts her shift. Frances is often bored and draws. One night, a boy named Devin comes in and innocently asks to see her drawing. Frances is friendly but not flirty since she already has a boyfriend, Leo. Even so, Devin comes in the next night with an expensive gift of pastels as an apology for bothering her the night before. Frances is uncomfortable about accepting the pastels, and is relieved when Leo comes to pick her up from work. After multiple run-ins with Devin, Frances realizes he is stalking her. He e-mails her pictures he has taken of her and sends flowers to her house. He also sends Leo a picture of her, making Leo believe that Frances was cheating on him.

The stalking comes to a climax when Devin forces Frances into the store's back room and locks the two of them in. He tells her that if he cannot have her, he will kill her. She stalls for time, offering to draw his picture, and then stabs him with her pencil. She escapes the back room right as Leo pulls in.

The novel ends with Devin going to trial for attempted murder. Frances claims that she will not let what happened to her keep her from going to art college and says, "But I have to admit, I'm scared. Maybe I should just stay in Lockeport for a while with Mom and Dad. And Leo. We'll see." The ending demonstrates how a young woman, even when she has money and ambition, can feel unsafe.

While this novel does not really focus on Frances's job, it does show the consequences of an unsafe work environment. Frances is a minor, yet she works the late shift completely alone. She has no means of protection against robbery, kidnapping, and attempted murder. It is important to note that Frances should have been provided with a safer work environment. It is also important to realize that this is not only true for a teenage girl, but for any employee. *Dead-End Job* is about how the work of young people, especially anyone in a service position, is trivialized and how that can create difficult situations in a society where money is necessary to succeed.

When Devin threatened Frances, she contemplated dying at the age of seventeen. She says "I felt sad for my father. He'd blame himself. He didn't like me working alone at a convenience store out on the highway. He'd tried to stop me, but I'd won. We both knew he didn't make enough money to pay for my college education. Somebody had to." *Dead-End Job* understands how hard it is to be a parent that is unable to support your children. The novel nurtures the maturity a teenager needs to understand this reality. Many people work hard and still do not have enough to afford everything they need, never mind the things they would like to have. Frances does not feel anger toward her father, since she understands he is doing the best he can.

Love and Other Perishable Items (2012) by Laura Buzo, is about a fifteen-year-old girl named Amelia. Amelia lives in Australia, goes to school, and works at a grocery store referred to as "The Land of Dreams." Amelia's coworker and trainer at work is twenty-one year-old Chris. Amelia has a huge crush on Chris, despite knowing their age difference makes it impossible for them to be together. Amelia tries to look and act more mature to get Chris to notice her. While it takes some time, Chris does notice Amelia, and he begins to wish she were older.

Both Amelia and Chris work while attending school and envy their classmates who are supported financially by their parents. Chris complains about having to work at the store, and he says that he could put more effort into schoolwork if he did not have to work. He resents that his friend Ro's parents gave him the down payment for a house and now his friend can live alone. Chris wants to rent an apartment, but his dad says paying rent is a waste of money. Chris argues that paying the money is worth the price of independence. Chris feels he cannot get ahead, saying "[I] can't run my own race. I'm constantly checking what's happening in the other lanes." Amelia understands Chris's frustration and chooses to work in order to be financially independent from her parents, but her long hours takes a toll. She is frequently tired and does not have time for a social life.

Amelia wakes up early, goes to school, and then works until nine o'clock every night. Then she has to finish all her schoolwork before going to bed. While she does not resent her parents for not having more money to give her, she does resent their unequal share of work around the house. While having a conversation with Chris about what Amelia hates, she confesses that she believes feminism has ruined her mother's life because she has to work at a job and at home. Amelia's dad also works but does not help with the cooking, cleaning, or taking care of the children.

Amelia works with people of all ages at the grocery store. While her work ethic is admirable, it may be worrisome for parents to see what Amelia is exposed to while working with older people. Amelia's coworkers ask her to smoke cigarettes and marijuana,

drink alcohol, and have sex. Admittedly, this could happen to Amelia under other circumstances. Buzo's message is that young adults need to be given the tools to make responsible, safe decisions when presented with opportunities to drink, smoke, and have sex.

Astrid, the protagonist in A. S. King's *Ask the Passengers*, works part-time at a catering company during her senior year of high school. Her parents are not good role models: her mother is an agoraphobic, workaholic, and her father is unemployed and smokes marijuana. Similar to the other protagonists, Astrid does not have much of a social life since she works weekends, and work becomes Astrid's social outlet and the setting of the novel's main conflict.

The novel deals primarily with the crush Dee, Astrid's coworker, has on Astrid. Astrid begins to question her own sexuality in the face of Dee's crush. She knows dating coworkers is generally taboo, but it is not at all uncommon, and Astrid, who does not have much time to meet people outside of work, starts a relationship with Dee.

In *Dairy Queen*, D. J. works on her family's farm in order to help support her family and keep the farm running. D. J. puts more effort into the farmwork than her homework, not because she likes farmwork, but because she feels she has no choice. Her family is thankful for her hard work, but D. J. becomes depressed and resentful of her family's expectations, causing tension between her and her parents. Eventually, D. J. realizes that she needs to find a balance between her work life and her social life. She cuts down on the farmwork and joins her school's football team. Her family realizes they were being unfair to D. J. and help pick up the extra work around the farm. *Dairy Queen* teaches the importance of hard work but also acknowledges the importance of recreation.

Reading these novels may help equip readers to handle difficult situations in the workplace. Readers should also appreciate being able to learn about jobs outside their own experience, as working at a grocery store is much different from working on a farm, but both require a good work ethic and self-motivation. It is beneficial for teens to develop a strong work ethic, but not at the cost of getting poor grades or putting oneself at risk, however.

Conclusions

Young adult fiction might be used to expand the perspective of young adults and teach them to empathize with the people around them. Reading about the work of others can prepare young adults for difficult situations they may encounter in the workplace.

Critics agree that young adult literature is becoming more prominent on the best sellers list, and more young people ages sixteen to twenty-nine are now reading these types of books. In each novel, the protagonist faces his or her precarious place in the workforce using different coping mechanisms, depending on the challenge each is confronted with. In *Dead-End Job*, Frances is forced into a job to provide for her future, but this puts her at risk of violence. Her labor, youth, and gender are connected vulnerabilities. According to critics these kinds of situations offer young adult readers "culture and contemporary realism."

In *Love and Other Perishable Items,* Amelia uses her sexuality to succeed in the workplace. She must keep in mind that she is working to become financially independent from her parents, which will require her to balance professionalism and her feelings for her coworker, Chris. Astrid is in a similar situation where she works with Dee, a coworker who has a crush on her, and Astrid must now examine her sexual identity, all while remaining professional. Critics believe that teens connect with this kind of story on a personal level.

D. J. is a victim of larger social issues. She has the most difficulty balancing work and school, as she takes it upon herself to keep the family farm going. She is concerned with the economics of self-employment due to her father's injury. D. J. must create her self-identity while working on the farm, and unlike other characters, she creates her own space for socializing, which forces her family to appreciate the work she does for them. It also changes her family's view of gender roles; D. J. is financially providing for the family, while her father does the cooking and baking.

The creation of self through work, and the resignation to its necessity by young adults is a major factor in these books. Providing for oneself and others is the most important and difficult aspect of growing up, and these books link that maturity to larger social issues. Valdes writes, "As situations get more desperate, so do the characters' reactions." These characters come to understand that though they are young, work is a necessity they have to face and accept.

Alexandra McBride, MA

Further Reading

Rev. *of Ask the Passengers*, by A. S. King. *Kirkus Reviews*. Kirkus Media, 15 Aug. 2012. Web. 12 May 2015. <https://www.kirkusreviews.com/book-reviews/as-king/ask-passengers/>.

Rev. of *Dairy Queen*, by Catherine Gilbert Murdock. *New York Times*. New York Times, 17 June 2006. Web. 2 May 2015. <http://www.nytimes.com/2006/06/18/books/review/18conni.html?_r=0>.

Rev. of *Love and other Perishable Items*, by Laura Buzo. *Kirkus Reviews*. Kirkus Media, 24 Oct. 2012. Web. 12 May 2015. <https://www.kirkusreviews.com/book-reviews/laura-buzo/love-and-other-perishable-items/>.

Bibliography

Barnes, Meredith. "How Young Adult Fiction Came of Age." Interview by David W. Brown. *Atlantic*. Atlantic Monthly Group, 1 Aug. 2011. Web. 12 May 2015. <http://www.theatlantic.com/entertainment/archive/2011/08/how-young-adult-fiction-came-of-age/242671/>.

Cart, Michael. "The Value of Young Adult Literature." *YALSA*. American Library Association, Jan. 2008. Web. 12 May 2015. <http://www.ala.org/yalsa/guidelines/whitepapers/yalit>.

Strickland, Ashley. "A Brief History of Young Adult Literature." *CNN*. CNN, 15 Apr. 2015. Web. 12 May 2015. <http://www.cnn.com/2013/10/15/living/young adult-fiction-evolution/index.html>.

Valdes, Marcela. "What Terrifies Teens in Today's Young-Adult Novels? The Economy." *NPR*. NPR, 30 Sept. 2013. Web. 12 May 2015. <http://www.npr.org/2013/09/30/226472708/whats-terrifying-teens-in-todays-ya-novels-the-economy>.

Love

Titles Discussed
Eleanor & Park by Rainbow Rowell
Sloppy Firsts by Megan McCafferty
Son of the Mob by Gordon Korman

Thematic Overview
Many teenagers experience their first romantic relationship during their adolescent years. Although it is rare for these romances to last beyond the end of high school, the

combination of bodily and hormonal changes through puberty and increased independence and emotional maturity makes the experience of adolescent love particularly intense. Hormonally, strong physical attraction triggers adrenaline, which increases excitement, and serotonin, which increases relaxation and blissful feelings. At the same time, the feeling of being in love affects testosterone in both men and women—while men experience lowered testosterone levels, female testosterone levels increase. For teenagers who are in the middle of experiencing drastic and disorienting changes in their bodies, this additional hormonal shift can feel especially intense, which in part explains the over-the-top, dramatic emotions often associated with the teenage concept of love and romance.

As so many people experience their first romantic relationships during adolescence, YA literature has consistently featured love as a major theme. While writers of the 1960s and 1970s were more likely to explore nonsexual and restrained relationships, limiting themselves to chaste kissing and longing, from the 1970s onward, authors were increasingly willing to craft characters who not only went on a few dates but initiated physical and sexual relationships of an intensity to match their emotional connection. Critically lauded novels such as Judy Blume's *Forever* (1975) and Nancy Garden's *Annie on My Mind* (1982) paved the way for sexualized romances as well as gay characters, facing constant censorship for the unapologetic choices of their young protagonists. At the same time, some of the best-selling novels of the 1980s and 1990s were series that focused primarily on young romance, such as Francine Pascal's Sweet Valley High series. Even YA novels not explicitly concerned with love often contain romantic subplots, with love providing motivation for characters across science fiction, fantasy, adventure, and similar subgenres.

While the intense emotions associated with love make romance a rich topic for writers, there are other reasons for its prevalence in YA novels. To fall in love is also widely considered a rite of passage into adulthood. This view is true despite the nature of the romance, from Megan McCafferty's *Sloppy Firsts* (2001), in which romance is more of an idea than a reality, to Gordon Korman's *Son of the Mob* (2002), in which love creates a conflict between the protagonist and the home. Even the healthy love at the center of Rainbow Rowell's *Eleanor & Park* (2013) is complicated by the pressures from both peers and adults. Romantic connections also provide teenagers with an opportunity to imagine an independent future—living as adults and possibly cohabitating with a romantic partner. As such, romance is not simply an obsession with another person but also an engagement with who the teenager might become in the future—how the adult self might be formed and impacted by the love of another.

Works

Sloppy Firsts is not so much a novel about experiencing first love as it is a novel about learning to recognize when the potential for love presents itself. The protagonist, Jessica Darling, is a withdrawn and moody teenager who retreats further from peers and family when her best friend, Hope, moves away during their sophomore year of high school. Jessica's remaining friends, whom she calls the Clueless Crew, are boy-obsessed girls who spend their lunch period going over fashion magazines. Writing sporadic letters to Hope, Jessica struggles to make any true connections at school, and while she nurtures a crush on a popular senior boy named Paul, she fails to find anyone she actually wants to date. Instead, her attention drifts among a number of boys who show varying forms of interest in her. There is an old friend, Scotty, who is obviously in love with her; Pierre, a somewhat nerdy freshman she nicknames Pepe Le Pew, whom she admires but does not take seriously as a prospect; and a drug-dealing troublemaker named Marcus, who suddenly begins to give her unexpected flirtatious attention but who was also involved in Hope's brother's drug overdose. As Jessica's sister prepares for marriage, Jessica finds herself more and more incapable of actual human connection, instead lingering on her disappointment with others and the fleeting ideas that Paul or Scotty might make a proper boyfriend. In junior year, however, Marcus returns to school a changed person, having been identified as a genius and moved into honors courses. There, Jessica and Marcus connect as friends, and by the end of the novel, she decides to be honest about her feelings and to enter into a relationship with him.

In contrast to many romantic, idealized depictions of first love and the joys it offers, Jessica's experience with romance is instead marked by pessimism, discomfort, and false starts—it is not until the very end of the novel, in fact, that she finally decides to actually get together with Marcus. For Jessica, this is a process by which she must first learn to be true to herself and to her own feelings in order to have a sincere, loving relationship with another person. She figures this out less by actually spending time with Marcus and instead by analyzing the variety of other insincere relationships she constructs in her life. The boy she feels she loves, for instance, is Paul, a senior she only knows from a distance. Therefore, she is able to idealize him as a perfect boyfriend. This construction fails, however, when Paul graduates high school and comes out as gay. She likewise considers her longtime admirer, Scotty, to be a safe option, always available as a boyfriend if she decides she needs one. When she finally does ask him on a date, however, Scotty has stopped carrying his torch for Jessica and has a girlfriend.

Even the platonic relationships Jessica has with her female friends are largely constructed out of lies and fantasy, as she purports to loathe the Clueless Crew yet realizes toward the close of the novel that one of those girls, Bridget, is actually a caring and attentive friend who feels similarly disconnected from the peer group. While Jessica has clear ideas about who she is and what romance should be, Marcus still manages to connect with her. Over time she realizes that the depth and honesty of the conversations they share matter much more than the sardonic ideals she has chosen to live her life by. In the end, she finds herself prepared, if not for love itself, then for the possibility of love with all of its risks and uncertainties. With Marcus having announced his feelings for her, she panics, but she is determined to pursue the relationship anyway.

Vincent, the protagonist of *Son of the Mob*, does not have trouble identifying the person he loves. Instead, he must navigate the differences in their lives and home environments in order to experience a truly loving relationship. Vincent's father, older brother, and relatives all work in organized crime. While Vincent refuses to go into the family business, he still sees his life constantly shaped by the family's illegal activities. After realizing during a football game that his opponents are afraid to tackle him because of his father's reputation, Vincent storms off the field and runs into Kendra, a classmate who writes for the school newspaper. Quickly, Kendra and Vincent realize they have feelings for each other, but just as quickly, Vincent learns that Kendra's father works for the Federal Bureau of Investigation (FBI) and has been investigating his own family for years. Hoping to keep the fact of the relationship secret from his family and his family's business secret from Kendra, Vincent nonetheless pursues the strong feelings he holds for her. He also finds himself wrapped up in organized crime after trying to help a hapless gambler in his father's debt,

only to end up being taken advantage of again and again. In the end, Vincent is able to find a way to help out the gambler, find an informant in the family (and help him escape safely), and impress his father. His competency and independence established, he reasserts his choice to stay out of organized crime while taking his relationship with Kendra public at last.

Through the compelling true-crime narrative, *Son of the Mob* draws attention to the fact that teenage romance typically marks a significant break between the family life at home and the independent life the young adult is beginning to establish. Although critical of organized crime, Vincent has also learned to establish a form of peace with his family's business over time, doing his best to ignore that reality so that he might pursue his own interests. With Kendra, however, this uneasy truce becomes impossible—in order for Vincent to pursue this new love, he actively puts his family and his new girlfriend at risk. Further, he realizes the necessity of severing his relationship to organized crime in order to develop a romantic relationship that is honest to himself.

The tension between FBI agent and organized crime boss, then, exaggerates many of the emotional considerations teenagers face when falling in love, with the act of turning away from the home life feeling like a betrayal of what came before. It is also, however, an opportunity for self-growth and positive change. Motivated by the love he feels for Kendra, Vincent realizes he must take action—driven by his own morals and goals—if he is to be with her. As such, he manages to reveal the relationship to his father through the same conversation in which he helps the FBI informant escape the city and clarifies that his involvement with the family business has ended. His maturity evidenced, he is able to return to Kendra, affirming his independence and his ongoing relationship with a home life he is leaving but still honoring with a complicated respect.

Home life likewise complicates the love that blossoms between the two protagonists of *Eleanor & Park*. For Eleanor, however, this is a process by which she must not only learn that she is deserving of love, but also that love can exist in a substantive and healthy way. Set in the 1980s, Eleanor and Park meet each other as two misfits in a small town, with Park offering Eleanor a seat on the bus during her first day of school. Eleanor had spent the past year staying with relatives, abandoned there by her mother, but has now returned to her tiny home, sharing a room with four siblings and living in constant fear of her abusive stepfather. When Park sees Eleanor's unconventional style (bright red hair and male clothes), he feels affection for her, and that affection blossoms through their shared love of music and comics.

Their romance is a rare point of happiness in their lives, particularly for Eleanor, who is bullied at school and tormented at home. While Park is quick to express his love for her, she does not find herself able to return it and even vocalizes doubt about the feasibility of young romance when reading William Shakespeare's *Romeo and Juliet* (1597) in class. At Park's home, she is safe from her family and witnesses Park's parents' stable and loving relationship, which feels foreign to her. When Eleanor's stepfather learns that she has been seeing Park, however, he flies into a rage, and Eleanor fears both violence and sexual assault from the alcoholic man. With the support of Park's family, the two teenagers drive Eleanor to the door of an uncle several states away. Although they say goodbye and Eleanor at first fails to return communication she receives from Park, she eventually mails him a postcard, with the end of the novel suggesting that it might finally announce her love for him.

While Eleanor has the more difficult home and school life by far, both she and Park find in each other a romance that signifies escape, safety, and understanding, rather than simply pure physical passion or immature fun. In this way, *Eleanor & Park* is about the ability of two teenagers to build a world together, apart not only from their troubled home lives, but from school and the bullying they experience from peers. The book emphasizes this concept through its third-person omniscient narration. At the start of the novel, the narrative voice lingers on one character at a time for multiple pages, revealing their troubled pasts as well as the attraction they feel for one another. As it progresses, however, the switches between characters come more and more frequently, until there are moments when sentences change focus so quickly it seems as though the narrator is in both of their minds at once. This is an intensity that, while fueled by physical longing, is not defined by sexuality.

In the end, the world that Eleanor and Park are able to create together does offer salvation from Eleanor's abusive home, even if it is a salvation that necessitates their separation from one another. Using a vehicle borrowed from Park's parents (symbolically, a loan from the best example of sustained and mutually respectful love in the novel), they are able to extend their safe and supportive bubble, placing Eleanor in a new and hopefully supportive home. While there is deep sadness in their separation, the postcard sent by Eleanor with the implied message of "I love you" also suggests optimism. In this ambiguity, there is the possibility that, safe from her stepfather, Eleanor has learned that she deserves and can express love. True to the complexity of the novel, however, this is kept not as a certainty but as a truth only shared by the two main characters.

Conclusions

In the era of massively popular YA novels and movie franchises like the Hunger Games, Harry Potter, and Twilight series, the inclusion of a love story seems to be all but a requirement. Romantic plotlines can be used to add an additional emotional complexity and sense of suspense to novels that are otherwise driven by action and adventure. Likewise, YA romances themselves remain a popular subgenre with readers, even as they receive less critical or academic attention, with Gossip Girls and similar series regularly charting on best seller lists.

As Park suggests when discussing *Romeo and Juliet* in class, there is a special thrill and joy that readers experience through narratives of first love. Emotional upheavals, bolstered independence, physical passion, and hormonal drives are all not only present in the lives of young adults, but present with an intensity that has likely never been felt before. For young adults in the twenty-first century, this experience often comes with altered implications than it did in the past. According to the Pew Research Center, only 51 percent of adults were married in 2011. Similarly, those who do get married are likely to have a number of romantic partnerships (including cohabitation) before marriage. As many young adults are also likely to engage in sexual relationships at earlier ages than was common throughout most of the twentieth century, the expectations of what love means, exactly, have clearly shifted. Rather than a disbelief in love, this signals an understanding that the emotional and physical intensity of love is valuable but not necessarily permanent, with the romantic love of adolescence likely to be only one instance of many loves throughout life.

For YA novels, this shifting perspective indicates a different type of maturity on the part of readers. Plots are less likely to focus exclusively on confusing feelings and promises of eternity, instead showing characters like those discussed above, cynical but also willing to take the dive into the complexities of romance. The emotional highs and lows of love are constants throughout literature and art. YA novels in the twenty-first century are no exception—they simply provide a wider range of skepticism, complexity, and hope than was offered to young adults in the past, and in turn celebrate a wider range of possibilities for what love can mean, one romance at a time.

T. Fleischmann, MFA

Further Reading

Fisher, Helen. *Why We Love: The Nature and Chemistry of Romantic Love.* New York: Holt, 2004. Print.

Hedeen, Katrina, and Rachel L. Smith. "What Makes a Good YA Love Story?" *Horn Book Magazine* May/June 2013: 48–54. *Literary Reference Center.* Web. 10 June 2015. <http://search.ebscohost.com/login.aspx?direct=true&db=lfh&AN=87024783&site=lrc-live>.

Bibliography

Cart, Michael. *Young Adult Literature: From Romance to Realism.* Chicago: ALA, 2011. Print.

Cohn, D'Vera. "Love and Marriage." *Pew Research Center.* Pew Research Center, 13 Feb. 2013. Web. 10 June 2015. <http://www.pewsocialtrends.org/2013/02/13/love-and-marriage/>.

Feiring, Candice. "Concepts of Romance in 15-Year-Old Adolescents." *Journal of Research on Adolescence (Lawrence Erlbaum)* 6.2 (1996): 181–200. *Academic Search Complete.* Web. 10 June 2015. <http://search.ebscohost.com/login.aspx?direct=true&db=a9h&AN=17699763>.

Nature and Survival

Titles Discussed

Hatchet by Gary Paulsen
Apocalypse by Tim Bowler
The White Darkness by Geraldine McCaughrean

Thematic Overview

The theme of nature and survival is not new to storytelling; many cultures have told stories that involve nature and the natural world and, particularly, humankind's struggle with and triumph over nature. In the latter half of the nineteenth century, realism became increasingly popular in literary storytelling in the United States. As Americans explored and settled the frontier, readers and writers moved away from the interests of the Romantic movement. In the last decade of the nineteenth century, a worldwide perspective emerged that made human beings the focus of its study. Naturalism emerged first in novels dealing with an urban setting. Regardless of setting, however, the concept was simple: to show objectively the human animal and how it behaves in relation to the world around it.

While urban settings became the ideal environment for writers such as Émile Zola to chart the survival of humans against indifference, violence, and the determinism of society, writers in the United States found a different setting to showcase the struggle of humankind. Reacting against the conceptions of nature set forth in previous decades by writers such as Ralph Waldo Emerson, Henry David Thoreau, and Walt Whitman, naturalist writers saw the vast landscape of the America as a natural force indifferent to the lives of human beings. In these spaces, individuals showed their true nature through their survival against the harsh, untamed world. Writer such as Stephen Crane, Frank Norris, and Jack London thrived as the twentieth century began, telling stories that showcased the triumph of individualism and free will in the American frontier and beyond.

While humankind's survival and triumph against nature set the stage historically for the theme of survival in the natural world, over the course of the twentieth century, new perspectives emerged on the relationship between humanity and nature. In the nineteenth century, the novel was predominantly seen as a form of entertainment and not an entirely serious literary endeavor. But as more serious authors began to write prose and more serious readers began to read novels, the novel began to be seen as a more serious literary form. However, adults were the audience for the majority of novels throughout the twentieth century, until the publication of S. E. Hinton's first novel, *The Outsiders*, in 1967. While literary works had been written for audiences of a variety of ages, not until the late 1960s did that form of young adult (YA) literature came into its own. For the first time, novels were written for and marketed to an adolescent audience, written from the perspective of a teenage protagonist and dealing with themes related to the transitory time period between childhood and adulthood.

YA literature quickly grew in the decade following Hinton's novel, finding its place within US and world literature, but it did not hit its true height until the 1990s and the first decades of the twenty-first century. Originally focused on realism and adolescent characters dealing with themes of identity, dating, love, and other difficult issues, YA literature began to splinter into subgenres. While there were a great variety of forms in YA literature, each was simply a different way to access and portray similar important issues of growing up.

The theme of nature and survival is one that became popular in YA literature nearly a century after its origins in American literature. The one distinct difference of this subgenre in the twentieth and twenty-first century is the relationship between human beings and their natural surroundings. Where the protagonists of books by authors such as Jack London found themselves pitted against nature in largely antagonistic relationships, the main characters of YA survival stories find a more holistic perspective. *Hatchet* (1987) by Gary Paulsen is one of the first YA novels dealing with the theme of nature and survival. Although written during the 1980s, when YA literature saw a brief dip in popularity, Paulsen's story became a popular and respected one. In the twenty-first century, writers Tim Bowler and Geraldine McCaughrean have followed Paulsen's lead and have added new perspective on the nature and survival theme through novels such as *Apocalypse* (2004) and *The White Darkness* (2005).

Works

Hatchet begins with the main character, Brian, on a small plane from New York to visit his father. Brian's parents have been separated for some time, but this trip marks the fact that they are getting a divorce, an idea that Brian cannot deal with as he sits in the copilot chair in the airplane. He feels hopeless, powerless, and alone, but before he has time to think too long about his circumstances, the pilot has a massive heart attack and Brian crash-lands the plane into a lake in the wilderness somewhere between New York and northern Canada. After Brian escapes from the plane, he learns to survive on his own in nature. With the hatchet that his mother gave him before the trip, Brian fends for himself. However,

Paulsen does not simply depict the theme of survival as the triumph of the individual against nature. Brian survives by learning to become a part of nature, by accepting his place, such as when he comes face to face with a wolf, which "knew Brian, knew him and owned him and chose not to do anything to him. But the fear moved then, moved away, and Brian knew the wolf for what it was—another part of the woods, another part of all of it." Brian sees everything as connected and natural, and by becoming a part of the woods himself, there is no longer conflict between him and the predators he had learned to fear.

Similarly, the juxtaposition of the city and nature becomes an important device in the story. In the beginning, Brian knows only the muted colors and sounds of the city; the natural surroundings are foreign. As he continues to learn from his environment, he also learns what does and does not belong, and he is able to make his own judgments about what is right for him, such as when he leaves the rifle from the plane: "Without the rifle he had to fit in, to be part of it all, to understand it and use it—the woods, all of it. With the rifle, suddenly, he didn't have to know; did not have to be afraid or understand." Brian learns to follow his own intuition. In the end, both his ability to survive and his understanding of himself are intricately connected. He survives exactly because he re-creates the agency and identity that he thought he had lost in his parents' divorce.

In *Apocalypse*, written by British author Tim Bowler, the protagonist of the story, Kit, is marooned on a small island with his parents after their yacht goes off course. The island is inhabited by a group of people known as Skaerlanders, who capture Kit's parents soon after they land on the island. Like Brian in *Hatchet*, Kit is forced to rely upon and trust in himself in the absence of his parents. He is aided by Ula, a local girl, as he attempts to find his parents and escape from the island. For the most part, though, he acts on his own, and in surviving, he realizes he is more than just a child: "He did not know how he had reached this place. . . . The boundaries of what he had believed in had long since fallen away." Yet while Kit comes into his own by being placed in extraordinary circumstances, the scope of the novel goes beyond the character of Kit. Through the beliefs of the Skaerlanders and the presence of a mysterious man on the island, Bowler also introduces the idea of good and evil and morality in general. In the end, Kit's survival redefines many of his previous assumptions about morality.

In early twentieth-century stories about nature and survival, writers wrote mostly about male protagonists. In general, these men faced direct, brutal competition with nature and found the independent determination to survive. In many ways, this tradition has continued in YA literature. Many novels with nature and survival at the heart of the story line revolve around young male protagonists. However, a growing number of writers have begun working with nature story lines that involve female protagonists as well. *The White Darkness* is one such story of a female protagonist finding empowerment and self-fulfillment in nature. As an author, Geraldine McCaughrean has found a voice telling and retelling favorite stories with empowered female characters. Her other works include *Not the End of the World* (2005), a version of the biblical flood and the story of Noah; *The Glorious Adventures of the Sunshine Queen* (2010); and *Gilgamesh the Hero* (2002), a retelling of the ancient Sumerian epic.

The White Darkness focuses on Symone Wates, a young girl who is obsessed with Lawrence Oates, a real-life British Antarctic explorer and whose life and family have always revolved around the mysterious continent. After Symone's father dies, a family friend known as Uncle Victor persuades her mother to let her go to Paris with him. However, this trip is motivated by devious ideas and devout beliefs. Victor takes her instead to Antarctica, where she is finally able to separate fact from fiction. Surviving in near-death conditions with her sanity slipping, she sees Oates as a regular human being (not an untouchable idol) and separates her childhood fantasies from the reality of her situation. She moves out of the past and starts her own life.

From the beginning of the novel, Symone is interested in adventure. It is a part of her family heritage and a part of herself, and an Antarctic adventure becomes a way for her to find herself by exploring the interests of her parents. Although she does not choose her adventure, nature and survival does not simply stir something within Symone as it does for Brian in *Hatchet*, but rather leads her to discover her identity. However, McCaughrean treats the theme of nature and survival as more than a vehicle for self-discovery, and this twist distinguishes her novel from other YA books that deal with nature and survival. By both surviving the brutal climate of Antarctica and challenging Victor, Symone is able to create an identity that makes her story a continuation of her father's and her ambitions both personal and part of a larger narrative. Symone is able to create something distinct and real for herself through the fulfillment of her personal dreams and her connection with Oates. By finally separating fact from myth in every aspect of her life, Symone can face the realities of her life.

The complexity of Symone's problems places her as the most mature protagonist of the three novels. In *Hatchet*, being lost in nature is the opportunity for Brian to become his own person and to make his own decisions. Kit experiences similar revelations on the island of Skaer. An extreme situation forces him to deal with problems that he might never choose to face on his own and gives perspective to his own problems. Through survival, Brian is empowered, which returns to him the power he thought he had lost because of his parents' divorce. Similarly, Kit looks for strength and finds knowledge of the world he is growing into, but his lessons are similarly basic compared to the deeper revelations that take place for Symone. By adding fantasy to the theme of nature and survival, McCaughrean creates a deeper and more substantial personal development for her character.

While employing theme of nature and survival in YA literature, each of these novels is also characteristic of each writer's body of work. Paulsen began his writing career in the late 1960s, making him one of the first YA writers. While Paulsen's earlier work focused on period pieces and Western stories, nature has always been a part of his books. *Hatchet* is one of Paulsen's most successful novels and the first book of the series known as Brian's Saga. *Apocalypse* is Tim Bowler's seventh novel and contains the themes of fantasy, the supernatural, and horror characteristic of Bowler's other novels. Bowler also employs a dark tone, aimed at older readers on the YA spectrum. *The White Darkness* is Geraldine McCaughrean's first contemporary YA novel, although its use of historical figures connects it with the other period pieces of McCaughrean's body of work. The long publication history of books that examine survival in nature means it will likely continue to be a successful subgenre of young adult fiction.

Conclusions

The continued success of Paulsen and the popularity of other novelists who make nature and survival central to their YA narratives suggests that this theme appeals to adolescent readers of any decade. Paulsen, Bowler, and McCaughrean have won awards for their works, but many novels using the nature and survival theme have not seen the same commercial or critical success as YA works such as the Harry Potter, Twilight, or Hunger Games series.

Even though nature and survival stories have not had the runaway successes of works in subgenres such as fantasy and science fiction, traces of this theme can be found in some successful YA series. For example, Suzanne Collins's *The Hunger Games* (2008) is a story about the survival of Katniss Everdeen. Similarly, James Dashner's *The Maze Runner* (2009) tells the story of protagonist Thomas's survival within a maze. Although the maze is built by humans, Thomas's relation to it seems to recall the indifferent nature faced by the protagonists of early American naturalism.

Audiences of YA literature are drawn to the struggles faced by adolescent protagonists. While audiences of the early twenty-first century are drawn to fantasy and other speculative-fiction subgenres, there continues to be a place for books that engage the theme of nature and survival. The theme of nature has a universal appeal beyond the genre of YA literature. Because of its characteristics—mysterious, intimidating, and terrifying but also hospitable—nature has long had a place in literature and storytelling.

Aaron Horton, MA

Further Reading

Falconer, Rachel. "Crossover Literature and Abjection: Geraldine McCaughrean's *The White Darkness*." *Children's Literature in Education* 38.1 (2007): 35–44. *Literary Reference Center*. Web. 28 May 2015. <http://search.ebscohost.com/login.aspx?direct=true&db=ehh&AN=23591178&site=ehost-live&scope=site>.

McCaughrean, Geraldine. "The Booklist Printz Interview: Geraldine McCaughrean." Interview by Stephanie Zvirin. *Booklist* 1 Mar. 2008: 65. *Literary Reference Center*. Web. 28 May 2015. <http://search.ebscohost.com/login.aspx?direct=true&db=1fh&AN=31388002&site=ehost-live&scope=site>.

Ringrose, Christopher. "Lying in Children's Fiction: Morality and the Imagination." *Children's Literature in Education* 37.3 (2006): 229–36. *Literary Reference Center*. Web. 28 May 2015. <http://search.ebscohost.com/login.aspx?direct=true&db=hlh&AN=21937114&site=ehost-live&scope=site>.

Bibliography

Gilbertson, Irvyn G. "McCaughrean, Geraldine." *Continuum Encyclopedia of Children's Literature* (2003): 529. *Literary Reference Center*. Web. 28 May 2015. <http://search.ebscohost.com/login.aspx?direct=true&db=1fh&AN=18776468&site=ehost-live&scope=site>.

Gross, Claire E. "Apocalypse." Rev. of *Apocalypse*, by Tim Bowler. *Horn Book* Nov.–Dec. 2005: 713–14. *Literary Reference Center*. Web. 28 May 2015. <http://search.ebscohost.com/login.aspx?direct=true&db=1fh&AN=18740327&site=ehost-live&scope=site>.

Lubar, David. "The History of Young Adult Novels." *ALAN Review* (2003): 117–22. DavidLubar.com. Web. 19 Mar. 2015. <http://www.davidlubar.com/ya-hist.htm>.

Reutter, Vicki. "Adventure and Survival." *School Library Journal* May 2004: 63. *Literary Reference Center*. Web. 28 May 2015. <http://search.ebscohost.com/login.aspx?direct=true&db=lfh&AN=13074087&site=lrc-live>.

Stowell, Theresa L. "Gary Paulsen." *Critical Survey of Long Fiction, Fourth Edition* (2010): 1–3. *Literary Reference Center*. Web. 28 May 2015. <http://search.ebscohost.com/login.aspx?direct=true&db=1fh&AN=103331CSLF14770141000075&site=lrc-live>.

Rev. of *The White Darkness*, by Geraldine McCaughrean. *Booklist* Jan. 2008: 14. *Literary Reference Center*. Web. 28 May 2015. <http://search.ebscohost.com/login.aspx?direct=true&db=lfh&AN=28833334&site=ehost-live&scope=site>.

Parent and Family Problems

Titles Discussed

A Brief Chapter in My Impossible Life by Dana Reinhardt
Homecoming by Cynthia Voigt
The Impossible Knife of Memory by Laurie Halse Anderson

Thematic Overview

As young adult novels were first recognized as a distinct genre of literature in the 1950s and 1960s, a large number of books focused on teenage protagonists who were in essence removed from their family unit. S. E. Hinton's 1967 novel *The Outsiders* features a group of orphan teenagers who rely on siblings and friends rather than parents to navigate the world; similarly, J. D. Salinger's *A Catcher in the Rye* (1951) and John Knowles's *A Separate Peace* (1959) both place their protagonists in boarding schools, where the parents are only able to have minimal influence. The popularity of these parent-free adolescents reflect the emphasis these novels placed on teenagers as independent figures, navigating the world from their unique position between childhood and adulthood; with parents absent from the picture, much more attention could be turned to interactions with peers, first romances, and other perennial topics of the genre.

By the 1970s, however, young adult novels began to shift their focus to social problems, and in turn parents became more common characters, especially when they represented problems such as divorce, alcoholism, poverty, and abuse. With some popular exceptions, a large number of novels through the 1980s still featured teenage protagonists exercising their independence outside of the family. However, rather than absent parents, these teenagers returned home to families that added further difficulty to their teenage years, often through violence and neglect. This can be seen in Cynthia Voigt's 1981 novel *Homecoming*, in which a mother abandons her children who then set out on an arduous journey to find relatives and a home. The sudden opportunity for young adult writers to depict social problems with realistic prose rather than forced optimism coupled with the changing face of American families at this time—divorce rates steadily rose, single mothers became more common, and the 1950s idealism of the nuclear family was not only less common as a lived reality but also less desirable, particularly to women who sought careers or men who wished to take on the domestic role of raising children. While parents entered the young adult novel more often during these decades, they were rarely loving and supportive figures and even more rarely were they portrayed as well-rounded and developed characters who played significant roles in the lives of their children.

The twenty-first century saw another significant change in the depiction of parents and family structures: while novels increasingly featured diverse families (including divorced and mixed families, gay and lesbian families, and families that blended cultural traditions), they also increasingly featured supportive and complex parent figures who were critical influences on the teenage protagonist. In part, this has to do with the increasing maturity of young adult novels and young adult readers—many adolescents do have significant and honest relationships with their parents, and as such, novels in which parents are rendered insignificant can appear false. Likewise, the increased diversity of family structures has also made conversations about family more comfortable for many readers (the shame associated with divorce in the 1950s, for example, is much less common in the twenty-first century). Dana Reinhardt's *A Brief Chapter in My Impossible Life* (2006), for instance, features two loving adoptive parents who encourage and support their daughter as she forms a relationship with her birth mother and explores her Jewish heritage. Even when parents are still reflective of social problems, they are more likely to appear as complicated and sympathetic characters with a significant presence in the lives of their children, as in Laurie Halse Anderson's *The Impossible Knife of Memory* (2014), in which a single father battles his post-traumatic stress disorder (PTSD) from serving in the Iraq War. Supportive or neglectful, married or single, parents in twenty-first-century young adult novels are no longer absent figures their children only occasionally recall, but instead they are presented as significant figures in the overall plot and themes of the novel, as involved in the lives of their children as the adolescents are involved in the complexities of the home.

Works

Homecoming tells the story of the four Tillerman children (between the ages of six and thirteen years), beginning when their mother abandons them in a parking lot. The oldest of the children, Dicey, decides they must travel to Bridgeport, where a relative they have never met named Aunt Cilla lives and where she hopes they might find their mother again. As Dicey knows that the government will separate the children from one another and place them in potentially unsafe foster homes if she contacts the police for help, she becomes something like the ersatz mother figure, trying her best to protect the young children on their journey. As the children sleep in abandoned houses and ration their little money for food, they encounter both friendly and malicious strangers, including a couple of college students who take them in for the night. Dicey is also distressed to see her younger brother Sammy regularly turning to crime, stealing in an effort to help the family out. When they reach Cilla's house, they find out their aunt is dead and instead are briefly taken in by her daughter, a religious woman who openly expresses her disinterest in raising the children and contemplates sending Sammy to the state rather than caring for him herself. Unhappy in this temporary home, the children again take to the road, having learned that their grandmother lives in Maryland. After another dangerous journey, they find their impoverished grandmother, who is reluctant to raise more children after all the difficulties she had faced with their mother. Eventually, however, the grandmother comes to accept the children, who feel that they might be happy at her farm despite the financial and emotional hardships it presents.

For the Tillerman children, family and parental problems are not simply one aspect of their lives, but rather the driving force in shaping their youth. However, the novel does not present the instability of the family as being any one person's fault, exactly, but rather the result of a number of other social factors, the largest among them being the mother's mental illness and the poverty passed generationally through the family. With the exception of recollections by the children, the mother is only present in the novel in that opening scene of abandonment, yet through the narrative the reader comes to learn of the extreme difficulties in her life, culminating in her becoming catatonic and being institutionalized. The fact that the children are aware of these hardships allows them to form a sophisticated understanding of what family can provide—they know, for instance, that state-sponsored organizations are likely to scatter the children into different homes and that although their religious cousin might provide them the stability of a roof and a comparatively steady income, she does not offer the honest love and support that the children need. Because of all this, the Tillerman children exhibit a much greater degree of independence than is typically seen in literature focusing on such young protagonists. The orphans and boarding-school children of 1950s young adult novels were free to explore their burgeoning adult identities with relative independence from their parents; the Tillermans, by contrast, have had the circumstances of their lives shaped by such extreme parental hardships that they are instead forced into adult roles and required to take mature actions in order to form a new, healthier sense of family. In the end, finding that the ideals of a stable family unit and financially secure home are unavailable to them, they instead define family based on the love and support shared among siblings, finding that this mutually dependent bond is strong enough to sustain them after all.

The protagonist of *A Brief Chapter in My Impossible Life*, Simone, lives in a family that is in many ways the polar opposite of the Tillerman family. Adopted as a baby, Simone's parents are happily married and supportive of both each other and their children. Simone's mother is the family breadwinner, and her father spends a lot of time caring for the children and cooking delicious meals for the family. Simone fits comfortably into this family unit, identifying herself as a liberal and an atheist just as her parents do, and she rarely thinks about her birth mother, Rivka. This changes, however, when Rivka contacts her one day. Although at first reluctant, Simone eventually agrees to meet Rivka, who reveals that she is dying of cancer. Simone then begins a process by which she learns about Rivka's life as well as about her diverse Jewish heritage, with Rivka identifying as an agnostic Jew after leaving the Hassidic family of her youth behind. Simone also begins to date her first boyfriend, a boy named Zack who comes from a practicing Jewish family. By the time Rivka dies at the end of the novel, Simone is confident enough to visit the home of her grandfather, to sit shiva, and to confront him about his relationship with his estranged daughter. In the end, Simone does not have clear answers about her own beliefs or future but optimistically faces the challenges of navigating an increasingly complex world with the support of her family.

While Simone faces challenges related to her family, she does so from a somewhat unique setting in young adult literature, with her own parents happily married and providing nothing but support and encouragement as she begins to explore her biological family and heritage. From the start of the novel, her parents are the ones who suggest Simone return the calls from Rivka, and her mother happily shares the story of the adoption when Simone decides she is ready to hear it. Likewise, her atheist parents do not discourage her new interest in Judaism, even as they had previously celebrated Simone's own involvement in her school's atheist club. Instead, they celebrate her new interest, accepting it without question and even hosting a Passover ceremony at their house when Rivka is too ill to do so herself. This narrative is a marked contrast to what many other young adult adoption novels represent, where conflicts between biological and adopted families (and particularly between cultural and religious differences) become a source of stress for adolescent protagonists. Free of this conflict and gifted with a biological mother and adoptive parents who fully support her independence, Simone is able instead to approach the emotional complexities concomitant with exploring her heritage and deepening her sense of personal identity. She describes this often through the metaphor of the family tree, remarking how slim and uncomplicated her own tree is at the beginning of the novel but celebrating it instead at the novel's end for its complexities and many branches. While in some ways the challenges Simone faces are about honestly facing her family heritage and history, then, they are just as importantly about her taking opportunities to reconsider her own sense of self and future path. By the end of the novel, she emerges confident and mature, happily pursuing her first romantic relationship and processing the loss of Rivka with the support of friends, family, and Judaic traditions.

Unlike the happy stability of Simone's life, Hayley, the protagonist of *The Impossible Knife of Memory*, has come to know nothing but radical and disruptive instability during her adolescent years. Raised by her single father, Andy, the two spent five years before the novel's opening traveling the country as Andy drove a commercial truck and Hayley homeschooled herself. A war veteran, Andy experiences constant struggles with post-traumatic stress disorder, suffering from hallucinations that drive him to violence and to alcohol and other substances in order to cope with the pain. When Andy and Hayley decide to settle into a home for a while, however, they face additional challenges—Hayley must learn how to interact with peers and to exist in the social environment of her new school, while Andy finds it harder to avoid his past when he is not in constant movement. Hayley eventually makes a friend named Gracie, who is often preoccupied with the divorce of her parents, and a boyfriend named Finn, whose sister is addicted to drugs and whose own home life is troubled. Hayley also receives some support for her father's worsening condition through his ex-partner Trish, although Trish's struggles with alcoholism previously caused her to abandon the family and both Trish and Hayley fear Andy will only make Trish's own condition worse. Eventually, Hayley opens up more to Finn about her family situation, and when her father attempts suicide, Finn is there to help her save him. At the novel's close, Hayley is cautiously optimistic, planning a future at college while her father seems to be improving through therapy and the support of others.

While the emotional instability of Hayley's home life makes her narrative resemble the wandering of *Homecoming* more than the supportive family of *A Brief Chapter of My Impossible Life*, her experience is defined as much by her commitment to her father as it is by the challenges he brings into her world. Hayley feels like she is actually the parent in the relationship with Andy, and her commitment to him is in fact much like the commitment of a mother to a child, with Hayley sacrificing her own needs and constantly convincing herself that Andy will not survive without her support. Because of this, Hayley's new life at the school presents her with unique challenges. On one hand, her enrollment in education and the family's choice to remain in one place represents a shift toward stability and future growth, yet at the same time, Hayley and Andy are so used to their constant travel as a coping mechanism that school life seems strange and impossible to Hayley, and she believes the move to be a major mistake at the start of the novel. In many ways, Hayley understands this through her focus on time—when the past (which includes her father's wartime service) becomes present in their life, her father becomes violent and incoherent. When they manage to stay in the present, however, avoiding both facing the past and planning for an unstable future, she believes that she and her father are fine. Yet once in school and developing relationships with peers that she hopes will last into the future, Hayley's strategy of avoidance and constant movement begins to fail her. These tensions come to a head when her father attempts suicide at the end of the novel. As he threatens to jump off a cliff, Hayley in turn threatens to follow him and jump herself, insisting that "I've been standing on the edge with you for years." More than a threat designed to make him live, Hayley's declaration is also an affirmation of their deep bond: they might face unimaginable challenges and traumas, but they also have the unshakable connection of familial love, and as such Hayley is only willing to pursue a future that includes Andy as well. While her life may be filled with the same radical instability that the Tillerman children face, Hayley's experience is also one relatively unique to contemporary young adult literature, in which the family problem is less something that must be overcome for total independence and instead a challenge that the teenage protagonist is willing to commit to, knowing that she and her father are strongest together.

Conclusions

The Impossible Knife of Memory has an additional quality that is rare in young adult novels—Hayley's father, Andy, receives several short chapters in which he narrates his own experiences, particularly the flashbacks to his time in war. The inclusion of these sections is indicative of the change in contemporary young adult literature, with parents and adult figures receiving increasing importance both in the lives of the teenage protagonists and the narrative in general.

The fact that Andy is portrayed as a complex and fully developed character could be taken as an indication that adolescent readers today are more likely to give their attention over to adult characters than they might have been in the past. At the same time, however, a number of popular novels rely upon and revive the trend of orphans and boarding schools that was popular in the middle of the twentieth century. Massively popular science-fiction and dystopian novels such as *The Maze Runner* and *The Hunger Games* go to elaborate lengths to remove parents from the narrative arcs of their main characters. In these examples, the focus on action, rebellion, and the independence of the protagonist renders family problems as nearly irrelevant, operating perhaps as a distant motivation for the main character but rarely entering the plot directly.

Ultimately, however, the tendency of young adult literature to address mature themes and plots of emotional and literary complexity has meant a boost in novels that address family problems. As families are often both the primary support network for teenagers and also the relationship against which teenagers rebel, the problems associated with the family can have tremendous ramifications for young adult development. While the stereotypical reaction of teenagers impulsively rebelling against their parents is still common, readers are more and more likely to find relationships like those shared between Hayley and Andy in *The Impossible Knife of Memory* or Simone and her parents in *A Brief Chapter of My Impossible Life*—relationships in which adolescents and adults face problems together, recognize their difficulties as being shared, and emerge with everyone (not just the teenage protagonist) having grown and learned.

T. Fleischmann, MFA

Further Reading

Ewing, Jack. "Cynthia Voigt." *Guide to Literary Masters and Their Works*. Pasadena: Salem, 2007. *Literary Reference Center*. Web. 13 July 2015. <http://search.ebscohost.com/login.aspx?direct=true&db=lfh&AN=103331LM76729790307616&site=lrc-live>.

Goldstein, Meredith. "Grown-Ups Make a Comeback in Young Adult Books." *Boston Globe*. Boston Globe Media Partners, 10 May 2014. Web. 13 July 2015. <https://www.bostonglobe.com/arts/books/2014/05/10/grown-ups-make-comeback-young adult-books/uiKSLYdTEq60ccIQ6FsO3L/story.html>.

Bibliography

Just, Julie. "The Parent Problem in Young Adult Lit." *New York Times*. New York Times, 1 Apr. 2010. Web. 13 July 2015. <http://www.nytimes.com/2010/04/04/books/review/Just-t.html>.

Lodge, Sally. "A Traumatic Family *Memory* Sparks New YA Novel." *Publishers Weekly* 20 Jan. 2014: 19. *Literary Reference Center*. Web. 13 July 2015. <http://search.ebscohost.com/login.aspx?direct=true&db=lfh&AN=94003305&site=lrc-live>.

Phillips, Tommy M. "The Influence of Family Structure vs. Family Climate on Adolescent Well-Being." *Child and Adolescent Social Work Journal* 29.2 (2012): 103–10. *Academic Search Premier*. Web. 13 July 2015. <https://search.ebscohost.com/login.aspx?direct=true&db=ccm&AN=2011485250&site=eds-live>.

Puberty

Titles Discussed
Are You There God? It's Me, Margaret by Judy Blume
Then Again, Maybe I Won't by Judy Blume
Unexpected Development by Marlene Perez

Thematic Overview
While the life of teens has been featured for decades in books and film and on television, the specifics of puberty have not. The Hardy Boys and Nancy Drew mysteries were first in print in the late 1920s. These novels focused entirely on teenagers who had adventures while solving mysteries. There was no mention of a first bra or uncontrollable bodily reactions. By the time the first book in Beverly Cleary's Beezus and Ramona series was published in the mid-1950s, the focus of the teen story had switched to sibling troubles and social activities.

In film from the 1930s to the 1950s, a young Mickey Rooney with an equally young Judy Garland at his side were wholesomeness and innocent love personified. During the early to mid-1960s, Annette Funicello and Frankie Avalon continued the image of wholesome love in their summer beach movies such as *Beach Blanket Bingo* (1965). Sandra Dee starred in the movie version of *Gidget* in 1959, with a television series of the same name starring Sally Field in the 1960s. None of these treatments delved into the changing bodies of the protagonists.

In 1970 Judy Blume's *Are You There God? It's Me, Margaret* changed everything. The book addressed the debate over interfaith marriage, and it explored puberty from the teen perspective, which was portrayed as a confusing time when changes in a body are too much, too little, too early, or too late. The following year, Blume published *Then Again, Maybe I Won't*, which is a book from an adolescent boy's perspective and described a boy's bodily changes in detail.

Blume's novels were a big switch from what had been presented to teens until that time. Many of her books have been banned from school and public libraries. In spite of any attempts to censor their content, they became enduring favorites among the intended audience—teen readers who were asking questions about themselves and the ways in which puberty was affecting them.

By discussing puberty in an open and unapologetic way, Blume and others who wrote the early young adult literature for adolescents and young teens, normalized a range of common behaviors that take place during puberty. As a result, the way was paved for authors such as Marlene Perez to write books for young adults that include the themes of incest, rape, teen pregnancy, and sexuality from a variety of perspectives.

Works

Puberty is a prominent theme in *Are You There God? It's Me, Margaret* (1970) by Judy Blume. Margaret is entering sixth grade, and she has also moved to a new town. She is faced with making new friends at the same time she is preparing for and experiencing the changes to her body that herald the start of womanhood.

Margaret and three other girls form a secret club. Part of the club is focused on which boy each girl likes. Because of this, each girl is required to keep a boy book and to bring it to each weekly meeting. The girls also vote to wear bras. Since none of them physically need a bra, not all of them have one. This leads to an amusing scene in which Margaret runs into another girl from the club at a department store where that girl is also purchasing her first bra. Each girl pledges to tell the others all about the experience of her first period, which they refer to as "menstroo-ation."

Margaret worries that she will be last to truly need a bra. She also worries that she will be last to get her period. When one girl lies and claims to have started her period—announcing it with "I GOT IT!!!" on a postcard mailed from Washington, DC—Margaret is more convinced than ever that she will not only be last and that she will never be normal.

After going to the movies one afternoon, Margaret and another girl from the club decide it is time for to purchase sanitary napkins so they will be ready "for the big day" when they first get their periods. After facing her fear of embarrassment, Margaret purchases the pads and takes them home to practice wearing them. When she is getting dressed to go to a party at Norman Fishbein's house, Margaret examines herself in the mirror. She notices that her breasts are not showing any growth, but she is happy to discover new body hair has been growing. She decides to put cotton balls into her bra, and when the party games that evening call for some time alone with boys, she worries she and the cotton balls will be found out.

Margaret talks to God often and asks for breasts and her period, explaining that she will be happy to have either and will take it as a sign that she is normal after all. The novel ends with Margaret getting her period for the first time, right before she heads off to camp for the summer.

> I locked the bathroom door and peeled the paper off the bottom of the pad. I pressed the sticky strip against my underpants. Then I got dressed and looked at myself in the mirror. Would anyone know my secret? Would it show? . . . I had to call Nancy and Gretchen and Janie right away. Poor Janie! She'd be the last . . . to get it. And I'd been so sure it would be me! How about that! Now I am growing for sure. Now I am almost a woman! *Are you still there God? It's me, Margaret. I know you're there God. I know you wouldn't have missed this for anything! Thank you God. Thanks an awful lot.* (171)

Are You There God? It's Me, Margaret tells the story of a girl who wants the physical changes of puberty to hurry up. There is a girl in the story who is taller and more developed than the other girls. She is treated like a fallen woman because the rumor is that she has been behind the local grocery story with some boys. Margaret never thinks to question the rumors or give the girl the benefit of the doubt. When she and the girl have a confrontation, Margaret learns she has not only been wrong, she has also been hurtful.

The theme of puberty is equally prominent in Blume's *Then Again, Maybe I Won't* (1971). Tony Miglione is looking forward to starting seventh grade, the first year of middle school, when everything changes. His father's invention has made them rich overnight. As a result, they have a new house in an affluent community, two new cars, and a swimming pool is being built. Tony cannot get used to having a new friend who lives next door and a brand new red ten-speed bike. Life should be great, but Tony is not so sure. He has always been a worrier, and he is discovering that there is even more for a rich kid to worry about.

For one thing, everyone in his family is changing. His older brother has decided to quit his teaching job and take a position at the firm his father now runs. Since Tony's mother hired a bossy housekeeper who insists the kitchen is her domain, his grandmother never leaves her room, not even to attend church. Tony's father traded his truck for a brand new car and, now that his invention has the family set for life, he never tries out new ideas. Even though there are more than enough bathrooms in the new house, his father does not have a workroom.

The biggest change is in Tony's mother. She is suddenly worried about what other people think, especially a woman named Mrs. Hoober. Tony explains that his mother can only see things on the surface, and because of that she cannot understand that the Hoobers are not the best example to follow. Tony's mom is hoping to become one of the country club ladies, something else Tony had never remotely imagined.

On the day he moved to the new house, Tony gave his former best friend the school pennant that belonged to Tony's older brother who was killed in Vietnam. The new house has all new furniture. Tony's grandmother has her own color television set and Tony's mother insists that his grandmother loves her new television so much that she's content to spend all her time in her bedroom. Tony is furious that his mother has taken away the one thing his grandmother loved to do—cook for the family—for the shallow reason that it will look bad to the neighbors. When his mother further rationalizes it by saying his grandmother deserves a rest, Tony is so upset he finds it difficult to remain silent.

Tony doesn't speak up very much and is more the type of person who holds his emotions inside. This causes him to have such bad stomach pains that he winds up in the hospital. The doctors who examine him assure him he is not dying, but he does need to talk to someone about his feelings. This embarrasses his mother, but Tony is pleased for the opportunity. He tells his psychiatrist everything, including everything that is puberty-related, and he is relieved to discover that he is normal.

Things that Tony is pleased to learn that it is normal to get erections that are beyond his control. He was embarrassed once at the blackboard during class when he was called upon to explain an answer in detail. All he wanted was to get back to his desk before anyone noticed. After that, he took to carrying a raincoat so he always had a cover-up handy. His mother makes him switch it for a jacket, but he believes that a jacket is better than nothing.

Tony has also discovered that watching his friend's older sister undress can cause him to be aroused. That doesn't concern the psychiatrist, nor does the news that Tony has requested binoculars so that he can see more clearly. The psychiatrist also remains unconcerned when Tony shares the details of his wet dream, a term he learned from his friends. Blume describes it in detail so that the mystery of that experience is dispelled for the reader. By the end of the book, Tony is more at peace with his family's new wealth, and his stomach hurts less often. He has also decided to put the binoculars away, but then again, maybe he won't.

In *Unexpected Development* (2004) by Marlene Perez, Megan has had a very full and complicated summer vacation. She has romanced the boy of her dreams, been harassed by a boss, grappled with whether or not to have breast reduction surgery, and has had sex. It was not an easy summer for Megan, who has had a difficult time since her breasts developed early and abundantly. Rather than be sympathetic toward Megan and what she is going through, the kids around her have assumed she is sexually active and that she enjoys the attention she gets because of her large breasts. That is hard enough for Megan, but when the attention comes from older men who assume Megan is ready for sex with them, all she can do is wish she could make herself invisible and flat-chested.

The most complicated part of the summer for Megan is determining whether the boy she likes only likes her because of her large breasts, as her mother suggests, or whether he likes her for being Megan. Megan laments that everyone seems to start with only noticing her breasts before they get to know the rest of her. She thinks this boy may be different because they knew each other as friends first.

Unlike Margaret, Megan's puberty journey is not one of too little development too slowly. It is one of unexpected abundance too early and too quickly. Megan is scrambling to adjust to the changes in her body while also contemplating breast reduction surgery. This is a big decision for such a young girl, but in Megan's case, it is a reasonable consideration.

Conclusions

These three books sold very well and were hugely popular with teens and parents alike for their sympathetic portrayal of teenagers going through puberty. *Unexpected Developments* was published in 2004 to generally positive reviews. Blume's books, though popular, were targets of censorship.

In the decade following the publication of *Are You There God? It's Me Margaret*, it was banned from schools and libraries across the United States. In a 1993 interview with *Index on Censorship*, Judy Blume says of the experience, "It never occurred to me, when I started to write that what I was writing was controversial. Much of it grew out of my own feelings and concerns when I was young. . . . The censors crawled out of the woodwork, seemingly overnight, organized and determined. Not only would they decide what their children could read, but what all children could read. Challenges to books quadrupled within months, and we shall never know how many teachers, school librarians, and principals quietly removed books to avoid trouble."

Then Again, Maybe I Won't was published in 1971, and it too was the subject of controversy and book banning in the 1980s. The frank description of Tony's difficulties when aroused, as well as his inability to control it, was too much for many parents. They objected to their younger children having access to this information, and they also did not want this information to be a topic of discussion for their older children.

In an interview with National Public Radio in 2011, Blume said of her role as champion for supporters of intellectual freedom for young people, "I'm saying to parents these days, 'Be careful. You know, you all want them to read the books that you read when you were growing up—often my books—and I say you will turn them off.' The best thing to do is leave the books around the house and from time to time say, 'I really don't think you're ready for that book.'"

Blume has written several other books that touch on puberty. On her website, she discusses reactions to these books, such as a male principal who decided *Are You There God? It's Me Margaret* should not be on the shelves in a school that went through sixth grade because the book discusses menstruation; a mother who cut the wet dream pages out of *Then Again, Maybe I Won't* so that her nearly thirteen-year-old son would not read them; and a young librarian who was instructed by her male principal to keep another July Blume title off the shelves because the main character, who is a girl, masturbates, which the principal said is normal for a boy but not for a girl. While her books are often banned or criticized for being inappropriate, as long as she writes about the young adult experience in real terms, she will continue to attract both young adult readers.

Gina Hagler, MBA

Further Reading

Blasingame, Nilsen. *Literature for Today's Young Adults*. 9th ed. Boston: Pearson, 2014. Print.

Cart, Michael. *Young Adult Literature: From Romance to Realism*. Chicago: Amer. Lib. Assn., 2012. Print.

Chance, Rosemary. *Young Adult Literature in Action: A Librarian's Guide*. 2nd ed. Santa Barbara: ABC-CLIO, 2014. Print.

Bibliography

Blume, Judy. "Places I Never Meant to Be." *Judy Blume on the Web*. Judy Blume, n.d. Web. 14 May 2015. <http://judyblume.com/censorship/places2.php>.

Bucher, Katherine, and KaaVonia Hinton. "Exploring Contemporary Realistic Fiction." *Young Adult Literature: Exploration, Evaluation, and Appreciation*. 3rd ed. New York: Pearson, 2014. 125–58. Print.

Cole, Pam B. *Young Adult Literature in the 21st Century*. New York: McGraw, 2009. Print.

Helms, Antje, Jan von Holleben, and Jen Metcalf. *Does This Happen to Everyone? A Budding Adult's Guide to Puberty*. Berlin: Little Gestalten, 2014. Print.

"Judy Blume: Often Banned, but Widely Beloved." *NPR*. National Public Radio, 28 Nov. 2011. Web. 14 May 2015. <http://www.npr.org/2011/11/28/142859819/judy-blume-banned-often-but-widely-beloved>.

Lynch-Brown, Carol G, Kathy G. Short, and Carl M. Tomlinson. *Essentials of Children's Literature*. 7th ed. Harlow: Pearson, 2014. Print.

Strickland, Ashley. "A Brief History of Young Adult Literature." CNN. Cable News Network/Turner Broadcasting System, 15 Apr. 2015. Web. 10 May 2015. <http://www.cnn.com/2013/10/15/living/young adult-fiction-evolution/>.

Race and Ethnicity

Titles Discussed

Ellen Foster by Kaye Gibbons
The Berlin Boxing Club by Robert Sharenow
Slave Day by Rob Thomas

Thematic Overview

To many Americans, it can seem as if the problems of racial discrimination are in the past, and this is especially true for young adults. When students read about the American Civil War, the internment of Japanese Americans during World War II, or the Holocaust, it is history. The problems couched in these events seem to belong to the past, and if a reader has never experienced racial tension, the politics of race can seem like they belong to a bygone era.

For other readers, the problems of race, anti-Semitism, systemic discrimination, or even violence are immediate. The feelings of powerlessness and the frustration to which they lead are present and pressing. The characters in these novels confront the problem of acting responsibly in societies designed to disempower them. They, like many young adults, have to figure out how to navigate their identities when that identity is in the minority.

As one of the high school characters of *Slave Day* puts it after his brother was killed in the First Gulf War, politics "don't change nothin'." The narrator of the chapter bemoans the apathy, wondering how their teacher can hope to engage the students with civil rights and history when politics sent this character's brother half way around the world to die.

The best-known novel that is taught and recommended to young adult readers in regard to race is Harper Lee's classic *To Kill a Mockingbird* (1960). As with *Ellen Foster*, the narrator is a young white girl caught up in legal battles with racial and classist tensions. *To Kill a Mockingbird*'s popularity has endured for decades not only because of how well it is written, full of vibrant characters and an engaging plot, but, as *Ellen Foster* does, the novel complicates social assumptions about

class and race, giving lie to the easy stereotypes of a social hierarchy favoring lighter-skinned people. The novel serves as a child's view of how American race relations often tragically play out.

Mildred D. Taylor's novel *Roll of Thunder, Hear My Cry* (1976) also follows children who are coming to grips with racial tension. Focusing on desegregation following *Brown v. The Board of Education of Topeka, Kansas*, black children in the South are taken from their familiar if lackluster schools and integrated into traditionally white public schools. While the children deal with the expected snide comments and playground bullying, they are also the targets of more overt violence, such as the firebombing of their school bus.

Slave Day also grapples with systemic violence against black students, though it takes place in the more egalitarian 1990s. Young adult literature often addresses the more overt racism of the civil rights movement, as in John Lewis's 2013 memoir *March*, which covers his time working with the movement. Young adult novels in general have tended to look at more violent racism, which lends itself to dramatic confrontations, rather than the more subtle experiences of systemic racism.

Gibbons's *Ellen Foster*, Sharenow's *The Berlin Boxing Club*, and Thomas's *Slave Day* address race and ethnicity within the context of everyday perspectives, taking the reader through different experiences of socially constructed identities. They take the theme of race to its most fundamental level, challenging both the notions of race existing apart from societal creation and "color blindness" to race.

Works

Ellen Foster by Kaye Gibbons shifts and bends race in the story of Ellen, a ten-year-old white girl surviving extreme poverty and an abusive family. The novel moves back and forth in Ellen's narration, oscillating between her life with her alcoholic and abusive father and subsequent custodies with various guardians and her "new mama," the foster family from whom Ellen takes her new surname.

The most direct address of race is the relationship between Ellen and her friend Starletta. At first, their friendship is one of convenience for Ellen. Both girls are dirt poor, so while Ellen assumes herself to be "better" than Starletta because she is white and Starletta is black, Ellen has no connections to white children, even in her extended family, because of the circumstances of her birth. She was born to a mean drunk father who drove her mother to suicide before drinking himself to death. Even though Ellen considers herself to be racially superior to Starletta, she envies Starletta's kind and loving family.

Ellen's father makes her life hell. Even after he dies—though not, as Ellen often fantasizes, by patricide—her affiliation with him continues to frustrate her attempts to be a member of her extended family. At her mother's funeral, Ellen's maternal grandmother calls her father racial slurs usually reserved for black people, even though he is white. When Ellen lives with her grandmother, the old woman compares Ellen's features to the "man who killed my girl," and so Ellen is lumped with her father. Within her family, she is, like Starletta, judged by her appearance.

Her father's racism against black people complicates the novel more than Ellen's biases, and without it the novel's story would stagnate as Ellen's coming of age centers on a new racial awareness. Her father's drinking buddies, who, when they come around, terrorize Ellen and wreck the house that only she cleans, are all black. They embody racial stereotypes, such as the aforementioned destructiveness and drunkenness, as well as a threatening sexuality. Ellen hears one of them explain to her father that she is nearly "ripe" and ready to have children or at least have sex.

These men contrast starkly against Mavis, a worker on Ellen's grandmother's farm, and Starletta, who goes from being a young girl who still wets herself to a self-assured young woman. Ellen watches these two women and understands that, despite what her father would have her believe, race does not affect a person's character.

Mavis, like Ellen and Starletta, is poor, living with her family in a shack on the edge of the fields. But, when Ellen sneaks down the old slave road to spy on Mavis, she sees her, her husband, and their children running around with each other, joking and laughing, eating together. Mavis's family, by enjoying each other, challenges Ellen's experience of family and her expectations of black people.

Starletta does the same, though she impresses Ellen through her ability to transform into a confident and capable young woman. Early in the novel, Starletta, despite being Ellen's age, still wets herself, cannot manage to produce the dollar for admission to a movie theater even though she has it on her somewhere, and cannot manage to speak much of the time.

By the end, Ellen is proud to invite Starletta to stay with her foster family for a weekend. Starletta confides in Ellen that she has a crush on a white boy, and Ellen realizes Starletta can and has rejected the usual racial politics of the South. The two of them connect more meaningfully than before as Ellen uses the weekend to try to cement herself in Starletta's mind as a real friend, not just another poor girl she happens to know.

At the end of the novel Ellen explains to Starletta, "I always thought I was special because I was white and when I thought about you being colored I said to myself it sure is a shame Starletta's colored. I sure would hate to be that way." Then, Ellen realizes, "Nobody but a handful of folks I know pays attention to rules about how you treat somebody anyway." She also now realizes that although she has faced difficulties in her life, that Starletta has faced even harder challenges and deserves to be treated as a respected friend, even if doing so breaks "the rules." Though the social mores have changed, they are still deeply ingrained in Ellen; she feels like she's breaking the law when she has Starletta come over and take a nap beside her.

It is an important distinction between realizing social mores regarding race and accepting a marginalized person as "one of the good ones." Karl Stern, the protagonist of *The Berlin Boxing Club*, comes upon the problem of being simultaneously accepted as a great athlete and reviled as a Jew in 1930s Germany.

The novel opens with an epigraph from Adolf Hitler's manifesto *Mein Kampf* (1925), "There is one kind of sport which should be especially encouraged, although many people . . . consider it brutal and vulgar, and that is boxing. . . . There is no other sport which equals this in developing the militant spirit, none that demands such a power of rapid decision or which gives the body the flexibility of good steel. . . . But, above all, a healthy youth has to learn to endure hard knocks." Hitler's quote provides a good introduction to the novel's themes, especially its irony. Hitler is arguing for the refinement of the German people, and that is what Karl Stern thinks of himself as: *Deutsche*. His family does not attend temple, observe the high holy days, or speak Yiddish.

This does not stop the people around Karl, especially the National Socialist club at his school, from identifying him as Jewish. The opening scene with the aspiring Brown Shirts demonstrates the complicated systems of power that marginalize "othered" people. The bullies pull down Karl's pants, using his circumcised penis to prove his Jewishness. When Karl continues to deny his ethnicity, one of the boys says, "There's only one thing worse than a Jew, and that's a Jew who tries to pretend he's not a Jew." A vague delineation is set up, where these boys seemingly admit, yes, the object of the racism is bad but not as bad as race traitors.

Karl suffers most from agreeing with his thuggish peers. He does not fit the stereotype of the self-hating Jew, but he does hate other Jews, especially Hasidic Jews. Their overt and separate racial identity is what offends Karl, whose family has assimilated into gentile German culture. But, as is the case when race becomes a binary, Karl still has Jewish ancestry. As far as Nazis are concerned, he is Jewish, and he has to defend himself against their anti-Semitism and violence.

The novel follows tropes of the race relations/sports movie, following in the footsteps of *Remember the Titans* (2000) or *Invictus* (2009), eschewing the more nuanced frustrations and anti-Semitism experienced by the Jewish characters in Michael Chabon's novel *The Amazing Adventures of Kavalier and Clay* (2000). The themes of race, identity, and survival become complicated as Karl grows closer to Max Schmeling, the historical boxer who serves in the novel as Karl's boxing instructor.

Despite the events of Kristallnacht, Karl is under the impression that, as long as he can box and not appear too Jewish, he will be safe. As an athlete, he is immune to the tempests of public opinion. Not so, Max teaches him. After Schmeling loses a match to African American boxer Joe Louis, he is ostracized from German high society. Joseph Goebbels, a high-ranking Nazi politician, no longer extends dinner invitations to Max. Instead, he finds himself drafted as a paratrooper, a job likely to kill him as a punishment for losing a boxing match to a black man.

Karl finds himself apart from his family, being the least Jewish-looking among them, and without his identity as a boxer and Max Schmeling's pupil. Karl decides to make his own identity, apart from his ethnicity, his country, or his vocation.

Sports culture has long complicated race relations, and *Slave Day* uses the microcosm of a Southern high school, its football team, and its traditions to address the problems of the relationships between black and white students as well as fragmented black identity. The novel follows a group of students and teachers at Robert E. Lee High School on Slave Day, when student council members are auctioned off to raise money for homecoming. The first-person accounts throughout the day come from young men and women, both black and white, and a white teacher, all offering glimpses into the

complicated justifications for racism, through history, tradition, and prejudice.

Keene, a black student, calls for a boycott of Slave Day, hoping the large black population of Robert E. Lee will side with him in denouncing the demeaning event. This does not hold water with his parents, who force Keene to cross his own picket lines and attend school on Slave Day. Making the best of a bad situation, he buys another black student, Shawn. Keene's idea is to embarrass the popular Shawn enough so that at least he will realize how degrading Slave Day is.

The problem with Keene's plan is that Shawn thinks "the Civil Rights movement ended 20 years ago," and that Slave Day is "good, clean fun." Keene making Shawn pick up a trail of cotton balls in the hallways does not do much to change Shawn's mind; he turns the chore into a joke, a minstrel show complete with "massa" and eye popping. It is not until later when Keene paraphrases Robert E. Lee in writing a speech for Shawn that Shawn sees the civil rights movement might not be so comfortably in the past.

As Keene and Shawn draw the attention of other, more militant black students, Keene is drawn into spreading rumors of racism in the school administration and exaggerating actual instances of bigotry. In the former, he accuses Marcus "Mr. History" Twilley of getting the only black woman in National Honor Society kicked out of the organization. As for the latter, he takes advantage of the black football players' quitting in protest of their coach's assertion that black players "fold" when they are hit. Keene uses this instance to demonize the coaches rather than support the fellow players.

Spurred on by his misinterpretation of Malcolm X's decree of "by any means necessary," Keene vandalizes Mr. Twilley's car. Looking at his work, he thinks of Laurence, the black student who is bound to be valedictorian. Keene realizes that by doing that, Laurence will do more for the black students of his high school than eggs and shoe polish on a teacher's car.

The struggle between Keene and Shawn typifies the question of blackness in America. The characters criticize each other for saying "cool . . . like it's 1980-something," or accusing each other of wanting to be white. They regulate each other's black identity, so when Keene is told to vandalize Twilley's car, he thinks to himself, "I don't want to be white."

While Keene is not proud of himself for that, he does dismantle Slave Day. The principal calls him in, bemoaning that an honor student ("one of the good ones") has made Slave Day such a hassle that it is not worth it. Even if it is a "fun tradition" in the eyes of many students and administrators, it ends.

Conclusions

Young adult novels dealing with race and ethnicity are part of a rich tradition including *Roll of Thunder, Hear My Cry* and *To Kill a Mockingbird*, with *Ellen Foster*'s use of ethnographic language reminiscent of Zora Neale Hurston's 1937 novel *Their Eyes Were Watching God*. The novels discussed here update these themes, examining the issues of racism and racial identity on this side of the civil rights movement. These novels take a past that is easy to condemn and reveal it in the present.

This consciousness-raising works as well as it does because contemporary readers can relate better to the covert and systemic racism of power systems, as opposed to bombing churches and burning crosses. Contemporary race politics in young adult literature needs to address how individuals understand race in relation to histories of economic inequality and prejudiced penal systems, especially as the gap between the American wealthy and poor expands.

Authors of young adult fiction may also revisit the central questions of the civil rights movement's philosophies. With the high-profile deaths of unarmed black men and the militarization of police, along with the increasing economization of politics, disempowerment becomes a fatal condition and the purview of socially conscious artists. As young people gain a better understanding of themselves and the world around them and are free to pursue their identities, they will look to literature as a template and sounding board for their most personal questions.

Alexandra McBride, MA

Further Reading

Doll, Jen. "The Ongoing Problem of Race in Y.A." *Wire*. Atlantic Monthly Group, 26 Apr. 2012. Web. 7 July 2015.

Osa, Osayimwense. *The All White World of Children's Books and African American Children's Literature*. Trenton: Africa World, 1995. Print.

Rev. of *The Berlin Boxing Club*, by Robert Sharenow. *Kirkus*. Kirkus, 4 Apr. 2011. Web. 16 May 2015. <https://www.kirkusreviews.com/book-reviews/robert-sharenow/berlin-boxing-club/>.

Rev. of *Ellen Foster*, by Kaye Gibbons. *Kirkus*. Kirkus, 15 May 1987. Web. 16 May 2015. <https://www.kirkusreviews.com/book-reviews/kaye-gibbons-6/ellen-foster/>.

Rev. of *Slave Day*, by Rob Thomas. *Kirkus*. Kirkus, 20 May 2010. Web. 16 May 2015. <https://www.kirkusreviews.com/book-reviews/rob-thomas/slave-day/>.

Bibliography

Chabon, Michael. *The Amazing Adventures of Kavalier and Clay: A Novel*. New York: Random, 2000. Print.

Lee, Harper. *To Kill a Mockingbird*. Philadelphia: Lippincott, 1960. Print.

Lewis, John, Andrew Aydin, Nate Powell, and Chris Ross. *March*. Marietta: Top Shelf, 2013. Print.

Taylor, Mildred D. *Roll of Thunder, Hear My Cry*. New York: Dial, 1976. Print.

School Life

Titles Discussed
The Disreputable History of Frankie Landau-Banks by E. Lockhart
Avalon High by Meg Cabot
Stargirl by Jerry Spinelli

Thematic Overview

It makes sense that school life would play a central role in literature for young adults, given that the bulk of their social life takes place during the school day. The things that happen in school matter deeply to the teens involved.

There are several aspects to the theme of school life. Social groups and peer pressure are one such aspect. To be in the right group may not be as important as not being in the wrong group, but being in no group is almost worse. The way the "right" and "wrong" groups manifest may vary from school to school, however.

Coursework and academic pressure are another major aspect of school life. At some high schools, it is routine to take a number of advanced-placement classes in preparation for college. Other high schools do not have that expectation of their students. The more demanding the curriculum, the more academic pressure there is. Dealing with that pressure can take up a lot of a student's time and energy, and it is often the case that young adults have limited free time and must choose their activities carefully.

Bullying is another part of school life that often appears in young adult literature. The bullying can occur in person or online—or both—and can be perpetrated by a group or by an individual. Whatever form it takes, it is disruptive to the student experiencing the bullying, and ignoring this common aspect of teenage social life would provide an incomplete picture of school life.

Administrators as parental figures comprise the final aspect of the school life theme in young adult literature. Parents are rarely a big part of these novels, but administrators are. They are the ones who decide on the discipline and hand down the consequences for poor decisions.

School life is not a new theme for young adult audiences. *The Breakfast Club* (1985) is a classic example of the theme, which has remained popular over the succeeding decades. The film focuses on a day of detention for five students from different cliques. The administrator thinks he knows all he needs to know about them, but over the course of the film they learn there is more to each of them than the others anticipated. *Ferris Bueller's Day Off*, starring Matthew Broderick, was released the following year. John Hughes directed these films back to back. In both of them, as in the works examined, school life is vital to the story line.

Works

School life is a major theme in *The Disreputable History of Frankie Landau-Banks* (2008), *Avalon High* (2006), and *Stargirl* (2000). The social dynamics of high school, among the students and sometimes between students and administrators, are a deciding factor in the plot and the growth of the main characters.

For Frankie Landau-Banks, entering Alabaster Prep gives her the opportunity to step out of the role her family has defined for her. At home she is the younger sister and not taken seriously. At boarding school, especially now that her older sister is away at college, she can be whomever she wants to be. The day-to-day rhythm of school life and the traditions that extend to the male students fuel this story.

Frankie is tired of being outside of the action. She wants to be the one making things happen. She wants to be involved with the group that has the power. To her dismay, however, that group takes the form of an all-male secret society. To make matters worse, the boys in

the society do not seem to appreciate the fact that they are lucky to have power. They seem to view it as their birthright if they give it any thought at all.

Frankie's father attended her boarding school and was a member of the secret society. Frankie has heard stories about his boarding school days all her life. She has also noticed that his friends and business contacts come from that pool of boys. She realizes that he has benefited from his time at school for many years and in ways that are not mentioned in the school literature.

Frankie wants the same easy nonchalance about her place in the world that the boys exhibit. From lunchtime, when she is afraid to take a seat at the regular table unless one of them is there first, to her shock when one girl is dumped by one of the boys and finds that her former friends no longer speak to her, Frankie is unsettled by the unspoken rules that govern these social interactions.

She decides to turn the boys' club on its head by taking it over and orchestrating the prank of a lifetime while concealing her identity. When the boys realize she has been the one making the decisions and plans the entire time, she believes, they will finally afford her equal respect. However, her plans do not turn out as she hopes.

Despite the fact that Frankie does everything the alpha male would have done, and does it better, she is not afforded the acclaim that would have gone to a boy under identical circumstances. She is angry and upset that the perks that should go to her are not going to her simply because she is female. Even the school administrators do not punish her as harshly as they would have punished a boy who had committed the same acts.

Frankie is left to consider her place in the school hierarchy and the implications of that place for the wider world. She understands that she is escaping a harsher punishment only because she is not seen as an equal to the boys in the first place. Now Frankie must determine if it is all boys (and men) who have this flaw or just the boys with the unlimited credit cards—the boys who were born to wealthy and powerful families, who take their place in the world for granted, and who will go on to benefit from their social position both at school and in the larger society regardless whether they do anything to earn that regard.

Avalon High is a world away from Alabaster Prep, being neither a boarding school nor a private school. It is a public high school located in Annapolis, Maryland. The only catch is that many of the students—and even some teachers—are reincarnations of characters from

Arthurian legend. Despite the fantasy element, however, *Avalon High* remains essentially a story of school life, with all its cliques and surface-level assessments of people.

The protagonist, Ellie, is the daughter of medievalists studying the legends of King Arthur, and so Ellie knows more about these tales than the average teenager. When Ellie and her parents move to Annapolis for her junior year of high school, it quickly becomes apparent to her that her new friend Will has a lot in common with King Arthur (and his girlfriend, Jennifer, and best friend, Lance, seem familiar, too). For his part, Will is certain he has met Ellie before. Thus, Ellie's normal concerns about fitting into a new school are made worse by the fact that her classmates' identities, and even her own, may not be what they seem, and the tragedies of the legends are beginning to repeat themselves. Even this remains relatable to the teenage reader, however; at heart, these tragedies have less to do with wizardry or the rise and fall of kingdoms than with betrayal by romantic partners and supposed friends or conflict within families. The students' discoveries of their past lives, meanwhile, provides a metaphor for a teenager's exploration and definition of his or her identity. Ellie, in particular, like Frankie, finds that entering a new school allows her an opportunity to redefine herself—to give herself a "total personality makeover," as her best friend from her old school says.

The world of *Stargirl* is still more remarkable, despite its lack of actual magic. Stargirl moves to a tiny town in Arizona. There she catches the attention of the protagonist, Leo Borlock. He has never met anyone like Stargirl; in fact, no one at the school has. She cannot help but change his view of the world from the moment he first sees her at lunch, wearing an oversized ruffled white dress and carrying a ukulele instead of a backpack.

Given the almost tyrannical need to conform in high school, it is hard at first to understand what drives Stargirl's need to be so different. It is also hard to understand how it is that she is happy in her nonconformity, apparently completely unconcerned with what her fellow students think of her. Indeed, she goes out of her way to be kind to them, even when they are less than kind to her, and gives cards and gifts to people she does not even know.

While Leo is mesmerized by Stargirl, Hillari Kimble is annoyed. She finds Stargirl irritating and says right out that she believes Stargirl is a scam orchestrated by the principal to bring more spirit to the school. By the time Hillari slaps Stargirl in the face, it is not a shock. It has been a long time coming. It is also not a shock that Stargirl reacts by kissing Hillari gently on the cheek. Stargirl's family moves soon after.

Stargirl has upset the careful balance of conformity at Mica Area High School for good. They have a ukulele in their band to this day. They have a club where members must do one nice thing each day for someone else. Her lessons on caring for others have stuck. Her lessons on being herself have fallen a bit flat. At least they have for Leo.

It was he who tried to get Stargirl to conform in the first place, so that he could associate with Stargirl without being shunned by his other friends. At first he does not realize the consequences of what he has done, saying, after Stargirl changes her name back to Susan, "she looked magnificently, wonderfully, gloriously ordinary. She looked just like a hundred other girls at Mica High . . . I had never been so happy and so proud in my life."

But Stargirl is unique in ways that transcend trite definition. The closest Leo ever comes to understanding her is when he meditates with her in the desert and reaches the point where he loses track of everything. As Stargirl explains, she is part of more than just the high school or the town. She is part of a much larger network that holds her and gives her energy.

The focus on the conformity aspect of school life helps the reader recognize the lifelong impact of a young adult's school life. Leo will never forget that he lost Stargirl by trying to make her like everyone else, even though what he valued about her was that she was not like everyone else.

Years later, Leo still cannot articulate what she meant to him. He knows from mutual friends that they still speak about her at the class reunions. They wonder where she is and ask each other if they did the bunny hop at the school dance right before Hillari slapped her. They wonder what Stargirl calls herself now and where she lives.

Leo, too, wonders what became of Stargirl, and continues to look for her in stories of kindness across the country. He feels her presence in his life: "Though I have no family of my own, I do not feel alone," he says. "The echo of her laughter is the second sunrise I awaken to each day." He is not incorrect that she still thinks of him; she even sends him a porcupine necklace for his birthday. But she is no longer physically present in his life, and he is left to reconcile his need to fit in with his schoolmates with the loss of the most remarkable person he has ever met.

Conclusions

These three works are all award-winning books by respected authors. Their work shares a common theme, but the worldview of the author shines through in each book. In *The Disreputable History of Frankie Landau-Banks*, E. Lockhart explores the influence of the collective will of the school. She has Frankie notice, wonder, and explore the implications of the behaviors that the other students adopt in order to conform to the school's overall ethos. These behaviors range from not taking a shortcut across the grass to knowing their place in the social hierarchy without having to be told outright.

Meg Cabot's *Avalon High* continues Cabot's pattern of writing about the trials of being a teenager with a fantastic twist—as in her earlier series, the Princess Diaries, where the protagonist is the princess of a small European principality but still struggles to fit in at school and fulfill her academic obligations despite the other stresses in her life. In *Avalon High*, Ellie may be the reincarnation of a mythological figure, but like many other teenagers, she deals with social conflicts and two-faced behavior at school and ultimately must decide whether to stand by a friend when other students turn against him.

Jerry Spinelli has written several books about school life and conformity. *Stargirl*, in particular, turns the concept of conformity on its ear. Stargirl is at once so different and captivating that at first the other students cannot help but notice her and want to emulate her—but this state of affairs does not last. The switch from respecting Stargirl to despising her comes about in a predictable and believable way, yet it is still startling in its swiftness. Spinelli has captured the nuance of the tyranny of school life in that moment. It is not enough to be popular. The popular girl must be popular in the right, safe ways—must stand out, but not too much—or she will be taken down as swiftly as she ascended.

These three works are an excellent sample of works with a serious and diverse treatment of school life. They ring true with a young adult audience because these readers know the underside of school life and recognize the validity of the portrayals in these works.

Gina Hagler, MBA

Further Reading

Blasingame, Nilsen. *Literature for Today's Young Adults*. Boston: Pearson, 2014. Print.

Cart, Michael. *Young Adult Literature: From Romance to Realism*. Chicago: Amer. Lib. Assn., 2010. Print.

Rev. of *Avalon High*, by Meg Cabot. *Guardian Children's Books*. Guardian News and Media, 12 Oct. 2011. Web. 11 May 2015. <http://www.theguardian.com/childrens-books-site/2011/oct/12/avalon-high-meg-cabot-review>.

Bibliography

Bucher, Katherine, and KaaVonia Hinton. "Exploring Contemporary Realistic Fiction." *Young Adult Literature: Exploration, Evaluation, and Appreciation*. 3rd ed. New York: Pearson, 2014. 125–58. Print.

Chance, Rosemary. *Young Adult Literature in Action: A Librarian's Guide*. Santa Barbara: ABC-CLIO, 2014. Print.

Cole, Pam B. *Young Adult Literature in the 21st Century*. New York: McGraw, 2009. Print.

Groban, Betsy. Rev. of *Stargirl*, by Jerry Spinelli. *New York Times Books*. New York Times, 17 Sept. 2000. Web. 9 May 2015. <https://www.nytimes.com/books/00/09/17/reviews/000917.rv110501.htm>.

Lynch-Brown, Carol G., Kathy G. Short, and Carl M. Tomlinson. *Essentials of Children's Literature*. Harlow: Pearson, 2014. Print.

Strickland, Ashley. "A Brief History of Young Adult Literature." *CNN*. CNN, 15 Feb. 2015. Web. 10 May 2015. <http://www.cnn.com/2013/10/15/living/young adult-fiction-evolution>.

Social Problems

Titles Discussed

American Born Chinese by Gene Luen Yang
The Outsiders by S. E. Hinton
Speak by Laurie Halse Anderson

Thematic Overview

Adolescence is the time during which many people first become seriously aware of social problems, particularly social problems that intersect with their lives and the lives of their peers and families. From first encounters with teenage pregnancy and sexual abuse to the realities of alcoholism and homophobia, teenagers are likely to encounter social problems not as broad and abstract concepts but as lived realities with real and immediate effects on their own lives.

Young adult novels began to seriously turn their attention to social problems shortly after the genre began to be recognized as distinct from children's literature. As the development of the young adult novel was a time during which major publishers and writers were first recognizing the maturity of teenage readers, many of the early young adult social-problem novels were in actuality moralistic tales that lacked the sophistication of other classics of young adult literature. Despite this, one of the first works to be described as a problem novel was S. E. Hinton's *The Outsiders* (1967), which explores the intersections of poverty, gang violence, and the daily lives of orphaned teenagers. Hinton's book is a superb example of literary complexity, developing nuanced and realistic characters while squarely confronting social realities that were rarely seen in young adult literature at the time. While the 1970s saw a number of poor imitations that attempted to re-create the crass language and dramatic plot structure of *The Outsiders* but failed to craft such engaging and thoughtful characters, the novel also paved the way for similarly realistic and valuable works for decades to come.

While there have been successful problem novels for decades, it is also true that the realities of social problems are in constant flux, and every generation of teenage readers encounters social realities that would be unfamiliar to the generation preceding them. Because of this, the advancement of different social justice movements has gone a long way toward making problem novels possible. Feminist activists in the 1970s and 1980s, for instance, helped make it acceptable for young adult novels to portray girls dealing realistically with pregnancy and sexuality, while the gay and lesbian rights movement has likewise made novels that deal with homophobia more acceptable for younger readers. While the issues might change, however, these novels are connected by the unique experience of adolescents confronting social problems in earnest. As teenagers begin to develop their adult identities outside of the home and gain new perspective on both their family life and the world in general, their understanding of personal and intimate experiences often shifts to become a more complicated understanding of the workings between the personal and the social.

In the twenty-first century, the vast majority of young adult novels deal with social problems in one form or another. Laurie Halse Anderson's *Speak* (1999), for instance, focuses on the reality of rape, while Gene Luen Yang's 2006 graphic novel *American Born Chinese* squarely confronts lived realities of racism and immigration from the perspective of a second-generation Chinese American teenager. As part of the trend toward realism and sophistication in contemporary young adult novels, however, even those works that do not focus their attention on a clear social problem are likely to include secondary characters facing divorce, substance abuse, poverty, misogyny, or other socially formed issues.

Works

S. E. Hinton's seminal young adult novel *The Outsiders* centers on its narrator, Ponyboy. Living with his brothers after the death of their parents in a car accident, Ponyboy finds an ersatz family unit in a gang called the Greasers. All boys from the impoverished part of town, the Greasers face constant harassment and violence from a richer gang called the Socials, or "Socs." After Ponyboy and some of the other Greasers hang out one evening with two girlfriends of the Socs, Ponyboy is attacked by a group of Socs who attempt to drown him in a park fountain. He is saved at the last minute by his best friend, Johnny, who stabs and kills one of the Socs. Ponyboy and Johnny go to hide out in an abandoned church for a while. When they return to their safe spot one day, they find it on fire, with some children trapped inside. While rushing inside to save children, Ponyboy and Johnny are both injured, and they end up in the hospital, with Johnny in critical condition. The Socials and the Greasers then agree to have a massive fight. When it is over, Ponyboy returns to the hospital to find that Johnny has died. Further worsening his emotional condition, a friend and fellow Greaser attempts to rob a grocery store and is killed by the police. Deeply distraught and uncertain of himself, Ponyboy begins to find comfort in his English class, where he sits down to write his own story.

While a number of social problems come into play during *The Outsiders*, from the alcoholism of family members to Ponyboy's reality as an orphan, the greatest social reality influencing the novel is the class disparity between the Greasers and the Socials. It is this disparity that sits at the heart of their constant battles, and it is also the poverty in which the Greasers live that leads to them being dismissed and judged by others in the town, teachers and police officers among them. Ponyboy is well aware of this reality; it is the reason he initially hides his interest in literature from others, believing that it is an inappropriate passion for someone of his class background. As the novel progresses and he spends more time interacting directly with the Socs and their girlfriends, however, he begins to understand these class barriers to be a false construct, enforced socially but not accurately representing either the Greasers or the Socs. Thus begins the process by which Ponyboy must reconcile his lived personal experiences of poverty with the socially constructed reality. In his younger years, he takes for granted many of the barriers and exclusions he faces because of his economic class, but as he begins to interact more with the world outside of himself and develop his adult identity, he begins to question his circumstances, integrating the social and the personal together into a more complex worldview. This new understanding allows him not only to fight more earnestly on behalf of his friends, defending them in the face of oppression, but also to develop a sense of sympathy for the Socs, understanding that they too are trapped in a class system that divides people unfairly. At the close of the novel, Ponyboy has experienced an incredible amount of loss as a result of these violent class divides, but he is now able to turn to literature for insight and solace, effectively crossing that class barrier in order to assert his own identity more fully.

The violence of social problems likewise shapes the life of Melinda, the protagonist of *Speak*, by Laurie Halse Anderson. Rather than facing her problem among a group of friends in similar positions, however, Melinda believes herself to be so totally alone that she cannot even acknowledge the reality of that violence to another person. The novel begins as Melinda is starting a new year of high school. Her old friends and social network have disappeared, and instead the entire school is mad at her for having called the police on a party the summer before. As Melinda falls into a deeper and deeper depression, she begins skipping class to hide in the janitor's closet and receiving uncharacteristically poor grades, with the slight exception of her art class. While she connects with a new student and befriends a boy in her science class, these connections prove tenuous until Melinda finally finds herself able to share her secret: she was raped at the party, resulting in the call to the police. She is motivated to overcome her silence in part by the realization that her former best friend, Rachel, had started to date her rapist, Andy. Although Andy becomes violent again, Melinda is empowered by sharing her

story, and as she slowly regains the acceptance of her classmates, she also shares her story with her art teacher, hoping to prevent Andy from committing further acts of violence.

The violence Melinda experiences creates a radical rift between her personal, interior world and the social world from which the violence was born, a rift that is itself reflected in the narrative style and voice of the novel. Her first-person narration makes this clear in a number of ways, not least among them the fact that she is able to articulate large parts of her daily experience to the reader, yet is unable to acknowledge the reality of the rape throughout most of the novel or to say more than a few brief words to her peers or teachers. Melinda further enforces this rift by referring to others primarily by nicknames; Andy, in particular, is known only as "IT" through most of the novel. Just as the social problems of poverty and gang violence cause Ponyboy to reconsider the relationship between his own life and the social structure of his town, the social problem of rape makes it impossible for Melinda to live as a functional and active member of the social world of her high school.

Because Melinda so rarely interacts in a meaningful way with others, the novel stays largely observational throughout, with any action muted and filtered through Melinda's internal narration. The interiority of Melinda's narration has another important implication, serving as a reminder that adolescents can never truly know what their friends and peers are experiencing. Even Rachel, Melinda's former best friend, is quick to judge Melinda and to cast her aside in favor of personal social gain, and when Melinda finally shares the truth with her, she struggles to accept it. The divide that Melinda creates between herself and her classmates becomes a tool that helps her finally accept that she was raped—it is only in an imagined scene with talk-show host Oprah Winfrey that she fully admits the reality to herself—which in turn allows her to bridge the divide between personal pain and social problems in order to live as an outgoing, socially connected teenager again.

Although it features less graphic violence than *Speak* and *The Outsiders*, Gene Luen Yang's *American Born Chinese* likewise focuses on a protagonist who finds his self-identity ruptured by social problems. The main character is this three-pronged story is Jin, a son of Chinese immigrants who is raised in an overwhelmingly white town. Constantly teased because of his race and the immigration status of his parents, Jin has only one true friend, a Taiwanese boy named Wei-Chen. Their friendship suffers when Jin kisses Wei-Chen's girlfriend, which Jin is motivated to do after a popular white boy tells him that he should not date a white girl at their school. Jin then fantasizes about being transformed into a blond-haired white boy named Danny. Danny is relatively popular at school until his Chinese cousin, Chin-Kee, visits, constantly embarrassing him in social spaces (Chin-Kee is drawn as a stereotype of a Chinese immigrant, complete with an exaggerated accent and traditional outfits). Danny finally gets into a fight with Chin-Kee, who then reveals himself to be the mythical Monkey King, a powerful martial artist who has come to Earth to keep an eye on his son, Wei-Chen. With the encouragement of the Monkey King, Danny returns to his true identity as Jin and makes amends with Wei-Chen, realizing the importance of their friendship both despite and because of the prejudice they both face.

Jin's need to reconcile social problems with his internal sense of self is initiated not by an act of overt violence but rather by countless smaller acts of racism, anti-immigrant sentiment, and similar aggressions. People, including his teachers, frequently mispronounce his name, for instance, and he avoids hanging out with a Japanese student named Suzy (Wei-Chen's eventual girlfriend) after they are teased that they must be in an arranged marriage. The relentless acts of racism at first cause Jin to internalize and recreate the social problems with which he struggles. When Wei-Chen shows up at school and is clearly a new immigrant, Jin redirects the teasing he has experienced onto his new friend, saying that he must be "fresh off the boat" and putting him down for any behaviors that Jin views as stereotypically Asian. The process of overcoming these social problems is a largely internal one, with Jin spending less time challenging the racism perpetuated by others and more time cleansing his own attitudes of anti-Asian sentiments. To render this visually, the graphic novel incorporates the magical story of Danny and the Monkey King. Rather than suggesting that Wei-Chen is actually the son of the Monkey King, this mythical narrative instead brings a deep sense of Chinese cultural heritage into the present moment of the American school. By engaging with this narrative and learning from the Monkey King, Jin goes through the

internal process of growth that allows him to again enter the social world of the school and affirm his bond with Wei-Chen. While the racism of his environment still exists, Jin's new self-confidence allows him to be more fully himself, just as Melinda finally learns to speak again after acknowledging the truth of her rape and as Ponyboy allows himself to write after realizing how false the divides of the class system truly are.

Conclusions

The term "social problems" can refer to an incredible range of cultural realities. While some are consistent over time—racism, misogyny, and poverty have remained constant problems since before the first young adult novels were published—other problems arise in new forms with shifting cultural attitudes and political realities. Online bullying, for instance, reflects the ongoing reality of bullying while presenting new challenges through the specificity of social media.

Because of these shifting realities, teenagers constantly experience social problems that previous generations might not have experienced, or might have experienced in radically different forms. For young adult novels, this means that contemporary social problems are a fruitful and consistent topic. More importantly, however, this reality highlights the unique experience of independence and autonomy that many teenagers feel as they first interact with problems that are not entirely personal, but also not entirely social. Confronting a social problem is not simply about finding a better life for the individual, as Melinda, Ponyboy, and Jin all manage to do. Rather, it is about improving the world for peers and for future generations as well. Melinda, for instance, demonstrates incredible bravery in speaking openly about her rape, and in doing so she helps protect other girls from experiencing the same violence. Jin likewise manages to improve his own social standing by confronting his internalized racism, while also paving the way for a fuller, healthier relationship with Wei-Chen and Suzy.

While novels focusing on social problems are often difficult reads due to their honest portrayals of violence and challenging subject matter, they are also often novels of strength and endurance, demonstrating that adolescents are as capable of changing the world and directing the future as adults are. As new problems continue to arise with which adults have little familiarity, teenage protagonists confronting social realities prove themselves again and again to be valuable, complex characters in the genre of young adult literature, showing that the transition to adulthood is less about accepting the world as it is and more about making the world what it should be.

T. Fleischmann, MFA

Further Reading

Alsup, Janet. "Politicizing Young Adult Literature: Reading Anderson's *Speak* as a Critical Text." *Journal of Adolescent and Adult Literacy* 47.2 (2003): 158–66. *Literary Reference Center*. Web. 7 July 2015. <http://search.ebscohost.com/login.aspx?direct=true&db=lfh&AN=11455383&site=lrc-live>.

Sardina, Martel. "*The Outsiders*." *Masterplots*. Ed. Laurence W. Mazzeno. 4th ed. Vol. 2. Pasadena: Salem, 2010. *Literary Reference Center*. Web. 7 July 2015. <http://search.ebscohost.com/login.aspx?direct=true&db=lfh&AN=103331MP424609820000724&site=lrc-live>.

Bibliography

Davis, Rocío G. "Childhood and Ethnic Visibility in Gene Yang's *American Born Chinese*." *Prose Studies* 35.1 (2013): 7–15. *Literary Reference Center*. Web. 7 July 2015. <http://search.ebscohost.com/login.aspx?direct=true&db=lfh&AN=87070527&site=lrc-live>.

Snider, Jessi. "'Be The Tree': Classical Literature, Art Therapy, and Transcending Trauma in *Speak*." *Children's Literature in Education* 45.4 (2014): 298–309. Print.

Tribunella, Eric L. "Institutionalizing *The Outsiders*: YA Literature, Social Class, and the American Faith in Education." *Children's Literature in Education* 38.2 (2007): 87–101. *Academic Search Premier*. Web. 7 July 2015. <https://search.ebscohost.com/login.aspx?direct=true&db=ehh&AN=24486924&site=eds-live>.

Sports

Titles Discussed

Dairy Queen by Catherine Gilbert Murdock
Darius & Twig by Walter Dean Myers
Heart of a Champion by Carl Deuker

Thematic Overview

Sports have been a part of every human culture, ranging from leisure (croquet) to martial training (fencing). It follows that sports, which are structured forms of play, should be so important to adolescents. Which teams teenagers follow and what sports they play often informs their identities, as, for many young adults, sports are both their entertainment and pastime.

Before the advent of the YA novel, the literary canon did not often concern itself with sports and games. However, as YA novels have increased in popularity and are aimed at teenagers, probably the most likely demographic to play sports on a regular basis, sports have become a more popular subject. This popularity can be linked to a general push to get boys to read, since a book about something they like—basketball, for instance—is likely to catch their attention.

The rise of sports as a subject of YA novels has also coincided with wider attention paid to athletes. Going back to baseball heroes such as Babe Ruth and Mickey Mantle, all the way to modern celebrity athletes such as Michael Jordan and sisters Venus and Serena Williams, popular culture has been interested in sports and the people who play them. This creates a more casual audience for novels in the genre, as opposed to the more coverage-based sports writing found in newspapers and online. In long form, such as YA novels, sports stories become about the personalities of athletes and the struggles they face in their personal lives. These stories are then related to athletic success. Furthermore, through sports, stories may also examine social and political issues.

While sports stories are about more than simply sports, these stories do lend themselves to a handful of themes suited to the subject. Many of these are perfect for the YA audience, as most readers can identify with underdog stories, the need to persevere, and the tensions of balancing school, hobbies, friends, and family. The values of sports—such as physical strength, endurance, and focus—mirror the characters' internal growth in these same areas. Teams are microcosms of society, coaches become parental figures, and winning represents becoming a well-rounded person.

Sports, then, serve as a group of metaphors in YA literature. In *Darius & Twig* (2013), both track and writing are used as metaphors for the struggle to succeed despite racial and economic encumbrances. The titular characters try to excel at their fields while trying to survive inner-city life. *Dairy Queen* (2006) frames sports, specifically football, as a way of forming identity both outside gender norms (its main character is a girl on the football team) and as part of a family, since her older brothers were also football players. *Heart of a Champion* (1993) is less interested in using baseball as a metaphor than using the most American of sports to typify all-American kids. While baseball plays a large role in the novel, the true message is a warning against the dangers of substance abuse.

Works

Murdock's *Dairy Queen* uses sports to promote hard work, humility, gender equality, and individuality. Darlene Joyce "D. J." Schwenk, the protagonist of *Dairy Queen*, is a fifteen-year-old girl burdened with the responsibility of keeping her family dairy farm running while living under the shadow of her football-star brothers. D. J. works hard, complains little, and does what she is told. In a sense, she is like a mindless cow trudging through life among the herd. She "started thinking that maybe everyone in the whole world was just like a cow, and we all go along doing what we're supposed to without complaining or even really noticing, until we die."

D. J. is asked to train Brian, the quarterback of the rival high school football team. She realizes she does not want to be like a cow and longs to play football. At first she does not consider playing football herself, but as she practices with Brian on her handmade football field, she realizes what she really wants to do is try out for her own school's team.

D. J.'s friends and family praise her for her ability to work hard, but Brian criticizes her for allowing her family to take advantage of her hard work around the farm. D. J. wants to do the right thing and help her family, but her family is unable to see how much her work costs her emotionally, mentally, and academically. D. J. is depressed, frustrated, and failing her classes. She does not want to work on the farm forever but resigns herself to her fate. She feels she is too dumb to get into college, and she cannot get football scholarships like her brothers.

D. J. and Brian are able to help each other. D. J. helps Brian improve his work ethic, train harder, and take responsibility for his mistakes. Brian helps D. J. to see she is living "like a cow" by following the herd and worrying about meeting expectations. Their friendship gives D. J. the confidence to pursue her dreams. Consequently, she stands up to her parents, cuts her hair to fit under a football helmet, and tries out for the football team.

D. J. defies gender norms by making the team without much trouble, as every team member but one is happy to have her on the team. Her brothers' reputations for football prowess and work ethic precedes her. The real emotional issues surface when Brian discovers D. J. has made the team. Brian feels betrayed, thinking she helped him over the summer only to gain information on his playing style. The two make amends, but their friendship does not change their rivalry. *Dairy Queen* is largely about how shared experiences create bonds between people.

Darius & Twig tells the story of two teenage boys making a name for themselves so they can leave Harlem and lead better lives. Darius, an African American, and Twig, a Dominican American, both grew up marginalized by the larger culture and in a community as familiar with sounds of gunshots as the honking of car horns. One of Darius's short stories is about to be published in a literary magazine, and he hopes to get a college scholarship. Twig is a record-breaking runner who wants a scholarship so he can escape the inner city.

Rather than encouraging Darius and Twig, authority figures try to get them to quit. Darius's guidance counselor tells him that he does not have shot at a scholarship. Twig's uncle wants him to work for free in his bodega. Both boys are targeted by gang members who mug and bully them.

The story Darius hopes will earn him a scholarship is about a boy with a crippled leg who tries to swim out to a distant island. The boy nearly drowns during his first attempt but is rescued by dolphins. At the end of the story the boy tries one last time to reach the island, but it is unclear if he drowns or is again rescued. The magazine editors tell Darius they want to publish his story but need to know the end of the story. Darius searches for the answer throughout the novel by drawing from his own experiences.

When Twig reads the final draft he says, "Now the story is clearer because the kid is looking for something inside of himself, and that's what it's all about . . . I like the fact that at the end, he still has a bad leg and stuff isn't just wonderful. He's still got all the problems in his life and he's still got to deal with them." Thus, the story Darius that has written parallels his own life.

Darius's mother accuses him of living vicariously through Twig's athletic achievements, but he does not care. Darius feels that if Twig can succeed and build a good life for himself then so can he. He refuses to let

Twig give up even though Twig draws unwanted attention to himself because of his athletic ability. In Twig's case, bullies pay attention to him when he succeeds in track, much as they do to Darius when his writing is noticed. For them, success is not wealth or fame but getting out of a neighborhood where gang violence in rampant.

Heart of a Champion is a simple but heart-wrenching story that uses high school baseball as a framing device for the relationship between two boys and focuses on the dangers of drinking alcohol. Seth, the narrator, meets Jimmy while the latter and his dad are playing baseball. Jimmy's dad is training him, and Seth is shocked by how strict and critical he is of his son. They ask Seth to play, and he is relieved when Jimmy's dad is friendly and helpful toward him.

Jimmy explains that his dad is so hard on him because he wants him to be the best he can be. While harsh, the tactics used by Jimmy's dad seem to be working. Jimmy is indeed a talented baseball player and could realistically play in the majors. Seth decides he wants to be serious about baseball too and spends the rest of his teenage years trying to catch up to Jimmy's skill.

For the most part, jealousy does not come between the boys, except for a few minor instances, such as when Jimmy becomes angry when Seth hits a home run. The larger problems occur when Seth and Jimmy begin to drink beer at a teammate's house. A few beers quickly turn into a lot more for Jimmy. This surprises Seth because of Jimmy's discipline when it comes to baseball. Jimmy's dad is an alcoholic and has been known to drive after drinking. Despite promising Seth to prioritize school and baseball, Jimmy begins to emulate his father's behavior.

Jimmy's coach catches him drinking and suspends him from the team. When Jimmy's suspension is up, he drinks again. This worries Seth. Their coach has a "three strikes" rule that jeopardizes Jimmy's place on the team.

Jimmy does not get another chance: he dies in a drunk-driving accident before the team's championship game. The team decides to play despite their grief and dedicates the game to Jimmy. The people around Jimmy thought only "bad kids" drink and drive, but they learn that even stars such as Jimmy can suffer an addictive personality.

Seth is left to question the role of death in his life. He thinks of both his late father and Jimmy, and he contemplates his own death. He realizes death does not have to make sense. It can happen to the young or old, sick or healthy. There is no explanation for why some people die while others live. Death, like life, is unfair.

Heart of a Champion teaches readers to identify risky behavior and urges readers to talk about difficult issues rather than dismiss them, even if talking about them causes trouble. While it was not Seth's responsibility to ensure that Jimmy not drink, he could have told their coach or parents what was going on so that Jimmy could get help.

While all three novels differ greatly, they do contain some similarities, such as their emphasis on family. In *Dairy Queen*, D. J. does not expect her family to support her decision to play football, but having them do so makes her feel valued and loved. Twig needs the support of his uncle but does not always receive it. Jimmy does not have much positive support from his family, even when it might have saved his life.

Conclusions

The importance of sports in YA literature lies not in the sports themselves but in what they are used to talk about. Sports open up avenues for dialog about family, economic disparity, and camaraderie, among many other topics.

In each of these novels, the protagonists weigh their responsibilities to their teammates with those they have toward their families, finding ways to belong in these support systems. In *Dairy Queen*, D. J. balances her responsibilities on her family's farm with those of her football team. Twig, whose sport is an individual one, has to decide to pursue either track or working for his uncle in his bodega. Jimmy chooses to emulate his father's destructive behavior instead of embracing the friendships of his baseball team.

In these novels, sports invite the reader to understand these characters' lives better through the simplification of games. Teammates, like families, depend on each other. This means sticking up for one another in the face of difficulty or injustice, be it the chauvinism D. J. faces from an opposing team or the pressures on Twig to quit track.

Sports provide characters with a place to belong and to assert their identity. While characters rely on their teammates, they ultimately learn to rely on themselves. Their responsibilities and athleticism spur them to follow their own desires, rather than what people expect of them. Sports are the crucible that equips these characters to survive the challenging aspects of life.

All three novels portray the reality of marginalized people using athletics to gain social capital. While D. J. will probably never make money playing football after high school, she still benefits emotionally from knowing she pursued her dream. Twig is able to use his speed and perseverance to gain the attention of college scouts and become something more than a bodega owner or a gang member. Seth and Jimmy use baseball to improve themselves. Jimmy does not want to just be a great baseball player; he wants to be the best person he can be.

Even with their emphasis on athletics, all three novels make clear that education is just as important as sports. D. J. must pass her English classes in order to play on the team; Darius and Twig must do well in school to be considered for scholarships; and Seth manages to keep up good grades in all AP classes while also playing baseball. Jimmy's coach reprimands him for slacking on his studies and tells him to bring up his grade point average or be forced off the team. In American culture, academics and athletics are assumed to go together, and students are taught that higher education is a way to reach success. In most cases, as these novels show, sports are a way to reach a new tier of learning.

Alexandra McBride, MA

Further Reading

Conniff, Ruth. "'Dairy Queen,' by Catherine Gilbert Murdock." Rev. of *Dairy Queen*, by Catherine Gilbert Murdock. *New York Times*. New York Times, 18 June 2006. Web. 11 June 2015. <http://www.ny-times.com/2006/06/18/books/review/18conni.html?_r=0>.

"Darius and Twig." Rev. of *Darius & Twig*, by Walter Dean Myers. *Kirkus Reviews* 15 Mar. 2013: 111. *Literary Reference Center*. Web. 12 June 2015. <http://search.ebscohost.com/login.aspx?direct=true&db=lfh&AN=86039328&site=lrc-live>.

Schafer, Elizabeth D. "Carl Deuker." *Guide to Literary Masters and Their Works* (2007): 1. *Literary Reference Center*. Web. 11 June 2015. <http://search.ebscohost.com/login.aspx?direct=true&db=lfh&AN=103331LM24969790302027&site=lrc-live>.

Bibliography

Brown, Alan, and Chris Crowe. "Ball Don't Lie: Connecting Adolescents, Sports, And Literature." *ALAN Review* 41.1 (2013): 76–80. *Education Research Complete*. Web. 12 June 2015. <http://search.ebsco-host.com/login.aspx?direct=true&db=ehh&AN=91644481&site=ehost-live&scope=site>.

Crowe, Chris. *More than a Game: Sports Literature for Young Adults*. Lanham: Scarecrow, 2004. Print.

Eitle, Tamela McNulty. "Race, Cultural Capital, and the Educational Effects of Participation in Sports." *Sociology of Education* 75.2 (2002): 123–46. *FRANCIS*. Web. 11 June 2015. <http://search.ebscohost.com/login.aspx?direct=true&db=fcs&AN=13605684&site=ehost-live&scope=site>.

Muwakkil, Salim. "Race, Sports, and the Big Bucks." *Chicago Tribune*. Chicago Tribune, 5 July 1999. Web. 11 June 2015. <http://articles.chicagotribune.com/1999-07-05/news/9907050055_1_black-communities-athletic-success-african-american-communities>.

Schneider, Dean. "What Makes A Good Sports Novel?" *Horn Book Magazine* 87.1 (2011): 68–72. *Literary Reference Center*. Web. 12 June 2015. <http://search.ebscohost.com/login.aspx?direct=true&db=lfh&AN=57049561&site=lrc-live>.

Tracy, Allison J. "Gender and Race Patterns in the Pathways from Sports Participation to Self-Esteem." *Sociological Perspectives* 45.4 (2002): 445–46. *SocINDEX with Full Text*. Web. 11 June 2015. <http://search.ebscohost.com/login.aspx?direct=true&db=sih&AN=8570503&site=ehost-live&scope=site>.

Whiteside, Erin, et al. "'I Am Not a Cow': Challenging Narratives of Empowerment in Teen Girls Sports Fiction." *Sociology of Sport Journal* 30.4 (2013): 415–34. *Education Abstracts (H.W. Wilson)*. Web. 12 June 2015. <http://search.ebscohost.com/login.aspx?direct=true&db=eax&AN=93749853&site=ehost-live&scope=site>.

Substance Abuse

Titles Discussed

Beneath a Meth Moon by Jacqueline Woodson
Go Ask Alice by Beatrice Sparks
Stoner & Spaz by Ronald Koertge

Thematic Overview

Substance abuse became a prominent topic in young adult novels during the 1970s. In part, the sudden interest in drugs and alcohol reflected the cultural shift that began in the 1960s. While experimentation with drugs and alcohol was not unheard of prior to the 1960s, the rise of the counterculture that accompanied the Vietnam War meant both that an increasing number of adolescents were using substances like marijuana, LSD, and cocaine, and that mainstream culture was more aware of the realities of substance use. Popular countercultural books written for adults, including Jack Kerouac's influential 1957 novel *On the Road* and the poetry of Beat writer Allen Ginsberg, centered drug usage as formative aspects of youth counterculture. The success of these and similar works extended the popularity of illegal drugs among youth cultures while furthering the anxiety older generations often had about adolescent substance abuse.

For YA novels, the 1970s were also defined by the popularity of the problem novel—realistic fiction that explored adolescent protagonists navigating social problems such as physical abuse, poverty, teenage pregnancy, and substance abuse. Problem novels often functioned as morality tales, intended to educate adolescent audiences and to dissuade young readers from following the paths of their main characters. Because of this, the many novels that featured substance abuse rarely included nuanced characters, complex plots, or artful literary techniques. Instead, one-dimensional characters and unsophisticated plot lines dominated the genre, resulting in sensationalist novels that sold well but lacked depth and were not relatable for teens who might already be struggling with these issues. The 1971 novel *Go Ask Alice*, for instance, is a graphically explicit account of one girl's descent into drug addiction and prostitution, its plot given over primarily to sordid and shocking details rather than character development.

In the 1980s and 1990s, however, YA novels increasingly shifted their focus away from the morality-based structure of problem novels and into more sophisticated plot and characterization. During this time, substance abuse began to appear more regularly not as a central concern of a novel, but as one of a number of issues with which main or secondary characters might contend. Depiction of, for instance, social drinking or casual marijuana use might occur over the course of a narrative without receiving heightened attention. At the same time, the social fabric of drug use shifted, with popular attention focusing more on the use of crack cocaine and similar stimulants in urban populations than on the use of psychedelics among suburban youth. As the specifics of drug usage in the United States continue to shift over

time, new versions of problem novels are also published, addressing the realities of popular contemporary drugs, yet with more nuance and sympathy than their earlier counterparts. This can be seen in Jacqueline Woodson's 2012 *Beneath a Meth Moon*, which deals frankly with addiction to crystal methamphetamine while also employing poetic literary devices and complex character development. Increased public awareness about substance abuse has also meant fewer shocking portrayals of severely damaged teenagers, as seen in *Go Ask Alice*. Instead, novels like Ronald Koertge's 2002 *Stoner & Spaz* feature intelligent and kind-hearted characters who struggle with substance abuse as only one aspect of their adolescent experience. Still recognized as difficulties for many adolescents, substance abuse or experimentation with drugs are also presented as problems that might be overcome with sensitivity and determination.

Works

Wildly controversial and popular among readers, *Go Ask Alice* purports to be the diary of a young girl who succumbs to drug abuse and, as such, was originally published as an anonymous work. After significant controversy surrounding its truthfulness, however, it began to be billed as fiction, and Beatrice Sparks, who at first claimed to have edited the diary for publication, was credited with authorship. (Other writers may also have contributed, but Sparks is the sole copyright-holder.)

The story follows a fifteen-year-old girl (unnamed in the book, but often referred to as Alice due to the book's title) who is lonely and depressed after her family's move to a new town. When she is tricked into drinking a soda laced with LSD at a party, she begins to spiral out of control, experimenting with amphetamines and promiscuous sex. While Alice has some anxiety about what her family (and particularly her ailing grandfather) will think of her behavior, she quickly abandons herself completely to the countercultural world where she first found drugs, selling LSD to elementary school children in order to make money and fleeing to San Francisco to begin a new life. There, Alice begins to use heroin with her new friends, suffers the trauma of a violent rape, and is arrested for drug possession. Attempting to become sober again, Alice travels around the country, but in no time begins using while turning to prostitution to support her habit. After another attempt to quit and a psychotic break due to an LSD overdose, Alice is institutionalized and sent to counseling. The novel ends with a note that, three weeks after her final diary entry, she was found dead of an overdose.

Go Ask Alice is unequivocally an antidrug novel, intended less to explore the complex realities of drug use and abuse and instead to frighten teenage and adult readers, presenting the countercultural world associated with substance use as a nightmarish place. The fact that the novel is written as a diary (and that many readers believe it to be a true account) goes a long way toward accomplishing this goal. The first-person narrative is immediate and uncensored, with Alice relying on obscenities and crass language to a degree that was rarely seen in YA novels of the 1970s.

As her entire journey is constructed through the lens of her first accidental encounter with LSD, all of her subsequent experiences are presented as the result of that unfortunate event—Alice's rape and her decision to turn to prostitution, for instance, would in theory have never occurred had someone not tricked her into using LSD. The effect of this narrative device is to conflate a number of social issues under the overarching theme of substance abuse, which sensationalizes Alice's struggle with drugs and addiction and further scares readers away from any experimentation with illicit substances. At the same time, Alice is provided with a loving and respectable family, which wants nothing more than to help her get past her new addictions and is waiting to welcome her with open arms no matter how many times she runs away. These characters, however, are rendered with minimal detail, and appear more as generic sketches of "good" people—the effect, again, is to demonize experimentation with drugs while suggesting that no amount of good might save a teenager like Alice from the tragic end she faces. The heavy-handed morality is made most explicit with the closing note of the diary—although Alice has committed herself fully to recovery and received the support of professionals, friends, and family alike, the temptations of drug use prove too much, and her final overdose is described as being somewhere ambiguously between an accident and suicide.

In contrast to the narrative of doomed Alice and her unavoidable death, the main characters of *Stoner & Spaz* have a more nuanced understanding of the dangers and pleasures that drugs bring into their lives. The story is told from the point of view of Ben, a boy who lives with cerebral palsy and who has no friends, relying instead on movies and the companionship of his overprotective grandmother to fill his life. One day, however, he meets Colleen, a girl well known in his school for using and selling marijuana, as well as other drugs. While at first Ben is shocked that Colleen even talks to him, the two quickly form a tight and romantically charged friendship. While Ben makes Colleen feel like a normal teenager and encourages her to use fewer substances, Colleen forces Ben to become more social, bringing him to see bands play and getting him to try marijuana for the first time. With each other's support, Ben begins to work on a short film and Colleen begins to cut back on her substance abuse, and eventually they engage in a short-lived sexual relationship. The novel ends on a somewhat ambiguous note, with Colleen slipping and beginning to use drugs again and Ben declining to join her as she heads to the club, preferring instead to stay at the opening for his film. While the two part ways, however, their bond is also affirmed, with both characters having learned about themselves from their connection.

Colleen's life, like Alice's, is defined by her dependence on illicit substances and the countercultural world that surrounds them. Unlike Alice, however, her choice to use these drugs does not guarantee a doomed future of violence and death, but rather represents an unhealthy choice that she must navigate in order to become a happier version of her true self. Because of this, the narrative itself makes a clear distinction between experimentation with drugs and addiction. Early on in their new friendship, Colleen offers Ben a hit of marijuana, which he accepts despite never having considered experimenting with drugs in the past. Ben's experience is entirely positive, with the marijuana both alleviating the discomfort of his cerebral palsy and allowing him to experience freedom from the social anxiety that usually defines his interactions with others. While Ben does not choose to become a regular user of drugs, he does understand marijuana to be a potentially beneficial substance, albeit only if he uses it sparingly and does not go on to try other drugs (he regularly declines Colleen's offer of cocaine, for instance). At the same time, Ben's grandmother displays a more conservative take on drug abuse, reminiscent of that of Alice's parents—she does not understand why Colleen would rely on drugs and feels that her choice to do so makes her friendship unfit for Ben. By the novel's end, Colleen is returning to her old, unhealthy patterns, making it clear that ending an addiction is not a simple task. At the same time, however, it is Ben's ability to engage with Colleen without judging her choices (and indeed to explore those choices for himself) that allows them to connect in the first place. Thus, acceptance, rather than demonization, of drug users might be the healthiest choice and might have the most to offer teenagers who encounter substance abuse as part of their daily social lives.

Contemporary novels may still rely on the narrative of substance abuse destroying lives, but they often display more nuanced and sympathetic views than those of *Go Ask Alice*, as can be seen in *Beneath a Meth Moon*. This novel tells the story of fifteen-year-old Laurel, a girl who loses her beloved mother and grandmother during Hurricane Katrina, then relocates to a new town with her single father and younger brother. Soon after relocating and before being able to properly process the trauma of the deaths, Laurel is offered crystal methamphetamine by one of the most popular boys in school. The drug offers Laurel both a reprieve from the pain of the hurricane and a rush of acceptance and love, as she begins dating the boy and finds her social status rising. Soon, however, she is addicted rather than casually using, and eventually she runs away from home in search of the drug. Living on the street in a nearby city, she scrounges for whatever meth she can find, making friends with a teenage boy named Moses who paints the sides of buildings with figures of teenagers who overdosed on the drug. Laurel ends up hospitalized and near death because of her addiction, and her father brings her back home after a long, painful period of recovery. Again surrounded by her surviving family, Laurel is both aware of the incredible challenges ahead of her and determined to survive into a better future.

Beneath a Meth Moon shifts back and forth among three different time periods: Laurel's life on the street, the trauma of Hurricane Katrina, and her introduction to meth and addiction. This narrative structure makes clear connections between the events Laurel experiences while avoiding a direct causal relationship. While the tragedy of the death of her mother and grandmother contributes to her desire to escape into substance abuse, Laurel herself never suggests that she is an addict because of this trauma, nor does she entirely blame the boyfriend that introduces her to the drug. Instead, readers are given a realistically complex set of motivations—the harsh and addictive reality of the drug, the fabric of teenage social life in her small town, the emotional

anguish of Hurricane Katrina, and her own personality all conspire to create the circumstances in which addiction becomes her reality. While Alice has a happy life that is immediately destroyed when she accidentally ingests hallucinogens, Laurel is able to recognize drugs as a malicious force while also understanding some of the reasons she might have turned to them in the first place, a subtlety that does not place the blame for addiction on any single cause. In this way, *Beneath a Meth Moon* operates somewhere between the tradition of the problem novel and the trend for more sophisticated and complex YA novels that have emerged during the twenty-first century. It employs explicit and realistic prose in its exploration of the social problem of crystal meth abuse, yet it resists any easy answers or morality lessons, favoring instead the development of complex characters who describe their own experiences with honesty.

Conclusions

A 2014 survey from the University of Michigan shows that use of most illegal drugs has fallen among teenagers from the rates it reached in the early 2000s. While roughly 35 percent of twelfth-grade students had used marijuana in the past year, fewer than 5 percent of students the same age had used hallucinogens, MDMA, cocaine, and almost all other illicit or prescription drugs during that time. At the same time, fewer than 40 percent of twelfth-grade students considered marijuana use to pose any significant risk to their lives, a view that corresponds to a larger societal shift in attitudes toward marijuana.

Overall, these trends suggest several realities that are reflected in YA novels that depict substance abuse. While a number of adolescents will experiment with substances during their lifetimes, and some of those will begin lifelong struggles with addiction during their teenage years, the majority of teenagers are relatively well-educated about the risks and realities of substance use compared to the generation that grew up reading *Go Ask Alice* and similar sensationalized novels. This does not mean that substance abuse is not a problem among teenagers, as indeed the realities of increased social pressures, adolescent anxiety and depression, and similar challenges associated with the teenage years can significantly increase risk for substance abuse and addiction. It does mean, however, that teenagers are much more receptive to novels in which substance abuse is rendered with complexity and nuance. Characters like Colleen, lovable and problematic but ultimately a positive influence in the lives of her friends, are becoming commonplace. The specifics of drug and alcohol abuse change with every generation of young people—different drugs are introduced or become popular, and generational attitudes toward use and addiction shift rapidly. Regardless of these changes, however, contemporary novels are increasingly able to face new realities with honesty and compassion, providing tools in understanding the emotional complexity of drugs and alcohol for readers who are sensitive and attuned enough to receive them.

T. Fleischmann, MFA

Further Reading

Garbett, Ann D. "Ronald Koertge." *Guide to Literary Masters & Their Works* (2007): 1. *Literary Reference Center*. Web. 30 June 2015. <http://search.ebscohost.com/login.aspx?direct=true&db=lfh&AN=103331LM45139790304222&site=ehost-live>.

Quina, James. "Go Ask Alice." *Masterplots II: Juvenile & Young Adult Fiction Series* (1991): 1–2. *Literary Reference Center*. Web. 30 June 2015. <http://search.ebscohost.com/login.aspx?direct=true&db=lfh&AN=103331JYF11509270000153&site=ehost-live>.

Bibliography

"DrugFacts: High School and Youth Trends." *National Institute of Drug Abuse*. Natl. Institutes of Health, Dec. 2014. Web. 30 May 2015. <http://www.drugabuse.gov/publications/drugfacts/high-school-youth-trends>.

Gershowitz, Elissa. "What Makes a Good 'Bad' Book?" *Horn Book Magazine* 89.4 (2013): 84–90. *Literary Reference Center*. Web. 30 June 2015. <http://search.ebscohost.com/login.aspx?direct=true&db=lfh&AN=88842868&site=ehost-live>.

Mathys, Cécile, William J. Burk, and Antonius H. N. Cillessen. "Popularity as a Moderator of Peer Selection and Socialization of Adolescent Alcohol, Marijuana, and Tobacco Use." *Journal of Research on Adolescence* 23.3 (2013): 513–23. *Academic Search Premier*. Web. 30 June 2015. <http://search.ebscohost.com/login.aspx?direct=true&db=aph&AN=89768892&site=ehost-live>.

Teen Pregnancy and Parenthood

Titles Discussed
After by Amy Efaw
The First Part Last by Angela Johnson
Someone like You by Sarah Dessen

Thematic Overview

One of the first young adult novels specifically focusing on teenage pregnancy was published in 1968, and by the 1970s, pregnancy and parenthood had become popular topics for young adult literature. As publishers turned their attention to problem novels exploring social issues, these early works typically attempted to educate teenagers on the risks and downsides associated with teenage sexual activity, presenting pregnancy as a disastrous outcome that could be avoided with proper behavior. These novels were almost always written from the perspective of the teenage girl, included limited information on birth control, and framed pregnancy as a reality that prevents future happiness in relationships, education, and careers.

Influenced in part by the feminist movement of the 1970s and advancements in women's rights such as the US Supreme Court's landmark decision in *Roe v. Wade*, which legalized abortion in the United States in 1973, and the increased popularity of the birth control pill in the same decade, teen pregnancy and parenthood novels in the following decades began to shift their focus away from didactic and moralistic tales and to instead feature a greater variety of perspectives on the teenage pregnancy experience. Although teenage pregnancy and parenthood are rarely celebrated in novels from the 1980s and beyond, pregnant teenage characters are more often presented as complex characters navigating a challenging situation rather than simply as people who have committed an unforgivable lapse in judgment. Likewise, the widening range of options available to teenage girls who find themselves pregnant, including abortion and social services, has widened the scope of the genre. At the same time, while teenage birth rates peaked in the late 1950s (at nearly one hundred births for every one thousand teenage girls aged fifteen to nineteen), that number has since steadily declined with only a few brief spikes, reaching less than twenty-seven births for every one thousand teenage girls in 2013. Fewer contemporary teenagers experience pregnancy and parenthood directly, and therefore fewer have direct knowledge of what pregnancy can mean.

As teenage pregnancy novels remain popular into the twenty-first century, a larger number also avoid painting teenage sexuality itself as inherently problematic, and characters are less likely to experience pregnancy or parenting as a punishment for their actions. Sarah Dessen's 1998 *Someone Like You*, for instance, features a protagonist whose own exploration of her sexuality is influenced by her relationship with her pregnant best friend. Similarly, Angela Johnson's *The First Part Last* (2003) focuses on a teenage father who consciously decides to raise his child despite having other options available to him. Finally, Amy Efaw's 2009 novel *After* features a teenage girl who throws her baby into the trash in a desperate act of denial. Rather than demonizing this main character, however, the novel presents her plight with sympathy and compassion. In all of these cases, as in the best presentations of teenage pregnancy and parenthood, the choices of the characters are not framed as moral lessons for teenage readers but rather as literary explorations of difficult and life-changing choices.

Works

Someone Like You is told from the perspective of Halley, a teenage girl whose life is shaped by her relationship with her best friend, Scarlett. As the novel opens, Halley is away at summer camp when Scarlet calls and tells her that the boy Scarlett has been secretly dating, Michael, has died in a motorcycle accident. As Halley comforts Scarlett throughout the funeral, she meets Macon, Michael's best friend, and the two begin a romance. Halley increasingly feels distant from her mother, especially when her mother disapproves of the new relationship despite never meeting Macon. Eventually, Scarlett tells Halley that she is pregnant with Michael's child. While Scarlett's family sets up an appointment for an abortion, Scarlett decides she wants to keep the baby, and Halley supports her decision. Halley's relationship with Macon continues to progress, and Macon regularly pressures Halley to have sex, which she does not feel ready to do. After another fight about their sexual relationship, Halley and Macon get in a car accident, and Halley is seriously injured. The accident causes Halley to break up with Macon and also initiates a conversation with her mother, during which the two decide they need to stop arguing and work on becoming close again. While Halley is at prom, Scarlett goes into labor, and Halley accepts a ride from Macon to the hospital. After Scarlett's baby is born, Halley sees herself surrounded by supportive friends and family, and she begins to feel optimistic about the future once again.

Dessen's novel is notable for the amount of agency and intelligence it bestows on the teenage main characters,

both of whom rely on the support and insight of one another in order to make major decisions in their lives. This is made clear from the moment Scarlett decides to keep her baby rather than perform the abortion her mother has scheduled for her; already at the clinic, it is Halley she contacts to take her home, and while Halley at first offers some confusion about Scarlett's choice, she also instantaneously decides that she must support Scarlett above all else. Scarlett's pregnancy then progresses along many plot lines that are familiar themes of problem novels—the two characters visit doctors together, the pregnancy is discovered by other students at the school, and a good deal of information about reproductive health is shared with the reader. What distinguishes it, however, is that both Scarlett and Halley maintain their agency throughout this process. Even when they confront difficulties or struggle with the realities of what pregnancy and parenthood might mean, they always prove themselves (rather than their parents or doctors) to be the best authorities on what is preferable for their lives and their bodies. For Halley, this agency is reflected back to her own sense of her sexuality; while she makes a different choice than the choice Scarlett made when she declines to have sex with her boyfriend, this decision is also treated as the "right" decision and likewise is made with the confidence and trust of her best friend. In the end, both girls do turn again to their families for support, realizing that the wisdom and guidance offered by their parents is also valuable. However, their journey through first romance and through pregnancy is never defined by anyone but themselves, and as such both the consequences and rewards of their choices are presented not as warnings to keep teenage readers on any one particular path but as realistic explorations of what it means to navigate sexuality as an adolescent.

Like Scarlett, Bobby, the main character of *The First Part Last*, also chooses to raise his baby, despite having other options available to him. Bobby's story is told in chapters that alternate between a present in which he is in New York City and raising his baby, Feather, on his own and a past in which he and his girlfriend Nia face the reality of her pregnancy. Early on, Bobby and Nia both face the diverse reactions of their friends and family, who judge the teenagers while also showing sincere care and love for them. As Bobby attempts to hold on to his childhood self in the past sections, the present sections show him dealing with the reality of being a single father, including the exhaustion he constantly faces and the seeming impossibility of maintaining his efforts in school, let alone his social life. The past sections reveal Bobby and

Nia deciding on adoption for their child, which their parents support. In the future, Bobby increasingly feels like he has become an old person and that no one (including his teachers or family) will be capable of properly understanding or supporting him through fatherhood. Finally, the novel reveals that Nia had suffered eclampsia during the pregnancy, which put her in an irreversible coma. Immediately after the birth, Bobby meets Feather and realizes he wants to raise the baby, foregoing the adoption. As the novel ends, Bobby realizes that New York is not where he wishes to raise Feather, and he moves to live with his brother in Heaven, Ohio.

The First Part Last is a rare example of a teenage parenthood novel that focuses on the father, and, furthermore, one that focuses on a father who chooses to be involved in the life of his child rather than abandon the baby and mother, as is often the case in novels warning of the dangers of teen pregnancy. In order to explore this character, the novel alternates between chapters in which we see Bobby the father dealing with the reality of his life and Bobby the teenager dealing with the possibilities that pregnancy presents. For Bobby, this change is inseparable from his conception of himself as a man as he becomes responsible for his own decisions. In the chapters that precede the birth of Feather, his energy and attention are focused squarely on spending time with his friends and getting enjoyment out of life whenever possible. As soon as Feather enters his world, however, the gravity of the situation dramatically shifts his priorities: school suddenly becomes important, as he believes he needs good grades to provide for his baby; while he misses his friends desperately, he knows that any spare time must be spent with Feather; and perhaps most important, he decides that he should give up living in the city he loves in order to provide a more stable environment for Feather's childhood. Bobby also narrates a good deal of his emotions and thought process in internal monologues, stressing the things he feels he cannot say out loud to friends, family, and medical professionals, including the pain he feels regarding his sacrifices and the joy he experiences from the love Feather gives him. On a whole, then, the novel accomplishes a complex portrait of a changing person, someone who remains a mystery even to those closest to him. Parenthood is no one thing to Bobby, but rather it is a nuanced experience in which an old self he loves is lost and a new self, equally as loved, emerges.

While Bobby is an easily likable character in his choice to love and support his child, the main character of *After*, Devon, presents readers with a teenager who at first seems monstrous, even evil. As the novel opens, Devon sits on her couch in a haze, home sick from school. In quick succession, her mother returns home and the police arrive, having found a newborn baby abandoned in a trash can nearby. Devon's mother pulls Devon's blanket off of her, revealing that she is soaked in blood, and Devon is immediately arrested and taken to the hospital. The novel unfolds from within the juvenile detention center where Devon is placed, and as she talks to her lawyer and a psychiatrist, she slowly recalls the events of her pregnancy and the traumatic birth. As Devon's mother has always been promiscuous and provided Devon with an unstable, often unloving home, Devon had promised herself that she would never have sex, believing it to be the cause of her mother's problems. Eventually, she admits that she had broken that rule once, and her subsequent denial spiraled out of control, leading her to hide the pregnancy, even from herself, and abandon the baby. Although Devon's mother does not visit her at all in prison, she does arrive for the hearing, in which a judge decides whether Devon will be tried as an adult (facing life in prison) or a juvenile (facing five years). Through confronting her mother and hearing the testimony of others, Devon finally accepts the truth of what she had done and decides at the novel's close to plead guilty to the charges.

At first glance, *After* is reminiscent of the 1970s problem pregnancy novels, in which the choices of the main character (particularly to be sexually active) lead to horrible and life-altering consequences. Rather than a morality tale meant to dissuade teenagers, however, *After* is a sympathetic exploration of a character who made an unthinkable choice, and its main function as a novel is in leading readers to see Devon as a complex and even likable character. In large part, this is done through the narrative device of Devon's fractured memory. Readers only gain as much knowledge about Devon's past as she can summon at any one time. At the novel's opening, this means that she comes across as an emotionally stunted and cruel teenager, watching television without a care while her child suffers and nearly dies in a trash can outside. As she slowly recalls the unloving environment in which she was raised as well as the deeply traumatic experience of being pregnant alone, however, readers begin to understand why she might have been lead to such a violent action, and she transforms from a selfish villain into a teenager dealing with incredibly difficult challenges entirely on her own. In this regard, the core tension of *After* is not much different from that of *Someone Like You*, despite the situations being radically different from one another.

While Scarlett made some unwise choices throughout her pregnancy, she also had the support and love of Halley, which lead her to happiness at the novel's end. Had Devon even one person in whom she could confide the truth of her circumstance (or indeed, who even took the time to notice she was pregnant), she likely would not have made the decision to abandon her child. *After* does not hide from the more gruesome aspects of its story, rendering the night of the birth and Devon's shocked reaction in vivid detail. Rather than scaring readers into avoiding pregnancy or sexual activity, however, the power of these scenes ultimately lies in their insistence on the need for teenagers to receive support and guidance no matter the choices they have made.

Conclusions

A large number of pregnancy and parenthood novels for young adults still linger around tropes that have been present since the 1970s: girls who engage in sexual activity out of naïveté, boys who abandon their pregnant partners, and adoption as the only nonparenting option at the novel's end. While some valuable novels have been written that engage with these basic plot points, the novels that diverge from this script are increasingly popular among teenage readers, many of whom have the sophistication and life experience to know that pregnancy and parenthood are incredibly varied experiences.

In part, the tension between the problem novels and the more nuanced, realist novels reflects another cultural tension, that between abstinence-only sexual education and comprehensive sexual education, which educates teenagers about birth control and other reproductive health options. Evidence shows that comprehensive sexual education is the most successful at lowering pregnancy rates among teenagers, and indeed, as comprehensive education becomes more popular, the rate of teenage pregnancy in the 2010s is at one of the lowest points it has been in the past century. While these broader social realities shape the way writers present pregnancy and parenthood to teenage readers, they also mean that representations of pregnancy in teenage novels are sometimes inconsistent with what pregnancy means in the lives of contemporary teenagers. A literature review by Kristen Nichols in an article for the *ALAN Review* found that, in novels published after 1990, only 10 percent of pregnant teenager characters chose to get an abortion, while 40 percent of actual pregnant teenagers in that time elected for an abortion. Similarly, while only 3 percent of teenagers in reality give their baby up for adoption, an incredible 35 percent of teenagers in novels made that same choice.

On a whole, these statistics show young adult novels have some way to go in honestly addressing pregnancy and parenting as it exists in the lives of teenagers. While the emotional complexity of characters such as Devon, Bobby, and Scarlett is engaging and while their stories manage to explore their difficult choices without the moralistic undertones of many problem novels, the genre of young adult pregnancy novels on whole still fails to provide teenagers with adequate representation of the choices and challenges they face. Regardless of the broader problems with representation, however, the rare novels that do succeed in crafting literary explorations of pregnancy from the perspective of adolescents have been wildly successful with readers and educators and will certainly continue to flourish as the genre expands to include more stories, more diversity, and more choices.

T. Fleischmann, MFA

Further Reading

Chance, Rosemary. *Young Adult Literature in Action: A Librarian's Guide*. Santa Barbara: Libraries Unlimited, 2014. Print.

Coffel, Cynthia Miller. "Strong Portraits and Stereotypes: Pregnant and Mothering Teens in YA Fiction." *ALAN Review* 30.1 (2002): 15–20. Web. 13 July 2015. <http://scholar.lib.vt.edu/ejournals/ALAN/v30n1/pdf/coffel.pdf>.

Davis, Joy B., and Laurie MacGillivray. "Books about Teen Parents: Messages and Omissions." *English Journal* 90.3 (2001): 90–96. Print.

Nichols, Kristen. "Facts and Fictions: Teen Pregnancy in Young Adult Literature." *ALAN Review* 34.3 (2007): 30–38. Web. 13 July 2015. <http://scholar.lib.vt.edu/ejournals/ALAN/v34n3/nichols.pdf>.

Bibliography

Cowley, Carol, and Tillman Farley. "Adolescent Girls' Attitudes toward Pregnancy." *Journal of Family Practice* 50.7 (2001): 603–7. *Academic Search Premier*. Web. 13 July 2015. <https://search.ebscohost.com/login.aspx?direct=true&db=mnh&AN=11485709&site=eds-live>.

"Teen Pregnancy: Trends and Lessons Learned." *Guttmacher Report on Public Policy* 5.1 (2002): N. pag. Web. 13 July 2015. <https://www.guttmacher.org/pubs/tgr/05/1/gr050107.html>.

Younger, Beth. *Learning Curves: Body Image and Female Sexuality in Young Adult Literature*. Lanham: Scarecrow, 2009. Print.

GENRES OF YOUNG ADULT LITERATURE

Apocalyptic and Postapocalyptic

Titles Discussed
How I Live Now by Meg Rosoff
Life as We Knew It by Susan Beth Pfeffer
The Maze Runner by James Dashner

General Overview

The word "apocalypse" is an ancient Greek term referring to an unveiling of new knowledge, typically used in the context of the destruction of the world in the Judeo-Christian traditions of the end-time. While the apocalypse and the "end of the world" as religious and mythological concepts have existed across cultures for centuries, the modern sense of apocalyptic fiction truly became popular following World War II, when the use of nuclear weapons made the possibility of worldwide destruction seem a newly viable threat. From the mid-twentieth century onward, advancing weapons technologies, the human impact on the environment, resource scarcity, and similar contemporary threats fueled the public interest in apocalyptic fiction. Novels explored diverse scenarios, from Kurt Vonnegut's *Cat's Cradle* (1963) and its imagined world where all water freezes at room temperature to Cormac McCarthy's *The Road* (2006) and its devastated landscape following an apocalypse of unspecified origin. Apocalyptic movies and television shows have likewise flourished, particularly following a number of popular science-fiction apocalypse movies in the 1970s, including *Omega Man* (1971), *Mad Max* (1979), and the various sequels to 1968's *Planet of the Apes*.

Young adult apocalyptic and postapocalyptic novels have similarly become increasingly popular, beginning roughly in the second half of the twentieth century. While the high entertainment value of the genre makes it a good fit for many younger readers—most apocalyptic novels are action focused, with plenty of suspense, and feature characters in a constant struggle for survival—there are also some clear metaphorical overlaps between the young adult experience and the apocalyptic experience. In the apocalypse, older generations have gone astray, resulting in the destruction of the earth, and surviving characters are left to survive and rebuild. Young adults likewise stand on the edge of inheriting society, and the apocalyptic scenario heightens the danger they face, the failings of older generations, and the potential for absolute change (or rebuilding).

In the twenty-first century, postapocalyptic novels such as James Dashner's *The Maze Runner* (2009) have become best sellers and are often adapted into popular film franchises. Other novels, such as Meg Rosoff's *How I Live Now* (2004) and Susan Beth Pfeffer's *Life as We Knew It* (2006), take an different approach, focusing less on action and more on the emotional adjustments the characters face. In all three of these novels, the cause of the apocalypse remains obscure, redirecting the focus to the survival of the teenage protagonists and their future rather than the specific politics of their pre-apocalypse world.

Works

The Maze Runner is written in the tradition of many science-fiction apocalyptic narratives that center on action, suspense, and entertainment. Rather than explore the apocalypse itself, the novel takes place in a seemingly postapocalyptic world about which readers and characters both know very little. The main character, Thomas, awakes one day in a mysterious Glade at the center of a towering Maze. The Glade is filled with other teenage boys who, like Thomas, remember nothing of their lives before they entered this landscape. The other boys have developed a new society, with strict rules, a loose government, and defined roles for everyone. As Thomas learns about this new reality and navigates the Maze's many dangers, however, the Maze itself begins to change, eventually pushing him to escape with a small number of other teenagers. Once free, they find the Creators of the Maze, but only moments pass before soldiers enter and kill the Creators. At the novel's end, Thomas is told that a disease is threatening all of humanity, leaving him with as many questions as answers.

From the opening scene in which Thomas enters the Glade to the final, confusing moments of violence as the Creators die, the experiences of the characters in *The Maze Runner* are defined by their lack of information. As apocalyptic scenarios typically involve a sudden absence of power structures, with governments and other societal forces crumbling, Thomas finds himself in a familiar trope, struggling to establish order and reason in a world where both seem to have disappeared. As the novel progresses, the challenges facing Thomas become not simply about the violent creatures in the Maze but about the process of reconstructing order with the other teenagers trapped there, as cooperation and trust are necessary for their safety. However, the former societal powers (mysterious as they are) are revealed to have survived whatever apocalyptic scenario rages outside the Maze, so the moment of freedom and escape turns out instead to be only a moment in which the characters are thrown into yet another apocalyptic scenario. This creates a constant tension between the young protagonists, struggling to build a society from a new logic, and the older figures of power who manipulate and exploit the teenagers. As a metaphor for the young adult experience of forming a better society as older generations pass, this makes the revelation of the novel's end particularly troubling, suggesting that adults will endlessly continue to intervene and require the young adult characters to overthrow them.

The presence of adults in *How I Live Now* likewise has the potential to stifle and destroy younger communities, although their absence results in an idyllic setting rather than the terrifying reality of the Glade. Focusing on fifteen-year-old Daisy, the novel is split into two parts. In the first, Daisy is sent from New York to England to live with her cousins in a remote region, her father wanting her to be safe in the face of an impending global war. When her aunt leaves on an extended work vacation, the teenagers and children are left on their own. Daisy finds herself in a pastoral world of beauty where she falls in love with her cousin Edmond, their romance bringing greater joy without the scrutiny of adults. Eventually, however, the war intrudes, at first in the form of food shortages from distant battles. Soon after, soldiers of unknown origin come and take over the farm, splitting up Daisy and Edmond by sending them to separate group homes. After the brutal violence of the war, the narrative moves forward five years, with Daisy returning to England a changed person and finding Edmond emotionally devastated by the war years. Together and older, they must heal each other and build a new life.

Although both sections are narrated by Daisy, they are written in markedly different styles, with changes in the character's voice indicating the emotional toll the war has taken on her sense of self. In the idyllic, rural opening, Daisy speaks with constant slang and sarcasm; even the beautiful setting of the countryside is given cynical treatment, the home life described as one that does not "exactly remind you of *Little Women* even on our best day." By the second half, Daisy is less likely to rely on humor or vernacular language. Instead, although she is brought back to the beauty of the rural environment and is reunited with her first love, her voice remains mature, steady, and serious. This split suggests that it is not the country home itself that allowed the

youthful joy and cooperation of the prewar days but rather the absence of adult influence. Now that the war (and the adults who are behind it) have permanently altered the landscape and the interior world of the characters, Daisy and Edmond are unable to simply return to their old mode of existence. While Thomas and the characters of *The Maze Runner* find themselves thrown into one apocalyptic scenario after the next, the challenge for Daisy is instead how to live a postapocalyptic life, one in which it seems that the damaging influence of adults will never be undone.

In *Life as We Knew It*, the apocalyptic violence comes in the form of natural disasters, which displaces the sense of adult failure and instead creates a small family unit of mixed ages struggling to survive together. The fifteen-year-old protagonist, Miranda, lives in a Pennsylvania town, and her greatest concerns are her crush on a boy from the swim team and an ankle injury that has made it impossible for her to ice-skate. When an asteroid hits the moon and causes massive environmental disasters on Earth, these concerns seem minor as she slowly finds herself fighting to survive alongside her family and friends. As a long, cold winter settles, Miranda and her family struggle to ration food, stay warm, and fend off disease. While the survival of individuals and of society itself suddenly becomes uncertain, Miranda bonds more tightly with her family, finding hope through mutual support.

The apocalypse as it unfolds in *Life as We Knew It* is in many ways an inversion of several popular contemporary apocalypses. With no human origin for the disaster, the need to overthrow previous generations is gone, and as such, the characters largely turn to already existing modes of survival and strength in order to sustain themselves rather than inventing entirely new ways to be. Notably, while it still presents a scenario in which Miranda must rise to fulfill adult responsibilities, her task is not to reinvent society but simply to exhibit strength and optimism when she is the only member of her family to avoid a potentially deadly virus that sweeps through town. Ultimately, *Life as We Knew It* is an apocalypse story that affirms its characters and their ways of life rather than insisting on revolutionary actions. Solutions and methods from the past must be drawn from in order to achieve an optimistic ending.

All three of these apocalyptic scenarios draw on different contemporary political realities: government surveillance and control in *The Maze Runner*, war and terrorism in *How I Live Now*, and natural disaster in *Life as*

We Knew It. While the novels allow readers to confront these fears, each novel remains focused on the choices that its respective protagonist must make. The books do not provide clear answers for how to live in a new reality; Miranda's answers turn to family and Thomas's to rebellion against authority, and both come with their own advantages and their own dangers. What the stories do reveal is a glimpse of the emotional growth and turmoil an apocalypse might bring about—turmoil that echoes the general anxieties inherent in entering adulthood and staking a claim in the world, apocalyptic or not.

Conclusions

Although nearly every culture exhibits fears of an apocalyptic event or events, those concerns seem especially heightened in Western society in the early twenty-first century. Political debates about the possibility of natural disasters due to global climate change, of nuclear- or chemical-fueled terrorist attacks, and of devastating scarcity and droughts all present these cataclysmic visions as viable realities.

Young adults, then, increasingly must consider the possibility that they will inherit a devastated world and that their future will involve rebuilding society rather than continuing it as it was. The genre of apocalyptic literature will likely hold its popularity, especially as the action-oriented nature of many apocalyptic plots make them easy source material for mainstream movies. While some critics fear that the popularity of apocalyptic and postapocalyptic literature indicates a pessimistic, doomed mentality in younger generations, it is also important to remember that young adults almost always serve as symbols of hope and future for these worlds. Even in the violence-drenched ending of *Maze Runner* and the emotionally shattered reality of *How We Live Now*, the youth still represent the possibility that things might be not only be different in the future, but improved. Because of this, the young adult fixation on apocalypses also indicates an insistence on optimism despite seemingly desperate political and cultural realities, the literature prepping younger generations to persevere no matter how broken or harsh the world they inherit becomes. This sense of survival ultimately aligns the genre with the biblical sense of the apocalypse, with the younger generation experiencing the unveiling of truth that will lead to a better world, even if that world exists as nothing more than hope in the novel itself.

T. Fleischmann, MFA

Further Reading

Craig, Amanda. "It's No Fun Being a Girl." Rev. of *Dirty Work*, by Julia Bell, and *Life as We Knew It*, by Susan Beth Pfeffer. *Times* 10 Mar. 2007, Features sec.: 15. *Newspaper Source*. Web. 30 Apr. 2015. <http://search.ebscohost.com/login.aspx?direct=true&db=nfh&AN=7EH0485454597&site=ehost-live>.

Paik, Peter Y. *From Utopia to Apocalypse: Science Fiction and the Politics of Catastrophe*. Minneapolis: U of Minnesota P, 2010. Print.

Reeve, Philip. "The Worst Is Yet to Come." *School Library Journal* Aug. 2011: 34–36. *Academic Search Complete*. Web. 30 Apr. 2015. <http://search.ebscohost.com/login.aspx?direct=true&db=a9h&AN=64135267&site=ehost-live>.

Bibliography

Hammond, Jeffrey. "The Sense of an Ending: Farewell to the Apocalypse." *River Styx* 88 (2012): 8–17. *Literary Reference Center*. Web. 30 Apr. 2015. <http://search.ebscohost.com/login.aspx?direct=true&db=lfh&AN=83530753&site=ehost-live>.

Miller, Laura. "Fresh Hell." *New Yorker*. Condé Nast, 14 June 2010. Web. 30 Apr. 2015. <http://www.newyorker.com/magazine/2010/06/14/fresh-hell-2>.

Watkins, Susan. "Future Shock: Rewriting the Apocalypse in Contemporary Women's Fiction." *LIT: Literature Interpretation Theory* 23.2 (2012): 119–37. *Literary Reference Center*. Web. 30 Apr. 2015. <http://search.ebscohost.com/login.aspx?direct=true&db=lfh&AN=76142945&site=ehost-live>.

Christian and Spiritual

Titles Discussed
A Time to Love by Walter Dean Myers
There You'll Find Me by Jenny B. Jones
If We Survive by Andrew Klavan

Genre Overview
The beginning of contemporary young adult Christian fiction dates to the 1950s and 1960s. Between 1950 and 1956, Oxford professor and Anglican theologian C. S. Lewis published his seven-volume series *The*

Chronicles of Narnia. Perennial favorites among young people as well as adults, the books relate the adventures of children who are magically transported to the mythical land of Narnia, which is a realm populated by talking animals, courageous heroes, and treacherous villains. The land is ruled by Aslan, a wild but benevolent lion, who needs the help of "sons and daughters of Eve" to rid Narnia of evil doers. Although Lewis denied that the stories were allegorical in nature, the novels highlight Christian themes, including sacrifice, death, resurrection, and rebirth.

C. S. Lewis's friend and Oxford colleague J. R. R. Tolkien published his own fantasy series beginning with *The Hobbit* in 1937, and continuing with the three-volume *The Lord of the Rings,* published between 1954 and 1955. Although Tolkien's works are not considered Christian allegories, his powerful portrayal of the battle between good and evil and the sacrificial actions of some of his main characters reflect his strong Catholic beliefs.

The cosmic battle between light and darkness is also prominent in Madeleine L'Engle's *A Wrinkle in Time* series published in 1962. Blending her interest in quantum mechanics with her Christian faith, L'Engle tells the story of thirteen-year-old Meg Murry's interplanetary search for her absent scientist father with the help of three eccentric old women who are angels in disguise. In contrast to Lewis and Tolkien, L'Engle specifically quotes Christian scripture and speaks openly about faith in her stories. The works of all three authors are beloved by children, teenagers, and adults, and, in the case of Lewis and Tolkien, have been successfully adapted to feature films.

The popularity of Lewis's, Tolkien's, and L'Engle's novels has endured among Christian and mainstream readers, but it was not until the 1970s and 1980s that young adult Christian fiction came into its own. The rise of the modern evangelical movement in the United States spawned a demand for values-driven, faith-based literature targeted to the adolescent market. Authors responded by penning narratives that specifically address issues that Christian teenagers find relevant to their personal lives. Contemporary adolescent concerns such as dating, depression, drug and alcohol abuse, family conflict, bullying, eating disorders, and other challenges often appear in young adult Christian literature. In addition, classic motifs, including the cycle of birth, death, and rebirth; the Edenic myth of original sin; the hero's journey; coming of age through a test or trial; and the quest for personal and spiritual identity, inform the plots.

Although these concerns and themes are found in mainstream young adult fiction as well, the emphasis on faith-based values is what separates Christian young adult literature from its secular counterpart. The degree to which these values shape the plot varies. For example, novels and short stories written for the evangelical young adult population adhere to the belief that the authority of the Bible is absolute, that salvation is attained only through Jesus Christ, that Christian prayer is central to addressing life's challenges, and that believers should not cross biblically mandated moral boundaries. Other works reflect a more tolerant view of moral issues yet still reflect the core message of salvation through Christ. Still others—similar to the works of Lewis and Tolkien—treat biblical themes less overtly. Although the degree to which Christianity informs various story lines may differ, the values of love, faith, hope, sacrifice, and a commitment to living a moral and just life are common threads running through the body of young adult Christian literature.

Works

Combining text by Walter Dean Myers and mixed-media illustrations by his son, Christopher, *A Time to Love* is composed of six short stories based on familiar and less well-known Old Testament tales. Each story is told by teen narrators, some of whom are secondary characters in the original texts. The first-person narratives lend an immediacy to the ancient stories, making them feel fresh and relevant to the lives of contemporary young adults. The title of the book points to the overarching theme in Christian literature of love, but within that theme, Myers explores specific facets of love, including sexual attraction, familial relationships, and friendship. Relationships between adults and children in Myers's stories are often problematic, resulting in significant moral and spiritual dilemmas for the adolescent narrators. However, Myers intends to "remind us that God *is* love, and the way to face life's challenges, and the best expression of our faith . . . is through love." Far from being a childish sentimental reaction, love is a mature response to the difficulties of an uncertain world.

In the opening story, fifteen-year-old Delilah tells how she is urged by her greedy father to collaborate with the Philistines to discover the secret of Samson's strength. Rather than cast her as a calculating seductress, Myers portrays her as vulnerable, unsure, and caught between her attraction to Samson and her duty to her people. Betrayal does not come easily to her, but eventually the love between Delilah and Samson—who has betrayed his Nazarite vow—redeems them both.

Betrayal is a prominent theme in the tale of brothers Reuben and Joseph. As the drama of sibling rivalry unfolds, Reuben admits his dislike of Joseph's haughty attitude, and yet he's reluctant to go along with his brothers' plan to kill Joseph. As the oldest, Reuben's opinion carries weight, and his brothers agree to sell Joseph into slavery instead. Years later, Joseph, a powerful official in Pharaoh's court, forgives his brothers and welcomes them to Egypt. His loving response bespeaks a spiritual maturity that far surpasses his siblings' childish jealousy.

Myers continues to focus on difficult family relationships in the story of Zillah and Lot. Myers's reimagining of the tale delves into the family dynamics between a strict, straight-laced father, a more tolerant mother, and their daughter who is trying to make sense of the twisted world of Sodom. In a moment of misguided hospitality, Lot offers Zillah and her sister to the people of Sodom in place of the three "holy men" who are guests in Lot's house. Her father's callousness shocks her, and Zillah is bitterly disappointed in the one adult whom she believed loved and cherished her.

In contrast to Zillah's disillusionment with her father, Isaac's faith in his father, Abraham—and God—never falters. One questions Abraham's actions as he prepares to sacrifice his only son in obedience to what he perceives as God's command. Is he really hearing the voice of God, or is he delusional? Isaac willingly and passively accepts the role of the lamb, even to the point of excusing Abraham when he exclaims, "I love you, Father. I know it is God's will." The relationship between Abraham and Isaac is disturbing considering that Abraham, like Lot, is willing to deceive his child in order to follow what he considers to be a higher ideal. Yet Abraham's unbending obedience and Isaac's passive acceptance can also be interpreted as love at its most radical.

There You'll Find Me by Jenny B. Jones is an example of a one of the most popular genres among young adult Christian girls, teenage romance. The plot follows a predictable formula—a young couple meet, are simultaneously attracted and repelled by each other, find themselves reluctantly falling in love, try to work out their differences, and decide they are meant for each other after all. In struggling to understand their relationship, they rely on God to show them the way. However, the path to a love is a rocky one for the narrator, Finley Sinclair, because she is dealing with a crisis of faith after the death of her beloved brother Will.

An heiress and former party girl, eighteen-year-old Finley decides to study abroad. She chooses Ireland because Will left a journal detailing his travels in that country. In contrast to the deep faith her brother expresses in his diary, Finley has nearly abandoned her own faith because of the crushing grief and loneliness she feels in the wake of Will's death. She is under added pressure because she is struggling to finish a violin composition in time for her upcoming audition at the New York Conservatory. She is hoping that visiting Ireland will help her to find emotional and spiritual peace. On the plane, she meets Hollywood superstar and bad boy Beckett Rush, who is on his way to Ireland to finish his latest vampire film. Their relationship gets off to a rough start. The acrimony between them accelerates when she discovers that he is staying at the bed-and-breakfast run by her host family.

Finley remains unimpressed by Beckett's celebrity, which heightens his attraction to her. Eventually he asks her to be his dialogue coach on the film set. Meanwhile, Finley's teacher requires her to perform a community service project. Finley's subject, Mrs. Sweeney, is a grumpy, nursing home patient who is dying from cancer. The stress Finley experiences as she deals with her composition deadline, her developing romance with Beckett, and her difficult relationship with Mrs. Sweeney manifests itself in an eating disorder. As her life shatters, Finley searches for God—and the Celtic cross appearing in the last photo of Will's journal. Her quest for both ends when Beckett, who is rediscovering his own dormant faith, brings her to an ancient graveyard. There she reconnects with God and finds the inspiration for completing her audition piece.

Transformation from seeker to believer is a familiar theme in both adult and young adult Christian fiction. Losing sight of God after her brother's death, Finley is often blinded by her fears and insecurities. Her faith hangs by a thread but is bolstered by Romans 8:37, a Bible verse given to her by her counselor after Will's death: "We are more than conquerors through him who loved us." It is a promise that Finley is unable to claim until she finally accepts that she needs help to overcome anorexia. She also discovers that it often takes a loving community of believers to bring about an individual's transformation. In Finley's case, the love of Beckett, her host family, and Mrs. Sweeney help her deal with her grief and re-establish her relationship with God.

The ability of a Christian community to strengthen and nurture faith is highlighted in Andrew Klavan's adventure story, *If We Survive*. The novel is set in the fictional Central American country of Costa Verdes, where five people from an American church group—a youth pastor, his assistant, and three teenagers—arrive to help villagers construct a schoolhouse. The first chapter ends with Will, the sixteen-year-old narrator, ominously observing, "We came to Costa Verdes to build a wall. I just wish I could tell you that all of us made it home alive."

When they are about to head home, the group is kidnapped by Communist-style revolutionaries who hold them as bargaining chips in a government take-over plan. Their well-meaning pastor, Ron, becomes a martyr in the hope that his death will persuade the rebels to let the others go. Meredith, Ron's fearless assistant, assumes responsibility for the teenagers: Will; Nicki, who is outwardly attractive by inwardly shallow; and Jim, the socialist intellectual. They are eventually joined by Palmer Dunn, a sardonic ex-Marine bush pilot who has promised to help them escape but whose loyalties are suspect.

The plot is faced-paced, suspenseful, and at times violent. Fall from innocence is a persistent theme, especially when Will is confronted with a rebel who is intent on killing him and his friends. Will is unsure whether he can pull the trigger of the machine gun he has stripped from the body of a dead revolutionary, but he is surprised to discover that he can kill if necessary to protect those he loves. As the situation escalates, Will notes that the only reason they came to Costa Verdes was "to build a wall." In effect, he is saying, "I'm only a kid." In order to hold on to hope throughout the ordeal, Will calls to mind two quotes he remembers. The first is Ernest Hemingway's definition of cowardice as "a lack of ability to suspend the functioning of the imagination." The second is something Pastor Ron quoted from the Bible, "Don't worry about anything—instead pray about everything." These principles guide Will as he deals with his involuntarily initiation into the adult world of war and violence.

Conclusions

In a culture where consumerism, technology, materialism, and violence are commonplace, many Christians fear that the moral deterioration of American society will negatively affect the future and faith of their children. The rise of secular humanism and atheism are perceived as a threat to the established church, and teenagers, as well as adults, increasingly identify themselves

as "spiritual" rather than declare allegiance to a specific Christian denomination. Major surveys show that most Millennials (those born between 1980 and 2000) who were raised as Christians no longer read the Bible, attend worship services, or pray.

Young adult Christian literature often serves an evangelical function. In the twenty-first century, young adults are exposed to complex challenges that previous generations did not encounter. Many of them are searching for guidance as they deal with peer pressure, bullying, eating disorders, broken families, drug and alcohol abuse, and other issues. Young adult Christian literature provides "unchurched" teenagers with a nonthreatening, entertaining way to become acquainted, and in some cases reacquainted, with Christian beliefs and values.

Young adult Christian literature also reinforces the religious beliefs of Christian teenagers as they journey from adolescence to adulthood. Reading about how teenage characters successfully make their way in a world that is perceived as hostile to Christian values can be both encouraging and affirming. As teenagers identify with the characters' failings and strengths, they begin to understand the vital role faith can play in helping them to confront and overcome moral obstacles in their own lives, obstacles that may prevent them from attaining spiritual and psychological maturity.

It is important to note that young adult Christian literature has been considered controversial, and some critics argue that a socially and politically conservative agenda often influences contemporary adult and young adult Christian fiction. While neither *A Time to Love* nor *There You'll Find Me* deals with political issues, Klavan's *If We Survive* portrays Jim as a young, out-of-touch liberal intellectual whose ideology blinds him to the obvious evil intentions of the rebels who capture him and his friends. Jim defends the revolutionaries and their leader—whose book he has read—claiming that their brutal actions are necessary in order to bring peace, prosperity, and social equality to the country. By the end of the book, Jim believes the revolution is a sham. While some readers may applaud Jim's new outlook, others might take offense at Klavan's portrayal. However, the political overtones are overshadowed by the sacrifice, faith, and heroism of the characters.

Pegge Bochynski, MA

Further Reading

Auguste, Margaret. "Those Kinds of Books: Religion and Spirituality in Young Adult Literature." *Young Adult Library Services* 11.4 (2013): 37–40. *Academic Search Complete*. Web. 19 June 2015. <http://search.ebscohost.com/login.aspx?direct=true&db=a9h&AN=89132688>.

Brown, Devin. *The Christian World of the Hobbit.* Nashville: Abingdon, 2014. Print.

Bibliography

Byle, Ann. "Christian YA Fiction: Coming into Full Bloom." *Publishers Weekly*. PWxyz, 27 Aug. 2012. Web. 23 May 2015. <http://www.publishersweekly.com/pw/by-topic/new-titles/adult-announcements/article/53700-religion-update-fall-2012-christian-ya-fiction-coming-into-full-bloom.html>.

Hill, Rebecca. "God on the Shelf: The Influence of Christian Young Adult Literature." *Voice of Youth Advocates* (2010): 322–32. Print.

Walker, Barbara J. *The Librarian's Guide to Developing Christian Fiction Collections for Children.* New York: Neal-Schuman, 2005. Print.

Coming of Age and Bildungsroman

Titles Discussed

The Outsiders by S. E. Hinton
Just Listen by Sarah Dessen
Fangirl by Rainbow Rowell

General Overview

In its broadest contemporary use, bildungsroman refers to a coming-of-age novel in which an adolescent protagonist experiences moral, psychological, and often physical maturation on the journey to adulthood. When the term was first coined in Germany in 1819, however, it referenced a much more formulaic plot in which a sensitive teenage boy (often an orphan) leaves a rural life in order to strike out on his own in a city. There, he feels excluded from society but, through the help of an older friend, learns to find his place in the world, emerging at the novel's end as a full adult.

Particularly because of the focus on teenage protagonists, it is no surprise that bildungsromans have often been popular among young adult readers through generations—including many classics of twentieth-century

literature, such as Harper Lee's *To Kill a Mockingbird* (1960) and J. D. Salinger's *The Catcher in the Rye* (1951). The modern young adult genre, as it is commonly understood, began around the publication of S. E. Hinton's 1967 bildungsroman *The Outsiders*. Published when Hinton was only seventeen, it tells the story of a young gang member's maturation in a gritty and violent world. Following *The Outsiders*, increasing attention was placed on young adult publishing by both publishers and authors, and as such the number of bildungsromans written specifically for young adult readers increased sharply.

The bildungsroman remains popular in the twenty-first century. It is important to note, however, that not all young adult novels fit into this categorization, despite the fact that almost all young adult novels feature teenage protagonists during the mental and physical formation process. Rather, it is the emergence into adulthood and the concomitant change in self-identity that typically define the genre. Almost every other qualification from that earliest definition has fallen away. Modern bildungsromans are as interested in young women as young men, for instance, and the sense of "successfully" entering society is less important as young adult fiction increasingly celebrates characters for their differences from, rather than similarities to, others. It is because of this evolution that novels like Sarah Dessen's *Just Listen* (2006) and Rainbow Rowell's *Fangirl* (2013) stand as acclaimed works in the bildungsroman genre.

Works

Hinton's *The Outsiders* has arguably had a greater impact on the development of modern young adult literature than any other novel, in large part because it established the first real young adult market through its honest depictions of the young protagonist's life—violence, obscene language, and teenage smoking and alcohol consumption are all present, despite being taboo subjects at the time. These honest depictions are also integral to the success of the novel as a bildungsroman, as the societal problems shape the protagonist's maturation.

The main character, Ponyboy, begins the narrative as a fourteen-year-old gang member, raised by his two older brothers after their parents' death in a car crash. Tough beyond his years, over the course of the novel, his gang of poor teenagers, the Greasers, comes into conflict with a gang of wealthier teenagers, the Socs, and the battles between the two lead to several deaths and serious injuries. While Ponyboy at one point collapses in a nervous state, exhausted from the constant violence and danger, he eventually returns to school, where he decides the important thing is to write down the story he has experienced.

Ponyboy does not emerge at the end of the story as a full adult, yet he experiences significant psychological maturation. Since that change is the primary focus of the novel, *The Outsiders* fits firmly into the subgenre of entwicklungsroman, a bildungsroman in which the protagonist comes shy of reaching adulthood. Hinton emphasizes his growth through a significant narrative device—rather than being simply a first-person narration, the ending reveals that the novel is in fact the text that Ponyboy sets down to write in order to process the violence he has experienced, with the final line of the novel also serving as its first. Because of this narrative choice, Ponyboy is able to explore his original feelings as the events occurred while also hinting at the growth he experiences and his altered perception from the other side of the violence. When he first meets the Socs, for instance, he assumes that their higher economic class indicates a lack of problems in their lives, yet he tells the readers that he was wrong in that same moment. As the two gangs become entwined in violence and he sees them acting out of the same confusion and desperation as the Greasers, he ultimately comes to feel empathy for and finally camaraderie with them, fulfilling the change in perspective first foreshadowed with his admission of misjudgment.

In the end, then, it is the writing by Ponyboy of *The Outsiders* and the turn to literature that allows him to grow out of the violent trap of the gangs. While the earliest bildungsromans would have ended with Ponyboy as a functional member of liberal society, this more modern entwicklungsroman resists that happy ending. It is the growth that matters most, and while readers hope Ponyboy will find a happier and safer life for himself at some point, the focus on the novel itself (and the return to its opening with that final repeated line) directs readers' attention not to the end result of Ponyboy's change, but to the ongoing process of change itself.

The possibilities opened up by the realism and candor of *The Outsiders* helped make books like *Just Listen* possible. At the novel's start, Annabel is entering her junior year of high school and finds herself isolated and withdrawn: at school, she has been ostracized by her best friend Sophie, and at home, her sister struggles with an eating disorder while her mother constantly pushes Annabel toward a modeling career she does not desire.

Annabel slowly makes friends with another loner and, through the friendship and time with a therapist, begins to talk about the fact that Sophie's boyfriend raped her. When the boyfriend rapes another girl, Annabel gathers the strength to speak at his trial. Soon after, she finds herself more and more comfortable at home and at school, her relationships stronger when she can honestly share her struggles.

As with *The Outsiders*, it is the telling of a difficult experience that marks a significant change for the protagonist and narrator, as Annabel's therapist encourages her to write her life story in order to make sense of it. Once again, this provides a narrative distance in which change takes place. At first, Annabel is unable to write about the rape, then after writing it she is unable to tell it to others, and finally, after sharing with loved ones, she gains the strength to speak publicly about what happened. This telling is also a mark of her growing process, with the Annabel of the opening pages a reserved person who believes she must make it entirely on her own in the world, and the Annabel of the ending a young woman who has learned to rely on other people and to see her problems as both personal challenges and aspects of society at large. The Annabel of the modern bildungsroman enters a society that is flawed——both a solution to and a cause of her problems—but that she is also invested in changing.

Rowell's novel *Fangirl* similarly tracks a withdrawn young woman who emerges into a social world, although for the protagonist Cath, writing first serves as an escape from that reality rather than a way to truly communicate with others. Cath is a first-year college student who excels as a writer of fan fiction based on a fantasy novel series, Simon Snow, earning countless online admirers for her work. However, she struggles to leave her room for anything but classes, overwhelmed with social anxiety. She encounters other social problems that are common in young adult novels after *The Outsiders*, including her twin sister's alcohol abuse and the reality of her mother abandoning the family years ago. Overall, Cath's struggles are much more internal, with the possibility of new friends and a crush eventually drawing her out of her imagined world and into the social and academic life of her university.

Rowell emphasizes the divide between Cath's interior world of imagination and childlike fancy and the exterior, adult world of the college by inserting brief excerpts from Simon Snow novels as well as occasional excerpts of Cath's fan fiction. The tension created between these narratives suggests the differences between them (the problems of her twin's alcohol abuse, for instance, seem more urgent when compared to the escapism of the fantasy series). The binary of Simon Snow and university life, then, is a clear reflection of the bildungsroman binary of adolescence and adult life, with Cath's task being the migration from one to the other. Just as importantly, however, *Fangirl* operates as a *Künstlerroman*, another subgenre of the bildungsroman in which the protagonist develops as an artist as well as an adult. As Cath struggles in her fiction-writing course throughout the novel, the success of her final short story is significant in that it is also one of her first attempts to write original fiction instead of stories set in the Simon Snow universe.

Cath's academic and social successes—acquiring a boyfriend around the same time she finishes her final story—dovetail to show the interconnected nature of each. She has entered an adult life fully, her concerns turned away from imagination and the interior and pointing outward toward the questions and concerns of the broader world, all to the benefit of her emotional health and her art. While Ponyboy in his entwicklungsroman has not fully reached this level of societal engagement by the end of his novel, the fact that he has started to tell his story to others is the first sign of this ongoing process. While all of these protagonists, then, have entered society in the literary tradition of the bildungsroman, in the modern tradition of the young adult novel initiated by Hinton, these societies are themselves imperfect, the characters not saved by others, but rather able to see themselves as people both changed by and capable of changing their flawed worlds.

Conclusions

Considering its long importance in Western literary traditions and its clear overlap with young adult literature, the bildungsroman has a firmly established place in both the publishing and education worlds. Young adult readers are quick to pick up books that feature characters experiencing similar challenges that they face on a daily basis, and the endless complexities of the transition to adulthood provide ample subject matter for authors and critics alike.

In fact, nearly all of the most popular and critically acclaimed young adult novels of the twenty-first century reflect some qualities of the bildungsroman,

including massive best sellers such as the Harry Potter fantasy series by J. K. Rowling and Stephenie Meyer's Twilight series. Since publication of the Harry Potter books spanned about ten years, many young fans of the book could have spent their entire adolescence reading them, experiencing their own real-world coming-of-age stories parallel to the characters in the books.

At the same time, societal ideas about adulthood and the boundary between childhood and adulthood have continued to change. Innovations in social media, shifting timelines for first careers and financial independence, and other twenty-first-century factors drastically alter what it means to be a young adult entering adult society in the contemporary world. Just as the bildungsroman has evolved from the story of a sensitive young boy leaving home to make it on his own in the city into the diverse novels of young adults entering and changing the social landscape, the genre will certainly evolve alongside its multifaceted society in the near future, earning the attention of both teenage and adult readers along the way.

T. Fleischmann, MFA

Further Reading

Noomé, Idette. "Shaping the Self: A *Bildungsroman* for Girls?" *Literator* 25.3 (2004): 125–49. *Literary Reference Center*. Web. 8 Apr. 2015. <http://search.ebscohost.com/login.aspx?direct=true&db=lfh&AN=18587956&site=lrc-live>.

Trites, Roberta Seelinger. *Disturbing the Universe: Power and Representation in Adolescent Literature.* Iowa City: U of Iowa P, 2000. Print.

Bibliography

Boyle, Brendan. "The *Bildungsroman* after McDowell: Mind, World, and Moral Education." *Journal of Aesthetics & Art Criticism* 69.2 (2011): 173–84. *Academic Search Premier*. Web. 8 Apr. 2015. <http://search.ebscohost.com/login.aspx?direct=true&db=vth&AN=60313852&site=ehost-live&scope=site>.

Castle, Gregory. *Reading the Modernist Bildungsroman.* Gainesville: UP of Florida, 2006. Print.

Jones, Leisha. "Contemporary Bildungsromans and the Prosumer Girl." *Criticism* 53.3 (2011): 439–69. *Literary Reference Center*. Web. 8 Apr. 2015. <http://search.ebscohost.com/login.aspx?direct=true&db=lfh&AN=69713568&site=lrc-live>.

Contemporary Realism

Titles Discussed
Looking for Alaska by John Green
Where Things Come Back by John Corey Whaley
In Darkness by Nick Lake

Genre Overview
Realism, as a literary concept, has prevailed since humans have attempted to faithfully record impressions received through the five senses. The object of realism, now as in the past, is to provide a vicarious experience of sights, sounds, smells, tastes, and feelings described so that readers can be fully involved in a fictional story that could plausibly happen in real life.

As a literary movement, realism was a mid-nineteenth-century reaction against romanticism, a rejection of the idealized in favor of the actual. The focus of fiction also shifted from stories set among the upper classes to the plight of commonplace individuals further down the economic scale: factory workers, tradespeople, farmers, beggars, and others at the fringes of society. In Europe, realism began with such authors as Honoré de Balzac, Gustave Flaubert, and Charles Dickens. In the United States, prominent realistic writers during the first heyday of the genre (ca. 1850–1900) included William Dean Howells, Henry James, and Mark Twain. Late in the nineteenth century, realism evolved into the subgenre of naturalism, which used realistic settings and characters to explore "nature versus nurture" as primary influences on human behavior. Naturalism was a literary movement (ca. 1880–1930) that produced such American authors as John Steinbeck, Jack London, and Upton Sinclair.

Though other literary movements (surrealism, Beat literature, etc.) have flourished and died since then, realism has seldom entirely fallen out of favor and, in the early twenty-first century, appears more popular than ever. Realism has become especially prevalent in young adult fiction as desire has increased to spotlight subject matter formerly ignored, merely suggested, or occurring offstage. Adolescent readers—seeking alternatives to escapist fantasies or speculative fiction beyond actual modern experience—have gravitated toward works that accurately reflect activities of conflicted, three-dimensional characters. Protagonists in genuine-feeling environments cope with real-life problems that teens might encounter: drug abuse, troubled family relationships, sexuality and sexual identity, bullying, prostitution, and

suicide. Such twentieth-century pioneers in young adult contemporary realism as S. E. Hinton (*The Outsiders*, 1967), Robert Cormier (*The Chocolate War*, 1974), and Judy Blume (*Tiger Eyes*, 1981) helped pave the way. Twenty-first-century authors have expanded upon the genre. Writers John Green (*Looking for Alaska*), John Corey Whaley (*Where Things Come Back*), and Nick Lake (*In Darkness*) each produced debut, Printz Award–winning novels that—though dealing with vastly different protagonists in diverse settings and confronting widely dissimilar contemporary issues—all have the ring of truth.

Works
John Green's first young adult novel *Looking for Alaska* (2005) is semiautobiographical. As the author has noted in interviews, as a teen he attended a boarding school near Birmingham, Alabama, much like the fictional Culver Creek that provides the plot setting. Green uses factual material from personal experience—filtered through the sensibilities of adolescents—as a starting point to produce a compelling story that explores the fragility of relationships, the nature of humanity, and the inevitability of death.

Core characters are quickly introduced. Protagonist and narrator Miles Halter, a tall, skinny sixteen-year-old from Florida, reads biographies to collect the dying words of famous authors; his favorite is François Rabelais's "I go to seek a Great Perhaps." Miles's roommate is short, muscular Chip "the Colonel" Martin, a memory whiz who gives nicknames Miles the ironic nickname of Pudge. Takumi Hikohito is a thin Japanese classmate and computer buff. All the boys, especially Miles, are smitten with Alaska Young, a beautiful, vivacious, intelligent young woman who, though she already has an older, off-campus boyfriend, flirts enough to give potential suitors hope. Alaska also has a dark side, often referring to the possibility of premature death: "I may die young, but at least I'll die smart." Despite romantic tension, the group—which later incorporates Romanian sophomore Lara Buterskaya—forms a close bond. The five students share various classes, including Religious Studies under aged Dr. Hyde, where they learn the various attributes of Buddhism, Islam, and Christianity. The friends regularly congregate to smoke, drink, participate in activities, and plan and carry out elaborate pranks.

Antagonists are various "Weekday Warriors," wealthy students who go home on weekends; a bunch of warriors haze Miles after his arrival by duct-taping him and throwing him into a lake. Mr. Starnes, "the Eagle," is the dean and a major opponent of all students. He lives on campus and vigilantly watches for individuals who flout school rules and regulations.

The novel is divided roughly in half. The first part is titled "before," and contains breaks like diary entries ("one hundred thirty-six days before," "fifty-two days before"), which in counting down build an impending sense of doom, causing the reader to ask, "Before what?" The second part, labeled "after," immediately answers the question: Alaska has been killed in a car wreck while driving drunk. Subsequent entries ("four days after," "one hundred thirty-six days after") detail actions of the surviving friends in coming to grips with her death, searching for clues indicating whether the fatal crash was accidental or a successful suicide attempt, and plotting one last hilarious prank to pull to commemorate her.

Beneath the surface of the plot of *Looking for Alaska* are several interrelated themes dealing with honor and truth and with fate and memory, and there is a strong, thought-provoking religio-philosophical undercurrent. The symbolism of a labyrinth as a metaphor for life's suffering recurs throughout the story. Author Green has since demonstrated understanding, empathy, and an ability to realistically frame young adult concerns in his subsequent novels, *An Abundance of Katherines* (2006), *Paper Towns* (2008), and *The Fault in Our Stars* (2012).

Where Things Come Back (2011), likewise a first novel (author Whaley published a second young adult novel, *Noggin*, in 2014), takes a different approach in examining more abstract subjects such as death, hope, and resurrection, and specific real-life issues like bullying, child abduction, religious fanaticism, and suicide.

The plot is presented along two seemingly unrelated alternating story lines. One thread is humorously realistic and slangy, in first-person viewpoint of seventeen-year-old Arkansas high school student Cullen Witter. The other thread, in third-person, is serious and religious in tone as it follows eighteen-year-old Benton Sage, an Atlanta church missionary to Ethiopia.

The story opens with Cullen in the Little Rock morgue, identifying his cousin Oslo, who has died of a drug overdose. As Cullen returns to Lily, his dull hometown, he thinks about his quirky, look-alike younger brother, Gabriel, "the most interesting person I've ever known." Cullen, who keeps a journal to record ironic potential novel titles, is eager to reunite with Lucas

Calder, his sturdy best friend who protects the nerdish Witter boys from school bullies.

Meanwhile, in Africa, a doubting Benton works with local contact Rameel in passing out food and water while ostensibly converting natives to Christianity. From Rameel, Benton learns about Archangel Gabriel—mentioned in the Ethiopian Orthodox Bible's Book of Enoch—who banished fallen angels that mated with humans on earth and killed their children, giants called Nephilim.

Back in Arkansas, the slumbering town of Lily awakens: a bird long thought extinct, the Lazarus Woodpecker, may have been spotted nearby. Oregon naturalist John Barling comes to town to document the rediscovery. The search spawns a carnival atmosphere—complete with woodpecker haircuts and fast-food Lazarus burgers—as birdwatchers flock into town. During the hoopla, Gabriel disappears. Despite efforts of police and a psychic, no trace of Gabriel is discovered, and it is thought he may have run away.

Benton, relieved of his missionary duties, returns home to the disappointment of his strict, religious father. He enters a university and rooms with philosophy major Cabot Searcy. Shunned by his family as a failure, Benton commits suicide at Christmas by jumping from a church tower. Gathering Benton's possessions for his indifferent family, Cabot finds Benton's diary, begins reading, and becomes obsessed with the Book of Enoch.

In Lily, Lucas arranges a date for Cullen with Alma Ember, soon to be divorced. Cullen makes love with Alma but breaks up with her not long afterward. He subsequently takes up with beautiful Ada Taylor, the former girlfriend of school bully Russell Quitman, who has been paralyzed in a car accident. Ada later breaks up with Cullen to care for Russell.

Ultimately, the two separate threads come together, as author Whaley manipulates story chronology and withholds information to increase suspense. It is finally revealed that Alma was married to and separated from Cabot. Jealous, Cabot travels to Lily to find Alma and learns she dated Cullen. Enraged, Cabot intends to confront Cullen but encounters Gabriel at the Witter house. Mistaking Gabriel for his brother, Cabot kidnaps and holds him prisoner. An increasingly crazed Cabot imagines teenaged Gabriel as the reincarnation of Archangel Gabriel and grills him on theology. Though the woodpecker hunt proves to be a bust, the story ends on a positive note: clever Gabriel, having given appropriate answers to the maniacal Cabot, is released and returns to his hometown.

In Darkness (2012), similar in structure to *Where Things Come Back* in its use of alternating chapters in different voices, employs genuine settings, real historical figures, and an actual natural disaster to tackle a number of highly charged issues of relevance to young adults.

The first voice, in present tense (headed "Now"), belongs to fictional fourteen-year-old Shorty. He is a member of a drug-dealing gang operating out of a slum in contemporary Port-au-Prince, Haiti. Shorty, wounded in a shootout, is recuperating in a hospital when the 2010 earthquake strikes. Shorty survives but is trapped beneath falling debris. As he waits for rescue, he reviews his life. Readers experience images of the slum's grinding poverty; the brutality that claims Shorty's father, a murder victim; his angelic twin sister, Marguerite, a kidnap victim; and the young killer's own assassinations of rivals, carried out under orders from leaders Dread Wilmè and Biggie, who were themselves cut down prematurely. As his physical and mental health deteriorates, Shorty hallucinates, imaging the time of Haiti's creation as a nation.

The second voice, in past tense, in alternating third-person sections (headed "Then") is that of the middle-aged Toussaint l'Ouverture, a historic figure who led a successful slave revolt in Haiti between 1791 and 1804. A brilliant military strategist despite his illiteracy, Toussaint thrashed the forces of the white-dominated government, trained French armies, and invading professional English troops to gain freedom for oppressed black Haitians. Betrayed and imprisoned in France in a dark dungeon, he weakens and dies of starvation while imagining the sights and sounds of the future: "rolling metal carriages with wheels . . . great machines with blades spinning" (317).

The two narrators are linked by numerous factors. Though both grew up in poverty, in a hopelessly unequal society, each character dares to hope. Both have experienced extreme violence firsthand. Both have, and lose, twin sisters. Both become trapped in darkness, in situations beyond their control, in which each contemplates the existence of the other. Most importantly, both live in environments influenced by vodoun (voodoo), a religion originally from Africa that involves the conjuring of spirits, protective charms, and belief in zombis (zombies), and both are personally affected by the religion in unexpected ways.

Author Nick Lake has since written a second young adult novel, *Hostage Three* (2013), which deals with contemporary issues against the backdrop of a topical event: the kidnapping of the wealthy by Somali pirates.

Conclusions

Realism appears relatively immune to literary trends, at least in adult fiction. The story is quite different for works aimed at young adults, particularly in the United States. Prior to the 1950s, juvenile novels were quite tame, reflecting idealized rather than realistic adolescent lifestyles, free of emotional troubles, personality-altering problems, or life-altering situations. Few youthful characters smoked or drank or engaged in willful behavior. Sex was a taboo subject and homosexuality never discussed, as though it did not exist. Anyone of an ethnicity other than white was seen as different, and their characterization was often offensively stereotypical.

By the mid-twentieth century, the paradigm for young adult literature began changing. Following the popularity of J. D. Salinger's *The Catcher in the Rye* (1951)—which has been continually challenged for protagonist Holden Caulfield's profanity, sexual references, immorality, and other issues—similarly rebellious teenage characters began cropping up with greater frequency. Abetted by such films as *The Wild One* (1953) and *Rebel without a Cause* (1955), young adult literature opened discussion of gang activities, communication difficulties with adults, and romantic angst. *West Side Story* (1961) helped introduce written works that focused on the differences—as well as the strengths and unique problems—of ethnic minorities, ushering in a period of multiculturalism that dominated into the 1990s.

Following a late-twentieth-century slump in realism (blamed in part on the saturation of confession-style television shows) and the subsequent boom of supernatural, horror, and dystopian teen fiction, young adult contemporary realism experienced a renaissance in the early twenty-first century. This was due in part to more exact marketing from publishers and more efficient exchange of information among a sophisticated youthful audience savvy to modern electronic social media.

While adults will always resist their children's loss of innocence (most of John Green's novels, for example, have been widely challenged for various reasons), the future for young adult contemporary realism is positive. It may be presumed that as long as authors play to the strengths of the genre—with settings that feel genuine, characters that come to life, factual details that underpin the story, and subjects that matter to adolescents—realism will continue to remain relevant and hold its appeal for a growing audience of young readers.

Jack Ewing

Further Reading

Corbett, Sue. "New Trends in YA: The Agents' Perspective. *Publishers Weekly*. PWxyz, 27 Sept., 2013. Web. 11 Apr. 2015. <http://www.publishersweekly.com/pw/by-topic/childrens/childrens-industry-news/article/59297-new-trends-in-ya-the-agents-perspective.html>.

Jensen, Kelly. "The Next Big Thing: Contemporary/Realistic Fiction. *YALSA: The Hub*. Amer. Lib. Assn., 10 Oct. 2012. Web. 11 Apr. 2015. <http://www.yalsa.ala.org/thehub/2012/10/10/the-next-big-thing-contemporary-realistic-fiction>.

Bibliography

Alter, Alexandra. "John Green and His Nerdfighters Are Upending the Summer Blockbuster Model." *Wall Street Journal*. Dow Jones, 14 May 2014. Web. 11 Apr. 2015. <http://www.wsj.com/articles/john-green-and-his-nerdfighters-are-upending-the-summer-blockbuster-model-1400088712>.

Cart, Michael. *Young Adult Literature: From Romance to Realism*. Chicago: ALA, 2010. Print.

Corbett, Sue. "How Reality Became the Hot New Thing in YA." *Publishers Weekly*. PWxyz, 2 May 2014. Web. 11 Apr. 2015. <http://www.publishersweekly.com/pw/by-topic/childrens/childrens-book-news/article/62116-kids-getting-real.html>.

Dystopian and Science Fiction

Titles Discussed

Feed by M. T. Anderson
The Giver by Lois Lowry
The Hunger Games series by Suzanne Collins

Genre Overview

Writing that features teenaged protagonists is, to varying degrees, inherently concerned with the experience of losing childhood innocence and gaining adult agency. This is often a process in which the shelter and protection of the family unit give way to the challenges and problems of the outside world, one through which young adults learn to see themselves as active members of a changing society. It is no surprise, then, that dystopian literature has been a popular subgenre of young adult literature for decades. In presenting nightmarish future societies that are based on contemporary culture and politics, dystopian literature aligns with the young adult experience, offering a sort of hyperreality in which the challenges of the teenage protagonist are magnified in proximity to the dystopian social landscape.

Young adults have been reading science-fiction dystopian novels in various forms for many decades. Classic novels such as Aldous Huxley's *Brave New World* (1932) and George Orwell's *Nineteen Eighty-Four* (1949), although written for adults, have long been mainstays of the high school English classroom, while popular science fiction and its many dystopian worlds have consistently earned the attention of young readers. It was not until Lois Lowry published *The Giver* in 1993, however, that a book crafted as a young adult science-fiction dystopia found such wide critical and popular acclaim. This success in turn only hinted at the massive popularity to come for Suzanne Collins's Hunger Games trilogy, which has sold tens of millions of copies and has been adapted as a popular movie series. As dystopian series flourished, stand-alone titles such as M. T. Anderson's *Feed* became fast sellers while also earning significant critical praise; *Feed* itself was a finalist for the National Book Award for Young People's Literature. By the first decade of the twenty-first century, science-fiction dystopias had become arguably the most popular, or at least best-selling, subgenre of young adult literature.

Critics point to any number of factors to explain this new popularity, most commonly citing the rapid technological innovations that have taken place since the 1990s, in particular the rise of social media. Young adults turn to technology while forming their identity and connecting with broader culture and peers, a phenomenon that allows new forms of connectivity and sociality while also introducing new concerns and potential problems. Science fiction allows writers to explore extremes of government surveillance and control, conformity and individuality, and consumerism through exaggerated versions of these technologies. As the contemporary political world faces ongoing wars, threats of terrorism and extremism, and potential environmental collapse, the future as it appears to young adults in the twenty-first century poses unique social questions that are particularly suited to the dystopian science-fiction genre.

Works

Lois Lowry's 1993 novel *The Giver* is a "false utopia," meaning it is set in a world that strives to exist as a perfect society but is revealed over the course of the novel to instead be a dystopian reality. This world attempts to achieve its utopian elements through an extreme form of equality: people no longer see color, the climate is always the same, families and careers are decided by government committees, and memories of experiences such as pain and death have been removed from the population. Like all members of this society, the main character, Jonas, is untroubled by his lack of privacy and individuality, obeying all rules until he is assigned to be the next "Receiver." In this position, he will absorb the memories of the past, becoming one of the only people in his society to know that colors, death, war, snow, and many other banned things ever existed. Upon gaining this knowledge, Jonas questions whether the equality of the current world is worth the sacrifice of beauty, individuality, and self-determination. He ultimately chooses to reject the community and flee for "Elsewhere."

It is through the shift from apparent utopia to actual dystopia that *The Giver* explores its main themes. The third-person narration is tied closely to Jonas, and readers only gain knowledge that is also available to him. His family unit, for instance, at first looks idealized by conventional Western standards: a mother, father, son, and daughter living together with steady jobs and plenty to eat. The reader learns, however, that their connection as a family was not through birth or choice but rather through government assignment, a fact that contrasts with contemporary Western reality and introduces questions of individuality and the role of communities and governments. When Jonas inherits memories from what readers will recognize as their present (or very recent past) and is shocked to discover love, these questions are thrown into much greater relief. Finally, Jonas learns that his father's community-assigned career is not to peacefully release babies into a new life, as he had always believed, but rather to kill those with health problems or physical differences. This final revelation completely undoes any utopian

ideals from that early family vision, confirming instead the nightmarish reality of the happy father who daily leaves a wife he does not love in order to go to work and kill babies.

Many dystopian science-fiction novels can be somewhat heavy handed in putting forward their political views, and entries in the young adult genre tend to be especially pedantic in this regard. While *The Giver* has faced some criticism from scholars for pushing its political point too hard, its shift from utopia to dystopia also encourages readers to draw their own conclusions. By the end of the novel, Jonas has fled the community, risking his life in order to pursue freedom and electing to change the world rather than accept it as is, although even he has expressed doubts. The memories he inherited, after all, contain both the horrors of war (an impossibility in his planned community) as well as the heights of beauty and love. *The Giver* has a clear political position, but it also encourages its readers to ask questions about difference, conformity, and memory, with the emphasis more on the asking of the questions than on answering them.

Eschewing the false utopia, M. T. Anderson's 2002 novel *Feed* instead presents a reality that quickly reveals its dystopian elements to the reader. The novel is told from the perspective of Titus, a teenager in a world where most people are connected via biological implants to a massive computer network called Feednet. Though similar to modern social networks, Feednet is much more highly advanced; people can telepathically communicate with one another, corporations constantly gather information directly from the brain, advertisements intrude on everyday consciousness, and entertainment is immediately available. Titus begins dating a teenage girl, Violet, whose feed malfunctions, eventually leading to her death. While their romance plays out, Feednet also gives Titus occasional information about his world, including updates on a devastating environmental collapse and a war between the United States and an international Global Alliance—a war the president is helpless to stop, as corporations hold all the real power.

In *Feed*, technological advancements not only have disastrous effects on the global environment and corporate power but also radically reshape language and self-identity, as is shown through Titus's narration. The first-person narration is addressed directly to the reader, with Titus assuming that his audience has knowledge of his fast-paced world; slang, technology, and other science-fiction elements are not explained but simply presented as a given and natural element of his existence. As Titus is fairly immature and only interested in his own interior existence, however, *Feed* also relies on an unreliable narrator, a device that is further magnified by the constant intrusions of Feednet advertisements and announcements into the text. The end result is that readers are encouraged to sympathize with Titus while remaining aware of his failings, the most obvious of which is the way his obsession with consumerism and his feed prevent him from either caring for Violet or taking seriously the threats of environmental collapse and war that surround him. This disconnect between Titus's feed-driven mind and the lives of others becomes especially clear when Violet is days away from death. Unable to show her any compassion, Titus returns home and obsessively orders pair after pair of the same pants from Feednet. It is clear that the world is collapsing around him, but unlike with *The Giver*, the reader is not able to champion him as a hero and believe he will fight to change it. Instead, his identity is complicit in the destruction of his world, and the novel ends with little suggestion of hope.

The Hunger Games trilogy by Suzanne Collins likewise provides a first-person narration from the perspective of the main character, in this case a young woman named Katniss Everdeen who manages to fight against the group mentality of her dystopia in pursuit of positive change. The novels in the trilogy—*The Hunger Games* (2008), *Catching Fire* (2009), and *Mockingjay* (2010)—all take place in Panem, a future version of the United States in which society is partitioned into districts that divide the population based on class and occupation, with the ridiculously wealthy ruling class living in the Capitol. Katniss lives in one of the poorest districts, and it is from there that she is selected for the Hunger Games, a yearly event in which two youths from each district are placed in an arena to fight to the death. The games serve a dual purpose, providing both entertainment for the masses and punishment for a rebellion against the Capitol many years previous. Katniss somewhat unwittingly becomes a symbol of a new rebellion, and over the course of the trilogy she evolves from a victor of the Hunger Games to a leader and propaganda device of the rebels. In the end, Katniss must again assert her independence—this time by killing the leader of the rebellion, a woman who has proved herself to be as cruel and power hungry as the previous rulers in the Capitol.

The Hunger Games trilogy is ultimately concerned with Katniss as a young woman who must learn to trust herself while realizing how little she can trust those in power, whether in government or in the rebellion. The novel shares many of the themes and devices with previous dystopian science-fiction works. The Hunger Games themselves are an exaggeration of reality television, for instance, in the same way that Feednet is an exaggeration of social media. Similarly, the strict rules and stratification of her society recall the heavily controlled reality of *The Giver*, albeit with a significant difference: in Panem, only those in the Capitol might live with the illusion that their society is utopian, while Katniss, like the majority of the population, sees its dystopian elements from the start.

What most distinguishes the Hunger Games series is the way that Katniss develops her adult identity in a world that is duplicitous and untrustworthy. Romantically, she finds herself in the middle of a love triangle, drawn to two young men yet unable to make sense of her feelings in the complex power struggle of the Hunger Games and the subsequent rebellion. Politically, she aligns herself firmly with the aims of the rebellion, her own life being so strongly shaped by the oppression and poverty of her district, yet learns quickly that this new government is going to reenact the oppressive and violent behaviors of the Capitol, even initiating a new Hunger Games for the children of the old Capitol leaders. As her actions and defiance inspire the population of Panem to take control over their own lives and fight the powers that be, Katniss craves only simplicity and safety, yet knows that these things can only be achieved by fighting.

Katniss, Titus, and Jonas are all born into worlds that seem horrifying to contemporary readers, and all three assume different strategies to navigate these realities. Jonas flees his community for a life elsewhere, Katniss elects to stay and fight, and Titus merely succumbs to the inhumanity and numbness of Feednet. There is no right or wrong way to navigate the science-fiction dystopia, and all three characters falter as often as they succeed. They all, however, exemplify that characteristic young adult experience: as they assume adulthood and express their own agency, it becomes clear that they cannot truly stand alone but instead must learn to understand themselves as members of a complex and evolving society, no matter how horrifying it might be.

Conclusions

With the massive successes of series such as the Hunger Games, Veronica Roth's Divergent trilogy (2011–13), and James Dashner's Maze Runner series (2009–16), science-fiction dystopian literature appears to have a firm footing in the young adult marketplace. Rapid advancements in social-media technology and mass communication continue to alter the lives of young adults, in particular the relationship between newly independent teenagers and the political and social reality they will soon inherit. For this reason, the genre remains well suited to continue exploring these themes, transforming potential problems into horrible realities through the exaggerated world of the dystopia.

Some critics, however, have questioned both the sustainability of the genre and the lasting power of recent publications. Young adult novels are written largely by adults, and as such the writers behind these stories are viewing new technologies from a radically different perspective than their young readers. A social-media news feed, for instance, might seem terrifying to some, with its overload of information, advertisement, and surveillance, but for many young readers it is a given and natural part of their world, present from the early moments of childhood consciousness. Just as Titus in *Feed* and Jonas in *The Giver* seem to passively accept their world at first, technologies rarely seem terrifying to those who have always known them. As more people enter the world comfortable with social media and other technological advances, some of the fears inherent in these science-fiction dystopias might seem dated or illogical in the years to come. Regardless, the best entries in this genre gain their power not as much through their reimagining of the contemporary world as through the dynamic characters they create, characters that reflect the struggles and opportunities of adolescence no matter what reality they find themselves inheriting.

T. Fleischmann, MFA

Further Reading

Bradford, Clare. "'Everything Must Go!': Consumerism and Reader Positioning in M. T. Anderson's *Feed*." *Jeunesse* 2.2 (2010): 128–37. *Literary Reference Center*. Web. 7 Apr. 2015. <http://search.ebscohost.com/login.aspx?direct=true&db=lfh&AN=59286336&site=lrc-live>.

Day, Sara K., Miranda A. Green-Barteet, and Amy L. Montz, eds. *Female Rebellion in Young Adult Dystopian Fiction*. Burlington: Ashgate, 2014. Print.

Gross, Melissa. "*The Giver* and *Shade's Children*: Future Views of Child Abandonment and Murder." *Children's Literature in Education* 30.2 (1999): 103–17. *Literary Reference Center*. Web. 7 Apr. 2015. <http://search.ebscohost.com/login.aspx?direct=true&db=lfh&AN=11305742&site=lrc-live>.

Bibliography

Basu, Balaka, Katherine R. Broad, and Carrie Hintz, eds. *Contemporary Dystopian Fiction for Young Adults: Brave New Teenagers*. New York: Routledge, 2013. Print.

Bullen, Elizabeth, and Elizabeth Parsons. "Dystopian Visions of Global Capitalism: Philip Reeve's *Mortal Engines* and M. T. Anderson's *Feed*." *Children's Literature in Education* 38.2 (2007): 127–39. *Literary Reference Center*. Web. 7 Apr. 2015. <http://search.ebscohost.com/login.aspx?direct=true&db=lfh&AN=24486923&site=lrc-live>.

Hintz, Carrie, and Elaine Ostry, eds. *Utopian and Dystopian Writing for Children and Young Adults*. New York: Routledge, 2003. Print.

Epistolary

Titles Discussed

Angus, Thongs, and Full-Frontal Snogging by Louise Rennison
Sloppy Firsts by Megan McCafferty
Feeling Sorry for Celia by Jaclyn Moriarty
The Perks of Being a Wallflower by Stephen Chbosky

Genre Overview

The epistolary genre, in which books are written as a series of documents, gained popularity in Europe with novels such as Bram Stoker's *Dracula* (1897) and Mary Shelley's *Frankenstein* (1818). People in the nineteenth century were avid diarists, and since diaries are extremely personal and are kept private at all cost, it was a relatable form to readers of that era. Epistolary novels can be written in the form of letters between multiple people (as in *Dracula* and *Frankenstein*) or as diary or journal entries. These novels are unique in that the reader is able to connect directly with the narrator on a much more personal level, especially with diary entries, by being invited in to the narrator's most personal correspondence. Epistolary literature appeals to a reader's voyeuristic nature since it can be thrilling to be privy to a narrator's most private thoughts, ideas, and experiences.

Rosbottom states in his review of Thomas O. Beebee's *Epistolary Fiction in Europe: 1500–1800* (1999) that epistolary fiction helped pave the way for the formation of the novel and realist fiction as popular genres. Beebee also states that reading epistolary works can be therapeutic, especially for contemporary readers. Letters can provide "a space for 'inappropriate' commentary in an increasingly surveilled society" (Rosbottom 232). This is what makes young adult epistolary fiction so problematic for those wishing to censor such works because it is expected that teenagers who are writing letters to each other—or who are writing in diaries that are not intended to be read by anyone else—would discuss sex, drug use, and problems with their families and the world at large.

Most popular young adult (YA) epistolary novels are written as diary entries from the perspective of a young girl. Some early YA epistolary novels, such as *Are You There God? It's Me Margaret* (1970) by Judy Blume, were challenged or banned in some libraries and schools for inappropriate sexual references and for promoting what was perceived to be immoral, anti-Christian behavior. Those who tried to censor the books were personally offended by the content and believed that authors or readers of YA epistolary novels were incapable of handling such mature and potentially damaging material in a healthy way. However, the epistolary form spoke to young readers who felt unable to voice their own concerns over issues such as their bodies, their faith, and their world at large. Although many schools and libraries in the 1980s required parental permission to read books like *Are You There God? It's Me Margaret*, censorship has become much less prevalent. Students now have greater access to books that speak to their experiences and problems.

More recent examples of young adult epistolary works utilize diary or journal entries and/or letters that are written by a teenager. These novels allow the reader to sympathize with the narrator and relate his or her experiences to their own lives. For example, both *Angus, Thongs, and Full-Frontal Snogging* and *Sloppy Firsts* portray girls who write about high school, good and bad times with friends, the struggle of puberty, and first crushes. *Feeling Sorry for Celia* also portrays a teenage

girl but deals with more serious issues such as running away and suicide. *The Perks of Being a Wallflower* is unique in that it is written from the perspective of a teenage boy, but the issues the novel addresses of sexual identity, bullying, and dating abuse are universal.

Works

Angus, Thongs, and Full-Frontal Snogging by Louise Rennison exemplifies the modern-day young adult epistolary novel. The narrator is a fifteen-year-old girl living in England who is primarily concerned with disguising her large nose and making herself up to get the attention of a boy she refers to as Sex God.

Rennison's narrative follows the chronology of a diary down to the time of day. Such references to time help show how often the narrator writes and how much time has passed between events. Rennison's writing style is humorous and her characterization prioritizes personality over intellect and power, which she accomplishes through the romance-themed plot and the conversational tone with its sometimes short snippets of text and amicable voice. Although Rennison makes her narrator likable through humor, she also uses the diary style to make a ground-level argument about cultural shallowness. The narrator's failed attempts at applying makeup and dyeing her hair are poignant in that they show how much effort and emotion go into a chance to attract another's attention despite the risk that it will all be for nothing.

While the tone of *Sloppy Firsts* is humorous like *Angus, Thongs, and Full-Frontal Snogging*, it is much less lighthearted and deals with more serious issues like depression and drug abuse. Jessica Darling is a high school sophomore whose best friend, Emily, has just moved away after the death of her brother to a drug overdose. Jessica does not have a positive disposition most of the time, but losing Emily makes it even worse.

Because of Jessica's last name, people, especially authority figures like teachers, expect her to be polite, friendly, and "darling." Jessica does well in school, but she suffers from depression, which makes it challenging for her to relate to people other than Emily, who has moved away, and a boy named Paul, on whom she has a crush. Jessica's loneliness and disregard for the majority of her world make it hard for her to enjoy life. She loses interest in almost everything except writing letters to Emily and jogging. The stress of her life choices causes her to develop health issues, and although Jessica acknowledges that she could be more popular by being friendly and by showing an interest in events like the prom, she refuses to engage and instead chooses to maintain her loner persona.

Eventually Jessica attracts the attention of Michael who is a known drug user. He seems to understand that she is different from others, and Jessica is intrigued by him at the same time as she is put off by his drug use. Jessica is subconsciously drawn to Michael because she feels he sees her for who she truly is.

About midway through *Sloppy Firsts* Jessica questions if anyone will ever read her words, "Who is this for, anyway? Who are you? Who actually found this notebook and cares enough to read it? You must have little to do. Wait. Are you me twenty-five years from now? Too weird. Stop thinking, Jessica," and the reader understands that the book is a series of Jessica's journal entries. Up to this point the reader may have felt empathy and a certain comradery for Jessica and her problems, but once it is understood that these pages are from Jessica's diary, the reader perhaps feels slightly empowered: Jessica's words are being read, which means that someone (the reader) is interested enough to care about what she has to say.

Although Georgia, the narrator of *Angus, Thongs, and Full-Frontal Snogging*, is funny, *Sloppy Firsts*' Jessica is the more plausible character. The reader gains an uncomfortable intimacy with Jessica's conflicts, anxieties, and depression. Georgia and her parents engage in what many may view as typical disagreements between parents and teenagers, but Georgia's portrayal of her parents is so comical that the issues don't seem quite as real or important. Jessica, on the other hand, has a hard time communicating with her family and with most everyone else except for Emily. Jessica's father criticizes her running form and her mother cannot connect with a daughter uninterested in shopping or lunch dates. While Jessica holds on to some angst over the arguments with her parents and sometimes cries because of it, Georgia turns everything into a joke, thus sharing her coping mechanism with the reader.

Elizabeth Clarry, the protagonist and narrator of Jaclyn Moriarty's *Feeling Sorry for Celia*, also has a humorous view of life, but the content of Moriarty's novel deals with serious issues similar to the ones found in *Sloppy Firsts*. *Celia* is constructed of Elizabeth's letters written to a girl named Christina, who goes to another school and has been paired with Elizabeth as part of a school assignment. In the letters, Elizabeth voices her worries to Christina about her friend Celia, who has run away. Elizabeth is worried Celia will be the victim of sexual violence or will give in to her suicidal thoughts. Moriarty uses the epistolary style to make it seem like Elizabeth receives bullying letters from various sources in school that are actually a part of her subconscious, which in turn provides the reader with insight into how Elizabeth views herself. By the end of the novel, Elizabeth writes to the bullies and demands they stop writing, and even if they ignore her and write more letters anyway, she will not open them. This shows Elizabeth's transformation: her confidence level has increased and her sense of self has evolved throughout the course of the book. She is no longer her own worst enemy but has become her greatest fan. Elizabeth's externalization of her feelings in *Feeling Sorry for Celia*, which takes something closer to the form of chain mail, shows that Moriarty's novel is both cathartic for the protagonist and for the reader and aligns with Rosbottom and Beebee's opinion on epistolary novels as being therapeutic.

The Perks of Being a Wallflower by Stephen Chbosky is another example of a cathartic epistolary novel. The main character, Charlie, goes from having no friends to getting close with two older high schoolers. In the process, he realizes he is capable of receiving love, loving himself, and, thanks to an encouraging and supportive English teacher, has a potential future as a writer. Charlie's letters are not written to a specific person but rather are addressed to "friend," allowing the reader to feel a direct connection to the difficulties Charlie experiences as he comes of age. He encounters and works through common high school problems, such as girls, classes, and family disagreements, but he must also bear the weight of heavier issues such as his friend's closeted homosexuality and his own survival of sexual abuse. This level of honesty allows the reader to connect with the character Charlie, sublimating their most hurtful memories in his story.

Conclusions

In young adult epistolary fiction, the reader is the direct recipient of the narrator's most personal thoughts and feelings and is therefore invited into the realizations and self-deceptions (willful or not) of the protagonist. These novels are designed to ameliorate the reader's anxieties, be they concerns about body image (*Angus, Thongs, and Full-Frontal Snogging*), struggling with mental illness (*Sloppy Firsts*), or sexual abuse and loneliness (*Feeling Sorry for Celia*). In "receiving" these letters and diary entries, the reader may then subconsciously "write back" by relating their own experiences to those of the narrator's, even and especially if the experiences are uncomfortable or difficult to process internally. The young adult epistle has a rich tradition of this, and these honest portrayals of characters grappling with such sensitive and deeply personal issues invites the reader to take comfort in knowing they are not alone in their turmoil and struggles.

Catharsis, however, does not need to have a heavy tone, which is seen especially in *Angus, Thongs, and Full-Frontal Snogging* and *Feeling Sorry for Celia*. The authors of these books give readers space and permission to work through their feelings through humor. Comedy is used to externalize and work through the character's and reader's emotions. The narrator's trivialization of their problems asks the reader to also put theirs in perspective.

Most epistolary novels for young adults feature female protagonists. This creates a feminine space in a culture that has little open discourse for young women. While the openness and honesty of these novels has drawn criticism from people who want to keep young readers from being exposed to events that many perceive to be disturbing or unpleasant, these novels help teenagers ease into their own coming of age by connecting with voices they recognize.

Alexandra McBride, MA

Further Reading

Bower, Rachel. "Epistolary Craft and the Literary Field." *Journal of Commonwealth Literature* 49.3 (2014): 315–31. Print.

Thein, Amanda Haertling, and Mark A. Sulzer. "Illuminating Discourses of Youth through the Study of First-Person Narration in Young Adult Literature." *English Journal* 104.3 (2015): 47. Print.

Bibliography

"Banned and Challenged Books: The Who, What, When, Where, and Why." *Delete Censorship*. Half Price Books, 2014. Web. 5 May 2015. <http://www.deletecensorship.org/downloads/booklist_hpb.pdf>.

"Feeling Sorry for Celia." *Kirkus*. Kirkus Media, 20 May 2010. Web. 5 May 2015. <https:www.kirkusreviews.com/book-reviews/>.

Rosbottom, Ronald C. "Epistolary Fiction in Europe: 1500–1850." *Philosophy and Literature* 24.1 (2000): 230–33. *Muse*. John Hopkins UP, 2000. Web. 5 May 2015. <https://muse.jhu.edu/journals/philosophy_and_literature/v024/24.1rosbottom.html>.

Fantasy

Titles Discussed

Dodger by Terry Pratchett
The Goblin Wood series by Hilari Bell
Harry Potter series by J. K. Rowling

Genre Overview

The fantasy genre has been a mainstay of children's literature since before the time of the Brothers Grimm. While books such as Mother Goose's fairy-tale collections and the works of Theodor Seuss Geisel, better known as Dr. Seuss, have become modern childhood staples, other works have crossover appeal for adults as well. Both children and adults can enjoy Lewis Carroll's *Alice's Adventures in Wonderland* (1865), Roald Dahl's *Charlie and the Chocolate Factory* (1964) and *James and the Giant Peach* (1961), Susan Cooper's The Dark Is Rising series (1965–77), and C. S. Lewis's The Chronicles of Narnia (1949–54).

Another fantasy mainstay popular with readers of all ages is J. R. R. Tolkien, whose works, including *The Hobbit* (1937), *The Lord of the Rings* (1954–55), and *The Silmarillion* (1977), have had a dedicated following since they were first published. Tolkien's work is considered to be high fantasy, with a richly imagined world that includes several of its own fully realized languages. Immersion in his world requires knowledge of several lands and types of creatures. The fantasy world in Tolkien's work is rich in detail and wide in breadth and has long appealed to both young adult and adult readers.

The quiet popularity of Tolkien's work did not prepare the world for the arrival of Harry Potter. Several other notable fantasy series had been published since *The Hobbit*, but nothing that shook the world of children's literature quite so much as J. K. Rowling's Harry Potter series (1997–2007), especially at a time when most experts were sure that the children of the late twentieth century were losing interest in reading altogether. The Potter phenomenon brought the young adult fantasy genre to the forefront of the publishing world, paving the way for countless more fantasy works targeted at young adult readers, including Hilari Bell's Goblin Wood series (2003–11) and Terry Pratchett's historical fantasy novel *Dodger* (2012).

Works

Harry Potter and the Philosopher's Stone, the first book in J. K. Rowling's Harry Potter series, made its debut in the United Kingdom in 1997. It hit bookstores in the United States in September 1998, retitled *Harry Potter and the Sorcerer's Stone* for the US market, and rose to the top of the New York Times best sellers list by the following August, where it remained for most of that year and the next. In fact, it is the enduring popularity of the Harry Potter series that led to the creation of separate best seller lists for children and adults. New books in the series were anticipated with such enthusiasm that bookstores stayed open past midnight on their release dates, and children and their parents waited in line to buy the latest in the seven-volume series as soon as it became available. Over the years, Harry Potter's fans aged along with him. As he entered puberty, so did they; as he went on to graduate and look toward his future, so did they. Those who picked up the first volume as children were high school or college students with an appreciation for a well-told fantasy tale by the time the series was complete.

The Harry Potter series is an important contribution to young adult literature for both its fantasy aspect and the depth of its literary roots. While it may be argued that the later books in the series are more commercial in nature, the series overall certainly was not conceived as such. It was not written as a fantasy with the primary purpose of attracting a broad audience with a high concept and plenty of action. In this series, the fantasy world is instead used as the outward manifestation of Harry's confusion over who he is and what his place in the world will be.

At their core, the Harry Potter books are literary novels. They rest heavily on the recognized body of classical literature, due in large part to J. K. Rowling's own studies in classical literature. The books variously incorporate, make reference to, or are influenced by Joseph Campbell's hero's journey, mythological creatures and their roles in literature, and the structures of works such as Homer's *Odyssey*, the novels of Tolkien and Jane Austen, and William Shakespeare's plays, among other elements. They are not one-note books with a single layer of meaning. Rather, they are filled with nuance and make use of the conventions of both fantasy and traditional literature.

The story of Harry Potter unfolds over the course of seven books. Each book has a narrative arc of its own while also occupying a space in the overall series arc. In the first book, *Harry Potter and the Philosopher's Stone*, readers meet Harry and learn along with him that he is no ordinary boy. He is the son of two very powerful and celebrated wizards who lost their lives while defending him from the evil Lord Voldemort. Harry has a lightning-shaped scar on his forehead that was left behind by Voldemort's attack, instantly identifying him to anyone in the wizarding community. This community hopes that Harry will be the one to defeat Voldemort once and for all.

Over the course of the series, Harry becomes close friends with Hermione and Ron. Hermione is intelligent, bookish, and strong willed. Ron, the second-youngest of his family, with five older, more accomplished brothers, wants to do something to distinguish himself—he just is not sure what that might be.

Harry, Ron, and Hermione tend to favor the underdog, befriending the house goblin, the gamekeeper, and the more unpopular students at the school. They form a vicious rivalry with fellow student Draco Malfoy and the boys who follow him. Harry becomes an honorary member of Ron's family, a role he treasures for the novelty of its normality. As the series unfolds, the three heroes scuffle with Malfoy, Voldemort (in various forms), and other wizards who are out to ruin Harry. They stick together and fight off giant poisonous spiders, enormous snakes with deadly stares, and armies of creatures intent on helping Voldemort claim victory over the wizarding world.

Harry greatly respects Albus Dumbledore, the headmaster of the Hogwarts School of Witchcraft and Wizardry. He is a loyal supporter of Dumbledore, and there are several scenes showcasing their devotion to one another. In one such scene, Harry sits before a mirror that shows the viewer his or her greatest desire. Harry, who sees himself with his parents, begins spending more and more time in front of the mirror, longing for what can never be. Dumbledore realizes that Harry is spending his time in this way and gently advises him that the mirror has been hidden because those who choose to sit and stare at what could be do not often go on to create what will be. Harry is bright enough and strong enough to take the hint and tear himself away. In another scene, a phoenix comes to Dumbledore, enabling him to assist Harry when Harry is in dire need. Dumbledore explains that the phoenix would only have sought him out if someone had been extraordinarily loyal to him. With this statement, Harry knows that Dumbledore understands the depth of his feelings for him.

The Goblin Wood, by Hilari Bell, is another well-received fantasy series. It consists of three books: *The Goblin Wood* (2003), *The Goblin Gate* (2010), and *The Goblin War* (2011). The series features an ongoing political struggle that necessitates warfare and intrigue. The story line calls for the reader to keep track of various shifting alliances and fortunes while also respecting the rules of the wood. In order to fully engage with the characters and the action, the reader must take the time to learn the many layers of fantasy and tradition at work in this series.

The Goblin Wood series uses a fantasy world as the backdrop for a political drama. The politics that unfold will decide the fate of the protagonist, Makenna. The series opens with the execution of Makenna's mother for witchcraft, and throughout the series, Makenna's fate hangs in the balance. The series is set in medieval times, so that the mores of that time also play a key role in the experience for the reader.

This series features a strong female protagonist in Makenna, who floods the village upon her mother's death and then works actively to prevent the ruling hierarchy from carrying out its pogrom against magic. Friendship also plays a central role in this series. Makenna and Tobin think at first that they know all they need to of each other. However, because their fates are linked without their consent, they must learn more about one another and then find a way to overcome their previous biases and work together.

Dodger, by Terry Pratchett, takes the fantasy genre in an entirely different direction by putting Dodger into direct contact with real people from the Victorian era. The fantasy aspect of this novel lies not in wizardry or mythical creatures; instead, it takes the form of a world in which the line between reality and imagination is not clearly drawn, or even noted at all. For those young adults who do not have an interest in or understanding of history, it is possible that an important level of meaning will go unappreciated. For those who are interested in history and literature, this aspect will add a deeper level of complexity to the work.

A fanciful approach to the possibilities of a fanciful life brings Dodger to life. In this book, the titular young thief becomes involved in romance, friendship, and unlikely meetings with notable figures of the time. The details are true to the period, even if Dodger is a fictional character playing a part in a historically accurate past.

In the end, Dodger becomes the hero who saves the day. Through his adventures, he has grown to be a caring person. His fame has brought him the information he needs to protect Simplicity, the mysterious girl whose initial rescue by Dodger kicks off the plot. When Dodger and Simplicity—now calling herself Serendipity—return to London and meet with the Queen, Dodger is more than ready to take on the new role of spy that is offered to him.

Conclusions

The message in the Harry Potter books is that whether or not Harry is destined for greatness—which is not a given—it is up to Harry to fulfill that destiny. The choice of whether or not to defeat Voldemort is his. Fundamentally, Harry is just a boy who lost both of his parents as an infant and grew up in an unloving and emotionally abusive environment. All he wants is to have a place where he belongs. He is utterly unaware of the expectations the wizarding community has for him when he arrives at Hogwarts, and when he learns of them, he is not at all convinced that he is up to the task.

The fantasy aspects of the series allow the reader to feel both Harry's confusion and his growing confidence. If there were no fantasy elements and Harry's story was simply that of a boy who has suffered a loss and must find his place in the world, it would not evoke as strong a response in the reader. The use of fantasy allows the reader to travel Harry's journey of self-discovery with him, step by step, for better or for worse.

The Goblin Wood series and *Dodger* also portray friendship, loyalty, and romantic love as integral to the plot and to character development. Their respective historical settings similarly take readers out of their comfort zone, forcing them to learn about this new milieu. While it is true that Harry is learning about a new setting along with the reader, the fact that the reader still must make this effort ensures that he or she is invested in the character's plight. The fantasy elements add another layer of meaning to the works, as fantastical creatures stand in for humans in ways that cause the reader to rethink their potential biases.

All of these fantasy novels are, at their heart, stories of the journey to adulthood. By setting them in previously unknown or unfamiliar worlds and equipping these worlds with creatures and characters that cause the reader to stretch past their assumptions about distinctions of gender, race, or class, the authors help bring readers to a new understanding of themselves.

Gina Hagler, MBA

Further Reading

Cart, Michael. *Young Adult Literature: From Romance to Realism.* Chicago: ALA, 2011. Print.

Chance, Rosemary. *Young Adult Literature in Action: A Librarian's Guide.* 2nd ed. Santa Barbara: ABC-CLIO, 2014. Print.

Nilsen, Alleen Pace, et al. *Literature for Today's Young Adults.* 9th ed. Boston: Pearson, 2013. Print.

Bibliography

Bucher, Katherine T., and KaaVonia Hinton. *Young Adult Literature: Exploration, Evaluation, and Appreciation.* 3rd ed. New York: Pearson, 2014. Print.

Cole, Pam B. *Young Adult Literature in the 21st Century.* New York: McGraw, 2009. Print.

Rabey, Melissa. *Historical Fiction for Teens: A Genre Guide.* Santa Barbara: Libs. Unltd., 2011. Print.

Sanchez, Matt. "Fantasy." *Genre Fiction as Literature.* Author, 2005. Web. 5 May 2015. <http://iml.jou.ufl.edu/projects/Spring05/Sanchez/fantasy.htm>.

Short, Kathy G., Carol Lynch-Brown, and Carl M. Tomlinson. *Essentials of Children's Literature.* 8th ed. Harlow: Pearson, 2014. Print.

Strickland, Ashley. "A Brief History of Young Adult Literature." *CNN.com.* Cable News Network, 15 Apr. 2015. Web. 10 May 2015. <http://www.cnn.com/2013/10/15/living/young-adult-fiction-evolution/>.

Graphic Novels

Titles Discussed

American Born Chinese by Gene Luen Yang
Azumanga Daioh by Kiyohiko Azuma
Runaways by Brian K. Vaughan
Smile by Raina Telgemeier

General Overview

The term "graphic novel" first came into popular use in the late 1970s to describe book-length works that used comic-book formats and sequential illustrations to tell their stories. The term became more popular in the 1980s and 1990s as graphic novels garnered increased attention from critics, with Art Spiegelman's *Maus* (1991) earning the Pulitzer Prize, and superhero narratives such as Frank Miller's four-issue miniseries *Batman: The Dark Knight Returns* (1986) featuring increasingly dark, adult subject matter. This marked a shift for many readers, as the format was no longer automatically associated with cheap superhero and adventure stories for children reminiscent of *Archie* and *Superman*, which for decades had exemplified the prevailing opinion of popular comics.

Young adults, of course, have been reading graphic novels since the early decades of the twentieth century, both mainstream superhero comics and underground, independently published works that dealt with more realistic narratives. It took some years, however, for the publishing industry and educational institutions to catch up to the potential inherent in promoting serious works of literature in graphic-novel formats for young adult readers. In the 1990s and the early twenty-first century, a large number of graphic novels were published that were both accessible to young adult readers and exhibitive of literary and artistic qualities praised in other genres; Marjane Satrapi's *Persepolis* (2000) and Alison Bechdel's *Fun Home* (2006) in particular met with critical and popular acclaim. Simultaneously, Japanese-created comics, known as manga, began to flourish in translation in the Western world, with libraries and bookstores responding to the demand from young readers. By this time, graphic novels had solidified their place and were recognized both for their wide popularity with young adult audiences and their capacity to stand as serious literary works.

By necessity, any young adult graphic novel must exist in several genres at once and must be judged by its format and illustrations as well as its narrative content. Because of this, the term "graphic novel" refers not exclusively to novels but also to historical works, memoirs, and any other genre that might exist in nongraphic literature. Raina Telgemeier's *Smile* (2010), for instance, is based on the author's adolescent life, while Gene Luen Yang's *American Born Chinese* (2006) blends a classic Chinese novel with a modern narrative set in the United States. As nonfiction graphic novels have become particularly popular, however, it is also important to note that superhero and manga stories have not been left behind, as novels such as Brian K. Vaughan's superhero series *Runaways* (2003–9) and Kiyohiko Azuma's manga *Azumanga Daioh* (1999–2002) have also found critical and popular success.

Works

Azumanga Daioh is popular in English translation for largely the same reasons that it found a wide Japanese audience: it centers on the lives of a group of high school girls, and it emphasizes character and mood ahead of plot and conflict. The girls themselves are eccentric individuals rather than normative members of a group mentality, such as the gentle but intimidatingly tall Sakaki, who is obsessed with cute animals, and the incredibly competitive yet incredibly nonathletic Tomo. While they interact with other students and teachers from time to time, the manga remains focused on their daily lives, particularly emphasizing their relationships with one another and the humor that results from their varied personalities.

Most of the stories take place in *yonkoma* format, in which four large horizontal panels of equal size fill the page. This format lends itself to visual jokes while also limiting the length of the story (although some narratives will carry across several pages). This contrasts with the traditional style of Western superhero comics, where the pages embrace dynamic layouts of varied panel shapes in order to emphasize action over many pages. As a result, many of the vignettes in *Azumanga Daioh* are slower paced, allowing readers to get to know the girls through the accruing moments of everyday life. While the constant visual gags and bizarre behavior of the characters make the novel appear to be light entertainment at first, those same characters prove themselves over many stories to be complex, changing personalities. By the conclusion of the series, the light and entertaining narrative mode has remained, but the girls themselves (and the relationships between them) have evolved in intricate, subtle ways.

Similarly, Brian K. Vaughan's superhero series *Runaways* provides a character-driven narrative in the familiar format of the superhero comic. The series focuses on a group of teenagers who discover that their parents are secretly supervillains; realizing that they, too, have supernatural powers, the teenagers form a superhero group to defeat their parents and fight for justice. After their first triumphant victory, they promise

to stay diligent in order to ensure that new villains do not rise up in their parents' place, leading to ongoing battles and an occasionally shifting cast of young, dedicated heroes. As the superhero narrative is so well developed and standardized by this point, Vaughan often chooses to forgo typical explanations and plot points, directing his attention instead to the characters. The team, for instance, eschews code names, costumes, and secret identities; they simply fight in whatever clothes they happen to be wearing and call one another by their original names. In place of the typical action-oriented superhero plot is a plot examining what it means for these particular young people to transform from regular teenagers into teenagers who hold immense power and rely on each other to understand the ramifications of the superhero life for their identities, moralities, and futures.

American Born Chinese also uses the graphic-novel format to explore the coming-of-age story of its teenage protagonist in conjunction with fantastical plotlines. The main character, Jin, is raised in a suburban American town by his parents who emigrated from China. One of the only Asian American students in his largely white school, he regularly struggles to find social acceptance and friendship. When he does gain a friend, Wei-Chen, he damages their friendship by kissing Wei-Chen's girlfriend. His story is woven together with two other narratives. In one, the legendary Monkey King, a kung-fu master, fights to become a deity but instead becomes a monk's disciple; in the other, white, blond teenager Danny loses what little bit of popularity he has when his cousin, a Chinese student named Chin-Kee, visits and embarrasses him. In the end, the narratives combine when it is revealed that Danny is Jin, transformed into a different body by magic, and that Chin-Kee is both the Monkey King and Wei-Chen's father. The Monkey King convinces Danny to revert back to being Jin. Once in his original body, Jin is able to repair his friendship with Wei-Chen.

The overlapping narratives of *American Born Chinese* create an interplay between Jin's different perceptions of himself, as well as the various ways that others perceive him. The racism and exclusion he faces from other students is manifested in the character of Chin-Kee, a teenager who personifies negative Chinese stereotypes (which are exaggerated through the drawing style), while the blond character of Danny embodies everything Jin wishes he could be—namely, not different from his classmates. At the same time, the Monkey King is a powerful figure and a source of wisdom. Taken from classic Chinese literature, he stands in for the power and beauty of Jin's heritage, and it is that power that allows Jin to reject the idealization of Caucasians, as symbolized by Danny, and return to his true self in order to repair his friendship with Wei-Chen. The graphic-novel format allows these narratives to exist side-by-side, told as separate stories for the majority of the novel before being united at the conclusion. The novel does not need to go to great lengths to explain itself, relying instead on images to do the majority of the work. Characters from the different narratives enter each other's worlds while maintaining their unique drawing styles. This echoes the multiplicity of identities that Jin experiences; he struggles to feel a sense of self while experiencing life through the intertwining prejudices and encouragements of others until, through his maturation, he is able to unite his different self-conceptions and shed the weight of racism.

Smile, in contrast, avoids supernatural or fantastic elements and instead uses the graphic-novel format to tell a story from the author's life. In sixth grade, Raina falls and breaks her two front teeth, leading to a long and painful series of surgeries as well as social embarrassment, especially as she needs to wear various types of gear to protect her mouth at the same time she enters adolescence. Expected young adult experiences, including her first crush and the challenges of beginning to establish her independence, are complicated by the self-consciousness and occasional social rejection that result from her dental injury. What transforms a fairly typical young adult story into a successful novel is the way that the drawing style and narrative work together. The illustrations are brightly colored with rounded lines, almost resembling a cartoon, so that even the most stressful moments of social rejection are lightened and palatable for younger readers. While the graphic novel does not hide from the gorier aspects of the dental procedure, it portrays them in that same gentle (albeit bloody) style. In this way, *Smile* is both heartfelt and honest, with its stories of young adulthood allowed to stand as they are: difficult and stressful at times, but ultimately no more than obstacles to be overcome.

These four graphic novels represent four radically different styles, both in literary voice and in artwork. They fall into markedly different genres and were even all first published in different venues: *Azumanga Daioh*

was serialized in a magazine, *Runaways* was a monthly comic-book series published over several years, and *Smile* was a series of web comics posted on the author's website; only *American Born Chinese* was initially published in the graphic-novel format that the others later adopted. Yet all rely heavily on the interplay of image and text to tell their stories. It is because of this that graphic novels are not simply books with illustrations added; they are a unique genre, telling stories that could exist no other way.

Conclusions

The concept of literacy has evolved in the twenty-first century, with adults increasingly expected to not only comprehend and analyze text but to apply those same skills to a range of multimedia. This shift has been driven by changes in information and communication technology, and as such, younger people are often familiar with navigating and understanding diverse forms of media at once.

The graphic novel is an especially contemporary genre because to fully engage with it requires multiple forms of literacy. From an educational perspective, growing numbers of teachers and librarians at the young adult level are turning to these novels in order to engage students and expand on their critical reading skills through analyzing the novel. While some educators still stand by their belief that graphic novels are easier and simpler to read than text-only novels, more and more recognize the complexity of the form.

This increased appreciation from educators will continue to bolster the respectability of graphic novels as representations of the diversity of readers and publishers represented in the genre. While many previously considered superhero comics to be for boys only, graphic novels—both superhero and not—draw large female audiences as well, and many regularly feature strong, independent female characters. The influx of manga from Japan has created a strong cross-cultural conversation as well, as there is arguably no other genre of literature that young adults read so much of in translation. As teenage audiences continue to live in an increasingly global world that they come to understand through nuanced readings of visual information, it is likely that young adult graphic novels will only continue to grow in popularity.

T. Fleischmann, MFA

Further Reading

Burns, Charles, et al. "Panel: Graphic Novel Forms Today; Charles Burns, Daniel Clowes, Seth, Chris Ware." *Critical Inquiry* 40.3 (2014): 151–68. *Literary Reference Center*. Web. 30 Apr. 2015. <http://search.ebscohost.com/login.aspx?direct=true&db=lfh&AN=96688991&site=ehost-live>.

Goldstein, Lisa, and Molly Phelan. "Are You There God? It's Me, Manga: Manga as an Extension of Young Adult Literature." *Young Adult Library Services* Summer 2009: 32–38. *Academic Search Premier*. Web. 30 Apr. 2015. <http://search.ebscohost.com/login.aspx?direct=true&db=aph&AN=43913377&site=ehost-live>.

MacDonald, Heidi. "How Graphic Novels Became the Hottest Section in the Library." *Publishers Weekly* 6 May 2013: 20–25. *Literary Reference Center*. Web. 30 Apr. 2015. <http://search.ebscohost.com/login.aspx?direct=true&db=lfh&AN=87499984&site=ehost-live>.

Bibliography

Abbott, Michael, and Charles Forceville. "Visual Representation of Emotion in Manga: Loss of Control Is Loss of Hands in *Azumanga Daioh* Volume 4." *Language and Literature* 20.2 (2011): 91–112. Print.

Davis, Rocío G. "Childhood and Ethnic Visibility in Gene Yang's *American Born Chinese*." *Prose Studies* 35.1 (2013): 7–15. *Literary Reference Center*. Web. 30 Apr. 2015. <http://search.ebscohost.com/login.aspx?direct=true&db=lfh&AN=87070527&site=ehost-live>.

Sabin, Roger. *Comics, Comix & Graphic Novels: A History of Comic Art*. New York: Phaidon, 2001. Print.

Historical Fiction

Titles Discussed

A Moment Comes by Jennifer Bradbury
A Northern Light by Jennifer Donnelly
Fever 1793 by Laurie Halse Anderson

Genre Overview

Historical fiction is a popular genre within young adult literature. From early works like *Johnny Tremain* (1943), set in Boston during the American Revolution, to *Sarah, Plain and Tall* (1986), about life on the American prairie during the 1800s, young readers have long been drawn to stories about the past. Historical fiction is beguiling because the act of writing it is akin to filling in the margins of a history book. "Historical fiction is a hybrid form, halfway between fiction and nonfiction," Larissa MacFarquhar wrote for the *New Yorker*. "It is pioneer country, without fixed laws." E. L. Doctorow, the award-winning author of the novel *Ragtime* (1975), has been criticized for taking too many liberties with the lives of historical figures. In an interview with writer George Plimpton for the *Paris Review* in 1986, Doctorow defended himself and praised the way Shakespeare and Tolstoy also "fiddled" with history. "History is a battlefield," he said. "It's constantly being fought over because the past controls the present. History is the present. That's why every generation writes it anew."

The majority of historical fiction novels center on periods of trauma, great change, or uncertainty. Lois Lowry's award-winning novel, *Number the Stars* (1989) takes place in Copenhagen during the Holocaust and World War II. Markus Zusak's *The Book Thief* (2006) takes place in Germany around the same time. John Boyne's *The Boy in the Striped Pajamas* (2006) is also set during World War II and is about the son of a Nazi prison guard. *Out of the Dust* (1997) by Karen Hesse is set in Oklahoma during the Dust Bowl years in the 1930s. *Copper Sun* (2006) by Sharon M. Draper and *Hang a Thousand Trees with Ribbons* (1996), a fictional account of the life of poet Phyllis Wheatley, both feature African protagonists who are kidnapped and sold into American slavery.

All three of the books discussed in this article—*A Moment Comes* by Jennifer Bradbury (2013), *A Northern Light* by Jennifer Donnelly (2003), and *Fever 1793* by Laurie Halse Anderson (2000)—feature women living in three different regions during three different eras in which societal attitudes toward gender directly conflict with their goals. Patriarchy, slavery, and colonialism have altered the way we talk about race and gender, and changing mores in regard to these legacies and institutions are evident in modern stories about the past. These novels provide a provocative lens through which to view the past; they slyly draw parallels between the past and present in order to invite readers to question accepted ways of thinking about the events portrayed within the pages.

Works

Laurie Halse Anderson's novel *Fever 1793* takes place in Philadelphia in the summer of 1793, when an outbreak of yellow fever ravaged the young city, which was then the largest in the United States, killing nearly 10 percent of the population. Anderson's protagonist is a fourteen-year-old girl named Matilda who is the daughter of widowed coffeehouse owner. Before the outbreak, Matilda works from sun up to sun down to help her mother and their African American cook and friend, Eliza, run the coffeehouse. Her prospects involve more drudgery and perhaps someday an advantageous marriage. Her mother hopes for the latter, more so than Matilda, who doesn't appreciate these plans until her mother falls ill. Matilda's father died when she was young, and her mother has been toiling to makes ends meet with the shop ever since. The life of a poor, eighteenth-century woman was difficult; the life of a poor, eighteenth-century widow was worse. "Had she ever enjoyed anything," Matilda wonders, looking at her sleeping mother early in the book (68). "Had every day been a struggle?"

"Outbreak" is an appropriate word for the nature of the epidemic of yellow fever that year—the sickness literally broke the bonds of the society it ravaged. Matilda was afforded freedoms that would have been denied her in a well society, as was Philadelphia's African American population, as exemplified by Eliza. Anderson suggests that some of these changes became permanent when, at the end of the book, Matilda and Eliza become business partners and take over the coffeehouse themselves.

Matilda has only a passing interaction with real figures of the time. In fact, the only historical figure she comes in contact with is George Washington, whom she sees from afar. Her beau, however, is apprenticed to Charles Willson Peale, the famous portrait artist, and Matilda recovers from her own bout with the fever at Bush Hill, an actual place that was transformed by Stephen Girard, a French American war hero who saved lives during the epidemic by making French methods of treatment widely available. American doctors (like the one who treats Matilda's mother) advocated blood-letting as a form of treatment—a "cure" from which many patients never recovered. One of the more curious misconceptions about yellow fever in 1793 was the idea that people of African descent were immune to the disease. The African Americans of the Free African Society served as primary caregivers to the sick, even after many of them were infected themselves. Eliza is a caregiver and member of the society and brings Matilda, who had been cured and could not contract the fever again, to care for the sick and dying.

Jennifer Donnelly's award-winning novel *A Northern Light* takes place in rural, upstate New York in 1905 and 1906. Like *Fever 1793*, the fictional story is intertwined with a true historical event, which in this case is an infamous murder. In the summer of 1906, a man named Chester Gillette engineered the drowning murder of Grace Brown, a girl whom he had impregnated and refused to marry, despite the proper custom of the time. Gillette was soon arrested for her death, and his trial was one of the most sensational of the twentieth century. He was convicted and executed in 1908. So thoroughly did Gillette's treachery capture the national imagination, that in 1925, Theodore Dreiser wrote a famous novel about the case called *An American Tragedy*. The novel in turn inspired two films including the Academy Award–winning *A Place in the Sun* (starring Elizabeth Taylor as Gillette's other, wealthier paramour) in 1951. After reading Brown and Gillette's letters, which came to light during his trial, Donnelly felt compelled to create Mattie Gokey, the sixteen-year-old protagonist of *A Northern Light*, to explore the crushing injustice—and yet, incredible possibility—of being a young woman in America in the 1900s. "Mattie was born, in part, because I wanted to change the past," Donnelly wrote in a short interview at the end of her novel. "I wanted Grace's death to have meaning. And I wanted her death to allow someone else to escape her confining circumstances and live her life, even though Grace herself didn't get that chance."

Donnelly's story has an intricate relationship with known historical figures. Mattie, the eldest daughter of a poor, widowed farmer, already has a slew of her own problems when she meets a nervous woman named Grace. Mattie is working a summer job at Big Moose Lake, a resort in the Adirondacks. She doesn't want to cause any trouble. She just wants to blend in and earn money for either college in New York City or more likely it seems, a dowry. Donnelly's decision to have Grace and Mattie meet is provocative; her decision to then have Grace hand Mattie a sheath of letters and ask her to burn them (before being summoned out to a boat and her ultimate death) is fairly explosive. Mattie, whose own story is told in flashbacks, must decide whether to keep her promise to Grace or turn the letters over to the police after's Grace's body is discovered in the lake. By putting Mattie squarely in the historical action, Donnelly creates a powerful metaphor about having the courage to take control of one's own life.

Jennifer Bradbury's *A Moment Comes* takes place in India in 1947, during the months that the British Raj prepares to leave India and in so doing, formally divides it into two countries: India (predominantly Hindu) and Pakistan (predominantly Muslim). Sikhs, a distinct religious sect, were politically aligned with Hindus at this time. Bradbury tells her story from the perspective of three characters: Tariq, an eighteen-year-old Muslim who dreams of going to college at Oxford University in England; Anupreet, a teenage Sikh girl; and Margaret, a wealthy Caucasian girl from England whose father is a civil servant tasked with dividing up the ancient country. The partition, as it became known, was far more serious than just lines on a map. It was a horrendous undertaking borne of a political quagmire that forced many Indians to migrate. It introduced a period of extreme violence unlike any previous event in the region's history. People who had once been neighbors, friends, and family turned against one another for land. Bradbury's characters struggle from their relative safety to understand the escalating violence.

It is significant that Bradbury chose to tell her story from the conflicting perspectives of a Sikh, a Muslim, and a British citizen. Through Tariq the reader sees how Muslims were forced out of their homes and businesses and how frustration can turn to violence under the influence of the mob. Through Anupreet, the reader sees how dangerous it was for a young woman to survive when rape is deployed as a weapon of war and victims of sexual violence are socially maligned. And finally, through Margaret, the reader sees the folly of British colonial rule and how power and racism blinded the empire, tricking the British people into thinking that their presence in India and their subsequent exit, was somehow a display of benevolence toward the Indian people. While none of the characters mentioned are real, Bradbury has explained that the character of Margaret was based on a teenager named Pamela Mountbatten, who was the daughter of the last viceroy of India. Pamela and her mother make an appearance in the novel when Pamela confides to Margaret that her mother, Lady Mountbatten, has developed a deep emotional attachment to Jawaharlal Nehru, the first prime minister of India. This relationship—reportedly never consummated—is true and thematically touches on Margaret's confusion regarding her own crush on Tariq.

Conclusions

The three novels discussed provide a provocative lens through which to contemplate the present through a view to the past. In *Fever 1793*, a horrific epidemic allows a young girl—who was to be married off to her wealthiest suitor—to escape the strictures and customs of early American life and achieve her dream of running her own coffeehouse. In *A Northern Light*, a young girl painfully breaks a promise to her dying mother (and with it, the hearts of her father and sisters) to avoid a life with an unloving husband and pursue her dream of becoming a writer. In *A Moment Comes*, a young Muslim boy kills a Sikh man to protect a Sikh girl from being raped, and an English girl is forced to reckon with her own views about race and love. The novels draw subtle comparisons between the past and present. In *Fever 1793*, Anderson highlights the fact that the brunt of the epidemic was borne by the poor and by African Americans. Those with money and power fled the city to save themselves. In *A Northern Light*, Mattie quickly learns that her desires—whether or not she wants to be kissed, for example—are totally meaningless to her suitor. In *A Moment Comes*, an army of wealthy, white civil servants do wrong in another country by attempting to do right; modern readers will recognize in the former British India notes of Western wars in Asia and the Middle East.

These novels are well-researched but unmistakably of the twenty-first century, having all been written in the 2000s. They ask readers to contemplate historical events from the perspectives of the people less likely to have had the chance to share their view of those events: women, African Americans, Muslims, Sikhs, and the young. Chandra L. Powers, in an essay for *Research in the Teaching of English* called this "presentism." Rather than merely inflict modern views on the past, presentism utilizes a more encompassing view of humanity to provide a richer understanding of history.

Molly Hagan

Further Reading

Collins, Fiona M., and Judith Graham. *Historical Fiction for Children: Capturing the Past*. New York: Routledge, 2013. Print.

Rycik, Mary Taylor, and Brenda Rosler. "The Return of Historical Fiction." *Reading Teacher* 63.2 (2009): 163–66. Print.

Bibliography

Johnson, Sarah. "Defining the Genre: What Are the Rules for Historical Fiction?" *Historical Novel Society*. Historical Novel Society, Mar. 2002. Web. 3 June 2015. <https://historicalnovelsociety.org/guides/defining-the-genre/defining-the-genre-what-are-the-rules-for-historical-fiction/>.

MacFarquhar, Larissa. "The Dead Are Real." *New Yorker*. Condé Nast, 15 Oct. 2012. Web. 3 June 2015. <http://www.newyorker.com/magazine/2012/10/15/the-dead-are-real>.

Mallon, Thomas. "Never Happened: Fictions of Alternative History." *New Yorker*. Condé Nast, 21 Nov. 2011. Web. 3 June 2015. <http://www.newyorker.com/magazine/2011/11/21/never-happened>.

Mantel, Hilary. "Booker Winner Hilary Mantel on Dealing with History in Fiction." *Guardian*. Guardian News and Media, 16 Oct. 2009. Web. 3 June 2015. <http://www.theguardian.com/books/2009/oct/17/hilary-mantel-author-booker>.

Plimpton, George. "E. L. Doctorow, The Art of Fiction No. 94." *Paris Review*. Paris Review, Winter 1986. Web. 4 June 2015. <http://www.theparisreview.org/interviews/2718/the-art-of-fiction-no-94-e-l-doctorow>.

Power, Chandra L. "Challenging the Pluralism of Our Past: Presentism and the Selective Tradition in Historical Fiction Written for Young People." *Research in the Teaching of English* 37.4 (2003): 425–66. Print.

Horror

Titles Discussed

Bonechiller by Graham McNamee
The Diviners by Libba Bray
Miss Peregrine's Home for Peculiar Children by Ransom Riggs
The Monstrumologist by Rick Yancey

Genre Overview

Before the Victorian period in Great Britain and the United States, when children's literature became its own profitable enterprise, children of all ages read literature written for adults. Gothic novels thrilled readers with haunted castles, twisted villains, and innocent heroines. In the United States, Charles Brockden Brown's *Wieland; or, the Transformation* (1798) gained popularity as one of the earliest examples of the American gothic novel, while in Britain, Ann Radcliffe published numerous gothic tales that were snapped up by the public. The trend for these stories was so enticing that one stormy night in 1816, three vacationing British writers—Lord Byron, Mary Shelley, and Percy Bysshe Shelley—decided to see who could write the most frightening story. The most famous work from this session is Mary Shelley's psychological horror story *Frankenstein*, first published in 1818.

In the decades that followed, the popularity of horror tales, specifically ghost stories, reached all audiences, and classic authors such as Henry James and Charles Dickens wrote ghost stories that are still read today. These stories led to new directions for scares, and Bram Stoker and Robert Louis Stephenson introduced new kinds of monsters (Dracula, Mr. Hyde) with which to scare their audiences.

The horror genre continued to flourish. In the early twentieth century, American writer H. P. Lovecraft introduced a new take on the gothic novel, the cosmic horror story, spawning a sprawling mythos of gods and monsters that led to his being called the "father of modern horror." Years later, in 1974, a then-unknown writer published his first novel, *Carrie*, about a teenage girl whose psychic powers manifest in a slaughter of cataclysmic proportions. The novel made Stephen King a household name, and readers of all ages gobbled up his tales of monsters, creepy phenomena, and frightening places.

The horror genre, like other genres, is not limited to just one type of story. Subgenres of horror include gothic tales, mysteries, science fiction, fantasy, paranormal romance, and historical fiction. Horror versions of other genres, such as mystery and science fiction, make use of the same tropes and characterizations as the non-horror versions, but they take them a step further by twisting those familiar aspects with an element of evil. Even horror stories with happy endings often leave readers unsettled, suspicious of the resolution and wondering what will happen next, and questions of morality arise as characters commit or are the victims of horrible acts. As a new generation of writers started producing horror specifically for young adults, many seemed to agree that such works, especially novel-length tales, should end with some sense of optimism.

Though some children's horror series, such as R. L. Stine's Goosebumps series (1992–97) or Jonathan Rand's Michigan Chillers (2000–) and American Chillers (2001–) books, may give the impression that horror writers lack depth, there are many well-written horror books for young adults. Psychological elements add to the characterization and the horror. Monsters become real whether they look like the person next door or something that could only exist in a nightmare. Works such as Graham McNamee's *Bonechiller* (2008), Rick Yancey's *The Monstrumologist* (2009), and Ransom Riggs's *Miss Peregrine's Home for Peculiar Children* (2011) feature less traditional monsters, while *The Diviners* (2012), by Libba Bray, introduces a ghostly evil. Whatever the subgenre, modern works of horror continue to appeal to readers because they cross genre boundaries, drawing in those who would otherwise choose romance, mystery, or even humor.

Works

Libba Bray's novel *The Diviners* opens in 1926 in Manhattan, where a naïve eighteen-year-old girl pulls out a haunted Ouija board to liven up her birthday party. The party soon turns to horror as the guests unwittingly unleash a spirit, and though they quickly put the incident out of their minds, it is too late: "Something moves again in the shadows. A harbinger of much greater evil to come. Naughty John has come home. And he has work to do" (9).

After this frightening setup, the novel primarily follows the life of Evie O'Neill, a young woman from Ohio who has been sent to New York to stay with her uncle after her psychic powers revealed a dark secret of one of her hometown's most popular sons. Once in New York, Evie makes new friends while dealing with her strange uncle's fascination with the occult. Drawn into the murders as an apprentice of sorts to Uncle Will, who has been asked to help by the police, Evie learns that she must rely on her powers to help solve the mystery.

Set in the 1920s, Bray's novel introduces readers to a setting that is reminiscent of F. Scott Fitzgerald's *The Great Gatsby* (1925). A party atmosphere follows Evie, in many cases highlighting her flaws, but also contrasting drastically with the dark actions of Naughty John and the supernatural fascination of Uncle Will's museum of occult artifacts. The novel's focus shifts between Evie and several other characters who have experienced strange dreams and the onset of individual psychic powers, adding an extra layer of confusion that exacerbates the horror in the story.

In contrast, *Bonechiller*, by Graham McNamee, is set in a small town in present-day Canada. Danny and his father have been wandering since his mother's death, and Danny has finally settled somewhere long enough to make friends. Ash, Howie, and Pike are military brats, so they understand Danny's nomadic life. After hanging out with his friends one night, Danny is attacked by a creature unlike anything he has ever seen. When Howie is attacked as well, the friends discover that teenagers have been disappearing for years. The disappearances escalate during the coldest winters when the creature apparently comes out of hibernation.

Confused about why the creature did not kill them, Danny and Howie soon start to notice that they are experiencing strange side effects from their attacks. They are both immune to the cold, despite subzero temperatures, and they are sharing dreams that also include the creature. Knowing they must find a way to survive, the friends discover where the creature lives and plan its destruction.

Miss Peregrine's Home for Peculiar Children, by Ransom Riggs, jumps in time from present day to one specific day in the past—the day when the home that Miss Peregrine had created as a safe harbor for children with odd powers was bombed during World War II in a German air raid. The story begins with sixteen-year-old Jacob Portman recalling his relationship with his grandfather. As a child, Jacob was fascinated by his grandfather's stories; once he reaches a certain age, he rejects them as fairy tales and forgets them until the day his grandfather dies. As he holds the dying old man in his arms, two things happen: his grandfather passes on a cryptic message, telling him, "Find the bird. In the loop. On the other side of the old man's grave. September third, 1940" (33); and Jacob sees a monster. In the months after his grandfather's death, Jacob believes he is going crazy.

On a search for the truth, Jacob and his father travel to Cairnholm Island in Wales, where Jacob's grandfather stayed during the war. One day, while exploring the ruins of his grandfather's childhood refuge,

Jacob finds an old trunk that contains photographs of the same children his grandfather had claimed as friends. While he is looking through the photos, he encounters a group of children. Strangely, though, these are the same children in the photographs, the same children whom his grandfather knew, the same children who were reportedly killed when the house was bombed. As he tries to catch the children, Jacob stumbles into a time loop where the island is still pristine, the children are still alive, and it is always September 3, 1940. The loop is maintained by Miss Peregrine, a bird shape-shifter. The horror comes to light as Jacob discovers the monsters he sees are real and are trying to kill Miss Peregrine and the children.

In *The Monstrumologist*, author Rick Yancey takes readers back in time to nineteenth-century New England. Twelve-year-old Will Henry is the assistant to Pellinore Warthrop, a scientist who studies monsters. One night a grave robber brings Warthrop a gruesome pair of bodies, one of which belongs to a monster classified by the scientist as a member of the genus *Anthropophagi*. This horrifying creature has no head, and its favored food source is human flesh.

After being attacked by a group of these monsters when they return to the graveyard, Warthrop and Will go on a search to discover why a group of these creatures would appear on the shores of America. The stories they hear along the way point to Warthrop's father as the culprit, so the two join forces with a monster hunter to get rid of the creatures. However, the monster hunter arrives too late to prevent the slaughter of a local family. Will's graphic description of the massacre makes it one of the most horrifying scenes in the novel. The novel climaxes with a monster hunt in which even the evil of men is revealed. The hunters succeed in demolishing the pack of *Anthropophagi*, but Will Henry's innocence is lost.

One aspect that all four of these novels has in common is that each character has lost someone close, and that loss plays an important role in the ensuing story. In *The Diviners*, Evie's older brother died serving the country during World War I. His death comes back to haunt her as she encounters him in her dreams, where he sends her warnings that she struggles to understand. In *Bonechiller*, Danny is only in Harvest Cove, Canada, because his father has not come to terms with his mother's death from brain cancer two years earlier, and the two have been traveling around the country

on a nomadic quest to find a place where they can escape the memories and begin to heal. The death of Jacob's grandfather sets him up for his adventure in *Miss Peregrine's Home for Peculiar Children*; the old man's dying message and the mysterious creature that Jacob sees while holding him in his arms send Jacob on a quest to understand his grandfather's life. In *The Monstrumologist,* Will Henry became Pellinore Warthrop's ward because both of his parents died in a fire that can be indirectly connected to Warthrop's scientific studies.

Outside of the loss of a major loved one, the three novels with male protagonists differ quite a bit from Bray's novel in terms of characterization. Though *The Diviners* focuses on Evie, she never really matures, and readers may grapple with her flighty and often unkind personality. Further, the novel's shifting point of view can confuse a reader's expectation and understanding of the plot and empathy for the characters, as it is not just Evie who is being terrorized by the horrific murders.

In contrast, the other novels feature strong side characters who support the protagonists and experience the horror along with them. McNamee's *Bonechiller* pulls Danny's friend Howie right into the nightmare as both boys have been attacked by the ancient creature that lives under the lake. Both Danny and, to a lesser extent, Howie change as the novel progresses and they work their way through their fear of death at the hands of a monster that has been murdering children for decades. Danny learns that life does go on after the death of a loved one and that he must stand up for himself if both he and his father are ever going to heal, while Howie changes from a timid, easily frightened boy into a more mature young man capable of handling challenges without fear. In *Miss Peregrine's Home for Peculiar Children*, Jacob finds a place where he can belong, even though it means giving up all that he has known. His choice to stay with Miss Peregrine, Emma, and the other children shows a sense of maturity and self-sacrifice for the greater good. Will Henry's growth in *The Monstrumologist* is a bit more limited due to his age; he is only twelve, while Evie, Danny, and Jacob are all older teenagers. Will's age, however, only contributes to the horror. Despite the limitations on his ability to change, Will does grow in his understanding of his relationship with his mentor, and this interdependence is the one bright note in the novel.

A final contrast between the novels is the nature of the horror element. *The Diviners* uses the ghost of Naughty John along with Uncle Will's connection to the occult as the main avenues for fear. The tone is more eerie and mysterious than horrifying. The other three novels all feature monstrous creatures: the Bonechiller in *Bonechiller*, the Hollowgast in *Miss Peregrine*, and the *Anthropophagi* in *The Monstrumologist*. These monsters are frightening for the damage they can do. The Bonechiller's horrifying appearance, ability to inhabit dreams, and decades of child murder combine to make it truly frightening, and the Hollowgast's desire to gain power in order to transform from a physically revolting monster into a human one adds a layer of psychological terror. Yancey's *Anthropophagus*, though, is the most horrifying of these beasts, due to its horrific physical bearing and its grotesque desire for human flesh.

Conclusions

Young adult horror continues to grow in popularity, as evidenced by the fact that all but one of the above-mentioned novels is the first in a series (*Bonechiller* being the exception). The adaptation of young adult horror for film and television and the continued popularity of authors such as Mary Downing Hahn and R. L. Stine, who write horror for younger readers, will help generate new audiences. The appeal of young adult novels for adults will also continue to contribute to the genre's health.

The twenty-first century has seen an upsurge in popularity of young adult horror. Many well-written horror novels starring young adult characters cross genre lines, pulling in fans of romance, mystery, and science fiction who crave the excitement, the terror, the emotional connections, and the adventures. As long as young adult authors continue to produce solid literary works that capture attention in original ways, horror fiction will continue to flourish.

Stephen King once argued that people desire horror fiction for several reasons: to challenge themselves to face their fears; to assure themselves that they are normal; and to find a safe outlet for the evil within themselves and the frustrations of everyday life. In essence, his premise is that the vicarious experience of evil acts allows people to exorcise their souls.

Theresa L. Stowell, PhD

Further Reading

Bucher, Katherine T., and KaaVonia Hinton. *Young Adult Literature: Exploration, Evaluation, and Appreciation.* 3rd ed. Boston: Pearson, 2014. Print.

Fann, Kelly. "Tapping into the Appeal of Cult Fiction." *Reference and User Services Quarterly* 51.1 (2011): 15–18. *Academic Search Complete.* Web. 4 June 2015. <https://search.ebscohost.com/login.aspx?direct=true&db=aqh&AN=65556763&site=eds-live>.

Bibliography

Bray, Libba. *The Diviners.* New York: Little, 2012. Print.

King, Stephen. "Why We Crave Horror Movies." *The Bedford Guide for College Writers: With Reader, Research Manual, and Handbook.* Ed. X. J. Kennedy, Dorothy M. Kennedy, and Marcia F. Muth. 9th ed. Boston: Bedford, 2011. 559–61. Print.

Lyga, Barry, Robin Wasserman, and Brenna Yovanoff. "Monsters, Murder, and Morality: A Graveside Chat about YA Horror Fiction." Interview by Daniel Kraus. *Booklist* 15 May 2014: 62–63. *Literary Reference Center.* Web. 4 June 2015. <https://search.ebscohost.com/login.aspx?direct=true&db=lfh&AN=96074059&site=eds-live>.

Riggs, Ransom. *Miss Peregrine's Home for Peculiar Children.* Philadelphia: Quirk, 2011. Print.

Humor

Titles Discussed

Beauty Queens by Libba Bray
Me and Earl and the Dying Girl by Jesse Andrews
Swim the Fly by Don Calame

Genre Overview

People of all ages in all times and all places enjoy laughing. This fact was discovered early in human history, and writers began taking advantage of that knowledge more than three thousand years ago. The ancient Greek poet Homer included comic passages in his *Iliad* and *Odyssey* to lighten the dramatic tension in his epics; in the fifth century BCE, the playwright Aristophanes produced such bawdy lampoons of human nature as *The Clouds* and *Lysistrata*; and ancient Roman playwrights such as Plautus and Terence continued the humorous tradition with theatrical farces.

In medieval Europe, works such as Giovanni Boccaccio's *Decameron* (1353), Geoffrey Chaucer's *Canterbury Tales* (late fourteenth century), and François Rabelais's *Life of Gargantua and Pantagruel* (ca. 1532–64) kept audiences in stitches. During the Renaissance, English playwright William Shakespeare made skillful use of puns, inside jokes, humorous devices such as mistaken identity, and comical figures such as Sir John Falstaff and various laughter-inducing fools and jesters, both liberally in such comedies as *Love's Labour's Lost* (ca. 1597) and *All's Well That Ends Well* (ca. 1604–5) and in smaller doses to leaven his more serious tragedies and history plays, such as *Hamlet* (ca. 1599–1601), *King Lear* (ca. 1606), and *Henry IV*, parts 1 and 2 (ca. 1596–99). During the eighteenth century, comic and satirical authors such as Jonathan Swift (*Gulliver's Travels*, 1726), Voltaire (*Candide*, 1759), and Henry Fielding (*Tom Jones*, 1749) paved the way for later humorous works such as Jane Austen's *Pride and Prejudice* (1813) and Charles Dickens's *The Pickwick Papers* (1836–37).

In the United States, nineteenth-century author Mark Twain exercised significant and long-lasting influence on both written and performed comedic works. The advent of newspaper comic strips in the late nineteenth century helped spread visual humor throughout the country. In the early twentieth century, radio ruled, giving birth to the sitcom, before television became the dominant medium in the 1950s.

Humor has long been an effective element in children's and young adult literature. The inclusion of funny scenes and comical characters helps account for the enduring popularity of such early twentieth-century works as L. Frank Baum's Oz series (1900–1920) and A. A. Milne's *Winnie-the-Pooh* (1926) and *The House at Pooh Corner* (1928). Comical descriptions, offbeat protagonists, humorous dialogue, creative use of linguistic techniques, and outrageous, unpredictable plots are prominent in contemporary young adult fiction, where they serve to soften the sharp edges of such serious real-life issues as sexual attraction, drug abuse, dysfunctional families, depression, and the possibility of early death. Humor, employed naturally and realistically, helps motivate adolescents to read, and the potential for laughter helps the reader identify intimately with the characters when they can share a sense of humor. Modern novels such as Don Calame's *Swim the Fly* (2009), Libba Bray's *Beauty Queens* (2011), and Jesse Andrews's *Me and Earl and the Dying Girl* (2012) employ a variety of techniques to elicit laughter while addressing traditionally sober topics such as competition, survival, romance, and death.

Works

Swim the Fly, by Don Calame, deals humorously with the qualities of friendship and the resiliency of youth while underlining the importance of making worthwhile choices. Longtime pals Matt, Cooper, and Sean set a goal each summer; at age fifteen, they vow to see "a real, live naked girl" and set their sights on the buxom Mandy Reagan. The boys are members of a swimming team of perennial losers led by uninspiring, lumpy coach Ms. Luntz. In order to impress their new team member, attractive backstroker Kelly West, Matt volunteers to replace the team's injured butterfly specialist and "swim the fly." He has no upper-body strength, likening his attempts at the stroke to "a palsied whippet struggling for its life." Matt will compete against champion butterflier Tony "The Gorilla" Grillo, whom Kelly has dated.

Sean hatches a plan to see Mandy naked. The boys use Sean's twin sister Cathy's clothes and makeup to dress like girls and enter the women's locker room at the community center where Mandy works out. The plan goes awry after Matt, having ingested a laxative that he mistook for protein powder, experiences a comically explosive reaction in the women's locker room.

At the first swim meet, Sean gets Matt out of competition by stuffing himself with junk food and vomiting into the pool. At night Matt sneaks into a country-club pool to practice swimming and runs into European martinet Ulf, who forces Matt into his grueling advanced lifesaving class and teaches him the rudiments of the butterfly stroke. Still unprepared, Matt ducks out of the next meet by faking appendicitis. A second attempt by the boys to glimpse Mandy naked at a party goes wrong when they are discovered spying from a bedroom closet and chased in a slapstick-like sequence. They do eventually see a naked woman at a nudist beach: flabby Ms. Luntz, a sight that the boys find eye-gougingly horrible.

Over time, Matt learns that Kelly is shallow—she cannot even remember his name, referring to him instead as "Mark"—and has returned to dating Tony. Matt gravitates towards Kelly's redheaded friend Valerie, who is smart, pretty, and funny and likes him enough to kiss him and hold his hand.

Ultimately, Matt cannot avoid competing and is entered in the hundred-yard butterfly championships, facing off against chiseled Tony and chubby swimmer Ernie. Despite finishing with the extremely slow time of three minutes and forty-six seconds, Matt ends up winning the race—because Cooper sabotaged Tony's Speedo, causing it to fall apart and resulting in Tony's disqualification.

Swim the Fly, Calame's semiautobiographical debut novel, offers tender moments between its farcical episodes. The book is aided considerably by comical subplots involving secondary characters such as Matt's love-struck grandfather, who keeps trying to connect romantically with a widowed neighbor.

Where *Swim the Fly* is a light-hearted farce, Libba Bray's *Beauty Queens* is a fierce satire. The novel takes aim at multiple targets, especially so-called reality television, corporate conglomerates, advertising, and beauty pageants. *Beauty Queens* opens with a plane carrying fifty girls, contestants for the annual Miss Teen Dream pageant, crashing on a remote tropical island, a scene that echoes such novels as William Golding's *Lord of the Flies* (1954) and such television shows as *Survivor* (2000–) and *Lost* (2004–10). All the adults—pilots, chaperones, photographers—are killed, along with most of the contestants. The thirteen teenage survivors, including a lesbian, two "ethnic" girls, and a member of a popular boy band disguised as a girl who wants to undergo sex reassignment surgery, must overcome rivalries and work together to fend for themselves until help arrives.

Meanwhile, unbeknownst to the teens, a military compound is hidden underground on the island, and a clandestine operation is in the works. The company that sponsors the beauty pageant, referred to throughout as simply "The Corporation," wants to deal arms to MoMo "The Peacock" ChaCha, an Idi Amin–like dictator with a penchant for Elvis, in exchange for permission to expand its business into the Republic of ChaCha. It is feared the presence of the teens will quash the arms deal, so Ladybird Hope, former Miss Teen Dream–turned–Corporation executive with aspirations of becoming US president, announces on television that the girls have all perished.

The plot is further complicated when a reproduction pirate ship, crewed by Sinjin St. Sinjin and the rest of the cast of the popular television show *Captains Bodacious*, runs aground on the island. Relationships immediately form between the boys and the girls. As the young adults slowly become more aware of what is transpiring on the island, they bond to foil the nefarious scheme, bringing down the treacherous Ladybird and thwarting the sinister Corporation in the process.

Beauty Queens is structured like a collision between two types of television programs, with the survivors' story representing reality television and the Corporation's schemes representing scripted shows. The novel heavily borrows and then reworks numerous adventure clichés; the island paradise contains perils such as giant snakes, a volcano, quicksand, and vegetation that causes hallucinations when ingested. Short narrative scenes are frequently interrupted by commercials for a range of Corporation products, including the Git R Done 447 handgun and lip-hair remover Lady 'Stache Off, both of which also serve as humorous plot devices. There are many promotions and insertions, such as the "Miss Teen Dream Fun Facts Pages," which highlight each contestant, and excerpts from television shows. Humorous footnotes explain the mostly invented cultural references. Beneath the madcap hilarity and the broad satirical strokes, however, is a semiserious message: appearances are deceptive. Though all the beauty queens are uniformly pretty on the outside, on the inside they are individuals, with secret hopes and desires, which, as the epilogue reveals, they mostly achieve.

Jesse Andrews's *Me and Earl and the Dying Girl* is a humorously nostalgic tale of teenage angst and uneasy friendships between dissimilar individuals founded on shaky common interests. The novel is told from the cynical, self-deprecating perspective of Greg Gaines, an overweight, pale, Jewish senior at an inner-city high school in Pittsburgh, Pennsylvania. Greg's middle-class family includes his befuddled college-professor father, his strong-willed mother, and two younger sisters. Throughout his existence, Greg has attempted to remain invisible and anonymous in order to avoid involvement. He does not join any school group—jocks, stoners, goths, theater kids, or band kids—but maintains access to them all via improvisational witticisms, because his life goal is "to not be ostracized by *anyone*."

Greg, having earlier experienced a series of dating disasters, suppresses his secret crush on a pretty, curvaceous, and vapid girl named Madison Hartner. His only friend is Earl Jackson, a short, profane, athletic African American boy who lives in a run-down house with an Internet-obsessed mother, no male adults, two brothers, and three drug-dealing, violence-prone gangster stepbrothers. Greg and Earl met in kindergarten, and both became interested in film at an early age. Over the years, they have made dozens of short films, mostly bad remakes of existing movies.

Things change when Greg learns that a girl he briefly dated in Hebrew school, Rachel Kushner, has been diagnosed with leukemia. Greg's mother asks him to spend time with Rachel, to help make a difference in her life. Greg, feeling obligated, is able to make the usually unresponsive Rachel snort with laughter, and Madison convinces Greg to make a movie just for Rachel.

Greg enlists Earl's aid, and they make several comical attempts to create films for Rachel—using documentary-style interviews, copying Ken Burns's style, using stop-action animation and sock puppets—that are equally awful. Eventually, they combine all their efforts with personal speeches (Earl's is considerably more heartfelt and sincere than Greg's), in what Greg considers "the worst film ever made." Rachel, however, appreciates the film, and because she is dying, the production is passed along to be shown during a pep rally as inspiration to the entire school. The exposure completely ruins Greg's low profile, and afterward, all of the various cliques uniformly hate him for subjecting them to such trash. After failing several classes, Greg holes up in his room, finally realizing how Rachel's unique essence was lost when she died. He and Earl drift apart for a time, and both destroy their personal copies of all their films. The two boys finally reunite, still friends but heading in different directions: Greg, finally comfortable with himself, will attend college (after making up his failed classes), while Earl starts working at a fast-food restaurant in an attempt to move out of his destructive home environment. Both will probably be forever affected by their shared experiences.

Conclusions

From the early twentieth century onward, moviegoers have flocked to films of all kinds, but the popularity of comedies has proved particularly enduring. Whether the silent comedy of *The Gold Rush* (1925) or the slapstick of *A Hard Day's Night* (1964), the musical humor of *Singin' in the Rain* (1952) or the dark satire of *Dr. Strangelove* (1964), the thought-provoking *All about Eve* (1950) or the difficult-to-define *The Grand Budapest Hotel* (2014), anything goes as long as it induces a smile, a snicker, or full-fledged bursts of roll-in-the-aisles laughter. Modern audiences have

a seemingly unquenchable appetite for that gift from vaudeville, live stand-up comics, and will eagerly accept a wide variety of offerings: insult and vulgar artists, ventriloquists, humorous jugglers and magicians, punsters, jokesters, and pratfallers. Since the 1950s, situation comedies have become a mainstay of network television. Sketch comedy is also alive and well, as demonstrated by the long-running *Saturday Night Live*, which premiered in 1975. Even surreal animated satire showcasing the antics of dysfunctional cartoon families has found a niche, as illustrated by the popular series *The Simpsons* (1989–).

Literature likewise allows for a broad range of styles and techniques to attract readers of all ages. Whether anecdotal, risqué, farcical, highbrow or sophomoric, parody or satire, slapstick or screwball, dark comedy or hyperbole, there is a place for every type of humor. Humor in written works serves a similar purpose as it does in film, live performances, and televised comedy. Particularly in young adult literature, it also helps defuse moral objections to scatological language or scenes dealing with otherwise taboo or socially uncomfortable subjects such as sex, sexuality, abortion, or child abuse.

Laughter is not only enjoyable but also, as a considerable body of medical research has revealed, beneficial to both mental and physical health; a whole field of study, gelotology, has been developed to study the physiological and psychological effects of laughter. A hearty guffaw has been shown to activate the brain's prefrontal cortex, producing endorphins that relieve pain. Sustained chortles can help dilate blood vessels to increase blood flow. Chuckling raises antibody production for stronger immunity. From infancy through adulthood, regular amusement eases tension and lessens stress on the heart, which suggests that humor is not only fun but also a necessary component for experiencing a long and satisfactory life.

Jack Ewing

Further Reading

Condren, Chelsea. "Genre Guide: Young Adult Humor." *The Hub: Your Connection to Teen Reads*. Amer. Lib. Assn., 29 July 2013. Web. 14 May 2015. <http://www.yalsa.ala.org/thehub/2013/07/29/genre-guide-young adult-humor/>.

Hogan, Walter. *Humor in Young Adult Literature: A Time to Laugh*. Lanham: Scarecrow, 2005. Print.

Bibliography

Attardo, Salvatore, ed. *Encyclopedia of Humor Studies*. Thousand Oaks: Sage, 2014. Print.

Bucher, Katherine T., and KaaVonia Hinton. *Young Adult Literature: Exploration, Evaluation, and Appreciation*. 3rd ed. Boston: Pearson, 2014. Print.

Davies, Stephanie. *Laughology: Improve Your Life with the Science of Laughter*. Bethel: Crown, 2013. Print.

Gillis, Bryan, and Joanna Simpson. *Sexual Content in Young Adult Literature: Reading between the Sheets*. Lanham: Rowman, 2015. Print.

Hill, Craig, ed. *The Critical Merits of Young Adult Literature: Coming of Age*. New York: Routledge, 2014. Print.

McClure, Amy A., Abigail V. Garthwait, and Janice V. Kristo. *Teaching Children's Literature in an Era of Standards*. Boston: Pearson, 2015. Print.

Roberts, Patricia L. *Taking Humor Seriously in Children's Literature: Literature-Based Mini-Units and Humorous Books for Children Ages 5–12*. Lanham: Scarecrow, 1997. Print.

LGBTQ

Titles Discussed

Annie on My Mind by Nancy Garden
Boy Meets Boy by David Levithan
Hard Love by Ellen Wittlinger

Genre Overview

John Donovan's novel *I'll Get There. It Better Be Worth the Trip.* (1969) is widely considered the first young adult novel to feature gay or lesbian content, not just positively but at all. It was published in the same year that the Stonewall riots, a series of spontaneous antipolice protests in New York City that is credited with sparking the modern lesbian, gay, bisexual, transgender, and queer (LGBTQ) rights movement, took place. While this coincidence speaks to the significant advancements in LGBTQ rights during that pivotal time, it also speaks to a divide; the LGBTQ culture and politics of adults had been fueled for decades by honest, powerful literature and works of art, yet the mere mention of homosexuality or gender variance to teenagers was (and, in some cases, still is) considered by many to be exceptionally taboo.

During the 1970s and 1980s, young adult novels featuring LGBTQ content occasionally found their way to major presses. In addition to the broader advancements of gay and lesbian rights during these decades, this increase can be credited to the popularity of "problem novels" for teenagers. Problem novels present difficult social issues to a teenage audience with frank language and realism, eschewing the preference for hyperbolic optimism and censorship that defined much of the previous young adult literature. S. E. Hinton's *The Outsiders* (1967), for example, deals with such topics as gang violence, teenage alcohol use, and physical abuse, while the anonymously published *Go Ask Alice* (1971) purported to be the diary of a real fifteen-year-old drug addict who turned to sex work to support her habit. In a publishing context that began to reward problem novels even as they faced censorship, LGBTQ content for teenagers suddenly seemed viable.

However, these trends also resulted in only a very slim range of narratives and representations of LGBTQ adolescents. These were characters who faced the harsh realities of homophobia, familial and societal rejection, peer-led violence, and emotional turmoil. Nancy Garden's novel *Annie on My Mind* (1982) is both an example of this plot, with the two main teenage girls struggling as much with society's judgment of their relationship as with their own internalized confusion, and one of the earliest to transcend it, employing more complex literary techniques and finding a happy ending for the main characters.

Continuing on through the 1980s, young adult LGBTQ novels largely dealt with issues associated with coming out, the characters first struggling to accept themselves and then, in some instances, announcing their identities to peers and family. In contrast, as the publication of LGBTQ young adult novels increased dramatically in the 1990s, more and more of them featured unabashedly positive portrayals of both the characters themselves and their circumstances. Novels began to feature protagonists who are already out of the closet and, because of this, are able to face additional questions—not simply "Am I gay?" but, for example, "What does it mean for me to be gay?" and "What kind of relationship do I want to have?" The range of identities also began to expand during this time, with characters navigating bisexual, queer, and transgender self-identifications as well. Ellen Wittlinger's *Hard Love* (1999), for instance, includes one straight male character and one lesbian character, a teenager who is out and proud from the start of the narrative.

In the twenty-first century, in alignment with the rapid advancement of LGBTQ rights and a publishing industry that is increasingly willing to address complex and previously taboo themes in young adult literature, more books than ever before feature sympathetic, strong LGBTQ teen characters. David Levithan's *Boy Meets Boy* (2003), for instance, presents a small town that unabashedly celebrates its many LGBTQ teenagers, including the transgender captain of the football team and other characters who do not fit easily into rigid identity categories of "gay" or "straight." While many LGBTQ teens still struggle like the characters in *Annie on My Mind*, modern LGBTQ young adult authors are free to approach a broad range of experiences, and LGBTQ characters are allowed to be as joyful, wrought, and complex as their straight counterparts.

Works

The dedication that opens *Annie on My Mind* reads, "For all of us." While on the surface this appears to be a simple invitation to young readers to consider themselves as members of a broader LGBTQ community, it also signals a distinguishing aspect of the novel: *Annie on My Mind* is written for, rather than about, LGBTQ teenagers.

This distinction is in part why *Annie on my Mind* is largely considered the first young adult novel to portray gay and lesbian characters who reach a happy ending. Previous novels in the genre still bowed to overwhelming social prejudice and the conventions of the problem novel, featuring gay and lesbian (rarely transgender or bisexual) characters who might experiment with their sexuality or briefly find a partner, but who typically found nothing more than violence, rejection, and isolation in the end.

In contrast, *Annie on My Mind* is told from the point of view of seventeen-year-old Liza, a young woman who never considered herself to be a lesbian before meeting Annie. The two take their time embarking on a romantic relationship, moving slowly from an obsessive friendship to a physically intimate connection, and a great deal of self-doubt and questioning floods Liza's mind. After their first kiss, Liza spirals with emotions and revelations, saying, "In the last two or three years, I'd wondered why I'd rather go to the movies with Sally or some other girl than with

a boy, and why, when I imagined living with someone someday, permanently I mean, that person was always female" (105). When she decides to commit to exploring the relationship, she joins Annie in bed, where the two end up "holding each other and sometimes kissing, but not really touching. Mostly just being happy. Still scared, though, too" (106). These moments find a place for the confusion and danger that often accompany young lesbian relationships in an often-hostile society, but they also emphasize the pleasure, safety, and happiness that the relationship will eventually bring to Liza.

The narrative of *Annie on My Mind* is designed to welcome young LGBTQ readers into a world defined by both optimism and honesty. This is further accomplished by an epistolary framing device, with chapters occasionally jumping into the future, where Liza struggles to write Annie a letter from college. These letters are important for several reasons. First, they let the reader know that Liza makes it out of high school without any real losses; when Annie and Liza get caught together and Liza fears expulsion from the school and the loss of her college acceptance, readers know that these fears will not ultimately be realized. Just as importantly, however, the letters provide the context of a slightly older, slightly wiser Liza to compare with the confused and sometimes-frightened Liza just beginning to date Annie. The most extreme moment of homophobia is likewise reframed. When two teachers are discovered to be in a lesbian relationship, the possibility of their influence on Liza is used as justification to fire them. At the time, Liza is awash in fear and despair at this occurrence. The letters, however, reveal the perspective of a Liza who has become more confident and assured in her sexual identity; she writes, *"I might have been able to help them; I could have said—I wanted to say—that they'd had no influence, that I'd have been gay anyway"* (225–26). On the whole, the novel serves to welcome young LGBTQ readers into a world that is marked by homophobia and misinformation, but also by love and self-respect, making it less of a problem novel and more a novel of celebration.

By the 1990s, the broader culture of the United States saw significant improvements in accepting and celebrating LGBTQ people. Young adult literature in this period began to include LGBTQ characters in novels that were not exclusively "about" the coming-out process. Ellen Wittlinger's *Hard Love*, for instance, is a novel about sexual awakening, navigating emotionally complex relationships, and asserting one's own identity in a world that can feel unwelcoming—all qualities that are present in *Annie on My Mind*. However, *Hard Love* is about a straight teenage boy, John, and a lesbian teenager, Marisol, who form a close friendship. From the start of the novel, Marisol is proudly and unambiguously out of the closet about her sexuality, and it is the ultimately straight John who briefly questions his attractions. In a social world with multiple gay and lesbian characters and almost no visible homophobia, Marisol proves to be more empowered and more self-aware than John, offering a sharp contrast to the confused and tentative Liza of *Annie on My Mind*.

Hard Love assumes several formal devices in order to explore its themes of self-awakening and honest expression, devices that further cast sexual identity as just one among many components of the teenagers' lives. John and Marisol meet through self-publishing zines—small magazines in which they can reveal their private thoughts to audiences of strangers—and excerpts from their zines are included throughout the novel. John, for instance, finds himself unable to talk about his family life with either of his divorced parents, while Marisol says of her accepting and gay-positive parents that she has "to escape from them, of course, as all children have to do, to escape from their understanding, their always tolerant love" (43). Because they connect first through the confessional anonymity of the zines, the two develop a friendship more intimate than any they had previously experienced, which in turn causes John to develop romantic feelings for Marisol. However, this sexual confusion is placed squarely on the shoulders of the straight character, with Marisol maintaining her uncompromising and confident self-identity while John wallows in confusion and shame after attempting to kiss her. Just as *Annie on My Mind* is significant for being written for LGBTQ teens rather than about them, *Hard Love* is one of the earliest examples of an LGBTQ narrative in which characters get to deal with conflicts and emotions unattached to the coming-out process, marking further progress toward novels that are inclusive and affirmative of LGBTQ people for all audiences.

While both of these narratives are powerful stories, significant for their insistence on honest portrayals of LGBTQ youth, it was not until the 2000s that young adult literature began to more regularly include a wider spectrum of the LGBTQ population. Just as the coming-out story and social rejection had dominated the genre

for years, so too had characters with fairly normative identities as gay and lesbian teenagers. *Boy Meets Boy*, by contrast, presents readers with a small California town with almost no homophobia, a place where, as the narrator announces, "there isn't really a gay scene or a straight scene" and "boys who love boys flirt with girls who love girls" (1). It tells the romantic tale of two boys, Paul and Noah, navigating love without the interference of homophobic parents or peers. Just as prominently, however, the plot includes Paul's ex-boyfriend Kyle, who is now dating a woman; Infinite Darlene, the transgender girl who is both homecoming queen and quarterback; Chuck, a popular jock who dates a cisgender girl but loves Infinite Darlene; and a range of characters with shifting desires and identities that do not fit neatly into categories of gay or straight.

As a story centered on positivity but with honest depictions of challenges—there is homophobia one town over, and characters do struggle with confusion over their desires at times—*Boy Meets Boy* resembles *Annie on My Mind*, in that both novels end in confident, blissful love. What has shifted, however, is who gets to experience that love and who will celebrate it with them. *Boy Meets Boy* ends with all the main characters in the woods together, dancing and celebrating the place at which they have all arrived, connected by both their similarities and their differences. It is a version of reality that, in all probability, is more optimistic and more inclusive than can be found in just about any high school in the United States. Yet it sticks close enough to reality to stay believable, further welcoming teenaged readers into the happiness promised "for all of us."

Conclusions

All three of the novels discussed above have earned literary awards as well as popular success, yet all three have also faced regular bannings and censorship challenges. This is sadly often the case when young adult literature depicts LGBTQ characters with honesty and integrity, and is sometimes the case when they are included at all. The genre, however, has not only survived and strengthened over the years but ultimately flourished, with multiple LGBTQ young adult titles published yearly to both popular and critical praise.

Which is not to imply that all LGBTQ literature for young adults is praiseworthy. Like all genres, it is by marked by as many misfires and problematic narratives as successes. Among *Annie on My Mind*'s contemporaries are many novels in which gay and lesbian young adults meet tragic, unhappy ends that are rendered with little literary merit, while *Boy Meets Boy* is a shining example of diverse sexualities and gender identities amid a number of novels that instead push for assimilation and "normal" gay sexualities. Yet there continue to be groundbreaking novels like the ones discussed above, skillfully employing literary techniques and deftly plotted narratives in the service of candid, affirmative portrayals of LGBTQ characters.

At the same time, it is important to remember that novels such as *Boy Meets Boy* do not signal an idealized "end point" for LGBTQ young adult literature. Contemporary understandings of gender and sexuality are constantly in flux, and new generations of young people face prejudices and challenges, as well as opportunities, that would have hardly seemed imaginable to the characters of *Annie on My Mind*. It is likely that new novels will continue to push forward, challenging heterosexism, transphobia, and other oppressive forces while finding new literary methods with which to affirm the identities of LGBTQ youth.

T. Fleischmann, MFA

Further Reading

Campbell, Patty. "The Sand in the Oyster." *Horn Book Magazine* Sept.–Oct. 1993: 568–572. *Literary Reference Center*. Web. 1 Apr. 2015. <http://search.ebscohost.com/login.aspx?direct=true&db=lfh&AN=9312031546&site=ehost-live>.

Cart, Michael, and Christine A. Jenkins. *The Heart Has Its Reasons: Young Adult Literature with Gay/Lesbian/Queer Content, 1969–2004*. Lanham: Scarecrow, 2006. Print.

Wilson, Martin. "Tireless Promoter of Gay-Themed Books for Young Adults." *Lambda Book Report* Mar. 2002: 5. *Literary Reference Center*. Web. 1 Apr. 2015. <http://search.ebscohost.com/login.aspx?direct=true&db=lfh&AN=6413429&site=ehost-live>.

Bibliography

Chuang, Laura, et al. "Out in Society, Invisible on the Shelves: Discussing LIS Literature about LGBTQ Youth." *Feliciter* Oct. 2013: 26–27. *Academic Search Complete*. Web. 1 Apr. 2015. <http://search.ebscohost.com/login.aspx?direct=true&db=a9h&AN=90624337&site=ehost-live>.

Garden, Nancy. *Annie on My Mind*. 1982. New York: Farrar, 2007. Print.

Levithan, David. *Boy Meets Boy*. New York: Knopf, 2003. Print.

Meixner, Emily. "Teacher Agency and Access to LGBTQ Young Adult Literature." *Radical Teacher* 76 (2006): 13–19. *Academic Search Complete*. Web. 1 Apr. 2015. <http://search.ebscohost.com/login.aspx?direct=true&db=a9h&AN=22214296&site=ehost-live>.

Wickens, Corrine M. "Codes, Silences, and Homophobia: Challenging Normative Assumptions about Gender and Sexuality in Contemporary LGBTQ Young Adult Literature." *Children's Literature in Education* 42.2 (2011): 148–64. *Literary Reference Center*. Web. 1 Apr. 2015. <http://search.ebscohost.com/login.aspx?direct=true&db=lfh&AN=60529017&site=lrc-live>.

Wittlinger, Ellen. *Hard Love*. New York: Simon, 1999. Print.

Middle Grade Literature

Titles Discussed
Better Nate Than Ever by Tim Federle
Mockingbird by Kathryn Erskine
The Thing about Luck by Cynthia Kadohata

General Overview
Books written for readers between eight and twelve years of age fall into a somewhat unique genre classification. While children's literature and young adult literature are both well-defined categories, up until the end of the twentieth century, many librarians, educators, and booksellers had a difficult time classifying what is now referred to as "middle-grade" literature, or, less commonly, "younger young adult" literature. While these books are often too advanced to be rightfully considered children's literature, they also largely shy away from the length, literary ambiguity, and mature subject matter that define much young adult literature.

This confusion of genre classification does not mean that middle-grade novels are new. Perennial favorites such as Madeleine L'Engle's *A Wrinkle in Time* (1962),

Louise Fitzhugh's *Harriet the Spy* (1964), and Lois Lowry's *The Giver* (1993) speak to the diversity of successful books that have targeted this age range. They did pose a unique problem, however, in that middle-grade readers often rely on adults—mainly parents, educators, and librarians—to acquire books for them. As the classification of middle-grade literature did not become common in libraries and bookstores until roughly around the turn of the twenty-first century, this made it unnecessarily difficult for young readers to connect with appropriate books for many decades, which in turn resulted in fewer middle-grade novels being published.

This scenario was compounded by the rapidity of the changes that preadolescents and adolescents experience, a fact that also illustrates the importance of understanding middle-grade literature as its own genre. While young adult literature typically features protagonists with developed or developing self-identities who are learning to navigate a complex world, middle-grade literature is more often concerned with the somewhat limited world of the home life and school, with protagonists just beginning to define their self-identities rather than testing how those identities might play out in the broader world. Similarly, middle-grade literature favors lighter more optimistic views of the world; characters might navigate their first crush, for instance, but are unlikely to encounter the complexities of a first sexual relationship. When trauma is present, it is almost always overcome. These distinctions might only last for a few years before middle-grade readers shift their attention to young adult novels, but they are crucial years in the development of literacy and self-identity.

More recent middle-grade books have continued to demonstrate that although there are considerations of appropriateness and literary complexity that must be taken into account when writing for younger readers, such novels are nonetheless able to employ smart literary techniques in confronting a broad range of subject matters. Kathryn Erskine's *Mockingbird* (2010) deals with a school shooting, while Cynthia Kadohata's *The Thing about Luck* (2013) addresses death and poverty, yet both are accessible to and appropriate for middle-grade readers (and both won the National Book Award for Young People's Literature). Similarly, Tim Federle's *Better Nate Than Ever* (2013) achieved critical and popular success with a decidedly lighthearted and optimistic narrative. While middle-grade literature as a genre has a unique set of expectations and boundaries attached to

it, the novels themselves are as diverse as young adult novels in general.

Works

Mockingbird, by Kathryn Erskine, covers some of the bleakest material readers are likely to find in middle-grade literature, although it does so with the same attention to sensitivity and accessibility that defines the genre as a whole. The novel is told in the present tense from the perspective of Caitlin, a fifth-grade girl with Asperger syndrome. Caitlin's brother Devon has recently been killed in a school shooting, and her mother died of cancer two years prior, leaving her father emotionally devastated and distant. In part because of her condition, Caitlin struggles to cope with her losses and the attendant social and family interactions, and she focuses much of her energy on her obsession with dictionaries and black-and-white drawings of birds. With the assistance of a school counselor, Caitlin spends the novel learning to process her feelings and form friendships with others affected by the shooting.

While her withdrawn father, the violent death of the brother, and the social ostracism Caitlin faces are all difficult subject matter for a middle-grade novel, *Mockingbird* portrays Caitlin as an empowered and healing individual rather than a girl disempowered by trauma. In part, this shift in focus is accomplished through the narration style. Caitlin's voice is influenced by her Asperger syndrome, and she renders her world in simple and often blunt sentences, explaining exactly how she sees these tragedies without sentimentality or melodrama. Discussing the fact that she is no longer allowed in her brother's room, for instance, she states, "So I can't go to my hidey-hole in Devon's room anymore and I miss it." Her loss is acknowledged, but it is treated more factually than emotionally—it is the place she hides, not Devon himself, that she mentions missing—which creates some distance for younger readers to process the trauma. Similarly, the book takes place after the immediate losses of mother and brother; combined with the present-tense narration, this places readers firmly in the healing process rather than in the moments of death. As the novel progresses and readers become more familiar with Caitlin's unique voice and perspective, the narrative develops a strong sense of empathy with her, and it becomes easier to understand the world as she experiences it. It is not unrealistic to assume that some younger readers will experience traumas similar to those Caitlin experiences. By presenting the traumas in this arc, from loss rendered at a remove to healing and closure found through other people, the subject matter is portrayed in a way that is both honest and accessible for its target audience while still ensuring a happy ending.

Difficult topics, including death, also permeate Cynthia Kadohata's *The Thing about Luck*, but here they are placed at a much greater distance, allowing the twelve-year-old narrator, Summer, to understand them without the sense of trauma present in *Mockingbird*. Summer's family experiences a year of "bad luck," with Summer almost dying of malaria, her parents returning to Japan to care for elderly relatives, and her grandparents taking her and her socially stunted younger brother to help them work the wheat harvest in order to make ends meet, as they are in danger of losing their home. While working the harvest, Summer increasingly takes on adult responsibilities, especially as her grandparents face their own health challenges that make physical labor impossible. Tied in with this narrative are Summer's first crush on a young boy and obsessions with mosquitoes and the harvesting process. When her grandfather ultimately finds himself unable to work, Summer uses her acquired knowledge to sneak out in the evening and drive the combine herself, effectively saving the family from losing their home.

In large part, the difficulties Summer faces are potential tragedies that she and her family manage to avoid, with the writing style further emphasizing the distance between her happy life and the dangers of the adult world. Her family struggles financially and risks losing their house, but they manage to earn enough through the harvest to avoid defaulting on their mortgage. Likewise, although malaria almost takes Summer's life before the novel begins, she lives without suffering any long-term effects. Summer displaces her engagement with these disasters, becoming obsessed with mosquitoes and with the wheat-harvesting process rather than with death and bankruptcy. She explains this displacement to the reader (ensuring that the text does not become too ambiguous in its meaning), saying of the mosquitoes, "I mean, if I saw one on my arm, I wouldn't hesitate to smash it or even run screaming down the highway. They terrified me. But still, we were inseparable." Her tone when discussing her near death from malaria is casual, even humorous. At the same time, she constantly writes about mosquitoes in her journal, allowing her to obsess over death without confronting the reality of it directly. These obsessions are revealed to have inherent worth when Summer operates

the combine and secretly saves her family, transforming the risk of bankruptcy into a moment of self-empowerment. While a young adult novel might require Summer to fully mature and face not only the loss of the family home and the impending deaths of her grandparents but also her own eventual death, in a middle-grade novel she only begins to explore these topics. There is still room for levity and optimism here, and it is a levity that Summer is learning to apply toward more difficult, more mature issues in her life.

Compared to Summer and Caitlin, the titular protagonist of Tim Federle's *Better Nate Than Ever* faces relatively mild challenges. Nate's friends and family tease him for his weight, his acne, his height, his effeminate qualities, and especially his obsession with musical theater. In the face of this teasing, however, Nate's sense of self-confidence begins to take shape, bolstered by his quick wit. When Nate learns that there is an open call in New York City for a musical based on the movie *E. T. the Extra-Terrestrial* (1982), he decides to run away from his Pennsylvania home for the afternoon and audition. Nate fumbles in navigating his adventure, with all the other young actors clearly more trained and professional than he is, and he must constantly fend off his furious parents at home. His unique charm, however, captures the attention of the casting team, and he gets pulled in for multiple callbacks. He also manages to connect with a long-lost aunt, and by the end of the novel, he has reunited his aunt and his mother and is waiting anxiously to find out if he has a part in a Broadway play.

While the difficulty Nate faces as a social outcast will be familiar to many middle-grade readers, his determination and sarcastic sense of humor, rendered through the first-person narration, allow him to transcend both his home life and school life. When some bullies tell him that he cannot leave the gym until he makes three three-point basketball shots in a row, he responds by asking if he can make "one nine-pointer and be done with it." He still faces bullying, but rather than experiencing it as deeply traumatic, as some middle-grade students will, his humor and narrative voice let readers know that he will be okay. These same skills apply in New York; when Nate finds himself cold and wandering the streets alone, he does not fall into physical danger; instead, he finds a giant coat on the street and muses, "If I get sent back to General Thomas Junior High, I should just wear this all day long: a padded bruise protector." In this way, young readers are able to experience the physical and social risks that Nate faces while remaining in the safe bubble of his charmingly defiant narrative. Importantly, the sarcastic nature of Nate's defiance also allows space for his own uncertainties and wounds. Regarding his sexuality, he states, "I am undecided. I am a freshman at the College of Sexuality and I have undecided my major." This is a uniquely middle-grade position to assume; while Nate is not ready to explicitly engage with any sexual identity, he still faces teasing because of his perceived homosexuality—presaging some challenges he might face in coming years—but is able to delay addressing the topic while simultaneously expressing defiance against the teasing through his humorous narrative voice.

Protagonists in middle-grade novels occupy a unique space. While their worlds are still largely defined by the social space of the school and the private space of home life, their experiences are also being shaped in a new way by the adult, outside world. All of these novels allow their main characters to encounter the complexity of that outside world while maintaining an important distance. Nate's sarcasm, Summer's obsessions, and Caitlin's emotional remove all serve them well in this regard. Just as important, they serve the middle-grade reader, providing a comfortable safety even as mature or even hostile forces begin to influence their lives.

Conclusions

Like young adult literature in general, middle-grade literature in the twenty-first century has increasingly incorporated more mature themes and language, with readers in their target demographic prepared for subject matter that would have seemed out of place in the genre in previous decades. Publishing companies and educational organizations have turned their attention to understanding the unique properties and opportunities of the middle-grade novel, a trend driven in part by the reality that young people between the ages of eight and twelve are emerging as a demographic that spends considerable amounts of money on entertainment.

These factors have all resulted in an upswing of high-quality middle-grade literature, with authors crafting works that lack the heightened literary ambiguity of young adult novels (which is often too difficult for middle-grade readers to process) but still embrace the challenges and complexities of middle-grade life in the twenty-first century. Some critics do take issue with

the influence of realistic fiction on the middle-grade genre, arguing that the social realities finding their way into these books might be too much for their intended readers and preferring the style of twentieth-century literature aimed at this age group, in which topics such as school shootings would have been inappropriate. These critics argue that although readers might be more likely to buy such novels, the maturing narratives rob them of their childhood innocence and optimism prematurely.

In contrast, those who praise these new, realistic novels point to the strength and success of the main characters. Middle-grade students, they argue, are encountering the adult world at younger ages than ever before, especially with ever-increasing access to social media and other communication technology. These critics believe that the solution is not to shield the readers from the world they are entering but rather to provide them with characters who not only survive in that world but thrive in it. The best of the middle-grade novels do just that, with the protagonists relying on the same optimism that has always characterized the genre in order to navigate their challenges, emerging by novel's end as characters who have gained confidence without having to sacrifice the joy of their youth.

T. Fleischmann, MFA

Further Reading

Birdsall, Jeanne. "Middle Grade Saved My Life." *Horn Book Magazine* May–June 2013: 27–30. *Literary Reference Center*. Web. 14 May 2015. <http://search.ebscohost.com/login.aspx?direct=true&db=lfh&AN=87024779&site=ehost-live>.

Dressel, Janice Hartwick. "Personal Response and Social Responsibility: Responses of Middle School Students to Multicultural Literature." *Reading Teacher* 58.8 (2005): 750–64. *Literary Reference Center*. Web. 14 May 2015. <http://search.ebscohost.com/login.aspx?direct=true&db=lfh&AN=16830263&site=ehost-live>.

Silvey, Anita, ed. *The Essential Guide to Children's Books and Their Creators*. New York: Houghton, 2002. Print.

Bibliography

Knickerbocker, Joan L., and James A. Rycik. "Reexamining Literature Study in the Middle Grades: A

Critical Response Framework." *American Secondary Education* 34.3 (2006): 43–56. *Academic Search Premier*. Web. 14 May 2015. <http://search.ebscohost.com/login.aspx?direct=true&db=aph&AN=22097244&site=ehost-live>.

Poray Goddu, Krystyna. "Good-Luck Charms." Rev. of *The Favorite Daughter*, by Allen Say, and *The Thing about Luck*, by Cynthia Kadohata. *New York Times*. New York Times, 14 June 2013. Web. 14 May 2015. <http://www.nytimes.com/2013/06/16/books/review/the-favorite-daughter-and-the-thing-about-luck.html>.

Rosen, Judith. "Middle Grade and YA: Where to Draw the Line?" *Publishers Weekly* 21 July 2014: 24–25. *Literary Reference Center*. Web. 14 May 2015. <http://search.ebscohost.com/login.aspx?direct=true&db=lfh&AN=97129996&site=ehost-live>.

Mystery and Thriller

Titles Discussed

The Body of Christopher Creed by Carol Plum-Ucci
Jellicoe Road by Melina Marchetta
Down the Rabbit Hole by Peter Abrahams
Paper Towns by John Green

Genre Overview

Crime, the basis for mysteries and thrillers, is as old as civilization. In the 3,500-year-old biblical book of Genesis depicts Cain's murder of his brother Abel. Likewise, the ancient *Epic of Gilgamesh* pits the titular hero against various natural and supernatural forces in one of the world's oldest thrillers.

Since those beginnings, criminals and people who write about the detection and solution of crimes have become more sophisticated. However, the primary motivations for committing crimes, especially murder, have remained consistent: greed, passion, jealousy, revenge, or insanity.

In more recent times, Edgar Allan Poe is generally credited as creator of the first modern amateur detective in fiction, C. Auguste Dupin, in "The Murders in the Rue Morgue" (1841). The genre was greatly advanced with the introduction in 1887 of Sir Arthur Conan Doyle's deductive detective Sherlock Holmes. In the mid-1920s, Dashiell Hammett (Sam Spade) and others invented hard-boiled professional private investigators. At the same time, Agatha Christie established the talented amateur female sleuth, Miss Marple. Marcia Muller created the first fictional female professional private detective, Sharon McCone, in the 1970s.

Since the late twentieth century, mysteries have been classified according to tone or focus under various subgenres: cozies, amateur sleuth, private investigator, police procedural, romantic suspense, legal, historical, noir. Thrillers are similarly categorized as psychological, crime, spy, erotic, or paranormal.

Mysteries and thrillers meet at a common element: suspense, which plays upon the reader's curiosity about what will happen next. A mystery generally involves the solution to a crime already committed, whereas a thriller generally involves prevention of a crime yet to happen. In mysteries, the criminal is usually unknown at the beginning; in thrillers, the antagonist is frequently revealed early. Mysteries often unfold in leisurely fashion, thrillers typically move at breakneck speed, and both ratchet up tension as the conclusion approaches.

Mysteries specifically aimed at young adults have been popular for more than a century, thanks to the late-nineteenth-century rise of public education and the spread of literacy. Book packager Edward L. Stratemeyer took advantage of this trend by introducing several long-running series featuring teens involved in crime-solving. Most popular were amateur sleuths the Bobbsey Twins (1904), the Hardy Boys (1927), and Nancy Drew (1930).

Contemporary young adult mysteries, while drawing upon tradition, are more realistic than their predecessors in language and subject matter. In the twenty-first century, young adult mysteries, employing modern innovations like smartphones, computers, and social media, focus upon personal aspects of the adolescent experience—concerns about identity, relationships, family issues, substance abuse, bullying, or suicide—while telling the story. Because of the youth of the protagonist, the most plausible subgenre is still amateur sleuth. The novels *The Body of Christopher Creed* (2000), *Jellicoe Road* (2008; previously published in Australia as *On the Jellicoe Road*, 2006), *Down the Rabbit Hole* (2005), and *Paper Towns* (2008) illustrate the different ways authors develop unique stories from a similar plot starting point: a young person attempting to solve a conundrum.

Works

Carol Plum-Ucci's Printz Award–winning *The Body of Christopher Creed* presents the amateur sleuth in a frame story, with short opening and conclusion bracketing a long flashback. Narrator Victor "Torey" Adams, completing his high school senior year in a new town, recalls the previous year, when he lived in Steepleton, New Jersey, was popular, and had a girlfriend, a garage band, and a relatively stable life. Then he lost everything.

The catalyst was Torey's obnoxious, universally despised classmate Christopher "Chris" Creed, who suddenly vanishes after sending an e-mail to the school principal hinting that he might commit suicide. Torey, who had been cruel to Creed, feels guilty about his possible role in the disappearance and begins gathering clues to the whereabouts of Creed, or his body. A bandmate hacks a computer to retrieve Creed's note, which leads to further evidence. Torey forms an alliance with Ali McDermott, a girl with a bad reputation. She is dating petty criminal Bo Richardson, a "boon"—a student from a poor, rural environment—who is more responsible than he appears and who contributes special skills to the search. The unlikely trio uncovers clues that not only suggest what happened to Creed, but also tie to an earlier disappearance.

The amateur investigation reveals a multitude of secrets beneath Steepleton's placid exterior. The town police chief is having an affair. Creed's supposedly upstanding parents are exposed as delusional and vindictive. Individuals in Torey's circle of friends demonstrate by their actions they are shallow and unfeeling. Christopher Creed is shown to have been sexually active. The widely denigrated boons prove to have more honor than the townspeople.

In the denouement, Torey simultaneously solves one riddle and experiences a natural phenomenon—"immaculate decomposition"—that traumatizes him and drives him to a new location, still obsessing about Creed, who leaves tantalizing clues that suggest he is still alive.

Author Plum-Ucci, who wrote a sequel in 2011, weaves religiously symbolic names and images throughout the novel. Creed ultimately becomes a Christlike figure sacrificed for the good of an unworthy town riddled with hypocrisy.

Another Printz-winner, *Jellicoe Road*, takes a different approach to the amateur sleuth motif. Teenage protagonist-narrator Taylor Markham, abandoned by her drug-abusing mother and housed at an orphanage school in the rural Australian town of Jellicoe, is haunted by dreams and memories. Nearby, thirty-something Hannah Schroeder, her guardian, is writing a novel that she allows Taylor to read.

Taylor and the school are girding for the annual territory wars, a contest to control local landmarks. The battle is waged among three groups: Houses, orphanage-school students who are under leaders like Taylor; Townies, local students at a neighboring school who are led by Chaz Santangelo; and Cadets, visiting military school members under the command of the Brigadier. The conflict is complicated by shifting loyalties: Taylor is infatuated with Cadet Jonah Griggs, and Raffaela, who attends Taylor's school, is a Townie. A subplot involving a serial child killer operating in the area serves as a red herring, heightening suspense.

Taylor acts as reluctant investigator, initially attempting to resolve personal issues. Her activities are punctuated with passages gleaned from Hannah's manuscript, which Taylor pieces together. She eventually comes to an understanding that permeates the novel thematically: past events influence the present and future in unexpected ways.

Taylor's history is linked to a tragedy that happened two decades earlier: a car crash orphaned four children at Jellicoe who, drawn together by circumstance, invented the territory wars. She learns the identity of the orphans. Among them were Hannah and Taylor's mother, Tate. Hannah's brother, Webb, later accidentally killed, impregnated Tate.

The revelations yield several benefits. The relationships Taylor helps forge (including her own with Cadet Jonah) defuse the territory wars. Hannah—who turns out to be Taylor's aunt and no longer has to hide her love for the Brigadier, her childhood friend Cadet Jude Scanlon—helps Taylor realize the value of family, allowing her to reconcile with her mother.

Author Melina Marchetta, a long-time teacher, uses a school setting and realistically placed contemporary social references to illuminate the behavior of young adults and to explore fluid personal relationships, as she also did in *Looking for Alibrandi* (1992) and *Saving Francesca* (2003).

Mystery and thriller author Peter Abrahams's *Down the Rabbit Hole* is the first of three entries to date in the Echo Falls mystery series, his first series for young adults. Like *The Body of Christopher Creed* and *Jellicoe Road*, it features an amateur sleuth: thirteen-year-old protagonist Ingrid Levin-Hill, who eagerly embraces her role as detective. Told in third-person limited point of view following

Ingrid's perspective, the plot revolves around her incidental encounter with local character, Katherine Eve Kovac, known as Cracked-Up Katie, who is subsequently murdered. Ingrid breaks into Katie's house in search of clues, nearly running into an intruder wearing paint-spattered sneakers. She also breaks into the neighboring apartment of two street people suspected of the crime, finds evidence they are innocent, and decides she will solve the murder.

Ingrid cultivates classmate Joey Strade and his father, police chief Gilbert L. Strade, as conduits to inside information. Ingrid and Chief Strade, both Sherlock Holmes fans, quote from the Doyle canon: "There is nothing more deceptive than an obvious fact." Through the chief, Ingrid learns Katie was once engaged to wealthy Phillip Prescott, who left town years before. From the local historian, Ingrid learns Prescott's parents died in a boating accident and that Prescott squandered his inheritance.

A talented thespian, Ingrid auditions for a production of *Alice in Wonderland* staged at Prescott Hall, now undergoing major renovation. Ingrid wins the title role. Among the cast is a stranger called Vincent Dunn. The play's director is seriously injured in a piano-moving accident, and Vincent, an experienced actor, takes over production.

Ingrid, looking for clues, discovers Vincent, in paint-spattered sneakers, digging up a human skull in the basement of Prescott Hall. Vincent, actually an obscure actor, murdered and buried Phillip Prescott long ago. Fearing discovery during the hall's renovation, he has returned to clean up his crime. He chases Ingrid, and they fall into the river. The villain dies going over Echo Falls, while Chief Strade arrives in a police boat to rescue Ingrid.

Down the Rabbit Hole contains many references to typical teenage concerns: self-image, budding romance, and other issues she discusses with friends via instant messaging. The novel is full of allusions to Sherlock Holmes, including Chief Gilbert L. Strade, who echoes Doyle's Inspector Lestrade, and Ingrid's dog, Nigel, who is named for Nigel Bruce, the actor who played Dr. Watson in many Sherlock Holmes movies.

Edgar Award–winning *Paper Towns* begins with a profound shared experience. As children, playmates Margo Roth Spiegelman and Quentin "Q" Jacobsen stumble across the body of a man who committed suicide. By the time they are high school seniors ready to graduate, the next-door neighbors in Orlando, Florida, have followed divergent paths. Attractive, popular Margo has a boyfriend. Studious Quentin, still a virgin, hangs out with nerds Ben Starling and Marcus "Radar" Lincoln, and worships Margo from afar.

Quentin is astonished when late one night Margo shows up and convinces him to accompany her. Her boyfriend has been sleeping with her best friend, and Margo wants revenge. Together, they carry out a series of pranks involving spray-painted graffiti, the planting of rotting catfish, the application of Vaseline to doorknobs, and other stunts. The night is capped by a visit to a building where they overlook the city. Margo flirts with Quentin, telling him, "Here's a tip: you're cute when you're confident." She calls Orlando a phony "paper town," a reference that takes on additional significance as the novel unfolds.

The next day Margo has vanished. Following a visit from a police detective familiar with Margo's history (she has run away before, always leaving clues), Quentin feels obligated to find her. He recruits friends Ben and Radar in the search, and Margo's best friend, Lacey Pemberton, joins them in the quest.

The amateur detectives uncover and connect a multitude of potential clues—a poster of Woody Guthrie, a song, Walt Whitman's poetry, a map—and take many wrong turns before finding a deserted mini-mall where Margo hid out. They come to a possible solution: Margo may be at Agloe, New York, a paper town: a cartographic device in which a fictional location is inserted into a map as a means to detect plagiarizing map-makers.

The four sleuths subsequently drive nonstop north and find Margo in a deserted barn, all of Agloe that ever existed. Margo had simply fled her stifling environment and intends to go to New York City. She admits she had a crush on Quentin, but he always seemed two-dimensional until he agreed to participate in the prank night. Their friendship renewed, Q and Margo part company but promise to keep in touch.

Conclusions

According to a 2014 Pew Research Center study, young adults have a healthy interest in reading for entertainment. Teens absorb written stimulation via the printed page or on screens through more modern methods (smartphones, tablets, laptops, or e-readers), which, thanks to integral technology, are beginning to provide feedback about individual reading habits. A 2015 *Publishers Weekly* report suggests that when it comes to fiction, the reading preferences of young adults standing on the threshold of adulthood are similar to those who have already made that passage. With 2014 book sales exceeding 34 million units (a slight slump from the previous year, due largely to the e-book's capture of a significant market share of publishing), adult readers kept mystery/detective (more than 14 million units) and related suspense/thriller (more than 20 million units) as highly popular collective genres.

There is good evidence that the strength of the mystery/thriller genre will continue. Young adults, wearying of the plethora of paranormal, dystopian, and apocalyptic series (Hunger Games, Divergent, Harry Potter, Twilight, Maze Runner, and others) that came into vogue in the early years of the twenty-first century, will probably opt to read more realistic fiction. This trend should add to the already dominant romantic suspense subgenre as young adults approach the age when lasting relationships form. Another factor helping to solidify the mystery/thriller genre is the tendency among contemporary authors to delve into personal issues (self-image and sexual identity, family matters like coping with infidelity or divorce, thoughts of suicide, or incipient mental illness) with genuine emotion in the course of presenting an intriguing puzzle to solve. Though young adult mysteries and thrillers are defined by their teenaged protagonists, many deal imaginatively with grown-up issues as explored by fully rounded characters in convoluted plots layered with symbolic meaning and can thus be enjoyed equally by youngsters and adults.

Such qualities are not, however, universally appreciated. As noted in an American Library Association report, protective parents continually challenge individual works on the basis of sexual content, drug use, violence, offensive language, unsuitability for the age group, perceived promotion of homosexuality, antireligious philosophy, or other matters. Parental objections have resulted in the banning of works by some of the world's best known writers, from Shakespeare, Mark Twain, and George Bernard Shaw to Ernest Hemingway, Boris Pasternak, and John Steinbeck. In the twenty-first century, banned

works have included titles by authors John Green and Carol Plum-Ucci, who nonetheless continue to thrive.

Jack Ewing

Further Reading

"Frequently Challenged Books of the 21st Century."*American Library Association*. Amer. Lib. Assn. 2015. Web. 23 Mar. 2015. <http://www.ala.org/bbooks/frequentlychallengedbooks/top10>.

Milliot, Jim. "The Hottest (and Coldest) Book Categories of 2014. *Publishers Weekly*. PWxyz, 23 Jan. 2015. Web. 23 Mar. 2015. <http://www.publishersweekly.com/pw/by-topic/industry-news/bookselling/article/65387-the-hot-and-cold-categories-of-2014.html>.

Bibliography

Alter, Alexandra. "Your E-Book Is Reading You." *Wall Street Journal*. Dow Jones, 19 July 2012. Web. 24 Mar. 2015. <http://www.wsj.com/articles/SB10001424052702304870304577490950051438304>.

Corbett, Sue. "New Trends in YA: The Agents' Perspective." *Publishers Weekly*. PWxyz, 27 Sept. 2013. Web. 24 Mar. 2015. <http://www.publishersweekly.com/pw/by-topic/childrens/childrens-industry-news/article/59297-new-trends-in-ya-the-agents-perspective.html>.

Wolitzer, Meg. "Look Homeward, Reader." *New York Times*. New York Times, 17 Oct. 2014. Web. 24 Mar. 2015. <http://www.nytimes.com/2014/10/19/fashion/a-not-so-young-audience-for-young adult-books.html?_r=0>.

Zickuhr, Kathryn, and Lee Rainie. "Younger Americans' Reading Habits and Technology Use." *Pew Research Center Internet & Tech*. Pew Research Center, 10 Sept. 2014. Web. 24 Mar. 2015. <http://www.pewinternet.org/2014/09/10/younger-americans-reading-habits-and-technology-use>.

Mythology

Titles Discussed

Percy Jackson and the Olympians series by Rick Riordan
Psyche in a Dress by Francesca Lia Block
Starcrossed by Josephine Angelini

Genre Overview

Variations of mythological stories have long been shared in book form for readers of all ages. Historically, mythology was used to explain mysteries such as natural phenomena and the motivations for human behavior. Such explanatory stories, sometimes called *pourquoi* stories (after the French word for "why"), are a common form of mythology that appeals to children who question why things happen. Understanding the desire to know, children's authors have incorporated various cultural traditions to explain simple natural actions, such as why mosquitoes buzz—a question "answered" by the classic 1975 children's book *Why Mosquitoes Buzz in People's Ears*, by Verna Aardema, who adapted the story from a West African legend.

For more mature readers, Greek and Roman mythology is a traditional part of many middle school curricula. Seventh- and eighth-grade students learn about Zeus and Hera (or Jupiter and Juno) as well as their sons and daughters, brothers and sisters, lovers and rivals. The stories are just exciting, romantic, or twisted enough to capture the attention of an audience of young teenagers. Themes of revenge, power, good versus evil, and life and death hold universal appeal, as do action-packed adventures filled with strange creatures, mysterious journeys, interfering gods, and strong emotions. Many contemporary writers find inspiration in such tales for their own imaginative stories, crafting fresh, original takes on age-old characters, tropes, and themes.

Mythological stories come in many forms, including heroic tales, epic poems, folklore, and legends. Heroic tales are stories that focus on the bravery of a particular character as he or she goes on an adventure. Epic poems are long narrative poems that generally follow an archetypal hero through a series of adventures; well-known examples include the Old English epic *Beowulf*, Homer's *Iliad* and *Odyssey*, and the Akkadian *Epic of Gilgamesh*. Folklore encompasses folktales, fairy tales, tall tales, and fables, while legends are historical narratives that, though partly or wholly fictional, possess some degree of verisimilitude. The English tales of King Arthur and Robin Hood are examples of legends.

Young adult authors in the twentieth and twenty-first centuries have drawn inspiration from the mythologies of many different cultures. Susan Cooper delved into Celtic myth and Arthurian legend for her series The Dark Is Rising (1965–77). Cindy Pon's *Silver Phoenix* (2009) is rooted in Chinese legend and myth, while Jay Kristoff's *Stormdancer* pulls from Japanese mythology and feudal tales. Egyptian mythology features heavily in Rick Riordan's Kane Chronicles trilogy (2010–12) and Kiersten White's *The Chaos of Stars* (2013). Ingrid Paulson's *Valkyrie Rising* (2012) and Wendy Delsol's Stork Trilogy (2010–12) are based on Norse mythology.

Greek and Roman tales are the most common fodder for modern novels based in mythology. The Percy Jackson and the Olympians series (2005–9), by Rick Riordan; *Psyche in a Dress* (2006), by Francesca Lia Block; and *Starcrossed* (2011), by Josephine Angelini, are all contemporary works that incorporate some aspects of Greek mythology.

Works

Rick Riordan's Percy Jackson and the Olympians series consists of five books—*The Lightning Thief* (2005), *The Sea of Monsters* (2006), *The Titan's Curse* (2007), *The Battle of the Labyrinth* (2008), and *The Last Olympian* (2009)—that follow the adventures of Percy Jackson, the modern-day adolescent son of the Greek god Poseidon. In addition to the series' more obvious use of Greek mythology, each individual book, as well as the series as a whole, follows the template of the hero's journey as described by Joseph Campbell in *The Hero with a Thousand Faces* (1949), his seminal work on mythology. According to Campbell, the hero's journey, also called the "monomyth," consists of seventeen distinct steps that describe a circular path. These steps are divided into three main stages: the departure, during which the hero is called to action and sets off on a journey; the initiation, during which the hero undergoes a number of trials and experiences before achieving the goal of the quest; and the return, during which the hero returns to his or her everyday life, wiser and irrevocably transformed. Along the way, the hero will meet and interact with a number of helpers and monsters.

Percy's journey in the book follows this same path. First, Percy begins the series as an unexpected hero with uncommon powers he knows nothing about. This is not unusual; as evidenced by other mythological figures such as Theseus, Jason, and Odysseus, classical heroes are usually a bit different from the people around them and do not fit in well. This is often a result of the hero's divine parentage, as it is in Percy's case. Percy's ADHD is one indicator that he is different, and his interactions with the other children on his field trip show how poorly he fits into the world in which he lives. Also during this trip, he encounters the world of fantasy creatures, and his adventure begins. The adventure really takes off as

Percy learns that he is the son of Poseidon and so must straddle two worlds: the ordinary world, where he lives with his mother and goes to school, and the world where Greek mythology comes to life. His first journey begins when he is sent to Camp Half-Blood to develop this new part of his life. While there, Percy realizes that his friend Grover is actually a satyr (which explains a lot about the way he walks); makes new friends, including Annabeth Chase, a daughter of Athena; and finds a mentor in Chiron, a centaur who had been posing as Percy's Latin teacher, Mr. Brunner. These characters all play a role in helping Percy understand his first quest: to find out who stole Zeus's lightning bolt and thus prevent a war on Olympus. Ultimately, Percy is able to defeat his true enemy, regain the lightning bolt, and return it to Olympus, thus (at least temporarily) saving the Greek gods from a war for power. He repeats the pattern four more times as he experiences new adventures in the subsequent books of the series.

The connection to the characters of mythology is clear in the stories. Once Percy arrives at Camp Half-Blood, readers learn that "Percy" is in fact a nickname, not for Percival, but for Perseus. In Greek mythology, Perseus was the son of Zeus and the human woman Danaë, best known for killing Medusa with the help of the gods Athena and Hermes. The connection between Percy and Perseus is further reinforced when Percy becomes friends with Athena's daughter Annabeth and Hermes's son Luke, then is made explicit when Percy kills Medusa. The main change is that Riordan has made to Perseus's story is that Percy is the son of Poseidon rather than Zeus. As Athena's daughter, Annabeth is understandably intelligent and brave, and her strategic command further reflects her mother's influence. Luke Castellan is the son of Hermes; though Hermes is known for being a protector in many version of the Greek myths in which he appears, he is also considered a trickster. It is in the role of the trickster that Riordan casts Luke, who is eventually revealed to be the titular lightning thief of the first novel. His theft of Zeus's lightning bolt sets Olympus up for a war for supremacy between Zeus and the Titan Kronos, and the battle between the Olympic gods and the Titans becomes central to the other stories in the series.

Josephine Angelini's novel *Starcrossed*, the first in a trilogy of the same name, also follows a familiar pattern based on mythological tales. Angelini's story is based on the doomed love story of Helen of Troy. According to myth, Helen's legendary beauty attracted a slew of suitors, including the Spartan king Menelaus, who defeated her other suitors in competition and won her as his wife. Though Helen married Menelaus, she was later enchanted by the god Aphrodite to fall in love with Paris, a prince of Troy. Paris's perceived kidnapping of her led to the outbreak of the Trojan War, the subject of Homer's epic poem the *Iliad*. Helen was never able to really experience the depth of emotion brought on by true love; every time her life seemed to be working out, a new obstacle was thrown in her path. She was doomed to a star-crossed love, one that would be constantly hindered by forces she could not control.

Angelini's novel brings a variation of this doomed love story to contemporary times. The novel stars Helen Hamilton, a sixteen-year-old girl living on Nantucket Island with her father. The teenager's beauty, like that of the legendary Helen, captures the attention of all who see her. When a new family moves to the island, Helen struggles with strong negative feelings about Lucas Delos, one of the sons. Eventually, the teens realize they are meant to be together, but obstacle after obstacle is placed in their paths. The play on the mythological story from the *Iliad* becomes clear as the characters are identified as demigods, children of a mortal and a god, and as the Furies and the Fates begin interfering in their love story. The basic premise suggests that a love affair between Lucas and Helen will result in a repetition of the Trojan War. Their desire to break the bonds of fate brings the story solidly into the present day and creates a strong appeal for a contemporary audience.

As in Riordan's novels, the inclusion of characters based on Greek mythology stands out clearly in this novel. Angelini also uses specific names from myth, Helen of course being the most obvious. Characters named Hector, Ariadne, and Cassandra further connect the story to its mythological origins.

Psyche in a Dress, by Francesca Lia Block, takes the connection to Greek mythology in a different direction. Written in verse to mimic the epic-poem format, this story breaks away from the familiar patterns of the hero's journey or romantic tales of doomed love. Also unlike Riordan and Angelini, Block does not shy away from the graphic content of the original myths. Though the existence of demigods in Riordan's and Angelini's novels presupposes sexual relationships between gods and humans, the implication is the extent of their depiction. Block, in contrast, clearly feels that the graphic nature of myth is a necessary part of the formula. From the start, violent images are not hidden, as evidenced by the second stanza, when Psyche says, "My father had me mutilated twice / He had my mother and sisters murdered more than once." In the next two stanzas, Psyche speaks frankly of her sexuality and how it is exploited by her film-director father:

> *They say he does things with me*
> *to work through issues he had with my mother*
> *I look just like her in the early films but*
> *now she is gone*
>
> *In the first film I had to take off my top*
> *I stood there, shivering*
> *with my hands covering my breasts*
> *as the cameras were rolling*
> *A million caterpillars crawled over my bones*
> *and my stomach was filled with the wings of dying*
> *   moths*
> *But I knew what I had to do*

Like Riordan and Angelini, Block uses a specific myth as the basis of her story but twists the details to suit her own purposes. In the first Percy Jackson novel, *The Lightning Thief*, there is a loose sense of Perseus's battle with Medusa, and *Starcrossed* is a modern-day retelling of the Trojan War. Similarly, *Psyche in a Dress* reproduces the story of Psyche and Eros. However, while the mythological Psyche was fully human, Block's modern-day version is the daughter of Zeus. Aphrodite plays a role in the novel as Zeus's jealous lover, echoing the goddess's envy of Psyche's beauty in the original story. Eros is Psyche's lover in the myth, as he is in the novel; in both versions, he is also Aphrodite's son. The mythological Eros is better known in modern Western culture by his Roman name, Cupid.

Whether contemporary young adult authors adopt their characters, plots, and formulas straight from mythology or fashion new stories based on the popularity of these traditional tales, young adult readers continue to enjoy reading these old conventions in a new light.

Conclusions

As long as people enjoy exciting stories, emotional characterization, and universally recognized themes, mythology will remain a popular inspiration for young adult literature, aided by film and television adaptations of mythological novels. The fact that novels based on mythology cross genre boundaries almost by definition further advances the genre's potential for continued growth.

Though scientific discoveries have lessened humanity's desire for mythological explanations of how the world has evolved, the need for common connections persists, and mythological stories, characters, and themes help fulfill this need. Ultimately, mythology showcases how far humans can go, how much they can achieve, and how they relate to each other and the world around them. These universal issues do not change regardless of how many questions are answered by science, so the appeal of literature that illustrates these ideas will remain.

Swiss psychiatrist Carl Jung's idea of a collective unconscious suggests that all humans base their knowledge and actions on a shared a set of ideas. Mythology plays a major part in this concept, and it continues to be studied in educational institutions around the world. Many university programs in specific literatures, comparative literature, world religions, and even psychology encourage the continued study of mythology at all levels. Whether young adults have read the original mythological versions or the contemporary novels based on those versions, their awareness of these stories will ensure the continued attractiveness of such programs. Purists may not like the twisting of the original myths, but teachers of young people will appreciate how their appeal encourages interest in reading as well as in ancient and historical cultures.

Theresa L. Stowell, PhD

Further Reading

Diessner, Rhett, and Kayla Burke. "The Beauty of the Psyche and Eros Myth: Integrating Aesthetics into Introduction to Psychology." *Journal of Aesthetic Education* 45.4 (2011): 97–108. *Philosopher's Index.* Web. 4 June 2015. <https://search.ebscohost.com/login.aspx?direct=true&db=edspmu&AN=edspmu.S1543780911400060&site=eds-live>.

Helbig, Alethea K., and Agnes Regan Perkins. *Myths and Hero Tales: A Cross-Cultural Guide to Literature for Children and Young Adults.* Westport: Greenwood, 1997. *eBook Collection (EBSCOhost).* Web. 14 July 2015. <https://search.ebscohost.com/login.as

px?direct=true&db=nlebk&AN=77748&site=eds-live>.

Roisman, Hanna M. "Helen and the Power of Erotic Love: From Homeric Contemplation to Hollywood Fantasy." *College Literature* 35.4 (2008): 127–50. *Literary Reference Center*. Web. 4 June 2015. <http://search.ebscohost.com/login.aspx?direct=true&db=lfh&AN=34632981&site=lrc-live>.

Bibliography

Block, Francesca Lia. *Psyche in a Dress*. 2006. New York: Harper, 2008. Print.

Campbell, Joseph. *The Hero with a Thousand Faces*. 3rd ed. Novato: New World, 2008. Print.

"An Epic Chart of 162 Young Adult Retellings." *Epic Reads*. Harper, 26 Feb. 2014. Web. 4 June 2015. <http://www.epicreads.com/blog/an-epic-chart-of-162-young adult-retellings/>.

Galda, Lee, et al. *Literature and the Child*. 8th ed. Belmont: Wadsworth, 2014. Print.

Nonfiction

Titles Discussed

Charles and Emma: The Darwins' Leap of Faith by Deborah Heiligman
Steve Jobs: The Man who Thought Different by Karen Blumenthal
Bomb: The Race to Build—and Steal—the World's Most Dangerous Weapon by Steve Sheinkin
The Notorious Benedict Arnold: A True Story of Adventure, Heroism, & Treachery by Steve Sheinkin

Genre Overview

In their 1992 article, "Young adult Nonfiction: Meeting the Needs and Curiosities of Today's Youth," education and writing professor John H. Bushman and high school English teacher Kay Parks Bushman stated that young adult nonfiction is "one of the fastest growing areas within young adult literature" (74). The authors also suggest a list of titles that will help young adults to "explore issues relevant to their own lives and to satisfy their curiosity" (74). This list includes books on dealing with anxiety, depression, and AIDS, as well as books on psychology and biology. While there is a range of subjects, none of the books seem geared toward entertaining the reader. Rather, they are books with serious subjects that are written for young adults. For example, *Don't Be S.A.D.: A Teenage Guide to Handling Stress, Anxiety, and Depression* (1992) by Susan Newman discusses several age-appropriate, real-life scenarios and offers several suggestions for dealing appropriately with each "problem." Another book, *Teenage Fathers* (1992) by Karen Gravelle and Leslie Peterson, was written to provide help and information for young fathers since there was already a large market of information and resources for teenage mothers.

As a genre, young adult nonfiction has changed considerably since 1992. Books within the genre have become more interesting and are written to not only inform and educate but to entertain as well. The increasing popularity of crossover novels (young adult books being read by adults) have ensured that young adult literature continues to grow in popularity and demand. Young adult nonfiction particularly has seen an increase in crossover interest among adult readers.

While the early examples of young adult nonfiction were geared toward informing readers and providing opportunities for self-help, young adult nonfiction titles of the twenty-first century offer a promise of excitement, thrill, and interest. For instance, Steve Sheinkin's *Bomb: The Race to Build—and Steal—the World's Most Dangerous Weapon* accurately relates the early history of the first atomic bomb, but it reads like a fictional espionage novel complete with suspense, deceit, and international intrigue. Another young adult nonfiction novel written by Sheinkin, *The Notorious Benedict Arnold: A True Story of Adventure, Heroism, & Treachery*, is, on the surface, a biography of Revolutionary War general Benedict Arnold. However, Sheinkin writes in a way unlike any textbook and uses a writing style that infuses excitement into the instruction. *Charles and Emma: The Darwins' Leap of Faith* by Deborah Heiligman teaches readers about the life and theories of nineteenth-century evolutionist Charles Darwin while artfully and respectfully exploring the debate between creationism and evolutionism through the story of Darwin's courtship, marriage, and the resulting inner debate he struggled with in his love for Emma, who was deeply religious. Journalist and children's nonfiction writer Karen Blumenthal not only presents an entertaining and instructive biography of Apple cofounder and CEO Steve Jobs, but she also weaves in the history of computers and computing.

Works

Deborah Heiligman creates an interesting and enjoyable reading experience in her portrayal of Charles Darwin's marriage and family life in *Charles and Emma*. This in turn makes the biography less dry and more relatable for a younger audience. Heiligman's scientific explanations are easy to understand, especially for those with limited scientific background.

Charles Darwin's *On the Origin of Species*, which was published in 1859, introduced evolutionary theory to the Victorians. The work sparked a long and ongoing debate about evolution versus creationism, and many school systems are still unsure as to how to handle teaching the subject and whether either or both theories should be presented in the classroom. Heiligman's approach, however, allows for the ability to listen to and respect each side. "The debate between evolution and religion continues, too. [Darwin] and Emma would certainly say that people from both worlds should keep talking to each other."

Heiligman's portrayal of Darwin and Emma and the manner in which she relates their story presents both the religious and scientific sides of the debate without judgment or room for heated debate. As Darwin began to realize that his theories disproved the teachings of the Bible, he grew concerned about whether he could find a wife. Rather than hide his religious doubts as his father suggested, Darwin told his first cousin Emma the truth. They agreed to disagree as long as they respected each other and took a "leap of faith." The two married and had ten children.

While their marriage was not always happy, especially with the death of three of their children, the couple worked together despite their divergent beliefs. Darwin let Emma take the children to church every Sunday while he walked around town. Emma read all of his work and urged him to be the best writer he could be.

Emma feared that she and Darwin would be separated in death, believing that she would go to heaven and that Darwin would not. Their marriage was unique to the time as it was not only between a man and a woman but also between science and religion. In the foreword, Jonathan Weiner states that readers will "understand in the most vivid, intimate, and personal way how shocking Darwin's ideas were for the people of his time, including some of the people who were closest to him."

Heiligman's life parallels Charles and Emma's in the sense that she majored in religious studies in college and her husband is a science writer, but explains that her husband inspired her to "fall in love with science," which allowed her explore her own beliefs and identity in the creative treatment of the Darwins' marriage. Her personalization allows history, science, and religion to come together in a narrative of romance and relationship.

In *Bomb: The Race to Build—and Steal—the World's Most Dangerous Weapon* Steve Sheinkin relates the history of the first atomic bomb and the repercussions its creation caused for the scientists who developed it and for the world. As with *Charles and Emma*, the science behind the story is explained clearly and is pedagogically suitable for young adult readers. However, the book grounds its storytelling in the lives of the scientists who researched and created atomic weaponry and the aftermath of their discoveries.

Sheinkin was at one time a textbook author, but he enjoys relating history in a more personal, creative, and less formal way. He calls himself a story detective, and he has written several other historical nonfiction works for young adults. He enhances the story of *Bomb* with authentic black-and-white photos and source documents that help personalize history and bring it to life. The book reads like a fast-paced spy novel and is full of subterfuge, betrayal, and high stakes international politics.

Although the science behind the creation of the atomic bomb is touched upon in *Bomb* and explained, it is Sheinkin's descriptions and his stories of the scientists behind the project as well as their reactions to their discovery that are what will resonate with young adults. As Sheinkin explains, "It was the chill of knowing [the scientists] had used something they loved—the study of physics—to build the deadliest weapon in human history." Sheinkin relates the words of the project's technical director J. Robert Oppenheimer: "We knew the world would not be the same. A few people laughed, a few people cried. Most people were silent," and also how the bomb's creation reminded Oppenheimer of a line from ancient Hindu scripture: "Now I am become death, the destroyer of the world." Sheinkin notes US president Harry S. Truman's indecision to use the bomb on the Japanese. The full weight of the device and its position in history is contextualized by the hard choices of these people. None of these decisions were made lightly; the decision to build and use the atom bomb changed the lives of everyone involved, tormenting most of the scientists. Readers learn the personal side of history along with the facts.

Sheinkin also wrote *The Notorious Benedict Arnold: A True Story of Adventure, Heroism, & Treachery* which won the 2012 Young Adult Library Services Association (YALSA) Award for Excellence in Nonfiction for Young Adults. As with *Bomb*, *Benedict* is well researched, thrilling to read, and presented in a story-like fashion. The book, which is a biography of General Benedict Arnold's life, contextualizes history with Arnold's personal relationships as well as with such well-known Revolutionary figures as George Washington.

Arnold was a talented spy and played a large role in bringing about the American Revolution. As with *Bomb*, the historical account of the events borrows the style of spy genre. *Benedict* succeeds by engaging readers while educating them about the American Revolution and many of its key players without presenting information and facts in a dry, scholarly manner. The story flows by characterizing historical figures and by showing readers that, in history as well as in present-day life, there are not always clear heroes and villains. Sheinkin extols Arnold's courage in serving the colonies and sympathizes with his reasons for betraying them.

Karen Blumenthal's *Steve Jobs: The Man Who Thought Different* is both an autobiography of Apple cofounder and CEO Steve Jobs and a history of the birth of computers. Blumenthal writes the book within the context of the commencement address Jobs gave at California's Stanford University in 2003. This personalizes the book's subject and allows readers to feel engaged in it, almost as if the reader is having a conversation directly with Jobs.

There were aspects of Jobs's life that may not be appropriate for a young adult audience, and in an interview with Amanda Margis for YALSA, Blumenthal explained that her biggest challenge was to write about a "very adult life" for young adults. Rather than avoid potentially difficult subject matter, Blumenthal writes an honest biography of Steve Jobs and does so without criticism or judgment. She does not speak down to her readers and includes computer jargon throughout the book but also adds a detailed glossary for readers' reference.

Conclusions

Journalist and children's book author Alexandra Alter discusses current trends in young adult nonfiction and expects more adult nonfiction to have young adult editions in the future. Alter believes that young adult nonfiction has become popular because it is written in a way that is more capable of grabbing and holding the attention of younger adults. She believes current young adult nonfiction is becoming more popular with adults because the genre is less lengthy and easier to read than nonfiction that is written and marketed for adults.

The difficulty with young adult nonfiction is that many issues need to be toned down and content has to be, as Alter terms it, "sanitized" in order to make it more appropriate for the young adult audience. While Alter's article discusses sanitizing and simplifying young adult content, she does not condone censoring it. Rather, potentially terrifying and disturbing material, such as torture, should be touched on rather than explored in-depth. Alter concedes that it "can be hard to maintain the drama and nuance of historical narratives while targeting the under-13 crowd."

Another controversy Alter discusses is whether there needs to be a young adult nonfiction genre at all. Many young adults are capable of reading adult nonfiction and would benefit from the more forthcoming versions. Alter shares that Chris Shoemaker, YALSA president, chooses the adult version if he feels the young adult version is oversimplified or if controversial topics have been removed (Alter). Yet young adult nonfiction is extremely popular. While most of the publishing industry has experienced a slump in sales, sales of children's and young adult books have been increasing.

Alter points out the varying subgenres among young adult nonfiction such as memoirs and self-help books, which is a departure from the traditional standbys of animal- and science-themed books. Many young adults no longer have to feel intimidated by grabbing a "hard to read" adult book and now have a range of more accessible options.

Young adult nonfiction books give young adult and adult readers more options to learn as well as to be entertained. Younger readers who feel capable of reading adult versions can and will do so, and adults who want a lighter read have that option too.

Alexandra McBride, MA

Further Reading

Kaplan, Jeffrey S. "The Changing Face of Young Adult Literature." *Teaching Young Adult Literature Today: Insights, Considerations, and Perspectives for the Classroom Teacher* (2012): 19. Print.

Reiman, Laura, and Ellen Greenblatt. "Censorship of Children's and Young Adult Books in Schools and

Public Libraries." *Serving LGBTIQ Library and Ar-chives Users: Essays on Outreach Service, Collections, and Access* (2011): 247–65. Print.

Tveit, Ase Kristine. "Reading Habits and Library Use among Young Adults." *New Rev. of Children's Literature and Librarianship* 18.2 (2012): 85–104. Print.

Bibliography

Alter, Alexandra. "To Lure Young Readers, Nonfiction Writers Sanitize and Simplify." *New York Times*. New York Times, 7 Oct. 2014. Web. 6 May 2015. <http://www.nytimes.com/2014/10/08/business/media/laura-hillenbrand-jon-meacham-adapt-titles-for-children.html>.

Barcott, Bruce. "The Darwins' Prenup." Rev. of *Charles and Emma: The Darwins' Leap of Faith*, by Deborah Heiligman. *New York Times*. New York Times, 6 May 2009. Web. 6 May 2015. <http://www.nytimes.com/2009/05/10/books/review/Barcott-t.html?_r=0>.

Blumenthal, Karen. "An Interview with Nonfiction Finalist Karen Blumenthal." By Amanda Margis. *YALSA*. American Library Assoc., 25 Jan. 2013. Web. 6 May 2015. <http://www.yalsa.ala.org/thehub/2013/01/25/an-interview-with-nonfiction-finalist-karen-blumenthal/>.

Rev. of *Bomb: The Race to Build—and Steal—the World's Most Dangerous Weapon*, by Steve Sheinkin. *Kirkus*. Kirkus Media, 18 July 2012. Web. 6 May 2015. <http://www.kirkusreviews.com/book-reviews/steve-sheinkin/bomb/>.

Bushman, John H., and Kay Parks Bushman. "Young adult Nonfiction: Meeting the Needs and Curiosities of Today's Youth." *English Journal* 81.1 (1992): 74. *Academic Search Complete*. Web. 27 May 2015. <http://search.ebscohost.com/login.aspx?direct=true&db=eric&AN=EJ454172&site=edslive>.

Flowers, Mark. "YALSA Nonfiction, Part Two: The Notorious Benedict Arnold." *YALSA*. Amer. Lib. Assoc., 16 Dec. 2011. Web. 6 May 2015. <http://www.yalsa.ala.org/thehub/2011/12/16/yalsa-nonfiction-part-two-the-notorious-benedict-arnold/>.

Rev. of *Steve Jobs: The Man Who Thought Different*, by Karen Blumenthal. *Kirkus Reviews* 15 Feb. 2012: 386–87. *Literary Reference Center*. Web. 6 May 2015. <http://search.ebscohost.com/login.aspx?direct=true&db=lfh&AN=71952989&site=lrclive>.

Novels in Verse

Titles Discussed
Crank by Ellen Hopkins
Fishtailing by Wendy Phillips
Keesha's House by Helen Frost
True Believer by Virginia Euwer Wolff

Genre Overview
Although young adult literature has existed as a distinct genre since the mid-twentieth century, the verse novel is a relatively new form of the genre that began to gain popularity in the 1990s. The appearance of works written for readers of different ages is nothing new in world literature. There have long been fables, nursery rhymes, and other forms of short stories written specifically for children, and especially since the rise in popularity of the modern novel, English-language stories have increasingly been written for specific audiences. Nevertheless, it was not until the 1960s that the modern young adult genre came about, a development that many agree coincided with the publication of S. E. Hinton's novel *The Outsiders* in 1967. In the following decade, young adult literature—that is, literature told from the perspective of teenage protagonists, written for and, perhaps more significantly, marketed to adolescents roughly between the ages of twelve and eighteen—saw a strong surge in popularity.

While many young people were reading during these early years, the scope of the genre was still relatively limited. Perhaps for this reason, the 1980s saw a decline in the popularity of young adult literature. Another problem arose near the end of the decade and the start of the 1990s as schools and libraries faced budgetary cutbacks. While young adult novels were partially marketed to their intended readers, they were also aimed at the adults making the purchases for libraries. With those libraries' sudden lack of resources, publishers needed to market directly to teenagers in order to sell their literature. As a result, in the 1990s, young adult literature saw not just a resurgence of the genre but also a broadening of its scope.

The verse novel was introduced for wider market consumption in the 1990s, with early examples including *Judy Scuppernong* (1990) by Brenda Seabrooke and *Soda Jerk* (1990) by Cynthia Rylant. However, it was not until the latter part of the decade that the genre found a footing in young adult literature. The end of the twentieth century saw authors, readers, and critics more interested in realistic and intense narratives that went beyond stories of romance and great friendships to focus on real, important issues faced by teens. Young adult literature focused on issues such as death, drugs, drinking, teen pregnancy, violence, and even suicide. With these new themes came a new interest in their impact on the teenage mind, as many young readers were dealing with these same issues in their own lives.

Poetry became a way for readers to enter a space that had been relatively closed off in prose fiction: the mind of the adolescent protagonist. The verse novel, drawing from the tradition of young adult realism, thus became a medium through which readers could experience the emotional consequences of major, life-changing events. Novels such as Ellen Hopkins's *Crank* (2004) and its two sequels, *Glass* (2007) and *Fallout* (2010), laid bare the rough world and emotional turbulence of teenage drug addiction, while Virginia Euwer Wolff's *True Believer* (2001) showed the impact that violence can have on love, family, and religion. *Keesha's House* (2003), by Helen Frost, is one of the first and most graphic depictions of issues surrounding teen pregnancy, drinking, abuse, and problems with the legal system. *Fishtailing* (2010), by Wendy Phillips, similarly gives readers a look into the struggles of multiple protagonists.

Works

While young adult novels vary widely in their choices of protagonist, setting, tone, and even mood, they tend to share many of the same plot details that echo those surrounding the lives of adolescents. Love interests and teenage romance play a role in many of these story lines, although often these scenes serve to add to the mood of the story rather than playing a pivotal role. Although romance has become something of cliché within the genre, it is also a key factor in the life of many, if not most, burgeoning adults, and verse novels tend to focus on challenges that many adolescents need to face and overcome. What makes these four novels—*Crank*, *True Believer*, *Keesha's House*, and *Fishtailing*—central to the verse-novel genre is that the obstacles they present are not ones that will necessarily help the protagonists become members of society but rather ones that they must overcome simply to survive. Yet in doing

so—in overcoming these obstacles, in continuing to move forward—the protagonists help form the most integral part of themselves: their identity. As one of the key conflicts for any young adult, this important theme is well suited for the verse-novel genre, where readers can experience the inner thoughts of the characters and see how such situations may be dealt with.

Virginia Euwer Wolff is one of the top names in young adult verse novels, in part for making an early contribution to the nascent genre with *Make Lemonade* in 1993. It is the first novel of a trilogy told from the perspective of fourteen-year-old Verna LaVaughn as she deals with class struggles, family issues, violence, and most importantly identity, and it is notable for being one of the foundational American young adult verse novels. Wolff's skill as a writer of verse was fully recognized with the publication of the second novel of the trilogy, *True Believer* (2001), which won the 2001 National Book Award for Young People's Literature. In it, Wolff focuses on the effects of violence on the adolescent mind. While LaVaughn is a witness to individual violence in the first novel, *True Believer* explores the consequences of living in a society of violence. Individual violence is the violence between people, the violence that can be observed every day, and LaVaughn's situation in life forces her to confront this violence. However, *True Believer* is also interested in institutional violence—that is, the pervasive culture, situations, and atmosphere that condone, or at least enable, individual acts of violence. Wolff does not attempt to shield the reader from the rawness of these actions; LaVaughn's place in society shows her this violence every day:

> Robby ran in the way of his mother's pimp,
> and Shyrelle got held in front of her big brother
> when the gang gun went off
> and she lived for 6 days
> before dying of all that violence and dumbness.
>   (Wolff 30)

But the book is about overcoming obstacles, and the obstacles LaVaughn faces are more than just her circumstances.

Love plays a role in the strong ties between characters in Wolff's novel, and it is also the driving force of Ellen Hopkins's novel *Crank*. Like *True Believer*, *Crank* holds very little back in its depiction of teenage use of methamphetamine hydrochloride, better known as crystal meth; it is so open in its depiction of drug use, sex, and addiction that it has been challenged and banned in many different school and districts. Hopkins, who is the mother of a crystal meth addict, has been recognized for her insight into the teenage mind and her skill as a poet. Written in the first person from the perspective of teenage addict Kristina, her verse mirrors the speech patterns of adolescents, setting the rhythm and timing of a particular mindset and making the reader seem more deeply connected to Kristina's personal thoughts.

Identification is one of the essential parts of the verse novel and one that is used frequently in *Keesha's House* by Helen Frost, a story about multiple young people with serious life issues who are attempting to put their lives in order. Frost begins by almost immediately revealing each character's situation, connecting with the reader through exposing lines of poetry that are both personal and attractive in their cadence, language, and rhythm. Through this connection, readers have a part in and can experience more directly the issues that the protagonists must overcome and the lost sense of identity that they struggle to regain over the course of the novel.

While *True Believer* and *Crank* are both told from the first-person perspective of a single main character—LaVaughn and Kristina, respectively—*Keesha's House* and *Fishtailing* both switch between multiple characters and perspectives. In *Keesha's House*, this is done by separating the story into eight parts of seven poems each, with the poems in each part representing seven different characters' points of view. The titular character's story begins in the third poem of part 1, "I Found a Place":

> Stephie walked by this afternoon, holding
> her umbrella in front of her face.
> When it rains like this, all day, into the night,
> that's when you need a home
> more than you need your pride. She still
> goes home to her folks, but she's scared
> of something. (Frost 6, lines 1–7)

Notably, Keesha is not the first but the third to speak, and her first lines are not about herself but rather about somebody else. In this way, *Keesha's House* gives readers a more external, and thus somewhat more objective,

view of its characters and their stories, working within the first-person perspective of one character to reveal more information about another.

In Wendy Phillips's *Fishtailing*, as in *Keesha's House*, each poem is told from a particular character's point of view. Although the arrangement of the poems is less ordered than in *Keesha's House*, each character's perspective is further differentiated by font choice and text justification. Tricia's and Miguel's poems are set in different serif fonts, for example, while Natalie's and Kyle's fonts are sans serif; Tricia's, Miguel's, and Natalie's poems are all flush left, while Kyle's are flush right. In addition, *Fishtailing* goes beyond inner monologues, looking to capture the feeling of different types of writing. While some of the poems are internal, others are evidently written for school assignments and are followed by notes from the English teacher, Mrs. Farr, which provide an outside perspective on both the poems and the students themselves. Phillips uses the structured form of poetry to represent a more holistic experience of high school, incorporating other text types, such as teachers' notes and administrative e-mails, to fill in details about the characters' lives without disrupting the narrative flow of the story.

The literary styles of these four works are very similar to one another and characteristic of the genre as a whole. Here, as in many verse novels written for young adults, free verse is the dominant form. As poetry is often read and experienced more personally than prose, it does seem natural that it can be used to share a character's inner mind with the reader.

The power of verse lies in more than just the arrangement of words. Poetry can use form and the page itself to make a point—for example, by using negative space to make writing stand out more, or as a way to emphasize defiance of authority. Form can also be used to make a point more dramatic, as in "Just before the Drop," one of the poems in Hopkins's *Crank*, in which Kristina explains:

> You know how you
> stand and stand and stand
> in line for the most
> gigantic incredible roller
>
> coaster
> you've ever dared attempt. (Hopkins 88, lines 1–6)

The indentation and line breaks help connect the form and structure of the lines and make the metaphor of crystal meth use as a roller-coaster ride more dramatic.

Yet while form and content are able to work together when the placement of words on the page become a part of the art, language itself is also very important to the expression of characters' inner thoughts. Hopkins defines a good verse novel as one that uses "startling imagery and elevated language, such as metaphor, alliteration, assonance," to connect the reader subconsciously with the text and make it more personally relatable (Shahan). The metaphor of the roller coaster above is one example of how poetic devices can create more vivid images and therefore stronger bonds with the reader. In *Fishtailing*, Tricia's first poem begins,

> Her glance
> across the crowded classroom
> speaks louder
> than the droning recital
> of paragraph structure. (Phillips 9, lines 1–5)

The abstract language used in the comparison, and even the brief uses of alliteration ("crowded classroom") and assonance ("crowded," "classroom, "louder"), works to remove the language from simple, realistic description into a more dreamlike, mental state. While this technique creates intensity for the reader on the emotional level, many writers of the verse-novel genre choose to contrast this with the intensity of the graphic, raw description of the lives that their main characters face. In the first poem of *Keesha's House*, titled "Now This Baby," pregnant teenager Stephie thinks,

> Jason said, You could get rid of it. I thought of how he
>   tossed
> the broken condom in the trash, saying, Nothing
>
> will happen. Now this baby is that nothing,
> growing fingers in the dark, growing toes, a girl
> or boy, heart pulsing. Not something to be tossed
> aside, not nothing. . . . (Frost 2, lines 5–7)

Very few genres of young adult literature have relied so heavily on the literary conventions of poetry. However, it is these conventions, including the focus on rhythm, the need to mirror natural patterns of speech, and the use of poetic devices to appeal to the more

subconscious parts of the reader's mind, that develop a reader's personal connection with the main characters. In turn, readers can more directly experience the often intense emotional issues that many adolescents face, issues that arise from these very real situations, and can identify with the protagonists' need for a stable, secure identity.

Conclusion

It is difficult to exactly delineate any style or specific genre of writing, but the verse novel aimed at young adult readers can be said to be a creation of the twenty-first century. The genre has found a place within the corpus of young adult literature since its inception in the 1990s, having come to represent the general trend of young adult literature toward depicting the most important and intense issues that adolescents face in their family, school, and personal lives.

While the uniqueness of this genre comes partly from its form, its most original element is the introspection and voyeuristic perspective that it offers to readers. While novels and authors throughout the history of young adult literature have faced the possibility of being banned for what some may consider too-graphic or too-adult depictions of problems, the verse novel takes these ideas to new levels. The verse novel is a genre that more than any other combines content with form, and in both aspects it can be said to be quite experimental. In general, modern poetry has been a medium of experimentation and expression unlike any other type of literature, and the verse novel is no exception. Many writers, especially those discussed above, have taken the opportunity to combine new and radical depictions of serious teenage problems with the experimental aspects of the poetry and novel forms.

This genre has offered new perspectives on serious issues such as addiction, drug use, abuse, suicide, and teen pregnancy. The internal, personal points of view from which these issues are addressed have made the verse novel a significant and worthy form of young adult literature. It is a genre that holds back very little from the readers, and for this reason it is both celebrated and reviled.

Unfortunately, poetry is still relatively unpopular among young readers. While some types of poetry have found younger audiences, particularly in performative contexts such as poetry slams and spoken-word performances, the form itself can be off-putting for many readers. However, this is balanced by the sheer intensity that authors are bringing to the genre. Sales of verse novels continue to climb, and the form has proven itself more than just a trend from the late twentieth century. As already-recognized authors find their works adapted to alternative mediums, such as film, and new authors find ways to share their perspectives, this still-young genre may continue to gain popularity. Truth is what adolescent readers want, and the verse novel has proved to be one of the best vehicles for it.

Aaron Horton, MA

Further Reading

Alexander, Joy. "The Verse-Novel: A New Genre." *Children's Literature in Education* 36.3 (2005): 269–283. *Literary Reference Center*. Web. 7 Apr. 2015. <http://search.ebscohost.com/login.aspx?direct=true&db=lfh&AN=18140560&site=lrc-live>.

Lubar, David. "The History of Young Adult Novels." *The ALAN Review* Spring 2003: 117–122. Print.

Sullivan, Ed. "Fiction or Poetry?" *School Library Journal* Aug. 2003: 44–45. *Literary Reference Center*. Web. 7 Apr. 2015. <http://search.ebscohost.com/login.aspx?direct=true&db=lfh&AN=10441660&site=lrc-live>.

Bibliography

Cart, Michael. "The Renaissance Continues: Young Adult Literature for the 21st Century." *Catholic Library World* 74.9 (2009): 279–85. *Poetry & Short Story Reference Center*. Web. 7 Apr. 2015. <http://search.ebscohost.com/login.aspx?direct=true&db=prf&AN=41423480&site=prc-live>.

Franzak, Judith, and Elizabeth Noll. "Monstrous Acts: Problematizing Violence in Young Adult Literature." *Journal of Adolescent & Adult Literacy* 49.8 (2006): 662–672. *Literary Reference Center*. Web. 7 Apr. 2015. <http://search.ebscohost.com/login.aspx?direct=true&db=lfh&AN=20913657&site=lrc-live>.

Frost, Helen. *Keesha's House*. 2003. New York: Farrar, 2007. Print.

Hopkins, Ellen. *Crank*. New York: Simon, 2004. Print.

Phillips, Wendy. *Fishtailing*. Regina: Coteau, 2010. Print.

Shahan, Sherry. "A Fresh Approach to YA Novels: Learn How the Young adult Novel-in-Verse Offers Unique Opportunities for Emotional Insight." *Writer* Feb. 2009: 34+. *Literary Reference Center*. Web. 7 Apr. 2015. <http://search.ebscohost.com/login.aspx?direct=true&db=lfh&AN=36183184&site=lrc-live>.

Strickland, Ashley. "A Brief History of Young Adult Literature." *CNN.com*. Cable News Network, 17 Oct. 2013. Web. 7 Apr. 2015. <http://www.cnn.com/2013/10/15/living/young-adult-fiction-evolution>.

Wolff, Virginia Euwer. *True Believer*. New York: Atheneum, 2001. Print.

Paranormal

Titles Discussed

Blood and Chocolate by Annette Curtis Klause
The Twilight series by Stephenie Meyer
Midwinterblood by Marcus Sedgwick
Far Far Away by Tom McNeal

Genre Overview

Paranormal describes anything that has some supernatural element that cannot be scientifically or logically explained. Although there is crossover between paranormal and a variety of other genres, such as horror, fantasy, science fiction, and romance, the distinguishing element of this genre is the introduction of something supernatural as a unifying element for the story. Categorization of a work as paranormal, rather than one of these complementary genres, is appropriate when authors make the supernatural a primary focus of the story. The facets of paranormal activity can include a variety of powers, such as telepathy, telekinesis, precognition, immortality, time travel, or reincarnation. As a result, unlike horror literature, paranormal works are not always frightening. Instead, they can be humorous or romantic. They may be more concerned with illustrating how a character develops despite an abnormal ability or how normal humans interact with the supernatural. These supernatural characters might include shape-shifters, werewolves, vampires, witches, ghosts, zombies, angels, or demons.

The interest in the supernatural has been a part of literature for centuries, starting as early as oral tradition with mythology and varying in popularity throughout the centuries. Eighteenth- and nineteenth-century Gothic novels were among the most popular literature of the time and were so influential that the works of Ann Radcliffe, a pioneering Gothic novelist and the author of *The Mysteries of Udolpho* (1794), were parodied by such authors as Jane Austen. Ghost stories were one of the most popular genres for Victorian audiences, and works such as Charles Dickens's *A Christmas Carol* (1843) remain popular today. Later Victorian authors such as Oscar Wilde, who wrote *The Picture of Dorian Gray* (1891), and Bram Stoker, who wrote *Dracula* (1897), incorporated paranormal events and characters as essential elements of their stories. Although popular literature of the early twentieth century did not pull as freely from paranormal influences, by the second half of the century, television programs such as *Bewitched* (1964–72) and *I Dream of Jeannie* (1965–70) introduced a lighthearted and often romantic component. An influx of paranormal romances in the later part of the twentieth century, including the television show *Charmed* (1998–2006) and books such as Annette Curtis Klause's *Blood and Chocolate* (1997), heralded a resurgence of paranormal fiction's popularity, with appeal to young female audiences in particular.

Works

Blood and Chocolate by Annette Curtis Klause is an example of a contemporary paranormal romance written for young adult audiences. Like many of the other books discussed here, the novel describes a girl's growth into emotional and sexual maturity. The story begins with main character Vivian Gandillon watching as her family home burns to the ground with her father trapped inside. The fire is a revenge strike against Vivian's werewolf pack because Vivian and her four friends killed a local human and the pack's neighbors became suspicious of their involvement. Forced to move away, Vivian is struggling with fitting into a new school, grieving for her father, and understanding her place in the pack.

Her mother's flirtations with twenty-four-year-old Gabriel, one of the strongest werewolves in the pack, introduce a graphic and sometimes disturbing theme of sexual activity that runs throughout the novel. This sexual awareness clearly carries over to sixteen-year-old Vivian, who becomes interested in a human boy at her high school. A relationship with gentle Aiden is appealing to Vivian, who longs for emotional support. When Aiden refers to her as "sweetheart," she thinks, "Sweetheart. He'd called her his sweetheart. She'd been a main squeeze, an ol' lady, and a piece of tail, but she'd never

been a sweetheart before. The word bubbled through her like champagne." On a night that Aiden sets up for a romantic first sexual encounter, Vivian decides to show him who she really is and, as he lies in bed waiting for her, she changes into a werewolf. His immediate rejection crushes and confuses Vivian, and Vivian is thrust onto an emotional rollercoaster that leads her to believe that she is a danger to her pack. The sexual development continues as Gabriel becomes leader of the pack, and Vivian is inadvertently named his queen. Despite the six-year age difference and his previous involvement with her mother, the two end the novel in each other's arms.

The paranormal in this novel is primarily in the focus on werewolves. Not only is Vivian a werewolf, but her parents and everyone in her immediate vicinity is as well. The paranormal elements of the story highlight Vivian's conflict over belonging to this group of outsiders as well as her feral characteristics that overwhelm her personality and make it difficult to fit in with the human teens around her. She turns away from her true nature until she is forced to accept her identity. The politics of Vivian's werewolf pack plays a leading role in the novel, with two violent competitions for supremacy, one between the men of the pack and one between the women.

Stephenie Meyer's Twilight series roared onto the literary scene in 2005 with the publication of the first book in the series, *Twilight*. The book introduces Bella Swan, a teenage girl who moves to the small town of Forks, Washington, to live with her father after her mother remarries. Within days of starting at the local high school, Bella is drawn to an unusual young man, Edward Cullen. The two are drawn into a relationship that quickly introduces Bella to the world of the supernatural when she finds out that Edward and his family are vampires. The series follows Bella for several years, culminating in her marriage to Edward and the birth of their child in the final novel, *Breaking Dawn* (2008).

Meyer's series shares a romantic theme with Klause's earlier novel, but the Twilight series is much less graphic than *Blood and Chocolate*. Though Bella's and Edward's romance is the central focus of the whole series, which follows their ups and downs, the two do not engage in sexual activity until the final novel after Bella has reached adulthood and they are married. Like Vivian, though, Bella is torn between two men. While Vivian ultimately chooses the werewolf Gabriel, Bella's continuous choice is Edward, even when he rejects her in a misplaced show of protectiveness. The conflict over whether Bella should choose Edward or her friend Jacob provides much of the drama in the series.

Edward and Jacob ultimately provide the paranormal connection in the novels. Edward is a vampire, while Jacob is a werewolf. A battle between the two paranormal groups alongside the romantic conflict over which love Bella will choose pulls readers into a description of their political systems. Like Klause does in her novel, Meyer establishes these groups as self-supporting and self-policing entities with their own rules, leadership, villains, and heroes. Much of the length of the series is spent establishing an understanding of this hidden world.

In his 2014 novel *Midwinterblood*, author Marcus Sedgwick takes the paranormal in a completely different direction than Klause or Meyer. The story begins and ends with Eric Seven, a journalist who travels to a small island with the idea of writing an investigative piece on the strangely long life spans of some of the island's citizens. Once there, he is shut off from the outside world, so when the islanders begin to provide him with a tea made from a rare local flower, he begins to suspect something is wrong, but he cannot figure out what it is or how to overcome it. While on the island, he is strangely attracted to a woman named Merle, one of the island's self-proclaimed protectors or wards. This chapter ends with his death in a strange occultist ritual. Overall, the novel consists of seven stories, each featuring a reincarnation of Eric and Merle, who have been tied to one another since primitive times. Eric and Merle experience a variety of relationships throughout the ages, as lovers, parent and child, siblings, and friends.

Though one of the short narratives that make up the whole of the novel does have a vampire as the central character, the principal paranormal element is reincarnation. The cycle begins when King Eirikr is sacrificed to provide his community with a return of healthy crops. As he dies, his wife, Melle, declares, "I will live seven times, and I will look for you in each one. We will always be together." Her question "Will you follow?" becomes the thread that ties their lives together for centuries, and as Eric Seven faces death in the epilogue, he knows his fate: "I have lived this before, but I will not live it again. He knows that this is his last life." Outside of the change in paranormal focal point, the format of this piece is unique. While *Blood and Chocolate* is a

standalone novel and Twilight is a series of four novels, *Midwinterblood* is one novel made up of seven short stories.

Tom McNeal's 2014 novel *Far Far Away* introduces yet another aspect of the paranormal. The novel starts with a blatant connection to the supernatural as the narrator of the story states, "What follows is the strange and fateful tale of a boy, a girl, and a ghost. The boy possessed uncommon qualities, the girl was winsome and daring, and the ancient ghost . . . well, let it only be said that his intentions were good."

Jeremy Johnson Johnson is one of the main characters of the novel. Jeremy has always been a bit different, primarily because he can talk to ghosts, a fact he mistakenly shared with a classmate when he was seven years old. In the years that followed, Jeremy became the laughingstock of his community, until Ginger Boultinghouse, a lovely popular girl, started to build a friendship with him. While McNeal develops a sweet romance between the two teens, in some ways reminiscent of Bella and Edward's innocent relationship, he pulls in the paranormal through the revelation of Jeremy's relationship with a ghost companion. This ghost companion, named Jacob Grimm, watches over Jeremy and narrates the story.

The story itself is ultimately a retelling of Hansel and Gretel. Though the budding romance between Jeremy and Ginger is one of the key elements of the tale, and the paranormal is focused primarily on the ghost, there is a villain. Unlike the aforementioned novels that share the political concerns of groups such as werewolves and vampires or the reincarnation theme in Sedgwick's novel, the conflict in McNeal's novel is centered on a desire for friendship. The villain, local baker Sten Blix, is a grandfatherly figure who looks like Santa Claus, so it is shocking when he kidnaps the children. Frank Bailey, another local boy who has been locked up by the baker, tells Jeremy and Ginger, "It's like he wants you to be his friend or something.'" Despite this twist on the theme of friendship, the story does provide a positive lesson on judging others, making friends, and taking care of family.

Whether the paranormal element is a werewolf, a vampire, or a ghost, the inclusion of supernatural elements in young adult fiction can speak to adolescents' feelings of estrangement and otherness from those around them, their anxieties and fears, and their need to keep secrets or desire to hide their perceived flaws.

Conclusions

The broad spectrum of paranormal characteristics allows writers of young adult literature so many avenues for creative outlet that the popularity of the genre seems guaranteed. Readers who are looking for romance can find flawed characters who can be redeemed when the right person comes along. Those who want an escape from the reality of everyday life can find strange new worlds where supernatural abilities and societal outcasts are normal. Romance literature with paranormal elements offers a platform for young adult readers to explore their sexuality. As long as young adult readers desire a way to safely escape from reality, paranormal literature for this age group will continue to flourish.

In addition to the appeal to readers, the visual attraction of paranormal stories has fascinated Hollywood. Film adaptations of *Blood and Chocolate* and the Twilight series have been turned profits that encourage further exploration of the genre for new inspiration. Though the box office income from the 2007 film of Klause's book grossed a disappointing $3.5 million in the United States, Meyer's Twilight saga blossomed into five films that earned more than $1.3 billion. Other young adult paranormal works that have been turned to film include *Beautiful Creatures* (2013) by Kami Garcia and Margaret Stohl and *Warm Bodies* (2013) by Isaac Marion. Television has also jumped on the bandwagon of using paranormal literature for young adults with series such as *The Vampire Diaries* (2009–), which is based on the book series of the same name by L. J. Smith.

One of the strongest aspects of paranormal literature that will keep it fresh is that huge range of topics that the genre covers. Even when vampires get old for the current audience, other paranormal creations like zombies or demons can take their place. When the walking dead are no longer romantic, witches and ghosts can make a comeback. As a result, this genre is likely to maintain a large following for years to come due its variety and versatility.

Theresa L. Stowell, PhD

Further Reading

Gaarden, Bonnie. "Twilight: Fairy Tale and Feminine Development." *Extrapolation* 53.2 (2012): 205–32. Print.

Silver, Anna. "Twilight Is Not Good for Maidens: Gender, Sexuality, and the Family in Stephenie Meyer's Twilight Series." *Studies in the Novel* 42.1/2 (2010): 121–38. *Literary Reference Center*. Web. 18 June 2015. <http://search.ebscohost.com/login.aspx?direct=true&db=lfh&AN=52945189&site=lrc-live>.

Bibliography

Baker, Deirdre F. Rev. of *Far Far Away*, by Tom McNeal. *Horn Book Magazine* 89.4 (2013): 139–40. *Literary Reference Center*. Web. 18 June 2015. <http://search.ebscohost.com/login.aspx?direct=true&db=lfh&AN=88842929&site=lrc-live>.

Rev. of *Blood and Chocolate*, by Annette Curtis Klause. *Kirkus*. Kirkus, 20 May 2010. Web. 8 June 2015. <https://www.kirkusreviews.com/book-reviews/annette-curtis-klause/blood-and-chocolate>.

Bodart, Joni Richards. *They Suck, They Bite, They Eat, They Kill: The Psychological Meaning of Supernatural Monsters in Young Adult Fiction*. Lanham: Scarecrow, 2012. Print.

Colfer, Eoin. "Seven Stories." Rev. of *Midwinterblood*, by Marcus Sedgwick. *Sunday Book Review*. New York Times, 8 Feb. 2013. Web. 8 June 2015.

Schall, Lucy. *Genre Talks for Teens: Booktalks and More for Every Teen Reading Interest*. Westport: Libraries Unlimited, 2009. Print.

Poetry

Titles Discussed
A Wreath for Emmett by Marilyn Nelson
19 Varieties of Gazelle Poems of the Middle East by Naomi Shihab Nye
How to (Un)cage a Girl by Francesca Lia Block

Genre Overview
Poetry written for children and adolescents is no new addition to the tradition of Western literature and poetry in general. Nor was the convention of writing about or from the perspective of a young adult anything revolutionary in the late twentieth century. English poet William Blake and other Romantics, for example, wrote many poems centered on the experiences of young poor workers in an effort to highlight and eliminate what they saw as social injustice within English and European society. Yet even these poems were not targeted at a younger audience. It was not until the late twentieth century and early twenty-first century that young adult poetry, as a literature written about teenagers and

addressed and marketed to a teenage audience, found a voice in Western literature.

Young adult literature as a genre is generally accepted to have gained popularity in the United States in the late 1960s. Since then, the genre has been defined largely by adolescent protagonists dealing with a range of issues, from becoming adults and a part of society to finding a place and identity in a larger social structure. The genre went through a period of popularity in the 1970s in which narratives tended to focus on real-life issues faced by protagonists navigating the world of high school social structures and undergoing puberty. While the next decade saw a sharp decline in the sales of young adult books, the genre resurged in the 1990s, exploding with a wealth of new subgenres such as fantasy, historical fiction, supernatural fiction, and mystery. Realism took a back seat to the more popular genres and books such as the Harry Potter series (1997–2007); however, realism was still a major subgenre for young readers. The problem that authors faced at the end of the twentieth century was finding subject matter that could hold readers' attention.

Adolescent readers did not simply want stories about innocent teen romance or learning to get along with a stepparent. Now that libraries and schools were faced with budgetary cuts, librarians were making fewer purchasing choices. Publishers and authors had to market directly to young readers, and so they needed to focus on new, exciting, difficult, and sometimes taboo subjects. The subgenre of realism looked to adult themes such as death, addiction, pregnancy, drugs, violence, and even depression and suicide, issues that teenagers were facing themselves more than ever.

While novels and short stories were able to focus on young protagonists dealing with these issues, poetry became a vehicle through which readers could experience the interiority of a character, dealing almost directly with the emotional consequences speakers and characters faced as a result of real-world situations. Novels written in verse, such as *Judy Scuppernong* (1990) by Brenda Seabrooke and *Soda Jerk* (1990) by Cynthia Rylant, marked the start of this new perspective in the 1990s, which was then continued with seminarrative works such as *Crank* (2004) by Ellen Hopkins, which deals with methamphetamine addiction, and *True Believer* (2001) by Virginia Euwer Wolff, a story of how to deal with and overcome violence.

As young adults took their place in an increasingly globalized world that continues to broaden and encompass disparate cultures, poetry reflecting the many voices of the international community has taken a place in young adult poetry of the twenty-first century. Poets such as Naomi Shihab Nye, Marilyn Nelson, and Francesca Lia Block have become representatives of the new era in young adult literature, sharing perspectives that epitomize and embrace the new era of pluralism.

Works

One of the marks of young adult literature in general is the incredibly wide range of protagonists who make up the multitude of narratives. Key to the appeal of these different perspectives is the idea of identity. Unique identity is both conventionally something adolescents seek to define for themselves and something that makes literature engaging. In modern young adult poetry, poets tap into their own unique pasts, cultures, ethnicities, and perspectives to show how individualism has its place within the new culture of pluralism.

Marilyn Nelson is an example of a poet who brings her own perspective to modern coming-of-age narratives. As an African American growing up during the height of the civil rights movement in the United States, her poetry seeks to reintroduce the perspective from when she was a child into twenty-first-century culture, where young readers have only secondhand experience of what US culture in the 1950s and 1960s was like for minorities.

Nelson's collection of poetry *A Wreath for Emmett Till* (2005) is a meditation on the past, individual and cultural memory, and the relevance of each in the twenty-first century. In the title poem of the collection, Nelson brings life back to a fourteen-year-old child whose murder was one of the sparks of the civil rights movement, "His mother had finally bought / that White Sox cap . . . she'd packed dungarees, T-shirts, underwear . . . Her only child. A body left to bloat." While the details of Emmett's desire for a baseball cap and his mother packing his bag clearly establish him as a child, the warmth of this scene is cut short by the reminder that his body was dumped in a river in Mississippi by his murderers. This poem allows modern young readers to identify with Emmett as a young adult and offers a stark reminder of the past.

Memory is also an important device within the poetry of Naomi Shihab Nye. As the daughter of a Palestinian refugee and an American of European descent, Nye grew up at the intersection of many different cultures, although her poetry focuses largely on the Middle East. Her poetry seeks to capture the voice of a girl defining her identity between the traditional and contemporary, the past and the present, and the East and the West. Her book *19 Varieties of Gazelle: Poems of the Middle East* (2002) is a collection of poems that focus on identity and duality. In the poem "Different Ways to Pray," the narrator begins, "There was the method of kneeling, a fine method . . . Women dreamed wistfully . . . their prayers . . . small calcium words uttered in sequence." Here, through memory, she focuses on the idea of tradition and its beauty but also its difficulty. While it is the cornerstone of identity, it is also calcifying and hard to break. Even for men tradition can bind: "There were men who had been shepherds so long / they walked like sheep." Nye's poems assert that there needs to be a fusion, a meeting where nothing is forgotten but nothing stays the same.

Yet while many poets offer their own voice and unique background to modern young adult poetry by focusing on world cultures and backgrounds, some also seek to add complexity to the identity of the traditional American teenager. In pop culture, far too often American teenagers are simplified and homogenized into a bland conglomeration of pop culture. Poets such as Francesca Lia Block seek to add interiority and complexity to her American characters, in the process demonstrating to young adults that intelligence and depth are desirable and attainable traits. *How to (Un)cage a Girl* (2008) is a collection of poetry from the perspective of a teenage girl in the process of finding her own voice and identity in a society that seems to elevate physical beauty, complacency, and popularity above anything else. In the poem "the little oven," the speaker is listening to her teacher talk about Nazis while the boys of the class make fun of her looks: "my body so thin / i had chopped off / my pretty brown hair / my skin charred and blistered." Without using capitalization, mirroring the language of texting, Block reveals the inner mind of the speaker and the brutality that the smallest comments can carry for a young woman.

The language of these poets can vary dramatically. Whereas Block attempts a direct line to the interiority of her characters through language more suited to an adolescent, poets such as Nye and Nelson use descriptive, complex language in order to convey more complex concepts.

Food is a major theme in Nye's poetry that helps accent the pluralism of her characters. Through various descriptions she is able to use the concept of food as something that both unites and contrasts. Between those of the same culture, it is a symbol of community, as in "Different Ways to Pray": "At night men ate heartily, flat bread / and white cheese, / and were happy." Or, as in "My Father and the Fig Tree," food is used as a symbol of culture, tradition, and individuality within a larger system. At the end of the poem, the poet's father, after many years in the United States, finds a fig tree like he had when he was a child, and to him it is "assurance / of a world that was always his own." Particularly with cultures from the Middle East, food is different from traditional food in the United States, and so the contrast in tastes becomes symbolic of the contrast in cultures, but these contrasts are brought together under something emotional, both in one's personal ties to food itself and its part in individual and cultural historical significance.

Nelson's poetry involves a similar connection to individual and cultural memory, although the catalyst for most of these connections is not food but nature and natural imagery. Drawing at some points from the idea of American regionalism, particularly the description of scenery in the Deep South, Nelson often employs imagery with a hint of nostalgia for her own past and a view of the past for a culture that was constantly marred by the brutality of some of its people. In "Pierced by the Screams of a Shortened Childhood," the narrator listens "to the songs of creature life, which disappears / and comes again to the music of the spheres." For two hundred years the narrator understands death and sees it in nature, until the "slaughter axed one quiet summer night." The quiet, serene landscapes of the South, particularly at night, come to symbolize an innocence that was shattered for the author and for the country as a whole. Though years have passed, the memory and past come quickly back, shattering the innocence and nostalgia that are comforting but not the whole truth.

While Nye and Nelson emphasize individualism through membership to different distinct communities, Block's poetry works on finding a voice within the dominant cultural sphere of US society. In a poem entitled "Popular Girl," the speaker meditates on this high school figure, "What are you going to be when you grow up? / are you still going to be beautiful? /

with good hair?" The narrator has both an innocence about her and a certain maturity, showing some awareness that life will be change drastically after high school and that those with high status in one social sphere are at once imbued with power within that sphere yet are powerless beyond its boundaries. Yet as with other poets of this genre, the speaker and author work together to both ask and answer the most important questions of a young reader trying to make sense of his or her world and to create some sense of identity and a way to approach the impending move to adulthood.

Conclusion

The influence of young adult poetry within the broader genre of young adult literature is not majorly significant. Young adult poetry, like poetry in general, does not have a broad readership base compared to prose. However, in every way it is still a legitimate form of literature and should not be judged artistically for its lack of commercial success. Poetry has always had a place and will always have a place in literature, and the uniqueness of the form makes it a crucial addition to young adult writing. In the future, as more poets write to and for an adolescent audience, there will be more voices and more perspectives to which teens can turn.

The more unique voices there are, the more of a chance there is that readers will find poets who explore the interior thoughts of a young person just like them. Novels will never be able to fully capture the intensity of this introspection nor the deep look into the mind that poetry can offer. It is a form that holds little back from the reader and this should become more popular as teens look for more direct insight into their own problems.

As long as the celebration of the plurality in US and world culture continues, many young adult poets will find their work being read, and there is space for many more voices to be heard within the genre. Even though it may be difficult to directly market poetry to younger audiences, schools and teachers continue to look for literature that is multicultural, intelligent, accessible, and engaging. Thus, through the efforts of schools, young adult poetry's popularity will likely continue to increase, even if it does not follow the path that many young adult novels have taken since the 1990s. In the end, young adults want literature that tackles complex and difficult concepts, and poetry remains one of the most direct ways to reveal ideas of the world.

Aaron Horton, MA

Further Reading

Alexander, Joy. "The Verse-Novel: A New Genre." *Children's Literature in Education* 36.3 (2005): 269–83. *Literary Reference Center*. Web. 29 Mar. 2015. <http://search.ebscohost.com/login.aspx?direct=true&db=lfh&AN=18140560&site=lrc-live>.

Fors, Nils Olov. "Words at Play: Diction and Context in Naomi Shihab Nye's *Remembered*." *Explicator* 69.1 (2010): 45–7. *Literary Reference Center*. Web. 25 Apr. 2015. <http://search.ebscohost.com/login.aspx?direct=true&db=lfh&AN=78222578&site=lrc-live>.

Campbell, Patricia J. "People Are Talking about . . . Francesca Lia Block." *Horn Book Magazine* 69.1 (1993): 57–64. *Literary Reference Center*. Web. 25 Apr. 2015. <http://search.ebscohost.com/login.aspx?direct=true&db=lfh&AN=9303010400&site=lrc-live>.

Bibliography

Cart, Michael. "The Renaissance Continues: Young Adult Literature for the 21st Century." *Catholic Library World* 74.9 (2009): 279. Print.

Lubar, David. "The History of Young Adult Novels." *ALAN Review* Spring 2003: 117–22. Print.

Holmes, Daryl Y. "Marilyn Nelson." *Guide to Literary Masters & Their Works* Jan. 2007: n.p. *Literary Reference Center*. Web. 25 Apr. 2015. <http://search.ebscohost.com/login.aspx?direct=true&db=lfh&AN=103331LM77329790307677&site=lrc-live>.

Low, Bernadette Flynn. "Naomi Shihab Nye." *Critical Survey of Poetry*. 2nd ed. Ipswich: Salem, 2002. 1–3. *Literary Reference Center*. Web. 25 Apr. 2015. <http://search.ebscohost.com/login.aspx?direct=true&db=lfh&AN=103331CSP14500160000701&site=lrc-live>.

Mercer, Lorraine, and Linda Strom. "Counter Narratives: Cooking Up Stories of Love and Loss in Naomi Shihab Nye's Poetry and Diana Abu-Jaber's 'Crescent.'" *Melus* 32.4 (2007): 33–46. *Literary Reference Center*. Web. 25 Apr. 2015. <http://search.ebscohost.com/login.aspx?direct=true&db=lfh&AN=28601305&site=lrc-live>.

Dziemianowicz, Stefan. "Francesca Lia Block." *Guide to Literary Masters & Their Works* Jan. 2007: n.p.

Literary Reference Center. Web. 25 Apr. 2015. <http://search.ebscohost.com/login.aspx?direct=true &db=lfh&AN=103331LM18939790300875&site=1 rc-live>.

Problem Novels

Titles Discussed

Between Shades of Gray by Ruta Sepetys
A Step from Heaven by An Na
Tears of a Tiger by Sharon M. Draper

General Overview

In the late 1960s, writers and publishers of young adult fiction began to shift their focus away from romanticized novels, which tended to shelter adolescent readers from mature or troubling subject matter, and increasingly publish realistic fiction that addressed ominous, more adult themes with candor. A number of social realities informed this shift, among them the cultural and sexual revolutions of the 1960s. Novels with realistic themes quickly became best sellers, popular with young readers even as some critics decried their depressing subject matter, and by the 1970s young adult novels consistently addressed topics such as abortion, drug use, alcoholism, suicide, teen runaways, physical abuse, and sex—all of which had been largely taboo only a decade before.

Although sometimes used as a synonym for realistic fiction, "problem novels" are more specifically novels that focus on a particular social problem or problems that are experienced as a personal struggle by the protagonist. One of the most famous works to first receive recognition as a problem novel was 1971's *Go Ask Alice*, written by an "anonymous" author (although commonly credited to Beatrice Sparks). In it, the unnamed main character accidentally ingests LSD at a party, which leads her to spirals out of control, becoming a drug addict and runaway and turning to prostitution to support herself. After briefly coming back to her family, she ultimately dies of a drug overdose.

Go Ask Alice is emblematic of the genre in several ways. The novel focuses as much on the social issues as on character development; taboo subject matter, such as prostitution and drug use, is rendered in explicit detail; the voice of the first-person narrator is casual, with regular use of slang and profanity; and instead of a happy ending, the realities of the social problem take

a great toll on the protagonist and those that love her. As problem novels continued to flourish throughout the 1970s and 1980s, these qualities resulted in a significant amount of negative attention from critics. In addition to the appropriateness of the subject matter (many popular problem novels faced censorship), some critics questioned the literary merit of the writing and the actual social value of the narratives, which they argued veered toward voyeurism of scandalous topics at the expense of redemption or inspiration.

While it is true that a good number of problem novels published during this time had little literary merit, an increasing number of gifted writers also turned their attention to the genre. Sharon M. Draper's *Tears of a Tiger* (1994) won two different awards from the American Library Association (ALA), while did An Na's *A Step from Heaven* (2001) was awarded the ALA's Michael L. Printz Award for the year's best novel for teens. Other writers employed the genre to write not about broad social issues but about particular political realities; Ruta Sepetys's *Between Shades of Gray* (2011), for instance, explores the genocide of Baltic people under Soviet dictator Joseph Stalin. Young adult literature, like all literature, is capable of addressing themes both uplifting and horrifying, rendering the protagonists' lives with honesty no matter how difficult it may be to face those realities. Problem novels serve as an important tool for writers seeking to expand the range of topics that young adult literature addresses.

Works

As is the case with many problem novels, Sharon M. Draper's *Tears of a Tiger* concerns itself not just with one social problem but with the intersection of several problems in the lives of its main characters. The novel begins with a group of friends out celebrating a high school basketball win by drinking beer and driving around town. Soon, the boys confront their first tragedy when the central character, Andy, crashes the car, killing his best friend, Robert. Andy slips into a deep depression over the course of the novel, visiting a therapist to seek help while withdrawing from his social circle and his girlfriend. This depression is further compounded as Andy sees the effects of racism on his black family and friends. The pain his friends experience following the accident is likewise complicated by their social and personal struggles; in particular, his friend Gerald must endure physical abuse from his stepfather while trying to heal emotionally from the car accident. In the end, a final social problem common to teenagers is introduced when Andy succumbs to his depression and commits suicide, leaving his friends to deal with one more loss.

Problem novels typically favor a first-person narrator, a literary device that heightens the emotional appeal of the characters and the immediacy of the narrative. *Tears of a Tiger* is somewhat unique in this regard—while still told in the first person, the perspective switches from character to character rather than staying with Andy. This narration style shifts the focus of the novel, allowing readers to understand the realities of drunk driving, physical abuse, depression, racism, and suicide not simply as singular issues that negatively affect an individual but as interrelated problems that are both personal and social in nature. This device allows room, for instance, for an essay Gerald writes in English class. While Gerald is devastated by the accident, his mind is equally preoccupied with the physical abuse in his home and the racism of everyday life. Writing about what he would change in the world, he wishes to eliminate Band-Aids (which only come in the color of white skin, but which he must wear regularly because of the abuse) and five-dollar bills (the type of bill he used to get beer on the night of the accident and the bill his stepfather uses to get drunk before beating him). In Gerald's essay, the social problems most affecting his own life become entwined in the symbols of the Band-Aid and the five-dollar bill; while the tragedy of the accident has devastated him, that devastation does not earn him a reprieve from the other social problems that shape his world. By the time of Andy's suicide at the end of the novel, the full complexities of these problems become evident, with a number of major characters expressing their conflicting emotions in a series of letters to the deceased central character.

A Step from Heaven, by An Na, likewise makes use of first-person narration in order to weave together various social problems, with the challenges of immigration to the United States being the most central. The novel begins when its narrator, Young Ju, is four years old, immigrating with her parents to the United States from Korea. As language and cultural barriers place constant strain on the family, Young Ju also faces misogyny in her home environment, with her father, Apa, discouraging her many talents in favor of praising her younger brother. The stresses of living in a new country contribute to Apa's escalating alcoholism and anger, resulting first in a DUI and eventually in regular physical abuse. After a particularly awful evening, a now-teenage Young Ju calls the police on Apa, who returns to Korea after being released from jail. In the end, Young Ju readies herself to leave for college, feeling that her mother and brother might finally have a better life without Apa around.

Rather than focusing on the immediate impact of traumatic social problems, such as the drunk-driving death and suicide in *Tears of a Tiger*, *A Step from Heaven* is concerned with the ongoing effects of social problems as they occur over many years. Young Ju's life is shaped in many ways by immigration, in particular by the prejudices and challenges she and her family face as outsiders in the United States. At the same time, she struggles with the constant misogyny and abuse she experiences from her father, including his insistence that she not become "too American" (a demand that shows how deeply Young Ju's experience as a cultural outsider and experience with family-based misogyny influence one another). The realities of these challenges unfold slowly and episodically over the course of the novel. Events are rendered not in a clear chronology, with obvious cause-and-effect logic, but rather through fleeting, impressionistic scenes. This creates an expanse of time over which readers are encouraged to focus less on plot than on the development of Young Ju's voice and sense of self in the context of these social problems. The early Young Ju is a passive girl, her life shaped by the violent forces of racism and misogyny and the exclusion of living in a culture that feels foreign to her; by the end of the novel, she has grown in subtle ways, not exactly triumphing above the social problems that defined her young life (their effects still shape her personality in many ways) but gaining the agency and confidence to challenge them by calling the police on her father and leaving home for an independent life at college.

While *Tears of a Tiger* and *A Step from Heaven* both center on social problems that might be experienced by contemporary young adults, Ruta Sepetys's novel *Between Shades of Gray* instead focuses on a historical problem—in this case, the mass deportations and deadly imprisonment of Lithuanian citizens under Joseph Stalin. Told from the perspective of fifteen-year-old Lina, the novel opens as Soviet soldiers enter her home in the middle of the night, splitting up her family and sending Lina, her mother, and her younger brother on a perilous journey to Siberian prison camps. Starving in the frigid weather, Lina is forced to grow vegetables for soldiers to eat and to live in a rickety shack her family builds of scrap wood. The people she meets expose her to a range of cruelties and kindnesses, including a horrific scene in which a man has his teeth removed with pliers and the realization that a friend's mother has been forced into prostitution. While Lina survives her deportation, the happiness of her survival is countered by the death of her mother and the treacherous political reality she faces upon returning home.

By applying the literary techniques of the problem novel to a historical tragedy, *Between Shades of Gray* manages to focus on its emotional and personal ramifications. Also narrated in the first person, it is primarily concerned with Lina's interior life as it unfolds in the context of the exterior horrors she faces. There is some distance provided, with Lina telling the story retrospectively, a move that both allows her some reflection and promises to the reader that she will survive. However, Lina's telling is still primarily concerned with recreating the immediate emotional effects of these horrors in straightforward, unembellished prose; the opening line of the novel, for instance, states simply and terrifyingly, "They took me in my nightgown." This choice allows readers to understand Lina as a teenager who is in many ways typical (she even develops a crush and young romance over the course of the novel) while also better understanding the horrific reality she endures. *Between Shades of Gray* is never educational at the expense of narrative or emotional development, yet it does include brief glimpses into a dimension of Soviet history with which many readers are likely to be unfamiliar. On the whole, it enacts the primary mode of the problem novel, humanizing a broad social problem (albeit one removed by history) by exploring it through the first-person narration of a teenage protagonist and refusing to censor even the most graphic or challenging details.

All three of these novels feature teenage protagonists who must deal not only with the expected challenges of entering adulthood and forming new self-identities but also with the additional challenges of damaging and sometimes deadly social problems. In large part, the reason they all succeed is because they treat the coming-of-age process and the social problem not as separate topics but as deeply related experiences. Just as the adult identity Gerald forms in *Tears of a Tiger* is shaped by the violence and death in his young life, so too are the horrors of Soviet oppression in *Between Shades of Gray* only comprehensible through Lina's

own maturation. Although dark and often depressing, the value of these novels comes not from the redemption of the characters or the defeat of the social problem but from the honest exploration of what it means to live in these realities.

Conclusions

Critics and academics continue to debate the worth of problem novels, with some preferring to draw a distinction between the "problem novels" of the 1970s and 1980s and the realistic fiction, much of it of exceptional literary merit, that became popular in the following decades. These distinctions aside, however, teenage readers have for decades consistently favored books that address difficult or taboo subject matter directly and without sugarcoating, and problem novels and realistic fiction have often become best sellers in the young adult marketplace.

The strict formula favored in problem novels of the 1970s and 1980s is rare in the twenty-first century, just as the writers discussed above filled their novels with literary techniques, changes of perspective, and lyric language that would have been unusual in the genre's early days. What remains similar, however, is that there seems to be no end to new problems facing teenagers. While perennial troubles such as depression and alcoholism have not changed much, there are also new social issues affecting teenagers, from cyberbullying on social media to increasingly diverse family structures and global terrorism. As the social and cultural fabric of the world constantly changes, talented authors will continue to craft complex young adult characters to explore new social problems. Simply addressing taboo or controversial subject matter is no indication of literary value, but neither is it proof of sensationalism. As young adult literature on the whole finds audiences of adult readers as well as the expected teenage ones, problem novels are increasingly received by sophisticated readers who are willing to enter depressing or even horrifying territory in the service of better understanding our world.

T. Fleischmann, MFA

Further Reading

Miller, Laura. "A Good Book Should Make You Cry." *New York Times*. New York Times, 22 Aug. 2004. Web. 14 May 2015. <http://www.nytimes.com/2004/

08/22/books/essay-a-good-book-should-make-you-cry.html>.

Nilsen, Alleen Pace. "That Was Then . . . This Is Now: Reflections on the 25th Anniversary of the YA Problem Novel." *School Library Journal* Apr. 1994: 30–33. *Literary Reference Center*. Web. 14 May 2015. <http://search.ebscohost.com/login.aspx?direct=true&db=lfh&AN=9404207503&site=ehost-live>.

Rafael, Lucy. "Are Problem Novels A Problem?" Rev. of *Welcome to Lizard Motel*, by Barbara Feinberg. *Independent School* Winter 2005: 98–100. *Academic Search Premier*. Web. 14 May 2015. <http://search.ebscohost.com/login.aspx?direct=true&db=aph&AN=18062963&site=ehost-live>.

Bibliography

Burling, Alexis. "Beyond the 'Problem Novel.'" *Publishers Weekly* 20 Oct. 2014: 24–26. *Literary Reference Center*. Web. 14 May 2015. <http://search.ebscohost.com/login.aspx?direct=true&db=lfh&AN=98983087&site=ehost-live>.

Cart, Michael. *Young Adult Literature: From Romance to Realism*. Chicago: ALA, 2011. Print.

Sturm, Brian W., and Karin Michel. "The Structure of Power in Young Adult Problem Novels." *Young Adult Library Services* Winter 2009: 39–47. *Academic Search Premier*. Web. 14 May 2015. <http://search.ebscohost.com/login.aspx?direct=true&db=aph&AN=36206383&site=ehost-live>.

Romance

Titles Discussed

Just One Day by Gayle Forman
Anna and the French Kiss by Stephanie Perkins
This Lullaby by Sarah Dessen

Genre Overview

The history of mainstream young adult literature began in the United States in the late 1960s with the publication of S. E. Hinton's novel *The Outsiders* (1967), which centers on a group of adolescent protagonists and is told from the perspective of a teenage boy. While many novels had been written about teenagers before, and other stories may have been written for an adolescent audience, *The Outsiders* marks the official start of a genre

that was written for and marketed to a teenage audience and told from the perspective of a teenage protagonist. This relatively new genre is also marked by a specific set of themes, such as identity, social pressures, dating, love, coming of age, and finding one's place within society. In the decade following the publication of Hinton's work, young adult literature became popular worldwide. In the beginning, the genre generally focused on teenagers dealing with real-life issues within the setting of traditional high schools and social situations, making realism the key feature. But in the 1980s, interest in young adult literature began to fade as libraries and schools faced budgetary issues. It wasn't until the 1990s that interest in the genre found a resurgence as publishers started marketing directly to parents and teens. With a new direct audience and even more popularity, a host of new subgenres entered into the scene. Fantasy, science fiction, mystery, and the supernatural became popular, and titles like the Harry Potter series and the Hunger Games series became worldwide best sellers.

Romance has always had a place within young adult literature. Love is and always has been an important topic for readers of any age. For adolescents who in middle and high school are usually exploring the notion of attraction and the idea of a relationship for the first time, the theme has been particularly popular. It is usually a key plot point in many novels, even those that may be better placed in other subgenres. For example, the relationship between Bella and Edward is central to the storyline of the Twilight series, although it is more easily placed within the supernatural subgenre. In fact, young adult literature as a whole is known for its melding of many of the more traditional subgenres of literature.

As a theme, romance can be said to hold a place of significance within the great majority of stories written for young adults. Nevertheless, as a genre of young adult literature, romance is distinct itself. The key is the centrality of love and relationships to the plot of the novel. As with traditional adult romance novels, young adult romance novels focus on the relationship between two individuals. However, what makes young adult romance novels unique is the impact that love has on the protagonist as a human being. Love in young adult romance novels is important in itself, but it is also a device that allows the protagonist to explore issues related to his or her self, including identity, self-acceptance, and finding a place within a larger community (whether that is at a school, university, or adult society). The genre became increasingly popular during the 1990s; however, its height of popularity was the twenty-first century. While books focusing on high-school-age characters like Stephenie Meyer's Twilight series and *The Fault in Our Stars* (2012) by John Green met with huge success in part because of the centrality of love to their plots, romance stories began placing a stronger emphasis on the independence of their protagonists. In 2002, Sarah Dessen wrote *This Lullaby* (2002), a story about an eighteen-year-old dealing with love while her own parents are too busy trying to make sense of their own relationships to care much about their daughter. *Anna and the French Kiss* (2010) by Stephanie Perkins and *Just One Day* (2013) by Gayle Forman are other defining examples of the romance genre where imperfect female teenage protagonists face the challenges of love as they struggle with becoming adults.

Works

At the center of any novel within the romance subgenre of young adult literature is love or one relationship. Sometimes these relationships work out for the protagonist, and sometimes they do not. What all romance novels have in common, however, is that this relationship acts as a catalyst for other issues related to growing up and becoming an adult. Through romance, the authors can address many of the main themes of the young adult genre. Sarah Dessen's *This Lullaby* illustrated this notion through the character of eighteen-year-old Remy.

From her mother's many failed relationships with men and the death of her father, Remy has become bitter toward the idea of a positive, lasting relationship. Even her own experience with short romances throughout high school has proven to her that love is not worth anything, and she is confident that she knows everything there is to know about relationships. However, when Remy enters into a relationship with Dexter, everything she thinks she knew is questioned. "I stood in the front yard, at the bottom of the stairs, feeling for the first time in a long while that things were completely out of my control. How had I let this happen?" It is destabilizing for her, but through this instability, she finds her own identity, deals with issues of her father and her past, and finally learns to accept challenges in her own life. It is not Dexter specifically who creates these changes, but rather the inner questions that are raised and answered by Remy herself that lead to her personal development.

While the stability and potential length of Remy's relationship with Dexter is the focus of Dessen's novel, Gayle Forman takes a different approach in *Just One Day* (2013). The romance at the center of the novel lasts for only one day, but the story follows the effects of that day for a year afterward. Allyson, the protagonist, always does the right thing, but on the last night of her vacation in Europe, she meets Willem and they spend one day together. For the next year, nothing seems to work out for Allyson. She is constantly mired and caught up in her first year of college. All of the questions and doubts from the time with Willem still stay with her, and it is not until she confronts those issues that she can take control of her own life. "Maybe that's the thing with liberation. It comes at a price. Forty years wandering in the desert." She abandons everything she is supposed to be doing, goes against the wishes of her parents, and finally finds her own way in life.

Parents, it seems, are generally not positive influences in young adult romance. The idea behind this genre is that a young protagonist progresses through a journey of self-discovery independent of his or her parents yet through their experiences of being in a relationship with another person, usually a contemporary. This relationship and the resulting lessons learned are the catalyst to the main character becoming an adult, and so often in the genre, parents are either background characters or are sometimes not present at all. In Stephanie Perkins's *Anna and the French Kiss*, the protagonist Anna Oliphant is sent away to a French boarding school in her senior year of high school. Without the direct influence of her parents, she is forced to develop her own relationships with the people around her. Although there are rules and discipline at the school, Anna has no mentor to help her, and it is through the people she meets at the school that she begins to understand herself better. The romance at the center of this story is slightly different from many within the romance genre because for most of the novel, it is played out initially through fantasy. However, it is through Anna's trust in herself that she finds the confidence to turn her fantasy into something real.

One of the major themes of *Just One Day* is connected to the many references within the novel to the works of Shakespeare, particularly *Twelfth Night*. It is after Allyson sees Willem perform in the play that she accepts his invitation to go to Paris, and this is not where acting, playing roles, and performance ends in the novel. Coming to terms with her own identity, Allyson must reconcile herself to the roles she plays and the true identity she needs to find in the midst of everything. Remy faces a similar issue in *This Lullaby*, although the problem she faces is in breaking down the barrier she has constructed for herself through the cold, cynical persona she has adopted. Much of the novel is the process Remy faces seeing what parts of herself are truly her and those she created in order to protect herself.

Travel is another major plot element that appears frequently in young adult romance novels. In both *Anna and the French Kiss* and *Just One Day*, travel, although perhaps not the central device within the plot, holds a key role. It is used in *Just One Day* to first drive Allyson to follow her desire to spend one day with Willem, something that she might not otherwise have done if she was in the comfort of her normal life. Travel also serves as a way to introduce physical separation, an issue that is one of the central catalysts for Allyson's personal reflection. Similarly, Anna's travel to Paris in *Anna and the French Kiss* is the main device that tests her self-confidence, drives her to approach and view life as an adult without the protection of her parents, and forces her to find her own identity.

Perhaps the most important theme in these three novels and in young adult romance genres as a whole is the theme of personal relationships. Without a doubt, the romantic relationship stands at the center of the romance novel; however, closely connected to the strength and value of this relationship is the main character's relationships with the people around her. For example, at the beginning of *Anna and the French Kiss*, Anna sees Etienne and instantly has a crush on him. But to her he is unattainable. He is beautiful and unavailable, and so she can only fantasize about their relationship. However, as the novel progresses, Anna develops deeper relationships with many people around her. As she learns the value of these relationships, her perspective of Etienne and the possibility of a more realistic romance develops. Similarly, the relationships that Remy has with her stepfathers and her own mother have determined much of how she approaches her own romantic relationships in life. It is only through a revaluation of the important relationships in her life that she is finally able to develop her relationship with Dexter.

Romance authors in general write and publish novels primarily within the romance genre. Authors of young adult literature are no different, and many authors write novels that take place in the same world. That is to say, often novels by the same author may share the same settings or even the same characters. For example, Gayle Forman wrote *Just One Year* (2013) after the publication of *Just One Day*. With the success of the first book, Forman wrote the sequel to Allyson and Willem's romance, but from the perspective of Willem. Stephanie Perkins and Sarah Dessen also include many sequels to their most popular stories and often with the same characters but from a different perspective. Romance writers appear to have strong connections to their characters—a sentiment that is also shared with readers of the genre.

Conclusions

The romance subgenre in young adult literature is very similar to its counterpart of romance novels written for an adult audience: The subgenre has a definite and somewhat large group of loyal readers. Traditionally, as part of the "genre fiction" group of novels and generally filed under "trade fiction," romance has been considered a less serious form of writing, a form of entertainment rather than a literary art form. However, in recent years this conception has begun to change and works within the young adult genre are similarly being recognized for their literary merit. The fact that young adult romance novels entail so many other themes and issues revolving around adolescent life and identity has opened the genre up to a wider audience more quickly than adult romance novels.

Nevertheless, romance is still a rather specific subgenre of young adult literature. Many titles, especially those under the emerging age label called "new adult," are written for an older audience, older high-school age and college. For this reason, the audience is limited within the young adult genre. However, the subject matter is simply another aspect of the genre that limits its readership. While many young adult novels transcend the traditional limits of subgenres, romance is generally recognized for its focus on one relationship. Even novels that have a romantic relationship at the center of the plot tend to be placed in other subgenres the more popular the story becomes. Until this changes, romance will continue to have a dedicated readership, even it if remains relatively small within the scope of young adult literature.

Aaron Horton, MA

Further Reading

Brookover, Sophie, Elizabeth Burns, and Kelly Jensen. "What's New about New Adult?" *Horn Book Magazine* 90.1 (2014): 41–45. *Literary Reference Center.* Web. 17 May 2015. <http://search.ebscohost.com/login.aspx?direct=true&db=lfh&AN=93250682&site=lrc-live>.

Donahue, Deirdre. "New Adult Fiction Is the Hot New Category in Books." *USA Today*. Gannett, 15 Apr. 2013. Web. 17 May 2015.

Lubar, David. "Everything: The History of Young Adult Novels." *Alan Review Spring* (2003): 19. Digital file. <http://scholar.lib.vt.edu/ejournals/ALAN/v30n3/pdf/lubar.pdf>.

Bibliography

"Anna and the French Kiss." *Kirkus Reviews* 78.21 (2010): 1110. *Literary Reference Center*. Web. 17 May 2015. <http://search.ebscohost.com/login.aspx?direct=true&db=lfh&AN=55096100&site=lrc-live>.

Dessen, Sarah. "An Interview with Sarah Dessen." By Roger Sutton. *Horn Book Magazine* 85.3 (2009): 243–50. *Literary Reference Center*. Web. 17 May 2015. <http://search.ebscohost.com/login.aspx?direct=true&db=lfh&AN=37925708&site=lrc-live>.

"Gayle Forman." *Baker & Taylor Author Biographies* (2000): 1. *Literary Reference Center*. Web. 17 May 2015. <http://search.ebscohost.com/login.aspx?direct=true&db=lfh&AN=49643833&site=lrc-live>.

"Sarah Dessen." *Baker & Taylor Author Biographies* (2000): 1. *Literary Reference Center*. Web. 17 May 2015. <http://search.ebscohost.com/login.aspx?direct=true&db=lfh&AN=49347700&site=lrc-live>.

Kelley, Ann. "Just One Day." *Booklist* 109.9/10 (2013): 108. *Literary Reference Center*. Web. 17 May 2015. <http://search.ebscohost.com/login.aspx?direct=true&db=lfh&AN=84769769&site=lrc-live>.

Roback, Diane, et al. "*This Lullaby* (Book)." *Publishers Weekly* 249.20 (2002): 66. *Literary Reference Center*. Web. 17 May 2015. <http://search.ebscohost.com/login.aspx?direct=true&db=lfh&AN=6695746&site=lrc-live>.

Strickland, Ashley. "A Brief History of Young Adult Literature." CNN. Cable News Network. Turner Broadcasting System, 17 Oct 2013. Web. 15 March 2015. <http://www.cnn.com/2013/10/15/living/young adult-fiction-evolution/>.

Steampunk

Titles Discussed

Airborn by Kenneth Oppel
Leviathan by Scott Westerfeld
Worldshaker by Richard Harland

Genre Overview

Steampunk as a genre first began to appear in the 1960s or 1970s, though it did not acquire its name, or indeed a unifying concept, until the late 1980s. Author K. W. Jeter coined the term in a 1987 letter to *Locus* magazine as a tongue-in-cheek takeoff on "cyberpunk"—another subgenre of science fiction, codified around 1980 or so and characterized as much by its subject matter as by its neo-noir, if not fully dystopian, worldview.

Steampunk was a logical extension of cyberpunk. Both use existing technology—computer and information technology (cyberpunk), steam-powered engines (steampunk)—as a starting point from which to extrapolate hypothetical advancements and their potential effects on a society on the verge of a technology revolution. Steampunk addresses the same interests and concerns as cyberpunk, engaging similarly with issues of empire, imperialism, globalization, futurity, and progress, albeit with a more optimistic attitude than is generally found in cyberpunk.

A classic example of steampunk is *The Difference Engine* (1990), by cyberpunk legends William Gibson and Bruce Sterling, a carefully constructed triptych of interlocking narratives set in an alternate 1855. In this time line, computer pioneer Charles Babbage actually succeeded in constructing his difference engine, an early mechanical computer that the real-life Babbage designed but never built. A fully realized alternate history, *The Difference Engine* makes many references to actual history, with archaeologists, politicians, and writers of the era popping up in ways recognizable but altered by the different chain of events. Within this structure, Gibson and Sterling are free to investigate the nature of the future and modernity: the Crimean War is fought by soldiers in camouflage uniforms, the British Empire covertly manipulates American politics, and scientists debate the nature of evolution.

Steampunk began attracting mainstream attention in the early twenty-first century, primarily as a visual aesthetic, although its growing prominence in popular culture translated to increased interest in steampunk as a media genre as well. This trend was particularly apparent in literature, and young adult novels were no exception. Oft-cited examples of young adult steampunk literature include *Airborn* (2004) by Kenneth Oppel; *Leviathan* (2009), by Scott Westerfeld; and *Worldshaker* (2009), by Richard Harland. All three are the first books in their respective series and feature young protagonists.

Works

Leviathan, by Scott Westerfeld, is set at the start of World War I. As the story opens, Europe is gearing up for war, and the fifteen-year-old prince of the Austro-Hungarian Empire is fleeing his own people. Both the Austro-Hungarians and the Germans are armed with Clankers, steam-powered iron machines bearing guns and cannons, while in Great Britain, the Darwinists instead fight using genetically modified animals as both weapons and "airbeasts"—artificially constructed animals that serve as giant airships. Clearly this is not the World War I that readers recall from history class. This time in history is pure fantasy with a bit of technology thrown in to give the entire world a spin into steampunk.

Deryn Sharp is a British commoner who wants to serve on an airbeast. This opportunity is closed to her because of her gender, so she disguises herself as a boy named Dylan Sharp and sets out to prove herself. Deryn uses a Huxley, a jellyfish-like creature that is lighter than air due to its hydrogen-derived fuel, to prove her abilities. When a storm hits and Deryn is blown out over the North Sea, she is rescued by the ultimate airbeast: the *Leviathan*, a massive flying whale. The *Leviathan* is an excellent example of a creation of the steampunk genre—fanciful in nature, on a scale that is beyond the limits of the technology of the time, yet with a shard of reality in the fact that it is a hydrogen-fueled vessel. This combination of fact and whimsy is representative of steampunk.

As is typical of the steampunk genre, the facts of World War I are in place. The technology is pure science fantasy that fits within the steampunk aesthetic. The alternate history arises from the combination of history and technology, with fanciful machines playing a large part. Some would argue that *Leviathan* is not truly an alternative history, even though the events underlying World War I remain the same, because the Austro-Hungarian Empire was never set to pass from father to child (as it is in the novel) but rather was an allegiance of convenience. Since this is the case, the argument can be made that there is no clear point of divergence that would lead to an alternate historical record. Others would argue that there is an alternative historical record, as evidenced by the difference in who wins and who loses.

Airborn, by Kenneth Oppel, is the story of a cabin boy named Matt Cruse who lives aboard the airship *Aurora*. One day, Matt spies a damaged balloon that turns out to be carrying an ailing old man. The old man mumbles something about "beautiful creatures" before he dies. A year later, Matt meets the man's granddaughter, Kate de Vries, when she comes aboard the *Aurora*. Kate is determined to locate the creatures that her grandfather drew in his journal—flying creatures that Matt describes as "half bird, half panther" (76), with massive, featherless wings. Because these animals most likely live their lives in the air, Kate must be airborne in order to find them.

Aspects of the steampunk genre are included from the start in this work. One aspect is the fact that the *Aurora* runs on hydrium—an obsolete name for hydrogen that here refers to a fictional chemical element. Another steampunk aspect is that Kate arrives by ornithopter, a machine that Leonardo da Vinci envisioned but never built. The ornithopters in *Airborn* are equal parts real and fanciful. Both of these aspects are portrayed as normal parts of everyday life, as is to be expected in this genre.

Not long after Kate boards, pirates attack the *Aurora*, destroying its communication abilities in the process. Shortly thereafter, a storm leaves Matt to steer the ship to safety on an island, which turns out to be the island Kate's grandfather wrote about in his diary. Kate convinces Matt to explore the island with her. They find a skull from one of the flying animals, which Matt dubs "cloud cats," as well as a living, injured animal. Along the way, Matt realizes there is hydrium on the island.

The pirates are on the island as well. Matt and Kate escape from them by inflating Kate's pants with hydrium. Freeing the *Aurora* is more complicated, but in the end, the pirates are defeated and Matt delivers the ship to safety. Months later, Matt meets Kate in Paris. She is lecturing about the cloud cats and will soon begin study as a zoologist. Matt will use his reward money from their adventures to attend the Airship Academy and fulfill his wish to become a pilot.

The steampunk genre is represented in the latter half of *Airborn* as well. Inflating Kate's pants as a means of escape is at once ingenious and swashbuckling. The fact that the cloud cats exist and can be studied is, once again, that half-step away from reality; zoology is a science, yet cloud cats exist in this version of that time. Matt's future as an airship captain, as well as the very fact that there is an airship academy, is also in keeping with the steampunk genre.

In *Worldshaker,* by Richard Hartland, history takes a turn during the Napoleonic Wars. In Hartland's version of history, Napoleon did not engage in a doomed naval battle at Trafalgar. Instead, he dug a tunnel underneath the English Channel, defeated the British, and ushered in a period of war and industrialization that resulted in the era of the juggernauts.

Juggernauts are tremendously huge mobile cities. Quintessentially steampunk, they also represent the potential negative side of industrialization, in which power is used for purposes that do not benefit the common good. Yet on the surface, this type of industrialization—the kind that leads to roving cities—is a perfect steampunk extravaganza, well within the genre's aesthetic. It is up to the reader to determine whether this is industrialization for some crass commercial purpose or for the purpose of the public good.

Hartland's novel tells of the impact of the first large rumblings of discontent in the society. Col, a member of the elite, lives on the upper decks of the juggernaut *Worldshaker*. Chosen to be next supreme commander of *Worldshaker*, Col finds his world upended when a girl Filthy, one of the underclass workers who keep the ship running, escapes from Below and appears in his cabin. The girl begs, "Don't let 'em take me" (4), stunning Col—all his life, he has been taught all his life that Filthies are little more than beasts, unable to understand or speak human language. In light of this revelation, Col is faced with a decision that will change his life: he can ignore the girl and go about his life as planned, or he can open his eyes and deal with the world as it really is. This dilemma is not a traditionally steampunk dilemma, but it is common in young adult literature that deals with a loss of innocence.

Conclusion

In his 1987 letter to *Locus* magazine, Jeter claims to have been the first of "the [Tim] Powers/[James] Blaylock/Jeter fantasy triumvirate" to write in the "gonzo-historical manner" of steampunk, as evidenced by the 1979 publication of his novel *Morlock Night*. While Jeter did not directly apply the term "steampunk" to the genre, he was the one who coined the word, suggesting that "steampunks" could be "a fitting collective term for Powers, Blaylock and myself" ("Birth").

According to librarian Jonathan Greyshade, "The steampunk written today is part of a fourth wave. . . .

A review of classic steampunk smashes many current tropes." Greyshade excoriates so-called steampunk novelists who merely parrot back the "fantasies of their target audience," claiming that this practice engenders "creative stagnation on both sides." Although each work discussed above has received multiple awards and recognition, it remains to be seen whether they are truly steampunk or a diluted version of the genre for young adults. It is possible that steampunk in the form of works such as *Leviathan*, *Airborn*, and *Worldshaker* will lay the foundation for an enduring genre in young adult literature.

Gina Hagler, MBA

Further Reading
Cart, Michael. *Young Adult Literature: From Romance to Realism*. Chicago: ALA, 2011. Print.

Chance, Rosemary. *Young Adult Literature in Action: A Librarian's Guide*. 2nd ed. Santa Barbara: ABC-CLIO, 2014. Print.

Nilsen, Alleen Pace, et al. *Literature for Today's Young Adults*. 9th ed. Boston: Pearson, 2013. Print.

Bibliography
"The Birth of Steampunk." *Letters of Note*. Ed. Shaun Usher. TinyLetter, Mar. 2011. Web. 30 June 2015. <http://www.lettersofnote.com/2011/03/birth-of-steampunk.html>.

Bucher, Katherine, and KaaVonia Hinton. *Young Adult Literature: Exploration, Evaluation, and Appreciation*. 3rd ed. New York: Pearson, 2014. Print.

Cole, Pam B. *Young Adult Literature in the 21st Century*. New York: McGraw, 2009. Print.

Greyshade, Jonathan. "The Nine Novels That Defined Steampunk." *The Steampunk Workshop*. Jake von Slatt, 29 Apr. 2013. Web. 10 May 2015. <http://steampunkworkshop.com/nine-novels-defined-steampunk>.

Laming, Scott. "Steampunk 101: From Sci-Fi Sub-genre to Cultural Phenomenon." *AbeBooks*. AbeBooks, n.d. Web. 10 May 2015. <http://www.abebooks.com/books/victorian-fiction-jeter-robots/steampunk-literature.shtml>.

Rabey, Melissa. *Historical Fiction for Teens: A Genre Guide*. Santa Barbara: Libs. Unltd., 2011. Print.

Sambuchino, Chuck. "Everything You Would've Asked about Steampunk, Had You Known It Existed." *Writer's Digest*. F+W, 13 Aug. 2013. Web. 10 May 2015.

<http://www.writersdigest.com/editor-blogs/guide-to-literary-agents/everything-you-would've-asked-about-steampunk-had-you-known-it-existed>.

Strickland, Ashley. "A Brief History of Young Adult Literature." *CNN*. Cable News Network, 15 Apr. 2015. Web. 10 May 2015. <http://www.cnn.com/2013/10/15/living/young adult-fiction-evolution>.

Urban

Titles Discussed

Homeboyz by Alan Lawrence Sitomer
The Fight by L. Divine
Dope Sick by Walter Dean Myers

Genre Overview

Urban literature is also known as ghetto fiction, street lit, and hip-hop fiction. Urban literature depicts life on the streets and includes themes such as crime, drug use, and gang involvement and contains references to hip-hop and its subgenre gangsta rap. Young adult urban literature features the lives of young, primarily black men and women living and learning to thrive in spite of their environment and circumstances.

Laura Ryan for the *Seattle Times* gives a brief history of the origins of urban literature in her article "Hip-hop Fiction Drawing More Readers to Black Lit." She states that the roots of urban literature began in the 1920s and 1930s with the Harlem Renaissance, continued through the Black Arts movement in the 1970s, and is an integral part of the new Black Renaissance today.

Popular urban fiction writer Donald Goines (1936–74) is known as one of the founding fathers of the street novel and published more than ten books in four years, including *Black Gangster* in 1972. Sister Souljah (b. 1964) continued to make the genre popular into the twenty-first century when she published her debut novel, *The Coldest Winter Ever* (1999). Despite being separated by several decades, *Black Gangster* and *The Coldest Winder Ever* both deal with the harsh realities of life on the streets and include characters involved with crime and drugs. Urban literature is based on authenticity and often on the writer's own life experiences. It is primarily semiautobiographical.

Urban literature did not become mainstream until the early 2000s, despite its popularity among black youth. Prior to that, many writers wrote for themselves, self-published their books independently, and then sold the books out of trunks of cars, street carts, and small convenience stores. *The Coldest Winter Ever* was one of the first urban books to be chosen by a major publisher and was one of the biggest sellers in the genre during the early 2000s.

Young adult urban literature is a quickly growing genre, but librarians are often leery about putting street-lit books on library shelves. The books contain themes many feel are inappropriate for teens and there are concerns that the themes of drug use, prostitution, and criminal activity are romanticized. Writers of urban literature often choose to forgo conventional grammar, spelling, and punctuation, and some educators and critics feel the books read more like early drafts of novels rather than finished works. Despite these concerns, librarians admit that urban literature is bringing in many new readers.

At first one might view Alan Lawrence Sitomer's *Homeboyz* as promoting gangs and the gang lifestyle, but that notion is dispelled as the reader follows Teddy's journey to avenge the murder of his little sister. *Dope Sick* by Walter Dean Myers portrays the harsh and disturbing effects and consequences of heroin addiction and the criminal lifestyle that so often accompanies it, yet the book also shows readers the value of second chances. *The Fight* by L. Divine is a lighthearted take on teenage urban life and depicts a young Jayd Jackson from the Los Angeles neighborhood of Compton and her drama-filled high school exploits.

Works

L. Divine's *The Fight* is the first book in the Drama High series, which follows the life of Jayd Jackson, a teenage girl from Compton who travels a great distance each day in order to attend high school in a wealthy section of Los Angeles. Jayd lives with her grandparents, whom she calls Mama and Daddy, and stays with her mother on weekends. The series portrays life in gang-led city neighborhoods and juxtaposes those neighborhoods with the suburbs and suburban schools.

As with all the books in the series, *The Fight* depicts the daily dangers in Jayd's neighborhood, such as when Jayd witnesses a fatal drive-by shooting on her way to buy snacks. Jayd is only momentarily affected by the shooting, however, and is soon more concerned that her boyfriend KJ will break up with her. Critics have compared Drama High to the 1983–2003 Sweet Valley High series by Francine Pascal that features the high school exploits of blonde twin girls. While that series was popular, today's youth crave protagonists who are more universal and relatable.

Despite the neighborhood that Jayd lives in, she values family and education over the gang lifestyle. She is a teen and therefore spends a lot of time focusing on boys, but she also does her homework, gets good grades, and abstains from alcohol, drugs, and casual sex.

The Fight brings mystical elements into play despite Divine's use of a real-world setting. Jayd's grandmother is called "Voodoo Queen," and she teaches Jayd spiritual work. The grandmother is also a Christian, and she often prays with her rosary beads and reads the Bible. Jayd keeps these aspects of herself separate from her friends and does not discuss her spiritual homework outside of her family.

Dope Sick by Walter Dean Myers also includes fantasy and spiritual elements and follows the present and past of a young man named Jeremy Dance who goes by the street name Lil J. The book opens with Lil J running from the police and trying to hide in an abandoned building. On his way up to the building's roof, he comes upon a man sitting in a chair watching television. Lil J and the reader soon realize that the man is watching what is happening outside the building as well as Lil J trying to get to the roof.

This television shows the past, present, and future and is used to help Lil J find the moment in time that he could change in order to get him out of his current predicament. The reader learns that Lil J is experiencing the effects heroin withdrawal, which is also referred to as being dope sick. The scenes from his past show how he first began getting involved with gangs and criminal activity as well as his failed relationship with his girlfriend and their son.

The man in the chair persuades Lil J to be more honest about his addiction and take responsibility for his actions. This man is a Jesus-like figure seeking to save Lil J from jail or a premature death by suicide, overdose, or at the hands of the police. At the end of the novel the man sacrifices himself to save Lil J and to give him a second chance at a better life.

Lil J is saved by the end of the book, despite not having chosen a past moment he would have changed. The message is clear, however, that although Lil J is saved in the short term from the police and death, it is up to him in the long run to save himself and restore a life for himself. Lil J seems to realize this, and it appears to be his hope that he will be able to turn his back on drugs and crime, find a job, and begin to rebuild a life for himself and his family.

Dope Sick is successful at deglamorizing the gangster lifestyle. Drugs do not make Lil J super human and his life is not enviable. He uses drugs to escape his memories and his troubles and to allow him to continue the path of crime. Lil J reasons that his drug use is not bad because as long as he does not take as many drugs as the next person, then he does not have a problem.

Rather than describe the symptoms and effects of painful opiate withdrawal, Myers describes those who are dope sick as being not only physically ill but also stupid, irrational, and even violent. Myers shows that running from the police is not exciting or glamorous or heroic but terrifying. Lil J is not strong and brave. He is scared, hurt, and tired. He constantly wishes he could have a normal life with a simple home, but the never ending cycle of crime and addiction seems inescapable.

Homeboyz is the third book in Alan Lawrence Sitomer's Hoopster trilogy and shows the consequences of crime. Teddy is a young black man unaffiliated with any gangs, which is noteworthy considering that he lives in the middle of warring gang zones. When Teddy's younger sister is killed in a drive-by shooting, he makes it his mission to avenge her death.

Sitomer uses Teddy to explain the basic rules of gang life and to show how easy it is for underprivileged kids to fall into a criminal lifestyle due to lack of good education and role models. Teddy ends up becoming a role model for a "high risk" kid named Micah as part of his probation. Despite Micah's young age he already has a lengthy criminal record. Eventually the two bond over food and family, but everything changes when Micah reveals he knows the truth behind who killed Teddy's sister.

Teddy must decide if he wants to throw his, and Micah's, life away in the name of revenge, but in the end Teddy arranges it so the guilty party is arrested. The novel does not end with Teddy choosing to put his trust and faith in the justice system. Instead, Teddy, who is extremely bright and has advanced computer skills, hacks into the jail's database and arranges for the man responsible for his sister's death to be placed in a cell with rival gang members. The man is quickly killed by the inmates, and Teddy moves on with his life and his parents take Micah in.

While *Homeboyz* is a cautionary tale, it does romanticize the desire for vengeance, and the novel's message is one of "Don't get caught." Teddy may be a criminal, if not a gangster, but there is hope that Micah will choose to live a better and more peaceful life. Furthermore, Sitomer appears to put much of the blame of Teddy's choices onto corrupt school and justice systems. Kids are not born bad, Sitomer seems to say, but often the hard life is chosen when there are few other options available.

Conclusions

Urban literature holds value for young readers in its relevance and themes. In his article "The Value of Young Adult Literature." Michael Cart states that "young adult literature is made valuable not only by its artistry but also by its relevance to the lives of its readers. And by addressing not only their needs but also their interests, the literature becomes a powerful inducement for them to read." Urban literature creates new readers because it reaches out for the audience that has trouble relating to much else. Cart states that literature for young adults needs "to offer readers an opportunity to see themselves reflected in its pages." He also believes that it is important for readers to read about lives unlike their own. This then discourages feelings of "us" and "them" and helps to join different people and cultures together.

Amy Pattee believes that street literature "walks a fine line between social criticism and profanity." It is most likely this fine distinction that makes urban literature hard to place in libraries. In 2006, Calvin Reid stated that many librarians felt uncomfortable purchasing urban literature because they were unfamiliar with the genre as a whole and the lack of reliable reviews in general.

Authors Emlen, Grenke, Lassen, and Raffensberger show that librarians are becoming more comfortable buying urban literature but are unsure of where to place it. The authors believe that the biggest problem for marketing the genre is that it is not easy to find within the library's stacks: Many young adult titles are placed in the adult sections and others are in a separate section unto themselves. Luckily more and more libraries are including respectable quantities of urban titles within their collection and bringing in more readers by doing so.

Despite the genre's early history of self-publication, more urban fiction titles seem to be getting optioned by mainstream and highly respectable publishers, and the more titles that are marketed and released, the larger the audience will be.

Alexandra McBride, MA

Further Reading

"Dope Sick." Rev. of *Dope Sick* by Walter Dean Myers. *Kirkus Reviews*. Kirkus Media, 20 May 2010. Web. 3 June 2015. <https://www.kirkusreviews.com%2Fbook-reviews%2Fwalter-dean-myers%2Fdope-sick%2F>.

"HOMEBOYZ by Alan Lawrence Sitomer." Rev. of *Homeboyz* by Alan Lawrence Sitomer. *Kirkus Reviews*. Kirkus Media, 20 May 2010. Web. 03 June 2015. <https://www.kirkusreviews.com/book-reviews/alan-lawrence-sitomer/homeboyz/>.

Bibliography

Cart, Michael. "The Value of Young Adult Literature." *YALSA*. American Library Association, Jan. 2008. Web. 3 June 2015. <http://www.ala.org/yalsa/guidelines/whitepapers/yalit>.

Emlen, Nina, Karen Grenke, Christopher Lassen, and Kristy Raffensberger. "What Librarians Say about Street Lit." *School Library Journal*. SLJournal, 4 Feb. 2009. Web. 3 June 2015. <http://www.slj.com/2009/02/collection-development/what-librarians-say-about-street-lit/>.

Patrick, Diane. "Urban Fiction." *Publishers Weekly*. PWxyz, 19 May 2003. Web. 3 June 2015. <http://www.publishersweekly.com/pw/print/20030519/24060-urban-fiction.html>.

Pattee, Amy. "Street Fight: Welcome to the World of Urban Lit." *School Library Journal*. SLJ, 1 July 2008. Web. 3 June 2015. <http://www.slj.com/2008/07/collection-development/street-fight-welcome-to-the-world-of-urban-lit/>.

Reid, Calvin. "Selling Urban Fiction." *Publishers Weekly*. PWxyz, 20 Jan. 2006. Web. 3 June 2015. <http://www.publishersweekly.com/pw/print/20060123/17726-selling-urban-fiction.html>.

Ryan, Laura T. "Hip-hop Fiction Drawing More Readers to Black Lit." *Seattle Times*. Seattle Times, 22 Feb. 2005. Web. 3 June 2015. <http://www.seattletimes.com/entertainment/hip-hop-fiction-drawing-more-readers-to-black-lit/>.

Wright, David. "Streetwise Urban Fiction." *Library Journal*. Lifestyle Theme on Genesis Framework, 15 July 2006. Web. 3 June 2015. <http://reviews.libraryjournal.com/2006/07/collection-development/streetwise-urban-fiction/>.

Timeline

1927
Notable Books:
> *The Tower Treasure*, by Franklin W. Dixon (the first book in the "Hardy Boys" series)

1930
Notable Books:
> *The Secret of the Old Clock*, by Carolyn Keene (the first book in the "Nancy Drew" series)

1936
News:
> Chartered Institute of Library and Information Professionals (CILIP) establishes the Carnegie Award for children's and young people's literature

1942
Notable Books:
> *Seventeenth Summer*, by Maureen Daly

1945
Notable Books:
> *Going on Sixteen*, by Betty Cavanna

1948
Notable Books:
> *Touchdown Pass*, by Clair Bee

1949
Notable Books:
> *Practically Seventeen*, by Rosamund Du Jardin
> *And Both Were Young*, by Madeleine L'Engle

1950
Notable Books:
> *Hot Rod*, by Henry Gregor Felsen

1951
Notable Books:
> *The Catcher in the Rye*, by J.D. Salinger

1962
Notable Books:
> *A Wrinkle in Time*, by Madeleine L'Engle

1965
Notable Books:
> *Over Sea, Under Stone*, by Susan Cooper (first novel in the "Dark is Rising" series)

1966
News:

Young Adult Library Services Association establishes annual "Best Books for Young Adults" list

1967
Notable Books:

The Outsiders, by S.E. Hinton
The Contender, by Robert Lipsyte

1968
Notable Books:

Dragonflight, by Anne McCaffrey (first novel in the "Pern" series)
The Pigman, by Paul Zindel
A Wizard of Earthsea, by Ursula K. Le Guin (first novel in the "Earthsea" series)

1971
Notable Books:

Then Again, Maybe I Won't, by Judy Blume
The Planet of Junior Brown, by Virginia Hamilton

1972
Notable Books:

A Teacup Full of Roses, by Sharon Bell Mathis
Dinky Hocker Shoots Smack! by M.E. Kerr
The Farthest Shore, by Ursula K. Le Guin

1973
Notable Books:

Deenie, by Judy Blume
I Know What You Did Last Summer, by Lois Duncan
A Hero Ain't Nothin' But a Sandwich, by Alice Childress

1974
Notable Books:

The Chocolate War, by Robert Cormier

1975
Notable Books:

Rumble Fish, by S.E. Hinton
Forever, by Judy Blume

1976
Notable Books:

Are You in the House Alone? by Richard Peck

1977
Notable Books:

One Fat Summer, by Robert Lipsyte

1979
Notable Books:
>   *Daughters of Eve*, by Lois Duncan
>   *The Young Landlords*, by Walter Dean Myers

1980
Notable Books:
>   *The Pigman's Legacy*, by Paul Zindel

1983
Notable Books:
>   *Dicey's Song*, by Cynthia Voigt
>   *Running Loose*, by Chris Crutcher
>   *The Colour of Magic*, by Sir Terry Pratchett (first novel in the "Discworld" series)
Media Adaptations:
>   *The Outsiders* (film)
>   *Rumble Fish* (film)

1985
Notable Books:
>   *Slumber Party*, by Christopher Pike
>   *Beyond the Chocolate War*, by Robert Cormier
>   *Ender's Game*, by Orson Scott Card
News:
>   *Perfect Summer*, by Francine Pascal ("Sweet Valley High" series) becomes the first young adult book to appear on the New York Times list of bestselling books

1986
Notable Books:
>   *Izzy, Willy-Nilly*, by Cynthia Voigt

1987
Notable Books:
>   *Motown and Didi*, by Walter Dean Myers
>   *Hatchet*, by Gary Paulsen

1988
Media Adaptations:
>   *The Chocolate War* (film)
Award Winners:
>   S.E. Hinton wins the Margaret A. Edwards Award
News:
>   Margaret A. Edwards Award established by the Young Adult Library Services Association

1989
Notable Books:
>   *The New Girl*, by R.L. Stine (first novel in the "Fear Street" series)
>   *Weetzie Bat*, by Francesca Lia Block
Award Winners:
>   Richard Peck wins the Margaret A. Edwards Award

1991
Notable Books:

The Vampire Diaries, Vol. I: The Awakening, by L.J. Smith
The Vampire Diaries, Vol. II: The Struggle, by L.J. Smith
The Vampire Diaries, Vol. III: The Fury, by L.J. Smith

Award Winners:

Robert Cormier wins the Margaret A. Edwards Award

1992
Notable Books:

The Vampire Diaries, Vol. IV: The Reunion, by L.J. Smith

Award Winners:

Lois Duncan wins the Margaret A. Edwards Award

1993
Award Winners:

M.E. Kerr wins the Margaret A. Edwards Award

1994
Notable Books:

I Hadn't Meant to Tell You This, by Jacqueline Woodson

Award Winners:

Walter Dean Myers wins the Margaret A. Edwards Award

1995
Award Winners:

Cynthia Voigt wins the Margaret A. Edwards Award

1996
Award Winners:

Parrot in the Oven, Mi Vida, by Victor Martinez wins National Book Award for Young People's Literature
Judy Blume wins the Margaret A. Edwards Award

News:

National Book Foundation establishes category of "Young People's Literature" to award young adult novels

1997
Notable Books:

The Facts Speak for Themselves, by Brock Cole

Award Winners:

Dancing on the Edge, by Han Nolan wins National Book Award for Young People's Literature
Gary Paulsen wins the Margaret A. Edwards Award

1998
Notable Books:

Harry Potter and the Sorcerer's Stone, by J.K. Rowling (U.S.)

Award Winners:

Holes, by Louis Sachar wins National Book Award for Young People's Literature
Madeleine L'Engle wins the Margaret A. Edwards Award

1999
Notable Books:
>*Harry Potter and the Chamber of Secrets*, by J.K. Rowling (U.S.)
>*Harry Potter and the Prisoner of Azkaban*, by J.K. Rowling (U.S.)
>*Ender's Shadow*, by Orson Scott Card
>*Speak*, by Laurie Halse Anderson

Award Winners:
>*When Zachary Beaver Came to Town*, by Kimberly Willis Holt wins National Book Award for Young People's Literature
>Anne McCaffrey wins the Margaret A. Edwards Award

2000
Notable Books:
>*Monster*, by Walter Dean Myers
>*Harry Potter and the Goblet of Fire*, by J.K. Rowling (U.S.)

Award Winners:
>*Homeless Bird*, by Gloria Whelan wins National Book Award for Young People's Literature
>*Monster*, by Walter Dean Myers wins Printz Award
>Chris Crutcher wins the Margaret A. Edwards Award

News:
>Michael L. Printz Award for young adult literature established by the Young Adult Library Services Association

2001
Notable Books:
>*The Amazing Maurice and His Educated Rodents*, by Terry Pratchett

Media Adaptations:
>*Harry Potter and the Sorcerer's Stone* (film)

Award Winners:
>*Kit's Wilderness*, by David Almond wins Printz Award
>*True Believer*, by Virginia Euwer Wolff wins National Book Award for Young People's Literature
>Robert Lipsyte wins the Margaret A. Edwards Award

2002
Notable Books:
>*Gossip Girl*, by Cecily von Ziegesar (first book in the "Gossip Girl" series)

Media Adaptations:
>*Harry Potter and the Chamber of Secrets* (film)

Award Winners:
>*A Step From Heaven*, by An Na, wins Printz Award
>*The House of the Scorpion*, by Nancy Farmer wins National Book Award for Young People's Literature
>Paul Zindel wins the Margaret A. Edwards Award

2003
Notable Books:
>*Harry Potter and the Order of the Phoenix*, by J.K. Rowling (U.S.)

Award Winners:
>*Postcards from No Man's Land*, by Aiden Chambers, wins Printz Award
>*The Canning Season*, by Polly Horvath wins National Book Award for Young People's Literature
>Nancy Garden wins the Margaret A. Edwards Award

2004
Media Adaptations:
> *Harry Potter and the Prisoner of Azkaban* (film)

Award Winners:
> *The First Part Last*, by Angela Johnson, wins Printz Award
> *Godless*, by Pete Hautman wins National Book Award for Young People's Literature
> Ursula K. LeGuin wins the Margaret A. Edwards Award

2005
Notable Books:
> *Twilight*, by Stephanie Meyer
> *Harry Potter and the Half-Blood Prince*, by J.K. Rowling (U.S.)
> *Looking for Alaska*, by John Green

Media Adaptations:
> *Harry Potter and the Goblet of Fire* (film)

Award Winners:
> *How I Live Now*, by Meg Rosoff, wins Printz Award
> *The Penderwicks*, by Jeanne Birdsall wins National Book Award for Young People's Literature
> Francesca Lia Block wins the Margaret A. Edwards Award

2006
Notable Books:
> *New Moon*, by Stephanie Meyer

Award Winners:
> *Looking for Alaska*, by John Green, wins Printz Award
> *The Astonishing Life of Octavian Nothing, Traitor to the Nation, Vol. 1: The Pox Party*, by M.T. Anderson wins National Book Award for Young People's Literature
> Jacqueline Woodson wins the Margaret A. Edwards Award

2007
Notable Books:
> *Eclipse*, by Stephanie Meyer
> *Harry Potter and the Deathly Hallows*, by J.K. Rowling (U.S.)

Media Adaptations:
> *Harry Potter and the Order of the Phoenix* (film)
> *Gossip Girl* (TV show)

Award Winners:
> *American Born Chinese*, by Gene Luen Yang, wins Printz Award
> *The Absolutely True Diary of a Part-Time Indian*, by Sherman Alexie wins National Book Award for Young People's Literature
> Lois Lowry wins the Margaret A. Edwards Award

2008
Notable Books:
> *Breaking Dawn*, by Stephanie Meyer
> *The Hunger Games*, by Suzanne Collins
> *Paper Towns*, by John Green

Media Adaptations:
> *Twilight* (film)

Award Winners:

The White Darkness, by Geraldine McCaughrean, wins Printz Award

What I Saw and How I Lied, by Judy Blundell wins National Book Award for Young People's Literature

Orson Scott Card wins the Margaret A. Edwards Award

2009

Notable Books:

Paper Towns, by John Green

Catching Fire, by Suzanne Collins

Beautiful Creatures, by Kami Garcia and Margaret Stohl

Vampire Diaries: The Return: Nightfall, by L.J. Smith

Media Adaptations:

Harry Potter and the Half-Blood Prince (film)

Twilight Saga: New Moon (film)

Vampire Diaries (TV show)

Award Winners:

Jellicoe Road, by Melina Marchetta, wins Printz Award

Claudette Colvin: Twice Toward Justice, by Phillip Hoose wins National Book Award for Young People's Literature

Laurie Halse Anderson wins the Margaret A. Edwards Award

2010

Notable Books:

Mockingjay, by Suzanne Collins

Beautiful Darkness, by Kami Garcia and Margaret Stohl

Vampire Diaries: The Return: Shadow Souls, by L.J. Smith

Media Adaptations:

Harry Potter and the Deathly Hallows, Part I (film)

Twilight Saga: Eclipse (film)

Award Winners:

Going Bovine, by Libba Bray, wins Printz Award

Mockingbird, by Kathryn Erskine wins National Book Award for Young People's Literature

Jim Murphy wins the Margaret A. Edwards Award

News:

Best Books for Young Adults list re-named Best Fiction for Young Adults

2011

Notable Books:

Divergent, by Veronica Roth

Beautiful Chaos, by Kami Garcia and Margaret Stohl

Vampire Diaries: The Return: Midnight, by L.J. Smith

Media Adaptations:

Harry Potter and the Deathly Hallows, Part II (film)

Twilight Saga: Breaking Dawn, Part I (film)

Award Winners:

Ship Breaker, by Paolo Bacigalupi, wins Printz Award

Inside Out and Back Again, by Thanhha Lai wins National Book Award for Young People's Literature

Sir Terry Pratchett wins the Margaret A. Edwards Award

2012
Notable Books:

> *Insurgent*, by Veronica Roth
> *The Fault in Our Stars*, by John Green
> *Eleanor and Park*, Rainbow Rowell
> *Beautiful Redemption*, by Kami Garcia and Margaret Stohl

Media Adaptations:

> *The Hunger Games* (film)
> *Twilight Saga: Breaking Dawn, Part II* (film)

Award Winners:

> *Where Things Come Back*, by John Corey Whaley, wins Printz Award
> *Goblin Secrets*, by William Alexander wins National Book Award for Young People's Literature
> Susan Cooper wins the Margaret A. Edwards Award

News:

> *New York Times* best sellers list establishes a "young adult" category

2013
Notable Books:

> *Allegiant*, by Veronica Roth
> *Fangirl*, by Rainbow Rowell

Media Adaptations:

> *The Hunger Games: Catching Fire* (film)

Award Winners:

> *In Darkness*, by Nick Lake, wins Printz Award
> *The Thing About Luck*, by Cynthia Kadohata wins National Book Award for Young People's Literature
> Tamora Pierce wins the Margaret A. Edwards Award

2014
Notable Books:

> *Four: A Divergent Collection*, by Veronica Roth

Media Adaptations:

> *The Hunger Games: Mockingjay, Part I* (film)
> *Divergent* (film)
> *The Fault in Our Stars* (film)

Award Winners:

> *Midwinterblood*, by Marcus Sedgwick, wins Printz Award
> *Brown Girl Dreaming*, by Jacqueline Woodson wins National Book Award for Young People's Literature
> Marcus Zusak wins the Margaret A. Edwards Award

2015
Media Adaptations:

> *The Hunger Games: Mockingjay, Part II* (film)
> *Insurgent* (film)
> *Paper Towns* (film)

Award Winners:

> *I'll Give You the Sun*, by Jandy Nelson, wins Printz Award
> *Challenger Deep*, by Neal Shusterman wins National Book Award for Young People's Literature
> Sharon Draper wins the Margaret A. Edwards Award

Resources

Young Adult Literature Overviews, Encyclopedias, and Reference Works

Beacham's Guide to Literature for Young Adults. Washington, DC: Beacham Publishing and Detroit, MI: Gale Research, 1989 – present.

Cart, Michael. *Young Adult Literature: From Romance to Realism*. Chicago: ALA Editions, 2010.

Children's Literature Review. Detroit, MI: Gale Research, 1976 – present.

Cullinan, Bernice E., Bonnie L. Kunzel, and Deborah A. Wooten (Ed.). *The Continuum Encyclopedia of Young Adult Literature*. NY: Continuum, 2005.

Drew Bernard A. *100 More Popular Young Adult Authors: Biographical Sketches and Bibliographies*. Greenwood Village, CO: Libraries Unlimited, 2002.

Drew, Bernard A. *The 100 Most Popular Young Adult Authors*. Englewood, CO: Libraries Unlimited, 1996.

Gillespie, John. *The Children's and Young Adult Literature Handbook: A Research and Reference Guide*. Santa Barbara, CA: Libraries Unlimited, 2005.

Gillespie, John and Corinne J. Naden. *Characters in Young Adult Literature*. Detroit, MI: Gale Research, 1997.

Nilsen, Alleen Pace and Don. L.F. Nilsen. *Names and Naming in Young Adult Literature*. Lanham, MD: Scarecrow Press, 2007.

Something About The Author. Detroit, MI: Gale Research, 1972 – present.

Young Adult Literature Textbooks

Bucher, Katherine T. and KaaVonia M. Hinton. *Young Adult Literature: Exploration, Evaluation, and Appreciation*, 3rd ed. Boston, MA: Pearson, 2013.

Cole, Pam. *Young Adult Literature in the 21st Century*. NY: McGraw-Hill, 2008.

Nilsen, Alleen Pace, James Blasingame, Kenneth L. Donelson, and Don L.F. Nilsen. *Literature for Today's Young Adults*, 9th ed. Boston, MA: Pearson, 2012.

Short, Kathy, Carl M. Tomlinson, Carol M. Lynch-Brown, and Holly M. Johnson. *Essentials of Young Adult Literature*, 3rd ed. Boston, MA: Pearson, 2014.

International Awards Recognizing Young Adult Literature

Astrid Lindgren Memorial Award
<http://www.alma.se/en/>

Canadian Library Association's Young Adult Book Award
<http://cla.ca/cla-at-work/awards/young-adult-book-award/>

Chartered Institute of Library and Information Professionals (CILIP) Carnegie Award
<http://www.carnegiegreenaway.org.uk/carnegie/index.php>

Children's Book Council of Australia Book of The Year—Older Readers
<http://cbca.org.au/index.htm>

Hans Christian Andersen Awards (International Board on Books for Young People)
<http://www.ibby.org/273.0.html>

U.S. Awards Recognizing Young Adult Literature
American Indian Youth Literature Award (American Indian Library Association)
<http://ailanet.org/activities/american-indian-youth-literature-award/>

Arab American Book Awards (Arab American National Museum)
<http://arabamericanmuseum.org/bookaward>

Asian/Pacific American Award for Literature (Asian/Pacific American Librarians Association)
<http://www.apalaweb.org/awards/literature-awards/>

Children's Choice Book Awards Teen Book of the Year (Children's Book Council)
<http://www.cbcbooks.org/ccba/>

Coretta Scott King Book Awards (Ethnic and Multicultural Exchange Round Table of the American Library Association)
<http://www.ala.org/emiert/cskbookawards>

Lambda Literary Awards—LGBT Children's/Young Adult (Lambda Literary Foundation)
<http://www.lambdaliterary.org/awards/>

Michael L. Printz Award for Excellence in Young Adult Literature (Young Adult Library Services Association)
<http://www.ala.org/yalsa/printz>

National Book Award for Young People's Literature (National Book Foundation)
<http://www.nationalbook.org/>

Pura Belpré Award (Association for Library Service to Children)
<http://www.ala.org/alsc/awardsgrants/bookmedia/belpremedal>

Schneider Family Book Awards—Teen Book category (American Library Association)
<http://www.ala.org/awardsgrants/schneider-family-book-award>

Stonewall Young Book Awards (Gay, Lesbian, Bisexual, Transgender Round Table of the American Library Association)
<http://www.ala.org/glbtrt/award>

Teens' Top Ten (Young Adult Library Services Association)
<http://www.ala.org/yalsa/teenstopten>

Blogs Addressing Themes and Topics in Young Adult Literature

The Brown Bookshelf: Founded by a group of African American authors and illustrators, The Brown Bookshelf highlights writing for children and young adults by African Americans
<http://thebrownbookshelf.com/>

Disability in Kidlit: edited by Corinne Duyvis, Kayla Whaley, Natasha Razi, and Kody Keplinger, this blog features reviews and discussion of books for young people that include characters with disabilities or address disability
<http://disabilityinkidlit.com/about/>

Diversity in YA: created by authors Cindy Pon and Malinda Lo, this blog and accompanying Tumblr spotlights diversity and offers commentary on diverse representation in young adult literature
< http://www.diversityinya.com/>

I'm Here, I'm Queer, What the Hell do I Read?: Written by blogger Lee Wind, this blog features lists of recommended titles with LGBTQIA content as well as commentary and interviews with authors and people in the youth publishing community
<http://www.leewind.org/>

Reading Rants: Librarian and book reviewer Jennifer Hubert Swann's blog includes reviews of individual YA titles as well as uniquely themed booklists ("Boy Meets Book" and "Fanging Around" are two examples) recommending young adult novels
<http://www.readingrants.org/>

Someday My Printz Will Come: hosted by *School Library Journal* and written by Karyn Silverman, Sarah Couri, and Joy Piedmont, the posts on this blog focus on award-winning and potentially award-winning young adult novels
<http://blogs.slj.com/printzblog/>

Bibliography

"A Long Way from Chicago." Rev. of *A Long Way from Chicago*, by Richard Peck. *Kirkus*. Kirkus, 1 Sept. 1998. Web. 8 May 2015.

"A Long Way from Chicago: A Novel in Stories." Rev. of *A Long Way from Chicago*, by Richard Peck. *Publisher's Weekly*. PWxyz, 1 Sept. 1998. Web. 8 May 2015.

"A Year Down Yonder." Rev. of *A Year Down Yonder*, by Richard Peck. *Publisher's Weekly*. PWxyz, 1 Oct. 2000. Web. 8 May 2015.

"About Darren." *Darren Shan*. Darren Shan, 2014. Web. 10 Mar. 2015.

"About Madeleine L'Engle." *Madeleine L'Engle*. Crosswicks, n.d. Web. 4 June 2015.

"About Maud." *The Official Website of the Lucy Maud Montgomery Society of Ontario*. LMMSO, n.d. Web. 1 May 2015.

Abbott, Michael, and Charles Forceville. "Visual Representation of Emotion in Manga: Loss of Control Is Loss of Hands in *Azumanga Daioh* Volume 4." *Language and Literature* 20.2 (2011): 91–112. Print.

Abrams, Sara. Rev. of *The Maze Runner*, by James Dashner. *Journal of Adolescent & Adult Literacy* 54.2 (2010): 158–59. *Literary Reference Center*. Web. 10 Feb. 2015.

ACT for Youth Center for Excellence. "U.S. Teen Demographics." *ACT for Youth Center for Excellence*. ACT for Youth Center for Excellence, n.d. Web. 25 February 2016.

Adams, Lauren. "Looking for Alibrandi." *Horn Book* 75.3 (1999): 334–35. *Literary Reference Center*. Web. 15 June 2015.

Adler, Margot. "Author Uncertain about *Dark* Leap to Big Screen." *NPR*. NPR, 1 Oct. 2007. Web. 2 June 2015.

"Aidan Chambers." *British Council: Literature*. British Council, 2011. Web. 18 Feb. 2015.

ALA. "Teens Choose Divergent as Their Favorite Book in YALSA's Teens' Top Ten." *ALA*. ALA, 15 October 2012. Web. 20 February 2016.

Alexander, Jonathan. "The Career of David Levithan: It Gets Better and Better." *Los Angeles Review of Books*. LARB, 22 Apr. 2014. Web. 13 Sept. 2015.

Alleva, Richard. "Restless Spirits." Rev. of *The Lovely Bones*, dir. Peter Jackson, and *A Single Man*, dir. Tom Ford. *Commonweal* 12 Feb. 2010: 18–19. *Literary Reference Center*. Web. 12 May 2015.

Alter, Alexandra. "John Green and His Nerdfighters Are Upending the Summer Blockbuster Model." *Wall Street Journal*. Dow Jones, 14 May 2014. Web. 11 Apr. 2015.

Alter, Alexandra. "To Lure Young Readers, Nonfiction Writers Sanitize and Simplify." *New York Times*. New York Times, 7 Oct. 2014. Web. 6 May 2015.

Alter, Alexandra. "Your E-Book Is Reading You." *Wall Street Journal*. Dow Jones, 19 July 2012. Web. 24 Mar. 2015.

"An Epic Chart of 162 Young Adult Retellings." *Epic Reads*. Harper, 26 Feb. 2014. Web. 4 June 2015.

Anderson, John. "Jesse Andrews Learns on the Fly to Write *Me and Earl and the Dying Girl*." *New York Times*. New York Times, 5 June 2015. Web. 15 Dec. 2015.

Anderson, Laurie Halse. "#Speak4RAINN: An Interview with Author Laurie Halse Anderson." Interview by Becca Rose. *HelloGiggles*. HelloGiggles, 18 Apr. 2013. Web. 12 May 2015.

Anderson, Laurie Halse. "Author Revealed." *Simon & Schuster*. Simon, n. d. Web. 12 May 2015.

Anderson, Laurie Halse. "Q & A with Laurie Halse Anderson." Interview by Sally Lodge. *Publishers Weekly*. PWxyz, 5 Dec. 2013. Web. 12 May 2015.

Anderson, M. T. "Him." *MT-Anderson*. M. T. Anderson, n.d. Web. 7 May 2015.

Anderson, M. T. "Q & A with M. T. Anderson." Interview by John A. Sellers. *Publisher's Weekly*. PWxyz, 16 Oct. 2008. Web. 7 May 2015.

Andronik, Catherine M. "Author Profile: Melina Marchetta." *Library Media Connection* 29.5 (2011): 30–32. *Literary Reference Center*. Web. 15 June 2015.

"Angela Johnson." *MacArthur Foundation*. John D. and Catherine T. MacArthur Foundation, 5 Oct. 2003. Web. 1 Dec. 2015.

"Anna and the French Kiss." *Kirkus Reviews* 78.21 (2010): 1110. *Literary Reference Center*. Web. 17 May 2015.

"Announcing New Faculty." *Hamline University*. Hamline U, 2012. Web. 31 Oct. 2015.

Atkinson, Frances. Rev. of *On the Jellicoe Road*, by Melina Marchetta. *Age*. Age, 13 Oct. 2006. Web. 15 Sept. 2015.

Attardo, Salvatore, ed. *Encyclopedia of Humor Studies*. Thousand Oaks: Sage, 2014. Print.

"Author Richard Peck '56 Wins Coveted Newbery Medal." *DePauw University*. DePauw University, 16 Jan. 2001. Web. 7 May 2015.

Bachelder, Linda, Patricia Kelly, Donald Kenney, and Robert Small. "Young Adult Literature: Looking Backward: Trying to Find the Classic Young Adult Novel." *The English Journal* 69.6 (Sept. 1980): 86–89.

Baker, Deirdre F. Rev. of *Far Far Away*, by Tom McNeal. *Horn Book Magazine* 89.4 (2013): 139–40. *Literary Reference Center*. Web. 18 June 2015.

Baker, Deirdre F. Rev. of *How I Live Now*, by Meg Rosoff. *Horn Book Magazine* 80.5 (2004): 597–80. *Literary Reference Center*. Web. 24 Nov. 2015.

Baker, Dierdre F. "Airheads." *Horn Book Magazine* 80.6 (Nov./Dec. 2004): 681–692.

"Banned and Challenged Books: The Who, What, When, Where, and Why." *Delete Censorship*. Half Price Books, 2014. Web. 5 May 2015.

Banned Books Resource Guide, Robert P. Doyle, and ALA. "Why Have These Books Been Banned/Challenged?" *American Library Association*. ALA, 2007. Web. 18 Mar. 2015.

Barcott, Bruce. "Off the Rez." *New York Times*. New York Times, 10 Nov. 2007. Web. 10 May 2015.

Barcott, Bruce. "The Darwins' Prenup." Rev. of *Charles and Emma: The Darwins' Leap of Faith*, by Deborah Heiligman. *New York Times*. New York Times, 6 May 2009. Web. 6 May 2015.

Barnes, Meredith. "How Young Adult Fiction Came of Age." Interview by David W. Brown. *Atlantic*. Atlantic Monthly Group, 1 Aug. 2011. Web. 12 May 2015.

Barth, F. Diane. "Social Media and Adolescent Development: Hazards, Pitfalls and Opportunities for Growth." *Entering the Digital World: Cybertechnology and Clinical Social Work Practice*. Ed. Laura W. Groshong and Faye Mishna. Spec. issue of *Clinical Social Work Journal* 43.2 (2015): 201–8. Print.

Bartyzel, Monika. "Girls on Film: How *The Thin Man*'s Nora Charles became Hollywood's 'Perfect Wife.'" *The Week*. The Week, 30 May 2014. Web. 21 May 2015.

Basu, Balaka, Katherine R. Broad, and Carrie Hintz, eds. *Contemporary Dystopian Fiction for Young Adults: Brave New Teenagers*. New York: Routledge, 2013. Print.

Bates, Dan. Rev. of *Island of the Blue Dolphins*, dir. James B. Clark. *Film Quarterly* 18.1 (1964): 61. Print.

Beardwood, Valerie. "Scott O'Dell and *Island of the Blue Dolphins*." *Elementary English* 38.6 (1961): 373–76. Print.

"*Beastly*." *IMDb*. IMDb.com. 4 Mar. 2011. Web. 13 Mar. 2015.

"Beatle Meets Destiny." Rev. of *Beatle Meets Destiny*, Gabrielle Williams. *Kirkus Reviews*. Kirkus Media, 31 Aug. 2010. Web. 16 Apr. 2015.

Beauchamp, Emma. Rev. of *The Midnight Zoo*, by Sonya Hartnett. Sept.–Oct. 2011: 61. *Literary Reference Center*. Web. 19 Sept. 2015.

Beck, Julie. "The Adult Lessons of YA Fiction." *The Atlantic*. The Atlantic Monthly Group, 9 June 2014. Web. 28 February 2016.

Beckerman, Marty. "A Year without Ned Vizzini: Brilliant YA Author, 'Teen Wolf' Writer, and My Best Friend.'" *MTV*. Viacom International, 18 Dec. 2014. Web. 11 Dec. 2015.

Belluci, Elizabeth. "Alice Sebold's 'The Lovely Bones.'" *Literary Contexts in Novels* (2012): 1. *Literary Reference Center*. Web. 13 May 2015.

Benson, Sheila. "Movie Review: Probing the Darkness in 'The Chocolate War.'" *Los Angeles Times*. Los Angeles Times, 23 Nov. 1988. Web. 30 Nov. 2015.

Bernardo, Anthony. "Something Wicked This Way Comes." *Masterplots II: American Fiction Series, Revised Edition* (2000): 1–3. *Literary Reference Center*. Web. 3 Nov. 2015.

Bernardo, Susan M., and Graham J. Murphy. *Ursula K. Le Guin: A Critical Companion*. Westport: Greenwood, 2006. Print.

"Best Books of 2011." *Goodreads*. Goodreads, n.d. Web. 20 February 2016.

"Best Books of 2012: Results for Best Young Adult Fantasy and Science Fiction." *Goodreads*. Goodreads, n.d. Web. 20 February 2016.

"Best Books of 2013 Winners: Results for Best Young Adult Fantasy and Science Fiction." *Goodreads*. Goodreads, n.d. Web. 20 February 2016.

Biddlecombe, Sarah. "J. K. Rowling: Life after Harry Potter." *Telegraph*. Telegraph Media Group, 1 Feb. 2015. Web. 31 Mar. 2015.

Biedenharn, Isabella. "Gayle Forman to Write First Novel for Adults—Exclusive." *Entertainment Weekly*. Entertainment Weekly, 23 June 2015. Web. 14 Sept. 2015.

Billard, Mary. "Lois Duncan: Revisiting the Classics of an Earlier Generation." *New York Times*. New York Times, 2 Oct. 2013. Web. 7 Apr. 2015.

"Bio." *Ellen Oh*. Author, n.d. Web. 11 Dec. 2015.

"Biography." *Aidan Chambers*. Aidan Chambers, 2011. Web. 18 Feb. 2015.

"Biography." *SharonDraper.com*. Draper, n.d. Web. 16 June 2015.

"Biography: Laurie Halse Anderson." *Scholastic*. Scholastic, n. d. Web. 12 May 2015.

Bishop, Rudine Sims. "Mirrors, Windows, and Sliding Glass Doors." *Perspectives: Choosing and Using Books for the Classroom* 6.3 (Summer 1990). Web. 27 February 2016.

Black, Sharon. "The Magic of Harry Potter: Symbols and Heroes of Fantasy." *Children's Literature in Education* 34.3 (2003): 237–47. *Literary Reference Center*. Web. 6 Apr. 2015.

Blatt, Ben. "Why Do So Many Schools Try to Ban *The Giver*?" *Slate*. Slate Group, 14 Aug. 2014. Web. 30 Mar. 2015.

Block, Francesca Lia. "A Conversation with Francesca Lia Block." Interview by Alan Fox. *Rattle*. Rattle Foundation, 5 Mar. 2014. Web. 31 Mar. 2015.

Block, Francesca Lia. "An Interview with *Weetzie Bat* Author Francesca Lia Block." Interview by Denise Hamilton. *Los Angeles Times*. Los Angeles Times, 15 Nov. 2008. Web. 31 Mar. 2015.

Block, Francesca Lia. "Empathy, Love and the LGBT Characters in My Books." *Huffington Post*. TheHuffingtonPost.com, 23 Oct. 2013. Web. 31 Mar. 2015.

Block, Francesca Lia. "The Rumpus Interview with Francesca Lia Block." Interview by Lauren Eggert-Crowe. *Rumpus*. Rumpus, 4 Aug. 2014. Web. 31 Mar. 2015.

Block, Francesca Lia. *Psyche in a Dress*. 2006. New York: Harper, 2008. Print.

Blume, Judy. "Judy Blume on the *Tiger Eyes* Film, What She's Reading, and Why Moms Can't Get Their Daughters to Read Her Books." Interview by Andrea Cuttler. *Vanity Fair*. Condé Nast, 6 June 2013. Web. 15 May 2015.

Blume, Judy. "Judy Blume: Often Banned, but Widely Beloved." Interview by Neal Conan. *Talk of the Nation*. NPR, 28 Nov. 2011. Web. 31 Mar. 2015.

Blume, Judy. "Places I Never Meant to Be." *Judy Blume on the Web*. Judy Blume, n.d. Web. 14 May 2015.

Blume, Judy. *Forever . . . .* Scarsdale: Bradbury, 1975. Print.

Blumenthal, Karen. "An Interview with Nonfiction Finalist Karen Blumenthal." By Amanda Margis. *YALSA*. American Library Assoc., 25 Jan. 2013. Web. 6 May 2015.

Bodart, Joni Richards. *They Suck, They Bite, They Eat, They Kill: The Psychological Meaning of Supernatural Monsters in Young Adult Fiction*. Lanham: Scarecrow, 2012. Print.

Bogino, Jeanne. "Zombie Fiction." Rev. of *Warm Bodies*, by Isaac Marion. *Library Journal* 136.15 (2011): 70–71. *Literary Reference Center*. Web. 16 May 2015.

"'Book Thief' Hits Two Million in US Sales." *Publishers Weekly*. PWxyz, 15 Dec. 2011. Web. 10 May 2015.

"100 Books That Shaped the Century." *School Library Journal*. Media Source, Inc, 1 January 2000. Web. 23 February 2016.

Booth, Coe. "A Bronx Tale." Interview by Rick Margolis. *School Library Journal* Feb. 2007: 32. *Academic Search Complete*. Web. 31 Oct. 2015.

Booth, Coe. "Everything You Need to Know about Me (Well, Not Really!)." *Coe Booth*. Author, 2014. Web. 29 Sept. 2015.

Borrelli, Christopher. "Veronica Roth the next literary superstar?" *Chicago Tribune*. Chicago Tribune, 21 October 2013. Web. 8 February 2016.

Bowles, Scott. "Concept for 'I Am Number Four' Is Anything but Alien." *USA Today* 17 Feb. 2011: n. pag. *NewsBank*. Web. 16 Apr. 2015.

Boyle, Brendan. "The *Bildungsroman* after McDowell: Mind, World, and Moral Education." *Journal of Aesthetics & Art Criticism* 69.2 (2011): 173–84. *Academic Search Premier*. Web. 8 Apr. 2015.

Bradshaw, Peter. "Stormbreaker." Rev. of *Alex Rider: Stormbreaker*, dir. Geoffrey Sax. *Guardian*. Guardian News and Media, 20 July 2006. Web. 30 Nov. 2015.

Bradshaw, Peter. Rev. of *Angus, Thongs, and Perfect Snogging*. *Guardian*. Guardian News and Media, 24 July 2008. Web. 31 Mar. 2015.

Bradshaw, Peter. Rev. of *Ender's Game*, dir. by Gavin Hood. *Guardian*. Guardian News and Media, 24 Oct. 2013. Web. 2 Apr. 2015.

Bradshaw, Peter. Rev. of *Hugo*, dir. Martin Scorsese. *Guardian*. Guardian News and Media, 1 Dec. 2011. Web. 3 Apr. 2015.

Bradshaw, Peter. Rev. of *It's Kind of a Funny Story*, dir. Ryan Fleck and Anna Boden. *Guardian*. Guardian News and Media, 6 Jan. 2011. Web. 26 Nov. 2015.

Bradshaw, Peter. Rev. of *Youth in Revolt*, dir. Miguel Arteta. *Guardian*. Guardian News and Media, 4 Feb. 2010. Web. 7 Dec. 2015.

Brady, Thomas J. "Mute Character Said a Lot to Her Creator." *Philadelphia Inquirer* 16 Apr. 2000: K02. Print.

Bray, Libba. "About Libba." *Libba Bray*. Libba Bray, n.d. Web. 7 Apr. 2015.

Bray, Libba. *The Diviners*. New York: Little, 2012. Print.

Breeding, Lucinda. "Fantastic Voyages." *Denton Record Chronicle* [TX] 18 Apr. 2004: 4A+. PDF File.

Breznican, Anthony. "'Eleanor & Park': DreamWorks Picks up Film Rights to Rainbow Rowell Novel." *Entertainment Weekly*. Entertainment Weekly, 2 Apr. 2014. Web. 14 Sept. 2015.

Breznican, Anthony. "Author Andrew Smith Keeps YA Weird with *Grasshopper Jungle* and *The Alex Crow*." *Entertainment Weekly*. Entertainment Weekly, 5 Mar. 2015. Web. 22 Oct. 2015.

Brockes, Emma. "John Green: Teenager, Aged 36." *Intelligent Life*. Economist, 1 May 2014. Web. 5 Mar. 2015.

Brodesser-Akner, Taffy. "Francesca Lia Block and Her Post-Apocalyptic Year." *Los Angeles Times*. Los Angeles Times, 22 Aug. 2013. Web. 31 Mar. 2015.

Brown, Alan, and Chris Crowe. "Ball Don't Lie: Connecting Adolescents, Sports, And Literature." *ALAN Review* 41.1 (2013): 76–80. *Education Research Complete*. Web. 12 June 2015.

Brown, Cat. "Authors raise 200,000 for refugees in 24 hours." *The Telegraph*. Telegraph Media Group Limited, 4 September 2015. Web. 5 February 2016.

Brown, Eric C. "Popularizing Pandaemonium: Milton and the Horror Film." *Milton in Popular Culture*. Eds. Laura Lunger Knoppers and Gregory M. Colon Semenza. New York: Palgrave, 2006. 85–97. *eBook Collection (EBSCOhost)*. Web. 3 Nov. 2015.

Brown, Helen. "Page in the Life: Philip Pullman." *Telegraph*. Telegraph Media Group, 17 Oct. 2011. Web. 4 June 2015.

Brown, Jennifer M. "From Outsider to Insider." *Publishers Weekly*. PWxyz, 11 Feb. 2002. Web. 19 Mar. 2015.

Brown, Jennifer M. and Cindi DiMarzo. "Why So Grim?" *Publishers Weekly* 245.7 (16 February 1998): 120–124.

Brown, Michael. "A Geographer Reads *Geography Club*: Spatial Metaphor and Metonym in Textual/ Sexual Space." *Cultural Geographies* 13.3 (2006): 313–39. *Literary Reference Center*. Web. 16 Nov. 2015.

Brown, Monica R., Kyle Higgins, and Kim Paulsen. "Adolescent Alienation: What Is It and What Can Educators Do about It?" *Intervention in School and Clinic* 39.1 (2003): 3–9. *Academic Search Premier*. Web. 14 May 2015.

Brown, Noel. *The Hollywood Family Film: A History, from Shirley Temple to Harry Potter*. London: Tauris, 2012. Print.

Bruni, Frank. "Bodies and Souls." Rev. of *Every Day*, by David Levithan. *New York Times*. New York Times, 23 Aug. 2012. Web. 13 Sept. 2015.

Bucher, Katherine T., and KaaVonia Hinton. *Young Adult Literature: Exploration, Evaluation, and Appreciation*. 3rd ed. New York: Pearson, 2014. 125–58. Print.

Bucher, Katherine, and KaaVonia M. Hinton. "Exploring Contemporary Realistic Fiction." *Young Adult Literature: Exploration, Evaluation, and Appreciation*. 3rd ed. New York: Pearson, 2014. 125–58. Print.

Buckwalter, Ian. "How *Perks of Being a Wallflower* Breaks an Old Filmmaking Curse." *Atlantic*. Atlantic Media Group, 21 Sept. 2012. Web. 3 June 2015.

Bullen, Elizabeth, and Elizabeth Parsons. "Dystopian Visions of Global Capitalism: Philip Reeve's *Mortal Engines* and M. T. Anderson's *Feed*." *Children's Literature in Education* 38.2 (2007): 127–39. *Literary Reference Center*. Web. 7 Apr. 2015.

Bullen, Elizabeth, Kim Toffoletti, and Liz Parsons. "Doing What Your Big Sister Does: Sex, Postfeminism and the YA Chick Lit Series." *Gender and Education* 23.4 (2011): 497–511. *Academic Search Premier*. Web. 8 June 2015.

Burling, Alexis. "Beyond the 'Problem Novel.'" *Publishers Weekly* 20 Oct. 2014: 24–26. *Literary Reference Center*. Web. 14 May 2015.

Burnett, Matia. "'Stay'-ing Power." *Publishers Weekly* 28 July 2014: 15. *Literary Reference Center*. Web. 15 Apr. 2015.

Burr, Ty. "Hide from *The Seeker*." Rev. of *The Seeker*, dir. David L. Cunningham. *Boston.com*. New York Times, 5 Oct. 2007. Web. 2 June 2015.

Burr, Ty. "Life, Above All: Close-Up View of a Courageous Preteen." Rev. of *Life, Above All*, dir. Oliver Schmitz. *Boston Globe*. Globe Newspaper Company, 4 Aug. 2011 Web. 3 Dec. 2015.

Burrows, Victoria. "Rolling with the Punches." *South China Morning Post* 1 Mar. 2009: 3. Print.

Burton, Dwight L. (1951). "The Novel for the Adolescent." *The English Journal*, 40.7 (1951): 363–369

Bushman, John H., and Kay Parks Bushman. "Young adult Nonfiction: Meeting the Needs and Curiosities of Today's Youth." *English Journal* 81.1 (1992): 74. *Academic Search Complete*. Web. 27 May 2015.

Byle, Ann. "Christian YA Fiction: Coming into Full Bloom." *Publishers Weekly*. PWxyz, 27 Aug. 2012. Web. 23 May 2015.

Cabot, Meg. "Author Chat with Meg Cabot." Interview. *New York Public Library*. New York Public Library, 25 Aug. 2005. Web. 9 June 2015.

Cabot, Meg. "Children's Bookshelf Talks with Meg Cabot." Interview by Sue Corbett. *Publishers Weekly*. PWxyz, 17 Jan 2008. Web. 9 June 2015.

Cabot, Meg. "Meg Cabot: Find Out What Meg Cabot Was Like at Seventeen." *Seventeen*. Hearst Communications, 25 Dec. 2007. Web. 31 May. 2015.

Cabot, Meg. "The Princess Diaries Vol. 1." *Meg Cabot*. Meggin Cabot, n.d. Web. 28 February 2016.

Cabot, Meg. Interview. *Readers Read*. Writers Write, 2015. Web. 9 June 2015.

Cabot, Meg. Interview. *YARN*. Young Adult Review Network, 19 Apr. 2010. Web. 9 June 2015.

Cabot, Meg. *The Princess Diaries*. New York: HarperCollins, 2000. Print.

Cahill, Bryon. "Magic and Dragons and Writing . . . Oh, My!" *Writing* Jan. 2007: 18–20. *Literary Reference Center*. Web. 25 Mar. 2015.

Caldwell, Thomas. Rev. of *Tomorrow, When the War Began*, dir. Stuart Beattie. *Cinema Autopsy*. Cinema Autopsy, 30 Aug. 2010. Web. 2 Dec. 2015.

"Cath Crowley Biography." *BookBrowse*. BookBrowse, 26 Aug. 2010. Web. 31 Oct, 2015.

Campbell, Joseph. *The Hero with a Thousand Faces*. 3rd ed. Novato: New World, 2008. Print.

Campbell, Patricia J. *Robert Cormier: Daring to Disturb the Universe*. New York: Delacorte, 2006. Print.

Campbell, Patty. "The Lit of Chick Lit." *Horn Book Magazine* 82.4 (July/August 2006): 487–491.

Campbell, Patty. "The Sand in the Oyster." *Horn Book* 70.2 (March/April 1994): 234–240. *Library and Information Science Source*. Web. 27 February 2016.

Canby, Vincent. "Cher's the Mother (Don't Eat the Snacks)." Rev. of *Mermaids*, dir. Richard Benjamin. *New York Times*. New York Times, 14 Dec. 1990. Web. 23 Nov. 2015.

Canby, Vincent. "Perfection and a 'Love Story': Erich Segal's Romantic Tale Begins Run." Rev. of *Love Story*, dir. by Arthur Hiller. *New York Times*. New York Times, 18 Dec. 1970. Web. 5 Mar. 2015.

Card, Orson Scott. Introduction. *Ender's Game*. New York: Tor, 1991. Print.

Carlson, Dale. Rev. of *Dinky Hocker Shoots Smack!*, by M. E. Kerr. *New York Times* 11 Feb. 1973: BR36. Web. 31 Mar. 2015.

Carlson, Daniel. "*Fat Kid Rules the World* Review: Don't Call It a Comeback, I Been Here for Years." Rev. of *Fat Kid Rules the World*, dir. Matthew Lillard. *Pajiba*. Pajiba, 5 Oct. 2012. Web. 1 Nov. 2015.

Cart, Michael and Christine A. Jenkins. *The Heart Has Its Reasons: Young Adult Literature with Gay/Lesbian/Queer Content, 1969–2004*. Lanham, MD: Scarecrow Press, 2006. Print.

Cart, Michael. "Making noise about chaos." *Booklist* 107.5 (2010): 42.

Cart, Michael. "The Renaissance Continues: Young Adult Literature for the 21st Century." *Catholic Library World* June 2009: 279–85. *Poetry & Short Story Reference Center*. Web. 19 Mar. 2015.

Cart, Michael. "The Renaissance Continues: Young Adult Literature for the 21st Century." *Catholic Library World* 74.9 (2009): 279–85. *Poetry & Short Story Reference Center*. Web. 7 Apr. 2015.

Cart, Michael. "The Renaissance Continues: Young Adult Literature for the 21st Century." *Catholic Library World* 74.9 (2009): 279. Print.

Cart, Michael. "The Value of Young Adult Literature." *YALSA*. American Library Association, Jan. 2008. Web. 12 May 2015.

Cart, Michael. "The Value of Young Adult Literature." *YALSA*. American Library Association, Jan. 2008. Web. 3 June 2015.

Cart, Michael. *From Romance to Realism: 50 Years of Growth and Change in Young Adult Literature*. NY: Harper Collins, 1996.

Cart, Michael. Rev. of *Paper Towns*, by John Green. *Booklist* 1 June 2008: 79. *Literary Reference Center*. Web. 17 Dec. 2015.

Cart, Michael. *Young Adult Literature: From Romance to Realism*, 2010. Chicago: ALA, 2011. Print.

Cart, Michael. *Young Adult Literature: From Romance to Realism*. Chicago: ALA, 2011. Print.

Carter, Ally. "Rich Kids, Greasers and the Life-Changing Power of 'The Outsiders.'" *National Public Radio*. NPR, 28 Jan. 2013. Web. 25 May 2015.

Carton, Debbie. Rev. of *A Little Wanting Song*, by Cath Crowley. *Booklist* 1 May 2010: 77. *Literary Reference Center*. Web. 16 Oct. 2015.

Castellitto, Linda M. "Sharon M. Draper: This Is the Sound of Courage." *BookPage*. BookPage, Jan. 2015. Web. 16 June 2015.

Castle, Gregory. *Reading the Modernist Bildungsroman*. Gainesville: UP of Florida, 2006. Print.

Castleberry, Kristi Janelle. "Elaine of Astolat / The Lady of Shalott." *The Camelot Project*. Rossell Hope Robbins Lib., U of Rochester, n.d. Web. 27 Oct. 2015.

Catsoulis, Jeannette. "Yes, She Has a Sweet Tooth, But She's a Major Carnivore." Rev. of *Blood and Chocolate*, dir. Katja von Garnier. *New York Times*. New York Times, 27 Jan. 2007. Web.5 Mar. 2015.

Caughey, Shanna. *Revisiting Narnia: Fantasy, Myth and Religion in C. S. Lewis' Chronicles*. Dallas: BenBella, 2005. Print.

Chabon, Michael. *The Amazing Adventures of Kavalier and Clay: A Novel*. New York: Random, 2000. Print.

Chambers, Aidan. "Reading: 'The Heart of English'; An Interview with Aidan Chambers." Interview by Anne Fairhall. *English Drama Media* Feb. 2011: 35–42. *Literary Reference Center*. Web. 27 Feb. 2015.

Chambers, Veronica. "Where We Enter." Rev. of *Brown Girl Dreaming*, by Jacqueline Woodson. *New York Times*. New York Times, 22 Aug. 2014. Web. 18 Mar. 2015.

Chance, Rosemary. *Young Adult Literature in Action: A Librarian's Guide*. Santa Barbara: ABC-CLIO, 2014. Print.

Chang, Justin. "Film Review: 'If I Stay.'" Rev. of *If I Stay*, dir. R. J. Cutler. *Variety*. Variety Media, 19 Aug. 2014. Web. 15 Apr. 2015.

Charaipotra, Sona. "*Eleanor & Park* Author Rainbow Rowell Talks about Her Latest Novel, *Fangirl*." *Parade*. Athlon Media Group, 11 Sept. 2013. Web. 14 Sept. 2015.

Chbosky, Stephen. "Interview: *The Perks of Being a Wallflower* Director Stephen Chbosky Talks Finding the Perfect Cast and Changing Teens' Lives." Interview by Tara Aquino. *Complex*. Complex Media, 22 Sept. 2012. Web. 3 June 2015.

Chbosky, Stephen. "Q&A: *Perks of Being a Wallflower*'s Stephen Chbosky on Emma Watson's Casting, High School Yearning, and 'Heroes.'" Interview by Bruce Handy. *Vanity Fair*. Condé Nast, 5 Oct. 2012. Web. 3 June 2015.

Chbosky, Stephen. *The Perks of Being a Wallflower*. New York: MTV, 1999. Print.

Child, Ben. "Ender's Game Sequel No Longer Likely after Unspectacular US Box Office." *Guardian*. Guardian News and Media, 5 Nov. 2013. Web. 2 Apr. 2015.

Child, Ben. "Will *Seventh Son* Bear Only a Faint Family Resemblance to the Books?" *Guardian*. Guardian News and Media, 12 July 2013. Web. 31 Oct. 2015.

"Chris Columbus Biography." *Biography.com*. A&E Television Networks, n.d. Web. 10 Nov. 2015.

Chuang, Laura, et al. "Out in Society, Invisible on the Shelves: Discussing LIS Literature about LGBTQ Youth." *Feliciter* Oct. 2013: 26–27. *Academic Search Complete*. Web. 1 Apr. 2015.

Churchill, David. Rev. of *I Know What You Did Last Summer*. *The School Librarian* 30.1 (June 1982): 151-152. In *Children's Literature Review*. Ed. Gerard J. Senick. Vol. 29. Detroit: Gale, 1993. *Children's Literature Review Online*. Web. 26 February 2016.

Clare, Cassandra. "Q&A: Cassandra Clare." Interview by Angelina Benedetti. *Library Journal* 1 June 2013: 66. Print.

Clark, Noelene. "'Ender's Game' Director Gavin Hood on Why He Changed Ender's Age." *Hero Complex*. Los Angeles Times, 31 Oct. 2013. Web. 2 Apr. 2015.

Clark, Noelene. "Gory *Razorhurst* by Justine Larbalestier Mixes Noir and Ghosts." Rev. of *Razorhurst* by Justine Larbalestier. *Los Angeles Times*. Tribune, 12 March, 2015. Web. 21 Dec. 2015.

Cline, Rich. "*Looking for Alibrandi*." Shadowsonthewall. co.uk. Shadows on the Wall, 2000. Web. 15 May 2015

Clute, John. "McCaffrey, Anne." *The Encyclopedia of Science Fiction*. Ed. John Clute, David Langford, Peter Nicholls, and Graham Sleight. Gollancz, 13 Nov. 2014. Web. 24 Feb. 2015.

Cochrane, Kira. "Stephenie Meyer on *Twilight*, Feminism and True Love." *Guardian*. Guardian News and Media, 11 Mar. 2013. Web. 4 June 2015.

Cohn, D'Vera. "Love and Marriage." *Pew Research Center*. Pew Research Center, 13 Feb. 2013. Web. 10 June 2015.

Cole, Pam B. "Romance, Humor, and Sports." *Young Adult Literature in the Twenty-First Century*. New York: McGraw, 2009. 163–81. Print.

Cole, Pam B. *Young Adult Literature in the 21st Century*. Boston: McGraw, 2009. Print.

Cole, Pam B. *Young Adult Literature in the 21st Century*. New York: McGraw, 2009. Print.

Colfer, Eoin. "Seven Stories." Rev. of *Midwinterblood*, by Marcus Sedgwick. *Sunday Book Review*. New York Times, 8 Feb. 2013. Web. 8 June 2015.

Collins, Suzanne. "A Killer Story: An Interview with Suzanne Collins, Author of 'The Hunger Games.'" Interview with Rick Margolis. *School Library Journal*. School Library Journal, 1 Sept. 2008. Web. 8 June 2015.

Collins, Suzanne. "An Interview with Suzanne Collins." Interview by James Blasingame. *Jour. of Adolescent & Adult Literacy* 52.8 (2009): 726–27. *Literary Reference Center*. Web. 31 Jan. 2015.

Collins, Suzanne. Interview with James Blasingame. *Journal of Adolescent & Adult Literacy* 52.8 (May 2009): 726–27. Print.

Columbus, Chris. "Christopher Columbus Remembers Harry Potter." Interview with Helen O'Hara. *Empire*. Bauer Consumer Media, n. d. Web. 28 Feb. 2015 .

Cooper, Susan. *The Dark Is Rising*. 1973. New York: Aladdin, 1999. Print.

Coppola, Francis Ford, and Stewart Copeland. "How We Made . . . Francis Ford Coppola and Stewart Copeland on Rumble Fish." Interview by Jack Watkins. *Guardian*. Guardian News and Media, 13 Aug. 2012. Web. 3 May 2015.

Corbett, Sue. "'Tiger Eyes': A Family Film." *Publishers Weekly* 6 May 2013: 17. *Literary Reference Center*. Web. 15 May 2015.

Corbett, Sue. "How Reality Became the Hot New Thing in YA." *Publishers Weekly*. PWxyz, 2 May 2014. Web. 11 Apr. 2015.

Corbett, Sue. "In praise of 'chaos.'" *Publishers Weekly* 257.28 (2010 July 19): 26–27. Print.

Corbett, Sue. "Meg Cabot in Margaritaville." *Publishers Weekly*. PWxyz, 14 July 2006. Web. 9 June 2015.

Corbett, Sue. "New Trends in YA: The Agents' Perspective." *Publishers Weekly*. PWxyz, 27 Sept. 2013. Web. 24 Mar. 2015.

Corbett, Sue. "What's New in YA? Mashups." *Publishers Weekly* Oct. 2012: 24–31. *Literary Reference Center*. Web. 14 Apr. 2015.

Corbett, Sue. "Writing for Risk Takers: Andrew Smith." *Publishers Weekly*. PWxzy, 13 Feb. 2015. Web. 22 Oct. 2015.

Corbett, Sue. *Gary Paulsen*. New York: Cavendish, 2014. *eBook Collection (EBSCOhost)*. Web. 23 Mar. 2015.

Cormier, Robert. Interview by Anita Silvey. Rpt. *Horn Book Magazine* 16 Aug. 2013: n. pag. *Horn Book*. Web. 11 June 2015.

Covert, Colin. "Paranormal Heart Beats in *Mortal Instruments*." *Star Tribune*. StarTribune, 23 Aug. 2013. Web. 9 May 2015.

Cowden, Tami D., Caro LaFever, and Sue Viders. *The Complete Writer's Guide to Heroes and Heroines: Sixteen Master Archetypes*. 2000. Las Vegas: Archetype, 2013. Print.

Cowley, Carol, and Tillman Farley. "Adolescent Girls' Attitudes toward Pregnancy." *Journal of Family Practice* 50.7 (2001): 603–7. *Academic Search Premier*. Web. 13 July 2015.

Crook, John. "Young Rape Victim Fights to Reclaim Her Life in 'Speak.'" *Buffalo News* [New York] 4 Sept. 2005: TV37. Print.

Crowder, Courtney. "Chicago Novelist Sells Film Rights." *Chicago Tribune*. Chicago Tribune, 20 April 2011. Web. 16 February 2016.

Crowe, Chris. *More than a Game: Sports Literature for Young Adults*. Lanham: Scarecrow, 2004. Print.

Crowley, Cath. "Cameron Wolfe, Lost and Found." *Age* 14 May 2003: 5. Print.

Crown, Sarah. "You're 10, a refugee in a foreign country. What the hell do you do?" *The Guardian*. Guardian, 18 December 2015. Web. 5 February 2016.

Crowther, Bosley. Rev. of *The Yearling*, dir. Clarence Brown. *New York Times*. New York Times, 24 Jan. 1947. Web. 25 Nov. 2015.

Crutcher, Chris. "Godspeed Ned Vizinni." *Huffington Post*. TheHuffingtonPost.com, 31 Dec. 2013. Web. 15 Dec. 2015.

Crutcher, Chris. Interview. "Author Chat with Chris Crutcher—Transcript of Live Chat." *New York Public Library*. New York Public Lib., 24 July 2002. Web. 18 Mar. 2015.

Crutcher, Paige. "Gayle Forman Concludes *Just One Day* and *Just One Year* with the E-Novella *Just One Night*." *Publishers Weekly*. PWxyz, 6 May 2014. Web. 14 Sept. 2015.

Curry, Alice. *Environmental Crisis in Young Adult Fiction: A Poetics of Earth*. New York: Palgrave, 2013. Print.

Curwood, Jen Scott. "Redefining Normal: A Critical Analysis of (Dis)Ability in Young Adult Literature." *Children's Literature in Education* 44.1 (March 2013): 15–28.

Dargis, Manohla A. "Horror through a Child's Eyes." *New York Times*. New York Times, 6 Nov. 2008. Web. 1 May 2015.

Dargis, Manohla. "Bloody Trouble at School." Rev. of *Vampire Academy*, dir. Mark Waters. *New York Times*. New York Times, 9 Feb. 2014. Web. 25 Feb. 2015.

Dargis, Manohla. "Burdened in a Ravaged South Africa." *New York Times*. New York Times, 14 July 2011. Web. 3 Dec. 2015.

Dargis, Manohla. "Ding Dong! The Witch Is Cute." Rev. of *Beautiful Creatures*, dir. Richard LaGravenese.

New York Times. New York Times, 13 Feb. 2013. Web. 20 Mar. 2015.

Dargis, Manohla. "He's in Love; Excuse His French." Rev. of *Youth in Revolt*, dir. Miguel Arteta. *New York Times*. New York Times, 7 Jan. 2010. Web. 7 Dec. 2015.

Dargis, Manohla. "In *Divergent*, Jolted Awake by Fear and Romance." Rev. of *Divergent*, dir. Neil Burger. *New York Times*. New York Times, 20 Mar. 2014. Web. 2 May 2015.

Dargis, Manohla. "Inventing a World, Just Like Clockwork." Rev. of *Hugo*, dir. Martin Scorsese. *New York Times*. New York Times, 22 Nov. 2011. Web. 6 Apr. 2015.

Dargis, Manohla. "What Oscar Nominees Do to Pass the Time." Rev. of *Seventh Son*, dir. Sergey Bodrov. *New York Times*. New York Times, 5 Feb. 2015. Web. 31 Oct. 2015.

Davies, Stephanie. *Laughology: Improve Your Life with the Science of Laughter*. Bethel: Crown, 2013. Print.

Davis, Rocío G. "Childhood and Ethnic Visibility in Gene Yang's *American Born Chinese*." *Prose Studies* 35.1 (2013): 7–15. *Literary Reference Center*. Web. 7 July 2015.

Davis, Rocío G. "Childhood and Ethnic Visibility in Gene Yang's *American Born Chinese*." *Prose Studies* 35.1 (2013): 7–15. *Literary Reference Center*. Web. 30 Apr. 2015.

De Lint, Charles. "Aquamarine (Book)." Rev. of *Aquamarine*, by Alice Hoffman. *Fantasy & Science Fiction* 102.2 (2002): 37. *Literary Reference Center*. Web. 19 June 2015.

Deahl, Rachel. "David Levithan: The Happy Editor-Writer." *Publisher's Weekly*. PWxyz, 18 Feb. 2008. Web. 13 Sept. 2015.

Deahl, Rachel. "Self-Pubbed Book Finds Homes in Hollywood, New York." *Publishers Weekly* 257.7 (2010): 8. *Literary Reference Center*. Web. 16 May 2015.

Dean Myers, Walter. "Talking with Walter Dean Myers." Interview by Cyndi Giorgis. *Booklist* 1 Jan. 2014: 16–19. *Literary Reference Center*. Web. 10 June 2015.

Dean Myers, Walter. "The Importance of Literacy: A Q&A with Author Walter Dean Myers." Interview by Earl Martin Phalen. *Huffington Post*. HuffingtonPost.com, 10 May 2012. Web. 10 June 2015.

Dean Myers, Walter. "Walter Dean Myers: *Lockdown*." Interview by Eisa Ulen. *National Book Foundation*. Natl. Book Foundation, n.d. Web. 10 June 2015.

Dean, Michelle. "Our young adult dystopia." *New York Times Magazine*. The New York Times Company, 31 January 2014. Web. 8 February 2016.

Debruge, Peter. "Film Review: 'Geography Club.'" Rev. of *The Geography Club*, dir. Gary Entin. *Variety*. Variety Media, 25 Mar. 2014. Web. 18 Nov. 2015.

Debruge, Peter. Rev. of *Seventh Son*, dir. Sergey Bodrov. *Variety*. Variety Media, 17 Dec. 2014. Web. 31 Oct. 2015.

Denby, David. "Dangerous Liaisons." Rev. of *Beautiful Creatures*, dir. Richard LaGravenese. *New Yorker*. Condé Nast, 4 Mar. 2013. Web. 19 Mar. 2015.

Dessen, Sarah. "An Interview with Sarah Dessen." By Roger Sutton. *Horn Book Magazine* 85.3 (2009): 243–50. *Literary Reference Center*. Web. 17 May 2015.

Dickerson, Justin. "An Inside Look at 'The Outsiders.'" *USA Today*. USA Today, 19 Sept. 2005. Web. 4 Mar. 2015.

Dickison, Cynthia. "While Not Innovative, *Maze Runner* Themes Deftly Mined." Rev. of *The Maze Runner*, dir. Wes Ball. *Star Tribune* [Minneapolis] 17 Sept. 2014: n. pag. *Points of View Reference Center*. Web. 10 Feb. 2015.

Dobbins, Amanda. "Chasing Katniss: Divergent Author Veronica Roth Builds Her Dystopian Empire." *New York* 7 October 2013. Academic One File. Web. 16 February 2016.

Dobrez, Cindy. Rev. of *Kendra*, by Coe Booth. *Booklist* 1 Nov. 2008: 34. *Literary Reference Center*. Web. 19 Sept. 2015.

Doll, Jen. "Reading Lois Lowry's 'The Giver' as an Adult." *Wire*. Atlantic Monthly Group, 23 Aug. 2012. Web. 30 Mar. 2015.

Dominus, Susan. "Suzanne Collins's War Stories for Kids." *New York Times Magazine*. New York Times, 8 Apr. 2011. Web. 8 June 2015.

Dominus, Susan. "What Happened to the Girls in Le Roy." *New York Times*. New York Times, 7 Mar. 2012. Web. 13 May 2015.

Donelson, Kenneth, and Alleen Pace Nilsen. *Literature for Today's Young Adults*. Glenview: Scott, 1980. Print.

Draper, Sharon M. "Interview with Award-Winning and Bestselling Author Dr. Sharon M. Draper." Interview by Bianca Shulze. *Children's Book Review*. Children's Book Review, 22 Aug. 2013. Web. 16 June 2015.

"DrugFacts: High School and Youth Trends." *National Institute of Drug Abuse*. Natl. Institutes of Health, Dec. 2014. Web. 30 May 2015.

"Duncan, Lois (1934-)." *Major 21st-Century Writers*. Ed. Tracey Matthews and Tracey Watson. Vol. 2. Detroit: Gale, 2005. *Gale Virtual Reference Library*. Web. 27 February 2016.

Duncan, Lois. "An Interview with Lois Duncan." Interview by Joan Kaywell. *Journal of Adolescent & Adult Literacy* 52.6 (2009): 545–47. *Literary Reference Center*. Web. 7 Apr. 2015.

Duncan, Lois. "An Interview with Lois Duncan." Interview by Joan Kaywell. *Journal of Adolescent & Adult Literacy* 52.6 (2009): 545–7. *Literary Reference Center*. Web. 6 Mar. 2015.

Dziemianowicz, Stefan. "Francesca Lia Block." *Guide to Literary Masters & Their Works* Jan. 2007: n.p. *Literary Reference Center*. Web. 25 Apr. 2015.

"Eating Disorders Statistics." *National Association of Anorexia Nervosa and Associated Disorders*. ANAD, 2015. Web. 13 May 2015.

Ebert, Robert. Rev. of *Rumble Fish*, dir. Francis Ford Coppola. *RogerEbert.com*. Ebert Digital, 26 Aug. 1983. Web. 3 May 2015.

Ebert, Roger. "Something Wicked This Way Comes." Rev. of *Something Wicked This Way* Comes, dir. by Jack Clayton. *RogerEbert.com*. Ebert Digital, 29 Apr. 1983. Web. 23 Oct. 2015.

Ebert, Roger. "Twilight." Roger Ebert. Ebert Digital, 19 Nov. 2008. Web. 10 May 2015.

Ebert, Roger. Rev. of *City of Ember*, dir. Gil Kenan. *RogerEbert.com*. al, 8 Oct. 2008. Web. 6 May. 2015.

Ebert, Roger. Rev. of *Harry Potter and the Prisoner of Azkaban*. *RogerEbert.com*. Ebert Digital, 3 June 2004. Web. 28 Feb. 2015.

Ebert, Roger. Rev. of *Holes*. *RogerEbert.com*. Ebert Digital, 18 Apr. 2003. Web. 28 Feb. 2015.

Ebert, Roger. Rev. of *Howl's Moving Castle*, dir. Hayao Miyazaki. *RogerEbert.com*. Ebert Digital, 9 June 2005. Web. 30 Apr. 2015.

Ebert, Roger. Rev. of *Life, Above All*, dir. Oliver Schmitz. *RogerEbert.com*. 31 Aug. 2011. Web. 3 Dec. 2015.

Ebert, Roger. Rev. of *Mermaids*, dir. Richard Benjamin. *RogerEbert.com*. Ebert Digital, 14 Dec. 1990. Web. 10 Nov. 2015.

Ebert, Roger. Rev. of *Mrs. Doubtfire*, dir. Chris Columbus. *RogerEbert.com*. Ebert Digital, 24 Nov. 1993. Web. 23 Nov. 2015.

Ebert, Roger. Rev. of *Nick and Norah's Infinite Playlist*, dir. Peter Sollett. *RogerEbert.com*. RogerEbert.com, 2 Oct. 2008. Web. 21 May 2015.

Ebert, Roger. Rev. of *Stardust*, dir. Matthew Vaughn. *RogerEbert.com*. Ebert Digital, 9 Aug. 2007. Web. 30 Nov. 2015.

Ebert, Roger. Rev. of *The Perks of Being a Wallflower*, dir. by Stephen Chbosky. *RogerEbert.com*. Ebert Digital, 26 Sept. 2012. Web. 5 June 2015.

Ebert, Roger. Rev. of *The Spectacular Now*, dir. James Ponsoldt. *RogerEbert*. Ebert Digital, 2 Aug. 2013. Web. 30 Dec. 2015.

Ebiri, Bilge. "The DUFF Is a New High-School Comedy Classic." *Vulture*. New York Media, 20 Feb. 2015. Web. 31 Oct. 2015.

Ehrlich, Hannah. "The Diversity Gap in Children's Publishing, 2015." *The Open Book*. Lee and Low Books, 5 March 2015. Web. 23 February 2016.

Eitle, Tamela McNulty. "Race, Cultural Capital, and the Educational Effects of Participation in Sports." *Sociology of Education* 75.2 (2002): 123–46. *FRANCIS*. Web. 11 June 2015.

"Elizabeth Hall: Author, Psychologist, Voyager." *Elizabethhall*. Elizabeth Hall, 11 June 2009. Web. 25 May 2015.

Eldridge, Alison. "Terry Pratchett." *Encyclopaedia Britannica*. Encyclopaedia Britannica, 12 Mar. 2015. Web. 4 June 2015.

Elwes, Cary, and Joe Layden. *As You Wish: Inconceivable Tales from the Making of* The Princess Bride. New York: Touchstone, 2014. Print.

"Ender's Game." Rev. of *Ender's Game*, by Orson Scott Card. *Kirkus Reviews*. Kirkus Media, 2 Nov. 2011. Web. 16 Apr. 2015.

Emlen, Nina, Karen Grenke, Christopher Lassen, and Kristy Raffensberger. "What Librarians Say about Street Lit." *School Library Journal*. SLJournal, 4 Feb. 2009. Web. 3 June 2015.

Englander, Elizabeth Kandel. *Bullying and Cyberbullying: What Every Educator Needs to Know*. Cambridge: Harvard Education P, 2013. Print.

Erickson, Hal. "*The Yearling* Synopsis." *Fandango*. Fandango, 2015. Web. 25 Nov. 2015.

Evarts, Lynn. "Trans by the Light of the Moon." *Lambda Book Report* 13.3 (2004): 13. *Academic Search Complete*. Web. 17 Dec. 2015.

Ewing, Jack. "Anne Fine." *Guide to Literary Masters & Their Works (*2007): 1. *Literary Reference Center*. Web. 16 Nov. 2015.

"FAQ." *We Need Diverse Books*. We Need Diverse Books, n.d. Web. 11 Dec. 2015.

Farber, Stephen. Rev. of *The Seeker*, dir. David L. Cunningham. *Hollywood Reporter*. Hollywood Reporter, 4 Oct. 2007. Web. 2 June 2015.

"Feeling Sorry for Celia." *Kirkus*. Kirkus Media, 20 May 2010. Web. 5 May 2015.

Feiring, Candice. "Concepts of Romance in 15-Year-Old Adolescents." *Journal of Research on Adolescence (Lawrence Erlbaum)* 6.2 (1996): 181–200. *Academic Search Complete*. Web. 10 June 2015.

Fike, Matthew A. *The One Mind: C. G. Jung and the Future of Literary Criticism*. New York: Routledge, 2014. Print.

"Film Review: The Geography Club." Rev. of *The Geography Club*, dir. Gary Entin. *FilmJournal Intl.* FilmJournal Intl., 15 Nov. 2013. Web. 18 Nov. 2015.

Fine, Anne. "Major Awards." *AnneFine.com*. Anne Fine, n.d. Web. 10 Nov. 2015.

Fine, Marshall. Rev. of *Life, Above All*, dir. Oliver Schmitz. *HuffPost Entertainment*. TheHuffingtonPost.com, 13 July 2011. Web. 3 Dec. 2015.

Flake, Sharon. "More Nonwhite Characters are Needed." *New York Times*. New York Times, 28 March 2012. Web. 22 February 2016.

Flood, Alison. "A Life in Writing: Terry Pratchett." *Guardian*. Guardian News and Media, 14 Oct. 2011. Web. 4 June 2015.

Flood, Alison. "Twilight Author Stephenie Meyer 'Can't Write Worth a Darn,' says Stephen King." *Guardian*. Guardian News and Media, 5 Feb. 2009. Web. 10 May 2015 .

Flood, Allison. "Patrick Ness wins Carnegie medal for second year running. *The Guardian*. Guardian, 14 June 2012. Web. 5 February 2016.

Flowers, Mark. "YALSA Nonfiction, Part Two: The Notorious Benedict Arnold." *YALSA*. Amer. Lib. Assoc., 16 Dec. 2011. Web. 6 May 2015.

Folkart, Burt A. "Scott O'Dell, 91: 'Writer of Books That Children Read.'" *LA Times*. Los Angeles Times, 18 Oct. 1989. Web. 25 May 2015.

Ford, Elizabeth A., and Deborah C. Mitchell. *The Makeover in Movies: Before and After in Hollywood Films, 1941–2002*. Jefferson: McFarland, 2004. Print.

Forman, Gayle. "Q&A with Gayle Forman." Interview by Sue Corbett. *Publishers Weekly*. PWxyz, 30 Apr. 2009. Web. 14 Sept. 2015.

Forman, Gayle. "Teens Crave Young Adult Books on Really Dark Topics (And That's OK)." *Time*. Time, 6 Feb. 2015. Web. 13 May 2015.

Forman, Gayle. Interview by Mike French. *The View from Here*. View from Here, 1 Nov. 2014. Web. 14 Sept. 2015.

Fowkes, Katherine A. *The Fantasy Film*. Malden: Wiley, 2013. Print.

Fox, Margalit. "Anne McCaffrey, Author of 'Dragonriders' Fantasies, Dies at 85." *New York Times*. New York Times, 24 Nov. 2011. Web. 22 Feb. 2015.

Franzak, Judith, and Elizabeth Noll. "Monstrous Acts: Problematizing Violence in Young Adult Literature." *Journal of Adolescent & Adult Literacy* 49.8 (2006): 662–672. *Literary Reference Center*. Web. 7 Apr.2015.

Freedman, Carl, ed. *Conversations with Ursula K. Le Guin*. Jackson: UP of Mississippi, 2008. Print.

Freitas, Donna. "How to Be Bad." Rev. of *The Disreputable History of Frankie Landau-Banks*, by E. Lockhart. *New York Times*. New York Times, 15 Aug. 2008. Web. 1 Mar. 2015.

Friedman, Robin. "The Write Stuff: A Young Adult Author's (Almost) Infinite Playlist." *New Jersey Jewish News*. New Jersey Jewish News, 2 July 2009. Web. 13 Sept. 2015.

Frost, Helen. *Keesha's House*. 2003. New York: Farrar, 2007. Print.

Fry, Erin. "Veronica Roth." *Publishers Weekly* 258.25 (2011): 25. Business Source Complete. Web. 16 February 2016.

Gaiman, Neil, and Amanda Palmer. "An Evening with Neil Gaiman and Amanda Palmer: Ask Us Anything. Go On. You Know You Want To." *Reddit*. Reddit, 19 Nov. 2013. Web. 3 Dec. 2015.

Gaiman, Neil. "Quint Has a Long Chat with Neil Gaiman about *Stardust, Beowulf, Coraline, Sandman, Death*, and Comic-Con!!!" Interview by Eric Vespe. *Ain't It Cool News*. Ain't It Cool News, 14 June 2007. Web. 30 Nov. 2015.

Galda, Lee, et al. *Literature and the Child*. 8th ed. Belmont: Wadsworth, 2014. Print.

Garden, Nancy. *Annie on My Mind*. 1982. New York: Farrar, 2007. Print.

Gardner, Lyn. "Robert Cormier." *Guardian*. Guardian News and Media, 5 Nov. 2000. Web. 2 June 2015.

Gavin, Adrienne E., ed. *Robert Cormier*. New York: Palgrave, 2012. Print.

"Gayle Forman." *Baker & Taylor Author Biographies* (2000): 1. *Literary Reference Center*. Web. 17 May 2015.

Genzlinger, Neil. "Closeted High School Romances." Rev. of *The Geography Club*, dir. Gary Entin. *New*

York Times. New York Times, 14 Nov. 2013. Web. 18 Nov. 2015.

Genzlinger, Neil. "For One Teenager, the Party's Over." *New York Times*. New York Times, 5 Sept. 2005. Web. 10 June 2015.

Gershowitz, Elissa. "What Makes a Good 'Bad' Book?" *Horn Book Magazine* 89.4 (2013): 84–90. *Literary Reference Center*. Web. 30 June 2015.

Gilbertson, Irvyn G. "McCaughrean, Geraldine." *Continuum Encyclopedia of Children's Literature* (2003): 529. *Literary Reference Center*. Web. 28 May 2015.

Gillis, Bryan, and Joanna Simpson. *Sexual Content in Young Adult Literature: Reading between the Sheets*. Lanham: Rowman, 2015. Print.

Gilman, Priscilla. "Midnight in Paris." Rev. of *Just One Day*, by Gayle Forman. *New York Times*. New York Times, 11 Jan. 2013. Web. 14 Sept. 2015.

Gilman, Priscilla. Rev. of *Just One Year*, by Gayle Forman. *Kirkus Reviews* 1 Oct. 2013: 201. *Literary Reference Center*. Web. 14 Sept. 2015.

Gleiberman, Owen. Rev. of *Beautiful Creatures*, dir. Richard LaGravenese. *Entertainment Weekly*. Entertainment Weekly, 28 Feb. 2013. Web. 19 Mar. 2013.

Going, K. L. "Michael L. Printz Honor Speech." *Young Adult Library Services* 3.1 (2004): 28–41. *Education Source*. Web. 17 Nov. 2015.

Going, K. L. "Q&A with K. L. Going." Interview by Sue Corbett. *Publishers Weekly*. PWxyz, 12 Feb. 2009. Web. 1 Nov. 2015.

Going, K. L. *K. L. Going*. K. L. Going, n.d. Web. 1 Nov. 2015.

Goldberg-Sloan, Holly. "'Stella by Starlight' and 'Moonpenny Island.'" Rev. of *Stella by Starlight*, by Sharon M. Draper. *New York Times*. New York Times, 6 Feb. 2015. Web. 16 June 2015.

Goldman, William. *The Princess Bride: S. Morgenstern's Classic Tale of True Love and High Adventure; The "Good Parts" Version, Abridged*. 1973. Orlando: Harcourt, 2007. Print.

Goldstein, Gary. Rev. of *Geography Club*, dir. Gary Entin. *Los Angeles Times*. Los Angeles Times, 21 Nov. 2013. Web. 9 Nov. 2015.

Goldstein, Patrick. "Dark 'Chocolate War' Sweet Debut for Director Gordon." *Los Angeles Times*. Los Angeles Times, 29 Nov. 1988. Web. 7 Dec. 2015.

Gopnik, Adam. "The Dragon's Egg." *New Yorker* 5 Dec. 2011: 86–89. *Literary Reference Center*. Web. 25 Mar. 2015.

Gordon, Keith. "DVD Finally on the Way!/Comment on Ending." *IMDb*. IMDB.com, 6 Feb. 2006. Web. 30 Nov. 2015.

Gottlieb, Amy. "Judy Blume." *Jewish Women's Archive*. Jewish Women's Archive, 2015. Web. 31 Mar. 2015.

Govan, Sandra Y. "Alice Childress's Rainbow Jordan: The Black Aesthetic Returns Dressed in Adolescent Fiction." *Children's Literature Association Quarterly* 13.2 (Summer 1988): 70–74.

Graham, Ruth. "Against YA." *Slate*. The Slate Group, 5 June 2014. Web. 28 February 2016.

Graser, Marc, and Dave McNary. "'Frozen' Director Jennifer Lee to Adapt 'A Wrinkle in Time' for Disney." *Variety*. Variety, 5 Aug. 2014. Web. 30 Nov. 2015.

Green, Amanda. "How Rainbow Rowell Went from Newspaper Reporter to Superstar Novelist." *Mental Floss*. Mental Floss, 1 Sep. 2014. Web. 14 Sep. 2015.

Green, John, and David Levithan. *Will Grayson, Will Grayson*. New York: Dutton, 2010. Print.

Green, John. "Fighting for Their Lives." *New York Times*. New York Times, 14 May, 2006. Web. 10 May 2015.

Green, John. "How John Green Wrote a Cancer Book but Not a 'Bullsh*t Cancer Book.'" Interview by Rebecca J. Rosen. *Atlantic*. Atlantic Monthly, 25 Feb. 2013. Web. 13 May 2015.

Green, John. Interview by Rebecca J. Rosen. *Atlantic* Feb. 2013: n. pag. Print.

Green, John. Online posting. *John Green's Tumblr*. Tumblr, 9 Aug. 2013. Web. 30 Nov. 2015.

Green, Melody. "Jesus, Girard, and Twentieth-Century Fantasy for Young Adults." *Studies in the Literary Imagination* 46.2 (2013): 19–33. *Literary Reference Center*. Web. 6 Apr. 2015.

Greene, Maxine. *Releasing the Imagination: Essays on Education, the Arts, and Social Change*. San Francisco: Jossey, 1995. Print.

Greene, Meg. *Louis Sachar*. New York: Rosen, 2004. Print.

Greenway, Betty. "Chris Crutcher—Hero or Villain?" *ALAN Review* 22.1 (1994): n. pag. Web. 18 Mar. 2015.

Greenway, Betty. *Aidan Chambers: Master Literary Choreographer*. Lanham: Scarecrow, 2006. Print.

Gresh, Lois H. *The Mortal Instruments Companion: City of Bones, Shadowhunters, and the Sight*. New York: St. Martin's, 2013. Print.

Greyshade, Jonathan. "The Nine Novels That Defined Steampunk." *The Steampunk Workshop*. Jake von Slatt, 29 Apr. 2013. Web. 10 May 2015.

Grice, Elizabeth. "Sir Terry Pratchett: 'I Thought My Alzheimer's Would Be a Lot Worse than This by Now.'" *Telegraph*. Telegraph Media Group, 10 Sept. 2012. Web. 4 June 2015.

Grinberg, Emanuella. "'Speak' Author: 'We as Adults Struggle to Talk to Kids Honestly about Sex.'" *CNN*. CNN, 12 Apr. 2014. Web. 10 June 2015.

Groban, Betsy. Rev. of *Stargirl*, by Jerry Spinelli. *New York Times Books*. New York Times, 17 Sept. 2000. Web. 9 May 2015.

Gross, Claire E. "Apocalypse." Rev. of *Apocalypse*, by Tim Bowler. *Horn Book* Nov.–Dec. 2005: 713–14. *Literary Reference Center*. Web. 28 May 2015.

Gross, Claire E. "From Page to Screen: *Inkheart* the Movie." Rev. of *Inkheart*, dir. Iain Softley. *Horn Book Magazine*. Horn Book, n.d. Web. 6 Apr. 2015.

Gross, Claire E. Rev. of *Butterfly*, by Sonya Hartnett. *Horn Book Magazine* July–Aug. 2010: 108–9. *Literary Reference Center*. Web. 19 Sept. 2015.

Gruner, Elizabeth Rose. "Telling Old Tales Newly: Intertextuality in Young Adult Fiction for Girls." *Telling Children's Stories: Narrative Theory and Children's Literature*. Ed. Mike Cadden. Lincoln: U of Nebraska P, 2011. 3–21. Print.

Hall, Sandra. Rev. of *Angus, Thongs and Perfect Snogging. Sydney Morning Herald*. Fairfax Digital, 18 Sept. 2008. Web. 31 Mar. 2015.

Hammond, Jeffrey. "The Sense of an Ending: Farewell to the Apocalypse." *River Styx* 88 (2012): 8–17. *Literary Reference Center*. Web. 30 Apr. 2015.

Hartlaub, Peter. "Ho-Hum Spy Caper Would Be Barely Worth TiVo-ing." Rev. of *Alex Rider: Operation Stormbreaker*, dir. Geoffrey Sax. *SFGate*. Hearst Communications, 13 Oct. 2006. Web. 8 Dec. 2015.

Harty, Kevin J. "Cinema Arthuriana." *A History of Arthurian Scholarship*. Ed. Norris J. Lacy. Cambridge: Brewer, 2006. 252–60. Print.

Harvey, Dennis. "*Seeker* Hides Cooper's Fantasy in a Flurry of F/X." Rev. of *The Seeker*, dir. David L. Cunningham. *Variety* 8–14 Oct. 2007: 54+. *Biography Reference Bank*. Web. 2 June 2015.

Hawker, Phillipa. "DVD Review: *The Mortal Instruments City of Bones*." *Newcastle Herald*. Fairfax Media, 22 Aug. 2013. Web. 9 May 2015.

Helms, Antje, Jan von Holleben, and Jen Metcalf. *Does This Happen to Everyone? A Budding Adult's Guide to Puberty*. Berlin: Little Gestalten, 2014. Print.

Henthorne, Tom. *Approaching the Hunger Games Trilogy: A Literary and Cultural Analysis*. Jefferson: Mc-Farland, 2012. Print.

Heppermann, Christine M. Rev. of *Beauty Queens*, by Libba Bray. *Horn Book Magazine* 87.4 (2011): 140–41. *Literary Reference Center*. Web. 14 Apr. 2015.

Heritage, Stuart. "Who Killed Off *The Golden Compass*?" *Guardian*. Guardian News and Media, 15 Dec. 2009. Web. 31 Oct. 2015.

Hill, Crag. *The Critical Merits of Young Adult Literature*. New York: Routledge, 2014. Print.

Hill, Craig, ed. *The Critical Merits of Young Adult Literature: Coming of Age*. New York: Routledge, 2014. Print.

Hill, Rebecca A. "GLBT Young Adult Fiction." *School Library Monthly* 27.8 (2011): 20–21. *Academic Search Complete*. Web. 17 Dec. 2015.

Hill, Rebecca. "God on the Shelf: The Influence of Christian Young Adult Literature." *Voice of Youth Advocates* (2010): 322–32. Print.

Hinton, S. E. "American Icons: The Outsiders." Interview by Kurt Anderson. *Studio 360*. Studio 360, 4 May 2012. Web. 17 Feb. 2015.

Hintz, Carrie, and Elaine Ostry, eds. *Utopian and Dystopian Writing for Children and Young Adults*. New York: Routledge, 2003. Print.

Hirsch, Lee, and Cynthia Lowen. *Bully: An Action Plan for Teachers, Parents, and Communities to Combat the Bullying Crisis*. New York: Weinstein, 2012. Print.

Hodge, Diana. "Young Adult Fiction's Dark Themes Give the Hope to Cope." *Conversation*. Conversation, 12 June 2014. Web. 12 May 2015.

Hodge, Diana. "Young Adult Fiction's Dark Themes Give the Hope to Cope." *Conversation*. Conversation, 12 June 2014. Web. 15 May 2015.

Holden, Stephen. "Fleeing a Dying Civilization, toward Hope and Sunlight." Rev. of *City of Ember*, dir. Gil Kenan. *New York Times*. New York Times, 9 Oct. 2008. Web. 6 Apr. 2015.

Holden, Stephen. "When Stars (Celestial) Fall, and Stars (Hollywood) Fly." Rev. of *Stardust*, dir. Matthew Vaughn. *New York Times*. New York Times, 10 Aug. 2007. Web. 30 Nov. 2015.

"Holes." Rev of *Holes*, by Louis Sachar." *Kirkus Reviews*. Kirkus Media, 20 May 2010. Web. 16 Apr. 2015.

Holmes, Daryl Y. "Marilyn Nelson." *Guide to Literary Masters & Their Works* Jan. 2007: n.p. *Literary Reference Center*. Web. 25 Apr. 2015.

Honan, William H. "Robert E. Cormier, 75, Author of Enduring Books for Teenagers." *New York Times.* New York Times, 5 Nov. 2000. Web. 2 June 2015.

Honeycutt, Kirk. Rev. of *Beastly*, dir. Daniel Barnz. *Hollywood Reporter.* Hollywoodreporter.com. 2 Mar. 2011. Web. 13 March 2015.

Hong, Terry. "Ellen Oh's Prophecy Trilogy and Why #WeNeedDiverseBooks." *Bloom.* Bloom, 8 Sept. 2014. Web. 9 Dec. 2015.

Hopkins, Ellen. *Crank.* New York: Simon, 2004. Print.

Horn, Caroline. "Carnegie winner attacks Gove." *Bookseller* 5486 (2011): 10. Business Source Complete. Web. 5 Feb. 2016.

Hornaday, Ann. 'If I Stay' Movie Review: An End-of-Summer Tear-Jerker." Rev. of *If I Stay*, dir. R. J. Cutler. *Washington Post.* Washington Post, 21 Aug. 2014. Web. 15 Apr. 2015.

Hornaday, Ann. "'How to Deal': Angst in Spades." Rev. of *How to Deal*, dir. Clare Kilner. *Washington Post.* Washington Post, 18 July 2003. Web. 9 Mar. 2015.

Horning, Kathleen T. "Children's Books: Still an All-White World?" *School Library Journal.* Media Source, Inc, 1 May 2014. Web. 25 February 2016.

"How I Live Now: When Love Means Survival." *Mag Pictures.* Magnolia Pictures, n.d. Web. 10 Nov. 2015.

Howe, Andrew. "*Looking for Alibrandi.*" Efilmcritic. com. Efilmcritic, 14 May 2000. Web. 10 May 2015.

"Howl's Moving Castle." *Box Office Mojo.* IMDb.com, n.d. Web. 30 Apr. 2015.

"'Hunger Games' Author Suzanne Collins Graduated from IU." *IU News Room.* Indiana U, 22 Mar. 2012. Web. 8 June 2015.

Hunt, Jonathan. Rev. of *Monsters of Men*, by Patrick Ness. *Horn Book* Nov./Dec. 2010: 99. Print.

Hutcheon, Jane. "Australian Author and Educator John Marsden on Children, Parents and Relationships." *ABC News: One plus One.* ABC, 21 May 2015. Web. 14 Dec. 2015.

Hylton, Jaime. "Exploring the 'Academic Side' of Cynthia Voigt." *ALAN Review* 33.1 (2005): 50–55. PDF file.

Isenberg, Robert. "The Perks of Being a Pittsburgher." *Pittsburgh Magazine.* Wiesner Media, 3 Oct. 2012. Web. 5 June 2015.

"In Memoriam: Anne McCaffrey (1926–2011)." *SFWA.* Science Fiction and Fantasy Writers of America, 22 Nov. 2011. Web. 24 Feb. 2015.

"In 'Red Pyramid,' Kid Heroes Take on Ancient Egypt." *NPR Books.* NPR, 19 Dec. 2012. Web. 31 May 2015.

"Interview with Meg Cabot." *Scholastic Book Club Kids.* Scholastic Ltd., n.d. Web. 28 February 2016.

*Issitt, Micah. "Divorce Rate: Overview." Points of View: Divorce Rate (2014): 1. Points of View Reference Center. We*b. 31 May 2015.

It Gets Better Project. "What Is the It Gets Better Project?" *It Gets Better Project.* n.d. Web. 26 February 2016.

Jackson, Peter. "Peter Jackson: 'Lovely Bones' Was Lovely to Make." Interview by Scott Bowles. *USA Today.* USA Today, 19 Apr. 2009. Web. 12 May 2015.

Jacobs, Matthew. "The Quirky Heartbreaker *Me and Earl and the Dying Girl* Is Summer's Signature Teen Movie." *Huffington Post.* TheHuffingtonPost.com, 14 June 2015. Web. 24 Nov. 2015.

Jemtegaard, Kristi Elle. "The Gospel according to Larry/Vote for Larry (Book)." Rev. of *The Gospel according to Larry*, by Janet Tashjian. *Horn Book Magazine* 80.5 (2004): 610. *Academic Search Complete.* Web. 1 July 2015.

Jenkins, Mark. "A 'Funny Story' of Just the Right Kind." Rev. of *It's Kind of a Funny Story*, dir. Ryan Fleck and Anna Boden. *NPR.* NPR, 8 Oct. 2010. Web. 26 Nov. 2015.

Johanson, MaryAnn. Rev. of *Now Is Good*, dir. Ol Parker. *FlickFilosopher.com.* MaryAnn Johanson, 21 Sept. 2012. Web. 6 Nov. 2015.

"John Corey Whaley—Who Is This Guy?" *John Corey Whaley, Author & Friend.* Author, 2013. Web. 22 Oct. 2015.

"John Green's Biography." *JohnGreenBooks.com.* John Green Books, n.d. Web. 15 Apr. 2015.

Johns, Nikara. "Third 'The Sisterhood of the Traveling Pants' Film in Development." *Variety.* Variety Media, 23 Apr. 2014. Web. 30 Apr. 2015.

Johnson, Alaya Dawn, and Carole McDonnell. "Multicultural Fantasists Alaya Dawn Johnson and Carole McDonnell." Interview by K. Tempest Bradford. *Fantasy Magazine.* Fantasy Magazine, 2007. Web. 30 Nov. 2015.

Johnson, Alaya Dawn. "#TTBF14 Interview: Alaya Dawn Johnson." *Texas Teen Book Festival.* Texas Teen Book Festival, 18 Oct. 2014. Web. 30 Nov. 2015.

Johnson, Alaya Dawn. "Alaya Dawn Johnson: Dreaming Stories." *Locus Online.* Locus, 18 Mar. 2011. Web. 30 Nov. 2015.

Johnson, Alaya Dawn. "Alaya Dawn Johnson: The Interfictions 2 Interview." Interview by Christian

Desrosiers. *Interstitial Arts Foundation.* Interstitial Arts Foundation, 2009. Web. 30 Nov. 2015.

Johnson, Alaya Dawn. "All Futures Are Political: A Q&A with Spec-Fic Author Alaya Dawn Johnson." Interview by Vann R. Newkirk II. *Gawker.* Gawker Media, 12 May 2015. Web. 30 Nov. 2015.

Johnson, Alaya Dawn. "Interview with Alaya Dawn Johnson: Transcript." *Gay YA.* Gay YA, 23 Oct. 2014. Web. 30 Nov. 2015.

Johnson, Alaya Dawn. "Questions for Alaya Dawn Johnson, Author of 'The Summer Prince.'" Interview by Petra Mayer. *NPR Books.* NPR, 15 Feb. 2013. Web. 30 Nov. 2015.

Johnson, Alaya Dawn. Interview. *Lightspeed.* Lightspeed, Aug. 2013. Web. 30 Nov. 2015.

Johnson, Angela. "Real Moments: An Interview with Angela Johnson." Interview by Andrea Maxworthy O'Brien. *Cooperative Children's Book Center.* Friends of the CCBC, U of Wisconsin-Madison, 2005. Web. 1 Dec. 2015.

Johnson, Angela. Interview. *Brown Bookshelf.* Brown Bookshelf, 8 Feb. 2009. Web. 1 Dec. 2015.

Johnson, Joanna Webb. "Chick Lit Jr.: More Than Glitz and Glamour for Teens and Tweens." *Chick Lit: The New Woman's Fiction.* Ed. Suzanne Ferriss and Mallory Young. New York: Routledge, 2006. 141–58. Print.

Johnson, Sarah. "Defining the Genre: What Are the Rules for Historical Fiction?" *Historical Novel Society.* Historical Novel Society, Mar. 2002. Web. 3 June 2015.

Jones, Diana Wynne. "He Saw My Books from the Inside Out." Interview by Nick Bradshaw. *Telegraph.* Telegraph Media, 23 Sept. 2005. Web. 30 Apr. 2015.

Jones, Diana Wynne. "Leaping Off the Page." Rev. of *Inkheart,* by Cornelia Funke. *Guardian.* Guardian News and Media, 21 Nov. 2003. Web. 6 Apr. 2015.

Jones, Jami L. "Freak Out or Melt Down: Teen Responses to Trauma and Depression." *Young Adult Library Services* 7.1 (2008): 30–34. *Academic Search Premier.* Web. 3 May 2015.

Jones, Leisha. "Contemporary Bildungsromans and the Prosumer Girl." *Criticism* 53.3 (2011): 439–69. *Literary Reference Center.* Web. 8 Apr. 2015.

Jones, Nicolette. "Whole truth for teenagers: Patrick Ness's novels have attracted acclaim, awards—and censure." *Independent.* Independent, 23 June 2011. Web. 5 February 2016.

Jones, Patrick. "Nothing to Fear." *Collection Management* 25.4 (2001): 3–23.

"Judy Blume: Often Banned, but Widely Beloved." *NPR.* National Public Radio, 28 Nov. 2011. Web. 14 May 2015.

Just, Julie. "The Parent Problem in Young Adult Lit." *New York Times.* New York Times, 1 Apr. 2010. Web. 13 July 2015.

"Justine Larbalestier." *JustineLarbalestier.com.* Web. December 15, 2015.

Kakutani, Michiko. "Up from the Depths of Pulp and into the Mainstream." *New York Times.* New York Times, 6 June 2012. Web. 23 Oct. 2015.

Kaplan, David A. "A Most Unusual Father-Daughter Professional Pairing." *Fortune.* Time, 29 Aug. 2012. Web. 4 Mar. 2015.

Karolides, Nicholas J., Lee Burress, and John M. Kean, eds. *Censored Books: Critical Viewpoints.* Lanham: Scarecrow, 2001. Print.

Kaywell, Joan. "An Interview with Lois Duncan." Journal of Adolescent and Adult Literacy 56.2 (March 2009): 545. *Literature Resource Center.* Web. 26 February 2016.

Kehr, Dave. "A Teenager Struggles to Star in Her New Town." Rev. of *Confessions of a Teenage Drama Queen,* dir. Sara Sugarman. *New York Times.* New York Times, 20 Feb. 2004. Web. 19 Mar. 2015.

Kelley, Ann. "Just One Day." *Booklist* 109.9/10 (2013): 108. *Literary Reference Center.* Web. 17 May 2015.

Kelly, Kate. "The New Animated Film 'Happy Feet' Doesn't Dance Around Serious Issues." *Wall Street Journal.* Dow Jones, 17 Nov. 2006. Web. 19 Mar. 2015.

Kennedy, Marina. "Mermaids, Starfish, and Goldfish: Patty Dann's Real Life Inspires Her Books." *Woman around Town.* Woman around Town, 16 June 2014. Web. 10 Nov. 2015.

Kenny, Glenn. "The Rise and Fall (and Rise?) of Teen Horror Movies." *Salon.* Salon Media, 3 May 2010. Web. 6 Mar. 2015.

Kenny, Glenn. Rev. of *How I Live Now.*" *RogerEbert.* Ebert Digital, 8 Nov. 2013. Web. 10 Nov. 2015.

Kenny, Glenn. Rev. of *Seventh Son,* dir. Sergey Bodrov. *RogerEbert.com.* Ebert Digital, 6 Feb. 2015. Web. 31 Oct. 2015.

Kermode, Jennie. Rev. of *Angus, Thongs and Perfect Snogging. Eye for Film.* Eye for Film, 21 July 2008. Web. 31 Mar. 2015.

Kerr, M. E. "M.E. Kerr (A.K.A. Mary James & Vin Packer)." *Balkin Buddies*. Catherine Balkin, n.d. Web. 30 Mar. 2015.

Kerr, M. E. Interview by Terry Gross. *Fresh Air*. NPR, 19 June 2003. Web. 3 Apr. 2015.

Kerr, M. E. *Me Me Me Me Me: Not a Novel*. New York: HarperCollins, 1983. Print.

Kidd, James. "'I don't want smut on the page:' Divergent author Veronica Roth on sex and teen fiction. *The Independent*. The Independent, 4 January 2014. Web. 8 February 2016.

Kidd, Kenneth. *Freud in Oz: At the Intersections of Psychoanalysis and Children's Literature*. Minneapolis, MN: University of Minnesota Press, 2011.

Kilner, Clare. Interview by Danny Manus. *Script*. F+W, 23 Apr. 2013. Web. 9 Mar. 2015.

King, Stephen. "Why We Crave Horror Movies." *The Bedford Guide for College Writers: With Reader, Research Manual, and Handbook*. Ed. X. J. Kennedy, Dorothy M. Kennedy, and Marcia F. Muth. 9th ed. Boston: Bedford, 2011. 559–61. Print.

"King of the Geeks." Rev. of *Youth in Revolt*, dir. Miguel Arteta. *Alberta Local News*. Black Press, 5 Jan. 2010. Web. 10 Dec. 2015.

Kinson, Sarah. "Why I Write—Markus Zusak." *Guardian*. Guardian News and Media, 28 Mar. 2008. Web. 6 May 2015.

Kipp, Jeremiah. "The Chocolate War." *Slant*. Slant, 15 Apr. 2007. Web. 30 Nov. 2015.

Klause, Annette Curtis. "What Did This YA Author Do to Get Banned from School Libraries?" Interview by Brenna Ehrlich. *MTVNews*. Viacom International, 26 Sept. 2014. Web. 6 Mar. 2015.

Kloves, Steve. "'Harry Potter' Countdown: Steve Kloves on a 'Haunting Moment' in 'Half-Blood Prince.'" Interview with Denise Martin. *Hero Complex*. Los Angeles Times, 17 June 2009. Web. 28 Feb. 2015.

Knapp, Bettina. *Machine, Metaphor, and the Writer: A Jungian View*. University Park: Pennsylvania State UP, 1989. Print.

Knickerbocker, Joan L., and James A. Rycik. "Reexamining Literature Study in the Middle Grades: A Critical Response Framework." *American Secondary Education* 34.3 (2006): 43–56. *Academic Search Premier*. Web. 14 May 2015.

Knoth, Maeve Visser. Rev. of *Sleeping Dogs*, by Sonya Hartnett. *Horn Book Magazine* Mar.–Apr. 1996: 207. *Literary Reference Center*. Web. 15 Oct. 2015.

Kokkola, Lydia. "Virtuous Vampires and Voluptuous Vamps: Romance Conventions Reconsidered in Stephenie Meyer's 'Twilight' Series." *Children's Literature in Education* 42.2 (2011): 165–79. *Literary Reference Center*. Web. 16 June 2015.

Koppelman, Susan. "Alice Childress: An Appreciation." *Belles Lettres: A Review of Books by Women* 10.1 (Fall 1994): 6. Literature Resource Center. Web. 25 February 2016.

Kraus, Daniel. Rev. of *I Am Number Four*, by Pittacus Lore. Booklist 106.19/20 (2010): 53. *Literary Reference Center*. Web. 13 Apr. 2015.

Kraus, Daniel. Rev. of *Insurgent*. *Booklist* 108.14 (15 March 2012): 59.

L. M. Montgomery Research Centre. U of Guelph, 12 Mar. 2009. Web. 1 May 2015.

L'Engle, Madeleine. "I Dare You." *Newsweek*. Newsweek, 6 May 2004. Web. 30 Nov. 2015.

L'Engle, Madeleine. "Madeleine L'Engle." Interview by Bob Abernethy. *Religion and Ethics Newsweekly*.

L'Engle, Madeleine. *A Wrinkle in Time*. New York: Bantam, 1973. Print.

La Bella, Laura. *Philip Pullman*. New York: Rosen, 2014. Print.

Laing, Olivia. "Stephenie Meyer: A Squeaky-Clean Vampire Queen." *Guardian*. Guardian News and Media, 14 Nov. 2009. Web. 4 June 2015.

Laming, Scott. "Steampunk 101: From Sci-Fi Sub-genre to Cultural Phenomenon." *AbeBooks*. AbeBooks, n.d. Web. 10 May 2015.

Lapidos, Juliet. "The 'Ender's Game' Boycott." *New York Times*. New York Times, 20 July 2013. Web. 1 Apr. 2015.

Larrick, Nancy. "The All-White World of Children's Books." *Saturday Review*. 11 September 1965. UNZ. org. Web. 24 February 2016.

LaSalle, Mick. "It's Easy to Dig 'Holes.'" *SFGate*. SFGate, 18 Apr. 2003. Web. 28 Feb. 2015.

Lawler, Kelly. "Book Buzz: Meg Cabot Returns to 'Princess Diaries' World." *USA Today*. Gannett, 5 May 2014. Web. 9 June 2015.

Le Guin, Ursula K. "Ursula K. Le Guin: Still Battling the Powers That Be." Interview by John Joseph Adams and David Barr Kirtley. *Wired*. Condé Nast, 25 July 2012. Web. 10 June 2015.

Le Guin, Ursula K. Interview by John Wray. *Paris Review*. Paris Review, 2013. Web. 10 June 2015.

Lederman, Marsha. "In *Life, Above All* Canadians Tell the Story of AIDS in Africa." *Globe and Mail*. Globe and Mail, 12 July 2011. Web. 3 Dec. 2015.

Lee, Harper. *To Kill a Mockingbird.* Philadelphia: Lippincott, 1960. Print.

Lee, Nathan. "Alex Rider: Operation Stormbreaker (2006)." Rev. of *Alex Rider: Operation Stormbreaker*, dir. Geoffrey Sax. *New York Times.* New York Times, 13 Oct. 2006. Web. 30 Nov. 2015.

Lehmann, Megan. Rev. of *Tomorrow, When the War Began*, dir. Stuart Beattie. *Hollywood Reporter.* Hollywood Reporter, 14 Oct. 2015. Web. 2 Dec. 2015.

Leighton, Alexander. "Re-Discovering Mythology: Adaptation and Appropriation in the Percy Jackson and the Olympians Saga." Spec. issue of *Mousaion* 32.2 (2014): 60–73. Print.

Lemire, Christy. Rev. of *Divergent*, dir. Neil Burger. *RogerEbert.com.* Ebert Digital, 21 Mar. 2014. Web. 2 May 2015.

Lemire, Christy. Rev. of *The DUFF*, dir. Ari Sandel. *RogerEbert.com.* Ebert Digital, 20 Feb. 2015. Web. 31 Oct. 2015.

Leopold, Wendy. "A book contract already!" *Northwestern University News.* Northwestern University, 10 May, 2010. Web. 8 February 2016.

Leverich, Kathleen. "Children's Books." Rev. of *Homecoming*, by Cynthia Voigt. *New York Times.* New York Times, 10 May 1981. Web. 6 Mar. 2015.

Levithan, David. "About Me." *David Levithan.* n.d. Web. 26 February 2016.

Levithan, David. *Boy Meets Boy.* New York: Knopf, 2003. Print.

Lewin, Tamar. "Tales of Raw Misery for Ages 12 and Up." *New York Times* 30 July 2000. ProQuest Historical Newspapers. Web. 27 February 2016.

Lewis, C. S. *Surprised by Joy: The Shape of My Early Life.* 1955. New York: Mariner, 2012. Print.

Lewis, John, Andrew Aydin, Nate Powell, and Chris Ross. *March.* Marietta: Top Shelf, 2013. Print.

Lewis, Jon. *Whom God Wishes to Destroy: Francis Coppola and the New Hollywood.* Durham: Duke UP, 2012. Print.

"LGBT Rights Milestones Fast Facts." *CNN.* Cable News Network, 30 Oct. 2015. Web. 18 Nov. 2015.

"Liar." Rev. of *Liar* by Justine Larbalestier. *Publisher's Weekly.* PWxyz, n.d. Web. December 15, 2015.

Lillard, Matthew. "Matthew Lillard on Why *Fat Kid Rules the World* Isn't about Being Fat." Interview by Rebecca Ford. *Hollywood Reporter.* Hollywood Reporter, 12 Oct. 2015. Web. 1 Nov. 2015.

Linshi, Jack. "*Insurgent* Tops Weekly Box Office but Misses *Divergent* Mark." Rev. of *Insurgent*, dir. Robert Schwentke. *Time.* Time, Mar. 22, 2015. Web. 2 May 2015.Lippman, Laura. "The Story behind *Last Summer* Writer: Lois Duncan Will Use the Film Version of Her Book, *I Know What You Did Last Summer*, to Draw Attention to the Murder of Her Daughter." *Baltimore Sun.* Tribune Interactive, 19 Nov. 1997. Web. 7 Apr. 2015.

Liptak, Andrew. "The Left and Right Hands of Ursula K. Le Guin." *Kirkus.* Kirkus Media, 14 Aug. 2014. Web. 11 June 2015.

Lo, Malinda. "Diversity in 2013 New York Times Young Adult Bestsellers." *Diversity in YA.* Malinda Lo and Cindy Pon, 21 April 2014. Web. 23 February 2016.

Lo, Malinda. "One Thing Leads to Another: An Interview with Malinda Lo." Interview by Julie Bartel. *Hub.* Amer. Lib. Assn., 27 June 2013. Web. 30 Nov. 2015.

Lo, Malinda. "Q & A with Malinda Lo." Interview by Donna Freitas. *Publishers Weekly.* PWxyz, 7 Apr. 2011. Web. 30 Nov. 2015.

Lockhart, E. "Biography." *E. Lockhart.* E. Lockhart, 2014. Web. 1 Mar. 2015.

Lodge, Guy. Rev. of *Now Is Good*, dir. Ol Parker. *Variety.* Variety Media, 17 Sept. 2012. Web. 20 Nov. 2015.

Lodge, Sally. "A Traumatic Family *Memory* Sparks New YA Novel." *Publishers Weekly* 20 Jan. 2014: 19. *Literary Reference Center.* Web. 13 July 2015.

Lodge, Sally. "Lois Duncan Thrillers Get an Update." *Publishers Weekly.* PWxyz, 23 Sept. 2010. Web. 6 Mar. 2015.

"Lois Lowry." *Biography Today* (2010): 1. *Biography Reference Center.* Web. 13 Apr. 2015.

Lovelace, Sunnie. "Warrior: A Prophecy Novel." Rev. of *Warrior*, by Ellen Oh. *School Library Journal* 60.2 (2014): 110. Print.

Low, Bernadette Flynn. "Naomi Shihab Nye." *Critical Survey of Poetry.* 2nd ed. Ipswich: Salem, 2002. 1–3. *Literary Reference Center.* Web. 25 Apr. 2015.

Low, Jason T. "Where is the Diversity in Publishing? The 2015 Diversity Baseline Survey Results." *The Open Book.* Lee and Low Books, 26 January 2016. Web. 22 February 2016.

Lowry, Lois. Interview. *Reading Rockets.* WETA Public Broadcasting, 2015. Web. 27 Mar. 2015.

Lubar, David. "Everything." *ALAN Review* Spring/Summer 2003: n. pag. *Virginia Tech Digital Library and Archives.* Web. 6 Apr. 2015.

Lubar, David. "The History of Young Adult Novels." *ALAN Review* (2003): 117–22. DavidLubar.com. Web. 19 Mar. 2015.

Lyga, Barry, Robin Wasserman, and Brenna Yovanoff. "Monsters, Murder, and Morality: A Graveside Chat about YA Horror Fiction." Interview by Daniel Kraus. *Booklist* 15 May 2014: 62–63. *Literary Reference Center*. Web. 4 June 2015.

Lynch-Brown, Carol G, Kathy G. Short, and Carl M. Tomlinson. *Essentials of Children's Literature*. 7th ed. Harlow: Pearson, 2014. Print.

Macadam, Alison. "Fear of the Dark: A Favorite Novel Goes Hollywood." *NPR*. NPR, 1 Oct. 2007. Web. 2 June 2015.MacFarquhar, Larissa. "The Dead Are Real." *New Yorker*. Condé Nast, 15 Oct. 2012. Web. 3 June 2015.

Madden, Mary, et al. *Teens, Social Media, and Privacy*. Washington: Pew Research Center, 2013. *Pew Research Center: Internet, Science & Technology*. Web. 22 June 2015.

Mafi, Tahereh. "Meet *Shatter Me* Author Tahereh Mafi." *Seventeen*. Hearst Communications, 12 Jan. 2012. Web. 27 Oct. 2015.

Mafi, Tahereh. "Not Just for Kids: Author Tahereh Mafi Discusses *Shatter Me*." Interview by Susan Carpenter. *Jacket Copy*. Los Angeles Times, 28 Nov. 2011. Web. 30 Oct. 2015.

Mafi, Tahereh. "Unraveling Tahereh Mafi." Interview by Tatin Yang. *Inquirer.net*. Inquirer.net, 16 Mar. 2013. Web. 30 Oct. 2015.

MaggieStiefvater.com. Maggie Stiefvater, 2015. Web. 11 Dec. 2015.

Mahood, Ramona Madson. "Deenie." *Masterplots II: Juvenile and Young Adult Literature Series Supplement*. Ed. Tracy Irons-Georges. Pasadena: Salem, 1997. *Literary Reference Center*. Web. 13 May 2015.

"Making Her Presence Known." *Publishers Weekly* 9 Feb. 2015: 14. *Literary Reference Center*. Web. 8 Oct. 2015.

O'Malley, Sheila. Rev. of *Me and Earl and the Dying Girl*, dir. Alfonso Gomez-Rejon. *RogerEbert.com*. Ebert Digital, 12 June 2015. Web. 24 Nov. 2015.

Mallon, Thomas. "Never Happened: Fictions of Alternative History." *New Yorker*. Condé Nast, 21 Nov. 2011. Web. 3 June 2015.

Mansky, Jacqueline. "Perk Creator Credits Versatility to USC." *Daily Trojan*. U of Southern California, 2 Oct. 2012. Web. 5 June 2015.

Mantel, Hilary. "Booker Winner Hilary Mantel on Dealing with History in Fiction." *Guardian*. Guardian News and Media, 16 Oct. 2009. Web. 3 June 2015.

Marchetta, Melina. Interview by Cris Menendez. *El Templo de las Mil Puertas*. El Templo de las Mil Puertas, Dec. 2012. Web. 15 Sept. 2015.

Marchetta, Melina. Interview by Judith Ridge. *Viewpoint: On Books for Young Adults*. Misrule.com.au, 1992. Web. 15 Sept. 2015.

Marsh, Calum. Rev. of *Tomorrow, When the War Began*, dir. Stuart Beattie. *Slant Magazine*. Slant Magazine, 21 Feb. 2012. Web. 2 Dec. 2015.

Martin, Douglas. "Madeleine L'Engle, Writer of Children's Classics, Is Dead at 88." *New York Times*. New York Times, 8 Sept. 2007. Web. 4 June 2015.

Martinez, Gladys, Casey E. Copen, and Joyce C. Abma. *Teenagers in the United States: Sexual Activity, Contraceptive Use, and Childbearing, 2006–2010 National Survey of Family Growth*. Washington, DC: GPO, 2011.*Centers for Disease Control and Prevention*. Web. 8 June 2015.

Martocci, Laura. *Bullying: The Social Destruction of Self*. Philadelphia: Temple UP, 2015. Print.

Maslin, Jane. Rev. of *Mrs. Doubtfire*, dir. Chris Columbus. *New York Times*. New York Times, 24 Nov. 1993. Web. 10 Nov. 2015.

Maslin, Janet. "Marriage Gone Sour? Go Home to Ma Bell." Rev. of *Landline*, by Rainbow Rowell. *New York Times*. New York Times, 9 July 2014. Web. 14 Sept. 2015.

Maslin, Janet. "Matt Dillon Is Coppola's *Rumble Fish*." Rev. of *Rumble Fish*, dir. Francis Ford Coppola. *New York Times*. New York Times, 7 Oct. 1983. Web. 3 May 2015.

Maslin, Janet. "Something Wicked This Way Comes (1983): Disney's Bradbury." Rev. of *Something Wicked This Way Comes*, dir. by Jack Clayton. *New York Times*. New York Times, 29 Apr. 1983. Web. 3 Nov. 2015.

Maslin, Janet. "The Chocolate War (1988)." *New York Times*. New York Times, 27 Jan. 1989. Web. 30 Nov. 2015.

Mason-Jones, Hugh, and Augusta Zeeng. "Looking for Alibrandi, Kate Woods, 2000." *Media Reloaded*. Melbourne: Cambridge UP, 2012. 41–45. Print.

Masters, Kim. "How 'Hugo's' Massive Losses Are Straining Producer Graham King's Partnerships." *Hollywood Reporter*. Hollywood Reporter, 25 Apr. 2012. Web. 6 Apr. 2015.

Mathieson, Craig. "The Spectacular Now Review: Love Changes Everything." Rev. of *The Spectacular Now*, dir. James Ponsoldt. *SMH*. Fairfax Media, 1 Dec. 2013. Web. 30 Dec. 2015.

Mathys, Cécile, William J. Burk, and Antonius H. N. Cillessen. "Popularity as a Moderator of Peer Selection and Socialization of Adolescent Alcohol, Marijuana, and Tobacco Use." *Journal of Research on Adolescence* 23.3 (2013): 513–23. *Academic Search Premier*. Web. 30 June 2015.

Matson, Nancy. "Review: Book Recalls the Tumult of the Teen Years." Rev. of *Speak*, by Laurie Halse Anderson. *CNN*. CNN, 29 Nov. 1999. Web. 10 June 2015.

Mattson, Jennifer. Rev. of *Beastly*, by Alex Flinn. *Booklist* Feb. 2008. *Literary Reference Center*. 30 Mar. 2015.

Mayer, Petra. "'Boxers & Saints' & Compassion: Questions for Gene Luen Yang." *NPR Books*. NPR, 22 Oct. 2013. Web. 31 Oct. 2015.

McClure, Amy A., Abigail V. Garthwait, and Janice V. Kristo. *Teaching Children's Literature in an Era of Standards*. Boston: Pearson, 2015. Print.

McCrum, Robert. "Dæmon Geezer." *Guardian*. Guardian News and Media, 27 Jan, 2002. Web. 4 June 2015.

McCurdy, Eric C. "The Pop Culture Effect: Trends in Young Adult Literature." Diss. University of Central Missouri, 2013. Web. 19 Mar. 2015.

McCurdy, Eric C. *The Pop Culture Effect: Trends in Young Adult Literature*. Diss. U of Central Missouri, 2013. Digital file.

McDonnell, Christine. "New Voices, New Visions: Chris Crutcher." *Horn Book Magazine* 64 (May 1988): 332–335.

McInally, Kate. "Who Wears the Pants? The (Multi)Cultural Politics of *The Sisterhood of the Traveling Pants*." *Children's Literature in Education* 39.3 (2008): 187–200. *Literary Reference Center*. Web. 8 June 2015.

McKinley, Jesse. "Keeping Options Open, Novelist Tows Museum on Road to Dream." Rev. of *Youth in Revolt*, dir. Miguel Arteta. *New York Times*. New York Times, 25 Jan. 2010. Web. 10 Dec. 2015.

McLuhan, Marshall, and Wilfred Watson. *From Cliché to Archetype*. 1970. Ed. W. Terrence Gordon. Berkeley: Gingko, 2011. Print.

McNamee, Gregory. "Appreciations: Scott O'Dell's 'Island of the Blue Dolphins.'" *Kirkus*. Kirkus, 12 Feb. 2014. Web. 25 May 2015.

McNary, Dave. "Sharon Draper's 'Out of My Mind' YA Novel Set for Movie Adaptation." *Variety*. Variety Media, 27 Apr. 2015. Web. 16 June 2015.

"Meg Cabot." *Teen Reads*. Book Report Inc., 2015. Web. 9 June 2015.

"Meg Cabot." Contemporary Authors Online. Detroit: Gale, 2010. *Literature Resource Center*. Web. 27 February 2016.

"Meg Rosoff." *Baker & Taylor Author Biographies* (2000): 1. *Literary Reference Center*. Web. 16 Nov. 2015.

"Meg Rosoff." *British Council: Literature*. British Council, 2015. Web. 10 Nov. 2015.

Meixner, Emily. "Teacher Agency and Access to LGBTQ Young Adult Literature." *Radical Teacher* 76 (2006): 13–19. *Academic Search Complete*. Web. 1 Apr. 2015.

Meloni, Christine. "Teen Chick Lit." *School Media Connection* 25.2 (October 2006): 16–19.

Mercer, Lorraine, and Linda Strom. "Counter Narratives: Cooking Up Stories of Love and Loss in Naomi Shihab Nye's Poetry and Diana Abu-Jaber's 'Crescent.'" *Melus* 32.4 (2007): 33–46. *Literary Reference Center*. Web. 25 Apr. 2015.

Merry, Stephanie. "'The Spectacular Now' Movie Review." Rev. of *The Spectacular Now*, dir. James Ponsoldt. *Washington Post*. Washington Post, 8 Aug. 2013. Web. 30 Dec. 2015.

Merry, Stephanie. "*Vampire Academy* Movie Review: A Lazy, Bloody Tale." Rev. of *Vampire Academy*, dir. Mark Waters. *Washington Post*. Washington Post, 7 Feb. 2014. Web. 26 Feb. 2015.

Meyer, Stephenie. "Interview with Vampire Writer Stephenie Meyer." Interview by Gregory Kirschling. *Entertainment Weekly*. Entertainment Weekly, 5 July 2008. Web. 4 June 2015.

Michaud, Jon. "S. E. Hinton and the Y. A. Debate." *New Yorker*. Condé Nast, 14 Oct. 2014. Web. 17 Feb. 2015.

Michaud, Jon. "That Was Then, This Is Now: S. E. Hinton in the Twitter Age." *New Yorker*. Condé Nast, 8 Nov. 2013. Web. 23 May 2015.

Miller, Laura. "'The Fault in Our Stars' Has Been Unfairly Bashed by Critics Who Don't Understand It." *Salon*. Salon Media, 6 June 2014. Web. 5 Mar. 2015.

Miller, Laura. "Fresh Hell." *New Yorker*. Condé Nast, 14 June 2010. Web. 30 Apr. 2015.

Ming, Cui, and Frank D. Ficham. "The Differential Effects of Parental Divorce and Marital Conflict on

Young Adult Romantic Relationships." Personal Relationships 17.3 (2010): 331–43. *Academic Search Premier. We*b. 31 May 2015.

Minkel, Elizabeth. "[Heart] for the 'The Lover's Dictionary.'" *New Yorker*. Condé Nast, 14 Feb. 2011. Web. 13 Sept. 2015.

Mirabito, Roger. "Stories of Inspiration: Laurie Halse Anderson, '81." *Continuum*. Onondaga Community College, 30 Jan. 2015. Web. 12 May 2015.

Mitchell, Elvis. "*The Princess Diaries* (2001) Film Review: Pygmalion for Another Fair Lady.*" New York Times*. New York Times, 3 Aug. 2001. Web. 31 Mar. 2015.

Miyazaki, Hayao. "A 'Positive Pessimist.'" Interview by Devin Gordon. *Newsweek*. Newsweek, 19 June 2005. Web. 30 Apr. 2015.

Modenait, Mr. "Ender's Game by Orson Scott Card." Rev. of *Ender's Game*, by Orson Scott Card. *Guardian*. Guardian News and Media, 14 May 2012. Web. 16 Apr. 2015.

Molland, Judy. "How Many Young Adult Novels Feature Transgender Characters?" *Care2*. Care2.com, 15 June 2015. Web. 17 Dec. 2015.

Montgomery, Lucy Maud. *The Alpine Path: The Story of My Career*. Don Mills: Fitzhenry, 1974. Print.

Moran, Rod. "Beauty amid the Carnage." *West Australian* 16 Oct. 2006: 10. Print.

Munley, Kyle. "Challenged and Banned: *A Wrinkle in Time*." *Suvudu*. Random House, 2 Oct. 2008. Web. 30 Nov. 2015.

Murray, Gail S. *American Children's Literature and the Construction of Childhood*. NY: Twayne, 1998.

Muwakkil, Salim. "Race, Sports, and the Big Bucks." *Chicago Tribune*. Chicago Tribune, 5 July 1999. Web. 11 June 2015.

Mydans, Seth. "Thai Protestors Are Detained after Using 'Hunger Games' Salute." *New York Times*. New York Times, 20 Nov. 2014. Web. 26 Feb. 2015.

Myers, Walter Dean. "Where are the People of Color in Children's Books?" *New York Times*. New York Times, 15 March 2014. Web. 23 February 2016.

Nashawaty, Chris. Rev. of *Ender's Game*, dir. by Gavin Hood. *Entertainment Weekly*. Entertainment Weekly, 17 Jan. 2015. Web. 2 Apr. 2015.

O'Neill, Phelim. Rev. of *Now Is Good*, dir. Ol Parker. *Guardian*. Guardian News and Media, 20 Sept. 2012. Web. 6 Nov. 2015.

"Ness, Patrick 1971–." *Something About the Author*, 2013. Print.

Ness, Patrick. "We two boys together clinging." *The Guardian*. Guardian, 23 June 2006. Web. 5 February 2016.

Ness, Patrick. *Patrick Ness*. Web. 5 February 2016.

Ness, Patrick. Rev. of *Dying to Know You*, by Aidan Chambers. *Guardian*. Guardian News and Media, 15 Jun. 2012. Web. 15 Feb. 2015.

"New Brief Biography." *ChrisCrutcher.com*. ChrisCrutcher.com, n.d. Web. 18 Mar. 2015.

"New Line Merged with Warner Bros Pictures." *Guardian*. Guardian News and Media, 29 Feb. 2008. Web. 31 Oct. 2015.

Nilsen, Alleen Pace. "Alice Childress: Overview." *Twentieth-Century Young Adult Writers*. Ed. Laura Standley Berger. Detroit: St. James Press, 1994. Literature Resource Center. Web. 26 February 2016.

Nilsen, Alleen Pace. "Books for Young Adults: Grandly Revolutionary? Or Simply Revolting?" *The English Journal* 64.6 (September 1975): 80–83.

Noffsinger, John, et al. "Still Good Reading: Adolescent Novels Written before 1967." *English Journal* 81.4 (1992): 87–90. Print.

Norton, Eric. Rev. of *Divergent. School Library Journal* 57.6 (June 2011): 133.

"On Robert Cormier's The Chocolate War." *PEN America*. PEN American Center, 15 Oct. 2012. Web. 11 June 2015.

O'Sullivan, Michael. "*Divergent* Movie Review: Better Than the Book? Believe It." Rev. of *Divergent*, dir. Neil Burger. *Washington Post*. Washington Post, 20 Mar. 2014. Web. 2 May 2015.

Office for Intellectual Freedom of the American Library Association. "100 Most Frequently Challenged Books: 1990–1999." *OIF/ALA*. ALA, n.d. Web. 23 February 2016.

Oh, Ellen. Interview by Natalie Aguirre. *Literary Rambles*. Literary Rambles, 7 Jan. 2013. Web. 9 Dec. 2015.

Olsen, Mark. Rev. of Beastly, dir. Daniel Barnz. *Los Angeles Times*. Los Angeles Times, 4 Mar. 2011. Web. 30 Mar. 2015.

Olweus, Dan. *Bullying at School: What We Know and What We Can Do*. Hoboken: Wiley, 1993. Print.

Ordona, Michael. "Romance Charms with a Teen Beat." *Los Angeles Times*. Los Angeles Times, 3 Oct. 2008. Web. 21 May 2015.

Pambid, Diadem. "*The Mortal Instruments Movie*: Five Reasons Why It Isn't a Twilight Rip Off.'" *International Business Times*. IBT Media, 26 Aug. 2013. Web. 9 May 2015.

Paolini, Christopher. "Christopher Paolini: Inspiration Strikes about Once Every Blue Moon." Interview. *Guardian*. Guardian News and Media, 16 Nov. 2011. Web. 25 Mar. 2015.

Paolini. "Christopher Paolini's Amazing Success: For the Bestselling Author of the Inheritance Cycle, It All Came Together Thanks to Discipline and Learning How to Structure and Pre-Plot a Story." Interview by Philip Martin. *Writer* May 2012: 24–26. *Literary Reference Center*. Web. 30 Mar. 2015.

"Paper Towns." *Box Office Mojo*. IMDb.com, 2015. Web. 17 Dec. 2015.

Parker, Ian. "Mugglemarch: J. K. Rowling Writes a Realist Novel for Adults." *New Yorker*. New Yorker, 1 Oct. 2012. Web. 31 Mar. 2015.

Patrick, Diane. "Urban Fiction." *Publishers Weekly*. PWxyz, 19 May 2003. Web. 3 June 2015.

"Patrick Ness's Biography." *Scholastic*. Scholastic, n.d. Web. 5 February 2016.

"Patrick Ness writing new Doctor Who spinoff series called Class." *Writers Write*. Writers Write, Inc., 3 October 2015. Web. 5 February 2016.

Pattee, Amy. "Street Fight: Welcome to the World of Urban Lit." *School Library Journal*. SLJ, 1 July 2008. Web. 3 June 2015.

"Patty Dann." *PattyDann.com*. Patty Dan, n.d. Web. 10 Nov. 2015.

Paulsen, Gary, and Jim Paulsen. Interview by Sally Lodge. "Q&A with Gary Paulsen and Jim Paulsen." *Publisher's Weekly*. PWxyz, 6 Dec. 2012. Web. 3 Mar. 2015.

Peck, Dale. "'The Outsiders': 40 Years Later." *New York Times*. New York Times, 23 Sept. 2007. Web. 17 Feb. 2015.

Peitzman, Louis. "Gene Luen Yang: Teacher, Dad, Graphic Novelist." *SFGate*. Hearst Communications, 29 Apr. 2010. Web. 31 Oct. 2015.

Pekoll, Kristin. "Why Gay Characters Matter." *Huffington Post*. TheHuffingtonPost.com, 22 Sept. 2014. Web. 17 Dec. 2015.

"Percy Jackson's World." *Rick Riordan*. Rick Riordan, n.d. Web. 10 May 2015.

Perenic, Laura. "Book to Movie: Before I Die and Now Is Good." *Hub.com*. YALSA, 17 July 2013. Web. 6 Nov. 2015.

Peters, Julie Anne. *Julie Anne Peters*. Julie Anne Peters, 2000. Web. 17 Dec. 2015.

Pheasant-Kelly, Frances. *Fantasy Films Post 9/11*. New York: Palgrave, 2013. Print.

Phillips, Michael. "Filmmaking Duo Good Even Not at Their Best." Rev. of *It's Kind of a Funny Story*, dir. Ryan Fleck and Anna Boden. *Chicago Tribune*. Chicago Tribune, 7 Oct. 2010. Web. 26 Nov. 2015.

Phillips, Michael. Rev. of *Youth in Revolt*, dir. Miguel Arteta. *Los Angeles Times*. Los Angeles Times, 8 Jan. 2010. Web. 8 Dec. 2015.

Phillips, Tommy M. "The Influence of Family Structure vs. Family Climate on Adolescent Well-Being." *Child and Adolescent Social Work Journal* 29.2 (2012): 103–10. *Academic Search Premier*. Web. 13 July 2015.

Phillips, Wendy. *Fishtailing*. Regina: Coteau, 2010. Print.

Phipps, Keith. "Alex Rider: Operation Stormbreaker." Rev. of *Alex Rider: Operation Stormbreaker*, dir. Geoffrey Sax. *A.V. Club*. Onion, 12 Oct. 2006. Web. 30 Nov. 2015.

Plimpton, George. "E. L. Doctorow, The Art of Fiction No. 94." *Paris Review*. Paris Review, Winter 1986. Web. 4 June 2015.

Pondiscio, Robert. "The Hunger Games Is a Civics Lesson." *Wall Street Journal*. Dow Jones, 4 Dec. 2013. Web. 26 Feb. 2015.

Poray Goddu, Krystyna. "Good-Luck Charms." Rev. of *The Favorite Daughter*, by Allen Say, and *The Thing about Luck*, by Cynthia Kadohata. *New York Times*. New York Times, 14 June 2013. Web. 14 May 2015.

Porter, Roy. *Madness: A Brief History*. Oxford: Oxford UP, 2003. Print.

Power, Chandra L. "Challenging the Pluralism of Our Past: Presentism and the Selective Tradition in Historical Fiction Written for Young People." *Research in the Teaching of English* 37.4 (2003): 425–66. Print.

Pratchett, Terry. "Terry Pratchett Interview: A Fantasy Writer Facing Reality." Interview by Tom Chivers. *Telegraph*. Telegraph Media Group, 12 Mar. 2015. Web. 4 June 2015.

Pratchett, Terry. "Terry Pratchett: My Case for a Euthanasia Tribunal." *Guardian*. Guardian News and Media, 1 Feb. 2010. Web. 4 June 2015.

"2004 Printz Award." *YALSA*. Amer. Lib. Assn., 2004. Web. 8 Dec. 2015.

Pullman, Philip. "Philip Pullman: A Life in Writing." *Guardian*. Guardian News and Media, 3 Mar. 2011. Web. 4 June 2015.

Pullman, Philip. "The Inventory: Philip Pullman." Interview with Hester Lacey. *FT Magazine*. Financial Times, 16 Mar. 2012. Web. 4 June 2015.

Pullman, Philip. *The Golden Compass*. New York: Knopf, 1996. Print.

Pung, Alice. Rev. of *Looking for Alibrandi*, by Melina Marchetta. Reading Australia. Copyright Agency, 2013. Web. 18 June 2015.

"Q&A with Richard Peck." Interview by Heather Vogel Frederick. *Publisher's Weekly*, PWxyz, 24 Sept. 2009. Web. 7 May 2015.

Rabey, Melissa. *Historical Fiction for Teens: A Genre Guide*. Santa Barbara: Libs. Unltd., 2011. Print.

Rabin, Nathan. "I'm Sorry for Coining the Phrase 'Manic Pixie Dream Girl.'" *Salon*. Salon Media Group, 15 July 2014. Web. 17 Dec. 2015.

Rabin, Nathan. "The Bataan Death March of Whimsy Case File #1: *Elizabethtown*." Rev. of *Elizabethtown*, dir. Cameron Crowe. *AV Club*. Onion, 25 Jan. 2007. Web. 17 Dec. 2015.

Raglan, FitzRoy Richard Somerset, Baron. *The Hero: A Study in Tradition, Myth, and Drama*. 1936. Mineola: Dover, 2011. Print.

Rainer, Peter. *Christian Science Monitor*. Christian Science Monitor, 8 Nov. 2008. Web. 1 May 2015.

Ramirez, Cindy. "El Paso Author Benjamin Alire Sáenz Wins PEN/Faulkner Award for Fiction." *El Paso Times*. El Paso Times, 19 Mar. 2013. Web. 16 Feb. 2015.

Ramos, Miguel. "10 Things You Did Not Know about Tahereh Mafi." *Philippine Star*. Philstar, 10 Mar. 2013. Web. 27 Oct. 2015.

Rapold, Nicolas. "The Spectacular Now." Rev. of *The Spectacular Now*, dir. James Ponsoldt. *New York Times*. New York Times, 1 Aug. 2013. Web. 30 Dec. 2015.

Reid, Calvin. "Selling Urban Fiction." *Publishers Weekly*. PWxyz, 20 Jan. 2006. Web. 3 June 2015.

Rentería, Ramón. "Author Ben Saenz Transcends, Inspires." *El Paso Times*. El Paso Times, 5 Mar. 2010. Web. 23 Feb. 2015.

Reutter, Vicki. "Adventure and Survival." *School Library Journal* May 2004: 63. *Literary Reference Center*. Web. 28 May 2015.

Rev. of *Blood and Chocolate*, by Annette Curtis Klause. *Kirkus*. Kirkus, 20 May 2010. Web. 8 June 2015.

Rev. of *Bomb: The Race to Build—and Steal—the World's Most Dangerous Weapon*, by Steve Sheinkin. *Kirkus*. Kirkus Media, 18 July 2012. Web. 6 May 2015.

Rev. of *Dark Sons*, by Nikki Grimes. *Kirkus Reviews* 73.15 (2005): 848. *Academic Search Complete*. Web. 16 May 2015.

Rev. of *Dying to Know You*, by Aidan Chambers. *Horn Book Magazine* May–June 2012: 78–79. *Literary Reference Center*. Web. 18 Feb. 2015.

Rev. of *Froi of the Exiles*, by Melina Marchetta. *Kirkus*. Kirkus, 18 Jan. 2012. Web. 15 Sept. 2015.

Rev. of *Godless*, by Pete Hautman. *Kirkus Reviews* 72.9 (2004): 442. *Academic Search Complete*. Web. 16 May 2015.

Rev. of *Graffiti Moon*, by Cath Crowley. *Publishers Weekly* 19 Dec. 2011: 54. *Literary Reference Center*. Web. 14 Oct. 2015.

Rev. of *Grasshopper Jungle*, by Andrew Smith. *Publishers Weekly* 4 Nov. 2013: 68. *Literary Reference Center*. Web. 22 Oct. 2015.

Rev. of *I Am Number Four*, by Pittacus Lore. *Publishers Weekly* 257.28 (2010): 131. *Literary Reference Center*. Web. 13 Apr. 2015.

Rev. of *Jellicoe Road*, by Melina Marchetta. *Kirkus*. Kirkus, 20 May 2010. Web. 15 Sept. 2015.

Rev. of *Kinda Like Brothers*, by Coe Booth. *Kirkus Reviews* 12 July 2014: 1. *Academic Search Complete*. Web. 31 Oct. 2015.

Rev. of *Miracle's Boys*, by Jacqueline Woodson. *Publishers Weekly*. PWxyz, 24 Apr. 2000. Web. 19 Mar. 2015.

Rev. of *More Than This*, by Patrick Ness. *Kirkus Reviews* 81.17 (2013): 107.

Rev. of *Nick and Norah's Infinite Playlist*, by Rachel Cohn and David Levithan. *Kirkus*. Kirkus Media, 23 May 2006. Web. 21 May 2015.

Rev. of *Noggin*, by John Corey Whaley. *Publishers Weekly* 20 Jan. 2014: 58. *Literary Reference Center*. Web. 22 Oct. 2015.

Rev. of *Passenger*, by Andrew Smith. *Kirkus Reviews* 2 Dec. 2012: 80–81. *Literary Reference Center*. Web. 22 Oct. 2015.

Rev. of *Saving Francesca*, by Melina Marchetta. *Publisher's Weekly*. PWxyz, n.d. Web. 15 Sept. 2015.

Rev. of *Steve Jobs: The Man Who Thought Different*, by Karen Blumenthal. *Kirkus Reviews* 15 Feb. 2012: 386–87. *Literary Reference Center*. Web. 6 May 2015.

Rev. of *Tex*, by S. E. Hinton. *Kirkus Reviews*. Kirkus Media, 1 Oct. 1980. Web. 25 May 2015.

Rev. of *The Kissing Game*, by Aidan Chambers. *Kirkus* 15 Feb. 2011: 304. *Literary Reference Center*. Web. 15 Feb. 2015.

Rev. of *The Meaning of Consuelo*, by Judith Ortiz Cofer. *Publishers Weekly*. PWxyz, 1 Nov. 2003. Web. 15 May 2015.

Rev. of *The Patron Saint of Butterflies*, by Cecilia Galante. *Kirkus Reviews* 76.8 (2008): 424. *Academic Search Complete*. Web. 16 May 2015.

Rev. of *The White Darkness*, by Geraldine McCaughrean. *Booklist* Jan. 2008: 14. *Literary Reference Center*. Web. 28 May 2015.

Rev. of *Uglies*, by Scott Westerfield. *Guardian*. Guardian News and Media, 23 June 2012. Web. 14 May 2015.

Rev. of *Warm Bodies*, by Isaac Marion. *Kirkus Reviews* 79.5 (2011): 357–58. *Literary Reference Center*. Web. 16 May 2015.

Rev. of *Warrior*, by Ellen Oh. *Kirkus Reviews* 81.21 (2013): 37. *Literary Reference Center*. Web. 14 Dec. 2015.

Rev. of *Where Things Come Back*, by John Corey Whaley. *Kirkus Reviews* 15 Apr. 2011: 702. *Literary Reference Center*. Web. 22 Oct. 2015.

Reynolds, Christopher. "Once Upon a Time: There Was a Little Girl Stranded on a Channel Island." *LA Times*. Los Angeles Times, 13 Dec. 1990. Web. 25 May 2015.

Richards, Linda. "Judy Blume: On Censorship, Enjoying Life, and Staying in the Spotlight for 25 Years." *January Magazine*. January Magazine, n.d. Web. 31 Mar. 2015.

Riggs, Ransom. *Miss Peregrine's Home for Peculiar Children*. Philadelphia: Quirk, 2011. Print.

Riordan, Rick, ed. *Demigods and Monsters: Your Favorite Authors on Rick Riordan's Percy Jackson and the Olympians Series*. Expanded ed. Dallas: Benbella, 2013. Print.

Riordan, Rick. "Rick Riordan Answers All Your Questions." *Guardian*. Guardian News and Media, 3 May 2011. Web. 31 May 2015.

Riordan, Rick. "Talking with Rick Riordan." Interview by Jeanette Larson. *ALA*. Amer. Library Assn., May 2009. Web. 31 May 2015.

Ritter, Cynthia K. Rev. of *I Am Number Four*, by Pittacus Lore. *Horn Book Magazine*. 86.5 (2010): 82–83. *Literary Reference Center*. Web. 16 Apr. 2015.

Roback, Diane, et al. "*This Lullaby* (Book)." *Publishers Weekly* 249.20 (2002): 66. *Literary Reference Center*. Web. 17 May 2015.

Robehmed, Natalie. "The World's Top-Earning Authors." *Forbes* 17 August 2015. Business Source Complete. Web. 16 February 2016.

Roberts, Patricia L. *Taking Humor Seriously in Children's Literature: Literature-Based Mini-Units and Humorous Books for Children Ages 5–12*. Lanham: Scarecrow, 1997. Print.

Robey, Tim. Rev. of *Angus, Thongs and Perfect Snogging*. *Telegraph*. Telegraph Media Group, 25 July 2008. Web. 31 Mar. 2015.

Robey, Tim. *Telegraph*. Telegraph Media Group, 12 Sept. 2008. (Web) 1 May 2015.

Robinson, Tasha. Rev. of *Stardust*, dir. Matthew Vaughn. *A. V. Club*. Onion, 10 Aug. 2007. Web. 30 Nov. 2015.

Robshaw, Brandon. Rev. of *Before I Die*, by Jenny Downham. *Independent.co.uk*. Independent, 22 Oct. 2011. Web. 20 Nov. 2015.

Rosbottom, Ronald C. "Epistolary Fiction in Europe: 1500–1850." *Philosophy and Literature* 24.1 (2000): 230–33. *Muse*. John Hopkins UP, 2000. Web. 5 May 2015.

Rosen, Judith. "Middle Grade and YA: Where to Draw the Line?" *Publishers Weekly* 21 July 2014: 24–25. *Literary Reference Center*. Web. 14 May 2015.

Rosen, Michael. "Lizzie McGuire Meets Queer as Folk." Rev. of *Boy Meets Boy*, by David Levithan. *Guardian*. Guardian News and Media, 15 Apr. 2005. Web. 13 Sept. 2015.

Rosen, Rebecca J. "How John Green Wrote a Cancer Book but Not a 'Bulls—— Cancer Book.'" *Atlantic*. Atlantic Monthly, 25 Feb. 2013. Web. 15 Apr. 2015.

Rosenberg, Alyssa. "From 'Harry Potter' to 'Twilight,' the Enduring Draw of Young Adult Fiction." *Atlantic*. Atlantic Monthly Group, 31 May 2011. Web. 23 June 2015.

Rosenberg, Liz. "Where the Coolest Kids Are, Like, Undead." *Boston.com*. Boston Globe Media Partners, 28 June 2009. Web. 26 Feb. 2015.

Rosenberg, Melissa. "Interview: 'Twilight' Scribe Melissa Rosenberg on 'Breaking Dawn' & Feminism." By Roth Cornet. *ScreenRant*. Screen Rant, 18 Nov 2011. Web. 10 May 2015.

Rosenberg, Merri. "Children's Books; Teen-Agers Face Evil." *New York Times*. New York Times, 5 May 1985. Web. 2 June 2015.

Rosin, Hanna. "How Hollywood Saved God." *Atlantic* 300.5 (2007): 68–79. *Literary Reference Center*. Web. 24 Nov. 2015.

Ross, Ashley. "These Are the Biggest Differences between the *Paper Towns* Movie and Book." *Time*. Time, 24 July 2015. Web. 30 Nov. 2015.

Roth, Veronica. "About the End of Allegiant (Spoilers)." *Veronica Roth*. 28 October, 2013. Web. 22 February 2016.

Roth, Veronica. "FAQs: About that next book." *Veronica Roth*. n.p., 4 December 2015. Web. 8 February 2016.

Roth, Veronica. "How Many Drafts Did You Go Through . . . ?" *Veronica Roth*. n.p., 14 October 2015. Web. 8 February 2016.

Rowell, Rainbow. Interview by Amanda Green. "The Rumpus Interview with Rainbow Rowell." *Rumpus*. Rumpus, 17 Oct. 2014. Web. 14 Sept. 2015.

Rowell, Rainbow. Interview by Julie Bartel. "One Thing Leads to Another: An Interview with Rainbow Rowell." *Hub*. Young Adult Library Services Association, 27 Feb. 2014. Web. 14 Sept. 2015.

Rowell, Rainbow. Interview by Nolan Feeney. "*Eleanor & Park* Author Rainbow Rowell Talks *Fifty Shades* and Franzen." *Time*. Time, 19 Feb. 2015. Web. 14 Sept. 2015.

Rowling, J. K. "The Fringe Benefits of Failure, and the Importance of Imagination." *Harvard Magazine*. Harvard Magazine, 5 June 2008. Web. 31 Mar. 2015.

Rubin, Kenneth, Bridget Fredstrom, and Julie Bowker. "Future Directions in . . . Friendship in Childhood and Early Adolescence." *Social Development* 17.4 (2008): 1085–96. *Academic Search Premier*. Web. 8 June 2015.

Ryan, Laura T. "Hip-hop Fiction Drawing More Readers to Black Lit." *Seattle Times*. Seattle Times, 22 Feb. 2005. Web. 3 June 2015.

S., R. Rev. of *Kendra*, by Coe Booth. *Horn Book Magazine* Nov.–Dec. 2008: 696–97. *Literary Reference Center*. Web. 19 Oct. 2015.

Sabin, Roger. *Comics, Comix & Graphic Novels: A History of Comic Art*. New York: Phaidon, 2001. Print.

Sachar, Louis. "An Interview with Louis Sachar." Interview by Julie Just. *New York Times*. New York Times, 15 Jan. 2006. Web. 30 Apr. 2015.

Sachar, Louis. "Louis Sachar Interview Transcript." *Scholastic*. Scholastic, 23 Feb. 2006. Web. 30 Apr. 2015.

Sachar, Louis. "Q & A with Louis Sachar." *Publishers Weekly*. PWxyz, 6 May 2010. Web. 30 Apr. 2015.

Sachar, Louis. "Younger Audiences." Interview by Elizabeth Farnsworth. *PBS Newshour*. Newshour Productions, 25 Nov. 1998. Web. 30 Apr. 2015.

Sachs, Nina. Rev. of *Insurgent. School Library Journal* 58.6 (June 2012): 136.

Sáenz, Benjamin Alire. "Discovering Sexuality through Teen Lit." Interview by Michel Martin. *NPR Books*. NPR, 20 Feb. 2013. Web. 16 Feb. 2015.

Sáenz, Benjamin Alire. "Just This Side of Tragic: An Interview with Benjamin Alire Sáenz." Interview by Daniel Olivas. *Los Angeles Review of Books*. Los Angeles Review of Books, 6 May 2013. Web. 23 Feb. 2015.

Salzer, Maureen. "Francesca Lia Block." *Popular Contemporary Writers*. Ed. Michael D. Sharp. Vol. 2. Tarrytown: Marshall, 2006. 209–18. Print.

Sambuchino, Chuck. "Everything You Would've Asked about Steampunk, Had You Known It Existed." *Writer's Digest*. F+W, 13 Aug. 2013. Web. 10 May 2015.

Sanchez, Matt. "Fantasy." *Genre Fiction as Literature*. Matt Sanchez, 2005. Web. 5 May 2015.

"Sarah Dessen." *Baker & Taylor Author Biographies* (2000): 1. *Literary Reference Center*. Web. 17 May 2015.

Scafaria, Lorene. "Lorene Scafaria Interview, *Nick and Norah's Infinite Playlist*, Toronto 2008." Interview by Kevin Kelly. *Indiewire*. Indiewire.com, 2008. Web. 21 May 2015.

Schager, Nick. "Film Review: 'The Duff.'" *Variety*. Variety Media, 20 Feb. 2015. Web. 31 Oct. 2015.

Schager, Nick. "YA Dystopian Films Have Become What They Hate." *New York Magazine*. New York Media, 21 Nov. 2014. Web. 2 Apr. 2015.

Schall, Lucy. *Genre Talks for Teens: Booktalks and More for Every Teen Reading Interest*. Westport: Libraries Unlimited, 2009. Print.

Schillinger, Liesl. "Children's Books/Young Adult: Eclipse." *New York Times*. New York Times, 12 Aug. 2007. Web. 10 May 2015.Schneider, Dean. "What Makes A Good Sports Novel?" *Horn Book Magazine* 87.1 (2011): 68–72. *Literary Reference Center*. Web. 12 June 2015.

Schwartz, John. Rev. of *The Invention of Hugo Cabret: A Novel in Words and Pictures*, by Brian Selznick. *New York Times*. New York Times, 11 Mar. 2007. Web. 3 Apr. 2015.

Schwartzapfel, Beth. "Two Teens, One Name." *Brown Alumni Magazine*. Brown Alumni Magazine, 1 July 2010. Web. 13 Sept. 2015.

Schweiger, Larry J. "Kids and Wildlife—A Perfect Big Screen Combination." *National Wildlife Federation*. Natl. Wildlife Federation, 10 Apr. 2006. Web. 19 Mar. 2015.

Scorsese, Martin. "Martin Scorsese's Magical 'Hugo.'" Interview by John Bowe. *New York Times Magazine*. New York Times, 2 Nov. 2011. Web. 6 Apr. 2015.

Scott, A. O. "A Coming-of-Age Tale, Set among the Sad." Rev. of *It's Kind of a Funny Story*, dir. Ryan Fleck and Anna Boden. *New York Times*. New York Times, 7 Oct. 2010. Web. 27 Nov. 2015.

Scott, A. O. "A Cursed Teenager Turns 90. Let the Adventures Begin." Rev. of *Howl's Moving Castle*, dir. Hayao Miyazaki. *New York Times*. New York Times, 10 June 2005. Web. 30 Apr. 2015.

Scott, A. O. "Amid Vampires, Boy Meets Girl, Complete with Monkey's Tail." Rev. of *Cirque du Freak: The Vampire's Assistant*, dir. Paul Weitz. *New York Times*. New York Times, 22 Oct. 2009. Web. 10 Mar. 2015.

Scott, A. O. "For Muddled Youth, Music to Live By." Rev. of *Nick and Norah's Infinite Playlist*, dir. Peter Sollett. *New York Times*. New York Times, 2 Oct. 2008. Web. 21 May 2015.

Scott, A. O. "*Holes* (2003) Film Review; Not Just for Children, a Suspenseful Allegory of Greed, Fate, and Racism." *New York Times*. New York Times, 18 Apr. 2003. Web. 28 Feb. 2015.

Scott, A. O. "Pimples Are the Least of This Girl's Worries." Rev. of *How to Deal*, dir. Clare Kilner. *New York Times*. New York Times, 18 July 2003. Web. 9 Mar. 2015.

Scott, A. O. "Review: In *Me and Earl and the Dying Girl*, a Comfort Zone That Cannot Last." Rev. of *Me and Earl and the Dying Girl*, dir. Alfonso Gomez-Rejon. *New York Times*. New York Times, 11 June 2015. Web. 24 Nov. 2015.

"Screenwriter and Novelist Stephen Chbosky: Rebel with a Cause." *Script Magazine*. FW, 21 Sept. 2012. Web. 5 June 2015.

Seed, David. *Ray Bradbury*. Urbana: U of Illinois P, 2015. *eBook Collection (EBSCOhost)*. Web. 3 Nov. 2015.Sette, Sunnie. Rev. of *Prophecy*, by Ellen Oh. *School Library Journal* 59.2 (2013): 111. Print.

Sexton, Colleen A. *J. K. Rowling*. Minneapolis: Twenty-First Century, 2008. Print.

Shahan, Sherry. "A Fresh Approach to YA Novels: Learn How the Young adult Novel-in-Verse Offers Unique Opportunities for Emotional Insight." *Writer* Feb. 2009: 34+. *Literary Reference Center*. Web. 7 Apr. 2015.

Shan, Darren. "The Master of Horror." Interview by Michael Mullooly. *University Times*. Trinity Coll. Dublin, 11 Feb. 2015. Web. 10 Mar. 2015.

Shan, Darren. Interview by Lisa Morton. *Nightmare* Apr. 2014: n. pag. Web. 30 Mar. 2015.

Sharkey, Betsy. "Strong Acting Can't Right Topsy-Turvy Priorities in 'The DUFF.'" *Los Angeles Times*. Los Angeles Times, 19 Feb. 2015. Web. 31 Oct. 2015.

Sharkey, Betsy. Rev. of *Cirque du Freak: The Vampire's Assistant*, dir. Paul Weitz. *Los Angeles Times*. Los Angeles Times, 23 Oct. 2009. Web. 10 Mar. 2015.

Sharkey, Betsy. Rev. of *It's Kind of a Funny Story*, dir. Ryan Fleck and Anna Boden. *Los Angeles Times*. Tribune, 8 Oct. 2010 Web. 26 Nov. 2015.

Sharp, Michael D., ed. *Popular Contemporary Writers*. Vol. 7. Tarrytown: Marshall, 2006. Print.

Sheckels, Theodore: "The Complex Politics and Rhetoric of John Marsden's 'Tomorrow' Series." *Antipodes* 28.2 (2014): 436–49. *Literary Reference Center*.Web. 17 Dec. 2015.

Sheldon, Dyan. Interview. *LitPick*. LitPick, n.d. Web. 19 Mar. 2015.

Sherman, Chris. Rev. of *The Princess Diaries*. *Booklist* 97.2 (15 September 2000): 233.

Shippey, Tom. "Orson Scott Card's Three-Decade Run." *Wall Street Journal*. Dow Jones, 22 Jan. 2011. Web. 2 June 2015.

Short, Kathy G., Carol Lynch-Brown, and Carl M. Tomlinson. *Essentials of Children's Literature*. 8th ed. Harlow: Pearson, 2014. Print.

Sibley, Brian. *The Golden Compass: The Official Illustrated Movie Companion*. New York: Scholastic, 2007. Print.

Silvey, Anita, ed. *Children's Books and Their Creators*. New York: Houghton, 1995. Print.

Simon, Rachel. "Laurie Halse Anderson on 'Speak,' Censorship, and 'The Impossible Knife of Memory.'" *Bustle*. Bustle.com, 6 Jan. 2014. Web. 10 June 2015.

Sims, Andrew. "'Divergent' Trilogy Holds Top Three Places on *USA Today*'s Best-Selling Books List." *Hypable*. Hypable, 9 January 2014. Web. 20 February 2016.

Smith, Andrew. "One Thing Leads to Another: An Interview with Andrew Smith." Interview by Julie Bartel. *Hub*. YALSA, 9 Oct. 2014. Web. 22 Oct. 2015.

Smith, Dinitia. "An Outsider, Out of the Shadows." *New York Times*. New York Times, 7 Sept. 2005. Web. 23 May 2015.

Smith, Kyle. "Bad Harry Day." Rev. of *The Seeker*, dir. David L. Cunningham. *New York Post*. NYP Holdings, 5 Oct. 2007. Web. 2 June 2015.

Smith, Robin. Rev. of *Tyrell*, by Coe Booth. *Horn Book Magazine* Jan.–Feb. 2007: 62–63. *Literary Reference Center*. Web. 19 Oct. 2015.

smith, s.e. "Review: *Marcelo in the Real World* by Francisco X. Stork." *Disability in Kidlit*. 1 July 2013. Web. 23 February 2016.

Snider, Jessi. "'Be The Tree': Classical Literature, Art Therapy, and Transcending Trauma in *Speak.*" *Children's Literature in Education* 45.4 (2014): 298–309. Print.

Snow, Shane. "Orson Scott Card Talks Ender's Game in Rare Interview." *Wired.* Condé Nast, 31 Oct. 2013. Web. 2 June 2015.

Snyder, Christopher A. "The Use of History and Archaeology in Contemporary Arthurian Fiction." *Arthuriana* 19.3 (2009): 114–22. *Literary Reference Center.* Web. 27 Oct. 2015.

Somers, Joseph Michael. "Gary Paulsen." *Magill's Survey of American Literature.* Rev. ed. Ipswich: Salem, 2006. *Biography Reference Center.* Web. 23 Mar. 2015.

"Sonya Hartnett Wins £400,000 Prize for Children's Writing." *Bookseller* 6 June 2008: 8. *Literary Reference Center.* Web. 15 Oct. 2015.

"Sonya Hartnett." *Literature Matters.* British Council of Lit., 2011. Web. 26 Sept. 2015.

Spencer Holley, Pam. Rev. of *Graffiti Moon*, by Cath Crowley. *Booklist* 15 May 2012: 70. *Literary Reference Center.* Web. 14 Oct. 2015.

Spencer, Liv. *Navigating the Shadow World: The Unofficial Guide to Cassandra Clare's The Mortal Instruments.* Toronto: ECW, 2013. Print.

Spisak, April. "Dystopian Novel?" *Horn Book Magazine* May–June 2012: 55–60. *Literary Reference Center.* Web. 10 Feb. 2015.

Spitz, Marc. "John Hughes and the Soundtrack to Our Lives." *SPIN.* SPIN Media, 7 Aug. 2009. Web. 21 May 2015.

Springen, Karen. "Fall 2009 Flying Starts: Malinda Lo." *Publishers Weekly.* PWxyz, 21 Dec. 2009. Web. 30 Nov. 2015.

"Stardust." *Box Office Mojo.* IMDB.com, 2015. Web. 30 Nov. 2015.

Stein, Ruthe. "Review: 'Sisterhood of the Traveling Pants 2.'" Rev. of *Sisterhood of the Traveling Pants 2*, dir. Sanaa Hamri. *SFGate.* Hearst Communications, 6 Aug. 2008. Web. 30 Apr. 2015.

Stein, Ruthe. "Review: Teen on Mission to Save Universe in *The Seeker.*" Rev. of *The Seeker*, dir. David L. Cunningham. *SFGate.* Hearst Communications, 4 Oct. 2007. Web. 2 June 2015.

Stelloh, Tim. "Who Killed Lois Duncan's Daughter?" *BuzzFeed News.* BuzzFeed, 30 May 2014. Web. 6 Mar. 2015.

Stern, Mark Joseph. "Neural Nostalgia." *Slate.* Slate, 12 Aug. 2014. Web. 21 May 2015.

Stewart, Debbie. Rev. of *The Princess Diaries. School Library Journal* 46.10 (October 2000): 155.

Stiefvater, Maggie. "One Thing Leads to Another: An Interview with Maggie Stiefvater." Interview by Julie Bartel. *Hub.* YALSA, 9 Jan. 2014. Web. 11 Dec. 2015.

Stiefvater, Maggie. "Q & A with Maggie Stiefvater." Interview by Sue Corbett. *Publishers Weekly.* PWxyz, 6 Oct. 2011. Web. 11 Dec. 2015.

Stone, Susan. "L'Engle's 'A Wrinkle in Time' to Make TV Debut." *All Things Considered.* NPR, 9 May 2004. Web. 30 Nov. 2015.

Stott, Jon C. "Narrative Technique and Meaning in *Island of the Blue Dolphins.*" *Elementary English* 52.4 (1975): 442–46. Print.

Stowell, Theresa L. "Gary Paulsen." *Critical Survey of Long Fiction, Fourth Edition* (2010): 1–3. *Literary Reference Center.* Web. 28 May 2015.

Strauss, Valerie. "A Farewell to 'It's Kind of a Funny Story' Author." *Washington Post.* Washington Post, 25 Dec. 2013. Web. 26 Nov. 2015.

Strickland, Ashley. "A Brief History of Young Adult Literature." *CNN.* Cable News Network, 17 Oct 2013. Web. 15 Mar. 2015.

Strickland, Ashley. "A Brief History of Young Adult Literature." CNN. Cable News Network, Turner Broadcasting System, 15 Feb. 2015. Web. 10 May 2015.

Strickland, Ashley. "A Brief History of Young Adult Literature." *CNN.* Cable News Network, 15 Apr. 2015. Web. 15 May 2015.

Strickland, Ashley. "A Brief History of Young Adult Literature." *CNN.* CNN, 15 Apr. 2015. Web. 12 May 2015.

Strickland, Ashley. "A Brief History of Young Adult Literature." CNN. Cable News Network/Turner Broadcasting System, 15 Apr. 2015. Web. 10 May 2015.

Strickland, Ashley. "A Brief History of Young Adult Literature." *CNN.com.* Cable News Network, 17 Oct. 2013. Web. 7 Apr. 2015.

Strickland, Ashley. "A Brief History of Young Adult Literature." CNN. Cable News Network. Turner Broadcasting System, 17 Oct 2013. Web. 15 March 2015.

Sturm, Brian W., and Karin Michel. "The Structure of Power in Young Adult Problem Novels." *Young Adult Library Services* Winter 2009: 39–47. *Academic Search Premier.* Web. 14 May 2015.

Subramanian, Mathangi. *Bullying: The Ultimate Teen Guide.* Lanham: Rowman, 2014. Print. It Happened to Me.

Sutton, Roger. "A Second Look: Annie on My Mind." *Horn Book* 83.5 (Sept./Oct. 2007): 543–546. Print.

Sutton, Roger. Rev. of *Bronxwood*, by Coe Booth. *Horn Book Magazine* Nov.–Dec. 2011: 93–94. *Literary Reference Center*. Web. 19 Oct. 2015.

Swain, Rebecca. Rev. of *Paper Towns*, by John Green. *Shakespeare's Coffee*. Orlando Sentinel, 11 Oct. 2008. *Internet Archive: Wayback Machine*. Web. 17 Dec. 2015.

Swanson, Clare. "The Bestselling Books of 2014." *Publishers Weekly*. PWxyz, LLC, 2 January 2015. Web. 20 February 2016.

Syme, Rachel. "'The Fault in Our Stars': Love in a Time of Cancer." Rev. of *The Fault in Our Stars*, by John Green. *NPR Books*. Natl. Public Radio, 17 Jan. 2012. Web. 15 Apr. 2015.

Tackett MacDonald, Jessica. Rev. of *I Was Here*, by Gayle Forman. *Horn Book Magazine* 1 Jan. 2015: 80–81. *Literary Reference Center*. Web. 8 Oct. 2015.

Talbot, Margaret. "The Teen Whisperer." *New Yorker*. Condé Nast, 9 June 2014. Web. 4 Mar. 2015.

Tan, Monica. "John Marsden Is Reminded of His Reply to the Fan Letter I Sent Him When I Was 14." *Guardian*. Guardian News and Media, 12 Feb. 2015. Web. 14 Dec. 2015.

Taylor, Ella. "A 'Life' Where HIV and Ignorance Are Twin Epidemics." *National Public Radio*. NPR, 22 July 2011. Web. 3 Dec. 2015.

Taylor, Mildred D. *Roll of Thunder, Hear My Cry*. New York: Dial, 1976. Print.

"Teen Pregnancy: Trends and Lessons Learned." *Guttmacher Report on Public Policy* 5.1 (2002): N. pag. Web. 13 July 2015.

"The Birth of Steampunk." *Letters of Note*. Ed. Shaun Usher. TinyLetter, Mar. 2011. Web. 30 June 2015.

"The Chocolate War." *Box Office Mojo*. IMDB.com, 2015. Web. 30 Nov. 2015.

"The Life of C. S. Lewis Timeline." *CSLewis.org*. C. S. Lewis Foundation, 2015. Web. 25 Feb. 2015.

"The Michael L. Printz Award for Excellence in Young Adult Literature." *ALA*. Amer. Lib. Assn., 2007. Web. 31 Oct. 2015.

"The Princess Bride." *Box Office Mojo*. IMDB.com, n.d. Web. 31 Oct. 2015.

"*The Seeker: The Dark Is Rising*." *Box Office Mojo*. IMDB.com, 2007. Web. 2 June 2015.

"The Sisterhood of the Traveling Pants." *Box Office Mojo*. IMDb.com, n. d. Web. 30 Apr. 2015.

"The Sisterhood of the Traveling Pants 2." *Box Office Mojo*. IMDb.com, n. d. Web. 30 Apr. 2015.

"*The Yearling*." *Teach with Movies*. TeachWithMovies. com, 2 Aug. 2010. Web. 25 Nov. 2015.

"*The Yearling* (1947)." *TCM.com*. Turner Entertainment Networks, 2015. Web. 25 Nov. 2015.

Thompson, Eliza. "The New 'Princess Diaries" Book May or May Not Include Sex in the Throne Room." *Cosmopolitan*. Hearst Communications, Inc., 13 May 2015. Web. 28 February 2016.

Thompson, Howard. "*Island of Blue Dolphins* Has Premiere." Rev. of *Island of the Blue Dolphins*, dir. James B. Clark. *New York Times*. New York Times, 4 July 1964. Web. 27 Oct. 2015.

Thompson, Raymond H., and Norris J. Lacy, eds. "The Arthurian Legend in Literature, Popular Culture and the Performing Arts, 2004–2008." *Arthurian Literature*. Vol. 26. Ed. Elizabeth Archibald and David F. Johnson. Cambridge: Brewer, 2009. 171–214. *eBook Collection*. Web. 27 Oct. 2015.

Thomson, David. "Bring Out Your Dead." Rev. of *Warm Bodies*, dir. Jonathan Levine. *New Republic* 244.3 (2013): 60–62. *Academic Search Premier*. Web. 16 May 2015.

Tracy, Allison J. "Gender and Race Patterns in the Pathways from Sports Participation to Self-Esteem." *Sociological Perspectives* 45.4 (2002): 445–46. *SocINDEX with Full Text*. Web. 11 June 2015.

Tribunella, Eric L. "Institutionalizing *The Outsiders*: YA Literature, Social Class, and the American Faith in Education." *Children's Literature in Education* 38.2 (2007): 87–101. *Academic Search Premier*. Web. 7 July 2015.

Tribunella, Eric. *Melancholia and Maturation: The Use of Trauma in American Children's Literature*. Knoxville: U of Tennessee P, 2010. Print.

Trites, Roberta Seelinger. *Disturbing the Universe: Power and Repression in Adolescent Literature*. Iowa City, IA: University of Iowa Press, 2000.

Tucker, Ken. "Movie Review: Worldwide Pants." Rev. of *Sisterhood of the Traveling Pants*, dir. Ken Kwapis. *NYMag.com*. New York, 2005. Web. 30 Apr. 2015.

Tyson, Edith S. *Orson Scott Card: Writer of the Terrible Choice*. Lanham: Scarecrow, 2003. Print.

Valdes, Marcela. "What Terrifies Teens in Today's Young-Adult Novels? The Economy." *NPR*. NPR, 30 Sept. 2013. Web. 12 May 2015.

Vasquez, Felix, Jr. Rev. of *Avalon High*, dir. Stuart Gillard. *Cinema Crazed*. Author, 17 Nov. 2010. Web. 28 Oct. 2015.

"Veronica Roth." *Contemporary Authors Online*. Detroit: Gale, 2015. Literature Resource Center. Web. 8 February 2016.

Vineyard, Jennifer. "Geoffrey Rush on *The Book Thief*, Magic Tricks, and Nazi Movies." *Vulture*. New York Media, 5 Nov. 2013. Web. 10 May 2015.

Voigt, Cynthia. "A Chat with Cynthia Voigt." Interview by Raymond Baartmans. *Time for Kids*. Time, 16 Oct. 2013. Web. 6 Mar. 2015.

Voigt, Cynthia. "Author Biography." *Cynthia Voigt*. Author, n.d. Web. 6 Mar. 2015.

Voigt, Cynthia. "Biography: Cynthia Voigt." *Scholastic*. Scholastic, n.d. Web. 6 Mar. 2015.

Voigt, Cynthia. "Cynthia Voigt Interview Transcript." *Scholastic*. Scholastic, n.d. Web. 6 Mar. 2015.

Voigts, Cynthia. "Cynthia Voigt Learns the Rhythms of a Different Life." Interview by Eugenia Williamson. *Boston Globe*. Boston Globe Media Partners, 27 Dec. 2014. Web. 6 Mar. 2015.

Wainwright, Natalie. "'Divergent:' A best-seller built in Evanston." *Evanston Round Table*. Evanston Round Table, LLC, 2011 July 5. Web. 8 February 2016.

Walker, Barbara J. *The Librarian's Guide to Developing Christian Fiction Collections for Children*. New York: Neal-Schuman, 2005. Print.

Walton, Alice G. "The Psychological Effects of Bullying Last Well into Adulthood, Study Finds." *Forbes*. Forbes, 21 Feb. 2013. Web. 25 June 2015.

Walton, Jo. "Australian Fantasy: Justine Larbalestier's *Magic or Madness*." *Tor.com*. Macmillan, 12 Apr. 2013. Web. 21 Dec. 2015.

Watkins, Susan. "Future Shock: Rewriting the Apocalypse in Contemporary Women's Fiction." *LIT: Literature Interpretation Theory* 23.2 (2012): 119–37. *Literary Reference Center*. Web. 30 Apr. 2015.

Way, Niobe. "Boys' Friendships during Adolescence: Intimacy, Desire, and Loss." *Journal of Research on Adolescence* 23.2 (2013): 201–13. *Academic Search Premier*. Web. 8 June 2015.

Weitzman, Elizabeth. "*ity of Ember* oes Underground." Rev. of *City of Ember*, dir. Gil Kenan. *New York Daily News*. NYDailyNews.com, 9 Oct. 2008. Web. 30 Apr. 2015.

Welsh, Kate Linnea. "How to Make Young Adult Fiction More Diverse." *Atlantic*. Atlantic Monthly, 2 June 2011. Web. 30 Nov. 2015.

Whaley, John Corey. "Author Interview: John Corey Whaley." Interview by Kate Pickett. *Hub*. Young Adult Lib. Services Assn., 12 Jan. 2012. Web. 22 Oct. 2015.

Whaley, John Corey. "Flying High: The Improbable True Tale of Debut Novelist John Corey Whaley." Interview Interview by Ed Spicer. *School Library Journal*. Lib. Jours., 1 May 2012. Web. 22 Oct. 2015.

Whaley, John Corey. "John Corey Whaley, 28, Discusses His Printz Award and What's Next." Interview by Susan Carpenter. *Los Angeles Times*. Tribune, 23 Jan. 2012. Web. 22 Oct. 2015.

Whaley, John Corey. "Printz Award Winner John Corey Whaley Talks *Noggin*. Also, See the Cover—Exclusive." Interview by Stephan Lee. *EW.com*. Entertainment Weekly, 13 June 2013. Web. 17 Sept. 2015.

Whaley, John Corey. "Wouldn't You Like to Know . . . John Corey Whaley." Interview by Stacey Hayman. *VOYA*. VOYA, 21 July 2015. Web. 22 Oct. 2015.

Wheeler, Jill C. *Gary Paulsen*. [N.p.]: ABDO, 2015. *eBook Collection (EBSCOhost)*. Web. 23 Mar. 2015.

White, Claire E. "A Conversation with Libba Bray." *Internet Writing Journal*. Writers Write, Feb. 2004. Web. 7 Apr. 2015.

Whiteside, Erin, et al. "'I Am Not a Cow': Challenging Narratives of Empowerment in Teen Girls Sports Fiction." *Sociology of Sport Journal* 30.4 (2013): 415–34. *Education Abstracts (H.W. Wilson)*. Web. 12 June 2015.

Whitworth, Melissa. "Judy Blume's Lessons in Love." *Telegraph*. Telegraph Media Group, 3 Feb. 2008. Web. 31 Mar. 2015.

"Who is Orson Scott Card?" *Hatrack River*. Hatrack River Enterprises, n.d. Web. 2 June 2015.

Wickens, Corrine M. "Codes, Silences, and Homophobia: Challenging Normative Assumptions about Gender and Sexuality in Contemporary LGBTQ Young Adult Literature." *Children's Literature in Education* 42.2 (2011): 148–64. *Literary Reference Center*. Web. 1 Apr. 2015.

Wigginton, Catherine. "Too Hot to Handle." *Village Voice*. Village Voice, 7 Nov. 2006. Web. 15 Dec. 2015.

Williams, Mary Elizabeth. "It's John Green's World Now—and That's a Good Thing." *Salon*. Salon Media, 2 June 2014. Web. 5 Mar. 2015.

Williams, Sally. "Percy Jackson: My Boy's Own Adventure." *Guardian*. Guardian News and Media, 8 Feb. 2010. Web. 31 May 2015.

Winfrey, Kerry. "Ruby Oliver Rules: 'The Boyfriend List' by E. Lockhart." *Hello Giggles*. HelloGiggles, 24 Aug. 2013. Web. 1 Mar. 2015.

Wittenberg, Ed. "Award-Winning Author Sharon Draper Helps Celebrate Newly Renovated Library at Memorial Junior High School in South Euclid." *Sun Messenger* [Cleveland]. Plain Dealer and Northeast Ohio Media, 3 Mar. 2011. Web. 16 June 2015.

Wittlinger, Ellen. *Hard Love*. New York: Simon, 1999. Print.

WNET, 10 Feb. 2012. Web. 4 June 2015.

Wolf, Shelby Anne. *Handbook of Research on Children's and Young Adult Literature*. New York: Routledge, 2011. Print.

Wolff, Virginia Euwer. *True Believer*. New York: Atheneum, 2001. Print.

Wolitzer, Meg. "Look Homeward, Reader." *New York Times*. New York Times, 17 Oct. 2014. Web. 24 Mar. 2015.

Woodley, Shailene. "The 100 Most Influential People: John Green." *Time*. Time, 23 Apr. 2014. Web. 17 Apr. 2015.

Woodside, D. Blake, et al. "Comparisons of Men with Full or Partial Eating Disorders, Men without Eating Disorders, and Women with Eating Disorders in the Community." *American Journal of Psychiatry* 158.4 (2001): 570–74. Web. 29 May 2015.

Woodson, Jacqueline. "Jacqueline Woodson on Growing Up, Coming Out and Saying Hi to Strangers." Interview by Terry Gross. *Fresh Air*. NPR, 10 Dec. 2014. Web. 18 Mar. 2015.

Wopperer, Emily. "Inclusive Literature in the Library and the Classroom: The Importance of Young Adult and Children's Books that Portray Characters with Disabilities." *Knowledge Quest* 39.3 (Jan./Feb. 2011): 26–35.

Wright, David. "Streetwise Urban Fiction." *Library Journal*. Lifestyle Theme on Genesis Framework, 15 July 2006. Web. 3 June 2015.

YALSA. "2012 Best Fiction for Young Adults." *YALSA*. ALA, n.d. Web. 20 February 2016.

YALSA. "2012 Teens' Top Ten." *YALSA*. ALA, n.d. Web. 20 February 2016.

YALSA. "2013 Teens' Top Ten." *YALSA*. ALA, n.d. Web. 20 February 2016.

Yardley, William. "Ned Vizzini, 32, Dies; Wrote Teenage Novels." *New York Times*. New York Times, 20 Dec. 2013. Web. 11 Dec. 2015.

Yin, Maryann. "Libba Bray Reveals Title & Release Date for *The Diviners* Sequel." *GalleyCat*. AdWeek, 23 Mar. 2015. Web. 14 Apr. 2015.

Young Adult Library Association. "2003 Margaret A. Edwards Award Winner." *YALSA*. ALA, n.d. Web. 23 February 2016.

Younger, Beth. "Pleasure, Pain, and the Power of Being Thin: Female Sexuality in Young Adult Literature." *NWSA Journal* 15.2 (2003): 45–56. *Literary Reference Center*. Web. 13 May 2015.

Younger, Beth. *Learning Curves: Body Image and Female Sexuality in Young Adult Literature*. Lanham: Scarecrow P, 2009. Print.

Zeises, Lara M. *Anyone but You*. 2005. New York: Laurel-Leaf, 2007. Print.

Zickuhr, Kathryn, and Lee Rainie. "Younger Americans' Reading Habits and Technology Use." *Pew Research Center Internet & Tech*. Pew Research Center, 10 Sept. 2014. Web. 24 Mar. 2015.

Index